Handbook of
INTERVIEW
RESEARCH

International Advisory Board

Handbook of
INTERVIEW
RESEARCH
Context & Method

Editors

Jaber F. Gubrium
University of Florida

James A. Holstein
Marquette University

A SAGE Reference Title

Sage Publications
International Educational and Professional Publisher
Thousand Oaks ▪ London ▪ New Delhi

For information:

Sage Publications, Inc.
2455 Teller Road
Thousand Oaks, California 91320
E-mail: order@sagepub.com

Sage Publications Ltd.
6 Bonhill Street
London EC2A 4PU
United Kingdom

Sage Publications India Pvt. Ltd.
M-32 Market
Greater Kailash I
New Delhi 110 048 India

Printed in the United States of America

Library of Congress Cataloging-in-Publication Data

Handbook of interview research: Context & method / [edited] by Jaber F. Gubrium and
　　James A. Holstein.
　　　　p.　cm.
　　Includes bibliographical references and indexes.
　　ISBN 978-0-7619-1951-3 (cloth: acid-free paper)
　　1. Interviewing-Handbooks, manuals, etc.　 I.　Gubrium, Jaber F.
II. Holstein, James A.
　　H61.28 .H36　2001
　　158'.39—dc21　　　　　　　　　　　　　　　　　　00-013201

This book is printed on acid-free paper.

　　　　　　　　　　　　　09　7　6　5

Acquisition Editor:	C. Deborah Laughton
Editorial Assistant:	Veronica Novak
Production Editor:	Sanford Robinson
Copy Editor:	Judy Selhorst
Editorial Assistant:	Cindy Bear
Typesetter/Designer:	Janelle LeMaster
Indexer:	Molly Hall
Cover Designer:	Michelle Lee

CONTENTS

PREFACE

The *Handbook of Interview Research* is both an encyclopedia and a story. An encyclopedia is a text that "circles" all aspects of its subject matter. We cannot promise that the *Handbook* is completely comprehensive regarding interviewing, because interviewing has far too rich and varied a history across the myriad disciplines in which it is practiced and across its professional applications to make that possible. Virtually all researchers and professionals who deal with people now make use of some form of interviewing. What we do promise is that this *Handbook* provides good coverage of the methodological issues now surrounding interview practice, including its varied forms, concerns centered on distinctive respondents, special institutional applications, technical matters related to data processing, analytic strategies, and representational questions. The *Handbook* is, indeed, quite a "circle" of knowledge for what has become the method of choice for obtaining experiential information from individuals.

The encyclopedically oriented reader has a distinct style of textual consultation. He or she moves directly to topics of interest. Someone about to organize a research project on early life, for example, might well consult only the chapter of the *Handbook* that discusses interviewing with children and adolescents. Someone else who is considering altering the kinds of interviewing he or she is conducting in professional practice might move directly to Part III, which focuses on how specific auspices orient to and complete the interviewing process. Such encyclopedic readings aim to capture information needed for specific purposes outside the text. For the reader's convenience, the editors have added cross-referencing between chapters with this in mind.

But the *Handbook* is also a story, which invites a different kind of reading. A story differs from an encyclopedia in that the story has a plot and theme of its own; it is something more than a compilation of "state-of-the-art" knowledge. Those who consult a text encyclopedically typically aim to develop their own stories, utilizing the information that their consultation provides. The *Handbook,* unlike most encyclopedias, also spins a particular tale of interviewing, one that moves from the commonly recognized individual interview to what we call "the interview society."

This is the gist of the *Handbook's* opening chapter, but the theme resonates throughout. No longer should we regard the interview as simply an instrument of data gathering technology; it is also an integral part of society—now more decidedly than ever. That is the *Handbook's* leading theme.

The theme is articulated in different ways across the various chapters. The more technical chapters convey the message that the part that interviewing now plays in society operates with growing efficiency and sophistication. The more conceptual chapters provide glimpses of the ways interviewing permeates, and gives shape to, our experience and identities. We provide short introductions to the various parts into which the *Handbook* is divided to highlight the theme and relate it to more specific discussions. Although we would not advise a reader to consult most encyclopedias as stories in their own right, the *Handbook* does offer the added dimension of being framed by a general perspective on the interview within contemporary society. We

invite readers to approach the text with this orientation also in mind.

Being both an encyclopedia and a story, the *Handbook* draws upon a vast reservoir of intellectual resources. We thank our many contributors on both counts. Each of them, in his or her own way, has furnished encyclopedic knowledge to us and to the reader, and has done so with consummate expertise and professionalism. The results are evident in the text. We also are grateful to the many contributors who offer food for thought regarding the leading theme in their chapters. This is our collective story, one that resonates throughout the volume.

Our advisory editors have been unstintingly supportive. They not only provided leads to potential contributors, but alerted us to new developments and suggested ways of thinking alternatively about old ones.

A long list of distinguished scholars reviewed the *Handbook* chapters. Many thanks to the following reviewers:

*   *   *

Lila Abu-Lughod	Joshua Gamson	Gale Miller
Pertti Alasuutari	Peter Grahame	Nancy Naples
Leon Anderson	Bill Gronfein	Virginia Olesen
H. Russell Bernard	Gisli Gudjonsson	Susan Ostrander
Joel Best	Tony Hak	Melvin Pollner
Spencer Cahill	Jeff Hearn	Shulamit Reinharz
Douglas Caulkins	Sally Hutchinson	Paul C. Rosenblatt
Kathy Charmaz	James R. Jarrett	Nora Cate Schaeffer
Susan E. Chase	David Karp	Joseph Schneider
Jeffrey Chin	Gary Kenyon	Howard Schuman
Christopher R. Corey	Michael Kimmel	David Silverman
Mick P. Couper	Ray Lee	Bruce Stave
Arlene Kaplan Daniels	Yvonna S. Lincoln	Barrie Thorne
Norman K. Denzin	Lyn Lofland	Barbara Truesdell
Robert Dingwall	Donileen Loseke	Carol A. B. Warren
Robert Emerson	George Marcus	Willi Wiesner
Glenn Firebaugh	Mike McDaniel	Harry Wolcott
James H. Frey	Janice M. Morse	Robert L. Young

Several friends and colleagues provided other kinds of support, from strategic advice to expert opinions on the state of the field in their areas. They include Pertti Alasuutari, Mitch Allen, Russ Bernard, Norman Bradburn, Ben Crabtree, Chris Corey, Mick Couper, Arlene Daniels, Norm Denzin, Giampietro Gobo, Steve Golant, Adam Hochschild, Michael Kimmel, Michael Messner, Steve Motowidlo, Howard Schuman, Clive Seale, David Silverman, and Bob Weiss.

Finally, we offer our heartfelt thanks to Peter Labella and C. Deborah Laughton, our editors at Sage Publications. Peter broached the idea for the *Handbook* and got the project off the ground, and then when Peter moved on to other projects, C. Deborah stepped in with unflagging enthusiasm and followed the *Handbook* through to completion. Production editor Sanford Robinson was the consummate professional in shepherding the *Handbook* into print. We appreciate all the help that they, and many others at Sage, have lavished on the project.

INTRODUCTION

1

FROM THE INDIVIDUAL INTERVIEW TO THE INTERVIEW SOCIETY

◆ Jaber F. Gubrium
James A. Holstein

At first glance, the interview seems simple and self-evident. The interviewer coordinates a conversation aimed at obtaining desired information. He or she makes the initial contact, schedules the event, designates its location, sets out the ground rules, and then begins to question the interviewee or "respondent." Questions elicit answers in more or less anticipatable format until the interviewer's agenda is completed and the interview ends.

The respondent provides the answers. She or he is usually well aware of the routine and waits until questions are posed before answering. The respondent's obligation is not to manage the encounter or to raise queries, but to offer information from his or her personal cache of experiential knowledge. Respondents are relatively passive in their roles, which are delimited by

the interviewer's coordinating activity and the available repository of answers. Should a respondent ask questions in his or her own right, the interviewer typically treats these questions as requests for clarification. The interviewer's responses are merely a means of keeping the interview and the respondent on track.

This is the familiar asymmetrical relationship that we recognize as interviewing. Except for technical nuances, we are conversant with either role in the encounter. Most educated urbanites, for instance, would know what it means to interview someone and would be able to manage the activity adequately in its broad details, from start to finish, if asked to do so. Likewise, most of us readily respond to demographic questionnaires, product-use surveys, public opinion polls, and health

◆ 3

inventories in considerable detail; we are willing and able to provide all sorts of information to strangers about the most intimate aspects of our lives. We carry out such encounters time and again with little hesitation and hardly an afterthought. The individual interview has become a commonplace feature of everyday life.

◆ The Democratization of Opinion

As familiar as it seems today, the interview, as a procedure for securing knowledge, is relatively new historically. Indeed, individuals have not always been viewed as important sources of knowledge about their own experience. Of course, we can imagine that particular forms of questioning and answering have been with us since the beginning of talk. As long as parental authority has existed, for example, fathers and mothers have undoubtedly questioned their children regarding their whereabouts; children have been expected to provide answers, not questions, in response. Similarly, suspects and prisoners have been interrogated for as long as suspicion and incarceration have been a part of human affairs. Healers, priests, employers, journalists, and many others seeking immediate, practical knowledge about everyday life have all undertaken interviewlike activity.

Nevertheless, not so long ago it would have seemed rather peculiar for an individual to approach a complete stranger and ask for permission to discuss personal matters. Daily life was more intimate; everyday business was conducted on a face-to-face basis between persons who were well acquainted with one another. According to Mark Benney and Everett Hughes (1956), there was a time when the interview simply didn't exist as a social form; they noted more than 40 years ago that "the interview [as we now refer to it] is a relatively new kind of encounter in the history of human

relations" (p. 139). Benney and Hughes were not saying that the activity of asking and answering questions was new, but rather that information gathering did not always rely upon the interview encounter. Although centuries ago a father might have interrogated his children concerning their whereabouts, this was not interviewing as we have come to know it today. The interview emerged only when specific information-gathering roles were formalized. This encounter would hardly be recognizable in a world of close relationships where the stranger was more likely to signify danger and the unknown than to be understood as a neutral conduit for the transmission of personal knowledge (Benney and Hughes 1956).

The modern interview changed all of this. Especially after World War II, with the emergence of the standardized survey interview, individuals became accustomed to offering information and opinions that had no immediate bearing on their lives and social relations. Individuals could forthrightly add their thoughts and feelings to the mix of "public opinion." Indeed, it became feasible for the first time for individuals to speak with strangers about all manner of thoughts concerning their lives, because these new strangers (that is, interviewers) didn't tell, at least in personally recognizable terms. Individuals—no matter how insignificant they might seem in the everyday scheme of things—came to be viewed as important elements of populations. Each person had a voice and it was imperative that each voice be heard, at least in principle. Seeking everyone's opinions, the interview has increasingly democratized experiential information.

THE MODERN TEMPER

David Riesman and Benney (1956) considered the interview format to be the product of a changing world of relationships, one that developed rapidly following the war years. The new era gradually accepted routine conversational exchanges between strangers; when people encountered interview situations, they were not immediately defensive about being asked for information about their lives, their associates, or their deepest sentiments, even though, in certain quarters, defensiveness was understandable because of perceived linkages between interviewing and oppression. Within this world, we have come to recognize easily two new roles associated with talking about oneself and one's life with strangers: the role of the interviewer and the role of the respondent—the centerpieces of the familiar interview.

This is an outgrowth of what Riesman and Benney called "the modern temper," a term that we take to have both cultural and interpersonal resonances. Culturally, it denotes a shared understanding that the individual has the wherewithal to offer a meaningful description of, or set of opinions about, his or her life. Individuals, in their own right, are accepted as significant commentators on their own experience; it is not just the "chief" community commentator who speaks for one and all, in other words, or the local representative of the commonwealth whose opinions are taken to express the thoughts and feelings of every mind and heart in the vicinity.

This modern temper is also interpersonal, in that it democratizes the interpretation of experience by providing a working space and means for expressing public opinion. Everyone—each individual—is taken to have significant views and feelings about life that are accessible to others who undertake to ask about them. As William James ([1892] 1961) noted at the end of the 19th century, this assumes that each and every individual has a sense of self that is owned and controlled by him- or herself, even if the self is socially formulated and interpersonally responsive. This self makes it possible for everyone to reflect meaningfully on individual experience and to enter into socially relevant dialogue about it. The modern temper has made it reasonable and

acceptable to turn to a world of individuals, most of whom are likely to be strangers, as a way of understanding the social organization of experience.

Just as the interview itself is a recent development, the selection of ordinary individuals as sources of information and opinions is also relatively new (see Kent 1981; Oberschall 1965; Selvin 1985). As Pertti Alasuutari (1998) explains, it was not so long ago that when one wanted to know something important about society or social life, one invariably asked those considered to be "in the know." In contrast to what seems self-evident today—that is, questioning those individuals whose experiences are under consideration—the obvious and efficient choice for very early interviewers was to ask *informed* citizens to provide answers to their questions. Alasuutari provides an example from Anthony Oberschall's work:

> It was natural that the questions were posed to knowledgeable citizens, such as state officials or church ministers. In other words, they were informants in expert interviews. For instance, in a survey of agricultural laborers conducted in 1874-1875 in Germany (Oberschall 1965: 19-20), question No. 25 read: "Is there a tendency among laborers to save money in order to be able to buy their own plot of land later on? Does this tendency appear already among the unmarried workers or only after marriage?" . . . The modern survey would of course approach such questions quite differently. Instead of asking an informed person whether married or unmarried workers have a tendency to save money to buy their own plot of land, a sample of workers would be asked about their marital status, savings, and plans about how to use them. (Pp. 135-36)

Those considered to be knowledgeable in the subject matter under consideration, Alasuutari notes, were viewed as infor-

mants, not respondents, the latter being su-
perfluous under the circumstances.

AN INDIVIDUALIZING
DISCOURSE

The research consequence of the subsequent democratization of opinion was part
of a trend toward increased surveillance in
everyday life. The growing discourse of individuality combined with an increasingly
widespread and efficient apparatus for information processing. Although interviewing and the resulting production of public
opinion developed rapidly after World War
II, the widespread surveillance of daily life
and the deployment of the category of the
individual had begun centuries earlier.

Michel Foucault's (1973, 1975, 1977,
1978) iconoclastic studies of the discursive
organization of subjectivity shed fascinating light on the development of the concepts of the personal self and individuality.
Time and again, in institutional contexts
ranging from the medical clinic and the asy-
lum to the prison, Foucault shows us how
what he calls "technologies of the self" have
transformed the way we view the sources
and structure of our subjectivity (see Dreyfus and Rabinow 1982; Foucault 1988).

We use the term *subjectivity* here to indicate the type(s) of subject(s) that individuals and cultures might comprehend and embody. With respect to the interview, we are
referring to the putative agent who stands
behind the "facades" of interview participants, so to speak, the agent who is held
practically and morally responsible for the
participants' words and actions. Most of us
are so familiar with the contemporary
Western image of the individualized self as
this agent that we find it difficult to comprehend alternative subjectivities. Clifford
Geertz (1984), however, points out that
this is "a rather peculiar idea within the
context of the world's cultures" (p. 126). In
other societies and historical periods,
agency and responsibility have been articu-

lated in relation to a variety of other social
structures, such as the tribe, the clan, the
lineage, the family, the community, and the
monarch. The notion of the bounded,
unique self, more or less integrated as the
center of awareness, emotion, judgment,
and action, is a very recent version of the
subject.

Foucault offers us new insights into how
this sense of subjectivity evolved. Technologies of the self, in Foucault's terms, are the
concrete, socially and historically located
institutional practices through which a relatively new sense of who and what we are as
human beings was constructed. These practices advanced the notion that each and every one of us has an ordinary self—the idea
being that each one could acceptably reflect
on his or her individual experience, personally describe it, and communicate opinions
about it and its surrounding world in his or
her own terms. This transformed our sense
of human beings as subjects. The now
self-evident view that each of us has opinions of public significance became intelligible only within a discourse of individuality.

Foucault argues that the newly formed
technologies of surveillance of the 18th and
19th centuries, the quintessential manifestation of which was Jeremy Bentham's
all-seeing panopticon, did not just incorporate and accommodate the experiences of
individual subjects who populated the contemporary social landscape, but, instead,
entered into the construction of individual
subjects in their own right. Foucault poignantly exemplifies this transformation in
the opening pages of *Discipline and Punish*
(1977), a book that is as much about the individuation of society as it is about "the
birth of the prison" (its subtitle). In the
opening pages, we cringe at a vivid account
of the torture of a man condemned to death
for attempting to assassinate King Louis
XV of France. We despair as the man's body
is flayed, burned, and drawn and quartered
in public view. From contemporary commentary, Foucault (1977) describes the
events:

On 2 March 1757 Damiens the regicide was condemned "to make the *amende honorable* before the main door of the Church of Paris," where he was to be "taken and conveyed in a cart wearing nothing but a shirt, holding a torch of burning wax weighing two pounds"; then, "in the said cart, to the Place de Grève, where, on a scaffold that will be erected there, the flesh will be torn from his breasts, arms, thighs and calves with red-hot pincers, his right hand, holding the knife with which he committed the said parricide, burnt with sulphur, and, on those places where the flesh will be torn away, poured molten lead, boiling oil, burning resin, wax and sulphur melted together and then his body drawn and quartered by four horses and his limbs and body consumed by fire, reduced to ashes and his ashes thrown to the winds." (P. 3)

Foucault asks why criminals were subjected to such horrible bodily torture. Why were they made to beg for forgiveness in public spectacles? His answer is that the spectacle of torture was an event whose political culture was informed by a sense of the seamless relations among the body of the king (the crown), social control, and subjectivity. As all people were, Damiens was conceived literally and legally as a subject of the king; his body and soul were inseparable extensions of the crown. An assault on the body of the king had to be attacked in turn, as a red-hot iron might be used to cauterize a festering wound. The spectacle of torture did not revolve around an autonomous agent who was regarded as an independent subject with a self, feelings, opinions, and experiential reality uniquely his own. This might have caused others sympathetically to consider Damiens's treatment to be cruel and unusual punishment, to put it in today's terms.

The disposition of the times, however, offered no sympathy for what Damiens might have been "going through." In the eyes of others, Damiens's feelings and opinions had no standing apart from the man's station in relation to the sovereign. The spectacle of punishment rested on a discourse of knowledge and power that lodged all experiential truth in the sovereign's shared embodiment. As Hubert Dreyfus and Paul Rabinow (1982) explain: "The figure of torture brings together a complex of power, truth, and bodies. The atrocity of torture was an enactment of power that also revealed truth. Its application on the body of the criminal was an act of revenge and an art" (p. 146). The idea that a thinking, feeling, consequential subject occupied the body of the criminal was simply beyond the pale of contemporary understanding. Individuality, as we know it today, did not exist as a recognizable social form.

A few pages later in *Discipline and Punish*, Foucault presents the new subject who comes into being as part of a discourse that is more in tune with "the modern temper." Discussing the evolution of penal reform, he describes the emergence of the "house of young prisoners" in Paris a mere 80 years after Damiens's death. Torture as a public spectacle has gradually disappeared. The "gloomy festival of punishment" is dying out, along with the accused's agonizing plea for pardon. It has been replaced by a humanizing regimen, informed by a discourse of the independent, thinking subject whose criminality is correctable. Rehabilitation is replacing retribution. Scientific methods of scrutiny and courses of instruction are viewed as the means for returning the criminal to right reason and back to the proper fold of society. The subject is no longer a selfless appendage of a larger entity; this is a new agent, one with a mind and sentiments of his or her own. With the proper regimen, this new agent is incited to individual self-scrutiny and responds to corrective action.

In time, this same subject would duly offer his or her opinions and sentiments within the self-scrutinizing regimens of what Foucault calls "governmentality," the archipelago of surveillance practices suffusing modern life. As James Miller (1993: 299) points out, governmentality extends well beyond the political and penal to include pedagogical, spiritual, and religious dimensions (see also Garland 1997). If Bentham's original panopticon was an efficient form of prison observation, panopticism in the modern temper becomes the widespread self-scrutiny that "governs" all aspects of everyday life in the very commonplace questions and answers posed about ourselves in both our inner thoughts and our public expressions. These are seemingly daily inquiries about what we personally think and feel about every conceivable topic, including our deepest sentiments and most secret actions.

We can readily view the individual interview as part of modern governmentality, impressed upon us by myriad inquiries into our lives. Indeed, the interview may be seen as one of the 20th century's most distinctive technologies of the self. In particular, it gives an "objective," "scientific" cast to the notion of the individual self, terms of reference that resolutely echo modern times. As Nikolas Rose (1990, 1997) has shown in the context of the psychological sciences, the private self, along with its descriptive data, was invented right along with the technologies we now associate with measurement.

"Scientific surveillance" such as psychological testing, case assessments, and, of course, individual interviews of all kinds have created the experiencing and informing respondent we now take for granted. The category of "the person" now identifies the self-reflective constituents of society (see Carrithers, Collins, and Lukes 1985; Lidz 1976); if we want to know what the social world is like, we now ask its individual inhabitants. The individual interview on a personal scale and the social survey on the societal level serve as democratizing agents, giving voice to individuals and, in the process, formulating "public" opinion.

LEARNING FROM STRANGERS

The title of Robert Weiss's (1994) book on interviewing, *Learning from Strangers*, points to the shared expectations that surround the face-to-face experience of interviewing, as the book lays out "the art and method of qualitative interview studies." Although qualitative interviews especially are sometimes conducted with acquaintances (see Warren, Chapter 4, this volume), much of Weiss's advice on how an interviewer should proceed is based on the premise that the interviewer does not know the respondent. Behind each bit of advice about how to interview effectively is the understanding that each and every stranger-respondent is someone worth listening to. The respondent is someone who can provide detailed descriptions of his or her thoughts, feelings, and activities, if the interviewer asks and listens carefully enough. The trick, in Weiss's judgment, is for the interviewer to present a caring and concerned attitude, expressed within a well-planned and encouraging format. The aim of the interviewer is to derive, as objectively as possible, the respondent's *own* opinions of the subject matter in question, information that the respondent will readily offer and elaborate when the circumstances are conducive to his or her doing so and the proper methods are applied.

The full range of individual experiences is potentially accessible, according to Weiss; the interview is a virtual window on that experience, a kind of universal panopticon. In answering the question of why we interview, Weiss offers a compelling portrayal of the democratization of opinion:

> Interviewing gives us access to the observations of others. Through interviewing we can learn about places we have not been and could not go and about settings in which we have not lived. If we have the right informants, we can learn about the quality of neighborhoods or what happens in families or how organizations set their goals. In-

terviewing can inform us about the nature of social life. We can learn about the work of occupations and how people fashion careers, about cultures and the values they sponsor, and about the challenges people confront as they lead their lives.

We can learn also, through interviewing, about people's interior experiences. We can learn what people perceived and how they interpreted their perceptions. We can learn how events affect their thoughts and feelings. We can learn the meanings to them of their relationships, their families, their work, and their selves. We can learn about all the experiences, from joy through grief, that together constitute the human condition. (P. 1)

The opportunities for knowing even strangers by way of their opinions are now ubiquitous. We find interviews virtually everywhere. We have come a very long way from the days when individuals' experiences and voices simply didn't matter, a long way from Damiens's "unheard" cries. The interview itself has created, as well as tapped into, the vast world of individual experience that now constitutes the substance of everyday life.

◆ The Interview Society

If the interview has helped to constitute the modern individual, has it simultaneously transformed society? It certainly has transported the myriad details of the most personal experience into the public domain. Indeed, it has established these realms as important sites for securing answers to what it means to be part of everyday life. Our social world now comprises viable and consequential individual opinions, assembled and offered up by actively agentic subjects, whose responses convey the individual particulars of modern society. With the spread of the discourse of individualized

subjectivity, we now are prepared as both questioners and answerers to produce readily the society of which we are a part. The modern temper gives us the interview as a significant means for realizing that subjectivity and the social contexts that bring it about.

THE MEDIATION OF CONTEMPORARY LIFE

Interviewing of all kinds mediates contemporary life. Think of how much we learn about today's world by way of interviews conducted across a broad spectrum of venues, well beyond research practice. Interviews, for example, are a source of popular celebrity and notoriety. Television interview host Larry King introduces us to politicians and power brokers who not only share their thoughts, feelings, and opinions with a mass audience but cultivate their celebrity status in the process. This combines with programming devoted to exposing the deepest personal, not just political or social, sentiments of high-profile figures. Celebrity news commentators/interviewers like Barbara Walters plumb the emotional depths of stars and pundits from across the media spectrum. To this, add the likes of talk-show hosts Oprah Winfrey, Geraldo Rivera, Ricki Lake, and Jerry Springer, who daily invite ordinary men and women, the emotionally tortured, and the behaviorally bizarre to "spill their guts" in front of millions of television viewers. Referring to all of these, the interview is becoming the experiential conduit par excellence of the electronic age. And this is only the tip of the iceberg, as questions and answers fly back and forth on the Internet, where chat rooms are now as intimate as back porches and bedrooms.

Interviews extend to professional practice as well. As the contributions to Part III of this *Handbook* indicate, myriad institutions employ interviewing to generate useful and often crucial information. Physicians conduct medical interviews with their patients in order to formulate diagnoses and monitor treatment and progress (see Zoppi and Epstein, Chapter 18). Employers interview job applicants (see Latham and Millman, Chapter 23). Psychotherapy has always been a largely interview-based enterprise. Its varied psychological and psychiatric perspectives have perhaps diversified the interview more than any other professional practice. As Gale Miller, Steve de Shazer, and Peter De Jong show in their essay on the therapy interview (Chapter 19), this ranges from traditional forms of in-depth interviewing to more contemporary solution-focused encounters that center on "restorying" experience. Even forensic investigation has come a long way from the interview practices of the Inquisition, where giving the "third degree" was a common feature of interrogation (see McKenzie, Chapter 21).

As interviewing has become more pervasive in the mass media and in professional practice, the interviewing industry itself has developed by leaps and bounds. Survey research, public opinion polling, and marketing research lead the way. Survey research has always been conducted for academic purposes, but today it is increasingly employed in service to commercial interests as well (see Platt, Chapter 2, this volume). The interviewing industry now extends from individual product-use inquiries to group interviewing services, where focus group discussions quickly establish consumer product preferences. Movie studios even use focus groups to decide which versions of motion picture finales will be most popularly received. Indeed, the group interview is among the most rapidly growing information-gathering techniques on the contemporary scene (see Morgan, Chapter 7, this volume).

The ubiquity and significance of the interview in our daily lives has prompted David Silverman (1997) to suggest that "perhaps we all live in what might be called an 'interview society,' in which interviews seem central to making sense of our lives"

(p. 248; see also Silverman 1993). Silverman's reasoning underscores the democratization of opinion that interviewing has enhanced. Silverman (1997) identifies three conditions required by an interview society. First, an interview society requires a particular informing subjectivity, "the emergence of the self as a proper object of narration." Societies with forms of collective or cosmic subjectivity, for example, do not provide the practical basis for learning from strangers. This is possible only in societies where there is a prevalent and shared sense that any individual has the potential to be a respondent and, as such, has something meaningful to offer when asked to do so.

Second, Silverman points to the need for an information-gathering apparatus he calls the "technology of the confessional." In other words, an interview society needs a practical means for securing the communicative by-product of "confession." This, Silverman (1997) points out, should commonly extend to friendship not only "with the policeman, but with the priest, the teacher, and the 'psy' professional" (p. 248).

Third, and perhaps most important, an interview society requires that a mass technology be readily available. An interview society is not the product of the age-old medical interview, or of the long-standing practice of police interrogation; rather, it requires that an interviewing establishment be recognizably in place throughout society. Virtually everyone should be familiar with the goals of interviewing as well as what it takes to conduct an interview.

Silverman argues that many contemporary societies have met these conditions, some more than others. Not only do media and human service professionals utilize interviews, but it has been estimated that fully 90 percent of all social science investigations exploit interview data (Briggs 1986). Internet surveys now provide instant questions and answers about every imaginable subject; we are asked to state our inclinations and opinions regarding everything from presidential candidates to which characters on TV serials should be retained or ousted. The interview society, it seems, has firmly arrived, is well, and is flourishing as a leading context for addressing the subjective contours of daily living.

THE ROMANTIC IMPULSE

Paul Atkinson and Silverman (1997) point out that the confessional properties of the interview not only construct individual subjectivity but, more and more, deepen and broaden the subjects' experiential truths. We no longer readily turn to the cosmos, the gods, the written word, the high priest, or local authorities for authentic knowledge; rather, we commonly search for authenticity through the in-depth interview. The interview society not only reflexively constructs a compatible subject, but fully rounds this out ontologically by taking us to the proverbial heart of the subject in question.

This reveals the romantic impulse behind the interview and the interview society. If we desire to "really know" the individual subject, then somehow we must provide a means to hear his or her genuine voice. Superficial discussion does not seem to be adequate. Many interviewers explore the emotional enclaves of the self by way of "open-ended" or "in-depth" interviewing. Although, technically, "open-endedness" is merely a way to structure the interview process, Atkinson and Silverman suggest that the term also flags a particular social understanding, namely, that the true, internal voice of the subject comes through only when it is not externally screened or otherwise communicatively constrained.

But, as Atkinson and Silverman advise, authenticity in practice is not an ultimate experiential truth. It is itself a methodically constructed social product that emerges from its reflexive communicative practices. In other words, authenticity, too, has its

constructive technology. Recognizable signs of emotional expression and scenic practices such as direct eye contact and intimate gestures are widely understood to reveal deep truths about individual selves (see also Gubrium and Holstein 1997; Holstein and Gubrium 2000). In in-depth interviews, we "do" deep, authentic experiences as much as we "do" opinion offering in the course of the survey interview. It is not simply a matter of procedure or the richness of data that turns researchers, the interview society, and its truth-seeing audiences to in-depth and open-ended interviewing. It is also a matter of collaboratively making audible and visible the phenomenal depths of the individual subject at the center of our shared concerns.

THE LEADING THEME

It would therefore be a mistake to treat the interview—or any information-gathering technique—as simply a research procedure. The interview is part and parcel of our society and culture. It is not just a way of obtaining information about who and what we are; it is now an integral, constitutive feature of our everyday lives. Indeed, as the romantic impulses of interviewing imply, it is at the very heart of what we have become and could possibly be as individuals.

That is the leading theme of this *Handbook:* "No method of research can stand outside the cultural and material world" (Silverman 1997:249). Whereas some would view the interview primarily as a research technique, we would do well also to consider its broader social, institutional, and representational contours. At the same time, we must be cautious lest the latter overshadow the interview's information-gathering contributions, which have been brilliantly and extensively developed by interview researchers for decades. To recognize, elaborate, and deconstruct the broad contours of the interview is not at all to suggest that we pay less attention to its technology in the conventional sense of the term. Rather, it implies just the opposite; we must think carefully about technical matters because they produce the detailed subject as much as they gather information about him or her. Taken together, the chapters of this *Handbook* provide a balance of related concerns, extending from aspects of the conventional technology of the interview—including forms of interviewing and diverse data gathering and analytic strategies—to the various ways interviewing relates to distinctive respondents, its institutional auspices, and representational issues.

◆ The Subjects behind Interview Participants

We began this introductory chapter by noting that the interview seems simple and self-evident. In actual practice, this is hardly the case. If the technology of the interview not only produces interview data but also simultaneously constructs individual and public opinion, what are the working contours of the encounter? What does it mean, in terms of communicative practice, to be an interviewer? What is the presumed subjectivity of this participant? Correspondingly, what does it mean to be a respondent? What is the presumed subjectivity of that participant? These, of course, are procedural questions, to a degree, and several authors who contribute to this *Handbook* address them in just these terms. As the chapters that follow show, there is nothing technically simple about the contemporary practice of asking and answering interview questions. But the questions also broker discursive and institutional issues related to matters of contemporary subjectivity. This complicates things, and it is to these issues that we turn in the rest of this chapter as a way of providing a more nuanced context for understanding the in-

dividual interview and the interview society.

Let's begin to unpack the complications by examining competing visions of the subjects who are imagined to stand behind interview participants. Regardless of the type of interview, there is always a working model of the subject lurking behind the persons assigned the roles of interviewer and respondent (Holstein and Gubrium 1995). By virtue of the kinds of subjects we project, we confer varying senses of epistemological agency upon interviewers and respondents. These, in turn, influence the ways we proceed technically, as well as our understanding of the relative validity of the information that is produced.

As we noted at the outset, interviewing typically has been viewed as an asymmetrical encounter in which an interviewer solicits information from an interviewee, who relatively passively responds to the interviewer's inquiries. This commonsensical, if somewhat oversimplified, view suggests that those who want to find out about another person's feelings, thoughts, or activities merely have to ask the right questions and the other's "reality" will be revealed. Studs Terkel, the legendary journalistic and sociological interviewer, makes the process sound elementary; he claims that he merely turns on his tape recorder and asks people to talk. Using his classic study *Working* (1972) as an example, Terkel claims that his questions merely evoke responses that interviewees are all too ready to share:

> There were questions, of course. But they were casual in nature . . . the kind you would ask while having a drink with someone; the kind he would ask you. . . . In short, it was a conversation. In time, the sluice gates of damned up hurts and dreams were open. (P. xxv)

As unsophisticated and guileless as it sounds, this image is common in interviewing practice. The image is one of "mining" or "prospecting" for the facts and feelings residing within the respondent. Of course, a highly sophisticated technology tells researcher/prospectors how to ask questions, what sorts of questions not to ask, the order in which to ask them, and ways to avoid saying things that might spoil, contaminate, or bias the data. The basic model, however, locates valued information inside the respondent and assigns the interviewer the task of somehow extracting it.

THE PASSIVE SUBJECT BEHIND THE RESPONDENT

In this rather conventional view, the subjects behind respondents are basically conceived as passive *vessels of answers* for experiential questions put to them by interviewers. Subjects are repositories of facts, feelings, and the related particulars of experience. They hold the answers to demographic questions, such as age, gender, race, occupation, and socioeconomic status. They contain information about social networks, including household composition, friendship groups, circles of care, and other relationships. These repositories also hold a treasure trove of experiential data pertinent to beliefs, feelings, and activities.

The vessel-like subject behind the respondent passively possesses information the interviewer wants to know; the respondent merely conveys, for better or worse, what the subject already possesses. Occasionally, such as with sensitive interview topics or with recalcitrant respondents, interviewers acknowledge that the task may be especially difficult. Nonetheless, the information is viewed, in principle, as the uncontaminated contents of the subject's vessel of answers. The knack is to formulate questions and provide an atmosphere conducive to open and undistorted communication between interviewer and respondent.

Much of the methodological literature on interviewing deals with the facets of these intricate matters. The vessel-of-answers view leads interviewers to be careful in how they ask questions, lest their method of inquiry bias what lies within the subject. This perspective has prompted the development of myriad procedures for obtaining unadulterated facts and details, most of which rely upon interviewer and question neutrality. Successful implementation of disinterested practices elicits objective truths from the vessel of answers. Validity results from the successful application of these techniques.

In the vessel-of-answers model, the image of the subject is not of an agent engaged in the production of knowledge. If the interviewing process goes "by the book" and is nondirectional and unbiased, respondents can validly proffer information that subjects presumably merely store within. Contamination emanates from the interview setting, its participants, and their interaction, not from the subject, who, under ideal conditions, is capable of providing accurate, authentic reports.

THE PASSIVE SUBJECT BEHIND THE INTERVIEWER

This evokes a complementary model of the subject behind the interviewer. Although not totally passive, the interviewer/subject nonetheless stands apart from the actual "data" of the field; he or she merely collects what is already there. To be sure, the collection process can be arduous, but the objective typically is to tap into information without unduly disturbing— and, therefore, biasing or contaminating— the respondent's vessel of answers. If it is not quite like Terkel's "sluice gates" metaphor, it still resembles turning on a spigot; the interviewer's role is limited to releasing what is already in place.

The interviewer, for example, is expected to keep the respondent's vessel of answers in plain view but to avoid shaping the information that is extracted. Put simply, this involves the interviewer's controlling him- or herself so as not to influence what the passive interview subject will communicate. The interviewer must discard serious self-consciousness; the interviewer must avoid any action that would imprint his or her presence onto the respondent's reported experience. The interviewer must resist supplying particular frames of reference for the respondent's answers. To the extent such frameworks appropriately exist, they are viewed as embedded in the subject's world behind the respondent, not behind the researcher. If the interviewer is to be at all self-conscious, this is technically limited to his or her being alert to the possibility that he or she may be contaminating or otherwise unduly influencing the research process.

Interviewers are generally expected to keep their "selves" out of the interview process. *Neutrality* is the byword. Ideally, the interviewer uses his or her interpersonal skills merely to encourage the expression of, but not to help construct, the attitudes, sentiments, and information in question. In effect, the image of the passive subject behind the interviewer is one of a facilitator. As skilled as the interviewer might be in practice, all that he or she appropriately does in principle is to promote the expression of the actual attitudes and information that lie in waiting in the respondent's vessel of answers.

In exerting control in this way, the interviewer limits his or her involvement in the interview to a specific preordained role—which can be quite scripted—that is constant from one interview to another. Should the interviewer go out of control, so to speak, and introduce anything but variations on specified questions into the interview, the passive subject behind the interviewer is methodologically violated and neutrality is compromised. It is not this passive subject who is the problem, but rather the interviewer who has not adequately regulated his or her conduct so as to facilitate the expression of respondent information.

ACTIVATING INTERVIEW SUBJECTS

As researchers have become more aware of the interview as a site for the production of meaning, they have increasingly come to appreciate the activity of the subjects projected behind both the respondent and the interviewer. The interview is being reconceptualized as an occasion for purposefully animated participants to *construct* versions of reality interactionally rather than merely purvey data (see Holstein and Gubrium 1995). This trend reflects an increasingly pervasive appreciation for the constitutive character of social interaction and of the constructive role played by active subjects in authoring their experiences.

Sentiments along these lines have been building for some time across diverse disciplines. Nearly a half century ago, for example, Ithiel de Sola Pool (1957), a prominent critic of public opinion polling, argued presciently that the dynamic, communicative contingencies of the interview literally activated respondents' opinions. Every interview, Pool suggested, is an "interpersonal drama with a developing plot" (p. 193). The metaphor conveys a far more active sense of interview participation than the "prospector for meaning" suggests. As Pool indicated:

> The social milieu in which communication takes place [during interviews] modifies not only what a person dares to say but even what he thinks he chooses to say. And these variations in expression cannot be viewed as mere deviations from some underlying "true" opinion, for there is no neutral, non-social, uninfluenced situation to provide that baseline. (P. 192)

Conceiving of the interview in this fashion casts interview participants as virtual *practitioners* of everyday life who work constantly to discern and designate the recognizable and orderly features of the experience under consideration. It transforms the subject behind the respondent from a repository of information and opinions or a wellspring of emotions into a productive source of knowledge. From the time a researcher identifies a research topic, through respondent selection, questioning and answering, and, finally, the interpretation of responses, interviewing is a concerted interactional project. Indeed, the subject behind the respondent now, more or less, becomes an imagined product of the project. Working within the interview itself, subjects are fleshed out, rationally and emotionally, in relation to the give-and-take of the interview process, the interview's research purposes, and its surrounding social contexts.

Construed as active, the subject behind the respondent not only holds the details of a life's experience but, in the very process of offering them up to the interviewer, constructively shapes the information. The active respondent can hardly "spoil" what he or she is, in effect, subjectively constructing in the interview process. Rather, the activated subject pieces experiences together before, during, and after occupying the respondent role. This subject is always making meaning, regardless of whether he or she is actually being interviewed.

An active subject behind the interviewer is also implicated in the production of knowledge. His or her participation in the process is not viewed in terms of standardization or constraint; neutrality is not figured to be necessary or achievable. One cannot very well taint knowledge if that knowledge is not conceived as existing in some pure form apart from the circumstances of its production. The active subject behind the interviewer thus becomes a necessary, practical counterpart to the active subject behind the respondent. Interviewer and, ultimately, researcher contributions to

the information produced in interviews are not viewed as incidental or immaterial. Nor is interviewer participation considered in terms of contamination. Rather, the subject behind the interviewer is seen as actively and unavoidably engaged in the interactional co-construction of the interview's content.

Interactional contingencies influence the construction of the active subjectivities of the interview. Especially important here are the varied subject positions articulated in the interview process, which need to be taken into account in the interpretation of interview material. For example, an interview project might center on the quality of care and quality of life of nursing home residents (see Gubrium 1993). This might be part of a study relating to the national debate about the organization and value of home versus institutional care. Careful attention to the way participants link substantive matters with biographical ones can vividly reveal a highly active subject. For instance, a nursing home resident might speak animatedly during an interview about the quality of care in her facility, asserting that, "for a woman, it ultimately gets down to feelings," invoking an emotional subject. Another resident might coolly and methodically list specifics about her facility's quality of care, never once mentioning her gender or her feelings about the care she receives. Offering her own take on the matter, this respondent might state that "getting emotional" over "these things" clouds clear judgment, implicating a rationalized subject. When researchers take this active subject into account, what is otherwise a contradictory and inconclusive data set is transformed into the meaningful, intentionally crafted responses of quite active respondents.

The standpoint from which information is offered continually unfolds in relation to ongoing interview interaction. In speaking of the quality of care, for example, nursing home residents, as interview respondents, not only offer substantive thoughts and feelings pertinent to the topic under consideration but simultaneously and continuously monitor who they are in relation to themselves and to the person questioning them. For example, prefacing her remarks about the quality of life in her facility with the statement "Speaking as a woman," a nursing home resident actively informs the interviewer that she is to be heard as a woman, not as someone else—not a mere resident, cancer patient, or abandoned mother. If and when she subsequently comments, "If I were a man in this place," the resident frames her thoughts and feelings about the quality of life differently, producing an alternative subject: the point of view of a man as spoken by a female respondent. The respondent is clearly working up experiential identities as the interview progresses.

Because the respondent's subjectivity and related experience are continually being assembled and modified, the "truth" value of interview responses cannot be judged simply in terms of whether those responses match what lies in an ostensibly objective vessel of answers. Rather, the value of interview data lies both in their meanings and in how meanings are constructed. These *what* and *how* matters go hand in hand, as two components of practical meaning-making action (see Gubrium and Holstein 1997). The entire process is fueled by the reality-constituting contributions of all participants; interviewers, too, are similarly implicated in the co-construction of the subject positions from which they ask the questions at hand (see in this volume Schaeffer and Maynard, Chapter 28; Briggs, Chapter 44).

The multiple subjects that could possibly stand behind interview participants add several layers of complication to the interview process as well as to the analysis of interview data. Decidedly different procedural strictures are required to accommodate and account for alternating subjects. Indeed, the very question of what constitutes or serves as data critically relates to these issues of subjectivity. What research-

ers choose to highlight when they analyze interview responses flows directly from how the issues are addressed (see Gubrium and Holstein 1997; see also Baker, Chapter 37, this volume).

◆ Empowering Respondents

Reconceptualizing what it means to interview and to analyze interview material has led to far-reaching innovations in research (see the contributions to this volume by Fontana, Chapter 8; Riessman, Chapter 33; Cándida Smith, Chapter 34; Denzin, Chapter 40; Ellis and Berger, Chapter 41; Richardson, Chapter 42; Rosenblatt, Chapter 43). It has also promoted the view that the interview society is not only the by-product of statistically summarized survey data, but is constituted by all manner of alternative interview encounters and information, the diverse agendas of which variably enter into "data" production. In the process, the political dimensions of the interview process have been critically underscored (see Briggs, Chapter 44, this volume).

The respondent's voice has taken on particular urgency, as we can hear in Eliot Mishler's (1986) poignant discussion of the empowerment of interview respondents. Uncomfortable with the evolution of the interview into a highly controlled, asymmetrical conversation dominated by the researcher (see Kahn and Cannell 1957; Maccoby and Maccoby 1954), Mishler challenges the assumptions and implications behind the "standardized" interview. His aim is to bring the respondent more fully and actively into the picture, to make the respondent more of an equal partner in the interview conversation.

Following a critique of standardized interviewing, Mishler (1986) offers a lengthy discussion of his alternative perspective, one that questions the need for strict control of the interview encounter. The approach, in part, echoes our discussion of the activation of interview participants. Mishler suggests that rather than conceiving of the interview as a form of stimulus and response, we might better view it as an interactional accomplishment. Noting that interview participants not only ask and answer questions in interviews but simultaneously engage in other speech activities, Mishler turns our attention to what the participants, in effect, are doing with words when they engage each other. He makes the point this way:

> Defining interviews as speech events or speech activities, as I do, marks the fundamental contrast between the standard antilinguistic, stimulus-response model and an alternative approach to interviewing as discourse between speakers. Different definitions in and of themselves do not constitute different practices. Nonetheless, this new definition alerts us to the features of interviews that hitherto have been neglected. (Pp. 35-36)

The key phrase here is "discourse between speakers." Mishler directs us to the integral and inexorable speech activities in which even survey interview participants engage as they ask and answer questions (see Schaeffer and Maynard, Chapter 28, this volume). Informed by a conversation-analytic perspective (see Sacks 1992; Sacks, Schegloff, and Jefferson 1974), he points to the discursive machinery apparent in interview transcripts. Highlighting evidence of the ways the interviewer and the respondent *mutually* monitor each other's speech exchanges, Mishler shows how the participants ongoingly and jointly construct in words their senses of the developing interview agenda. He notes, for example, that even token responses by the interviewer, such as "Hm hm," can serve as confirmatory markers that the respondent is on the "right" track for interview purposes. But, interestingly enough, not much can be done to eliminate even token responses, given that a fundamental rule of conversational exchange is that turns must be taken in the unfolding interview process. To eliminate even tokens or to refuse to take one's turn, however minimally, is, in effect, to stop the conversation, hence the interview. The dilemma here is striking in that it points to the practical need for interview participants to be linguistically animated, not just standardized and passive, in order to complete the interview conversation.

It goes without saying that this introduces us to a pair of subjects behind the interviewer and the respondent who are more conversationally active than standardization would imply, let alone tolerate. Following a number of conversation-analytic and linguistic arguments (Cicourel 1967, 1982; Gumperz 1982; Hymes 1967; Sacks et al. 1974), Mishler (1986) explains that each and every point in the series of speech exchanges that constitute an interview is, in effect, open to interactional work, activity that constructs communicative sense out of the participants as well as the subject matter under consideration. Thus, in contrast to the modeled asymmetry of the standardized interview, there is considerable communicative equality and interdependence in the speech activities of all interviewing, where participants invariably engage in the "joint construction of meaning," no matter how asymmetrical the informing model might seem:

> The discourse of the interview is jointly constructed by interviewer and respondent. . . . Both questions and responses are formulated in, developed through, and shaped by the discourse between interviewers and respondents. . . . An adequate understanding of interviews depends on recognizing how interviewers reformulate questions and how respondents frame answers in terms of their reciprocal understanding as meanings emerge during the course of an interview. (P. 52)

THE ISSUE OF "OWNING" NARRATIVE

Mishler's entry into the linguistic and conversation-analytic fray was fundamentally motivated by his desire to valorize the respondent's perspective and experience. This was, to some extent, a product of Mishler's long-standing professional interest in humanizing the doctor-patient encounter. His earlier book *The Discourse of Medicine: Dialectics of Medical Interviews* (1984) is important in that it shows how medical interviews can unwittingly but systematically abrogate the patient's sense of his or her own illness even in the sincerest doctor's search for medical knowledge. As an alternative, Mishler advocates more open-ended questions, minimal interruptions of patient accounts, and the use of patients' own linguistic formulations to encourage their own articulations of illness. Similarly, in the context of the research interview, Mishler urges us to consider ways that interviewing might be designed so that the respondent's voice comes through in greater detail, as a way of paying greater attention to respondent relevancies.

According to Mishler, this turns us forthrightly to respondents' stories. His view is that experience comes to us in the form of narratives. When we communicate our experiences to each other, we do so by storying them. When, in turn, we encourage elaboration, we commonly use such narrative devices as "Go on" and "Then what happened?" to prompt further storylike communication. It would be difficult to imagine how an experience of any kind could be conveyed except in narrative format, in terms that structure events into distinct plots, themes, and forms of characterization. Consequently, according to this view, we must leave our research efforts open to respondents' stories if we are to understand respondents' experiences in, and on, their own terms, leading to less formal control in the interview process.

Applied to the research interview, the "radical transformation of the traditional approach to interviewing" (Mishler 1986:117) serves to empower respondents. This resonates with a broadening concern with what is increasingly referred to as the respondent's *own* voice or authentic story (see the contributions to this volume by Platt, Chapter 2; Warren, Chapter 4; Fontana, Chapter 8; Riessman, Chapter 33; Ellis and Berger, Chapter 41). Although *story, narrative,* and the respondent's *voice* are the leading terms of reference, an equally key, yet unexplicated, usage is the term *own.* It appears throughout Mishler's discussion of empowerment, yet he gives it hardly any attention.

Consider several applications of the term *own* in Mishler's (1986) research interviewing text. In introducing a chapter titled "The Empowerment of Respondents," he writes, "I will be concerned primarily with the impact of different forms of practice on respondents' modes of understanding themselves and the world, on the possibility of their acting in terms of their *own* interests, on social scientists' ways of working and theorizing, and the social functions of scientific knowledge" (pp. 117-18; emphasis added). Further along, Mishler explains, "Various attempts to restructure the interviewee-interviewer relationship so as to empower respondents are designed to encourage them to find and speak in their *own* 'voices'" (p. 118; emphasis added). Finally, in pointing to the political potential of narrative, Mishler boldly flags the ownership in question: "To be empowered is not only to speak in one's *own* voice and to tell one's *own* story, but to apply the understanding arrived at to action in accord with one's *own* interests" (p. 119; emphasis added).

Mishler is admittedly being persuasive. Just as in his earlier book on medical interviews he encourages what Michael Balint (1964) and others (see Silverman 1987; Zoppi and Epstein, Chapter 18, this volume) have come to call *patient-centered medicine,* in his research interview book he advocates what might be called *respondent-centered research.* Mishler constructs a preferred version of the subject behind the respondent, one that allegedly gives voice to the respondent's own story. The image is one of a respondent who owns his or her experience, who, on his or her own, can narrate the story if given the opportunity. It is a story that is uniquely the respondent's in that only his or her own voice can articulate it authentically; any other voice or format would apparently detract from what this subject behind the respondent more genuinely and competently does on his or her own. Procedurally, the point is to provide the narrative opportunity for this ownership to be expressed, to reveal what presumably lies within.

But valorizing the individual's ownership of his or her story is a mere step away from seeing the subject as a vessel of answers. As we discussed earlier, this subject is passive and, wittingly or not, taken to be a mere repository of information, opinion, and sentiment. More subtly, perhaps, the subject behind the respondent who "owns" his or her story is viewed as virtually possessing what we seek to know about. Mishler's advice is that we provide respondents with the opportunity to convey these stories to us on their own terms rather than deploy predesignated categories or other structured formats for doing so. This, Mishler claims, empowers respondents.

Nevertheless, the passive vessel of answers is still there in its essential detail. It is now more deeply embedded in the subject, perhaps, but it is as passively secured in the inner reaches of the respondent as the vessel informing the survey respondent's subjectivity (see Johnson, Chapter 5, this volume). We might say that the subject behind the standardized interview respondent is a highly rationalized version of the romanticized subject envisioned by Mishler, one who harbors his or her own story. Both visions are rhetorics of subjectivity that have historically been used to account for the "truths" of experience. Indeed, we might say that the standardized interview produces a different narrative of experience than does the empowered interviewing style that Mishler and others advocate. This is not meant to disparage, but only to point out that when the question of subjectivity is raised, the resulting complications of the interview are as epistemological as they are invidious.

It is important to emphasize that the ownership in question results from a preferred subjectivity, not from an experiential subject that is more essential than all other subjects. It is, as Silverman and his associates remind us, a romanticized discourse of its own and, although it has contributed immensely to our understanding of the variety of "others" we can be, it does not empower absolutely (see Silverman 1987, 1993; Atkinson and Silverman 1997). Rather, it empowers in relation to the kinds of stories that one can ostensibly own, that would seem to be genuine, or that are otherwise accountably recognized as fitting or authentic to oneself in the particular times and places they are conveyed.

A DISCOURSE OF EMPOWERMENT

Invoking a discourse of empowerment is a way of giving both rhetorical and practical spin to how we conduct interviews. Like all discourses, the discourse of individual empowerment deploys preferred terms of reference. For example, in the discourse of the standardized survey interview, the interview encounter is asymmetrical and the operating principle is control. Participants have different functions: One side asks questions and records information, and the other side provides answers to the questions asked. Procedurally, the matter of control is centered on keeping these functions and their roles separate. Accordingly, an important operating rule is that the interviewer does not provide answers or offer opinions. Conversely, the respondent is encouraged to answer questions, not ask them. Above all, the language of the enterprise locates knowledge within the respondent, but control rests with the interviewer.

The terms of reference change significantly when the interview is more symmetrical or, as Mishler puts it, when the respondent is empowered. The interviewer and respondent are referred to jointly as interview *participants,* highlighting their collective contribution to the enterprise. This works against asymmetry, emphasizing a more fundamental sense of the shared task at hand, which now becomes a form of "collaboration" in the production of meaning. One procedure for setting this tone is to make it clear that all participants in the interview can effectively raise questions related to the topics under consideration. Equally important, everyone should understand that answers are not meant to be conclusive but instead serve to further the agenda for discussion. The result, then, is more of a team effort, rather than a division of labor, even though the discourse of empowerment still aims to put the narrative ball in the respondent's court, so to speak.

Assiduously concerned with the need to "redistribute power" in the interview encounter, Mishler (1986) argues compellingly for the more equalized relationship he envisions. Seeking a redefinition of roles, he describes what he has in mind:

> These types of role redefinitions may be characterized briefly by the following terms referring respectively to the relationship between interviewee and interviewer as informant and reporter, as research collaborators, and as learner/actor and advocate. Taking on the roles of each successive pair in this series involves a more comprehensive and more radical transformation of the power relationship inherent in traditional roles, and each succeeding pair of roles relies on and absorbs the earlier one. (Pp. 122-23)

The use of the prefix *co-* is commonplace in such discussions, further signaling symmetry. Participants often become "coparticipants" and, of course, the word *collaboration* speaks for itself in this context. Some

authors even refer to the interview encounter as a "conversational partnership" (Rubin and Rubin 1995).

Mishler's discourse of collaboration and empowerment extends to the representation of interview material, taking *co-* into new territory. In discussing the role of the advocate, for instance, Mishler describes Kai Erikson's (1976) activity as a researcher hired by attorneys representing the residents affected by the 1972 dam collapse in the Buffalo Creek valley of West Virginia. Erikson was advocating for the surviving residents, several of whom he interviewed, but not the local coal company from which they were seeking damages. The researcher and the sponsor clearly collaborated with each other in representing interview materials.

Others are not as forthrightly political in their corepresentations. Laurel Richardson (see Chapter 42, this volume), for example, discusses alternative textual choices in relation to the presentation of the respondent's "own" story. Research interviews, she reminds us, are usually conducted for research audiences. Whether they are closed- or open-ended, the questions and answers are formulated with the analytic interests of researchers in mind. Sociologists, for example, may wish to consider how gender, race, or class background shapes respondents' opinions, so they will tailor questions and interpret answers in these terms. Ultimately, researchers will represent interview material in the frameworks and languages of their research concerns and in disciplinary terms. But, as Richardson points out, respondents might not figure that their experiences or opinions are best understood that way. Additionally, Richardson asks us whether the process of coding interview responses for research purposes itself disenfranchises respondents, transforming their narratives into terms foreign to what their original sensibilities might have been (see also Briggs, Chapter 44, this volume).

Richardson suggests that a radically different textual form can help us to represent the respondent's experience more inventively, and authentically. Using poetry rather than prose, for example, capitalizes on poetry's culturally understood role of evoking and making meaning, not just conveying it. This extends to poetry's alleged capacity to communicate meaning where prose is said to be inadequate, in the way that folk poetry is used in some quarters to represent the ineffable (see Gubrium 1988). It is not uncommon, for instance, for individuals to say that plain words can't convey what they mean or that they simply cannot put certain experiences into words, something that, ironically, poetry might accomplish in poetic terms.

How, then, are such experiences and their opinions to be communicated in interviews? Must some respondents literally sing the blues, for example, as folks traditionally have done in the rural South of the United States? Should some experiences be "performed," rather than simply translated into text? Do mere retellings of others' experiences compromise the ability of those who experience them to convey the "scenic presence" of the actual experiences in their lives? A number of researchers take such issues to heart and have been experimenting, for several years now, with alternative representational forms that they believe can convey respondents' experience more on, if not in, their own terms (see Clifford and Marcus 1986; Ellis and Flaherty 1992; Ellis and Bochner 1996; Reed-Danahay 1997; see also in this volume Fontana, Chapter 8; Ellis and Berger, Chapter 41). The border between fact and fiction itself is being explored for its empowering capacity, taking empowerment's informing discourse firmly into the realm of literature (see Rosenblatt, Chapter 43, this volume).

◆ Voice and Ownership

When we empower the respondent (or the informing coparticipant) in the interview encounter, we establish a space for the respondent's *own* story to be heard—at least this is the reasoning behind Mishler's and others' aims in this regard. But questions do arise in relation to the voices we listen to when we provide respondents the opportunity to convey their own stories. Whose voices do we hear? From where do respondents obtain the material they communicate to us in interviews? Is there always only one story for a given respondent to tell, or can there be several to choose from? If the latter, the question can become, Which among these is most tellable under the circumstances? And, as if these questions weren't challenging enough, do the queries themselves presume that they are answerable in straightforward terms, or do answers to them turn in different directions and get worked out in the very course of the interview in narrative practice?

SUBJECT POSITIONS AND RELATED VOICES

An anecdote from Jaber Gubrium's doctoral supervision duties speaks to the heart of these issues. Gubrium was serving on the dissertation committee of a graduate student who was researching substance abuse among pharmacists. The student was especially keen to allow the pharmacists being interviewed to convey in their own words their experiences of illicitly using drugs, seeking help for their habits, and going through rehabilitation. He hoped to understand how those who "should know better" would account for what happened to them.

When the interviews were completed, the student analyzed the interview data thematically and presented the themes in the dissertation along with individual accounts of experience. Interestingly, several of the themes identified in the pharmacists' stories closely paralleled the familiar recovery rubrics of self-help groups such as Alcoholics Anonymous (A.A.) and Narcotics Anonymous (N.A.). Gubrium noted this, and it turned out that many, if not all, of the pharmacists had participated in these recovery groups and evidently had incorporated the groups' ways of narrating the substance abuse experience into their "own" stories. For example, respondents spoke of the experience of "hitting bottom" and organized the trajectory of the recovery process in relation to that very important low point in their lives. Gubrium raised the issue of the extent to which the interview material could be analyzed as the pharmacists' "own" stories as opposed to the stories of these recovery programs. At a doctoral committee meeting, he asked, "Whose voice do we hear when these pharmacists tell their stories? Their own or N.A.'s?" He asked, in effect, whether the stories belonged to these individuals or to the organizations that promulgated their discourse.

The issue of voice is important because it points to the subject who is assumed to be responding in interviews (Gubrium 1993; Holstein and Gubrium 2000). Voice references the subject position that is taken for granted behind speech. Voice works at the level of everyday life, whereas subject positions are what we imagine to be their operating standpoints. This is the working side of our earlier discussion of the subjects behind interview participants. The possibility of alternative voicings and varied subject positions turned researchers' attention to concerns such as how interview participants collaborate to construct the interview's shifting subjectivities in relation to the topics under consideration.

Empirically, the concept of voice leads us to the question of who—or what subject —speaks over the course of an interview and from what standpoint. For example, does a 50-year-old man offer the opinions of a "professional" at the apex of his successful career, or might his voice be that of a husband and father reflecting on what he has missed as a result in the way of family life? Or will he speak as a church elder, a novice airplane pilot, or the "enabling" brother of an alcoholic as the interview unfolds? All of these are possible, given the range of contemporary experiences that he could call upon to account for his opinions.

At the same time, it is important to entertain the possibility that the respondent's subjectivity and variable voices emerge out of the immediate interview's interaction and are not necessarily preformed in the respondent's ostensible vessel of answers. Indeed, topics raised in the interview may incite respondents to voice subjectivities never contemplated before.

As noted earlier, at times one can actually hear interview participants indicate subject positions. Verbal prefaces, for example, can provide clues to subject position and voice, but they are often ignored in interview research. Phrases such as "to put myself in someone else's shoes" and "to put on a different hat" are signals that respondents employ to voice shifts in position. Acknowledging this, in an interview study of nurses on the qualities of good infant care, we probably would not be surprised to hear a respondent say something like, "That's when I have my RN cap on, but as a mother, I might tell you a different story." Sometimes respondents are quite forthright in giving voice to alternative points of view in precisely those terms, as when a respondent prefaces remarks with, say, "Well, from the point of view of a . . . ." Such phrases are not interview debris; they convey the important and persistent subjective work of the interview encounter.

In the actual practice of asking interview questions and giving answers, things are seldom so straightforward, however. An interview, for example, might start under the assumption that a father or a mother is being interviewed, which the interview's introductions might appear to confirm. But there is no guarantee that particular subjectivities will prevail throughout. There's the matter of the *ongoing* construction of subjectivity, which unfolds with the give-and-take of the interview encounter. Something said later in the interview, for example, might prompt the respondent to figure, not necessarily audibly, that he really had, "all along," been responding from a quite different point of view than was evident at the start. Unfortunately, shifts in subjectivity are not always evident in so many words or comments. Indeed, the possibility of an unforeseen change in subjectivity might not be evident until the very end of an interview, if at all, when a respondent remarks for the first time, "Yeah, that's the way all of us who were raised down South do with our children," making it unclear which subject had been providing responses to the interviewer's questions—the voice of this individual parent or her regional membership and its associated experiential sensibilities.

Adding to these complications, subject position and voice must also be considered in relation to the perceived voice of the interviewer. Who, after all, is the interviewer in the eyes of the respondent? How will the interviewer role be positioned into the conversational matrix? For example, respondents in debriefings might comment that an interviewer sounded more like a company man than a human being, or that a particular interviewer made the respondent feel that the interviewer was "just an ordinary person, like myself." Indeed, even issues of social justice might creep in and position the interviewer, say, as a worthless hack, as the respondent takes the interviewer to be "just one more token of the establishment," choosing to silence her own voice in the process (see Dunbar, Rodriguez, and Parker, Chapter 14, this volume). This raises the possibility that the respondent's working subjectivity is constructed out of the unfolding interpersonal reflections of the interview participants' attendant historical experiences. It opens to consideration, for example, an important question: If the interviewee had not been figured to be just an "ordinary" respondent, who (which subject) might the respondent have been in giving voice to his or her opinions?

As if this doesn't muddy the interview waters enough, imagine what the acknowledgment of multiple subjectivities does to the concept of sample size, another dimension figured to be under considerable control in traditional interview research. To decompose the designated respondent into

his or her (multiple) working subjects is to raise the possibility that any single element of a sample can expand or contract in size in the course of the interview, increasing or decreasing the sample n accordingly. Treating subject positions and their associated voices seriously, we might find that an ostensibly single interview could actually be, in practice, an interview with several subjects, whose particular identities may be only partially clear. Under the circumstances, to be satisfied that one has completed an interview with a single respondent and to code it as such because it was formally conducted with a single embodied individual is to be rather cavalier about the complications of subjectivity and of the narrative organization of sample size.

As Mishler (1986) has pointed out, such matters have traditionally been treated as technical issues in interview research. Still, they have long been informally recognized, and an astute positivistic version of the complexities entailed has been theorized and researched with great care and insight (see, for example, Fishbein 1967). Jean Converse and Howard Schuman's (1974) delightful book on survey research as interviewers see it, for instance, illuminates this recognition with intriguing case material.

There is ample reason, then, for some researchers to approach the interview as a set of activities that are ongoingly accomplished, not just completed. In standardized interviewing, one would need to settle conclusively on matters of who the subject behind the respondent is, lest it be impossible to know to which population generalizations can be made. Indeed, a respondent who shifts the subject to whom she is giving voice would pose dramatic technical difficulties for survey researchers, such that, for example, varied parts of a single completed interview would have to be coded as the responses of different subjects and be generalizable to different populations. This takes us well beyond the possibility of coding in the traditional sense of the term, a point that, of course, Harold Garfinkel (1967) and Aaron Cicourel (1964), among others, made years ago and that, oddly enough, inspired the approach Mishler advocates.

OWNERSHIP AND EMPOWERMENT

Having raised these vexing issues, can we ever effectively address the question of who owns the opinions and stories expressed in interviews, including both the standardized interview and the more open-ended, narrative form? Whose "own" story do we obtain in the process of interviewing? Can we ever discern ownership in individual terms? And how does this relate to respondent empowerment?

Recall that ownership implies that the respondent has, or has title to, a story and that the interview can be designed to bring this forth. But the concept of voice suggests that this is not as straightforward as it might seem. The very activity of opening the interview to extended discussion among the participants indicates that ownership can be a joint or collaborative matter, if not rather fleeting in designation. In practice, the idea of "own story" is not just a commendable research goal but something participants themselves seek to resolve as they move through the interview conversation. Each participant tentatively engages the interactive problems of ownership as a way of sorting out the assumed subjectivities in question and proceeds on that basis, for the practical communicative purposes of completing the interview.

When a respondent such as a substance-abusing pharmacist responds to a question about the future, "I've learned [from N.A.] that it's best to take it one day at a time; I really believe that," it is clear that the pharmacist's narrative is more than an individual's story. What he owns would seem to have wended its way through the informing voices of other subjectivities: Narcotics Anonymous's recovery ideology, this particular respondent's articulation of that ideology, the communicative twists on both discourses that emerge in the give-and-take of the interview exchange, the project's own framing of the issues and resulting agenda of questions, the interviewer's ongoing articulation of that agenda, and the reflexively collaborative flow of unforeseen voiced and unvoiced subjectivities operating in the unfolding exchange. What's more, all of these together can raise metacommunicative concerns about "what this [the interview] is all about, anyway," which the respondent might ask at any time. Under the circumstances, it would seem that ownership is something rather diffusely spread about the topical and processual landscape of speech activities entailed in the interview.

Respondent empowerment would appear to be a working, rather than definitive, feature of these speech activities. It is not clear in practice how one could distinguish any one respondent's own story from the tellable stories available to this and other respondents, which they might more or less share. Putting it in terms of "tellable stories" further complicates voice, subjectivity, and empowerment. And, at the other end of the spectrum of what is tellable, there are those perplexing responses that, in the respondent's search for help in formulating an answer, can return "power" to the very source that would hold it in the first place. It is not uncommon to hear respondents remark that they are not sure how they feel or what they think, or that they haven't really thought about the question or topic before, or to hear them actually think out loud about what it might mean personally to convey particular sentiments or answer in a specific way—and ask the interviewer for assistance in doing so.

Philosophically, the central issue here is a version of Ludwig Wittgenstein's (1953) "private language" problem. Wittgenstein argues that because language—and, by implication, stories and other interview responses—is a shared "form of life," the idea that one could have available exclusively to oneself an unshared, private language would not make much sense. Given the reflexive duality of self-consciousness, one could not even share an ostensible private language with oneself. In more practical terms, this means that whatever is conveyed by the respondent to the interviewer is always subject to the question of what it means, in which case we're back to square one with shared knowledge and the various "language games" that can be collaboratively engaged by interview participants to assign meaning to these questions and responses. Empowerment in this context is not so much a matter of providing the communicative means for the respondent to tell his or her "own" story as it is a matter of recognizing, first, that responses or stories, as the case might be, are collaborative accomplishments and, second, that there are as many individual responses or stories to tell as there are recognizable forms of response. This, of course, ultimately brings us full circle to the analytically hoary problem of whose interests are being served when the individually "empowered" respondent speaks, implicating power in relation to the broader social horizons of speech and discourse.

Kirin Narayan and Kenneth George (Chapter 39, this volume) inform us further that empowerment is also a cultural prerogative, something that the interviewer does not expressly control and, given the opportunity, cannot simply choose to put into effect. Cultures of storytelling enter into the decision as to whether there is even a story to convey or relevant experiences to highlight. Although the democratization of opinion potentially turns interviewers toward any and all individuals for their accounts, not all individuals believe that their opinions are worthy of communication. The Asian Indian women Narayan interviewed, for example, did not think they had opinions worth telling unless they had done "something different" with their lives. It had to be something "special"; as one woman put it, "You ate, drank, slept, served

your husband and brought up your children. What's the story in that?" This powerfully affected the stories that were heard in the area, tying ownership to the local relevance of one's narrative resources.

GOING CONCERNS AND DISCURSIVE ENVIRONMENTS

Where do tellable stories and other forms of response come from if they are not owned by individuals? How do they figure in what is said in interview situations? It was evident in the previous discussion of the pharmacist drug abuse research that respondents were making use of a very common notion of recovery in today's world, one that seems to have percolated through the entire troubles treatment industry (Gubrium and Holstein 2001). Do this industry and other institutions dealing with human experiences offer us a clue to the question of narrative ownership? Do Narayan's respondents proffer agendas of social, not just individual, relevance?

Erving Goffman's (1961) exploration of what he calls "moral careers" provides a point of departure for addressing such questions. Goffman was especially concerned with the moral careers of stigmatized persons such as mental patients, but the social concerns of his approach are broadly suggestive. In his reckoning, each of us has many selves and associated ways of accounting for our thoughts and actions. According to Goffman, individuals obtain senses of who they are as they move through the various moral environments that offer specifications for identity. A mental hospital, for example, provides patients with particular selves, including ways of presenting who one is, one's past, and one's future. The moral environment of the mental hospital also provides others, such as staff members, acquaintances, and even strangers, with parallel sensibilities toward the patient. In other words, moral environments deploy localized universes of choice for constructing subjectivity, relatedly providing a shared format for voicing participants' selves, thoughts, and feelings. Goffman's view is not so much that these environments govern who and what people are as individuals, but that individuals—everyday actors—strategically play out who and what they are as the moral agents of particular circumstances.

Goffman is mainly concerned with the face-to-face situations that constitute daily life; he is less concerned with institutional matters. Still, his analysis of moral careers in relation to what he calls "total institutions" points us in an important direction, toward what Everett Hughes ([1942] 1984) calls the "going concerns" of today's world. This is Hughes's way of emphasizing that institutions are not only concerns in having formal and informal mandates; they are social forms that *ongoingly* provide distinct patterning for our thoughts, words, sentiments, and actions.

From the myriad formal organizations in which we work, study, pray, play, and recover to the countless informal associations and networks to which we belong, to our affiliations with racial, ethnic, and gendered groupings, we engage a panoply of going concerns on a daily basis. Taken together, they set the "conditions of possibility" (Foucault 1988) for identity—for who and what we could possibly be. Many of these going concerns explicitly structure or reconfigure personal identity. All variety of human service agencies, for example, readily delve into the deepest enclaves of the self in order to ameliorate personal ills. Self-help organizations seem to crop up on every street corner, and self-help literature beckons us from the book spindles of supermarkets and the shelves of every bookstore. "Psychobabble" on radio and TV talk shows constantly prompts us to formulate (or reformulate) who and what we are, urging us to give voice to the selves we live by. The self is increasingly *deprivatized* (even if it never was private in Wittgenstein's terms in the first place), constructed and interpreted under the auspices of these decidedly public going concerns (Gubrium and Holstein 1995, 2000; Holstein and Gubrium 2000).

Since early in the 20th century, social life has come into the purview of countless institutions whose moral function is to assemble, alter, and reformulate our lives and selves (see Gubrium and Holstein 2001). We refer to these as *discursive environments* because they provide choices for how we articulate our lives and selves. Discursive environments are interactional domains characterized by distinctive ways of interpreting and representing everyday life, of speaking about who and what we are. Institutions such as schools, correctional facilities, clinics, family courts, support groups, recreational clubs, fitness centers, and self-improvement programs promote particular ways of speaking of life. They are families of language games, as it were, for formulating our opinions. They furnish discourses of subjectivity that are accountably put into discursive practice as individuals give voice to experience, such as they are now widely asked to do in interviews.

These going concerns pose new challenges to the concept of the individual respondent, to voice, and to the idea of empowerment. They are not especially hostile to the personal; indeed, they are often in the business of reconstructing the personal from the ground up. Rather, today's variegated landscape of discursive environments provides complex options for who we could be, the conditions of possibility we mentioned earlier. This is the world of multiple subjects and of ways to give voice to them that respondents now increasingly bring with them into interviews, whose discursive resources also figure significantly in marking narrative relevance.

In turn, these environments also provide the source of socially relevant questions that interviewers pose to respondents. Those who conduct surveys, for example, are often sponsored by the very agents who formulate these applicable discourses. The collaborative production of the respondent's own story is therefore shaped, for better or worse, in response to markets and concerns spread well beyond the give-and-take of the individual interview conversation.

This brings us back, full circle, to the interview society. The research context is not the only place in which we are asked interview questions. All the going concerns mentioned above and more are in the interviewing business, all constructing and marshaling the subjects they need to do their work. Each provides a social context for narrative practice, for the collaborative production of the identities and experiences that come to be viewed as the moral equivalents of respondents and interview responses. Medical clinics deploy interviews and, in the process, assemble doctors, patients, and their illnesses (see Zoppi and Epstein, Chapter 18, this volume). Personnel officers interview job applicants and collect information that forms the basis for employment decisions (see Latham and Millman, Chapter 23, this volume). Therapists of all stripes conduct counseling interviews, and now increasingly assemble narrative plots of experiences, which are grounds for further rehabilitative interviewing (see Miller et al., Chapter 19, this volume). The same is true for schools, forensic investigation, and journalistic interviewing, among the broad range of institutional contexts that shape our lives through their collaborative speech activities (see in this volume Altheide, Chapter 20; McKenzie, Chapter 21; Tierney and Dilley, Chapter 22).

The interview society expands the institutional auspices of interviewing well beyond the research context. Indeed, it would have been mistakenly restrictive to limit the purview of this *Handbook* to the research interview alone. Social research is only one of the many sites where subjectivities and the voicing of individual experience are undertaken. What's more, these various going concerns cannot be considered to be independent of one another. As our pharmacist anecdote suggests, the discursive environments of therapy and recovery can be brought directly into the research interview, serving to commingle an agglomeration of institutional voices.

Interview formats are themselves going concerns. The group interview, for example, can take us into a veritable swirl of subject formations and opinion construction, as participants share and make use of narrative material from a broader range of discursive environments than any single one of them might muster to account for his or her experience alone (see Morgan, Chapter 7, this volume). Life story and oral history interviews extend the biographical particulars of the subject and subject matter in time, producing respondents who are incited to trace opinion from early to late life and across eras, something that can be amazingly convoluted when compared to the commonly detemporalized information elicited from cross-sectional survey respondents (see in this volume Atkinson, Chapter 6; Cándida Smith, Chapter 34). The in-depth interview extends experience in emotional terms, affectively elaborating the subject (see Johnson, Chapter 5, this volume).

Identity politics, too, forms going concerns. Although we now might consider that both men and women are proper subjects for interviews, the contributions to this volume on men as respondents, by Michael Schwalbe and Michelle Wolkomir (Chapter 10), and on women as respondents, by Shulamit Reinharz and Susan Chase (Chapter 11), present men and women as "distinctly" historical, if not political, subjects. The idea of interviewing men as men, for example, and not simply assuming that they are general respondents, is of recent vintage, and undoubtedly also is a gendered political response to feminist self-consciousness, according to Schwalbe and Wolkomir. The same can be said for the other "distinctive" respondents discussed in Part II of this *Handbook*. The point here is that, whether responses give voice, say, to children as such, or to gays and lesbians, particular ethnic and racial groups, older people, social elites, or the seriously ill, they are products of the rubrics we bring to bear in prompting ourselves or in being prompted by others to give voice to experience, not just the products of individual empowerment.

◆ Artfulness and Narrative Practice

Lest we socially overdetermine subjectivity, it is important to emphasize that the practice of interviewing does not simply incorporate wholesale the identities proffered by institutionalized concerns and cultural relevancies. Interview participants themselves are actively involved in how these subjectivities are put into play. Although varied institutional auspices provide particular resources for asking and answering questions, prescribe the roles played by interview participants, and privilege certain accounts, interview participants do not behave like robots and adopt and reproduce these resources and roles in their speech activities. If participants are accountable to particular circumstances, such as job interviews, medical diagnostic encounters, or journalistic interviews, they nonetheless borrow from the variety of narrative resources available to them. In this regard, they are more "artful" (Garfinkel 1967) than automatic in realizing their respective roles and voices. This extends to all interview participants, as both interviewers and respondents collaboratively assemble who and what they are in narrative practice.

Our pharmacist anecdote is an important case in point. Although the interviews in question were formal research encounters, it was evident that respondents were not only reporting their "own" experiences, but were interpolating their "own" stories, in part, in N.A. recovery terms. They drew from their experiences in recovery groups to convey to the interviewer what it felt like to be "taken over" by drugs. Several respondents used the familiar metaphor of "hitting bottom" to convey a trajectory for the experience. But these respondents were not simply mouthpieces for Narcotics Anonymous; they gave their own individual spins to the terminology, which, in turn, were selectively applied in their responses. For example, "hitting bottom" meant different things to different respondents, depending on the biographical particulars of their lives. How hitting bottom narratively figured in one respondent's comments was no guarantee of how it might figure in another's.

Interviewers, too, are artful in coordinating the interview process, even in the context of the standardized survey, which employs rather formalized procedures (see in this volume Schaeffer and Maynard, Chapter 28; Baker, Chapter 37). In some forms of interviewing, such as in-depth interviews, interviewers may use all of the personal narrative resources at their disposal to establish open and trusting relationships with respondents (see Johnson, Chapter 5, this volume). This may involve extensive self-disclosure, following on the assumption that reciprocal self-disclosure is likely.

Taking this a step farther, a growing postmodern trend in interviewing deliberately blurs the line between the interviewer and the respondent, moving beyond symmetry to a considerable overlap of roles (see Fontana, Chapter 8, this volume). Although this may have been characteristic of in-depth interviewing for years, postmodern sensibilities aim for an associated representational inventiveness as much as deep disclosure. Artfulness extends to the representation of interviewers' and researchers' own reflective collaborations in moving from respondent to respondent as the project develops, as Carolyn Ellis and Leigh Berger show in their contribution to this volume (Chapter 41). Of course, interviewers and their sponsoring researchers have always collaborated on the design of interviews and offered collaborative feedback to one another on the interview process. But there is a distinct difference here:

Ellis and Berger choose not to separate this from their interview materials. In layered writing, they provide us with an intriguing account of how interviewers interviewing each other artfully and fruitfully combine the interview "data" with their own related life experiences to broaden and enrich the results. Their reflections collaboratively impel them forward to complete additional interviews and revisit old ones in new and interesting ways. The separation in conventional research reports of interviewers' experiences from those of respondents, they argue, is highly artificial and produces sanitized portrayals of the "data" in question. According to Ellis and Berger, researchers may capture collaborative richness by forthrightly presenting the full round of narrative practices that generate responses. Artfulness derives from the interpretive work that is undertaken in mingling together what interviewers draw upon to make meaning in the interview process and what respondents themselves bring along.

Further blurring boundaries, Narayan and George (Chapter 39, this volume) provide a delightful jaunt through the artful relationship between what they call personal narratives and folk narratives. The former allegedly are the idiosyncratic individual stories that anthropologists regularly encounter in their fieldwork, accounts of experience considered to be peculiar to their storytellers. Folk narratives, in contrast, are ostensibly those shared tales of experience common to a group or culture. They are part of the narrative tradition and, in their telling, are a cultural accounting of the experiences in question. But, as Narayan and George explain, in their respective attempts to obtain life stories from respondents in various parts of the globe, what was personal and what was folk was never clearly demarcated. Individual respondents made use of what was shared to represent themselves as individuals, so that, narratively, who any "one" was, was mediated artfully by various applications of common usage. In turn, the cultural particulars embodied in folktales were constantly being applied in both old and new ways in personal accounts. Biography and culture, in other words, were mutually implicative and alive in their narrative renderings; their interviews both reproduced and invented participants' lives (see also Abu-Lughod 1993; Behar 1993; Degh 1969; Narayan 1997).

In some sense, then, although the aim of empowering respondents is certainly attractive and to be encouraged in principle, interview participants are always already "empowered" to engage artfully in a vast range of discursive practices. Even "asymmetrical" interview conversations require the active involvement of both parties. Although interview preferences and politics move in various directions, interview participants nonetheless actively and artfully engage the auspices of the interview and their own biographies at many levels. As Foucault might put it, power is everywhere in the interview's exploration and explication of experience. Even the standardized survey interview, which seemingly allocates all power to the researcher, deploys it elsewhere in the collaboratively constructive vocalization of "individual" opinion.

◆ Interviewing as Cultural Production

The interview is certainly more than what it seemed to be at the start of this chapter; we have taken it well beyond a simple and self-evident encounter between interviewer and respondent. As we moved from the individual interview to the interview society, we noted that the interview is among our most commonplace means for constructing individualized experience. We recognized, too, that by virtue of our widespread participation in interviews, each and every one of us is implicated in the production of who and what we are as the collection of individual subjects that populate our lives.

Of course, interviewing is found in places where it has been for decades, such as in applying for jobs, in clinical encounters, and in the telephone surveys of public opinion polling. But it has also penetrated formerly hidden spaces, such as the foothills of the Himalayas and the everyday worlds of children and the seriously ill. Interviews are everywhere these days, as researchers pursue respondents to the ends of the earth, as we offer our opinions and preferences to pollsters, in Internet questionnaires, and to marketing researchers, as we bare our souls to therapists and healers in the "privacy" of the clinic as well as in the mass media.

With its penetration and globalization, the interview has become a worldwide form of cultural production. Regardless of social venue or geographic location—characteristics that were once argued to be empirically distinct or interpersonally isolating—the methodical application of interview technology is bringing us into a single world of accounts and accountability. Despite its community borders and national and linguistic boundaries, it is a world that can be described in the common language of sample characteristics and whose subjectivities can be represented in terms of individualized voices. Whereas we once might have refrained from examining Asian village women's stories in relation to the accounts of their urban European counterparts—because the two groups were understood to be culturally and geographically distinct—the women's ability to respond to interviews now makes it possible for us to compare their experiences in the same methodological terms.

The interview is such a common information-gathering procedure that it seems to bring all experience together narratively. Of course, there are technical challenges and local narrative solutions that cannot be overlooked. But technology is only the procedural scaffolding of what is a broad culturally productive enterprise. More and more, the interview society provides both a sense of who we are and the method by which we represent ourselves and our experiences. This returns us to the leading theme of this *Handbook:* The interview is part and parcel of society, not simply a mode of inquiry into and about society. If it is part of, not just a conduit to, our personal lives, then we might well entertain the possibility that the interview's ubiquity serves to produce communicatively and ramify the very culture it ostensibly only inquires about.

It is in the spirit of this cultural, as well as its constituent technical, activity that this *Handbook* is presented. As the contributors deftly describe the interview's varied modalities, distinctive respondents, technical dimensions, auspices, analytic strategies, and reflections and representations, they also specify the most common procedural facilitator for the expression of experience of our times.

■ *References*

Abu-Lughod, L. 1993. *Writing Women's Worlds: Bedouin Stories.* Berkeley: University of California Press.

Alasuutari, P. 1998. *An Invitation to Social Research.* London: Sage.

Atkinson, P. and D. Silverman. 1997. "Kundera's *Immortality*: The Interview Society and the Invention of Self." *Qualitative Inquiry* 3:304-25.

Balint, M. 1964. *The Doctor, His Patient, and the Illness.* London: Pitman.

Behar, R. 1993. *Translated Woman: Crossing the Border with Esperanza's Story.* Boston: Beacon.

Benney, M. and E. C. Hughes. 1956. "Of Sociology and the Interview." *American Journal of Sociology* 62:137-42.

Briggs, C. L. 1986. *Learning How to Ask: A Sociolinguistic Appraisal of the Role of the Interview in Social Science Research.* Cambridge: Cambridge University Press.

Carrithers, M., S. Collins, and S. Lukes, eds. 1985. *The Category of the Person.* Cambridge: Cambridge University Press.

Cicourel, A. V. 1964. *Method and Measurement in Sociology.* New York: Free Press.

———. 1967. "Fertility, Family Planning, and the Social Organization of Family Life: Some Methodological Issues." *Journal of Social Issues* 23:57-81.

———. 1982. "Interviews, Surveys, and the Problem of Ecological Validity." *American Sociologist* 17:11-20.

Clifford, J. and G. E. Marcus, eds. 1986. *Writing Culture: The Poetics and Politics of Ethnography.* Berkeley: University of California Press.

Converse, J. M. and H. Schuman. 1974. *Conversations at Random: Survey Research as Interviewers See It.* New York: John Wiley.

Degh, L. 1969. *Folktales and Society: Story Telling in a Hungarian Peasant Community.* Translated by E. M. Schossberger. Bloomington: Indiana University Press.

Dreyfus, H. L. and P. Rabinow. 1982. *Michel Foucault: Beyond Structuralism and Hermeneutics.* Chicago: University of Chicago Press.

Ellis, C. and A. P. Bochner, eds. 1996. *Composing Ethnography: Alternative Forms of Qualitative Writing.* Walnut Creek, CA: AltaMira.

Ellis, C. and M. G. Flaherty, eds. 1992. *Investigating Subjectivity: Research on Lived Experience.* Newbury Park, CA: Sage.

Erikson, K. T. 1976. *Everything in Its Path: Destruction of Community in the Buffalo Creek Flood.* New York: Simon & Schuster.

Fishbein, M., ed. 1967. *Readings in Attitude Theory and Measurement.* New York: John Wiley.

Foucault, M. 1973. *Madness and Civilization: A History of Insanity in the Age of Reason.* New York: Vintage.

———. 1975. *The Birth of the Clinic: An Archeology of Medical Perception.* New York: Vintage.

———. 1977. *Discipline and Punish: The Birth of the Prison.* Translated by A. M. Sheridan. New York: Vintage.

———. 1978. *The History of Sexuality,* Vol. 1, *An Introduction.* Translated by R. Hurley. New York: Vintage.

———. 1988. *Technologies of the Self.* Edited by L. H. Martin, H. Gutman, and P. H. Hutton. Amherst: University of Massachusetts Press.

Garfinkel, H. 1967. *Studies in Ethnomethodology.* Englewood Cliffs, NJ: Prentice Hall.

Garland, D. 1997. " 'Governmentality' and the Problem of Crime." *Theoretical Criminology* 1:173-214.

Geertz, C. 1984. " 'From the Native's Point of View': On the Nature of Anthropological Understanding." Pp. 123-37 in *Culture Theory,* edited by R. A. Shweder and R. LeVine. Cambridge: Cambridge University Press.

Goffman, E. 1961. *Asylums: Essays on the Social Situation of Mental Patients and Other Inmates.* Garden City, NY: Doubleday.

Gubrium, J. F. 1988. "Incommunicables and Poetic Documentation in the Alzheimer's Disease Experience." *Semiotica* 72:235-53.

———. 1993. "Voice and Context in a New Gerontology." Pp. 46-63 in *Voices and Visions of Aging: Toward a Critical Gerontology,* edited by T. R. Cole, W. A. Achenbaum, P. L. Jakobi, and R. Kastenbaum. New York: Springer.

Gubrium, J. F. and J. A. Holstein. 1995. "Qualitative Inquiry and the Deprivatization of Experience." *Qualitative Inquiry* 1:204-22.

———. 1997. *The New Language of Qualitative Method.* New York: Oxford University Press.

———. 2000. "The Self in a World of Going Concerns." *Symbolic Interaction* 23:95-115.

———, eds. 2001. *Institutional Selves: Troubled Identities in a Postmodern World.* New York: Oxford University Press.

Gumperz, J. J. 1982. *Discourse Strategies.* Cambridge: Cambridge University Press.

Holstein, J. A. and J. F. Gubrium. 1995. *The Active Interview.* Thousand Oaks, CA: Sage.

———. 2000. *The Self We Live By: Narrative Identity in a Postmodern World.* New York: Oxford University Press.

Hughes, E. C. [1942] 1984. *The Sociological Eye: Selected Papers.* Chicago: Aldine.

Hymes, D. 1967. "Models of the Interaction of Language and Social Setting." *Journal of Social Issues* 33:8-28.

James, W. [1892] 1961. *Psychology: The Briefer Course.* New York: Harper & Brothers.

Kahn, R. L. and C. F. Cannell. 1957. *The Dynamics of Interviewing: Theory, Technique, and Cases.* New York: John Wiley.

Kent, R. 1981. *A History of British Empirical Sociology.* Farnborough, England: Gower.

Lidz, T. 1976. *The Person.* New York: Basic.

Maccoby, E. E. and N. Maccoby. 1954. "The Interview: A Tool of Social Science." Pp. 449-87 in *Handbook of Social Psychology,* Vol. 1, edited by G. Lindzey. Reading, MA: Addison-Wesley.

Miller, J. 1993. *The Passion of Michel Foucault.* Garden City, NY: Doubleday.

Mishler, E. G. 1984. *The Discourse of Medicine: Dialectics of Medical Interviews.* Norwood, NJ: Ablex.

———. 1986. *Research Interviewing: Context and Narrative.* Cambridge, MA: Harvard University Press.

Narayan, K., in collaboration with U. D. Sood. 1997. *Mondays on the Dark Night of the Moon: Himalayan Foothill Folktales.* New York: Oxford University Press.

Oberschall, A. 1965. *Empirical Social Research in Germany.* Paris: Mouton.

Pool, I. de S. 1957. "A Critique of the Twentieth Anniversary Issue." *Public Opinion Quarterly* 21:190-98.

Reed-Danahay, D. E., ed. 1997. *Auto/Ethnography: Rewriting the Self and the Social.* New York: Berg.

Riesman, D. and M. Benney. 1956. "Asking and Answering." *Journal of Business of the University of Chicago* 29:225-36.

Rose, N. 1990. *Governing the Soul: The Shaping of the Private Self.* London: Routledge.

———. 1997. *Inventing Ourselves: Psychology, Power, and Personhood.* Cambridge: Cambridge University Press.

Rubin, H. J. and I. S. Rubin. 1995. *Qualitative Interviewing: The Art of Hearing Data.* Thousand Oaks, CA: Sage.

Sacks, H. 1992. *Lectures on Conversation,* Vols. 1-2. Edited by G. Jefferson. Oxford: Blackwell.

Sacks, H., E. A. Schegloff, and G. Jefferson. 1974. "A Simplest Systematics for the Organization of Turn-Taking for Conversation." *Language* 50:696-735.

Selvin, H. C. 1985. "Durkheim, Booth and Yule: The Non-Diffusion of an Intellectual Innovation." Pp. 70-82 in *Essays on the History of British Sociological Research,* edited by M. Bulmer. Cambridge: Cambridge University Press.

Silverman, D. 1987. *Communication and Medical Practice.* London: Sage.

———. 1993. *Interpreting Qualitative Data: Methods for Analysing Talk, Text and Interaction.* London: Sage.

———. 1997. *Qualitative Research: Theory, Method and Practice.* London: Sage.

Terkel, S. 1972. *Working: People Talk about What They Do All Day and How They Feel about It.* New York: Pantheon.

Weiss, R. S. 1994. *Learning from Strangers: The Art and Method of Qualitative Interview Studies.* New York: Free Press.

Wittgenstein, L. 1953. *Philosophical Investigations.* New York: Macmillan.

2

THE HISTORY OF THE INTERVIEW

◆ Jennifer Platt

The "interview" has existed, and changed over time, both as a practice and as a methodological term in current use. However, the practice has not always been theorized or distinguished from other modes of acquiring information; there have been some cases of practices that we would today describe as interviewing, although contemporaries did not. Interviewing has sometimes been treated as a distinct method, but more often it has been located within some broader methodological category, such as "survey," "case study," or "life story."

At each stage, more fully institutionalized practices have been less likely to be written about in detail, except for trainees; we must therefore exercise caution in generalizing from the prescriptive literature to current practice. In principle, my aim in this chapter is to look at both the theorization and the practice of the interview, without assuming that there has always been a close correspondence between the two. But interview *practice* has been very unevenly described. It is most common for interview practice to be described when some aspect of that practice becomes salient because what has been done is seen as novel, or unconventional. Even then, what is described is commonly a policy or strategy rather than the actual practice, which in reality may not always conform to the stated policy. This creates a problem of data, so for this historical account I must draw largely on prescriptions for practice as it should be.

I have decided to concentrate here on the book literature, although many articles have appeared on aspects of interviewing. It is my assumption that the main points in the journal literature are soon taken up in books if they are practically influential, so an emphasis on the book literature should be adequate for a broad overview of the pattern of development. It is with regret that I have also decided, given the limitations of space, to focus entirely on the U.S. experience. For the pre-World War II period, especially its earlier part, this is quite misleading, as other national sociologies

Table 2.1 GENRES OF BOOKS RELATED TO INTERVIEWING

Genre	Examples
Practitioner textbooks	Garrett, *Interviewing: Its Principles and Method* (1942)
Polling and market research practice	Gallup, *A Guide to Public Opinion Polls* (1944); American Marketing Association, *The Technique of Marketing Research* (1937)
Social science methods textbooks	Goode and Hatt, *Methods in Social Research* (1952)
Instructions to survey interviewers	University of Michigan, Survey Research Center, *Manual for Interviewers* (1954)
Critiques of method, general or particular	Christie and Jahoda, *Studies in the Scope and Method of "The Authoritarian Personality"* (1954); Cicourel, *Method and Measurement in Sociology* (1964)
Empirical work discussing its methods	Kinsey, Pomeroy, and Martin, *Sexual Behavior in the Human Male* (1948)
Handbooks	Denzin and Lincoln, *Handbook of Qualitative Research* (2000)
Monographs on special groups, novel approaches	Dexter, *Elite and Specialized Interviewing* (1970); Douglas, *Creative Interviewing* (1985)
Philosophical/theoretical discussion	Sjoberg and Nett, *A Methodology for Social Research* (1968)
Reports of methodological research	Hyman, *Interviewing in Social Research* (1954)

had some of their own distinct traditions and discussion. From about 1945 to 1960, U.S. social science and the survey became so hegemonic elsewhere that the U.S. literature can perhaps be treated as representing the whole; after the high period of hegemony, that becomes less reasonable.[1] Because I am a sociologist, this chapter is unavoidably written from a sociologist's perspective; the most likely bias is one toward work that sociologists have used and treated as important, whether or not the authors were sociologists. The choices of work to review might well differ somewhat if I were equally familiar with anthropology, political science, and psychology; scholars from other backgrounds are invited to supplement my examples with their own.

The U.S. book literature on interviewing can be broken down into a number of categories, of which some illustrative examples are listed in Table 2.1. (Where possible, these are chosen from works not extensively discussed below, to indicate more of the range of material drawn on.) There are a number of relatively distinct intellectual and practical traditions, despite overlaps and some strong influences across traditions, and that needs to be taken into account in any discussion of the stances and concerns of single texts.

It is not always easy to decide what in the literature should be treated as a part of interviewing as such; for instance, some discussions of questions to be put in an interview are only about the construction of schedules, without reference to how those are presented to the respondent, and many discussions of the interviewer's role include sections about sampling decisions that may fall to the interviewer. For the purposes of this chapter, my focus is on what happens while the interviewer is in contact with the respondent.

I concentrate here on social scientific interviewing, but that has not always been distinguished from the interviewing techniques of psychiatrists, social caseworkers, or personnel managers. When distinctions have been made in the literature, social scientists still have often drawn upon work in such fields. But the character of the literature has changed historically. The earliest relevant work was not specifically social scientific. As new practices and bodies (such as polling and survey organizations) emerged, they generated writing that expressed their concerns, and their professional commitment to work in the same area led to methodological research concerning issues in which they were interested.

Once an orthodoxy was established, there was room for critiques of it and declarations of independence from it. Those working on special groups developed special ways of dealing with them; then, with an understandable lag, theorists began to take an interest in more philosophical aspects of interviewing. Textbooks regularly strove to keep up with the main developments, whereas authors of empirical studies wrote about the special experiences and needs of their particular topics. In later times, as quantitative and qualitative worlds became increasingly separate, discussions of interviewing diverged correspondingly. The quantitativists carried forward an established tradition with increasing sophistication, from time to time taking on technical innovations such as telephone interviewing, while qualitative workers blossomed out into focus groups, life histories, and own-brand novelties. However, an interesting recent link has been reestablished between the qualitative and quantitative camps in the use by surveyors of conversation-analytic techniques to analyze what is happening in their questions and answers.

In the rest of this chapter, I sketch the trajectory of the field of interviewing by using selected examples of such writings, starting with the prescriptive methodological literature and going on to empirical work that has been treated as methodologically important. I then review some key analytic themes in the literature. I consider the literature of research on interviewing as much for what the issues reflected there show us about the researchers' focuses of interest as for what the findings have been, although research has surely influenced practice. I briefly explore the interlinked issues of changing interest in and thinking about validity, the conceptions held of appropriate social relations between interviewer and respondent, and the types of data sought by those working in different styles; I make a particular effort to draw out points of potential interest to researchers whose concern is less with the history as such than it is with informing their own practice. Finally, I draw the strands of the discussion together to present a synthetic account of the ways in which interviewing and thinking about it have changed over time.

◆ The Trajectory of Change in Methodological Writing

To give a sense of the broad trajectory of change in methodological writing about interviewing, I present below, in order of historical appearance, descriptions of some arguably representative accounts of interviewing, its forms and purposes. I outline key points of content and assumptions, and briefly place each in its context.

HOWARD W. ODUM AND KATHARINE JOCHER

An Introduction to Social Research (1929)

Odum and Jocher's volume is one of the first general social science methods textbooks. In it, in addition to *interview*, the terms *schedule* (an instrument to be used by an enumerator) and *questionnaire* (an instrument to be answered unaided) are mentioned; for these, there is discussion of questions and presentation, but nothing on interviewing as such. (During this period the conduct of structured interviews was not treated as at all problematic, and so was hardly discussed.) Odum and Jocher state:

> An interview is made for the purpose of securing information . . . about the informant himself, or about other persons or undertakings that he knows or is interested in. The purpose may be to secure a life history, to corroborate evidence got from other sources, to secure . . . data which the informant possesses. [It] . . . may also be the means of enlisting the informant's cooperation . . . in the investigation, or . . . advice . . . in the procedure to be followed. . . . If the student is not acquainted with the informant, some method of introduction through a mutual acquaintance should be secured. (Pp. 366-67)

They note also that the interviewer should request permission to take notes.

In the 1920s and 1930s, an "interview" was often, as here, assumed to be with a key informant or gatekeeper, rather than with a respondent who is merely one member of a sample (see Bingham and Moore 1931; Fry 1934). The implicit model of the old, fact-finding "survey" in the tradition of Charles Booth was still in the background, and Booth's data on the family in the street was provided by middle-class visitors (Bales 1991). The interviewee was thus seen as an informant about the situation studied, as much as or more than as being part of what was studied. Thus the respondent might be of status superior to the interviewer, another reason for an unstructured approach. This does not mean that no questionnaires were being used with mass samples, although these were not common yet in aca-

demic social science; rather, the use of questionnaires was seen as a distinct method. (The lack of development of theories of sampling meant that successful contact with previously identified mass respondents was not yet felt as a need.) It was often recommended that notes should not be taken during the interview, or only to a minimal extent; rather, recording should be done as soon as possible afterward. Questions might not be revealed, or might be written on the back of an envelope to appear informal and spontaneous (see Converse 1987:51). Clearly the role of respondent was not felt to be sufficiently institutionalized for no concealment of the mechanics to be necessary.

PAULINE V. YOUNG

Scientific Social Surveys and Research (1939)

In Young's very successful general methods textbook, *interview* is again distinguished from *schedule* and *questionnaire*, which are dealt with separately. Young distinguishes between respondents who are adequate sources on factual matters and those who are of interest as subjects individually or in relation to the larger situation. A personal introduction to the subject is still seen as desirable: "The interview proper does not begin until a considerable degree of rapport has been established. . . . The most important touchstone is probably the mutual discovery of common experiences" (p. 189).

What does Young see as the value of the interview?

> The personal interview is penetrating; it goes to the "living source." Through it the student . . . is able to go behind mere outward behavior and phenomena. He can secure accounts of events and processes as they are reflected in personal experiences, in social attitudes. He can check inferences and external observations by a vital account of the persons who are being observed. . . .

> the field worker . . . needs to know in a general way why he is interviewing this particular person or group and what he intends asking. Too rigid definition is, of course, fatal to any scientific pursuit; the mind of the interviewer needs to be open to unforeseen developments. . . . Before the interview proceeds very far the interviewer should aim to learn the interviewees' point of view, their habitual reactions to the social situations under consideration, their opportunities for and degree of familiarity with these situations, their ability to give an accurate and unbiased account. (Pp. 175, 179)

She advises that the interviewer ask as few questions as possible:

> When people are least interrupted, when they can tell their stories in their own way . . . they can react naturally and freely and express themselves fully. . . . [Interruptions and leading questions are likely to have the effect that] . . . the adventure into the unknown, into uncharted and hitherto undisclosed spheres, has been destroyed. (P. 190)

Young notes that it is rarely advisable to complete an interview at one sitting (p. 195). She also asserts that it is better for the interviewer not to take notes, except maybe a few key words, and states that there is some controversy as to whether the interviewer should record the interview in first or third person and whether a verbatim account is to be preferred to a summary by the interviewer (pp. 196, 200).

Young was at the University of Southern California, which was oriented toward the training of practitioners; her *Interviewing in Social Work* (1935) was widely cited in sociology when there were few other such sources available. Its perceived relevance owed something to the widespread use by sociologists of case histories collected by social workers, especially at the University

of Chicago, where Young was trained; this connects with the idea of the case study and of the significance of life history data, which are clearly the contexts she has in mind in the passages quoted above (Platt 1996:46). One may also perhaps detect formative traces of the participant observation she used in her doctoral work. George A. Lundberg's (1942) important—and intellectually far superior—textbook takes a similar approach, although with a slight twist in the direction of the more modern concern with personality and psychoanalytic interests. Lundberg's own tastes were strongly scientistic, but it is interesting that he still offered advice on ways of gaining the confidence of the informant (see below) of a kind that would soon be regarded as thoroughly unacceptable.

In the 1949 edition of her text, Young mentions the modern survey, although she is still far from treating it as the paradigm:

> A specialized form of the interview is useful in the collection of personal data for quantitative purposes. This type of interview aims to accumulate a variety of uniform responses to a wide scope of predetermined specific questions. (Generally these questions appear on a printed form.) (P. 244)

This distanced account was in effect one of the last traces of an older conception of the interview.

CHARLES F. CANNELL AND ROBERT L. KAHN

"The Collection of Data By Interviewing" (1953)

Cannell and Kahn produced this chapter for what became one of the standard general-methods textbooks, written by a group from the Institute for Social Research (ISR) at the University of Michigan. Cannell and Kahn, a clinical and a social psychologist, were members of a team that started in the Department of Agriculture before the war, became the wartime Division of Program

Surveys (DPS), and after the war transformed itself into the ISR. In this chapter they attempt to go beyond current rules of thumb and to draw on work in counseling and communication theory to understand the psychology of the interview. (Their later book *The Dynamics of Interviewing* carries this forward, coming to the formulation of objectives and questions only after three chapters on the interviewing relationship; Kahn and Cannell 1957.)

Note, in the following quotation, the relatively qualitative orientation, which nonetheless goes with a strong commitment to scientific procedure; one may detect some tension between the two:

> Even when the research objectives call for information which is beyond the individual's power to provide directly, the interview is often an effective means of obtaining the desired data [e.g., Adorno et al.'s rating of anti-Semitism or personality features]. . . . Bias and lack of training make it impossible for an individual to provide such intimate information about himself, even if he is motivated to the utmost frankness. But only he can provide the data about his attitudes towards his parents, colleagues, and members of minority groups from which some of his deeper-lying characteristics can be inferred. . . . Considering . . . the interviewing process as a scientific technique implies that we are able, through the application of a specific instrument in a specific manner, to achieve identical results in given situations . . . [but] the interviewer cannot apply unvaryingly a specified set of techniques, because he is dealing with a varying situation. . . . [Given that] we cannot tailor the question for each respondent, the best approximation to a standard stimulus is to word the question at a level which is understandable to all respondents and then to ask the question of each respondent in identical fashion. . . . The only instance in which the interviewer is permitted to vary this procedure is when

> an individual is unable to understand the question as worded. . . . the interviewer's role with respect to the questionnaire is to treat it as a scientific instrument designed to administer a constant stimulus to a population of respondents. This technique is necessary when quantifiable data are desired. (Pp. 332, 358)

Cannell was a research student of Carl Rogers, recruited by Rensis Likert to the DPS to draw on what he had learned with Rogers about nondirective styles of questioning. It is assumed in the book of which Cannell and Kahn's chapter is a part that an interview schedule is used, but this heritage was shown in the team's long-term commitment to more open-ended questions than those favored by other teams and explains some of the assumptions made here about interviewing. At an early stage there was controversy between the proponents of closed- and open-ended questions, contrasted by one participant within the DPS as the "neat reliables" and the "sloppy valids." This was reflected in a classic paper by Paul F. Lazarsfeld (1944) in which he aimed to resolve the conflict between two wartime research outfits with divergent styles. Converse (1987:195-202) shows that the dispute was as much about the costs of more open-ended work, and whether the gains were worth it, as it was about validity. It became evident even to those committed in principle to the open style that it not only created coding problems, it was impossible to sustain when less educated interviewers were used, and interviewers were based all across the country, so that training and supervision were difficult.

CLAIRE SELLTIZ, MARIE JAHODA, MORTON DEUTSCH, AND STUART W. COOK

Research Methods in Social Relations (1965)

This classic textbook, written by psychologists, has passed through many editions. Selltiz et al. still distinguish between *interview* and *questionnaire,* seeing the interview, which may be structured or unstructured, as practically advantageous because it does not require literacy, has a better response rate than postal questionnaires, and is the more flexible and "the more appropriate technique for revealing information about complex, emotionally laden subjects, or for probing the sentiments that may underlie an expressed opinion" (p. 242). However, much of the discussion concerns question wording, with no distinction made between interview and questionnaire, and clearly a standard survey interview, by now well established, is what the authors have in mind. They note that the interviewer should put the respondent at ease and create a friendly atmosphere, but "must keep the direction of the interview in his own hands, discouraging irrelevant conversation and endeavouring to keep the respondent to the point" (p. 576); the interviewer must ask the questions exactly as worded and not give impromptu explanations. Complete verbatim recording is needed for free-answer questions, "aside from obvious irrelevancies and repetitions" (p. 580).

This shows development well beyond the approach of George Gallup (1944) in early work conducting the simple political poll designed for newspaper rather than academic publication. The interview there was unequivocally designed for quantification of the responses made to fixed questions by members of the general public. The need for accuracy and precision was emphasized, but uniformity of stimulus was not given the importance that it later acquired; reliability was seen primarily in terms of getting the public predictions right. Many of those involved in the early development of polling and market research into the survey were psychologists, and for them the experiment was usually the model, so they laid great emphasis, as here, on the importance of applying a uniform stimulus.

GIDEON SJOBERG AND ROGER NETT

A Methodology for Social Research (1968)

This book represents quite a new genre of work, reflecting wider movements in sociology. Sjoberg and Nett were not closely involved with survey units and were writing not a conventional methods text but a textbook/monograph with a standpoint: "The scientist who employs . . . [structured interviews] is usually intent upon testing an existing set of hypotheses; he is less concerned with discovery per se. And, of course, standardization greatly enhances reliability" (p. 193). Standardization also saves time and money. However, it has the drawback of imposing the investigator's categories on informants:

> The unstructured type is most useful for studying the normative structure of organizations, for establishing classes, and for discovering the existence of possible social patterns (rather than the formal testing of propositions concerning the existence of given patterns). (P. 195)

Sjoberg and Nett describe four types of unstructured interviews: the free-association method interview, the focused interview, the objectifying interview, and the group interview. Of these, they prefer the objectifying interview:

> The researcher informs the interviewee from the start . . . concerning the kinds of information he is seeking and why. The informant is apprised of his role in the scientific process and is encouraged to develop his skills in observation (and even in interpretation). . . . Besides examining his own actions, the interviewee is encouraged to observe and interpret the behavior of his associates in his social group. Ideally, he becomes a peer with whom the scientist can objec-

tively discuss the ongoing system, to the extent that he is encouraged to criticize the scientist's observations and interpretations. (P. 214)

Throughout the discussion, Sjoberg and Nett stress the social assumptions built into different choices of questions. They discuss status effects in the interview situation and the consequences of varying cultural backgrounds, especially for work in the Third World.

These authors approach the matter from a theoretical and—in a turn characteristic of the period—sociopolitical perspective; they propose to involve the respondent as an equal, not so much for instrumental reasons of technical efficacy as because they see a nonhierarchical, nonexploitative relationship as intrinsically right. It is also notable that this is a sociologists' version; there is no orientation to psychologists' usual concerns, and the topics envisaged are sociological ones. Although Johan Galtung (1967) and Norman K. Denzin (1970) wrote books that are more like conventional methods texts, theirs have key features in common with Sjoberg and Nett's: more theoretical and philosophical interests, a more distanced approach to surveys and their mundane practicalities, and a clearly sociological frame of reference. Interviewing of various kinds had by this period become a standard practice to which even those with theoretical interests related their ideas.

STEVEN J. TAYLOR AND ROBERT BOGDAN

Introduction to Qualitative Research Methods (1984)

Taylor and Bogdan produced a specialized methods textbook, again with a strong standpoint:

In stark contrast to structured interviewing qualitative interviewing is flexible and dynamic. . . . By in-depth qualitative interviewing we mean repeated

face-to-face encounters between the researcher and informants directed toward understanding informants' perspectives on their lives, experiences, or situations as expressed in their own words. The in-depth interview is modeled after a conversation between equals, rather than a formal question-and-answer exchange. Far from being a robotlike data collector, the interviewer, not an interview schedule or protocol, is the research tool. The role entails not merely obtaining answers, but learning what questions to ask and how to ask them. (P. 77)

Taylor and Bogdan note that without direct observation to give context to what people say in an interview, their responses may not be adequately understood, and there may be problems of deception and distortion; it is important, therefore, to interview in depth (see Johnson, Chapter 5, this volume),

getting to know people well enough to understand what they mean and creating an atmosphere in which they are likely to talk freely. . . . it is only by designing the interview along the lines of natural interaction that the interviewer can tap into what is important to people. In fact, the interviewer has many parallels in everyday life: "the good listener" "the shoulder to cry on," "the confidante." . . . there has to be some exchange in terms of what interviewers say about themselves. . . . The best advice is to be discreet in the interview, but to talk about yourself in other situations. You should be willing to relate to informants in terms other than interviewer/informant. Interviewers can serve as errand-runners, drivers, babysitters, advocates. (Pp. 83, 101)

This reaction against "robotlike" standard survey interviewing is part of the growth of a separate "qualitative" stream that recommends many practices that have previously been anathema to surveyors. It will be noted that the rhetoric is very distant from that of science. These authors often refer to the "Chicago school" as a model, drawing on a widely current image of it—if one more useful for ideological than for historical purposes (Platt 1996: 265-69). The ideal is clearly participant observation or ethnography, and this type of interviewing again blurs the boundary with that. It could not be adapted to large representative samples and makes implicit assumptions about what kinds of topic are of interest, which, one somehow infers, exclude (for instance) the demographic or economic. Other representatives of this broad tendency are Jack D. Douglas (1985) and James A. Holstein and Jaber F. Gubrium (1995).

Many feminists have practiced and argued in favor of similar styles on feminist grounds. Shulamit Reinharz (1992) suggests that interviewing appeals to feminists because it

> offers researchers access to people's ideas, thoughts and memories in their own words rather than in the words of the researcher. This asset is particularly important for the study of women because [this] . . . is an antidote to centuries of ignoring women's ideas altogether or having men speak for women. (P. 19)

Reinharz points out, however, that declared feminists have also done positivistic research, and concludes by suggesting that close relations with every subject are not practicable, and that too much emphasis on rapport may limit the range of topics covered unduly (see Reinharz and Chase, Chapter 11, this volume). It is notable that the work she cites in the chapter from which I quote above is almost all on such topics as rape and hysterectomy. Others have pointed out that many of the arguments used by feminists as though they were specific to the study of women can be seen as equally applicable to men.

One might speculate on how much of this tendency rests on the increased availability of good-quality portable tape recorders; the assumptions made about what it is practical to record have not been much examined, and research on the consequences for practice of changing techniques and technologies for the recording of free answers is strikingly absent.

◆ Empirical Work and Its Influence

Important contributions to the discussion of interviewing have also been made by authors whose primary concerns were with their substantive topics; these do not necessarily relate directly to the professional methodological discussion and cannot be explained by their location within that. Below, I review some of these. It is probably not by chance that the empirical exemplars that come to mind, as well as much methodological research, are mainly from work done in the period 1935-55. This was the time when the modern survey was emerging, and so the problems that its practice raised were live ones being confronted and disputed for the first time, while its high profile and popularity also encouraged those with criticisms, or alternatives suited to less usual topics, to write about them. None of the exemplars employs a conventional, standardized survey because, where there is a structured schedule, the tradition has been to provide a copy of it without describing the interviewing process; what took place is implicitly assumed (not always rightly) to have been determined, and sufficiently described, by the schedule.

F. J. Roethlisberger and William J. Dickson ([1939] 1964) made an early contribution to unstructured interviewing technique —although the intellectual responsibility for this arguably lies more with Elton Mayo, who led the work. Mayo's ideas on method were influenced both by his interest in Jungian psychoanalysis and by his friendship with the anthropologist and fieldwork pioneer Bronislaw Malinowski, whom he met in Australia.[2] Roethlisberger and Dickson began their interviewing program to collect employees' views about their work (for use in improving supervisor training) but found that the workers often wanted to talk about "irrelevant" material, so in 1929 the decision was made to adopt an "indirect approach," following the workers' leads without changing the subject and asking only noncommittal questions. Interviews were now recorded as far as possible verbatim, rather than under target headings, and the data were seen as information not so much on real problems as on the meanings that the workers gave to the realities. "Rules of Performance" were set up, such as "Listen in a patient, friendly but intelligently critical manner" and "Do not display any kind of authority," but these rules were to be treated as flexible: "If the interviewer understands what he is doing and is in active touch with the actual situation, he has extreme latitude in what he can do" (Roethlisberger and Dickson [1939] 1964:286-87). Years of training were necessary for such interviewing. The interviewing program was not initially intended for social scientific purposes, but it came to be used for social science.

W. Lloyd Warner and Paul S. Lunt (1941) said that in their work they used techniques suggested by Roethlisberger and Dickson, although their research, an intensive community study, was of a very different character. However, Warner was an anthropologist by training, and the anthropological fieldwork tradition seems more relevant to its general style. Many of Warner and Lunt's "interviews" were done without the subjects' awareness of being interviewed, and interviewing shaded over into observation: "The activity of the investigator has been classed as observation when the emphasis fell on the observer's seeing behavior of an individual; as interviewing, when emphasis fell on listening to what was said" (p. 46). These authors expressed great skepticism about the utility of questionnaires, which they saw as liable to take items out of their social context and useful only when one is already familiar with the general situation from interviews (pp. 55-56). Although they described their main method as interviewing, this should probably be regarded primarily as part of the history of what we now call participant observation.

The next example, Alfred C. Kinsey, Wardell B. Pomeroy, and Clyde E. Martin's *Sexual Behavior in the Human Male* (1948), is more idiosyncratic. Kinsey was a professor of zoology and devised techniques to suit his special topic. There was a list of items to be covered in the interview, but no fixed order or standardized wording for them. Additional questions were designed for subjects with uncommon ranges of experience. The questions placed the burden of denial of sexual practices on the subject and were asked very rapidly to increase the spontaneity of answers (pp. 50-54). Interviewer neutrality was not valued:

> Something more than cold objectivity is needed in dealing with human subjects. . . . The interviewer who senses what these things can mean . . . is more effective, though he may not be altogether neutral. The sympathetic interviewer records his reactions in ways that may not involve spoken words but which are, nonetheless, readily comprehended by most people. . . . These are the things that . . . can never be done through a written questionnaire, or even through a directed interview in which the questions are formalized and the confines of the investigation strictly limited. (P. 42)

The researchers' aims were not at all concealed from respondents, and if a respondent appeared not to be answering truthfully, the interview was broken off. Very lengthy training was again seen as necessary for the interviewers, who were also required, in the interests of confidentiality, to memorize a large number of codes to record respondents' answers. Any use of this method by others has not been identified in the mainstream sociological literature; Kinsey et al.'s reasoning suggests that it would be applicable only in areas posing the same problems as research into sexual behavior.

Radically different, almost equally famous, and more influential in social science method was Theodor W. Adorno, Else Frenkel-Brunswik, Daniel J. Levinson, and R. Nevitt Sanford's *The Authoritarian Personality* (1950). Here again there was a schedule, but interviewers were not expected to stick closely to its questions or order. The model followed was that of the psychotherapeutic encounter, and the instructions distinguished "underlying" and "manifest" questions. It was taken that "the subject's view of his own life . . . may be assumed to contain real information together with wishful—and fearful—distortions," and consequently methods were needed "to differentiate the more genuine, basic feelings, attitudes, and strivings from those of a more compensatory character behind which are hidden tendencies, frequently unknown to the subject himself, which are contrary to those manifested or verbalized on a surface level" (p. 293). Kinsey, too, distrusted overt statements of attitudes, but his solution was to ask only about behavior and (unless untruths were suspected) to accept what was offered at face value.

Perhaps surprisingly, given the lack of social scientific precedent for Kinsey's approach, Adorno and his associates were treated more harshly in published critiques. Kinsey et al. were criticized, but critics concluded that empirical evidence to show that their results were less valid than those of researchers who used alternative approaches was not available (Cochran, Mosteller, and Tukey 1954:78-79). Adorno and his colleagues, however, were accused of inconsistency and speculative overinterpretation of data not appropriate for their uses (Christie and Jahoda 1954:97, 100).

What might be seen as a more social version of such an approach, used to generate large ideas about historical change in American society, is shown in other work from the same period by David Riesman and associates. They carried out many interviews, but certainly did not take them at face value: "Everything conspired to lead to an emphasis not on the interview itself but on its interpretation . . . such a method . . . requires repeated reading of the interview record . . . in search of those small verbal nuances and occasional Freudian slips that might be clues to character" (Riesman and Glazer 1952:14-15). Of course, character as a topic hardly lends itself to direct questions of a factual nature, but the extent of "interpretation" here goes strikingly beyond the literal data. It is interesting that there are two books from the project: the main interpretive one, Riesman, Glazer, and Denney's *The Lonely Crowd* (1950), which contains almost no direct interview data, and Riesman and Glazer's *Faces in the Crowd* (1952), consisting mainly of raw interview data without analysis. The issue of how well the data support the interpretation is thus avoided.[3]

The genre of publication of raw interview data is one with a history—sometimes, like the work of Studs Terkel, a history not within academic social science, even if social scientists refer to it. However, material that looks raw may be at least lightly cooked. Terkel describes his own procedure: "*The* most important part of the work, is the editing of the transcripts . . . the cutting and shaping of it into a readable result. The way I look at it is I suppose something like the way a sculptor looks at a block of stone: inside it there's a shape which he'll find" (quoted in Parker 1997:169). Thus to treat the published version as showing just what took place in the interview would be quite misleading. Whole "life stories" have been published in sociology, although sometimes written by their subjects rather than elicited through interviewing;[4] the genre was treated as of central importance in the interwar period, and much more recently has been revived.

Some recent work on life stories takes a similar approach, on the one hand putting a very high value on the subject's own version of events, but on the other hand permitting the interviewer a considerable editorial role (e.g., Atkinson 1998; see also Atkinson, Chapter 6, this volume). Note that this, interestingly, shifts the stage intended as active researcher intervention from data elicitation, as with a questionnaire or interview guide, to data presentation. The version presented is, however, nearer to raw data than are the figures and tables of the quantitative tradition.

Topics of research have their own traditions and intrinsic needs (Platt 1996:129-30), and so some methodological ideas arise from the substance of the work being done: Kinsey et al.'s conceptions of interviewing technique followed directly from what they saw as the needs of work on sexual behavior. (On the other hand, Adorno et al.'s ideas followed as much from their general intellectual backgrounds as from the substantive topic.) One might expect the influence of such work to follow the same paths, although whether or not it has cannot be explored here. It is clear that the choices of method did not simply follow from the current state of methodological discussion, although the results fed into that, if only by evoking criticism. The level of attention paid to the methods of such work has depended on the extent to which it has departed from the survey paradigm as well as on the general interest in its substantive content.

◆ Some Analytic Themes

Discussions of empirical work take us a little nearer to what has happened in practice. Research on interviewing gives us one of the other windows through which we may see something of the actual conduct of the interview, as distinct from the prescriptions for it. Practice has often been indeed distinct. Interviewers are repeatedly shown to use their own ways of dealing with problems in eliciting the data wanted. Julius Roth (1966) long ago documented a few cases where research employees had, for their own reasons, departed from the investigator's plan in ways that damaged it. He argued that this was only to be expected when interviewers were employed as "hired hands," with no personal commitment to the research goal or control over content and methods.

More recent authors have also identified interviewer cheating. Jean Peneff (1988) observed some of the most experienced and valued interviewers working for a French governmental survey organization, all highly motivated, and found that they regularly adapted their behavior and language to the social context: "They intuitively improvised a blend of survey norms and field-work practices" (p. 533). He offers a less pessimistic perspective, querying whether departure from specifications should be regarded as "cheating"—although it tended to make what was intended as standard survey work more "qualitative." It sounds as though there was an implicit bargain between interviewers and their supervisors, in which good-quality work was exchanged for lack of close inquiry into the way in which the quality was achieved. (The great underresearched and undertheorized area of interviewing is that of the social relations between employed interviewers and their supervisors, and the consequences of those relations.) We do not know how far such patterns as those found by Peneff have held more widely, but we ought not to be surprised if sometimes they do.

But Roth's and Peneff's work is unusual. Research on interviewing has come overwhelmingly from those active in specialist survey units. (A list of main book sources presenting research on interviewing is given in Table 2.2.) It is not surprising that it should be those with continuing reason for professional concern with the matter who do such work, but this does mean that the research has been skewed toward their distinctive preoccupations. What was

Table 2.2 **KEY WORKS PRESENTING RESEARCH AND ANALYSIS ON INTERVIEWING**

1947	Hadley Cantril, *Gauging Public Opinion*
1954	Herbert H. Hyman, *Interviewing in Social Research*
1965	Stephen A. Richardson, Barbara Snell Dohrenwend, and David Klein, *Interviewing: Its Forms and Functions*
1969	Raymond L. Gorden, *Interviewing: Strategy, Techniques, and Tactics*
1974	Jean M. Converse and Howard Schuman, *Conversations at Random: Survey Research as Interviewers See It*
1979	Norman M. Bradburn and Seymour Sudman, *Improving Interview Method and Questionnaire Design*
1981	Charles F. Cannell, Peter Miller, and Lois Oksenberg, "Research on Interviewing Techniques"
1984	Charles Turner and Elizabeth Martin, eds., *Surveying Subjective Phenomena*
1990	Lucy Suchman and Brigitte Jordan, "Interactional Troubles in Face-to-Face Survey Interviews"
1991	Paul P. Biemer et al., eds., *Measurement Errors in Surveys*

problematic about interviewing for them can be seen from the topics researched, and it is from that point of view that some of their themes are considered.

A major preoccupation over the years has concerned the variation in answers elicited by different interviewers. This is commonly taken as the measure of "error," implying that validity is defined as arriving at the correct overall figures rather than as fully grasping individuals' meanings or correctly identifying their real opinions. Cantril (1947) suggested, for instance, that researchers could deal with the problem of interviewer biases by selecting interviewers with canceling biases. Other writers have seen careful selection of interviewers for their personal characteristics, whether of race or of personality, as valuable—although they often faced the fact that the real labor market made this difficult. Fowler (1991:260) points out that the conventional definition of "error" that he uses makes standardization across interviewers

tautologically necessary to reduce error; this approach inevitably ignores the possibility that some nonstandardized interviewers might be better than others. In the earlier work, there was a strong tendency to blame the interviewers for problems, and to see greater control over interviewers as the answer to those problems.

An extreme of this definition of the situation is suggested by Norman Bradburn and Seymour Sudman's (1979) chapter on interviewer variations in asking questions, where the nonprogrammed interviewer behavior studied through tape recordings included such minutiae as stuttering, coughing, false starts, and corrected substitutions.[5] Converse and Howard Schuman (1974), in contrast, studied the interviewers' point of view and were not concerned primarily with their errors and how to control their behavior—which may owe something to the fact that the interviewers in question were graduate students, members of "us" rather than "them." Consequently,

Converse and Schuman emphasize the tensions their interviewers experienced between conflicting roles and expectations.

Later work, however, more often recognizes respondents' contributions and takes the interview as interaction more seriously. For Cannell, Peter V. Miller, and Lois Oksenberg (1981), the aim was to decrease error in reporting due to the respondent rather than to the interviewer. Because their study was on topics appearing in medical records—which could, unlike attitudes, be checked—they were able to identify some clear factual errors made by respondents. They found that interviewers were giving positive feedback for poor respondent performance, in the supposed interests of rapport, so that correction of this, and clearer guidance to respondents on what was expected of them, improved performance.

More recent writing about "cognitive" interviewing has revived the issue of accuracy in ways that deal seriously with the issue of validity, if only in relation to "factual" questions. Lucy Suchman and Brigitte Jordan (1990), anthropologists using a conversation-analytic perspective, stress the extent to which "the survey interview suppresses those interactional resources that routinely mediate uncertainties of relevance and interpretation" (p. 232), so that reliability is bought at the cost of validity. They recommend encouraging interviewers to play a more normal conversational role, so that respondents may correctly grasp the concepts used in the questions asked. Suchman and Jordan's article, which appeared in the *Journal of the American Statistical Association,* raised considerable discussion; perhaps its ideas would not have seemed so novel to the readership of a more social-scientific journal.

Nora Cate Schaeffer (1991) balances such considerations against the need for some uniformity if the answers are to be added to give a total. She points out that "artificiality" in the interview situation does not necessarily mean that the answers given are less valid, but that to elicit them as intended, the researcher needs to bear in mind the rules of interaction that the respondent brings to the situation. Michael Schober and Frederick Conrad (1997) have shown that less standardized and more conversational interviewing can markedly increase the accuracy of the responses given —by, for instance, allowing interviewers to help respondents fit their relatively complicated circumstances into the categories of answers provided. Schober and Conrad illustrate the self-defeating extremes to which the pursuit of the uniform stimulus has gone, with researchers forbidding interviewers even to provide guidance that would ensure that the meanings the researchers sought were indeed conveyed in the answers chosen.

Presumably, training for practice will follow the latest findings. It is notable, however, that most of the examples used in these recent discussions have been drawn from large-scale national surveys, often carried out for governmental purposes and with fact-finding as a key aim. This reflects the increasing tendency for academics to use data of high quality that they have not gathered for their own purposes, which has led discussion in the directions suitable to the character of such work, but not equally applicable to the whole range of potential surveys.

Schober and Conrad's study exemplifies a recurrent pattern, in which research shows that commonly taught practices do not necessarily have the intended effects. That the limited benefits of "rapport" for data quality have repeatedly been (re)discovered suggests that, for whatever reasons, practice has not always followed research-based conclusions, and that the folklore of the field has been powerful. Recommendations on the relations between interviewer and respondent have changed considerably, whether the aim is "rapport" or just access. One of the earliest statements on this topic was made by Walter Bingham and Bruce Moore (1931): "The interviewee is frank when he feels that his own point of view is appreciated and respected, that the interviewer has some right to the information, and that the questions are relevant and not impertinent" (p. 11). This is rationalistic, corresponding to the assumption that the respondent is of relatively high status and is being approached for factual information; it is not typical of later discussion with other assumptions.

When the interview is seen as deep and richly qualitative, or as a large-scale survey interview with members of the general public, other approaches follow. The early survey literature typically suggested that interviewers need to establish rapport to get access and cooperation, but that they should also, when questioning, appear unshockable, have no detectable personal opinions, and, behind the front of friendliness, be objective and scientific.[6] Not every writer offered as businesslike a conception of rapport as William J. Goode and Paul K. Hatt (1952): "A state of rapport exists between interviewer and respondent when the latter has accepted the research goals of the interviewer, and actively seeks to help him in obtaining the necessary information" (p. 190). But the ideal was clearly an instrumental relationship.

Before the modern survey was fully developed, it was often not seen as so important to keep the interviewer as a person out of the picture. Lundberg (1942) suggests several ways of getting an informant "started": "refer to important friends of the informant as if one were quite well acquainted with them; . . . tell of one's own experiences or problems and ask the informant's advice or reactions to them" (pp. 365-66). These are just the kinds of techniques that survey organizations trained their interviewers to avoid. I have quoted above Kinsey et al.'s (1948) advocacy of a less impersonal and unbiased style. Elements of such an approach have now come around again in recent qualitative work, where there has often been a sociopolitical commitment to treating the respondent as an equal. This is taken to imply the researcher's not playing a detached role while expecting the other partner to reveal him- or herself:

> We can no longer remain objective, faceless interviewers, but become human beings and must disclose ourselves, learning about ourselves as we try to learn about the other.
> . . . As long as . . . researchers continue to treat respondents as unimportant, faceless individuals whose only contribution is to fill one more boxed response, the answers we . . . will get will be commensurable with the questions we ask and with the way we ask them. (Fontana and Frey 1994:374)

This line can, however, be presented in a more manipulative way. In Douglas's (1985) unique style:

> Creative interviewing . . . involves the use of many strategies and tactics of interaction, largely based on an understanding of friendly feelings and intimacy, to optimize cooperative, mutual disclosure and a creative search for mutual understanding. . . . Most Goddesses feel the need for a significant amount of self-disclosure before they will . . . reveal their innermost selves in their most self-discrediting aspects. When they seem to be proceeding to the inner depths with reluctance, I normally try to lead the way with a significant bit of self-discrediting self-disclosure. (P. 122)

Research on the partners' perceptions of each other has shown that respondents do not necessarily detect interviewers' biases or manipulative strategies; to that extent the impulse is moral or political rather than scientific. The barrier between the role and the self is broken down—or is it? Is this just another mode of instrumental presentation of self, as fellow human rather than as detached professional?

A method of data collection that cannot make plausible claims to validity is of no use, so it is surprising that widely discrepant levels of concern for validity, and conceptions of it, have been shown in relation to interviews. It has commonly been agreed that less rigidly structured methods may score higher on validity, although this has to be traded off against the greater reliability of more structured methods. But concern with the problem has come more from those who employ other people to do their interviews; those who carry out their own have usually seemed to regard their validity as self-evident, not requiring checks. This sometimes reflects a hostility toward "science" or "positivism" prevalent among qualitative researchers. However, in some of the literature on the standard survey there has also been surprisingly little concern about validity as such. The question of the substantive meaningfulness of the data, except on purely factual questions, somehow gets elided in the concern over interviewer error and questionnaire improvement.

Of course it is difficult in the survey, as in other contexts, to demonstrate validity, although some authors have suggested ways of doing so. Eleanor E. Maccoby and Nathan Maccoby (1954) proposed a traditional measure: "It remains to be seen whether unstandardized interviews have sufficiently greater validity so that ratings based upon them will predict criterion variables better than will ratings based on standardized interviews" (p. 454). Where there is a clear criterion to use as the standard of prediction, as in voting results, that standard has been used. But for many topics there are no criteria. There has been some discussion in terms of whether the respondent is telling the truth. Kinsey et al. (1948) take an inimitably robust stand on this:

> It has been asked how it is possible for an interviewer to know whether people are telling the truth. . . . As well ask a horse trader how he knows when to close a bargain! The experienced interviewer knows when he has established a sufficient rapport to obtain an honest record. (P. 43)

Even if one accepts the horse-trading approach as adequate, it could be applied only in relatively deep and unstructured types of interviews, where the interviewer has time to establish a relationship. For the in-depth or psychoanalytic interview, of course, the issue of validity has not arisen in the same sense, because the focus has been on the interpretations made by the analyst rather than on correct factuality. Warner and Lunt (1941) take a different approach:

> The information gathered about social relations is always social fact if the informant believes it, and it is always fact of another kind if he tells it and does not believe it. If the informant does not believe it, the lie he tells is frequently more valuable as a lead to understanding his behavior or that of others than the truth. (P. 52)

Warner and Lunt assume that the researcher will have ways of *knowing* that the respondent is lying. In intensive, long-term studies of a community, like Warner and Lunt's, that is a relatively plausible assumption; Arthur Vidich and Joseph Bensman (1954) have also reported detecting much intentional misrepresentation. Plainly, however, this assumption would not be met in many other cases.

Galtung (1967) is one of the earliest representatives of what might be seen as a truly sociological position, even if not one that exactly solves the problem:

> The spoken word is a social act, the inner thought is not, and the sociologist has good reasons to be most interested and concerned with the former, the psychologist perhaps with the latter. But this only transforms the problem from the problem of correspondence between words and thoughts to the problem of how representative the in-

terview situation is as social intercourse. (P. 124)

Holstein and Gubrium (1995), writing much more recently, take this one step further and, informed by ethnomethodological perspectives, stop worrying about such representativeness:

> One cannot expect answers on one occasion to replicate those on another because they emerge from different circumstances of production. Similarly, the validity of answers derives not from their correspondence to meanings held within the respondent but from their ability to convey situated experiential realities in terms that are locally comprehensible. (P. 9)

This assumes that there is no stable underlying reality to identify, thus, in a sense, abolishing the problem.

Elliot Mishler's (1986) emphasis on the interview response as a narrative in which the respondent makes sense of, and gives meaning to, experience has a similar stance. The issue has thus moved from the interview as an adequate measure of a reality external to it to the content of the interview as of interest in its own right. This is a long way from the concerns of some survey researchers to get correct reports concerning such matters as bathroom equipment and medical treatment received. All of the extreme perspectives on "the interview" have different paradigms in mind, as well as different research topics; each has shown little interest in the problems relevant to the needs and concerns of the others.

◆ The Historical Pattern

Not all of the work on interviewing fits into a clear historical pattern, and empirical studies may be idiosyncratic in relation to the methodological literature. Nonetheless, below I sketch a broad trajectory that summarizes major lines of thinking. The dates suggested are not meant to be precise, given that different workers move at different speeds.

Up to the late 1930s, *interview* was distinguished from *questionnaire*, which generally connoted a self-completed instrument; if an interview was administered by an interviewer, that person's contribution was not seen as requiring serious attention. The interview was unstructured, if with an agenda, and wide ranging; the interviewer was likely to be the researcher. Subjects were often used as informants with special knowledge to pass on, rather than as units to be quantified. This kind of interview was not strongly distinguished from interviews for job selection or journalism or, when "interviewing down," for social casework. (Indeed, data from social work interviews in particular were widely used by social scientists at a time when the idea that professors might themselves go into the field was a new one.) Little concern was shown for reliability or validity; a few rules of thumb were suggested for success. It was assumed that subjects might not accept overt interviewing of the modern kind, so some concealment was necessary. In parallel to this, however, much of what we might today call interviewing was done under such rubrics as "life history," "fieldwork," and "case study." For these, there was serious discussion of technical matters, such as how to keep the respondent talking without affecting the direction of the conversation too much (see, for example, Palmer 1928: 171-75).

Meanwhile, political polling and market research were developing. Here interviews were carried out by crews of interviewers instructed and supervised from the center. The private research agency came into existence, alongside developments within government. The modern survey began to emerge, and hence concern with the technique of interviewing within a relatively elaborate fixed schedule. Often, the work done was to be published in newspapers or was of direct commercial interest to the client, which meant that predictions might be testable, and numerical accuracy became important. There were also repeated studies of similar kinds carried out by the same agencies. Reliability began to be taken seriously as the data to evaluate it became available, and this led to concern with "interviewer effects" and the control of the interviewing force.

The development of ideas about sampling was also important because it was only when, in the late 1930s, it began to be seen as desirable to have nationally representative samples that the issue of how to control a large, scattered, and not very highly trained body of interviewers came to the fore. Whatever the intellectual preferences of the surveyors, the realities of dealing with such a labor force had weight. Less was left to the interviewer's initiative, and training became more detailed and serious. Much of the work was done by psychologists, so an experimental and stimulus-response model was influential, and attitudes rather than factual information became a focus of interest.

The hothouse atmosphere of wartime research brought different strands of work together, and the modern survey emerged fully. There were controversies concerning structured versus unstructured approaches and open-ended versus closed questions, and different teams developed different styles, but there was much cooperation and consensus on many practical and technical issues. Nonexperimental aspects of psychology were prominent as inspiration; on the level of technique, Rogers's "nondirective" approach and psychoanalytic approaches were popular sources in the more qualitative styles. For those in the lead on survey research, however, question construction, sampling, and scaling became of more interest than interviewing as such. Researchers not in the survey world developed their own detailed qualitative techniques, often designed to deal with their own particular subject matters; some were heavily criticized by methodologists from

the perspectives that they had now developed.

After the war, new practices were incorporated into textbooks and training procedures. Systematic research on interviewing started, and it showed that some of the folk wisdom was unfounded. Social scientists turned to the survey as a major method, and it became a standard practice. Those out of favor defended alternatives, often under the banner of "participant observation" (Becker and Geer 1957). They differentiated their perspective from the survey by stressing direct observation over questioning, although certainly much "conversation with a purpose" (a frequently cited definition of *interview*) was part of their observation. Discussions of participant observation technique have, however, given attention to the social relations involved in such conversation rather than to the fine detail of what takes place in the encounter; obviously, repeated contacts with the same subjects raise different issues (see Atkinson and Coffey, Chapter 38, this volume).

Soon surveys were widespread enough for nonmethodologists to take an interest in them—although this interest was often skeptical. From the late 1960s, the upheaval in political and theoretical interests of the time was related to interviewing, and work was done on the implicit assumptions of interviewing in such matters as epistemology. Much more interest was shown in the social relations of interviewing; this was the heyday of reflexivity and autobiographical accounts of research. Specialist work on interviewing with particular groups (children, elites) also started to be written as the general application of survey method brought to light the special problems involved (see the contributions to Part II of this *Handbook*).

By the 1970s, interviewing was being taken for granted as an established practice in the survey world; specialists continued with increasingly sophisticated methodological research and refined details of method yet further, often in relation to new technologies using telephones and/or computers. The qualitative world became ideologically more separate from quantitative research, and qualitative researchers developed their own discussions, which showed little concern with the technical issues they might have in common with the survey world. Social scientists active in the growing feminist movement often saw qualitative methods as particularly appropriate to women as subjects and developed ideas about the special requirements of a feminist approach. The barrier between interviewer and respondent was attacked, and efforts were made to define ways of co-opting respondents rather than using them; whether this has been successful, and how it feels from the respondent's point of view, has hardly been investigated.

There is a sense in which interviewing has come full circle. Although in its early beginnings the typical stance of the researcher toward mass respondents was that of the social worker rather than of the social equal, for some researchers the interviewer again has a high degree of freedom and initiative and may make direct use of personal experience in conversation with subjects.

In much of the survey world, however, the pattern has been different. From a starting point where the interviewer's behavior was not much programmed, it has gone through a phase of high programming with relatively unsophisticated techniques to one where the areas formerly left unspoken, such as probing, are themselves intended to be programmed. What really happened in the field might not live up to those hopes, but less was done "in the field" now. The coming of the telephone interviewing system opened up fresh possibilities of near-total surveillance and control of interviewer behavior. Thus the flexibility needed for adaptation to the respondent's needs became no longer an arena of initiative. But meanwhile, another strand of development, the "cognitive" approach, has reopened some of the earlier possibilities of

unprogrammed conversational initiative by the survey interviewer and shows an interesting convergence between otherwise very separate areas of work.

Nevertheless, the interview remains an area of richly diverse practice about which few convincing generalizations can be made. Some of the changes that have taken place over time have arisen internally, from methodological concerns—although just which methodological concerns have been salient has depended on the problems studied and on the organizational and technological frameworks within which particular studies have taken place. Other changes have responded to broader intellectual movements and to agendas defined in sociopolitical rather than methodological terms.

■ Notes

1. For readers who would like to look at some of the discussions within another national tradition, a few references to French work: Bizeul (1998), Blanchet and Gotman (1992), Demaziere and Dubar (1997), Mayer (1995), Michelat (1975). I am grateful to Jean Peneff and Pierre Fournier for drawing these references to my attention.

2. I am indebted to John Smith for details of Elton Mayo's background and methodological development.

3. Later, however, Riesman contributed, in his chapter in Lazarsfeld and Thielens's collection titled *The Academic Mind* (1958), what is in effect—although he does not present it as such —an extended research-based discussion of validity based on respondent reports on the experience of being interviewed.

4. James Bennett (1981) has suggested the circumstances under which some types of these appear appropriate.

5. Some kinds of error, such as mistakes in following the schedule's instructions regarding which question to ask next, have been eliminated by the computer-assisted methods now commonly used by survey organizations. Lars Lyberg and Daniel Kasprzyk (1991:257) point out, how-

ever, that errors specific to computer-assisted telephone interviewing (CATI) may also arise.

6. This is another area where CATI must have changed the issues, although it has been little written about from that point of view; perhaps the physical separation from the respondent has placed the focus on control of the interviewer rather than on understanding the respondent's reactions to the situation.

■ *References*

Adorno, T. W., E. Frenkel-Brunswik, D. J. Levinson, and R. N. Sanford. 1950. *The Authoritarian Personality*. New York: Harper & Row.

American Marketing Association. 1937. *The Technique of Marketing Research*. New York: McGraw Hill.

Atkinson, R. 1998. *The Life Story Interview*. Thousand Oaks, CA: Sage.

Bales, K. 1991. "Charles Booth's Survey of *Life and Labour of the People in London 1889-1903*." Pp. 66-110 in *The Social Survey in Historical Perspective 1880-1940*, edited by M. Bulmer, K. Bales, and K. Sklar. Cambridge: Cambridge University Press.

Becker, H. S. and B. Geer. 1957. "Participant Observation and Interviewing: A Comparison." *Human Organization* 16:28-32.

Bennett, J. 1981. *Oral History and Delinquency: The Rhetoric of Criminology*. Chicago: University of Chicago Press.

Biemer, P. P., R. M. Groves, L. E. Lyberg, N. A. Mathiowetz, and S. Sudman, eds. 1991. *Measurement Errors in Surveys*. New York: John Wiley.

Bingham, W. and B. Moore. 1931. *How to Interview*. New York: Harper.

Bizeul, D. 1998. "Le Récit des conditions d'enquête: Exploiter l'information en connaissance de cause." *Revue Française de Sociologie* 39:751-87.

Blanchet, A. and A. Gotman. 1992. *L'Enquête et ses méthodes: L'Entretien*. Paris: Nathan.

Bradburn, N. and S. Sudman. 1979. *Improving Interview Method and Questionnaire Design*. San Francisco: Jossey-Bass.

Cannell, C. F. and R. L. Kahn. 1953. "The Collection of Data by Interviewing." Pp. 327-80 in *Research Methods in the Behavioral Sciences*, edited by L. Festinger and D. Katz. New York: Dryden.

Cannell, C. F., P. V. Miller, and L. Oksenberg. 1981. "Research on Interviewing Techniques." Pp. 389-437 in *Sociological Methodology 1981*, edited by S. Leinhardt. San Francisco: Jossey-Bass.

Cantril, H. 1947. *Gauging Public Opinion*. Princeton, NJ: Princeton University Press.

Christie, R. and M. Jahoda, eds. 1954. *Studies in the Scope and Method of "The Authoritarian Personality."* Glencoe, IL: Free Press.

Cicourel, A. V. 1964. *Method and Measurement in Sociology*. New York: Free Press.

Cochran, W., F. Mosteller, and J. W. Tukey. 1954. *Statistical Problems of the Kinsey Report*. Washington, DC: American Statistical Association.

Converse, J. M. 1987. *Survey Research in the U.S.: Roots and Emergence, 1890-1960*. Berkeley: University of California Press.

Converse, J. M. and H. Schuman. 1974. *Conversations at Random: Survey Research as Interviewers See It*. New York: John Wiley.

Demazière, D. and C. Dubar. 1997. *Analyser les entretiens biographiques: L'Exemple de récits d'insertion*, Paris: Nathan.

Denzin, N. K. 1970. *The Research Act in Sociology*. Chicago: Aldine.

Denzin, N. K. and Y. S. Lincoln. 2000. *Handbook of Qualitative Research*. 2d ed. Thousand Oaks, CA: Sage.

Dexter, L. 1970. *Elite and Specialized Interviewing*. Evanston, IL: Northwestern University Press.

Douglas, J. D. 1985. *Creative Interviewing*. Beverly Hills, CA: Sage.

Fontana, A. and J. H. Frey. 1994. "Interviewing: The Art of Science." Pp. 361-76 in *Handbook of Qualitative Research*, edited by N. K. Denzin and Y. S. Lincoln. Thousand Oaks, CA: Sage.

Fowler, F. J., Jr. 1991. "Reducing Interviewer-Related Error through Interviewer Training, Supervision, and Other Means." Pp. 259-78 in *Measurement Errors in Surveys,* edited by P. P. Biemer, R. M. Groves, L. E. Lyberg, N. A. Mathiowetz, and S. Sudman. New York: John Wiley.

Fry, C. L. 1934. *The Technique of Social Investigation.* New York: Harper.

Gallup, G. 1944. *A Guide to Public Opinion Polls.* Princeton, NJ: Princeton University Press.

Galtung, J. 1967. *Theory and Methods of Social Research.* London: Allen & Unwin.

Garrett, A. 1942. *Interviewing: Its Principles and Methods.* New York: Family Service Association of America.

Goode, W. J. and P. K. Hatt. 1952. *Methods in Social Research.* New York: McGraw-Hill.

Gorden, R. L. 1969. *Interviewing: Strategy, Techniques, and Tactics.* Homewood, IL: Dorsey.

Holstein, J. A. and J. F. Gubrium. 1995. *The Active Interview.* Thousand Oaks, CA: Sage.

Hyman, H. 1954. *Interviewing in Social Research.* Chicago: University of Chicago Press.

Kahn, R. L. and Cannell, C. F. 1957. *The Dynamics of Interviewing.* New York: John Wiley.

Kinsey, A. C., W. B. Pomeroy, and C. E. Martin. 1948. *Sexual Behavior in the Human Male.* Philadelphia: W. B. Saunders.

Lazarsfeld, P. F. 1944. "The Controversy over Detailed Interviews: An Offer for Negotiation." *Public Opinion Quarterly* 8:38-60.

Lazarsfeld, P. F. and W. Thielens, Jr., eds. 1958. *The Academic Mind.* Glencoe, IL: Free Press.

Lundberg, G. A. 1942. *Social Research.* New York: Longman, Green.

Lyberg, L. E. and D. Kasprzyk. 1991. "Data Collection Methods and Measurement Error: An Overview." Pp. 237-57 in *Measurement Errors in Surveys,* edited by P. P. Biemer, R. M. Groves, L. E. Lyberg, N. A. Mathiowetz, and S. Sudman. New York: John Wiley.

Maccoby, E. E. and N. Maccoby. 1954. "The Interview: A Tool of Social Science." Pp. 449-87 in *Handbook of Social Psychology,* Vol. 1, edited by G. Lindzey. Reading, MA: Addison-Wesley.

Mayer, N. 1995. "L'Entretien selon Pierre Bourdieu." *Revue Française de Sociologie* 36:355-70.

Michelat, G. 1975. "Sur l'utilisation de l'entretien non-directif en sociologie." *Revue Française de Sociologie* 16:229-47.

Mishler, E. G. 1986. *Research Interviewing: Context and Narrative.* Cambridge, MA: Harvard University Press.

Odum, H. W. and K. Jocher. 1929. *An Introduction to Social Research.* New York: Holt.

Palmer, V. M. 1928. *Field Studies in Sociology: A Student's Manual.* Chicago: University of Chicago Press.

Parker, T. 1997. *Studs Terkel: A Life in Words.* London: HarperCollins.

Peneff, J. 1988. "The Observers Observed: French Survey Researchers at Work." *Social Problems* 35:520-35.

Platt, J. 1996. *A History of Sociological Research Methods in America, 1920-1960.* Cambridge: Cambridge University Press,

Reinharz, S. 1992. *Feminist Methods in Social Research.* New York: Oxford University Press.

Richardson, S., B. S. Dohrenwend, and D. Klein. 1965. *Interviewing: Its Forms and Functions.* New York: Basic Books.

Riesman, D. 1958. "Some Observations on the Interviewing in the Teacher Apprehension Study." Pp. 266-370 in *The Academic Mind,* edited by P. F. Lazarsfeld and W. Thielens, Jr. Glencoe, IL: Free Press.

Riesman, D. and N. Glazer. 1952. *Faces in the Crowd.* New Haven, CT: Yale University Press.

Riesman, D., N. Glazer, and R. Denney. 1950. *The Lonely Crowd: A Study of the Changing American Character.* New Haven, CT: Yale University Press.

Roethlisberger, F. J. and W. J. Dickson. [1939] 1964. *Management and the Worker.* New York: John Wiley.

Roth, J. 1966. "Hired Hand Research." *American Sociologist* 1:190-96.

Schaeffer, N. C. 1991. "Conversation with a Purpose—or Conversation? Interaction in the Standardized Interview." Pp. 367-91 in *Measurement Errors in Surveys,* edited by P. P. Biemer, R. M. Groves, L. E. Lyberg, N. A. Mathiowetz, and S. Sudman. New York: John Wiley.

Schober, M. and F. Conrad. 1997. "Does Conversational Interviewing Reduce Survey Measurement Error?" *Public Opinion Quarterly* 61:576-602.

Selltiz, C., M. Jahoda, M. Deutsch, and S. W. Cook. 1965. *Research Methods in Social Relations*. London: Methuen.

Sjoberg, G. and R. Nett. 1968. *A Methodology for Social Research*. New York: Harper & Row.

Suchman, L. and B. Jordan. 1990. "Interactional Troubles in Face-to-Face Survey Interviews." *Journal of the American Statistical Association* 85:232-41.

Taylor, S. J. and R. Bogdan. 1984. *Introduction to Qualitative Research Methods*. 2d ed. New York: John Wiley.

Turner, C. and E. Martin, eds. 1984. *Surveying Subjective Phenomena*. New York: Russell Sage Foundation.

University of Michigan, Survey Research Center. 1954. *Manual for Interviewers*. Ann Arbor: Institute for Social Research.

Vidich, A. and J. Bensman. 1954. "The validity of field data." *Human Organization* 13:20-27.

Warner, W. L. and P. S. Lunt. 1941. *The Social Life of a Modern Community*. New Haven, CT: Yale University Press.

Young, P. V. 1935. *Interviewing in Social Work*. New York: McGraw-Hill.

———. 1939. *Scientific Social Surveys and Research*. New York: Prentice Hall.

———. 1949. *Scientific Social Surveys and Research*. 2d ed. New York: Prentice Hall.

FORMS OF INTERVIEWING

The forms of interviewing discussed by the contributors to Part I of this *Handbook* represent the variety of ways the interviewing process is organized. The chapters move from the individual survey interview, through diverse iterations of qualitative interviewing, to the group interview, concluding with observations on postmodern trends in interviewing. The emphasis of this section of the volume is on the diversity found within research interviewing, although, as we see from the nonresearch auspices of interviewing considered in Part III, the interview has applications in venues as far-flung as therapy and forensic investigation.

A leading model of interviewing that is typical of survey research conceives of the interview as a face-to-face "conversation with a purpose" between two unacquainted individuals, one the interviewer and the other the interviewee or respondent. Their roles are viewed as distinct; one asks questions and the other provides the answers. Much of the conventional methodological wisdom bearing on this model is built on this distinction and largely centers on the role of the interviewer. Less attention is paid to the respondent; it is taken for granted that if the interviewer does a good job, the respondent's work will fall into place. The interviewer is provided the slate of questions and is afforded the latitude to probe or invite as detailed responses as are warranted. The interviewer's job is to bring the respondent's full attention to the task and to encourage him or her to answer honestly, but otherwise not to shape or influence the responses. The interviewer aims for neutrality and objectivity. His or her role is to facilitate responses that the respondent is primed to give. Standardization is key (see also Schaeffer and Maynard, Chapter 28, this volume).

Other forms of interviewing alter this design. The rules or expectations for the behavior of the interviewer are relaxed. Qualitative and in-depth interviewing are more exploratory, theory driven, and collaborative. The interviewer has greater freedom to raise topics, formulate questions, and move in new directions. The interviewer sees his or her relationship with the respondent as an extended, open-ended exchange, focused on particular topics and the related subject matter that emerges in the interview process. The exchange is designed not so much to collect *the* facts, as it were, as to gather information that meaningfully frames the configuration and salience of those facts in the interviewee's life.

The nuances of understanding and the depths of experience are especially important. The qualitative interview is, to put it simply, focused on the "qualities" of respondents' experiences. This is not construed primarily in evaluatory terms, as in measures of the quality of life or the quality of care, but rather rests on the assumption that whatever the subject matter, it can have diverse qualities or meanings in people's experience. The aim of qualitative interviewing is to ascertain those qualities and their social organization.

In-depth interviewing takes this into the emotional realm. Given that meanings that are not readily available to casual communication are commonly center stage—such as the deep self, hidden feelings, and the most heartfelt views and values—the interview setting and process must be conducive to what some call "deep disclosure." The formalities of interviewing are decidedly reduced to enable the exploration of deeply nuanced inner worlds. Exploring the depths of experience takes time and patience and, as a result, considerable attention is paid to the interviewer's getting acquainted with the respondent. If acquaintanceship is not developed within the interview, its groundwork is laid in rapport-building sessions between interviewer and respondent before the actual interviewing gets under way. Some in-depth interviewers believe that the establishment of rapport requires a personal commitment from the interviewer; they often emphasize mutual disclosure. The idea here is that the respondent is more likely to offer up what is otherwise hidden within if the interviewer also communicates his or her own inner truths or emotionality.

Two important new avenues for interviewing that move in other directions are the life story interview and focus group interviewing. Although the life story interview has a substantial history in social research, the genre is currently being revisited and has become very popular across the social and behavioral sciences, the humanities, and professional practice. Narrative approaches are at the cutting edge of endeavors as wide-ranging as therapeutic interviewing (see Miller, de Shazer, and De Jong, Chapter 19, this volume) and oral history interviews (see Cándida Smith, Chapter 34, this volume). Some life story interviewing is naturalistic, whereas other applications are constructivist, with implications for the roles of the interview participants and the substantive aims of the interview process. The more naturalistically inclined tend to approach the interview as a search for meaning and pattern within respondents' lives, whereas the more constructively inclined open the purview to the mechanisms of co-construction that take place as the interview encounter unfolds.

Social scientific researchers have recently embraced focus group interviewing, just as the business world has employed it for decades. The organization of this form of interviewing alters the face-to-face interview by expanding the number of interview participants, especially the number of respondents. The goal is not so much to gather experiential facts from individuals and generalize them to a population (clearly, such facts would be contaminated by the social interaction involved) as it is to explore the range and depth of shared meanings in an area. The assumption is that public opinion can be revealed in an environment where respondents are encouraged to communicate with each other about the common knowledge that informs their understandings. Facilitated by a group moderator, the focus group interview becomes a process of mutual interviewing, with the roles of interviewer and interviewee in effect becoming shared property in the give-and-take of the proceedings.

If these distinctions—between interviewer and interviewee, questions and answers, facts and meanings—are organized in different ways across these forms of interviewing, they are nonetheless distinctions that have come to characterize the interview enterprise. Researchers with postmodern inclinations question the need for these distinctions in the first place. For example, the distinction between interviewer and interviewee is blurred and role reversals are put into effect, or roles are combined into what some call "autoethnography." The premise is that answers raise new questions and, in turn, become the basis for eliciting new answers. Postmodernism's communicative repositionings and inventive realizations take us from conventional interviewing to reflexive conversations and radical representations of interview "data." Although a distinct form of postmodern interview is yet to be discerned—and indeed postmodern sensibilities would certainly work against any definitive formulation—there are decided trends in this direction.

3

SURVEY INTERVIEWING

◆ Royce A. Singleton, Jr.
Bruce C. Straits

U ntil recently, survey research was carried out via face-to-face or telephone interviews or by way of mailed questionnaires. Developments in computer-assisted interviewing (see Couper and Hansen, Chapter 27, this volume) and Internet-based surveys (see Mann and Stewart, Chapter 29, this volume), however, have challenged the traditional distinction between an interview survey and a mail survey. Now it is more appropriate to think of the various modes of data collection as falling along a continuum from the most to the least interactive. At one end of this continuum, involving all channels of communication, is the face-to-face interview; this is followed, in turn, by telephone interviews, Internet interviews, computer-assisted self-interviews, and self-administered questionnaires. In addition, some surveys employ a mixture of data collection modes, such as incorporating a confidential self-administered form within a face-to-face interview as a means of collecting sensitive information.

This chapter focuses on surveys conducted using face-to-face and telephone interviews—surveys in which a researcher or, more commonly, an agent of the researcher interacts directly with a respondent. Face-to-face interviews were the dominant mode of survey data collection until the 1970s, when improved methods and an increasing proportion of households with telephones made telephone interviewing more viable and practical. Today, many polling agencies rely exclusively on telephone interviews, whereas many large-scale academic and government surveys are still conducted with face-to-face interviews.

In the past half century, surveys have become ubiquitous data gathering devices serving many purposes (see Platt, Chapter 2, this volume). Through surveys, social scientists, federal government agencies, the mass media, and other commercial interests test models of human behavior, estimate population trends, gauge public opinion, and assess consumer preferences. Regardless of surveys' purposes, their value ultimately rests on how accurately they measure population characteristics.

Robert Groves's (1989) "total error perspective" identifies four types of error that threaten the accuracy of survey results. *Sampling error,* the difference between a population value and a sample estimate of that value, occurs because only a sample rather than a complete census of the population is surveyed. Because sampling error is primarily a function of sampling design, sample size, and population heterogeneity, and not a function of the data collection process, our focus here is on the three other, nonsampling, errors: *coverage error,* the failure to give some members of the target population any chance of being included in the sample; *nonresponse error,* the failure to obtain data from all sampled persons; and *measurement error,* inaccuracies in what respondents report.

In describing interviewing as a survey mode, we review current knowledge regarding sources of interviewer-related error and common procedures for minimizing interviewer effects. Interviewer effects became an issue early in the history of survey research, when studies demonstrated the influence of interviewer ideology (Rice 1929) and expectations (e.g., Hyman 1954) on responses. By the 1950s, survey practitioners had developed widely accepted, standard survey interviewing practices designed to reduce interviewer error. These practices, still dominant in interviewer training, emphasize the highly structured role of the interviewer, who reads questions as a neutral agent while the respondent passively answers them (for an extended discussion of the challenges of standardization, see Schaeffer and Maynard, Chapter 28, this volume). As improved methods lessened concerns about interviewer effects, survey researchers gradually shifted the focus from the role of the interviewer to the role of the respondent and developed a more complex view of the interaction between interviewer and respondent (O'Muircheartaigh 1997). This shift in perspective has renewed interest in interviewing techniques and has stimulated considerable research in recent years, which we discuss at several points in this chapter.

◆ *Initial Concerns*

In nearly all survey interviewing, one individual or group (the researcher) designs the survey and another group (the interviewers) collects the data. Once the goals of the survey are established, the researcher initially must (a) develop a sampling plan, (b) devise appropriate questions, and (c) select the survey mode. Selection of the survey mode depends on several factors, including study goals, nature of the questions, the target population, and funds and other available resources. The objective is to select the survey mode that maximizes data quality (that is, minimizes error) within cost and resource constraints.

Face-to-face interviews, in comparison to telephone interviews, offer more flexibility in terms of question content and target population, tend to generate higher response rates, are more appropriate for long interviews with complex questions, permit the use of visual aids in presenting questions and response options, and enable unobtrusive interviewer observations of the respondents and their surroundings. By comparison, telephone interviews are cheaper, easier to administer, require a shorter data collection period, and permit greater control over interviewer training, supervision, and data collection quality (Singleton and Straits 1999:255-58; see also Shuy, Chapter 26, this volume).

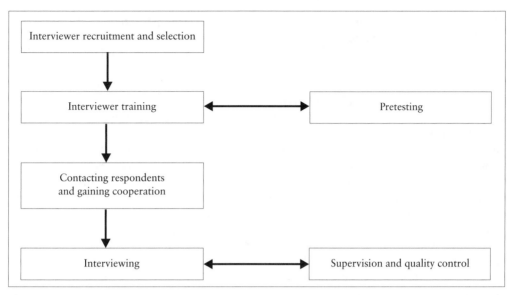

Figure 3.1. Steps in Survey Interviewing

Selection of a mode of data collection, development of a sampling design, and creation of a preliminary survey instrument complete the planning phase of the survey. The fieldwork phase then begins. This phase starts with the recruitment of interviewers, continues with interviewer training and instrument pretesting, and concludes with interviewing and field supervision. Figure 3.1 depicts the steps in survey interviewing.

◆ Interviewer Recruitment and Selection

Interviewer selection may influence the quality of surveys insofar as interviewer attributes affect an interviewer's ability to perform the job or the manner in which respondents interpret and answer questions. Consequently, survey researchers are concerned not only with hiring people who are competent to carry out interviewing tasks, but with identifying and controlling visible background traits that might affect responses. With regard to performance, reading and writing skills are clearly necessary

for interviewing; otherwise, researchers have found no consistent correlates between interviewer characteristics and the quality of interviewing (Fowler 1991). One meta-analysis of hundreds of studies showed only that interviewers under 25 years of age (mainly college students) produced more error than others (Sudman and Bradburn 1974); however, this appeared to be an artifact stemming from the inexperience and lack of training of student interviewers (Bradburn 1983).[1]

Regarding the impact of interviewer demographic characteristics on the answers obtained, two generalizations are consistent with research findings. First, despite an abundance of research, few studies have found any association; second, the few positive findings suggest that interviewer traits may have an effect when they stimulate respondents' apprehension about normatively appropriate responses (Fowler 1991). Several studies have shown, for example, that the race of the interviewer affects racially relevant responses (e.g., Schuman and Converse 1971; Hatchett and Schuman 1976; Anderson, Silver, and Abramson 1988b; Finkel, Guterbock, and Borg 1991). In general, blacks express fewer antiwhite sentiments to white than to black interviewers, and whites give fewer antiblack answers to black than to white interviewers. Less is known about whether other demographic variables, such as age, gender, and class, have the same effect as race, although this seems likely when a specific interviewer trait is particularly relevant. For instance, Emily Kane and Laura Macaulay (1993) found gender-of-interviewer effects on several items measuring gender role attitudes, with both male and female respondents tending to give more egalitarian responses to female than to male interviewers.

What are the implications of these findings for interviewer recruitment and selection? Because interviewer characteristics seldom have been found to affect responses, there is little basis for choosing one interviewer over another. The exception occurs when interviewer characteristics are particularly relevant to the survey topic, which is most apparent in questions pertaining to race. When race is a major survey topic, researchers often attempt to control for race-of-interviewer effects by matching the race of the interviewer with the race of the respondent. The assumption is that an interviewer who resembles the respondent will obtain more valid data than one who does not. Even race matching may be of limited utility, however, as evidence suggests that the interviewer's race makes little difference on most survey questions (Schuman and Converse 1971), and some research calls into question the assumption that race matching enhances validity (Anderson et al. 1988a).

The process of recruiting interviewers is basically the same as hiring for any job (Weinberg 1983). That is, positions are advertised, and applicants are screened and selected. Beyond minimum reading and writing skills, availability and readiness to meet job requirements are the principal selection criteria.[2] Other interviewer attributes are largely dependent on market forces. The majority of interviewers, according to data from a sample of interviewers at U.S. government statistical agencies,

do not regard their interviewing jobs as primary sources of income or as careers, perhaps because of the intermittent nature of the work (Groves and Couper 1998: 198). This work feature, as well as job requisites, also may account for the composition of the interviewer workforce, which is predominantly female, young to middle-aged, with above-average education. Given that such attributes are largely beyond the control of the researcher, it is fortunate that they appear to be much less important in determining the quality of a survey than the interviewer's ability achieved through careful training and experience.

◆ Interviewer Training

Interviewers receive training in general interviewing skills and techniques as well as in specific procedures required for particular survey projects. In practice, these two aspects of training often are combined, with survey-specific materials (e.g., questionnaire or sampling procedures) used for practical application (Weinberg 1983). The typical training program combines home study with a series of classroom sessions. The first session might begin with a general introduction to the study, followed by a presentation and instruction in basic interviewing skills and responsibilities. In the second session, the researcher might thoroughly familiarize interviewers with the survey questionnaire, conduct a demonstration interview, and then divide interviewers into pairs for supervised practice interviewing. Third and subsequent sessions might involve further practice, possibly including field experience, and further evaluation. Experienced interviewers generally receive survey-specific training through home study of the project's special interviewing procedures and survey instrument, followed by discussions or mock interviews with a field manager.

The length of the general training period varies, from less than one day in many surveys to three to five days in government and academic survey organizations (Fowler and Mangione 1990). Telephone interviewing also requires a shorter training period than does in-person interviewing. Two studies that examined the impact of training on interview skills suggest that less than one day of training is inadequate and three days may be optimal. Floyd Fowler and Thomas Mangione (1990) analyzed in-person interviews done by interviewers who were randomly assigned to four training programs of varying length. Those with less than one day of training were significantly worse than those with two or more days of training on several skills, such as reading questions correctly and probing when respondents gave incomplete or ambiguous answers. Analyses further suggested that supervised practice made the critical difference in interviewer skills, and that a protracted training period of 10 days was counterproductive, producing more interviewer-related error. Likewise, Jacques Billiet and Geert Loosveldt (1988) found that interviewers exposed to five three-hour training sessions were much better at handling questions requiring probing than those with only one three-hour session.

◆ Pretesting

Just as interviewers are trained to administer the survey effectively, the survey questions and instrument as a whole are evaluated to ascertain that they meet survey objectives and quality standards. Pretesting consists of one or more phases in the process of the design and evaluation of survey questions and procedures. An early stage in this process may entail focused discussions with small groups of participants (usually five to eight) led by a skilled interviewer. Before the discussions, the researcher will already have identified key topics and developed preliminary questions; the focus groups are then asked to share their perceptions of and reactions to these items. In this way, they can help evaluate the researcher's assumptions about reality and the appropriateness of the vocabulary (Fowler 1995). In the planning of a survey of sexual practices among teenagers, for example, teen focus groups could provide insight into how teens cognitively organize, label, and retrieve sexual information.

COGNITIVE LABORATORY INTERVIEWING

Once a draft of the survey instrument has been prepared, the next step is to evaluate the specific wording of questions to determine if respondents clearly understand and are able to answer them. Traditionally, such testing has been done solely "in the field," that is, in the homes of respondents drawn from the target population. However, sparked by recent interest in cognitive aspects of surveys (Jobe and Mingay 1991; Tanur 1992; Sirken et al. 1999), researchers have begun to test questions in the laboratory. The goal of cognitive laboratory interviewing is to understand the thought processes involved when respondents answer survey questions and to use this information to identify problems and formulate better questions. The cognitive laboratories established at the U.S. Census Bureau and other federal statistical agencies typically use paid subjects who are recruited to take part in intensive sessions lasting one to two hours. The primary methods are "think-aloud" interviews, probing questions, and paraphrasing follow-ups (for a more complete review, see Forsyth and Lessler 1991).

In think-aloud interviews, respondents are asked to think out loud, reporting everything that comes to mind, while arriving at answers to the questions. They verbalize their thought processes either concurrently, as they work out an answer to each question, or retrospectively, after they answer each question or complete the survey.

Here is an example of an improved question resulting from this procedure:

> One question asked, "How many times during the past twelve months have you stopped smoking for one day or longer?" The intent of this question was to measure attempts to quit smoking. However, the question was not always interpreted this way. Several respondents included instances when they had not smoked for at least one day because of illness, excessive drinking the previous day, or other extraneous circumstances. The revised version makes the intent clearer, asking specifically, "How many times during the past twelve months have you stopped smoking for one day or longer because you were trying to quit smoking?" (DeMaio and Rothgeb 1996:182-83)

A weakness of the think-aloud technique is that some respondents have great difficulty describing their thought processes verbally. Instead, an interviewer can focus on particular aspects of the cognitive processes by using special probes, such as "What did you think I meant by 'stopping smoking'?" Probes may directly follow each question (when the information used to answer the question is freshest in memory) or come at the end of the survey (to avoid reactivity or bias associated with the probing). Here is an example of probes used to pretest a question intended for elderly people:

Question: By yourself and without using special equipment, how much difficulty do you have bathing or showering, some, a lot, or are you unable to do it?

Probes: I said without using special equipment. What sort of things do you think would be special equipment? Do you use anything to help you bathe or shower? (Jobe, Keller, and Smith 1996:201)

Another technique, paraphrasing follow-ups, is to ask respondents to summarize or repeat a question in their own words. Not only is this a good test of whether respondents understand the literal and intended meaning of the question, it may also reveal better ways to word the question.

FIELD PRETESTING

The information gained through these cognitive diagnostic procedures gives direction to revision efforts. Often, several pretests and revisions of a questionnaire may be necessary to arrive at a good semifinal draft. Once the questionnaire is in this form, it is routinely tested in the field under more realistic interviewing conditions. This phase of pretesting may be carried out before or as part of interviewer training, with either experienced interviewers or interviewers in training. Typically, field pretesting is based on 25-50 interviews with a convenience sample of persons having characteristics similar to those in the target population. Interviewers both administer the questionnaire and observe the process to identify practical problems in following procedures as well as questions that respondents have trouble answering. Although they may take notes during the interviews or file reports afterward, their observations generally are conveyed in a group oral debriefing (Converse and Presser 1986).

Field pretests of this sort are standard in survey research, providing the ultimate "dress rehearsal" of the instrument and procedures. However, they have several limitations (Fowler 1995; Fowler and Cannell 1996): Playing the role of interviewer may interfere with the task of observing the process; each interviewer's observations are based on a small number of interviews, which may not be adequate for reliably assessing question problems; the standards for evaluation may not be well articulated or may be applied inconsistently, resulting in a lack of agreement about problem questions; and the recognition of question comprehension problems is limited to items in which respondents ask for clarification or give inappropriate answers. Some of these problems may be addressed through cognitive laboratory interviewing. Recently, however, several strategies have been applied to make field pretesting more systematic and reliable. These include behavior coding, respondent debriefings, interviewing ratings, split-panel tests, and response analysis.

Originally developed to evaluate interviewer performance (e.g., Cannell, Miller, and Oksenberg 1981), behavior coding consists of the systematic coding of the frequency of problematic respondent and interviewer behaviors with respect to each question in live or taped interviews. For example, one might code such behaviors as interviewers incorrectly reading or skipping questions, respondents interrupting interviewers before questions are completely read, respondents requesting that questions be repeated or clarified, and interviewers probing to follow up on inadequate answers (Fowler 1995:116-21). For instance, behavior coding revealed that a question commonly used in governmental health studies, "When was the last time you had a general physical examination or checkup?" elicited a high proportion (87 percent) of inadequate answers because respondents did not understand the meaning of "general physical examination or checkup" and whether the "when" was a request for a date, elapsed time, or their age at the time (Oksenberg, Cannell, and Kalton 1991:335).[3]

Although behavior coding is designed to identify question problems, it does not always reveal the sources of problems. One way to do this is to use the cognitive interviewing technique of special probes, sometimes called respondent debriefings, in field pretest interviews (see DeMaio and Rothgeb 1996:188-94). The results of cognitive laboratory interviews tend to be limited to very small, unrepresentative samples, but respondent debriefing can provide

researchers with a way to assess the generalizability of cognitive testing results. To apply this method successfully, however, "researchers must have a clear idea of potential problems in order to develop good debriefing questions" (DeMaio and Rothgeb 1996:190).

Researchers may seek another perspective on question-and-answer problems from the pretest interviewers. Although interviewer debriefings customarily entail informal group discussions with the interviewers, Fowler (1995:121-24) recommends that researchers have the interviewers fill out standardized ratings of each question prior to the debriefing session in order to collect more systematic information.

Finally, two other methods require somewhat larger pretest samples. Experimental manipulations of question ordering, wording, and formats, called split-panel or split-ballot tests, are a costly but effective way to check out suspected problems or weaknesses under field conditions. Split-panel tests require random assignment of adequate-sized samples of pretest respondents to the versions being tested. For example, the results of cognitive interviewing might suggest a serious problem of question-order effects. The researcher could test this suspicion experimentally by randomly assigning pretest respondents to two forms of the instrument in which the order of related questions differs and then comparing the responses on the two forms.

The responses of the pretest respondents also can be tabulated and examined for such problems as a low response rate to sensitive questions, the incidence of "don't know" responses, items on which nearly everyone makes the same response, and the adequacy of responses to open-ended questions. The generalizability of a response analysis is dependent upon the pretest sample size and the degree to which the pretest respondents resemble the target population.

Each of these pretesting techniques offers a slightly different window on the question-and-answer process: Behavior coding allows the researcher to see interviewer-respondent interaction under actual field conditions, respondent debriefings and other cognitive interviewing methods reveal problems from the respondent's perspective, interviewer debriefings expose problems from the interviewer's perspective, response analysis reveals problems from the researcher's perspective, and split-panel tests show differences among instrument versions. This suggests that some pretest methods are better than others at identifying particular types of question problems.

To test this idea, Stanley Presser and Johnny Blair (1994) systematically compared four pretest methods: conventional field pretesting with oral group debriefings, behavior coding of live pretest interviews, cognitive interviewing combining follow-up probes with concurrent and retrospective think-alouds, and panels of experts. Each method was applied to a single questionnaire in repeated trials. Results indicated that behavior coding was the most reliable and conventional pretesting the least reliable, expert panels identified the largest number of problems and were the least costly, experts and cognitive interviewing were the only methods likely to spot problems affecting the data analysis, and conventional pretesting and behavior coding were the only effective methods for spotting problems involving the interviewer.

Noting that the expert panel was the most cost-effective, Presser and Blair argued that questionnaire drafts should be routinely subjected to a peer review process. Their results also imply that questionnaires should be subjected to more than one form of pretesting. After reviewing an evaluation of the U.S. Current Population Survey, James Esposito and Jennifer Rothgeb (1997) concluded that the use of multiple techniques is critical to any comprehensive program of pretesting, as it capitalizes on the strengths of individual techniques while compensating for the unique weaknesses associated with each.

◆ Securing Respondents

The manner in which respondents are selected depends on the survey mode and the sampling design. Because only random samples provide unbiased estimates of population characteristics and the means of calculating the expected margin of sampling error, virtually all major surveys use some form of random or probability sampling. When there is no adequate list of the individuals in the population, such as for the adult population of the United States, sample selection proceeds in stages. It is common in face-to-face surveys to select individuals within randomly chosen households from randomly chosen blocks within sampled counties or metropolitan areas. Similarly, most telephone surveys use a technique called random-digit dialing (RDD) to choose telephone numbers randomly; for example, telephone prefixes (exchanges) within the target geographic area are sampled and then the last four digits of the telephone number are chosen or generated by computer randomly.

The interviewer's responsibility in the sampling process ordinarily consists of following specified rules to select an eligible respondent within each designated or telephone household. In most face-to-face interviews, prospective respondents first receive letters introducing them to the survey and notifying them that they will be contacted. Once someone answers the door, the interviewer introduces him- or herself, explains the purpose of the visit, presents credentials or other supporting documents (e.g., brochures, identification card), identifies the eligible household member, and asks for his or her cooperation. This scenario is similar in RDD telephone surveys except that prior notification is not possible and other means of legitimating the survey request are more limited.

To obtain responses, interviewers must contact or reach the sample person and then persuade him or her to cooperate by completing the survey. Noncontacts and refusals both contribute to nonresponse error or bias. Nonresponse error is a function of the proportion of noncontacts and refusals (nonresponse rate) and the difference between respondents and nonrespondents. Because the latter difference is almost always unknown, however, most surveys report the nonresponse rate as an indicator of sample quality. "The implicit assumption . . . is the higher the response rate, the lower the nonresponse bias" (Groves 1989:209).

Making contact with designated households is primarily a matter of persistence and overcoming barriers. To maximize the likelihood that respondents are at home at the time of the initial contact, some survey organizations limit the hours of contact to weekdays after 4:00 p.m. and all day on weekends. If no one is available, interviewers make repeated callbacks, typically at least 6 for face-to-face surveys and 10 or more for telephone surveys (Fowler 1993). To increase the odds of contacting persons with different at-home patterns, they also vary the times of calls among daytime, evenings, and weekends. Finally, interviewers may leave notes, ask neighbors or apartment managers when the target respondents are usually at home, and obtain telephone numbers to set up appointments.

Avoiding refusals is a more difficult problem with a more complex set of causes (Schwarz, Groves, and Schuman 1998; see also Adler and Adler, Chapter 25, this volume). Some of those causes lie in the social environment and in demographic characteristics of nonrespondents. For example, evidence of declining response rates in surveys (Steeh 1981; Hox and de Leeuw 1994; Groves and Couper 1998) has led to speculation about the negative impact of public opinion regarding survey participation and concerns over privacy and confidentiality (Singer, Hippler, and Schwarz 1992). Some studies also indicate that the elderly, lower-educated householders, those living alone, and those living in urban areas are more likely to refuse than their counterparts (DeMaio 1980; Groves 1989; Groves and Couper 1998). Other causes of refusals reside in characteristics of the interviewer, survey design and procedures, and interviewer-respondent interaction. Because survey design and interaction variables are under the control of the researcher or interviewer, they offer the most promising lines of inquiry for overcoming resistance to cooperation.

Many survey procedures that are intended to enhance the likelihood of gaining cooperation are based on a social exchange theory of human behavior (Goyder 1987; Dillman 2000). According to this view, the greater the perceived rewards relative to perceived costs of complying with an interview request, the more likely it is that an individual will cooperate. Among the ways that survey researchers attempt to provide rewards are showing positive regard for respondents, expressing appreciation, and pointing out the social utility of the survey; attempts to reduce costs include making the interview as short as possible and otherwise minimizing the burden of responding (Dillman 2000). Research also supports the utility of promising or giving respondents cash or token gifts (e.g., pens, calendars) when they are contacted. Eleanor Singer and associates' (1999) meta-analysis of 39 experiments in telephone and face-to-face interview surveys showed that both monetary and nonmonetary incentives increased response rates, even when the cash amount was relatively small (less than $10 U.S.) and the burden of the interview was low. Other research shows that respondents are more likely to comply when the survey topic is of high rather than low salience to them (Goyder 1987; Hox and de Leeuw 1994; Couper 1997), presumably because answering high-salience questions is more interesting and rewarding.

In survey interviews, it is the interviewer who ultimately mediates such design features. Indeed, the interaction between interviewer and respondent appears to play a large part in the decision to cooperate or refuse. According to Robert Groves and Mick Couper's (1996, 1998) theory of survey participation, in the initial moments of the survey encounter, the sample person is actively trying to comprehend the purpose of the interviewer's visit. He or she uses cues from the words, behavior, and physical appearance of the interviewer to arrive at an explanation (or identify a "script") and then evaluates the costs of continuing the conversation. Whether the person eventually agrees or refuses to participate depends on the interviewer's ability to judge the particular script reflected in the householder's initial response quickly and accurately and to react accordingly.

The theory is consistent with analyses of interviewer-householder interactions. For example, Robert Groves, Robert Cialdini, and Mick Couper (1992) found that experienced interviewers use two related strategies to convince respondents to participate. First, they tailor their approach to the sample unit, adjusting their dress, mannerisms, language, and arguments according to their observations of the neighborhood, housing unit, and immediate reactions of the householder. Second, they maintain interaction, which maximizes the possibility of identifying relevant cues for tailoring the conversation to present the most effective arguments. In a subsequent analysis, Groves and Couper (1996) concluded that the most effective interviewer adaptations were those that addressed the real concerns of the householder.

The theory of survey participation applies mainly to face-to-face interviews. The cues for tailoring are much richer and it is easier to prolong the conversation in face-to-face compared with telephone conversations. Fewer normative constraints for maintaining telephone conversations make telephone surveys easier to terminate, and refusals tend to occur in the first minute, before any argument for participating can be presented (Groves 1990). In telephone surveys, there are also fewer means of legitimating the survey request, as there is no opportunity to present identification badges or brochures, no visual contact with the interviewer, and (in RDD surveys) no advance contact through letters.

Given these more limited sources of influence, it is not surprising that refusal rates are higher and response rates consistently lower in telephone than in face-to-face surveys. Joop Hox and Edith de Leeuw (1994:335) found an average response rate of 70.3 percent in telephone and 73.5 percent in face-to-face surveys, based on a meta-analysis of 45 studies that compared the responses obtained across survey modes.[4] Some studies indicate that a prior letter to respondents in telephone surveys can reduce refusals (Dillman, Gallegos, and Frey 1976; Traugott, Groves, and Lepkowski 1987), but this technique requires the use of lists of telephone numbers, which invariably are outdated and exclude new and unlisted numbers. Consequently, the reduction in nonresponse error may be more than offset by an increase in coverage error.

Other research suggests that in telephone surveys, the interviewer's vocalization, apart from the content of the communication, may affect compliance rates. Lois Oksenberg and Charles Cannell (1988; see also Oksenberg, Coleman, and Cannell 1986) asked subjects to rate the tape-recorded voices of interviewers who were giving actual introductions to a telephone survey. Interviewers who obtained higher cooperation rates were perceived as speaking louder and more rapidly, as speaking with a standard American pronunciation and a falling intonation, and as sounding more confident and competent than those whose cooperation rates were lower. Moreover, the speech characteristics were highly correlated with the confidence and competence ratings. Apparently, impressions formed based on interviewer vocalization affected willingness to cooperate, leading Oksenberg and Cannell to propose the introduction of voice training into training programs for telephone survey interviewers.

Finally, survey practitioners utilize various methods to convert householders who are reluctant to cooperate when initially contacted. Most often, they assign more experienced interviewers or supervisors to recontact refusals, or they may employ highly effective interviewers known as "converters." Groves (1990) found that a conversion rate of 20-40 percent is common in telephone surveys, and one academic-based, national face-to-face survey reported successful conversions of 35-45 percent (Davis and Smith 1992). Another common practice is to mail special persuasion letters that reiterate the importance of the survey and the respondent's participation in it. Based on their theory of survey participation, Groves and Couper (1998) speculate that such letters are most likely to be successful if they acknowledge the legitimacy of the householder's comments and present appropriate counterarguments. For example, if a person has declined to participate because she is too busy, the letter could indicate the willingness of the interviewer to meet at any time that is convenient for her. Some researchers may buttress such appeals by offering respondents incentive fees to complete the survey (e.g., Laumann et al. 1994:56-57). Also, in telephone and mail surveys initially reluctant respondents may be contacted through a different, usually more expensive mode; thus face-to-face contacts sometimes are made with initial refusals in telephone surveys, and telephone contacts may be used to follow up nonreturns in mail surveys.

◆ Interviewing

Once the respondent has agreed to cooperate, the interviewer begins the process of asking questions and recording answers. At this point, the researcher's concern shifts to measurement error, or inaccuracies in responses to questions. The four principal sources of measurement error are the inter-viewers, the respondents, the questions, and the mode of data collection. Regarding survey mode, available evidence generally points to small differences between face-to-face and telephone interviews, suggesting that similar conclusions will be reached independent of the mode, provided that the surveys are implemented competently (Schwarz et al. 1998). A substantial literature exists on question design—the effects of question forms (e.g., open versus closed), types of questions (e.g., threatening versus nonthreatening), question wording, the order in which questions are asked (Schuman and Presser 1981; for a recent overview, see Schwarz et al. 1998). There also is a growing literature on respondents' question comprehension, memory, motivation, and judgment (Schwarz and Sudman 1994, 1996; Sudman, Bradburn, and Schwarz 1996). Here we examine the effects of the interviewer. One potential source of influence on respondents' answers, discussed earlier with respect to interviewer selection, is the interviewer's social background characteristics. In this section, we focus on the survey interviewer's role demands and variations in role behavior.

INTERVIEWING PRACTICES

Survey interviewing is generally synonymous with standardized interviewing. The goal of standardization is to expose each respondent to the same interview experience, so that any differences in recorded answers can be assumed to be due to differences among respondents "rather than differences in the process that produced the answer" (Fowler and Mangione 1990:14). To standardize the measurement process, survey researchers construct structured questionnaires consisting almost entirely of closed-ended questions that are presented to all respondents in the same order, and they carefully prescribe the procedures that interviewers must follow. Ideally, interviewers should be perfectly consistent, neutral intermediaries of the survey researcher (but see Schaeffer and Maynard, Chapter 28, this volume). In short, "the goal [of standardized interviewing] is nothing less than the elimination of the interviewer as a source of measurement error" (Groves 1989:358).

Although specific practices vary from one survey organization to another, the following four rules of standardized interviewing, according to Fowler (1991:264; see also Fowler and Mangione 1990), are given almost universally to interviewers:

1. Read the questions exactly as written.

2. If a respondent does not answer a question fully, use nondirective follow-up probes to elicit a better answer. Standard probes include repeating the question, prompting with "Tell me more," and asking such questions as "Anything else?" and "How do you mean that?"

3. Record answers to questions without interpretation or editing. When a question is open-ended, this means recording the answer verbatim.

4. Maintain a professional, neutral relationship with the respondent. Do not give personal information, express opinions about the subject matter of the interview, or give feedback that implies a judgment about the content of an answer.

Survey practitioners use several strategies to assure standardization. Most important, they train interviewers to follow the above rules; as noted earlier, research has shown that interviewers with insufficient training are not adept at applying standardized protocols, especially nondirective probing. Second, field supervisors monitor and provide feedback on interviewers' performance (see the discussion of supervision below).

Third, as Fowler and Mangione (1990) argue, training respondents in how to participate in the question-and-answer process facilitates the conduct of a standardized in-terview. If respondents have an understanding of their role, they will feel more comfortable and interviewers will feel less awkward in following the rules of standardization. To train respondents, interviewers can read a brief statement before the interview starts that describes the nature of a standardized interview, and they can remind respondents of their role when they fail to perform it appropriately.

Fourth, in a similar vein, Cannell et al. (1981) contend that respondents also need to be *motivated* to perform their role, especially the reporting task. They recommend and have tested three principal methods of promoting a good role performance: (a) adding instructional passages to the interview that explain to the respondent the importance of producing complete and accurate information and how to answer questions adequately, (b) providing differential verbal feedback that positively reinforces good performance and negatively reinforces poor performance, and (c) asking the respondent to make an overt agreement to answer questions conscientiously. To standardize the feedback process as much as possible, criteria for judging the respondent's performance and appropriate feedback statements are printed in the questionnaire, and interviewers are trained in their use. In experiments with both face-to-face and telephone interviews, Cannell and his associates showed that the use of these techniques improved the quality of reporting (Cannell et al. 1981; Miller and Cannell 1982). Despite their apparent value and relatively low cost, however, they do not appear to be widely used in surveys.

A fifth way to ensure standardization is to reduce the need for interviewers to clarify the meanings of questions for respondents. Thomas Mangione, Floyd Fowler, and Thomas Louis (1992) found that questions that produced the greatest variation among interviewers were those that required the use of follow-up probes to obtain adequate answers. Robert Groves and Lou Magilavy (1986) also found that interviewer error was correlated with the number of distinct answers to open-ended questions, due to variable probing behavior. Together, these results indicate that interviewer error is more likely to occur when questionnaire items are difficult to administer and to answer. One way of minimizing the impact of such questions is to specify more interviewer reactions to certain responses within the survey instrument. The best approach is to identify and correct poorly designed questions with cognitive laboratory and other pretesting techniques —before the survey is undertaken.

Finally, for the past three decades, survey practitioners have attempted to increase standardization through the application of computer technology that automates various data collection tasks (see Couper and Hansen, Chapter 27, this volume). Computer-assisted interviewing (CAI) techniques replace paper-and-pencil forms with a small computer or computer terminal. Interviewers (or respondents) read the survey questions as presented on the computer screen and enter the answers via the keyboard. The application of this technology began in the 1970s with the development of computer-assisted telephone interviewing (CATI), which is currently used widely to manage the sampling process, control and monitor interviewer tasks, and expedite data processing. Specifically, CATI systems can automatically dial phone numbers, schedule callbacks, and even screen and select the person to be interviewed at each sampled phone number; prompt the interviewer with appropriate introductions, probes, and questions in the proper sequence, skip irrelevant questions, and identify responses inconsistent with replies to earlier questions; alert the interviewer when an illegitimate code is entered and record responses into a computer data file; maintain records of interviewer productivity that are accessible to survey supervisors; and reproduce an interviewer's screen at a supervisor's terminal to allow for audio monitoring (Nicholls 1988).

With the advent of microcomputers in the 1980s, CAI was extended to face-to-face surveys. In computer-assisted personal interviewing (CAPI), the interviewer carries out the survey using a laptop computer that he or she brings to the respondent's home; in computer-assisted self-administered interviewing (CASI), the respondent records his or her own answers on a computer provided by an interviewer or researcher.[5] Noting that many large- scale government surveys in the United States are conducted with CAPI, Roger Tourangeau and Tom Smith (1996) claim that "CAPI has become perhaps the most commonly used method of face-to-face data collection today" (p. 276). CASI can be used with or without an interviewer present and either as an adjunct to personal interviewing or as a stand-alone method. Several studies have shown that self-administered surveys, including those conducted using CASI, increase the reporting of illegal or embarrassing activities, such as illicit drug use, alcohol consumption, and sexual activity (e.g., Aquilino 1994; Jobe et al. 1997; Tourangeau and Smith 1996). Given the trend for surveys to collect increasingly sensitive information (Tourangeau and Smith 1996), it seems likely that the use of CASI also will increase.

CAI methods offer several advantages apart from automating interviewer tasks. They can reduce the costs of data collection, speed up data delivery, and improve data quality by reducing item omissions and data inconsistencies (Weeks 1992; Baker, Bradburn, and Johnson 1995; Nicholls, Baker, and Martin 1997); they also make it easier to randomize question sequences and question wording for experimental tests. Based on their comprehensive review of studies comparing CAI surveys with paper-and-pencil interview (PAPI) surveys, William Nicholls and his colleagues (1997) concluded that both respondents and interviewers accept, often enthusiastically, the use of a computer during interviewing, that data entry errors are no more frequent with CAI than with PAPI, and that CATI enhances supervisory quality control. Despite the presumed potential of CAI to reduce measurement error, however, extant studies tend to show that CAI is at best marginally superior to PAPI.

In the end, Nicholls et al. (1997) deduced that comparisons of CAI and PAPI methods may become irrelevant "as CAI becomes the new standard for survey data collection." As this occurs, they argue, research on CAI methodology "should be refocused to inform choices of collection mode, questionnaire design, and field work procedures" (p. 242). Instrument design or layout, as Mick Couper and Sue Hansen note in Chapter 27 of this volume, is particularly important in CAI surveys because the computer exerts greater control over the flow of the interview and the interviewer becomes more dependent on the work of the designer.

EVALUATIVE STUDIES

Considerable empirical evidence and sound theoretical arguments justify standardization principles (Fowler 1991; Fowler and Mangione 1990). For example, if questions are not asked as worded, one cannot know what question was posed. Numerous experiments have shown that small changes in the wording of questions can alter the distribution of answers (Schuman and Presser 1981). Also, experiments have demonstrated that suggestive questioning (presenting only a subset of answer alternatives that are presumed to be relevant) and suggestive probing can affect response distributions and relationships with other variables (Smit, Dijkstra, and van der Zouwen 1997).

Indirect evidence of the effectiveness of standardization derives from studies of interviewer error in well-conducted surveys. When interviewer error is measured in terms of interviewer variation, or the extent to which answers to a question are cor-

related with the interviewer, the estimates tend to be relatively small (Groves 1989; de Leeuw and Collins 1997).[6] There is little direct evidence, however, on the relationship between prescribed interviewer behavior and data quality. On the one hand, observational studies applying behavior coding indicate that even well-trained interviewers often depart from standardized protocols. Fowler (1991) has reported studies that showed a range of 5 to 60 percent of questions at least slightly reworded and a range of 20 to 40 percent in the use of directive or leading probes (see, for example, Bradburn et al. 1979; Cannell and Oksenberg 1988; Fowler and Mangione 1990). On the other hand, few studies have connected such behavior to interviewer-related error and even fewer have found a significant correlation. For example, Groves and Magilavy (1986) found no relationship between errors in question reading and interviewer variability. One recent study, reportedly the first to test the effect of nonstandardized interviewer behavior on the *accuracy* of responses, analyzed audiotaped in-home interviews in a survey of health and health care utilization (Dykema, Lepkowski, and Blixt 1997). When the researchers compared responses with hospital records, they found no consistent relationship between interviewers' departures from the exact reading of questions and response accuracy. The only exception was an item in which changes in question wording produced *more* accurate reporting.

More information clearly is needed on what interviewer behaviors contribute most to interviewer-related error. Still, there is little doubt that standardization reduces the interviewer's contribution to measurement error. A more serious, long-standing concern—one that recently has resurfaced—is that presenting a standard stimulus in and of itself can produce measurement error. According to this view, standardized interviewing stifles interviewer-respondent communication in two ways: (a) It inhibits the ability to establish rapport, which motivates respondents to cooperate and give complete and accurate answers; and (b) it ignores the detection and correction of communication problems (Beatty 1995).

The issue of rapport received the most attention during the early development of standardization. By the mid-1970s, a smattering of evidence that personalizing interviews was counterproductive led survey researchers to discredit the value of rapport (Beatty 1995). Interest in the interviewer-respondent relationship survives today in research on different styles of interviewing. Wil Dijkstra (1987; see also van der Zouwen, Dijkstra, and Smit 1991) investigated the consequences of a personal versus formal style of interviewing with interviewers who maintained the general rules of standardization. Interviewers trained in the "personal" style were instructed to express a sympathetic attitude toward respondents by making such statements as "I understand what moving to this house meant for you" and "How nice for you!" Those trained in a "formal" style were instructed to be polite but neutral. Results indicated that respondents interviewed in a personal style gave more accurate answers on a map-drawing task, more socially undesirable answers, and fewer "don't know" responses than did those interviewed in a formal style. But interviewers trained in the personal style also were more likely than interviewers trained in a formal style to use leading probes and to accept incomplete answers. Thus respondent performance may be better with the personal style, but additional training and close supervision of interviewers may be necessary to offset the style's undesirable effects.

The second controversy—that standardization sidesteps communication problems—recently has gained the greatest notice. In a widely cited article, Lucy Suchman and Brigitte Jordan (1990) argue that standardization suppresses elements of ordinary conversation that are crucial for establishing the relevance and meaning of questions. Interviewers who are trained to read questions as written and to discourage elabora-tion are not prepared to listen carefully for misunderstandings and correct them. From videotapes of standardized interviews, Suchman and Jordan give several examples of miscommunication, such as an interviewer failing to correct a respondent who interprets "alcoholic beverages" to include hard liquor but to exclude wine, which led to invalid responses. Such problems could be resolved, these authors claim, if interviewers were granted the freedom and responsibility to negotiate the intended meanings of questions through ordinary conversational conventions.

While acknowledging the communication problems identified by Suchman and Jordan, advocates of standardized interviewing tend to disagree with them about causes and remedies. Some advocates contend that problems arise chiefly because of poorly worded questions, and whether respondents interpret questions consistently and accurately depends on adequate question pretesting (Kovar and Royston 1990). Detractors of standardization maintain that efforts to improve question wording are rarely, if ever, sufficient. Researchers need interviewers to help assure consistent interpretations, but this is unlikely unless interviewers are given a freer hand in communicating with respondents than standardization allows.

Paul Beatty (1995) notes that advocates on both sides of this debate tend to take extreme positions that seem incompatible. He argues, following Nora Cate Schaeffer (1991), that although the problems of standardization should not be overlooked, it also is foolish to ignore the merits. The real issue for Beatty is "How can researchers solve communication problems while harnessing the full benefits of standardization?" One means is the development of better questions; another may involve adapting the role of the interviewer. Both Beatty and Schaeffer (see Schaeffer and Maynard, Chapter 28, this volume) call for empirical research on interaction within the interview to investigate breakdowns in establishing mutual understanding.

At the least, the debate over standardization will continue to raise questions about restrictions on interviewer behavior. Michael Schober and Frederick Conrad's (1997) promising new line of research suggests, for example, that it may be beneficial to give interviewers more leeway in clarifying terms or concepts in survey questions. According to the most stringent view of standardization, interviewers should not attempt to define terms for respondents, even if scripted definitions are available, because this will make the stimulus inconsistent (Fowler and Mangione 1990). Initially, Schober and Conrad conducted a laboratory experiment comparing this form of standardized interviewing with a more flexible method that encouraged interviewers to paraphrase questions, provide definitions in their own words, and ask questions or intervene if they thought the respondent misunderstood the question. Experienced interviewers were trained in one of these two interviewing techniques after first receiving instruction on the key survey concepts. The questions were drawn from ongoing government surveys. So that response accuracy could be assessed, respondents were given fictional scenarios upon which to base their answers; in half the scenarios, the circumstances corresponded straightforwardly to government definitions of the terms in the question, and in half they did not. When the mapping between the scenario and question was straightforward, both interviewing methods produced nearly perfect accuracy. But when the mapping was complicated, response accuracy was much higher for the flexible than for the standardized interviewers. This increased accuracy came at a cost, however, as flexible interviewers took nearly three times as long to complete the interview.

In subsequent studies, Schober and Conrad replicated this basic finding—greater response accuracy but more lengthy interviews with flexible interviewing—when they measured natural interviewer deviations from standardization (Schober and Conrad 1999), when interviewers could clarify concepts with either scripted definitions or in their own words and the clarification was either solicited or unsolicited (Schober, Conrad, and Fricker 2000), and when respondents in a household telephone survey were reinterviewed and accuracy was inferred from measures of response change and explanations for answers (Conrad and Schober 2000). Although this research implies that different interviewing techniques may be appropriate under different circumstances (Schober and Conrad 1997:596), more research is needed to determine when and how best to implement the "conversational" interviewing approach.

THE INTERVIEW AS A SOCIAL OCCASION

Schober and Conrad's research draws upon theoretical analyses of the process of understanding in ordinary conversations. A key proposition of this theory is that addressees make sense of questions by relying on speakers to help interpret the question —that is, to make sure that the question was understood as intended (Schober 1999). From this perspective, the problem with strictly standardized interviewing is that interviewers are not supposed to help respondents interpret the questions, which leaves respondents to arrive at their own, sometimes erroneous, interpretations.

Schober and Conrad's theoretical focus is on the interview as an interactive process. Many other survey methodologists recently have begun to concentrate on the role of the respondent; in so doing, they also have drawn heavily on theories of conversational processes as well as on work in cognitive and social psychology (for detailed discussions, see Schwarz and Sudman 1996; Sudman et al. 1996; Sirken et al. 1999). Although, scientifically, the survey interview is an occasion to obtain valid responses to a series of questions, it also is a social occasion subject to the influences of the social world. Being interviewed is an uncommon, sometimes anxiety-provoking experience for many respondents. Unfamiliar with the canons of structured interviewing, they turn to the social and linguistic rules governing everyday conversation for guidance on how they should behave as respondents. In answering each question, they also attend to a sequence of cognitive tasks with a certain level of motivation. What can each of these perspectives tell us about survey interviewing?

From a conversational perspective, survey interviews are social encounters between highly trained interviewers and respondents who, at best, receive limited "on-the-job" training. In deciphering their proper role in answering questions, respondents may be unintentionally influenced by subtle aspects of the survey instrument and administration, such as prior questions, response formats, and other cues irrelevant to the intended purpose of the current question. In particular, respondents may rely upon the implied assumptions underlying ordinary conversations to make sense of survey interviews (Grice 1989:22-40). Seymour Sudman and his colleagues (1996: 247-48) suggest that many common types of response errors stem from respondents' adherence to H. P. Grice's (1989) principles of conversation:

1. Speakers should not say things that they believe to be false. [*Truthfulness*]

2. Speakers should make comments that are relevant to the purposes of the conversation. [*Relevance*]

3. Speakers should make their contributions as informative as possible and not repeat themselves. [*Nonredundancy*]

4. Speakers should express themselves as clearly as possible. [*Clarity*]

These principles imply that interviewers will ask only clear questions that respondents are capable of answering promptly. That is, asking the question presupposes

that it can and should be answered. Because respondents will perceive vague, ambiguous, and difficult questions as relevant, they will feel pressure to respond immediately, even if their replies are haphazard guesses or hasty estimates. Unless an explicit "don't know" option is part of an attitudinal question, people without opinions may feel obligated to provide some.

The methodological strategy of exploring complex topics by asking a series of related questions runs counter to the conversational principle that the same information will not be requested twice. Consequently, when a general question on a topic (e.g., general life satisfaction) follows a related specific one (e.g., marital satisfaction), respondents try to be informative by not reiterating information provided earlier in their responses to the specific question. That is, they interpret the second question as asking for new information about general life satisfaction apart from their marital satisfaction.

From the perspective of cognitive processing, obtaining reliable and valid responses requires that the respondents (a) comprehend the literal and intended meaning of the question, (b) retrieve the information requested from memory, (c) formulate a response in accord with the question and the information retrieved, and (d) communicate a response deemed appropriate (Sudman et al. 1996:58-75). The question-answer task breaks down when question wording is vague, when the purpose of the question is misunderstood, when there is insufficient time to access relevant information from memory, when the accessed information does not fit the response options provided in the question, and when the respondent modifies the information to project a favorable image to the interviewer.

Another theoretical perspective, rational choice theory, has been applied to understanding when respondents are motivated to expend the minimum ("satisficing") or the maximum ("optimizing") effort to generate acceptable answers to survey questions (Alwin 1991:17-18; Krosnick 1991). Theoretically, the likelihood of satisficing behavior increases with question difficulty and decreases with the respondent's motivation and ability to answer the question.

The aforementioned conversational, cognitive, and motivational processes are interdependent in the question-response task. If respondents perceive that a difficult question should be answered promptly, for example, they may not allow adequate time to search memory (satisficing strategy). Because they judge every aspect of the survey instrument to be relevant, respondents may draw upon prior, but unrelated, questions to infer the intended meaning of the current question.

Efforts to apply communication and cognitive theories to the survey process began in the 1980s. With a few notable exceptions (e.g., Groves and Couper's theory of survey participation), most applications thus far have been applied to questionnaire design, including the development of diagnostic procedures for pretesting, described earlier. The time now appears to be ripe for the integration of this work into a broader theory of survey interviewing that fully integrates the interviewer, the respondent, and the task.

◆ Supervision and Quality Control

Once the interviewing phase of the survey begins, the researcher or an interviewer supervisor oversees all aspects of the data collection. The supervisor's role involves three interrelated sets of activities: managing the work of the interviewers, monitoring interviewer performance, and administering quality control procedures. In their management role, supervisors provide materials, collect completed questionnaires, pay interviewers for work done, make themselves available to answer questions and provide help, identify and resolve problems, hold regular meetings with interviewers, and review and give feedback on interviewers' work.

To detect problems and review interviewers' progress, supervisors monitor their performance. In virtually all surveys, part of performance monitoring involves careful record keeping and evaluation of completed interviews. Records kept on the numbers of hours worked, amounts paid, numbers of eligible contacts, and numbers of refusals provide critical information on interviewer productivity, survey costs (e.g., time and dollars per interview), and survey quality (response and refusal rates). By reviewing completed questionnaires, supervisors also can clarify uncodable responses and check to see if interviewers are following instructions and recording answers appropriately. As Fowler and Mangione (1990:122) point out, however, none of this information is useful for assessing the quality of measurement, because it does not reveal what actually occurs during the question-and-answer process. To tell whether interviewers ask questions exactly as written, use neutral probes, and record answers correctly, many survey organizations also have supervisors monitor or observe the interview process.

In face-to-face interview surveys, supervisors may observe interviewers either by accompanying them on interviews or by having them make tape recordings of all or a sample of their interviews. Direct field observation is much more costly and possibly more intrusive, although it provides the most information, including what occurs from the initial contact to the beginning of the interview and nonverbal communication during the interview. The low-cost, portable tape recorders available today make it feasible for field monitoring to be practiced routinely. Respondents' permission is required for the tape recording of interviews, but respondents seldom object when interviewers explain that this is a standard part of the quality control process (Weinberg 1983:354).

Monitoring, as well as all other supervisory activities, is much simpler for telephone than for face-to-face interviewing. When a telephone survey is conducted from a central facility, special monitoring phones allow supervisors to listen to ongoing interviews without being heard by either the interviewer or the respondent. This allows for prompt feedback and retraining, if necessary, which helps to minimize interviewer error.

For both in-person and telephone monitoring, Fowler and Mangione (1990) recommend the use of systematic evaluation forms to make certain that observers attend to all aspects of interviewer performance. When they systematically varied the feedback that interviewers received from their supervisors, they found that the kinds of feedback they received affected interviewers' perceptions of the priorities of the survey organization. Interviewers who received feedback on their completed questionnaires or on tape-recorded interviews rated being a standardized interviewer as more important than did interviewers who received feedback only on productivity indicators such as costs, numbers of hours worked, and response rates.

Reviewing completed questionnaires and observing interviews are two mechanisms for controlling the quality of interviewers' work and thereby determining the quality of the data. Two other processes are retrieving missing data and validating interviews (Weinberg 1983). When data are missing, particularly for factual items that are critical to the survey, respondents may be recontacted to retrieve the information. Also, it is standard in all well-conducted surveys to verify that the interview actually took place and that the interviewer did not fabricate some responses or deviate from prescribed procedures. As evidence of the potential significance of this problem, one study found that 3-5 percent of interviewers at the U.S. Census Bureau committed some form of cheating between September 1982 and August 1985 (Biemer and Stokes 1989:25). Supervisors usually accomplish

validation by reinterviewing a sample of respondents for each interviewer; respondents may be asked a subset of items. In the case of in-person surveys, reinterviews often are carried out by telephone. For recurring surveys, supervisors may use reinterviews not only to detect cheating but to evaluate and provide feedback on interviewers' performance (Forsman and Schreiner 1991).

The supervision of interviewers is an extension of another form of quality control: interviewer training. Supervision cannot replace training, but it can reinforce the need for precision and accuracy (Weinberg 1983) and ensure that interviewers are using the skills they have learned (Fowler and Mangione 1990). Another important aspect of the supervisory role involves sustaining interviewers' motivation and enthusiasm and preventing interviewers from developing feelings of isolation. It is easy to assume that interviewers will do better work as they gain experience; however, studies have shown that the opposite may be the case. For example, validity studies of reports of hospitalizations and physician visits found that the more interviews an interviewer had done, the greater the problem of underreporting (Cannell, Marquis, and Laurent 1977). Thus supervisors should meet with interviewers regularly throughout the interviewing period, not only to provide continuing feedback and reinforcement of skills but to communicate the importance of good interviewing.

♦ Conclusions

In this chapter we have examined the essential steps in the fieldwork or data collection phase of interviewer-administered surveys. It is important, however, to consider again the broader survey process. Prior to collecting data, the researcher must formulate objectives, identify the population, design and draw a sample, translate concepts into appropriate questions, and select a data collection mode. Thus considerable planning must be accomplished before the first interview takes place. And even before the last interview is finished, the researcher will have begun to prepare for the postsurvey phase by editing and coding completed questionnaires or, in the case of centralized telephone surveys, by entering the data into a computer file. Finally, data processing and analysis, interpretation of findings, and dissemination of results complete the survey process.

Each step in the planning and fieldwork phases may influence subsequent stages in the survey, and each has implications for sources of error and, hence, the quality of the survey. Choice of survey mode, as we have seen, has an impact on nonresponse error, which tends to be greater in telephone than in face-to-face surveys. This affects follow-up efforts to reach respondents and efforts to convert initial refusals; it also affects postsurvey statistical adjustments and estimates of error. Throughout this chapter we have emphasized survey error and data quality. But further adding to the complexity, costs must be weighed against data quality at all stages of a project. For example, cost considerations may dictate the choice of survey mode (telephone surveys are less expensive than face-to-face surveys), the number of callbacks that can be made to reach respondents, and the time and effort that can be devoted to convert refusals, all of which affect nonresponse error.

A survey interview is both a type of survey and a type of interview. In this chapter we have emphasized the former, drawing attention to how interviewing operates to accomplish survey aims. It also is important, however, to consider the survey interview as a special case of conversation between individuals. Although the survey interview has a definite structure and rules of its own that differ from other conversations (Bradburn 1992), it has many elements in common with ordinary conversation (see Baker, Chapter 37, this volume), as we have seen in our discussion of the interview as a social encounter. By focusing on these common elements, in particular the cognitive, communicative, and social processes involved in answering questions, survey methodologists can gain important insights into interviewing practice as it relates to the quality of survey data.

■ Notes

1. Interviewer-related error has been measured in various ways. The most commonly used measure, the intraclass correlation, compares the variation in responses among different interviewers with the total variation in responses (see Groves 1989). The more alike the responses obtained by one interviewer relative to those obtained by another, the higher the correlation. Researchers also have calculated the association between interviewer traits (e.g., race, gender) and answers to particular questions. Finally, in rare instances, researchers have directly measured response accuracy associated with different interviewers by comparing survey answers against records or other behavioral evidence (e.g., Anderson, Silver, and Abramson 1988a).

2. Surveys of target populations with large percentages of non-English-speaking people may require the recruitment of bilingual interviewers. The need to conduct interviews in a foreign language raises numerous issues that are beyond the scope of the present chapter. Historically, most U.S. surveys, including virtually all of those reviewed here, have avoided such issues by limiting their target populations to those who speak English. Obviously, however, that solution may result in a large coverage error.

3. Ruth Bolton and Tina Bronkhorst (1996) recently have extended this approach by developing a coding scheme that can be applied automatically to electronically transcribed interviews.

4. Response rates are affected by many other factors, including the sponsoring organization. Commercial surveys tend to have a lower rate of response than government or academic surveys, and some government face-to-face surveys achieve response rates of well over 90 percent.

5. In addition to CAPI and CASI, new data collection technologies include audio computer-assisted self-administered interviewing and audio computer-assisted telephone surveys that use voice recording or Touch-Tone data en-

try. Internet surveys and on-line interviewing are also becoming increasingly common (see Mann and Stewart, Chapter 29, this volume).

6. Edith de Leeuw and Martin Collins (1997) report that the intraclass correlation averages round .02 in well-conducted face-to-face surveys and .01 in centrally controlled telephone surveys; however, the total error that is interviewer related is a function of both the intraclass correlation and the number of interviews conducted per interviewer.

■ References

Alwin, D. F. 1991. "Research on Survey Quality." *Sociological Methods & Research* 20:3-29.

Anderson, B. A., B. D. Silver, and P. R. Abramson. 1988a. "The Effects of Race of Interviewer on Measures of Electoral Participation by Blacks in SRC National Election Studies." *Public Opinion Quarterly* 52:53-83.

———. 1988b. "The Effects of Race of the Interviewer on Race-Related Attitudes of Black Respondents in SRC/CPS National Election Studies." *Public Opinion Quarterly* 52:289-324.

Aquilino, W. S. 1994. "Interview Mode Effects in Surveys of Drug and Alcohol Use." *Public Opinion Quarterly* 58:210-50.

Baker, R. P., N. M. Bradburn, and R. A. Johnson. 1995. "Computer-Assisted Personal Interviewing: An Experimental Evaluation of Data Quality and Cost." *Journal of Official Statistics* 11:413-31.

Beatty, P. 1995. "Understanding the Standardized/Non-Standardized Interviewing Controversy." *Journal of Official Statistics* 11:147-60.

Biemer, P. P. and S. L. Stokes. 1989. "The Optimal Design of Quality Control Samples to Detect Interviewer Cheating." *Journal of Official Statistics* 5:23-39.

Billiet, J. and G. Loosveldt. 1988. "Improvement of the Quality of Responses to Factual Survey Questions by Interviewer Training." *Public Opinion Quarterly* 52:190-211.

Bolton, R. N. and T. M. Bronkhorst. 1996. "Questionnaire Pretesting: Computer-Assisted Coding of Concurrent Protocols." Pp. 37-64 in *Answering Questions: Methodology for Determining Cognitive and Communicative Processes in Survey Research,* edited by N. Schwarz and S. Sudman. San Francisco: Jossey-Bass.

Bradburn, N. M. 1983. "Response Effects." Pp. 289-328 in *Handbook of Survey Research,* edited by P. H. Rossi, J. D. Wright, and A. B. Anderson. New York: Academic Press.

———. 1992. "What Have We Learned?" Pp. 315-23 in *Context Effects in Social and Psychological Research,* edited by N. Schwarz and S. Sudman. New York: Springer-Verlag.

Bradburn, N. M., S. Sudman, and Associates. 1979. *Improving Interview Method and Questionnaire Design: Response Effects to Threatening Questions in Survey Research.* San Francisco: Jossey-Bass.

Cannell, C. F., K. H. Marquis, and A. Laurent. 1977. *A Summary of Studies of Interviewing Methodology* (Vital and Health Statistics Series 2, Data Evaluation and Methods Research, No. 69). Rockville, MD: National Center for Health Statistics.

Cannell, C. F., P. V. Miller, and L. Oksenberg. 1981. "Research on Interviewing Techniques." Pp. 389-437 in *Sociological Methodology 1981,* edited by S. Leinhardt. San Francisco: Jossey-Bass.

Cannell, C. F. and L. Oksenberg. 1988. "Observation of Behavior in Telephone Interviews." Pp. 475-95 in *Telephone Survey Methodology,* edited by R. M. Groves, P. P. Biemer, L. E. Lyberg, J. T. Massey, W. L. Nicholls II, and J. Waksberg. New York: John Wiley.

Conrad, F. G. and M. F. Schober. 2000. "Clarifying Question Meaning in a Household Telephone Survey." *Public Opinion Quarterly* 64:1-28.

Converse, J. M. and S. Presser. 1986. *Survey Questions: Handcrafting the Standardized Questionnaire.* Beverly Hills, CA: Sage.

Couper, M. P. 1997. "Survey Introductions and Data Quality." *Public Opinion Quarterly* 61:317-38.

Davis, J. A. and T. W. Smith. 1992. *The NORC General Social Survey: A User's Guide.* Newbury Park, CA: Sage.

de Leeuw, E. D. and M. Collins. 1997. "Data Collection Methods and Survey Quality: An Overview." Pp. 199-220 in *Survey Measurement and Process Quality,* edited by L. E. Lyberg, P. P. Biemer, M. Collins, E. D. de Leeuw, C. Dippo, N. Schwarz, and D. Trewin. New York: John Wiley.

DeMaio, T. J. 1980. "Refusals: Who, Where and Why." *Public Opinion Quarterly* 44:223-33.

DeMaio, T. J. and J. M. Rothgeb. 1996. "Cognitive Interviewing Techniques: In the Lab and in the Field." Pp. 177-95 in *Answering Questions: Methodology for Determining Cognitive and Communicative Processes in Survey Research,* edited by N. Schwarz and S. Sudman. San Francisco: Jossey-Bass.

Dijkstra, W. 1987. "Interviewing Style and Respondent Behavior: An Experimental Study of the Survey-Interview." *Sociological Methods & Research* 16:309-34.

Dillman, D. A. 2000. *Mail and Internet Surveys: The Tailored Design Method.* 2d ed. New York: John Wiley.

Dillman, D. A., J. G. Gallegos, and J. H. Frey. 1976. "Reducing Refusal Rates for Telephone Interviews." *Public Opinion Quarterly* 40:66-78.

Dykema, J., J. M. Lepkowski, and S. Blixt. 1997. "The Effect of Interviewer and Respondent Behavior on Data Quality: Analysis of Interaction Coding in a Validation Study." Pp. 287-310 in *Survey Measurement and Process Quality,* edited by L. E. Lyberg, P. P. Biemer, M. Collins, E. D. de Leeuw, C. Dippo, N. Schwarz, and D. Trewin. New York: John Wiley.

Esposito, J. L. and J. M. Rothgeb. 1997. "Evaluating Survey Data: Making the Transition from Pretesting to Quality Assessment." Pp. 541-71 in *Survey Measurement and Process Quality,* edited by L. E. Lyberg, P. P. Biemer, M. Collins, E. D. de Leeuw, C. Dippo, N. Schwarz, and D. Trewin. New York: John Wiley.

Finkel, S. E., T. M. Guterbock, and M. J. Borg. 1991. "Race-of-Interviewer Effects in a Pre-election Poll: Virginia 1989." *Public Opinion Quarterly* 55:313-30.

Forsman, G. and I. Schreiner. 1991. "The Design and Analysis of Reinterview: An Overview." Pp. 279-301 in *Measurement Errors in Surveys,* edited by P. P. Biemer, R. M. Groves, L. E. Lyberg, N. A. Mathiowetz, and S. Sudman. New York: John Wiley.

Forsyth, B. H. and J. T. Lessler. 1991. "Cognitive Laboratory Methods: A Taxonomy." Pp. 393-418 in *Measurement Errors in Surveys,* edited by P. P. Biemer, R. M. Groves, L. E. Lyberg, N. A. Mathiowetz, and S. Sudman. New York: John Wiley.

Fowler, F. J., Jr. 1991. "Reducing Interviewer-Related Error through Interviewer Training, Supervision, and Other Means." Pp. 259-78 in *Measurement Errors in Surveys,* edited by P. P. Biemer, R. M. Groves, L. E. Lyberg, N. A. Mathiowetz, and S. Sudman. New York: John Wiley.

———. 1993. *Survey Research Methods.* 2d ed. Newbury Park, CA: Sage.

———. 1995. *Improving Survey Questions: Design and Evaluation.* Thousand Oaks, CA: Sage.

Fowler, F. J., Jr. and C. F. Cannell. 1996. "Using Behavioral Coding to Identify Cognitive Problems with Survey Questions." Pp. 15-36 in *Answering Questions: Methodology for Determining Cognitive and Communicative Processes in Survey Research,* edited by N. Schwarz and S. Sudman. San Francisco: Jossey-Bass.

Fowler, F. J., Jr. and T. W. Mangione. 1990. *Standardized Survey Interviewing: Minimizing Interviewer-Related Error.* Newbury Park, CA: Sage.

Goyder, J. 1987. *The Silent Minority: Nonrespondents and Sample Surveys.* Boulder, CO: Westview.

Grice, H. P. 1989. *Studies in the Way of Words.* Cambridge, MA: Harvard University Press.

Groves, R. M. 1989. *Survey Errors and Survey Costs.* New York: John Wiley.

———. 1990. "Theories and Methods of Telephone Surveys." *Annual Review of Sociology* 16:221-40.

Groves, R. M., R. B. Cialdini, and M. P. Couper. 1992. "Understanding the Decision to Participate in a Survey." *Public Opinion Quarterly* 56:475-95.

Groves, R. M. and M. P. Couper. 1996. "Contact-Level Influences on Cooperation in Face-to-Face Surveys." *Journal of Official Statistics* 12:63-83.

———. 1998. *Nonresponse in Household Interview Surveys.* New York: John Wiley.

Groves, R. M. and L. J. Magilavy. 1986. "Measuring and Explaining Interviewer Effects in Centralized Telephone Surveys." *Public Opinion Quarterly* 50:251-66.

Hatchett, S. and H. Schuman. 1976. "White Respondents and Race of Interviewer Effects." *Public Opinion Quarterly* 39:523-28.

Hox, J. J. and E. D. de Leeuw. 1994. "A Comparison of Nonresponse in Mail, Telephone, and Face-to-Face Surveys." *Quality and Quantity* 28:329-44.

Hyman, H. H. 1954. *Interviewing in Social Research.* Chicago: University of Chicago Press.

Jobe, J. B., D. M. Keller, and A. F. Smith. 1996. "Cognitive Techniques in Interviewing Older People." Pp. 197-219 in *Answering Questions: Methodology for Determining Cognitive and Communicative Processes in Survey Research,* edited by N. Schwarz and S. Sudman. San Francisco: Jossey-Bass.

Jobe, J. B. and D. J. Mingay. 1991. "Cognition and Survey Measurement: History and Overview." *Applied Cognitive Psychology* 5:175-92.

Jobe, J. B., W. F. Pratt, R. Tourangeau, A. K. Baldwin, and K. A. Rasinski. 1997. "Effects of Interview Mode on Sensitive Questions in a Fertility Survey." Pp. 311-29 in *Survey Measurement and Process Quality,* edited by L. E. Lyberg, P. P. Biemer, M. Collins, E. D. de Leeuw, C. Dippo, N. Schwarz, and D. Trewin. New York: John Wiley.

Kane, E. W. and L. J. Macaulay. 1993. "Interviewer Gender and Gender Attitudes." *Public Opinion Quarterly* 57:1-28.

Kovar, M. G. and P. Royston. 1990. "Comment." *Journal of the American Statistical Association* 85:246-47.

Krosnick, J. A. 1991. "Response Strategies for Coping with the Cognitive Demands of Attitude Measures in Surveys." *Applied Cognitive Psychology* 5:213-36.

Laumann, E. O., J. H. Gagnon, R. T. Michael, and S. Michaels. 1994. *The Social Organization of Sexuality: Sexual Practices in the United States.* Chicago: University of Chicago Press.

Mangione, T. W., F. J. Fowler, Jr., and T. A. Louis. 1992. "Question Characteristics and Interviewer Effects." *Journal of Official Statistics* 8:293-307.

Miller, P. V. and C. F. Cannell. 1982. "A Study of Experimental Techniques for Telephone Interviewing." *Public Opinion Quarterly* 46:250-69.

Nicholls, W. L., II. 1988. "Computer-Assisted Telephone Interviewing: A General Introduction." Pp. 377-85 in *Telephone Survey Methodology,* edited by R. M. Groves, P. P. Biemer, L. E. Lyberg, J. T. Massey, W. L. Nicholls II, and J. Waksberg. New York: John Wiley.

Nicholls, W. L., II, R. P. Baker, and J. Martin. 1997. "The Effect of New Data Collection Technologies on Survey Data Quality." Pp. 221-48 in *Survey Measurement and Process Quality,* edited by L. E. Lyberg, P. P. Biemer, M. Collins, E. D. de Leeuw, C. Dippo, N. Schwarz, and D. Trewin. New York: John Wiley.

Oksenberg, L. and C. F. Cannell. 1988. "Effects of Interviewer Vocal Characteristics on Nonresponse." Pp. 257-69 in *Telephone Survey Methodology,* edited by R. M. Groves, P. P. Biemer, L. E. Lyberg, J. T. Massey, W. L. Nicholls II, and J. Waksberg. New York: John Wiley.

Oksenberg, L., C. F. Cannell, and G. Kalton. 1991. "New Strategies for Pretesting Survey Questions." *Journal of Official Statistics* 7:349-65.

Oksenberg, L., L. Coleman, and C. F. Cannell. 1986. "Interviewers' Voices and Refusal Rates in Telephone Surveys." *Public Opinion Quarterly* 50:97-111.

O'Muircheartaigh, C. A. 1997. "Measurement Error in Surveys: A Historical Perspective." Pp. 1-25 in *Survey Measurement and Process Quality,* edited by L. E. Lyberg, P. P. Biemer, M. Collins, E. D. de Leeuw, C. Dippo, N. Schwarz, and D. Trewin. New York: John Wiley.

Presser, S. and J. Blair. 1994. "Survey Pretesting: Do Different Methods Produce Different Results?" Pp. 73-104 in *Sociological Methodology 1994,* edited by P. Marsden. San Francisco: Jossey-Bass.

Rice, S. A. 1929. "Contagious Bias in the Interview: A Methodological Note." *American Journal of Sociology* 35:420-23.

Schaeffer, N. C. 1991. "Conversation with a Purpose—or Conversation? Interaction in the Standardized Interview." Pp. 367-91 in *Measurement Errors in Surveys,* edited by P. P. Biemer, R. M. Groves, L. E. Lyberg, N. A. Mathiowetz, and S. Sudman. New York: John Wiley.

Schober, M. F. 1999. "Making Sense of Questions: An Interactional Approach." Pp. 77-93 in *Cognition and Survey Research,* edited by M. G. Sirken, D. Herrmann, S. Schechter, N. Schwarz, J. M. Tanur, and R. Tourangeau. New York: John Wiley.

Schober, M. F. and F. G. Conrad. 1997. "Does Conversational Interviewing Reduce Survey Measurement Error?" *Public Opinion Quarterly* 61:576-602.

———. 1999. "Response Accuracy When Interviewers Stray from Standardization." Pp. 940-45 in *Proceedings of the Joint Statistical Meeting of the American Statistical Association, Section on Survey Research Methods, 1998.* Alexandria, VA: American Statistical Association.

Schober, M. F., F. G. Conrad, and S. S. Fricker. 2000. "When and How Should Survey Interviewers Clarify Question Meaning?" In *Proceedings of the Joint Statistical Meeting of the American Statistical Association, Section on Survey Research Methods, 1999.* Alexandria, VA: American Statistical Association.

Schuman, H. and J. M. Converse. 1971. "Effects of Black and White Interviewers on Black Responses in 1968." *Public Opinion Quarterly* 35:44-68.

Schuman, H. and S. Presser. 1981. *Questions and Answers in Attitude Surveys: Experiments on Question Form, Wording, and Context.* San Diego: Academic Press.

Schwarz, N., R. M. Groves, and H. Schuman. 1998. "Survey Methods." Pp. 143-79 in *Handbook of Social Psychology,* 4th ed., Vol. 1, edited by D. T. Gilbert, S. T. Fiske, and G. Lindzey. New York: McGraw-Hill.

Schwarz, N. and S. Sudman, eds. 1994. *Autobiographical Memory and the Validity of Retrospective Reports.* New York: Springer-Verlag.

———, eds. 1996. *Answering Questions: Methodology for Determining Cognitive and Communicative Processes in Survey Research.* San Francisco: Jossey-Bass.

Singer, E., H.-J. Hippler, and N. Schwarz. 1992. "Confidentiality Assurances in Surveys: Reassurance or Threat?" *International Journal of Public Opinion Research* 4:256-68.

Singer, E., J. V. Hoewyk, N. Gebler, T. Raghunathan, and K. McGonagle. 1999. "The Effect of Incentives on Response Rates in Interviewer-Mediated Surveys." *Journal of Official Statistics* 15:217-30.

Singleton, R. A., Jr. and B. C. Straits. 1999. *Approaches to Social Research.* 3d ed. New York: Oxford University Press.

Sirken, M. G., D. Herrmann, S. Schechter, N. Schwarz, J. M. Tanur, and R. Tourangeau, eds. 1999. *Cognition and Survey Research.* New York: John Wiley.

Smit, J. H., W. Dijkstra, and J. van der Zouwen. 1997. "Suggestive Interviewer Behavior in Surveys: An Experimental Study." *Journal of Official Statistics* 13:19-28.

Steeh, C. G. 1981. "Trends in Nonresponse Rates, 1952-1979." *Public Opinion Quarterly* 45:40-57.

Suchman, L. and B. Jordan. 1990. "Interactional Troubles in Face-to-Face Survey Interviews." *Journal of the American Statistical Association* 85:232-41.

Sudman, S. and N. M. Bradburn. 1974. *Response Effects in Surveys: A Review and Synthesis.* Chicago: Aldine.

Sudman, S., N. M. Bradburn, and N. Schwarz. 1996. *Thinking about Answers: The Application of Cognitive Processes to Survey Methodology.* San Francisco: Jossey-Bass.

Tanur, J. M., ed. 1992. *Questions about Questions: Inquiries into the Cognitive Bases of Surveys.* New York: Russell Sage Foundation.

Tourangeau, R. and T. W. Smith. 1996. "Asking Sensitive Questions: Impact of Data Collection Mode, Question Format, and Question Context." *Public Opinion Quarterly* 60:275-304.

Traugott, M. W., R. M. Groves, and J. M. Lepkowski. 1987. "Using Dual Frame Designs to Reduce Nonresponse in Telephone Surveys." *Public Opinion Quarterly* 51:522-39.

van der Zouwen, J., W. Dijkstra, and J. H. Smit. 1991. "Studying Respondent-Interviewer Interaction: The Relationship between Interviewing Style, Interviewer Behavior, and Response Behavior." Pp. 419-37 in *Measurement Errors in Surveys,* edited by P. P. Biemer, R. M. Groves, L. E. Lyberg, N. A. Mathiowetz, and S. Sudman. New York: John Wiley.

Weeks, M. F. 1992. "Computer-Assisted Survey Methods Information Collection: A Review of CASIC Methods and Their Implications for Survey Operations." *Journal of Official Statistics* 8:445-65.

Weinberg, E. 1983. "Data Collection: Planning and Management." Pp. 329-58 in *Handbook of Survey Research,* edited by P. H. Rossi, J. D. Wright, and A. B. Anderson. New York: Academic Press.

4

QUALITATIVE INTERVIEWING

◆ Carol A. B. Warren

Qualitative interviewing is based in conversation (Kvale 1996), with the emphasis on researchers asking questions and listening, and respondents answering (Rubin and Rubin 1995). It is similar to standardized survey interviewing in this respect, but unlike the survey interview, the epistemology of the qualitative interview tends to be more constructionist than positivist. Interview participants are more likely to be viewed as meaning makers, not passive conduits for retrieving information from an existing vessel of answers (Holstein and Gubrium 1995). The purpose of most qualitative interviewing is to derive interpretations, not facts or laws, from respondent talk. Some researchers frame the qualitative interview as a "speech event" (see Mishler 1986), which is useful, for instance, in narrative or conversation analysis (see in this volume Baker, Chapter 37; Riessman, Chapter 33). Other researchers, such as myself, frame it more substantively and interactionally, aiming to understand the meaning of respondents' experiences and life worlds.[1]

The emphasis of this chapter is on the substantive and social contours of the qualitative interview. Following a brief note on the importance of participants' perspectives for an understanding of the process and the relevancies of qualitative interviewing, the chapter proceeds through three major sections. The first of these takes up some initial considerations the researcher might engage in preparing to do qualitative interviewing; the focus is on concerns that are preliminary to the actual interviewing process. The second section deals with the interview process itself, especially as it relates to meaning making. The third and final section takes up the matter of interpretation in relation to self and others. Throughout the chapter, I draw on various qualitative interview-based studies for illustration, especially my own.

◆ A Note on Perspective

Donna Luff (1999:701) refers to perspectives as "fractured subjectivities." Applied to interviewing, Luff's characterization suggests that participants—both researchers and respondents—speak to each other not from stable and coherent standpoints, but from varied *perspectives*. These include the structured and historically grounded roles and hierarchies of their society, particularly those of gender, race, and class (Campbell 1998). Extending this to more local considerations, it also suggests that the perspectives relevant to the qualitative interview encompass the social positions that emerge in the interview itself, apparent in talk and interaction between interviewer and respondent. For example, during an interview, the perspective of the respondent may shift from one standpoint in her experience to another, as she speaks, say, as a former child, then as a mother, as a caregiver, then as an employee, or even as one who watches the local news (Holstein and Gubrium 1995; see also Gubrium and Holstein, Chapter 1, this volume). Although situational, these perspectives shape the flow of the interview and, in its qualitative version, are taken into account by the interviewer in understanding the meaning-making process.

In most texts on qualitative interviewing, the perspective of the interviewer is taken to be that of the discipline: she or he is interviewing in order to write, publish, and contribute to a body of knowledge and literature. The ways in which this disciplinary task are conceived is historically grounded, with the planning, conduct, and interpretation of interviews shaped by changing rules and expectations. What was viewed as improper procedure at an earlier time might now be de rigueur, as changing concepts of the interview task become accepted (see in this volume Platt, Chapter 2, as well as all contributions to Part VI). Indeed, even the significance of perspectives is historically grounded, with the current recognition that perspectives other than those drawn from the discipline come into play for the interviewer as well as the respondent, especially in qualitative interviewing.[2]

Much has been written on the respondent's perspectives in the qualitative interview, especially in relation to gender (Arendell 1997; Warren and Hackney 2000). The chapters in Part II of this volume are, in some sense, an outline of an accumulated discourse on types of respondents, including the respondent as ethnic, gendered, aged, classed, and identified with one or another sexual community. An important point to emphasize here is that these are not only distinctive respondents but various perspectives that can be taken up by a single respondent within a single interview. Perspective is especially significant in qualitative interviewing, where meaning making is center stage in the interpretive process.

My own disciplinary and research experience, for example, forms a perspective, one that gives shape to how I present the qualitative interview.[3] I write this chapter from the perspective of a seasoned sociologist who has done qualitative interviewing and extensive writing about interviews. During the 1980s, I interviewed respondents for two projects, one on older women married to younger men (Warren 1996) and the other on patients, relatives, psychiatrists, and hospital administrators involved with electroconvulsive therapy (ECT), formerly known as electroshock therapy or EST (Warren and Levy 1991; Kneeland and Warren forthcoming). My ethnographic study of a gay community in the late 1960s also included interviewing (Warren 1972). In another study, I analyzed 30,000 pages of interviews with 17 women diagnosed as schizophrenic in the late 1950s and early 1960s, and their husbands. This was known as the Bay Area study (Sampson, Messinger, and Towne 1964), material from which I used to write a monograph titled *Madwives* on the intersection of psychiatry, gender, and marital roles during that era (Warren 1987). I drew on the interpretive, feminist perspectives of the 1980s for my reinterpretation of this material. I have also written or coauthored a number of methodological articles on interviewing based on *Madwives* and other research (Warren 1985; Harkess and Warren 1993; Karner and Warren 1995) and, like many of my colleagues, have supervised several generations of student research using qualitative interviewing and ethnography.[4] All of this shapes this presentation, which, together with other perspectives, both within and outside the qualitative interview, will bring up noteworthy points throughout the chapter.

◆ Preliminary Considerations

Qualitative interviewing is a kind of guided conversation (Kvale 1996; Rubin and Rubin 1995) in which the researcher carefully listens "so as to *hear the meaning*" of what is being conveyed (Rubin and Rubin 1995:7). James Spradley (1979:8) extends the concept of listening to include distinctly disciplinary concerns. According to Spradley, the purpose of interviewing is to make "cultural inferences," thick descriptions of a given social world analyzed for cultural patterns and themes. These are of typical anthropological interest, which is Spradley's own disciplinary context. Spradley explains that qualitative researchers make cultural inferences from three sources: what people say, the ways they act, and the artifacts they use. Taken together, these sources implicate qualitative interviewing's sister research genre, ethnography (see Atkinson and Coffey, Chapter 38, this volume.)

QUALITATIVE INTERVIEWING AND ETHNOGRAPHY

Qualitative interviewing has long been linked to ethnographic fieldwork, a tradi-tional staple of anthropological research. Today, it is linked to many other disciplinary contexts. Qualitative interviewing and fieldwork are often classified together, along with documentary analysis, as qualitative or interpretive methods (Kvale 1996:9; Rubin and Rubin 1995:34-35). Yet the "cultural inferences" that the qualitative methods of ethnography and interviewing provide give us subtly different lenses on the world. Ethnography's lens is that of lived experience, set in an eternal present. The lens of the intensive interview is verbal—what people say and mean—but its temporal range is biographical, extending into the past and the future. In this regard, contrast Erving Goffman's (1961) ethnography of a late-1950s mental hospital with my own interview-based study of mental patients (Warren 1987). From Goffman, we see staff-patient and patient-patient interaction in the context of that decade's eternal present. From my work, we see the meaning of mental-patienthood in the context of 1950s housewifery.

Researchers often choose qualitative interviews over ethnographic methods when their topics of interest do not center on particular settings but their concern is with establishing common patterns or themes between particular types of respondents. As Rubin and Rubin (1995) note, interview topics come from many sources: "employers; life experiences . . . the researcher's personality; from ethnic, racial, or sexual identity. Some subjects attract researchers' curiosity; others appeal to researchers' political or social values" (p. 49).

Where both settings and individuals are available, and are mutually pertinent, researchers often combine ethnographic data with interview data, illuminating both the culture and the biographical particulars of members' worlds. Social researchers use ethnographic interviews and other field-based methods to "fill in" the biographical meanings of observed interactions (Spradley and Mann 1975; Esterberg 1997).[5] These methods hearken back, in sociology, to the Chicago school and its methods, which combined surveys, case studies, documentary analysis, and qualitative interviewing. These methods were brought together in the service of understanding the varieties of experience that made up the Chicago urban experience in the 1930s and 1940s. Although Chicago school scholars were short on methodological treatises and ruminations (in general they just did their job, but see Palmer 1928), certain aspects of contemporary qualitative interviewing, and its penchant for ethnographic linkages, can be seen as linear inheritors of the Chicago school.

DESIGNING QUALITATIVE INTERVIEW RESEARCH

Steiner Kvale (1996) writes that the original Greek meaning of the word *method* is "a route that leads to the goal" (p. 4). Extending this concept by way of a traveler's metaphor to the qualitative interview researcher, Kvale adds, "The interviewer wanders along with the local inhabitants, asks questions that lead the subjects to tell their own stories of the lived world, and converses with them in the original Latin meaning of *conversation* as 'wandering together with' " (p. 4). The design of qualitative interview research, for Kvale, is open-ended in the sense that it is more concerned with being attuned to who is being traveled with, so to speak, than with setting out a precise route for all to follow, as in survey research.

As with ethnography in earlier decades, the wanderings of qualitative interviewing became systematized into texts and monographs during the 1990s (Arksey and Knight 1999; Holstein and Gubrium 1995; Kvale 1996; Rubin and Rubin 1995; Weiss 1994). Kvale (1996:88) proposes that, like Shakespeare's "man," interviewing has seven stages: thematizing, designing, interviewing, transcribing, analyzing, verifying, and reporting. By *thematizing*, he means thinking about the topic of interest to *the researcher* and its fit with the interview

method; qualitative interviewing is designed with the aim of thematizing *the respondent's* experience as well.

Of course, designing the research may involve reviewing the existing qualitative (and perhaps quantitative) literature on the topic to determine whether a new qualitative interview study would add anything to it. The researcher also considers the time available to complete the study, access to respondents, and the financial and emotional costs of conducting the study (Rubin and Rubin 1995:54). Emotional costs are particularly relevant in qualitative interviewing because of its open-ended, exploratory character; probing for details and depths of experiences (see Johnson, Chapter 5, this volume) can be stressful for all participants.

At the same time, beyond the standard issues such as reviews of the existing literature and the practical matters of time and access, qualitative researchers' concern with meaning making causes them to be rather skeptical of standard design strictures. For example, the constructionist epistemological leanings undergirding much of qualitative research beg the researcher to move ahead and interview open-endedly. The goal is to unveil the distinctive meaning-making actions of interview participants. As such, the design of qualitative interview research necessarily places limits on standardization and the working relevance of existing literature.

This is not to say that the research literature is unimportant. It is, but its relevance for the design of interviewing is confined to the first steps, if it is taken into account at all. From the "research questions" generated by a possible review of the literature, the interviewer develops 10 to 12 specific questions, together with a face sheet covering such descriptors as respondent age, race, and gender. Rubin and Rubin (1995: 145-46) note that the qualitative interview uses three kinds of questions: main questions that begin and guide the conversation, probes to clarify answers or request further examples, and follow-up questions that pursue the implications of answers to main questions. But, equally important, the qualitative interviewer remains flexible and attentive to the variety of meanings that may emerge as the interview progresses. This open stance includes being alert to developing meanings that may render previously designed questions *irrelevant* in light of the changing contexts of meaning.[6]

FINDING RESPONDENTS

Whom does one interview? In the logic of survey research, interviews are conducted with a representative sample of a larger population, drawn systematically in order that the findings will be generalizable to that population. In qualitative interview studies, respondents may be chosen based on a priori research design, theoretical sampling, or "snowball" or convenience design, or particular respondents may be sought out to act as key informants (Holstein and Gubrium 1995; Spradley 1979). In the Bay Area study, respondents were selected by a priori research design. Interviewers were to approach Caucasian, married women with children who were first admissions to Napa State Hospital within one week of their admission (Sampson et al. 1964; Warren 1987). Such a priori strictures, of course, do not always work out. One respondent was found to have had prior psychiatric admissions, but she was kept in the sample because, by the time this discovery was made, a great deal of time and effort had been expended in interviewing her.

Using a theoretical sampling strategy, the interviewer seeks out respondents who seem likely to epitomize the analytic criteria in which he or she is interested (see Glaser and Strauss 1967; see also Charmaz, Chapter 32, this volume). Because the object of qualitative interviewing is to discern meaningful patterns within thick description, researchers may try to minimize or maximize differences among respondents —say, according to race or class—in order to highlight or contrast patterns. In general, with one-time interviews, the more comparisons to be made between sets of patterns, the more respondents are likely to be interviewed. For example, a researcher studying male caregivers of elderly Alzheimer's patients may decide on 20 or 25 interviews, whereas a researcher comparing male and female caregivers may seek 35 or 40.[7]

Theoretical sampling may be carried out through a "snowball" process: One respondent is located who fulfills the theoretical criteria, then that person helps to locate others through her or his social networks (Arksey and Knight 1999:4; Biernacki and Waldorf 1981; Weiss 1994:25). But there are many other ingenious ways in which qualitative researchers find respondents to interview. For example, one sociology graduate student at the University of Southern California who was interested in the topic of interracial marriage approached her respondents during her working hours as a supermarket checker. Any time she checked the groceries of an apparently interracial couple, she asked them if they would be willing to be interviewed. Most of them agreed, to my supervisorly surprise.

One of the problems in seeking respondents for an interview study may be, in Hillary Arksey and Peter Knight's (1999:70) terms, not being able to find anyone to talk to. This can be a problem, especially when the topic of the interview is stigmatizing or when the occurrence of needed respondents is rare in a population. Both were true for our study of elderly ECT patients (Warren and Levy 1991). For other topics, such as that of Laurel Richardson's *The New Other Woman* (1985), finding respondents is less difficult, even if personally stigmatizing. As Richardson says:

> Finding "other women" to interview was not difficult. . . . I announced my research interest to nearly everyone I met—conferees, salesclerks, travel acquaintances, and so on. Women I met in these different circumstances volun-

teered to be interviewed, or put me in contact with women who were involved with married men. (P. x)

In ethnographic interviews, informants may be chosen for their communicative competence or access to information rather than their personal epitomization of some topic-related characteristic of interest to the researcher (Briggs 1986). As Spradley (1979) notes: "I use the term *informant* in a very specific way, not to be confused with concepts like subject, respondent, friend, or actor. . . . Informants are first and foremost *native speakers*" (p. 8), one connotation of which is that they have inside knowledge of some social world. Where interviewer and interviewee share the same life world, however, the selection of an informant may be based more on the particular standpoint from which the individual can interpret cultural meanings. As James Holstein and Jaber Gubrium (1995) state, "The term *informant* no longer conveys a distinct difference in narrative competence; instead it signals more a difference in point of view" (p. 24). Indeed, because of their interest in the construction, not just the substance, of meaning making, Holstein and Gubrium propose that, where there is a choice, qualitative interviewers should select "respondents because they are assumed to be capable of narrative production" (p. 24), thus dignifying them as people and orienting to the interview project as narrative collaboration.

Both positivist and constructionist discussions of respondent selection tend to assume that the interviewer and respondent will be strangers; indeed, the title of a recent text on qualitative interviewing is *Learning from Strangers* (Weiss 1994). However, this may not be the case. Richardson (1985), for example, included fellow conferees and acquaintances among her 55 respondents. In ethnographic studies, where the researcher is a member of the community she or he is studying, respondents may even be a part of the interviewer's own social circle. Kristin Esterberg

(1997) describes her theoretical sampling of members of a community with which she was quite familiar:

The initial interviewees were selected, in part, for their location in the community; I actively sought out those who were seen by others at the "center" and at the "margins" of community. I also sought out women, with varying degrees of success, in "under-represented" categories: old women, bisexual women, working-class women, and women of color. (Pp. 177-78)

In some cases, sampling begins with acquaintances and moves on to strangers. This is typical of snowball sampling. In the ECT study (Warren and Levy 1991), we initially posted flyers in nursing homes seeking respondents, with absolutely no luck. In discussing the study with colleagues and friends, however, we found that many had elderly relatives who had had ECT. Similarly, in our study of older women married to younger men, respondents included university colleagues, friends, and even a cleaning woman who worked for one of the researchers.

INFORMED CONSENT

As with other kinds of research involving human subjects, qualitative interviewing requires researchers to deal with professional ethical codes, in particular federal and university human subjects regulations. These have become more formalized over the past several decades, to the point where some say that they unduly constrain the conduct of social research or protect the researcher more than the subjects of the research (see Adler and Adler, Chapter 25, this volume). Institutional review boards (IRBs) translate federal policy into local standards for the protection of human subjects from physical and emotional harm by requiring researchers to obtain informed consent from research subjects.

From an IRB perspective, human subjects regulation of interview research seeks to protect respondents from such things as invasion of privacy, breaches of confidentiality or anonymity, and distress caused by topics raised in the interview process itself. But from the standpoint of understanding qualitative interviewing, what is interesting about these strictures is not so much the ways they are implemented by the researcher, but the ways they are interpreted by the respondent.

Among dangers or harms in intensive interviewing research from the perspective of the respondent is the act of listening itself. Listening to another speak, for example, is an act that reflects the self back to the respondent, and this may unfold in ways unforeseen by IRBs or researchers themselves. In reflecting on repeat interviews with ex-patients in the Bay Area conducted in the 1950s and Vietnam veterans in the 1990s, I found that

> the interviewer becomes dangerous by the simple act of listening: when the speaker has put on the mantle of a new self seeking to bury the old in an unmarked grave, yet must confront the presence of an interviewer who has knowledge of the past self. The listener is also dangerous as a participant in the retelling of the past by a respondent who feels unable to escape from that past and the self constituted by it. (Karner and Warren 1995:81)

Some subjects may not see written consent forms as at all protective. In a study conducted by a University of Southern California graduate student, respondents expressed repeated exasperation with consent forms. This particular study focused on lesbian identities. The researcher's requests for interviews—which included clear promises of confidentiality yet required signed consent forms—were uniformly met with exasperated refusals by prospective respondents. The contradiction between requiring signed consent forms, which prospective respondents perceived as going to the government funding agency, and promising confidentiality was too great. The researcher resolved the problem by shifting to oral, tape-recorded consent.

In the team qualitative interview study in which I participated in the late 1980s (Warren and Levy 1991), in which we sought interviews with elderly ECT recipients, their relatives, hospital psychiatrists, and hospital administrators, none of the patients or relatives took issue with the consent forms. But most of the hospital psychiatrists and administrators waved them away as "too official." They were willing to talk with us, but they were not willing to put their names to any documents that might involve them in future litigation. Curiously enough, such responses are often not discovered until *after* the interview process has begun, the start of which the consent form is meant to regulate.

The logic of informed consent presumes that the respondent will understand the intent of the research, as it is explained by the researcher or a consent letter. However, there are many indications in the literature on qualitative interviewing that the researcher's understanding may not match the interviewer's from the start, may shift over time, or may be "confused." The following extract from an interview with a Bay Area ex-patient—whom the researcher had interviewed at least 50 times over a 36-month period—illustrates the dynamics involved:

> She began by asking what kind of a psychologist I was. . . . "You said that you were working on a project. I was wondering what your field was. . . . at times, as I said, I was confused about what your interest was in the family, whether you were prying or whether you were just surveying to see how the family was getting along, with your connection with the hospital in your field, whether it has helped out or whether it was part

of it—it wasn't really that, it was just simple explanation of the confusement of it all." (Warren and Karner 1990: 123)

SETTING UP THE INTERVIEW

Once the researcher identifies respondents, she or he must ask them if they will agree to be interviewed, a process that usually accompanies obtaining informed consent. In particular, the time and place of the interview needs to be decided. The received wisdom on how to accomplish this is highly varied, with some commentators advising particular venues and specific kinds of scheduling (see Seidman 1998) and others leaving this largely an open question (for example, see Kvale 1996).

In my experience, the continuum of responses to these preliminary matters can range from outright refusal to welcoming agreement, with every variation in between. In the original Bay Area study, one husband refused to be interviewed at all. More generally, a willingness, even an eagerness, to talk about oneself in interviews is quite commonly reported, at least in the American context. Indeed, as Rubin and Rubin (1995) note:

> At a basic level, people like to talk about themselves: they enjoy the sociability of a long discussion and are pleased that somebody is interested in them. . . . you come along and say, yes, what you know is valuable, it should not be lost, teach me, and through me, teach others. (P. 103)

Setting up the interview and actually making it happen are two different things. Generations of qualitative interviewers have been admonished to schedule interviews at times and in places convenient to respondents, but they may find that even this is problematic. For example, an undergraduate sociology student at the University of Kansas had, with great difficulty, scheduled a focus group session for six students to talk about the issue of going to school and working at the same time. When the scheduled time for the group to meet expired, he ran into my office and breathlessly announced that not one of the six had appeared. Although this incident may be extreme, it is not uncommon for respondents to forget, simply not show up, or in other ways delay or prevent the actual completion of the interview.

But let us continue with those interviews that do move ahead. Armed with a list of questions, a fact sheet for demographic information, the informed consent letter, and the requisite tape recorder and backup pencil and paper, the interviewer meets the respondent at the agreed-upon location. The location itself may have been negotiated. In the Bay Area study, the female respondents, once out of the hospital, did not know quite where to meet their male interviewers. The home seemed out of the question—what would the neighbors say? And the same might be said for the coffee shop across the road. On the other hand, a journey to the researchers' offices, although far from the gaze of prying eyes, was logistically difficult, given child-care and household responsibilities. These ex-patient interviews were replete with discussion and discomfort over the issue of where to meet; in the summer, interviewers sometimes resolved the problem by meeting with respondents in the outdoors, in a garden or on a park bench. Most interviews were eventually completed, but their locations were far from being the result of a well-defined method of procedure. In retrospect, it is evident that the negotiation of perspectives on this matter filtered many of these preliminary issues, just as many seasoned qualitative researchers have noted that such negotiations indeed reverberate throughout the interview process itself.

A respondent is, by definition, someone who responds—someone who is willing and able to talk to the interviewer. But the respondent is also raced, classed, and gendered as well as being situated in the present moment, with anticipatory notions of what an interview might entail. All this, too, will reverberate in the forthcoming interview. Nancy Ammerman's (1987) ethnographic study of fundamentalist Christians, for example, illustrates the religious, class, and educational perspectives from which her respondents anticipated interviews:

> My role as an interviewer often placed an initial distance between me and my subjects that was not present in my role as a participant observer. . . . a good many people approached the interview full of apprehension about what it would be like to be interviewed by someone who was getting a Ph.D. from Yale. After they had cleaned their houses, prepared special food, and even bought new clothes, some still worried about whether they would know the "right" answers and why I had chosen them instead of someone who was a stronger Christian or had been in the church longer or who had a more interesting testimony. (P. 13)

Clearly, the procedural staging of the qualitative interview develops both extemporaneously and methodically within the social relations of the participants.

◆ The Qualitative Interviewing Process

We now turn to the interview process itself, in particular to the meaning making involved as it relates to the social interaction of the participants. This has been a common topic in the interview methods literature for years (see DeSantis 1980; Suchman and Jordan 1990; Peneff 1988). Meaning making is especially pertinent to qualitative researchers because their constructionist leanings bring the interview process itself

within the purview of the designated research topic. The social contexts of the interview process are not viewed as something to be controlled, as they are in standardized survey interviews, but instead are seen as an important part of meaning making in its own right. Qualitative researchers, in other words, treat the unfolding social contexts of the interview as data, not as something that, under ideal conditions, can be eliminated from the interview process.

To illustrate these unfolding social contexts, I begin at the very start of the interview, when the tape recorder is set up, and end after it is over, with the "echoes" that can follow the respondent and researcher into their other lives. Between the beginning and the echoes, interviews can take many directions. Here, I depict two such directions: currents of the clinical and the sociable—of loyalty and disloyalty—that occurred in situations where one interviewer interviewed spouses (separately), and issues of gender and power in feminist interviewing.

THE TAPE RECORDER AND ITS MEANINGS

The interview often begins as the interviewer's tape recorder is set up amid friendly greetings, creating a particular social context for the interview conversation. For several decades, the conventional wisdom has been that qualitative interviews should be audiotaped, and perhaps even videotaped (Holstein and Gubrium, 1995:78). But does the respondent remain basically unaffected by this? Not only might turning on a tape recorder alter the ensuing conversation, creating a particular context for what is said, but the meanings of audio- or videotaping may be different to different respondents, whose perspectives on the matter are likely to vary by social class and age, for example.

Tape recording has historical resonances. The tape recorder itself, ubiquitous in recent decades, was a novelty at the time of the Bay Area study; indeed, the first half of the study was conducted with the eight interviewers taking handwritten notes. When tape recorders were introduced, they were a source of exclamation and discussion on the part of the respondents, who would bring their children into the room to examine and discuss the then-bulky instruments. But times and expectations change. In my study of older women married to younger men, the one working-class Hispanic couple I interviewed met me at their front door with exclamations of disappointment over my small and insignificant tape recorder. Their concept of the "interview"—shaped by the TV program *Eye on L.A.*—had led them to expect me to arrive with a video camera, perhaps even a TV camera crew. What Paul Atkinson and David Silverman (1997) call "the interview society" seems to have constructed a new, postmodern, social context for interview data, perhaps making the interview itself the characteristic format for personal narratives (see Gubrium and Holstein, Chapter 1, this volume).

In the process of conducting qualitative interviews, many of us have encountered the "on and off the record" associations that respondents have with recording devices. In perhaps the majority of interviews that I have conducted, supervised, or analyzed, from the 1960s through the 1990s, respondents have continued to speak after the tape recorders have been turned off. This seems to occur for two reasons: (a) The respondent wants to talk about his or her own, rather than the interviewer's, concerns; and (b) the respondent does not want to talk "on the record" about issues that might be dangerous or personally damaging. For example, my notes from the Bay Area study show that an interview with one husband was extended past its conclusion, with the husband offering some telling remarks about ECT that had not been forthcoming in the interview proper:

As I packed up the tape recorder, Mr. W. asked me what ECT does for people. I muttered something about, "I wish I knew." He responded with, "Well, what's it *supposed* to do?"

In another instance, as I turned off the tape recorder in a 1980s interview with a hospital psychiatrist concerning ECT, the psychiatrist said, "Now that we can talk off the record, I will tell you about billing." It is a hallmark of qualitative interviewing that "unrecorded" data of this kind are as important as those derived from tape recordings.

SHIFTING CONTEXTS

Whatever the training and intentions of the interviewer, the social interaction of the qualitative interview may unfold in unexpected ways. This unfolding is even more complex when interviews are repeated over time. Once again, the interview process itself can be treated as an important source of data. In the Bay Area interviews, for example, "clinical" perspectives emerged in interviews with the women patients and ex-patients, whereas "distancing" perspectives emerged with both the ex-patients and their husbands after the wives' release from hospitalization. Although interviewers were trained to be nonpartisan with these husbands and wives, they nevertheless were at times treated as partisan.

In their training, the Bay Area study interviewers were instructed not to act as clinicians during the study. One psychiatrist warned that "any sort of regular relationship was bound to be therapeutic (or antitherapeutic) notwithstanding our 'intentions' " (Warren 1985:74). And from the point of view expressed in interviewers' accounts, it was apparent that this psychiatrist's warnings were appropriate. The women patients and ex-patients asked the researchers for help, advice, and opinions, as did their husbands. "Transference" also seemed to affect the interactions between respondents and interviewers (Laslett and Rapoport 1975; Warren 1985). After one interview with patient Joyce Noon on April 3, 1959, the interviewer commented:

> I had originally anticipated that I would stop the interview after about one tape, but since Joyce seemed to be getting some benefit from talking to me and expressing her feelings, I went on for another tape to give her further opportunity to do so. (Warren 1985:80)

In the ex-patient phase of the Bay Area study, the issue of the interviewer as dangerous listener was especially salient. Some of the women and their husbands sought to distance themselves from the women's "old selves," a distancing that extended to the researcher. This, in turn, affected the social interactions within these interviews. For example, ex-patient June Mark said that

> she cannot fully participate in the research simply because the research in itself signifies the stigma of deviance which she is struggling to avoid. . . . "You keep asking a lot of questions . . . things I want to forget about. . . . It's not normal, my talking to you. . . . It's just that I am reminded I'm a patient. If you're a patient, you're always a patient." (Field notes)

Despite her strong reservations, June continued to participate, as did all but one of the respondents. However, they did try to redirect the interviews into more sociable, everyday—in June Mark's word, "normal"—channels. For example, in response to one interviewer's "How are you?" the respondent answered "How are *you*?" in a pointed attempt at role reversal (Warren 1987:261). This rather explicit attempt at reconstructing the interaction not only altered the social context of the interview, changing it from an interview with an ex-patient to one with another person, it presented itself as data in the sense that it documented, on that occasion, the normalizing work of everyday life for this population. This is one of those many points in qualitative interviews when the interview becomes ethnographic.

Building a context for sociability, rather than data gathering, was especially apparent in posthospital interviews with Ann Rand. One of the interviewer's notes in this case reads:

> Repeated that she would only see [me] again if she would have her over to her house. While the interviewer was evasive, Ann said, "Then I suppose you still see me as a patient. To me you are either a friend or some kind of authority, now which is it? The way I see it, you either see me as a friend or a patient." (Warren 1987:261)

Another note, this one concerning Jack Oren's interview, reads, "Mr. Oren asked me if I wanted to join them for dinner, and was rather insistent about this despite my repeated declining" (Warren 1987:261).

Other respondents turned the psychiatric tables on the interviewers, interpreting *them* clinically, as the following note indicates:

> [Referring to the interviewer], Jack Oren said, "I think that you're a kid that missed happiness somewhere along the line." He then started speculating about my past life and thought that something had happened to me . . . to make me feel like that. Mr. Oren first was critical about my interviewing technique, then started to question me about my life, and so on. (Warren 1987:62)

But not all of the ex-patients sought to release themselves from the researcher's grasp on their past selves, or saw this as dangerous. Some continued to therapeutize the researcher and the interviews, as the following notes about two respondents suggest:

> I had the feeling that Irene James was desperately trying to gain some control over her feelings and thoughts by talk-

> ing about them to me. . . . Irene says that when I arrive for my interview that seems reassuring. (Warren 1987:262)

> I asked Shirley Arlen if she would see a psychiatrist and she said no, she couldn't afford it, then all she would do is talk, and she feels she would do better just talking to me. (Warren 1987:262)

In the Bay Area study, each of the eight female and male interviewers spoke with both the mental patients and their husbands. Each wife and husband knew that the other was being interviewed by the same person, forming a triadic relationship. One consequence of this arrangement was that the interviewer was incorporated into the respondents' attempts to find out and pass on information and opinions concerning, mainly, the wife's mental condition at the time. In such a situation, the interviewer is supposed to be, in Georg Simmel's (1950) words, a nonpartisan who either

> stands above the contrasting interests and opinions [of the dyad] and is actually not concerned with them, or . . . is equally concerned with them. . . . the non-partisan may make the interaction between the parties, and between himself and them, a means for his own purposes. (Pp. 149-50)

Regarding the latter point, it is characteristic of qualitative interviewing that it is structured to take these options seriously, generating new data in the process. It was clear in the Bay Area transcripts that respondents took varied perspectives in the interview, some of which were far from being neutral sources of information.

Interviewed husbands often asked the interviewer about their wives, and when they did not hear what they wanted, some became testy:

> Mr. Sand told me that he didn't see any point going on [with the interviews]. . . .

> He asked me if I had talked to his wife that day and when I did not answer at once he repeated the question and I finally told him that I did. . . . He told me that this wasn't going to help him anyway, and besides which, I knew things about what was going on at the hospital with his wife, and I didn't tell him a thing about it. (Warren 1987:266)

The respondents' varied perspectives in these triadic relationships—perhaps centered on secrecy in relation to oneself or loyalty in relation to another—are as significant for what they reveal or conceal, in terms of data, as they are indicators of interview rapport. Here, again, the ethnographic character of the qualitative interview is evident. For example, Bay Area ex-patient Joan Baker agreed to continue with her interviews but kept them secret from her husband. She felt he would interpret her being interviewed as evidence that she was still mentally ill (Warren 1987: 267). Similarly, in a different research context, a woman sociologist, commenting on a draft of an article on interviewing, conveyed her thoughts about an interview she had just completed and her husband's forthcoming one:

> I was conscious all through the interview of trying to be honest with [the interviewer] but not to say anything that would seem disloyal to [husband]. She was going to interview him next, and I kept wondering if she would say anything to him that might make him feel I had been disloyal to him. (Harkess and Warren 1993:334)

GENDER AS A SOCIAL CONTEXT

Although race, ethnicity, nationality, sexual orientation, and age have received increasing attention in the interviewing literature, it is gender to which qualitative researchers have been most attentive in sociology (Benney, Hughes, and Starr 1956;

Luff 1999). In the early years of the Chicago school, the authoritative, question-asking status of the interviewer was unproblematic, the gender of the interviewer either unacknowledged or presumptively male. In time, however,

> the interviewer with "no gender," like the ethnographer as "any person," ceded place during the century to the male interviewer interviewing both women and men (Kinsey's model. . .). . . . During the modern era, accounts of what made an interview go smoothly and produce valid data was contested terrain: any polite and dignified interviewer (Palmer 1928), a male interviewer (Cressey 1920/1986) or a female interviewer with a female respondent (Oakley 1981). . . . Not to mention the female "sociability specialist" of the 1980s wresting secret information from reluctant male and female nude beach habitués. (Warren and Hackney 2000:37-38, 42)

In a historical shift in disciplinary perspectives, feminist interviewers have sought, over the past several decades, to change the social interactions of the interview from being authoritative, sociable, or therapeutic to being expressly egalitarian. By the 1970s, women interviewers were being encouraged to interview other women from the empathic standpoint of gender. By the 1980s, it was commonplace to speak of a special genre of "feminist interviewing" (DeVault 1986; Oakley 1981). In the late 1990s, however, exceptions to, and critiques of, the idea of feminist interviewing appeared and the consideration of respondent subjectivity became more complex (see in this volume Reinharz and Chase, Chapter 11; DeVault and McCoy, Chapter 36). The standpoints of race, ethnicity, nationality, and sexual orientation were proposed as de-essentializing femaleness. Thus "women interviewing women" was complicated by whether or not one participant was Third World and one First, one lesbian

and one heterosexual, or one religious and radical right and the other left-leaning and feminist (Blee 1991; Luff 1999).

Even where both interviewer and respondent are women, interviews may not be with "those whose standpoints the researcher shares" in terms of "religious/secular, feminist/antifeminist, or liberal/heterosexist" (Luff 1999). For example, Luff (1999) discusses how her preconceptions affected her interviews with British "moral right" (what American sociologists might call "moral majority") women. She points out that the disciplinary perspectives of sociologists are often secular, feminist, antihomophobic, and politically left-leaning. Her respondents reversed all of these perspectives; they were religious, antifeminist, homophobic, and politically right-wing. Furthermore, as middle-class, semipublic figures, they were "relatively powerful" as well as potentially hostile (p. 687). Retelling "moments of rapport" in her research with these women, Luff concludes that "the researcher, as much as the participant, draws on her own conflicting, often contradictory aspects of identity as resources in the interaction," adding that

> the emphasis on power-sharing and the vulnerability of the researched that has characterized much feminist methodology . . . may come from tendencies within feminist research to study the "powerless" and therefore may not be transferable, indeed may be counter-productive, to the development of feminist theory and practice in research with the "powerful." (P. 692)

By the 1990s, some feminist researchers had come to recognize that women interviewing women might not work (Hertz 1996) or might be ethically problematic (Luff 1999). In her interviews with military men and their wives concerning gender integration in the military, Rosanna Hertz (1996) found that the men were uncomfortable "trying to explain . . . their position to the two female interviewers who were outside of male camaraderie" (p. 256). But Hertz also found that the women respondents had even less to say than the men; she surmised that this was because the status she shared with them as women was overshadowed by educational, social class, and marital differences (p. 256). Indeed, Luff (1999:698) points out that rapport—and trust-enhancing interview strategies such as not arguing, saying "I see" and "um," smiling, and maintaining a polite tone of voice—can make even (liberal) women interviewing (right-wing) women seem deceitful, "falling somewhere between the covert and overt" in social research.

There is general agreement in the qualitative interviewing literature that women interviewing men presents special problems, given the obduracy of the interpersonal dominance involved (Arendell 1997; Warren and Hackney 2000). This gender problem was exacerbated for Terry Arendell (1997) in a study where the topic of the interview was divorce. The topic created an interaction in which male respondents spoke forcefully of their betrayal by women to another woman who was the interviewer. Arendell found that from the initial point of contact, the interview became a proving ground for masculinity and a site for the exercise of male definitions and dominance displays against ex-wives (and sometimes against all women). These men immediately "took charge" of the interview process and topic and attempted to "place" Arendell as married or unmarried, available or not, male basher or nice girl. Their "assertion of superiority" involved both the denigration of women in general and the assumption that their knowledge and insights were superior to Arendell's. Their handling of the interview (for it was they who handled) ranged from chivalry to sexual harassment (Warren and Hackney 2000:37).

POSTINTERVIEW ECHOES

Like most things, qualitative interviews come to an end, with respondents and interviewers returning to their respective life worlds. For the respondent, there may be no more thoughts of the interview (DeSantis 1980); for the interviewer, the main thoughts may be of the way in which the interview fits into the overall analysis. But sometimes—perhaps especially where interviews are combined with ethnographic research—there may be echoes of the interview within the life worlds of the interviewer, the respondent, or both. This possibility was recognized in the 1970s and 1980s literature on feminist interviewing; Luff (1999) refers to this early "assumption that feminists can, or indeed should have a powerful affect [sic] on participants' lives" as "patronizing" (p. 692). Nevertheless, such echoes can occur.

Two lesbian sociology graduate students at the University of Kansas who did ethnographic and interview research on their own communities concluded that the interviewing experience created an emotional distance between themselves and their respondents. In one case, this extended to emotional distance between the researcher herself and her lesbian identity (Warren 2000). In the research on ECT recipients and their families (Warren and Levy 1991), several of our collaborators interviewed university colleagues—friends or acquaintances—concerning their elderly, hospitalized parents. In more than one instance during the interviews, divining our possible critique of the use of ECT on elderly mental patients, our colleagues became upset with us, accusing us of not understanding their situation and, in one case, of no longer being a friend. We suspected, too, that one or two respondents simply did not tell us the truth about their family members, avoiding the sort of confrontation we had had with others. In one case, a prior friendship between an interviewer and respondent was severely strained for many months following the interview.

Qualitative interviewing is distinctive in this regard. Interviewers do not necessarily end their relationships with respondents at the conclusion of their interviews, as is typically done in survey interviewing. Rather, the perspectives of, and information conveyed in, interviews echo in the ongoing relations of research participants.

◆ Interpretation, Self, and Others

The interviewer, like the respondent, participates in the interview from historically grounded biographical as well as disciplinary perspectives. Biographical perspectives may frame entire analyses or affect the selection of illustrative quotes. In her book *Worlds of Pain* (1976), for example, Lillian Rubin tells the reader that her interpretation of working-class life was shaped by her experiences as a working-class child, left-wing political activist, and clinical practitioner. She saw pain, and only pain, in working-class lives: "Often people implored, even commanded me, to believe they had happy home lives as children. I tried . . . [but the] dominant memories of childhood for me, as for the people I met, are of pain and deprivation" (p. 46).

When, in the late 1980s, I was analyzing transcripts of ECT experiences, I saw myself in respondents' comments, something that was highly emotional for me. In sifting through the many thousands of pages of interviews, I chose the following extract from ex-patient Shirley Arlen's case material to illustrate and exemplify the negative aspects of the biographical memory loss attendant upon EST:

> [Shirley Arlen], although she had been reminded by others of her son's existence, appeared to have lost her affective memory of him *as* her child: "I guess I feel sort of strange with him. . . . I just don't even feel like he's mine, for some reason. . . . I think he's nine months now . . . I really don't know. I can't even remember when he was born." (Warren 1988:295)

This comment was particularly poignant for me because while I was writing *Madwives* (Warren 1987) I was a new mother myself, and could imagine nothing more horrible than the emotional separation from a baby.

Extending the metaphor of the qualitative interviewer as a traveler to strange lands (Kvale 1996), we see that the interview, like the ethnography, is about self as well as other (Warren 2000). As Rubin (1976) says of her interview research about working-class pain: "No matter how far we travel, we can never leave our roots behind. I found they claimed me at unexpected times, in unexpected places" (p. 13).

As I noted at the start of this chapter, the purpose of qualitative interviewing (and associated fieldwork) is to understand others' meaning making. As many qualitative researchers report, I came early on to the point at which I viewed those meanings as intersecting with my own story. Yet, even with our knowledge of the different perspectives from which respondents and researchers talk and write, the empathic appreciation of others' meanings is not an easy task, especially across various cultural divides. In *Learning How to Ask* (1986), Charles Briggs cautions researchers against importing one set of linguistic and cultural assumptions into another when interviewing between cultures. But it is evident that even within the same culture, meanings that seem clear to the interviewer can be unshared (see in this volume Dunbar, Rodriguez, and Parker, Chapter 14; Briggs, Chapter 44). In a study of "affirmative action" in the South in the 1970s, an employer, when asked his definition of the term, replied:

> Uh . . . try to get a job done in as orderly a manner and please our customers . . . so it's firm as possible . . . to get a day's work for a day's pay. . . . And it would be affirmative action. And it's almost impossible. (Harkess and Warren 1994:273)

Indeed, even the most seemingly commonplace terms may vary surprisingly in meaning in the context of particular life worlds. In the Bay Area study, sociologist and interviewer Sheldon Messinger talked approximately 25 times between November 1957 and July 1958 with ex-patient Kate White (Messinger and Warren 1984). Among the "delusions" that precipitated Kate White's diagnosis and hospitalization was the idea that she and her husband were "homosexual." In the commonsense meanings of the 1950s, homosexuality referenced, as it does now, same-gender erotic preferences, attraction, or behavior (although there would be differences now in the social sensibilities associated with the category). But as Messinger delved into the meaning Kate assigned to the term, it became clear that what she was talking about was not desire or eroticism at all, but a social role. She wanted to work outside the home and men did that, so she talked of herself as homosexual. During her hospitalization, her husband had enjoyed keeping house and taking care of the children—ostensibly a woman's role—so perhaps he was also homosexual. For Kate White, homosexuality referenced gender roles, not sexual desire; in fact, she was having an extramarital heterosexual affair at the time she was interviewed.

Messinger and Warren (1984) also point out that stories such as that of Kate White's "homosexuality" are grounded in important relationships and adaptations that exist outside the purview of the interview. This observation, of course, highlights the necessity of using ethnographic linkages to flesh out the social contexts of meaning making. The social situation of the interview may not be the most important one for researchers who are trying to understand the meanings ("frameworks or labels") used by respondents. "These frameworks or labels must be examined in their interaction contexts. It is there that they do their work" (Messinger and Warren 1984:205), not in the interview or with the interviewer.

So we return full circle to the close relationship between qualitative interviewing and ethnography. I have always found experiences and stories such as Kate White's to point me in the direction of multiple rather than one-shot interviews, or of ethnography combined with interviews rather than interviews alone. But, as Holstein and Gubrium (1995) point out, even in the one-shot interview, the respondent may shift viewpoints and tell different tales.

In a 1970s ethnographic study of Weight Watchers (Laslett and Warren 1975), I had noticed that a large portion of each meeting was taken up with the discussion of food—what was permitted, how to cook, and so on. This came as no surprise to me. Flush with the then-current ardor for "triangulation," I embarked on interviews to "validate" my observations.[8] When I asked my first respondent, "Do you think that the meetings focus on food?" she responded, to my astonishment, with a definite "Oh no!" About one and a half hours later, however—much of which was spent discussing food—she said, "About that earlier question of yours—well, it does seem like we spend an awful lot of time discussing food doesn't it!" Among the ethnographic qualities of the qualitative interview itself is that the interview unfolds reflexively as each participant looks at the world through the other's eyes, incorporating both self and other into the process of interpretation.

Although asking, listening, talking, and hearing are important, so are seeing and feeling as means of apprehending the social world. Although the frame of talking and listening may be apt for conceiving telephone interviews, the frame of social interaction accords better with the face-to-face qualitative interview. In the social interaction of the qualitative interview, the perspectives of the interviewer and the respondent dance together for the moment but also extend outward in social space and backward and forward in time. Both are gendered, aged, and otherwise embodied, one person (perhaps) thinking about her topic, questions, rapport, consent forms, and the tape recorder, not to mention feeling nervous. The other is (perhaps) preoccupied with her relationships outside the interview, pressing tasks left undone, seeking information, getting help, or being loyal. These are the working selves and others at the center of qualitative interviewing. And that is just the beginning.

■ Notes

1. Although interviews may be conducted with more than one interviewer and more than one respondent, I confine this discussion to the dyadic interview situation. See Chapter 7 of this volume for a discussion of group interviewing.

2. Some approaches to interviewing, notably those taking a postmodern perspective, focus more on the interviewer's viewpoint than on the respondent's. Sometimes they fuse these perspectives. Norman Denzin's (1987) study of self-help groups of which the interviewer or ethnographer is a member is a case in point.

3. Consider the differences in presentation apparent in the following diversely authored depictions: Spradley (1979), Seidman (1998), Weiss (1994), Holstein and Gubrium (1995), Kvale (1996), and Rubin and Rubin (1995).

4. This research includes both one-shot interviews, which I suspect is the form encountered in most interview research, and repeat interviews, which can be considered a kind of longitudinal design.

5. In a section of his book titled "When Not to Interview," Kvale (1996) notes, "In recent social research there has been an inflationary use of interviews; also in areas better covered by other methods." He adds, "If you want to study people's behavior and their interaction with the environment, the observations of field studies will usually give more valid knowledge than merely asking subjects about their behavior" (p. 104).

6. Indeed, the folk wisdom of qualitative research regarding design includes the caution that researchers should not consult the literature until after the research has gotten under way and they have apprehended a sense of the subject matter. This, of course, works against design as formally understood.

7. Although there are few reasons set forth for the numbers of respondents appropriate in qualitative studies, there seem to be norms. To have a nonethnographic qualitative interview study published, the minimum number of interviews seems to fall in the range of 20 to 30. Respondent groups also generally come in round numbers, such as 20 or 35.

8. The idea of triangulation was discredited in the 1980s, but it is apparently staging a comeback (see Arksey and Knight, 1999; relatedly, see also Atkinson and Coffey, Chapter 38, this volume).

■ References

Ammerman, N. T. 1987. *Bible Believers: Fundamentalists in the Modern World.* New Brunswick, NJ: Rutgers University Press.

Arendell, T. 1997. "Reflections on the Researcher-Researched Relationship: A Woman Interviewing Men." *Qualitative Sociology* 20:341-68.

Arksey, H. and P. Knight. 1999. *Interviewing for Social Scientists: An Introductory Resource with Examples.* Thousand Oaks, CA: Sage.

Atkinson, P. and D. Silverman. 1997. "Kundera's *Immortality:* The Interview Society and the Invention of Self." *Qualitative Inquiry* 3:304-25.

Benney, M., E. C. Hughes, and S. Star. 1956. "Age and Sex in the Interview." *American Journal of Sociology* 62:143-52.

Biernacki, P. and D. Waldorf. 1981. "Snowball Sampling: Problems and Techniques of Chain Referral Sampling." *Sociological Methods & Research* 10:141-63.

Blee, K. M. 1991. *Women of the Klan: Racism and Gender in the 1920s.* Berkeley: University of California Press.

Briggs, C. L. 1986. *Learning How to Ask: A Sociolinguistic Appraisal of the Role of the Interview in Social Science Research*. Cambridge: Cambridge University Press.

Campbell, M. L. 1998. "Institutional Ethnography and Experience as Data." *Qualitative Sociology* 21:55-73.

Cressey, P. G. [1920] 1986. "Comparison of the roles of the 'sociological stranger' and the 'anonymous stranger" in field research." *Urban Life* 12:112-20.

Denzin, N. K. 1987. *The Recovering Alcoholic*. Newbury Park, CA: Sage.

DeSantis, G. 1980. "Interviewing as Social Interaction." *Qualitative Sociology* 2:72-98.

DeVault, M. L. 1986. "Talking and Listening from Women's Standpoints: Feminist Strategies for Analyzing Interview Data." Presented at the annual meeting of the Society for the Study of Symbolic Interaction, August, New York.

Esterberg, K. G. 1997. *Lesbian and Bisexual Identities: Constructing Communities, Constructing Selves*. Philadelphia: Temple University Press.

Glaser, B. G. and A. L. Strauss. 1967. *The Discovery of Grounded Theory: Strategies for Qualitative Research*. Chicago: Aldine.

Goffman, E. 1961. *Asylums: Essays on the Social Situation of Mental Patients and Other Inmates*. Garden City, NY: Doubleday.

Harkess, S. and C. A. B. Warren. 1993. "The Social Relations of Intensive Interviewing: Constellations of Strangeness and Science." *Sociological Methods & Research* 21:317-39.

———. 1994. "The Good Worker: Race and Gender in a 1970s Southern City." *Sociological Perspectives* 37:269-92.

Hertz, R. 1996. "Guarding against Women? Responses of Military Men and Their Wives to Gender Integration." *Journal of Contemporary Ethnography* 25:251-84.

Holstein, J. A. and J. F. Gubrium. 1995. *The Active Interview*. Thousand Oaks, CA: Sage.

Karner, T. X. and C. A. B. Warren. 1995. "The Dangerous Listener: Unforeseen Perils in Intensive Interviewing." *Clinical Sociology Review* 13:80-105.

Kneeland, T. and C. A. B. Warren. Forthcoming. *Pushbutton Psychiatry: A History of Electroshock in America*. Westport, CT: Greenwood.

Kvale, S. 1996. *InterViews: An Introduction to Qualitative Research Interviewing*. Thousand Oaks, CA: Sage.

Laslett, B. and R. Rapoport. 1975. "Collaborative Interviewing and Interactive Research." *Journal of Marriage and the Family* 37:968-77.

Laslett, B. and C. A. B. Warren. 1975. "Losing Weight: The Organizational Production of Behavior Change." *Social Problems* 23:69-80.

Luff, D. 1999. "Doing Social Research: Issues and Dilemmas." *Sociology* 33:687-703.

Messinger, S. L. and C. A. B. Warren. 1984. "The Homosexual Self and the Organization of Experience. Pp. 196-206 in *The Existential Self in Society*, edited by J. A. Kotarba and A. Fontana. Chicago: University of Chicago Press.

Mishler, E. G. 1986. *Research Interviewing: Context and Narrative*. Cambridge, MA: Harvard University Press.

Oakley, A. 1981. "Interviewing Women: A Contradiction in Terms?" Pp. 30-61 in *Doing Feminist Research*, edited by H. Roberts. London: Routledge & Kegan Paul.

Palmer, V. M. 1928. *Field Studies in Sociology: A Student's Manual*. Chicago: University of Chicago Press.

Peneff, J. 1988. "The Observers Observed: French Survey Researchers at Work." *Social Problems* 35:520-35.

Richardson, L. 1985. *The New Other Woman: Contemporary Single Women in Affairs with Married Men*. London: Collier Macmillan.

Rubin, H. J. and I. S. Rubin. 1995. *Qualitative Interviewing: The Art of Hearing Data*. Thousand Oaks, CA: Sage.

Rubin, L. B. 1976. *Worlds of Pain: Life in the Working-Class Family*. New York: Basic Books.

Sampson, H., S. L. Messinger, and R. D. Towne. 1964. *Schizophrenic Women: Studies in Marital Crisis*. New York: Atherton.

Seidman, I. 1998. *Interviewing as Qualitative Research: A Guide for Researchers in Education and the Social Sciences.* 2d ed. New York: Teachers College Press.

Simmel, G. 1950. *The Sociology of Georg Simmel,* edited and translated by K. H. Wolff. New York: Free Press.

Spradley, J. P. 1979. *The Ethnographic Interview.* New York: Holt, Rinehart & Winston.

Spradley, J. P. and B. J. Mann. 1975. *The Cocktail Waitress: Women's Work in a Man's World.* New York: John Wiley.

Suchman, L. and B. Jordan. 1990. "Interactional Troubles in Face-to-Face Survey Interviews." *Journal of the American Statistical Association* 85:232-41.

Warren, C. A. B. 1972. *Identity and Community in the Gay World.* New York: Wiley-Interscience.

———. 1985. "Clinical and Research Interviewing in Sociology." *Clinical Sociology Review* 3:72-84.

———. 1987. *Madwives: Schizophrenic Women in the 1950s.* New Brunswick, NJ: Rutgers University Press.

———. 1988. "Electroconvulsive Therapy, the Self, and Family Relations." *Research in the Sociology of Health Care* 7:283-300.

———. 1996. "Older Women, Younger Men: Self and Stigma in Age-Discrepant Relationships." *Clinical Sociology Review* 14:62-86.

———. 2000. "Writing the Other, Inscribing the Self." *Qualitative Sociology* 23:183-199.

Warren, C. A. B. and J. K. Hackney. 2000. *Gender Issues in Ethnography.* 2d ed. Thousand Oaks, CA: Sage.

Warren, C. A. B. and T. X. Karner. 1990. "Permissions and the Social Context." *American Sociologist* 21:116-35.

Warren, C. A. B. and K. A. K. Levy. 1991. "Electroconvulsive Therapy and the Elderly." *Journal of Aging Studies* 5:309-27.

Weiss, R. S. 1994. *Learning from Strangers: The Art and Method of Qualitative Interview Studies.* New York: Free Press.

5

IN-DEPTH INTERVIEWING

◆ John M. Johnson

The contributors to this volume describe many different types of interviewing. Each type has its distinct style, methods, advantages, and limitations. Each uses and builds on our commonsense knowledge about talking to others. Each type of interviewing uses our common cultural wisdom about people, places, manner, and contexts. Each is no better than the person using it. This chapter examines in-depth interviewing. In-depth interviews tend to be of relatively long duration. They commonly involve one-on-one, face-to-face interaction between an interviewer and an informant, and seek to build the kind of intimacy that is common for mutual self-disclosure. They tend to involve a greater expression of the interviewer's self than do some other types of interviews, as well as a personal commitment on the part of participants that spans several or many interview segments. In-depth interviewing offers great advantages, but it also entails some risks and dangers as well as some distinct ethical considerations.

In this chapter, I first describe in-depth interviewing as a social form and explain how this form is commonly used along with other methods of collecting data. I then discuss the goals and purposes of in-depth interviewing, emphasizing the importance of clarifying the research question in order to maximize the utility of this method, and describe some methods for locating informants. This is followed by an examination of the life cycle of an in-depth interviewing project. The chapter concludes with a discussion of some common ethical issues associated with in-depth interviewing.

AUTHOR'S NOTE: I wish to express my gratitude to the following persons who provided criticisms and suggestions to improve this chapter: David Altheide, Arlene Kaplan Daniels, Norman K. Denzin, Jack D. Douglas, and the editors of this volume.

◆ *In-Depth Interviewing as a Social Form*

In-depth interviewing involves a certain style of social and interpersonal interaction. As a social form, it differs from the kinds of interactions one usually finds in sales pitches, public lectures, job interviews, counseling sessions, sexual pickups, board meetings, monologues, or marital conflicts. To be effective and useful, in-depth interviews develop and build on intimacy; in this respect, they resemble the forms of talking one finds among close friends. They resemble friendship, and they may even lead to long-term friendship. But in-depth interviews are also very different from the kind of talking one finds between friends, mainly because the interviewer seeks to use the information obtained in the interaction for some other purpose.

A researcher who uses in-depth interviewing commonly seeks "deep" information and knowledge—usually deeper information and knowledge than is sought in surveys, informal interviewing, or focus groups, for example. This information usually concerns very personal matters, such as an individual's self, lived experience, values and decisions, occupational ideology, cultural knowledge, or perspective. When two close or "best" friends talk, there is no pragmatic purpose that transcends the friendship itself. That kind of talk is an end in itself. But when an in-depth interviewer talks to an informant, the goal is to collect data. Some specific ethical issues arise because of this difference.

In-depth interviews rarely constitute the sole source of data in research. More commonly, they are used in conjunction with data gathered through such avenues as lived experience of the interviewer as a member or participant in what is being studied, naturalistic or direct observation, informal interviewing, documentary records, and team field research. In many cases, researchers use in-depth interviewing as a way to check out theories they have formulated through naturalistic observation, to verify independently (or triangulate) knowledge they have gained through participation as members of particular cultural settings, or to explore multiple meanings of or perspectives on some actions, events, or settings. This was true in the famous case of anthropologist Margaret Mead's *Coming of Age in Samoa* ([1928] 1960). Mead supplemented her field experience, direct or naturalistic observations, and other interviews with in-depth interviews with informants (see Atkinson and Coffee, Chapter 38, this volume).

Years later, in his reexamination of Mead's research in *Margaret Mead and Samoa* (1983), however, Derek Freeman raised serious questions about these interviews. Freeman argues that Mead was misled by her female adolescent informants, even though she had lived in the Samoan villages for many months, because of the Samoan suspicion of outsiders and other contextual features of their recent contacts with Westerners. When Freeman later interviewed some of the same women who had been Mead's adolescent informants, they told him that they had told Mead what they thought she wanted to hear.

Another well-known case is represented by the studies of the Mexican village of Tepotzlan done over several decades by two different researchers, Robert Redfield (1930, 1941, 1960) and Oscar Lewis (1951). Redfield and Lewis made different inferences from their observations and interviews and drew diverse conclusions from their lengthy experiences of living in this small, remote village. Each justified and legitimated what he reported by referring to his heroic fieldwork and interviews. The two men's findings were different, however, in large part because of certain basic assumptions each made about the nature of "conflict" and "shared meanings" (or consensus) in everyday life, assumptions that predated their research observations and experiences.

Another heated debate arose recently concerning what is arguably the most famous sociological ethnography of all time, William Foote Whyte's *Street Corner Society* (1943, 1955, 1981, 1993), the classic study of an Italian American community in north Boston. Whyte also utilized in-depth interviewing in his study to supplement and complement other forms of data collection. Years later, W. A. Marianne Boelen (1992) returned to north Boston and reinterviewed virtually all of the people Whyte had interviewed; she then contested the truth of what he had reported (see Whyte 1992; Vidich 1992; Denzin 1992).

All of the studies noted above involved multiple research methodologies in addition to in-depth interviews. They illustrate that each research project involves the observer or interviewer as an active sense maker and interpreter of what is seen or heard in the research context. Each inevitably depends on the researcher's own standpoint and place in the community, as well as his or her own self-understandings, reflections, sincerity, authenticity, honesty, and integrity.

Whether in-depth interviewing should be used in research depends on the nature of the research question. Achieving clarity in the formulation and articulation of the research question commonly enhances the clarity of the methodological goals and objectives. If one is interested in an area of study in which the information sought is relatively limited, such as the marketing choices of individuals, then there is every reason to think that the use of focus groups or fixed-choice questionnaires might be appropriate. If one is interested in understanding forms of urban sociation, then direct observation would seem to be a reasonable approach to gathering data. But if one is interested in questions of greater depth, where the knowledge sought is often taken for granted and not readily articulated by most members, where the research question involves highly conflicted emotions, where different individuals or groups

involved in the same line of activity have complicated, multiple perspectives on some phenomenon, then in-depth interviewing is likely the best approach, despite its known imperfections. In-depth interviewing is often a very appropriate method to use in qualitative research (see Warren, Chapter 4, this volume), life story research (see Atkinson, Chapter 6, this volume), the gathering of personal narratives (see Riessman, Chapter 33, this volume) and oral histories (see Cándida Smith, Chapter 34, this volume), and the use of grounded theory methodology to analyze the accounts of members of some social setting (see Charmaz, Chapter 32, this volume). The important point is this: The nature of the research question determines whether or not the use of in-depth interviewing is advisable.

◆ The Goals and Purposes of In-Depth Interviewing

Many talented researchers have analyzed in-depth interviewing as a method or technique of collecting data (see Atkinson 1998; Cicourel 1964; Denzin 1989a, 1989b; Douglas 1985; Fontana and Frey 1994; Geertz 1988; Holstein and Gubrium 1995; Lofland and Lofland 1984, 1995; Merton, Fiske, and Kendall 1956; Rubin and Rubin 1995; Spradley 1979; Wax 1971). Many authors have taken up the issue of "how to do" qualitative or in-depth interviewing, and most additionally affirm the importance of the researcher's goals and purposes, the researcher's moral commitment to seek out what is true, and the researcher's ethical imperative to examine his or her own personal ideas, occupational ideologies, assumptions, common sense, and emotions as crucial resources for what he or she "sees" or "hears" in a particular research interview or project.

Many reflective parents have had to learn this important lesson from their children, often painfully: Children don't learn what their parents tell them, but what they are prepared and ready to hear. The same holds for in-depth interviewers: They don't necessarily "hear" what their informants tell them, but only what their own intellectual and ethical development has prepared them to hear. The Mead/Freeman, Lewis/Redfield, and Whyte/Boelen conflicts emphatically underscore this point. In each of the complicated community settings these researchers studied, it is not the case that there is just "one truth" that the observer or interviewer either does or does not "see" or "hear." Rather, each researcher implicitly draws upon his or her commonsense cultural knowledge—or "stock of knowledge," as Alfred Schutz (1967) terms it—and creates or constructs a truth or interpretation that will work for all practical (intellectual) purposes.

As the name implies, in-depth interviewing seeks "deep" information and understanding. The word *deep* has several meanings in this context. First, deep understandings are held by the real-life members of or participants in some everyday activity, event, or place. The interviewer seeks to achieve the same deep level of knowledge and understanding as the members or participants. If the interviewer is not a current or former member or participant in what is being investigated, he or she might use in-depth interviewing as a way to learn the meanings of participants' actions. In the words of the famous ethnographer and student of daily life Erving Goffman (1989), the goal here is one of "subjecting yourself . . . and your own social situation, to the set of contingencies that play upon a set of individuals, so that you can physically and ecologically penetrate their circle of response to their social situation, their work situation, or their ethnic situation" (p. 125).

In this respect, the informant would be a kind of teacher and the interviewer a student, one interested in learning the ropes or gaining member knowledge from a veteran informant. If the interviewer happens to be

a current or former member or participant in this activity, he or she may use in-depth interviews to explore or check his or her understandings, to see if they are shared by other members or participants. Former or returning members can fruitfully use in-depth interviews to check, stimulate, or inspire their own self-reflections and to see if their understandings are the same as those shared by others who are also members or participants.

Second, deep understandings go beyond commonsense explanations for and other understandings of some cultural form, activity, event, place, or artifact. In-depth interviewing is an irremediably commonsensical (or intersubjective) enterprise. It begins with commonsense perceptions, explanations, and understandings of some lived cultural experience (which include scientific explanations) and aims to explore the contextual boundaries of that experience or perception, to uncover what is usually hidden from ordinary view or reflection or to penetrate to more reflective understandings about the nature of that experience. For example, in one of my own current research projects I am using in-depth interviewing to explore the complicated phenomenon of "stalking"; I am seeking to learn how those who stalk others actually see or interpret their actions, as well as to explore the nature of the (often conflicted) emotions that lie underneath these actions.

Third, deep understandings can reveal how our commonsense assumptions, practices, and ways of talking partly constitute our interests and how we understand them. In his self-revealing book *Creative Interviewing,* for example, Jack Douglas (1985) tells how his own deeply hidden and conflicted emotions about his mother's prostitution influenced what he was able to "hear" in the in-depth interviews he conducted on the nature of love and intimacy (Douglas 1985, 1988).

Fourth, deep understandings allow us to grasp and articulate the multiple views of, perspectives on, and meanings of some activity, event, place, or cultural object. To illustrate with an example from my own current research with Beth McLin: We are currently seeking to understand the multiple perspectives on the death penalty. At a commonsense level, one might think this would include studying the views of those who advocate the death penalty and those who oppose it. Although this is a useful distinction for some limited purpose, it fails to grasp the variety among the many groups involved in this issue: death penalty abolitionists and protesters, executioners, death row prisoners' wives and other family members, victims' family members, prison guards, legislators, clerics, pro-death penalty demonstrators, wardens, prosecutors, defense lawyers, and death row prisoners. Knowing whether an individual is "for" or "against" the death penalty tells us little about the complicated, multifaceted perspectives on and meanings of capital executions. Jaber Gubrium (1975, 1988; Buckholdt and Gubrium 1985) is a longtime qualitative researcher who has successfully combined observations with in-depth interviewing in several settings in order to gain explicit understanding of the multiple interpretations of and perspectives on the activities and settings he investigated.

To gain clarity on the goals for conducting in-depth interviews, the researcher must achieve clarity on the research questions. An important issue is the researcher's relationship to member knowledge and lived experience. Is the researcher completely ignorant of and inexperienced in the issues to be addressed in the interviews? If so, the interviews will take on the nature of instruction, with the more experienced members teaching the novice interviewer. Such interviews are commonly very uneven in quality, with the early ones usually telling more about the novice's ignorance than about the phenomenon being studied. John Lofland and Lyn Lofland (1995) have observed that virtually all of such interviews will prove to be entirely worthless as empirical data. They may play an important role

in the education and learning curve of the neophyte interviewer, but it usually takes a long time for a novice to begin to "hear" what a veteran is saying about the important matters of lived experience. This aspect of interviewing is of such importance that the authors of a recent book elevate it to the very subtitle of their work: *Qualitative Interviewing: The Art of Hearing Data* (Rubin and Rubin, 1995).

In prior decades, social researchers who possessed experiential knowledge of some activity or scene that they were studying commonly elected to hide that fact to elude professional disrepute or even some more severe stigma. The many legendary examples (including quantitative researchers as well) provide fodder for the informal gossip one finds at professional meetings. These tales are commonly transmitted orally, and one begins to achieve "inside" or "member" status as a social science professional by learning these sad and joyous tales of heroism, cowardice, and perseverance in the face of adversity. In these earlier times, the professional ideal was that of "detachment" and "objectivity," which was taken to mean that actual lived experience or actual membership status could "taint" the research or its findings. John Irwin's perception that he had to conceal his nine-year prison sentence as an important experiential resource in the research that went into the writing of *The Felon* (1970) is a good example from this era. H. Laud Humphreys's concealment of his gay identity in his award-winning *Tearoom Trade* (1970) is another.

Lived experience and member status are no longer stigmatized among social scientists, and some even extol their relative merits (Ellis and Flaherty 1992; Denzin 1997; see also in this volume Dunbar, Rodriguez, and Parker, Chapter 14; Ellis and Berger, Chapter 41). Today there are many researchers who use their investigations and interviews to explore phenomena about which they have prior or current member-based knowledge. Jeffrey Riemer (1977), who terms this "opportunistic research," provides many examples of individuals who have conducted such research (see also Higgins and Johnson 1988). Lofland and Lofland (1995) advocate the advantages of "starting where you are," by which they mean potential researchers should seriously consider studying those social phenomena to which they have ready or advantaged access. Some of my own first research experiences and in-depth interviews fit this pattern. Making use of my knowledge and membership as a former U.S. Navy officer, I conducted in-depth interviews to explore others' perceptions and knowledge of routine bureaucratic record-keeping activities and "gundecking" (fudging) of official reports (Johnson 1972, 1980a, 1980b). Later, active participation in the battered women's shelter movement as a founder and worker in a shelter provided me with a foundation from which to conduct in-depth interviews with battered women about their experiences with domestic violence (Adhikari, Reinhard, and Johnson 1993; Ferraro and Johnson 1983; Johnson 1981, 1985, 1992; Johnson and Ferraro 1984; Johnson, Luna, and Stein forthcoming). And even today, my years of activist participation as a death penalty abolitionist serve to inform my work as I conduct in-depth interviews with respondents who hold multiple perspectives on these actions.

When charting a research project that includes in-depth interviewing, is it better to be an experienced veteran or a relatively ignorant novice? Each status has its strengths and advantages, and each its pitfalls and dangers. Novices are less inclined to possess hardened assumptions about what they are studying, but they often have more difficulty seeing the nuances or layered meanings of participating members. When undertaking a research project through in-depth interviews, they are likely to have a longer learning curve. Veterans with actual lived experience may already possess member knowledge, but they may also take that knowledge for granted. Additionally, their current or former status as

members may constitute a barrier when they interview others. It is important that researchers recognize these nuances in advance, so that they can undertake the planning of in-depth interviewing in a manner that will help them to assess these influences on the accounts and reflections collected during the interviewing process. Whether the researcher is a neophyte or a returning veteran, in-depth interviewing involves an interactive process in which both interviewer and informant draw upon and use their commonsense knowledge to create some intelligible sense of the questions posed and the ensuing discussions about them.

◆ Locating Informants

Planning and preparation are essential for successful in-depth interviews, but few researchers do everything they think they should before beginning them. Hardly anyone reads everything he or she feels should be read or achieves the kind of clarity he or she really wants on the protocol of questions. In their recent work on interviewing, Herbert Rubin and Irene Rubin (1995:42) liken the planning for an interviewing session to planning for a vacation—that is, making plans sufficient to meet practical and emotional expectations while at the same time providing for the possibility of "hanging loose," or altering the course of the interview to go where the informant wants to lead. At some point, the researcher must make a leap of faith and just dive into the process.

The research process is a learning process. Interviewers make mistakes; they make gaffs and alienate informants. They learn that their race, age, gender, social class, appearance, and even achieved statuses make one kind of difference with some informants and another kind of difference with other informants (see in this volume Schwalbe and Wolkomir, Chapter 10; Reinharz and Chase, Chapter 11;

Dunbar et al., Chapter 14). The point is that researchers can learn from all this—learn what makes a difference for their specific projects, learn their strengths and how to play to them, and how to cover or compensate for their weaknesses.

Individuals have performed the basic forms of asking questions and answering questions countless times before they ever come to their first formal, in-depth interviews. The role of informant is part of the cultural stock of commonsense knowledge for the vast majority of children and adults. As friends, we talk in an informal manner and engage in cooperative, mutual self-disclosure. Those who elect to conduct research in a more formal fashion draw upon and build upon these cultural forms and commonsense practices. When a researcher begins an in-depth interview, he or she behaves in a friendly and interested manner so as to help build trust and good rapport.

An in-depth interviewer begins slowly, with small talk (chitchat), explains the purposes of the research, and commonly begins with simple planned questions (often referred to as icebreakers) that are intended to "get the ball rolling" but not to move so quickly into the issues of the key interview questions as to jeopardize intimate self-disclosure (or trust). Good rapport is signaled by emotions that feel harmonious and cooperative, and trust can commonly be discerned through eye contact, facial expression, and bodily idiom.

In-depth interviewing differs from other forms because it involves a greater involvement of the interviewer's self. To progressively and incrementally build a mutual sense of cooperative self-disclosure and trust, the interviewer must offer some form of strict or complementary reciprocity. Strict reciprocity is possible only if the interviewer is a former or current member of the group under study, and would take the form of the interviewer's sharing with the informant his or her own views, feelings, or reflections on the topics being discussed.

It is more common for an interviewer to bring some form of complementary reci-procity to the informant—not a strict exchange of perceptions, feelings, or reflections, but rather some form of help, assistance, or other form of information. When I interviewed the women who came to the battered women's shelter that I helped establish in the late 1970s, for example, I could hardly offer them strict reciprocity for their views on battering, given that I was not a battered woman. Rather, I could share with them what many other women had told me they felt and said about their similar circumstances; after a while, I could even offer well-grounded advice on what they might do next (Ferraro and Johnson 1983; Johnson and Ferraro 1984). I did the same in two subsequent interview studies on the effectiveness of domestic violence protection orders (Adhikari et al. 1993; Johnson et al. forthcoming). In my current interviews with male stalkers, I cannot offer my informants the solace of strict reciprocity, given that I have never stalked anyone myself. I can, however, share the wisdom I have culled from working in the field of domestic violence for 30 years, including almost two decades of work and counseling with violent men.

In order to conduct in-depth interviewing, then, researchers must undertake considerable self-reflection to get to know themselves; they must also make a self-conscious effort to observe themselves in interaction with others. The development and cultivation of trust with informants is slow, incremental, and emotional, in most cases, and the relationship can change quickly (Johnson 1975). The ideal goal is that the informant become a collaborative partner with the researcher in the intellectual adventure at hand.

Gender is inevitably important in interviewing, but it is difficult to generalize about the precise nature of its importance. The nature of the research question is commonly the main issue. Some research questions may elicit responses or perspectives for which gender has great relevance, whereas others may not. Feminist scholars such as Carol Gilligan (1982) assert that many researchers interpret women's responses according to male standards (hierarchy, individualization, rationality) while neglecting women's relatively greater uses of relational categories and perspectives. Dorothy Smith (1987, 1990) notes that prevailing institutional priorities and agendas often devalue women's lived experiences in the world, and that the very formulation of the questions that animate a research project often implicitly contain hidden gender evaluations or perspectives. She proposes that researchers place the issue of women's daily lived experiences at the center of the research process itself. All researchers would be wise to develop a special sensitivity to the explicit or deeply obscured meanings of gender in any particular research topic.

The process of locating informants is simplified if members of the group of interest are usually or regularly located at the same place or scene; it is more complicated if potential informants do not regularly congregate at one locale. All those persons who are members of some scene or community, or who participate in some activity, are not equally valuable as informants. Informants differ greatly in their intelligence, knowledge, and ability to reflect. Informants also differ in their motivations to assist in or cooperate with an in-depth interview or series of interviews. Informants differ widely in their responses to specific individuals, whether because of racial, class, gender, age, or other characteristics, or perhaps just because of timing. It is realistic for the researcher to anticipate that this will happen. Because those who do in-depth interviews for research purposes have no interest in "counting" them or "adding them up," this reality of noncomparable interviews poses no problem.

Many research projects have been "made" by the researcher's finding that rare, reflective inside informant who seems to know just about everything that seems to be important and has thought about it and reflected on it for some considerable period of time before he or she ever meets an eth-

nographer or does an in-depth interview. Legendary examples include "Doc" (Dean Pecci), William Foote Whyte's key informant in his research for *Street Corner Society* (1943, 1955, 1981, 1993); "Tally," Elliot Liebow's key informant for *Tally's Corner* (1967); and "Vincent Swaggi," Carl Klockars's key informant for *The Professional Fence* (1974). The kinds or types of individuals who are likely to become key informants like this can be found in many settings. They are often marginal to the setting or scene being studied and are often seen by others in the setting as "lay intellectuals," thinkers, eggheads, or know-it-alls. Sometimes they are the politically ambitious individuals in the setting, those who have strenuously studied the setting and its personnel for the purposes of occupational or material gain or advancement. Sometimes they are the "outsiders" of the setting, stigmatized for some quality that is depreciated or deprecated.

Ethnographers and interviewers should always develop an awareness of such individuals and be ready to cultivate their trust and friendship for the purposes of gaining member knowledge. Marginal membership status in the setting or activity seems to provide many with an invitation to reflection and usually a certain sense of intellectual detachment from the "official line" among the membership. Finding such individuals and making them collaborators in the research process can yield wonderful results. Researchers should take care, however, to check out the observations and reflections of such individuals by getting independent verification through other interviews, if and when possible. Researchers who fail to do such checking can jeopardize the integrity of their research findings and possibly their own reputations.

Some informants are better than others. Not all members of a setting or community are equally valuable for purposes of in-depth interviews. Not all of those who participate in some activity have a sufficient motive or interest to be interviewed about it. The best informants are those who have been thoroughly enculturated in the setting or community, have recent membership participation, have some provisional interest in assisting the interviewer, and have adequate time and resources to take part in the interviews. The best informants are those who can describe a scene or setting or activity, those who can provide "thick description," as Clifford Geertz (1973, 1988) terms it, but not necessarily those who analyze or theorize. In some settings or situations, such individuals may "click" with the interviewer or they may not—this is inevitable. The issue of "sampling," or how researchers decided which informants to include and which to exclude, is one that is rarely addressed in research reports and publications. It is important for researchers to provide accounts or explanations of how this selection was done in specific projects, so that readers may assess the researchers' findings (Altheide and Johnson 1994: 494-95).

◆ Conducting In-Depth Interviews

The act of conducting the first in-depth interviews on a new study is often tinged with anxiety but also great anticipation and excitement. The first interviews usually yield great leaps forward in learning. The learning curve is steep at this point. It is best for the interviewer to begin with an actual protocol of questions: usually two or three introductory icebreakers to get the ball rolling; several transition questions, which may again explain the purposes of the interviewing project or elicit permission from the respondent to use a tape recorder; and then perhaps five to eight main or key questions that address the heart or essence of the research question(s). An in-depth interview commonly concludes with the interviewer summarizing some of the main points he or she has understood or giving the informant some information about what others have said about the issues dis-

cussed. Although interviewers might anticipate following such a nice, neat, rational plan before they begin interviewing, they inevitably find that the path, tone, and trajectory of actual interviews rarely follow this sequence.

As an interview progresses, it often takes unexpected turns or digressions that follow the informant's interests or knowledge. Such digressions or diversions are likely to be very productive, so the interviewer should be prepared to depart from his or her prepared plan and "go with the flow"— that is, consider following for a while where the informant wants to lead. It is essential that the interviewer be assertive enough to return the interview to its anticipated course when necessary, but not so rigid as to preclude his or her learning unexpected information. Go with the flow, be playful, and be open to an experimental attitude—these are all good pieces of advice for a novice in-depth interviewer in the early stages of a project.

USING THE TAPE RECORDER TO LEARN INTERVIEWING SKILLS

We now know with some certainty that a human being's individual memory does not remember what the person sees or hears, but rather organizes it into some intelligible coherence based on the individual's past experience. Thus it is essential that interviewers tape-record in-depth interviews to obtain verbatim records of those interviews. Handwritten field notes are important for any research project, and there exists considerable wisdom about how to make such notes (Emerson, Fretz, and Shaw 1995; Lofland and Lofland 1995; Strauss and Corbin 1990), but field notes are far inferior to tape recording for in-depth interviews.

One of the main goals of qualitative research has always been to capture the words and perceptions of informants, or, as Bronislaw Malinowski (1922) puts it, "to grasp the native's point of view, his relation to life, to realize his visions of his world" (p. 25). So obtaining a verbatim record is the ideal if the subsequent analysis is to be valid and meaningful. Whether or not the researcher tape-records an interview, it is imperative that he or she take process notes regarding the interview itself, to gain an understanding of the interview as a social occasion and how the questions and answers mutually constitute the sense of what is said. The questions asked guide and influence the answers given, and so it is important for the interviewer to grasp why the informant proffers one segment of talk as an answer rather than another.

Researchers can develop and cultivate the skills needed for in-depth interviewing with practice. Although in-depth interviewing is perhaps the form of interviewing closest to the kind of talking done between friends, the individual who conducts an in-depth interview exercises greater control over the flow and tone of the conversation than does the respondent. The beginning of the interview is different from the beginning of a conversation between friends in that the interviewer commonly explains the purposes of the research and, these days, perhaps gets the informant's signature on an informed consent statement. The turn taking is also different from that in a conversation between friends, with the interviewer deferring to the informant.

The asking and answering of questions is asymmetrical, with the interviewer having previously prepared a protocol of questions and the will to keep the informant on track, attending to the business at hand. The interviewer is more passive in the role of listener, and, if the interviewer is successful, the informant is more active as a speaker. During interviews, the rules for pausing are usually different from those in talks between friends, as are the rules for physical proximity. The interviewer's aim is to develop progressively with the informant the kind of mutual and cooperative self-disclosure that is associated with the building of intimacy and trust, but it takes great skill to accomplish this when one is working with asymmetrical communication norms very dissimilar to those one usually associates with building intimacy and trust, as in actual friendship. The interviewer's goal is to solicit the informant as a collaborative partner in the sense making and interpretations that flow from the interviewing process.

USING INTERVIEWS TO EXPLORE VERSUS USING INTERVIEWS TO VERIFY

In the early stages of a research project, the in-depth interviewer may feel relatively ignorant about what he or she is studying. After several interviews, however, the interviewer begins to build a stock of knowledge about the research questions, and in most cases feeds some of this information back to the informants in subsequent interviews, after those same questions have been covered. This information exchange becomes part of the complementary reciprocity so necessary to the continued building of intimacy, and it also begins the process of verification in the research process. Data collection and verification become inextricably intertwined in most in-depth interviewing projects. As the research develops, the interviewer should keep and review his or her own jottings and notes (see Emerson et al. 1995; Lofland and Lofland 1995) and should review prior interviews when possible, or when transcripts become available, and should begin progressively to focus the nature of the questioning and probing in later interviews. The later interviews of an in-depth interviewing project are usually more focused on specific probes and verification of what has been learned in earlier interviews.

In more traditional or standardized interviewing, interviewers are commonly told to stick to the questions on the research protocol, to ask the questions precisely as they are given, to probe for clarifications only in ways that will not influence the respondents' answers, and to record only what the respondents say (see, for example, Singleton and Straits, Chapter 3, this volume). Further, traditional interviewers are trained to be impersonal; that is, they are trained to avoid offering any kind of personal information or revelations about any of their own values, beliefs, or opinions that might influence respondents in any way (see, for example, Fowler and Mangione 1990). This is not a realistic ideal for in-depth interviewing, because the nature of the research question itself usually entails a deeper process of mutual self-disclosure and trust building.

Skilled in-depth interviewers may often deviate from the research protocol, to go where the informant seems to want to go or perhaps to follow what appear to be more interesting leads. The interviewer should record these moves in his or her process notes, so that he or she can see later how one set of interviewing actions influenced and thereby constituted what the informant said. The interviewer can use subsequent interviews with the same informant or other interviews with additional informants to check the interpretive validity of this strategy.

◆ The Life Cycle of In-Depth Interviewing

Excitement runs high when an interviewer is in the springtime of a research project. Genuine students are usually enthusiastic about gaining new knowledge from informants and learning what they have to teach. Eventually, however, the excitement begins to wane. The doldrums of the summer monsoons appear. The animating enthusiasm begins to lessen, and researchers find themselves using all sorts of excuses, rationalizations, and self-deceptions to alter their involvement with the research interviews. In some cases, boredom appears. This happens because the learning curve has peaked, and it is less satisfying to do all of the pragmatic work required to set up interviews when one learns progressively less

from them. Barney Glaser and Anselm Strauss (1967:120-45) refer to this as the "saturation point" of a research project. It is commonly in this context that the researcher begins to ask, How many interviews are needed? How many interviews are enough?

Interestingly, the academic literature on interviewing includes various answers to the question of how many interviews are needed. James Spradley (1979:51), an anthropologist usually interested in using interviews to understand cultural forms and members' perspectives, has noted, for example, that for him, one in-depth interview commonly involves six or seven one-hour sessions, and a given research project might include between 25 and 30 of these. Grant McCracken (1988:37), a researcher with a business background who uses in-depth interviews (which he terms "long interviews") to gain knowledge about marketing and business questions, says eight such interviews are usually enough. The progenitors of grounded theory methodology in qualitative research, Glaser and Strauss (1967), do not recommend a specific number of interviews or observations, but say that the researcher should continue until a state of *theoretical* saturation is achieved; the identification of this point, however, is left ambiguous in their writings on this issue. Many others have shared their opinions on this question, but as the researchers cited above illustrate, there is no specific, set answer.

The number of interviews needed to explore a given research question depends on the nature of that question and the kind or type of knowledge the interviewer seeks. To those students who have asked me how many interviews they need, I have often responded, "Enough." By this I mean that enough interviews must be conducted so that the interviewer feels he or she has learned all there is to be learned from the interviews and has checked out those understandings by reinterviewing the most trusted and most knowledgeable informants.

It has been a common ideal in in-depth interviewing for the interviewer to check out his or her understandings with one or more key informants since this practice was first articulated and reported by William Foote Whyte (1943:279-358); this is usually called the "member's test of validity." In research that uses interviewing as a basic form of data collection, whether the researcher is a neophyte or a returning member, early interviews will embody much more "grand tour" questioning (Lofland and Lofland 1984:78-86; Spradley 1979: 86-92) than will later interviews, which tend to be more focused on checking out and verifying research observations, analyses, and presumptive findings.

In a very important sense, all research is "team research" in that it occurs in social, interactional, and community contexts. Even in the case of the heroic "lone ranger," the individual who is for the most part working on his or her own out in the field, there is usually a social support system of family members and friends and a small coterie of professional colleagues who provide intellectual and social support for the project. Researchers usually acknowledge such ties in the introductions, prefaces, or notes of the reports they publish on their studies. In other cases, interviewers may work in teams on projects with other researchers and share the interviewing duties. The interpersonal dynamics among research team members can be a source of problems, from the beginning negotiations concerning the "research bargain" (the division of labor and reward) to the eventual analysis and report. Members of an interviewing team may feel violated or "ripped off" just as informants may feel violated or "ripped off" if their confidentiality is breached or if promises are not kept (Adler, Adler, and Rochford 1986; Douglas 1976). In one of the extensive team research projects on which I worked, proprietary rights to the interviewing records were specified in a divorce agreement.

In addition to the social relationships implicated in and by a particular research project, research reports claim membership in some kind of interpretive community. They do this through the idiom, language, and issues that they embody. Qualitative research is a diverse and multifaceted field. The editors of the *Handbook of Qualitative Research*, Norman Denzin and Yvonna Lincoln (2000a), identify "seven moments" of qualitative research; in their recent work, Jaber Gubrium and James Holstein (1997) identify four major "idioms" of qualitative method. However one classifies qualitative research communities, each implicates its own standards of acceptable and reportable truth. Researchers would be wise to make their connections to particular research communities explicit and to incorporate these into their research processes and reporting, so that competent readers may assess how standards were created and embodied in actual research situations.

◆ Ethical Issues Raised by In-Depth Interviewing

In-depth interviewing commonly elicits highly personal information about specific individuals, perhaps even about the interviewer. This information may include participants' personal feelings and reflections as well as their perceptions of others. It may include details about deviant or illegal activities that, if made known, would have deleterious consequences for lives and reputations. It may include expressions of private knowledge about some setting or occupation that goes against that setting or occupation's public front or public presentation. Collecting this kind of information raises some specific ethical issues.

HOW DEEP?

One ethical issue concerns how far an interviewer should go in probing informants' answers. As noted previously, in-depth interviewers should be prepared to follow where informants might lead, because this often leads to fruitful territory for those informants who wish to use the interviewing situation as an occasion for self-reflection and their own increased understanding. It is sometimes difficult, if not impossible, however, for a researcher to anticipate fully the consequences of such probing. In the case of one in-depth interview conducted by Rubin and Rubin (1995:98), an informant's suicide followed a revealing interview by a matter of weeks; the timing of this informant's death led the researchers to wonder if there was any connection between their interview and the suicide.

PROTECTING SUBJECTS

Professional social science organizations have traditionally addressed potentially difficult issues in their published codes of ethics (see Neuman 1994). One traditional ethical principle has been that the researcher must do whatever is necessary "to protect research subjects." There are several different ways in which such a principle can be interpreted, however, and so there exists some ambiguity about what is required of the researcher. One interpretation of this ethical principle is that the researcher should do what is necessary *to protect the specific individuals who have assisted him or her in the research, as individuals.* This means that a researcher or interviewer would feel obligated to take whatever steps are necessary to protect the individuals who have cooperated in the research from any misuses of the information they have shared.

In one well-known case, a researcher coded all his interview records and kept them in a safe deposit box in a bank located in a state different from the one where the research was conducted (Humphreys 1970). In another famous case, a researcher went to jail rather than yield research and interview materials to court officials (Brajuha and Hallowell 1986; Hallowell

1985). In that case, Mario Brajuha was a graduate student who was studying a restaurant that was "torched" (burned down), and when police investigators suspected mob arson, they went to the courts in an effort to obtain Brajuha's research records. Knowing about such potential complexities in advance should stimulate researchers to give prior consideration to their ethical commitments and the lengths to which they will go in order to protect research informants. In another case, a sociology graduate student spent five months in jail in order to protect his subjects in a sociological field project on ecoterrorism; his incarceration produced further reflections on this ethical dilemma (Scarce 1994, 1995, 1999).

PROTECTING COMMUNITIES

Another issue concerning the protection of research informants is whether researchers should feel any obligation to avoid causing harm to the reputation, social standing, or social prestige of their informants' professions, occupations, communities, or groups *as collectives*. Predicting future consequences of this kind is highly problematic, so it is exceedingly difficult to assess the risk of such harm with any certainty.

Another issue concerning the protection of informants is whether a research report will play some role in "deprivatizing" their lived experience (Gubrium and Holstein 1995). The risk of this is also very difficult to assess, and so it is reasonable to anticipate that different individuals will reach different ethical judgments, even individuals within the same support community or research team. This seems like one reasonable reading of what occurred when Carolyn Ellis (1986), an ethnographer, published an award-winning book about two fishing villages near the Chesapeake Bay. Ellis studied the villages over a period of 19 years, but when she returned in the early 1990s she discovered that her published accounts had offended some of the community members, leading her to express some reservations about the standards she had used in the research publication (Ellis 1995). It seems clear that Ellis did not use the criteria for privacy that existed in the communities she studied, but instead used a much broader standard familiar to most of the cosmopolitans who live and work in and around universities today. The problematic nature of such ethical judgments does not reduce the need for interviewers to face and address them as best they can.

TELLING THE TRUTH

The most important ethical imperative is to tell the truth. This issue has become especially important during the current period, which Denzin and Lincoln (2000b:3) call "the postmodern moment." This moment is defined by two crises: the crisis of representation and the crisis of legitimation (for qualitative research). One response to these crises is the advocacy of "standpoint epistemologies" (Denzin 1997:53-89), where the research interviewer not only *self-consciously empathizes* with the informants as individuals, but *self-consciously sympathizes* with the political or community goals of those informants *as a category or collective.*

John Lofland (1995), a strong advocate of analytic ethnography, heartily disagrees with this position, saying that it amounts to a promotion of "fettered research." Most of the complex settings or situations that the vast majority of social scientists are likely to study are highly variegated, pluralistic, and filled with multiple perspectives and interpretations, so the adoption of a standpoint epistemology does not address certain important ethical questions (Altheide and Johnson 1994).

In a situation with multiple perspectives or interpretations, whose standards or criteria of truth are to prevail in the final report? This is the critical ethical question for in-depth interviewing. In several recent

publications, Denzin discusses a short story written by Raymond Carver (1989) about a writer who returns to his home town to find out that everyone there is angry with him because of what he has written about them. Denzin (1997:285-87) interprets the import of this story to be that "a writer is always selling someone out," meaning that, in virtually all complex settings in today's world, all interpretations and voices are subject to conflict and dispute. To resolve this problematic dilemma, Denzin suggests "upping the ante" on the guilt and other professional consequences for not telling a defensible truth in one's writings.

Robert Emerson and Melvin Pollner (1992) advocate another way to address this issue: Take the final ethnographic report back to the informants and other members of the setting that was studied, not so much to verify the findings independently (as in Whyte's "member's test of validity") as to gain their impressions and feedback on what has been written about them. The goal is not necessarily to seek a consensus, but to open a dialogue on what is written in the final report. E. Burke Rochford (1992) is one researcher who has actually followed this path. His experiences indicate that this practice may be very problematic, however; it can lead to conflict among members who later dispute what even they will accept as a true interpretation, because of subsequent considerations about the consequences of publication.

Carl Klockars (1977) offers the opinion that "the true test of ethics of research with human beings is whether or not it forces the researcher to suffer with his subjects" (p. 225). This is an ambiguous standard, to be sure. And Jeffrey Reiman (1979:57) would add to this the consideration of whether the publication of the research results enhances the author's career or the informant's freedom. Even in a postmodern age characterized by little consensus on the answers to such ethical issues, the questions stay with us to haunt our enterprise.

■ *References*

Adhikari, R. P., D. Reinhard, and J. M. Johnson. 1993. "The Myth of Protection Orders." Pp. 294-311 in *Studies in Symbolic Interaction: A Research Annual,* Vol. 14, edited by N. K. Denzin. Greenwich, CT: JAI.

Adler, P. A., P. Adler, and E. B. Rochford. 1986. "The Politics of Participation in Field Research." *Urban Life* 14:363-76.

Altheide, D. L. and J. M. Johnson. 1994. "Criteria for Assessing Interpretive Validity in Qualitative Research." Pp. 485-99 in *Handbook of Qualitative Research,* edited by N. K. Denzin and Y. S. Lincoln. Thousand Oaks, CA: Sage.

Atkinson, R. 1998. *The Life Story Interview.* Thousand Oaks, CA: Sage.

Boelen, M. A. 1992. "*Street Corner Society:* Cornerville Revisited." *Journal of Contemporary Ethnography* 21:11-51.

Brajuha, M. and L. Hallowell. 1986. "Legal Intrusion and the Politics of Fieldwork: The Impact of the Brajuha Case." *Urban Life* 14:454-78.

Buckholdt, D. R. and J. F. Gubrium. 1985. *Caretakers.* Beverly Hills, CA: Sage.

Carver, R. 1989. "Intimacy." Pp. 444-53 in *Where I'm Calling From,* edited by R. Carver. New York: Vintage.

Cicourel, A. V. 1964. *Method and Measurement in Sociology.* New York: Free Press.

Denzin, N. K. 1989a. *Interpretive Interactionism.* Newbury Park, CA: Sage.

———. 1989b. *The Research Act: A Theoretical Introduction to Sociological Methods.* 3d ed. Englewood Cliffs, NJ: Prentice Hall.

———. 1992. "Whose Cornerville Is It, Anyway?" *Journal of Contemporary Ethnography* 21:120-32.

———. 1997. *Interpretive Ethnography: Ethnographic Practices for the 21st century.* Thousand Oaks, CA: Sage.

Denzin, N. K. and Y. S. Lincoln, eds. 2000a. *Handbook of Qualitative Research.* 2d ed. Thousand Oaks, CA: Sage.

———. 2000b. "Introduction: The Discipline and Practice of Qualitative Research." Pp. 1-28 in *Handbook of Qualitative Research,* 2d ed., edited by N. K. Denzin and Y. S. Lincoln. Thousand Oaks, CA: Sage.

Douglas, J. D. 1976. *Investigative Social Research.* Beverly Hills, CA: Sage.

———. 1985. *Creative Interviewing.* Beverly Hills, CA: Sage.

———. 1988. *Love, Intimacy, and Sex.* Newbury Park, CA: Sage.

Ellis, C. 1986. *Fisher Folk: Two Communities on Chesapeake Bay.* Lexington: University Press of Kentucky.

———. 1995. "Emotional and Ethical Quagmires in Returning to the Field." *Journal of Contemporary Ethnography* 24:711-13.

Ellis, C. and M. G. Flaherty, eds. 1992. *Investigating Subjectivity: Research on Lived Experience.* Newbury Park, CA: Sage.

Emerson, R. M., R. I. Fretz, and L. L. Shaw. 1995. *Writing Ethnographic Fieldnotes.* Chicago: University of Chicago Press.

Emerson, R. M. and M. Pollner. 1992. "Difference and Dialogue: Members' Readings of Ethnographic Texts." Pp. 79-98 in *Perspectives on Social Problems,* Vol. 3, edited by G. Miller and J. A. Holstein. Greenwich, CT: JAI.

Ferraro, K. J. and J. M. Johnson. 1983. "How Women Experience Battering." *Social Problems* 30:325-39.

Fontana, A. and J. H. Frey. 1994. "Interviewing: The Art of Science." Pp. 361-76 in *Handbook of Qualitative Research,* edited by N. K. Denzin and Y. S. Lincoln. Thousand Oaks, CA: Sage.

Fowler, F. J., Jr. and T. W. Mangione. 1990. *Standardized Survey Interviewing: Minimizing Interviewer-Related Error.* Newbury Park, CA: Sage.

Freeman, D. 1983. *Margaret Mead and Samoa: The Making and Unmaking of an Anthropological Myth.* Cambridge, MA: Harvard University Press.

Geertz, C. 1973. Thick Description: Toward an Interpretive Theory of Culture. Pp. 3-30 in C. Geertz, *The Interpretation of Cultures: Selected Essays.* New York: Basic Books.

———. 1988. *Works and Lives: The Anthropologist as Author.* Stanford, CA: Stanford University Press.

Gilligan, C. 1982. *In a Different Voice: Psychological Theory and Women's Development.* Cambridge, MA: Harvard University Press.

Glaser, B. G. and A. L. Strauss. 1967. *The Discovery of Grounded Theory: Strategies for Qualitative Research.* Chicago: Aldine.

Goffman, E. 1989. "On Fieldwork." *Journal of Contemporary Ethnography* 18:123-32.

Gubrium, J. F. 1975. *Living and Dying at Murray Manor.* New York: St. Martin's.

———. 1988. "Rationality and Practical Reasoning in Human Service Organizations." Pp. 103-17 in *Personal Sociology,* edited by P. C. Higgins and J. M. Johnson. New York: Praeger.

Gubrium, J. F. and J. A. Holstein. 1995. "Qualitative Inquiry and the Deprivatization of Experience." *Qualitative Inquiry* 1:204-22.

———. 1997. *The New Language of Qualitative Method.* New York: Oxford University Press.

Hallowell, L. 1985. "The Outcome of the Brajuha Case: Legal Implications for Sociologists." *Footnotes* 13:13.

Higgins, P. C. and J. M. Johnson, eds. 1988. *Personal Sociology.* New York: Praeger.

Holstein, J. A. and J. F. Gubrium. 1995. *The Active Interview.* Thousand Oaks, CA: Sage.

Humphreys, H. L. 1970. *Tearoom Trade: Impersonal Sex in Public Places.* Chicago: Aldine.

Irwin, J. 1970. *The Felon.* Englewood Cliffs, NJ: Prentice Hall.

Johnson, J. M. 1972. "The Practical Use of Rules." Pp. 145-62 in *Theoretical Perspectives on Deviance,* edited by R. A. Scott and J. D Douglas. New York: Basic Books.

———. 1975. *Doing Field Research.* New York: Free Press.

———. 1980a. "Battle Efficiency Reports as Propaganda." Pp. 205-28 in *Bureaucratic Propaganda,* edited by D. L. Altheide and J. M. Johnson. Boston: Allyn & Bacon.

———. 1980b. "Military Preparedness as Propaganda." Pp. 179-204 in *Bureaucratic Propaganda,* edited by D. L. Altheide and J. M. Johnson. Boston: Allyn & Bacon.

———. 1981. "Program Enterprise and the Official Co-optation of the Battered Women's Shelter Movement." *American Behavioral Scientist* 24:827-42.

———. 1985. "The Changing Meanings of Child Abuse." Pp. 123-40 in *The American Family and the State,* edited by J. Peden. San Francisco: Pacific Institute.

———. 1992. "The Church Response to Domestic Violence." Pp. 245-59 in *Studies in Symbolic Interaction: A Research Annual,* Vol. 13, edited by N. K. Denzin. Greenwich, CT: JAI.

Johnson, J. M. and K. J. Ferraro. 1984. "The Victimized Self: The Case of Battered Women." Pp. 119-30 in *The Existential Self in Society,* edited by J. A. Kotarba and A. Fontana. Chicago: University of Chicago Press.

Johnson, J. M., Y. Luna, and J. Stein. Forthcoming. "Victim Protection Orders and the Stake in Conformity Thesis." *Journal of Family Violence.*

Klockars, C. B. 1974. *The Professional Fence.* New York: Free Press.

———. 1977. "Field Ethics for the Life History." Pp. 210-26 in *Street Ethnography: Selected Studies of Crime and Drug Use in Natural Settings,* edited by R. S. Weppner. Beverly Hills, CA: Sage.

Lewis, O. 1951. *Life in a Mexican Village: Tepoztlan Restudied.* Urbana: University of Illinois Press.

Liebow, E. 1967. *Tally's Corner: A Study of Negro Street Corner Men.* Boston: Little, Brown.

Lofland, J. 1995. "Analytic Ethnography." *Journal of Contemporary Ethnography* 24:30-67.

Lofland, J. and L. H. Lofland. 1984. *Analyzing Social Settings.* 2d ed. Belmont, CA: Wadsworth.

Lofland, J. and L. H. Lofland. 1995. *Analyzing Social Settings.* 3d ed. Belmont, CA: Wadsworth.

Malinowski, B. 1922. *Argonauts of the Western Pacific: An Account of Native Enterprise and Adventure in the Archipelagoes of Melanesian New Guinea.* London: Routledge & Kegan Paul.

McCracken, G. 1988. *The Long Interview.* Newbury Park, CA: Sage.

Mead, M. [1928] 1960. *Coming of Age in Samoa: A Psychological Study of Primitive Youth for Western Civilization.* New York: Mentor.

Merton, R. K., M. Fiske, and P. L. Kendall. 1956. *The Focused Interview: A Manual of Problems and Procedures.* Glencoe, IL: Free Press.

Neuman, W. L. 1994. *Social Research Methods: Qualitative and Quantitative Approaches.* 2d ed. Boston: Allyn & Bacon.

Redfield, R. 1930. *Tepoztlan—A Mexican Village: A Study of Folk Life.* Chicago: University of Chicago Press.

———. 1941. *The Folk Culture of Yucatan.* Chicago: University of Chicago Press.

———. 1960. *The Little Community and Peasant Society and Culture.* Chicago: University of Chicago Press.

Reiman, J. H. 1979. "Research Subjects, Political Subjects, and Human Subjects." Pp. 33-57 in *Deviance and Decency: The Ethics of Research with Human Subjects,* edited by C. B. Klockars and F. W. O'Connor. Beverly Hills, CA: Sage.

Riemer, J. 1977. "Varieties of Opportunistic Research." *Urban Life* 5:467-77.

Rochford, E. B. 1992. "On the Politics of Member Validations: Taking Findings Back to Hare Krishna." Pp. 99-116 in *Perspectives on Social Problems,* Vol. 3, edited by G. Miller and J. A. Holstein. Greenwich, CT: JAI.

Rubin, H. J. and I. S. Rubin. 1995. *Qualitative Interviewing: The Art of Hearing Data.* Thousand Oaks, CA: Sage.

Scarce, R. 1994. "(No) Trial (but) Tribulation: When Courts and Ethnography Conflict." *Journal of Contemporary Ethnography* 23:123-49.

———. 1995. "Scholarly Ethics and Courtroom Antics: Where Researchers Stand in the Eyes of the Law." *American Sociologist* 26:87-112.

———. 1999. "Good Faith, Bad Ethics: When Scholars Go the Distance and Scholarly Associations Do Not." *Law and Social Inquiry* 24:1301-10.

Schutz, A. 1967. *The Phenomenology of the Social World.* Translated by G. Walsh and F. Lehnert. Evanston, IL: Northwestern University Press.

Smith, D. E. 1987. *The Everyday World as Problematic: A Feminist Sociology.* Boston: Northeastern University Press.

———. 1990. *Texts, Facts and Femininity: Exploring the Relations of Ruling.* London: Routledge.

Spradley, J. P. 1979. *The Ethnographic Interview.* New York: Holt, Rinehart & Winston.

Strauss, A. L. and J. Corbin. 1990. *Basics of Qualitative Research: Grounded Theory Procedures and Techniques.* Newbury Park, CA: Sage.

Vidich, A. J. 1992. "The Historical Context of *Street Corner Society.*" *Journal of Contemporary Ethnography* 21:99-119.

Wax, R. H. 1971. *Doing Fieldwork: Warning and Advice.* Chicago: University of Chicago Press.

Whyte, W. F. 1943. *Street Corner Society: The Social Structure of an Italian Slum.* Chicago: University of Chicago Press.

———. 1955. *Street Corner Society: The Social Structure of an Italian Slum.* 2d ed. Chicago: University of Chicago Press.

———. 1981. *Street Corner Society: The Social Structure of an Italian Slum.* 3d ed. Chicago: University of Chicago Press.

———. 1992. "In Defense of *Street Corner Society:* Response to Boelen." *Journal of Contemporary Ethnography* 21:52-68.

———. 1993. *Street Corner Society: The Social Structure of an Italian Slum.* 4th ed. Chicago: University of Chicago Press.

6

THE LIFE STORY INTERVIEW

◆ Robert Atkinson

Telling the stories of our lives is so basic to our nature that we are largely unaware of its importance. We think in story form, speak in story form, and bring meaning to our lives through stories. People everywhere are telling stories about some pieces of their lives to friends and strangers alike. The stories we tell of our lives carry ageless, universal themes or motifs and are always variations of one of the thousands of folktales, myths, or legends that have spoken to us for generations of our inner truths (see Narayan and George, Chapter 39, this volume). Stories connect us to our roots.

In traditional communities of the past, stories played a central role in the lives of the people. It was through story that the timeless elements of life were transmitted. Stories told from generation to generation carried enduring values as well as lessons about life lived deeply. Traditional stories followed a timeless and universal pattern that can be represented as separation, transition, incorporation (van Gennep 1960), birth, death, rebirth (Eliade 1954), or as departure, initiation, return (Campbell 1968). This pattern is like a blueprint, or an original form, within which the story communicates a balance between opposing forces. The pattern actually forms the basis for the plot of a story and aids the storyteller in remembering the elements of a story while keeping the story on the course on which it is meant to be.

The stories we tell of our own lives today are still guided by the same patterns and enduring elements. Our lives unfold according to an innate blueprint, following the pattern of beginning, muddle, and resolution, with many repetitions of this pattern. Our lives consist of a series of events and circumstances that are drawn from a well of archetypal experiences common to all other human beings. It is within this ageless and universal context that we can best begin to understand the importance and power of the life story interview and how it is fundamental to our very nature.

Storytelling is in our blood. We are the storytelling species. Stories were once the center of community life. We are recognizing more readily now that there is something of the gods and goddesses inside us, in the stories we tell of our own lives. Life storytelling gives us direction, validates our own experience, restores value to living, and strengthens community bonds.

The reasons we tell our stories today can be traced to the original functions of the earliest known stories. Myths and folktales have traditionally served four classic functions, bringing us into accord with ourselves, with others, with the mystery of life, and with the universe around us (Campbell 1970). A living mythology contains symbols, motifs, and archetypes that speak to us on a fundamentally human level; they reverberate beyond the personal and into the collective realm. They carry a power that connects with that deepest part of ourselves. Sacred, or traditional, stories touch a center of life that we all have within us.

Life stories, too, serve the same classic functions, by carrying the timeless themes and motifs found in a living mythology into our own lives. As we tell our life stories, ageless themes and motifs emerge that link us to our ancestors. Life stories serve these classic functions in four distinct realms. First, stories, with their deeply human elements and motifs, can guide us psychologically, stage by stage, through the entire life course. They foster an unfolding of the self and help us to center and integrate ourselves by gaining a clearer understanding of our experiences, our feelings about them, and their meaning for us. The stories we tell of our lives bring order to our experiences and help us to view our lives both subjectively and objectively at the same time while assisting us in forming our identities.

Second, stories can affirm, validate, and support our own experiences socially and clarify our relationships to those around us. They enforce the norms of a moral order

and shape the individual to the requirements of the society. Stories help us understand our commonalities and bonds with others as well as our differences. Stories foster a sense of community.

Third, stories can serve a mystical-religious function, by bringing us face-to-face with an ultimate mystery. Stories awaken feelings of awe, wonder, humility, respect, and gratitude in recognition of the mysteries around us. These feelings help us participate in the mystery of being. Stories take us beyond the here and now, beyond our everyday existence, and allow us to enter the realm of the spirit, the domain of the sacred.

And finally, stories can render a cosmology, an interpretive total image of the universe that is in accord with the knowledge of the time, a worldview that makes sense of the natural workings of the universe around us. Stories help us to understand the universe of which we are a part, and how we fit into it.

When our life stories are told in a way that follows this ageless pattern of transformation, they can carry the power and force of living myth for us and our listeners, by bringing about insights, sentiments, and commitments that can result in a new level of maturity, new responsibilities, and possibly even a new status. We seem to be recognizing more now that everyone has a story, even many, to tell about his or her life, and that the stories we have to tell are indeed important (Atkinson 1995, 1998; Kenyon and Randall 1997; Randall 1995; Gubrium and Holstein 1998).

◆ *Development of Interest in the Life Story*

People in many academic disciplines have been interviewing others for their life stories for longer than we often recognize. As far as I can determine, and as I use the term here, the life story interview has evolved from oral history, life history, and other ethnographic and field approaches. Life story interviewing is a qualitative research method for gathering information on the subjective essence of one person's entire life that is transferable across disciplines.

As a method of looking at life as a whole, and as a way of carrying out in-depth study of individual lives, the life story interview stands alone. It has become a central element of the burgeoning subfield of the narrative study of lives (Cohler 1988; Josselson and Lieblich 1993), for its interdisciplinary applications in understanding single lives in detail and how the individual plays various roles in society (Cohler 1993; Gergen and Gergen 1993).

The use of life narratives for serious academic study is considered to have begun in psychology with Sigmund Freud's (1957, 1958) psychoanalytic interpretation of individual case studies, although these were based on secondary documents. Freud used these narratives primarily in applying his psychoanalytic theory to individual lives. Gordon Allport (1942) used personal documents to study personality development in individuals, focusing on primary documents, including narratives, while also considering the problems of reliability and validity of interpretation associated with using such materials. This method reached its maturation in Erik Erikson's (1958, 1969) studies of Luther and Gandhi. Erikson (1975) also used the life history to explore how the historical moment influences lives.

Henry Murray (1938, 1955) was one of the first to study individual lives using life narratives primarily to understand personality development. The recent interest in story on the part of personality psychologists, other social scientists, and scholars in diverse disciplines reflects the broader interest in narrative as it serves to illuminate the lives of persons in society. Theodore Sarbin (1986) uses narrative for understanding human experience, identifying it as the "root metaphor" and placing it at the core of self-formation, whereas Jerome Bruner (1986) employs narrative as an important means for discovering how we "construct" our lives. The narrative study of lives, as presented in a series of books edited by Ruthellen Josselson and Amia Lieblich (1993, 1995, 1999; Josselson 1996; Lieblich and Josselson 1994, 1997), aims to further the theoretical understanding of individual life narratives through in-depth studies, methodological examinations, and theoretical explorations.

The life history has long been a primary methodology of anthropological field work. As James Spradley (1979) points out, some life histories are heavily edited by the ethnographer (often only 60 percent of the description is actually in the insider's own words or language), whereas others are presented in the same form in which they were recorded. The life history interview and the life story interview are very similar in their approaches and what they cover, but the specific information sought and final products can be very different. In folklore, the term *life story* is used much as *life history* is in anthropology, with the focus usually being on the role of the interviewee in the community as a tradition bearer (see Titon 1980; Ives 1986).

Because of the broad interdisciplinary use of the life story, as well as the particular approach of each interviewer or researcher, the final forms of life stories can vary greatly. On the one hand, a life story can read as mostly the researcher's own description of what was said, done, or intimated. On the other, it can be a 100 percent first-person narrative in the words of the person interviewed.

As a research tool that is gaining much interest and use in many disciplines today, the life story interview is employed by researchers who take two primary approaches: the constructionist and the naturalistic. Some narrative researchers conceive of the life story as a circumstantially mediated, constructive collaboration between the interviewer and interviewee.

This approach stresses the situated emergence of the life story as opposed to the subjectively faithful, experientially oriented account. In the constructionist perspective, life stories are evaluated not so much for how well they accord with the life experiences in question, but more in terms of how accounts of lives are used by a variety of others, in addition to the subjects whose lives are under consideration, for various descriptive purposes (see Gubrium and Holstein 1998; Holstein and Gubrium 2000a, 2000b).

My own approach to the life story, which is based in a naturalistic, person-centered view, has evolved from an interdisciplinary context, beginning more than 30 years ago with my graduate study of folklore, when I interviewed an elder tradition bearer for his life story. I went on to pursue a second master's degree in counseling, and I began to see the power not only in telling but in retelling, or composing and recomposing, recasting and reframing, one's own story, and especially in getting to one's deeper or larger story. In my doctoral work, which focused on cross-cultural human development, I further expanded this interest by using the life story interview to explore how cultural values and traditions influence development across the life cycle.

I have felt that it is important, in trying to understand other persons' experiences in life or their relations to others, to let their voices be heard, to let them speak for and about themselves first. If we want to know the unique perspective of an individual, there is no better way to get this than in that person's own voice. I am also interested in having the person tell his or her story from the vantage point that allows the individual to see his or her life as a whole, to see it subjectively across time as it all fits together, or as it seems discontinuous, or both. It is, after all, this subjective perspective that tells us what we are looking for in all our research efforts. This is what constitutes the individual's reality of his or her world. Storytellers are the first interpreters of the stories they tell. It is through their construction of their realities, and the stories they tell about those realities, that we, as researchers, learn what we want to from them.

Since creating the Center for the Study of Lives at the University of Southern Maine in 1988, I have tried to merge all these interests, not only in building bridges across disciplines but in building a growing archive of life stories, currently numbering over 500, to offer researchers with various purposes and interests a unique database. Most of the life stories in the archive were gathered by my graduate students for class projects designed for them to learn as much as possible about how one person views his or her own development over time and across the life cycle. The life stories in the archives are available to all researchers for secondary analysis and can be searched by topics or by categories on the cover sheets.

I believe that there is much in each life story to identify the unique value and worth of each life, and that there are many common elements, motifs, and issues that all life stories express, indeed that we all share as human beings, along with some differences that exist. As an example of how I have used life stories, I have looked for important life themes that emerge in a person's telling of his or her story. These might explain coherence, how and why the story holds together, even if it also contains disruptions. Life themes also highlight important influences and relationships. In a small group of life story interviews with elders, I looked for the life-as-a-whole perspective and explored how the themes of continuity, purpose, commitment, and meaning were expressed in their lives (Atkinson 1985).

Life stories have gained respect and acceptance in many academic circles. Psychologists see the value of personal narratives for understanding development and personality (Runyan 1982; McAdams 1993). Anthropologists use the life history, or individual case study, as the preferred unit of study for their measures of cultural similarities and variations (Spradley 1979; Langness and Frank 1981; Abu-Lughod 1993). Sociologists use life stories to understand and define relationships and group interactions and memberships (Bertaux 1981; Linde 1993). In education, life stories have been used as a new way of knowing and teaching (Witherell & Noddings 1991). Literary scholars use autobiographies as texts through which to explore questions of design, style, content, literary themes, and personal truth (Olney 1980). Historians find in using the oral history approach that life story materials are an important source for enhancing local history (Allen and Montell 1981).

The movement toward life stories, where we tell our own stories in our own words, is a movement toward acknowledging personal truth from the subjective point of view as well as a movement toward the validity of narrative. A life story narrative highlights the most important influences, experiences, circumstances, issues, themes, and lessons of a lifetime. As such, a life story narrative can be both a valuable experience for the person telling the story and a successful research endeavor for the one gathering the data.

This movement is championed by Bruner (1986, 1987, 1990, 1991), a cognitive psychologist who has illustrated that we actually construct personal meaning (and reality) during the making and telling of our narratives, that our own experiences take the form of the narratives we use to tell about them. According to Bruner, stories are our way of organizing, interpreting, and creating meaning from our experiences while maintaining a sense of continuity through it all. A promising direction is gerontologist James Birren's continuing use of "guided autobiography" as a source of psychological and social science research (see Birren and Birren 1996). Guided autobiography is the relating of a life by the one who has experienced it, but with the assistance of an experienced storyteller or writer (see Kenyon, Clark, and de Vries 2001).

◆ Defining a Life Story

An individual life and the role it plays in the larger community are best understood through story. We become fully aware, fully conscious, of our own lives through the process of putting them together in story form. It is through story that we gain context and recognize meaning. Reclaiming story is part of our birthright. Telling our stories enables us to be heard, recognized, and acknowledged by others. Telling a life story makes the implicit explicit, the hidden seen, the unformed formed, and the confusing clear.

A life story is the story a person chooses to tell about the life he or she has lived, told as completely and honestly as possible, what the person remembers of it and what he or she wants others to know of it, usually as a result of a guided interview by another. The resulting life story is the narrative essence of what has happened to the person. It can cover the time from birth to the present or before and beyond. It includes the important events, experiences, and feelings of a lifetime.

There is very little difference between a life story and a life history. The two terms are often used interchangeably. The difference between a life story and an oral history is usually emphasis and scope. An oral history most often focuses on a specific aspect of a person's life, such as work life or a special role in some part of the life of a community. An oral history most often focuses on the community or on what someone remembers about a specific historical event, issue, time, or place (see Cándida Smith, Chapter 34, this volume). When an oral interview focuses on a person's entire life, it is usually referred to as a life story or life history.

A life story can take a factual form, a metaphorical form, a poetic form, or any other creatively expressive form. What is important is that the life story be told in the form, shape, and style that is most comfortable to the person telling it. Whatever form it takes, a life story always brings order and meaning to the life being told, for both the teller and the listener. It is a way to understand the past and the present more fully, and a way to leave a personal legacy for the future.

A life story is a fairly complete narrative of an individual's entire experience of life as a whole, highlighting the most important aspects. A life story gives us a vantage point from which to see how one person experiences and understands life, his or her own especially, over time. It enables us to see and identify threads and links that connect one part of a person's life to another, that connect childhood to adulthood.

Life stories are told on many occasions. We are in fact continually telling others who we are and what we are about. Through the daily chores of life, and at every stage of life, we share pieces of ourselves with those we come in contact with. Whether it is the solitary, social, or dramatic play of childhood, a rite of passage of adolescence, a wedding, or a retirement banquet, we are continually telling episodes and chapters of our life stories, both as we live them and as we relive them in our everyday actions, behaviors, creations, and the words we speak about them.

We keep memories, experiences, and collective values alive by telling others about them or putting them in a form that may last longer than ourselves. In a life story interview, the interviewee is a storyteller, the narrator of the story of his or her own life; the interviewer is a guide, or director, in this process. The two together are collaborators, composing and constructing a story the teller can be pleased with.

As collaborator in an open-ended process, the researcher/guide is never really in control of the story actually told. The process may not always go as smoothly as hoped. The person asked to tell his or her story may be brief, unembellishing, and unemotional in the telling. This could result in a short listing of factual events that have occurred. In some cases there may be more

that can be done to help a storyteller to develop a more fully told, feeling-based story; in other cases a recitation of facts may be all an interviewer will be able to get.

At other times, the teller may present a conjured, fabricated, or strategic story. If this happens, the interviewer need not run out for a lie detector; it may be that this type of story will also serve his or her research interests. The researcher could ask, and include some interpretation about, why the individual chose a fabricated story—that is, what purpose this served for the storyteller.

A researcher may also use corroborators, or seek indicators of internal consistency. It may be that the researcher can use whatever story an interviewee tells to accomplish the research goals, finding an interpretation that will be useful. The point of the life story interview is to give the person interviewed the opportunity to tell his or her story in the way that person chooses to tell it. Coherence and honesty can be part of the collaborative process, if necessary, but achieving this will depend on how open the storyteller is to coherence and honesty in the first place.

◆ Benefits and Uses of the Life Story Interview

It is impossible to anticipate what a life story interview will be like—not so much the form it will take, but the power of the experience itself. I have found this to be the case over and over, as have my students, who have reported how meaningful it has been for them to have done particular interviews, especially those with individuals they were already close to, such as parents or spouses. Just witnessing—really hearing, understanding, and accepting, without judgment—another's life story can be transforming (Birren and Birren 1996).

PERSONAL BENEFITS

A woman who had just completed a life story interview with her father said, "There was no way I could have prepared for the emotional impact this experience had on me." She was completely overwhelmed by what she had learned about her father and later described having a great deal of "emotional residue" from that experience with him. After I read her father's life story, with all of the details of his having been raised during the Depression by a single mother as one of four children in poverty and with constant uprooting, of having witnessed the frontline horrors of World War II, and of struggling to enter the postwar working world with a grade school education, I thought I knew what she meant.

Another woman interviewed her father and had a similar experience. She later wrote:

> Sitting with my father for three hours listening to his life story was a wonderful experience for both of us. Our relationship has not been one of sharing feelings and innermost thoughts. I've always felt that he loves me, although he has seldom shown his love through words or behavior. What started out to be a slightly uncomfortable experience for both of us ended up being a very special time. It was like we had both been lifted out of our worlds and placed in this room together. Of course, I would have liked to hear more about how he felt about different life events, but I know that he shared more with me that day than he had in my entire lifetime. At the end of our three hours together we hugged each other. I told him that I loved him and was glad he was my father. He told me that he loved me and was glad that I was his daughter. Our eyes both filled up and then this special time ended, although the effects of this time together will stay with us. That door within him that was slammed shut when he was thirteen years old opened up a crack, and I was allowed to peek in and see my father from the inside out—and I am thankful for this.

There may be no equal to the life story interview for revealing the inner life of a person. Historical reconstruction may not be the primary concern in life stories; rather, it may be how the individuals see themselves at given points in their lives, and how they want others to see them. Life stories offer glimpses of the sometimes hidden human qualities and characteristics that make us all so fascinating, *and* fun to listen to.

I have found that the vast majority of people really want to share their life stories. All that most people usually need is someone to listen, or someone to show a sincere interest in their stories, and they welcome being interviewed. Even those who may be reluctant to be interviewed because they feel intimidated, embarrassed, ashamed, or simply unsure about it or uncomfortable with it (see Adler and Adler, Chapter 25, this volume) may be persuaded by the many valuable personal benefits that can come with sharing their life stories, if they can overcome their unwillingness:

1. In sharing our stories, we gain a clearer perspective on personal experiences and feelings, which in turn brings greater meaning to our lives.

2. Through sharing our stories, we obtain greater self-knowledge, stronger self-image, and enhanced self-esteem.

3. In sharing our stories, we share cherished experiences and insights with others.

4. Sharing our stories can bring us joy, satisfaction, and inner peace.

5. Sharing our stories is a way of purging, or releasing, certain burdens and validating personal experience; this is in fact central to the recovery process.

6. Sharing our stories helps create community, and may show us that we have more in common with others than we thought.

7. By sharing our stories, we can help other people see their lives more clearly or differently, and perhaps inspire them to change negative things in their lives.

8. When we share our stories, others will get to know and understand us better, in ways that they hadn't before.

9. In sharing our stories, we might gain a better sense of how we want our stories to end, or how we can give ourselves the "good" endings we want. By understanding our past and present, we derive a clearer perspective on our goals for the future.

Not everyone will experience the life story interview exactly in the same way, of course. Some may look back on certain parts of their lives with regret, and for some the interview can be a painful process. But even this kind of reaction can have eventual positive outcomes.

RESEARCH USES

The life story interview is inherently interdisciplinary; its many research uses directly parallel the four classic functions of sacred stories. The life story interview can help the teller, the listener, the reader, and the scholar to understand a broad range of psychological, sociological, mystical-religious, and cosmological-philosophical issues.

As for psychological uses, the remembering, shaping, and sharing of a life story can be a valuable text for learning about the human endeavor. There are many domains within psychology where the life story can be a helpful research tool. The life story narrative may be the most effective means for gaining an understanding of how the self evolves over time. Through an exami-

nation of the self-narrative process, the researcher can secure useful information and come to the desired understanding of the self as a meaning maker with a place in society, the culture, and history (Freeman 1992). Telling a life story can be one of the most emphatic ways to answer the question, "Who am I?" The researcher can determine if the story tells who the person really is, if there is a felt unity of experiences in the story told, how identity is defined, whether this is internally and externally consistent, and how these match with identity-formation models (Widdershoven 1993; Kroger 1993; Erikson 1963; Marcia 1966).

Telling a life story is not therapy, but the act of telling the story can often help clarify things for the teller that he or she might not have understood before, as noted earlier. After all, psychotherapy is known as the "talking cure." In therapy, individuals tell their stories to professionals who are trained to help them understand, interpret, and learn from their stories better than they could on their own. The narrative approach, when used by therapists or counselors as a guided means for assisting clients to get to the details of their lives, is a process of "storying" and/or "restorying" (White & Epston 1990), or creating new and possibly liberating narratives (see Miller, de Shazer, and De Jong, Chapter 19, this volume).

The life story interview is also one of the most helpful psychological research approaches available to enable researchers to gain a subjective perspective on and understanding of the broad scope of topics or issues that individuals experience. In telling their life stories, individuals follow a natural tendency of arranging the events and circumstances of their lives in ways that give those events a coherent order (Cohler 1988). The book series *The Narrative Study of Lives,* which explores questions of how we construct and make sense of our lives through narrative, is essential reading for any researcher using life stories (Josselson and Lieblich 1993, 1995, 1999; Lieblich and Josselson 1994, 1997; Josselson 1996).

The results of life story interviews also have sociological uses. Life stories can help the researcher become more aware of the range of possible roles and standards that exist within a human community. They can define an individual's place in the social order of things and can explain or confirm experience through the moral, ethical, or social context of a given situation. They can provide the researcher with information about a social reality existing outside the story that is described by the story (Bertaux 1981). They also can help explain the story itself as a social construct (Rosenthal 1993) as well as help explain an individual's understanding of social events, movements, and political causes, or how individual members of a group, generation, or cohort see certain events or movements (Stewart 1994).

The stories people tell about their lives all contain discourse units, degrees of coherence, and an overall linguistic structure. All of these are useful to researchers interested in determining the relation between language and social practice, the relation of self to others, and the creation of social identity (Linde 1993; Mkhonza 1995).

Regarding mystical-religious issues, life stories can provide clues to what people's greatest struggles and triumphs are, where their deepest values lie, what their quests have been, where they might have been broken, and where they have been made whole again. Life stories portray religion and spirituality as lived experience. Researchers can ask specific questions of a story, such as, What beliefs, or worldview, are expressed in the story? Is the transcendent expressed? In what way does community play a role in the life lived deeply? How does this spiritual autobiography compare to the lives of the classic spiritual leaders (Comstock 1995)?

Addressing questions of beliefs, values, customs, sacred traditions, and meaning in life, anthropologists regularly use life stories to get at shared cultural meanings, the insider's view of a community, and the dynamics of cultural change (Geertz 1973; Langness & Frank 1981). Folklorists know that life stories are the repositories of traditional lore, beliefs, customs, and practices, and that they can answer many questions about the process of keeping traditions alive (Titon 1980; Ives 1986).

As far as cosmological-philosophical issues are concerned, it is very likely that each life story will contain a personal worldview, a personal philosophy, a personal value system, and a personal ideology, as well as views on what is morally, if not politically, correct, how life is to be lived, and so on. Researchers could explore how life stories told currently fit with what we know of the universe today, or how people make sense of the world we now live in, or the "thickness" of connections across time, or the personal vision or interpretation of what life and reality is about for the person (Brockelman 1985).

The research applications of the life story interview are limitless. In any field, the life story itself could serve as the centerpiece for published research, or segments could be used as data to illustrate any number of research needs. The life story interview allows for the gathering of more data than a researcher may actually use, which is good practice and provides a broad foundation of information to draw upon. The life story approach can be used within the disciplines already mentioned, as well as for the examination of many substantive issues, as the following few examples illustrate.

Narratives are being given a central place in the search for fresh approaches to knowing and teaching. The life stories of educators can tell researchers how those individuals have found their own centers through their chosen work; they can illustrate the primacy, in both individual lives and educational practice, of the quest for life's meaning and the role of caring for persons (Witherell and Noddings 1991).

Life stories are central to human development, interactions between generations, and integrity in late life. It is now commonly recognized in gerontology that a primary developmental task for elders is the "life review" (Butler 1963). This is, in effect, the process of remembering and expressing the experiences, struggles, lessons, and wisdom of a lifetime, which can be of great value to the researcher. It was the role of elders to pass on their values and wisdom through their stories long before Robert Butler (1963) described the life review process and referred to it as the "elder function."

When the life review is purposeful and not a passive, fragmentary flickering of images from the past, the result can be transforming. Telling a life story, at any age, with much reflection, can help a person to clarify his or her "ultimate concerns" before it is too late (Tillich 1957; Erikson 1964). The life stories of elders can provide researchers with much significant information about the life course, the sequence of generations, our understanding of aging, and the role of stories across the life cycle, and can help us to determine ways to improve the quality of life (Birren et al. 1996).

To balance out the databases researchers have relied upon for so long in generating theory, more life stories of women and members of culturally diverse groups need to be recorded. We need to give the feminine voice more opportunities to be heard, analyzed, and theorized about, at least to see if there might be a female equivalent to the monomyth (Campbell 1968), so that researchers will be able to determine more effectively the similarities and differences between the male and female experience, and to seek a synthesis that would expand life story options for all and benefit both genders (Gergen and Gergen 1993). There is a wide range of uses and applications of narrative knowing in relation to gender issues (see especially Helle 1991; Lieblich and Josselson 1994). For similar reasons, because how we tell our stories is mediated by our cultures (Josselson 1995), we need to hear the life stories of individuals from underrepresented groups, to help establish a balance in the literature and expand the options for us all on the cultural level. Life stories of gay men and lesbians would also contribute to a more complete understanding of the issues related to change in people's lives (Boxer and Cohler 1989; Ben-Ari 1995).

◆ The Art and Science of Life Story Interviewing

Although a fairly uniform research methodology can be applied and many important data can be gathered from a life story, there may be more subjectivity, even chance, involved in doing a life story interview than common standards of objectivity would lead one to expect. The same researcher may use different questions with different interviewees, based on a number of variables, and still end up with a fairly complete life story of each person being interviewed. Different interviewers may also use different questions, depending on the particular foci of their projects. The life story interview is essentially a template that will be applied differently in different situations, circumstances, and settings.

For example, in The Life Story Interview (Atkinson 1998), I suggest more than 200 questions an interviewer can ask in obtaining a life story. These questions are not meant to be used in their entirety or as a structure that is in any way set in stone. They are merely suggested questions, and only the most appropriate few need be used for each person interviewed. There are times when a researcher might use a handful of these questions and other times when he or she might ask two or three dozen of them. From case to case, it is very likely that an interviewer will choose different sets of questions. The key to getting the best interview is for the interviewer to be flexible and able to adapt to specific circumstances.

There may be cases in which an interviewer will ask questions that are not on the list of those offered at all, when someone's life experience is best expressed or understood in an entirely different context than the standard domains of life.

In my view, the life story interview can be *approached* scientifically, but it is best *carried out* as an art. Although there may be a structure (a set of questions, or parts thereof) that can be used, each interviewer will apply this in his or her own way. Although theories may come into play to a varying degree throughout the process, the interview and the interpretation of it are highly subjective. Further, just as there are good and better artists, there are good and better interviewers. The execution of the interview, whether structured or not, will vary from one interviewer to another. The particular interviewee is another important factor. Life storytellers offer highly personal meanings, memories, and interpretations of their own, adding to the artful contours of their life stories.

Because life story interviewing itself is primarily an artful endeavor, the resulting interviews should be *interpreted* as an art form. The life story interview has its own standards of reliability and validity that are distinct from quantitative research methods. Qualitative research (including life story interviews) can be determined to be reliable or valid on its own merits. As works of art have their own standards of judgment, so too do research methods based primarily on subjectivity, flexibility, and inevitable human variables. A life story is first and foremost a text, to be read, understood, and interpreted on its own merit and in its own way.

THE PROCESS OF LIFE STORY INTERVIEWING

A life story interview unfolds in three stages. First is the planning or preinterview stage, which includes preparing for the interview and, especially, understanding why and how a life story can be beneficial. Second is the process of doing the interview itself, guiding a person through the telling of his or her life story while recording it on audio- or videotape. Third are the processes of transcribing and interpreting the interview material.

Because my own orientation is to the person telling the story, my inclination in transcribing narrative material is to leave the interviewer's questions and comments, as well as repetitions, out of the transcript, so that it becomes a flowing, connected narrative in the respondent's own words. I might then give the transcribed life story to the person to review and check over for any changes he or she might want to make in it, thus responding to the life story in the form of a subjective reaction or validity check. Still, the broader question of what to transcribe remains debatable, an issue I will return to in the next section.

What we end up with is a flowing life story in the words of the person telling it. The only editing necessary would be to delete repetitions or other completely extraneous information. It may be that some reordering of content will add to the clarity or readability of the story. If one does such reordering, the greatest advantage to the life story approach comes into play, which is that one can still consult the person whose story it is and give him or her the final say in what the life story will look like in its completed form, given that it is that person's story that is being told. The life storyteller can also address the internal consistency issue; that is, does the way things seem to be connected in narrative form make sense to him or her? The person telling the life story should always have the last word in how his or her story is presented in written form before it gets passed on to others or is published.

Life story interviews can vary considerably in length. Sometimes restrictive circumstances prevail and an interview may be limited to an hour or less. This is far from the ideal. For example, I have had to conduct a few life story interviews under such conditions, when interviewees were away from home and had other obligations at the time. In each case I had to revise my usual approach and carry out the interview looking primarily for the essence, or highlights, of the person's life, still trying to have the person include something from each stage of life. In such circumstances, a researcher may be able to get more in-depth life stories by sending transcripts of the interviews to the persons to see if they want to add anything. Usually such additions can be done by mail, if there is a problem of distance, but this again is not ideal; face-to-face involvement is always preferred.

More typical of the kind of life story interviewing being described here is a series of at least two or three interviews with the person, each an hour to an hour and a half in duration. Even this may be considered brief, but it is quite a bit longer than the one-time interview, and much can be learned about a person's life in a two- or three-part interview that extends over three hours. This is the length of interview I recommend for students especially, as it provides them with more than enough information to gain a good understanding of whatever they are seeking for purposes of a course. With the transcription time involved, it is also about all they can manage within the time constraints of a course.

Some life story interviews can go on for two or three dozen hours. Interviews of this length are typical of full-length assisted autobiography. I have done a life story interview of more than 40 hours for the purpose of writing an assisted autobiography with Babatunde Olatunji, the African drummer. The interviews took place over a three-year period, as we were able to fit our meetings into our respective schedules and to allow time for transcriptions and going over each section or chapter. Other longer life histories, such as Carl Klockars's (1974) study of a professional fence, can require closer to 100 hours. An average-length life story interview, however, is more in the range of three to five hours, consisting of many sittings.

◆ Issues and Challenges

The life story interview is a highly contextualized, highly personalized approach to the gathering of qualitative information about the human experience. It demands many spontaneous, individual judgments on the part of the interviewer while the interview is in progress. Its direction can be determined on the spur of the moment by unexpected responses to questions, or by the way a life is given its particular narrative structure. The quest in a life story interview is for the unique voice and experience of the storyteller, which is morally implicative and may also merge at some points with the universal human experience. As such, a number of important related issues need to be considered.

ETHICAL AND CONCEPTUAL ISSUES

Because those of us who conduct life story interviews are asking real people to tell us their true stories, and because we are attempting to assist and collaborate with them in this process and then take their stories to a larger audience, we have to ask ourselves and be able to answer satisfactorily several questions concerning ethical issues, including the following: How can we reconcile the benefits of the life story to our interviewees with the benefits to our research agenda? How do we make sure that we maintain consistency between our original intention and the final product, and that this is clear all the way through? These are not easy questions to answer, especially if we ask people for their stories and then write only *about* them, not using their own words to tell their stories (Josselson 1996). The issue centers on the uneasy relationship between the personal and the research relevance of life stories, especially as story details are likely to be taken beyond the purview of the respondents.

This leads to an important conceptual issue, that of voice. If you ask someone to tell his or her life story, will what you get be in that person's authentic voice, or in a voice that he or she thinks you might be looking for? The type or quality of the relationship between interviewer and interviewee may have something to do with what you get. A relationship in which a power differential is part of the equation may or may not affect the voice the story is told in. If the power factor puts the interviewee in a vulnerable position, that could affect not only the voice the story is told in, but the impact telling it has on the one doing the telling (see Briggs, Chapter 44, this volume). If the respondent has found his or her own voice, knows what it is, and is used to using that voice, it is hard to imagine that a certain changeable circumstance would alter or influence the voice that person uses to tell his or her story. My own experience shows that people tend to want to tell their stories the way they happened, in their own voices as best they know how, regardless of who is asking what questions. A related issue here is consistency. If people are *aware* of, and accept, their own stories, those are the ones they would normally want to tell anyone.

A related conceptual issue is clarity. Life stories can be extremely complex. Life story interviews can help people organize, synthesize, and present the events, circumstances, and perceptions of their lives. This raises the following questions: Do interviewees see themselves clearly or vaguely? Do their stories tell us who they see themselves as? Do their words, tone, mood, or style tell us anything about them? Do their own meanings come across clearly in their stories? Do their stories tell us why as well as what?

These questions illustrate the threefold complexity of every life story. First is the story's content, which relates to the "Who am I?" question, or what happened to make me who I am. Second is the story's construct, which answers the "How am I?" question, or how the story is told. And third is the story's meaning, which answers the "Why am I?" question, or what those things mean to me (de Vries & Lehman 1996). Each life story is complex in its own way, and each tells us something about the patterns, perceptions, and processes that contribute to our understanding of lives across time.

INTERPRETIVE CHALLENGES

This brings us to the interpretation of the life story. There are two steps in the postinterview stage of life story interviewing: transcription and interpretation. This is the point at which the researcher applies the interview itself, or the information gained from it, effectively and efficiently to achieve his or her original research goals. The ultimate aim of the narrative investigation of human life, which applies to life stories as well, is the interpretation of experience (Josselson and Lieblich 1995). This is a complex matter because both *interpretation* and *experience* are highly relative terms. Subjectivity is at the center of the process of life storytelling. This involves reaching for meaning through interpretation, as contrasted with experimental scientific approaches that aim for one-to-one correspondence between experience and its representation (Geertz 1973).

Transcription can be an interpretive issue in its own right when different methods are applied in making the information on interview tapes useful (see Poland, Chapter 30, this volume). Researchers in some oral history projects make final transcripts from the tapes, whereas others make only bare outlines; still others develop complete catalogs from the tapes and encourage individual researchers to listen to the tapes and make their own transcripts. The purpose of such partial secondary documents is essentially to facilitate finding material on the tapes (Ives 1974).

The approach taken at the Center for the Study of Lives, because its purpose is to tell the life stories of the people being interviewed in their own words, is to make complete transcripts of everything that interviewees say about their lives on the tapes. The primary goal in transcription is to ensure accuracy of meaning, to capture the meaning conveyed in the words used by the storyteller, thus the less editing, the better. Of course, the final transcript depends upon the research goal. If the researcher's purpose is linguistic, then it would be important to keep language usage, dialect, pauses, and other verbal idiosyncrasies intact in the transcript. Because the aim of the Center for the Study of Lives is to end up with flowing narratives in the words of the persons telling the stories, with their intended meanings as clearly specified as possible, the interviewers' questions and comments are left out of transcriptions; only the interviewees' words appear, put into sentence and paragraph form. The transcriptions may note significant emphases, actions, or sounds in brackets or as part of explanatory prefaces. Relistening to a tape while reading its transcript can also be interpretive, because the closer one can get to the text itself, the closer one is to its meaning.

Even though no interview can be perfectly controlled, just as no measuring instrument can be perfectly calibrated, there are still certain ways of determining how reliable and how valid a life story is. Reliability has to do with the extent to which questioning will yield the same answers whenever and wherever it is carried out. Validity is the extent to which inquiry yields the "correct" answers; this refers to the quality of fit between information received or observed and that expected (Kirk and Miller 1986; Holstein and Gubrium 1995).

It is not necessary to try to interpret a life story interview against quantitative standards of analysis. Categories of analysis will emerge from a review of each life story text itself, along with a complexity of patterns and meanings, rather than being set from the beginning as in quantitative studies (McCracken 1988). The researcher's objective is to have the storyteller elaborate, with feeling, upon what has happened in his or her life; thus the researcher is seeking the "insider's" viewpoint on the life being lived. A fundamental interpretive guideline is that the storyteller should be considered both the expert and the authority on his or her own life. This is based on the belief that the storyteller knows the story being told and will give a truthful and thorough representation of that story. This demands a standard of reliability and validity that is appropriate to the life story interview as a subjective reflection of the experience in question.

A life story interview is a highly personal encounter; an analysis of a life story is highly subjective. There are a multiplicity of perspectives possible, and the narratives arrived at by different interviewers will be representative of their own positions, just as a portrait painted from the side or from the front is still a faithful portrait (Frank 1980; Runyan 1982). A personal narrative is not meant to be read as an exact record of everything, or even what actually happened in the person's life (Riessman 1993). Historical truth is not the main issue in narrative; telling a story implies a certain, maybe unique, point of view. It is more important that the life story be deemed "trustworthy" than that it be "true." We are seeking the subjective reality, after all.

One of the most important measures here is internal consistency, but this also needs to be understood subjectively. According to Bert Cohler (1982), the way an individual recounts a personal narrative at any point in his or her life represents the most internally consistent interpretation of the way that person currently understands the past, the experienced present, and the anticipated future. This means that what a life storyteller says in one part of the narrative should not contradict what he or she says in another part. There *are* inconsistencies in life, and people may react to things one way at one time and different ways at others, but their stories of what happened and what they did should be consistent within themselves. Internal consistency is a primary quality check that can be used by both the interviewer and the storyteller to square or clarify earlier comments with recent insights if they appear to be different (McCracken 1988).

External consistency—where what the storyteller says conforms to what one may already know, or think one knows, about the person telling the story—is not always going to be a valid measure, either, because the life story interview does not necessarily seek historical truth, only the storyteller's version of or perspective on what he or she remembers happened. The narrative approach to the study of lives places emphasis upon internal coherence as experienced by the person, rather than external criteria of truth or validity.

Corroboration and persuasion are two other control measures of the validity of a life story interview. Subjective corroboration comes into play when the transcribed, edited life story is given to the storyteller to review. Does the person confirm or support what he or she said originally? External corroboration would be achieved if, upon reading the life story, a close relative of the storyteller, or someone else who is familiar with as much of that person's life as possible, confirms what was said as well. Persuasion is an objective measure of whether the life story seems reasonable and convincing to others. Does the story, or any part of it, strike a resonant chord with us, based on our own experience? If the experiences and events recounted are not familiar to us, does it seem possible or plausible that they could have happened to someone else (Riessman 1993)? Another aspect of persuasion is how a story involves us: Does the story compel, stimulate, delight, or invite us in any way (Gergen 1985)? This may be more a matter of storytelling ability than of truth telling, and the former is as much a criterion of validity as is the latter in life storytelling.

The standard being put forth here is that the life storyteller has the final say in telling the story, even after it has been transcribed, because he or she is the one telling the story in the first place and is the one to determine

how it all fits together, what sense it makes, and whether or not it is a valid story. The storyteller is the one who determines what gets told and whether something stays the same or is changed.

The question of meaning is vital to both the storyteller and the researcher. Life storytelling is a process of creating and re-creating a life. Each time a life story is told, the person telling it can find new or additional meaning. The key to meaning making through life storytelling, for the one telling the story, is reflective thinking. If this is not happening, more work may be required for meaning making to take place. To help a life storyteller to be reflective, to encourage him or her pull out the story's inherent meaning, the interviewer can ask direct questions aimed at discovering the meaning, especially the emotional, level of the story.

Whether life stories are used as a source of psychological or social science research material, as a source of historical material for family and community, as a means of promoting personal insight, or for any other disciplinary inquiry, interpretations of life stories—the meaning-making process —are usually of two kinds: those that are founded upon a theoretical basis and those that emerge from a personal frame of reference.

There are numerous discipline-based theories that can be used with life stories (see Holstein and Gubrium 2000a; Kenyon and Randall 1997). In my view, however, a theory should be applied to a life story only when and if it fits the story well—if the theory actually emerges out of the story itself. One quick example: In interpreting the life story of a 60-year-old man who emphasizes the importance of his relationship with his children and grandchildren, a researcher might want to make reference to Erikson's (1963, 1980) theory of human development, in which the stage of middle adulthood has as its core conflict "generativity versus stagnation."

Personal interpretations of life stories can be very important. The researcher's own personal frame of reference can be appropriate, as well. I would suggest three basic guidelines in this regard. First, the researcher should not judge, but, rather, make connections. Rather than assuming a stance "over and against" the person telling the story, analyzing, limiting, or classifying the storyteller in some way, the researcher should seek to find the personal relevance of the story. Second, a life story is a text like any other document or story in any other field. It can stand on its own, because it automatically and immediately evokes certain personal, subjective responses based on the experiences it describes or the perspective of the reader. Third, we are all each other's teachers. Like a novel or a poem, a life story has something to say to us about life. We often learn from the stories we hear or read. These are all reasons researchers need to take a personal, consider-one-life-at-a-time approach to interpreting life stories.

THE SCALE OF TRUTHFULNESS

As many disciplines take the narrative turn toward story and away from the immutable laws of nature, historians, social scientists, philosophers, and legal scholars have begun to celebrate the particularity and localism inherent in the medium of "the little story" (Arras 1997). This has created considerable differences of opinion about the use, value, and meaning of personal narratives.

Perhaps the most important question to ask here is, Is there a connection between the story being told and "the truth" being sought? One view is that the stories that convey the subjective quest of the person, even though they might be "evasive," "are their own truth" (Frank 1995). Another view is that each of us shades the truth or even intentionally distorts crucial facts in the stories we tell about our own lives (Arras 1997). My view, from my own experience with life story interviews, is that both of these perspectives can be accurate.

Truthfulness is a matter of scale. For example, the truths of "the little story" may be valid but perhaps questionable in relation to larger social questions, such as the typicality of a particular respondent's story in relation to others of similar backgrounds. It all depends on the interpretive context in question.

B. B. King, the great blues singer, has self-consciously addressed these views. In his autobiography *Blues All around Me,* he acknowledges:

> When it comes to my own life, others may know the cold facts better than me. Scholars have told me to my face that I'm mixed up. I smile but don't argue. Truth is, cold facts don't tell the whole story. Reading this, some may accuse me of remembering wrong. That's okay, because I'm not writing a cold-blooded history. I'm writing a memory of my heart. That's the truth I'm after—following my feelings, no matter where they lead. (King and Ritz 1996:2)

King wants to understand himself, so he remembers the best he can, and tells a story of the heart. This may be all we can ask of a person telling his own story without the aid of a photographic memory. This may be the best we can expect. But it still leaves us with the dilemma of not knowing whether it is King's actual experience or an experience of the heart that he tells about.

There are scales of validity for all life stories, all autobiographies, all interviews. People cannot be, and don't need to be, under oath when telling their life stories. Realistically, life story interviewers should remember that it is possible that what they are getting from those they interview is not the whole truth. They can be pretty sure, however, that what they are getting are the stories respondents want to tell. That in itself tells us a good deal about what we really want to know. As Arras (1997) points out, "We ought to favor such narratives, first, because we can't do any better."

◆ Conclusion

Whether they are gathered for research purposes on particular topics or questions or to learn more about human lives and societies from different individuals' perspectives, life stories serve as excellent means for understanding how people see their own experiences, their own lives, and their interactions with others. Researchers who employ the approach to the life story interview suggested here may avoid many typical research and publication dilemmas if they keep certain primary "values" in mind. If one sets out with clear intent to help people tell their stories in their own words, the results will be clear as well.

The essences of life stories told seriously and consciously, in the voices of the persons telling them, are timeless; settings and circumstances change, but motifs and the meanings they represent remain constant across lives and time. Life stories make connections, shed light on the possible paths through life, and, maybe most important, lead us to the human spirit, to our deepest feelings, the values we live by, and the eternal meaning of life.

More life stories need to be brought forth that respect and honor the personal meanings life storytellers give to their stories. We share our stories for the bond of understanding that is established between us through the telling. In this regard, there is an exciting future for life stories and the narrative study of lives. The more we share our own stories, the closer we all become.

■ References

Abu-Lughod, L. 1993. *Writing Women's Worlds: Bedouin Stories.* Berkeley: University of California Press.

Allen, B. and L. Montell. 1981. *From Memory to History: Using Oral Sources in Local Historical Research.* Nashville, TN: American Association for State and Local History.

Allport, G. W. 1942. *The Use of Personal Documents in Psychological Science.* New York: Social Science Research Council.

Arras, J. D. 1997. "Nice Story, but So What? Narrative and Justification in Ethics." In *Stories and Their Limits: Narrative Approaches to Bioethics,* edited by H. L. Nelson. New York: Routledge.

Atkinson, R. 1985. *Life Outcomes: Elderhood in a Bicameral Culture.* Ann Arbor, MI: University Microfilms International.

———. 1995. *The Gift of Stories: Practical and Spiritual Applications of Autobiography, Life Stories, and Personal Mythmaking.* Westport, CT: Bergin & Garvey.

———. 1998. *The Life Story Interview.* Thousand Oaks, CA: Sage.

Ben-Ari, A. 1995. "It's the Telling That Makes the Difference." Pp. 153-72 in *The Narrative Study of Lives,* Vol. 3, *Interpreting Experience: The Narrative Study of Lives,* edited by R. Josselson and A. Lieblich. Thousand Oaks, CA: Sage.

Bertaux, D. 1981. *Biography and Society.* Beverly Hills, CA: Sage.

Birren, J. E. and B. A. Birren. 1996. "Autobiography: Exploring the Self and Encouraging Development." Pp. 283-99 in *Aging and Biography: Explorations in Adult Development,* edited by J. E. Birren, G. M. Kenyon, J. E. Ruth, J. J. F. Schroots, and T. Svensson. New York: Springer.

Birren, J. E., G. M. Kenyon, J. E. Ruth, J. J. F. Schroots, and T. Svensson, eds. 1996. *Aging and Biography: Explorations in Adult Development.* New York: Springer.

Boxer, A. M. and B. Cohler. 1989. "The Life Course of Gay and Lesbian Youth: An Immodest Proposal for the Study of Lives." *Journal of Homosexuality* 17:315-55.

Brockelman, P. 1985. *Time and Self.* New York: Crossroads.

Bruner, J. 1986. *Actual Minds, Possible Worlds.* Cambridge, MA: Harvard University Press.

———. 1987. "Life as Narrative." *Social Research* 54:11-32.

————. 1990. *Acts of Meaning.* Cambridge, MA: Harvard University Press.

—. 1991. "The Narrative Construction of Reality." *Critical Inquiry* 18:1-21.

Butler, R. N. 1963. "The Life Review: An Interpretation of Reminiscence in the Aged." *Psychiatry* 26:65-67.

Campbell, J. 1968. *The Hero with a Thousand Faces.* New York: Meridian.

————. 1970. *The Masks of God,* Vol. 4, *Creative Mythology.* New York: Viking.

Cohler, B. 1982. "Personal Narrative and the Life Course." In *Life Span Development and Behavior,* Vol. 4, edited by P. B. Baltes and O. G. Brim. New York: Academic Press.

Cohler, B. 1988. "The Human Studies and Life History." *Social Service Review* 62:552-75.

Cohler, B. 1993. "Aging, Morale, and Meaning: The Nexus of Narrative." Pp. 107-33 in *Voices and Visions of Aging,* edited by T. R. Cole, W. A. Achenbaum, P. L. Jakobi, and R. Kastenbaum. New York: Springer.

Comstock, G. L. 1995. *Religious Autobiographies.* Belmont, CA: Wadsworth.

de Vries, B. and A. J. Lehman. 1996. "The Complexity of Personal Narratives." In *Aging and Biography: Explorations in Adult Development,* edited by J. E. Birren, G. M. Kenyon, J. E. Ruth, J. J. F. Schroots, and T. Svensson. New York: Springer.

Eliade, M. 1954. *The Myth of the Eternal Return.* Princeton, NJ: Princeton University Press.

Erikson, E. 1958. *Young Man Luther: A Study in Psychoanalysis and History.* New York: Norton.

————. 1963. *Childhood and Society.* New York: Norton.

————. 1964. *Insight and Responsibility.* New York: Norton.

————. 1969. *Gandhi's Truth: On the Origins of Militant Nonviolence.* New York: Norton.

————. 1975. *Life History and the Historical Moment.* New York: Norton.

————. 1980. *Identity and the Life Cycle.* New York: Norton.

Frank, A. W. 1995. *The Wounded Storyteller: Body, Illness, and Ethics.* Chicago: University of Chicago Press.

Frank, G. 1980. "Life Histories in Gerontology: The Subjective Side to Aging." In *New Methods from Old Age Research: Anthropological Alternatives,* edited by C. L. Fry and J. Keith. Chicago: Loyola of Chicago University Press.

Freeman, M. 1992. "Self as Narrative: The Place of Life History in Studying the Life Span." Pp. 15-43 in *The Self: Definitional and Methodological Issues,* edited by T. M. Brinthaupt and R. P. Lipka. Albany: State University of New York Press.

Freud, S. 1957. "Leonardo da Vinci and a Memory of His Childhood" [1910]. Pp. 59-137 in *The Standard Edition of the Complete Psychological Works of Sigmund Freud,* Vol. 11, edited and translated by J. Strachey. London: Hogarth.

Freud, S. 1958. "Psycho-analytic Notes on an Autobiographical Account of a Case of Paranoia" [1911]. Pp. 3-82 in *The Standard Edition of the Complete Psychological Works of Sigmund Freud,* Vol. 12, edited and translated by J. Strachey. London: Hogarth.

Geertz, C. 1973. *The Interpretation of Cultures: Selected Essays.* New York: Basic Books.

Gergen, K. J. 1985. "The Social Constructionist Movement in Modern Psychology." *American Psychologist* 40:266-75.

Gergen, M. M. and K. J. Gergen. 1993. "Narratives of the Gendered Body in Popular Autobiography." Pp. 191-218 in *The Narrative Study of Lives,* Vol. 1, *The Narrative Study of Lives,* edited by R. Josselson and A. Lieblich. Newbury Park, CA: Sage.

Gubrium, J. F. and J. A. Holstein. 1998. "Narrative Practice and the Coherence of Personal Stories." *Sociological Quarterly* 39:163-87.

Helle, A. P. 1991. "Reading Women's Autobiographies: A Map of Reconstructed Knowing." Pp. 48-66 in *Stories Lives Tell: Narrative and Dialogue in Education,* edited by C. Witherell and N. Noddings. New York: Teachers College Press.

Holstein, J. A. and J. F. Gubrium. 1995. *The Active Interview.* Thousand Oaks, CA: Sage.

————. 2000a. *Constructing the Life Course.* 2d ed. Dix Hills, NY: General Hall.

————. 2000b. *The Self We Live By: Narrative Identity in a Postmodern World.* New York: Oxford University Press.

Ives, E. 1974. *The Tape-Recorded Interview: A Manual for Field Workers in Folklore and Oral History.* Nashville: University of Tennessee Press.

————, ed. 1986. *Folklife Annual: Symposium on the Life Story.* Washington, DC: American Folklife Center.

Josselson, R. 1995. "Imagining the Real: Empathy, Narrative, and the Dialogic Self." Pp. 27-44 in *The Narrative Study of Lives,* Vol. 3, *Interpreting Experience: The Narrative Study of Lives,* edited by R. Josselson and A. Lieblich. Thousand Oaks, CA: Sage.

Josselson, R., ed. 1996. *The Narrative Study of Lives,* Vol. 4, *Ethics and Process in the Narrative Study of Lives.* Thousand Oaks, CA: Sage.

Josselson, R. and A. Lieblich, eds. 1993. *The Narrative Study of Lives,* Vol. 1, *The Narrative Study of Lives.* Newbury Park, CA: Sage.

————, eds. 1995. *The Narrative Study of Lives,* Vol. 3, *Interpreting Experience: The Narrative Study of Lives.* Thousand Oaks, CA: Sage.

————, eds. 1999. *The Narrative Study of Lives,* Vol. 6, *Making Meaning of Narratives in the Narrative Study of Lives.* Thousand Oaks, CA: Sage.

Kenyon, G. M., P. Clark, and B. de Vries, eds. 2001. *Narrative Gerontology.* New York: Springer.

Kenyon, G. M. and W. L. Randall. 1997. *Restorying Our Lives: Personal Growth through Autobiographical Reflection.* Westport, CT: Praeger.

King, B. B. and D. Ritz. 1996. *Blues All around Me: The Autobiography of B. B. King.* New York: Avon.

Kirk, J. and M. L. Miller. (1986). *Reliability and Validity in Qualitative Research.* Beverly Hills, CA: Sage.

Klockars, C. B. 1974. *The Professional Fence.* New York: Free Press.

Kroger, J. 1993. "Identity and Context: How Identity Statuses Choose Their Match." Pp. 130-62 in *The Narrative Study of Lives,* Vol. 1, *The Narrative Study of Lives,* edited by R. Josselson and A. Lieblich. Newbury Park, CA: Sage.

Langness, L. L. and Frank, G. 1981. *Lives: An Anthropological Approach to Biography.* Novato, CA: Chandler & Sharp.

Lieblich, A. and R. Josselson, eds. 1994. *The Narrative Study of Lives,* Vol. 2, *Exploring Identity and Gender: The Narrative Study of Lives.* Thousand Oaks, CA: Sage.

————, eds. 1997. *The Narrative Study of Lives,* Vol. 5, *The Narrative Study of Lives.* Thousand Oaks, CA: Sage.

Linde, C. 1993. *Life Stories: The Creation of Coherence.* New York: Oxford University Press.

Marcia, J. E. 1966. "Development and Validation of Ego Identity Status." *Journal of Personality and Social Psychology* 3:551-58.

McAdams, D. P. 1993. *Stories We Live By: Personal Myths and the Making of the Self.* New York: William Morrow.

McCracken, G. 1988. *The Long Interview.* Newbury Park, CA: Sage.

Mkhonza, S. 1995. "Life Histories as Social Texts of Personal Experiences in Sociolinguistic Studies: A Look at the Lives of Domestic Workers in Swaziland." Pp. 173-204 in *The Narrative Study of Lives,* Vol. 3, *Interpreting Experience: The Narrative Study of Lives,* edited by R. Josselson and A. Lieblich. Thousand Oaks, CA: Sage.

Murray, H. A. 1938. *Explorations in Personality.* New York: Oxford University Press.

————. 1955. "American Icarus." Pp. 615-41 in *Clinical Studies in Personality,* Vol. 3, edited by A. Burton and R. E. Harris. New York: Harper & Row.

Olney, J., ed. 1980. *Autobiography: Essays Theoretical and Critical.* Princeton, NJ: Princeton University Press.

Randall, W. L. 1995. *The Stories We Are: An Essay on Self-Creation.* Toronto: University of Toronto Press.

Riessman, C. K. 1993. *Narrative Analysis.* Newbury Park, CA: Sage.

Rosenthal, G. 1993. "Reconstruction of Life Stories: Principles of Selection in Generating Stories for Narrative Biographical Interviews." Pp. 59-91 in *The Narrative Study of Lives,* Vol. 1, *The Narrative Study of Lives,* edited by R. Josselson and A. Lieblich. Newbury Park, CA: Sage.

Runyan, W. M. 1982. *Life Histories and Psychobiography: Explorations in Theory and Method.* New York: Oxford University Press.

Sarbin, T. R. 1986. "The Narrative as Root Metaphor for Psychology." Pp. 3-21 in *Narrative Psychology: The Storied Nature of Human Conduct,* edited by T. R. Sarbin. New York: Praeger.

Spradley, J. 1979. *The Ethnographic Interview.* New York: Holt, Rinehart & Winston.

Stewart, A. J. 1994. "The Women's Movement and Women's Lives: Linking Individual Development and Social Events." Pp. 230-50 in *The Narrative Study of Lives,* Vol. 2, *Exploring Identity and Gender: The Narrative Study of Lives,* edited by A. Lieblich and R. Josselson. Thousand Oaks, CA: Sage.

Tillich, P. 1957. *Dynamics of Faith.* New York: Harper & Row.

Titon, J. 1980. "The Life Story." *Journal of American Folklore* 93:276-92.

van Gennep, A. 1960. *The Rites of Passage.* Chicago: University of Chicago Press.

White, M. and D. Epston. 1990. *Narrative Means to Therapeutic Ends.* New York: Norton.

Widdershoven, G. A. M. 1993. "The Story of Life: Hermeneutic Perspectives on the Relationship between Narrative and Life History." Pp. 1-20 in *The Narrative Study of Lives,* Vol. 1, edited by R. Josselson and A. Lieblich. Newbury Park, CA: Sage.

Witherell, C. and N. Noddings, eds. 1991. *Stories Lives Tell: Narrative and Dialogue in Education.* New York: Teachers College Press.

7

FOCUS GROUP INTERVIEWING

◆ David L. Morgan

A dozen or so years ago, few social scientists had even heard of focus groups. Now focus group interviewing is a widely accepted research method. The focus group interview can be defined as "a research technique that collects data through group interaction on a topic determined by the researcher" (Morgan 1996:130). This is a broad definition that includes most forms of group interviews, with the exception of observing naturally occurring conversations in ongoing interaction. Although some researchers do differentiate among varied kinds of group interviews (Frey and Fontana 1991; Kahn and Manderson 1992), the more common practice is to treat the focus group as a wide-ranging method in which the researcher has a variety of options for conducting the actual interviews. The fact that focus group interviewing is such a flexible data gathering technique is undoubtedly one of the reasons for its popularity.

In this chapter I examine the rapid growth of the use of focus groups in the social sciences, both to explore why researchers conduct focus groups in the way they do and to stimulate thinking about different ways to conduct them. The chapter falls into three major sections. The first addresses the growing popularity of focus groups in the social sciences, especially in terms of how developments in marketing have become increasingly attractive to social researchers. Turning next to focus group methodology, in the second section I consider various approaches to moderating, in particular the issue of how structured moderating should be. In the third section I compare individual and group interviews in relation to questions of validity and the interchangeability of these forms of interviewing as research procedures. The chapter concludes with a discussion of future directions for focus group interviewing.

◆ The Popularity of Focus Groups

The growth in social scientists' use of focus groups has been phenomenal. A search of both *Sociological Abstracts* and *Psychological Abstracts* reveals only a handful of publications about research that used focus groups during the 1980s, followed by a rapid upswing starting around 1990. By the end of the 1990s, the number of articles based on focus group research was well over 200 per year. Allowing for the lag between when a research project enters the field and when it gets published, the rising number of articles in the early 1990s points to an active experimentation with focus groups during the middle of the preceding decade. This corresponds to the first appearance of both methodological articles (e.g., Basch 1987; Morgan and Spanish 1984) and textbooks (e.g., Krueger 1988; Morgan 1988) that presented the method for a social science audience.

It is, of course, easier to describe the growing popularity of focus groups than it is to explain why this occurred. Social scientists have only recently begun to pay careful attention to the history of research in their disciplines (e.g., Converse 1987; Platt 1996; see also Platt, Chapter 2, this volume), hence it is challenging to answer the question of why there was such a dramatic increase in the use of a particular method. One way of understanding the evolution of research methods is to consider their strengths and weaknesses. For example, researchers during the 1950s were especially fascinated by the possibility of representing a whole country's beliefs through just a thousand or so survey interviews (Converse 1987). Similarly, the 1970s saw an increasing interest in the possibility of bringing about social change through the evaluation of experimental social service programs (Campbell 1969). These strengths ostensibly explain the methods' respective popularity.

If the strengths of a method are the primary force that guides its usage, then an examination of trends from roughly 1985 to 1990 in the social sciences, as well as in the larger society, should reveal an increasing interest in a set of research goals that called for the use of focus groups. By most accounts, the single most compelling purpose that focus groups served was to bridge social and cultural differences. Thus Richard A. Krueger and I urged our colleagues to "consider focus groups when you need a friendly research method that is respectful and not condescending to your target audience" (Morgan and Krueger 1993:18). This was matched by a broader interest in recognizing and understanding diversity, so it is not surprising that focus groups have become a prominent tool for quite literally giving voice to those outside the mainstream of society. (For summaries as well as critiques of this argument, see Johnson 1996; Cunningham-Burley, Kerr, and Pavis 1999.) It may be an overstatement, but there is undoubtedly a grain of truth to the contrast between using surveys to summarize the views of the entire nation during the 1950s and using focus groups to get closer to the thoughts and experiences of smaller and more specific segments of society in the 1990s.

THE MIGRATION OF FOCUS GROUPS FROM MARKETING

A different way of accounting for the shift toward focus groups is to trace the actual process through which they migrated from marketing and made their appearance in the social sciences. This approach replaces the seeming inevitability of focus groups with a more complex historical account of their rising popularity. Most important, it points to a set of circumstances that still are exerting an influence on how social science researchers use focus groups.

There is indeed a consensus that the current use of focus groups in the social sciences arose through contacts with marketing, where it had been a popular technique since the 1950s (Johnson 1996; Krueger 1994; Morgan 1998a). This is not the whole story of the origins of focus groups, of course, given that some of the most important early work was done by the well-known social scientists Robert Merton and Paul Lazarsfeld (see the introductory chapter in Merton, Fiske, and Kendall 1990). By the 1980s, however, that early work had been largely forgotten, and nearly all of the usage in the social sciences applied versions of focus groups that originated in the field of marketing.

Throughout most of their history in marketing, focus groups have been an applied technique that fell outside the boundaries of academic market research. Because market researchers in academic settings had ignored qualitative methods such as focus groups, there was very little in the way of research-based guidelines for the use of focus groups in marketing practice. Similarly, because focus groups were not included in the formal curriculum, most marketers learned how to do focus groups through informal, on-the-job training. Indeed, a review of my 1988 book *Focus Groups as Qualitative Research* in a marketing journal (McQuarrie 1990) suggested that if social scientists were paying more attention to focus groups, marketing researchers might also want to take them more seriously.

At first glance, this absence of academic attention to focus groups in marketing seems similar to the dominance of quantitative methods in the social sciences during this period. The key distinction, however, is that focus groups were widely used in *applied* marketing practice even if they were largely ignored in academic settings. This situation posed a dilemma for social scientists who were becoming interested in focus groups. Although there clearly was a substantial knowledge base about focus groups, this knowledge was not available through textbooks or the usual research literature.

One especially striking feature of the empirical reports of marketing focus groups prior to 1990 is their vague descriptions of methodology. From a social science point of view, this would be unacceptable. For the marketers who wrote these articles, however, the details of their methods were the product that they were selling to their clients. Whereas social scientists might be rewarded for publishing methodological articles that provided guidance about when and how to do focus groups, commercial marketers who did so would be giving away their "stock-in-trade."

So how did social scientists acquire the knowledge they needed to use focus groups? One important pathway was through the field of social marketing. Starting in the 1970s, a group of marketers sought to apply their techniques to "social problems," not just to the marketing of goods and services (Andreason 1995). This led to a partnership between the marketing firm of Potter-Novelli and a group of applied demographers who used focus groups to study fertility and contraception in Mexico (Folch-Lyon, de la Macorra, and Schearer 1981). This early linkage between social marketing and demography is a nice illustration of the importance of a particular context in the development of methods, because demographers, despite the quantitative dominance in that speciality, have continued to be an important influence on focus groups within academic research (e.g., Knodel 1993, 1995). More recently, social marketing techniques, including focus groups (Basch 1987), have been pursued by both academic and applied researchers in the field of public health, targeting a wide variety of health-related behaviors.

Another point of contact was the connection between survey researchers and pollsters. Ironically, Lazarsfeld was one of the most important sources for this continuing exchange between the more academic and more applied sides of survey research (Converse 1987). Within marketing, focus groups were often treated as the first stage in a research process that would be followed by surveys (Hayes and Tatham 1989). Indeed, many marketers asserted that the lack of statistical generalizability for focus group required confirmation by survey research. In practice, this meant that focus groups came to be treated as a valuable tool for creating survey questionnaires. As academic researchers became more aware of this practice, they began to experiment with the use of focus groups in the development of their own survey instruments. One illustration of this practice is the work of a group of researchers at the University of Michigan's Institute for Social Research who used focus groups to develop a survey on the sexual practices of gay men in one of the first social science studies on AIDS (Joseph et al. 1984). In that case, the inclusion of a qualitative method in the creation of a survey instrument was easily justified by the need to do exploratory work on a new topic in an understudied population. Since that time, focus groups have become a routine option in the development of survey instruments (Fowler 1995).

For both social marketing and survey research, there were existing pathways between marketing and applied research within the social sciences. Social scientists also gained exposure to focus groups through a number of less formal mechanisms. In some cases, social scientists who did consulting work added focus groups to the services they offered (Richard Zeller, personal communication). In other cases, conducting marketing focus groups provided employment for future graduate students in the social sciences (Robin Jarrett, personal communication). In my own case, I was designing a project to use group discussions as a source of qualitative data when a friend with exposure to marketing asked me why I was going to so much effort to reinvent focus groups (see the acknowledgments in Morgan 1988).

These were just a few of the points of connection that encouraged the crossover of focus groups from marketing to the social sciences. By the end of the 1980s, this process was occurring in any number of different places. For some fields, the nature of the connection was obvious, such as the use of focus groups in election campaigns and the subsequent interest among political scientists. In other fields, such as nursing, the source of the original connection remains less clear. What is clear is that the movement of focus groups into the social sciences was not something that happened just once. Similarly, it is probably not accurate to treat it as something that was championed by just a few advocates. Instead, the 1980s produced a growing interest in focus groups across a number of social science fields.

THE ACCEPTANCE OF FOCUS GROUPS IN THE SOCIAL SCIENCES

If the above discussion addresses some of the factors that affected how focus groups moved from marketing, what can be said about the context they moved into, namely, the social sciences during the 1980s? First of all, it is important to recognize that social scientists at that time considered marketing, especially applied marketing, to be well beneath them in terms of methodological rigor. This low-status origin may help to explain why few of the early social science articles on focus groups made more than passing mention of their debt to marketing (for an exception, see Morgan and Spanish 1984).

Most descriptions of the social sciences in this period (e.g., Denzin and Lincoln 1994) would show a quantitative dominance but would also mention an increasing interest in qualitative methods. This growing interest in qualitative methods was certainly a favorable influence, which helps to explain why focus groups reemerged in the social sciences at this point, after a lapse of some 30 years. Another relevant factor was the major reduction in funding for social science research in the United States that began during the Reagan administration. Without external funding, researchers needed to pursue smaller-scale projects in which they themselves did much of the work. Focus groups were well suited to this constraint.

The emphasis on evaluation research during this period also played an important role. Both the development of programs through "formative evaluation" and the assessment of programs through "summative evaluation" could benefit from in-depth knowledge about specific situations and specific client populations that focus groups provided (Krueger 1988, 1994). It was relatively easy to adapt focus groups to these tasks, because the existing procedures for generating discussions of commercial products could also fit discussions of social services.

Although there was a strong movement toward qualitative evaluation throughout this period (e.g., Patton 1990), focus groups frequently functioned as supplementary studies within projects based on quasi-experimental designs. This arrangement was beneficial in many ways, because it gave focus groups legitimacy as a research method at the same time it provided qualitative researchers with access to funding. Still, these "partnerships" were typically organized around the assumption that the quantitative aspects of the project were the most important. The same could be said about the uses of focus groups in survey research. They provided quantitative researchers with the opportunity to benefit from a supplementary qualitative method while largely remaining within the boundaries of their traditional approach.

All of this emphasis on the use of focus groups within quantitative research projects raises obvious questions about the reception of focus group interviewing among researchers who had been trained in the use of other qualitative methods. This is an area that I personally have addressed ever since my earliest work on focus groups (Morgan and Spanish 1984), and it is explicitly embodied in the title of my 1988 book, *Focus Groups as Qualitative Research*. In my conclusions to that brief volume, I stated that I was "optimistic about the ability of focus groups to establish a unique position within the existing array of methods for gathering qualitative data," and that "if we are to expand our horizons to include focus groups as a routine option, it will most likely happen through their adoption by those who already have a solid background in qualitative research" (pp. 76-77).

Although focus groups have indeed established their position as a qualitative method, the practitioners of other qualitative methods have had little to do with this success. In a few cases, qualitative researchers have encouraged the growth of the field, such as through sponsorship of a special issue on focus groups in the journal *Qualitative Health Research* (Carey 1995). In other cases, they have discounted focus groups, as in Michael Agar and James Mac-Donald's (1995) unfavorable comparison of focus group interviewing to ethnographic interviewing. By and large, however, established researchers with expertise in qualitative methodology have simply ignored focus groups. Because those with expertise in other qualitative methods have paid little attention to them, these researchers also have had little influence on the development of focus groups within the social sciences.

The movement of focus groups into the social sciences thus presents a contrast between rapid acceptance in a variety of applied fields and a more tepid reception from established qualitative researchers. The most obvious change that occurred through this contact was the use of focus groups as a qualitative method within fields that had traditionally relied exclusively on quantitative methods. The focus group method itself, however, did not undergo a great deal of change in its migration from marketing to the social sciences.

◆ Approaches to Moderating

Most treatments of focus group methodology emphasize the need to keep the discussion on topic while encouraging the group to interact freely. It is the moderator's job to walk this tightrope. Arguably, there are many possible ways to balance the demands of both keeping a focus group discussion on topic and allowing the participants to express their own interests. Yet most research projects rely on only a narrow range of moderating strategies.

To understand what moderators do, it is important to distinguish between the larger role that moderators frequently play and the specific activity of *moderating* the focus group discussion. Although it is common to think of the moderator's role solely in terms of what happens during group discussion, moderators almost always do more than that. In most focus group projects, the individuals who act as moderators also design and oversee the recruitment process that brings the participants to the groups. They write the questions that will guide the discussions. Following group discussion, it is usually the moderator's job to do the analysis and prepare the research reports. Elsewhere, I have argued that good recruitment, question writing, and analysis are just as essential to focus group research as good moderating, yet all of these activities are far less visible (Morgan 1995). Like an iceberg, the most obvious aspect of moderating is only part of the larger reality.

THE VALUE OF MORE STRUCTURED APPROACHES IN MARKETING

To understand why the marketing approach to focus groups often uses a more structured strategy, it helps to understand the broader role that the moderator serves in that field. Moderators typically perform a boundary-spanning role that connects what their clients want to know with what the participants say in the focus groups. One of the most interesting aspects of this effort to connect clients and participants occurs when the clients, behind a one-way mirror, watch a moderator lead a focus group (for fuller discussion of this arrangement, see Morgan 1998b). Even when marketing researchers do not have clients watching from behind mirrors, they routinely give videotapes of group proceedings to their clients, so that clients have a record of what the moderator did or did not do. Because moderating skills are one of the most costly things that clients are purchasing, being watched creates a strong incentive for moderators to prove their skills by taking a visible and active role in directing the group discussion.

This need to perform before a client who is paying the bills may be the single biggest difference between what moderators do in marketing and what they do in the social sciences. I had the opportunity to observe a group of marketers and social scientists as they came to grips with this issue during a panel at the annual conference of the American Sociological Association in 1998. The session was organized by a group of marketers who had university affiliations, whereas the audience consisted mostly of academic researchers. When the presenters discussed the routine (for them) aspects of renting professional facilities with one-way mirrors and dealing with the clients who were observing the proceedings from the "back room," it created quite a stir in the audience. Eventually, someone stood up and, in disbelief, asked the panel something like, "You mean to say that the people who pay you to do the research actually watch the groups from behind a mirror? What human subjects committee ever approved that?" The rest of the session amounted to an exercise in virtual cross-cultural communication as the marketers and the sociologists attempted to sort out their different assumptions about how to do focus groups.

For current purposes, the difference that matters most is that marketers tend to use a more structured approach whereas social

Table 7.1 COMPARISON OF MORE AND LESS STRUCTURED APPROACHES TO FOCUS GROUPS

More Structured Approaches	Less Structured Approaches
Goal: Answer researchers' questions.	Goal: Understand participants' thinking.
Researchers' interests are dominant.	Participants' interests are dominant.
Questions set the agenda for discussion.	Questions guide discussion.
Larger number of more specific questions.	Fewer, more general questions.
Specific amounts of time per question.	Flexible allocation of time.
Moderator directs discussion.	Moderator facilitates interaction.
Moderator "refocuses" off-topic remarks.	Moderator can explore new directions.
Participants address the moderator.	Participants talk to each other.

scientists frequently use a less structured one. This difference has a long history, going back at least to Merton's initial exposure to Lazarsfeld's use of group interviews in radio research. After observing his first group, Merton voiced his opinion that the hired moderator was "inadvertently guiding the responses" and "not eliciting spontaneous expressions," so Lazarsfeld had Merton demonstrate his preferred style of interviewing by moderating the next group (Merton et al. 1990:xv-xvii; Rogers 1994).

Table 7.1 summarizes the differences between more and less structured approaches to focus groups across the board, regardless of who is sponsoring the research. The left-hand column of the table lists the characteristics of more structured approaches, which center on the researchers' interests. The moderator's influence on the degree of structure begins well before the interview itself. The right-hand column lists the equivalent characteristics of a less structured approach, showing that participants' interests have a much greater impact on the course of the discussion. Taken together, the characteristics listed in the table indicate that the degree of structure has as much to do with the kinds of questions asked as with the way the moderator conducts the discussion of those questions.

In fairness, the "need to perform" for the client is only one reason marketers tend to use a more structured approach. In addition, marketing focus groups often involve members of the general public who have only weak attachment to the discussion topic. For many marketing topics, considerable effort must be expended not only to get the participants engaged initially but to keep them on topic during the subsequent discussion. It thus makes sense to organize the discussion around a well-defined set of concrete issues, such as what participants like or dislike about a product or service, how they would compare it to available alternatives, and what they might do to improve it.

There is thus a good fit between marketers' more structured approach to focus groups and their need to work with participants who have a low level of involvement with the research topic. The larger lesson is that this approach to moderating is driven by a specific set of needs and goals. When social scientists are operating in similar circumstances, they too can benefit from the strengths of a more structured approach to moderating. When the circumstances are different, however, they need to step back and consider whether this approach still meets their needs.

QUESTIONING THE VALUE OF STRUCTURED APPROACHES IN THE SOCIAL SCIENCES

Social scientists have a wider array of options for how they do focus groups because they pursue a broader range of goals across a number of different disciplines. This often leads them to work on topics that are quite different from those addressed in marketing research. One of the most important contrasts is that social scientists are more likely to work with participants who are closely connected to the research topic—such as my own work with recent widows (Morgan 1989) and with caregivers for family members with Alzheimer's disease (Morgan and Zhao 1993). When the participants in a focus group have a high level of personal commitment or emotional involvement with the topic, it is easier for them to start and maintain a discussion, so a less structured approach is a realistic option.

Yet social scientists have continued to emphasize a relatively structured approach to focus groups. This is particularly problematic in situations where more structured focus groups run the risk of limiting the discussion to the topics the researchers want to hear about rather than revealing the participants' own perspectives. If social scientists' reliance on more structured approaches to focus groups were simply an unquestioned inheritance from earlier practices in marketing, this would indicate a serious lack of critical thinking. The reality, of course, is more complex. As I have noted in the earlier historical discussion, social marketing, survey research, and evaluation research were some of the most important crossover points for the migration of focus groups from marketing into the social sciences. Like marketing, each of these fields typically works with participants who have a low level of involvement with the topic. Because the needs of this type of social science research matched the more structured approach that was already prevalent in marketing, there was little need to modify the existing techniques. Further, as these fields supplied many of the first uses of focus groups in the social sciences, their reliance on a relatively structured approach to interviewing served as a model that influenced later applications of focus groups.

This historical emphasis on structured approaches to interviewing is also present in nearly all of the books available about focus groups, which place a great deal of emphasis on the things the moderator should do to lead the group. There is considerable discussion of how to control difficult participants and how to get shy people talking, how to control overly talkative groups and breathe life into flat discussions, and the like. This kind of instruction makes it easy to conclude that focus groups will fail without the active direction of a highly skilled moderator. It is not surprising, then, that most novice moderators begin with assumptions that emphasize a more structured approach, so they are likely to perpetuate past practices unless they are exposed to alternatives.

One way that I have tried to offer that alternative—in addition to my published descriptions of less structured focus groups (Morgan 1997:39-42, 1998b:43-53)—is through training sessions that describe what I personally consider to be my "ideal focus group," which is based on a less structured approach. The ideal group would start with an opening question that was designed to capture the participants' interest, so that they themselves would explore nearly all of the issues that a moderator might have probed. Then, just as the allocated amount of time for that question was running out, one of the participants in the ideal group would spontaneously direct the others' attention to the topic for the second question by saying something like, "You know what really strikes me is how many of the things we're saying are connected to . . . ."

Anyone who has done much moderating has experienced this magic moment, as the group goes right where you want it to, without any help from you. When that happens, a less structured approach to moderating can keep the discussion going with little more than a smile and a nod. In my version of an ideal focus group, that kind of minimal response from the moderator would be all that was ever necessary, because the group itself would work through all the topics of the interview guide. Finally, 5 or 10 minutes before the session was supposed to be over, the discussion would begin to wind down, and the moderator could move toward closure with a typical wrap-up request, such as, "This has really been wonderful, and I'd like to finish by having each one of you summarize . . . ."

In this ideal version of a less structured group, the moderator would have to ask only the first and the last questions. Beyond that, the group itself would cover every topic on the interview guide. Although this may sound like a fantasy, I have come close to it on several occasions. The trick is to remember that there is much more to moderating than just what the moderator does during the group.

A less structured approach works best when the participants themselves are just as interested in the topic as the researcher is, so the first step is a recruitment process that carefully matches the participants to the research topic. Then the moderator has to write a guide in which the first question not only gets the discussion flowing but opens up a number of other topics that the participants will be eager to explore. So creating the possibility for a less structured focus group depends on a great deal more than the things that a moderator does or doesn't do during the discussion itself. Indeed, I like to say that the reason I have yet to moderate a group that fully matches my ideal has as much to do with my abilities at recruitment and question writing as with my moderating skills.

My version of this ideal may be appropriate for many social science research projects (including the kind of work that I myself do), but it is far less likely to work when the participants have a low level of involvement with the research topic. And imagine what would happen if someone used this moderating strategy for a consulting contract where the clients were watching from behind a one-way mirror. Wouldn't those clients have to wonder why on earth they were paying the moderator so much money to do "nothing"? Of course, the real work would have been done before group discussion got under way, in the recruitment process and the writing of the interview guide, but none of that would show up during the group itself.

Neither a more structured nor a less structured approach to focus groups is appropriate in every circumstance. Instead, researchers need to make well-informed decisions between these options. If my tracing of the historical development of focus groups in the social sciences is accurate, fields such as evaluation, social marketing, and survey research do indeed match some of the circumstances that lead marketers to use a more structured approach. In other areas, however, social scientists' reliance on more structured focus groups may be due to little more than their greater familiarity with that approach.

Viewing social science approaches to moderating in historical perspective leads to the conclusion that the established practices deserve to be continued in some cases and questioned in others. If researchers are going to question their established procedures, they need both a sense of what their options are and a set of guidelines for deciding when one choice would be preferred over others. Fortunately, the existing methodological knowledge about more and less structured approaches to moderating now provides a starting point for such decisions.

◆ Comparing Individual and Group Interviews

The existing expertise that social scientists have developed in individual interviewing might have served as a considerable resource for the development of focus groups as well. Instead, even the limited contact between these two seemingly similar methods has been relatively hostile. Much of this hostility has taken the form of questions about whether the data from focus groups are as "natural" or "valid" as the data from individual interviews. Further, the fear that focus groups not only produce poor data but can also be done more quickly than intensive interviewing has led to a belief, in some corners, that they pose a threat to "real" qualitative research.

This section addresses both charges about the adequacy of the data from group interviews and concerns that focus groups might be used as a substitute for more in-depth approaches to qualitative research. Responding to these concerns is only one goal. More important, researchers need to learn from these disputes and move past them. An emphasis on the mutually relevant aspects of individual and group interviews will benefit both methods.

ARE FOCUS GROUPS LESS NATURAL OR LESS VALID THAN INDIVIDUAL INTERVIEWS?

In both one-on-one and group interviews, the interviewer and the research participant(s) work together to create their conversation, but it is the interviewer who initiates the contact, determines the content of the conversation, asks the questions, and serves as the audience for the responses to those questions. From this perspective, Yvonna Lincoln and Egon Guba (1985) are right to speak of "naturalistic" inquiry, rather than treating any form of interviewing as truly natural. At the same time, however, Lincoln and Guba clearly claim that qualitative interviewing is *more* natural than survey interviewing; thus, even if all methods are at best naturalistic, some are apparently more natural than others. Unfortunately, the idea of a hierarchy of naturalness has also carried over to the idea that

even if focus groups are qualitative interviews, they are more artificial than individual, open-ended interviews.

I had a particularly memorable encounter with the idea that focus groups are less natural than individual interviews when I taught a workshop for several professors from the former Soviet Union, to help them study the transition to democracy in their home countries. My week of teaching about focus groups was preceded by a similar unit on autobiographical interviews taught by an anthropologist. On my second day of class, I was confronted with the opinion that focus groups are a contrived way of talking to people, at least in comparison to the techniques that had been presented the week before. In response, I asked the students how "natural" it is to have a complete stranger spend several hours talking about just the portions of his or her life that involved politics. In contrast, I asked whether it would be possible to bring together a group of neighbors to discuss how the politics in their country had changed since independence. They responded enthusiastically with remarks like, "You'd never be able to get them to go home!" By the end of the week, the students were engaged in a lively debate about the relative merits of individual and group interviews for the projects they were planning to do.

This simple example illustrates how even a small amount of prior familiarity with a technique can make it into a de facto standard for assessing what one encounters later. Although I personally believe that seniority is the main reason some people think of group interviews as less natural than individual interviews, there are several seemingly substantive reasons behind this claim, and it is instructive to examine them. One possible source of the sense that group interviews are more artificial is the effort involved in bringing together a number of people for a focus group, which is often more overt than the work that it takes to conduct a series of individual interviews. Thus a focus group appears to be more "staged" in comparison to each of the separate meetings in a set of individual interviews, even though it is the researcher who creates both kinds of conversations.

The highly visible role of the moderator in focus groups is another source for the claim that they are less natural than individual interviews. This matches a belief that group dynamics are more complex than the dynamics in one-on-one interviews, so the skillful management of the interview is more important to the success of focus groups. The problem with this claim is that it is based on an appeal to common sense rather than actual evidence. In fact, it is just as easy to argue the opposite—that group interviewing is easier. As I have illustrated in the previous section, a group of participants who are interested in a topic can keep a discussion going with very little direction from the interviewer. Of course, that approach requires participants who have a relatively high level of involvement with the topic. But what about interviewing people who have little interest in a topic? Would you really want to spend an hour interviewing someone about bar soap or car seats? Yet marketers routinely get *groups* of people to share and compare their thoughts about such mundane topics.

Another way to question commonsense assumptions about the naturalness of individual versus group interviews is to pose a counterfactual argument. What if social scientists had begun with group interviews and become interested in individual interviewing only at a later point—would that routine experience with focus groups lead them to think of focus groups as more natural and individual interviews as more problematic? Interestingly, this reversal of fortune is actually the situation in marketing research. There, focus groups are the better-established tool, whereas "one-on-ones" and "customer visits" (McQuarrie 1996) suffer by comparison to the well-established procedures and well-known value of focus groups. Thus the sense that one kind of interview is more natural than another may be a simple reflection of which of the two is more familiar.

From a claim that focus groups are less natural than individual interviews it is only a short step to the more serious assertion that they are less valid. According to this argument, people are more likely to say what they "really" think in individual interviews because the presence of other participants during a focus group will influence what everyone says. It certainly is true that the same people might say different things in individual interviews than they would in a group discussion, but that does not mean that one set of statements is distorted and the other is not. Instead, if people say different things in different contexts, that is an interesting fact that may well be worthy of study in its own right. Carefully designed studies in which the same people are asked about the same topics in both individual and group interviews are rare, but Daniel Wight (1994) provides a particularly useful example in his work on adolescent boys' behavior toward girls their age. When an adult male interviewed these boys individually, they displayed relatively sensitive understanding of what girls their age expect in a relationship. Yet when this same interviewer led the boys in group interviews, they exhibited noticeably more macho attitudes, bragging about how they could get girls to do anything that they wanted (see also Eder and Fingerson, Chapter 9, this volume).

Wight explains this difference by arguing that being around other boys brought a whole set of male-oriented norms into play for his respondents. Group interviews among adolescent boys are thus likely to invoke a particular aspect of their peer culture, but whether this is good or bad depends on what the research is about. For some purposes, observing the kind of macho behavior that boys bring out in each other might be crucial. For other purposes, this predictable group dynamic might get in the way. Rather than claiming that one set of results is more valid than the other, it makes more sense to treat each method as more useful for some purposes and less useful for others.

There is no denying the fact that the types of interviews that researchers conduct can shape the things they hear in interview conversations. Unfortunately, there is a gap in the basic knowledge that would predict when a researcher might hear one thing in group interviews and another thing from individuals. At this point, little more than generalities are available about the greater depth and detail to be gained from individual interviews and the possibility of observing social norms at work in group discussions. One way to improve the understanding of what each method can and cannot do would be to do more studies like Wight's that provide systematic comparisons of group and individual interviews. This would certainly be more productive than further debates about the relative naturalness and validity of the two methods.

ARE FOCUS GROUPS A SHORTCUT THAT CAN REPLACE INDIVIDUAL INTERVIEWS?

The most prominent claim that focus groups amount to a stripped-down, shortcut approach to qualitative research is undoubtedly Agar and MacDonald's (1995) critique, which appeared in the journal *Human Organization*. I agree that the typical practice of conducting three or four highly structured focus groups can never replace a series of in-depth, ethnographic interviews. What Agar and MacDonald ignore is the fact that focus groups that are done in this fashion typically serve very applied purposes that are quite different from the purposes of most ethnographic research.

Even if most focus groups are designed to serve other purposes, this still leaves the question of whether focus groups are interchangeable with individual interviews in that they produce data that have the same degree of depth and detail as those produced by individual interviews. I would ar-

gue that it is quite possible to use focus groups for such purposes. One example is the set of 53 focus groups that Jenny Kitzinger (1994) conducted to understand how people think about AIDS and why they think that way. Kitzinger worked with a variety of groups in which the participants were already acquainted with one another (including members of a retirement club, mothers from a preschool, prison officers, and male prostitutes). Using preexisting groups allowed her to hear how the participants used elements of their shared experiences to discuss a controversial topic. This kind of focus group research can indeed produce in-depth information about cultural understandings, but it is also quite different from small studies that serve narrow, applied purposes.

These broad responses address the basic concern that originally motivated Agar and MacDonald's critique, but they do not speak to the substantive conclusions that those authors draw from their experience with group and individual interviews. It is instructive to consider three of the major points that Agar and MacDonald raise:

◆ Because the group interview format requires the moderator to direct the discussion, focus groups produce a limited form of interaction that is as much like a meeting as it is like a conversation.

◆ Individual interviews encourage informants to explain their "folk knowledge" to the interviewer, whereas the participants in a group conversation simply use their "indexed knowledge" without any need to explain themselves to one another.

◆ Because of the limited kinds of interaction in focus groups, one must make a line-by-line analysis of detailed transcripts in order to understand the process that produced the data.

Agar and MacDonald's (1995) first point concerns their need to fall back on a directive style of moderating, despite their efforts to conduct a less structured group. With the benefit of hindsight, I submit that this problem was actually due to a flawed recruitment process, which Agar and MacDonald themselves characterize as a "comedy of errors" (p. 79). Although Agar and MacDonald sought seven or eight LSD users to discuss that drug, they ended up with just four respondents, only one of whom had extensive experience with LSD. As a result, they had trouble conducting an unstructured group among participants who had little experience with the topic they were supposed to discuss. By comparison, if the authors had intended to do an ethnographic interview, then locating only one experienced LSD user would have been sufficient. Even though Agar and MacDonald cite several focus group texts that emphasize the importance of recruitment, they seem to have followed a set of procedures that were more appropriate for individual interviewing. A pair of expert ethnographic interviewers managed to make one of the most common mistakes of novice focus group researchers.

Even though Agar and MacDonald's failure to follow the standard advice on recruitment did have a predictable effect on group dynamics, their violation of the received wisdom on focus group recruitment also produced some interesting insights. Because the participants had a wide range of backgrounds with respect to the core topic, their discussion showed that teenagers who lack experience with LSD share the adult community's simplistic notions about the drug. If Agar and MacDonald had successfully followed the textbook advice and created a homogeneous group of LSD users, this finding would have been "designed away." This use of a homogeneous group to create more manageable group dynamics is another procedure that the social sciences have borrowed in a relatively unquestioned fashion from marketing. As a consequence, focus group researchers have done little to investigate the possible advantages of more mixed groups. Thus one benefit of Agar

and MacDonald's inadvertent experiment with mixed groups is that it provides a reason to question traditional procedures in focus group research.

Agar and MacDonald's second point, that the conversations in focus groups tend to rely on shared knowledge that does not need to be explained to an interviewer, also arises from their failure to follow well-established procedures in focus group research. The problem here is that their focus group participants were already acquainted through their involvement in the same drug treatment program. Agar and MacDonald complain against the "rule" requiring strangers in focus groups, but they fail to grasp that focus group participants who do not know each other will make their "folk knowledge" explicit as they explore the range of opinions and experiences the other participants bring to the group. Focus group researchers have well-developed procedures for dealing with "folk knowledge" and "indexed talk," such as encouraging participants to explore the degree of consensus and diversity in the group by first "sharing" and then "comparing" their opinions and experiences (Morgan 1997). What is lacking is a conceptual framework for discussing these issues, so Agar and MacDonald's ability to pinpoint and examine issues related to folk knowledge is quite useful. This seems to be a case where individual and group interviewing have different ways of reaching the same goal, but research on individual interviews has gone farther in developing concepts that could be beneficial in focus groups as well.

The third point that Agar and MacDonald make concerns the need for detailed analysis of transcripts that capture some of the basic features of interaction in focus groups, such as pauses, overlapping speech, and "back-channel" responses (hmm, unh-hunh, yeah, and so on). I do not dispute the idea that this kind of analysis can offer certain advantages. I do, however, disagree with the assertion that only focus groups would benefit from the analysis of interaction. In fact, Agar and MacDonald

(1995) present only the bare text in their examples from individual interviews and justify this practice on the grounds that they "are no longer analyzing interaction" (p. 83). Even if group and individual interviews differ in their basic forms of interaction, there is still much to be learned from a comparative analysis of the kinds of interaction that they do share—such as starting a conversation, encouraging some responses and not others, and managing shifts in topic (see Schaeffer and Maynard, Chapter 28, this volume). Although Agar and MacDonald treat the need to analyze interaction as something that divides individual and group interviewing, I believe that it creates an opportunity for more dialogue between the two methods.

Overall, considering Agar and MacDonald's claims both reinforces some of the well-established principles behind why social science researchers do focus groups the way they do and calls some of those procedures into question. On the one hand, the mistakes that Agar and MacDonald made provide a cautionary tale against importing the assumptions associated with individual interviews into focus groups. On the other hand, some of their "mistakes" produced interesting data, and their efforts to understand the differences between the methods demonstrate a set of conceptual frameworks and analytic techniques that will be new to most focus group researchers. Viewed from this perspective, this encounter between group and individual interviewing does indeed serve the larger purpose of making social scientists aware of the need for both change and continuity in the ways they use their methods.

As I noted at the beginning of this chapter, the experience that social scientists already had with individual interviewing could have helped them in developing more innovative approaches to focus groups. Sadly, this possibility has been blocked by the need to address the kinds of issues that dominate this section. Further, the need to answer charges about the value of group interviewing has produced a de-

gree of defensiveness in focus group researchers. The need to justify the reasons for doing focus groups not only diverts energy that could have gone into innovation, it reinforces a reliance on tried-and-true procedures for doing group interviews. Instead of arguing about the supposed superiority or inferiority of either method, social science researchers would do better to channel their energies into understanding both the differences and the similarities between these two forms of interviewing.

Underlying several of the specific points discussed in this section has been the claim that many of the differences between focus groups and individual interviews in the social sciences arise from the different purposes that guide their use. It may be that these two methods will maintain their current division of labor, with more reliance on focus groups for relatively limited, applied projects and greater use of individual interviewing for studies that require more depth and detail. Even if these different roles do persist, researchers need to avoid the conclusion that this difference arises solely from the inherent strengths or weaknesses of either method. Instead, it is important to recognize that both methods can be adapted to serve a wide variety of purposes, and that the dominant direction that each has taken may be largely a result of historical circumstances.

◆ Finding New Directions

Paying serious attention to the argument that methods are shaped by the social and historical contexts in which they are used creates the possibility of revising and reinventing research methods. But doing so requires a reflexive awareness of why researchers use their methods in the ways that they do. As I noted at the outset, the very newness of focus groups in the social sciences presents an unusual opportunity in this regard, because this field has not yet felt the full weight of tradition. Hence I will devote my concluding comments to ways that future researchers can both build on existing knowledge about focus groups and create new ways of using focus groups.

CREATING CONTINUITY

Continuity does not just exist, it has to be created. The self-evident manner in which this occurs is through the unquestioned acceptance of existing assumptions. The most important way in which social scientists justify their procedures is through methodological research, so that they can offer evidence rather than tradition as the basis for their work. So it is not surprising that a group of social scientists who considered "future directions for focus groups" (Morgan 1993) came to the conclusion that the field needs a program of research on focus groups. The goal of that research would be to produce a better understanding of the difference it makes to do focus groups one way rather than another.

This kind of methodological work is beginning to appear (see the review in Morgan 1996), but it remains scattered and idiosyncratic. One major factor that limits such work is the difficulty of assessing outcomes. It is easy to design focus groups that vary in size or moderating style or mixed versus homogeneous composition, but what is the best way to characterize the differences that might result from these variations in research design? One promising set of tools for addressing this issue is based on earlier work in discourse analysis (Potter and Wetherell 1987). I refer to this as an "expanded version of discourse analysis," because most of the work that has applied this approach to focus groups has been relatively eclectic. For example, Greg Myers (1998) describes his method of analysis as a blend of conversation analysis, linguistically based discourse analysis, and the study of argument. What all of these approaches have in common is the same kind of close analysis of transcribed conversations that Agar and MacDonald (1995) recommend.

Consider three articles that illustrate this approach. Myers (1998) investigated both the ways that moderators handle the work of closing off versus extending exchanges among participants and the ways that participants can express disagreement without threatening group dynamics. Claudia Puchta and Jonathan Potter (1999) examined the perennial challenge of keeping a group on track while simultaneously encouraging open conversation, and their analysis shows how moderators managed this problem by elaborating on basic questions in ways that gave participants multiple options about how to respond. Finally, Myers and Phil Macnaughten (1999) researched the ways that participants created transitions between topics as well as the ways that the moderator's back-channel utterances influenced the group interaction.

It should be evident how this kind of work could help us to assess the potential effects of different ways of doing focus groups. For example, earlier in this chapter I mentioned my own preference for a moderating style that encourages a process of "sharing and comparing" among focus group participants (Morgan 1997:20, 1998a:12). In my own moderating, I have a series of things that I do to encourage the process of sharing and comparing, including the opening instructions that I give, the kinds of questions I use, and the way that I manage my own interaction with the participants. Through an expanded version of discourse analysis, it should be possible to find out which of these things really work. In fact, I believe that all interviewers have at least implicit explanations for why they conduct their interviews in the ways that they do, so discourse analysis is a way to find out whether the things that interviewers do truly make a difference.

I want to be clear, however, that I am advocating these tools primarily as ways to assess what happens during focus groups. Some of the articles cited above make the case for this expanded version of discourse analysis as a general-purpose approach to analyzing focus groups and other forms of interviews, but I believe that this remains an open question. Most of these authors readily admit that this sort of detailed analysis takes a great deal of time, and some of those who have tried it have found that the substantive returns simply did not justify the effort required (e.g., Gamson 1992). As with any method, researchers will have to decide on a case-by-case basis whether discourse analysis meets their needs. There is already, however, a strong case that these tools can help determine how specific research design decisions affect what actually happens in focus groups (see Schaeffer and Maynard, Chapter 28, this volume).

Discourse analysis is certainly not a panacea when it comes to researching the things that happen in focus groups. It does, however, offer researchers a way to get started on a program of research about focus groups. Perhaps the results will show that marketing researchers were right all along—that the traditions social scientists borrowed from that field really are the procedures that work most consistently. More likely, social science researchers will discover that the established techniques represent good "typical case" solutions, but there are also a variety of circumstances in which other ways of doing things are more useful.

ENCOURAGING INNOVATION

It should be obvious that the same tools that make it possible to examine existing procedures in focus groups can be just as useful for the assessment of proposed innovations. But it is one thing to assess the value of innovative ways to do focus groups and quite another to find those new approaches. Fortunately, there is a great deal of naturally occurring variation in the use of focus groups, so what amounts to standard practice in one part of the field can seem quite innovative elsewhere.

One promising example of this naturally occurring variation is the recent appearance of several articles describing the use of focus groups in participatory action research, most notably in a collection edited by Rosaline Barbour and Jenny Kitzinger (1999). There are many ways in which participatory action research differs from the typical project where the research team collects data from the participants and then departs; for present purposes, however, the most important difference lies in the relationships that unite the researchers and the participants. This basic modification of the research setting has implications for nearly every aspect of focus group research. For example, what does "recruitment" mean in this context, and does it even make sense to use "questions" as the basis for discussions that encourage empowerment? Certainly the moderating style in participatory action focus groups must be different from leading either structured or unstructured discussions for other purposes.

It would be nice to have answers to these questions, but at this point nearly all of the published articles on participatory action focus groups are devoted to the general merits of this approach. This lack of methodological detail is understandable in a form of research that is driven by its action orientation. Yet once the value of focus groups for participatory action research is well established, that should motivate the appearance of "how-to" articles specific to that field. When that happens, focus group researchers outside the field will also be able to benefit from these innovations. It may be the case that some of the procedures in participatory action research focus groups are context-bound and thus unlikely to find uses outside that field, but, with any luck, some of these procedures will be useful across a variety of contexts.

Participatory action research is, of course, just one example of how the field as a whole can benefit by borrowing procedures that were developed elsewhere. Cross-cultural variations in focus groups are another source of procedures that are well established in one setting but innovative in another. A British student in one of my focus group workshops taught me a valuable lesson in this regard. After I drew a diagram of a "typical" focus group setup, with the moderator and participants seated around a table, she wanted to know, "What's all this business about a table? I've done lots of focus groups, and we never use a table." True enough, it seems that focus groups in Britain emerged from a media-oriented form of marketing that relied on "living room discussions," where a group of neighbors would watch a television program together and then discuss it afterward (Lunt and Livingstone 1996). Consequently, British focus groups are more likely to be conducted in homes or home-like settings (for a comparable example from the United States, see Gamson 1992).

Cross-cultural variations on focus groups are not limited to the use of tables or viewing rooms with one-way mirrors. Over the years, I have heard any number of anecdotes about how focus group procedures have been adapted to both Western and non-Western cultures. What is lacking, however, is any systematic investigation of these naturally occurring innovations. Beyond simple descriptions of the variations, there needs to be an explanation of *why* things were done one way rather than another. Once other researchers understand the purpose that a particular procedure is supposed to serve, this can stimulate their methodological imaginations to think of other ways to use that innovation.

I want to close with a particularly radical suggestion. Social scientists need to go back to marketing and find out more about why they do the things they do. Although social scientists borrowed many of their current approaches to focus groups from marketing, there has been remarkably little continuing contact between the two fields. This creates a substantial opportunity for innovation. In making renewed contacts with marketing approaches to focus groups, social scientists should expect to have their own assumptions challenged, but that kind of learning is one of the great advantages of "cross-cultural contact."

As this reference to marketing should make clear, these recommendations for developments in group interviewing return to the original spirit of innovation that accompanied the migration of focus groups into the social sciences. Just as social scientists in the 1980s responded to the basic appeal of focus groups, current practitioners should be equally enthusiastic about locating new ways to do group interviews. The goal should be not only to use this method, but to develop it as well.

■ *References*

Agar, M. H. and J. MacDonald. 1995. "Focus Groups and Ethnography." *Human Organization* 54:78-86.

Andreason, A. 1995. *Marketing Social Change: Changing Behaviors to Promote Health, Social Development, and the Environment.* San Francisco: Jossey-Bass.

Barbour, R. S. and J. Kitzinger, eds. 1999. *Developing Focus Group Research: Politics, Theory and Practice.* London: Sage.

Basch, C. E. 1987. "Focus Group Interview: An Underutilized Research Technique for Improving Theory and Practice in Health Education." *Health Education Quarterly* 14:411-48.

Campbell, D. T. 1969. "Reforms as Experiments." *American Psychologist* 24:409-29

Carey, M. A. 1995. "Issues and Applications of Focus Groups: Introduction." *Qualitative Health Research* 5:413.

Converse, J. M. 1987. *Survey Research in the United States: Roots and Emergence, 1890-1960.* Berkeley: University of California Press.

Cunningham-Burley, S., A. Kerr, and S. Pavis. 1999. "Theorizing Subjects and Subject Matter in Focus Group Research." Pp. 186-99 in *Developing Focus Group Research: Politics, Theory and Practice,* edited by R. S. Barbour and J. Kitzinger. London: Sage.

Denzin, N. K. and Y. S. Lincoln, eds. 1994. *Handbook of Qualitative Research*. Thousand Oaks, CA: Sage.

Folch-Lyon, E., L. de la Macorra, and S. B. Schearer. 1981. "Focus Group and Survey Research on Family Planning in Mexico." *Studies in Family Planning* 12:409-32.

Fowler, F. J., Jr. 1995. *Improving Survey Questions: Design and Evaluation*. Thousand Oaks, CA: Sage.

Frey, J. H. and A. Fontana. 1991. "The Group Interview in Social Research." *Social Science Journal* 28:175-87.

Gamson, W. A. 1992. *Talking Politics*. New York: Cambridge University Press.

Hayes, T. J. and C. B. Tatham. 1989. *Focus Group Interviews: A Reader*. 2d ed. Chicago: American Marketing Association.

Johnson, A. 1996. "It's Good to Talk." *Sociological Review* 44:517-38.

Joseph, J. G., C. A. Emmons, R. C. Kessler, C. B. Wortman, K. J. O'Brien, W. T. Hocker, and C. Schaefer. 1984. "Coping with the Threat of AIDS: An Approach to Psychosocial Assessment." *American Psychologist* 39:1297-1302.

Kahn, M. E. and L. Manderson. 1992. "Focus Groups in Tropical Diseases Research." *Health Policy Planning* 7:56-66.

Kitzinger, J. 1994. "The Methodology of Focus Groups: The Importance of Interaction between Research Participants." *Sociology of Health and Illness* 16:103-21.

Knodel, J. 1993. "The Design and Analysis of Focus Group Studies: A Practical Approach." Pp. 35-50 in *Successful Focus Groups: Advancing the State of the Art*, edited by D. L. Morgan. Newbury Park, CA: Sage.

———. 1995. "Focus Groups as a Method for Cross-Cultural Research in Social Gerontology." *Journal of Cross-Cultural Gerontology* 10:7-20.

Krueger, R. A. 1988. *Focus Groups: A Practical Guide for Applied Research*. Newbury Park, CA: Sage.

———. 1994. *Focus Groups: A Practical Guide for Applied Research*. 2d ed. Thousand Oaks, CA: Sage.

Lincoln, Y. S. and E. G. Guba. 1985. *Naturalistic Inquiry*. Beverly Hills, CA: Sage.

Lunt, P. and S. M. Livingstone. 1996. "Rethinking the Focus Group in Media and Communications Research." *Journal of Communication* 46(2):79-98.

McQuarrie, E. F. 1990. "Review of Morgan, *Focus Groups as Qualitative Research*, and McCracken, *The Long Interview*." *Journal of Marketing Research* 13:114-17.

———. 1996. *The Market Research Toolbox: A Concise Guide for Beginners*. Thousand Oaks, CA: Sage.

Merton, R. K., M. Fiske, and P. L. Kendall. 1990. *The Focused Interview: A Manual of Problems and Procedures*. 2d ed. New York: Free Press.

Morgan, D. L. 1988. *Focus Groups as Qualitative Research*. Newbury Park, CA: Sage.

———. 1989. "Adjusting to Widowhood: Do Social Networks Really Make It Easier?" *Gerontologist* 29:101-7.

———. 1993. "Future Directions for Focus Groups." In *Successful Focus Groups: Advancing the State of the Art*, edited by D. L. Morgan. Newbury Park, CA: Sage.

———. 1995. "Why Things (Sometimes) Go Wrong in Focus Groups." *Qualitative Health Research* 5:515-22.

———. 1996. "Focus Groups." *Annual Review of Sociology* 22:129-52.

———. 1997. *Focus Groups as Qualitative Research*. 2d ed. Thousand Oaks, CA: Sage.

———. 1998a. *The Focus Groups Guidebook*. Thousand Oaks, CA: Sage.

———. 1998b. *Planning Focus Groups*. Thousand Oaks, CA: Sage.

Morgan, D. L. and R. A. Krueger. 1993. "When to Use Focus Groups and Why." Pp. 3-19 in *Successful Focus Groups: Advancing the State of the Art*, edited by D. L. Morgan. Newbury Park, CA: Sage.

Morgan, D. L. and M. T. Spanish. 1984. "Focus Groups: A New Tool for Qualitative Research." *Qualitative Sociology* 7:253-70.

Morgan, D. L. and P. Z. Zhao. 1993. "The Doctor-Caregiver Relationship: Managing the Care of Family Members with Alzheimer's Disease." *Qualitative Health Research* 3:133-16.

Myers, G. 1998. "Displaying Opinions: Topics and Disagreement in Focus Groups." *Language in Society* 27:85-111.

Myers, G. and P. Macnaughten. 1999. "Can Focus Groups Be Analysed as Talk?" Pp. 173-85 in *Developing Focus Group Research: Politics, Theory and Practice,* edited by R. S. Barbour and J. Kitzinger. London: Sage.

Patton, M. Q. 1990. *Qualitative Evaluation and Research Methods.* 2d ed. Newbury Park, CA: Sage.

Platt, J. 1996. *A History of Sociological Research Methods in America: 1920-1960.* Cambridge: Cambridge University Press.

Potter, J. and M. Wetherell. 1987. *Discourse and Social Psychology: Beyond Attitudes and Behaviour.* London: Sage.

Puchta, C. and J. Potter. 1999. "Asking Elaborate Questions: Focus Groups and the Management of Spontaneity." *Journal of Sociolinguistics* 3:314-35.

Rogers, E. M. 1994. *A History of Communication Study: A Biographical Approach.* New York: Free Press.

Wight, D. 1994. "Boys' Thoughts and Talk about Sex in a Working-Class Locality of Glasgow." *Sociological Review* 42:702-37.

8

POSTMODERN TRENDS IN INTERVIEWING

◆ Andrea Fontana

Postmodernism has changed our society, the way in which we conceive of it, and the way we see ourselves and relate to others. Whether we consider postmodernism a radical break from modernism or merely modernism's continuation, profound changes have occurred (see Best and Kellner 1991; Dickens and Fontana 1994). We are no longer awed by metatheories about the nature of society and the self (Lyotard 1984), theories that we now question and deconstruct. Today, we focus on smaller parcels of knowledge; we study society in its fragments, in its daily details (Silverman 1997). Postmodernism has affected many fields, from architecture to literary criticism, from anthropology to sociology. It has provided few answers but raised more questions, rendering the reality of the world extremely problematic. Postmodernism also has changed the very nature of experience. The everyday world and the world of media have been merged (Baudrillard 1983), and as the boundaries

between the two have collapsed, experience is mediated by the "hyperreality" of the likes of Disneyland, *Real TV*, and *The Jerry Springer Show*, where the imaginary becomes real and the real imaginary (see Denzin, Chapter 40, this volume).

Influenced by postmodern epistemologies, interviewing also has changed; ours has become "the interview society" (Silverman 1993; Atkinson and Silverman 1997). Interviewing is no longer reserved for social researchers or investigative reporters, but has become the very stuff of life as members of society spend much of their time asking questions, being asked questions themselves, or watching TV shows about people being asked questions and answering them in turn. They all seem to have routine knowledge of the rules of interviewing, with no need for instruction.

In this chapter, I discuss postmodern trends in interviewing. I begin by outlining some of the postmodern sensibilities that are relevant to interviewing. Although there is no such a thing as postmodern interviewing per se, postmodern epistemologies have profoundly influenced our understanding of the interview process, so that approaches increasingly take on a postmodern cast. Perhaps it is appropriate, then, given that postmodernism advocates the blurring and fragmentation of theories and methods, that I can present only fragments of postmodern-informed interviewing rather than an overarching, modernistic formulation of "the" postmodern interview.[1]

◆ Postmodernism and Its Influence

Postmodernism, which is not a unified system of beliefs, has been presented and interpreted in a diversity of ways. It can be seen as a crisis of representation in a great variety of fields, from the arts to the sciences, and more generally in society at large (Dickens and Fontana 1994). It has been conceptualized both as the continuation of modernism and as a break from it. In some views, postmodernism advocates abandoning overarching paradigms and theoretical and methodological metasystems (Lyotard 1984). Postmodernism questions traditional assumptions and deconstructs them (Derrida 1972); that is, it shows the ambiguity and contextuality of meaning. It proposes that, in the name of grand theorizing, we have suppressed this ambiguity in favor of a single interpretation, which is commonly touted as "the truth," rather than a choice among many possible truths. Postmodernism orients to theorizing and, indeed, to society itself, not as a monolithic structure but as a series of fragments in continuous flux. It persuades us to turn our attention to these fragments, to the minute events of everyday life, seeking to understand them in their own right rather than gloss over differences and patch them together into paradigmatic wholes (Silverman 1997).

POSTMODERN SENSIBILITIES AND INTERVIEWING

Postmodern sensibilities have greatly affected the methodologies used by social scientists. Researchers influenced by a postmodern agenda have come to display a greatly heightened sensitivity to problems and concerns that previously had been glossed over or scantily addressed. These can be briefly described as follows:

◆ The boundaries between, and respective roles, of interviewer and interviewee have become blurred as the traditional relationship between the two is no longer seen as natural (see Ellis and Berger, Chapter 41, this volume).

◆ New forms of communication in interviewing are being used, as interviewer and respondent(s) collaborate together in constructing their narratives.

◆ Interviewers have become more concerned about issues of representation, seriously engaging questions such as, Whose story are we telling and for what purpose?

◆ The authority of the researcher qua interviewer but also qua writer comes under scrutiny (see Briggs, Chapter 44, this volume). Respondents are no longer seen as faceless numbers whose opinions we process completely on our own terms. Consequently, there is increasing concern with the respondent's own understanding as he or she frames and represents an "opinion."

◆ Traditional patriarchal relations in interviewing are being criticized, and ways to make formerly unarticulated voices audible are now center stage.

◆ The forms used to report findings have been hugely expanded. As boundaries separating disciplines collapse, modes of expression from literature, poetry, and drama are being applied (see in this volume Ellis and Berger, Chapter 41; Richardson, Chapter 42; Rosenblatt, Chapter 43).

◆ The topic of inquiry—interviewing—has expanded to encompass the cinematic and the televisual. Electronic media are increasingly accepted as a resource in interviews, with growing use of e-mail, Internet chat rooms, and other electronic modes of communication (see in this volume Mann and Stewart, Chapter 29; Denzin, Chapter 40).

These sensibilities, some of which are now old and some new, provide a context for methodological exploration. Let us consider, initially, how these have informed and affected traditional interview roles. Note, especially, that some ostensibly postmodern trends have been close to the heart of qualitative inquiry for decades (see in this volume Warren, Chapter 4; Johnson, Chapter 5).

◆ From Traditional to Postmodern-Informed Interviewing

Traditional, structured interviewing establishes a priori categories and then asks pre-established questions aimed at capturing precise data that can be categorized, codified, and generalized (see Singleton and Straits, Chapter 3, this volume). The aim is to provide explanations about the social world. The method assumes that there is a set of discreet facts to be apprehended in the social world and that we can garner them through the use of rigorous techniques. The language of science permeates these techniques. The interviewer is not unlike a highly trained instrument and remains substantively detached from the situation and the respondent. Responses are quantifiable and allow generalizations

about society. Ideally, respondents can be viewed as "rational beings" in that they understand all possible choices presented to them and answer as comprehensively and truthfully as possible.

CRITIQUES OF THE DETACHED INTERVIEWER

Some critics claim that the method of traditional interviewing is much more like science fiction than science, a perspective that has not been lost on qualitative researchers. Herbert Blumer (1969), for one, prefaces the introduction of his book *Symbolic Interactionism* with an insightful critique of traditional methodologies. The seminal work of Aaron Cicourel also is a milestone in unveiling the myth of "scientific" interviewing. Cicourel (1964) refers to the hidden complexity of the interview situation:

> All social research includes an unknown number of implicit decisions which are not mirrored in the measurement procedures used. The abstraction process required to describe a set of properties, regardless of the measurement system, automatically imposes some amount of reification. (P. 80)

Discussing and quoting the work of Herbert Hyman and other survey researchers, Cicourel adds, "The authors are not aware that too much stress has been placed on asking questions and recording answers, and that the interviewer is overlooking . . . the many judgments *he made* in the process" (p. 91). Cicourel goes on to suggest that the interview is an interactional event based on reciprocal stocks of knowledge, a point I shall take up again in discussing phenomenological influences on postmodern trends.

The response of interactionist sociologists to problems inherent in structured interviewing was to move interviewers center stage as constructive agents and acknowledge their influence on interview outcomes. They also recognized the importance of feelings on the part of both the interviewer and the respondent, as well as the possibility of deceit in the interview situation. Jack Douglas (1985), in his book *Creative Interviewing,* advocates lengthy, unstructured interviews in which the interviewer uses his or her *personal* skills by adapting to the changing interactional situation of the interview. For Douglas, the creativity is cultivated by the interviewer, who attempts inventively to reach a mutual understanding and intimacy of feelings with the interviewee. Still, it has been pointed out that the interviewee remains a rather passive participant even in this context. Jaber Gubrium and James Holstein (1997; Holstein and Gubrium 1995) consider Douglas's interviewing techniques decidedly "romantic." As they explain, "Douglas imagines his subject, like the image implicit in survey research, to be a repository of answers, but in his case, the subject is a well guarded vessel of feelings not simply a collection of attitudes and opinions" (Gubrium and Holstein 1997:65).

EMERGING VOICES OF INTERVIEWEES

In the 1980s, new trends appeared in qualitative sociology, in both ethnography and interviewing, as researchers attempted to secure the constructive voices of research subjects. Some were concerned with the authorial voice of the researcher speaking for his or her subjects (Van Maanen 1988; Geertz 1988); others took a broader epistemological approach (Marcus and Fischer 1986).

George Marcus and Michael Fischer (1986) gave widely appreciated special attention to these issues. Marcus and Fischer were concerned with the authority of traditional ethnographic texts, commonly derived through a combination of ethnographic work and in-depth interviews. They also addressed problems of representation and selectivity generated by the privileged position of the researcher both as a field-worker and as an author. Marcus and Fischer felt that in "modernistic" interviewing, the researcher is in control of the narrative and highlights what best conveys, in his or her judgment, the social worlds of those being studied (see the discussion of "representational rights" in Briggs, Chapter 44, this volume).

Marcus and Fischer present postmodern alternatives in anthropology that allow diverse voices to come through. Some of these alternatives apply to interviewing as well as to ethnography. One is the need to take a "dialogic" approach, in which the focus is "on the dialogue between anthropologist and informant as a way of exposing how ethnographic knowledge develops" (Marcus and Fischer 1986:69). An exemplar of this work is Kevin Dwyer's (1982) *Moroccan Dialogues,* in which the interviews are only minimally edited and show the problematic nature of interviewing for all participants. Another is the use of "polyphony," which is "the registering of different points of views in multiple voices" (Marcus and Fischer 1986:71). The aim here is to reduce the editorial authority of the researcher. Another alternative is found in Vincent Crapanzano's (1980) ethnography *Tuhami: Portrait of a Moroccan,* where the author presents transcripts from interviews and minimizes his interpretation of them, inviting the reader to help in the process of interpretation. This is rendered more difficult by the informant, Tuhami, who uses complex metaphors in his communication with the researcher, mixing real events with fantasy, both of which Crapanzano takes as valid data.

In sociological work we find similar trends. Susan Krieger (1983) focuses on polyphony by presenting the various perspectives of respondents, highlighting discrepancies and problems rather than minimizing them. Allen Shelton (1995), in a study of victimization, social process, and resistance, uses the machine and other powerful metaphors to convey his message.

He mixes sociological data with stories from his past, using visual imagery from paintings to underscore his points. In another context, Shelton (1996) even goes back to the vespers to compellingly embellish his sociological findings.

Norman Denzin's work is a major impetus for applying postmodern sensibilities to research methodology (see Denzin, Chapter 40, this volume). Denzin (1989) focuses on "the meanings persons give to themselves and their life projects" (pp. 14-15). Key elements of the approach are the essentially *interpretive* nature of fieldwork and interviewing and the attempt to let the members *speak for themselves.* In particular, Denzin borrows the concept of epiphanies from James Joyce and orients to these as turning points that reshape people's lives, which, in turn, have significant implications for the selection of interview topics. By focusing on these existential moments, Denzin believes, we can gain access to the otherwise hidden feelings experienced by individuals and bring them to the fore for others to appreciate.

Denzin (1997) continues his dialogue with postmodernism in more recent work, but becomes more distinctly partisan. Here, again, he begins with Joyce and the concern for meaning as perceived by the members of society. However, he is no longer happy with just trying to understand and make these meanings visible. He has become more politically involved with his research subjects. He rejects the traditional canons of researcher noninvolvement and objectivity, and instead advocates "partnership" between researcher and subjects. He is especially partial to subjects' "underdog" status: "This model seeks to produce narratives that ennoble human experiences while facilitating civic transformation in the public (and private) spheres" (p. 277).

In summary, one path from traditional to postmodern-informed interviewing is that the so-called detached researcher and interviewer are recast as active agents in the interview process and attempts are made to deprivilege their agency. Another path is that the interviewee's agency is privileged and, in the name of the interviewee, all manner of experimentation is undertaken to make evident his or her own sense of identity and representational practices. I turn now to the influences of various theoretical perspectives on this trend; following that, I will consider how this has affected representational practices for interview material.

◆ Phenomenologically Informed Interviews

Phenomenological sociology first appeared in the 1960s, loosely based on the philosophy of Edmund Husserl and the writings of the social philosopher Alfred Schutz. It is in Cicourel's (1964) work that we see the tie between phenomenology and interviewing most clearly, even as in Harold Garfinkel's (1967) own project there is an added phenomenological influence through ethnomethodology.

Cicourel argues forcefully early on that the interview, no matter how technically perfected its execution, is grounded in the world of commonsense thinking (see Schaeffer and Maynard, Chapter 28, this volume). In fact, according to Cicourel, it must be so, for without the participants' ability to share common or overlapping social worlds and their related communicative understanding, the interview would not be possible. Cicourel follows in Schutz's (1962, 1964, 1966) footsteps here. Schutz discusses the way that members of society share a common stock of knowledge that allows them to understand and reciprocate actions. This extends to markedly mundane and shared knowledge, such as speaking in the same language, knowing that the sun will set, that peanut butter will stick to the roof of your mouth, that the Chicago Cubs will never win the World Series, and that Pamela Anderson's beauty is surgically enhanced.

Years later, following postmodern trends, Irving Seidman resurrects Schutz's sentiments in his book *Interviewing as Qualitative Research* (1991). Seidman explains that by establishing an "I-thou" relationship or reciprocity of perspectives, the interviewee (I) and the interviewer (thou) form a personal relationship. The result is that the interviewee is no longer objectified but becomes a comember of a communicative partnership. In fact, in some instances, this may blossom into a full "we" relationship, according to Seidman (for an example, see Denzin's 1997 model of "collaboration").

Robert Dingwall (1997) seems to be rediscovering these sentiments when he states:

> If the interview is a social encounter, then, logically, it must be analyzed in the same way as any other social encounter. The products of an interview are the outcome of a socially situated activity where the responses are passed through the role-playing and impression management of both the interviewer and the respondent. (P. 56)

Dingwall adds elements of Goffman's dramaturgical view to the basic notions, which he attributes to both Mead and Schutz. Both within and outside of the interview, action is mediated by others' responses and their co-contingent dramatic realizations. According to Dingwall, individuals in interviews provide organizing accounts; that is, they turn the helter-skelter, fragmented process of everyday life into coherent explanations, thus cocreating a situationally cohesive sense of reality.

ETHNOMETHODOLOGICAL IMPULSES

Ethnomethodologists put forward similar sentiments. They share a skeptical approach to standardized methodologies. Garfinkel (1967), for one, informs us that we cannot study social interaction except in relation to the interactive methods employed by social actors themselves to create and maintain their sense of reality. As such, the impulse in interview research would be to attend as much to *how* participants assemble their respective communications as to *what* is asked and answered (Boden and Zimmerman 1991; Maynard et al. 2001).

Recently, Holstein and Gubrium (1995) have directly linked ethnomethodology with these distinctive questions in their discussion of the "active interview." They specifically apply to interviewing the perspective that the interview is a social production between interviewer and respondent. In other words, it entails collaborative construction between two *active* parties. Because the interview is situationally and contextually produced, it is itself a site for knowledge production, rather than simply a neutral conduit for experiential knowledge, as traditionally believed.

Holstein and Gubrium are further inspired by the ethnomethodological distinction between *topics* (substantive elements of inquiry) and *resources* (procedures used to study the topics) (see Zimmerman and Pollner 1970). They point out that, in interviews, researchers focus too much on the *whats*, or substantive foreground, and tend to gloss over the *hows*, which "refer to the interactional, narrative procedures of knowledge production, not merely to interview techniques" (p. 4). Indeed, given the irremediably collaborative and constructed nature of the interview, a postmodern sentiment would behoove us to pay more attention to the *hows*, that is, to try to understand the biographical, contextual, historical, and institutional elements that are brought to the interview and used by both parties. The interview should be understood in light all of these elements, rather than as a discreet, neutral set of questions and ensuing responses, detached from both the interviewer's and the respondent's constructive and culturally informed agency.

Gubrium and Holstein (1998) continue this line of thinking in a discussion of personal narratives. Their point of departure is the argument that life comes to us in the form of stories, and personal narratives are approached as individualized constructions. In conveying life to us, respondents tell us stories about themselves, but they do not do so in a social vacuum (see Atkinson, Chapter 6, this volume). Rather, as Gubrium and Holstein explain, "personal accounts are built up from experience and actively cast in the terms of preferred vocabularies" (p. 164; compare Garfinkel 1967). A postmodern trend emphasizing social construction is evident in their goal: "We want to make visible the way narrative activities play out in everyday practice to both produce coherence and reveal difference" (p. 165).

Others share similar perspectives. The late Madan Sarup (1996), in analyzing the role of narrative in the construction of identity, distinguishes two parts to each narrative: "The story is the 'what' of the narrative, the discourse is the 'how' " (p. 170). And more: "When we talk about our identity and our life-story, we include some things and exclude others, we stress some things and subordinate others" (p. 16). Although Sarup's focus is identity, the message is much the same—the story (and its identities) is constructed in its communicative unfolding.

Dingwall (1997) takes this impulse further. Following Garfinkel, he states that interviews are "an occasion for the elicitation of *accounts*" and that "accounting is how we build a stable order in social encounters and in society" (pp. 56, 57). Applying this to interviews, Dingwall concludes: "An interview is a point at which order is deliberately put under stress. It is a situation in which respondents are required to demonstrate their competence in the role in which the interview casts them" (p. 58). Once more, we are directed to the collaborative production of contextually based accounts.

◆ Feminist Influences

In analyzing the images of a nude man with his arm raised in greeting and a nude woman imprinted on the *Pioneer* spacecraft, Craig Owens (1983) states: "For in this (Lacanian) image, chosen to represent the inhabitants of Earth for the extraterrestrial Other, it is the man who speaks, who represents mankind. The woman is only represented; she is (as always) already spoken for" (p. 61). It has been much the same in the methodological world of interviewing; women have always already been spoken for in the very structure of the traditional interview. This is exemplified in Earl Babbie's (1992) classic text on research, which has nothing to say about gender differences in interviewing. Indeed, as Carol Warren (1988) reports, female researchers in primitive patriarchal societies were, at times, temporarily "promoted" to the role of male in order to be allowed to witness events and ceremonies from which women were traditionally excluded (see Ryen, Chapter 17, this volume).

Not any longer. One of the significant influences on the postmodern trends in interviewing comes from feminist quarters (see Hertz 1997). An ongoing concern has been the elastic subject position of the respondent. A leading question here, for example, is, Do women always speak as women, or are other important subject positions part of their response repertoires? If feminists have focused on gender differences, they have not ignored other important factors, such as race.[2] For instance, Kim Marie Vaz (1997) has edited an interdisciplinary book about African and African American women to "unearth" their experiences by telling personal portraits, focusing on how both their gender and their race have affected them. Patricia Hill Collins (1990) uses interviews as well as autobiographical accounts, songs, images, and fiction to bring out the viewpoints of black women. Her interviews are hardly "detached," as they are shaped to provide a sympathetic context for making visible the experiences of being both black and women.

Kath Weston (1998) explores another traditionally silenced subjectivity, sexual nonconformity. As she recounts, "Back in graduate school, when I first decided to study lesbians and gay men in the United States, the faculty members who mentored me pronounced the project 'academic suicide' " (p. 190). Weston persevered nevertheless and, in her book *Long Slow Burn* (1998) she rejects the idea that sexuality is merely a sociological specialization; rather, she considers sexuality as being at the often silent heart of the social sciences, deeply implicating the subject. We infer from this that the interview that realizes alternative sexualities can serve to reveal the sexual contours of all subject positions (see Kong, Mahoney, and Plummer, Chapter 12, this volume).

Contrary to the traditional belief that the relation between interviewer and interviewee is neutral and the results of the interview can be treated as independent of the interview process as long as the interviewer is methodologically skilled, gender-consciousness changes the nature of interview results (Denzin 1989). Seidman (1991) shares this view:

> All the problems that one can associate with sexist gender relationships can be played out in an interview. Males interviewing females can be overbearing. Women interviewing men can sometimes be reluctant to control the focus of the interview. Male participants can be too easily dismissive of female interviewers. (P. 78)

If we are to overcome these and other potential problems, the traditional relationship between interviewer and interviewee must change, according to many feminists. The two must become equal partners in a negotiated dialogue. The woman/interviewee should be allowed to express herself freely. Rather than saying or implying, "Answer my question, but don't tell me anything else," interviewers should indeed encourage all respondents to express their feelings, their fears, and their doubts. As Kathryn Anderson and Dana Jack (1991) explain, "If we want to know what women feel about their lives, then we have to allow them to talk about their feelings as well as their activities" (p. 15).

Hertz (1997) urges us to blur the distinction between the interviewer and the respondent. As the interviewer comes to realize that she is an active participant in the interview, she must become reflexive, acknowledge who she is in the interview, what she brings it, and how the interview gets negotiated and constructed in the process. Doing so will alleviate an associated reification of methodological problems. But we need to go beyond methodology, as Hertz points out, to face the ethical problems associated with how much we are willing to become partners and disclose about ourselves (also see Behar 1996). As we turn the interviewee from a faceless member of a category to a person, how much should we divulge about her? How do we maintain her anonymity? Ruth Behar (1996) poses the matter succinctly: "Are there limits—of respect, piety, pathos—that should not be crossed, even to leave a record? But if you can't stop the horror, shouldn't you at least document it?" (p. 2).

A related ethical problem stems from researchers' traditional custom of using interviewees to gather material for their own purposes. As Daphne Patai (1987) explains, no matter how well-intentioned researchers are, if they use interview materials exclusively for their own purposes, they are exploiting the women they interview (Oakley 1981; Reinharz 1992; Smith 1987). As a result, some interviewers take the notion of partnership one step further and become advocates for those they interview (Gluck 1991); others turn interview narratives into political acts as they uncover the injustices to which those studies are subjected (Denzin 1999a).

◆ Virtual Interviewing

For traditional interviewing, the transition to the Internet would seem flawless, moving from telephone questionnaires to the use of e-mail, chat rooms, and Web sites. In one way or another, all of these remain "distant" interviewing, with little or no face-to-face contact. If only about 50 percent of American households have personal computers and about half of these have access to the Internet (Fontana and Frey 2000), new software programs facilitate electronic interviewing and provide the ability to obtain returns of almost 100 percent from some specialized groups (Schaefer and Dillman 1998). At the same time, new ethical problems are surfacing, because anonymity is not feasible in e-mail communication, although in chat rooms the use of pseudonyms is possible (see Mann and Stewart, Chapter 29, this volume).

The move to electronic interviewing is perhaps most problematic for in-depth interviewing. Rather than the parties to the interview being face-to-face, interaction centers on "virtual" respondents and "virtual" interviewers, to which we might add the "virtual" researcher, all of whose empirical groundings are unclear. Indeed, the lack of clarity portends a version of Baudrillard's (1983) "hyperreality," the melding together of everyday and media realities, confounding the traditional boundaries of text, identity, and other.

To explore some of these issues on-line, Annette Markham (1998) created on Internet site where she interviewed and conversed with other on-line media users. In particular, she and the others were "trying to make sense of what it means to be there" (p. 18). The participants, including Markham, were experimenting with their sense of self on-line: "By logging onto my computer, I (or part of me) can seem to (or perhaps actually) exist separately from my body in 'places' formed by the exchange of messages" (p. 17).

People exchanging messages on-line apply a text—on-line dialogue—to communicate with each other and create a sense of reality as well as a sense of on-line identity. According to Markham, despite the fact that communication takes place through fiber-optic cables, the interactants actually "feel *a sense of presence*" (p. 17) of the other: "We feel we meet in the flesh. . . . Everywhere we rub shoulders with each other" (Argyle, quoted in Markham 1998:17).

The identities that interactants create on-line may differ from their other identities, as the lack of visual communication allows one to create a practically new self if one so wishes. The interaction can also be very different from face-to-face communication, because the interactants, visually hidden as they are, can formulate "false nonverbals," claiming feelings and emotions that do not correspond to their demeanor. This type of interviewing takes away from one of the traditional strengths of qualitative research, which is perennially based on the claim, "I saw it, I heard it, I was there."

In a way, using on-line interviews is not very different from Crapanzano's (1980) use of Tuhami's dreams and lies as data, which he presents as just as valid as Tuhami's recounting of real events. Crapanzano found all of these elements to be of equal help in creating Tuhami's biography. Similarly, whatever elements help people communicating on-line to create and sustain a sense of on-line identity in their dialogue are an integral part of their working subjectivity.

Researchers' increased reliance upon computers has faced the criticism of social commentators for some time (see, among others, Dreyfus 1979; Searle 1984). These critics contend that computers are not mere aids that facilitate research; rather, they drastically change our lives and modes of communication. That modern-day "Luddite" Neal Postman (1993) states, "The fundamental metaphoric message of the computer, in short, is that we are machines —thinking machines, to be sure, but machines nonetheless" (p. 111). According to Postman, reliance on machines will increase human belief in scientism, with the result that we will try to scientize and cloak in the language of science the stories we tell. John Murphy (1999) echoes the sentiment. He sees qualitative researchers as being pressured by the ethos of the times and the demands of academia and granting agencies into the use of computers and software programs such as ETHNO, QualPro, and the Ethnograph (see Seale, Chapter 31, this volume). Murphy warns that computers will not merely help us to sort out the data, but will lead us to seek precise responses, removing ambiguity from interview material. Rather than created, negotiated, face-to-face narratives, we will be left with artificially derived categories that will reify our results and have little to do with the world of everyday life.

◆ Representational Practices

One of the most controversial areas of postmodern-informed interview research centers on the question of how empirical material should be represented. Traditionally, the writing of social science has mimicked the sparse prose of the natural sciences (see Geertz 1988). John Van Maanen (1988) has analyzed the more recent changes in reporting styles and found that they are moving toward the literary. With postmodern-informed reporting practices, writing engages new, experimental, and highly controversial forms of representation. Mindful of the postmodern collapse of disciplinary barriers, social researchers are using literature, poetry, and even plays to represent interview narratives.

AUTOETHNOGRAPHY

Carolyn Ellis (1995a), Jeffrey Riemer (1977), and others have been employing autoethnography to conflate the traditional distinction between the interviewer and the respondent. Ellis, for example, writes about her past experiences in what becomes a form of retrospective self-interview and narrative reconstruction of life events. The crucial difference between this work and traditional representation is that Ellis aims to recount her own feelings about interview topics that apply to her as a researcher and subject of the experience under consideration, thus combining the roles of interviewer and interviewee. As a result, we are witness to many personally conveyed epiphanic moments in her life, moments that could be our very own. For example, she has written about the agony of facing the death of her brother in an airplane crash (1993), her uneasy encounter with a friend dying of AIDS (1995b), and the slow spiral toward death of her beloved partner, who was stricken with a terminal illness (1995a). In the same vein, Laurel Richardson (1999) has written a personal narrative of her misadventures with paternalistic faculty colleagues after a car accident. Troy McGinnis's (1999) presentation "The Art of Leaving" is about his stumbling upon his wife and a best friend in an intimate situation, and Norman Denzin (1999b, 1999c) has written stories about his hideout in Montana. These are just a few of the many recent autoethnographic (self-interviewing) representations of experience.

POETRY

Laurel Richardson extends this trend to poetic representation (see Richardson, Chapter 42, this volume). After lengthy interview sessions with a southern, middle-aged, single mother, Richardson (1997) transformed the woman's sad and powerful tale into a poem, which she recites masterfully, in a sorrowful southern drawl. A segment follows, which in Richardson's view comes fully to life only in its recitation.

So, the Doctor said, "You're pregnant."

I was 41. John and I

had had a happy kind of relationship,

not a serious one.

But beside himself with fear and anger,

awful, rageful, vengeful, horrid,

Jody May's father said,

"Get an Abortion."

I told him,

"I would never marry you.

I would never marry you.

I would never." (P. 133)

Others have followed Richardson's lead into the realm of sociological poetry. For example, Patricia Clough's (1999) angst-filled poetic presentation "A Child Is Being Killed" took the place of the keynote address at a recent symposium of the Society for the Study of Symbolic Interaction.

STAGED PLAYS AND PERFORMANCES

Scripted performance also has been rallied to enhance the "scenic presence" (Holstein and Gubrium 2000) of interview-based reports of experience. Richardson, for example, not only constructs poetic accounts but uses plays to tell her stories, at times soliciting participation from her audience (see Richardson 1997). Indeed, dramatic realization has become a broadly popular mode of expression. Jim Miencza-

kowski and Steve Morgan (1998) have dressed as police officers to act out their counseling interviews, which were completed in Queensland, Australia. I personally donned black clothing and a white mask to portray Farinelli, the castrato, in reporting on a study of transsexuals (Fontana and Schmidt 1998, 1999). Robert Schmidt and I enlisted Jennifer O'Brien's help in producing a polyphonic play based on in-depth interviews with a lap dancer (Schmidt and Fontana 1998).

At times, however, performances have moved from the sublime to the studiously ridiculous. For example, I have witnessed sociologist Stephen Pfohl (1995) strip to black bikini bottoms at the culmination of his video-music play, and, more recently, I watched as a graduate student smeared himself with bean dip to convey the ironies of Latino identity. Postmodern trends have taken representation a long way from the guarded prose of research reports.

◆ Conclusion

Clearly, postmodernism has influenced interviewing, loosening it from many of its traditional moorings. Perhaps it has accomplished its goal—imploding traditional interviewing to leave it in fragments, each crying out to be appreciated in its own way. Some see this fragmentation as a healthy sign, because we have many groups with different approaches and methods all presenting their wares (Adler and Adler 1999). Others feel threatened by it and, in various ways, decry the ostensible chaos (Best 1995; Dawson and Prus 1993; Prus 1996; Sanders 1995; Shalin 1993). Yet another response strikes a balance between the modern and postmodern, staking a middle-ground approach to incorporate innovative postmodern ideas with more traditional precepts (Gubrium and Holstein 1998; Holstein and Gubrium 1995). And, finally, there are those who are oblivious to these trends, who continue to be guided by traditional rules of both qualitative and quantitative inquiry (Murphy 1999; Adler and Adler 1999).

Shadowing the differences is the prospect that the interview can no longer be viewed as a discreet event, the straightforward result of asking questions and receiving answers. Indeed, even the traditional "conversation with a purpose," which until recently was a way of conceptualizing the survey interview, has increasingly given way to evidence of the systematic communicative work that produces interview data (see Schaeffer and Maynard, Chapter 28, this volume). Survey researchers themselves are systematically discovering something they have always suspected: that both the interviewer and the respondent negotiate and work together to accomplish the interview, the resulting "data" being as much a product of interview participants' collaborative efforts as of the experiences under consideration. Postmodern trends in the area are seemingly coming full circle, back to where they began. Increasingly, we are learning that what Paul Rabinow (1977) said about informant and researcher in ethnography also applies to the interviewer and the respondent: "The common understanding they construct is fragile and thin, but it is upon this shaky ground that anthropological inquiry proceeds" (p. 39).

■ *Notes*

1. Following Lee Harvey (1987), I see ethnography and in-depth interviewing as much more intertwined than methodologists usually do. Indeed, fieldwork relies on a combination of both methods. Harvey points out that many of the works of the Chicago school, which are commonly referred to as "ethnographic," actually rely on in-depth interviews. As early as Malinowski's fieldwork in New Guinea, the two methods have been combined. In fact, Malinowski did not actually live in the village with the natives, but would go there only occasionally, with an interpreter, to interview them (Malinowski 1989; also see Lofland 1971).

2. Shifting subject positions have traditionally been glossed over in interview research. Seidman (1991) recounts that in his study of community college faculty, he was treated either with deference because of his affiliation with what was perceived to be a higher status institution (the university) or with suspicion because of his affiliation with the "ivory tower." The difference was important in how it mediated the organization of responses. In my study of poor elderly (Fontana 1977), the fact that I was young led to my being treated with extreme suspicion. This was because the elderly people I approached saw my explanation that I was conducting interviews for my dissertation as a cover for some kind of "con game," because some young men who had recently approached them "for similar reasons" were con men and pimps.

■ *References*

Adler, P. A. and P. Adler. 1999. "The Ethnographer's Ball—Revisited." *Journal of Contemporary Ethnography* 28: 442-50.

Anderson, K. and D. C. Jack. 1991. "Learning to Listen: Interview Techniques and Analyses." Pp. 11-26 in *Women's Words: The Feminist Practice of Oral History,* edited by S. B. Gluck and D. Patai. New York: Routledge.

Atkinson, P. and D. Silverman. 1997. "Kundera's *Immortality:* The Interview Society and the Invention of Self." *Qualitative Inquiry* 3:304-25.

Babbie, E. 1992. *The Practice of Social Research.* 6th ed. Belmont, CA: Wadsworth.

Baudrillard, J. 1983. *Simulations.* Translated by Paul Foss, Paul Patton, and John Johnston. New York: Semiotext(e).

Behar, R. 1996. *The Vulnerable Observer: Anthropology That Breaks Your Heart.* Boston: Beacon.

Best, J. 1995. "Lost in the Ozone Again." Pp. 125-30 in *Studies in Symbolic Interaction: A Research Annual,* Vol. 17, edited by N. K. Denzin. Greenwich, CT: JAI.

Best, S. and D. Kellner. 1991. *Postmodern Theory: Critical Interrogations.* New York: Guilford.

Blumer, H. 1969. *Symbolic Interactionism: Perspective and Method.* Englewood Cliffs, NJ: Prentice Hall.

Boden, D. and D. H. Zimmerman, eds. *Talk and Social Structure: Studies in Ethnomethodology and Conversation Analysis.* Berkeley: University of California Press.

Cicourel, A. V. 1964. *Method and Measurement in Sociology.* New York: Free Press.

Clough, P. T. 1999. "A Child Is Being Killed: The Unconscious of Autoethnography." Keynote address presented at the annual symposium of the Couch-Stone Society for the Study of Symbolic Interaction, February 5-7, Las Vegas.

Collins, P. H. 1990. *Black Feminist Thought: Knowledge, Consciousness, and the Politics of Empowerment.* New York: Routledge, Chapman & Hall.

Crapanzano, V. 1980. *Tuhami: Portrait of a Moroccan.* Chicago: University of Chicago Press.

Dawson, L. and R. Prus. 1993. "Interactionist Ethnography and Postmodern Discourse." Pp. 147-77 in *Studies in Symbolic Interaction: A Research Annual,* Vol. 15, edited by N. K. Denzin. Greenwich, CT: JAI.

Denzin, N. K. 1989. *Interpretive Interactionalism.* Newbury Park, CA: Sage.

———. 1997. *Interpretive Ethnography: Ethnographic Practices for the 21st Century.* Thousand Oaks, CA: Sage.

———. 1999a. "An Interpretive Ethnography for the Next Century." *Journal of Contemporary Ethnography* 28:510-19.

———. 1999b. "Performing Montana." Pp. 147-58 in *Qualitative Sociology as Everyday Life,* edited by B. Glassner and R. Hertz. Thousand Oaks, CA: Sage.

———. 1999c. "Performing Montana, Part II." Presented at the annual symposium of the Couch-Stone Society for the Study of Symbolic Interaction, February 5-7, Las Vegas.

Derrida, J. 1972. "Structure, Sign and Play in the Discourse of the Human Sciences." Pp. 247-72 in *The Structuralist Controversy,* edited by R. Macksey and E. Donato. Baltimore: Johns Hopkins University Press.

Dickens, D. R. and A. Fontana, eds. 1994. *Postmodernism and Social Inquiry.* New York: Guilford.

Dingwall, R. 1997. "Accounts, Interviews and Observations." Pp. 51-65 in *Context and Method in Qualitative Research,* edited by G. Miller and R. Dingwall. Thousand Oaks: Sage.

Douglas, J. D. 1985. *Creative Interviewing.* Beverly Hills, CA: Sage.

Dreyfus, H. 1979. *What Computers Can't Do: The Limits of Artificial Intelligence.* New York: Harper & Row.

Dwyer, K. 1982. *Moroccan Dialogues: Anthropology in Question.* Baltimore: Johns Hopkins University Press.

Ellis, C. 1993. " 'There Are Survivors': Telling a Story of Sudden Death." *Sociological Quarterly* 34:711-30.

———. 1995a. *Final Negotiations: A Story of Love, Loss, and Chronic Illness.* Philadelphia: Temple University Press.

———. 1995b. "Speaking of Dying: An Ethnographic Short Story." *Symbolic Interaction* 18:73-81.

Fontana, A. 1977. *The Last Frontier: The Social Meaning of Growing Old.* Beverly Hills, CA: Sage.

Fontana, A. and J. H. Frey. 2000. "The Interview: From Structured Questions to Negotiated Text." Pp. 645-72 in *Handbook of Qualitative Research,* 2d ed., edited by N. K. Denzin and Y. S. Lincoln. Thousand Oaks, CA: Sage.

Fontana, A. and R. Schmidt (with Jennifer O'Brien). 1998. "The Fluid Self." Presented at the annual meeting of the Society for the Study of Symbolic Interaction, August 22-23, San Francisco.

Fontana, A. and R. Schmidt. 1999. "Castrato: Predetermined to Fluid Self or a Dialogue/Performance Script Intended to Inform Garfinkel about the Possibilities of Gendering." In *Studies in Symbolic Interaction: A Research Annual,* Vol. 23, edited by N. K. Denzin. Greenwich, CT: JAI.

Garfinkel, H. 1967. *Studies in Ethnomethodology.* Englewood Cliffs, NJ: Prentice Hall.

Geertz, C. 1988. *Works and Lives: The Anthropologist as Author.* Stanford, CA: Stanford University Press.

Gluck, S. B. 1991. "Advocacy Oral History: Palestinian Women in Resistance." Pp. 205-20 in *Women's Words: The Feminist Practice of Oral History*. Edited by S. B. Gluck and D. Patai. New York: Routledge.

Gubrium, J. F. and J. A. Holstein. 1997. *The New Language of Qualitative Method*. New York: Oxford University Press.

———. 1998. "Narrative Practice and the Coherence of Personal Stories." *Sociological Quarterly* 39:163-87.

Harvey, L. 1987. *Myths of the Chicago School of Sociology*. Aldershot, England: Avebury.

Hertz, R., ed. 1997. *Reflexivity and Voice*. Thousand Oaks, CA: Sage.

Holstein, J. A. and J. F. Gubrium. 1995. *The Active Interview*. Thousand Oaks, CA: Sage.

———. 2000. *The Self We Live By: Narrative Identity in a Postmodern World*. New York: Oxford University Press.

Krieger, S. 1983. *The Mirror's Dance: Identity in a Women's Community*. Philadelphia: Temple University Press.

Lofland, J. 1971. *Analyzing Social Settings*. Belmont, CA: Wadsworth.

Lyotard, J.-F. 1984. *The Postmodern Condition: A Report on Knowledge*. Translated by G. Bennington and B. Massumi. Minneapolis: University of Minnesota Press.

Malinowski, B. 1989. *A Diary in the Strict Sense of the Term*. Stanford, CA: Stanford University Press.

Marcus, G. E. and M. M. J. Fischer. 1986. *Anthropology as Cultural Critique: An Experimental Moment in the Human Sciences*. Chicago: University of Chicago Press.

Markham, A. N. 1998. *Life Online: Researching Real Experience in Virtual Space*. Walnut Creek, CA: AltaMira.

Maynard, D. W., H. Houtkoop-Steenstra, J. van der Zouwen, and N. C. Schaeffer. 2001. *Interaction and Practice in the Survey Interview*. New York: John Wiley.

McGinnis, T. 1999. "The Art of Leaving." Presented at the annual symposium of the Couch-Stone Society for the Study of Symbolic Interaction, February 5-7, Las Vegas.

Mienczakowski, J. and S. Morgan. 1998. "Stop! In the Name of Love!" Presented at the annual symposium of the Couch-Stone Society for the Study of Symbolic Interaction, February 20-22, Houston, TX.

Murphy, J. 1999. "Computerized Ethnography: Fad and Disaster!" Presented at the annual symposium of the Couch-Stone Society for the Study of Symbolic Interaction, February 5-7, Las Vegas.

Oakley, A. 1981. "Interviewing Women: A Contradiction in Terms?" Pp. 30-61 in *Doing Feminist Research*, edited by H. Roberts. London: Routledge & Kegan Paul.

Owens, C. 1983. "The Discourse of Others: Feminists and Postmodernism." Pp. 57-82 in *The Anti-aesthetic: Essays on Postmodern Culture*, edited by H. Foster. Port Townsend, WA: Bay.

Patai, D. 1987. "Ethical Problems of Personal Narrative, or Who Should Eat the Last Piece of Cake?" *International Journal of Oral History* 8(1):5-27.

Pfohl, S. 1995. "Venus in Microsoft." Presented at the Gregory Stone Annual Symposium of the Society for the Study of Symbolic Interaction, May 19-21, Des Moines, IA.

Postman, N. 1993. *Technopoly: The Surrender of Culture to Technology*. New York: Vintage.

Prus, R. 1996. *Symbolic Interaction and Ethnographic Research*. Albany: State University of New York Press.

Rabinow, P. 1977. *Reflections on Fieldwork in Morocco*. Berkeley: University of California Press.

Reinharz, S. 1992. *Feminist Methods in Social Research*. New York: Oxford University Press.

Richardson, L. 1997. *Fields of Play: Constructing an Academic Life*. New Brunswick, NJ: Rutgers University Press.

———. 1999. "Jeopardy." Presented at the Forum Lecture Series, February 4, University of Nevada, Las Vegas.

Riemer, J. 1977. "Varieties of Opportunistic Research." *Urban Life* 5:467-77.

Sanders, C. 1995. "Stranger Than Fiction." Pp. 89-104 in *Studies in Symbolic Interaction: A Research Annual*, Vol. 17, edited by N. K. Denzin. Greenwich, CT: JAI.

Sarup, M. 1996. *Identity, Culture and the Postmodern World*. Athens: University of Georgia Press.

Schaefer, D. R. and D. A. Dillman. 1998. "Development of a Standard E-Mail Methodology." *Public Opinion Quarterly* 62:378-97.

Schmidt, R. and A. Fontana. 1998. "Deconstructing Peggy Sue." Presented at the annual symposium of the Couch-Stone Society for the Study of Symbolic Interaction, February 20-22, Houston, TX.

Schutz, A. 1962. *Collected Papers I: The Problem of Social Reality.* The Hague: Martinus Nijhoff.

———. 1964. *Collected Papers II: Studies in Social Theory.* The Hague: Martinus Nijhoff.

———. 1966. *Collected Papers III: Studies in Phenomenological Philosophy.* The Hague: Martinus Nijhoff.

Searle, J. 1984. *Minds, Brains and Science.* Cambridge, MA: Harvard University Press.

Seidman, I. 1991. *Interviewing as Qualitative Research: A Guide for Researchers in Education and the Social Sciences.* New York: Teachers College Press.

Shalin, D. 1993. "Modernity, Postmodernism and Pragmatist Inquiry." *Symbolic Interaction* 16:303-32.

Shelton, A. 1995. "The Man at the End of the Machine." *Symbolic Interaction* 18: 505-18.

———. 1996. "Vespers." Presented at the Gregory Stone Annual Symposium of the Society for the Study of Symbolic Interaction, May 19-21, Des Moines, IA.

Silverman, D. 1993. *Interpreting Qualitative Data: Methods for Analysing Talk, Text and Interaction.* London: Sage.

———, ed. 1997. *Qualitative Research: Theory, Method and Practice.* London: Sage.

Smith, D. E. 1987. *The Everyday World as Problematic: A Feminist Sociology.* Boston: Northeastern University Press.

Van Maanen, J. 1988. *Tales of the Field: On Writing Ethnography.* Chicago: University of Chicago Press.

Vaz, K. M., ed. 1997. *Oral Narrative Research with Black Women.* Thousand Oaks: Sage.

Warren, C. A. B. 1988. *Gender Issues in Field Research.* Newbury Park, CA: Sage.

Weston, K. 1998. *Long Slow Burn: Sexuality and Social Science.* New York: Routledge.

Zimmerman, D. H. and M. Pollner. 1970. "The Everyday World as a Phenomenon." Pp. 80-104 in *Understanding Everyday Life: Toward a Reconstruction of Social Knowledge,* edited by J. D. Douglas. Chicago: Aldine.

Part II

DISTINCTIVE RESPONDENTS

Interviewing has a long history of a "one-size-fits-all" approach. The push toward standardization has tended to homogenize the process further. As far as the role of interviewer is concerned, the desire has been to locate the kind of person to serve as an interviewer who will least influence the respondent's answers and, at the same time, help to maximize response rates and complete the interviews efficiently. The conventional wisdom has often been that educated, middle-aged females are the best candidates for the job; indeed, this has become a sort of working ideal.

Standardization also has served to homogenize the interview process itself. Standard operating rules govern the proceedings. For example, simple, complicated, and sensitive questions are posed at particular locations in the interview in order to facilitate the "flow" of information and to help build and sustain interviewer-respondent rapport. Question format, too, understandably has been conventionalized, so as to reduce variation that might be introduced into the interview process when questions are presented in different ways.

The vision of the respondent (and the subject behind the respondent) has added to the homogenization. Of course, years ago, many national populations were more homogeneous than they are today, racially, ethnically, and in terms of household composition, for example. This in itself worked to "standardize" the respondent within the sampling process. But aside from the demographic influences on respondent pools, there has always been a tacit understanding that the subjectivity of the respondent is constant throughout the interview process. Perhaps the most exaggerated instance of this came in researchers' taking for granted that an interview with the proverbial "head of household" actually reflected the experiences and opinions of everyone in the home. The head, it was presumed, could speak for everyone.

The human body has been a significant means for marking the constancy of the subject. It would not be unusual, for example, for a researcher to select a potential respondent who is demographically female and who presents as such in person and to figure that she embodies a female respondent. This respondent's interview, as a result, would accordingly be taken to represent a female's point of view. Or, for instance, the successfully interviewed racialized respondent, selected from a particular pool of potential respondents of color, is assumed to provide the responses of a person of color; data derived from this interview are interpreted as representing the standpoint of a member of a racialized population.

As the chapters in Part II show, this and other assumptions that bear on homogenization have changed dramatically. The one-size-fits-all approach, especially as it applies to an ostensible category of respondent, is now less the operating rule than it is a significant procedural and analytic issue. The subjective embodiment of the respondent is no longer so commonly taken for granted. Reflection on the questions broached in Chapter 1 of this *Handbook* can illustrate this point. Although the selected respondent might be female for all practical purposes, does this assure interviewers and researchers that the voice that comes through in the interview represents the beliefs and sentiments of "a" woman (see Reinharz and Chase, Chapter 11, this volume)? The female respondent, like most, holds many roles; she might also be African American and working-class. How do these standpoints figure in what she says in the interview? Indeed, this combination of identities, located at the intersection of their subject positions, each with specific social, historical, and cultural resonances, challenges procedural homogeneity. Simply moving along in the interview as if subject position does not matter—eliciting answers from, encouraging, acknowledging, and probing the respondent with an image of a constant subject behind the respondent in place—constructs homogeneity in its own right. Proceeding then to analyze the data as if they also were the responses of a constant subject only exaggerates the problem.

The contributors to this part of the *Handbook* argue—in their own ways—against the homogenization of the interview as this relates to distinctive respondents. Taken together, the chapters in Part II convey the message that we can no longer think in terms of "one size fits all." Interviewers can no longer rely upon old categories and identities as the basis for seeking and analyzing respondent standpoints (see Kong, Mahoney, and Plummer, Chapter 12).

The contributors present an equally important conventional awareness of the procedural challenges associated with the distribution of sampling characteristics in any designated respondent pool. For example, at the same time Donna Eder and Laura Fingerson offer a discussion of the methodological problems of interviewing children and adolescents, they are well aware that this category of respondents comprises a wide range of ages, from the toddler years to late adolescence. With this in view, the "distinctiveness" of this respondent pool becomes multidimensional, with significant methodological implications arising from that fact. In her chapter on interviewing older people, Clare Wenger raises the same issue for the other end of the life course, putting it in terms of researchers' need to attend critically to the research consequences of thinking homogeneously about *the* older person when this group can include individuals ranging in age from their 50s to their 90s and above.

Each of the chapters here also suggests that, when it comes to "distinctive" respondents, researchers would do well to combine interviewing with more ethnographic approaches. The aim is better understanding of the "distinctive"—as opposed to the ostensibly more familiar—respondent's experience in its often hidden or overlooked social contexts. In her chapter on interviewing the ill, Janice Morse not only tells us that the category "illness" can violate the chief characteristics of the good respondent—someone who can intelligibly present experiential particulars on his or her own—but suggests, as Wenger does in her chapter, that significant others can serve an important function in interview-based research. They can be "proxy" interviewees, providing information about respondents' worlds that the respondents may not be able to provide themselves. In their chapter on race, subjectivity, and the interview process, Christopher Dunbar, Dalia Rodriguez, and Laurence Parker take up this subject in relation to issues surrounding respondents' willingness, not their ability, to provide interviewers with pictures of their lives and worlds. As these authors show in compelling vignettes, knowledge of the lived social and historical environments of respondents, in this case poor persons of color, can help sensitize researchers to the potential meaning of what is or is not being expressed in interviews. Such knowledge can also suggest some reasons why members of such groups might resist becoming respondents in the first place. Working at the other end of the status spectrum, Teresa Odendahl and Aileen Shaw, in their chapter on interviewing elites, surprisingly enough offer similar advice regarding the mix of methods. They also point out the ramifications of different methods for successful recruitment of respondents. Here, too, methodological success works against a one-size-fits-all approach.

9

INTERVIEWING CHILDREN AND ADOLESCENTS

◆ Donna Eder
   Laura Fingerson

The task of interviewing children and adolescents presents researchers with unique opportunities and dilemmas. Although some researchers advocate participant observation and ethnography rather than interviewing in the study of children (Corsaro 1997; Prout and James 1997; Weisner 1996), we believe there is a place for the interview approach in such research. We have found that interviewing can be used successfully with children from preschool age (e.g., Davies 1989) through high school age (e.g., Eckert 1989). Although very young children may not be as comfortable as adolescents in one-on-one interviews with adults, most of the issues we present in this chapter are applicable to a range of age groups.

One clear reason for interviewing youthful respondents is to allow them to give voice to their own interpretations and thoughts rather than rely solely on our adult interpretations of their lives. For example, rather than forming our own views on the content of the media that children use, it is important that we find out how they are interpreting the messages they receive through books, television, movies, and magazines. Another reason for interviewing young people is to study those topics that are salient in their lives but do not occur in daily conversations or interactions. For example, although family relationships are very salient to many adolescents, they seldom discuss these relationships in their daily conversations with peers. Likewise, adolescents discuss topics such as sexuality and menstruation in joking or playful terms, if they discuss them at all, in public settings. Thus researchers interested in these topics have relied more extensively on interviews than on observations (Lees 1993; Tolman 1994). Finally, some topics that do occur naturally in young people's daily conversations do not occur on a regular enough basis to warrant the time it would take to study them through participant observation. For example, although some boys regularly discuss media events in their daily conversations, girls are much less likely to do so on a regular basis (Eder 1995; Milkie 1994). Thus for collecting girls' interpretations of media, conducting interviews with groups of girls is a much more efficient method than observation (see Fingerson 1999).

When interviewing children, it is essential that researchers begin by examining the power dynamics between adults and youth. Researchers do not always recognize that, in general, children have lower status than adults and lack power in Western societies. Berry Mayall (1999) advocates seeing children as their own minority group compared to the adults who order and control their lives, viewing them as lacking essential abilities and characteristics of adulthood. For Mayall, "child" is a relational category defining children as subordinate to the superordinate "adult." Ivar Frønes (1994) also argues that children are primarily seen as an "age group," which positions them low in the overall age-graded power structure, rather than as a group with its own culture and unique abilities. According to Suzanne Hood, Berry Mayall, and Sandy Oliver (1999), children are a socially disadvantaged and disempowered group, not only because of their age but because of their position in society as the "researched" and never the "researchers."

Interviewers need to be sensitive to this power imbalance. Gary Alan Fine and Kent Sandstrom (1988) argue that in any participation event with children, the adults cannot have equal status because "the social roles of the participants have been influenced by age, cognitive development, physical maturity, and acquisition of social responsibility" (p. 14). Children are taught

all their lives to listen to, respect, and obey adults. They are surrounded by teachers, parents, relatives, and adult friends who all have the power to command children's actions (Caputo 1995; see also in this volume Adler and Adler, Chapter 25; Briggs, Chapter 44).

Throughout this chapter, we will explore various ways in which researchers can address this power dynamic, our first theme, when interviewing children and adolescents. In the first section below, we argue that the adult researcher's power can be reduced while making the interviewing context more natural if children are interviewed as a group rather than as individuals. Thus, unlike in most other chapters in this *Handbook,* the reader should assume that we are referring to group interviews unless otherwise specified (see also Morgan, Chapter 7, this volume). In the next section, we emphasize reciprocity as a central means for responding to the potential power inequality between adult researchers and youthful respondents. We argue that the concept of reciprocity can be applied at several levels, from directly empowering respondents to using research findings to enrich and improve the lives of children through an action-oriented research focus. Finally, we return to the theme of power dynamics as we discuss how to represent youth in their own terms.

A second theme of this chapter is the importance of using multiple methods. Although some interviewers may seek only to collect interview data, we argue that a brief period of observation should precede the interviewing process, so that interviewers can identify natural contexts for interviewing and children's own speech routines (see in this volume Dunbar, Rodriguez, and Parker, Chapter 14; Atkinson and Coffey, Chapter 38). We also believe that a sociolinguistic approach can strengthen the validity of interviews as well as complement other modes of data analysis by showing *how* certain beliefs are acquired and communicated. Finally, we discuss how researchers can combine group interviews with single interviews and with content analysis of media to enhance our understanding of children and adolescents.

◆ Creating a Natural Context

One of the most important considerations in interview research with young people is the creation of a natural context for the interview. This can mean different things depending on the ages of the children being interviewed. Studies of peer culture among youth have emphasized the importance of social learning in the context of groups (Corsaro and Eder 1995; Eder 1995; Corsaro 1997). Children, especially young children, acquire social knowledge through interaction with others as they construct meanings through a shared process. This is also the most natural way for them to communicate social knowledge to others. Some researchers have found that African American children are more comfortable in group settings (Holmes 1998), and we have found that European American children are also relaxed and engage in typical peer routines when interviewed in groups (Simon, Eder, and Evans 1992; Eder 1995; Fingerson 1999).

The group setting is also important for minimizing the power differential between the researcher and those being studied. Power dynamics occur in all interview studies, in that the researcher has control over the research process as well as over much of the interview by virtue of being the one posing the questions. As noted previously, in studies of youth the researcher also has the added power associated with age. Both of these aspects can be minimized to some degree when interviewing takes place in group settings, as children are more relaxed in the company of their peers and are more comfortable knowing that they outnumber the adults in the setting. Also, there is less chance for a researcher to impose adult interpretations and language on the young people if they are interviewed collectively

and have the opportunity to develop and convey aspects of peer culture in their talk.

Group interviews grow directly out of peer culture, as children construct their meanings collectively with their peers. In group interviews (also referred to as focus groups), participants build on each other's talk and discuss a wider range of experiences and opinions than may develop in individual interviews (Morgan 1993). Also, the interaction in focus groups can elicit more accurate accounts, as participants must defend their statements to their peers, especially if the group is made up of individuals who interact on a daily basis. Although participants in focus groups are sometimes taken out of their natural settings, if an interview is conducted with an existing group of friends or peers, the conversations in the focus group are more indicative of those occurring in a natural setting (Albrecht, Johnson, and Walther 1993). As an alternative approach, some researchers have conducted whole-class interviews with elementary school students (Adler and Adler 1998). This technique allows interviewers to ask children from a variety of peer groups to discuss their different perspectives on issues of social power among peers.

The naturalness of the interview context can be furthered developed if the interview is placed within a larger activity with which the respondents are already familiar. According to Julie Tammivaara and D. Scott Enright (1986), researchers can reduce the artificiality of interviews by embedding them into everyday activities such as recess, "show and tell," "circle time," or sessions of ongoing small instructional groups. In some cases, interviewers might create new games that are similar to the types of games children naturally engage in, such as "Let's Pretend" or "Telling Stories," and embed their interviews in these meaningful activities. Robyn Holmes (1998) notes that she avoids formal interviews with children and instead conducts informal individual and group interviews during free-play time, while children take part in drawing activities, or on the playground. In addition, she has developed journalistic role-play scenarios in which she and the children take turns interviewing each other. Brenda Bryant (1985) conducted individual interviews with children while taking them on "neighborhood walks." The walks are intended to make the setting more inviting as well as to elicit cues and reminders to promote more accurate reporting of neighborhood experiences. In all of these cases, by avoiding decontextualized interview situations, researchers have been able to elicit more natural and valid responses from young respondents.

Another aspect of creating a natural context in the interview involves gaining an understanding of the communicative rules used by the youth being studied. Charles Briggs (1986) has argued that interview studies should be grounded in the discourse of those being interviewed. This is especially true in studies of youth, who often have their own discourse styles and peer culture. According to Briggs, the design, implementation, and analysis of interviews should emerge from an awareness of the nature of the respondents' communicative competence. The researcher can learn the communicative norms of the youth being studied through a combination of observation and informal interviewing prior to the formal interviewing process. In this observation period, the researcher should pay careful attention to the young people's sense of questions and the appropriateness of their timing and use in different contexts. Briggs also recommends that the researcher perform a microanalysis of a selected interview as a way to develop a clearer understanding of the respondents' discourse patterns. (We consider the topic of sociolinguistic analysis of interview data later in this chapter.)

One innovative approach to interview research with children is the use of children as interviewers. Tobias Hecht (1998), in a study of street children in Brazil, found success having kids take the tape recorder and interview other kids on their own. Through this method, Hecht discovered many modes of discourse and ways of referring to the home, family, and the street that were invaluable in his own interviewing and observations.

Another way in which a researcher can help respondents' norms to emerge is through the careful structuring of the interview itself. The best interview emerges from a state of egalitarian cooperation in which both the researcher and respondents form the discourse (Briggs 1986). Shulamit Reinharz (1992) advocates beginning the interview with very unstructured questions, to allow the respondents' concerns to emerge. She notes that the interviewer should be less concerned with getting his or her questions answered than with understanding the people being interviewed. In studies of youth, it is especially important for interviewers to emphasize nondirected, open, and inclusive questions (Tammivaara and Enright 1986). If the questions are open-ended, the children will have more opportunity to bring in the topics and modes of discourse that are familiar to them. Also, nondirected questions provide more opportunity for children in group interviews to collaborate in their answers and to expand on the responses of others. This type of interaction is typical of the discourse styles in many peer cultures and is reflective of children's natural way of developing shared meanings (Eder 1988, 1995).

In attempting to create a natural context for the interview, the researcher must also take care to avoid creating situations that remind youth of classroom lessons based on "known-answer" questions. Because many students are exposed to the type of lessons in which questions are asked for the purpose of getting correct answers (Tammivaara and Enright 1986), respondents in a research setting who are asked similar types of questions may seek to provide the answers they feel are expected of them rather than stating what they actually think or feel. In addition, Tammivaara and Enright (1986) suggest that interviewers should avoid certain controlling behaviors that might associate them with teachers, such as asking respondents to stop fidgeting or to stop being silly. Instead, they recommend that some of the interview time be taken up with playing with items or figuratively playing with questions; they observe that this will lead to more valid information in the end.

Another way the interviewer can avoid being associated with the classroom teacher is by resisting being the one to initiate all activities during the interview (Corsaro 1981; Tammivaara and Enright 1986). Lessons in which right answers are sought seldom include the opportunity for children to develop and ask their own questions. By inviting the children's questions and comments throughout the interview, the interviewer conveys a different context of developing knowledge. By encouraging respondents to initiate questions and comments, the interviewer breaks down the basic power dimension of the interview context by personalizing and humanizing him- or herself and empowering the respondents. In addition, when the interviewer gives respondents opportunities to introduce their own topics and concerns into the discussion, the knowledge shared and gained reflects the interests of the youth being studied as well as the interests of the researcher. Judith Cook and Mary Fonow (1986) note that feminist researchers who want to avoid treating their subjects as "objects of knowledge" use an interactive interviewing approach that allows their respondents to have a voice during the production of the data. In interview research with children, researchers can also report their findings back to the children to check the accuracy of the adults' interpretations (Mayall 1999). This allows the children to hear what the researchers think and to respond directly to researchers' interpretations of their lives.

One of the key aspects of the interview approach recommended here is flexibility. Although the researcher will have certain questions in mind to start, he or she must be willing to let the interview develop by allowing opportunities for new questions to emerge based on what is shared during the interview. These questions may arise from anyone, not just the researcher. Also, flexibility allows for changes in setting and procedure as the needs and interests of the youth being studied are revealed. It may become clear only as the interview process progresses that certain questions are inappropriate due either to ethical or substantive considerations, and these should then be omitted. On the other hand, new questions may emerge that better capture the experiences of the youth, and these might become the focus of an added stage of the research.

◆ Reciprocity as a Response to Power Dynamics

Current discussions of ethics regarding research on youth are too often limited to debates regarding the protection of children's rights. Although we support these concerns, we believe that this focus has limited the perception of ethical responsibility to that of guarding individual rights. We believe that in order to respond to the power dynamics in research with children, researchers must expand this ethical discussion to include a greater emphasis on reciprocity. The researcher's desire to gain information from child participants without giving something in return reflects an underlying sense of the adult researcher's privilege. However, by giving something in return for receiving this information, researchers can reduce the potential power inequality.

Reciprocity can take place on several levels. One important level is within the interview itself. Researchers can treat respondents in such a way that they receive something from participating in the study, whether it be a greater sense of empowerment, a greater understanding of their own life experiences, or both. Feminist researchers have discussed some general ways in which respondents may be empowered through interviews (Lather 1988; Reinharz 1992). For example, researchers can promote interactive interviews in which the researchers self-disclose along with participants. Researchers can also conduct multiple interviews with the same individuals, promoting a greater level of depth. Some feminist researchers also advocate the use of group interviews and the collective negotiation of interpretations. All of these strategies are designed to promote respondents' empowerment by encouraging respondents' self-reflection as well as researchers' deeper understanding of the respondents' situation in their worlds.

Some researchers who have interviewed adolescents have commented on the potential for adolescents to gain from the research experience. In a study of girls from different ethnic and social backgrounds, Jill Taylor, Carol Gilligan, and Amy Sullivan (1995) found that the individual interviews conducted by adult females provided these girls with opportunities to think through issues of importance to them by talking about them with interested adults. During these interviews the girls were less afraid of judgment, betrayal, misunderstanding, and anger than is generally the case when adolescents talk with adults. One respondent told the interviewer that she was able to speak freely because the interviewer was clearly interested in her. This led her to discuss things that she did not feel she could share with family members or even with friends. Some of the girls also said they were able to gain new insights about themselves during the course of their interviews. As one said: "But since the question came up, it let me know how I felt. I think that's good. I can do this forever you know . . . keep on going. I'll bring a lot up with just easy questions that you would ask anybody, you know. It lets you know about yourself" (p. 129).

Similarly, Penelope Eckert (1989) found that many participants thanked her for the opportunity to think and talk in a struc-

tured way about themselves and their high school issues. When she began her study, she was not prepared for the number of students who needed an interested adult to talk with about themselves. As the interview setting was both nonjudgmental and confidential, her respondents found their interviews to be safer than most conversations with adults.

Taylor et al. (1995) found that the adolescent girls they interviewed felt close to their mothers but did not feel they could talk to them about anything "important." White and Hispanic girls in particular have been found to have difficulty discussing issues of sexuality with their mothers (Ward and Taylor 1991). James Youniss and Jacqueline Smollar (1985) have reported that in discussions with their parents, compared to conversations with their friends, adolescents are more likely to be careful about what they say, are more likely to hide their true feelings, and are less likely to talk about doubts and fear. Given the difficulty adolescents have in talking with the adults to whom they are closest, it is not surprising that some interviewers have found their young respondents eager to be listened to in a nonjudgmental and accepting manner.

Reciprocity can also take the form of giving something back to the community in which the study takes place and/or including some form of social action or social change as part of the project. People of color have written about the importance of service in their respective ethnic communities. For example, Rayna Green (1990) says that what she does with her scholarship needs to work for people, to bring about change in some way. Patricia Hill Collins (1990) believes that thought and action should be tied closely together. For example, the struggle for self-definition among African American women includes a merging of thought and action to eliminate oppression. Creating safe communities is an important form of activism, but, Collins argues, it is not enough; broader forms of change are also needed, such as transformations in social institutions.

An interest in action-oriented research is growing among qualitative researchers. As they move away from the view that qualitative research is a detached science, researchers are realizing that they influence the participants in their studies and are in turn influenced by them (Lincoln and Denzin 1994). As researchers accept that such impacts are inevitable, many have begun to consider ways to make their influences more positive. This has led to the consideration of a new measure of validity, one that reflects the degree to which a given research project empowers and emancipates a research community (Lather 1988).

Researchers who interview youth are also calling for more action-oriented research as well as for more discussion on ethics, praxis, and qualitative work. Angela Valenzuela (1999) found a unique opportunity to assist one of the English teachers in the high school in which she was conducting research. The seasoned teacher was having difficulty controlling the classroom and asked Valenzuela to speak to his class. During her visit, she not only gathered valuable data, but was able to speak with the kids openly and honestly, diffuse the situation, and explain to the teacher the roots of the difficult classroom dynamics.

In her work with high school dropouts, Michelle Fine (1994) sought to represent the voices of African American and Hispanic adolescents in courts and public policy debates as well as in academic scholarship. She raises several dilemmas associated with this action-oriented work, including whether or not others resent her speaking on their behalf and whether she might be colluding with structures of domination when her white, middle-class translation of her respondents' words is given more authority than their own narratives. She advises that those who do such work need to create communities of friendly critical informants who can help determine whose voices and analyses are foregrounded.

Fine's experience highlights the fact that differences in culture and power make researchers' attempts at reciprocity especially challenging. What may be culturally appropriate in one context may not be in another. Also, any attempt to affect change by researchers who hold greater power due to their ethnicity and/or social class may be viewed negatively by others. In such cases it is crucial that researchers consult informants about the cultural norms of reciprocity and be willing to work collaboratively for change rather than as independent agents.

In our own research projects with young people, we have sought to include some aspect of service to the communities in which the research took place. In Laura Fingerson's case, she volunteered at "Girls Inc.," the organization in which she collected her data, both before interviewing the girls for her study and then for the following two years. During that time she brought many of her academic skills, such as knowledge of computing, into the environment to enrich the lives of the girls who had participated in her study as well as other girls in this setting. After completing her study of gender, status, and peer culture, Donna Eder applied much of what she and others have learned about peer culture in developing a conflict intervention program for the schools in the community she studied. KACTIS (Kids Against Cruel Treatment in Schools) relied primarily on speech routines that were natural aspects of children's own cultures, such as role-play and collaborative performances. During these familiar routines, children developed alternative approaches for dealing with conflict and abuse that they had witnessed in their school.

We believe that researchers should consider how they can best benefit the communities in which their research takes place by considering from the start possible applications of their research for action as well as for theory. Those involved in action-oriented research have, like Fine (1994), faced political issues and dilemmas related to their attempts to benefit others. For example, Christopher Goodey's (1999) research on assessing the needs of students with learning disabilities reveals the importance of using the concept of "difficulty" rather than "need":

> In qualitative work difficulties must be critically probed rather than just ticked off, whereas research methods based on a concept of need tend to forestall reflexivity or mutual understanding. The notion of difficulty thus has a clear interactive character. It enables us to see something not purely as a consequence of specific characteristics of the child, but of the encounter between the child and [context] and thus to question the supposed division between "special" (pathological) and normal needs. (P. 4)

In her discussion of research involving community intervention, Joan Sieber (1992) notes that researchers may be restricted as to what they can do by members of the community who seek to protect the rights of youth. She warns that researchers involved in community intervention should decide ahead of time who will have access to their data. They should also consider how they can avoid using certain terms in their studies that could potentially stigmatize children, such as *sexually promiscuous* and *at risk,* so that their participants do not face any additional labeling when their data are employed to benefit others in the community.

◆ Combining Interviews with Other Methods

A combination of methods is often useful in research because it is difficult for any single method to capture fully the richness of human experience (Denzin and Lincoln 1994). Because children's experiences are grounded in their own peer cultures and life experiences, it is especially important that researchers use interviews in combination with other methods, both to obtain more valid responses and to strengthen the analysis of interview data. In this section we look at research that has combined group interviews with field observation, content analysis of media, and individual interviews.

COMBINING INTERVIEWS WITH FIELD OBSERVATION

Field observation has often been combined with interviewing in studies of youth. In some cases, observation sets the ground for the interviews, which are the primary mode of data collection. In other cases, participant observation is the main methodology and interviews are used to complement the collection of field notes based on extensive observation. Finally, some studies draw equally on both methods or combine them with additional methods, such as the use of diaries, surveys, or recorded observations.

We believe that it is essential to begin an interview study with at least some type of field observation. This could take place over a few days or a much longer period, depending on the setting and the research agenda. Without such initial observation, the researcher will find it difficult to assess how to introduce the interviews into the setting in a natural manner. Through observation, the researcher can identify naturally occurring events during which interviews could take place as well as typical language routines in the setting. Observation also helps the researcher to assess some of the basic communicative norms and patterns that children of given ages and backgrounds are using, so that he or she can modify the interview format to include them. Finally, observation can increase the researcher's general understanding of the children's local culture and social structure.

Whether or not interviewing is the main methodology in a study, a period of field observation can enable the researcher to gain rapport with the children prior to interviewing them. Fingerson spent a month volunteering in the setting prior to interviewing girls in groups about their reactions to family television programs. Eder and her colleagues spent several months observing adolescent lunchtime and after-school activities before formulating certain questions that they then asked in interviews with groups of students during lunchtime. In both cases, the initial periods of observation allowed us to establish a high degree of rapport with respondents, so that we could join in their conversations during the interviews, making them seem extensions of their naturally occurring talk.

Just as observations are a useful supplement to an interview-based study, interviews can add important information to studies based primarily on participant or field observation. Although interviews have played an important role in many ethnographic studies of children and youth, only some ethnographers have taken the time to write directly about their interviewing decisions. Penelope Eckert (1989), who studied social categories and identities in high school, notes that she purposely allowed her group interviews to be highly unstructured. She formed her groups by asking a student she knew to gather a group of friends to talk about "stuff." When the group met, she let them talk about whatever topics they considered interesting or important, asking questions only to get the discussion under way.

Likewise, in his study of suburban youth, Ralph Larkin (1979) emphasized the importance of unstructured group interviews. Rather than asking predetermined questions in his interviews, he developed his role as that of a discussion facilitator to a student-based conversation. Larkin purposely avoided the use of more structured questions that would place the definitions of concepts and reality in the hands of the researcher. He wanted his interviews to tap into the students' own reality rather than force their experiences and ideas to fit predetermined categories.

In Eder's study of adolescent peer cultures, the researchers used group interviews to collect more information on concepts and processes that were clearly salient based on observations, but were not fully explained by them (Eder 1995; Simon et al. 1992). For example, although popularity and status hierarchy were obvious concepts, the researchers needed to ask students specifically: "What makes certain students more popular than others?" and "What does it mean to be popular?" These questions arose in part because the researchers associated popularity with being well liked, but the students' comments during natural conversations and during the interviews suggested that they did not. In addition, because romantic feelings toward boys were such a major preoccupation for some groups of girls, the researchers asked them several questions regarding their views on the importance of boys in their lives and the difference between concepts of "liking" and "going with" someone. These interviews ended up revealing a set of norms that girls more or less agreed upon regarding romantic feelings at their age. In both cases, the researchers used interviews primarily to help them understand the adolescents' perceptions and views of these concepts and processes, rather than relying solely on their own interpretations.

Although interviewing can add important information to participant observation studies, researchers should also be aware of the limitations of interviews. There are aspects of children's cultures that are difficult to put into words, and these aspects need to be captured through direct observation rather than interviews. For example, Bronwyn Davies (1989), who studied preschool children, says this about her experience observing their play:

> Sometimes the children would provide an explanation if they came to talk to me. But there was often no immediate answer, for neither they nor I could *say* what it was that was going on because we did not know how to find the words or concepts that would encapsulate the event. To this extent the children's world was as yet only partially shaped

by language, by linguistic symbolic forms. And for this reason learning to interact with them on their own terms was of central importance. (P. 39)

INTERVIEWS AS PART OF MEDIA INTERPRETATION STUDIES

Group interviewing of children is a particularly good method for gathering data for use in media reception analysis. Many studies examining media have focused only on media content rather than on how audiences interpret the media themselves (Greenberg 1980; Cantor 1991; Cantor and Cantor 1992). How audiences perceive and understand television, for example, is not determined solely by programmed content (Granello 1997); rather, viewers select from and assign significance to specific televised messages through social interaction and experience. Janice Radway (1984) terms the social groups in which viewers collectively interpret media texts "interpretive communities." These are the groups with which viewers discuss, evaluate, and interpret television programs. They include children's peer groups. Because watching television consumes such large amounts of their time, children discuss television meanings as a social activity, and through this interaction they create meanings out of the programs' messages and content (Peterson and Peters 1983; Milkie 1994; Gillespie 1995).

It is important that researchers examine the perceptions and interpretations that youth have of media rather than relying solely on their own adult interpretations, such as is done in content analysis studies. For example, Robert Hodge and David Tripp (1986) combined semiotic content analysis with audience reception analysis in a study of 8- to 12-year-old Australian children's responses to the cartoon *Fangface*. They specifically argue for the importance of language: "For these children it is as

though their own thoughts and feelings do not really exist unless they become public and visible through language: the language of others requiring attention and consciousness, their own language reinforcing or sometimes deforming their fluid, inchoate structures of meaning" (p. 66). We agree with this formulation, which emphasizes how important group processes and language are in enabling us to understand children's worlds.

In Fingerson's (1999) research, she used individual interviews combined with focus groups to uncover how middle school girls individually and collectively interpreted family television programs. In particular, she found it interesting to see what the girls focused on in their group discussions. For example, the individual interviews brought up a variety of different issues, but in the focus groups, the girls particularly enjoyed discussing issues of the body brought up in the television programs viewed.

In one group, the girls discussed how Tim, a character on the television program *Home Improvement*, slipped and fell into a portable toilet from the top of a high steel structure at a construction site. The girls expanded and elaborated on this scene in a sequence of collaborative talk dealing with issues of body control and bodily functions. One girl noted that Tim's falling into the portable toilet was realistic because "I can't even balance on a curb!" Body control was uncovered as a salient theme in their culture, possibly because growing limbs and changing centers of gravity leave many girls in their age group feeling unusually clumsy, like Tim. According to the culturalist approach (McRobbie 1991), one cannot summarily determine the effects and meanings of media programs through their content; rather, these effects and meanings are shaped by the individual viewer's attachment of salience to particular events and experiences. The use of group interviews in combination with individual interviews is an excellent way for researchers to access children's and adolescents' understanding of media.

Other studies of children's interpretations of media indicate that children sometimes interpret stories very differently than do adults. In her study of feminist stories, Davies (1989) was surprised to find that some of the preschool children she interviewed expressed viewpoints that did not initially make sense to her, as in the following example:[1]

B.D.: If you were Oliver and you hated all the boy's things and you wanted to do girl's things, would you want to go to dancing school?

Robbie: No.

B.D.: (reads about boys teasing Oliver) So what sort of boys are they?

Robbie: Big, they//

B.D.: Big boys, and should they say that to Oliver Button?

Robbie: Yes.

B.D.: They should? (surprised) . . . (reads about boys writing "Oliver Button is a Sissy" on the school wall) How does Oliver feel?

Robbie: Sad.

B.D.: He's very sad isn't he? So should the boys have written that on the wall?

Robbie: (nods)

B.D.: They should? (surprised) Why should they have written that on the wall?

Robbie: Because he, because he's a sissy doing tap dancing.

B.D.: (reads about Oliver practicing his dancing) So why do you suppose he keeps going though everybody gives him a hard time there?

Robbie: Because he just wants to.

B.D.: He just wants to and should you keep doing what you want to do even though everybody keeps giving you a hard time?

Robbie: (nods) (Pp. 27-28)

Davies notes several contradictions in Robbie's responses as viewed from an adult perspective. Robbie states that it is both right to tease someone who is deviating and right to keep doing what you want to do. Also, even though he knows the teasing makes Oliver sad, he believes that the teasing is okay. It is important to realize that what might be contradictory viewpoints for an adult might not be contradictory for a child. It is only through interviewing children about media that researchers can reveal these different perspectives.

COMBINING SINGLE AND GROUP INTERVIEWS

In this chapter we have advocated using group interviews with children, as these can nicely capture group interactive processes in an efficient way (Morgan 1993). Also, guided interviewing techniques used in focus groups can uncover specific concepts and feelings in the peer culture of interest to the researcher that are not always spoken about regularly in everyday settings. Finally, group interviews readily allow children's own conversational styles to appear.

Some researchers have also found success with individual interviews, such as Carol Gilligan in her studies of girls' self-esteem, confidence, and communication styles (Gilligan 1982; Gilligan, Lyons, and Hanmer 1990; Brown and Gilligan 1992; Taylor et al. 1995) and Youniss and Smollar (1985) in their research on adolescents' relations with their mothers, fathers, and friends. Although Lyn Mikel Brown and Gilligan (1992) note their concern about their respondents' possibly tailoring their answers to seek approval from the researchers, we find mixed evidence of this. As the example from Davies's (1989) study presented above shows, Davies found that children frequently gave answers that were different from those she expected or approved of, even when being interviewed alone. She notes that the children simply saw her as another person who needed to have the way the world really is explained to her.

Individual interviews are especially common in studies of sexuality and body issues. For example, Deborah Tolman (1994) interviewed girls about their experiences and feelings of sexual desire; Sue Lees (1993) interviewed mostly girls and some boys about their sexuality and how they experience their worlds; Michelle Fine and Pat Macpherson (1994) interviewed teenage girls on adolescent feminism, including femininity and sexuality; and Roberta Simmons and Dale Blyth (1987) interviewed both boys and girls on the combined impacts of pubertal change and changing school contexts on self-esteem and self-image.

Sharon Thompson (1995) interviewed girls individually about sexuality, love, and romance and found great success in assessing these girls' narratives of their experience through long, open-ended interviews. Most of these interviews were individual, although she interviewed some respondents in pairs or occasionally in groups. Thompson states: "Their accounts sometimes had a polished quality that made them seem rehearsed, and in a way they were. These were the stories that teenage girls spend hundreds of hours telling each other, going over and over detail and possibility, reporting, strategizing, problem solving, constructing sexual and existential meaning for themselves" (p. 4). Thompson was able to tap into an existing mode of talk for these girls—one-on-one conversations about their romantic and sexual experiences that they already do in their everyday lives with friends.

Using both single and group interviews in conjunction can be an effective method for uncovering social phenomena among older children and adolescents. Older children and adolescents have the developmental capacity to reflect upon their experiences in the manner needed to complete individual interviews successfully. By including single interviews in research, the investigator can examine the participants' individual attitudes, opinions, and contexts and use this information to understand more fully the discussion occurring in the group interviews. Peggy Orenstein (1994) conducted group interviews first in her study of eighth-grade girls in school and then selected individuals from those groups to interview alone in further depth to understand more about their individual contexts, feelings, and experiences.

In addition, some themes may be discussed in individual interviews that may not appear in group discussions but are still important and relevant to the participants and their individual understandings of their social worlds. In this way, the researcher can explore social interaction dimensions. For example, in Hecht's (1998) research with Brazilian street children, the children interviewed in group settings would often defend their mothers to others even though they were not living at home with them. In private conversations, however, they would often reveal feelings of rejection and abandonment by their mothers.

Fingerson (1999) used a combination of individual interviews and focus groups in her research on girls' interpretations of family television programs. Background questions asked in one-on-one settings are particularly necessary in reception analysis; in Fingerson's research, the answers to such questions were essential to her understanding of the unique context of each girl's television viewing and interpretation. For example, one of the girls in the study did not participate fully during the discussions of television programs other than the program viewed for the study and appeared to be quite frustrated about this. Fingerson knew that this was based in part on the strict television-watching rules in the girl's home, which meant that she had less experience with popular television shows than did the other girls.

Also, by conducting individual interviews first, Fingerson was able to see peer power influences in the group interviews. She found that girls reflected on their own opinions and beliefs in the individual interviews but would change those beliefs in the group interviews to be more congruent with their peers. In one of the focus groups, the girls agreed that the family shown in the television program was not realistic, even though they had said the opposite in the individual interviews. The instigator, however, was Alice, who was more popular at the girls' club and more socially powerful than the other girls in this particular group. Fingerson argues that the other two girls were deferring to Alice's higher status by changing their views without introducing the contrasting views they had expressed earlier individually.

In this incident, Alice's greater status allowed her response to carry more weight in the group discussions. This points to a potential problem with group interviews —that is, the power dynamics among peers may influence the nature of their responses. Although we see this as a possible bias in group interview data, the many advantages of group interviews generally outweigh this disadvantage. In fact, many studies based on field observation data in which children are observed interacting in peer groups would have a similar disadvantage in that socially constructed knowledge often is biased in favor of more powerful peers (Adler and Adler 1998). Thus, in seeking to create the most natural contexts possible, interviewers will often need to confront naturally occurring peer power dynamics.

However, in those interview situations where researchers have a particular interest in obtaining individual, unbiased perspectives, they have the option, as Fingerson did, of including individual interviews as part of the research design. Also, researchers can interview children in groups with other classmates or schoolmates who are not part of their smaller peer groups, as long as it is possible to create such group contexts. Finally, keeping groups small in size (three or four members) further helps to minimize the influence of peer power dynamics.

It is important to reflect on the order in which individual and group interviews are conducted. In Fingerson's (1999) research, she was interested in comparing individual responses with changes emerging in group discussion. In this context, it was important that she ask the girls their individual opinions first. In other research, it may be more appropriate to conduct group interviews first. For example, in dealing with sensitive topics, such as sexuality, the body, and intimate relationships, children and adolescents may feel more comfortable in a group. This places the respondents in a position of power as they outnumber the researcher and are among their own friends and peers. Then, after a comfort level has been reached in the group and the topics have been discussed in the open, they may feel more comfortable, confident, and relaxed in a one-on-one setting with the researcher.

◆ Issues in Data Analysis

We now turn from issues of data collection to issues of data analysis. We begin by examining the many uses of sociolinguistic analysis in interviewing studies. We then follow this examination with a discussion of the importance of representing youth in their own terms.

SOCIOLINGUISTIC ANALYSIS OF INTERVIEW DATA

Sociolinguistic analysis can help to uncover the discourse and conversational norms of the participants in a research project. This is all the more important when the focus of the study is on children, because children's conversational norms and patterns can differ substantially from those of adult respondents. Sociolinguistic analysis of interview data is also an important way to address the power dynamics between the researcher and participants so that the discourse styles of both are incorporated within the interview format (see Shuy, Chapter 26, this volume).

There are a number of ways in which a researcher can bring sociolinguistic analysis into an interview study. Briggs (1986) advocates the microanalysis of an interactional event (either a natural conversation or an initial informal interview) as a way to learn the communicative norms of the participants. Eder has conducted such an analysis in her current research on children's interpretations of animal teaching stories. In analyzing the first informal interview, Eder discovered that certain questions were picked up more often than others by the group of fourth- and fifth-grade students. Not only did they have many answers to these questions when first asked, but they continued to give answers to them at various points throughout the interview, suggesting that these questions were highly salient and fit into children's own modes of discourse as well.

Eder also noted that certain of her respondents could tell from changes in her pitch and pacing that a section of interviewing was about to end and she was ready to move on to the next story. They made a point of bringing up additional ideas before it was too late. Realizing that the interviewer has the power to end sequences prematurely, Eder modified her interviewing technique, asking the children for their comments and questions or telling them directly that she was about to finish a particular section, so that they would have the opportunity to express their viewpoints completely before moving on.

Another way of bringing sociolinguistic analysis into an interview study is to begin the analysis by looking at the interview itself as a communicative event (Briggs 1986; see also in this volume Schaeffer and Maynard, Chapter 28; Baker, Chapter 37). This involves first examining the communicative structure of the interview as a whole, so that the meanings of specific responses are considered in regard to the whole event. It is clear from Eder's analysis that children drew upon questions asked early in the interview to provide responses throughout the interview. They also referred back to earlier humorous or salient remarks. Thus if an interviewer wants to set a tone of informality, interest in hearing from all respondents, and interest in how they see the questions as applying to their lives, it is important that he or she introduce these discourse styles and strategies early in the interview.

Analyzing the discourse styles of respondents is also an important way of assessing the degree of rapport and validity achieved during the interview. If the dialect codes and styles of talking that respondents use during the interview are those they use with people they know well and with whom they are comfortable, the researcher can be assured that a high level of validity has been achieved. For example, in her research on Puerto Rican children, Ana Celia Zentella (1998) combined discourse analysis with individual interviews, observation, and analysis of letters. When she asked one respondent about her use of mixed languages, the girl explained:

> Depends who you're talkin' to. If you're talkin' to—if you're talkin' to someone that really understands it, it's not [incorrect], not if you know the differences. . . . Because I can speak to you mixed up because I know you [ACZ: Yeah] so I got that confidence. Now if someone I don't know, I will impress them. I'll talk the language of intelligence. [ACZ: Okay] 'Cause I know you I'll talk to you how I WANNA speak to you, 'cause I know you. Like, for exam-

ple, right now I'm talkin to you how I WANNA speak to you. [ACZ: Right] But if I don't know you, I'll give you that RESPECT. (P. 107)

Here the respondent feels free to switch dialectical codes during the interview because she knows the interviewer well and it is the mode of speaking with which she is most comfortable. She further acknowledges her ability to use a more standard code with people she does not know as well, as a way to convey respect. By discussing this topic directly, the interviewer gains further evidence that this young woman feels comfortable using her preferred mode of speech during the interview.

A researcher can also gain a sense of whether the language respondents use during an interview reflects the typical norms of their group by looking at the modes of talk they use while answering other questions in the interview. For example, in Fingerson's (1999) research, she found numerous examples of collaborative talk and many examples of playful discourse. Both modes are typical of the ways in which girls of that age develop shared knowledge and strengthen the cohesion of their groups (Eder 1988, 1995). The following is an illustration from the group members' answers to a question on how television shows compare to real family life:

Annette: Well, I think the difference between TV families and real life families if they're like TV families seem to get along really well.

Carolyn: Yeah.

Annette: Like on *Full House* or something well they always have a problem but they talk it out and then everyone goes back to being one big happy family. Heh heh.

Carolyn: Heh heh.

Annette: Real life doesn't work that way.

Carolyn: Sort of like a fairy tale, always like a happy ending, heh.

Shauna: Yeah, that's not the way it happens in my family.

Carolyn: No, heh heh.

Annette: Heh heh.

In this collaborative talk sequence, the girls build upon each other's ideas in the "cooperative overlap style" (Eder 1988). Carolyn gives supporting comments to Annette, such as "yeah," and laughs along with the previous speaker. Often in collaboration, the speakers will start with minimal comments such as "yeah" and then expand on the topic later. Carolyn's first expansion is when she talks about the television program being "like a fairy tale." Shauna then enters the discussion by agreeing and expanding. Then the other two girls laugh in shared humor about how their families do not get along as well as the TV family does. The existence of this collaborative talk suggests that the girls naturally talk about television among their peers and supports the validity of using focus groups to investigate collective interpretations of media content.

So far, we have discussed sociolinguistic analysis primarily as a way to strengthen and assess the degree of validity in interview data. However, more and more research of children's experiences is addressing *how* children develop their social knowledge as well as the content of that knowledge. This indicates that sociolinguistic analysis can be an important part of the ongoing analysis of interview data, in that it can offer insights concerning how meanings are developed and shared.

Several approaches have been suggested for how to incorporate this type of analysis into more typical interview analysis of *what* people think and believe. Jaber Gubrium and James Holstein (1997) note that one way to deal with the tension of two different analytic focuses is through "analytic bracketing." Here, one employs one type of analysis at a time, looking either at what is being said or at how it is being accomplished.

Another approach is to examine both aspects of the analysis organized around the content of the material. In Eder's collaborative research on romantic norms among adolescent girls, the researchers examined both the content of each norm and the processes by which the norm was constructed and shared (Simon et al. 1992). In a group interview, girls discussed the norm of having romantic feelings for only one boy at a time. Although this was an emerging norm in this group of girls, it was not yet shared by all. Thus when this topic came up, their playful challenges became more serious, as can be seen in the following example:

Ellen: We were sittin' there starin' at guys at church last night, me and Hanna were, and—

Hanna: And she saw one that looked just like Craig.

Natalie: But// I was—

Ellen: I wasn't starin' at him.

Hanna: That was groaty.

Natalie: You're going with Craig.

Ellen: I know. I stared at Steve. Heh, heh.

Hanna: I know, but he looks like him in the face,

Natalie: But, um, he just—

Peg: You// go to church for a different reason than that, Ellen!

Natalie: I// get stuck on one guy.

Peg: Then you shouldn't of been there.

In this episode, the girls begin by providing mild challenges regarding Ellen's action of staring at one boy while going with another. Hanna comments, "That was groaty" (gross), and Natalie reminds Ellen that she is going with Craig. Ellen treats these challenges in a humorous manner, showing that she is not taking this violation seriously, and Hanna collaborates with Ellen by saying again that the boys look alike. Peg then offers another reason for the inappropriateness of Ellen's behavior—that it occurred in church. This is a more serious challenge to Ellen. It is immediately followed by Natalie stating the normative rule as she follows it: "I get stuck on one guy." In this episode we see how mild and strong challenges can be mixed together as girls deliberate their views on the norms of romantic love. It also shows that girls' informal discourse includes both confrontations and collaborations, often side by side. In general, this interview extract demonstrates not only the content of the girls' peer culture, but some of the communicative styles used to develop and express the norms of this culture.

REPRESENTING YOUTH IN THEIR OWN TERMS

In research on children and adolescents, there are several strategies investigators can use to give their respondents a voice. For example, Barrie Thorne (1994) uses the term *kids* to describe the participants in her research rather than *children*, which is a term only adults use. They refer to themselves as kids, so she maintains their own language and terminology in her research presentation. It is important to represent youth in their own terms in data analysis and presentation. Not only does this help maintain their power in the research interaction, but it preserves their conceptions and meanings in the analysis and text.

Another way in which a researcher can represent children in their own terms is by actively bringing children's voices into the research project itself and any presentations of the research. This can be done through liberal use of direct quotes from interviews. Sara Shandler (1999) takes direct issue with adult representation of adolescent voices; she criticizes in particular the work of Mary Pipher (1994), who, in her best-selling book *Reviving Ophelia,* discusses adolescent girls and their difficulties with depression, eating disorders, addictions, and suicide attempts. Shandler, who wrote her book *Ophelia Speaks* while she was a high school student, argues that Pipher accurately uncovers issues of importance to Shandler and her friends, but notes her disappointment that the voices of the girls studied are not represented in Pipher's research. In response, Shandler solicited letters and essays from adolescent girls all over the United States; *Ophelia Speaks* is composed mostly of these unedited essays.

Other researchers have made conscious efforts to include participants' voices in their research presentations. Lees (1993) demonstrates her awareness of the importance of the language and discourse structures of the girls she studied through her open-ended and nondirective interview techniques as well as her liberal use of direct quotes in her book. She argues that "by focusing on the terms girls used to describe their world, and by looking across at the transcripts, light was thrown on the commonalities of the girls' lives and how individual experiences were socially structured" (p. 11). In a more direct approach, Hecht (1998) developed "radio workshops" in which the participants handled the audio recorder and asked each other questions. Then, in his analysis, he relied heavily on the children's questions as analytic categories. In general, researchers can use participants' own voices, which accurately express their views, and give them some power over the presentation of their voices as yet another way to combat the power differential inherent in the researcher-researched relationship.

◆ Conclusion

A theme throughout this chapter has been the importance of finding multiple ways of responding to the power differential between adult researchers and young participants. Some feminist researchers have come to the conclusion that regardless of any efforts a researcher makes, the researcher has the ultimate power in the interaction because he or she is the final distributor of the data and findings drawn from that data (Fonow and Cook 1991; Acker, Barry, and Esseveld 1991; Reinharz 1992). As Pamela Cotterill (1992) argues, the researcher and the researched both have power that fluctuates and shifts between the two during the interview; however, the researcher holds the final power because it is he or she who does the interpretation and presents the data to the wider world, and these data will most likely never reach the respondents or their everyday lives. The respondents are vulnerable because they have no control over the production or distribution of the research. In spite of this, we have argued that researchers can and should attempt to empower their respondents, particularly in research involving children, where there are inherent power differences between adult and child in addition to those between researcher and participant.

As Reinharz (1992) states, interviewing allows people access to the participants' ideas, thoughts, and memories using their own words, terminology, and language structure (see also Reinharz and Chase, Chapter 11, this volume). As interviewers, our goal is to learn about the participants' worlds in their own terms (Taylor and Rupp 1991). Rather than translating these words into our own language for data presentation, we should sustain the participants' language use, as it adds new perspectives and greater depth to the data and analyses. In particular, we need to let children and adolescents speak for themselves in the data, as their language and speech are often marginalized in adult culture.

By representing our research participants in their own language and in their own terms, we can avoid viewing them as a separate "Other" (Fine 1994; Lincoln and Denzin 1994). Yvonna Lincoln and Norman Denzin (1994) argue that social science is now in a crisis of representation, with researchers asking: "Who is the Other? Can we ever hope to speak authentically of the experience of the Other, or an Other? And if not, how do we create a social science that includes the Other?" (p. 577). They argue that the answer to these questions is that, as researchers, we must include the Other in our research processes and research presentations.

Michelle Fine (1994) believes that in order to resist Othering, we need to "work the hyphen." By this she means that we must actively understand and probe our relationships with those we study. We should bring the researcher into the text and interpret the negotiated relations between the researcher and the researched to avoid seeing the researched as a distant and separate Other. Fine asserts that we must acknowledge the researcher's context, including his or her race, class, gender, and voice. Understanding these relations and placing the researcher in the data, Fine argues, will give us better data, help us to be more true to the data and the participants, and engage us in an intimacy with our research participants that will help us to be more honest in our analyses, interpretations, and data presentation.

Hood et al. (1999) ask several questions that we as researchers must think about in our endeavors: "Whose interests are served by research? For whom is it undertaken? What research methods are appropriate? How can those researched find a voice in the research process?" It is particularly important that we ask the questions of research "for what and for whom" when we are conducting research on children, as they are among the least powerful of all research participants.

In interviewing with children and adolescents, the power imbalance between interviewer and interviewee is highlighted so that it is impossible to ignore. However, much of what we have discussed in this chapter is relevant to other interview contexts as well. Although children are perhaps the least powerful Others, women, people of color, lower-class people, and those with disabilities also lack power in our society. We have drawn on the writings of feminists and people of color for insights into how to deal with the power differential of age. In turn, we believe that many of the insights gained by those who have examined age as a power factor can be applied to other situations in which there are additional power differences between researchers and participants. Indeed, all interviewers could benefit from considering these issues, because interviewers, by virtue of their role in data collection and analysis, have a power advantage over their respondents. As we have stated throughout, this advantage is most problematic when interviewers fail to recognize it and fail to adopt strategies to minimize the power imbalance. By increasing awareness of this important issue, we hope in general to promote better interview data as well as better relationships between researchers and those they study.

■ Note

1. In the examples of discourse data, double slashes indicate where an interruption has occurred and material in parentheses describes nonverbal and paralinguistic behaviors. All names used in the examples are pseudonyms.

■ References

Acker, J., K. Barry, and J. Esseveld. 1991. "Objectivity and Truth: Problems in Doing Feminist Research." Pp. 133-53 in *Beyond Methodology: Feminist Scholarship as Lived Research*, edited by M. M. Fonow and J. A. Cook. Bloomington: Indiana University Press.

Adler, P. A. and P. Adler. 1998. *Peer Power: Preadolescent Culture and Identity*. New Brunswick, NJ: Rutgers University Press.

Albrecht, T. L., G. M. Johnson, and J. B. Walther. 1993. "Understanding Communication Processes in Focus Groups." Pp. 51-64 in *Successful Focus Groups: Advancing the State of the Art*, edited by D. L. Morgan. Newbury Park, CA: Sage.

Briggs, C. L. 1986. *Learning How to Ask: A Sociolinguistic Appraisal of the Role of the Interview in Social Science Research*. Cambridge: Cambridge University Press.

Brown, L. M. and C. Gilligan. 1992. *Meeting at the Crossroads: Women's Psychology and Girls' Development*. New York: Ballantine.

Bryant, B. K. 1985. "The Neighborhood Walk: Sources of Support in Middle Childhood." *Monographs of the Society for Research in Child Development* 50(3, Serial No. 210).

Cantor, M. G. 1991. "The American Family on Television: From Molly Goldberg to Bill Cosby." *Journal of Comparative Family Studies* 22:205-16.

Cantor, M. G. and J. M. Cantor. 1992. *Prime-Time Television: Content and Control*. Newbury Park, CA: Sage.

Caputo, V. 1995. "Anthropology's Silent 'Others': A Consideration of Some Conceptual and Methodological Issues for the Study of Youth and Children's Cultures," in *Youth Cultures: A Cross-Cultural Perspective*, edited by V. Amit-Talai and H. Wulff. London: Routledge.

Collins, P. H. 1990. *Black Feminist Thought: Knowledge, Consciousness, and the Politics of Empowerment*. New York: Routledge, Chapman & Hall.

Cook, J. A. and M. M. Fonow. 1986. "Knowledge and Women's Interests: Issues of Epistemology and Methodology in Feminist Sociological Research." *Sociological Inquiry* 56:2-27.

Corsaro, W. A. 1981. "Entering the Child's World: Research Strategies for Field Entry and Data Collection in a Preschool Setting." Pp. 117-46 in *Ethnography and Language in Educational Settings*, edited by J. Green and C. Wallet. Norwood, NJ: Ablex.

———. 1997. *The Sociology of Childhood*. Thousand Oaks, CA: Pine Forge.

Corsaro, W. A. and D. Eder. 1995. "The Development and Socialization of Children and Adolescents." Pp. 421-51 in *Sociological Perspectives on Social Psychology*, edited by K. S. Cook, G. A. Fine, and J. S. House. Boston: Allyn & Bacon.

Cotterill, P. 1992. "Interviewing Women: Issues of Friendship, Vulnerability, and Power." *Women's Studies International Forum* 15:5-6.

Davies, B. 1989. *Frogs and Snails and Feminist Tales: Preschool Children and Gender*. Boston: Allen & Unwin.

Denzin, N. K. and Y. S. Lincoln. 1994. "Introduction: Entering the Field of Qualitative Research." Pp. 1-17 in *Handbook of Qualitative Research*, edited by N. K. Denzin and Y. S. Lincoln. Thousand Oaks, CA: Sage.

Eckert, P. 1989. *Jocks and Burnouts: Social Categories and Identity in the High School*. New York: Teachers College Press.

Eder, D. 1988. "Building Cohesion through Collaborative Narration." *Social Psychology Quarterly* 51:225-35.

———. 1995. *School Talk: Gender and Adolescent Culture*. New Brunswick, NJ: Rutgers University Press.

Fine, G. A. and K. L. Sandstrom. 1988. *Knowing Children: Participant Observation with Minors*. Newbury Park, CA: Sage.

Fine, M. 1994. "Working the Hyphens: Reinventing Self and Other in Qualitative Research." Pp. 70-82 in *Handbook of Qualitative Research*, edited by N. K. Denzin and Y. S. Lincoln. Thousand Oaks, CA: Sage.

Fine, M. and P. Macpherson. 1994. "Over Dinner: Feminism and Adolescent Female Bodies." Pp. 219-46 in *Power/Gender: Social Relations in Theory and Practice,* edited by H. L. Radtke and H. J. Stam III. London: Sage.

Fingerson, L. 1999. "Active Viewing: Girls' Interpretations of Family Television Programs." *Journal of Contemporary Ethnography* 28:389-418.

Fonow, M. M. and J. A. Cook. 1991. "Back to the Future: A Look at the Second Wave of Feminist Epistemology and Methodology." Pp. 1-15 in *Beyond Methodology: Feminist Scholarship as Lived Research,* edited by M. M. Fonow and J. A. Cook. Bloomington: Indiana University Press.

Frønes, I. 1994. "Dimensions of Childhood." Pp. 145-64 in *Childhood Matters: Social Theory, Practice and Politics,* edited by J. Qvortrup, M. Bardy, G. Sgritta, and H. Wintersberger. Aldershot, England: Avebury.

Gillespie, M. 1995. *Television, Ethnicity and Cultural Change.* London: Routledge.

Gilligan, C. 1982. *In a Different Voice: Psychological Theory and Women's Development.* Cambridge, MA: Harvard University Press.

Gilligan, C., N. P. Lyons, and T. J. Hanmer, eds. 1990. *Making Connections: The Relational Worlds of Adolescent Girls at Emma Willard School.* Cambridge, MA: Harvard University Press.

Goodey, C. 1999. "Learning Disabilities: The Researcher's Voyage to Planet Earth." In *Critical Issues in Social Research: Power and Prejudice,* edited by S. Hood, B. Mayall, and S. Oliver. Philadelphia: Open University Press.

Granello, D. H. 1997. "Using *Beverly Hills, 90210* to Explore Developmental Issues in Female Adolescents." *Youth & Society* 29:24-53.

Green, R. 1990. "American Indian Women: Diverse Leadership for Social Change." Pp. 61-73 in *Bridges of Power: Women's Multicultural Alliances,* edited by L. Albrecht and R. M. Brewer. Philadelphia: New Society.

Greenberg, B. S. 1980. *Life on Television: Content Analyses of U.S. TV Drama.* Norwood, NJ: Ablex.

Gubrium, J. F. and J. A. Holstein. 1997. *The New Language of Qualitative Method.* New York: Oxford University Press.

Hecht, T. 1998. *At Home in the Street: Street Children of Northeast Brazil.* Cambridge: Cambridge University Press.

Hodge, R. and D. Tripp. 1986. *Children and Television: A Semiotic Approach.* Cambridge: Polity.

Holmes, R. M. 1998. *Fieldwork with Children.* Thousand Oaks, CA: Sage.

Hood, S., B. Mayall, and S. Oliver. 1999. "Introduction." In *Critical Issues in Social Research: Power and Prejudice,* edited by S. Hood, B. Mayall, and S. Oliver. Philadelphia: Open University Press.

Larkin, R. 1979. *Suburban Youth in Cultural Crisis.* New York: Oxford University Press.

Lather, P. 1988. "Feminist Perspectives on Empowering Research Methodologies." *Women's Studies International Forum* 11:569-81.

Lees, S. 1993. *Sugar and Spice: Sexuality and Adolescent Girls.* London: Penguin.

Lincoln, Y. S. and N. K. Denzin. 1994. "The Fifth Moment." Pp. 575-86 in *Handbook of Qualitative Research,* edited by N. K. Denzin and Y. S. Lincoln. Thousand Oaks, CA: Sage.

Mayall, B. 1999. "Children and Childhood." In *Critical Issues in Social Research: Power and Prejudice,* edited by S. Hood, B. Mayall, and S. Oliver. Philadelphia: Open University Press.

McRobbie, A. 1991. *Feminism and Youth Culture: From "Jackie" to "Just Seventeen."* Boston: Unwin Hyman.

Milkie, M. 1994. "Social World Approach to Cultural Studies: Mass Media and Gender in the Adolescent Peer Group." *Journal of Contemporary Ethnography* 23:354-80.

Morgan, D. L. 1993. "Future Directions for Focus Groups." In *Successful Focus Groups: Advancing the State of the Art,* edited by D. L. Morgan. Newbury Park, CA: Sage.

Orenstein, P. 1994. *School Girls: Young Women, Self-Esteem, and the Confidence Gap.* New York: Doubleday.

Peterson, G. W. and D. F. Peters. 1983. "Adolescents' Construction of Social Reality: The Impact of Television and Peers." *Youth & Society* 15:67-85.

Pipher, M. 1994. *Reviving Ophelia: Saving the Selves of Adolescent Girls.* New York: Ballantine.

Prout, A. and A. James. 1997. "A New Paradigm for the Sociology of Childhood? Provenance, Promise, and Problems." Pp. 7-33 in *Constructing and Reconstructing Childhood: Contemporary Issues in the Sociological Study of Childhood,* edited by A. James and A. Prout. London: Falmer.

Radway, J. 1984. "Interpretive Communities and Variable Literacies." *Daedalus* 113:49-73.

Reinharz, S. 1992. *Feminist Methods in Social Research.* New York: Oxford University Press.

Shandler, S. 1999. *Ophelia Speaks: Adolescent Girls Write about Their Search for Self.* New York: Harper Perennial.

Sieber, J. E. 1992. "Community Intervention Research on Minors." In *Social Research on Children and Adolescents: Ethical Issues,* edited by B. Stanley and J. E. Sieber. Newbury Park, CA: Sage.

Simmons, R. G. and D. A. Blyth. 1987. *Moving into Adolescence: The Impact of Pubertal Change and School Context.* New York: Aldine de Gruyter.

Simon, R., D. Eder, and C. Evans. 1992. "The Development of Feeling Norms Underlying Romantic Love among Adolescent Females." *Social Psychology Quarterly* 55:29-46.

Tammivaara, J. and D. S. Enright. 1986. "On Eliciting Information: Dialogues with Child Informants." *Anthropology and Education Quarterly* 17:218-38.

Taylor, J. M., C. Gilligan, and A. M. Sullivan. 1995. *Between Voice and Silence: Women and Girls, Race and Relationship.* Cambridge, MA: Harvard University Press.

Taylor, V. and L. J. Rupp. 1991. "Researching the Women's Movement: We Make Our Own History, but Not Just as We Please." Pp. 119-32 in *Beyond Methodology: Feminist Scholarship as Lived Research,* edited by M. M. Fonow and J. A. Cook. Bloomington: Indiana University Press.

Thompson, S. 1995. *Going All the Way: Teenage Girls' Tales of Sex, Romance, and Pregnancy.* New York: Hill & Wang.

Thorne, B. 1994. *Gender Play: Girls and Boys in School.* New Brunswick, NJ: Rutgers University Press.

Tolman, D. 1994. "Daring to Desire: Culture and Bodies of Adolescent Girls." In *Sexual Cultures and the Construction of Adolescent Identities,* edited by J. M. Irvine. Philadelphia: Temple University Press.

Valenzuela, A. 1999. *Subtractive Schooling: U.S.-Mexican Youth and the Politics of Caring.* Albany: State University of New York Press.

Ward, J. and J. Taylor. 1991. "Sex Education for Immigrant and Minority Students: Developing a Culturally Appropriate Curriculum." In *Sexuality and the Curriculum: The Politics and Practices of Sexuality Education,* edited by J. T. Sears. New York: Teachers College Press.

Weisner, T. S. 1996. "Why Ethnography Should Be the Most Important Method in the Study of Human Development." In *Ethnography and Human Development: Context and Meaning in Social Inquiry,* edited by R. Jessor, A. Colby, and R. A. Shweder. Chicago: University of Chicago Press.

Youniss, J. and J. Smollar. 1985. *Adolescent Relations with Mothers, Fathers, and Friends.* Chicago: University of Chicago Press.

Zentella, A. C. 1998. "Multiple Codes, Multiple Identities: Puerto Rican Children in New York City." Pp. 95-112 in *Kids Talk: Strategic Language Use in Later Childhood,* edited by S. M. Hoyle and C. T. Adger. New York: Oxford University Press.

10

INTERVIEWING MEN

◆ Michael L. Schwalbe
Michelle Wolkomir

For most of the history of social science, men were considered the standard, normal, unmarked category of human beings, and so it would have seemed odd, not that long ago, to write about interviewing *men,* as if doing so required special strategies or techniques. Some readers might be skeptical even now. Why, after all, isn't good technique enough? What is it about interviewing men that calls for anything more? Our answer is that good technique—as might befit the imaginary generic interview subject—does not adequately equip us to recognize and respond to problems that arise specifically from how men "do gender" in an interview. Working around these problems, and perhaps even turning them into useful data, requires seeing how they arise from men's efforts to signify, in culturally prescribed ways, a creditable masculine self.

Of course we are generalizing. All men, obviously, do not behave the same way in interviews. Much depends on who is inter-

viewing whom, how, about what, when, and where. To the extent, however, that men attempt to signify elements of what has come to be called *hegemonic masculinity,* and do so in conventional ways, their behavior will be patterned (Connell 1995). We might even say that although the category "men" is internally diverse in many ways, what gives it coherence at all is its members' recognizably similar patterns of self-presentation. Which is to say that if the creatures we call "men" did not do gender in roughly similar ways, we would not even know them as men. But, again, our claim is not that all men behave alike; rather, it is that a particular *cultural* prescription for self-presentation—when men feel compelled to abide by it—will generate a predictable set of problems in interviews.

The advice we offer for dealing with these problems applies mainly to intensive, flexible interviewing (see Johnson, Chapter 5, this volume). This is the kind of interviewing that is most likely to evoke the masculinity displays that block communication and call for interviewer skill in drawing out unarticulated meanings. Our advice may thus be of less use to researchers doing survey-style interviews that do not probe sensitive territory. We are also addressing mainly those who do inductive or quasi-inductive research, because our advice presumes that interviews are open to change over the course of a study. If the aim of strict hypothesis testing dictates no evolution in interview content and strategy, then our advice will apply mostly to the phase in which an interview protocol is devised.

If one's research has to do with gender, then there is another good reason to pay attention to masculinity displays: Such displays are not simply obstacles to obtaining the data one wants, they may in fact constitute part of the data one needs (see also Reinharz and Chase, Chapter 11, this volume). *How* men answer questions and *how they behave in an interview* are potentially valuable sources of data when the research has to do with gender or topics related to gender (e.g., division of household labor). To see these data, we have to recognize the kinds of verbal and physical behaviors that can be interpreted as signifying masculinity. Knowing what to look for, as we will show, makes it possible for us to see not only problems but more information and new paths for inquiry.

In the section below we lay out our perspective on gender enactments as problems and as resources in interviewing men. In the next section of the chapter, we examine specific problems and offer potential solutions. We then consider strategies for informal interviewing—the practice of interviewing by casual question. Finally, we offer several general suggestions for doing better interviews in field studies focusing on men. Our advice grows primarily out of our experiences as field-workers studying men, usually in an inductive or quasi-inductive fashion. We hope that readers whose research styles differ will find ways to adapt our suggestions to suit their purposes.

◆ The Masculine Self and the Interview Situation

Gender is socially constructed, in part, through the identity work we do that marks us as members of the category "men" or the category "women" (Kessler and McKenna 1978; West and Zimmerman 1987). As adults, our bodies do much of this identity work for us, although we also use speech, dress, and movement to corroborate the body's silent claims (Schwalbe and Mason-Schrock 1996). But it is not merely category membership, as if this were a matter of casual choice, that we must signify. The prevailing gender order requires that we also signify possession of an essentially gendered self that makes our placement in a particular category right and proper. This self is not a psychic entity that exists inside individuals; rather, it is a dramatic effect created by performance and interpretation.[1]

For men, the dramaturgical task is to signify possession of an essentially masculine self, a self with the desires and capacities that warrant membership in the dominant group (Brittan 1989). Precisely what must be signified, and how it must be done, will vary by age, ethnicity, social class, sexual orientation, local culture, and immediate circumstance. A masculine self is thus always the product of a performance tailored to the situation and audience at hand. Despite variations in the details of performance, we can see commonalities that arise from a pervasive cultural notion of the qualities and capacities men must signify to be fully creditable as men.

In Western culture, men who wish to claim the full privileges of manhood must distinguish themselves from women by signifying greater desires and capacities for control of people and the world, autonomous thought and action, rational thought and action, risk and excitement, and (hetero)sexual pleasure and prowess (Connell 1995). Obviously, we have put things in general and abbreviated terms. Each element could be unpacked, and arguments could be made about which is most important. Our purpose, however, is only to sketch the self that men's expressive behavior is often aimed, sometimes strategically and perhaps more often as a matter of unconscious habit, at creating. We can, with this sketch in mind, get a better understanding of what goes wrong in interviews with men.

THE INTERVIEW AS THREAT AND OPPORTUNITY

Every encounter, as Erving Goffman (1967:97-112) notes, is fraught with risk. The selves we try to create, the selves to which are attached some of our strongest feelings, can be sabotaged by our own gaffes or by the antagonistic acts of others. All selves are thus provisional; none is safe from the threat of discrepant information or disbelieving audiences. The harder it is to control the leakage of discrepant information, or the more incredulous the audience, the harder it will be to sustain a particular kind of self. A masculine self can be a tenuous construct for both reasons.

To sustain such a self requires, as noted previously, signifying desires and/or capacities for control, autonomy, rationality, risk taking, and heterosexual conquest. Acts that signify these qualities must be integrated into a performance recognizable as "being a man." The problem, however, is that reality often contradicts the performance. Most men have little control over their worlds; no man exists without ties to others; men's alleged rationality is usually a matter of post hoc rationalizing to mask the emotional basis of action; most men are conformists who take few significant risks of any kind; and most men do more sexual fantasizing than "conquesting." The manhood act, we might say, is performed rather worriedly in a field of discrepant information.

Audience cooperation is often problematic because the masculine self is crafted to evoke deference and compliance in members of the validating audience. This gives others incentive to be alert for flaws in the performance, for evidence that a particular masculine self warrants less deference. The others who are likely to be most alert in this regard are other men, whose success at crafting a masculine self depends, in part, on the lesser success of other men's efforts. Women, too, are a dangerous audience, although usually for different reasons. Even while they may help to sustain the masculine self, women, as witnesses to men's weaknesses and failures, know just how much of an illusion it is. Women thus often possess a great deal of potentially discrediting information. Heterosexual women may also have incentive to disrupt the performance of manhood because of the obstacle it presents to achieving intimacy.

It is understandable, then, that men can be insecure, anxious, and afraid even while striving to construct a self that is supposedly the antithesis of these emotions. Some situations, of course, will be more problematic than others, depending on the performance called for and the cooperativeness of the audience. In general terms, however, we can say that situations that make it difficult to signify control, autonomy, rationality, and sexual desirability may be especially anxiety provoking for men wedded to displaying hegemonic masculinity.[2] In such situations we might expect to see behaviors aimed at countering, or symbolically compensating for, the real or implied threat to the masculine self.

An interview situation is both an opportunity for signifying masculinity and a peculiar type of encounter in which masculinity is threatened. It is an opportunity to signify masculinity inasmuch as men are allowed to portray themselves as in control, autonomous, rational, and so on. It is a threat inasmuch as an interviewer controls the interaction, asks questions that put these elements of manly self-portrayal into doubt, and does not simply affirm a man's masculinity displays. We propose distinguishing between the *baseline threat* to masculinity posed by the interview situation and the *surplus threat* that arises because of who is asking whom about what.

The baseline threat is built into any intensive interview. The situation is usually defined as one in which a stranger sets the agenda, asks the questions, controls the flow of talk, and probes for information about internal or backstage realities. To agree to sit for an interview, no matter how friendly and conversational, is to give up some control and to risk having one's public persona stripped away. For these reasons, many people, men and women, find interviews discomfiting. But because male privilege is staked on signifying a masculine self, men may perceive a greater threat and may act in ways that give rise to predictable sorts of problems—even if the topics being explored are not in themselves terribly sensitive.

Surplus threat can arise from at least two sources. One is a line of questioning that might expose the masculine self as illusory. Questions calling for answers that put control, autonomy, or rationality into doubt, if only implicitly, may be experienced as threatening. The threat may be heightened if it seems that the interviewer is interested in gender, broadly construed, because this makes the subject's identity as a man more salient to the interaction. Surplus threat can also arise because of the interviewer's identity. The threat potential is likely to be different if, for example, a gay man interviews other gay men about sexual behavior, as opposed to a straight man asking the same questions. Other kinds of difference—most obviously along lines of race, class, and age—in combination with certain topics, can also heighten the threat potential of an interview (see also in this volume Kong, Mahoney, and Plummer, Chapter 12; Dunbar, Rodriguez, and Parker, Chapter 14).

We do not suppose that the threat potential of a line of questioning, a specific topic, or an interviewer's identity is always con-sciously perceived. More likely, it is perceived only vaguely. Reactions to such threat are also more likely to be matters of self-presentational habit than of conscious strategy. Most men, after all, are well practiced in adapting their signifying behavior to the situation at hand. A subject's conscious awareness of the threat to the masculine self is, however, beside the point. What matters is the *interviewer's* awareness of the threat potential, alertness for problems arising because of this threat, and ability to respond in a way that makes the interview successful.

Again, the category "men" is internally diverse, and therefore all generalizations about how men will perceive and respond to the threat potential of an interview are empirically suspect. But so too are generalizations about men in categories defined by sexual orientation, race, ethnicity, and class. These categories are not unitary, either. Not all men who identify as gay, or as black, or as working-class will experience the threat potential of an interview in the same way, even if all else is constant. Multiple category memberships, plus an interviewer's possible ignorance of the categories to which a subject belongs, can also complicate things. We thus propose that the best way for an interviewer to deal with diversity among men is also the best way to discover patterns among men: Avoid presuming very much based on membership in *any* categories and rely instead on the interview itself to reveal the individual.

In considering specific problems and possible responses, we assume that the interviewer's goal is to obtain accurate and complete information about whatever matters the research is concerned with. The problems we discuss in the next section are ones that impede communication and thus make it hard for the interviewer to get good data. In most cases, the interviewer can overcome these problems by using strategies that minimize threat to the masculine self. But it would be a loss, we think, to treat the identity work men do in interviews as noise that one must filter out in order to get at the "real" data. Instead, we suggest that this identity work be treated as data—the first step being to see it, in the form of how and when men try to signify masculinity in interviews. The opportunity here for researchers is not merely to get more data, but to get a kind of data that can help us develop more insightful analyses of men's lives as gendered beings.

◆ Problems and Strategies

The problems examined here have come up in our work or the work of colleagues. The strategies we suggest are, in most cases, ones we have used ourselves. Their effectiveness will depend, of course, on context and on who is interviewing whom about what. A strategy that works for a male interviewer might not work for a female interviewer, and vice versa. The keys to finding a strategy that works are, first, recognizing the nature of the masculinity threat that is evoking defensiveness and, second, careful review of tapes or transcripts yielded by alternative strategies. Without some analysis, *early in a study,* of what is going wrong in interviews, it is hard to see how to make things go right.[3]

THE STRUGGLE FOR CONTROL

The interview situation itself, as we noted earlier, is potentially threatening to the masculine self because the interviewee relinquishes control, the exercise of which is a basic way in which masculinity is signified. To open oneself to interrogation is to put oneself in a vulnerable position, and thus to put one's masculinity further at risk. It is not uncommon, then, in our experience, for men being interviewed to try to exert a sort of compensatory control over the interview situation. This behavior can take various forms, which can be more or less problematic. Three forms that can disrupt the interview process are what we call testing, sexualizing, and minimizing.

Testing is an attempt to expose a researcher's agenda and/or inferiority when it comes to grasping the matters being inquired about. Terry Arendell (1997), for example, describes how some of the divorced fathers she interviewed made a point of saying that, as a woman, she would be unable to understand men's experiences and to give them fair consideration. Michelle Wolkomir (1999) describes how, in a study of gay religious men, she was told that, as a heterosexual woman, she would not be able to face the indelicate facts of gay male sex. In these cases, subjects sought to test both the interviewer's legitimacy as an interrogator and the interviewer's ability to maintain control of the situation (see Dunbar et al., Chapter 14, this volume). If the interviewer is flustered, or concedes being in unfathomable waters, control shifts to the interviewee.

How the interviewer handles such testing will have consequences for how the interview unfolds. Losing poise or concentration because of a subject's efforts to reassert control can obviously be detrimental to the quality of an interview. Expecting and being prepared for these assertions of compensatory control—and understanding their meaning—can render them manageable and, in fact, useful as data. To manage, or perhaps even preempt them, an interviewer might employ a number of strategies:

◆ Allow *symbolic* expressions of control. For example, explain what kind of arrangement is needed for a good interview to occur, and then let the subject choose the time and place. If the subject proposes an unsatisfactory arrangement, ask, "I wonder if you could find us a place that is [quieter/more private/more accessible]?" This strategy allows the subject to feel in control even while this "control" serves the purpose of creating a good interview situation.[4]

◆ Let the subject ask the first question. We presume that the interviewer will offer some sort of preamble before launching into questions. A way to do this that lowers the threat to control is to say, "I appreciate your willingness to help me with my research. Before I ask any questions, I wonder if you'd like to know more about what it is I'm interested in." This lets men feel less like they are relinquishing control to a stranger with an unknown agenda and provides a chance for the them to test the researcher in a way that can generate useful data.

◆ Challenge the subject to take charge as an *expert*. The idea is to allow men to feel in control and powerful in a particular way: by providing useful information. This can be done with probes that altercast the subject as expert or teacher: Can you explain to me how . . . ? Can you help me understand how . . . ? What does that entail? In light of your experience, can you tell me more about _____? What's the most important thing to understand about _____?

◆ A variation on the preceding strategy is to preface a question with "I'm not sure how to ask this, but . . . ." This preface, which should be used sparingly, reduces threat by taking the interviewer out of the role of grand inquisitor. It also allows the subject to assume a triple expert role: as one whose experiences are not easily grasped by outsiders, as one who knows how questions ought to be asked to get at the heart of things, and as one who knows the answers.

◆ In the face of overt testing, adopt the stance of an investigator who is firmly and fearlessly determined to learn whatever is important to know about the subject's experience. For example, Wolkomir, in seeking access to an ex-gay men's Bible study group, was initially tested by the group leader, who told her that the men's frank talk of "fisting" and other sexual practices would be more than she could handle. She replied, "It's only sex, and it seems to bother you more than me." This response effectively stopped the leader's testing behavior and gained Wolkomir access to the group.

◆ When the opportunity presents itself, probe sensitive topics by saying, "Since you brought it up, I was wondering if you could tell me more about _____." This allows the subject to feel more in control of the flow of talk and also invokes the conversational norm that obligates the subject to say more about a topic he has brought up.

In metaphorical terms, we are suggesting a kind of research aikido—the martial art of turning the other's movement and energy to one's own advantage. This is not to say that we see all interviews as contests or struggles. We prefer, in fact, the metaphor of conversation (Briggs 1986; Mishler 1986). Be that as it may, in interviews with men the subtle threat to control, hence to masculinity, can generate a kind of struggle —of which men themselves may be only dimly aware. It is the interviewer's job, however, to possess this awareness and to use it to keep things from going awry.

Inappropriate *sexualizing* is a way that some heterosexual men try to reassert control when being interviewed by women. This can take the forms of flirting, sexual innuendo, touching, and remarks on appearance (Arendell 1997; Gurney 1985; Lee 1997; McKee and O'Brien 1983). Although some of this behavior might be construed as innocent and harmless, it can also be seen as aimed at diminishing a woman's legitimacy and power as an interrogator, thus preserving a man's control of the situation. It is as if to say, "You might be asking the questions here, but I won't let you forget that you're a woman and I'm a man, and therefore I have the status advantage."

Given the normality of sexualized interaction between women and men, it might be hard to see sexualizing as a problem.

Some interviewers might even see "flirting" as a way to establish rapport. Although this might work in some cases, it has the distinct disadvantage of encouraging a subject to try to create an impression of himself as sexually desirable—and therefore to conceal unflattering information. Sexualized rapport can thus turn out to be counterproductive for maximizing information gained from an interview. With that caveat made, all we can say is that researchers must decide for themselves, all things considered in the context of a given study, the degree to which sexualizing is a problem and needs to be discouraged.

Unfortunately, with men who habitually and aggressively use a sexualizing strategy to disempower women, there might be little that a researcher can do about it. But keeping in mind that sexualizing is often about control suggests some possible ways to preempt or reduce it. Allowing symbolic control, in the ways proposed earlier, might help reduce a subject's "need" to sexualize an interview situation. Researchers might also try the following:

◆ Dress in a style—befitting local culture and circumstance—that conveys a businesslike seriousness of purpose, without crossing into off-putting formality.

◆ Reward, with close attention, an interviewee's "on-task" answers while showing cool disinterest, perhaps even disappointment, in "off-task" remarks. This behavioral modification strategy may lead men to realize, or intuit, that they will be seen as desirable interactants only by performing well as sources of pertinent and original information, not tired come-ons. In general, keep turning the interview back to the subject's experience and reporting thereof.

◆ Hold interviews in businesslike or quiet public settings. Library or workplace conference rooms are possibilities, if they can be reserved. Clearly there are times and topics that demand special provisions for privacy and psychic comfort, and thus the subject's home may be the best venue. If so, the kitchen table —"because that's where I'll be more comfortable writing notes"—might be preferable to the living room. Where an interview is held conveys a message about what the interaction is about.

Sexualizing probably occurs more often to female researchers than straight male researchers realize. But again, the likelihood that it will occur depends on who is interviewing whom about what and on the threat potential of the interview. So it is quite possible that some female researchers will rarely have to deal with it. In any event, being ready for it increases the interviewer's chances of responding in a way that will keep the interview on track. We would also note that sexualizing, like any other kind of masculinity-signifying behavior in an interview, is data. See, for example, Deborah Lee (1997), who discusses how men's efforts to sexualize interviews gave her some insight into how they engaged in sexual harassment at work.

A subject who *minimizes* fails to take normal conversational cues to give expansive answers, instead offering terse answers that tell little. This kind of response pattern is typically seen as constituting a "bad interview" because a subject is simply not articulate. Although sheer inarticulateness can indeed be the problem, minimizing can also arise from a desire to protect a masculine self by maintaining control or by revealing no vulnerabilities and uncertainties. Male interviewers may thus be more likely to encounter minimizing, because they are the potential status competitors to whom revealing vulnerabilities and uncertainties is risky.

When minimizing becomes apparent— when none of one's questions are being answered in the kind of depth one had hoped for—it is tempting to write the interview off as a loss and hope that the next one goes better. It may be possible, however, for an interviewer to draw out a great deal more information through the use of strategies that are sensitive to the fear felt by the minimizer.

◆ If a subject persists in giving terse answers, despite cues and probes, let the interview proceed in exactly this way. This allows the minimizer to feel in control. But instead of ending the interview after the last question, *circle back*. Try saying, "I think that what you've said gives me a good overall picture, but I'm still unsure about a few of the more complicated issues you brought up. For instance, when you said _____." The interviewer thus admits uncertainty, affirms the subject's experience as complex, and puts the subject in the driver's seat. Often the subject will then feel comfortable enough to elaborate in a useful way.

◆ Invoke what other men have said. For example, "What you said about _____ was interesting. Other men have brought this up, but your experience seems to be somewhat different. I wonder if you could tell me a bit more about what that's been like for you." This kind of probe can make the revelation of further information seem less risky to the minimizer. After all, if other men have talked about these issues, then perhaps it is safe for him to do so. The hint of competition may also nudge the minimizer to try to outdo those other men who said more about their experience.

◆ Notepads and tape recorders are signs of an interviewer's power and can be intimidating. Minimizers will sometimes open up if these tools are set aside and the conversation is carried on in a more casual way. If a tape recorder is running, leave the notepad alone as long as possible. If a minimizer begins to speak more freely after the "official" interview is over and the tape recorder is put away, keep asking questions. Later, capture as much as possible in the form of field notes.

Our use of the term *minimizer* implies the possibility of a subject who uses a maximizing strategy—expounding vastly—to take control in an interview. It happens, we suppose. But maximizing is rarely a problem, because information is flowing freely, in which case the interviewer need only keep the interview on track. In our experience, it is much easier to steer a loquacious subject than to draw out a taciturn one.

NONDISCLOSURE OF EMOTIONS

In a classic article, Jack Sattel (1976) examines the problem of the "inexpressive male," concluding that in intimate relationships men's emotional reticence is a control strategy. According to Sattel, men conceal emotions to mask vulnerabilities and to maintain a negotiating advantage by implying readiness to leave a relationship if a partner demands too much. As suggested in our discussion of minimizing, inexpressivity may indeed be about control. But beyond control, the nondisclosure, or very limited disclosure, of emotions is a key part of signifying a (hegemonic) masculine self. This creates a problem when interviewers want to find out not only what it is that men think and do, but what they feel.

With a subject who seems unabashed, it may work to ask directly, "How did you feel about _____?" Sometimes a direct question will get one the data one hopes for. Often, however, the answer to such a question, in keeping with the strictures of masculine self-presentation, takes the form of "I guess I felt okay about it," with no further elaboration. And so it may be better, if it is crucial to obtain data about men's emotions, for the interviewer to try an indirect approach. Once again the idea is to lower the threat to the masculine self. An interviewer might accomplish this in several ways:

◆ Don't immediately try to probe emotionally loaded topics if a subject is hesitant to say more. Circle back to the topic later. Once trust has been established in an interview, a man may be more willing to share feelings. Return to a topic by saying, for example, "It seemed to me that when you talked about _____ you had some stronger feelings than you let on. I'd like to try to understand that, if it's something you can talk about."

◆ Instead of asking direct questions about emotionally loaded topics, ask for stories. For example, instead of asking, "How do you feel when you and your son argue about his performance in school?" ask for a story about a specific argument, and then, at the right time, ask, "How did you feel when your son said/did _____?" It may be easier for many men to report emotion that arose in the past than to give a report that implies an "emotional self" in the present.

◆ Invoke what other men have said. Again, this can help make the reporting of emotions seem safe and acceptable. If, for example, a man talks with no affect about an experience that seems likely to have evoked strong feelings, an interviewer might say, "Another man told me about a similar experience. For him it stirred up feelings of _____. I wonder if you felt anything like that?" This strategy can also help to get at emotional complexity. Often men will readily express anger or pride, but not admit fear or sadness. A useful probe for complexity might thus be, "Another man told of a similar experience. It made him angry too, but he said he also felt sad about it. Did anything like sadness come up for you?"

◆ Use elicitation devices. Reporting emotions in the absence of some concrete stimulus can seem to imply an unmanly degree of emotionality. An interviewer can often dispel this impression by focusing the subject's attention on an object that is seen as legitimately evocative of strong feelings. For instance, many men are more willing to describe—and to show—emotions when looking at photographs than when merely conversing. Maps, too, can be evocative, if they call up memories of places to which strong feelings are attached. But any object, if it is connected in a significant way to a subject's life, can be used to elicit reports of feelings (see Johnson and Weller, Chapter 24, this volume).

◆ Ask about thoughts, not feelings, then work back to feelings. Asking, "How do you feel about _____?" can pose a threat to the masculine self. Asking, "What do you think about _____?" can, in contrast, seem to offer an opportunity to signify masculinity. But then, as the subject expounds, the interviewer must be ready to probe: "It sounds like _____ makes you feel a bit [sad/angry/embarrassed/happy/etc.]." Once men feel that they have justified themselves—by saying what they think—they may be more willing to talk about what they feel.

Researchers interested in men's emotions must pay attention not only to what men say in interviews, but to *how* they say it and what they *do*. Tears do not show up on transcripts, but they ought to be noted. Our point is that emotions are expressed in all kinds of ways, and that these emotional expressions are data. Men's most assiduous efforts to conceal their emotions are data, too. To reveal or report no emotion when talking about what seem likely to be powerfully affecting experiences is an act of gender signification that cries out for analysis.

EXAGGERATING RATIONALITY, AUTONOMY, AND CONTROL

Researchers want accurate and thorough accounts of events and experiences in men's lives. In addition to every other problem that stands in the way of getting such accounts is the problem of men's tendencies to exaggerate rationality, autonomy, and control as part of signifying a masculine self. These tendencies often can be countered by sensitive questioning and probing. In some cases, however, interviewers may need first to allow the exaggerations before trying to get behind them.

Previously, we suggested a circling-back strategy, which is, in general, a good way to work around many of the problems presented by masculinity displays. Once men have been allowed to signify a creditable masculine self—in the course of initially answering a set of questions—they may be willing to return to topics and reveal more uncertainty, confusion, vulnerability, and weakness. That is, they may be more willing to give accurate accounts of their experiences. We suggest, therefore, that an interviewer employ the circling-back strategy whenever his or her intuition suggests that there is a deeper level of experience to be tapped, but the subject does not seem ready to talk forthrightly about it (see Arendell 1997:352).

There are other strategies that interviewers can use, at any point in an interview, to lower threats to the masculine self and elicit more revealing accounts of men's experiences. Suppose, for purposes of illustration, that we are interviewing men to find out how they make certain kinds of career-related decisions. We might expect, owing to a desire to signify a masculine self, some exaggeration of control, autonomy, and rationality in our subjects' accounts. The following strategies might help counter this tendency:

◆ If we want to know who the men talked to in trying to make their decisions, and we ask about this directly, we might hear, "I didn't talk to anyone; I just decided." Although this might be true, it might also be an account that exaggerates autonomy. Anticipating this, we might approach the matter indirectly, by asking, "Did a friend ever talk to you when he was trying to make a decision about his career?" If yes, probe for details. Then ask, "Did *you* talk to anyone when you were trying to make that kind of decision?" This strategy lowers the threat value of the line of questioning by implying that it is okay if men talk to others when trying to make difficult decisions.

◆ Asking directly about fears and worries a man had when making his decision might elicit accounts of the hyperrational "I knew what I wanted and went after it" variety. We might get more accurate accounts by focusing attention on process and by giving a man the opportunity to speak about a younger self. For example, "Back then, you obviously didn't know what you know now. So what was going through your mind when you were trying to decide about _____?" This can open the door for probing about fears, worries, and uncertainties.

◆ A variation on the above strategy is to emphasize risk, the taking of which is consistent with signifying a masculine self. For example, "No one could have been sure how things were going to turn out. So you were taking a chance back then. How did you decide to do it?" Again, this can open the door to probing about the feelings that underlay a risky decision, feelings that might otherwise be masked by an overly rationalized account.

◆ Another variation is to ask the subject to imagine advising his younger self. For example, "Looking back, if you could step into the past and give yourself advice about making that decision, what would you say?" The answer is likely to reveal what the subject, at the time of the decision, was most unsure about. So if a subject replies, "I would tell myself to think about how time is more important than money," a probe might be, "Is that something you wrestled with back then?"

◆ Shift the focus to the environment. As long as the focus is on the subject and his choices and actions, the tendency to exaggerate control will be strong. Shifting the focus to the *context* of the subject's action can turn this tendency to the interviewer's advantage. For example, asking, "What was going on around you at that time? What kinds of problems were you facing?" poses the environment as a source of challenges that had to be met—success in doing so being to a man's credit as a man. This strategy may make a subject feel more comfortable about elaborating on the problems and struggles that were part of his experience.

◆ Use the conversational norm of reciprocity. That is, offer an equivalent piece of information about yourself, thus obligating the subject to share a bit more about himself. This is a risky strategy, however, in that it opens the door for a subject who truly wishes not to disclose to "turn the interview around" and begin interviewing the interviewer. We suggest that this strategy is best used by male interviewers in cases where a subject seems likely to benefit from reassurance that it is acceptable for men to express doubts, fears, and vulnerabilities. (See also in this volume Warren, Chapter 4; Johnson, Chapter 5; Eder and Fingerson, Chapter 9; Reinharz and Chase, Chapter 11; Kong et al., Chapter 12; Dunbar et al., Chapter 14.)

Interviews that do not explore men's decision making may not give rise to the problems of exaggerated rationality, autonomy, and control in the ways we have suggested here. We think it unlikely, however, that any in-depth interviews in which men are asked to give accounts of their lives, experiences, actions, and so on will be free from problems of exaggeration. The important thing is for the interviewer to see where these problems are likely to arise and to devise questioning and probing strategies to get around them. Each of the strategies proposed above follows a logic of trying to lower the masculinity threat through indirect questioning, by affirming a masculine self-presentation and then circumventing it, or both. Researchers can use this logic to devise more effective questioning and probing strategies regardless of the research topic.

To recognize that men often exaggerate rationality, autonomy, and control is not to say that men's actions never genuinely reflect these qualities. Certainly they do; it is the degree to which they do that is often exaggerated. Nor is this recognition tantamount to saying that men never give truthful accounts. In fact, all of us, women and men, give selective, strategically crafted accounts of our lives and actions. The key for researchers is to realize how gender enactments bias these accounts and to know how to work around this bias so as to get at the experiential complexity behind the identity work.

BONDING PLOYS; OR, "YOU KNOW WHAT I MEAN"

At times in intensive interviews, subjects may be hesitant to say, or even to try to say, what they mean. The job of the researcher, of course, is to get at these meanings, perhaps even helping subjects to articulate them. But researchers often fail to do this because of their own desire to be accepted and maintain rapport. It is tempting for interviewers to nod or say, "Yeah, I know what you mean," especially when they know that by saying, "No, I *don't* know what you mean," they might disrupt the comfortable flow of talk. What ends up happening, then, is that crucial meanings are glossed over and lost. And it may turn out later that the interviewer really didn't know what a subject meant.

Obviously, this problem does not arise only in interviews with men. It can arise whenever an interviewer gets into territory that is difficult for a subject to talk about explicitly, for fear of making a discrediting statement. For example, a white subject speaking to a white interviewer might try to avoid appearing overtly racist by referring to "those women who have one baby after another so they can collect bigger welfare checks—you know what I mean" (see Blee 1998). In this case, it is pretty clear what the subject means, although a good interviewer will draw it out. This example also suggests that the subject may be trying to engage in some bonding around a common identity.

It seems that this kind of bonding, the kind that can allow crucial meanings to go unarticulated, is most likely to arise when men are interviewing men (Williams and Heikes 1993). Subjects, as we have said, may have a moral identity at stake, and may for that reason wish to avoid stating some things explicitly. But it may also be that a male interviewer does not want to say that he does not know what another man means, because to do so would put the interviewer's identity as a man into question. By using the bonding ploy, the subject communicates, in effect, "If you are man, you must know what I mean." By falling for this ploy, the interviewer gains acceptance and loses information.

Not every instance of "you know what I mean" is going to demand a strategic response. Sometimes, in the course of an extensive field study, a researcher might indeed know what the subject means and not feel a need to probe. Or it might be that, at the outset of a study, the researcher deems acceptance and rapport to be more important than the information he or she might gain from probing. Researchers must make their own judgments in these matters. Presuming, however, that at some point a researcher wishes to explore the meanings hidden by bonding ploys, the following strategies might be helpful:

◆ Circle back to what a subject presumed you understood. For example, "Earlier you said _____ . I just want to make sure I understood you. Did you mean _____ ?" Again, the circling-back strategy allows a subject to feel as if his self-presentation has been seen and appreciated, and thus he may be more willing to reveal information that he was hesitant to reveal initially. Asking, "Did you mean _____ ?" also allows the subject to take the masculinity-signifying role of corrector if the interviewer gets it wrong.

◆ Take a newcomer's license not to understand. If a subject says, "You know what I mean," a researcher can say, "I think I do, but I'd rather not presume anything before I've got a handle on what's going on here. So maybe you could clue me in." Often this is enough to induce a subject to elaborate. Again, it allows the subject to play the mentor who is showing the greenhorn the ropes.

◆ Try to articulate what the subject presumably means, then ask for corroboration, qualification, or correction. On the one hand, this can be as simple as saying, "Do you mean _____ ?" and having a subject say "Yes." On the other hand, getting such a yes might be too easy and may lead nowhere. Thus a better strategy is to say, "Do you mean _____ , or do you mean _____ ?" This presumes that it is possible to articulate plausible alternative meanings. If a researcher can do this, it invites the subject to say more about which meaning he intends.

◆ Try indirect approaches to matters that evoke bonding ploys. Suppose, for example, a man is apparently hesitant to admit that he believes women do not belong in what he construes as his properly all-male workplace, because of "well, because of how women are—you know what I mean." To crack this open, a researcher might come at the matter indirectly by asking, "What kind of jobs do women tend to be good at?" The subject's answer, whatever it might be, is likely to offer the researcher a chance to ask, "So how do you think women do/would do in your kind of job?" This indirect route gives the subject a chance to justify himself and may lead to an enthusiastic unpacking of "you know what I mean."

These strategies are best seen as ways to "crack open" an interview. Merely coming at something indirectly, if it is a transparently strategic maneuver on the interviewer's part, is unlikely to work, and may even backfire. The purpose of these moves of indirection is not to trick a subject into self-disclosure, but to lead a subject to a place where he will be comfortable enough to unpack his thoughts and feelings. This "place" is arrived at when a subject feels he has created a sufficiently durable image of himself—as a man and/or as a good person —that it will not be discredited by his saying more about some matter that was previously glossed, evaded, or unarticulated. In interviews as in life, we all want to make sure that some things about us are known first, so that others can put less flattering information into context. Interviewers who appreciate this will learn much more than those who do not.

The skill required of an interviewer is that of employing these strategies in a smooth, natural way to structure a conversation in which a subject can construct what he feels is a creditable masculine self and, against this background, share the information and articulate the meanings that will allow the researcher to see more deeply into his life. Paying attention to what is glossed, evaded, or reluctantly articulated is, of course, an important part of this. Every instance of "you know what I mean" is a piece of data.

Although the strategies suggested above are intended for use in intensive, flexible interviews, they can, to a lesser extent, be used to improve survey-style interviews (see Singleton and Straits, Chapter 3, this volume). Even in such interviews, researchers may have to deal with obstructive testing, inappropriate sexualizing, and mini-

mal responses to open-ended questions. Being able to respond effectively to this kind of behavior increases the interviewer's chances of getting thoughtful, accurate, and complete information, and of making the interview a congenial encounter. Skilled interviewers are those who have turned what we call strategies into a set of habits that they can call upon as the need arises, whether doing surveys or life histories.[5]

◆ Informal Interviewing

The stereotypical image of an interview is actually that of a *formal* interview, a peculiar occasion on which researcher and subject meet, by mutual agreement, for the express purpose of asking and answering questions. Whereas some studies rely almost entirely on this kind of data gathering procedure, field studies often involve more informal than formal interviews (see Atkinson and Coffey, Chapter 38, this volume). By an informal interview we mean any occasion, brief as it might be, when a researcher casually asks a question or two of someone in a field setting and gets an answer that constitutes usable data (see, e.g., Zurcher 1982, 1985). In studies of men, informal interviews may be especially revealing because, if they are handled properly, they may pose very little threat to the masculine self.

The formal, sit-down interview has the virtue of giving the researcher considerable control over the interaction. In interviewing men, however, this virtue is also a potential weakness, because the control that shifts to the researcher can threaten the masculine self and give rise to problems that impede communication. Although it has been our purpose to suggest how researchers can overcome these problems in formal interviews, we want also to suggest how researchers can get around many of these problems through informal interviewing. But "informal" does not mean haphazard; some strategizing is necessary here, too.

In most settings there are occasions when there is a break in the action and casual talk is appropriate. Good field researchers learn to use these occasions to obtain data they might not have gotten otherwise. A researcher can obtain a great deal of information by using only a few informal interviewing strategies:[6]

◆ Interview by comment. The proverbial example is the remark "Things sure have changed around here," which invites the other to expound on how he thinks things have changed. If this remark doesn't fit the situation, there are other possibilities: "I haven't seen anything quite like this before"; "It's interesting to think about how this all got started"; "There's more to this than a lot of people realize." Such a remark, in a well-chosen moment with a well-chosen informant, might yield more data than a pointed question in a formal interview.

◆ Preface a question with a statement that yields status to the informant. For example, "You seem to know what's going on here" cedes authority to the informant and invites help rather than competition. A good informal interview question might thus be, "You seem to know what's going on here. Have things always been like this/done like this?" This simple questioning strategy puts the subject in the superior position and safely invites a flow of informative talk.

◆ Link a question to a man's earlier talk or action (presuming it is not embarrassing). For example, in a field setting where the researcher is in a participant observer role, it is often possible for the researcher to ask, during a break in the action, "I heard you say/saw you do _____, and I wasn't sure I understood what that was about. Could you fill that in for me?" This can work because it invites a man to give a fuller account of

himself and underscores the significance of what he said or did. A request for help is also less threatening than transparent grubbing for information.

The trick to informal interviewing, if indeed there is one, is not so much a matter of knowing what to ask as it is knowing *whom* to ask and *when* to ask. As for *how* to ask, a few simple strategies, as suggested above, will often suffice. In the context of a field study, informal and formal interviews should also inform each other. What we learn in informal interviewing can help us to refine the questions we ask and the approaches we take in formal interviews. What we learn in the latter can also alert us to what we need to explore informally in the field. As a general rule, we ought to pay special attention to discrepancies between what we see and what we are told. Behind such discrepancies are often the doorways through which we must pass to figure out what is going on in a setting.

◆ *General Practice*

We began by saying that good interviewing technique does not fully equip us to deal with problems that can arise because of how men "do gender." As we have tried to show, it is also necessary to be aware of how men try to signify a masculine self in interviews, and to use questioning and probing strategies that reduce the threat to this virtual self. Most of the strategies we have suggested can be seen as conversational ploys that interviewers can use to elicit more information from subjects. There is, however, more to conducting good interview research than skilled questioning and probing. And so here, by way of conclusion, we would like to offer suggestions about the kind of research practice that can increase the payoff from applying our advice about interviewing men.

First, to underscore a point made earlier, interviews must evolve. If we are looking at an unfamiliar group, setting, or activity, it is unlikely that we are going to know precisely what to ask and how to ask it at the outset of a study (Becker 1970; Douglas 1985). More likely, we will have to learn, as we go along, what the right questions are and how to ask them effectively. We also have to learn when to ask, and what not to ask of whom. All of this may come to us as we gain an understanding of the setting and people under study. But we are likely to do a better job of developing this understanding if we allow our interviews to evolve systematically.

As we also suggested earlier, this requires early evaluation of what is happening in interviews. This means more than just looking for trouble spots. It means looking to see what kinds of patterns of responses are elicited by certain kinds of questions. In effect, this means beginning the analysis simultaneously with data collection. To delay analysis until "all the data are in" is to miss the chance to make midcourse adjustments and go after precisely the data needed to strengthen an emerging analysis (Kleinman and Copp 1993). We thus propose the *Twenty Percent Rule*: After 20 percent of the anticipated total number of interviews are completed, pause and develop a provisional analysis. After another 20 percent are done, pause again and revise the analysis. In this way, not only is the interview increasingly refined, but the analysis itself gains strength and focus as the study proceeds.

Second, just as field researchers are astutely advised to write analytic memos and "notes on notes" (Kleinman, Copp, and Henderson 1997), interviewers should do the same. Notes on notes constitute a running analytic commentary on the content of field notes. Writing such notes is a way to capture one's thoughts, insights, and analytic leads as a study proceeds. Every interview, just like every venture into the field, should lead to the writing of similar notes. The data may be captured on tape and, later, in a transcript for more detailed analysis. But a mix of potential data and

protoanalysis can exist in the form of "head notes" that the researcher needs to get onto paper immediately after an interview. Again, as we see it, this is an essential part of refining the focus of an inductive or quasi-inductive study, so that an analysis will come together not merely sooner, but stronger.

What should an interviewer reflect on in writing notes on interviews? In general terms, we advise writing down anything and everything that one's intuition even hints might be significant. More specifically, notes on interviews can be focused with a few self-posed questions:

◆ What did I feel and when did I feel it as the interview was unfolding?

◆ What kind of impression did the subject seem to be trying to create?

◆ What was said or not said that surprised me, and why was I surprised?

◆ About what did the subject seem to have mixed feelings?

◆ About what did the subject seem to be overly glib?

◆ What did the subject seem to have trouble articulating?

◆ What would I want to ask if I could do the interview over?

There is no guarantee that answers to these questions will, on any given occasion, contain gems of insight. It is a good bet, however, that without this kind of systematic reflection and written record, those gems will be harder to generate and harder to find later. Writing notes on interviews is a way to create resources for analysis before it is too late to put them to best use.

Third, interviews—even in pure interview studies—should be seen as occasions of fieldwork; that is, interviews can be opportunities to gather data through observation as well as through talk. What does a subject say and do before the interview begins? What does he wear? How does he move, stand, and sit? What does he say and do after the interview ends? All of these are potentially data and should be captured either in field notes or in interview notes. Although this might seem rather obvious advice to experienced field researchers, it is not uncommon for beginners to treat only the formal interview—the dialogue recorded on tape—as data and to ignore other pertinent information about the subject and the setting.

The suggestion that interviews be treated as occasions of fieldwork harks back to an earlier point about the signifying of masculinity as part of what is going on when we interview men. These acts of signification, whatever form they take—before, during, or after an interview—are potentially important data that can help us to understand who and what men are and how they experience their lives. If that kind of understanding is part of what a research project aims for, then the researcher needs to develop an awareness of what men do, and how they do it, to signify their identities as men. To put it another way, we cannot understand men's lives and experiences without paying attention to what men do to ensure that others perceive and treat them as men.

These matters of general practice, as well as the specific strategies discussed earlier, are not simply ways to wring more data out of research subjects. They are also ways to see, make sense of, and then see past the gender enactments we typically take for granted. Interviewers can thus be better equipped to carry on probing conversations with the men they study. A further prospect is that researchers will be equipped to learn more about how the reproduction of the gender order is a joint accomplishment—in interviews and everywhere else. Whenever we are studying men, there is the possibility, in other words, that we will learn not only about men, but

about the processes through which we create them.

■ Notes

1. From the dramaturgical perspective that we use here (Brissett and Edgley 1990:1-46; Goffman 1959), the self is an *imputed character* brought into being by expressive behavior and an audience's interpretation thereof. In this view, gendered selves are *virtual* realities created collaboratively in interaction. Such selves are thus fictions in one sense, yet are nonetheless enormously consequential because of the responses they evoke in actors and audiences.

2. Most men cannot construct a fully creditable *hegemonic* masculine self because, by definition, creating such a self requires expressive resources available only to members of the ruling group. But even if most men cannot create a hegemonic masculine self in its ideal form, they are still compelled, in a heterosexist society dominated by men, to seek privilege and avoid oppression by constructing some kind of masculine self (see, for example, Robert Connell's 1992 analysis of gay men doing "straight" masculinity). Thus any man—in fact, any person—who seeks, for whatever reason, to construct a masculine self in accord with the prevailing gender order will create for interviewers some of the problems discussed in this chapter.

3. If an interviewer never establishes rapport, if an interview feels tense and awkward from start to finish, or if a subject never opens up, then it is usually clear that something has gone wrong and a change of style or protocol is called for. It is also possible, however, for an interview to go smoothly and feel fine yet not yield much useful data. This is why we urge early review of transcripts (or at least of tapes). Often it is possible to look at a transcript and see that, although an interview did not seem to go at all wrong, it did not go as far or deep as it might have.

4. Although it should perhaps go without saying, we urge that researchers consider the safety of both parties to the interview when choosing a location.

5. Interviewing skills are developed not only in methods classes or in the course of research projects. The interviewing and probing strategies we recommend can be practiced at parties,

on airplanes, during academic conferences, and so on. A roomful of strangers is a fine place to work on forming conversational habits that are effective for getting to know people.

6. David Snow, Lou Zurcher, and Gideon Sjoberg (1982) provide a discussion of additional strategies for interviewing by comment.

■ References

Arendell, T. 1997. "Reflections on the Researcher-Researched Relationship: A Woman Interviewing Men." *Qualitative Sociology* 20:341-68.

Becker, H. S. 1970. "Interviewing Medical Students." Pp. 103-6 in *Qualitative Methodology*, edited by W. J. Filstead. Chicago: Rand McNally.

Blee, K. M. 1998. "White-Knuckle Research: Emotional Dynamics in Fieldwork with Racist Activists." *Qualitative Sociology* 21:381-99.

Briggs, C. L. 1986. *Learning How to Ask: A Sociolinguistic Appraisal of the Role of the Interview in Social Science Research.* Cambridge: Cambridge University Press.

Brissett, D. and C. Edgley. 1991. *Life as Theater: A Dramaturgical Sourcebook.* 2d ed. Hawthorne, NY: Aldine de Gruyter.

Brittan, A. 1989. *Masculinity and Power.* New York: Basil Blackwell.

Connell, R. W. 1992. "A Very Straight Gay: Masculinity, Homosexual Experience, and the Dynamics of Gender." *American Sociological Review* 57:735-51.

———. 1995. *Masculinities.* Berkeley: University of California Press.

Douglas, J. D. 1985. *Creative Interviewing.* Beverly Hills, CA: Sage.

Goffman, E. 1959. *The Presentation of Self in Everyday Life.* Garden City, NY: Doubleday.

———. 1967. *Interaction Ritual: Essays on Face-to-Face Behavior.* New York: Pantheon.

Gurney, J. N. 1985. "Not One of the Guys: The Female Researcher in the Male-Dominated Setting." *Qualitative Sociology* 8:42-62.

Kessler, S. J. and W. McKenna. 1978. *Gender: An Ethnomethodological Approach.* Chicago: University of Chicago Press.

Kleinman, S. and M. A. Copp. 1993. *Emotions and Fieldwork.* Newbury Park, CA: Sage.

Kleinman, S., M. A. Copp, and K. Henderson. 1997. "Qualitatively Different: Teaching Fieldwork to Graduate Students." *Journal of Contemporary Ethnography* 25:469-99.

Lee, D. 1997. "Interviewing Men: Vulnerabilities and Dilemmas." *Women's Studies International Forum* 20:553-64.

McKee, L. and M. O'Brien. 1983. "Interviewing Men: Taking Gender Seriously." Pp. 147-59 in *The Public and the Private*, edited by E. Garmarknikow, D. Morgan, J. Purvis, and D. Taylorson. London: Heinemann.

Mishler, E. G. 1986. *Research Interviewing: Context and Narrative.* Cambridge, MA: Harvard University Press.

Sattel, J. 1976. "The Inexpressive Male: Tragedy or Sexual Politics?" *Social Problems* 23:469-77.

Schwalbe, M. L. and D. Mason-Schrock. 1996. "Identity Work as Group Process." Pp. 113-47 in *Advances in Group Processes*, Vol. 13, edited by B. Markovsky, M. J. Lovaglia, and R. Simon. Greenwich, CT: JAI.

Snow, D. A., L. Zurcher, and G. Sjoberg. 1982. "Interviewing by Comment." *Qualitative Sociology* 5:285-311.

West, C. and D. Zimmerman. 1987. "Doing Gender." *Gender & Society* 1:125-51.

Williams, C. L. and J. E. Heikes. 1993. "The Importance of Researcher's Gender in the In-Depth Interview: Evidence from Two Case Studies of Male Nurses." *Gender & Society* 7:280-91.

Wolkomir, M. 1999. "Redeeming Identities: Ideology, Emotion, and the Creation of Moral Selves." Ph.D. dissertation, Department of Sociology, North Carolina State University, Raleigh.

Zurcher, L. 1982. "The Staging of Emotion: A Dramaturgical Analysis." *Symbolic Interaction* 5:1-22.

———. 1985. "The War Game: Organizational Scripting and the Expression of Emotion." *Symbolic Interaction* 8:191-206.

11

INTERVIEWING WOMEN

◆ Shulamit Reinharz and Susan E. Chase

The interdisciplinary field of women's studies has devoted much attention to defining the word *woman* (Lorber 1993, 1998; Oyěwùmí 1997; Butler 1990). On the one hand, feminist scholars resist an essentialist definition that implies that all women are the same. On the other hand, feminists agree that denying any shared properties among women is as absurd as ignoring the vast differences among us. As Mary Rogers (1988) states, "Women do face some odds that put us in the same big boat (if not on the same deck, let alone in the same cabin)" (p. 1). For example, most women, at least in Western societies, are likely to grow up with some negative notions about female bodies; to fear rape; to be treated as "mother confessors," at work or elsewhere; to earn less than equally educated men in the labor force; if partnered with a man, to do more than half of the domestic and nurturing work at home; and to need the services of men in positions of power and authority, such as doctors, religious leaders, and school or university ad-

ministrators (Rogers 1998:1-2). Women, in general, also share characteristics that many women experience as positive, most notably the potential for bearing children.

In short, gender shapes institutions, ideologies, interactions, and identities. At the same time, race, class, and other social dimensions intersect with the gendered contours of our worlds. We assume, then, that although all women's experiences are gendered, no two women's experiences are identical. Thus in this chapter we treat "women" as encompassing the greatest possible variety of people who self-define as women, including people of many ages (approximately 18 and older), cultures, nationalities, sexual orientations, classes, races, abilities, and physical conditions.

How does interview research in the social sciences deal with women? In this chapter, we look briefly at how traditional social science has rendered women invisible, and we explore a range of issues that arise when interview research focuses on women. Drawing on the rich methodological literature that feminists have developed since the early 1970s, we concentrate on the situations of women interviewing women and, to a lesser extent, men interviewing women.[1] All the while, we keep in mind that the interviewing of women is not a "one-size-fits-all" type of activity. Researchers need to attend not only to the intersections of race, class, and gender in women's lives, but also to the ideas that different groups of women may have about "the way we talk to strangers" or "the way we think about research" (see Marin and Marin 1991; Samovar and Porter 1991; Tixier y Vigil and Elsasser 1978). Finally, throughout this chapter, we are guided by our fundamental assumption that

> interviewing offers researchers access to people's ideas, thoughts, and memories in their own words, rather than in the words of the researcher. This asset is particularly important for the study of women because this way of learning from women is an antidote to centuries of ignoring women's ideas altogether or having men speak for women. (Reinharz 1992b:19)

◆ The Missing Tradition

Throughout the 19th century and for much of the 20th century, most male social researchers did not consider women worthy of study. One of the most blatant examples of the disregard of women as interview subjects is found in the work of Alexis de Tocqueville, who traveled throughout the United States in the early 1830s without interviewing women at all. Michael Hill (1990) describes a travel journal entry in which Tocqueville assumes he understands the thoughts of a woman he observed from afar. On the basis of such observations, Tocqueville ([1835] 1994) proclaimed that "morals are the work of woman," that American women are taught to think for themselves and to speak freely, and that

they display no "timidity or ignorance" (p. 198).

Concurrent with Tocqueville's study of the fledgling United States, Harriet Martineau (one of many underrecognized women social scientists of the 19th century) undertook her own inquiry and came to quite different conclusions (see Martineau [1837] 1962; Reinharz 1992a). Perhaps because she understood the importance of women's as well as men's lives, she included both women and men in her interviews. Martineau's contact with women led her to draw an analogy between the status of women and slaves, and to predict that women would eventually win the right to vote. By contrast, Tocqueville ([1835] 1994:201-3) believed that women were satisfied with their domestic lot. Yet only 15 years after his visit, a women's rights convention in Seneca Falls, New York, initiated the first wave of the women's movement in the United States.

Well into the 20th century, most major social science studies continued to be based primarily on men's experiences. This is true of many studies now considered classics: William Foote Whyte's *Street Corner Society* (1943), Peter Blau and Otis Dudley Duncan's *The American Occupational Structure* (1967), and Lawrence Kohlberg's *The Psychology of Moral Development* (1984), to name just a few. This exclusion of women, of course, was not unique to social science. Medicine, too, was oriented toward men; studies of diseases were done on male subjects and the results then generalized to women.

During the 1970s, feminist social scientists began to analyze the "gynopia" (Reinharz 1985)—the inability to see women—in both traditional social science and conventional social arrangements. For example, in 1975, Lyn Lofland wrote:

> Despite, or perhaps in part because of, their omni-presence, [women] remain, by and large, merely part of the scene. They are continually perceived, but rarely perceivers. They are part of the

furniture of the setting through which the plot moves. Essential to the set but largely irrelevant to the action. They are simply, there. (Pp. 144-45)

Exposing and redressing women's invisibility as social actors has been one of feminist researchers' important accomplishments. Interview studies have played a central role. In *Men and Women of the Corporation,* for example, Rosabeth Moss Kanter (1977) broke through the gynopia of earlier organizational sociology by investigating the situation of women as well as men who are pivotal in corporate life, including secretaries and the wives of high-ranking male executives. Arlene Kaplan Daniels's *Invisible Careers: Women Civic Leaders from the Volunteer World* (1988) brought to light the unremunerated but significant community work of upper-class women. In *Between Women: Domestics and Their Employers,* Judith Rollins (1985) demonstrated that gynopia is not only gendered but also race and class based. She found that middle- and upper-class white women frequently treat as invisible the working-class women of color who clean their homes.

Despite the explosion of feminist interview research over the past three decades, many groups of women continue to be unrecognized as competent social actors. For example, in her study of homeless women, Meredith Ralston (1996) writes:

The women I interviewed were people whom Maria Lugones and Elizabeth Spelman define as the most silenced; women who are not "white, middle-class, heterosexual, Christian women." The value of listening to these women's voices is the value of their testimony and experiences, which have been ignored and dismissed. The women know why they are homeless. They know why they are addicts. No one has thought to ask them about what they need or what would help them, either because people assume that they

do not know what their needs are; or because people assume that they are stupid and lazy and have no potential anyway; or because people think that welfare recipients do not deserve any choices or special treatment because it is their own fault they are on welfare in the first place. The words of the women refute all of the above beliefs and demonstrate the consequences for society of not listening to the needs of the recipients of welfare services. (P. xii)

Thus the "missing tradition" in the interviewing of women includes both gynopia and the holding of untested and unexamined assumptions about women's lives.

◆ Recovering Research on Women

Despite the lack of attention to women in the foundation of male-defined social science, some women researchers did study women using the interview method even before the advent of second-wave feminism. Many of these researchers are not remembered, but some, like Martineau, produced works that feminist scholars today are recovering (Reinharz 1992a).

In the 1930s, for example, Margaret Jarman Hagood, author of *Mothers of the South: Portraiture of the White Tenant Farm Woman* ([1939] 1977), carried out studies by using the role of "visitor":

The actual first-hand gathering of data consisted of repeated visits made by the writer to the tenant farm mothers during a sixteen months' period of field work. . . . [I] stated that [I] was interested in women who live in the country and their problems of bringing up children, and asked if [I] might visit for a little while. . . . in general, questioning was avoided. Topics on which an expression of attitudes was desired were approached obliquely, and the interview was kept as much as possible to a friendly, conversational, "just visiting." No notes were taken during the first visits to the North Carolina group, but the visit was written up as quickly as possible after the interview and much of the conversation was recorded practically verbatim. (P. 227)

Not only did Hagood produce a searing indictment of the effect of tenant farming practices on women, she also explained very carefully how such studies can be done.

In the 1950s, Mirra Komarovsky (1961), the second woman to become president of the American Sociological Association, conducted a study of working-class marriages that included interviews of men and women. She wrote:

We were struck with the openness of the women. Obviously not all were equally candid with us, but the great majority —usually during the second interview —were open enough to confide intimate feelings. Although 58 husbands did grant us interviews, more husbands than wives refused to cooperate. In fact, the initial response of many wives to our request for an interview with the husbands was "Oh, he won't be interested," or "I don't think he will talk to you," or "He's tongue-tied, he'll just say yes or no." . . .

The husbands talked easily enough about their jobs, but when the interviewer turned to the marriage relationship, many became noticeably uncomfortable. . . . We do not know whether the husbands would have spoken more freely to a male interviewer. But, in any event, we shall show that the reticence of the men cannot wholly be explained by the sex of the interviewer. (Pp. 13-14)

In the 1970s, Lillian Rubin (1976) continued the study of working-class marriages, interviewing both women and men without appearing more friendly to one group than the other. Because "women tend to discuss their feelings about their lives, their roles, and their marriages more freely when men are not present" (p. 11), she interviewed women and men separately.

These few examples show that women researchers have been concerned not only with including women in their studies, but also with addressing the impact of gender on the interview process itself. By contrast, "the traditional interview paradigm does not account for gendered differences" even though social scientists have always known that "gender filters knowledge" (Fontana and Frey 1994:369). Indeed, the classic text on interviewing, Robert Merton, Marjorie Fiske, and Patricia Kendall's *The Focused Interview: A Manual of Problems and Procedures* (1956), makes no reference to gender differences among interviewers or interviewees.

◆ Feminist Methodological Issues

Since the 1970s, feminist researchers have become avid students of women's experiences and have made good use of the interview method for collecting data. At the same time, they have developed a remarkable literature on feminist methodological issues.[2] In this section we draw on that literature as we consider the effects of interviewing on both interviewees and interviewers, the issues of interviewer self-disclosure and sisterly bonds in the research relationship, and the significance of interviewers' and interviewees' complex social locations and subjectivities.

THE IMPACT OF INTERVIEWING ON WOMEN INTERVIEWEES

An interview is typically a conversation between two people in which one asks questions and the other answers. In the case of open-ended interviewing, there may be a more spontaneous exchange between interviewer and interviewee. Although on the face of it this is not a remarkable activity, it may turn out to be an extraordinary experience for some women interviewees. This is so because some women still feel powerless, without much to say. In many societies girls are still raised to be pretty objects who should be seen but not heard or fecund reproducers whose intellect is devalued. In some religious traditions, women's voices must not be heard in public because they are defined as erotic and dangerous. Even well-educated women in managerial or professional occupations are not immune from self-censoring or silencing. For example, in her study of how parental leave is used in a major U.S. corporation, Mindy Fried (1998) remarks that "even the most forceful upper-level female manager I met was relatively soft-spoken when we met together with a group of upper-level male managers" (p. 12). Nadya Aisenberg (1994) helps to make sense of this situation: "For women there have been thousands of years of silencing. The speech-act itself is a rebellion against stifling social norms which call for women's silence" (p. 99).

Interpreting any particular woman's silence or speech is a complex task that requires a strong understanding of her social location, including her place within her community and society, the cultural constraints and resources shaping her everyday life, and her particular circumstances (Gal 1991; Collins 1990:92; Tannen 1993). Yet when an interviewer approaches a woman whose culture, religion, community, family, or work situation prescribes her silence in one way or another, and says, "I want to hear what you have to say," the interviewer may be creating a relatively new social situation for that woman. When the interviewer implies that what the woman has to say is important and that she will not be interrupted, the interviewee may have an epiphany, dramatic as this may sound. The reason is quite straightforward: "The si-

lence of women, whether self-imposed as a strategy of resistance or societally imposed as a tool of subordination, is a classic clinical symptom of depressive illness" (Aisenberg 1994:102).

Researchers who interview women should thus understand the possibly radical impact of the interview on the woman herself. She may discover her thoughts, learn who she is, and "find her voice." At the same time, researchers need to be aware that women who have never had an opportunity to express themselves may not know what to do when given that opportunity, as Mary Field Belenky and her colleagues (1986, 1997) discovered when they interviewed women who grew up in violent families and who had no external sources of support. Furthermore, under some circumstances, an interview may be traumatic. In studies about women's experiences of violence, for instance, both interviewer and interviewee need to be prepared for the distress, anxiety, and flashbacks participants may experience. The interviewer needs to be able to offer referrals to support resources in case the participant finds the interview overwhelming. Otherwise, the interview may be harmful (Brzuzy, Ault, and Segal, 1997).

Although there have been no systematic studies conducted to examine the impact of interview research on participants (Maynard and Purvis 1994:5), Ruthellen Josselson's (1996) description of what interviewees said about their experience of talking to her is not unusual (see also Rothman 1993:19-20; Phoenix 1994: 60-61; Reay 1995:211). Focusing on women's self-development over time, Josselson interviewed 30 women when they were in their early 20s, early 30s, and early 40s:

> Many said they told me things they have never divulged to anyone. In that sense, I am for them a kind of private diary. Others remarked that the interview was like therapy, where "I say things out loud that I've never said before." Some told me that our conversations have of-

ten been painful, especially when they reawakened buried loss, anger, or confusion. But there is something about our interaction that led these women to strive for naked truthfulness, and that has felt liberating—for both of us. (P. 13)

Interestingly, research on elite women (see Odendahl and Shaw, Chapter 15, this volume) may involve a completely different set of issues. Powerful women are much more likely than less powerful women to be accustomed to speaking and being heard, and so they may not find the interview experience psychologically empowering or therapeutic, as Josselson's interviewees did. In fact, they may have difficulty finding time to schedule an interview. Women with power may have less discretionary time than their male counterparts because such women usually have the additional responsibilities of "representing women" in various venues and managing (if not doing) domestic and nurturing work at home.

It is no surprise, then, that Nirmal Puwar (1997) found many women members of the British Parliament agreeing only grudgingly to be interviewed, treating the request as an imposition and a favor to the researcher (also see Adler and Adler, Chapter 25, this volume). Nonetheless, some elite women may consent to interviews because of their unique position and their ability to provide a fresh perspective. In her study of upper-class women, Susan Ostrander (1984) gained access to her respondents in part by appealing to them specifically as women. "I suggested that, while we know a good deal about the men from old and influential families, we know little about the women. This approach proved successful. I know of only two women who were unwilling to talk with me, pleading busy schedules" (p. 10; see also Ostrander 1995). In addition, high-achieving women in traditionally white- and male-dominated professions may feel that participating in research is part of their responsibility to women who aspire to follow in their footsteps (Chase 1995, 1996:46).

THE IMPACT OF INTERVIEWING ON WOMEN INTERVIEWERS

Mirroring the personal impact that interviewees sometimes mention, many researchers have discussed how the interviewing process has affected them personally (Luttrell 1997; Shostak 1989; Thompson 1990). For example, in her book about how men and women experience divorce, Catherine Riessman (1990) writes:

Not only did the interviewing process have an effect on them [interviewees], it also strongly affected me. I was divorced, as my mother and grandmother had been before me, and though I was aware that this personal history had stimulated my choice of the topic, I was not entirely prepared for my response. Listening to people's painful accounts of their marriages and trying to probe sensitively for their understandings of what had happened was sometimes difficult. It was difficult, too, when a few male interviewees asked for dates (this happened to both women interviewers) and when one threatened me when I refused. During the coding and analysis process, I had more trouble empathically interpreting men's experience than I did women's. (P. 225)

Sometimes researchers find that their interviews with women have reverberations long after their projects are done. After completing her study of identity and self-transformation in mothers' lives, Martha McMahon (1998) began rethinking her own life, especially when her mother died: "Learning to live with her death forced me to revisit my sociological story and to shift the focus from the meaning of motherhood in other women's lives to its meaning to me, a childless woman" (p. 187).

Some researchers intentionally use their personal reactions to the interview process as a source of knowledge about the topic under study. Alison Griffith and Dorothy Smith (1987) used this strategy in their project on mothers' work in relation to their children's schooling (how mothers help children with homework and how they interact with teachers). In the course of their interviews, Griffith and Smith sometimes found themselves reexperiencing the guilt and inadequacy they had felt while raising their children as single mothers and comparing themselves unfavorably to middle-class mothers who have more resources and time to help their children. They analyze these feelings—which they trace in many mothers' talk—as pointing to "a strongly moral dimension governing the relationship of mothers to the school, capable of generating an almost theological sense of guilt and anxiety" (p. 95; see also DeVault and McCoy, Chapter 36, this volume).

Daniels (1988) identifies another kind of personal and intellectual effect on herself as researcher. In an unusual preface to her study of upper-class women leaders in the volunteer world, she explains the negative bias she had toward participants while writing her book about them: "I accepted the somewhat negative stereotypes of women volunteers" (p. xii). The details she gives make us wonder why she includes the word "somewhat." Daniels was strongly influenced, however, by her participants' responses to her early analyses. "My informants helped me see the error of my ways. . . . I rewrote the study, adding new material that showed their work in a more serious and respectful light" (pp. xiv-xv). At this point, Daniels struggled with the tension between listening carefully to participants and analyzing their position sociologically.

Daniels concludes her discussion with a story about male colleagues and their wives whom she invited to dinner along with a prominent volunteer leader and her husband. The male colleagues were uninterested in, and unimpressed by, the volunteer; the colleagues' wives, however, felt privileged to meet "a woman of such spirit who had made so remarkable a career for herself" (p. xvi). Although she began with stereotypical perceptions like those of her male colleagues, Daniels ended up with a view closer to that of her colleagues' wives.

INTERVIEWER SELF-DISCLOSURE

Interviewer self-disclosure takes place when the interviewer shares ideas, attitudes, and/or experiences concerning matters that might relate to the interview topic in order to encourage respondents to be more forthcoming (see also in this volume Warren, Chapter 4; Johnson, Chapter 5; Eder and Fingerson, Chapter 9; Dunbar, Rodriguez, and Parker, Chapter 14). In a study of sexual harassment, for instance, the interviewer might disclose her own experience of having been harassed. Conventionally, qualitative research students are instructed not to disclose their experiences, feelings, or opinions about the research topic because "the interview is about the respondent, not about the interviewer. . . . It is usually enough for the interviewer to give business card information . . . along with the study's aims and sponsorship" (Weiss 1994:79).

Some feminists reject this stance because it assumes a distant and hierarchical relationship between the interviewer and participants. Moreover, many feminists choose research topics that are deeply personal, which tends to make the interview process emotionally intense for both interviewer and participant. These conditions can lead easily to the researcher's self-disclosure. In addition to humanizing and equalizing the research relationship, some argue, interviewer self-disclosure can put the interviewee at ease, thus helping the participant to tell her story (Oakley 1981; Reinharz 1992b:32-34).

In practice, however, it is difficult to know how much and what kind of disclosure is appropriate (Blum 1999:214). Indeed, there is very little literature about the impact of interviewer self-disclosure on the interview process or on the interviewee. One report by three social work researchers suggests that in some cases interviewees may feel constrained when interviewers talk about themselves. Marilyn Wedenoja, who was at first an interviewee and later a collaborator in the project, notes that

> personal sharing on [the interviewer's part] . . . was triggering off in me a self-censoring process. I began to second [guess] what she would want to hear and not want to hear based on my perception of the information about herself. . . . She was giving me . . . personal information as a way of equalizing the relationship . . . yet it seemed more out of her need to self-disclose rather than my need . . . to know about her. (quoted in Reinharz 1992b:33)

Rather than adopting an abstract commitment to self-disclosure, interviewers need to think carefully about whether, when, and how much disclosure makes sense in the context of particular research projects and with specific participants. If the research arises in part from the researcher's personal experiences or needs, to what extent—and why—should that personal connection play a role in the research relationship itself? Under what conditions might self-disclosure put the interviewee at ease or pressure her to adopt a particular point of view? When does self-disclosure indicate openness to the other's experience or a sharing of power within the interview relationship, and when does it indicate that the researcher prefers to speak rather than listen?

The issue of self-disclosure arises for researchers when they assume that their ex-

periences or points of view are similar to those of participants. But when researchers interview women whose perspectives are clearly different from their own, they may find a tight-lipped approach to be essential to gaining trust. For example, in *Women of the New Right,* Rebecca Klatch (1987) writes:

> I built trust by adopting a non-argumentative approach in the interviews. While I would push to clarify ideas and beliefs, I did not assert my own opinions, judgments or values nor did I try to debate ideas. If asked, of course, I would state my own doubts or disagreements, but generally I defined my own role entirely in terms of listening and absorbing the other world view. I believe this approach, more than anything else, bridged the gap between me and the women I interviewed. Because many activists on the right have been met with hostility and constant rebuttal by liberals and the media . . . , the fact that I conveyed an honest attempt to understand the opinions and values of the women I met in a non-aggressive manner was met with a welcome and open response. (P. 17)

SISTERLY BONDS

In 1981, Ann Oakley argued dramatically that interviewing women is a contradiction in terms. She claimed that women who interview women have an obligation to assist, remain in touch with, and otherwise revise the more passive, distant interviewing stance recommended by conventional research methodology.

When the researcher already knows participants, or when the study requires contact with participants over a long period, interviewers sometimes do develop connections with, and responsibilities toward, participants that extend beyond the research itself (Shostak 1989; Ellis, Kiesinger, and Tillman-Healy 1997). For example,

Laurel Richardson's (1985) study of single women involved with married men included several women whom she interviewed over the course of their affairs. Richardson invited the women to contact her if they wanted or needed to (p. 162), and some did:

> Interviews took place in private settings—the respondent's home or mine, a hotel room, or occasionally a private office. They lasted between two and five hours and were tape-recorded and transcribed. . . . Many of the women cried at some point in the interview. Nearly all of them thanked me for the "therapy" the interview provided, and several still phone me. (Pp. x-xi)

Because feminists seek to create nonexploitative research relationships, it might seem that developing sisterly bonds with participants should be a feminist goal. Indeed, some of the early feminist methodological literature gave the impression that women who interview women automatically like their interviewees and will easily form bonds of mutual understanding with them (Oakley 1981; Finch 1984). Problems encountered during research, however, led many feminists to reject this romanticization of the woman-to-woman interview and to explore the complexities of research relationships (Reay 1995, 1996; Cotterill 1992; Phoenix 1994).

A major drawback to treating sisterly bonds as the ideal research relationship is that this standard precludes studies of groups of women in which such bonds are unlikely to develop. Interview-based studies of women should not be limited to women who seek such bonds, to women who need help, or to women whom researchers perceive as like themselves or as potential friends. Indeed, even if researcher and interviewee share life experiences and ideological perspectives, there is no guarantee that they will like each other and want or need to continue a relationship after the research is complete. Furthermore,

to assume that interviewees want or need an extended relationship is condescending and "maternalistic" (Reinharz 1993).

We can begin to sort out the confusion surrounding this issue by distinguishing "rapport" from "intense bonding." Rapport is a necessary ingredient for interviewing, and many women may establish rapport easily, given that women typically are socialized to connect with others. However, rapport is more likely to be established by strong listening skills than by promises of future support or friendship. In many cases, it may be the very fact that the researcher is not regularly involved in the participant's life that allows the participant the freedom to express herself in ways she might not otherwise, even with a close friend (Cotterill 1992). This is especially true if the topic is highly personal or if the interviewee has rarely or never discussed the matter before. Under these circumstances, the bond of the intimate stranger may emerge (Simmel 1971:145).

Researchers have a responsibility to express as clearly as possible to participants their expectations and the boundaries of the research relationship. The process of securing informed consent can facilitate this. And yet, as in all relationships, what may transpire during interview relationships cannot always be predicted. When a participant seeks further contact that the researcher does not welcome, the researcher needs to reflect carefully on what is going on: Does the interviewee feel exploited or abandoned? If so, why? Did the interviewer lead her, directly or indirectly, to have certain expectations regarding the relationship? Has the interviewer fulfilled whatever promises she made for follow-up? Even if she has, are there other forms of gratitude or reciprocity that would satisfy the participant and resolve the problem (Daniels 1983; Lindsey 1997; Altork 1998)?

At the other end of the relationship spectrum, if an intense bond forms between interviewer and interviewee, that should be considered a serendipitous event. In most cases, the interviewer's purpose in conducting the interview is not to create such a bond but to elicit and listen closely to the interviewee's life experiences. The feminist methodological literature cogently criticizes the overdone and self-deceiving value-neutral stance of social science, but this critique should not lead to an unexamined assumption that a feminist research project is successful only if it creates sisterly bonds between researchers and participants (Reinharz 1992b:chap. 2).

COMPLEX SOCIAL LOCATIONS AND SUBJECTIVITIES

Social scientists generally agree that a person's social location shapes his or her identity, experiences, and perspectives. What difference, then, do the similar or different social locations of researcher and participant make to interview research? How, for example, should interviewers take into account their own and their interviewees' races, ethnicities, classes, sexual orientations, ages, and disabilities or abilities?

These questions arise even in the matter of constructing a sample of research participants. In criticizing the overrepresentation of white, middle-class women as subjects in feminist research, Lynn Weber Cannon, Elizabeth Higginbotham, and Marianne Leung (1988) argue that women of color and working-class women may be less able and less willing than more privileged women to volunteer for research because of their heavy responsibilities and their well-founded skepticism about the value of social research (see also Edwards 1990:483-85; Phoenix 1994:50-55). In order to make feminist research more inclusive, Cannon and her colleagues recommend that researchers recruit participants through face-to-face contact, and they encourage researchers to be flexible and persistent in arranging and rescheduling interviews. They also recommend the use of multiracial research teams. Similarly, Kath

Weston (1991) discusses her flexibility and persistence in scheduling interviews with lesbians and gay men, some of whom are reluctant to become research subjects because they construct very private lives and often fear that researchers will disrespect their identities or experiences (pp. 10-11; see also Kong, Mahoney, and Plummer, Chapter 12, this volume).

Conventional wisdom suggests that when interviewer and interviewee share similar social locations (such as sexual orientation and racial, ethnic, and class backgrounds), access, rapport, and understanding are relatively easy to achieve. Yet in recent years feminists have been most interested in exploring the instability of "insider" and "outsider" statuses (Reay 1995; Naples 1997). For instance, in her study of the ethnic identity of Chicanas in New Mexico, Patricia Zavella (1996) found that even though she and her interviewees had much in common (like them, she was an employed Chicana mother who faced family-work tensions; she also had New Mexican kin), many of the women were reluctant to talk about their ethnicity. Because Zavella was unfamiliar with their hesitancy as well as their use of the term *Spanish* (as opposed to *Chicana*), she had to struggle to understand the meanings the women imputed to their ethnicity (see in this volume Dunbar et al., Chapter 14; Ryen, Chapter 17; Narayan and George, Chapter 39).

Feminists also address the situation of researchers whose social locations clearly differ from those of their interviewees. Ann Phoenix (1994:55-56) notes that in several of her research projects some white interviewees were surprised to discover that she, the interviewer, is black. She suggests that this racial difference may have been both inhibitory and liberating for interviewees.

Similarly, in her study of working-class women returning to school as adults, Wendy Luttrell (1997) reflects on her social location and subjectivity in relation to two groups of participants: white working-class women in Philadelphia and African American working-class women in North Carolina. In both settings, she got to know the women as their teacher before she began her study; thus the research relationship was shaped by the participants' prior teacher-student contact as well as by their educational, class, and (with one group) racial differences. Luttrell carefully sorts through the emotions that the women's stories aroused in her—guilt, envy, shame—as a way of developing "a clearer picture of what it means to define one's womanhood against controlling gender-, race-, and class-based images, including images that I projected onto the women and they projected onto me" (p. 21).

The methodological lesson that Phoenix, Luttrell, and others offer is that uncertainty and discomfort are likely to arise for interviewers and interviewees whose social locations differ dramatically, and those aspects of the relationship need to be explored rather than ignored. Along these lines, Linda Blum (1999) states that during her interviews with African American women about their experiences of breast-feeding, "I learned most from those facets of African-American women's stories which I had the most trouble hearing" (p. 213; see also Rubin 1976, 1995; DeVault 1999:chap. 5; Pierce 1995; Reay 1996; Villenas 1998; Fordham 1996; Fine 1998; Riessman 1987).

In addition to race, ethnicity, and class, and to a lesser extent sexual orientation, age, and disability, feminist researchers discuss other significant aspects of their social locations and subjectivities. Several recent studies of women's experiences of motherhood, for instance, have been conducted by women who are not mothers (Hays 1996; McMahon 1995; Lewin 1993; Taylor 1996).

In her study of the self-help movement surrounding postpartum depression, Verta Taylor (1996) presents herself as both like and unlike her interviewees. Although she is not a mother, she has suffered a period of debilitating depression:

If over the course of this research I have come to understand depression in a more personal way, I have also come to terms with my own decision not to bear and raise children. I have never been sure exactly how or when I came to the conclusion that I did not want to be a mother. But perhaps as a sign of how women's self-definitions revolve less around motherhood than they once did, the women I got to know while doing this study never questioned my decision. Nor did they challenge my ability to understand and write about their lives because I never have mothered a child. (P. xvi)

Ellen Lewin (1998) comes to a somewhat different conclusion about the effect of her nonmotherhood on her interviews. Five years after publishing her study of lesbian mothers, Lewin, herself a lesbian, remarks:

By the time I unraveled the narratives mothers offered me, I began to understand that among other dynamics they had formulated their stories for a non-mother. The mothers tended to emphasize the moral attributes of motherhood and the central part motherhood played in the way they constructed and conceptualized their identities, highlighting the ways that they saw themselves as fundamentally different from women who did not have children. How their narratives would have been shaped had I also been a mother I cannot know, but I feel sure that they would have been different, if not in substance, then in emphasis. (Pp. 40-41)

By contrast, in her study of gay and lesbian commitment ceremonies, Lewin describes herself as the " 'insider' par excellence." Like her interviewees, she and her lesbian partner had a commitment ceremony. Lewin points out that this closeness to her topic raises its own issues of subjectivity: "I have tried earnestly to avoid the pitfalls of cheerleading or polemics, but the astute reader will no doubt detect my enthusiasm for and engagement with the phenomena I report on in these pages" (p. xix).

What feminist researchers share, regardless of their status as insider or outsider in relation to interviewees, is a commitment to reflecting on the complexities of their own and participants' social locations and subjectivities.

◆ Men Interviewing Women

The situation of men studying women raises particular issues concerning interviewers' and interviewees' social locations and subjectivities. Maureen Padfield and Ian Procter (1996) looked carefully at this situation in their joint study of 39 young women's work and family experiences and aspirations. From the outset, they attempted to minimize the differences their genders made by maximizing their commonalities: Both are middle-aged, experienced field-workers who are knowledgeable about feminist critiques of research methodology. They also had a common objective—encouraging women to talk freely in response to their questions.

In comparing their interviews (each interviewed half of the women), Padfield and Procter found no significant differences in their length or the women's attitudes, even on controversial topics such as feminism and abortion. However, women who had had abortions were much more likely to reveal that information to the woman (Padfield) than to the man (Procter). (The interviewer did not ask directly whether the woman had ever aborted a pregnancy; six women volunteered this information to Padfield, none to Procter.) In follow-up interviews, two of Procter's interviewees revealed that they had had abortions before the first interview, which suggests that the interviewer's gender did affect this voluntary sharing of personal experience.

During the follow-up interviews, Padfield and Procter also asked about the difference the interviewer's gender had made in the first interviews. The women's responses show that the salience of gender is not fixed, but shifts along with other dynamics:

> If the interviewee perceives herself as skilled in dealing with men then that can counter the implied influence of "maleness." If the interviewer puts aside "maleness" ["inappropriate features of masculinity (arrogance, not listening)" (Padfield and Procter 1996: 363)] then women could respond. (P. 362)

Along the same lines, Javier Treviño (1992) found that he had trouble getting interviews with women members of Alcoholics Anonymous until he made efforts to downplay his gender and desexualize the research encounter. For example, although he initially thought of his office as a neutral space, he discovered that some women were reluctant to meet with him there out of concern for their safety.

Because gender regulates access to space, gender can affect where interviews take place in another sense. When he studied the Ladies Professional Golf Association, for example, Todd Crosset (1992) was not allowed into the women's locker room, which "serve[s] as a private space for golfers and thus an excellent setting to collect data" (p. 44). Despite his limited access to interviewees, Crosset's rapport with them was enhanced by his ability to play golf, his general helpfulness and dedication to their work, and his status as a professional athlete.

In cases where research revolves around extremely sensitive gendered experiences, a man may decide not to do the interviews himself. For example, for his study of courtroom negotiations between judges and women who seek restraining orders, James Ptacek (1999) needed information from the women themselves. He was concerned, however, that he might cause the women harm by contacting them:

> Three types of potential harm exist. First, the conversation—even a brief conversation in which a woman declines to participate—can be upsetting. This is a very sensitive issue to discuss with anyone, let alone a stranger. Women may fear phone calls from strangers, particularly if they are no longer living with their abusive partners; abusive men often harass women by telephone and through myriad other means. . . .
>
> Second, if an interviewer telephones a woman but reaches an abusive man, there is the potential that the man may become suspicious and angry toward the woman. . . .
>
> A third type of danger concerns women who have children and fear losing their children either to their estranged abusive partner or to child-protection authorities. . . . Care must therefore be taken to establish trust in the telephone interview. . . .
>
> To protect against these risks, I had the interviews conducted by women who have experience as advocates on the issues of violence against women. (Pp. 189-90)

When men study women, then, the same general methodological principle applies as when women study women: It is crucial that the researcher take account of his or her own and the interviewee's social locations and how they might affect the research relationship.

◆ Concluding Thoughts: Interpreting Women's Words

The salience and meanings of gender, race, class, and other aspects of our social locations shift not only from study to study and across contexts, but also over time. Thus we need to continue our reflexivity even when we leave the field and turn our attention to interpretation. As social scientists, we spend years examining theory and conducting research. We assume we understand society, social structures, and a vast array of topics about everyday life, with an eye to the ways in which structures and cultures typically disadvantage most women. We also assume that people will benefit from our interpretations of these phenomena. Thus we approach our interpretive work with background, with conviction, and, yes, often with biases or "agendas" of our own (Anderson and Jack 1991).

Feminist researchers face a particular challenge when we interpret the words of women who reject feminism or other progressive movements. In such cases, it is tempting to attribute an interviewee's ideas to "false consciousness" and to discount what she says. The idea of false consciousness suggests that a person misunderstands his or her own situation, particularly with regard to self-interest (Bartky 1998). Feminists need to exercise self-control and reflexive thinking, for example, when we interview women who espouse a "pro-life" position or a submissive attitude toward men, or who embrace an apparently assimilationist ethnic identity (Andersen 1987; Zavella 1996). How are such women making reasonable decisions within the context of their particular circumstances?

Conflicts surface between researchers' and interviewees' perspectives in part because of the feminist commitment to reducing the hierarchy and inequality inherent in the conventional research relationship. Such conflicts come to light, for instance, when researchers share their analyses with interviewees before publication. In some cases, participants respond angrily (Krieger 1991:154), even requesting that they be taken out of the study (Sacks 1988:viii-ix). As we have seen, some researchers resolve such problems by altering their interpretations (Daniels 1988) or by making room within their publications for participants' autonomous responses to and critiques of researchers' interpretations (Andersen 1987; Stacey 1990; Borland 1991; Jackson 1999).

In addition to the question of what it means to listen well to perspectives different from our own, what is at stake in conflicts of this sort is "interpretive authority": To whom does it belong? How should it be negotiated? When is it appropriate for researchers to claim it for themselves (Chase 1996)? Although instances of conflict between researchers' and interviewees' perspectives may jolt researchers to reconsider their interpretations, researchers often find that they are more invested in their analyses than are their participants. Participants sometimes claim that the analysis is "your story, not mine" (Zavella 1996:154; Shostak 1989:233; Stacey 1990:273).

Rather than being seen as a failure of communication, this disjunction can be viewed in terms of the difference between individuals' interpretive work in narrating their lives and social scientists' interpretive work in articulating the social processes, ideologies, and structures embedded in interviewees' stories (Chase 1996; Cotterill 1992; Reay 1996; Holland and Ramazanoglu 1994). Thus interpreting women's words and stories requires a delicate and reflexive balancing act. We need to work at understanding and respecting participants' interpretations of their lives, particularly if those interpretations are different from our own. We need to identify how our acts of knowing—our interpretations of women's words—are socially situated, which includes reflecting on our complex social locations and subjectivities as well as our personal, political, and intellectual agendas. We need to embrace the value of feminist social scientific perspectives, the value of locating women's words within, among other things, gendered, racial, and class-based structures and cultures. Finally, we need to be open to the ways in which our interpretations, as well as those of research participants, may change over time.

■ Notes

1. A full discussion of the impact of gender on interview research would include the situations of men interviewing men (which much of social science is based on) and women interviewing men (see Arendell 1997; Williams 1995). It would also explore mixed-gender groups of interviewers and mixed-gender groups of interviewees. See Michael Schwalbe and Michelle Wolkomir's contribution to this volume (Chapter 10).

2. Recent contributors to this literature include Rebecca Campbell (1995), Marjorie DeVault (1999), Mary Maynard and June Purvis (1994), Virginia Olesen (1998), Shulamit Reinharz (1992b), Dorothy Smith (1987), and Diane Wolf (1996).

■ References

Aisenberg, N. 1994. *Ordinary Heroines: Transforming the Male Myth.* New York: Continuum.

Altork, K. 1998. "You Never Know When You Might Want to Be a Redhead in Belize." Pp. 111-25 in *Inside Stories: Qualitative Research Reflections,* edited by K. B. deMarrais. Mahwah, NJ: Lawrence Erlbaum.

Andersen, M. L. 1987. "Corporate Wives: Longing for Liberation or Satisfied with the Status Quo?" Pp. 179-90 in *Women and Symbolic Interaction,* edited by M. J. Deegan and M. Hill. Boston: Allen & Unwin.

Anderson, K. and D. C. Jack. 1991. "Learning to Listen: Interview Techniques and Analyses." Pp. 11-26 in *Women's Words: The Feminist Practice of Oral History,* edited by S. B. Gluck and D. Patai. New York: Routledge.

Arendell, T. 1997. "Reflections on the Researcher-Researched Relationship: A Woman Interviewing Men." *Qualitative Sociology* 20:341-68.

Bartky, S. L. 1998. "On Psychological Oppression." Pp. 43-52 in *Contemporary Feminist Theory: A Text/Reader,* edited by M. F. Rogers. New York: McGraw-Hill.

Belenky, M. F., B. M. Clinchy, N. R. Goldberger, and J. M. Tarule. 1986. *Women's Ways of Knowing: The Development of Self, Voice, and Mind.* New York: Basic Books.

———. 1997. *Women's Ways of Knowing: The Development of Self, Voice, and Mind.* 10th anniversary ed. New York: Basic Books.

Blau, P. and Duncan, O. D. 1967. *The American Occupational Structure.* New York: John Wiley.

Blum, L. M. 1999. *At the Breast: Ideologies of Breastfeeding and Motherhood in the Contemporary United States.* Boston: Beacon.

Borland, K. 1991. " 'That's Not What I Said': Interpretive Conflict in Oral Narrative Research." Pp. 63-76 in *Women's Words: The Feminist Practice of Oral History,* edited by S. B. Gluck and D. Patai. New York: Routledge.

Brzuzy, S., A. Ault, and E. A. Segal. 1997. "Conducting Qualitative Interviews with Women Survivors of Trauma." *Affilia* 12(1):76-83.

Butler, J. 1990. *Gender Trouble: Feminism and the Subversion of Identity.* New York: Routledge.

Campbell, R. 1995. "Weaving a New Tapestry of Research: A Bibliography of Selected Readings on Feminist Research Methods." *Women's Studies International Forum* 18:215-22.

Cannon, L. W., E. Higginbotham, and M. L. A. Leung. 1988. "Race and Class Bias in Qualitative Research on Women." *Gender & Society* 2:449-62.

Chase, S. 1995. *Ambiguous Empowerment: The Work Narratives of Women School Superintendents.* Amherst: University of Massachusetts Press.

———. 1996. "Personal Vulnerability and Interpretive Authority in Narrative Research." Pp. 45-59 in *The Narrative Study of Lives,* Vol. 4, *Ethics and Process in the Narrative Study of Lives,* edited by R. Josselson. Thousand Oaks, CA: Sage.

Collins, P. H. 1990. *Black Feminist Thought: Knowledge, Consciousness, and the Politics of Empowerment.* New York: Routledge, Chapman & Hall.

Cotterill, P. 1992. "Interviewing Women: Issues of Friendship, Vulnerability, and Power." *Women's Studies International Forum* 15:593-606.

Crosset, T. 1992. "Out Here: Sport and Gender on the Women's Professional Golf Tour." Ph.D. dissertation, Brandeis University.

Daniels, A. K. 1983. "Self-Deception and Self-Discovery in Fieldwork." *Qualitative Sociology* 6:195-214.

———. 1988. *Invisible Careers: Women Civic Leaders from the Volunteer World.* Chicago: University of Chicago Press.

DeVault, M. L. 1999. *Liberating Method: Feminism and Social Research.* Philadelphia: Temple University Press.

Edwards, R. 1990. "Connecting Method and Epistemology: A White Woman Interviewing Black Women." *Women's Studies International Forum* 13:477-90.

Ellis, C., C. E. Kiesinger, and L. M. Tillman-Healy. 1997. "Interactive Interviewing: Talking about Emotional Experience." Pp. 119-49 in *Reflexivity and Voice,* edited by R. Hertz. Thousand Oaks, CA: Sage.

Finch, J. 1984. " 'It's Great to Have Someone to Talk To': The Ethics and Politics of Interviewing Women." Pp. 70-87 in *Social Researching: Politics, Problems, Practice,* edited by C. Bell and H. Roberts. New York: Routledge.

Fine, M. 1998. "Working the Hyphens: Reinventing Self and Other in Qualitative Research." Pp. 130-55 in *The Landscape of Qualitative Research: Theories and Issues,* edited by N. K. Denzin and Y. S. Lincoln. Thousand Oaks, CA: Sage.

Fontana, A. and Frey, J. H. 1994. "Interviewing: The Art of Science." Pp. 361-76 in *Handbook of Qualitative Research,* edited by N. K. Denzin and Y. S. Lincoln. Thousand Oaks, CA: Sage.

Fordham, S. 1996. *Blacked Out: Dilemmas of Race, Identity, and Success at Capital High.* Chicago: University of Chicago Press.

Fried, M. 1998. *Taking Time: Parental Leave Policy and Corporate Culture.* Philadelphia: Temple University Press.

Gal, S. 1991. "Between Speech and Silence: The Problematics of Research on Language and Gender." Pp. 175-203 in *Gender at the Crossroads of Knowledge: Feminist Anthropology in the Postmodern Era,* edited by M. di Leonardo. Berkeley: University of California Press.

Griffith, A. I. and D. E. Smith. 1987. "Constructing Cultural Knowledge: Mothering as Discourse." Pp. 87-103 in *Women and Education: A Canadian Perspective,* edited by J. S. Gaskell and A. T. McLaren. Calgary, Alberta: Detselig.

Hagood, M. J. [1939] 1977. *Mothers of the South: Portraiture of the White Tenant Farm Woman.* New York: Norton.

Hays, S. 1996. *The Cultural Contradictions of Motherhood.* New Haven, CT: Yale University Press.

Hill, M. 1990. "The Methodological Framework of Harriet Martineau's Feminist Analyses of American Society." Presented at the annual meeting of the American Studies Association, New Orleans.

Holland, J. and C. Ramazanoglu. 1994. "Coming to Conclusions: Power and Interpretation in Researching Young Women's Sexuality." Pp. 125-48 in *Researching Women's Lives from a Feminist Perspective,* edited by M. Maynard and J. Purvis. London: Taylor & Francis.

Jackson, D. 1999. "Thoughtful Practice: Responding with Questions from the Superintendency." Pp. 217-19 in *Sacred Dreams: Women and the Superintendency,* edited by C. C. Brunner. Albany: State University of New York Press.

Josselson, R. 1996. *Revising Herself: The Story of Women's Identity from College to Midlife.* New York: Oxford University Press.

Kanter, R. M. 1977. *Men and Women of the Corporation.* New York: Basic Books.

Kohlberg, L. 1984. *The Psychology of Moral Development.* New York: Harper & Row.

Klatch, R. E. 1987. *Women of the New Right.* Philadelphia: Temple University Press.

Komarovsky, M. 1961. *Blue-Collar Marriage.* New York: Random House.

Krieger, S. 1991. *Social Science and the Self: Personal Essays on an Art Form.* New Brunswick, NJ: Rutgers University Press.

Lewin, E. 1993. *Lesbian Mothers: Accounts of Gender in American Culture.* Ithaca, NY: Cornell University Press.

———. 1998. *Recognizing Ourselves: Ceremonies of Lesbian and Gay Commitment.* New York: Columbia University Press.

Lindsey, E. W. 1997. "Feminist Issues in Qualitative Research with Formerly Homeless Mothers." *Affilia* 12(1):57-75.

Lofland, L. H. 1975. "The 'Thereness' of Women: A Selective Review of Urban Sociology." Pp. 144-70 in *Another Voice: Feminist Perspectives on Social Life and Social Science,* edited by M. M. Millman and R. M. Kanter. Garden City, NY: Anchor/Doubleday.

Lorber, J. 1993. "Believing Is Seeing: Biology as Ideology." *Gender & Society* 7:568-81.

———. 1998. *Gender Inequality: Feminist Theories and Politics.* Los Angeles: Roxbury.

Luttrell, W. 1997. *Schoolsmart and Motherwise: Working-Class Women's Identity and Schooling.* New York: Routledge.

Marin, G. and B. V. Marin. 1991. *Research with Hispanic Populations.* Newbury Park, CA: Sage.

Martineau, H. [1837] 1962. *Society in America.* Edited by S. M. Lipset. Garden City, NY: Anchor.

Maynard, M. and J. Purvis. 1994. "Doing Feminist Research." Pp. 1-9 in *Researching Women's Lives from a Feminist Perspective,* edited by M. Maynard and J. Purvis. London: Taylor & Francis.

McMahon, M. 1995. *Engendering Motherhood: Identity and Self-Transformation in Women's Lives.* New York: Guilford.

———. 1998. "Between Exile and Home." Pp. 187-200 in *Redefining Motherhood: Changing Identities and Patterns,* edited by S. Abbey and A. O'Reilly. Toronto: Second Story.

Merton, R. K., M. Fiske, and P. L. Kendall. 1956. *The Focused Interview: A Manual of Problems and Procedures.* New York: Free Press.

Naples, N. 1997. "A Feminist Revisiting of the Insider/Outsider Debate: The 'Outsider Phenomenon' in Rural Iowa." Pp. 70-94 in *Reflexivity and Voice,* edited by R. Hertz. Thousand Oaks, CA: Sage.

Oakley, A. 1981. "Interviewing Women: A Contradiction in Terms?" Pp. 30-61 in *Doing Feminist Research,* edited by H. Roberts. London: Routledge & Kegan Paul.

Olesen, V. L. 1998. "Feminisms and Models of Qualitative Research." Pp. 300-332 in *The Landscape of Qualitative Research: Theories and Issues,* edited by N. K. Denzin and Y. S. Lincoln. Thousand Oaks, CA: Sage.

Ostrander, S. A. 1984. *Women of the Upper Class*. Philadelphia: Temple University Press.

———. 1995. " 'Surely You're Not in This Just to Be Helpful': Access, Rapport, and Interviews in Three Studies of Elites." Pp. 133-50 in *Studying Elites Using Qualitative Methods*, edited by R. Hertz and J. B. Imber. Thousand Oaks, CA: Sage.

Oyĕwùmí, O. 1997. *The Invention of Women: Making an African Sense of Western Gender Discourses*. Minneapolis: University of Minnesota Press.

Padfield, M. and I. Procter. 1996. "The Effect of Interviewer's Gender on the Interviewing Process: A Comparative Enquiry." *Sociology* 30:355-66.

Phoenix, A. 1994. "Practicing Feminist Research: The Intersection of Gender and 'Race' in the Research Process." Pp. 49-71 in *Researching Women's Lives from a Feminist Perspective*, edited by M. Maynard and J. Purvis. London: Taylor & Francis.

Pierce, J. L. 1995. *Gender Trials: Emotional Lives in Contemporary Law Firms*. Berkeley: University of California Press.

Ptacek, J. 1999. *Battered Women in the Courtroom: The Power of Judicial Responses*. Boston: Northeastern University Press.

Puwar, N. 1997. "Reflections on Interviewing Women MPs." *Sociological Research Online* 2(1). Available Internet: http://www.socresonline.org.uk/socresonline/2/1/4.html

Ralston, M. L. 1996. *"Nobody Wants to Hear Our Truth": Homeless Women and Theories of the Welfare State*. Westport, CT: Greenwood.

Reay, D. 1995. "The Fallacy of Easy Access." *Women's Studies International Forum* 18:205-13.

———. 1996. "Insider Perspectives or Stealing the Words Out of Women's Mouths: Interpretation in the Research Process." *Feminist Review* 53:57-73.

Reinharz, S. 1985. "Feminist Distrust: Problems of Content and Context in Sociological Work." Pp. 153-72 in *The Self in Social Inquiry: Researching Methods*, edited by D. N. Berg and K. K. Smith. Beverly Hills, CA: Sage.

———. 1992a. "A Contextualized Chronology of Women's Sociological Work." Working Paper No. 1, Brandeis University Women's Studies Program.

———. 1992b. *Feminist Methods in Social Research*. New York: Oxford University Press.

———. 1993. "Neglected Voices and Excessive Demands in Feminist Research." *Qualitative Sociology* 16:69-75.

Richardson, L. 1985. *The New Other Woman: Contemporary Single Women in Affairs with Married Men*. New York: Free Press.

Riessman, C. K. 1987. "When Gender Is Not Enough: Women Interviewing Women." *Gender & Society* 1:172-207.

———. 1990. *Divorce Talk: Women and Men Make Sense of Personal Relationships*. New Brunswick, NJ: Rutgers University Press.

Rogers, M. F., ed. 1998. *Contemporary Feminist Theory: A Text/Reader*. New York: McGraw-Hill.

Rollins, J. 1985. *Between Women: Domestics and Their Employers*. Philadelphia: Temple University Press.

Rothman, B. K. 1993. *The Tentative Pregnancy: How Amniocentesis Changes the Experience of Motherhood*. New York: Norton.

Rubin, L. B. 1976. *Worlds of Pain: Life in the Working-Class Family*. New York: Basic Books.

———. 1995. *Families on the Faultline: America's Working Class Speaks about the Family, the Economy, Race, and Ethnicity*. New York: Harper Perennial.

Sacks, K. B. 1988. *Caring by the Hour: Women, Work, and Organizing at Duke Medical Center*. Urbana: University of Illinois Press.

Samovar, L. A. and R. E. Porter, eds. 1991. *Intercultural Communication: A Reader*. 6th ed. Belmont, CA: Wadsworth.

Shostak, M. 1989. " 'What the Wind Won't Take Away': The Genesis of *Nisa—The Life and Words of a !Kung Woman*." Pp. 228-40 in *Interpreting Women's Lives: Feminist Theory and Personal Narratives*, edited by Personal Narratives Group. Bloomington: Indiana University Press.

Simmel, G. 1971. "The Stranger." Pp. 143-49 in G. Simmel, *On Individuality and Social Forms: Selected Writings*, edited by D. N. Levine. Chicago: University of Chicago Press.

Smith, D. E. 1987. *The Everyday World as Problematic: A Feminist Sociology*. Boston: Northeastern University Press.

Stacey, J. 1990. *Brave New Families: Stories of Domestic Upheaval in Late Twentieth Century America*. New York: Basic Books.

Tannen, D., ed. 1993. *Gender and Conversational Interaction*. New York: Oxford University Press.

Taylor, V. 1996. *Rock-a-By Baby: Feminism, Self-Help, and Postpartum Depression*. New York: Routledge.

Thompson, B. 1990. "Raisins and Smiles for Me and My Sister: A Feminist Theory of Eating Problems, Trauma, and Recovery in Women's Lives." Ph.D. dissertation, Brandeis University.

Tixier y Vigil, Y. and N. Elsasser. 1978. "The Effects of the Ethnicity of the Interviewer on Conversation: A Study of Chicana Women." Pp. 161-70 in *Sociology of the Languages of American Women*, edited by B. L. Dubois and I. Crouch. San Antonio, TX: Trinity University.

Tocqueville, A. de. [1835] 1994. *Democracy in America*, Vol. 2. New York: Alfred A. Knopf.

Treviño, A. J. 1992. "Interviewing Women: Researcher Sensitivity and the Male Interviewer." *Humanity and Society* 16:504-23.

Villenas, S. 1998. "The Colonizer/Colonized Chicana Ethnographer: Identity, Marginalization, and Co-optation in the Field." Pp. 172-88 in *Contemporary Feminist Theory: A Text/Reader*, edited by M. F. Rogers. New York: McGraw-Hill.

Weiss, R. S. 1994. *Learning from Strangers: The Art and Method of Qualitative Interview Studies*. New York: Free Press.

Weston, K. 1991. *Families We Choose: Lesbians, Gays, Kinship*. New York: Columbia University Press.

Whyte, W. F. 1943. *Street Corner Society: The Social Structure of an Italian Slum*. Chicago: University of Chicago Press.

Williams, C. L. 1995. *Still a Man's World: Men Who Do Women's Work*. Berkeley: University of California Press.

Wolf, D. L., ed. 1996. *Feminist Dilemmas in Fieldwork*. Boulder, CO: Westview.

Zavella, P. 1996. "Feminist Insider Dilemmas: Constructing Ethnic Identity with Chicana Informants." Pp. 138-59 in *Feminist Dilemmas in Fieldwork*, edited by D. L. Wolf. Boulder, CO: Westview.

12

QUEERING THE INTERVIEW

◆ Travis S. K. Kong
Dan Mahoney
Ken Plummer

The challenge lies in what each of us chooses to do when we represent our experiences. Whose rules do we follow? Will we make our own? What is the nature of the "I," that so many of our prohibitions bury? How can we unearth some of the inner worlds that we learn so very well to hide? Are we willing to do this within social science? Do we, in fact, have the guts to say, "You may not like it, but here I am." (Krieger 1991:244)

These questions resonate with the challenges of many of the changes the 20th century saw in the cultural forms of Western same-sex experience. Such experiences shifted from being highly disparaged—stigmatized, psychiatrized, and criminalized—to being politicized, social, and "out." A new form of gayness emerged symbolically in 1969 around the Stonewall moment, the start of the Gay Liberation Front, or GLF, sparked by gay resistance to the police invasion of the Stonewall Tavern in New York City. It led on to what might be seen as a proliferation of de-essentialized "queer" forms by the start of the new century, an array of different types of experience with no clear common core. These shifts—in the changing organization of "the closet," in the structures of homophobia and heterosexism, in the blurring of boundaries and borders, in the arrival of AIDS as a major galvanizing and depressing force, in the globalization and the "glocalization" of gay experience, indeed in the postmodernization of homosexualities—have all now been much documented, discussed, and dissected in the huge literatures that constitute a lesbian/gay/bisexual/transgender/queer compendium of studies (e.g., Abelove, Barale, and Halperin 1993; Murray 1997; Nardi and Schneider 1998;

Seidman, Meeks, and Traschen 1999; Weeks 1977, 1999).

Our aim in this chapter is to address the sense that, as all of this has changed, so have the methodologies for approaching it. We are now in the midst of emerging forms of experience that are paralleled by shifting styles of interviewing and analysis. What we suggest is simply that *the sensibilities of interviewing are altered with the changing social phenomena that constitute "the interviewee."* Interviewer and interviewee are always connected by a social location or habitus. We start with a brief tour of the shifts in the interviewing of gays in North America and Europe over the past 100 years before turning to a discussion of how contemporary issues have necessitated a different procedural agenda for researching same-sex experience.

◆ Interviewing "Homosexuals"

Table 12.1 presents some of the key changes that have taken place in the interviewing of gays in the past century. The table should be seen as an unstable continuum, certainly involving much overlap, depicting trends, rather than as a designation of strict time periods.[1] Broadly, we can trace a movement from a highly positivist mode of research through one where the boundaries become weaker, and on to a situation where interviewing has been partially deconstructed.

THE EARLY DAYS: A TRADITIONAL WORLD OF RESEARCH

Traditional "homosexual" research relied on a form of positivism that drew a sharp distinction between the subjects of knowing (i.e., researchers) and the objects of study (i.e., interviewees).[2] Through standardized interviews, ostensibly disinterested researchers obtained seemingly objective accounts of the nature of homo-sexuality. Here, "homosexuals"—a term coined by Hungarian doctor Karoly Maria Benkert in the 1860s—were interviewed as the Other. Until the latter third of the 20th century "scientists" studied homosexuals, initially as perverted, then as sick, and finally as different persons. The interviews usually aimed at explaining the properties of sexuality by referring to "an inner truth or essence—a uniform pattern ordained by nature, not connected to values and emotions" (Stein 1997:203).

This dominant pattern of research unfolded in two waves. In both, homosexuals were incited to speak through interviews about what made them that way and just how different they were. But in one wave, the interview was clearly an instrument of pathological diagnosis—strongly dehumanizing, rendering homosexuals sick and diseased, and often serving as a specific means for placing homosexuals in prison, under treatment, or worse. Medicine and psychiatry dominated. This continued until 1973, when at least the American Psychiatric Association saw fit, under pressure, to demedicalize homosexuality (Bayer 1981). Prime examples of work in this vein include Richard von Krafft-Ebing's (1899) research, the studies of George W. Henry (1941), and, in the 1950s and 1960s the research of Irving Bieber (1962) and Charles Socarides (1968).

At the same time, another more benign tendency was taking place, one that was to play a more humanizing role. In this wave, the interview became a tool of modernist democratization and ultimately of social reform. To some extent, it can be found in Freud's openness to polymorphousness and bisexuality, but it is strongly present in the important interviews of Alfred Kinsey and his associates (Kinsey, Pomeroy, and Martin 1948; Kinsey et al. 1953) and Evelyn Hooker (1957) in the United States and of Michael Schofield, alias Gordon Westwood (1961), in the United Kingdom. This more benign approach humanized the deviant, advocated tolerance, and weakened the language of the exotic. It made the

Table 12.1   CHANGES IN INTERVIEWING REGARDING SAME-SEX EXPERIENCE

	Traditional	Modernizing	Postmodern
Kind of interviewer	Presumed heterosexual and objective interviewer	Closeted gay and heterosexual interviewers	An "out" gay or lesbian interviewer
Conception of same-sex relations	1. "Essential homosexual"; a clear type of person awaiting an interview 2. Strict closet	1. The arrival of "homosexualities"; diversities 2. Weakened closet; gradual "coming out"	1. De-essentialized homosexual; no clear type of person; multiple pathways and experiences 2. Old closets weakened; new closets grow
Types of respondents	1. Homosexual respondents hard to find; usually psychiatric patients, criminal samples 2. Exotic and stigmatized "outsider"	1. Respondents from within the gay community: often white and male 2. Homosexuals becoming "normalized"	1. Recognition of a range of experiences; queer, global, multicultural 2. Queers and gays; fracturing; a normalization of a mainstream gay with new groups on the "outside"
Questions posed	Etiology and pathology: What causes homosexuality and descriptions of pathologies and negative lives?	The "coming out" story detailing the classic life story and lifestyle	Fragmenting; de-essentialized questions; a wider range of questions, often going well beyond the issue of homosexualities; "queering the field"
Approach	Mainly clinical	Mainly psychological and sociological surveys	Much more active, reflexive, and reflective; the decentered, deconstructed, and self-aware interview
Wider discourses of same-sex experience	Disease discourse	Psychosocial discourses	Cultural and political discourses
Nature of interview	Subject as interview object; sometimes coercive; seen as other		Mutuality of interviewer and subject; seen as potential friend
Examples	Krafft-Ebing (1989), moving to Kinsey et al. (1948, 1953)	Bell & Weinberg (1978); Gagnon & Simon (1973)	Krieger (1983, 1991, 1996)
Politics	Traditional-conservative, often with interview as a tool of control	Modernist-liberatory, often with interview as a democratic liberalizing force	Postmodernist themes; fragmented, postmodern ethics; self-conscious, more localized, politics and change

interview a more pedestrian affair. Findings saw continua in sexuality, a strong overlap between gay and heterosexual experience. Such studies investigated social backgrounds, early homosexual experiences, attempts to combat personal troubles, work, leisure, law, and community integration, as well as sexual adjustment.

With the exception of the work of Kinsey and his colleagues, however, little overt attention was given to the problems of interviewing themselves. Of course, there were the standard obligatory considerations of where interviews should take place (preferably in the home of the "contact") and the nature of the sample. But there was no methodological reflexivity of any kind, any sense of "active interviewing" (Holstein and Gubrium 1995). Subjects were largely taken to be passive receptacles of information, and emphasis was placed on the presentation of objective data.

This was true of the major, massive surveys that were conducted in the 1960s by the Kinsey Institute, one in Chicago as a pilot and the other in San Francisco. These studies, headed initially by John Gagnon and William Simon, and later conducted by Martin Weinberg and Alan Bell, drew from a very large subject pool established by way of advertising and recruitment in bars, gay baths, public places, and organizations, and through personal contacts. Samples of approximately 1,000 gay and 500 heterosexual men and women were obtained, and an interview schedule of some 175 pages was used, which took two to five hours for the recruited graduate student interviewers to complete. This produced some of the most widely cited findings of the late 20th century (e.g., Bell and Weinberg 1978; Bell, Weinberg, and Hammersmith 1982). But again, interview methodology followed strictly in the positivist mold, applying research practices that had by then become well established (see in this volume Platt, Chapter 2; Singleton and Straits, Chapter 3).[3]

Much, if not all, of this tradition of research has been "essentialist" in approach (Plummer 1981:57-61), an orientation that was progressively critiqued by the so-called social constructionists, who became prominent during the 1970s and 1980s.[4] The latter argued that sexuality and sexual identity are social constructions, belonging less to the biological world than to the domain of culture and meaning (Epstein 1987). Constructionists relativized the conception of gay identity and argued that the late-20th-century Western experience of same-sex intimacies was historically unique, as they simultaneously sketched the different makings of the homosexual role. They argued that the modern homosexual role emerged with the appearance of male transvestite

social clubs and homosexual coteries in major cities such as London in the 17th century, with the experience of the wage labor sector and the growth of urban populations in the 18th century, and with the professionalization of medicine and the social organization of sexual "types" in the 19th century (Adam 1985; Foucault 1979).

"COMING OUT" AS A MODERNIST TALE

The rise of a lesbian and gay movement from the 1960s onward triggered a new understanding of homosexuality and a new research direction. With the redeployment of the 19th-century slang term *gay* to oppose the pathologizing term *homosexual,* the positivist approach was being slowly undone, as it was elsewhere in the social sciences. A hermeneutic or interpretive perspective emerged, and the interview increasingly became a tool for self-identification and "coming out." As researchers asked how respondents got to be gay and how they felt about it, a cultural event started to take shape through interviewing that led to the makings of the "coming out story."

These stories were typically "modernist tales," articulated in a causal language of linear progression and centered on an unproblematic identity. Interviews were presumed to be discovering the "truth" of the gay self. Starting in childhood and following through the life course in linear progression, gay interviews assumed the same sequenced and causal pattern featured in much modern biography. In gay stories, childhood was usually presented as an unhappy time, frequently the source of the individual's being gay or lesbian. There was often a strong sense of difference expressed: "I never felt as if I fit in. I don't know why for sure. I felt different. I thought it was because I was more sensitive" (Troiden 1988; cited in Savin-Williams 1990). A crucial moment appeared within this modernist narrative, usually in early adolescence, where problems led to a marked concern over being "gay." Personal difficulties abounded and were usually documented in detail: secrecy, guilt or shame, fear of discovery, and suicidal feelings. But they were then resolved in some fashion in a redemption tale, usually involving the person's meeting other lesbians or gays in the community. Finally, the individual achieved a sense of identity or self *as* gay or lesbian, along with a sense of community (see Dank [1971] in Nardi and Schneider 1998; Plummer 1995:83). This is a simplified version, but over and over again narratives of this kind were proffered in the many "coming out" interviews gathered in the 1970s and 1980s. Coming out became the central narrative of positive gay experience.

At the same time, more and more self-identified gay researchers engaged in the interview process, collapsing the old split between subject/researcher and the object/researched. Some researchers started to come out through their writings. If in some instances the interview process became a political act, it also started to imply that only gay and lesbian researchers could conduct this interviewing, because of their more authentic understanding of other gay men and lesbians. Putting it simply, the assumption was that only those who have been there can understand what it's like.

THE DRIFT TO REFLEXIVITY IN THE 1980s

Two major changes took place in the 1980s that extended these shifts in interviewing: the consolidation of feminist research practices and the arrival of AIDS research. Feminist research practices had been advocated since at least the mid-1970s. Feminists brought a heightened self-awareness and reflexivity to interview methodology, which led to a greater concern with subjects' lived and contradictory experience, along with an image of the in-

terview that was based more on friendly conversation than on "masculine" interrogation (see Reinharz and Chase, Chapter 11, this volume). This brought the researcher and the researched into greater contact and made the research process more expressly moral and political. Many feminist researchers also were lesbians, and they incorporated a mode of working that also touched specifically on lesbian issues (Krieger 1983, 1991, 1996; Stanley and Wise 1983, 1993).

AIDS and HIV research led to more community-based approaches to interviewing, although it must be said that much of this was carried out in the time-honored positivist manner, which researchers saw as the only way to gain funding. New, culturally specific practices were incorporated as gay researchers went into the field and interviewed in venues most frequented by gay men, using sexually explicit language and gay vernacular.

As a result, an interview context emerged that was based largely on gay (and lesbian) "sensibilities." Although this term may have an essentialist resonance, in practice this meant that the gay interviewer and gay interviewee could empathize around shared meanings and ways of knowing.[5] A safe environment where gay men felt at ease to talk about their sexual and relationship histories was constructed. The result was that the interview context was distinctively "gayed."

THE RISE OF QUEER THEORY AND A QUEER METHODOLOGY

It was but a few steps from this to a more developed "queer methodology." Drawing from some of the existing critical trends, but taking a lead from poststructuralism, some researchers mounted a challenge to traditional epistemologies by arguing that we have no way of accessing the reality where our theory can be grounded without some form of conceptual and linguistic ordering in which to understand experience.

Interpretation, writing, and speech acts are all practices both of and in an intertextual field. Poststructuralism radically rejected the notion of the possibility of obtaining objective reality, as it elided a reality "posited beyond the text with reference to which meaning can be stabilized among different subjects" (Smith 1996:174).

On the status of objective knowledge, the poststructuralist rejection of a one-to-one correspondence between a category and the object it denoted implied that language was no longer a transparent medium. Attention to the multiple discursivity that constituted social relations was the only alternative. On the status of subjectivity, poststructuralists rejected the notion of a unified disciplinary subject, because subjects are always "situated" or "positioned" when they enter the symbolic world. Poststructuralists thus urged us to recon- cile ourselves to our having multiple and fragmented, discursively constituted subjectivities, intersected significantly by gender, race, sexuality, and class, among the many and diverse subject positions that mediate everyday life and, of course, the interview.

Queer theory works toward deconstructing discourses, and, to the extent that interviewing is discursive, this means deconstructing the interview.[6] To quote Michael Warner (1993), this leads to a stark attack on "normal business in the academy" (p. xxv). One result is the adoption of a "scavenger methodology that uses different methods to collect and produce information on subjects who have been deliberately or accidentally excluded from traditional studies of human behavior." In its most general form, this entails a refusal to abide orthodox methodology, encouraging a "certain disloyalty to conventional disciplinary methods" (Halberstam 1998:9, 13).

In this context, the traditional "scientific" interview is devalorized and takes a much more down-to-earth role alongside any and all other methods. The very idea that various types of people named homosexuals or gays or lesbians can simply be called up for interviews becomes a key problem in itself. Instead, the researcher becomes increasingly open and sensitive to how sexuality, among a broad range of identities, is anchored in fleeting ways within the discursive contours of interviewing. The many social worlds that can, as a result, contextualize what is said during interviews are not immediately transparent, whereas others are amorphously nascent and forming. It is not always possible to see what is forming, producing subjective domains and identities that Plummer (1995) has called the worlds of "imagining-visualising-empathising" (p. 126).

The subject of inquiry ("the homosexual"), the nature of the inquiry ("the interview"), and the inquirers themselves have all become problematized and open to deconstruction. The result is that new procedural issues are being seriously considered in relation to how interviewing gets done. One of these relates to matters of *subjective representation.*[7] Here the problem arises of literally who and what is being heard through the interview. Specifically, who are these "homosexuals" being interviewed, how do they come to find their voice, and what indeed is that voice? If one is successfully coaxed into giving voice to one's experience in an interview, what are the chances that one will become the Other in the process? Homosexuals, gays, bisexuals, transgenders, lesbians, even "queer" subjects have typically been homogenized and cast into some role of Other and thus seriously misrepresented, their thoughts, language, and sentiments collapsed into categories foreign to, if not destructive of, experience. Indeed, how often are these voices mere reproductions of white, middle-class, Western gay men, as if there were indeed no other subjectivities to consider? As far as representation is concerned, doing interviews now more urgently than ever requires us to investigate simultaneously who has been excluded. And this leads to the questions of who can speak for the other, from what position, and on what basis

(Denzin 1994; Lincoln and Denzin 1994:577).

This raises a second procedural issue centered on *legitimation*. This relates to the old problem of the validity of interviews, although now the problem becomes to sense the legitimacy of "constructing an interview" and how results get composed into a "research text." When, therefore, we come to a text about gay lives that is composed through interviews, we want some sense of how faithful it is "to the context and the individuals it is supposed to represent" (Lincoln and Denzin 1994:578).

A third and related issue is *reflexivity*, which centers on the problem of locating the connectedness between the (gay?) interviewer and (gay? bisexual? lesbian? queer?) interviewee. This alerts us to questions of whether researchers should be part of the communities they study, and to the emotional responses interviews provoke in their subjects, indeed to their erotic involvements as well. The full assembly of academic and intellectual conventions around interviewing is broached, conventions that can actually work to obscure, not discover, knowledge.

And, finally, there is the matter of interviewing's *politics, morality, and ethics*. Closely linked to all of the above is the crucial recognition that interviewing involves human dimensions. Although it may be cozy to see interviews as simply a matter of "gathering data," a deconstruction of interviewing that derives from firmly sensing what has been done to "homosexuals" through interviews in the past must be at the forefront of what it now means to "queer" the interview. We need to take account of the distinct possibility that, within the research process itself, interviews are moral and political interventions through and through, and we need to represent our findings as such.

Of course, these problems are not peculiar to the interviewing of homosexuals. The latter highlight them in different ways in relation to distinct subjectivities. In what follows, we take up the issues in greater detail as they specifically relate to possibilities for queering the interview process.

◆ The Problem of Representation

Who is being re-presented in the interview? Posing the question in this way leads to the consideration of how the gay person being interviewed may become the Other within the context of being a respondent. Indeed, if we are to take Michel Foucault seriously, our interviews may show nothing but our will to power as interviewers. An interview could never really "represent" the gay or lesbian who is being interviewed as such; rather, it is one more technical display of a disciplined regimen of interviewer/author power over subjects. From this perspective, representation is a kind of authorial and cultural self-re-presentation. Interviewees' presentations are always already directly connected to the situated interviewing self of an author/researcher and his or her project (Krieger 1991).

Can the interview stories we hear from lesbians and gays and that appear in texts as diverse as Arlene Stein's *Sex and Sensibility* (1997), Gary Dowsett's *Practicing Desire* (1996), and Richard Parker's *Beneath the Equator* (1999) really represent the worlds of those studied? What does the interview come to represent? Can it reveal, legitimately, the experience of interviewees? Or does it implicate, instead, the narrower, more restricted world of the researcher, which would say more about Arlene Stein, Gary Dowsett, and Richard Parker than about their subjects themselves? Do these texts address the interests of those studied?

The key status of the interviewer/author is now put into question. Whether or not the interviewer's voice is manifest, it always deploys a unique self in the interview and claims to have some pervasive authorial functions over other subject matters that are being interpreted. Even having the research subjects as authors does not completely solve the problem, for we are left asking under what institutional constraints they can come to be authors and under what historical limitations they can speak and write. Just when and how can stories of such lives be told? (See Plummer 1995; see also Briggs, Chapter 44, this volume.)

This makes interviewing and the texts that flow from it much more problematic than the authors of the earlier studies of gay life could have figured. New strategies for handling matters of representation have to be found (see in this volume Denzin, Chapter 40; Ellis and Berger, Chapter 41; Richardson, Chapter 42). One way may involve a greater focus on specialized and localized knowledges, another may focus on the creation of new modes of writing the interview.

THE INTERVIEW AS A SITE OF LOCALIZED KNOWLEDGE

Because epistemology has traditionally been the legacy of white, straight men, it has had to be challenged by more specialized and marginalized knowledges. From diverse positions—Foucauldian, standpoint theoretical, postmodern, and postcolonial —new voices have started to be heard telling their stories (Foucault 1984; Harding 1991; Spivak 1994). The missing voice of "authentic" (a word with a host of problems and that we use advisedly) gays and lesbians under the sign of compulsory heterosexuality in the sex/gender regime of society can become a key to new forms of local knowledge. The heterosexual/homosexual binary is recognized as a master rhetoric, not an essential framework, for constructing the self, sexual knowledge, and social institutions. This binary sex system, or power/knowledge regime, is critically assessed for how it creates rigid psychological and social boundaries that inevitably give rise to systems of dominance and hierarchy (Sedgwick 1990; Fuss 1991; Butler 1990; Warner 1993).

AIDS interview research has, perhaps of necessity, only partially given way to this critical consciousness. Rather than interviewing self-identified gay men as the sole sources to learn about the sexual practices of same-sex experience, researchers interview "MSM" (men who have sex with other men)—a distinction that seems to terminologically suspend the issue of the interviewee's identity. This recognition of the "collapse of identity and difference" links up queer with AIDS activism (Edelman 1995). Although coming out of the closet is often viewed as a gay empowerment strategy and as a supreme political act to affirm gay visibility from heterosexism, the division between individuals who are "in" the closet and those who are "out" has its costs, as this not only narrowly defines the sexual experiences of lesbians and gay men, but also stigmatizes the former, who are "in," as living unhappily and privileges the latter, who are "out," as presumably now more satisfied with their lives and identities (see Seidman et al. 1999).

The recent critique from "queer theorists" also receives its attention in anthropology, as Kath Weston (1998) argues. Many lesbians and gay men do not offer the "best" natives for study. In representation, if not in action, they appear too modern, too urban, too here and now, too wealthy, and too white. Below the perceptual horizon are queers with rural origins, immigrant status, empty pocketbooks, racial identities at variance with the Anglo. Ironically, the gay movement's problematic tendency is to draw analogies between sexual and racial identity, as though all gays were white and people of color could not be gay (Weston 1998:194).

Last but not least, localization is extended as postcolonial theorists examine the intertwining relationship between race and sexuality.[8] Drawing heavily on the legacy of poststructuralism, queer theory, and postcolonialism, postcolonial queer theorists contend that homosexuality is often viewed as a white European experience, and gay Asian British/American identity seems to be contradictory. These theorists argue that postcolonial gay identities are not merely the additive experiences of race, gender, class, and sexuality, or simply another variation of the Western homoerotic experience; rather, they are the result of multifarious and contradictory sets of oppression within specific institutional arenas. We must understand sexual identity in terms of this "politics of difference" in order to avoid suppressing the multiple ways of experiencing homosexual desires (Takagi 1996; Hanawa 1994; Jackson and Sullivan 1999; Leong 1996; Kong 2000). Interviewing in relation to such differences can reveal and, at the same time, dissolve into multiplicities, the many ways there are to experience same-sexedness.

THE INTERVIEW AS A SHIFT IN WRITING STRATEGY

Many experiments with writing have been undertaken, pioneered by feminist researchers who have emphasized how personal experience can be used as evidence in research (see in this volume Ellis and Berger, Chapter 41; Richardson, Chapter 42). The standard mode, of course, is to use interview extracts in such a way that the representative text becomes littered with examples of first-person speech drawn out of interview findings. In this mode of representation, the interviewed gay or lesbian is engrossed by the author's own writing and scholarly authority.

What is required is a shift in style that shows textually how interviews of gay men and lesbians can be led by the researcher's vested interest. This effort would help to create a new way of looking at things by blurring representational distinctions (e.g., between philosophy and literary) and subject matters (e.g., between "hard-core" sociological writing and autobiography). Researchers can explore this shift in style by using "fictionalized" interview material to express issues of representation, subjectivity, and critique for social research (Banks

and Banks 1998; see also Rosenblatt, Chapter 43, this volume). They may also explore by experimenting with the use of autovideo—that is, turning the camera back onto interviewer and interviewee (Juhasz 1995). Researchers may further explore this shift through renditions of social science that see it as drama, poetry, diary, documentaries, interactive Web sites, and more.

Ironically, at the same time, the author can often lose his or her own voice in favor of a more "subjective" one. In a series of studies and observations, Susan Krieger has pondered just how she "had a right to say something that was mine," reflecting the perspective of researchers and interviewers who figure they have no right at all to bring themselves and their feelings into their work. In several studies, such as *The Mirror Dance* (1983), *Social Science and the Self* (1991), and *The Family Silver* (1996), Krieger has tried to find ways in which she can do research and yet allow her own presence and experiences to be felt. During her research reported in *The Mirror Dance*, for example, she lived in a community of lesbians, seeing her year's participation with the group she studied as an active emotional reengagement process. Krieger describes how an understanding of her own self, worked through over time, helped her to clarify what could otherwise have been just "data."

◆ The Problem of Legitimation

Another key problem of interviewing centers on issues of legitimation and authenticity, what used to be called validity. At the simplest level, gays and lesbians may tell lies or just set out to please the interviewer to gain positive evaluations. Even if they are assumed to give authentic answers, problems still exist. As a large part of gay and lesbian interviews are usually retrospective accounts, interviewees are required to reconstruct their pasts actively in order to make sense of their present selves. Problems of memory and accounting enter here (Plummer 2001). Even questions that do not directly ask about the past, such as "What does it mean to be gay?" and questions concerning interviewees' current opinions on love and/or sex still demand that lesbians and gays create some kind of coherent account of their responses, implicating the past. Of course, these problems are not unique to lesbian and gay interviews, but they do suggest problems that are trickier than the older ways of putting this in terms of validity and reliability.

Any attempt to overcome this authenticity problem, as it relates to narrative, risks falling back into the trap of positivism, where it is assumed that the "truth" of the past can be revealed through objective methods of investigation. How can this be overcome? Various kinds of postmodern sensibilities for "queer interviewing" suggest themselves.

One is overtly political. Foucault's (1984) subversive genealogy is a strategy that exposes how power and discourse operate together and how subordinated knowledges can be used to resist any validity-as-authority claims. Thus studying gay and lesbian identity may disturb the prevailing rigid familial, gender, and moral systems of society, but this may also reify the very categories of lesbian and gay that may fix or control conduct.

Another recent leap of the imagination may be found in Judith Halberstam's (1998) work. In examining "female masculinity," Halberstam argues that although we have started to recognize the varieties of masculinities that are linked to men, we have signally failed to develop ways of seeing that can grasp the different kinds of masculinities that women have revealed both in the past and in the present. According to Halberstam, there are aristocratic European cross-dressing women of the 1920s, butch lesbians, dykes, drag kings, tomboys, black butch-in-the-hood rappers, trans-butches, tribades, gender inverts, stone butches, female-to-male transsexuals

(FTMs), and raging bull dykes. Halberstam also detects, through examination of films as diverse as *Alien* and *The Killing of Sister George,* at least six prototypes of the female masculine: the tomboy, the predator, the fantasy butch, the transvestite, the barely butch, and the postmodern butch.

This research brings to the surface social worlds only dimly articulated hitherto, suggesting that there are more, many more, to be formulated. As far as interviewing is concerned, it signals the hugely diverse, mixed, hybridized, and newly imagined subjectivities around which questions could be prepared, responses offered, and interview material interpreted—which a single category of female, male, or even female masculinity itself would collapse into homogenized subjective meaninglessness.

The task is to subvert the unified notion of gay and lesbian identity and to paint a picture of multiple and conflicting sexual/gendered experiences. Further to the point, in these times of globalization, we can present postcolonial queer identities that offer new insights by troubling the hegemonic Western formulation of "being gay." The queer interview can be composed discursively to cause trouble.[9] Such complicated assumptions behind interviewing are made clearer, for example, by Travis Kong, one of the authors of this chapter. Kong comes from Hong Kong, has self-identified as a gay man, has been living in London for a couple of years, and works in English. Although he shares with the other two authors a sense of being a gay academic man, his postcolonial and sexual statuses inevitably affect his formulation of gayness under a Western hegemonic knowledge regime. For example, as a sexual and racial minority in a white and heterosexual society, the Chinese gay man is imagined as an exotic/erotic fantasy, as the "golden boy," as an infantilized (age), feminized (gender), and golden (race) persona who seems to suffer different forms of subordination under the hierarchies of domination in both the straight and gay worlds (Kong 2000, forthcoming).

Assumptions are usually made about what it means to be gay in the West, not the East. The Chinese construction of the individual as a "relational self" seems to be in conflict with the Western idea of coming out, in which outed gay figures are usually without blood-family ties. The possibility of leading a satisfactory life outside the family seems to be inconceivable in Asian countries, and so the problem is how to reconcile gay identity with the institution of the neo-Confucian family (see Berry 1996; Kong 2000). In the Chinese context, coming out is not a common way of asserting one's gayness, and desires do not seem to be framed in terms of political interests. Rather than the term *homosexual* (a Western medical term), *gay* (a Western construction), or even *queer* (a Western deconstruction), the term *tongzhi* (literally "comrade") has gained in popularity within gay circles in Hong Kong because of its ambiguous nature.[10] Because *tongzhi* also carries no direct sexual connotation, Hong Kong gay men feel comfortable using it. This and other kinds of non-Western "trouble" provide a culturally sensitive pretext for *normalizing* family-oriented questions in interviews with gays. Needless to say, the coming out narrative in this context might very well signal domestic reconciliation or transformation more than disengagement.

◆ Self-Reflection in the Interview Process

Another concern for gay and lesbian interviewing has to be the increased awareness of the need for self-reflexivity. Pierre Bourdieu, in *An Invitation to Reflexive Sociology* (1992), suggests that reflexivity provides a much greater awareness of the entire intellectual process. We need to look at (a) the subject of the research along with (b) the social locations in which research knowledge is produced, as well as (c) a much fuller sense of the spaces—personal,

cultural, academic, intellectual, historical—that the researcher occupies in building that knowledge. There has to be an attentiveness to what people take into research situations and take out of them, as well as to feeling, identity, and the body.

This is of particular importance in the case of in-depth interviews on gay men's private lives. Before being interviewed, many gay men want to know where both the researcher and the teller of that life are coming from, what kind of relationship they are having together, and how intimate details will be used and represented. Dan Mahoney, another of the authors of this chapter, found this self-reflexive process to be an effective strategy when he was recruiting a gay couple for an interview. In his field notes, Mahoney (2000) writes:

Our drive back to their home outside London went particularly well. It became clear that Adam and I would get on. We both took the opportunity to ask and respond to each other's questions in a way that felt appropriate and polite. I was careful to come across as an interested and sincere person. I wanted to give the impression that I wasn't the type of researcher who was overbearing or full of myself. I felt it was important that I set the stage for the interview. I also felt that Adam was doing some preliminary assessing on his own. . . .

Adam produced the fax I sent him and went about asking for clarification about the nature of the research and what I meant by storytelling. I took the opportunity to speak about the book I was writing on gay men and their families, and my interest in writing about experiences of gay men we haven't heard about before. James [Adam's partner] sat and took it all in. Adam continued to ask me questions. He wanted to know about my personal background, why I was studying in England, and why on earth I was living in Colchester. I gave him a short biography of my life. More disclosures about my life precipitated more answers and questions about me and my research interests. I was getting the impression that they were warming up to the idea of being interviewed.

REFLEXIVITY, EMOTIONS, AND THE RESEARCHER'S SELF

The doing of interviews is personal, interactional, and emotional. It is embodied work that can have implications for the researcher as well as the researched. How does the researcher present him- or herself? How is the interaction embodied? How are feelings presented and managed (see Coffey 1999; Kleinman and Copp 1993)? In earlier work on sexual life stories, Ken Plummer (1995) describes a situation he encountered in doing life story interviewing that wasn't gay but fetishistic, and then reflects on just what the doing of such an interview meant. Plummer comments on a so-called foot fetishist:

I travel to the North of England where I meet a young man in his early twenties in a hotel lobby. We go to my hotel room, and he tells me in enormous detail of his desire to be trod upon by women in high heels. As this happens, he fantasizes a dagger being plunged into his stomach. It is a long story, which takes me through his childhood memories of this and the "driven" nature of his "single" adult life. I record the conversation, and respond very sympathetically to him; he seems a nice enough man. Back at my university, the tape is transcribed and makes fascinating reading. The secretary (of the research) names him Jack (a pseudonym, but interestingly her husband is called Jack!). This transcript is sent to Jack, who comments profusely on it. A short correspondence is set up, and I send him a copy of a key book in this field, *The Sex Life of the Foot and Shoe*. For

the past ten years, the transcript and its commentary sits in my filing cabinet. I have lost contact with him. (P. 10)

After this brief description, so much more could have been said. So Plummer continues asking questions of himself about what he was actually doing, implicating a number of his own identities in the process —as tolerant researcher, as a coparticipant in self-disclosure, and as representer of the experience under consideration.

What brought me to seek out a man who wanted to talk about his "unusual" sexual life? Why should I, in the name of Holy Social Science, want to coax anyone to tell me about their sexual lives? What brought him to the hotel room to tell me all about it? How could he produce such stories, and how did my "tolerant" responses to him actively encourage him to tell a certain sort of story? He could sense very early on that I was not going to be shocked or censorious in any way. But didn't that make him say certain things rather than others? And to leave endless undetected absences? How much of his story was a performance of a dress rehearsal he had practised many times in solitude before? What, then, was the relationship of my transcribed interview to his actual life? And how was I to write this? In his voice, or in my voice, or in his voice through my voice, or even in my voice through his voice? And then, once read by others—including me and him— what multiple interpretations would it be open to? Would there perhaps be a correct reading which would finally get us all to the truth of such foot fetishists? Or would it be used as an occasion for condemnation, curiosity, or simple titillation, or as a guide for someone else to locate their sexual nature? What would it do to Jack once published? And indeed, what has it done to him since it has *not* been published, but sits unread in a filing cabinet? And so it goes on.

The questions proliferate. I became more and more aware of these questions at the time of doing the research, and they slowly incapacitated me. Just what *are* these sexual stories gathered for research? (P. 12)

THE BIG SILENCE: ON SEXING THE INTERVIEW

What starts to be sensed are all the typically silenced questions around an interview that more and more need to be brought to the fore. We can take all this one stage further, into slightly dangerous, certainly controversial, territory. Here we turn to the hidden dimensions of romance, passion, and sexuality that must impinge on some, maybe much, research, even if rarely spoken about. It is curious, not to say disingenuous, to find that most research is written as if such experiences quite simply never happen in people's lives. From fieldwork to interviews, as people come and go, nothing much ever appears to unfold in erotic mode. Just where is it?

Recently, a number of researchers have started to make this erotic dimension more explicit. For example, in a wonderful account of Kay, a lesbian in her 80s and one of Esther Newton's (1993) key informants at the lesbian community of Cherry Grove, Newton makes her passion and involvement very clear:

This morning I introduced myself to a woman of eighty plus, whom I'd been wanting to meet, as she rolled toward me in her electric chair. Not only was she receptive, she clasped my arm in an intimate embrace and practically pulled me into her while we talked . . . and my heart quite turned over. Such are the perils of fieldwork. . . .

. . . the beauty of it is I adore her even though I need her and have ulterior professional motives. (Pp. 12-14)

There surely have been other cases when, in interviews concerning sex, having actual sexual experiences could be strongly justified. Some years back, Joseph Styles (1979) wrote about how his personal sexual experiences of gay bathhouses helped him to understand others' sexualities. In the wake of an explosion of sex research around AIDS, one leading anthropologist, Ralph Bolton (1992), has indeed positively advocated sex with respondents if what the interviewer wishes to understand is their sexuality. Of course, this is a controversial area, but it is one that surely needs to be confronted and scrutinized rather than methodologically and morally silenced. Certainly, all the authors of this chapter can recall moments of feeling passion for persons we were busy interviewing, and we keep quiet about saying whether it went any further. Such stories need to be told and discussed.

◆ Toward an Ethical Strategy in Gay Interviewing

Gay interviewing often brings with it a kind of gay and lesbian sensibility that informs the questions asked, the types of relationships formed, and our ways of knowing. For some researchers, this finely tuned aesthetic facilitates the process of building a collaborative, communicative experience between interviewer and interviewee, and it suggests the need for a greater ethical awareness of this relationship. Thus many gay men, lesbians, and bisexual and transgendered people will speak about their personal experiences only when they feel safe. Getting gay men to speak openly about their subjective experiences can be very much like asking them to go through another form of coming out (Seidman et al. 1999).

Investigating the complex nature of this queer subjectivity, for some, requires the researcher to adopt a pragmatic ethical strategy. The adoption of such a perspective places emphasis on the specific cultural meanings that gay people and their communities bring to their intimate arrangement and argues against any moral imperative that values one set of experiences over another. As Seidman (1992) suggests:

> Our starting point should be an understanding of the basic assumptions of a particular society with regard to sexuality, the relationship between sex, identity, and private and public life. The existing sexual and social patterns of the society one is addressing need to be accorded a certain respect and legitimacy; these patterns should be seen as growing out of, and fitted in some useful way, to the lives of the various individuals and groups who share a history, culture and social structural position. A minimal level of respect therefore needs to be accorded existing patterns as they reflect, in part, a creative adaptation to individual or group. (P. 192)

This pragmatic of adopting an ethical strategy when investigating gay subjectivity usually comes about on a number of fronts and can be thought of as a process. Although being members, or keen supporters, of particular gay communities may provide researchers with some important insider contacts, this is no assurance that the researchers' location within these communities will mark the beginning of successful research recruitment. What appears to be more important is that researchers begin by first constructing ethical identities in the communities they wish to study, so that individuals, groups, and networks in those communities begin to see the researchers as trusted insiders (or trusted outsiders, as the case might be) who are not out to misrepresent them in their research write-ups.

Gay research can generate innovative interview practices. For example, Dan Mahoney's preferred style relies heavily on his participating as a member in gay social groups, allowing him to get to know individuals, as well as the norms, practices, and cultural nuisances of their particular community, slowly, over time. This also provides the community members the opportunity to form their own opinions and judgments of him. In such research, it is particularly important during the initial phases that the researcher be transparent about the reasons (both interpersonal and work related) he or she has become a member of the group, as well as about the point of the research and the tools and resources he or she has brought to the research context. Such interactions allow individuals and communities to make informed choices about whether they want to participate in the research. The construction of an ethical researcher in the field is an important methodological tool for building trust and cooperation.

THE ART OF AN ETHICAL STRATEGY

Forming an ethical strategy is as much art as science and figures as much in personally sensitive research of any kind as it does in the interviewing of gay people. One facet of this centers on self-presentation. The researcher's management of his or her research identity comes about through ongoing internal dialogue, as well as through the researcher's conversations with research participants. Key questions the researcher should ask him- or herself include the following: Am I describing the research correctly? Does this person understand the concepts/language I am putting forward? Am I presenting enough information about myself and my research in order for this person to make an informed choice?

A second facet relates to the interviewer's empathic stance. Adopting an ethical strategy also suggests that the interviewer constructs an empathic, emotional orientation during the interview process. When interviewers ask gay people to engage in a potentially lengthy process of disclosure, the respondents need to know that the interviewer will be open to their lived experiences and is prepared to cofacilitate the interpretations of those events. Establishing such empathic rapport in an interview is always context specific, of course. However, deep levels of disclosure will come about only if the subject senses shared understanding from the interviewer (Josselson 1995).

Herbert Rubin and Irene Rubin (1995) present a hermeneutic model of interviewing that is well suited for this style of interviewing. In their view, interviewers must understand what they have seen, heard, or experienced in the subject's terms. According to Rubin and Rubin, what interviewers hear is affected by the ongoing interpersonal relationship between themselves and their informants, a perspective we share. The research process is indeed personal, not objectively detached, as a result. This interview context makes collaboration more open to interpretation while emphasizing the active participation of the researcher in the process.

A third facet concerns borders and boundaries. It is important that interviewers be able to sense the boundaries and limitations that are associated with these relationships. Interpretive interview methods often require that gay and lesbian researchers seek out other gays and lesbians toward whom they have some affinity; otherwise, the construction of intense, ongoing interpersonal contexts is difficult. However, it is important to remember that an interview context where "friendship" is constructed can be contrived and artificial. The scheduled nature of research projects often means that interview relationships have very short life spans (Crick 1992; Coffey 1999; El-Or 1997). These fieldwork relationships are often deep and intense, but not long lasting, which places unusual boundaries on the research's interpersonal dimensions.

Interpersonal borders can shift to inhibit the research process. There are times during the interview process when subjects do not respond well to an empathic, interac-tive process, or are not be willing to explore feelings and emotions. There also may be clashes of personalities between the interviewer and interviewee, making the construction of an interactive context impossible. The combination of these factors can be quite disastrous. It is often at this stage that the interviewer and/or interviewee begins to disengage from the interview process, and a loss of empathy and shared understanding occurs. An ethical strategy requires the researcher to acknowledge and be more open to examining these shifts as they relate to the feelings and behaviors participants bring to the interview context (Kleinman and Copp 1993; see also Johnson, Chapter 5, this volume).

Interviewers need to become more aware of their own feelings and, in turn, use them to guide the research process. For example, Mahoney (2000) found that further distancing himself during the interview process resulted in a lost opportunity. He made note of the consequences of this experience in his dissertation research:

In Richard's story, I was confronted with the realisation that I didn't care for this person very much, in fact I had little empathy for him. I couldn't relate to his snobbery and I certainly couldn't relate to a person who wasn't more up front about their feelings. After much reflection and journal writing, I was able to acknowledge this discomfort openly. Acknowledging these feelings and concerns helped me to recognise the assumptions, beliefs, and life experiences I brought to this experience. It allowed me to question my own values and expectations around power relations between myself and my research collaborators. Perhaps, most importantly, it got me to acknowledge the distancing that took place between myself and Richard. This distancing prevented me from becoming more interactive in the discussion, which further prevented an expansion of our knowledge construction of his story.

Much of this bears on the ethical imperative of what might be viewed as a methodology of friendship, moving beyond the roles of traditional research procedure. The research aims at building a quite special relationship founded partly on research goals but equally on friendship. But there is a downside to this, as a number of feminists have recently noted. All is not always so well when research turns into a friendship: "As researchers and participants get acquainted, establish trust and friendship, they become vulnerable to misunderstanding, disappointment, and invaded privacy. It can lead amongst other things to false intimacies, fraudulent friendships, a deceptiveness over equal relationships, and a masking of power" (Kirsch 1999:26).

◆ *Conclusion*

In this chapter, we have been concerned to show, in the first instance, how interviews are not fixed in time but change with historical moments. Interviewing "gays and lesbians" at the start of the 21st century is very different indeed than interviewing "them" was at the end of the 19th century. We are now much more sensitive to issues of othering and how we construct representation. We now consciously contend with the challenges of legitimation, with what it is that is being claimed and written and how that is accomplished. Issues of reflexivity, involvement, and ethics come forth in ways that were not possible at the start of the 20th century. We have suggested that findings and research practice are bound together; what is found in an interview depends upon the historical shape of the interview. With the arrival of postmodern, poststructural, and queer sensibilities, new forms of interviewing and indeed new kinds of findings may well be in the making.

The lessons of this chapter, however, go well beyond an account of lesbian and gay interviewing. Although the changes described are striking, we would suggest that this sense of radical historicity should now be seen as a necessary feature of all interviewing. Interviewing must be viewed as recursive: It feeds out of a historical, cultural moment from which questions and methodological strictures are mediated. In this context, interviewing is also a cultural form, providing a new cultural text of "findings," in which questions and answers become self-validating circles (Cicourel 1964; Gubrium and Holstein 1997). The short history of interviewing gays—a subjectivity that appeared only in the last decades of the 20th century with any pervasiveness—echoes this.

■ *Notes*

1. Terminology is always a problem. In short, *homosexual* is a term of the past, *gay* and *lesbian* are contemporary terms, and *queer* is a recent, more radical term. It is generally argued that these various terms do not depict the same phenomena, but in popular parlance they do, while highlighting key contrasting nuances.

2. There are major exceptions to this classification. The classic studies by Magnus Hirschfield in Germany in the early 20th century do not quite fit the theme of "exotic outsider." Hirschfield was a homosexual, his research was sympathetic to gays, and he was a victim of the Nazi purges. Likewise, in the 1990s, some of the major sex surveys conducted around AIDS were not conducted by gays.

3. There were other linked traditions. We are thinking especially of the urban ethnographic tradition that blossomed in the 1960s and is perhaps most keenly exemplified in the notorious work of the late Laud Humphreys (1970). He conducted interviews as well. Carol Warren (1974) was not interested in etiology, but found that her respondents in fact spent a great deal of time telling her their stories of "how they got to be this way." Warren notes, "The tales had a uniformity; they tallied well with all kinds of deterministic social science theories of dominant mothers, environment, traumas, and seduction." Warren slowly realized that "these social science rhetorics were being put to good use in the con-

struction of members' current identities and commitments" (p. 176).

4. International conferences were organized around this theme.

5. Although the term *gay sensibility* can lead to an essentialist understanding of a common core of meaning, we wish to make it clear that it is a form of historically specific "local knowledge" and not a universal, time-free sensitivity.

6. Often distinctions are made among queer theory, queer politics, and queer culture. Here we are referring mainly to queer theory (see Stein and Plummer 1996).

7. In this and the next section, our key source of inspiration is Yvonna Lincoln and Norman Denzin's (1994) discussion of issues of representation and legitimation.

8. Examples include Edward Said's (1978) and Franz Fanon's (1970) critiques of Western representations of non-Western cultures, which show how Western abstractions (e.g., human, man, masculinity) are produced at the expense of non-Western, colonized, and localized specificities (e.g., the other, the native, femininity). In her essay "Can the Subaltern Speak?" (1994), Gayatri Chakravorty Spivak concludes that it is impossible for the subaltern to speak because she is a "female subaltern from an underprivileged third-world nation." The composition of gendered, class, and racial subordination is the ulti-

mate silent/silenced bearer of the burdens of centuries of Western imperialist history. Contrasting with Spivak's pessimistic conclusion that "the natives have gone forever," other postcolonial theorists advance a notion of minority discourse (Deleuze and Guattari 1990) or the option of hybridity (Bhabha 1994).

9. As Jacques Derrida (1976) has noted, writing itself is a "wandering outcast" of the Western logocentric tradition, because it is always spoken rather than written language that is privileged. But writing also is a political act. Certain questions—Who is writing? Can everyone write? What does it mean to write? Write to whom? To dispatch what?—are not simply interrogative; they are questions of power.

10. The term *queer* is not commonly used in the gay community in Hong Kong. Its popularity seems to be restricted to academic circles. The term *tongzhi* was originally used by the Chinese national father Sun Yi Xian, who encouraged Chinese people to fight against the imperialist regime of the early 20th century. He said, "Evolution has not been successful; comrades should fight against it until the end." The term is believed to have been first appropriated as a synonym for gays, lesbians, and other sexual minorities after the first gay and lesbian film festival, held in 1991, which was referred to as the Tongzhi Film Festival.

■ *References*

Abelove, H., M. A. Barale, and D. M. Halperin, eds. 1993. *The Lesbian and Gay Studies Reader.* New York: Routledge.

Adam, B. 1985. "Structural Foundations of the Gay World." *Comparative Study of Society and History* 27:658-71.

Banks, A. and S. P. Banks, eds. 1998. *Fiction and Social Research: By Ice or Fire.* Walnut Creek, CA: AltaMira.

Bayer, R. 1981. *Homosexuality and American Psychiatry.* New York: Basic Books.

Bell, A. and M. S. Weinberg. 1978. *Homosexualities: A Study of Diversity among Men and Women.* London: Mitchell Beazley.

Bell, A., M. S. Weinberg, and S. K. Hammersmith. 1982. *Sexual Preference: Its Development in Men and Women.* Bloomington: Indiana University Press.

Berry, C. 1996. "Sexual DisOrientations: Homosexual Rights, East Asian Films, and Postmodern Postnationalism." Pp. 157-82 in *In Pursuit of Contemporary East Asian Culture,* edited by X. Tang and S. Snyder. Boulder, CO: Westview.

Bhabha, H. K. 1994. *The Location of Culture.* London: Routledge.

Bieber, I. 1962. *Homosexuality: A Psychoanalytic Study of Male Homosexuality.* New York: Basic Books.

Bolton, R. 1992. "Mapping Terra Incognita: Sex Research for AIDS Prevention—An Urgent Agenda for the 1990s." Pp. 124-58 in *The Time of AIDS: Social Analysis, Theory, and Method,* edited by G. H. Herdt and S. Lindebaum. Newbury Park, CA: Sage.

Bourdieu, P. 1992. *An Invitation to Reflexive Sociology.* Chicago: University of Chicago Press.

Butler, J. 1990. *Gender Trouble: Feminism and the Subversion Identity.* London: Routledge.

Cicourel, A. V. 1964. *Method and Measurement in Sociology.* New York: Free Press.

Coffey, A. 1999. *The Ethnographic Self: Fieldwork and the Representation of Identity.* London: Sage.

Crick, M. 1992. "Ali and Me: An Essay in Street-Corner Anthropology." In *Anthropology and Autobiography,* edited by J. Okely and H. Callaway. London: Routledge.

Deleuze, G. and F. Guattari. 1990. "What Is a Minor Literature?" In *Out There: Marginalization and Contemporary Cultures,* edited by R. Ferguson, M. Gever, Trinh T. M., and C. West. Cambridge: MIT Press.

Denzin, N. K. 1994. "The Art and Politics of Interpretation." Pp. 500-515 in *Handbook of Qualitative Research,* edited by N. K. Denzin and Y. S. Lincoln. Thousand Oaks, CA: Sage.

Derrida, J. 1976. *Of Grammatology.* Translated by G. C. Spivak. Baltimore: Johns Hopkins University Press.

Dowsett, G. W. 1996. *Practicing Desire: Homosexual Sex in an Era of AIDS.* Stanford, CA: Stanford University Press.

Edelman, L. 1995. "Queer Theory: Unstating Desire." *GLQ: A Journal of Lesbian and Gay Studies* 1:343-46.

El-Or, T. 1997. "Do You Really Know How They Make Love? The Limits on Intimacy with Ethnographic Informants." In *Reflexivity and Voice,* edited by R. Hertz. Thousand Oaks, CA: Sage.

Epstein, S. 1987. "Gay Politics, Ethnic Identity: The Limit of Social Constructionism." *Socialist Review* 93/94:9-54.

Fanon, F. 1970. *Black Skins, White Masks.* London: Paladin.

Foucault, M. 1979. *The History of Sexuality,* Vol. 1, *An Introduction.* Harmondsworth: Penguin.

———. 1984. "What Is Enlightenment?" In M. Foucault, *The Foucault Reader.* Edited by P. Rabinow. New York: Pantheon.

Fuss, D., ed. 1991. *Inside/Out: Lesbian Theories, Gay Theories.* New York: Routledge.

Gagnon, J. and W. Simon. 1973. *Sexual Conduct: The Social Sources of Human Sexuality.* Chicago: Aldine.

Gubrium, J. F. and J. A. Holstein. 1997. *The New Language of Qualitative Method.* New York: Oxford University Press.

Halberstam, J. 1998. *Female Masculinity.* Durham, NC: Duke University Press.

Hanawa, Y., ed. 1994. "Circuits of Desire (special issue). *Positions: East Asia Cultures Critique* 2(1).

Harding, S. 1991. *Whose Science? Whose Knowledge? Thinking from Women's Lives.* Ithaca, NY: Cornell University Press.

Henry, G. W. 1941. *Sex Variants: A Study in Homosexual Patterns,* 2 vols. New York: Hoeber & Sons.

Holstein, J. A. and J. F. Gubrium. 1995. *The Active Interview.* Thousand Oaks, CA: Sage.

Hooker, E. 1957. "The Adjustment of the Male Overt Homosexual." *Journal of Projective Techniques* 21:17-31.

Humphreys, H. L. (1970). *Tearoom trade: Impersonal sex in public places.* Chicago: Aldine.

Jackson, P. A. and G. Sullivan, eds. 1999. "Multicultural Queer: Australian Narratives" (special issue). *Journal of Homosexuality* 36(3-4).

Josselson, R. 1995. "Imagining the Real: Empathy, Narrative, and the Dialogic Self." Pp. 27-44 in *The Narrative Study of Lives,* Vol. 3, *Interpreting Experience: The Narrative Study of Lives,* edited by R. Josselson and A. Lieblich. Thousand Oaks, CA: Sage.

Juhasz, A. 1995. *AIDS TV: Identity, Community and Alternative Video.* Durham, NC: Duke University Press.

Kinsey, A. C., W. B. Pomeroy, and C. E. Martin. 1948. *Sexual Behavior in the Human Male.* Philadelphia: W. B. Saunders.

Kinsey, A. C., W. B. Pomeroy, C. E. Martin, and P. Gebhard. 1953. *Sexual Behavior in the Human Female.* Philadelphia: W. B. Saunders.

Kirsch, G. E. 1999. *Ethical Dilemmas in Feminist Research: The Politics of Location, Interpretation, and Publication.* Albany: State University of New York Press.

Kleinman, S. and M. A. Copp. 1993. *Emotions and Fieldwork.* Thousand Oaks, CA: Sage.

Kong, T. S. K. 2000. "The Voices in Between . . . : The Body Politics of Hong Kong Gay Men." Ph.D. thesis, Department of Sociology, University of Essex.

———. Forthcoming. "The Seduction of the Golden Boy: The Body Politics of Hong Kong Gay Men." *Body and Society.*

Krafft-Ebing, R. von. 1899. *Psychopathia Sexualis.* London: Rebman.

Krieger, S. 1983. *The Mirror Dance: Identity in a Women's Community.* Philadelphia: Temple University Press.

———. 1991. *Social Science and the Self: Personal Essays on an Art Form.* New Brunswick, NJ: Rutgers University Press.

———. 1996. *The Family Silver: Essays on Relationships among Women.* Berkeley: University of California Press.

Leong, R., ed. 1996. *Asian American Sexualities: Dimensions of the Gay and Lesbian Experience.* London: Routledge.

Lincoln, Y. S. and N. K. Denzin. 1994. "The Fifth Moment." Pp. 575-86 in *Handbook of Qualitative Research,* edited by N. K. Denzin and Y. S. Lincoln. Thousand Oaks, CA: Sage.

Mahoney, D. 2000. Unpublished field notes for Ph.D. thesis, Department of Sociology, University of Essex.

Murray, S. O. 1997. *American Gay.* Chicago: University of Chicago Press.

Nardi, P. M. and B. E. Schneider, eds. 1998. *Social Perspectives in Lesbian and Gay Studies: A Reader.* London: Routledge.

Newton, E. 1993. "My Best Informant's Dress: The Erotic Equation in Fieldwork." *Cultural Anthropology* 8:3-23.

Parker, R. 1999. *Beneath the Equator: Cultures of Desire, Male Homosexuality, and Emerging Gay Communities in Brazil.* London: Routledge.

Plummer, K. 1981. "Homosexual Categories: Some Research Problems in the Labelling Perspective of Homosexuality." Pp. 53-75 in *The Making of the Modern Homosexual,* edited by K. Plummer. London: Hutchinson.

———. 1995. *Telling Sexual Stories: Power, Change and Social Worlds.* London: Routledge.

———. 2000. *Documents of Life—2.* London: Sage.

Rubin, H. J. and I. S. Rubin. 1995. *Qualitative Interviewing: The Art of Hearing Data.* Thousand Oaks, CA: Sage.

Said, E. W. 1978. *Orientalism.* London: Routledge & Kegan Paul.

Sedgwick, E. K. 1990. *Epistemology of the Closet.* Berkeley: University of California Press.

Seidman, S. 1992. *Embattled Eros: Sexual Politics and Ethics in Contemporary America.* London: Routledge.

Seidman, S., C. Meeks, and F. Traschen. 1999. "Beyond the Closet? The Changing Social Meaning of Homosexuality in the United States." *Sexualities* 2:9-34.

Smith, D. E. 1996. "Telling the Truth after Postmodernism." *Symbolic Interaction* 19:171-202.

Socarides, C. 1968. *The Overt Homosexual.* New York: Grune & Stratton.

Spivak, G. C. 1994. "Can the Subaltern Speak?" In *Colonial Discourse and Post-colonial Theory: A Reader,* edited by P. Williams and L. Chrisman. Cambridge: Cambridge University Press.

Stanley, L. and S. Wise. 1983. *Breaking Out Again: Feminist Ontology and Epistemology.* London: Routledge.

———. 1993. *Breaking Out Again: Feminist Ontology and Epistemology.* 2d ed. London: Routledge.

Stein, A. 1997. *Sex and Sensibility: Stories of a Lesbian Generation.* Berkeley: University of California Press.

Stein, A. and K. Plummer. 1996. " 'I Can't Even Think Straight': 'Queer' Theory and the Missing Sexual Revolution in Sociology." Pp. 129-44 in *Queer Theory/Sociology,* edited by S. Seidman. Cambridge, MA: Blackwell.

Styles, J. (1979) "Outsider/Insider: Researching Gay Baths." *Urban Life* 8:135-52.

Takagi, D. Y. 1996. "Maiden Voyage: Excursion into Sexuality and Identity Politics in Asian America." In *Queer Theory/Sociology,* edited by S. Seidman. Cambridge, MA: Blackwell.

Warner, M. "Introduction." Pp. vii-xxxi in *Fear of a Queer Planet: Queer Politics and Social Theory,* edited by M. Warner. Minneapolis: University of Minnesota Press.

Warren, C. A. B. 1974. *Identity and Community in the Gay World.* London: John Wiley.

Weeks, J. 1977. *Coming Out: Homosexual Politics in Britain from the Nineteenth Century to the Present.* London: Quartet.

———. 1999. *Making Sexual History.* Cambridge: Polity.

Weston, K. 1998. *Long Slow Burn: Sexuality and Social Science.* New York: Routledge.

Westwood, G. 1961. *A Minority: A Report on the Life of the Male Homosexual in Great Britain.* London: Longmans.

13

INTERVIEWING OLDER PEOPLE

◆ G. Clare Wenger

It is important to start by asking two questions: Who are older people, and who are they older than? When I entered the field of gerontology more than 20 years ago, this growing area of study tended to focus on people over 65 years old. In those countries with established pension schemes, pressures existed for the field to include those "over retirement age," but differential retirement ages for men and women and, in some countries, differences in retirement policies among occupations complicated the issue. As a result, in many instances, government statistics were based on retirement ages, whereas academic researchers stuck to research on those 65+ or 60+, so that samples of men and women— then referred to as *the elderly*—would be directly comparable.

The study of gerontology, while projecting its objectivity, has been haunted by the specter of ageism. If ageist attitudes are more easily observed among health and social care professionals, they have from the outset remained only lightly disguised among academics. Referring to older people as *the elderly* had the effect of setting apart a significant proportion of the population on the basis of age, even though that proportion could include two generations. This was recognized in the introduction of such subcategories as *the young elderly* (those aged 65-75), *the old elderly* (aged 75+), and, subsequently, *the oldest old* (aged 85+).

In a climate of growing consciousness of discrimination on the basis of ascribed characteristics and the emergence of political correctness, "the elderly" came to be perceived as a stigmatizing category. More astute readers will recognize the inherent ageism in this perception. Why should being older than others be stigmatizing, unless being old is somehow a disadvantage? We learned to refer to *elderly people*. This group was still generally considered to be those aged 65+, and so we also talked about *younger elderly people* and *older elderly people*. In the United States, the terms *elders* and *seniors* were introduced, but these never achieved general popularity outside North America, although the first is often used in the United Kingdom to refer to older members of minority ethnic groups.

At the same time, the field of gerontology (and allied service disciplines) was expanding to include concerns about preretirement, early retirement, menopause, and the impacts of aging on the social and physical aspects of people's lives. Papers presented at international gerontological conferences gradually began to focus on a much wider age range, from circum-menopausal women to centenarians. In parallel with this expansion in the definition of the field of study of gerontology, life expectancy was extending, birthrates were diminishing, and morbidity was becoming more and more concentrated into the last few years of life. Active life well into retirement became the norm for growing proportions of people, many of whom did not conform with the image of "elderly people" at all.

With a field of study or concern that includes people of roughly ages 45 to 100, the term *elderly people* began to sound embarrassingly patronizing. We were already learning to refer to children as *younger people,* and gradually *older people* and *older adults* crept into the politically correct terminology used to refer to those subject to developmental changes that occur after approximately the age of 45 or 50. These terms are not entirely satisfactory either, because everyone is older than someone. A helpful editor once changed every reference I had made to "elderly people" in a paper to "older people"—a term I had used in the same paper to refer to those aged 80 or over within the sample I was discussing—successfully destroying both the argument and the sense of the paper.

◆ Interviewing and Heterogeneity

I have raised this problem of definition in detail at the start of this chapter to alert the reader to the semantic as well as procedural problems that exist. It is also my intent to draw attention to the fact that getting older tends to be derogated and perceived by others as stigmatizing or embarrassing. Although we all want to live long and fulfilling lives, and wish for the same for all those whom we love, we have a tendency to see those who are achieving this goal as somehow diminished, irrespective of how these aging individuals experience the aging process.

Interviewing older people for the most part involves ascertaining what their experience of aging is like. In this chapter, I adopt the currently accepted term *older people,* but first I would like to say something about the wide heterogeneity of age and experience that this term embraces, as this affects the forms that interviewing will take. The point is that interviewing older people should not be conceived as a one-size-fits-all set of procedures; rather, it is a form of inquiry that should take into account the diverse subjects older people are now known to be. It is also important that those who interview older people try not to become preoccupied with age; they should not assume that everything under consideration is age related (Kaufman 1986; Duffy 1988).

As I noted above, those described as older people may be aged anywhere from 45 to 100 or more. This wide age range can include three generations and normally includes at least two. This fact was brought home to me vividly some years ago when I went to interview a housebound widow of 68 who was living alone in a sheltered bungalow. I was 46, and the woman's daughter, who seemed to be about my age or older, was just leaving when I arrived. Early in the lengthy interview, the 68-year-old woman commented that I had interviewed her mother the previous week. I was sure that she was mistaken and wondered whether her cognitive function was impaired. But I soon figured out that she was right; I had indeed interviewed her 92-year-old mother, and her mother had telephoned her and told her all about me. What is significant about this anecdote is not only the generational span included in our current definition of "older" people, but also my assumption that the interviewee could be impaired despite the accuracy of her observation. I will return to this aspect of interviewing older people later in the chapter.

Because the later years of life are characterized by losses of different kinds, the age range includes a broad heterogeneity. The older people become, the more likely they are to become widowed, to lose brothers and sisters, to live alone, to suffer from mobility problems, to need to use the services of health and social care providers, to lose age peers (friends and neighbors) through disability or death, to become frail, and to move into sheltered or long-term care facilities. Clearly, interviewing well people in their 60s and 70s is comparable to interviewing younger well adults, whereas interviewing frail and impaired people in their 80s and 90s calls for an approach that is sympathetic to the physical and mental energies of the respondents (see Eder and Fingerson, Chapter 9, this volume).

Other aspects of the heterogeneity of the group we call older people reflect the patterns of the individuals' earlier lives, and as people age the potential differences between them are accentuated and increase as each represents the sum of all that has gone before. Not all older people have been married, and some who married did not bear children, so not all are parents. Some older people had many brothers and sisters, whereas others were only children. Those who had no brothers, sisters, or children also have no nieces, nephews, or grandchildren. Their life experiences have been different from those of individuals who have been members of large and growing families. The life experiences of men and women are also different (see in this volume Schwalbe and Wolkomir, Chapter 10; Reinharz and Chase, Chapter 11). Men are less likely than women to become widowed and more likely to have worked full-time for a large part of their adult lives. They are more likely than women to be receiving an occupational pension. With increasing age, more older people are women and more are middle-class as a result of differential survival. Approximately three-fourths of those aged 85+ are women, and a similar proportion of surviving men and women come from middle-class backgrounds.

All societies distinguish between those older people who are able to live independently and those who have become dependent on others for help (Amoss and Harrell 1981). In traditional societies, which have neither the concept of retirement nor pensions, old age is often defined by the ability to look after oneself. The lives of older people who must depend on others (family members, neighbors, friends, or formal services) are very different from those of individuals who remain independent. Self-image and self-esteem are affected by decline in physical capacities and by changes in personal appearance. There is no one recommended approach to interviewing older people across such differences. Although interviewers may be more likely to encounter some situations when interviewing older people than when interviewing individuals in other age groups, they should keep in mind that, as with all age groups, each older interviewee is one person, and they need to respond to each interviewee on an individual basis (Patterson and Dupree 1994).

◆ Sampling and Heterogeneity

Given the heterogeneity of the group designated as older people, it is clear that interviewing older people involves researchers in interactions with a wide range of interviewees. In addition, older people can be the subjects of a variety of types of interviewing, from clinical, therapeutic, and assessment interviews—which are more common than in other age groups (Patterson and Dupree 1994)—to research interviews. Types of interviewing are addressed elsewhere in this volume, and I will not deal with them again here, although it is worth pointing out that cognitive interviewing has been found to work better than other types in eliciting information from older people (Jobe, Keller, and Smith 1996; Mello and Fisher 1996; see also Johnson and Weller, Chapter 24, this volume).

Reflecting the great heterogeneity among older people, the range of reasons for interviewing is equally broad. Professionals conduct clinical or assessment interviews in order to intervene to ameliorate problems in an older person's life. Such interviews are, therefore, personal and relate to the interviewee only. They may continue over several time periods and may take a variety of forms (Edelstein and Semenchuk 1996). Interviewing skills for multidimensional assessment of older people are taught in many professional areas (Robins and Wolf 1989; Morrow-Howell 1992; Nelson 1992). In other situations, interviews are conducted as part of research projects, to gain information. The nature of the research question determines the nature of the sample and the type of interview, in addition to age heterogeneity.

The selection of samples of older people is arguably more complex than sample selection with other age groups. Population samples need to be representative of the general population of older people. However, because at any one time a small proportion of older people will be in residential care of one sort or another, population samples are often limited to "older people living in the community." Thus the oldest age groups, of which larger proportions are living in residential establishments, are often undersampled. Even if institutional residents are included in a sample, there are always some who are too mentally or physically impaired to be interviewed (see Morse, Chapter 16, this volume). The problems of interviewing older people in residential care have been identified, and the need for researchers to use observational data in addition to interviews has been stressed (West, Bondy, and Hutchinson 1991).

Even interviewing older people living in the community can be difficult, as relatives often try to avoid involvement of their oldest family members if they are at all frail. This further limits the representation of the oldest, most impaired, and family-dependent individuals. So the achievement of a truly representative population sample is difficult. Other, more purposive, samples may be easier to compile, such as samples of patients, clients, service users, sufferers of particular conditions, grandparents, those who never married, and the oldest old.

◆ Gaining Access

Having identified a sample, the interviewer must accomplish the next step: attaining access to potential interviewees. Where assessment interviews are concerned, access is part of the role relationship between the older person and a service provider, and so is usually straightforward. Where there is no formal service involvement (for instance, with doctors, community nurses, social workers, residential homes), the interviewer may approach older persons directly. An initial approach may be made by letter or by telephone, or by cold calling in person. The choice will be determined by the nature of the research, but the approach will come directly from the researcher/interviewer. Whatever approach is used, this forms the first step in the establishment of the interview relationship.

Approach by letter can take several forms. The interviewer might invite potential interviewees to participate and ask them to notify him or her of their willingness to do so, at which time the interviewer will make contact to arrange a time and place for the interview. Or the interviewer can tell potential interviewees that they have been selected and that an interviewer will call on them unless they express their unwillingness to be involved. In the latter case, the interviewer might suggest a particular date for a meeting in the initial letter.

There are several disadvantages to an initial approach by letter. The older persons contacted may not clearly understand the reason for the requested visit. They may feel uneasy or wary about admitting a stranger into their homes or of committing themselves without knowing more about the study or the interviewer. It is therefore easier for them not to volunteer or to decline. Some older people may consult relatives or ask them to read the letter—particularly where the older person's vision is impaired—and these individuals may become concerned about the implications of the interview. They may feel that it would be irresponsible for them to encourage their older relatives (usually parents) to admit a stranger to their homes. They may be concerned about the authenticity of the approach, or, if the topic of the study has to do, for instance, with family relationships or sources of support, they may be concerned that their older relatives will put them in a bad light, whether deserved or undeserved. Approach by letter makes it relatively easy for older persons or their agents to refuse.

Telephone interviewing is becoming increasingly popular as a research technique, particularly where research topics are sufficiently well defined and interviews are likely to be short. It is less easy to reject a friendly voice on the telephone. Cultural constraints of politeness, helpfulness, and, in the case of some people, loneliness make it likely that potential interviewees will enter into conversation. The skillful interviewer will establish rapport before broaching the asking of specific questions. Older people are less likely to refuse to answer questions asked over the telephone unless they seem too intrusive or personal, or are related to money or property. Unless someone else answers the telephone, the intervention of relatives is unlikely.

However, not all older people use the telephone, and thus resulting samples are likely to be biased away from poorer respondents or consumers. Hearing loss is a problem of old age that increases with the years. Older people with a hearing loss may be reluctant to establish conversation on the telephone, may misinterpret what is said to them and give misleading answers, or do not answer incoming calls. This effect biases achieved samples toward younger respondents. Tests of telephone interviewing against face-to-face data collection produce highly correlated results. Telephone interviewing is more convenient and less expensive than in-person interviewing and is considered a practical method for collecting data from older people about function and affect (Morishita et al. 1995; see Shuy, Chapter 26, this volume).

Experience suggests that, handled sensibly, direct approaches to older people are most successful in gaining access. Direct approaches vary, from the market researcher with a clipboard filling her quota of older people on the street, through approaches made through social, sports, or religious organizations, to knocking on the door of the older person's home. Approaches made in public places and group situations are obviously different from the individual approach. However, what all these direct approaches have in common is that the potential interviewee can see the interviewer and form an impression of him or her. The interviewer has a face and an apparent personality. It is harder to reject someone face-to-face than to decline an invitation by letter or to hang up the telephone.

When calling on older persons at home, interviewers should bear in mind that older people may at times have difficulty with mobility or hearing, and may take a long time to respond to a doorbell or knock on the door. On the other hand, especially in rural areas, they may call, "Come in!" When this happens, it can put the interviewer in a quandary, because the potential interviewee may never have seen him or her before. It also raises issues of security. I usually instruct interviewers to show older respondents their identification cards, even if the respondents do not ask to see them. My hope is that this will alert the older persons to the appropriateness of seeing identification, so they might be more inclined to ask for it in the future. Moreover, anxious relatives may ask the older persons if they checked identification and remonstrate with them if they did not. This can dissuade them from agreeing to subsequent interviews.

Where the approach is made in a public place or in a group situation, the older person is more likely to feel that he or she is being included in something rather than left out. In group situations, potential respondents see others agreeing to be interviewed and again want to be included, or are at least intrigued to know what it is all about. When the approach is made on the doorstep, the presentation of the interviewer is more important. Even if the timing is inconvenient, the interviewer may be able to establish rapport and negotiate an appointment to return at a mutually convenient time.

Older people are more likely to admit women than men into their homes, although they may also be suspicious of very young women. Interviewers are also more likely to be successful if they are conventionally dressed. Based on my own experience, the interviewers with the highest success rates in acceptance by older interviewees are middle-aged or older women with outgoing personalities. The oldest interviewer I have used was 82. Other researchers have also used older interviewers and have found that, compared with interviews conducted by students, those conducted by older persons were "qualitatively and empirically more complete and useful" (Prager 1995).

Early in my career, although I already suspected that women would be more acceptable on the doorstep, particularly in isolated rural areas, I sought interviewing help from two male colleagues. At that point in the research, the interview was brief and could be conducted on the doorstep if necessary; the interviewer did not need to go into the house. Some months later in that same community, a 77-year-old woman I was interviewing said to me:

> I want to give you a piece of advice, my dear. You made a great mistake when you sent those young men round asking questions. They frightened a lot of people. Everyone was talking about them. Next time you go yourself. You're a nice young woman [actually, I was 40+] and people trust you.

The two "young men" in question were in their mid- to late 30s, established academics with very gentle personalities, and I was hard-pressed to imagine that either of them could be perceived as threatening, but to these old women living alone, men clearly could not be trusted. The only other time I used a male research assistant to do interviews, his refusal rate was higher than those of any of the women interviewers I used. On the other hand, male professional carers have commented on the fact that many older women tell them how nice it is to have a young man in the house. The professional role is clearly protective in both directions.

There can also be constraints that make older men reluctant to admit women into their homes. This may be marked in Muslim communities. On more than one occasion, men living alone explained to me that they were happy to be interviewed but they thought I ought to know they were alone in the house before they admitted me. In one case, a man I interviewed left his outside door open to protect my reputation. There is a tendency for younger people to assume that once past retirement age, older people cease to be sexual beings (Archibald and Baikie 1998). Clearly, this does not always extend to older people's own self-images.

The importance of putting respondents at ease is covered in most books on methodology (e.g., Fetterman 1998). The more common experience of interviewers who knock on the doors of older persons is that, once the interviewers have demonstrated their friendliness and eagerness to talk by showing the potential interviewees that they have information the interviewers value, the prospect of distraction and company they offer makes access easy. Although most older people are obligingly interested and pleased to help, however, interviewers do occasionally encounter reluctance or outright refusal (see Adler and Adler, Chapter 25, this volume).

When a potential respondent expresses reluctance, the skillful interviewer can often overcome that reluctance if he or she can establish the reason for it. Sometimes, a request to answer questions is anxiety provoking (perhaps particularly if the interviewer has identified him- or herself as being from a university) because questions are associated with tests, and many older persons have had only a very basic education. One woman told me that she felt she could tell me nothing. I explained that although she might feel that way, all I wanted to do was to find out about the experiences of older people, and without people like her answering questions, this was impossible to know. She then said, "But what if I give the wrong answers?" Another explanation that there were no wrong answers and a few examples of the types of questions to be asked, such as "When did you last visit the doctor?" convinced her that she could help after all. She remarked, "Oh, is that all? Why didn't you say? Come in!" Often the interviewer's offering to make an agreement with a potential interviewee that no question must be answered and that he or she can terminate the interview at any time will be enough to gain acceptance that an interview can at least be started.

In other situations, older persons' reluctance or refusal is based on the admonishment of an adult child that "I mustn't let anyone I don't know into the house." It is possible that this is also the reason for refusals when no reasons are given. Once an interviewer has established rapport with a potential interviewee, he or she may be able to overcome this reluctance by explaining that, having seen the interviewer's identity card and received a business card, the older person does know who the interviewer is; further, the interviewer can suggest that he

or she meet with the adult child to explain the study and discuss the interview. In many cases, it is clear that the older person is willing to help and would really like the company and experience but is constrained by not wanting to cause family conflict. However, it is never appropriate for the interviewer to push too hard. Discussion and negotiation are acceptable, but no must mean no in the final analysis.

Where the sample is to be drawn from service caseloads or from among the residents of a hospital or residential care home, in most developed countries access by researchers to older persons as a result of their contact with professionals must be negotiated by way of an ethics committee. Such committees are set up to protect vulnerable people from being approached by (unscrupulous) interviewers, to protect the confidentiality of the clinical or assessment interview, and to guard professionals from complaints that could be made by patients/clients or members of their families. In these sorts of situations, once ethical approval is granted, interviewers may approach older persons in their doctors' offices, in hospitals, in residential homes, or in other therapeutic contexts and seek their participation in an interview. Ethical approval is more easily achieved where research is being conducted in partnership with professionals to answer questions in which they have an interest.

In other instances, where older persons are to be interviewed independent of treatment/intervention settings, identifying individuals as, for instance, patients or sufferers of particular conditions could be seen as a breach of confidentiality. In these cases, the professionals involved may be unable to divulge the names and addresses of vulnerable people without first gaining their consent to interview. This procedure needs to be described in detail in any application for ethical approval. A professional representative then acts as an intermediary by securing the agreement of the older person before identifying him or her to the potential interviewer.

There are several difficulties associated with these types of interviews. It is sometimes impossible to get ethical approval if the committee feels that the research might undermine the profession in any way or bring to light inadequacies in a service. Much evaluation research, if it involves questions regarding current patterns of treatment or care, may be turned down because it is seen to threaten practice accepted by the profession or potentially to question the competence, sensitivity, or reliability of professionals. Generating a sample through professional approaches to patients/clients can also lead to bias in the sample. The researcher has no control over who is approached to participate, and professionals may seek to exclude especially vulnerable, sick, critical, or difficult older people because they feel they should not be bothered, would make poor interviewees, have communication difficulties, or might express negative views about the service or its providers.

◆ Confidentiality

Researchers, of course, have their own codes of ethics. Confidentiality must be maintained at all times. Most academic professional associations and institutions have their own guidelines. Once access has been granted, the researcher must protect all types of data; this includes protecting the data from access by other members of the respondents' families and service providers. There are some particular situations, however, that are more critical in the context of interviewing frail older people. Any access by unauthorized people to data that make clear that the interviewee is physically, mentally, or financially vulnerable to exploitation or abuse puts that person at risk.

Maintaining confidentiality sounds more straightforward than it is. Ethnographic approaches rely heavily on what respondents tell researchers—what others might call gossip. Gossip is a reciprocal activity, and interviewees are likely to both volunteer information and ask questions about others they know to be part of the study. It is often difficult for interviewers to curb their spontaneity and keep the exchange of the relationship on track while also maintaining discretion about other participants. This is particularly taxing when you know that they know what they know you know and ask you about it! The other side of this coin, however, is that interviewers can, in the course of an interview, become privy to situations of risk that are not known to others.

There are many types of risk or emergency situations that interviewers can discover in the course of their contact with an older person. Some of these are straightforward. For instance, if an interviewer arrives at an older person's house to find that he or she has fallen and is in pain, the interviewer's calling an ambulance does not compromise confidentiality. For other kinds of concerns, it is advisable for researchers to develop written codes of conduct in advance. If possible, an interviewer should ask the older person's permission to seek professional help for him or her. In most cases, the older person will be relieved that somebody is taking that initiative (see below).

As rapport is established, the interviewee may divulge information that makes the interviewer become concerned about the older person's safety. In cases where the older person is at risk but is not willing for the interviewer to take any action, the interviewer needs to have a prearranged code to follow in discussion with colleagues. Such cases could involve suspected physical, psychological, or financial abuse of the older person or unmet needs for medical or instrumental assistance. Where an interviewer encounters reluctance or outright refusal of intervention, he or she may need to discuss the matter with the research director and come to a joint decision about what to do. In such instances discretion is of the utmost importance; the interviewer may have incurred an ethical or legal responsibility, but the bottom line must be the safety of the older person.

◆ Special Challenges

Older people are "just like us but they've been alive longer," as one of my interviewers once commented. Many of the general statements made about interviewing techniques in other chapters in this volume apply also to older people. In this chapter, I limit my discussion to the challenges of interviewing older people that in my experience seem different from those encountered in interviewing members of other populations, or are more likely to occur with older people. This means that I may seem to be concentrating on the "problems" of old age, but the reader should keep in mind that most older people do not suffer from infirmities that interfere with the interview process. Remember that "older people" can be any age from 45 up.

RESPONDENTS WITH SENSORY IMPAIRMENTS

Among the practical challenges that researchers may encounter in interviewing older people, impaired hearing is one of the most common. Poor hearing may make an older person less willing to be interviewed. If an individual is wearing a hearing aid or is clearly having hearing problems, the interviewer should acknowledge this and explain that he or she will speak clearly and slowly. The interviewer should tell the potential interviewee that he or she is prepared to take the time to make sure the respondent understands everything the interviewer says, and that the interview will be ended if it becomes too tiring for the interviewee.

In interviewing a person with hearing problems, the interviewer should try to ensure that the respondent can see his or her face. It is helpful in such a case for the interviewer to face the light; even if they are not aware of it, most older persons with impaired hearing gain additional information from seeing facial expressions and lip reading. It may be necessary for the interviewer to sit very close to the respondent, almost knee-to-knee, particularly if the respondent also has impaired vision. My experience has been that when the interviewer is prepared to be patient and to make the effort to be understood, the older person relaxes, enjoys the interview and the interaction, and is frequently very grateful for the efforts made on his or her behalf. If a potential interviewee is profoundly deaf and uses sign language, the researcher may need to find someone who signs to conduct the interview. An alternative to this, if appropriate, is for the interviewer to read from a questionnaire or interview schedule as the interviewee follows the printed text.

Impaired vision can reduce an older person's willingness to let anyone into the house, although it does not interfere with the comprehension of questions. Interviewers should be prepared for respondents with poor sight to move close to their faces in order to try to make out their features more clearly. This can be disconcerting, particularly in most Western cultures, where people have expectations of a generous amount of personal space. The interviewer's stepping back in such a case, however, may make the older person feel threatened, as if the interviewer may have something to hide.

In the context of some illnesses—for instance, if the older person has suffered a stroke or is in the advanced stages of Parkinson's disease—speech may be affected. With goodwill and patience, it is possible to interview speech-impaired people. When a speech-impaired respondent realizes that the interviewer is prepared to be patient, the older person is likely to relax and to become more coherent. It is often useful in such situations for the interviewer to ask someone who is close to the person and understands him or her to be present during the interview, to act as an interpreter. An interviewer may be tempted to put words in a speech-impaired respondent's mouth by finishing his or her sentences. This can lead to misinformation, as it may be easier for the interviewee to agree rather than to struggle to put the interviewer right. On the other hand, sometimes such interviewer intervention can ease the experience for the interviewee by reducing the effort he or she must make to consciously form each word.

People with speech impairments are quickly tired by the effort of speaking. It is important for interviewers to remember that even if a person's speech is impaired, his or her understanding and hearing may not be. Unless the interviewer has evidence to the contrary, he or she should never ignore or shout at such a respondent. Interviewing speech-impaired persons is one of the situations in which it is probably often advantageous to interview by proxy.

USING INTERVIEW PROXIES

It is often useful to employ proxies in interviews with older people in order to ensure the representativeness of the sample. If all those who are too impaired or too ill are omitted on compassionate grounds, the sample becomes biased. In most cases, proxies for older respondents should be spouses or close relatives. Where that is not possible, the proxy should be the individual who is closest to the older person. When conducting proxy interviews, researchers should ask only questions of fact (e.g., "Can X get up and down steps without help?"), not questions requiring subjective answers involving feelings or attitudes (e.g., "Does X feel lonely often?"). On the other hand, it is valid for interviewers to record proxies' interpretations of given situations as long as they take care to analyze those interpretations as the responses of carers, friends, or spouses.

It is sometimes necessary for an interviewer to bring an interview to a close before he or she has gained all the information he or she might have wished because it is clear that the interviewee is struggling with illness or fatigue. If the older person was enjoying the exchange, the interviewer and interviewee can plan another time to meet and continue, but if the older person's effort seems to be inappropriate or pressured, the interviewer may find it better to continue with a proxy.

Interviewers should resort to proxy interviews with people with impaired hearing only if all their efforts to make themselves understood have failed. With respondents who are blind or partially sighted, proxy interviews are usually not necessary unless the respondents' hearing is also impaired. Proxy interviews with close relatives may be indicated where respondents have speech difficulties and find the effort to speak tiring and debilitating. However, interviewers should address persons with speech difficulties directly and give them the opportunity to respond or to counter their proxies' responses. When using a proxy, the interviewer should explain to the older person that this might make the interview easier for him or her. The interviewer should also ask the older person to indicate his or her agreement or disagreement with the proxy's responses. This not only results in better data but gives the older person the chance to be involved in the interview, something many speech-impaired people enjoy.

RESPONDENTS WITH COGNITIVE IMPAIRMENT

Cognitive impairments affect approximately 7 to 10 percent of older people in the developed world, with some national variation (Saunders et al. 1989). Among those aged 80 plus, approximately 20 percent have some cognitive impairment. It is possible that greater longevity is increasing the incidence and prevalence of dementia (Melzer, Ely, and Brayne 1997). Interviewers working with older people are likely to encounter various forms of cognitive impairment, and this is one of the most difficult areas for interviewing. There are indications that different types of data collection have varied impacts on results—structured interviews have been shown to result in lower prevalence rates than physicians' clinical diagnoses based on assessment interviews (Fichter et al. 1995)—although it is not obvious why this might be. It is not possible to interview older people who are in the final stages of dementia, but it may be possible to communicate with them in other ways, and it is always possible to observe them, which may be a more appropriate way to collect data.

Most older people who are in the early stages of dementia are able to respond to interviews, although they may experience lapses in memory or word recall. A great deal depends on the subject matter. As the disease progresses, long-term memory is more resilient than short-term memory. Respondents may be able to recall accurately most of the names of the children who were in their first-grade classes at school but be unable to remember the names of all their own grandchildren.

Sometimes, interviewers may not realize that their interviewees are affected by cognitive impairments. Such individuals might present well, demonstrate good social and communication skills, and respond with answers to most questions. Their "don't knows" or "can't remembers" might seem to be perfectly plausible. However, interviewers who work with older persons must be on their guard: It is possible to conduct an entire interview and be completely unaware that most of what one has been told is inaccurate.

The following anecdote illustrates this phenomenon. At the start of a longitudinal study, a never-married woman, Miss R, had been interviewed by one of our interviewers. Subsequently, one of Miss R's friends was a subject in an intensive study of a small subsample, which I conducted. I therefore heard much about Miss R from her friend, including about the friend's disappointment when Miss R entered residential care and her friend could not see her anymore.

Eight years after the study began, I went to interview Miss R in residential care. She was sitting in her wheelchair and looking out the window of the dining room when I arrived. A care assistant took me in and said, "You have a visitor, Miss R." She had not met me before, but she looked up and said, "Oh, hello, my dear, how nice to see you. You're from the book club aren't you?" I explained who I was and why I had come. She graciously agreed that she remembered an earlier interview and was willing to talk to me. Prior to my visit, I had briefed myself by reading through her file.

I first asked her about how long she had been in the residential home and then asked about whether she had visitors. She assured me that she had regular visits from her friends and from her brother, who looked after all her affairs. I was a bit disconcerted at that, because I had read in her file that her only brother had died a few years before. It is rare, but it is always possible that there is a relative who has not been mentioned previously. She was able to tell me where her brother lived, how often he came, and when he had last been to visit.

I then asked her how she had come to be admitted to residential care. She became tearful and said that she couldn't live alone in the house after her mother died. At that point I knew that she was cognitively impaired, because her mother had died before she had moved to the village where she was originally interviewed. She became more and more distressed and told me in great detail about how she had cared for her mother for umpteen years and had promised her that she would never have to go into a nursing home. She went on to explain that when her own health failed, she had had to put her mother in a home, and that she felt she had really let her down. She was not entirely clear, but it seemed that she thought that her admission to residential care was associated with this in some way.

After Miss R recovered and we talked about other things for a while, I left. Our leave-taking was as courteous and gracious as my arrival. She thanked me for coming to see her and said how much she had enjoyed our chat. Before I left the home, I spoke with the person in charge. I felt very sad that Miss R still felt guilt about her mother. I asked about the brother. My memory was accurate—she had had only one brother and he had died long before she had entered care. "Did she tell you about her mother?" the person in charge asked. I told her that she had and commented on how sad it was that she was still feeling guilt. "But it's not true," said the staff member. "It's more tragic than that. She nursed her mother at home and her mother died in her arms. She was never in a nursing home." Somehow Miss R's admission appeared to have been transmogrified into her mother's admission. She wept about it every day.

Not only was Miss R's speech perfectly coherent throughout the interview, but her social skills were intact and she was very convincing. Had I not known anything about her previously, I would have accepted everything she told me about her brother. I was also convinced that her feelings of guilt were based on a real occurrence, even though I realized that her admission to long-term care had nothing to do with her mother's death.

The point of this anecdote is that some people with cognitive impairment can continue to present with entirely appropriate behavior and to answer questions convincingly. On the other hand, if an interviewee's answers sometimes seem incongruous, as did those mentioned in my earlier anecdote, an interviewer cannot automatically assume that the speaker is cognitively impaired. This is one of the more difficult aspects of interviewing older people. Even in the case of diagnostic interviews for dementia, some researchers have identified a need for a second witness (Walstra and van Gool 1995).

I have sometimes asked interviewers working with very old people to record how confident they are about the responses they were given. Where doubts are evident, it is often desirable, if the possibility exists, for the interviewer to check with a relative of the interviewee or with a member of resi-dential staff; in such instances, however, the interviewer must pay attention to matters of confidentiality. Perhaps the best situation is for a relative of the older person to be present during the interview, so that he or she can indicate by a shake of the head when responses are not accurate. The interviewer can then check out those questions with the relative or others after the interview has ended. Many inaccuracies have to do with older persons' not remembering whether or not particular persons are still alive.

Still, it bears repeating that the presence of cognitive impairment or deficiency is not a reason to assume that interviewing is impossible. Although interviewing people who suffer from cognitive impairments and learning difficulties can be a challenge, researchers who treat such individuals sensitively and appropriately can be successful in completing interviews and recording useful data (McVilly 1995).

TAPE RECORDING AND COMPUTER ASSISTANCE

Sometimes it may be considered appropriate for interviewers to tape-record interviews. This is often desirable with open-ended interviews, where the discussion is free-flowing and ranges over many topics, some of which are unpredictable. Most of the older people I have interviewed have had no problem with this. As soon as the interview moves beyond the first few exchanges after the tape recorder is set up, they tend to forget it is there and are often startled when they hear the click indicating the end of a tape. Occasionally, respondents may have misgivings about being recorded. It often seems inappropriate to ask them why; they have every right to refuse. It is important in any case that the interviewer explain why he or she wants to tape the interview, to what use the tape will be put, and who else might hear it. Confidentiality must be assured.

In at least one instance when I was trying to negotiate the use of a tape recorder, the respondent told me that she did not want to be recorded because she thought her English was not very good. I reminded her that only I and perhaps a colleague would ever hear the tape, and I would have heard her speaking in any case. She was still reluctant, although she said that she wanted to be helpful. So I suggested that we record the interview, and when it was over, I would play it back to her. If at that point she did not like it, I would either erase it or leave the tape with her. She was happy with this arrangement and the interview went ahead. She had never heard her own voice before, and when I played back the tape, she kept saying, "That's right!" When I reminded her that the voice she was hearing was hers, she said, "Well, I'm not so bad in English am I? Let's hear some more." She let me keep the tape.

In survey research, interviewees' responses are often recorded on paper interview schedules, although the use of laptop computers for this purpose is becoming more common (see Couper and Hansen, Chapter 27, this volume). In such computer-assisted interviewing, the computer is programmed so that the interviewer can click on or type in responses. The program then automatically skips to the next relevant question, thus saving interviewer time. The main advantage of this method is that data can be entered into the data set as they are received. This method also reduces margins of error, because the data are not transferred again after they are recorded. Furthermore, researchers can perform partial exploratory analyses before all the data are collected.

When my colleagues and I first planned to use laptops in our research, we received a lot of criticism to the effect that the machine and its unfamiliar technology would create a barrier between the older person and the interviewer. It was also suggested that older respondents living on fixed incomes would be concerned about our using their electricity to run our computers. Our experiences were quite the opposite. The older people were fascinated by the laptops. For most of them, it was their first close contact with a computer. They seemed to be impressed that such advanced technology was being used to record their responses. In some cases, respondents came to sit next to the interviewers and soon started to respond before the interviewers could read out the questions. This was a real benefit for those with hearing impairments. Where it seemed that the cost of electricity to run the computer might be significant, we used or offered to use batteries ("I could plug this in or if you prefer we can run it on the batteries"). In other cases, we believed it would be inappropriately demeaning to indicate that we felt cost might be an issue.

USING MATERIAL CLUES

The homes of older people tend to give clues to their earlier lives. Photographs of members of several generations may be on display, for example. These clues are a useful way into discussions of topics that the interviewer wishes to explore. In the context of qualitative data collection, a comment on a picture of a grandchild can serve as a trigger for discussions about the whole family—children, grandchildren, and great-grandchildren—including all their ages, places of residence, and frequency of contact. Photographs of parents and brothers and sisters can offer similar starting places for family histories. Interviewers might also ask older people if they have pictures of themselves when they were young. Most older people enjoy reminiscing in this way and will give interviewers extensive information about their pasts (see Johnson and Weller, Chapter 24, this volume).

If the interview is focused on a particular craft or skill, comments on tools of the trade in evidence can also be useful: How were they used? What did you do then?

Who made the tools? What are they called? It is often better for interviewers to look at the products of crafts and ask questions about them than to ask respondents to talk about such things in the abstract. Interviewers may also gather useful data by photographing some of their respondents' artifacts, but only after receiving the respondents' permission.

Taking photographs of older people themselves is more controversial. Some older people are happy to be photographed, whereas others are reluctant to be pictured warts and all. Women are more likely than men to be reluctant, and reluctance often increases with greater frailty. On the other hand, photographs enrich the textual data, remind the interviewer of the respondent, and often include interesting life clues for analysis. Interviewers should never photograph respondents without their permission, and they should take care to be tactful in requesting that permission.

The laws of copyright and privacy differ from country to country. In the United Kingdom, a photograph and its copyright are the property of the photographer. However, this does not mean that courtesies can be overlooked. Most of the older people my colleagues and I have photographed have been happy, even delighted, to have their likenesses used to illustrate our work. However, these have usually been posed portrait photographs. It is important that researchers employ sensitivity in using photographs of recognizable people to illustrate dependency, impairment, and other less positive aspects of old age.

INTERPERSONAL RELATIONS

One challenge of interviewing respondents of any age is to make an interview feel like a conversation. One of the normative expectations of conversation is that the interlocutors take turns and match self-disclosure with self-disclosure. Interviews tend to be one-sided, with one person doing all the asking and the other person doing all the answering. The subjects of interviews may feel that they are giving much away without getting anything in return. It is common for older people, who may be less familiar than other respondents with the concept of the research interview, to expect to exchange information with an interviewer, as they would in ordinary conversation. When interviewers ask older interviewees about how many children they have, where their children live, and what they do, this often raises the interviewees' curiosity about the interviewers' own children.

The interview's interpersonal relations are likely to vary over time. Conversation in the early stages of a relationship is structured around getting to know one another. Self-disclosure on the part of the interviewer encourages the interviewee to continue the exchange. Resistance to self-disclosure by the interviewer, on the other hand, can create a feeling of imbalance and increase the distance between interlocutors. There needs to be giving as well as receiving in these exchanges. Reciprocity is needed to maintain the relationship. For example, I have found that when I tell respondents that I have been divorced, they sometimes amend information they have previously given me about married sons or daughters, admitting that they too have been separated or divorced. The establishment of a reciprocal relationship is particularly important in the context of in-depth interviewing (Kaufman 1994; see also Johnson, Chapter 5, this volume). It has, however, been suggested that such relationships raise ethical dilemmas about the exploitation of respondents (Hart and Crawford-Wright 1999). It is a matter of conscience for each interviewer to decide this for him- or herself.

Where interviewing continues over an extended period of time, the relationship between interviewer and interviewee often shifts in tone. Friendship can develop, with the accretion of the norms and responsibilities associated with that relationship.

Greater familiarity leads to an expectation of more disclosure and participation on the part of the interviewer. Older people may ask an interviewer for advice or help with small tasks. My own inclination is to enter freely into such relationships. There is an opposing viewpoint that suggests that growing familiarity and closeness with respondents affect the objectivity with which the researcher can view the data. This is a real concern and, again, one that each interviewer has to recognize and negotiate for him- or herself. Doctors do not treat members of their own families, but they seek to influence the behavior of their patients. Researchers, on the other hand, may need to be careful not to influence behavior, because this distorts the data.

CULTURAL SENSITIVITY

It is important that interviewers be sensitive to the different values, concerns, and expectations of respondents from different cultures, ethnic groups, and religious traditions, whatever the age of the respondents (see in this volume Dunbar, Rodriguez, and Parker, Chapter 14; Ryen, Chapter 17). In the context of the aging process, researchers should take pains to ascertain what the expectations, assumptions, and practices associated with advancing age are for the specific groups they are working with. It is possible here to cover only a few of the challenges that can arise.

In cultures where women are secluded, such as in most traditional Muslim communities, it can be difficult for interviewers to gain access to older women, who are often unlikely to venture outside the household. Women interviewers are essential for the study of women in such communities, because it is culturally inappropriate for a woman to be alone with a man who is not a relative. It is sometimes difficult even for a woman interviewer to interview a woman alone. Her husband or adult son may expect to be present and to answer most of the questions for her. Women interviewers need to be diplomatic to ensure that they are able to talk to Muslim women alone. It may be useful for the interviewer to intimate that it is women's talk—concerning specific health matters, for instance—that is to be undertaken, where it might be inappropriate for any man to be present.

Likewise, even though it is easier for both male and female interviewers to gain access to Muslim men, it is advisable that male interviewers be used. Even older respondents may not feel that they are being taken seriously if interviewed by a woman, and, in the worst-case scenario, a woman who tries to interview a man could be placed in a stigmatized category and treated accordingly.

From the Middle East to the Far East, responsibilities toward aging parents rest with sons, in contrast to the West, where daughters are more likely to be expected to provide care for frail parents. These responsibilities are deeply embedded in Eastern cultures. Unmarried women are the responsibility of their fathers and subsequently other senior male relatives, wives are the responsibility of their husbands, and widows are the responsibility of their sons. In some cultures, married women cease to belong to their families of socialization upon marriage.

In Eastern cultures, an interviewer's asking an older woman about seemingly straightforward matters of household composition can be a source of embarrassment, shame, or loss of face if the appropriate relative has not fulfilled his responsibilities to her. This was brought home forcefully to me when I visited China. While I was visiting a woman in her 70s at home, where she lived with her married son, daughter-in-law, and two adult granddaughters, she asked me (through an interpreter) about my own children. When I told her that I had three sons, she asked, "And which one do you live with?" When I told her that I did not live with any of them, she was mortified and embarrassed because she felt that she had committed a faux pas by causing a guest to lose face. My having to admit that I did not live with one of my sons was seen as the equivalent of admitting that I had not been a good mother, which was shameful and had caused the embarrassment of a guest.

Similarly, once when I was in rural India, everyone present was embarrassed when I asked an older woman how many children she had. In India, a country where arranged marriages are common, virtually everyone marries. For a woman to remain childless is both shaming and a source of sadness. The woman told me she had no children. This meant that she was dependent on the good-will of a nephew for food and shelter. All the other women present were uncomfortable at this exchange, and my hosts apologized to me for not being aware of this in advance and warning me, so that a difficult situation could have been avoided.

These two incidents illustrate how an interviewer's lack of knowledge of cultural implications and values can inadvertently lead to embarrassment when he or she asks questions that are perceived as insensitive or inappropriate. They underline the importance of the interviewer's having a good understanding of the cultural backgrounds of the individuals in the target sample. When interviewers are working with ethnic groups other than their own, it is important that they learn as much as possible about the cultures of those groups before they begin to interview. In most cases, it is better for interviewers to be of the same ethnic group as the interviewees. In all cases, interviews with older people should be conducted in the respondents' first languages or own dialects whenever possible (Matsuoka 1993; Goldstein et al. 1996).

Other sensitive issues related to old age are death (on suicide, see Hendren 1990) and difficulties involving age-related historical experiences (on the Nazi Holocaust, see Kahana, Harel, and Kahana 1989). For example, it is inappropriate for interviewers to discuss suicide with older Chinese, as they are likely to interpret this as a sugges-

tion that they remove the burden of their care from their families. Likewise, interviewers working with older Jews and European Gypsies need to be aware that the Holocaust is a most sensitive subject with these groups. All social groups, of course, have topics that are "not spoken about." Researchers need to identify such topics and approach them carefully. Among other subjects that are especially age sensitive are incontinence, sexuality, physical impairment, mental illness, cognitive deterioration, inheritance, accumulated income, intergenerational conflict, divorce, and residential care. For example, in the United Kingdom most refusals relate to questions about income. In Japan, questions that could reveal tensions with daughters-in-law are difficult. Chinese elders do not display likenesses or photographs of living relatives, only of the deceased. Jews do not name grandchildren after grandparents who are still alive. If you think about the way in which older people in your own social group might feel about talking with a stranger about some of these topics related to themselves, you can start to see how important it is for interviewers to understand about different cultures. All of these kinds of knowledge can facilitate the cultural sensitivity of interviewing.

◆ Ending the Interview

With older respondents, interviewers can often find it difficult to end their interviews and take their leave. In some cases, being interviewed can be tiring, upsetting, or debilitating; interviewers need to be aware of how the effort is affecting their interviewees, even though they may appear to be enjoying themselves. Older people often want to help; this can be especially important to those whose mobility is impaired, because their opportunities to contribute have already been reduced. Finding that they cannot do what they want to do can be upsetting, and they often want to continue with interviews even though they are feeling a strain.

My experience is that it is usually best for the interviewer to be quite straight with a tiring interviewee. The interviewer can explain that he or she is concerned that the respondent is getting tired, and then, taking a cue from the context, suggest either that he or she come back later, preferably saying or negotiating when, or that perhaps he or she could speak with the respondent's spouse or daughter and gain agreement to this. Of course, if a respondent does not want the interviewer to talk to a proxy, the interviewer must respect this. In certain circumstances, using subterfuge may be justified. For instance, if it is clear that an interview is proving hard work for the older person but he or she is determined to go on, the interviewer can claim to have another appointment to keep, end the interview, and set a time to return and continue. Not only will this ensure that the interviewee is not overtired, but it will inevitably result in the rested interviewee's later providing more detailed and far-ranging information.

In cases where the older person is in good health, ending the interview can be difficult because the interviewee may have few opportunities to talk to someone so obviously interested as the interviewer. Just when the interviewer thinks it is time to leave, the respondent employs some delaying tactic: "Oh, before you go, I just want to show you something!" or "Now you will have a cup of tea, won't you?" Having taken up the older person's time, the interviewer may find it difficult to refuse such requests. My feeling is that interviewers have to be prepared to be generous with their time if their respondents have been generous with theirs. Many older persons may get few opportunities to chat about themselves. They may be lonely, and they may get a boost to their self-esteem by being able to make a contribution.

As noted earlier, good interviews take the form of natural conversation. There needs to be some exchange and the estab-

lishment of common ground or rapport. For lonely older persons who may not get out as much as they would like and thus have reduced opportunities for meeting people, an interview can be a highlight in their week. By the end of many interviews, the two people have developed warm feelings toward each other and mutual understandings. For the interviewer leaving may be routine, as he or she moves on to another interview, to reflect on the interview content as data, or to return to professional or family life. The older person, on the other hand, may be left alone to think over the experience and to wonder if he or she will ever see the interviewer again. The older respondent may feel a sense of loss, missing the recent interest shown by the interviewer and the company. The experience may raise feelings of regret in the older person that he or she does not have many visitors.

Clearly, the interviewer needs to establish his or her role at the beginning of the interview, but that does not prevent the respondent from having expectations or desires for further contact. In many instances, the interviewer will not be returning. In some cases, an interviewer may return frequently over a short period of time or infrequently over a longer period. In either case, a relationship inevitably develops. Ending even an embryonic relationship can be hard for vulnerable people. Where repeat interviewing has led to the development of closeness, disengagement raises ethical as well as difficult social and psychological questions. Interviewers need to give serious thought to how they handle such withdrawal.

In conducting a longitudinal study over 20 years, I formed what became socially intimate relationships with some of the respondents, on the basis of our growing knowledge of each other, although I saw most only once every 4 years. This was particularly so with older women, as women's informal interactions and friendships, compared with men's, tend to be based more on mutual exchange and disclosure. The question "When are you coming back?" was appropriate when this was the third interview. Saying "In 4 years" was often hard to do, as it seemed socially inappropriate to leave the relationship for so long. On more than one occasion, respondents told me that I should try to come back soon, as they would not live forever, or some similar sentiment. For those respondents in the intensive phase of this study with whom I became closer, disengagement after 4 years was not possible in all cases. By the end of 4 years, half the intensive sample had died, but I continued to keep in touch with some of the others who had few contacts on account of mutual affection and a sense of responsibility. If I had not done so, I felt I would not have fulfilled an obligation that I had created.

◆ Summary and Conclusion

Many of the topics covered in this chapter are also covered by other contributors to this volume. Interviewing older people is not a very different undertaking from interviewing members of any other social groups. Most interviews are exchanges between two individuals, and it is the individuality of the interviewee to which the interviewer must relate. With older people, paradoxically perhaps, it is important that the interviewer not approach the task as specifically an encounter with old age. Rather, the interviewer should see the event primarily as an encounter with another person. As I noted at the start, those described as "older people" can now include anyone aged 45 or more. If we exclude those still in full-time education, that probably means half of all adults.

Nonetheless, there are some specific considerations of which interviewers need to be aware with respect to interviewing those who, as a result of advancing age, suffer from various sensory, physical, and mental impairments. In addition to interfering with communication, these factors may also render the frail older person vulnerable, both in terms of the possible stress of the interview situation and in terms of exploitation, not only by researchers but by unscrupulous persons who could gain illicit access to the data. Researchers need to take these age-related factors into account when interviewing frail older people. Although they do not apply to the majority of people aged 45-100 plus, they are more prevalent among those over 80. Of course, researchers need to afford consideration to all those who are vulnerable as a result of physical or mental impairment, irrespective of age.

People over the age of 70 constitute the majority of those who use health and social care services. Much of the interviewing of older people, therefore, is aimed at clinical assessment or seeking information about their needs for and use of services. The problem orientation of much of the research requiring interviewing of older people has no doubt contributed to the stereotypes of older persons as vulnerable, dependent, and in ill health. However, representative population samples should include appropriate proportions of people in their 60s, 70s, and older age groups. Interviewers need to be encouraged to see interviewing older people in the same way they see interviewing younger people; that is, they should see each interviewee as a separate individual and should accommodate vulnerabilities and disadvantages as appropriate, no matter what the age of the interviewee. It is not age that makes older people different from other categories of people, it is the higher incidence of sensory and physical impairment, widowhood and other bereavements, mobility problems, reduced incomes, and negative self-image among individuals in this group that lead to their being seen as different from younger age groups. As I noted at the beginning, most older people are just like everyone else, except that they have been around longer.

■ References

Amoss, P. T. and S. Harrell. 1981. "Introduction: An Anthropological Perspective on Aging."
Pp. 1-24 in P. T. Amoss and S. Harrell, *Other Ways of Growing Old: Anthropological Perspectives.*
Stanford, CA: Stanford University Press.

Archibald, C. and E. Baikie. 1998. "The Sexual Politics of Old Age." Pp. 222-36 in *The Social Policy
of Old Age: Moving into the 21st Century,* edited by M. Bernard and J. Phillips. London: Centre
for Policy on Ageing.

Duffy, M. 1988. "Interviewing Older Adults." Pp. 160-78 in *Systematic Interviewing: Communication Skills for Professional Effectiveness,* edited by J. M. Dillard and R. R. Reilly. Columbus, OH:
Merrill.

Edelstein, B. A. and E. M. Semenchuk. 1996. "Interviewing Older Adults." Pp. 153-73 in *The Practical Handbook of Clinical Gerontology,* edited by L. L. Carstensen and B. A. Edelstein. Thousand
Oaks, CA: Sage.

Fetterman, D. M. 1998. *Ethnography: Step by Step.* 2d ed. Thousand Oaks, CA: Sage.

Fichter, M. M., I. Meller, H. Schroeppel, and R. Steinkirchner. 1995. "Dementia and Cognitive Impairment in the Oldest Old in the Community: Prevalence and Comorbidity." *British Journal of
Psychiatry* 166:621-29.

Goldstein, A. E., L. Safarik, W. Reiboldt, and L. Albright. 1996. "An Ethnographic Approach to Un-
derstanding Service Use among Ethnically Diverse Low Income Families." Pp. 297-321 in *The
Methods and Methodologies of Qualitative Family Research,* edited by J. F. Gilgun and M. B.
Sussman. New York: Haworth.

Hart, N. and A. Crawford-Wright, A. 1999. "Research as Therapy, Therapy as Research: Ethical Dilemmas in New-Paradigm Research." *British Journal of Guidance and Counselling* 27:205-14.

Hendren, R. L. 1990. "Assessment and Interviewing Strategies for Suicidal Patients over the Life Cycle." Pp. 235-52 in *Suicide over the Life Cycle: Risk Factors, Assessment, and Treatment of Suicidal
Patients,* edited by S. J. Blumenthal and D. J. Kupfer. Washington, DC: American Psychiatric Press.

Jobe, J. B., D. M. Keller, and A. F. Smith. 1996. "Cognitive Techniques in Interviewing Older People." Pp. 197-219 in *Answering Questions: Methodology for Determining Cognitive and Communicative Processes in Survey Research,* edited by N. Schwarz and S. Sudman. San Francisco:
Jossey-Bass.

Kahana, B., Z. Harel, and E. Kahana. 1989. "Clinical and Gerontological Issues Facing Survivors of
the Nazi Holocaust." Pp. 197-211 in *Healing Their Wounds: Psychotherapy with Holocaust Survivors and Their Families,* edited by P. Marcus and A. Rosenberg. New York: Praeger.

Kaufman, S. R. 1986. *The Ageless Self: Sources of Meaning in Late Life.* Madison: University of Wisconsin Press.

———. 1994. "In-Depth Interviewing." Pp. 123-36 in *Qualitative Methods in Aging Research,* edited
by J. F. Gubrium and A. Sankar. Thousand Oaks, CA: Sage.

Matsuoka, A. K. 1993. "Collecting Qualitative Data through Interviews with Ethnic Older People."
Canadian Journal on Aging 12:216-32.

McVilly, K. R. 1995. "Interviewing People with a Learning Disability about Their Residential Service." *British Journal of Learning Disabilities* 23:138-42.

Mello, E. W. and R. P. Fisher. 1996. "Enhancing Older Adult Eyewitness Memory with the Cognitive
Interview." *Applied Cognitive Psychology* 10:403-17.

Melzer, D., M. Ely, and C. Brayne. 1997. "Cognitive Impairment in Elderly People: Population Based
Estimate of the Future in England, Scotland and Wales." *British Medical Journal* 315:462.

Morishita, L., C. Boult, B. Ebbitt, and M. Rambel. 1995. "Concurrent Validity of Administering the
Geriatric Depression Scale and the Physical Functioning Dimension of the SIP by Telephone."
Journal of the American Geriatrics Society 43:680-83.

Morrow-Howell, N. 1992. "Multidimensional Assessment of the Elderly Client." *Families in Society*
73:395-407.

Nelson, G. M. 1992. "Training Adult-Service Social Workers in the Public Sector: A Core Curriculum
for Effective Geriatric Social Work Practice." *Educational Gerontology* 18:163-76.

Patterson, R. L. and L. W. Dupree. 1994. "Older Adults." Pp. 373-97 in *Diagnostic Interviewing*, 2d ed., edited by M. Hersen and S. M. Turner. New York: Plenum.

Prager, E. 1995. "The Older Volunteer as Research Colleague: Toward 'Generative Participation' for older adults." *Educational Gerontology* 21:209-18.

Robins, L. S. and F. M. Wolf. 1989. "The Effect of Training on Medical Students' Responses to Geriatric Patient Concerns: Results of a Linguistic Analysis." *Gerontologist* 29:341-44.

Saunders, P. A., J. R. M. Copeland, M. E. Dewey, C. Gilmore, B. A. Larkin, H. Phateperkar, and A. Scott. 1989. "The Prevalence of Dementia, Depression and Neurosis in Later Life: Findings from the Liverpool MRC-ALPHA Study." *International Journal of Epidemiology* 22:838-47.

Walstra, G. J. M. and W. A. van Gool. "The Need for a 'Second Witness' in Diagnosing Dementia." *Journal of the American Geriatrics Society* 43:1176-77.

West, M., E. Bondy, and S. Hutchinson. 1991. "Interviewing Institutionalized Elders: Threats to Validity." *Image: Journal of Nursing Scholarship* 23:171-76.

RACE, SUBJECTIVITY, AND THE INTERVIEW PROCESS

◆ Christopher Dunbar, Jr.
Dalia Rodriguez
Laurence Parker

The only ethic I can find that you can hang your hat on says:
Now that I have the material, how do I treat my subjects? Do I accord
them all the humanity they deserve or do I write a crude and simplistic exposé?

David Simon, June 2000

David Simon, former reporter for the *Baltimore Sun*, goes directly to the heart of the interview process when he pointedly asks, "How do I treat my subjects?" (quoted in Scott 2000). This question focuses our attention on the subject that is taken to lie behind the interview respondent. Does the researcher/interviewer approach the respondent as if he or she were simply a vessel of answers—a mere interviewee—who can provide the information needed for a particular story or the data for a research project, or does the in-terviewer treat the respondent as a subject replete with a full complement of histori-cal, biographical, and social sensibilities (see Holstein and Gubrium 1995; see also Gubrium and Holstein, Chapter 1, this vol-ume)? Where interpretations of interview data are concerned, are we merely to report our findings and write our stories as if what we have heard is "objective" fact, or are we obligated, as C. Wright Mills (1959) pas-sionately argues, to link the personally bio-graphical with the social and historical?

In this chapter, we argue and present case material to show that the interview process and the interpretation of interview material must take into account how social and historical factors—especially those associated with race—mediate both the meanings of questions that are asked and how those questions are answered. Responsibility lies primarily with the interviewer and his or her sponsor, but all participants in the interview process are ultimately implicated in these concerns.

Although there is always an envisioned subject behind an interview respondent, this subjectivity—the subject or agent who produces meaningful, contextualized interview responses—becomes especially problematic when the respondent is a member of a "nonmainstream" group or population. If there are myriad assumptions made about mainstream respondents, they commonly emanate from presumed similarities between interviewer and interviewee. For nonmainstream respondents—whether they are persons of color, members of culturally distinct or enigmatic groups, or persons of nonconformist political persuasions or lifestyles, for example—the complications and uncertainties of how such subjects will be constituted virtually multiply. A common consequence, as Simon implies in the remarks quoted above, is that "crude and simplistic" portrayals of complex and nuanced experience emerge, because subjects are not accorded their due respect as distinctly situated individuals.

Here we focus on race as a distinct dimension of subjectivity. In the contemporary context of American and Western European society, being "white" is the unreflected-upon standard from which all other racial identities vary. But the meaning and consequence of that variation itself often goes unnoted. Frequently, persons of color are thought of as nonmainstream subjects in relation to a white standard—people whose social and/or personal characteristics do not reflect those that are taken for granted as "conventional" in the general population. What this might possibly mean is glossed over by attempts to standardize or normalize research perspectives and procedures.

As subjects, persons of color share the experience of other groups who have not traditionally been accorded viable subjectivities in their own right. For example, until recently, few interviewers figured that when interviewing women, they needed to take account of these respondents as special subjects distinct from the population at large (see Reinharz and Chase, Chapter 11, this volume). This was also true of interviewing men (see Schwalbe and Wolkomir, Chapter 10, this volume). Interviewers viewed both men and women simply as "respondents" for the most part, and proceeded to interview them as such, not particularly formulating questions in terms of special social or historical experiences that distinguished them as subjects. The rise of feminist consciousness and, in turn, the emergence of gender self-consciousness for men transformed female and male subjects from being generic mainstream respondents into subjects with considerable distinctions. The upshot for research, and especially interviewing, is that we are now increasingly procedurally conscious of femaleness and maleness as subject positions from which respondents may or may not speak in interview situations; we take this into account in relating to both the interview process and the interpretation of interview material. (For a discussion of "queering" as a further specification of gendered subjectivity, see Kong, Mahoney, and Plummer, Chapter 12, this volume.) We argue for a similar procedural consciousness with regard to race.

It is our view that such a sensibility as it applies to the subjectivity of racialized populations requires very special attention and needs to be heightened throughout the research process. Researchers and interviewers cannot simply apply technical skills and be straightforwardly "objective," as if respondents were people whose subjectivity could be taken for granted. Race is a category of the subject that has traditionally struck so many negative social and historical resonances that interviewers must always be vigilant for the ways it becomes insinuated into all aspects of identity and self-presentation, either by assertion or through silence. Once again following Simon, we suggest that the only *ethic* that properly applies in interviewing is one that accords the subject all the humanity he or she deserves. As we will show, it is an ethic that necessarily directs us to the racialized subject behind the respondent. Knowledge of this subject is immeasurably significant for an interviewer's understanding of what the respondent is saying, why he or she might remain silent in relation to particular interview topics, and how the interviewer might proceed to influence the context for openness and the respondent's willingness to speak honestly about his or her experiences.

This chapter proceeds in three parts. The first is a brief overview of literature on race and the interview process. It is not exhaustive; rather, we present this overview to show how a procedural consciousness in the matter of a racialized research subject has emerged. The second part of the chapter draws from Dalia Rodriguez's field research on interviewing nonwhite subjects in educational settings. As Rodriguez shows, the everyday, noninterview contexts surrounding an interview situation can help a researcher to gain deep insight into what he or she needs to take into account in approaching and interacting with respondents behind whom racialized subjects are to be found. A central proposition that emerges is that interviewing nonwhite subjects may require a researcher to conduct extensive ethnographic fieldwork, both before and during the interview process. This fieldwork should center on how the lived experiences of the members of the particular subject category under consideration can inform participants' conversation in the interview situation. Rodriguez is quite proactive in articulating an ethic of procedural consciousness as she turns methodological matters into concerted, re-

flexive practice that has direct implications for the meaning of being a subject/respondent.

The third part of the chapter builds on these themes to offer insights into, and suggestions for, the interviewing of persons of color. Using as a point of departure some of the experiences Christopher Dunbar, Jr., has had in his research with African American youth, we propose some special sensibilities that might inform interview research where race is concerned. Among other things, Dunbar's experience as an African American male researcher attempting to study younger African American males suggests that the simple common ground of race provides no guarantee that the expressed subjects behind these respondents will honestly relate their experiences as black youth. The lesson, as we will show, is that respondents themselves recognize the subtleties and complexities of identity—of race and other subject positions—and this affects the kinds of subjects/respondents they will be if they choose to be interviewed.

◆ Interviewing and Race

Interviewing has always been a major methodological component of both qualitative and quantitative social research and of journalistic reporting. The art and science of hearing data has been at the center of how researchers obtain information, get the story right, and offer readers with insights into the social world of interviewees (Casey 1996; Rubin and Rubin 1995). However, the interview process, especially interviewing using "standardized" methods, has always been problematic with respect to nonmainstream subjects, especially in the area of race. Discussions of race currently center on how it plays out as a social construct, either in color-blind discourse and whiteness or from critical race perspectives and interpretations such as critical race theory, critical race feminism, Latina/o critical race theory (LatCrit), Asian/Pacific Islander positions, Tribal Nation perspectives, and race's intersections with other aspects of identity and issues of power (see, for example, Crenshaw et al. 1995; Delgado and Stefancic 1997; Ladson-Billings 1998; Lipsitz 1998; Omi and Winant 1994; Tate 1997). The debates in this area mirror conflicts in qualitative and quantitative research regarding the interview process and race. Historically, researchers have asked why interviews are done on "racial- ized" populations, for what purpose, and by whom (Andersen 1993; Stanfield 1993; Foster 1994).

HORIZONS OF RACIAL INTERVIEWING

The types of interviews related to race range from polls that are conducted to determine racial attitudes to in-depth focus groups and oral life histories. For example, a recent survey of racial perceptions in the United States gathered many of its data on race from organizations such as the National Opinion Research Center and the Institute for Social Research (Schuman et al. 1998). A *New York Times* poll measuring race relations in the United States (Sack and Elder 2000) was conducted through telephone interviews with 2,165 adults, with African Americans sampled at a higher rate than normal to permit analysis of black attitudes in greater depth. The results of these interviews indicated that both whites and blacks see some progress in the area of race relations. Many whites who were interviewed, however, expressed fatigue with race as an issue and said that they thought too much time and energy are devoted to it. This finding corresponds with the findings of other interview research conducted on the racial attitudes of white European Americans, in which whites indicated that they believed racism to be a thing of the past (Berger 1999). White respondents said they themselves were not racist, and very few respondents revealed honest, in-depth,

or self-critical feelings about race. However, in the *New York Times* poll and other interview studies (see, for example, Feagin 1992), African Americans in general have said that they see race as a determining factor in their lives, especially in the areas of education, housing, and employment.

These views on race have focused on the "black/white" paradigm that has been central to race-based discourse, law, and social policy. However, some have called for a broader discussion of race that includes perspectives and intersections with ethnicity. Critical race theory and its progressions into LatCrit and Asian American critical legal perspectives have been helpful with respect to providing a legal, social policy, and culturally sensitive framework from which to view race, power, and authority in the 21st century. For example, Cheryl Harris (1993) examined the role of law in shaping how white, as a race, is associated with property and power, over and against Native Americans and African Americans. The connection of "whiteness" to property rights has been used against Native Americans in the confiscation of Native lands and the relegation of indigenous populations to reservations and subordinate status. Harris notes how the connection of "whiteness" to property also has been used legally against African Americans with regard to slavery and white ownership of African chattel.

Another example of the expanding perspectives on race is the work of Robert Chang (1994) and others featured in a 1994 special issue of the *Asian Law Journal* of the *California Law Review* devoted to critical Asian American legal scholarship. Some of the articles in this issue examine the "honorary white" status of Asian Americans at various points in U.S. legal history, juxtaposing this status with discriminatory actions taken at other times, such as the forced relocation and internment of Japanese during World War II. Edward Park and John Park (1999) have called for new perspectives on race theory not just to be inclusive, but to alter fundamentally the lens through which researchers analyze Asian

American and Latino racial realities. A critical race theory position here would account for their differences related to Asian American/Pacific Islander American ethnicity, culture, and language and how this is also linked to transnational issues and racial status. It would also consider how the concepts of race and racial groups are constructed by the larger society, taking factors such as immigration and U.S. foreign policy into account in the monolithic ways Asian American populations are viewed and treated in the United States. Finally, the LatCrit movement has been important in shaping theory and documenting the racialization of Latino/a and Chicano/a groups. It has shown how the myth of assimilation has been held out to these groups, but also how they, in turn, have had to face the reality of laws and social hostility directed at them through such anti-immigration and affirmative action measures as Propositions 187 and 209 in California ("LatCrit Theory" 1997; Martinez 1999).

Interviews have emerged as one of the main ways of documenting the lived experience undergirding critical race theory. Topical oral histories, life histories, and evaluation interviews show that racism and racial discrimination play important roles in recent challenges to the prevailing notion of legal neutrality and race in the civil rights desegregation era. The thick descriptions and interviews characteristic of case study research not only serve illuminative purposes, but can be used to document institutional racism as well as stories of overt personal racism. The interviewing process yields narratives that can be used in building cases against racially biased policies and discriminatory practices, as shown in the historical and personal testimonies of African American expert witnesses in *Knight v. State of Alabama* (1991). In that case, the court found the state of Alabama guilty of perpetuating a dual, and racially discriminatory, segregated higher-education system. Interviews related to race can serve important purposes in that descriptions of discrimination can form an integral and in-

valuable part of the historical and current legal evidence in such cases.

REFLEXIVITY AND RACE

Another issue related to the interview process and race involves reflexivity in research (Pillow 2000). Too often, qualitative researchers have neglected discussions of the subjective lenses through which they view their research (Van Maanen 1988). But that has begun to change as qualitative researchers and ethnographers in particular are making efforts to write about the researcher's position and how the researcher is affected by the fieldwork and field relationships. This is especially noteworthy regarding how race and race relations shape the research and its implications (see Behar 1995; Cochran-Smith 2000). Yet this too is not without controversy, as some reflexive accounts have been criticized for being too focused on the personal tales of the researcher or for dealing too much with self-therapy as the researcher engages in ethnic or racial narcissism and confessional tales related to mistakes made in the field, rather than more directly addressing matters related to race, representation, and the reporting of data or its implications for social justice and validity (Buford and Pattillo-McCoy 2000; Deyhle and Swisher 1997).[1]

John Stanfield (1993, 1994) and Michelle Foster (1994) have criticized the use of interview data as narratives in research with respect to how they are used to describe various aspects of black life and the African American community. Both of these authors argue that narrative descriptions by white European American researchers are fraught with problems of subject exploitation. They assert that white researchers often neglect diverse discourse styles in their interview protocols and fail to deal with the plethora of power struggles that can take place between the researchers and "subjects" of color (see also Briggs, Chapter 44, this volume). Part of this criticism has led researchers to try to paint more nuanced portraits of African American life (e.g., Anderson 1990) and the experiences of other groups of color. For example, John Langston Gwaltney's (1980) interviews with African Americans reveal complexities of urban life and depths of black experience not previously told by most white researchers.

Many ethnographies have reflexively elaborated how the researchers have conducted their interviews to reflect the racial reality of aspirations and expectations concerning how to address racism in everyday life (see MacLeod 1995; Noblit 1999).[2] Nevertheless, researchers' reflections on the nuances of subject-interviewer interaction have often failed to identify important factors that revolve around race. For example, it is likely that white researchers have frequently been deliberately misled by the "trickster" discourse of African Americans and Native Americans as well (Vizenor 1988; Jeffries 1994). The trickster is an imagined amalgamative figure who uses comic discourse and language as a game to tell stories that challenge conformity and existing norms with multiple meanings. Some groups have typically used trickster discourse in relating to outsiders. For example, Native Americans have used such discourse to fool traditional anthropologists who have tried to interpret the meanings of tribal nation folklore; during slavery, the trickster was the defiant representative of African Americans against the oppression of the masters. The trickster disrupts the idea that we can know another group if we are outsiders (or, in some cases, insiders). The trickster can play a significant role in interview dialogue and data surrounding the experiences of members of groups of color and what they say about their racial experiences (Buendia 2000).

Other reflexive concerns are decidedly epistemological. Much recent research builds on the work of Maxine Baca Zinn (1979) and her insights related to insider-outsider qualitative studies with women of color. A related Chicana feminist episte-

mology underpins a wave of new research into the postcolonial identities that emerge as young women struggle with race, class, and gender issues growing up in Mexico and the United States (see Delgado Bernal 1998; Gonzalez 1998; Pizarro 1998; Villenas 1996).

Matters of social context and interviewing have moved in varied directions. For example, issues of race and reflexivity bear on sexual nonconformity. When analysis of race has been combined with sexual orientation, the use of narrative has been problematic for gays and lesbians of color because their stories have been used against them within homophobic institutional/political structures (Tanaka and Cruz 1998). Other issues relate to researchers of color studying and interviewing whites and examining their perspectives on race and racism (Parker 1998; Roediger 1998). Another concern for researchers is how formal interview settings may restrict more idiomatic forms of racial/cultural expression, leading to considerations of how researchers can conduct interviews in a group format/setting to facilitate talk among the participants, including the interviewer (Meacham 2000). The emerging critical race perspective and its connection, through interviews, to qualitative research has created powerful frameworks from which researchers can analyze and illustrate the larger context of the social construction of race.

◆ Understanding the Racialized Subject

Given the growing sensitivity to race in interview research, it is imperative that we examine how the racialized subject can be understood by way of interviews. The social context of racialized experience provides the backdrop against which the interview subject is constituted and understood as the interviewer attempts to elicit a full and authentic version of the interviewee's story. But what subject will be activated by interview questions? Whose voice might be heard or silenced? And how can the interviewer anticipate the narratives that will emerge and what they mean in the ongoing lives of respondents?

Dalia Rodriguez, a Latina graduate student from a working-class family in the U.S. Midwest, conducted a field study of overt and perceived racism encountered by students of color on a college campus and at the annual professional and student development conference held by the professional group Latinos in Higher Education. In the following subsections, Rodriguez presents both informal interview narratives and ethnographic descriptions of the social contexts that inform her understanding of what she hears her respondents say. In the process, she provides readers with information that gives shape to the subject behind the interview respondent. Her first-person accounts display the reflexive interplay between background knowledge derived ethnographically and experientially and the personal narratives generated by way of interview questions. This interplay fleshes out the subjects of her research; in documenting her related research experiences, Rodriguez adds rich and significant social detail as it relates to what her respondents could mean by what they say.

PROCEDURAL UNDERSTANDING

I run down the hall with my bag half open, frantically double-checking to see whether I have extra batteries for my tape recorder, extra tapes, and my interview guide. I rush into the "dungeon," the graduate student T.A. office, filled with rows of battered desks piled with old exams and papers. Okay, he's not here yet. I sit in front of my desk deciding whether or not to start grading my students' papers. Just as I pick up my pen, in walks J.R., an African American undergraduate student; he is about six feet tall, muscular, with long dreadlocks. I

start by asking him about what he's studying and about his future plans. He has come back to school after taking a few years off and plans to finish his bachelor's degree in December.

We then move on to the meat of the interview, and I ask him about his experience as an African American on campus. He responds:

> When I first came to this campus . . . it's just a shame that I was grouped into a group that had to prove that I belonged here. It wasn't like I was accepted with open arms by professors. Ya know, they see me . . . as a big black guy. Just having to prove myself to people, constantly . . . [I want to] start a rebellion against the status quo. Like my rhetoric professor, I used to hate going to that class. She used to dog me out about how I talk, cuz I was just fresh out of high school, and I used to speak a lot of slang then and I would turn papers in and she would say things were wrong with the paper. She told us we could pick any subject we wanted and then I wrote about my relationship with my girlfriend versus my friend. One time I was five minutes late for her class, and she marked my paper an entire grade. Since that experience I questioned myself and thought, "Man, maybe I don't belong in school." . . . You do end up second guessing yourself.

Hearing J.R. express self-doubts reminds me of my own trepidations. I think about my first year in graduate school and the constant doubting. No "hellos" in the hallway from professors, no "How ya doing?" When a professor did speak to me, it was to say, "Your work isn't good enough," or "Why is *that* [studying race] significant? *Everyone* studies race, do something different." I was constantly doubting myself, my abilities, and feeling like perhaps I'm not cut out to be an academic. I recall Jonathan, a graduate student, asking me one day, "Notice that there aren't *any* American racial/ethnic minorities in this new year's cohort?" Yes, I had heard through another graduate student of the many reasons that African Americans and Latinas/os were not being admitted that year, because the department was trying to improve its national ranking and admitting racial/ethnic minorities who were "doomed to fail" would only bring down the reputation of the program. After all, Latinos represent such a small percentage of Ph.D. recipients. Surprised to see myself and two other minorities in the program come back to finish our second year, one professor said, "Oh! You guys are back?!?! That's a surprise." I know they expected me to fail.

Hearing J.R. doubt himself angers me because I know that he deserves better, and I make every effort to encourage J.R. to continue his education. I ask him, "What are you planning on doing after you get your degree?" He responds, "I was thinking about graduate school . . . but, I don't know. . . . I don't think I have that great of a GPA, I mean I'm no A student." I can hear some confidence, along with doubt—doubt that I know he shouldn't have.

Breaking the methodological "rule" of not giving an interviewee your own personal views, I tell J.R., "I have also doubted myself . . . a lot. . . . Ya know, I study race/ethnicity issues, not simply because it's an interesting topic but also because of my personal experiences." He deserves to hear that he can make it. "You don't have to be an all-A student to apply to graduate school. That's great that you want to attend graduate school, you should still apply. . . . I'm sure that you already know this, but as an African American male, you will encounter so much more racism at every level, and don't *ever* let anyone tell you that you're not good enough. When you get ready to apply to graduate school, please call me, we'll work on your application, okay?" I scribble down my number as well as my e-mail address and tell him to contact me.

* * *

This instance of empathy and self-disclosure might be viewed in conventional research terms as "contamination," but one could also argue that, in this case, it further encouraged the respondent—now conceived as a capable and deserving subject—to elaborate on the racialized aspects of his student experience. Employing an approach similar to what Jack Douglas (1985) calls "creative interviewing," the interviewer forges common ground to share with the respondent, so that the subjects behind both interviewee and interviewer share a familiar, if sometimes uncomfortable, narrative space (see also in this volume Eder and Fingerson, Chapter 9; Reinharz and Chase, Chapter 11). In order to cultivate a climate of mutual disclosure, Douglas suggests to the researcher, "know thyself" (p. 51).

By reflexively constituting and engaging a racialized subject with whom she shares an appreciation for what it means to be a student of color, the interviewer provides empirical grounds for elaboration on the respondent's narrative. She thus forms a relevant procedural understanding of the respondent. J.R. continues:

> A lot of times when I walk into an administrative office, they [administrators] keep asking me if I'm in a "special program," an assisting type of program, and I have never seen them ask a white student that. There will be a white student in front of me and they ask him, "Your name, social security number, college you belong to" and that's it. Whereas every time I go up there I gotta be in some special program.

J.R. goes on to tell about constantly being questioned and having administrators and professors make assumptions about him as a black student, about how they constantly assume that he's "not good enough."

> I even had a professor tell me something about my hair, cuz ya know, I have dreadlocks. My professor told me, "I

like your hair, but a lot of professors can be intimidated by that and that maybe when you go talk to a professor, maybe you should dress up." I'm thinking, "I'm in college and everyone dresses in T-shirts and jeans and it's not like I'm at a conference, where I would dress accordingly."

Reflexively playing off her own experiences and feelings about what she is being told, the interviewer interactively crafts the subject of her interview into one to be appreciated rather than trivialized, compartmentalized, or derided. In this form of active interviewing (Holstein and Gubrium 1995), she conveys a personal appreciation for the subject's racialized experience, which in turn cultivates further narrative disclosure. Although the interviewer's building J.R.'s confidence with respect to graduate school may reap long-term benefits for J.R., the more immediate research consequence is that he continues to be forthcoming in the context of the interview; J.R. poignantly elaborates the details of how considerations of race infuse his university experience—even though race may only hover in the background of research conversations.

In this instance, the interviewer draws upon her own experience as a person of color and minority student—her autobiography and autoethnography, so to speak—to fill in some of the "humanity" that is necessary for a nuanced portrayal of the subject. Moreover, she uses her general sensitivities to racial issues—acquired experientially and ethnographically—to provide a framework for asking about, listening to, and understanding stories about the impact of race on the lives of students of color. Not only does she empathize with the respondent, she "activates" a racialized subject behind the respondent, inciting narratives that reveal the implications of race that might not otherwise become available. Following a proactive research ethic that aims to empower the racialized subject, Rodriguez is well aware of the need to support

the formation of a respondent who will forthrightly speak to his racialized experiences. She attempts to introduce a kind of procedural consciousness to the interview process. Although her active engagement in the interview interaction may violate strictures of standardization, the anticipated trade-off is the likelihood of deeper and more complete, meaningful disclosure.

SPEAKING OUT AND BEING SILENCED

Being attuned to both the lived and procedural complexities of a racialized subject can help an interviewer to draw that subject out in the course of an interview. Why do some respondents nonetheless remain silent or inarticulate regarding race? Is it that they have nothing to say? Do they have no relevant experience to recount? Rodriguez's experiences with other students of color tell us that there are alternative explanations, as we hear in the following narrative and in her interactions in other educational settings.

*   *   *

Whenever students discussed issues in class, they, including the professor, would turn to me and ask, "What do Latinos think?" I tried to tell them, hey, yeah, sure . . . I'm Mexican, but I'm also a true cowboy! My home consists of horses and a ranch back at home—so, there's a lot more to me than being Mexican.

Although I understand the importance of speaking out, I can't help but think about one semester when I assisted in an "Introduction to Women's Studies" course. An African American student approached me about feeling exactly the same way. The prior week we had a discussion about *Skin Deep* (Hoffman 1995), a documentary film about college students of color who get together for a retreat to confront each other's attitudes about issues of race/ethnicity. I started the discussion by announcing the many events and symposia offered on campus. Because we had been discussing body image issues the previous week, I decided to offer extra credit to anyone who would attend the Latina body image issues workshop held at La Casa, the Latina/o cultural center on campus. As I continued with the announcements, I heard Linda and Jen, both sitting in the front row, right in front of me, whispering something. Linda, blonde with bright red lipstick, covered her mouth with one hand, but I distinctly heard her tell Linda, "Well, if we go you know that we'll be the only white people there," laughing underneath her breath. "Umhhh. . . . Do you have something you'd like to share with the class?" I asked, trying not to sound angry. "No," they responded. Linda and Jen looked at each other and began to laugh, while I looked at them intently and inquiringly. "No, never mind."

The task for the day was to get students to open up about issues of race, an all-too-familiar challenge I meet every single semester in every class I teach. However, I felt confident that my students would eventually talk about these sensitive issues, because we had spent weeks repeatedly discussing theoretical paradigms and sociological concepts: social conflict theory, structural functionalism, symbolic interactionism, internalized racism, and blaming the victim. I began by asking them what their initial reactions were to the film they had seen. One student commented that she really enjoyed the film and that she felt that she could relate to it because the setting was on a college campus. Others nodded in agreement.

But the students still seemed hesitant to "really talk." I kept hearing "Yes, great film," over and over again, but no one offered any specific thoughts about *why* it was a good film. Keeping in mind my pedagogical rules for getting people to "talk more," I did not ask, "Why?" but instead asked, "What about the film did you like, specifically?" Dead silence. Hesitantly, Es-

ther, an incoming freshman who usually sat quietly in the front row, said, "Well, I thought it was interesting to see how white students feel when they're the only ones in the room. I mean, it's more common to hear that from racial/ethnic minorities, but not from white students."

"Yes!" Tracy jumped in. "One time I was in a fashion show for an Asian American cultural event and I just remember feeling as if everyone there kept staring at me. I mean, I know they were wondering, 'How did this white girl get into this fashion show? What is *she* doing here?' "

"Yes!" other white female students chimed in. "It is alienating being the only white person in a room, you feel like everyone's staring at you." Esther again expressed how glad she was to have seen the film, because she had never "thought about how it would be to be the only white person in a room. I never realized this before but you [indicating me], Ana, and Lindsay are the only minorities in this room." All 23 white female students stared at me, waiting for me to reply.

As Beverly Daniel Tatum (1997) has noted, "Fear is a powerful emotion, one that immobilizes, traps words in our throats, and stills our tongues" (p. 194). People do not speak out about issues of race and racism for many reasons: fear of isolation from friends and family, fear of being ostracized, fear of rejection by those who are offended by what they have to say, fear of the loss of privilege that may come with speaking in support of the marginalized (Tatum 1997). Some are afraid of their own ignorance.

Karla, another student, mentioned that there was something about the film that she couldn't understand: "I couldn't understand why all of those people of color were so angry." I noticed that none of my students of color responded, nor did any of my white students. The students continued talking about being the only white students in certain situations. I finally decided that we had to address the issue of anger. I know that the reality on a predominantly white campus is that students of color are often "the only ones" in classes, at talks, and in most facets of university life. The only thing that came to mind was bell hooks's (1995) insight into how black rage has been pathologized, that there's no room even to think that African Americans (or other people of color) can feel anger because of the racism and discrimination they experience. "Rage is not necessarily pathological nor are we victims if we choose to become enraged," hooks says. "In fact, denying that rage . . . can create a cultural climate where the psychological impact of racism can be ignored and where race and racism become topics that are de-politicized" (p. 26).

"Let's go back to the issue Karla brought up, the issue of anger—what about that anger? Why do you think that the students of color were so angry?" Linda responded:

> Well, I don't know, I thought that the only thing the students of color wanted was an apology from the white students. They were so angry and I just didn't think it was fair that they yell like that. And, when they didn't get it they were pissed off. I thought that was uncalled for. Personally, I think it's ridiculous that I have to apologize for being white. I can't help it that I have what I have. I have no problem recognizing my white skin privilege, but I refuse to apologize to *anyone* for the position I'm in.

No one else seemed to want to talk about it; students began to look down at their feet or at the wall, avoiding the issue altogether. Then, one of my white liberal students spoke up:

> Well, I just don't see why people of color aren't more pissed off. I mean, really, they have every right to be. To be treated so horribly, in the past and now even, if I were them I would've done a lot more than just yell at white students. You guys were talking about being the only white person in a group; can you imagine what people of color feel like *every day* at this university?

After our discussion of the film, one of my students who is African American thanked me for establishing a comfortable class environment. She apologized profusely for not speaking very much in class, adding that she was simply "tired of being expected to represent all black people." It is clear that "speaking up" and "representing my racial group" are big burdens that many members of racial/ethnic minority groups carry. I can understand why students of color don't want to speak up.

* * *

Active, thoughtful subjects lurk behind even the most taciturn respondents. What we make of the silent (or silenced) respondent, however, involves more than recording "no opinion" on an interview code sheet. Rodriguez shows us how her own experiences with public discussions involving persons of color and topics of race shape her understanding of why respondents might be less than forthcoming in interview situations. In light of such experience, the interviewer must be especially conscious of the implications of what potential respondents might or might not say when asked interview questions. An interviewer's experiences outside the interview situation inform what he or she might hear (or not hear) within it. Equally important, they can cast experiential light on the broader social meanings of silence and speaking out on topics of race. Again, a proactive research ethic would aim to empower the subject to "speak up" concerning these matters, even when the "natural" impulse is to remain silent. The result is that the sensitive and astute researcher tries to look past and into the silences that greet interview questions in order to understand the possible categorical sources of silence.

◆ *Procedural Sensibilities*

Taken together, the preceding observations suggest that interviewers must be deeply familiar with the lives of potential respondents in order to cultivate and activate fully the subjects that figuratively stand behind them. Indeed, one might infer that interviewers need to be "insiders" in order to conduct productive, insightful, nuanced, and revealing interviews. Ethnographic fieldwork might provide researchers with the sorts of background knowledge they need to establish this familiarity, but actual membership in the subject groups under consideration is another avenue to the sorts of human portrayals that interview researchers often seek. This clearly implies the often-heard argument that only members of a group or a race are capable of truly understanding and representing the experiences of members of that group or race.

In this section we take issue with that view, suggesting some procedural sensibilities that even members need to take into account in seeking to know and recognize racialized subjects. Christopher Dunbar, Jr., adds to the accounts Dalia Rodriguez presents above by presenting some of his research experiences with young African American males, revealing further complexities in the study of race. Dunbar, an African American, has conducted ethnographic and interview research in a rural community in the Midwest for several years. His study focuses on school-aged African American males' encounters with schools and the criminal justice system. His insights echo Rodriguez's in many respects, and they also propel our considerations of race and the interview process in new directions, revealing the interactive subtleties of interviewing and race.

* * *

Education is like, for a black man you have to fight to stay free, you have to fight to have freedom, you got you fight to stay out of jail, you got to fight to get your education. That's for a black man. For a white man you don't got to do nothing but do it. (Bobby, quoted in Dunbar 1999:138)

Bobby, a 14-year-old African American male and a student in an alternative school, sat up from a slouched position on the floor to respond to a question about what education means to him. His analysis of his environment and perceived plight prompted him to stand up as he articulated his assessment of what it was like for him to be black and male and to live in America. He articulated his belief that success and education are inextricably linked and that a litany of obstacles stand in the way of his effort to obtain an education. His response also suggests his perception that racism is the leading cause of these blockages.

Two thoughts come to mind as I reflect on this response. First, would Bobby have responded the same way if I were someone other than an African American male? Second, could someone other than an African American male understand how profound a statement this young boy had made and its implications for him, a student who had been expelled from school?

SUBJECTS NEED TO KNOW THE RESEARCHER

I recently told a white colleague that I had been asked to coauthor a chapter on interviewing people of color. He responded jokingly that the first thing you have to do is "be a person of color." He went on to tell me a story about another professor who had attempted to interview African American students. The professor, it seems, was unable to penetrate cultural barriers despite his best efforts. The circumstances that surround this situation are unknown to me, but it has been my experience when I interview African Americans students that, in order to have a meaningful dialogue, I have to spend time in the school so that students get to know me. That is, I need to spend time to develop and subsequently nurture a relationship with the students.

Too often, the emphasis in research efforts is disproportionately placed on the researcher's getting information from the interviewee. The greater effort is given over to uncovering or discovering some aspect of the individuals being studied. The problem with this approach is that it includes little or no exchange or disclosure about the life of the researcher. The researcher enters a situation wanting to learn everything about the interviewees without disclosing anything about him- or herself. Being approached by someone with such intentions would make many of us suspicious, yet it is the practice of many researchers. I think it is important to the success of the interview for the researcher to disclose something about him- or herself to the interviewees. This is foundation work; that is, it tells the interviewee where the researcher is coming from (see Douglas 1985).

Self-disclosure on the part of the interviewer is especially important when he or she is interviewing people of color, because, like other marginalized individuals, people of color tend to regard outsiders with suspicion. Years of misrepresentation and misinterpretation have legitimated skepticism and distrust. The question most often asked of interviewers by interviewees of color is "Who are you?" The second most frequently asked question is "Why should I talk to you?" This is clearly understandable if the researcher has not provided interviewees with any reason they should psychologically disrobe in front of strangers.

While in schools as a participant observer, I would often notice students watching me closely and listening to me. It was important for them to gauge my reactions and interactions with their peers and teachers so that they could assess whether I was someone they would talk with. For some students, it was important to determine if they could "shake me." For example, I asked one student his name, and he responded, "Eatdees." Thinking the name unusual, I asked "Eatdees what?" The student replied, "Eatdees [expletive]," referring to parts of his anatomy. I retorted, "You don't have any." The student and his peers laughed, surprised at my response. Had I responded any other way, my credibility may have gone out the window. This middle school student and his cohort determined at that moment that I was "straight" (translation: I was okay to talk with). The student immediately apologized, stopped what he was doing, and became my tour guide and informant throughout the study. From that moment on, I became an ally rather than a foe. The student took me directly to the computer room and began to pull up information on rap star Tupac Shakur, who had recently been killed. This was his effort to show me two things. First, he wanted to show off his computer skills, which he had acquired despite the fact that he was enrolled in an alternative school, where students are not typically considered to be academically inclined. Second, it was another way of saying that I was okay. This episode broke the ice, so to speak. When his peers saw him spending time with me, it provided a virtual stamp of approval.

Did my prior knowledge of the "tough-guy image" played out by these boys help me know how to respond in the situation? Did the fact that I was African American, male, and inextricably linked to "the black experience" prepare me to respond appropriately to the test imposed by these youngsters? I address these questions below.

SHARING THE SUBJECT'S EXPERIENCES

As an African American male, I shared the same race and gender as the students I interviewed. Apparently, race would not be an issue. However, it quickly became apparent that the students were deeply concerned with "who I was," well beyond my demographic characteristics. I came to the alternative school as a graduate student from a campus where many of these students had been barred. (It seems that any student placed on probation was forbidden from entering the campus unsupervised. This was a condition of probation. Most of the students in the study were on probation and therefore were barred from the campus.) So, here I was, an African American from the campus that was off-limits to them.

Many were suspicious of me; that was only reasonable. As far as many of them were concerned, I represented someone who probably did not have their interests at heart. I was simply another of the many researchers who had come and gone in their lives, intruding into their affairs until I got what I wanted. They suspected that I would eventually leave without showing a hint of gratitude for their temporary unpacking of layers of protection against further abuse (Dunbar 1999). Why would I be any different from the rest? Yes, I was indeed African American, but they were convinced that their experiences were completely different from mine. That is, our cultural and class experiences were different. In this instance, by *culture and class* I mean "the way we do things around here." Even if we were racially similar, the students had no good reason to believe that I would appreciate "the way they do things." I was a stranger to their way of life.

In fact, I grew up in a "traditional" working-class family, where I observed my parents waking up on time every day and going to work. My sisters and I went to school every day, too. That is how things were done around our house. Many of the students I interviewed were living in "nontraditional" family structures. For example, some students were being reared by grandparents or other extended family members. Others were being raised in foster homes. The ways things were done in their respective homes were often very different from my own experiences. This posed a quandary for me. It was incumbent upon me to acknowledge these "real" differences, yet I also wanted to hold on to the

notion that "we" (African Americans) are all the same, that we all suffer the same indignities.

My self-perceptions have been shaped by my social and political experiences, which are not dissimilar to those that my subject, Bobby, has experienced. His words rang loud in my ear. Bobby heard what I heard as a child. Words from my grandma —"You must work twice as hard as the white man in order to succeed"—rang in concert with Bobby's predilection.

Different family structures often result in different cultural experiences. However, some social and political influences cross cultural barriers. Do you have to share the same race to understand the nuances of differences that exist among different cultures? In many instances, probably not; however, it can work to your advantage.

LISTENING, OBSERVING, AND COMMUNICATING

Most of the literature on interviewing techniques discusses the art of asking and listening but stops short of considering the use of personal reflections and experiences as these relate to the research (but see in this volume Johnson, Chapter 5; Fontana, Chapter 8; Schwalbe and Wolkomir, Chapter 10; Kong et al., Chapter 12; Adler and Adler, Chapter 25; Ellis and Berger, Chapter 41). Being "objective" is a major tenet of most interviewing techniques. My experience in interviewing people of color conflicts with this. The notion that the researcher should shelve his or her experiences, values, and beliefs to maintain objectivity does not always serve us well in the pursuit of rich interview data.

The notion of objectivity is problematic for me on two counts. First, my passion and interest for the subject matter of my research makes it difficult for me to sever my beliefs and values from my convictions. I do, however, maintain the capacity to check them. Second, especially when I have interviewed African American educators, I have found many of them looking to me to share *my* perceptions because they view me as a former teacher (this information I share early on) as well as a researcher. My providing this information opens opportunities for meaningful dialogue. Educators want to know if others in like positions face similar situations. They look to me not only as a researcher but as a resource. There is an expected exchange. Otherwise, it becomes a situation of "all give and no get." Mutual disclosure is often a more productive strategy (see Douglas 1985; see also in this volume Warren, Chapter 4; Johnson, Chapter 5; Eder and Fingerson, Chapter 9; Reinharz and Chase, Chapter 11).

Sometimes when I interview persons of color, there seems to exist an unstated expectation that because I am a researcher—even though I am an African American—I will not understand the messages my subjects convey. I think some of this has to do with the fact that I am "the researcher" and therefore respondents think that I am "out of touch" with circumstances that exist in "their" communities. They seem to assume automatically that there are social and economic differences between us. They view me as someone "outside the loop."

To counteract this, I usually try to relate some aspect of my own experiences to potential respondents, to establish common experiential ground. Discerning what that common ground might possibly be requires close listening on the part of both interviewer and interviewee. I listen to respondents' answers to my inquiries not just for informational purposes but for procedural purposes as well. I listen to pick up the colloquial. I also listen for implicit nuances and respond accordingly, in order to indicate my understanding of what has been said. What subjects reveal conveys their perception of who they think I am and how they think I am receiving their response. They listen and watch in order to discern the way I understand their messages. When I pull from my own experience as it relates to the subject, it conveys to them the message that I "really" understand. This two-way communication process within the interview suggests that respondents themselves recognize the subtleties of identity—of race as a subject position, not as a fixed demographic category. This, in turn, affects the kinds of subjects they will be, as well as what kind of subject they take me to be as the interviewer.

TAKING NOTE OF SUBTLE CUES

Observing facial expressions, vernacular voice intonations, nonverbal cues, and other forms of body language is an important part of interviewing African Americans. Important cues may come from a respondent's nodding his or her head or changing facial expressions that convey a look that says "I don't understand" or "I disagree," or from verbal expressions that use few words yet convey much meaning. Also, when an interviewer nods and says, "I hear ya" or, in today's vernacular, "I'm feelin' you," this can go a long way toward communicating to the respondent that the interviewer understands the point being made. It also displays a circumscribed degree of cultural familiarity without making it appear that the interviewer is "trying too hard" to fit in.

It has been my experience in interviewing African Americans that when some respondents become excited, their voices become louder. This does not signal anger; it simply means that the interview has touched on a point that is especially important to them. When Bobby began to explain what education meant to him, his voice became louder because he became excited about being asked to express himself about something of consequence to him. When he began saying, "A black man has to . . . ," I could hear the rhythm and intonation in his voice. This was an issue important to him and one that warranted further probing. His excitement indicated the importance of the question to him.

BEING AWARE OF CULTURALLY SENSITIVE QUESTIONS

When interviewees offer only short responses, it may indicate several problems. First, the question may seem too simple to the interviewee. It may appear rhetorical, or it may have been asked in a way that does not conform to the way the interviewee is accustomed to being asked such a question. The interviewer's charge is not only to ask culturally sensitive questions, but to ask questions in a culturally relevant and explicit manner.

"Wat yu trying to say, Mr. Dunbar, dat dare's somtin' wrong with my famly?" This was Bobby's response when I asked him if there was anyone at home to help him do his homework and to make sure he was in bed at a reasonable hour. Many poor African American children have been interviewed, tested, incarcerated, restrained, denied, abused, lied to, and misled so often that they have developed a keen ear for what is being asked *implicitly* (Dunbar 1999:138). Some will respond accordingly —that is, they may tell the interviewer what they think he or she wants to hear—and others will question the question. Some children have developed savvy that far exceeds their age. The art of interviewing entails framing questions in a way that allows interviewees (in this case children) to maintain their dignity while they tell the stories that are important to them. This means allowing subjects their humanity.

CAPTURING AND PRESENTING THE STORY

Had I not listened to Bobby as he lamented his educational plight, and had I not acquired prior knowledge of his cultural experiences, which were influenced by both social and political forces, and had I paid less attention to Bobby's body language as he sat up to begin his story, and were I not an African American male, perhaps I would have walked out of this interview thinking not only that Bobby was angry, but that he was particularly angry with me. However, having developed some useful sensibilities with respect to interviewing persons of color, I came away feeling excited—excited that I had struck an important chord with Bobby as a thoughtfully engaged subject. The interview ceased to be an interview. It became a conversation. It evolved into a dialogue. It became the story of a rich, nuanced, and important life.

When I set out to learn about the experiences of African American males in an alternative school, I didn't figure on writing stories. I set out to write a traditional ethnography. I planned to collect data, code themes, conduct an analysis, and write up my findings. Instead, as stories began to surface, they illuminated new dimensions of the lives of these students. I spent time with them as they were shuffled from detention center to foster care, to extended family members and back home, only to repeat the cycle. This, in turn, enriched my understanding of their interview narratives. My observations and experiences with the students reflexively informed, and were informed by, what the students themselves told me.

Stories and performance texts helped me to represent these experiences in an evocative way (see in this volume Ellis and Berger, Chapter 41; Richardson, Chapter 42). This approach allowed me to rework the data so that they highlighted the triumphs and tragedies that constituted the lives of these children. My intent was to bring their experiences to life for the reader rather than simply attempt to explain them. Turning simple tales of suffering, loss, pain, and victory into evocative performances sometimes moves audiences beyond just emotional catharsis, to reflective critical action (Denzin 1997). I wrote collective stories from the data in an effort "to give voice to silenced people to represent them as historical actors" (Richardson 1997:15).

Dramatic and nondramatic performances also emerged from the data that interrogated the meanings of the lived experiences of these students (Denzin 1997). The dramatic text evolved into poems and plays, and the nondramatic texts evolved from conversations turned into natural performances (Denzin 1997). These were simply recountings of events, tellings, and interpretations from the field. Performance texts allowed me to expose and challenge conventional understandings that are underpinned by systems of realistic interpretation and meaning. They provided me with a way "to turn the chaotic, unstructured, spontaneous moments of students into evocative performances" (Denzin 1997:94).

Using this approach to represent the experiences of these students allowed me to put faces on these children and to provide an enlightened glimpse into their lives. It further gave me an opportunity to present a critical view of alternative education that is filled with sociological implications without ostentatiously parading them as such, doing more to obfuscate than to reveal.

◆ Conclusion

The accounts of interviewing people of color presented in this chapter are just the tip of a social and historical iceberg. The biographical material expressed in interviews draws from, and is mediated by, experiences from well beyond the interview situation and any one respondent's life. These experiences vary from overt racism to subtle racism. Students of color face a constant struggle as they routinely must work to overcome obstacles—in the classroom, with other students, with professors, administrators, law enforcement officers, and judges. To do justice to their experience, interviews must reflexively engage subjects in terms that can capture these complexities of their lives.

The perspective on interviewing that we have tried to present in this chapter focuses on the connections that can form between lived experiences and interview activities, which in traditional interviewing and conventional representation remain hidden behind shields of research practice. Emerging critical theoretical perspectives on racialized subjectivity have done much to reveal the actual, lived, racialized experiences of persons of all colors by providing both the procedural pretext for interviewing differently and an ethic to support such actions.

We have focused here on racialized youth cultures, but we believe it is important for researchers to have prior knowledge when studying racialized cultures of any kind. As we enter the field, we now find ourselves at the intersection of social class, gender, race, and other subjective sensibilities; the task is now to describe this intersection in all its complexity, not gloss it in tired and trite conventional terms. The operating principle here should be, "Do not assume that the subject behind the respondent is merely there for the asking." Rather, we must take the subject to have a biography that is socially and historically mediated, and proceed accordingly.

Equally important, as we have tried to illustrate, research practices that ostensibly only report "what's there" and ignore matters of procedural consciousness—or nonconsciousness, as the case has traditionally been—serve to suppress nonmainstream (often racialized) subjectivities. Conceiving of a "standardized" subject behind the respondent casts the subject as a mere vessel of answers that can be expressed only in conventional terms, in relation to the standards that are assumed to be in place. This cheats the experiences of those whose lives are not lived in accord with, or may even be lived against, the standard. Research practices that respect and reveal the social world of the lived subject are an important procedural step toward decomposing "standards" into the variety of historically and socially relevant experiences that characterize a diverse society.

■ Notes

1. Donna Deyhle and Karen Swisher (1997: 183) argue for research validity with regard to methods seriously grounded in social justice on tribal nation terms and long-term commitment to and involvement in challenging white supremacy over Native American affairs.

2. Jay MacLeod (1995:300) notes in his appendix how in some ways the "brothers" wanted to "look good" in terms of what they would and would not reveal about their status; he speculates that this may have been due to these interviewees' trying to put the best possible face on bad situations related to racism.

■ References

Andersen, M. L. 1993. "Studying across Difference: Race, Class, and Gender in Qualitative Research." Pp. 39-52 in *Race and Ethnicity in Research Methods,* edited by J. H. Stanfield II and R. M. Dennis. Newbury Park, CA: Sage.

Anderson, E. 1990. *Streetwise: Race, Class, and Change in an Urban Community.* Chicago: University of Chicago Press.

Behar, R. 1995. "Writing in My Father's Name: A Diary of *Translated Woman's First Year." Pp.* 65-82 in *Women Writing Culture,* edited by R. Behar and D. A. Gordon. Berkeley: University of California Press.

Berger, M. 1999. *White Lies: Race and the Myths of Whiteness.* New York: Farrar, Straus & Giroux.

Buendia, E. 2000. "Race, Method, and Narrative Structure: The Place of Trickster Discourses in Representing Whiteness." Presented at the annual meeting of the American Educational Research Association, April 24-28, New Orleans.

Buford, R. A. and M. Pattillo-McCoy. 2000. "Do You See What I See? Examining a Collaborative Ethnography." *Qualitative Inquiry* 6:65-87.

Casey, K. 1996. "The New Narrative Research in Education." Pp. 211-54 in *Review of Research in Education,* Vol. 21, edited by M. W. Apple. Washington, DC: American Educational Research Association.

Chang, R. 1994. "Toward an Asian American Legal Scholarship: Critical Race Theory, Poststructuralism, and Narrative Space." *Asian Law Journal–California Law Review* 1:3-82.

Cochran-Smith, M. 2000. "Blind Vision: Unlearning Racism in Teacher Education." *Harvard Educational Review* 70:157-90.

Crenshaw, K., N. Gotanda, G. Peller, and K. Thomas, eds. 1995. *Critical Race Theory: The Key Writings That Formed the Movement.* New York: New Press.

Delgado, R. and J. Stefancic. 1997. *Critical White Studies: Looking Behind the Mirror.* Philadelphia: Temple University Press.

Delgado Bernal, D. 1998. "Using a Chicana Feminist Epistemology in Educational Research." *Harvard Educational Review* 68:555-79.

Denzin, N. K. 1997. *Interpretive Ethnography: Ethnographic Practices for the 21st Century.* Thousand Oaks, CA: Sage.

Deyhle, D. and K. G. Swisher. 1997. "Research in American Indian and Alaska Native Education: From Assimilation to Self-Determination." Pp. 113-94 in *Review of Research in Education,* Vol. 22, edited by M. W. Apple. Washington, DC: American Educational Research Association.

Douglas, J. D. 1985. *Creative Interviewing.* Beverly Hills, CA: Sage.

Dunbar, C., Jr. 1999. "Three Short Stories." *Qualitative Inquiry* 5:130-40.

Feagin, J. 1992. "The Continuing Significance of Racism: Discrimination against Black Students in White Colleges." *Journal of Black Studies* 22:546-78.

Foster, M. 1994. "The Power to Know One Thing Is Never the Power to Know All Things: Methodological Notes on Two Studies of Black American Teachers." Pp. 129-46 in *Power and Method: Political Activism and Educational Research,* edited by A. Gitlin. New York: Routledge.

Gonzalez, F. E. 1998. "Formations of Mexicananess: Trenzas de Identidades Multiples/Growing Up Mexicana: Braids of Multiple Identities." *International Journal of Qualitative Studies in Education* 11:81-103.

Gwaltney, J. L. 1980. *Drylongso: A Self-Portrait of Black America.* New York: Random House.

Harris, C. 1993. "Whiteness as Property." *Harvard Law Review* 106:1707-91.

Hoffman, D. 1995. *Skin Deep* (film). San Francisco: Iris Films, California Newsreel.

Holstein, J. A. and J. F. Gubrium. 1995. *The Active Interview.* Thousand Oaks, CA: Sage.

hooks, b. 1995. *Killing Rage: Ending Racism.* New York: Henry Holt.

Jeffries, R. B. 1994. "The Trickster Figure in African American Teaching Pre- and Postdesegregation." *Urban Review* 26:289-304.

Knight v. State of Alabama, 787 F. Supp. 1030 (N.D. Ala. 1991).

Ladson-Billings, G. 1998. "Just What Is Critical Race Theory and What Is It Doing in a 'Nice' Field Like Education?" *International Journal of Qualitative Studies in Education* 11:7-24.

"LatCrit Theory: Latinas/os and the Law" (symposium). 1997. *California Law Review* 85(4).

Lipsitz, G. 1998. *The Possessive Investment in Whiteness: How White People Profit from Identity Politics.* Philadelphia: Temple University Press.

MacLeod, J. 1995. *Ain't No Makin' It: Aspirations and Attainment in a Low-Income Neighborhood.* Boulder, CO: Westview.

Martinez, G. A. 1999. "Latinos, Assimilation and the Law: A Philosophical Perspective." *Chicano Latino Law Review* 20:1-34.

Meacham, S. J. 2000. "Black Self-Love, Language, and the Teacher Education Dilemma: The Cultural Denial and Cultural Limbo of African American Preservice Teachers." *Urban Education* 34:571-96.

Mills, C. W. 1959. *The Sociological Imagination.* New York: Oxford University Press.

Noblit, G. W. 1999. *Particularities: Collected Essays on Ethnography and Education.* New York: Peter Lang.

Omi, M. and H. Winant. 1994. *Racial Formation in the United States: 1960-1990.* 2d ed. New York: Routledge.

Park, E. J. W. and J. S. W. Park. 1999. "A New American Dilemma? Asian Americans and Latinos in Race Theorizing." *Journal of Asian American Studies* 2:289-309.

Parker, L. 1998. "Who Is the Master and What Are the Tools? A Critical Conversation on Race, Class, Gender, Postcolonialism and Other Standpoints in Educational Research." Presented at an interactive symposium at the annual meeting of the American Educational Research Association, April 19-24, San Diego, CA.

Pillow, W. S. 2000. "Exposed Methodology: The Body as a Deconstructive Practice." Pp. 199-220 in *Working the Ruins: Feminist Poststructural Theory and Methods in Education,* edited by E. A. St. Pierre and W. S. Pillow. New York: Routledge.

Pizarro, M. 1998. "Chicana/o Power! Epistemology and Methodology for Social Justice and Empowerment in Chicana/o Educational Communities." *International Journal of Qualitative Studies in Education* 11:57-80.

Richardson, L. 1997. *Fields of Play: Constructing an Academic Life.* New Brunswick, NJ: Rutgers University Press.

Roediger, D. R. 1998. *Black on White: Black Writers on What It Means to Be White.* New York: Schocken.

Rubin, H. J. and I. S. Rubin. 1995. *Qualitative Interviewing: The Art of Hearing Data.* Thousand Oaks, CA: Sage.

Sack, K. and J. Elder. 2000. "Poll Finds Optimistic Outlook but Enduring Racial Division." *New York Times,* July 11, pp. A1, A23.

Schuman, H., C. Steeh, L. Bobo, and M. Krysan. 1998. *Racial Attitudes in America: Trends and Interpretations.* Rev. ed. Cambridge, MA: Harvard University Press.

Scott, J. 2000. "Who Gets to Tell a Black Story?" *New York Times,* June 11, pp. 1, 16, 17, 18.

Stanfield, J. H., II. 1993. "Methodological Reflections: An Introduction." Pp. 3-15 in *Race and Ethnicity in Research Methods,* edited by J. H. Stanfield II and R. M. Dennis. Newbury Park, CA: Sage.

————. 1994. "Ethnic Modeling in Qualitative Research." Pp. 175-88 in *Handbook of Qualitative Research*, edited by N. K. Denzin and Y. S. Lincoln. Thousand Oaks, CA: Sage.

Tanaka, G. and C. Cruz. 1998. "The Locker Room: Eroticism and Exoticism in a Polyphonic Text." *International Journal of Qualitative Studies in Education* 11:137-53.

Tate, W. F., IV. 1997. "Critical Race Theory and Education: History, Theory, and Implications." Pp. 195-250 in *Review of Research in Education*, Vol. 22, edited by M. W. Apple. Washington, DC: American Educational Research Association.

Tatum, B. D. 1997. *"Why Are All the Black Kids Sitting Together in the Cafeteria?" and Other Conversations about Race*. New York: Basic Books.

Van Maanen, J. 1988. *Tales of the Field: On Writing Ethnography*. Chicago: University of Chicago Press.

Villenas, S. 1996. "The Colonizer/Colonized Chicana Ethnographer: Identity, Marginalization, and Co-optation in the Field." *Harvard Educational Review* 66:711-31.

Vizenor, G. 1988. *The Trickster of Liberty: Tribal Heirs to a Wild Baronage*. Minneapolis: University of Minnesota Press.

Zinn, M. B. 1979. "Field Research in Minority Communities: Ethical, Methodological and Political Observations by an Insider." *Social Problems* 27:209-19.

15

INTERVIEWING ELITES

◆ Teresa Odendahl
Aileen M. Shaw

Elite individuals and groups occupy the top echelons of society. They are integral to every community, government, occupation, and religion, as well as to other institutional spheres (Mills 1956; Pareto 1935). Elites generally have more knowledge, money, and status and assume a higher position than others in the population. The privileges and responsibilities of elites are often not tangible or transparent, making their world difficult to penetrate. Sometimes, a cloak of privacy, or even secrecy, masks their activities. The composition of many elite groups is relatively fluid and changes over time. Moreover, there are important intersections among different types of elites, as well as between elites and other groups (Keller 1963; Marcus 1983).

Social scientists commonly acknowledge elites but less frequently study them, opting instead to investigate those without influ-

ence, over whom power is exercised rather than society's decision makers. There are practical reasons for this preference. Elites are difficult to identify and often are inaccessible, much less open to being the subjects of scrutiny. They ably protect themselves from outsiders. Barriers to reaching elites are real and include the difficulty of identifying who they are; getting past gatekeepers such as personal assistants, advisers, lawyers, and security guards; and accessing exclusive physical spaces including boardrooms, clubs, and domiciles surrounded by walls.

Underlying any study dealing with elites is a particular understanding of wealth and power in society. Our discussion in this chapter is based on our own extensive experiences in studying elites in the nonprofit or philanthropic sector. Our focus is on interviewing wealthy elites, who are identifiable by their distinctive cultural and class characteristics. Our research interest has been in determining to what extent these elites are open and accessible to the diverse society in which they operate and over which philanthropy exercises enormous influence. We emphasize here the importance of researchers' clarifying the designation of elite status as a point of departure for research, and we present a workable framework for elite studies based on interviews.

◆ Interview Methodology

Personal interviews are an effective method of data collection for research on elite subjects and culture, but there is a shortage of methodological literature on applicable research practices. Guides and manuals dedicated to interview techniques seldom differentiate elite from nonelite subjects; if they do, they make cursory reference to any specialized approaches (Kvale 1996:101). There is one edited volume, Rosanna Hertz and Jonathan B. Imber's *Studying Elites Using Qualitative Methods* (1995), dedicated to methodological issues in interviewing elites as such. The essays in Hertz and Imber's collection take an ethnographic approach and are organized according to traditional sector categories—business, community, and political elites—as well as the more recent delineation of professional elites. Chapters cover interviews with clergy, corporate executives, Hollywood star makers, nonprofit leaders, and women elites, for example, primarily with a U.S. focus. The contributors reflect on their experiences in gaining access to elites, the maneuverings they have found necessary to negotiate the otherwise closed worlds occupied by elites, and the ethical issues they have faced in analyzing and reporting their research findings.

Using a broader international and cross-disciplinary approach, George Moyser and Margaret Wagstaffe, in their earlier edited volume *Research Methods for Elite Studies* (1987a), examine how and why to research elites from both theoretical and methodological perspectives. Their collection illustrates the importance of establishing the procedural dimensions of any given inquiry into elites: "It is almost axiomatic that the success of any given research project is closely associated with the appropriateness of the chosen methodology" (Wagstaffe and Moyser 1987:201). Moyser and Wagstaffe's contributors come from a variety of disciplines—economics, political science, and sociology—and consider a range of settings, including Northern Ireland, Eastern Europe, and Taiwan. The collection is divided into conventional (political) elites, economic elites, and what the editors term "defensive" elites, that is, people or groups who are threatened by, have little to gain from, or are otherwise reluctant to place themselves under scrutiny. Despite extreme differences in the research settings considered, the various chapters show that similar procedural issues and dilemmas arise in studies with elites, including problems of identification, access, and power relations.

The literature in the area of elite studies includes materials that approach elite interviewing from specialized perspectives, yet careful attention to methodology reveals that the operational tools used can be applied to a variety of disciplines and areas of inquiry. A collection of essays in a 1998 issue of *Environment and Planning,* for example, takes a geographic approach to studying elites and the "connection of people and places in the construction of elites" (Hughes and Cormode 1998:2100). The authors of these essays on elites and elite spaces offer guidelines on the practical issues, obstacles, and dilemmas encountered that echo less specialized discussions of the same issues. For example, in an essay on her experiences in interviewing high-status workers in London's merchant banks, Linda McDowell (1998) offers a particularly insightful discussion of the tactics of control that the typically supplicant researcher might employ in interviewing powerful people.

◆ Designating Elites

Although meager information is available on interviewing elites, the conceptual literature on elites is extensive and yet mainly outside of the purview of this chapter's focus on interviewing. Nevertheless, some understanding of the history and scope of elite theory, especially as it bears on designating elites, is necessary to an exploration of the varied methods for choosing and conducting a study of elite subjects and designating those to be studied.

The term *elite* is closely linked with abstract notions of power and privilege, generally in connection with certain identifiable individuals or groups of individuals. Indeed, as described by George Marcus (1983), the ability to evoke images of "specifiable groups of persons" is what differentiates *elite* from other concepts such as class. At the same time, the ambiguity of the term makes for an elusive indicator:

> Clear in what it signifies, but ambiguous to its precise referents, the concept of elite in general usage has a certain force. . . . Only when *elite* is elaborated as an interest of social theory and research, which address as their purpose the empirical referents of the concept, does the inherent vagueness of the concept become a major difficulty. (P. 7)

The designation of elites depends on broader understandings of power and society. For the purposes of determining criteria for selection, researchers tend to classify elites into sector categories, such as business elites, political elites, and community elites. Of course, these delineations are not mutually exclusive; indeed, there tends to be substantial overlap among them. However, in order to operationalize the term

elite and to ascribe particular attributes to the subjects under study, researchers must define the parameters of the group in question.

The designation of who or what is elite varies according to the area of inquiry, and part of the investigative process is determining the scope of inquiry. For instance, is the subject of study the individuals, groups, associations, or sectors considered elite? What geographic boundaries should be identified—international, national, regional, state, or local? Are the elites under study viewed in isolation or as intertwined in a simple or complex way? Are elites to be considered in relation to a broader examination of a field, sector, system, or society?

Those studying elites have developed many different typologies. Early classifications include C. Wright Mills's (1956) economic, military, and political elites and Siegfried Nadel's (1956) social, specialized, and governing elites. Suzanne Keller (1963) differentiates between levels of elites:

> Whereas elites are important in some social and psychological contexts, only some are important for society as a whole. These must somehow be distinguished from the rest. There is, in effect, a hierarchy among elites: some elites are more elite than others. Beauty queens, criminal masterminds, champion bridge players, and master chefs all hold top rank in certain pyramids of talent or power. But not all are equally significant in the life of society. Certain elites may arouse momentary attention, but only certain leadership groups have a general and sustained social impact. . . . these groups [are] *strategic elites*. (P. 20)

Keller's strategic elites are found in the worlds of business, politics, diplomacy, and defense. Recently, the study of professional elites—academics, celebrities, members of the clergy, lawyers, and physicians—has burgeoned. The use of additional demographic variables, such as gender (Ostrander 1980, 1984) and religion (Birmingham 1967), in conjunction with elite status has further specified elite subjects and communities. Political and corporate elites can constitute the primary subjects of study (Hertz and Imber 1995; Putnam 1976). In one recent study of American elites, members of this group are defined primarily by their occupations (Lerner, Nagai, and Rothman 1996). The 12 categories of analysis include elites from the traditional business and cultural sectors as well as "elite members of new occupations," including religious leaders, labor leaders, and media leaders.

William Domhoff (1967, 1970, 1980, 1983; Domhoff and Dye 1987; Zweigenhaft and Domhoff 1998), a prominent researcher of the power elite, has developed indicators of social class according to club membership, educational pedigree, lineage, and inclusion in local social registers. In their recent book *Diversity in the Power Elite* (1998), Richard Zweigenhaft and Domhoff question whether the power elite has diversified in terms of gender, ethnicity, race, sexual orientation, and class. Taking issue with those who argue that the "old" power elite identified by Mills as white, male, and Christian has been replaced by a new, culturally diverse group, Zweigenhaft and Domhoff ask, Has the power elite gone multicultural? Mills studied the career paths and social backgrounds of those who occupied the highest positions in what he identified as the three major branches of power: the corporations, the executive branch of the federal government, and the military. He contended that great wealth and power were embodied in those institutional hierarchies and the people who run them. More than four decades later, Zweigenhaft and Domhoff explored the social, educational, and occupational backgrounds of top leaders in these areas. Although this power elite shows considerable diversity compared to the 1950s, its core group continues to be wealthy, white, Christian, and male. The diverse newcom-

ers share common values and class backgrounds that are unlikely to "rock the boat." They are often accepted in response to pressure and serve a buffer function that benefits the old guard. Those who have succeeded have done so through "identity management," recognition of the importance of education, and high social origins. Affirming Mills's earlier findings, Zweigenhaft and Domhoff conclude that diverse groups have had little effect on the way the power elite functions or on the class structure on which it is based.

The establishment of criteria for elite standing is central to any research undertaking concerning elites. Deciding on the evidence of elite status will direct the researcher to the relevant sources for identification. Typically, studies of elites have focused on economic and social backgrounds, which, although these include the sizes of individuals' fortunes, are not the only or indeed the primary variables in the determination of elite status. Also significant in characterizing elites is a shared set of attributes, behavior, values, and lifestyles. For example, if a researcher were to equate simple economic power with elite status, he or she would seek wealthy respondents to interview. Economic elites are, after all, individuals in our society with the greatest fortunes at their disposal. Yet the factors that characterize elite standing are usually based on more than money; these include what Nelson Aldrich (1988) has aptly labeled the "class curriculum," namely, schools, colleges, clubs, museums, welfare charities, and the like. Taking such characteristics into account, a researcher would cast a wider net in discerning a respondent pool.

Each year, *Forbes* magazine publishes a list of the 400 wealthiest Americans. This list and other types of "registers" of elites (for example, legislative rosters for political elites) can serve as starting points in interview research. However, in the two decades since *Forbes* began publication of its list, sources of individual wealth have changed dramatically. The proportion of the fortunes of the nation's richest coming from inheritance dropped from 85 percent to 39 percent between 1982 and 1996, whereas that coming from investment in software or computers increased from 4 percent to 26 percent. Thus the creation of vast new wealth in the 1990s has blurred the lines of demarcation in what had been a useful framework for researchers to use in selecting traditional elite subjects. Indeed, in today's world, being a millionaire may only be an indication of semi-elite economic status.

Although part of the selection methods for designating elites might rely on quantitative data such as rankings and numerical indexes, these alone are not sufficient. It is important that researchers view these indicators as maps to a reality that can unfold only through broader knowledge of evolving patterns of wealth and power in the social context under consideration. The criteria for inclusion of a subject in an interview sample are set as the result of a complex process that depends on the types of elites being studied and the theoretical perspectives of the researchers. There is no magic formula independent of this process.

PHILANTHROPIC ELITES

We define philanthropic elites as wealthy people, representatives of institutions of wealth, such as foundations, and their leaders. The definition includes not only donors but also "professionals," such as personal advisers and private foundation staff, who often take on the values shared by the elites they serve.

Charitable foundations are primary vehicles of giving for wealthy individuals, families, and groups. Since 1980, the number of such foundations in the United States has doubled, from 22,000 to more than 44,000. Private foundations derive their funds from single sources, such as an individual, family, or corporation. In recent years, largely due to the boom in the stock market and the creation of substantial new

wealth, there has been unprecedented growth in the nation's largest foundations. Adjusted for inflation, foundations give away more than three times more today than they did in 1982, whereas their assets have grown more than fivefold. Most of the giving benefits education, the arts, and the humanities.

Under the foundation system, a wealthy individual or small group gives up certain income or assets to be used for charitable purposes at the discretion of a body of decision makers selected by the donor. The most common reason individuals cite for setting up foundations involves the tax advantages that doing so offers (Odendahl 1987); funds donated to foundations would otherwise be available to the government for taxation. Foundation trustees are donors, their family members, friends, business associates, advisers, and, in some instances, experts on particular issue areas for grant making. Within the ranks of a foundation, the highest level of professional staff is the chief executive officer (CEO), followed by program officers who recommend or make decisions on funding priorities. Like trustees, foundation staff are generally handpicked by the donors and tend to mirror the donors' beliefs, attitudes, and, often, social status.

Convinced of the importance of what anthropologist Laura Nader (1972) calls "studying up," Teresa Odendahl (1990) has identified a culture of philanthropy among a subset of the wealthy in the United States. Odendahl's research, conducted as part of a larger study housed at Yale University, is based on interviews with 140 millionaire philanthropists and 100 foundation staff members and personal advisers. The elite who participate in the culture of philanthropy share behavior and manners, economic status, and sociocultural institutions as well as attitudes, ideas, perceptions, and values.

One of her first interviews conducted for the Yale study, with a middle-aged woman, was among Odendahl's most memorable. She vividly recalls her first introduction into the private world or "sub-culture" of the philanthropic elite as well as the opportunities for observational analysis provided by the interview setting:

> We had met at a conference on philanthropy. When the wealthy woman learned about the project, she kindly invited me to visit her. After an exchange of letters and phone calls, the arrangements were made. I drove through beautiful, wooded countryside into what I knew to be one of the wealthiest counties in the United States. At one juncture I passed through a stone gateway that I had been told would mean I was close to her house. I had not expected the mansion that awaited me.
>
> The woman opened the door herself. She was dressed elegantly but informally. I was wearing my "interview outfit," a subdued brown business suit and a silk blouse, and carrying a leather attaché case. We exchanged pleasantries, and she asked if I would like a tour of the house. She explained that the downstairs was intended for formal entertaining and was not regularly used by the family. We walked through a large entry hall, adorned with a tropical flower arrangement. . . . My hostess waved vaguely toward a doorway at the end of the room and said that was the "big" kitchen. She did not offer to show it to me but steered me toward the "music room," which was parallel to the dining room and about the same size. A grand piano graced one end of this area, with plenty of space for a small audience. I have to admit that I started thinking about the board game "Clue." I just was not sure that everything around me was real, and I was nervous enough to wonder when the crime would be committed. Later in the research I became more accustomed to the trappings of wealth.
>
> She did not show me the "private" area of the house. She offered coffee and got it herself. . . . I oriented myself

> and placed my tape recorder next to a small vase of spring flowers on the coffee table. It struck me that if I had not just come through the formal part of the mansion, it would have seemed as if I were sitting in a well-appointed suburban house. The upstairs decor reminded me of many of my parents friends' (middle-class) homes. It was tasteful, yet did not appear terribly expensive. The interview was conducted in this room. . . . My hostess was charming, gracious, and helpful, all aspects of philanthropic style. (Pp. 6-7)

Interviewing elites calls into question issues of control, power, and accessibility. The dynamics that operate during the interaction are strong and prescient, often constrained by the demands of time and place. The environment where any interview takes place has a bearing on the richness of the data collected. As with the instance described above, some of the best, most informative meetings held during Odendahl's research, where sensitive or subtle ideas were expressed, were conducted in people's homes.

We have collaborated over the past five years on two additional interviewing projects with elites in the philanthropic field. This chapter also draws on that research, conducted at the National Network of Grantmakers, a membership organization of employees and trustees of foundations, major donors, and philanthropic advisers. For a study of grant-making "best practices," we analyzed 100 interviews with board and staff members of foundations nationwide (Shaw 1997). Our primary interest was in examining the decision-making processes that determine the distribution of vast amounts of public money. Through telephone interviews, in-person interviews, and case studies, we reviewed governance and grant-making practices at a range of institutions and explored the processes by which foundations open up their decision-making structures in order to share power and make themselves more accessible. In a study currently under way, we are part of a team engaged in research concerning diversity among board and staff members in the philanthropic field.[1]

For the most part, interviews with elites in these studies take place in offices. As part of the diversity study, we interviewed the relatively new CEO of a large public foundation. This interview subject is one of the few Latina executives of a major grant-making organization. She hustled us into her spacious office, glanced at her watch, and announced that she had less than an hour. "What is this all about?" she asked. Of course, we had previously sent her detailed materials concerning our purpose and the scope of the research. Her demeanor was pleasant and businesslike; her manner did not invite chitchat. The respondent's assistant had scheduled a two-hour meeting for which we had prepared extensively. She gave us 45 minutes. Therefore, we improvised, cutting less essential questions out of our formal interview schedule as the conversation progressed. Our interview subject was an impressive person, clearly accustomed to exercising authority. She was knowledgeable and gave us excellent information. She took a personal phone call during the interview—a subtle reminder both of the demands on her time and that she had a life outside the institution.

Such interviewing experiences can help researchers to gain invaluable insights that can serve them as they design research on elites. We offer practical guidance in the following sections based on our own experiences in philanthropy, as well as from the methodological literature covering a range of fields of sociological study.

◆ Locating and Contacting Respondents

One of the first steps in any interview study is to locate respondents. The process of identifying and gaining access to elite subjects calls for the incorporation of strategies that include a mixture of ingenuity, social skills, contacts, careful negotiation, and circumstance.

Computers have dramatically changed the methods researchers might employ for locating elite respondents. For example, the *Forbes* 400 list mentioned previously is now a searchable database on the Internet, a tool that allows researchers to identify such criteria as names, states, industries (including agriculture, engineering, technology, oil and gas, entertainment), ages, and sources of wealth (inherited, self-made, or built up). Profiles of individuals with histories of family fortunes are readily available.

Researchers may be daunted initially by what they may consider barriers to information. But whatever the elite group, material is more readily accessible than one might assume. Elite individuals and groups are popular subjects in the mass media. *Business Week, Forbes, Fortune, Newsweek, Worth,* and the *Economist* are all extensive sources of information on wealthy individuals and families. Many of these periodicals have Internet sites that make articles available on-line, and many are available in most public or university libraries. Within the business community, chief executives are easily identified because, by law, companies are required to make public certain information on their top officers and executives. Directories such as *Who's Who,* annual reports, and business almanacs provide information on the salaries, educations, backgrounds, and affiliations of corporate executives. Researchers will also find database searches of newspapers and magazines at the national, regional, and state levels useful for locating and obtaining information on elites.

The identification of individual elites and the compilation of subject pools are only the beginning of a protracted process involving several layers of additional research. For example, when Odendahl and her colleagues began their study of America's philanthropic wealthy, they used the *Forbes* list and cross-referenced individuals and families on it with directories published by the Foundation Center and the Taft Corporation. From this painstaking process, they extracted information on which of the wealthy were serving on foundation boards and which were contributing substantial amounts of money to nonprofit causes. They simultaneously reviewed the biographies and histories of wealthy families as well as journalistic accounts in leading newspapers such as the *New York Times, Washington Post,* and *Los Angeles Times.*

In our current research on diversity in philanthropy, we have relied on the leading trade associations in the foundation field for our initial interview sample. Large trade associations have research departments that compile statistics on a wide range of data. Researchers must cultivate personal contacts within such organizations. We used unpublished data from the Council of Foundations (CoF) to assist us in the selection of foundation executives and trustees for our sample in the diversity research. Every two years, the CoF surveys its membership, gathering information on the age, gender, and racial and ethnic characteristics of board and staff members; the CoF also conducts extensive analyses of the foundations it surveys, by, for example, assets size and foundation type. Although the philanthropic field remains a nexus of the power elite, our interest is in how foundations become more diverse and less exclusive in their board compositions and in their staffing and funding patterns. The CoF data provided the base against which we could rank and select interview subjects.

We created two indexes. One consisted simply of the percentage of minority members and the percentage of women on a foundation board, added together to produce a "board diversity score." We constructed another index by adding together the percentage of minorities on a foundation's board, the percentage of women on the board, and the percentage of minorities on the foundation's staff. We then sorted the foundations by their scores. The final sorting resulted in a list of foundations with the highest scores in terms of diversity at the top of the list. We identified the executives of these top foundations as good candidates for interviews.

Score alone was not sufficient, however. We used these rankings as guidelines only. We also tried to ensure that the foundations we chose for interviews not only had high diversity scores, but varied in terms of regions, foundation types, and assets sizes.

Identifying a subject pool is more than a matter of generating lists of potential respondents. Contacting potential respondents and convincing them to participate is, needless to say, the key to moving ahead. As with any social circle, those who have contacts with members of philanthropic groups tend to be the best sources of information on power and influence within their own sphere. The researcher seeking to become part of these groups is imbued with a certain legitimacy if she or he enters with personal information gleaned from insiders or from those who have personal contacts with insiders. Although Odendahl and her colleagues started with the *Forbes* list and foundation directories, their next step was to investigate and locate contacts who were acquaintances of the individuals they sought for interviews. Several members of the research team had previously worked in foundations or were trustees and personally knew philanthropists. Even so, it took one year of background research and various attempts to make contacts before the first formal interview was conducted.

◆ Access and Preparation

In practice, many research activities tend to occur simultaneously: culling lists, reviewing the literature available, and cultivating contacts. In our experience, success in studying elites is predicated upon the researcher's overall knowledge of the elite culture under study, in combination with the personal status and institutional affiliation of the interviewer or project director. Gaining permission to interview an elite subject typically requires extensive preparation, homework, and creativity on the part of the researcher, as well as the right credentials and contacts.

However, luck also plays a role. In discussing her study of London elites, McDowell (1998) observes:

> Somehow you have to get in there, and although we often, in writing up our results talk blandly of our samples or our case studies, letting the reader assume that the particular industry, location, site, and respondents were the optimal or ideal for investigating the particular issue in which we were interested, we all know that the "reality" . . . is a lot messier. A great deal depends on luck and chance, connections and networks, and the particular circumstances at the time. (P. 2135)

Frequently, the original or most important contact who leads to a series of introductions may seem to appear almost by chance. Yet such chance events require that the researcher be at the right place at the right time, making the subject of interest clear to persons who might be in a position to help.

Early in a research project, it is extremely useful for a researcher to acquire one or more key informants. These are individuals or "insiders" with whom the researcher is able to establish considerable rapport and trust and who are willing to spend time familiarizing the investigator with the elite culture under consideration. A bit of old-fashioned ethnographic fieldwork is tremendously useful at this point (see in this volume Warren, Chapter 4; Atkinson and Coffey, Chapter 38). A researcher may identify key informants during the interview pretest phase of the study, or he or she may have known the individuals previously; the project sponsor may

even be a key informant. Alternatively, during the course of the study, certain interview subjects may develop particular interest in the research and agree to serve in this capacity. If a key informant is prominent within his or her circle, this can help to establish the researcher's credibility.

Elite groups are often characterized by intricate interpersonal networks that include influential actors behind the scenes or others who control access to those scenes. Acquiring the right key informant can set the course of the research, because "who knows whom" matters. The best entrée to elite individuals for interviews is provided by members of the elites' own groups, or, as a substitute, their "gatekeepers." Gatekeepers to the philanthropic elite are generally professionals such as accountants, bank trust officers, financial and estate planners, foundation employees, lawyers, and investment counselors, as well as the potentially more influential family office directors, personal assistants, and philanthropic advisers. Such individuals can be significant sources of advice, guidance, and background information about the subjects of study. Many such retainers have well-established reputations and status in their own right; they often move in the same social circles as the elites they serve. In addition to providing access to their clients, gatekeepers may serve as key informants, and thus can be candidates for interviews themselves (Moyser and Wagstaffe 1987b:16-17; Odendahl 1990: 209-31).

Generally, an elite individual or gatekeeper who is centrally positioned can direct the researcher to other individuals in his or her network, or agree to contact potential subjects and even make introductions on the researcher's behalf. Candidacy for elite interviews often cannot be planned for adequately in advance of the project; rather, it emerges as part of the fieldwork. As in most ethnographically oriented interview studies, "access is negotiated and renegotiated throughout the research process" (Burgess 1991:43).

One tactic researchers commonly use in attempting to identify and gain access to subjects is to attend events or gatherings frequented by the groups or individuals under study (Daniels 1988; Hunter 1995). In the case of elites, such activities may range from conferences to fund-raisers and awards dinners, or, even better, strictly social events. By attending these events, the researcher can observe the group's dynamics and arrange to be introduced to potential contacts or subjects.

Albert Hunter (1995) has argued that "in the actual act of studying elites, the ethnographer cannot ignore the elite's power and must not ignore his or her own power in the relationship" (pp. 151-52). As he recalls:

On two different occasions, it happened in field settings that a key informant, acting as shepherd and host, proudly introduced me to fellow elites as "the professor" . . . who was interested in studying their community. On one of these occasions, my host . . . rushed over to me, grabbed me by the arm, and led me to the front of the receiving line where he proudly introduced me in a formal voice sufficiently loud for all around to hear. . . . His grown son, sitting at the family banquet table, [later] leaned over to me and whispered, "He said you're writing a book about us. Watch out. Now everyone will want to talk to you." By observing how I was defined and used as an "object" within these interactions, subtleties of power and deference were revealed that would have been masked had I self-consciously ignored "the self" as but an intrusive methodological error. (P. 160)

Not to be underestimated, then, are researchers' own personal and professional contacts, particularly academic, community, nonprofit, and religious affiliations. We all know people who know others, who can help us gain access. Researchers' own reputations, as well as their positions and status on university faculties or within organizations, can assist them in gaining access to the elite.

Whether or not an introduction has been made, it is incumbent upon the interviewer or study director to invite respondents officially to participate in interviews. We have found it essential to extend such invitations through formal written communications, printed on institutional or personal letterhead, that include background on the researchers' credentials and an accompanying description of the project. The use of Yale University letterhead proved particularly effective in Odendahl's research, given the fact that in the year it began, one-third of the people on the *Forbes* list of wealthiest Americans had graduated from that institution. In our present study, although several cosponsoring organizations are involved, we decided that the academic standing of a university would enhance our access to interview candidates. Whatever the auspices under which the research is conducted, we recommend full disclosure to potential subjects of the true goals and intended uses of the findings. Some researchers and most academic institutions require written agreements of informed consent between participants. Such "contracts" can prove useful when confusion or disputes arise over the use of data gleaned from an interview (Ostrander 1995).

◆ The Interview

Scheduling interviews with elite individuals is labor-intensive, typically requiring several telephone calls with personal assistants or other gatekeepers. We prefer to conduct in-person interviews, but in some cases, when several months have gone by and logistical constraints have prevailed, we have resorted to telephone interviews instead. Occasionally, we have offered recalcitrant subjects this option, although we generally glean more information from face-to-face exchanges, where the interviewer can assess the personality of the subject as well as the nuances, gestures, omissions, and dynamics taking place.

TIME AND VENUE

In almost all cases, the location of the interview is chosen for the subject's convenience. Unless the respondent is local, the interviewer must make travel and lodging arrangements, often at considerable expense. Despite the amount of advance preparation that often takes place as the interviewer works to confirm and reserve a meeting time of sufficient length, in our experience subtle power dynamics frequently come into play; the elite subject may keep the interviewer waiting beyond the appointed interview time, may announce at the onset of the conversation other demands on his or her schedule, and may interrupt the interview to conduct other business. Such dynamics create less-than-ideal interview conditions and shorten the time available for the interview itself.

With elite subjects, it is important that the researcher make the most of the time allotted. He or she should find out as much as possible beforehand about the particular individual to be interviewed or the organization of interest (through annual reports, policy papers, statements, press clippings) in order to conserve time with the respondent for the gathering of information that is otherwise unattainable. The savvy interviewer can also use such background information during the meeting to demonstrate familiarity with the person or institution, to stimulate discussion, or to spark reactions. Given the time constraints within which elites operate, we have found that it is advantageous to provide a copy of the interview protocol or general questions in advance to the respondent so that he or she can be prepared to speak directly to the issues of interest (although there is no assurance that the respondent will actually read

any documents provided in advance). In addition, when the interviewee understands the scope of inquiry, he or she may independently supply relevant materials to the researcher prior to or at the meeting.

Establishing how much time the subject has available at the beginning of the interview allows the researcher to adapt if there is less time than would seem to be required. Odendahl once traveled some distance to see a particular multimillionaire who, upon her arrival, indicated that he could give her only 20 minutes of his time. He kept strictly to his word. He glanced at his watch when she entered the office. His answers were brief but to the point. The meeting was interrupted by a telephone call from the man's wife; he timed the telephone conversation, apparently took the time into account in his calculations, and, as he was hanging up, told Odendahl how many minutes she had left. She came out of the interview mentally catching her breath but considered it a success. The respondent had been brusque yet friendly and had not hesitated to provide detailed and specific information.

Other elite participants in the same study, in contrast, spent several hours—in a few cases, full days—talking with Odendahl or other interviewers. Some had smiles on their faces and a sparkle in their eyes; others appeared affectless, with deadpan demeanors. A few were obsessed with every possible boring detail. Several were incredibly shy and halting in their manner of speech. Yet all displayed impeccable manners.

INTERVIEW FORMAT

In the course of our work, we have experimented with several interview formats. These have included structured, semistructured, and unstructured instruments. As Moyser and Wagstaffe (1987b) note:

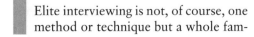 Elite interviewing is not, of course, one method or technique but a whole fam-

ily comprising varied alternatives. One principal axis along which such alternatives differ is the degree of structure or directiveness employed by the interviewer. . . . This helps to identify three major variants: the fully structured, the semi-structured and the unstructured interview, the first two having been more extensively utilized in the study of elites than the last. The choice between them is ultimately a decision about which data-generation strategy best fits the particular research design and theoretical problems being addressed. (P. 18)

We have ultimately preferred a semi-structured instrument derived from our research questions. We begin to develop the instrument in the pretest phase, in which we identify both which issues can be broached and which are potentially off-putting. For example, in the Yale study, which was directly concerned with family wealth and its uses, the researchers found the topics of income and net worth to be taboo among their elite subjects. People would more readily speak of their sex lives than of the details of their personal finances. Questions about income, which originally were included in the interview guide, stood to jeopardize rapport with potential informants and had to be removed from the instrument.

In all three of the research projects from which we draw examples in this chapter, the coinvestigators first formulated detailed, highly structured interview instruments, which they then modified over time. As the studies evolved, patterns emerged in the data and interviewers concurrently became more adept at asking questions and more discriminating in the questions they asked. By the time the projects were completed, the interviewers had virtually internalized the instruments; they could intuitively allow subjects to talk, following a less structured format, leading them to the relevant issues. In a few cases respondents obviously preferred a less structured approach, and the interviewers adapted, prompting only when necessary.

INTERVIEW DYNAMICS

Customs of courtesy, friendliness, and professional demeanor are much appreciated by elites. In the social upper class, these attributes are even more valued and expected than in the wider society (Aldrich 1988; Daniels 1988). Our interviews with elite respondents have typically been quite businesslike. We have rarely engaged in social or unguarded conversation with elite subjects, yet we have remained conscious of the need to acknowledge and indeed engage in a certain amount of sociability. Although a researcher may find it a pleasant surprise to be treated cordially by a respondent, this can also be somewhat disarming to the researcher with "difficult" questions to pose. After all, it is "not nice" to tackle a person when one is the recipient of that person's hospitality.

Interviewing people who are accustomed to exercising power and imbued with elite social status calls for particular strategies on the part of the interviewer, although researchers do not necessarily concur on which strategies are most effective. The issue of control is fundamental to the elite interview and extends from the physical location of the meeting to the type of interview format used to elicit information, as well as to the interviewer's presentation of self. Interviewing elites inevitably leads to questions about the researchers' own identity and status, which are often investigated in advance. It is not uncommon for elite interviewees or their gatekeepers to conduct background checks on researchers' credentials prior to agreeing to meet.

At the outset of the interview, the interviewer should expect to be questioned again on the purposes, goals, and uses of the proposed research, even if he or she has already submitted to such questioning in order to get to the person of interest. In general, if the end product will be something that the subject's organization can use, or if it will place the institution or individual in a favorable light, the interviewee is more likely to be cooperative, as one might expect. In order to obtain information from respondents, it helps if the researcher can offer something in exchange that will be of practical use to the agency, person, or institution featured, such as the likely generation of favorable publicity or a report that can have positive uses internally.

The dynamics of interaction between the elite interviewee and the generally nonelite researcher can play out in various ways. For both our best practices and diversity research, we selected individuals for interviews based on their positions within institutions, especially those deemed to possess exemplary or emulatory reputations. We emphasized this in contacting the individuals, and our flattering approach doubtless led to more forthcoming responses. In writing about interviewing corporate elites, Robert Thomas (1995) acknowledges feeling "like a supplicant granted audience with a dignitary. I must admit to have felt 'honored' to be granted time with a well-known executive and to be tempted to be less assertive than I might have been with someone less newsworthy" (p. 7). In our own research, we have also been intimidated by elite individuals and their surroundings. We have learned to gird ourselves psychologically for each situation by knowing as much as possible beforehand about the organizational culture. Such preparation includes details that might appear to be trivial, from conforming closely in our styles of dress to those we are interviewing to the substance and degree of formality of our introductory conversation.

Nevertheless, the interviewer must establish his or her own authority to ensure a productive exchange. There are subtle ways in which an interviewer can communicate expertise either in the field under study or in knowledge of other prominent players within it. These may range from immediately handing over a business card that indicates higher degrees, institutional position, and title to name-dropping around either individuals or projects that can validate the interviewer to the subject. Many elite people may also be impressed by established publication records or the potential for the interview to appear in print. In all instances, the interviewer needs to read the situation and the individual concerned so as not to self-aggrandize, appear arrogant, or, conversely, be ingratiating.

Susan Ostrander (1995), who has studied upper-class women, elite charity executives, and philanthropists, reminds us that elites are accustomed to "being in charge" and to "having others defer to them. They also are used to being asked what they think and having what they think matter in other people's lives" (p. 143). Such characteristics can be an advantage when a researcher is seeking a participant to engage in an interview, but a detriment when the interviewer is trying to guide the subject through a focused instrument.

In our experience, flexibility and a certain degree of opportunism are helpful. The interviewer should be prepared to adapt to the scenario and personality at hand, rather than determined to stick robotlike to an established script (see Schaeffer and Maynard, Chapter 28, this volume). If, for example, the interview is conducted in an office where there is artwork displayed, a well-placed compliment on the art can serve as a useful conversational icebreaker. The demeanor of the respondent, whether or not and how he or she greets the interviewer, and even how firm the handshake can reveal the course the interviewer might take in the conversation. The interviewer's intuition is paramount.

Gender also is an issue in many interview exchanges (Gurney 1991; Oakley 1981; Pierce 1995; see also in this volume Schwalbe and Wolkomir, Chapter 10; Reinharz and Chase, Chapter 11). Women interviewers of elite subjects invariably recognize greater pressure to accommodate the prejudices of others, play off their gender, and establish a clearer degree of control. As McDowell (1998) describes it:

> I developed a way of relating to the different respondents that depended on a quick initial assessment of a range of visual and verbal clues and an establishment of a relationship as we progressed through the interview. . . . In some interviews I seemed to fall into the classic male-female pattern, for example with an older charming but rather patriarchal figure I found myself to some extent "playing dumb"; with an older and extremely fierce senior woman I was brusquely efficient . . . with younger men I was superfast, well informed, and definitely not to be patronized. (P. 2138)

Age and reputation, as well as the respect these confer, can create their own dynamics (see Wenger, Chapter 13, this volume). A big age differential, where the researcher is considerably younger than the respondent, can make it difficult for the interviewer to be taken seriously. Conversely, an interviewer who is older than the subject may be able to establish greater authority. In interviewing elites over two decades, Odendahl has noticed changes over time in the reactions of respondents that relate to their respective ages. In retrospect, she now believes that when she was younger many older elite subjects spoke more candidly, possibly because they discounted her capacity to do much with the information. After she had published more critical and widely read accounts about the motivations of philanthropic elites and her reputation grew, subjects seemed to become more guarded in their comments. Still, at the same time, as Odendahl's reputation has grown, her access to elite subjects has increased.

Social status is important to elites. Manifestations of hierarchy and the appearance of exchanges between peers play a part in the interview interchange. During one interview with a CEO of one of the nation's largest foundations, undertaken as part of our diversity research, one of the principal investigators was accompanied by a younger female colleague, whom the CEO apparently assumed to be an assistant or simply a note taker. As the events soon demonstrated, this inadvertently elevated the status of the interviewer in the eyes of the CEO. The interviewer's self-presentation and the presence of an "assistant" served to convey to the CEO that he was talking to an equal, who, like him, had a bevy of subordinates. In fact, the CEO proceeded to make a point of calling in "his" people to make copies and generally assist with administrative tasks throughout the meeting.

Typically, elite respondents want to communicate at some point with the director of the project or some other "known" entity. It is useful, we have found, if the interviewer is not the project's principal investigator, for the interviewer to be accompanied by a peer of the subject, such as a board member or another elite individual. While interviewing individuals on the topic of best practices for grant-making research, Shaw (1997) was fortunate to have a member of a wealthy family on the advisory committee who actually joined her on the research team. This person's presence proved invaluable in establishing rapport and making the interviews less guarded. People, regardless of their status, like to converse with others with whom they feel comfortable.

Having two interviewers present can be helpful in other ways as well. Apart from the obvious logistical advantages, there are situations in which it may be useful for interviewers to play off against each other, to shift ground when the questioning seems to waver or become uncomfortable, and to rely on the interpretations of two minds. Especially if the interview is not being taped, the use of a two-interviewer team allows one person to pose the questions and direct the conversation while the other concentrates on taking notes. These roles can be reversed in the course of the interview.

The issue of psychologically separating the person being interviewed from the institution he or she represents can be especially challenging with elite subjects. Respondents within institutions are likely to present the kinds of statements or promote the kinds of company images developed in conjunction with the organizations' public relations advisers, press departments, and, in some instances, speechwriters. Thomas (1995) recommends that the interviewer pose the issue under discussion in terms that personalize it, putting it in various ways, such as "What do *you* think?" This approach not only supplies a compelling reason for the interviewer to be granted access to the person rather than to one of his or her subordinates, it also has the advantage of differentiating that individual from the institution, thereby circumventing the formalized responses with which people at the top tend to communicate with the press and the public.

For our interviews with foundation CEOs for the diversity study, we adopted a similar strategy. After leading with questions on the institution's approach to diversity, for instance, we asked the CEO, "Are *you* satisfied with the level of staff and board diversity?" and "In *your* experience, what are the best hiring and recruitment practices?" This way, we were able to get beyond the stock organizational answers.

In the course of our work, we have come across many individuals who represent elite institutions yet whose personal or political identities may not reflect the values of those institutions. Usually, the interviewer is unaware of such sentiments in advance of the meeting. These informants may be the best sources, because they yearn to tell the full story. Almost like whistle-blowers who know their identities will not be revealed, alienated or disenchanted informants sometimes air what others consider to be "dirty laundry," information that can shed

considerable light on particular areas of elite activity.

CONFIDENTIALITY

Confidentiality is especially important in the interviewing of high-profile subjects. Many of those interviewed enjoy considerable visibility in their communities and may be readily identifiable even when their names are omitted from published reports. Hence it is important that researchers not disclose personal traits or organizational affiliations through which their respondents could be easily identified. Strategies such as the use of composites in the presentation of findings can help to maintain subjects' anonymity. Odendahl (1990) explains her own use of these strategies:

> This method of presentation [composites and pseudonyms] does not reveal the identities of study participants but allows a closer look at patterns and nuances of beliefs and behavior. The personal features and life experiences are factual and realistic. They have been combined from the accounts of several people who are similar in age and gender . . . and the same generation removed from the families original wealth. At least one and generally several individuals have each of the attributes reported in a composite vignette. They were selected for presentation because of common activities, outlook, and philosophy. I use actual quotations from these people, but in any one composite, several different study participants are quoted with remarks representative of a number of the individuals in the group. Pseudonyms were invented for each of the composite characters. (P. 79)

Some elite respondents do not require confidentiality. Nevertheless, they generally request prior approval of or the opportunity to review any text before the use of their names, references to their organizational affiliations, and any direct quotations can go to press. In the grant-making research best practices study, which involved 92 individuals at 28 organizations, Shaw extricated all references to the institution or individual in the draft report and sent these, along with a release form, to any person being quoted. In many instances, faced with the reality of the material appearing in print, respondents substantially modified their original remarks. In some cases, this necessitated renegotiation of consent between the author and the person interviewed (or that person's supervisor).

◆ Interpretation Beyond Interviews

In this chapter we have focused on the problems associated with and techniques for identifying, gaining access to, and interviewing elites. We have reviewed the sparse methodological literature on the topic and have provided examples from our own experiences in studying philanthropic elites. Our goal has been to provide practical advice to colleagues and students involved in interviewing elites across a broad spectrum of research interests. Although located in a specific privileged community of philanthropic elites, the constraints, barriers, and insights we have encountered are pertinent to the work of any researcher investigating elites.

A theoretical rationale exists for the necessity of incorporating the elite perspective into economic, political, and sociological inquiry. Our perception is based on the assumption that socio-economic or class identities distinguish philanthropic elites from others within their sphere of operation. We have observed that, among elites, those in the upper class are the least investigated by researchers, especially in the United States. The notion of class is often

ignored. Domhoff's latest work is one of the few to look for class indicators in the examination of elites. Perhaps due to the peculiarly American adherence to the ideal of equal access, there is a reticence to name, much less study, elites. Therefore in attempting to document the inner workings of particular communities, sectors or societies, researchers neglect to study those very individuals or groups that are central to or, at a minimum, influence, the functioning of entire structures.

The only way to permeate the workings of any given institution is through an analysis of the power base within. Too often, what appear to be democratic, open, and accessible institutions are revealed to be closed structures operated at the behest of a few individuals. This is particularly true among philanthropic elites. Despite the existence of organizations set up to serve the public good, in the governance and operation of foundations, the idiosyncrasies of the donors are paramount.

In arguing for the importance of inquiry on elites, we would encourage the study of these subjects in relation to other groups in society, especially research concerning how power is exercised in relation to nonelites. Elites should not be studied in isolation from the communities and organizational contexts in which they operate. Interviews with elite subjects at institutions, although informative, may provide only the "top" part of a top-down perspective. It is critical, therefore, that researchers substantiate elite interviews with additional nonelite interviews.

In our current research on diversity on foundation boards and staffs, our interest is in determining how much diversity in race, ethnicity, gender, sexual orientation, and physical ability is represented in foundation administrations and in grant-making patterns. After conducting interviews with several CEOs at foundations with good reputations for diversity, we found that more than half proved to be white men. Based on our conviction that interview findings can be validated only through interviews across institutional structures, which can provide "reality checks" against which to interpret the views of elites, we interviewed additional layers of staff. These interviews offered balance to the original findings as well as furnished the kinds of detailed information, from the perspective of those actually affected by efforts to diversify, that the CEOs were unable to supply. Interestingly, as we probed deeper into the structures of foundations, we found a disconnect between policy and practice. The interviews revealed that despite having in place policies and standards that indicate adherence to high standards of diversity, foundations often do not incorporate such policies and standards into institutional practice.

The term *elite* is closely linked with the operation of power and privilege. Any analysis of elites also depends on broader interpretations of hegemony and society, and on an understanding of the intersection between elites and nonelites, and their respective environments. This calls for elite studies—and interviewing—that are linked with theoretical understandings of power, status, and society.

■ Note

1. The study, which is being conducted by Lynn Burbridge, Bill Diaz, Terry Odendahl, and Aileen Shaw, is titled "The Meaning and Impact of Board and Staff Diversity in the Philanthropic Field."

■ References

Aldrich, N. 1988. *Old Money: The Mythology of America's Upper Class.* New York: Vintage.

Birmingham, S. 1967. *"Our Crowd": The Great Jewish Families of New York.* New York: Harper & Row.

Burgess, R. G. 1991. "Sponsors, Gatekeepers, Members, and Friends: Access in Educational Settings." Pp. 43-52 in *Experiencing Fieldwork: An Inside View of Qualitative Research,* edited by W. B. Shaffir and R. A. Stebbins. Newbury Park, CA: Sage.

Daniels, A. K. 1988. *Invisible Careers: Women Civic Leaders from the Volunteer World.* Chicago: University of Chicago Press.

Domhoff, G. W. 1967. *Who Rules America?* Englewood Cliffs, NJ: Prentice Hall.

———. 1970. *The Higher Circles: The Governing Class in America.* New York: Vintage.

———, ed. 1980. *Power Structure Research.* Beverly Hills, CA: Sage.

———. 1983. *Who Rules America Now? A View for the '80s.* Englewood Cliffs, NJ: Prentice Hall.

Domhoff, G. W. and T. R. Dye, eds. 1987. *Power Elites and Organizations.* Newbury Park, CA: Sage.

Gurney, J. N. 1991. "Female Researchers in Male-Dominated Settings: Implications for Long-Term versus Short-Term Research." Pp. 53-61 in *Experiencing Fieldwork: An Inside View of Qualitative Research,* edited by W. B. Shaffir and R. A. Stebbins. Newbury Park, CA: Sage.

Hertz, R. and J. B. Imber, eds. 1995. *Studying Elites Using Qualitative Methods.* Thousand Oaks, CA: Sage.

Hughes, A. and L. Cormode. 1998. "Guest Editorial: Researching Elites and Elite Spaces." *Environment and Planning A* 30:2098-100.

Hunter, A. 1995. "Local Knowledge and Local Power: Notes on the Ethnography of Local Elites." Pp. 151-70 in *Studying Elites Using Qualitative Methods,* edited by R. Hertz and J. B. Imber. Thousand Oaks, CA: Sage.

Kvale, S. 1996. *InterViews: An Introduction to Qualitative Research Interviewing.* Thousand Oaks, CA, Sage.

Keller, S. 1963. *Beyond the Ruling Class.* New York: Random House.

Lerner, R., A. K. Nagai, and S. Rothman. 1996. *American Elites.* New Haven, CT: Yale University Press.

McDowell, L. 1998. "Elites in the City of London: Some Methodological Considerations." *Environment and Planning A* 30:2133-46.

Marcus, G. E. 1983. " 'Elite' as a Concept, Theory, and Research Tradition." Pp. 7-28 in *Elites: Ethnographic Issues,* edited by G. E. Marcus. Albuquerque: University of New Mexico Press.

Mills, C. W. 1956. *The Power Elite.* New York: Oxford University Press.

Moyser, G. and M. Wagstaffe, eds. 1987a. *Research Methods for Elite Studies.* London: Allen & Unwin.

———. 1987b. "Studying Elites: Theoretical and Methodological Issues." In *Research Methods for Elite Studies,* edited by G. Moyser and M. Wagstaffe. London: Allen & Unwin.

Nadel, S. F. 1956. "The Concept of Social Elites." *International Social Science Bulletin* 8:413-24.

Nader, L. 1972. "Up the Anthropologist: Perspectives Gained from Studying Up." Pp. 284-311 in *Reinventing Anthropology,* edited by D. Hymes. New York: Pantheon.

Oakley, A. 1981. "Interviewing Women: A Contradiction in Terms?" Pp. 30-61 in *Doing Feminist Research,* edited by H. Roberts. London: Routledge & Kegan Paul.

Odendahl, T., ed. 1987. *America's Wealthy and the Future of Foundations.* New York: Foundation Center.

———. 1990. *Charity Begins at Home: Generosity and Self-Interest among the Philanthropic Elite.* New York: Basic Books.

Ostrander, S. 1980. "Upper-Class Women: Class Consciousness as Conduct and Meaning." Pp. 73-96 in *Power Structure Research,* edited by G. W. Domhoff. Beverly Hills, CA: Sage.

———. 1984. *Women of the Upper Class.* Philadelphia: Temple University Press.

———. 1995. " 'Surely You're Not in This Just to Be Helpful': Access, Rapport, and Interviews in Three Studies of Elites." Pp. 133-50 in *Studying Elites Using Qualitative Methods,* edited by R. Hertz and J. B. Imber. Thousand Oaks, CA: Sage.

Pareto, V. 1935. *Mind and Society.* Edited by A. Livingstone. New York: Harcourt, Brace.

Pierce, J. 1995. "Reflections on Fieldwork in a Complex Organization: Lawyers, Ethnographic Authority, and Lethal Weapons." Pp. 94-110 in *Studying Elites Using Qualitative Methods,* edited by R. Hertz and J. B. Imber. Thousand Oaks, CA: Sage.

Putnam, R. 1976. *The Comparative Study of Political Elites.* Englewood Cliffs, NJ: Prentice Hall.

Shaw, A. 1997. *Preserving the Public Trust: A Study of Exemplary Grantmaking Practices in Grantmaking.* San Diego, CA: National Network of Grantmakers.

Thomas, R. 1995. "Interviewing Important People in Big Companies." Pp. 3-18 in *Studying Elites Using Qualitative Methods,* edited by R. Hertz and J. B. Imber. Thousand Oaks, CA: Sage.

Wagstaffe, M. and G. Moyser. 1987. "The Threatened Elite: Studying Leaders in an Urban Community." In *Research Methods for Elite Studies,* edited by G. Moyser and M. Wagstaffe. London: Allen & Unwin.

Zweigenhaft, R. and G. W. Domhoff. 1998. *Diversity in the Power Elite: Have Women and Minorities Reached the Top?* New Haven, CT: Yale University Press.

16

INTERVIEWING THE ILL

◆ Janice M. Morse

Can those who are not ill understand the illness experience? Physicians, who may be considered experts in *disease* processes and who come into daily contact with the sick, may have had little personal experience with being ill. They often are surprised, even shocked, when they find themselves in the role of patient and experience illness from this perspective (Viner 1994). For several hundred years, medicine has very successfully investigated disease causation, processes, and treatments with the goal of curing. Yet, despite their understanding of disease processes, practicing physicians still know little about the human responses to illness. Although they easily identify the manifestation of symptoms, they have limited knowledge, in comparison, of what it is like to live with those symptoms.

Those who are ill often complain that they are poorly understood and that "nobody knows what it is like to be sick." Ris-

ing to this challenge, qualitative researchers have been exploring the illness experience for more than five decades, ever since the classic work of Talcott Parsons (1951, 1975) on the sick role. These researchers now constitute a large and cohesive subgroup of qualitative health researchers, and their modes of inquiry are making an increasingly significant contribution to the knowledge base on health behaviors and responses to illness in the health science disciplines.

My own experience of research with the ill arises from more than two decades of qualitative exploration of health behaviors, such as adolescent responses to menarche, breast-feeding, childbirth, all phases of illness and injury from trauma care to rehabilitation, and care practices such as the removal of restraints from the elderly and the prevention of falls. From this experience and the literature on the illness experience, I take this opportunity to discuss in broad terms what it means to qualitative researchers to engage those who are sick in the interview process.

It is interesting to consider why qualitative health researchers have formed such a specialist subgroup. I would suggest that it is because illness presents extraordinary challenges for the researcher, the heart of which is the interview itself. In order to make this case, I first address the assumptions underlying the qualitative interview and explore how interviewing the ill necessarily violates these assumptions. Next, I discuss various interviewing strategies and researcher suitability. Finally, I offer a concluding comment.

◆ Violating the Usual Assumptions

The researcher's purpose in conducting the qualitative interview is to obtain data that will enable him or her to understand the experience and interpret the everyday world of the respondent and to communicate the respondent's experience, in all its rich detail, to others (see Warren, Chapter 4, this volume). Two assumptions underlie qualitative interviewing: (a) Those interviewed must be familiar with their everyday worlds and can be viewed as experts on the interview's subject matter, and (b) good participants are those who can reflect on and articulate their experiences and describe their everyday worlds (Morse 2000). These two factors enable the researcher to interpret the respondent's experience and to communicate it to others.

When the researcher's participants are the acutely ill or seriously injured, however, these assumptions usually do not apply. The acutely ill are frequently silenced by their disease or injury and muted by their treatments, and can be in shock or in severe pain. The rapidity of the physical and/or mental changes they experience places them in an unfamiliar and often frightening environment—frightening because of the

intensity of pain (Madjar 1998) and the threat to life and self-integrity (Morse 1997). For such persons the nature of reality itself may change, owing to physiological disruption (Estroff 1981) or drug-induced psychosis (see Richman 2000).

SILENCED BY DISEASE

The first principle of qualitative sampling is that the researcher purposefully selects those to be interviewed on the basis of their ability to provide information necessary for the study (Fontana and Frey 1994). Yet when a researcher is interviewing the ill, an entire group of individuals within that category do not fit Spradley's (1979) criteria of a good informant. The ill and the seriously injured are often unable to be interviewed because they have undergone physical changes caused by their illness or injury that inhibit their ability to speak. An individual may have a disease or condition that directly interferes with speech or makes speech impossible, such as Guillain-Barré syndrome, Parkinson's disease, stroke, surgery to the neck, or simply a sore throat (Boss 1991). Even communication at the most basic level can be a challenge with such an individual, but sometimes, with ingenuity, barriers to communication may be overcome. The person may learn to communicate with pencil and paper or by signaling with nods or winks. Such forms of communication can make for tedious and often very poor interviews, but sometimes these techniques can be extended, such as with the use of an alphabet board on which the person can spell words out. With effort, the person who cannot speak may have some means of self-expression restored. Indeed, with the ability to move only one eyelid, Jean-Dominique Bauby (1997) has written a biography of his illness by applying such techniques.

In the case of some psychiatric illnesses, the interview can become an interactionally compromising endeavor. The interviewer's questions may compete with other voices a respondent hears, to which he or she needs to respond. For instance, in her exploration of the experience of discharge from a psychiatric hospital, Beverly Lorencz (1991) found that when interviewing schizophrenic patients, she had to wait sometimes for more than a minute for them to respond to her questions—but eventually responses were forthcoming. Sometimes participants responded verbally to the voices they heard, and Lorencz had to sort out which responses were to her own questions. Of course, the feasibility of a researcher's obtaining information that made sense in an interview with a mentally ill participant would depend on the type and severity of the mental illness itself.

Interviewing becomes nearly impossible when the participant's illness prohibits his or her ability to express thoughts. With Alzheimer's disease, for instance, communication is impeded by the inability of the sufferer to find the correct words. Sentences become muddled and meaning is lost as speech becomes increasingly garbled and incomprehensible (Lee 1991). With advanced Parkinson's disease, the sufferer is unable to articulate words, with the silent stutter of spastic and rigid dysarthria preventing even the formation of speech. In such cases, interviewing as a data collection strategy is not feasible; researchers need to consider other methods for data collection, such as observation and biography.

MUTED BY TREATMENT

When an individual is critically injured, medical treatment takes priority. Interference by the researcher is not possible, even to ask for permission to observe or to ask questions. In certain cases, even if the person could respond, interviewing is out of the question. The patient may be too ill, too breathless, or in too much pain to be disturbed.

Medical treatments may subsequently interfere with an ill person's ability to communicate. Most obviously, if the person is on a respirator, articulation is impossible. A person who has a tracheotomy can speak on expiration and so may be interviewed, but the process is slow and can be quite tiring for the patient (Menzel 1998).

Drugs may interfere with a patient's ability to be interviewed, transforming a potential respondent from an expert on his or her experience to a stranger to it. Sedation can make a patient too drowsy to think clearly about otherwise familiar matters. Drugs can interfere in other ways, too, from changing the person's affect (Estroff 1981) to making his or her mouth dry, so that speech is difficult and uncomfortable. In the latter instance, it is a good idea for the interviewer to be sure that drinking water is handy. Because an individual in such circumstances is likely to have difficulty in articulating and to have a soft voice, later transcription of the tape-recorded interview may be difficult.

STUNNED BY SHOCK AND PAIN

When patients are severely ill or critically injured, they usually experience some type of shock. Particularly in the acute phase, they are in a state of disbelief that what has happened has really taken place. The severity of their pain demands their full attention, and their focus is primarily on maintaining self-control (Morse 1997). They may be focused on their breathing —breathing in and breathing out—or on moving or not moving. They struggle to keep track of treatments, of the time of day, and even of the day of the week (Morse and Carter 1995). Some try to sleep to rid themselves of reality. Then they try to awaken to rid themselves of nightmares, only to find that their nightmares are true, reminding them that the reality of their illness is more frightening than the nightmare itself. Sleep deprivation adds to the risk of a patient's developing psychosis, further inhibiting their ability to communicate.

Such experiences are often new to patients, and, as a result, they do not have the vocabulary to describe them. Some struggle to find words to convey the nature and intensity of their pain, and may use descriptive phrases and comparative statements that are unfamiliar to interviewers. Others simply give up for lack of the ability to make sense of things. For example, in one of my studies, a burn patient remarked, "This pain is too great to even try and describe" (Morse and Carter 1995:41).

The result is that the patient enters a state of enduring the illness and of suppressing emotions. He or she remains present focused, trying to "hold on" and attempting not to lose control. The normal biographical competence of the respondent is on hold. The intense moment-by-moment concern with the present prevents the patient from realizing the future ramifications of the illness or injury and limits reflection on the past and the realization that the healthy body is lost. This state of enduring an illness may be prolonged beyond the most acute phases into the rehabilitation period.

◆ The Chronically Ill and Handicapped

Given all of these difficulties, it is no coincidence that much qualitative research on the ill has been conducted with those who have chronic conditions or who are handicapped. The two assumptions listed earlier do not hold as tenaciously for these individuals as they do for the acutely ill and seriously injured. The onset of chronic illness is not as rapid as the onset of acute illness; indeed, it may be insidiously slow. Time gives sufferers the opportunity to become familiar with and to adapt to their worlds from the perspective of sick or handicapped persons, and they are usually able to reflect on and adapt to their illness.

As a result, the content of interviews with chronically ill and handicapped respondents is different from that of other interviews. These individuals often report in considerable detail the shape of even minor events and daily routines. Indeed, the long-term adaptation experience of the chronically ill and handicapped can make them highly reflective respondents. Many significant qualitative studies of chronic illness have been published, several of which offer influential models based on these particular illness experiences. Among these models are Juliet Corbin and Anselm Strauss's (1998) chronic illness trajectory model; Kathy Charmaz's (1991) constructionist approach, which is presented in her book *Good Days, Bad Days: The Self in Chronic Illness and Time*; the illness constellation model, which I developed with Joy Johnson (Morse and Johnson 1991); and theories of normalization (Thorne and Robinson 1989; Morse, Wilson, and Penrod 2000).

Once the work of rehabilitation begins, the interview process may be a welcome distraction for the patient. Patients begin to endure treatments and learn to live with their disabled bodies (Morse and Carter 1995, 1996). They have the capability to begin to respond emotionally to their changed situation and to understand that their future will be different. In other words, they begin the suffering process. They try to make sense of what happened to them. If they were critically ill or injured and were resuscitated, they seek to find out what happened to them while they were unconscious or semiconscious. They ask relatives or medical staff, "What happened?" "How did I get here?" and "How did I behave?" They may experience flashbacks as they gradually piece together their stories and learn to make sense of their condition.

This is an excellent time to interview such patients. In fact, it is not uncommon for rehabilitating patients to comment that the interview process helped them to piece together what had happened to them. Patients have told me that the experience of being interviewed enabled them to make sense of the overall illness experience. Family members and counselors may hear patients' stories only piecemeal, as their illness progresses bit by bit. But as patients tell their stories in unstructured interviews, they have the opportunity to assess what has happened more fully and to understand it on their own terms. From the researcher's perspective, this is important because these accounts have had a chance to mature, to become fleshed with detail, and to deepen in perspective.

How can retrospective interviews be reliable and valid, when the researcher is interested in a time when the person was overwhelmed with pain and the suddenness of the event, and the drugs make forgetting likely? An important point also is that the process of interviewing itself triggers memories for the participants about the period when they were critically ill. The interviewer should expect the respondent to cry and should be prepared to offer comfort and tissues to wipe the tears. Researchers who are new to interviewing may be afraid to commiserate or to console, for fear that such actions will "contaminate the data" or "lead the participant." Our own experience shows this to be unlikely. The interviewer should respond humanly and kindly when the participant becomes emotional; the interviewer can ask the participant if she or he would like a break and then continue with the interview when the respondent is ready to do so.

The interviewer might also consider alternative means of addressing the respondent, other than the traditional face-to-face, sit-down interview. For example, in one of our studies, a farmer whose son had died volunteered to be interviewed. However, the student who was to interview the farmer reported that he was so overcome with sadness each time he began his story that he could not continue. With some patience, this student managed to conduct the interview. She gave the farmer a lapel microphone, placed the tape recorder in his pocket, and walked with him on his farm while he told his story.

Patients' stories may be supplemented with observational data (Gordon 1980). "Shadowing" or accompanying the respondent on his or her daily rounds can be quite enlightening for the researcher, especially if the respondent casually addresses and comments on what he or she is doing and what it means in the context of illness or injury. If the course of the illness is long, the research design may incorporate both retrospective and prospective interviews, or interviews that focus on special events, such as walking unaided for the first time; particular topics, such as weaning from a respirator; or especially meaningful moments, such as discharge.

◆ The Surrounding World

Patients usually do not experience their illnesses alone. There are many others involved, including caregivers, intimate acquaintances, and friends. There also is the surrounding care environment, including both the home and institutional venues. All play into the interviewing process.

THE CAREGIVER'S WORLD

The literature describing the experiences of caregivers and the significant others of ill or injured patients is now huge and another important source of information about the illness experience (see Brubaker 1987; Abel and Nelson 1990; Gubrium and Sankar 1990; Biegel, Sales, and Schulz 1991). The experiences described include those of professional caregivers, such as physicians and nurses, and those of lay caregivers, such as patients' family members and friends. This important body of research has produced such theoretical constructs as caregiver burden, burnout, and compassion and has distinguished various forms of caring.

The comments and feelings of the others surrounding the seriously ill and dying are important when we consider that the ill individuals are often unable to speak for themselves. Researchers can be left with no option but to collect reports of others' observations of the illness experience. Such reports are necessarily one step removed from data obtained directly through interviews with patients themselves, but they nonetheless offer perspective on illness and can also provide information of which patients themselves are unaware or cannot offer on their own. Observational data can also complement interview data.

Like interviewing the ill, interviewing caregivers and significant others of the ill, and observing their surrounding worlds, can have a trenchant impact on the researcher. Observing pain and suffering may result in a shared response of pain and distress, or the *compathetic* response (Morse, Mitcham, and Van der Steen 1998). This can impede data collection, as the researcher may find him- or herself crying during interviews, being preoccupied by visual disturbances, or unable to sleep. Of course, the researcher's experience is directly affected by the nature of the illness and the relationship between the caregiver and the ill person, which can bring things closer emotionally or distance the researcher from the illness experience, as the case might be.

INSTITUTIONAL CONTEXT

Qualitative health research has explored both the health care institution as a whole and the ward as the unit of analysis. This broadens research topics from the individual's or family member's experience of the illness to the interactions and the groups involved. Much of this kind of research combines interviewing with participant observation.

When conducting ethnography, the researcher may use unstructured interviews and include them in the final report as case or life histories. When interviews are combined with observation, the pacing of the interviews and the questions asked can be quite different from individual interviews. Rather than focusing on attitudes or beliefs, the ethnographic interviewer commonly converses casually with the respondent as he or she goes about daily tasks. The purpose of ethnography is to describe the culture, the milieu, or "what is going on" rather than the experience of a sample of individuals over time.

When ethnographers are new to a social setting, they must observe and learn the ropes. In this case, interviews as such tend to come about later in the data gathering, with the researcher moving toward interviewing as he or she becomes a part of the scene (Spradley 1979; Agar 1996). Initially, the researcher employs very casual interviewing to learn quickly about the processes or mechanics of the setting. In time, the researcher works toward eliciting knowledge of more subtle patterns of experience, at which point the interviewing typically grows more structured (see Johnson and Weller, Chapter 24, this volume).

Special difficulties are associated with conducting interviews in hospital units. If the patient is bed-bound and shares the room with another person, it is virtually impossible for the participants to obtain the privacy necessary for an individual interview. In such a case, the interviewer can ask hospital staff whether it might be possible to gain some privacy by moving one of the patients temporarily. If the interviewee is able to get about using a wheelchair or can walk, the interviewer may be able to find a quiet office in which to conduct the interview. Of course, he or she should be certain to tell the patient's nurse or ward clerk where the patient will be, in case treatments need to be administered. Sensitive tape recorders can pick up all of the background noises typical of the hospital ward, including the sounds of television sets, the white noise of air conditioners, and the ward's general clatter. To obtain as clear a recording as possible, the interviewer should try to remove or steer clear of such noises.

Examples of ethnographies of institutions that combine participant observation with interviewing the ill are Jaber Gubrium's *Living and Dying at Murray Manor* (1975, 1997), Jeanie Kayser-Jones's *Old, Alone, and Neglected* (1990), Carol Germain's *The Cancer Ward* (1979), and Lorna Rhodes's *Emptying Beds* (1995). Examples of grounded theories (see Charmaz, Chapter 32, this volume) of institutional care, where interviewing serves the purpose of continuous theory formation, are reported in Anselm Strauss et al.'s *Chronic Illness and the Quality of Life* (1984) and Sally Hutchinson's "Creating Meaning Out of Horror" (1984). All of these studies are oriented to the surrounding, institutionalized care environment as an important factor in the illness experience.

There can be numerous gatekeepers between the hospitalized patient and the researcher. Because health care institutions are responsible for protecting their patients' privacy, research may not be conducted in hospitals or nursing homes without institutional permission. Thus, in addition to ethical clearance from his or her university, a researcher must receive administrative clearance from the institution in which he or she wants to conduct a study. There is also the matter of obtaining ethical clearance in the institutional venue itself. Ethical approval is required because the institution is responsible for patients' lives and well-being, and administrative approval is needed because the administration must ensure that the staff and patients can take the time to accommodate the needs of the researcher.

When first entering a hospital to begin data collection, the researcher should always confirm his or her appointment with the staff. They will then assist the researcher in identifying patients who may be willing to participate in the study. If staff members know what time the researcher will be coming to see a given patient, they will often attempt to get the patient's care completed before then and check with the patient's visitors so that they can arrange their schedule around the interview, or vice versa.

How does a researcher go about "fitting in" when interviewing in a hospital? Once at the unit, the researcher should check in with the head nurse and the patient's primary nurse, so that they are aware of the researcher's presence and the need to respect the privacy of researcher and patient during the interview. In the hospital, managing interruptions may be difficult, especially if the patient is in a shared room and cannot be moved to a more private area for the interview. If possible, the researcher might place a do-not-disturb sign on the patient's door to warn others that an interview is in progress. Nevertheless, such measures may only be temporary, as interruptions may be necessary at any time for medical attention. The researcher needs to bear in mind that medical personnel have priority. They may approach the patient at any time to assess his or her condition. Nursing staff may enter to provide essential treatments, but cleaning staff may respect the do-not-disturb sign and return later. In clinical areas, the researcher should use batteries to run the tape recorder rather than connecting to the electrical main, because there are standards regulating the use of electrical equipment in hospitals. During the interview, the researcher should observe the patient's condition and offer to stop the interview if he or she appears tired. Several shorter interviews may be necessary under such regularly intrusive institutional conditions.

◆ Interviewing Strategies

What do patients who are enduring pain and suffering look like? When being interviewed, their faces are without expression and appear wooden, they barely move their lips to speak, and they commonly communicate in a monotone. They are present focused, using the present tense when talking. If asked about past events, they typically give brief responses, presenting brief facts in expressionless voices.

How does a person who is enduring illness respond during an interview? In my own research exploring the experience of trauma, we planned to interview patients on discharge from the intensive care unit and admitted to the general surgical floors. At the time, patient after patient responded to questions in monosyllables, presenting rote accounts of what had happened to them in monotones, devoid of expression. This information was of no more use to us than reading a police report or a hospital chart. So we changed strategies and waited to interview each person until he or she had moved into rehabilitation, approximately six months after injury. By that time the person was able to articulate reflections on his or her suffering, and the interviews were all as we had hoped for, richly experiential (Morse 2000).

The observation that the quality of the interview changes with the stage of illness has important ramifications for research practice. It means that if the researcher plans to learn what the experience is like for patients or ill persons, he or she must conduct the interviews when those experiencing illness are able to comprehend and successfully communicate what has happened and is happening to them. An effective way of collecting these data is to conduct unstructured, retrospective interviews some time after the acute event.

UNSTRUCTURED INTERVIEWING

The unstructured interview is a research strategy that permits the persons being interviewed to tell their stories at their own pace, in their own ways, and within their own time frames (see in this volume Warren, Chapter 4; Johnson, Chapter 5; Atkinson, Chapter 6). When setting up the appointment for the interview, the researcher informs the interviewee about the purpose of the interview, how long it will take, and that the interview will be tape-recorded. The researcher tells the respondent that when the interview is completed it will be transcribed word for word, and that some of what the respondent has said

may appear in articles, but that all respondents' individual identities will be protected. If the researcher has not already mailed a copy of the consent form to the participant, he or she may give the form to the participant at this point to read and consider.

The course of an unstructured interview is commonly retrospective, and responses are often conveyed in linear form. The interviewer typically begins simply by asking the person to "tell me about . . . ." Occasionally, if the interviewee asks, "Where should I begin?" the interviewer might reply, "Tell me from the beginning" or "Wherever you wish" (Morse and Johnson 1991). In turn, the story of an illness is typically delineated with a distinctive beginning, middle, and end. The person conveys his or her account as one thread, weaving all of the associated events that are relevant into a sequential tale.

The respondent may start tentatively, providing some contextual details, but then quickly become engrossed in the story (see Mishler 1986). The person's gaze may become unfocused as he or she relives the experience. Respondents often cry, and many laugh, as they recount what happened to them, as the interview process brings forth the emotions they endured in the period under consideration (Gordon 1980). As they bring their stories up to date, respondents may convey a sense of relief or completeness. Indeed, it is not uncommon for respondents to report that they never before had the opportunity to tell their stories in their entirety, or to reflect on their experiences all at once, and that the opportunity to do so has provided them with a genuine sense of satisfaction or closure (see in this volume Johnson, Chapter 5; Atkinson, Chapter 6). Interviews often end with light-hearted small talk about irrelevant things. Although some ethical review committees may require that a stand-by counseling service be available for respondents who may become distraught, in the 20 years I have been conducting such interviews I have never found such a referral necessary.

Rather, commonly, the opposite is true. As one participant told me, "I had expected to cry, but I had not expected it to be fun!"

During the interview, the researcher assumes a stance of active listening. Few formal questions are presented in interviewing of this kind; other than possibly asking a participant to clarify certain points, the interviewer asks very little, so that the participant can tell his or her story with minimal interruption. Instead of asking questions immediately at pertinent points during the interview, the interviewer may "stack" questions at the back of his or her mind to ask when the story is completed. If the interview becomes too long, the interviewer may ask the participant to come back for a second or even a third time (see McCracken 1988). The interviewer may use such second and third interviews to ask probing questions or to obtain additional details or ancillary accounts.

Ancillary accounts are accounts that are not central to the interviewee's main story line. For example, such an account may refer to how the interviewee/patient perceived his wife's ability to cope or the responses of other patients. Sometimes a respondent comes to what I call a "critical juncture" and elects to tell one "branch" of the story (Morse and Johnson 1991). At the end of the interview or during a second interview, the researcher may take the participant back to the critical juncture by asking, for instance, "Remember when you said that one of your kids responded by clinging to you whenever he visited? Can you tell me how the others responded?"

The course of the interview may take different paths. Occasionally, the story line will have a loop, with the respondent diverting to a side story and then coming back to the main story exactly where he or she left off. Some respondents will present their stories in several parallel accounts. For instance, a respondent may first give the "medical story," relating information about doctor visits, tests, medications, and surgeries from the beginning of the illness up to the present. Next, he or she may re-late the "illness story," reporting from the beginning to the present time how he or she felt about and responded to being sick, how it affected his or her life. This may be followed by the "family's story," an account that describes what happened to the ill person's family. Alternatively, the participant may tell the story in a comparative fashion, constantly weighing and linking the acute phase of illness to the present convalescent period or to the period of time before the illness, providing a comparison of health status before and after the onset of the disease or injury.

The risks of conducting unstructured interactive interviews with those who have been critically ill or injured are minimal, and the guidelines of the U.S. Public Health Service allow expedited review for such research. In Canada and Britain, however, many institutional review boards require full review. Committees are concerned that distress arising from interviewing or any associated depression may overwhelm the patient and result in the need for counseling or psychiatric help. But such incidents are undocumented; there is a need for a survey of ethical review committees and researchers to determine the incidence of such untoward effects of the interview process.

THE STRUCTURED INTERVIEW

Researchers use structured interviews when they already have considerable knowledge about the research topic but need further information in specific areas. Research using structured questionnaires differs from research using an unstructured approach in the following ways: (a) The questionnaire is prepared before data collection commences and does not change during data collection, (b) all participants are asked the same questions in the same order, and (c) data are not collected and analyzed simultaneously but are analyzed all at once at the end of data collection (see Singleton and Straits, Chapter 3, this volume).

The data collected through structured interviews are often not as rich and as in-depth as data collected using unstructured interviews. Structured interviewing also requires larger samples, often including dozens or even hundreds of participants. When studying individuals in a particular disease category, researchers can use semistructured interviews only when the disease is sufficiently commonplace or when participants can be readily identified by means of well-known characteristics of the illness or injury.

Researchers have found that the key to using more structured forms of interviewing is to develop questions that will elicit fairly descriptive responses and to provide interviewees with adequate time to react completely to the often detailed response options presented. Explicit probes are important and may be prepared beforehand and printed on the interview schedule or questionnaire. Questionnaires may be administered by interviewers, with the interviews tape-recorded and transcribed, or they may be mailed to respondents, who then provide the answers in writing and return the questionnaires by mail.

SUPPLEMENTARY DATA

Both unstructured and structured interview data may be supplemented by published autobiographical accounts of illness from secondary sources (for example, see Ellis 1995; Frank 1991; Lear 1980). Some of the most useful of these have been written from the perspective of the patient (see, in addition, Grealy 1994; Kaysen 1993; Murphy 1990; Olson 1993). There is also helpful information available in the form of illness narratives presented from the perspectives of significant others, who are often also caregivers (see, for instance, Baier and Schomaker 1986; Lear 1980; Peabody 1986).

Such sources differ from interview data in several ways. They can be more detailed than individual interview data. They can present more of a "public face" for the indi-

vidual in question, with the more personal and private aspects of illness omitted. Interview data are sometimes criticized because respondents may tell interviewers only what they want the interviewers to know; this criticism may be even more valid when applied to published autobiographical accounts. Published accounts are more public than interview data in that they are not typically published anonymously. This autobiographical information can be an important source of research inspiration because it is often highly reflective. As such, it can offer rich insights and suggest new and intriguing directions for interview research.

RESEARCHER SUITABILITY

Given the stressful nature of communicating with the ill and the problems of institutional access and hospital protocol, who is best suited to conduct research on the ill? Should the researcher belong to the health care professions, or can illness research be adequately conducted by a researcher with general social science training?

In my view, there is much room in this field for both types of researchers. Both bring important procedural perspectives and their own theoretical understanding (see Thorne 2000). Nonnurse and nonphysician social science researchers bring psychological, sociological, and cultural frameworks to bear that can differ significantly from the ameliorative and therapeutic focus of nurses and physicians. They can have contrasting research agendas and draw different conclusions from their work. All of this can be useful for uncovering the complex character of what it means to be ill.

Moreover, who should conduct the interviews in such research? If the interviewing duties are not undertaken by the researcher, they should be assigned to a trained assistant—one who is mature enough to handle the painful nature of the interview content and, if necessary, console participants. Similarly, the persons who transcribe the interviews should be understanding and should be given the opportunity to debrief following their work (Gregory, Russell, and Phillips 1997). It is the responsibility of the principal investigator, along with the rest of the team, to monitor and support all team members in what can be a very difficult, but rewarding research experience.

◆ Conclusion

Interviewing the critically and chronically ill and the severely injured presents unique challenges for the qualitative researcher. As I have noted above, the assumptions inherent in qualitative inquiry do not necessarily hold for research with this population, and this presents unique problems. Researchers may overcome many of these problems with forethought and training. For example, the quality of the data gathered can be improved through the use of retrospective rather than prospective interviews. At the end of the day, however, interviewing these distinctive respondents is much like interviewing the members of any vulnerable population—it requires a combination of good research practice and special attention to the human characteristics and frailties of the participants in question.

■ References

Abel, E. K. and M. K. Nelson. 1990. *Circles of Care: Work and Identity in Women's Lives.* Albany: State University of New York Press.

Agar, M. H. 1996. *The Professional Stranger: An Informal Introduction to Ethnography.* 2d ed. San Diego, CA: Academic Press.

Baier, S. and M. Z. Schomaker. 1986. *Bed Number Ten.* Boca Raton, FL: CRC.

Bauby, J.-D. 1997. *The Diving Bell and the Butterfly: A Memoir of Life in Death.* Translated by J. Leggatt. New York: Random House.

Biegel, D. E., E. Sales, and R. Schulz. 1991. *Family Caregiving in Chronic Illness.* Newbury Park, CA: Sage.

Boss, B. J. 1991. "Managing Communication Disorders in Stroke." *Nursing Clinics of North America* 26:985-96.

Brubaker, T. H., ed. 1987. *Aging, Health, and Family: Long-Term Care.* Newbury Park, CA: Sage.

Charmaz, K. 1991. *Good Days, Bad Days: The Self in Chronic Illness and Time.* New Brunswick, NJ: Rutgers University Press.

Corbin, J. and Strauss, A. L. 1998. "Illness Trajectory Model: An Update." *Scholarly Inquiry for Nursing Practice* 12(1):33-41.

Ellis, C. 1995. *Final Negotiations: A Story of Love, Loss, and Chronic Illness.* Philadelphia: Temple University Press.

Estroff, S. E. 1981. *Making It Crazy: Ethnography of Psychiatric Clients in an American Community.* Berkeley: University of California Press.

Fontana, A. and J. H. Frey. 1994. "Interviewing: The Art of Science." Pp. 361-76 in *Handbook of Qualitative Research,* edited by N. K. Denzin and Y. S. Lincoln. Thousand Oaks, CA: Sage.

Frank, A. W. 1991. *At the Will of the Body: Reflections on Illness.* Boston: Houghton Mifflin.

Germain, C. 1979. *The Cancer Ward: Ethnography.* Wakefield, MA: Nursing Resources.

Gordon, R. L. 1980. *Interviewing Strategy, Techniques, and Tactics.* Homewood, IL: Dorsey.

Grealy, L. 1994. *Autobiography of a Face.* Boston: Houghton Mifflin.

Gregory, D., C. K. Russell, and L. R. Phillips. 1997. "Beyond Textual Perfection: Transcribers as Vulnerable Persons." *Qualitative Health Research* 7:294-300.

Gubrium. J. F. 1975. *Living and Dying at Murray Manor.* New York: St. Martin's.

———. 1997. *Living and Dying at Murray Manor.* Expanded ed. Charlottesville: University Press of Virginia.

Gubrium, J. F. and A. Sankar, eds. 1990. *The Home Care Experience: Ethnography and Policy.* Newbury Park, CA: Sage.

Hutchinson, S. 1984. "Creating Meaning Out of Horror." *Nursing Outlook* 32(2):86-90.

Kaysen, S. 1993. *Girl, Interrupted.* New York: Vintage.

Kayser-Jones, J. S. 1990. *Old, Alone, and Neglected: Care of the Aged in Scotland and the United States.* Berkeley: University of California Press.

Lear, M. W. 1980. *Heartsounds.* New York: Simon & Schuster.

Lee, V. K. 1991. "Language Changes and Alzheimer's Disease: A Literature Review." *Journal of Gerontological Nursing* 17(1):16-20.

Lorencz, B. 1991. "Becoming Ordinary: Leaving the Psychiatric Hospital." Pp. 140-200 in *The Illness Experience: Dimensions of Suffering,* edited by J. M. Morse & J. L. Johnson. Newbury Park, CA: Sage.

Madjar, I. 1998. *Giving Comfort and Inflicting Pain.* Edmonton, Alberta: Qual Institute Press.

McCracken, G. 1988. *The Long Interview.* Newbury Park, CA: Sage.

Menzel, L. 1998. "Factors Related to the Emotional Responses of Intubated Patients Being Unable to Speak." *Journal of Acute Critical Care* 27(4):245-52.

Mishler, E. G. 1986. *Research Interviewing: Context and Narrative.* Cambridge, MA: Harvard University Press.

Morse, J. M. 1997. "Responding to Threats to Integrity of Self." *Advances in Nursing Science* 19(4):21-36.

———. 2000. "Researching Illness and Injury: Methodological Considerations." *Qualitative Health Research* 10(5).

Morse, J. M. and B. J. Carter. 1995. "Strategies of Enduring and the Suffering of Loss: Modes of Comfort Used by a Resilient Survivor." *Holistic Nursing Practice* 9(3):33-58.

———. 1996. "The Essence of Enduring and the Expression of Suffering: The Reformulation of Self." *Scholarly Inquiry for Nursing Practice* 10(1):43-60.

Morse, J. M. and J. L. Johnson. 1991. "Toward a Theory of Illness: The Illness Constellation Model." Pp. 315-42 in *The Illness Experience: Dimensions of Suffering,* edited by J. M. Morse and J. L. Johnson. Newbury Park, CA: Sage.

Morse, J. M., C. Mitcham, and V. Van der Steen. 1998. "Compathy or Physical Empathy: Implications for the Caregiver Relationship." *Journal of Medical Humanities* 19(1):51-65.

Morse, J. M., S. Wilson, and J. Penrod. 2000. "Mothers and Their Disabled Children: Refining the Concept of Normalization." *Health Care for Women International* 21(8):659-76.

Murphy, R. F. 1990. *The Body Silent.* New York: Norton.

Olson, C. T. 1993. *The Life of Illness: One Woman's Journey.* Albany: State University of New York Press.

Parsons, T. 1951. "Illness and the Role of the Physician." *American Journal of Orthopsychiatry* 21:452-60.

———. 1975. "The Sick Role and the Role of the Physician Reconsidered." *Milbank Memorial Fund, Health and Society* 53:257-78.

Peabody, B. 1986. *The Screaming Room: A Mother's Journal of Her Son's Struggle with AIDS—A True Story of Love, Dedication, and Courage.* New York: Avon.

Rhodes, L. A. 1995. *Emptying Beds: The Work of an Emergency Psychiatric Unit.* Berkeley: University of California Press.

Richman, J. 2000. "Coming Out of Intensive Care Crazy: Dreams of Affliction." *Qualitative Health Research* 10:84-102.

Spradley, J. P. 1979. *The Ethnographic Interview.* New York: Holt, Rinehart & Winston.

Strauss, A. L., J. Corbin, S. Fagerhaugh, B. G. Glaser, D. Maines, B. Suczek, and C. L. Wiener. 1984. *Chronic Illness and the Quality of Life.* St. Louis, MO: C. V. Mosby.

Thorne, S. 2000. "Angle of Vision: The Impact of Disciplinary Perspective on Qualitative Interpretation." Keynote address presented at the Sixth Qualitative Health Research Conference, Banff, Alberta.

Thorne, S. and C. Robinson. 1989. "Guarded Alliance: Health Care Relationships in Chronic Illness." *Image: Journal of Nursing Scholarship* 21:153-57.

Viner, E. D. 1994. "A Physician's Personal Experience of Critical Illness." *Trends in Health Care, Law and Ethics* 9(2):42-45.

Part III

AUSPICES OF INTERVIEWING

"How-to" books for academically oriented readers take for granted that interviewing is conducted under the auspices of social research. Discussions of the preliminaries to survey interviewing—for example, issues of concept development and hypothesis formation, sampling design, interviewer training, and interviewer-respondent rapport—are presented with the assumption that research matters are at stake. Theoretical concerns may frame the significance of forthcoming responses, in which case results are discussed in terms of what they tell researchers about existing conceptualizations or new understandings. At the very least, research guidelines are concerned with what generalizations are justified in particular circumstances. They offer advice for interviewer training that centers on the twin goals of being objective and being facilitative. The interviewer's job is to elicit factual, unbiased responses from interviewees, who have given their informed consent to be approached in this way.

More qualitatively oriented how-to books carry a version of the same message. In this case, advice usually centers on the sole researcher/interviewer, because much qualitative interviewing is undertaken by the researcher him- or herself. Samples are almost always smaller than in survey interviewing and, although the goal of seeking unbiased responses prevails, the methods by which this is accomplished can differ considerably. The facilitative function, for example, can overshadow the objective one, the idea being that mutually engrossing interactions between interview participants are more likely than reserved interactions to encourage "richly textured" responses.

Across the board, research guidelines pay little or no attention to the particular auspices or institutional sponsorship of research interviewing. They are virtually blind to the fact that the interview at the heart of their concerns is being done for research purposes and not for some other

end. But what if the auspices change, so that interviewing is conducted for some other purpose, under different sponsorship? What can we learn by comparing research interviews to interviews conducted for other reasons?

Today, many kinds of interviewing—formal and recognizable interpersonal inquiry between strangers—are being done under diverse auspices, with myriad alternative goals. Some of these kinds of interviewing, such as medical interviewing (see Zoppi and Epstein, Chapter 18, this volume) and forensic investigative interviewing (see McKenzie, Chapter 21, this volume), are much older than the research interview, having been conducted for centuries. Indeed, in the burgeoning interview society, myriad institutions and going concerns have, for many years, sponsored all manner of interview activities. From television talk shows, market-oriented focus groups, and journalistic interviews to therapeutic encounters, medical history taking, and job interviews, interviewing now has more varied sponsors and purposes than ever before.

It is instructive to consider how auspices shape the procedural considerations and normative dimensions highlighted in research-oriented texts. The issue of whether the procedural strictures of interviewing are as much artifacts of their auspices as they are general methodological warrants is a significant one. For example, the securing of informed consent of the interviewed, which might now seem to be virtually sacred in the context of research interviewing, has been historically trivial for forensic investigative interviewing. As Ian McKenzie points out in his chapter in this section, the "third degree" once was the option of choice when "consent" was not forthcoming. But as McKenzie also explains, there have been recent convergences with informed consent ideals in this area. The U.S. Supreme Court's *Miranda* ruling, which led to the common police practice of reading crime suspects their rights before interviewing them, was inspired by concern regarding the violation of suspects' due process rights, given the belief that a person is "innocent until proven guilty." Similarly, a growing public debate in both the United States and the United Kingdom over police brutality and investigatory excess has led to various humanizing efforts in forensic interviewing. McKenzie notes that, based on the evidence, investigative interviews that are governed more by the aims of objectivity and facilitation—which are standard research aims—are less likely to produce errors in testimony than are those conducted with force. Clearly, the institutional auspices surrounding such interviewing, along with changing public sentiments bearing on forensic investigation, have affected what it means to conduct proper investigative interviewing.

Although research "how-to" books do not usually consider the possibility that research interviews may be subject to the same institutional effects and public sentiments, we might return to the early decades of research interviewing for a contrasting view. As we have noted in Chapter 1, early in the history of interviewing, those individuals whose experience was under consideration were not always considered to be ideal respondents; rather, those who were believed to have expert knowledge in the particular area were often the respondents of choice. More recent history is also instructive. Requirements for informed consent, which developed largely in relation to ethical issues surrounding medical intervention and experimentation, have spread into all research areas involving human subjects. But the question remains: Who in this process benefits most, the researcher or the researched? It has been suggested that the institutionalization of the informed consent process and its resulting perfunctory application can reduce the concern for the research subject below levels that existed when professional ethics and the subject's well-being were the watchdogs (see Adler and Adler, Chapter 25, this volume).

When we consider auspices broadly, many of the how-to manuals that we are accustomed to reading with research interviewing in mind appear in a different light. We begin to take into consideration the possibility that interview methodology is *institutionally* rationalized, not subject to universal application or evaluation. As the leading theme of this *Handbook* would suggest, methodology is part of society, not just a procedure for learning about society. A comparison of auspices suggests the possibility that the institutional sponsors and going concerns that engage in interviewing construct the interview participants they need to do their work at the same time that they gather "facts" pertinent to the participants' particular activities. Whether it is a research or nonresearch context, the enterprise that sponsors the gathering of institutionally pertinent facts simultaneously *constructs* facts that are ostensibly attributed to, say, respondents, job seekers, patients, suspects, and celebrities, among the wide range of interviewees that we encounter today.

Limiting the consideration of interview methodology to research auspices can shortchange potentially useful procedural possibilities, which is reason enough to compare auspices. Take the interests of the respondent in the interview process, for example. Research "how-to" books pay little attention to the respondent's interests, other than to offer advice about how to legitimate the research or how to otherwise enlist the respondent's cooperation. As Roger Shuy suggests in Chapter 26 of this volume, researchers have not seriously addressed the question of what respondents themselves might want to get out of interviews. To be sure, qualitative researchers especially have debated the issue of what the interviewer eventually comes to owe his or her subjects, which is often a natural outcome of the intimate acquaintanceship spawned in this form of interviewing (see in this volume Warren, Chapter 4; Johnson, Chapter 5; Wenger, Chapter 13; Richardson, Chapter 42), but this has not led to the rationalization of respondent interest, as it has, say, in the job interview. Countless "how-to" books are now available that inform job applicants about ways of successfully navigating job interviews—this stands as a counterweight to research on how the employer can complete unbiased interviews (see Latham and Millman, Chapter 23, this volume). The comparison of auspices allows us to consider what might alternatively be possible in a research context.

17

CROSS-CULTURAL INTERVIEWING

◆ Anne Ryen

In recent decades there has been vast growth in cross-cultural studies, one indication of which has been the increasing numbers of publications in the area. Close to 40 percent of all cross-cultural studies published to date were published in the 1980s; 75 percent were published in the 1970s and 1980s combined. The trend will undoubtedly continue in the new millennium, propelled by the globalization of capital and business and by huge leaps in cross-cultural communication and negotiations (Tse and Francis 1994; Habib 1987; Shenkar and Zeira 1990; Bilbow 1996). This has resulted in a rapid increase in new research periodicals; topics centered on cross-cultural studies are now covered by close to 80 journals (Ember and Levinson 1991).

Accompanying this growth, researchers have pointed to the methodological diffi-

culties of transporting experiential data across cultures. Field-workers have been faced with such perennial problems as understanding local nuances in the languages and cultures of their respondents (Deutscher 1968; Wax 1960) and the difficulties associated with using interpreters (Freeman 1983; Berreman 1962). Researchers have had constant personal reminders that in the eyes of those they study, the role of researcher is not always the most salient one for them. As a bachelor in India, M. N. Srinivas (1979) found that the Indian villagers he studied went out of their way to look for a bride for him; they were as much concerned for his welfare as he was with understanding their lives. British African researcher Kate Crehan (1991) found that because she was perceived as foreign in Zambian society, the villagers she studied coped with her unmarried status by assign-

AUTHOR'S NOTE: My grateful thanks to David Silverman, department colleagues, the two *Handbook* reviewers, and the editors, who all read and commented on an earlier draft of this chapter. I would also like to thank the Norwegian Research Council for funding.

ing her a "functional male" role. This role was denied her when she was doing fieldwork among "her own" people in Britain, where she was seen as indigenous and needed to deal with related limited female rights and responsibilities. The "insider-outsider" problem of doing cross-cultural research clearly reverberates in many directions.

Although these challenges are particularly prevalent in participant observation studies, a substantial amount of data collected in such studies come from interviewing in the field (Lofland 1971). It is this particular aspect of cross-cultural research that is the focus of this chapter. Although cross-cultural interviewing is often combined with other methodologies (see Spradley 1979), in this chapter I will focus on the communicative challenges of interviewing as it is mediated by the relation between interviewer and interviewee, who in the case of cross-cultural encounters often inhabit vastly different worlds or engage each other with sharply contrasting aims.

Traditionally, *cross-cultural interviewing* refers to the collection of interview data across cultural and national borders. However, there are many research examples that show this to be too narrow a delimitation. Several fieldwork reports describe insider-outsider challenges faced by researchers conducting ethnic interviews within their own societies (Warren 1977; Montero 1977). Even indigenous researchers studying their own people in societies with class, ethnic, and sectarian divisions have reported challenges arising from the insider-outsider problem, among them Jharna Nath (1991) from her fieldwork in Bangladesh, S. Kamil (1991) in Pakistan, Masliana Bangun (1991) in Indonesia, Anne Abeyewardene (1991) in Sri Lanka and Minako, and M. Kurokawa Maykovich in the United States and Canada (1977). Such challenges have also been found in studies where researchers have conducted interviews with fellow ethnics who constitute minorities within larger societies, such as Constantinos Phellas's (2000) in-depth in-terview study of male Anglo-Cypriot residents in London and Kalivant Bhopal's (2000) research involving interviews with South Asian women in East London. In many ways, the insider-outsider problem is generic to all forms of interviewing conducted under the auspices of cultural difference, whether ethnicity or culture writ large mediates the relation between interviewer and interviewee.

Much of the literature dealing with the insider-outsider problem rests on naturalistic assumptions about culture and communication (see Gubrium and Holstein 1997). These assumptions both positively inform the methodological literature in the area, especially as it bears on interviewing, and, in their deconstruction, present the opportunity for research to move in a different direction. The argument here is that the naturalistic assumptions pose insider-outsider challenges because of how culture and communication are viewed as a nexus for interviewing.

The naturalistic view is characterized by a belief that, in principle, social reality is transparent in people's words and actions. Given that the researcher follows certain technical guidelines in the interviewing, he or she is assumed to have access to data reflecting this transparent reality.[1] The data are regarded as preproduced, culturally stored, and independent of the interviewer-interviewee relationship. The challenge, then, is first to get the interviewee to cooperate and then to get hold of the data in the form they are stored in the interviewee's cultural reservoir (see Gubrium and Holstein, Chapter 1, this volume). The large share of literature on cross-cultural interviewing is thus informed, the methodological imperatives of which move in the direction of overcoming the communicative hurdles put in place by cultural differences. This firm belief in a preexisting cultural reality is the epistemological basis for the demand that the researcher catch or grasp that reality as closely as possible to the way the interviewee does.

◆ Communicative Challenges

The naturalistic challenges of cross-cultural interviewing are usually presented as problems of communication. Both nonverbal and verbal challenges have been identified that relate to the problems of maintaining rapport between interviewer and interviewee.

ESTABLISHING AND MAINTAINING RAPPORT

Textbooks on fieldwork and interviews all stress the importance of interviewers' establishing good relations in the field in general and with interviewees in particular. As Steinar Kvale (1996) points out: "In a research setting it is up to the interviewer to create in a short time a contact that allows the interaction to get beyond merely a polite conversation or exchange of ideas. The interviewer must establish an atmosphere in which the subject feels safe enough to talk freely about his or her experiences and feelings" (p. 125). The interviewer's ability to develop trust and rapport and establish relationships with interviewees facilitates valid data collection. The challenge for the researcher is to make staying in the field and keeping the good relations already established acceptable to those being studied. A common recommendation to researchers is that they should "gain the trust of the community by openness and frankness; participate in community activities whilst retaining an independent stance on local controversies and disputes" (Casley and Lury 1987:69).

In traditional studies using in-depth interviews, the research is dependent on the researcher's establishing relationships that allow him or her to get access to the respondents' own perspectives, and this is not necessarily quickly achieved (see Johnson, Chapter 5, this volume). The problem is exacerbated in cross-cultural studies. Indeed, the researcher is often quickly reminded that confirmed rapport with a group of interviewees or with particular persons is a necessity to valid cultural understanding. Rapport, however, is the outcome of communication and is not established once and forever. Rather, and especially in cross-cultural contexts, it is mediated by the complex external and internal ingredients of day-to-day involvement. In research situations that often entail researchers' staying for extended periods in cultures other than their own, the importance of rapport cannot be overestimated. If researcher and subjects have established good rapport, subjects will be cooperative and will have enough confidence in the researcher to pass on information about themselves ranging from the details of daily life to sensitive matters (Shaffir 1991; Dean, Eichhorn, and Dean 1969; Wax 1971). The cross-cultural researcher will also learn that the roles available or enacted, which are sometimes quite vague at the start, develop as the project unfolds. Especially in "noninterview societies" (see Atkinson and Silverman 1997), researchers often need to work out their roles in the very process of conducting the research, as the work by Srinivas (1979) and Crehan (1991) mentioned above suggests.

Alternatively, field data can be regarded as "constructs of the process by which we acquire them" (Rabinow 1977:xi). In Paul Rabinow's (1977) reflections on the relationship between the informant and the anthropologist, or the insider and the outsider, in his own fieldwork in Morocco, he says:

> This highlighting, identification, and analysis also disturbed Ali's [an informant] usual patterns of experience. He was constantly being forced to reflect on his own activities and objectify them. Because he was a good informant, he seemed to enjoy this process and soon began to develop an art of presenting his world to me. The better he became at it, the more we shared together. But the more we engaged in

such activity, the more he experienced aspects of his own life in new ways. Under my systematic questioning, Ali was taking realms of his own world and interpreting them for an outsider. This meant that he, too, was spending more time in this liminal, self-conscious world between cultures. (P. 38).

Rabinow later adds, "Things become more secure as this liminal world is mutually constructed but, by definition, it never really loses its quality of externality" (p. 153). From this perspective, fieldwork and interviewing are parts of a constantly developing process.

Rapport building is difficult enough between research participants who hail from the same culture; the cross-cultural context adds the complexities and the vicissitudes of relatively enduring research encounters. Cross-cultural researchers frequently refer to the importance of the researcher's relationship with community members. M. N. Panini (1991) notes in this regard: "In a way, the fieldworker's search for the status of an 'insider' is like chasing a mirage. In societies comprising . . . class, ethnic, and factional divisions, a fieldworker cannot be accepted as an insider of every section of society" (p. 8). Hilda Tadria (1991) conveys this in reference to her own fieldwork experiences in Uganda. One woman recommended to Tadria that if she wanted to get unprejudiced data, she needed to stop dressing "like a government employee." However, after she bought and dressed in some secondhand clothes, she notes, "people were saying that I was disguising myself as a peasant because I was a spy" (p. 90), whereupon she decided to go back to wearing her original clothing.

The role of the ostensible insider generates its own problems in the long term, the duration often required in cross-cultural research. Mario Rutten (1995, 1996) recalls that in order to secure prolonged field relations, he had to socialize with his interviewees, who were small-scale entrepreneurs in Malaysia, India, and Indonesia. In

Malaysia, he visited a karaoke bar for the first time in his life, and his alcohol consumption was involuntarily raised during his fieldwork among Chinese businessmen, who told him, "If you want to join us in the evening, you have to drink as much as we do." Things became more delicate, however, when he was confronted with their expectations that he join them in "womanizing." [2] (See also Jayaraman 1979:272 on fieldwork in Sri Lanka.)

This relates to the experiences of some women researchers who have faced sexual overtures from male interviewees while doing fieldwork; sexual innuendo can be exaggerated in cross-cultural encounters. Sexual activity, propositions, and actual physical molestation are not infrequent themes in field reports, such as Mary Ellen Conaway's (1986) description of being physically molested and Eva Moreno's (1995) of being raped. Colin Thurnbull (1986) has described his relationship with a local woman during his fieldwork with the Mbuti of Africa, and Ruth Landes (1986) has written about her dilemmas as an unattached woman in the field. In a contrasting turn of events, Dona Davis (1986) found that people in the Newfoundland community she studied seemed friendlier and more at ease after they discovered she was having an affair.

Researchers are sometimes unwilling to write about their erotic experiences in the field (see Kong, Mahoney, and Plummer, Chapter 12, this volume). The reasons for this are varied and include issues of ethics, gendered effects, and potential implications for career chances. Some researchers may also be unwilling to confront the issues of positionality, hierarchy, exploitation, and that racism that such experiences may raise (see Kulick and Willson 1995). For example, Evelyn Blackwood (1995:68) asserts that an erotic attraction between a researcher and a person in the field will not necessarily dissolve differences between them, but may serve instead to highlight those differences. This topic has also been related to the reflexive turn within anthropology and theorizing the self (Probyn 1993; Wengle 1988; Newton 1993).

Researchers doing fieldwork often report attempts by the natives to get them to conform to local norms. For example, the Nahua Indians tried to get Peggy Golde (1986) married. As noted earlier, a landlord and trader in India tried to find a bride for Srinivas (1979). Nancie Gonzalez (1986) has written about the difficulties she encountered as a divorced woman doing fieldwork in Roman Catholic Guatemala. Similarly, Srinivas (1979) comments on the impact of his role as a bachelor on his access to parts of the field. Carol Warren (1988) describes this aspect of fieldwork: "The man or woman entering a strange culture becomes a stranger. . . . Their place in the society . . . is negotiated from the existing cultural stock of knowledge and action available to define and cope with strangers" (p. 189). She also points to the dicey dynamics involved in negotiating roles after one has established a place in a strange culture.

If the insider-outsider dilemma looms large in cross-cultural studies, it can also lead in surprising directions. Jayaraman (1979) found that his belonging to the Brahman caste and the caste system of their home country made his informants reluctant to disclose information. Because of Sunanda Patwardhan's (1979) language, the untouchables in her study saw her as an outsider and not as a Brahman. This fortunately protected her from hostile reactions. Anand Chakravarti (1979), as an urban Indian doing research in rural India, found caste membership to be vital to her interviewees. Because there was no equivalent in the field to her caste, her interviewees related to the caste of her fiancé, who was a Brahman. Veena Dua (1979) notes how she, as an unmarried woman, used local categories to manage the hostility of wives to her spending time with their husbands as interviewees.[3]

Resembling an insider can dissipate the advantage of naïveté, reducing the investigatory advantages of the novice. Regarding his fieldwork among the Tharu, a tribal community in the Himalaya, Triloki Pandey (1979) states:

> My first fieldwork introduced me to a people who were not much different from the lower caste members I had known in my natal village as a child. Whenever I asked my Tharu friends questions about their religion, their response was: "What sort of a Brahmin are you that you are asking us questions about religion? You should know all this and tell us about them." (P. 260)

Rapport and data collection also relate to power differences and local norms of reciprocity. Not everybody in the field appreciates the curiosity of a field-worker or interviewer.[4] (See the discussion of the institutionalization of the stranger in Gubrium and Holstein, Chapter 1, this volume.) Pandey (1979) recalls that he was asked to help an interviewee by lying. Dua (1979) illustrates the complications of doing fieldwork in castes of different status. Srinivas (1979) remembers how he was trapped due to his naïveté, and A. M. Shah (1979) reports how the research team's field notes were inspected by villagers. The local social elite may try to give advice, actively interfere in research projects, and even monopolize the field-worker's time. (For several examples from India, see Srinivas 1979; on development projects in general, see Uphoff 1991.)

If rapport triggers prolonged relationships and a seemingly open road to "good" data, the expectations concerning reciprocity between the researcher and his or her informants or interviewees can pose their own hazards. For example, Maren Bellwinkel's (1979) impoverished respondents expected her to give them gifts and loans. B. S. Baviskar (1979) was asked to collect systematic data for his informants on productivity in local sugar factories. A researcher's local landlord may be discontented with the rent he or she is paying (Pandey 1979), or the researcher may wind up providing information to interviewees that they would otherwise find difficult to obtain.[5]

Lest we take the insider-outsider problem too far as it relates to rapport building, we should bear in mind that cross-cultural differences are increasingly being homogenized by globalization. There is considerable unevenness in this development, of course, and there are always local particulars to consider, but the vast cultural divides that the traditional methodological literature seemingly cautions about concerning issues of rapport may be gradually disappearing. Indeed, as more and more cultures around the globe are coming to resemble interview societies (Atkinson and Silverman 1997), the problems of cross-cultural interviewing may very well reflect a historical epoch.

Globalization through television and the Internet is arguably dissolving former identities and loyalties based on geography or places. Men and women do business, work, and marry across international borders, and because of television and the Internet, children are raised in the generalized place of nowhere, so to speak (see Denzin 1997 on "hyperreality"). A study of cross-national perspectives on photographs, for example, points to the possible impact of Western mass media on visual perceptions (McIsaac and Ozkalp 1992), which bears on the internationalization of elicitation techniques for interviews (see Johnson and Weller, Chapter 24, this volume).[6]

However, because of the uneven distribution of telecommunication throughout the world, internationally this process will likely also be very uneven. The future prospects and relevance of this development for the rapport needs and related communicative considerations of cross-cultural interviewing are still unclear. A paradox is observed in the comment that "increasing transnational flows of culture seem to be producing, not global homogenization, but the growing assertion of heterogeneity and local distinctivity" (Sibley 1995:183-84;

see also Friedman 1994; Harrison 1999). And, as Birgit Meyer and Peter Geschiere (1999) note, there is also the possibility that one outcome of "global flows" of culture may be reactive attempts at "cultural closure," in which case we might have to continue to keep one foot on square one in considering matters of rapport building for cross-cultural interviewing.

Rapport building also has confronted the varied critiques of poststructuralist commentators, who certainly would not envision the problems of cross-cultural interviewing in chiefly procedural terms. Power and perspective are center stage here. For example, poststructuralist critics have accused studies of communities and groups in Third World countries of Western ethnocentrism, imputing to the researchers a variety of vested interests and underlying motives (Asad 1973; Marcus and Fischer 1986; Szwed 1972). They have accused researchers of undertaking studies on minorities from the perspective of the dominant group. (For critiques of orthodox social science perspectives on representations of African American experiences and feminist critiques of Western social science, see Stanfield 1994.) Poststructuralists have criticized the norms and values of dominant ethnic groups for constructing the very realities researchers figured they were only studying (Stanfield 1993; Hymes 1972; Gubrium and Holstein 1997; Vidich and Lyman 1994). As a result, John Stanfield (1994), for one, has called for alternative ethnic modeling in qualitative research.

Feminist researchers have put forth parallel views (see Olesen 1994). Both Ruth Behar (1993) and Lila Abu-Lughod (1990) have argued that to liberate ethnography from the domination linked to its colonial past, self/other distinctions need to be dissolved, or at the very least critically reappraised. Researcher bias in particular is related to this issue of subjectivity. In her book *Writing Women's Worlds* (1993), Abu-Lughod presents women's stories and conversations as narrative chapters; as a way of critiquing ethnographic typification, she drops the traditional formal conclusion to avoid reestablishing the authority of the expert's voice. (For references to self and othering, reflexivity, co-constructions, and the ethnographic encounter, see Riesman 1977; Crapanzano 1980; Dwyer 1982; Rosaldo 1986; Dumont 1992; Clough 1992; Behar 1993.) The point is to draw critical attention to the scientistic claims of traditional ethnographic studies, including data generated from cross-cultural interviews, as they relate to the problem and meaning of rapport building.

NONVERBAL COMMUNICATION

As Walburga von Raffler-Engel (1988) notes, nonverbal communication is an often unarticulated obstacle to cross-cultural interaction: "When two people of different cultures talk with each other in one of the two languages familiar to both of them, they automatically assume that they also share the extra-linguistic features of communication" (p. 74). She asserts that the most extensive disequilibrium in cross-cultural encounters comes from the features that lie below consciousness.

Two common forms of nonverbal communication problems are often noted: lack of comprehension and misunderstanding. In cases of the former, the receiver misses the information evident in the nonverbal signal; in cases of the latter, the receiver misinterprets the signal. In his work on misunderstandings in multicultural Israel, for example, Rafael Schneller (1988) found that different cultural groups use similar gestures, but with different meanings intended. He notes that the problems caused by misinterpreted signals are accentuated by implicit messages, such as gestures dominating explicit messages in the form of words when the two are in conflict. An illustration of a gesture that has different meanings is the head nod; in most parts of Europe, nodding signifies agreement, whereas in certain southern areas, such as in parts of Greece, nodding means no.

Such communicative problems extend to material culture. As Mary Douglas and Baron Isherwood (1996) note, "It is standard ethnographic practice to assume that all material possessions carry social meanings and to concentrate a main part of cultural analysis [and we would presume interviewing] upon their use as communicators" (p. 38). Goods are used to make visible and stable the categories of culture, not just for subsistence and competitive display. Edward E. Evans-Pritchard's (1940) account of the Nuer's cattle shows how rules stated in terms of cattle were basic to the network of kinship and provides a perspective on the cattle's double role. Cattle provided subsistence but also were used to draw the lines of social relationships. It is this approach to goods that Douglas and Isherwood assert is a proper route to cultural understanding. In an important message for cross-cultural interviewers, they advise us that commodities are "good for thinking; treat them as a non-verbal medium for the human creative faculty" (pp. 40-41).

Marcel Mauss's essay *The Gift* (1990), which centers on the social organization of gift exchange, makes explicit the theme of consumption and especially goods and rituals as maps of social order (see also Appadurai 1986; Bourdieu 1984). According to Don Slater (1997), "As communicators, goods are primarily 'markers' that indicate social relationships and classifications." He continues, "Through the use of goods we can construct and maintain an intelligible social universe, since by classifying, comparing, and ordering the things we have and use we make sense of and organize our social relations, classifying persons and events" (p. 150). Consequently, goods can also be used for exclusion and inclusion.[7] The latter relates to rapport, of course, and is dependent on knowledge of material categories; this virtually demands that an interviewer establish a place in the information network from which to gain knowledge of the meaning of goods.[8] The implication for cross-cultural interviewing is that interviewing must be accompanied by ongoing ethnographic knowledge of material culture, especially as that bears on cultural communication. The rub, of course, is that entering a new field usually implies that the researcher has limited information about the categories that particular goods mark in the community. The implication here is that, to conduct effective cross-cultural interviewing, a researcher must have sufficient time to establish a modicum of community membership (Ryen 2000).

Breaks and silences are another challenging aspect of cross-cultural communication with obvious consequences for interviewing. In some countries, it is regarded as inappropriate to talk during meals (Dahl and Habert 1986); in others, long pauses are an integral part of everyday social interaction, not signals for turn taking, such as invariably occurs in interview exchanges (Ryen 2000). Compared to speech patterns in some cultures in the Third World, the fast pace of Western speech hardly provides room for long breaks during talk. Thus Western interviewers risk interrupting interviewees' accounts by starting to talk in the middle of their sentences or stories. In some Asian cultures, silences and pauses are active parts of communication. These can be differentiated and operate as forms of respect, agreement, or disagreement (Smutkupt and Barna 1976). Helmut Morsbach's (1988a, 1988b) work on silence and bowing in Japan, comparing Japanese with Americans' and Australians' interpretations of silent periods in everyday discourse, is relevant to interviewing. This also has been discussed in the context of marketing research, another field in which cross-cultural communication is important (Tung 1984; Tse et al. 1988; Graham and Gronhaug 1989; Stewart, Hecker, and Graham 1987).

Nonverbal communication constitutes a vital part of intercultural encounters. Indeed, as Kvale (1996) notes, one problem with the analysis of qualitative interviews —the form that cross-cultural interviewing often takes—is researchers' usual tendency to focus on purely verbal communication while ignoring bodily expressions and other unverbalized texts.[9]

CONTEXT AND VERBAL COMMUNICATION

Social reality and how we talk about reality are intertwined. Reality varies according to the context of its articulation, and this by implication presents a challenge especially for cross-cultural, interview research. In low-context languages, for example, the interactional context has little impact upon the meaning of what is said; the message, in effect, is in the words. This is exemplified by Germanic languages; speakers of these languages are viewed as having faces without expressions and make economical use of body language. In the high-context Latin languages, in contrast, messages cannot be interpreted literally, but have to be linked to performances (Hall 1976, 1988).

Moving from a low-context to a high-context language can be interactionally complicated. Acquiring the ability to speak another language for purposes of cross-cultural interviewing thus requires that interviewers learn more than vocabulary and grammar. (Blum-Kulka, House, and Kasper 1989 provide a useful overview of publications on such aspects of "cross-cultural pragmatics"; on the role of affect in cross-cultural negotiations, see George, Jones, and Gonzalez 1998.) As John Gumperz (1982; Gumperz and Cook-Gumperz 1982) explains in his work on the cultural specificity of speech act behavior, "Cross-cultural differences in expectations of linguistic behavior, interpretative strategies, and signaling devices can lead to breakdowns in interethnic communication" (cited in Blum-Kulka et al. 1989:6).

Gumperz's work on the communicative shape of ethnic communication is pioneering and directly pertinent to cross-cultural interviewing. The extract below from his

6	A:	I have done my graduate certificate in Education from L. Uni-
7		versity. I had been teaching after getting that teacher's training in
8		H., in H.
9	B:	Oh, so you have *done* some teaching
10	A:	Some [I have done I have done some [teaching
11	B:	[in H. [I see
12	A:	Um . . . I completed two terms . . . uh, unfortunately I had to
13		leave from that place because [uh I was appointed only
14	B:	[oh
15	A:	for two terms
16	B:	Oh so you did not get to finish your probation, I suppose
17	A:	(sighs) so that is uh [my start was alright but later
18	B:	[oh
19	A:	on what happened it is a mi-a great chaos, I don't know
20		where I stand or what I can do . . . um, [after
21	B:	[and now you find
22		you can't get a job
23	A:	No, this is not actually the situation, [I have not
24	B:	[oh
25	A:	completely explained [my position
26	B:	[yes

linguistic material illustrates how the interpretation of speakers' meanings is an interactional and collaborative activity. Linguistic contextualization processes mediate informational and verbal messages.[10] Gumperz's (1977, 1978, 1979) analyses of interactions between British English and Indian English speakers in England show that differences in cues resulted in systematic miscommunication. Gumperz asserts that the problems were the result of differences in systems of conversational inference and cues for signaling speech acts. At the same time, the results are notably embodied in the interactional machinery and style of the speakers' encounter, which constructs cultural data of its own, a point I will take up in the next section of this chapter.

An illustration is drawn from an interview-counseling session recorded in an industrial suburb in London (Gumperz 1982:183). The communication is between English-speaking persons. The client is a male Pakistani teacher of mathematics, born in South Asia but with a university degree from England. The counselor is a female staff member of a center funded by the Department of Employment, which deals with interethnic communication problems in British industry. The participants are said to agree on the general definition of the event but to differ in expectations and on what needs to be done.

The extract above shows how misinterpretation is an interactional and collaborative activity, and how linguistic contextualization processes mediate verbal messages. A, the Pakistani teacher, has been unable to secure permanent employment and has been told that he lacks the necessary communicative skills for high school teaching, for which he has been referred to the center. B is a center counselor. The extract illustrates misunderstandings and a failure to negotiate a common frame of reference despite repeated attempts.

B's focus on "done" (line 9) is an indirect probe for more information about A's

working experience.[11] A's (12-15) next remark can be interpreted as intended to lead
to a longer narrative, but his contextualization invites problems. His voice drops
and the tempo of his account speeds up, followed by what may be assumed to be the
main point in his argument. However, here
it starts with "unfortunately" (12). In England, new graduates often begin with pro-
bationary short-term appointments. B's
"oh" (14) and response (16) indicates that
she assumes A is talking about such a post,
from which he later was dismissed. This is
assumed to be justified by his use of the
word "unfortunately." But when A says that
his "start was alright" (17), B interjects another surprised "oh" (18) that can be
viewed as a form of repair or correction.
A's words and prosody run counter to the
expectations of English speakers. Repairs
and corrections imply that new or non-
shared information is to be introduced and
usually marked by accent or rise in pitch
and transitions such as "Oh" or "I mean."
He then seems inconsistent and is not responding to B's reply, which explains her
second interjection (18). A's "I don't know
where I stand or what I can do" (19 and 20)
is spoken with a contoured intonation that
by Indian English speakers is interpreted as
a signal that what is to come is important to
the speaker. However, he finds himself being interrupted by B (22). His reply (23)
suggests annoyance before he eventually
starts his narrative (29, not shown).

Throughout, B seems to be trying to
make A concentrate on what she thinks is
the point of the interview, which is more
training. As Gumperz (1982) notes:

> The interaction is punctuated by long
> asides, misunderstandings of fact and
> misreadings of intent. A, on the other
> hand, finds he is not being listened to
> and not given a chance to explain his
> problem. . . . in spite of repeated at-
> tempts, both speakers utterly fail in
> their efforts to negotiate a common
> frame in terms to decide on what is be-
> ing focused on and where the argument
> is going at any one time. (P. 185)

Gumperz summarizes by quoting an Indian
English speaker: "They're on parallel
tracks which don't meet."

Differences in systems of conversational
inferences and cues for signaling speech
acts combine into distinctive interactional
styles. This is why problems often arise
when speakers from different speech communities interact. "Only by looking at the
whole range of linguistic phenomena that
enter into conversational management can
we understand what goes on in an interaction" (Gumperz 1982:186).[12]

Short of becoming community members
themselves, some researchers make use of
local interpreters. But still issues arise related to the ways in which individuals use
language, the connotative meanings of
words, pronunciation problems or problems with specific sounds, and challenges
associated with linguistic styles in different
contexts. The problem may not necessarily
be a matter of posing the right questions,
but one of the researcher's communicating
questions to the interpreter in culturally appropriate ways that invite further communication. It is of vital importance that
words and concepts be interpreted in the
same ways by interviewers, interpreters,
and respondents to avoid violating validity.

For interpreters, English is often their
second language, and there is a high probability that people for whom English is a second, or even a third, language will use English in different ways from native speakers.
The same applies to local interpreters of
any language when the speakers in question
belong to different cultures. The further
the distance between the cultures, the more
an interpreter has to transform language to
convey the same content. For example, the
word *yes* has often proved to be a problematic response in interviews and other information-seeking contexts. In certain cultures, *yes* is heard as agreement, whereas in
others it is simply a response confirming

that the question has been heard. Such differences have proved problematic in negotiations of business contracts, for example, where unsavvy interpretations can produce unfortunate results. Agreements that one side understood to be confirmed with a yes may never be implemented, with the result that the partners are seen as unreliable. In Asian cultures, an explicit no to a request is often seen as rude, or as threatening to the opposite party's face when subordinates are present (Dahl and Habert 1986). However, in these cultures closer relationships seem to allow greater tolerance of linguistic directness (Bilbow 1998; Brown and Levinson 1978).

International business is increasingly dependent on cross-cultural interviewing, to which many of the issues noted above apply. In my own work in this area in Tanzania, humor proved to be a way around miscommunication. In interview research focused on fringe benefits, for example, I posed a question to coresearchers about the "cold lunch" as a fringe benefit in Tanzania. My Tanzanian coresearchers laughed in a friendly way and told me that a cold lunch is given only to one's enemies. In another instance, a publishing company that wanted to market its products in India by using the owl as a symbol of wisdom eventually learned that among Indians this bird is associated with "bad fortune." Another company tried to introduce its animal feed products to the Muslim areas of Arab countries, but unfortunately the company's advertising brochure pictured on its cover a well-fed pig, an animal that Muslims consider to be unclean. These are only a few examples of how local symbolic relevancies mediate meaning, any of which can apply in the interview encounter.

Norms also vary among cultures concerning how and when it is appropriate for two parties to begin serious business (Dahl and Habert 1986; Hall 1988). Indeed, gaps may be found between any two cultures, not only between the traditional exotic and nonexotic groups, as A. Bennett (1986) has shown in his work on relatedly specialized

training for foreign managers in the United States.[13]

As business and corporate organizational concerns increasingly penetrate cross-cultural communication, seemingly straightforward matters such as questions about quality, quantity, and frequency are increasingly raised in interviews. Poor communication in this regard may erode rapport in the very process of interviewing, with unfortunate economic consequences. The researcher may be cut off from prompting or asking detailed follow-up questions to elaborate or clarify numerical information, for example. The problem probably looms larger in short-term projects than in long-term, traditional participant observation studies. Indeed, Hein Streefkerk (1993) found that in his research he could collect data on quantities, numbers of workers, and wage levels only in indirect ways over long periods of time, because employers avoided giving him exact information on these and other important economic data.[14]

◆ *Cultural Data as Collaborative Accomplishment*

Lest we dwell exclusively on the communicative problems that derive from a naturalistic view of cultural facts, let us briefly consider how a perspective on shared meaning as a locally collaborative accomplishment relates to cross-cultural interviewing. Because little work has focused on collaborative accomplishment in cross-cultural interviewing, I will use my own data from e-mail communication with an Asian businessman in East Africa as an illustration of how this is done (Ryen and Silverman 2000; relatedly, see also in this volume Mann and Stewart, Chapter 29; Baker, Chapter 37). In the following exchanges, AR (the researcher) and Sachin (the Kenyan entrepreneur) work at achieving acceptable forms of "sign-offs" or closings at the ends of their e-mail messages. Taken together, these exchanges illustrate how both parties achieve mutual understanding about the preferred interpersonal relationship on a turn-by-turn basis, which I would argue accomplishes a form of cultural understanding *within* the interview process itself.

Sachin ends his first message as follows:

> tell me more about yourself in your next email. . . .
> love
> Sachin (Ending of first message
> dated October 26, 1998)

AR replies, among other things:

> I am married and have two small children. (October 30, 1998)

Presumably, even if she is married, AR does not necessarily have to mention it. In categorizing herself as "married" with "two small children," she also categorizes the other person, who in the next few exchanges becomes a "friend" or something "more," not a potential lover. Moreover, AR does not use "love" as a closing, but *"hilsen"* (Norwegian for "greetings"). Sachin has apparently monitored the category-bound implications here, for his next message ends with "regards Sachin" (November 5, 1998).

In later messages, Sachin no longer uses "love," but rather "well regards" (November 17, 1998), "well cheerio" (December 10, 1998), and "cheeeers" (December 26, 1998). In her later correspondence, AR relaxes the interpersonal distance of her preceding closings from her somewhat impersonal *"hilsen"* to *"beste hilsen"* (November 23, 1998) and then *"Kjaere* [dear] Sachin" (December 22, 1998). Despite her self-

identification as sexually unavailable, AR responds to Sachin's information that he intends to get married soon by writing, "Lucky woman to marry you,—tell me more!" (November 10, 1998). This recontextualizes Sachin's sexual availability to his future bride. AR intentionally uses such banter to maintain a friendly relationship with a respondent who is, after all, giving his time freely to help her. As we see above, flattery ("lucky woman") is a verbal reward that researchers can offer their research subjects and that helps to facilitate a continuing exchange. A researcher might use such friendly, noninstrumental framing to preface a whole message. So one of AR's e-mails begins, "Sachin, this time I have no research questions" (November 30, 1998).

Sachin's grandmother died a few days before AR actually visited him. Religious tradition demanded that she cancel parts of her research agenda, and much of their talk referred instead to the family. So one of his next e-mail messages began:

> Dear ANNI,
> hope you and the entire family is in the best of the health and spirits by the grace of the almighty. . . . How are your kids. . . . I bet they must be giving you a run for your money. . . . and your husband . . . is he ok. (July 11, 1999)

This set of exchanges shows how AR and Sachin negotiate the shared parameters of their relationship, invoking a range of paired identities: researcher-researched, female-male, married woman-single man, friend-friend. They don't simply arrive, in good methodological order, at some preexisting set of culture-bound roles and start the interview process. Their subject positions as interview participants, in other words, are not preset by culture, but emerge in ongoing interaction (see Gubrium and Holstein, Chapter 1, this volume). AR begins by implying her sexual unavailability, and Sachin's recognition of this is evidenced in his modification of his e-mail sign-off. However, conscious of the rewards that research subjects rightly may expect, AR later uses what Harvey Sacks (1992a, 1992b) calls a "category-modifier" to show her respondent that just because she is "unavailable" does not mean that she cannot treat him as a friend or that, indeed, she is unaware of his attractiveness to other women.

These exchanges show that interview researchers must be very careful how they use categories. Sacks (1992a) puts the issue succinctly:

> Suppose you're an anthropologist or sociologist standing somewhere. You see somebody do some action, and you see it to be some activity. How can you go about formulating who is it that did it, for the purposes of your report? Can you use at least what you might take to be the most conservative formulation —his name? Knowing, of course, that any category you choose would have the[se] kinds of systematic problems: how would you go about selecting a given category from the set that would equally well characterise or identify that person at hand? (Pp. 467-68)

In a chapter titled "Pursuing Members' Meaning," Robert Emerson, Rachel Fretz, and Linda Shaw (1995) argue that "deeper, fuller memos and analyses in a final ethnography require examining not simply what terms members use, but when, where, and how they use them and how they actually categorize or classify events and objects in specific situations" (p. 126). This implies that the analysis of cultural particulars should also focus on how meaning is collaboratively produced within the interview. Sacks (1992a) shows how one cannot resolve such problems simply "by taking the best possible notes at the time and making

your decisions afterwards" (p. 468). Sacks (1992a) quotes from two linguists who appear to have no problem in characterizing particular (invented) utterances as "simple," "complex," "casual," or "ceremonial" and explains that such rapid characterizations of data assume "that we can know that without an analysis of what it is [they] are doing [with words]" (p. 429), a viewpoint that shortchanges the local accomplishment of the characterization.

Let us try to follow Sacks's argument on this and consider how it might relate to cross-cultural interviewing. First, the conclusion that studying other cultures can open our minds to our own is commonplace. Indeed, it can lead in a Durkheimian direction, where differences are simply "explained" as a product of "culture" or "common knowledge" without problematizing the communicative "machinery" involved. Second, a focus on the natural "thereness" of culture deflects our attention from how meaning is locally assembled. For example, Sacks (1992a) points out how, in Evans-Pritchard's work on the Nuer, Evans-Pritchard asserts that "the Nuer tend to define all social processes and relationships in terms of cattle." But, as Sacks goes on to say, "it's one thing to say that every conversation ends up about cattle and another to show how that's so" (p. 389).

The interviewer who is alert to the collaborative accomplishment of culture relates to the life of the interview as storied and managed by and through narratives and participants. The focus is on *how* the interview is narratively constructed. Narrative shifts, for example, produce different contexts, and it is within these different contexts that questions are asked and answered and, most significantly, meaning produced in the process. Interviewers' questions, cues, and prompts are not simply stimuli to empty the interviewee's reservoir of cultural data; rather, they actively contribute to the contexts in which experiences are narrated. Both interviewer and interviewee actively co-construct meaning and, notably, also who and what they represent to each other in the process. This differs from considerations of the communicative challenges of cross-cultural interviewing discussed earlier. The problems seen as the integral role dilemmas of cross-cultural interviews—the insider-outsider issue—are here regarded as *indigenous* parts of meaning construction in ongoing social interaction. The insider-outsider problem is transformed into something research participants themselves accomplish and resolve rather than merely cope with or suffer from.

How far is culture reducible to members' ongoing categorization practices? If collaborative accomplishment constructs cultural understanding, how can related explanatory purchase be obtained for concepts such as "culture," "cultural differences," and "cross-cultural communication"? Sacks again provides direction. Put crudely, for Sacks, if "culture" has any salience, it is not as a source of explanation —as it might be when we approach it as the cause of miscommunication—but as a member's method. In this sense, "culture" is best approached as what Sacks (1992a) calls an "inference-making machine" (p. 119). This refers to a locally employed descriptive apparatus that can be documented for how descriptions are used and administered in specific contexts, such as took place in the "cross-cultural" communication between AR and Sachin described above. Orienting to culture as an interactive resource, both AR and Sachin used categories available to them to position each other within the interview context and, as a result, constructed the interactive and moral contours of their relationship. They did not simply correctly or incorrectly appropriate external categories to organize their relationship as interviewer and interviewee. In skillfully using these categories, they constructed the social organization of the interview process in the course of ongoing social interaction.

In this regard, consider the external reality of ostensible "coincidences," for example. To the layperson, coincidence may be the product of some mysterious external reality. To the social researcher, a focus on coincidence may seem to be a feature of particular cultures or subcultures, as in accounts of cultures of poverty where the poor are seen to stress coincidence or luck rather than rational behavior. However, Sacks (1992b:237-40) shows that it could be that people *package* their accounts in terms of coincidence in order to produce "relevant-at-that-moment tellable stories." This is directly pertinent to Emanuel Schegloff's (1992) comment that Sacks proposes that "much of the observable orderliness of the world may be better understood as the by-products of ambient organizations which are quite unconcerned with those outcomes rather than as products which were the design target of some explanation" (p. xxiv). If we take Schegloff seriously, it is also worth pursuing the "ambient social organization" demonstrably attended by interview participants. The result for cross-cultural interviewing would be that we would begin by bracketing the concept of "culture" in order to build our knowledge of how interviewer and interviewee collaboratively use and assemble accounts of "cultures" in communicative practice. This would serve to reveal the constructive, as much as the procedural, contours of the interviewing in question.

■ Notes

1. According to Gubrium and Holstein (1997; Holstein and Gubrium 1995), traditional approaches portray subjects as rather passive "vessels of answers." It is assumed that the researcher will be able to get access to this store of data by establishing rapport with subjects and by posing questions in what is seen as the correct, neutral way.

2. Rutten conveyed this information to me in a personal communication.

3. By calling the women *bhabi,* Dua (1979) took on the role of their men's sister. By excluding herself from being a sister-in-law, she was protecting herself from local norms that give men sexual liberties with their wives' sisters.

4. Streefkerk (1993) reports about his difficulties in getting access to data on quantitative "facts" from his entrepreneurs: "Many entrepreneurs did not like my efforts to count the number of workers and they gave incomplete information and tried to hinder my attempts to visit shop floors" (p. 18). This kind of problem is accentuated by the low quality of public statistics in many countries, which often rules out triangulation. Respondents can also be skillful at circumventing the informational needs of interviewers. Ahmed (1984; cited in Rutten 1995), for example, discusses how researchers tried to cross-check data on small-scale industries in Bangladesh by repeating certain questions from their last visit. However, most of the industrialists who were questioned simply asked the researchers to copy down information from their previous visit.

5. This also applies to myself sending Web addresses with information on comparable Western products, brochures, information on production gear when setting up new productions, and so on. Also, in cultures where it is regarded as impolite to oppose a guest, interviewees may accept researchers' requests to find materials or documents for them, but never follow through. This happened in my own experience in communicating with an Asian entrepreneur. In one of his e-mails he wrote, "The questions that you have asked me have been answered in the package i sent you . . . so if you have more please email them to me" (July 11, 1999). That package never arrived, and I never asked him about it.

6. McIsaac and Ozkalp (1992) studied American and Turkish women's perceptions of body positions of male and female models as shown in slides.

7. See Slater (1997:152) for his criticism of Douglas on modern consumption culture, where he comments that Douglas too easily translates her perspective on the relationship between meanings and rituals of consumption and social order. He also points to the impact of vested commercial interests. See also Bourdieu (1984).

8. This also applies to the researcher. During fieldwork with entrepreneurs in East Africa, my African colleagues claimed that the entrepreneurs watching this white, Western person arriving in a LandCruiser were initially more interested in the potential funding than in the interviews.

9. However, the growing interest in the analysis of videotapes does begin to address this problem.

10. The text is an illustration of the "naturally occurring data" traditionally preferred in ethnomethodological studies. For a discussion, see Silverman (1993).

11. All of my comments here are closely based on Gumperz (1982).

12. This makes context-bound interpretive preferences an alternative perspective on attitudes and stereotypes. This is a perspective Gumperz (1982) has employed in teaching sessions to improve relations between staff and supervisors in workplaces that employ members of different ethnic groups (see also Gumperz 1978). However, analyses also show that participants may lose nuances of meaning without communication breaking down, due to a high level of linguistic tolerance in close relationships (Bilbow 1996).

13. In general, representatives from different cultures may respond differently to the same phenomena (Johnson et al. 1996; Mangione, Fowler, and Louis 1992), and the definitions of particular words may vary, such as the definitions of *family* and *sister* in Western compared with African cultures. Further, in some cultures certain phenomena are given special terms, such as *parastatal sector* (Bureau of Statistics and Labour Department 1993), and phenomena that are important in some cultures, such as witchcraft and medicine men, are regarded as nonexistent in others.

14. For discussions of some special problems related to cross-cultural data on quantity, see Claudia Zaslavsky's (1990) work on comparing numbers and on number superstition, P. H. Gulliver's (1958) on age and social organization, and Andreas Fuglesang's (1982:55, 65) on ethnocentrism in Western tests of mental development and on comparing models for assessing quantity by visual perception.

■ References

Abeyewardene, A. 1991. "Familial versus Professional Responsibilities: Fieldwork Experiences in Sri Lanka." Pp. 52-58 in *From the Female Eye: Accounts of Women Fieldworkers Studying Their Own Communities,* edited by M. N. Panini. Delhi: Hindustan Publishing.

Abu-Lughod, L. 1990. "Can There Be a Feminist Ethnography?" *Women and Performance* 5:7-27.

———. 1993. *Writing Women's Worlds: Bedouin Stories.* Berkeley: University of California Press.

Ahmed, Q. K. 1984. "Rural Industries Study Project (RISP); An Introduction." *Bangladesh Development Studies* 12(1-2):iii-xi.

Appadurai, A., ed. 1986. *The Social Life of Things: Commodities in Cultural Perspective.* Cambridge: Cambridge University Press.

Asad, T. 1973. *Anthropology and the Colonial Encounter.* New York: Humanities.

Atkinson, P. and D. Silverman. 1997. "Kundera's *Immortality:* The Interview Society and the Invention of Self." *Qualitative Inquiry* 3:304-25.

Bangun, M. 1991. "Sensitive Social Relationships: An Urban Professional Woman in a Village Setting." Pp. 81-87 in *From the Female Eye: Accounts of Women Fieldworkers Studying Their Own Communities,* edited by M. N. Panini. Delhi: Hindustan Publishing.

Baviskar, B. S. 1979. "Walking on the Edge of Factionalism: An Industrial Cooperative in Rural Maharashtra." Pp. 184-201 in *The Fieldworker and the Field: Problems and Challenges in Sociological Investigation,* edited by M. N. Srinivas, A. M. Shah, and E. A. Ramaswamy. Bombay: Oxford University Press.

Behar, R. 1993. *Translated Woman: Crossing the Border with Esperanza's Story.* Boston: Beacon.

Bellwinkel, M. 1979. "Objective Appreciation through Subjective Involvement: A Slum in Kanpur." Pp. 141-52 in *The Fieldworker and the Field: Problems and Challenges in Sociological Investigation,* edited by M. N. Srinivas, A. M. Shah, and E. A. Ramaswamy. Bombay: Oxford University Press.

Bennett, A. 1986. "American Culture Is Often a Puzzle for Foreign Managers in the U.S." *Wall Street Journal,* February 20.

Berreman, G. D. 1962. *Behind Many Masks: Ethnography and Impression Management in a Himalayan Village.* Ithaca, NY: Cornell University Press.

Bhopal, K. 2000. "Gender, 'Race' and Power in the Research Process: South Asian Women in East London." Pp. 67-79 in *Research and Inequality,* edited by C. Truman, D. M. Mertens, and B. Humphries. London: UCL.

Bilbow, G. T. 1996. "Managing Impressions in the Multicultural Workplace: An Impression Management-Based Model for Cross-Cultural Discourse Analysis and Awareness Training for the Workplace." Ph.D. dissertation, City University of Hong Kong.

———. 1998. "Look Who's Talking: An Analysis of 'Chair-Talk' in Business Meetings." *Journal of Business and Technical Communication* 12:157-99.

Blackwood, E. 1995. "Falling in Love with an-Other Lesbian: Reflections on Identity in Fieldwork." Pp. 51-76 in *Taboo: Sex, Identity, and Erotic Subjectivity in Anthropological Fieldwork,* edited by D. Kulick and M. Willson. London: Routledge.

Blum-Kulka, S., J. House, and G. Kasper. 1989. "Investigating Cross-Cultural Pragmatics: An Introductory Overview." Pp. 1-34 in *Cross-Cultural Pragmatics: Requests and Apologies,* edited by S. Blum-Kulka, J. House, and G. Kasper. Norwood, NJ: Ablex.

Bourdieu, P. 1984. *Distinction: A Social Critique of the Judgement of Taste.* Translated by R. Nice. Cambridge, MA: Harvard University Press.

Brown, P. and S. C. Levinson. 1978. "Universals in Language Usage: Politeness Phenomena." Pp. 256-58 in *Questions and Politeness: Strategies in Social Interaction,* edited by E. N. Goody. Cambridge: Cambridge University Press.

Bureau of Statistics and Labour Department. 1993. *Tanzania (Mainland): The Labour Force Survey, 1990/91.* Dar es Salaam: Author.

Casley, D. J. and D. A. Lury. 1987. *Data Collection in Developing Countries.* New York: Oxford University Press.

Chakravarti, A. 1979. "Experiences of an Encapsulated Observer: A Village in Rajasthan." Pp. 38-57 in *The Fieldworker and the Field: Problems and Challenges in Sociological Investigation,* edited by M. N. Srinivas, A. M. Shah, and E. A. Ramaswamy. Bombay: Oxford University Press.

Clough, P. T. 1992. *The End(s) of Ethnography: From Realism to Social Criticism.* Newbury Park, CA: Sage.

Conaway, M. E. 1986. "The Pretense of the Neutral Researcher." Pp. 52-63 in *Self, Sex and Gender in Cross-Cultural Fieldwork,* edited by T. L. Whitehead and M. E. Conaway. Urbana: University of Illinois Press.

Crapanzano, V. 1980. *Tuhami: Portrait of a Moroccan.* Chicago: University of Chicago Press.

Crehan, K. 1991. "Listening to Different Voices." Pp. 99-106 in *From the Female Eye: Accounts of Women Fieldworkers Studying Their Own Communities,* edited by M. N. Panini. Delhi: Hindustan Publishing.

Dahl, Ø. and K. Habert. 1986. *Møte mellom kulturer: Tverrkulturell kommunikasjon.* Stavanger, Norway: Universitetsforlaget.

Davis, D. 1986. "Changing Self-Image: Studying Menopausal Women in a Newfoundland Fishing Village." Pp. 240-61 in *Self, Sex and Gender in Cross-Cultural Fieldwork,* edited by T. L. Whitehead and M. E. Conaway. Urbana: University of Illinois Press.

Dean, J. P., R. L. Eichhorn, and L. R. Dean. 1969. "Establishing Field Relations." Pp. 68-70 in *Issues in Participant Observation: A Text and Reader,* edited by G. J. McCall and J. L. Simmons. Reading, MA: Addison-Wesley.

Denzin, N. K. 1997. *Interpretive Ethnography: Ethnographic Practices for the 21st Century.* Thousands Oaks, CA: Sage.

Deutscher, I. 1968. "Asking Questions Cross-Culturally: Some Problems of Linguistic Comparability." Pp. 318-41 in *Institutions and the Person,* edited by H. S. Becker, B. Geer, D. Riesman, and R. Weiss. Chicago: Aldine.

Douglas, M. and B. Isherwood. 1996. *The World of Goods: Towards an Anthropology of Consumption.* London: Routledge.

Dua, V. 1979. "A Woman's Encounter with Arya Samaj and Untouchables: A Slum in Jullundur." Pp. 115-26 in *The Fieldworker and the Field: Problems and Challenges in Sociological Investigation,* edited by M. N. Srinivas, A. M. Shah, and E. A. Ramaswamy. Bombay: Oxford University Press.

Dumont, J.-P. 1992. *The Headman and I: Ambiguity and Ambivalence in the Fieldworking Experience.* Prospect Heights, IL: Waveland.

Dwyer, K. 1982. *Moroccan Dialogues: Anthropology in Question.* Baltimore: Johns Hopkins University Press.

Ember, C. R. and D. Levinson. 1991. "The Substantive Contributions of Worldwide Cross-Cultural Studies. *Behavior Science Research* 25:79-141.

Emerson, R. M., R. I. Fretz, and L. L. Shaw. 1995. *Writing Ethnographic Fieldnotes.* Chicago: University of Chicago Press.

Evans-Pritchard, E. E. 1940. "The Nuer." Pp. 17-19 in E. E. Evans-Pritchard, *The Political Institutions of a Nilotic People.* Oxford: Clarendon.

Freeman, D. 1983. *Margaret Mead and Samoa: The Making and Unmaking of an Anthropological Myth.* Cambridge, MA: Harvard University Press.

Friedman, J. 1994. *Cultural Identity and Global Process.* London: Sage.

Fuglesang, A. 1982. *About Understanding: Ideas and Observations on Cross-Cultural Communication.* Uppsala: Dag Hammarskjøld Foundation.

George, J. M., G. R. Jones, and J. A. Gonzalez. 1998. "The Role of Affect in Cross-Cultural Negotiations." *Journal of International Business Studies* 29:749-72.

Golde, P. 1986. "Odyssey of Encounter." Pp. 67-93 in *Women in the Field: Anthropological Experiences,* edited by P. Golde. Berkeley: University of California Press.

Gonzalez, N. 1986. "The Anthropologist as Female Head of Household." Pp. 84-100 in *Self, Sex and Gender in Cross-Cultural Fieldwork,* edited by T. L. Whitehead and M. E. Conaway. Urbana: University of Illinois Press.

Graham, J. L. and K. Gronhaug. 1989. "Ned Hall Didn't Have to Get a Haircut, or Why We Haven't Learned Much about International Marketing in the Last 25 Years." *Journal of Higher Education* 60:152-87.

Gubrium, J. F. and J. A. Holstein. 1997. *The New Language of Qualitative Method.* New York: Oxford University Press.

Gulliver, P. H. 1958. "Counting by the Fingers by Two East African Tribes." *African Notes* 51:259-62.

Gumperz, J. J. 1977."Sociocultural Knowledge in Conversational Inferences." In *28th Annual Round Table Monograph Series on Language and Linguistics*. Washington, DC: Georgetown University Press.

———. 1978. "The Conversational Analysis of Interethnic Communication." In *Interethnic Communication*, edited by E. L. Ross. Athens: University of Georgia Press.

———. 1979. "The Sociolinguistic Basis of Speech Act Theory." In *Speech Act: Ten Years After*, edited by J. Boyd and S. Ferra. Milan: Versus.

———. 1982. *Discourse Strategies*. Cambridge: Cambridge University Press.

Gumperz, J. J. and J. Cook-Gumperz. 1982. "Interethnic Communication in Committee Negotiations." Pp. 145-62 in *Language and Social Identity*, edited by J. J. Gumperz. Cambridge: Cambridge University Press.

Habib, G. M. 1987. "Measures of Manifest Conflicts in International Joint Ventures." *Academy of Management Journal* 30:808-16.

Hall, E. T. 1976. *Beyond Culture*. Garden City, NY: Doubleday.

———. 1988. "The Hidden Dimensions of Time and Space in Today's World." Pp. 145-52 in *Cross-Cultural Perspectives in Nonverbal Communication*, edited by F. Poyatos. Toronto: C. J. Hogrefe.

Harrison, S. 1999. "Cultural Boundaries." *Anthropology Today* 15(5):10-13.

Heritage, J. C. 1997. "Conversation Analysis and Institutional Talk: Analysing Data." Pp. 161-82 in *Qualitative Research: Theory, Method and Practice*, edited by D. Silverman. London: Sage.

Holstein, J. A. and J. F. Gubrium. 1995. *The Active Interview*. Thousand Oaks, CA: Sage.

Hymes, D., ed. 1972. *Reinventing Anthropology*. New York: Pantheon.

Jayaraman, R. 1979. "Problems of Entry: Sri Lanka, Zambia and Australia." Pp. 266-75 in *The Fieldworker and the Field: Problems and Challenges in Sociological Investigation*, edited by M. N. Srinivas, A. M. Shah, and E. A. Ramaswamy. Bombay: Oxford University Press.

Johnson, T., D. O'Rourke, S. Sudman, and R. Warnecke. 1996. "Assessing Question Comprehension across Cultures: Evidence from the United States." Presented at the Essex '96 Conference, Essex, England.

Kamil, S. 1991. "Maidenhood, Marriage and Fieldwork: Experiences in India and Pakistan." Pp. 36-40 in *From the Female Eye: Accounts of Women Fieldworkers Studying Their Own Communities*, edited by M. N. Panini. Delhi: Hindustan Publishing.

Kulick, D. and M. Willson, eds. 1995. *Taboo: Sex, Identity, and Erotic Subjectivity in Anthropological Fieldwork*. London: Routledge.

Kvale, S. 1996. *InterViews: An Introduction to Qualitative Research Interviewing*. Thousand Oaks, CA: Sage.

Landes, R. 1986. "A Woman Anthropologist in Brazil." Pp. 119-39 in *Women in the Field: Anthropological Experiences*, edited by P. Golde. Berkeley: University of California Press.

Lofland, J. 1971. *Analyzing Social Settings*. Belmont, CA: Wadsworth.

Mangione, T. W., F. J. Fowler, Jr., and T. A. Louis. 1992. "Question Characteristics and Interviewer Effects." *Journal of Official Statistics* 8:293-307.

Marcus, G. E. and M. M. J. Fischer. 1986. *Anthropology as Cultural Critique: An Experimental Moment in the Human Sciences*. Chicago: University of Chicago Press.

Mauss, M. 1990. *The Gift: The Form and Reason for Exchange in Archaic Societies*. New York: Norton.

Maykovich, M. K. 1977. "The Difficulties of a Minority Researcher in Minority Communities." *Journal of Social Issues* 33(4):108-19.

McIsaac, M. S. and E. Ozkalp. 1992. "Crossnational Perspectives on Gender Differences and Perspectives of Professional Competence in Photographs." *International Journal of Instructional Media* 19:349-66.

Meyer, B. and P. Geschiere. 1999. "Introduction." Pp. 1-15 in *Globalization and Identity: Dialectics of Flow and Closure*, edited by B. Meyer and P. Geschiere. Oxford: Blackwell.

Montero, D. 1977. "Research among Racial and Cultural Minorities: An Overview." *Journal of Social Issues* 33(4):1-10.

Moreno, E. 1995. "Rape in the Field: Reflections from a Survivor." Pp. 219-51 in *Taboo: Sex, Identity, and Erotic Subjectivity in Anthropological Fieldwork*, edited by D. Kulick and M. Willson. London: Routledge.

Morsbach, H. 1988a. "The Importance of Silence and Stillness in Japanese Nonverbal Communication: A Cross-Cultural Approach." Pp. 201-18 in *Cross-Cultural Perspectives in Nonverbal Communication,* edited by F. Poyatos. Toronto: C. J. Hogrefe.

———. 1988b. "Nonverbal Communication and Hierarchical Relationships: The Case of Bowing in Japan." Pp. 189-99 in *Cross-Cultural Perspectives in Nonverbal Communication,* edited by F. Poyatos. Toronto: C. J. Hogrefe.

Nath, J. 1991. "A Bengali Woman in Three Different Field Situations." Pp. 59-65 in *From the Female Eye: Accounts of Women Fieldworkers Studying Their Own Communities,* edited by M. N. Panini. Delhi: Hindustan Publishing.

Newton, E. 1993. "My Best Informant's Dress: The Erotic Equation in Fieldwork." *Cultural Anthropology* 8:3-23.

Olesen, V. 1994. "Feminisms and Models of Qualitative Research." Pp. 158-74 in *Handbook of Qualitative Research,* edited by N. K. Denzin and Y. S. Lincoln. Thousand Oaks, CA: Sage.

Pandey, T. N. 1979. "The Anthropologist-Informant Relationship: The Navajo and Zuni in America and the Tharu in India." Pp. 246-65 in *The Fieldworker and the Field: Problems and Challenges in Sociological Investigation,* edited by M. N. Srinivas, A. M. Shah, and E. A. Ramaswamy. Bombay: Oxford University Press.

Panini, M. N. 1991. "Introduction: Reflections in Feminism and Fieldwork." Pp. 1-10 in *From the Female Eye: Accounts of Women Fieldworkers Studying Their Own Communities,* edited by M. N. Panini. Delhi: Hindustan Publishing.

Patwardhan, S. 1979. "Making My Way through Caste Images: Untouchables in Poona." Pp. 153-60 in *The Fieldworker and the Field: Problems and Challenges in Sociological Investigation,* edited by M. N. Srinivas, A. M. Shah, and E. A. Ramaswamy. Bombay: Oxford University Press.

Phellas, C. N. 2000 "Cultural and Sexual Identities in In-Depth Interviewing." Pp. 52-64 in *Research and Inequality,* edited by C. Truman, D. M. Mertens, and B. Humphries. London: UCL.

Probyn, E. 1993. *Sexing the Self: Gendered Positions in Cultural Studies.* London: Routledge.

Rabinow, P. 1977. *Reflections on Fieldwork in Morocco.* Berkeley: University of California Press.

Riesman, P. 1977. *Freedom in Fulani Social Life.* Chicago: University of Chicago Press.

Rosaldo, R. 1986. "Ilongot Hunting as Story and Experience." Pp. 97-138 in *The Anthropology of Experience,* edited by V. W. Turner and E. M. Bruner. Urbana: University of Illinois Press.

Rutten, M. 1995. *Farms and Factories: Social Profile of Large Farmers and Rural Industrialists in West India.* Delhi: Oxford University Press.

———. 1996. "Business Strategy and Life-Style: Owners of Combine-Harvesters in North Malaysia." *Kajian Malaysia* (Journal of Malaysian Studies) 14(1-2):112-50.

Ryen, A. 2000. "Colonial Methodology? Methodological Challenges to Cross-Cultural Projects Collecting Data by Structured Interviews." Pp. 220-35 in *Research and Inequality,* edited by C. Truman, D. M. Mertens, and B. Humphries. London: UCL.

Ryen, A. and D. Silverman. 2000. "Marking Boundaries: Culture as Category Work." *Qualitative Inquiry* 6:107-27.

Sacks, H. 1992a. *Lectures on Conversation,* Vol. 1. Edited by G. Jefferson. Oxford: Blackwell.

———. 1992b. *Lectures on Conversation,* Vol. 2. Edited by G. Jefferson. Oxford: Blackwell.

Schegloff, E. A. 1992. "Introduction." In H. Sacks, *Lectures on Conversation,* Vol. 2. Edited by G. Jefferson. Oxford: Blackwell.

Schneller, R. 1988. "The Israeli Experience of Cross-Cultural Misunderstanding: Insights and Lessons." Pp. 153-73 in *Cross-Cultural Perspectives in Nonverbal Communication,* edited by F. Poyatos. Toronto: C. J. Hogrefe.

Shaffir, W. B. 1991. "Managing a Convincing Self-Presentation: Some Personal Reflections on Entering the Field." Pp. 72-96 in *Experiencing Fieldwork: An Inside View of Qualitative Research,* edited by W. B. Shaffir and R. A. Stebbins. Newbury Park: Sage.

Shah, A. M. 1979. "Studying the Present and the Past: A Village in Gurajat." Pp. 29-37 in *The Fieldworker and the Field: Problems and Challenges in Sociological Investigation,* edited by M. N. Srinivas, A. M. Shah, and E. A. Ramaswamy. Bombay: Oxford University Press.

Shenkar, O. and Y. Zeira. 1990. "International Joint Ventures: A Tough Test for HR." *Personnel Journal* 67(1):26-31.

Slater, D. 1997. *Consumer Culture and Modernity.* Cambridge: Polity.

Sibley, D. 1995. *Geographies of Exclusion: Society and Difference in the West.* London: Routledge.

Silverman, D. 1993. *Interpreting Qualitative Data: Methods for Analysing Talk, Text and Interaction.* London: Sage.

Smutkupt, S. and L. M. Barna. 1976. "Impact of Non-verbal Communication in an Intercultural Setting: Thailand." *International and Intercultural Annual* 3:130-38.

Spradley, J. P. 1979. *The Ethnographic Interview.* New York: Holt, Rinehart & Winston.

Srinivas, M. N. 1979. "The Fieldworker and the Field: A Village in Karnataka." Pp. 19-28 in *The Fieldworker and the Field: Problems and Challenges in Sociological Investigation,* edited by M. N. Srinivas, A. M. Shah, and E. A. Ramaswamy. Bombay: Oxford University Press.

Stanfield, J. H., II. 1993. "Methodological Reflections: An introduction." Pp. 3-15 in *Race and Ethnicity in Research Methods,* edited by J. H. Stanfield II and R. M. Dennis. Newbury Park, CA: Sage.

———. 1994. "Ethnic Modeling in Qualitative Research." Pp. 175-88 in *Handbook of Qualitative Research,* edited by N. K. Denzin and Y. S. Lincoln. Thousand Oaks, CA: Sage.

Stewart, D. W., S. Hecker, and J. L. Graham. 1987. "It's More Than What You Say: Assessing the Influence of Nonverbal Communication in Marketing." *Psychology and Marketing* 4:303-22.

Streefkerk, H. 1993. *On the Production of Knowledge: Fieldwork in South Gurajat, 1971-1991.* Amsterdam: VU University Press.

Szwed, J. F. 1972. "An American Anthropological Dilemma: The Politics of Afro-American Culture." Pp. 153-81 in *Reinventing Anthropology,* edited by D. Hymes. New York: Pantheon.

Tadria, H. M. K. 1991. "Challenges of Participation and Observation: Fieldwork Experience among Some Peasants of Uganda." Pp. 88-98 in *From the Female Eye: Accounts of Women Fieldworkers Studying Their Own Communities,* edited by M. N. Panini. Delhi: Hindustan Publishing.

Thurnbull, C. M. 1986. "Sex and Gender: The Role of Subjectivity in Field Research." Pp. 17-27 in *Self, Sex and Gender in Cross-Cultural Fieldwork,* edited by T. L. Whitehead and M. E. Conaway. Urbana: University of Illinois Press.

Tse, D. K. and J. Francis. 1994. "Cultural Differences in Conducting Intra- and Intercultural Negotiations: A Sino-Canadian Comparison." *Journal of International Studies* 25:537-56.

Tse, D. K., K. Lee, I. Vertinsky, and D. A. Wehrung. 1988. "Does Culture Matter? A Cross-Cultural Study of Executives' Choice, Decisiveness and Risk Adjustment in International Marketing." *Journal of Marketing* 52(4):81-95.

Tung, R. I. 1984. "How to Negotiate with the Japanese. *California Management Review* 26(4):62-77.

Uphoff, N. 1991. "Fitting Projects to People." Pp. 467-511 in *Putting People First: Sociological Variables in Rural Development,* edited by M. M. Cernea. New York: Oxford University Press.

Vidich, A. J. and S. M. Lyman. 1994. "Qualitative Methods: Their History in Sociology and Anthropology." Pp. 23-59 in *Handbook of Qualitative Research,* edited by N. K. Denzin and Y. S. Lincoln. Thousand Oaks, CA: Sage.

von Raffler-Engel, W. 1988. "The Impact of Covert Factors in Cross-Cultural Communication." Pp. 71-104 in *Cross-Cultural Perspectives in Nonverbal Communication,* edited by F. Poyatos. Toronto: C. J. Hogrefe.

Warren, C. A. B. 1977. "Fieldwork in the Gay World: Issues in Phenomenological Research." *Journal of Social Issues* 33(4):93-107.

———. 1988. *Gender Issues in Field Research.* Newbury Park, CA: Sage.

Wax, R. H. 1960. "Twelve Years Later: An Analysis of Field Experiences." Pp. 166-78 in *Human Organization Research: Field Relations and Techniques,* edited by R. N. Adams and J. J. Preiss. Homewood, IL: Dorsey.

———. 1971. *Doing Fieldwork: Warnings and Advice.* Chicago: University of Chicago Press.

Wengle, J. L. 1988. *Ethnographers in the Field: The Psychology of Research.* Tuscaloosa: University of Alabama Press.

Zaslavsky, C. 1990. *Africa Counts: Number and Pattern in African Culture.* New York: Lawrence Hill.

18

INTERVIEWING IN MEDICAL SETTINGS

◆ Kathleen A. Zoppi
Ronald M. Epstein

Clinical conversations (Stephens 1994) do not occur in isolation; the nature of patient concerns and the multiple contexts of family, medical care organizations, financial reimbursement systems, and regulatory structures create limitations and conflicting priorities for patient care. Research on the patient-physician interview also must be understood in context; the questions asked are driven by patient and health systems factors, and the interactions observed inform medical education and health policy. In this chapter, we identify the ways context affects both the patient-physician relationship and the research agenda.

As medical educators, researchers, and practitioners, we are interested in both theories about medical interviewing and their application, but we emphasize research on patient-physician interactions that has practical implications for clinical care. During clinicians' visits with patients, the clini-

cians' knowledge about the structure of the medical interview and context is relegated to subsidiary awareness, as caring for the patient becomes primary (Crabtree and Miller 1992; Polanyi 1974). In this chapter, we address several important questions:

1. What are the purposes of the medical interview?

2. How do patients and physicians define a successful medical interview?

3. What effects does the patient-physician relationship have on communication?

4. How do patients and physicians handle differences in power, perspectives, and goals in medical interactions?

5. What common situations lead to difficulties in medical interviews?

6. What is known about the structure and process of the medical interview?

7. How do the people involved, the setting in which interviews take place, and systems of health care define and limit the ways that patients and physicians work with each other?

8. How is the medical interview linked to important health outcomes?

9. What research methods, used alone or in combination, can effectively answer questions such as these?

10. What future directions in the study of the patient-physician interview will be useful?

Research into the medical encounter and the patient-physician relationship is enriched by an understanding of the subjective experience of the ill person. Descriptive research can enlighten us about the structures, observed processes, and outcomes of patient-physician interactions. The studies conducted to date concerning patient-physician communication have been heterogeneous; most have been characterized by either a theoretical or an empirical framework for collecting and examining data and either a qualitative (e.g., observational studies, discourse analysis, conversation analysis) model or a quantitative (coding systems or distributional analyses) model. Because of the limitations of each, we advocate the use of combined methods to create a more coherent picture of the communication process.

In this chapter we employ a "patient-centered" (Stewart et al. 1995) or "relationship-centered" model (Tresolini and Pew-Fetzer Task Force 1994), both because of the attention such a model pays to the patient's subjective experience and shared decision making and because of the increasing use of such models for physician evaluation, credentialing, and licensure internationally. Although other theoretical approaches are also heuristically useful, those of most value to clinicians are those that are most directly applicable to patient care and linked to health care outcomes.

The patient-physician relationship and patient-physician communication are broad areas of research and writing, and we cannot do justice to the breadth of these topics in a short chapter. Many fine speculative and empirical pieces have been written, and we will not be able either to duplicate or to survey all of them here. Other authors have reviewed the history of the medical interview (DiMatteo and Friedman 1979; Stoeckle and Billings 1987) and the state of medical teaching and education research (Carroll 1995; Stewart et al. 1999), so we will not attempt to repeat these tasks. In some instances, in areas of specific interest we will direct the reader to the work of authors who review the patient-physician encounter in detail (e.g., Maynard and Heritage forthcoming). Furthermore, excellent reviews of research in patient-physician interaction have been done, and we encourage the reader to refer to these overviews (Boon and Stewart 1998; Inui and Carter 1985). In each of the following sections, we address one of the pertinent questions listed above, briefly reviewing the existing literature relevant to the question as well as what is not yet researched. Finally, we review the research methods that have created our current view of the medical encounter and speculate about what future innovations might bring.

◆ What Are the Purposes of the Medical Interview?

The purposes of the medical interview are to promote healing relationships, to allow for the exchange of information, and to promote the relief of suffering. The encounter, then, can lead to specific, active, purposeful interventions designed to prevent, cure, or palliate illness, as well as the nonspecific healing effects of the patient-physician relationship itself (Cassell 1985). The physician has a moral imperative to establish a healing relationship with the patient and to alleviate suffering. If the purpose of medical care is to accomplish both therapeutic and relational tasks, the process of interaction between patient and physician must include multiple, simultaneously occurring activities. The traditional split between the task and relationship functions of the medical interview is a false dichotomy, mostly an artifact of the methods applied to studying the process. Research on interviews in general has often focused on their verbal content, which has sometimes resulted in a de-emphasizing of nonverbal dimensions and outcomes. More important, most methods for evaluating interviews currently in use do not allow for the study of both content and process levels in a simultaneous and integrated manner (Street and Cappella 1985).

The ways in which the "layers" of an interview affect one another and interact is not clear; for example, a patient's mere expression of symptoms and experiences to the physician may, in fact, be both psychologically relieving and physiologically beneficial to the patient (Berry and Pennebaker 1993). In order to promote healing, the relationship may need to be mutually satisfying to both patient and physician, to represent a positive connection between caregiver and patient (Candib 1995; Matthews, Suchman, and Branch 1993). In the words of Michael Balint (1964), an effective interaction may offer the "doctor as drug." The biopsychosocial model developed by George Engel (1977) promotes the idea that the physician's interaction with the patient is central to the process of healing. Although this may seem obvious, this interaction was not made an explicit subject of research until recent years.

◆ How Do Patients and Physicians Define a Successful Interview?

We do not yet understand all the criteria patients and physicians use to define a successful medical interview, although research indicates that patients, physicians, and observers do not find the same aspects of the medical interview to be important (Stewart et al. 2000; Street 1992). At minimum, however, patients anticipate that physicians will complete information gathering and effect a treatment. This expectation is different from some other professional interviews, in that purposeful activity is expected of the physician at the time of the visit; the expectation is that, in addition to observing, listening, and gathering information, the physician will perform a physical examination, touch, treat, test, prescribe, and perform procedures. The implicit pressure to *do* may be one of the defining features of medical care, as well as one of the forces acting as a barrier to physicians' abilities to listen effectively without prematurely moving to action. The tension among multiple goals that both physician and patient contribute to the visit undergirds the entire interview structure and process (Jaén, Stange, and Nutting 1994; Kleinman 1988; Mishler 1984; Smith et al. 1998).

As currently practiced, the medical interview is often ineffective in eliciting and responding to patients' reasons for coming to the physician (Korsch, Gozzi, and Francis 1968; Francis, Korsch, and Morris 1969; Beckman and Frankel 1984; Starfield et al. 1979). The history-taking model most widely used by clinicians is a highly structured model that presumes one chief complaint expressed first by the patient as the reason for the visit (Stoeckle and Billings 1987). Evidence to refute this assumption is abundant. Typically, patients arrive for visits with three or four major concerns (Starfield et al. 1979, 1981; Freidin, Goldman, and Cecil 1980), usually do not present the most important of their concerns first (Beckman, Frankel, and Darnley 1985; Barsky 1981), and often leave the physician's office without having their most important concerns addressed to their satisfaction.

Physicians tend to use methods of questioning that serve to allow them to keep directing the flow of the interview, rather than allowing patients to speak freely. (For a comprehensive review of the ways in which physicians exert interactional control, see Candib 1995; Cecil and Killeen 1997; Marvel et al. 1999.) Affect and emotion are minimized, and the context of the patient's life, the health care setting, and the work and personal contexts of the physician are frequently not discussed, or, if they are, discussed only in a superficial manner. Poor communication begets poor outcomes. As a consequence, patients may fail to adhere to treatment recommendations, change physicians, seek alternative treatments, sue physicians (Levinson et al. 1997), and remain ill (Greenfield, Kaplan, and Ware 1985). Because medical encounters involve multiple, complex, and competing demands, resulting gaps between patient and physician expectations can be dramatic. Simple congruence or agreement between patient and physician about the reason for a medical visit immediately after the visit has been shown to be poor, with patient and physician agreeing about the major topic less than half the time (Freidin et al. 1980; Starfield et al. 1979, 1981). If accord about the reason for a just-completed visit is difficult to achieve, how much more difficult is agreement about a complex treatment plan?

The consequences of faulty communication processes between patients and physicians can be dramatic, even life threatening. Research interest in this area has developed over the past 25-50 years because challenges and barriers to effective communication are great and may be growing. From his standpoint as an ethicist, Jay Katz (1984) describes how the vulnerability of patients, the desire for help and healing, the need to trust one's physician, and the desire to retain control in the face of severe illness are unspoken themes in many patient-physician discussions. As managed care and other economic forces pull physicians in different directions, the ability of physicians to win the confidence and trust of

their patients becomes even more challenged than in past decades.

◆ What Effects Does the Patient-Physician Relationship Have on Communication?

It is not clear which models of patient-physician relationships describe the most useful and satisfactory relationships. Several models of patient-physician relationships have been advanced (Candib 1995; Doherty and Baird 1983; Emanuel and Emanuel 1992; Kleinman, Eisenberg, and Good 1978; May 1975; Stewart et al. 1995; Szasz and Hollender 1956); these are summarized in Table 18.1.

The domains of relationships can also be described along several continua, such as closeness-distance, empathy-detachment, autonomy-authority, family or community focus-individual focus, collaboration-coercion, and relationship centered-diagnosis centered. Although relationship-centered, empathic, collaborative, and autonomy-supportive care has been promoted as an ideal (Tresolini and Pew-Fetzer Task Force 1994), in actual practice, most clinicians find that different situations require different types of relationships. For example, in an emergency, such as treating an unconscious patient after an accident, medical authority is required. Paranoid patients may become fearful if they feel that they have been too well understood and may fear being touched by the physician. Although social warmth is often useful, a cooler, more detached interaction may be desirable at times; a patient who has been sexually abused, for example, may require a more temperate and even relationship to feel safe. Sometimes coercion is necessary when a patient is a danger to him- or herself or others, such as the compulsory hospitalization of suicidal patients. But all situations share the imperative of respect for the pa-

Table 18.1   MODELS OF THE PATIENT-PHYSICIAN RELATIONSHIP

Model	Physician's Role	Values and Assumptions
Activity/passivity (controlling)	Does something to the patient without patient involvement (e.g., unconscious patient, emergency treatment).	Physician knows best; patient cannot participate in care.
Guidance/cooperation (paternalistic)	Tells patient what to do in order to help patient; uses reassurance rather than explanation.	Physician knows best how to promote patient's best interest; values are shared between physician and patient.
Consumer/informative	Helps patient to help him- or herself. Physician is technical expert who informs patient of options; patient chooses.	Patient bases decisions on his or her own values, of which he or she is aware.
Interpretive	Counsels patient to make decisions in keeping with patient's values.	Patient needs help from the physician to clarify his or her values. Physician does not try to change patient's values.
Deliberative	Engages patient in discussion to develop values; suggests a course of action.	Patient values are malleable; physician's duty is to persuade (not coerce) patient to adopt healthy values.
Contractual/covenantal	Provides a philanthropic, consensual, negotiated, and mutually beneficial relationship with patient.	Values are discussed openly. Moral responsibility is shared between physician and patient in the context of an acknowledged power differential.
Family systems	Cares for patient in context of family unit. Physician helps patient help him- or herself and helps the family help the patient.	Individual and family values are taken into account. Moral responsibility is shared among physician, patient, and patient's family.
Ethnographic	Discovers, with patient, personal and cultural meanings of illness.	Cultural values are embedded in illness and must be addressed comprehensively.
Patient centered	Finds common ground with patient on which to base medical decision making.	Illness must be understood from the patient's perspective as well as from a diagnostic perspective. Physician has a moral obligation to share power and show a human face.

SOURCE: Adapted from Epstein (1996).

tient's autonomy; the physician must allow the patient maximum involvement in his or her own health care.

A patient-centered model embodies the values of autonomy, respect, collaboration, nonabandonment, honesty, charity, and commitment (McWhinney 1997). Respect, in clinical settings, means nonjudgmental acknowledgment of the patient's experience of illness, willingness to find common ground, and acknowledgment of the patient's attempts to heal, whether or not the clinician and patient agree entirely on the nature of the problem or the patient's choices (Rogers 1961). The autonomy-supportive clinician helps the patient to make informed decisions and provides support for follow-through (Miller and Rollnick 1991; Williams et al. 1998). Nonabandon- ment conveys the notion that the physician has a commitment to stay with the patient and continue to help with problem solving, even if medical treatments are no longer the curative (Quill 1983). Honesty means that the clinician lets the patient know what he or she thinks when asked. Charity, as Ian McWhinney (1997) puts it, is "giving with love despite the presence or absence of affection for the patient." These qualities often develop and deepen over time in well-functioning patient-physician relationships; they are most imperiled when things go wrong (Candib 1995; Tresolini and Pew-Fetzer Task Force 1994). "Relationship centered" may be a better descriptor of this model, because it emphasizes the development of a relationship through interaction, rather than a focus on either patient or physician.

Empathy, the cognitive and emotional understanding of another's experience, is crucial to relationship building (Zinn 1993). Physician and patient, in their conversations with each other, transfer information as well as develop frames of reference for interpretation of that information. These frames of reference are sometimes shared between physician and patient; often they are not. Cultural, personal, family, cognitive, language, disability-related, and educational factors are some of the possible barriers to understanding that clinicians commonly encounter (Quill 1989). Empathy is the bridge that clinicians can use to surmount those barriers. Physicians at times feel moments of intense connection with patients that can be transformative for both the patients and the physicians (Matthews et al. 1993). However, the sharing of empathy can be a much less dramatic event. A physician can express "bodily empathy" (Rudebeck 1992) by touching his or her own head while listening to a patient describe a severe migraine, or by nonverbally acknowledging the sensitivity of the part being examined during a physical examination. Affective resonance through subtle nonverbal gestures builds a relationship. Often, however, a physician's explicit verbal acknowledgment of the patient's suffering is the key to helping that patient feel understood. Because physicians commonly do not express empathy, training in this area may be helpful (Suchman et al. 1997), with the caveat that expressions of empathy ultimately must be authentic personal responses to patients' emotional states; otherwise, they may be perceived as inauthentic (Candib 1995).

◆ How Do Patients and Physicians Handle Differences in Power, Perspectives, and Goals in Medical Interactions?

In interactions, relational and task dimensions are consistently present and simultaneous, and these dimensions influence each other (Watzlawick, Beavin, and Jackson 1967). Taking this view, "one cannot not communicate"; every action (or absence), every word (or silence) is potentially subject to the interpretation of others. In particular, the detaching of relational control from topical (content) control is conceptually important to our thinking (Cecil 1998; Cecil and Killeen 1997; Folger and Poole 1982): Each act of communication, whether nonverbal or verbal, is a bid for a relationship definition.

Relational bids have typically been described along two dimensions: control (dominance/submission) and affiliation (hostile or affiliative). Clearly, however, they are more complex than that. In one conceptualization, any relational bid can be made and accepted (indicating you have the right to ask me what you did), rejected (indicating you have no right to ask me what you did), or disconfirmed (not responding to the relationship message, leaving ambiguous the person's right to ask what he or she did), all of which contribute to the process of defining the relationship (Millar, Rogers-Millar, and Courtwright 1979). Acceptance of a relational bid is not the same as agreement (at the level of the content), nor is it equivalent to dominance or submission. An example of how a submissive bid exerts control over the definition of the relationship might be when a patient acquiesces during a physician's sequence of specific questions. This move is the patient's implicit granting of permission to the physician to continue, rather than attempting to reroute the direction of the discussion. Both participants, however, are not equally free to exercise relational control; power differences between participants in any interaction may lead to more frequent submissive or dominant bids (Candib 1995; Cecil and Killeen 1997). Both Anthony Suchman (in Suchman, Botelho, and Hinton-Walker 1998) and Lucy Candib (1995) have made a case that the paradigm of relationship is a stronger model for promoting health and healing than is a model emphasizing control.

Collaboration between physicians and patients in clinical care involves the sharing of power, so that physicians can utilize their expertise and patients can make informed choices. Some have called this process *negotiation* (Lazare 1995), but we believe that the process of reaching common ground is more complex than the reconciling of two contrasting positions. The processes of mutual exploration and understanding of opinions and beliefs are essential to both successful negotiation and relationship building. Ezekiel Emanuel and Linda Emanuel (1992) suggest using the term *deliberation;* however, they do not discuss the

processing of emotions, which we feel is central to the relationship and shifts the focus of the clinical exchange to the patient's well-being and away from a value-neutral contract of mutual interest.

In order for physician and patient to achieve common ground about the illness and its treatment, both must understand the patient's interests and goals, and the patient must know that he or she has been understood. Often, patients' and physicians' interests are stated in generalities: "I want to get better" or "I want to help you get better." But "getting better" may mean different things to physician and patient. Some patients may include in "getting better" unrealistic hopes for cure of a terminal illness, whereas for others "getting better" might mean being well enough to attend a family event. Mutual understanding of the goals of treatment facilitates discussion of means to achieve them. In contrast, disagreements about treatment methods and noncompliance have their roots in lack of agreement about the nature of the problem and goals of treatment, or other conflict in the patient-physician relationship (Lazare, Putnam, and Lipkin 1995). Collaboration also involves agreement about roles and expectations. Who will be responsible for taking the next step? Does the patient want reminders? Would the patient like more information? How much does the patient want to know? Would he or she prefer for the physician to make all the decisions?

Religious and spiritual dimensions of health care are important to most patients and to many physicians (Maugans and Wadland 1991). Most people describe themselves as having a spiritual life, which may or may not be connected directly to religious belief. Even when physician and patient do not share the same religion and values, some patients view positively their physicians' inquiries into their patients' beliefs, faith, and expectations. In the absence of explicit discussions about religious beliefs and practices, there are often spiritual dimensions to the patient-physician relationship as well, and physicians have described a variety of ways in which they have shared transcendent experiences with patients (Matthews et al. 1993). Most cultures have healing traditions that invoke faith, and most traditional healers invoke the imagination to promote healing. Similarly, physicians use their shamanistic or ritualistic power routinely, with the laying on of hands and the rituals of an office visit. Respectful use of spiritual power, initiated with open-ended inquiry and guided by the patient's (and not the physician's) needs, can help the patient-physician relationship to grow and can enhance the patient's body's own healing powers by employing the "placebo effect" (Brody 1992). Clearly, such power has potential for abuse and coercion.

For most of history, interaction between patient and physician has been seen within the context of the interactants' social surroundings, setting, culture, or health care system. As early as the time of Plato, doctors were described as skilled caregivers who saw the development of a therapeutic relationship as essential to good doctoring, yet in Western medical education, the concept of patient empowerment or patient-focused medical care is not yet pervasive or dominant.

The patient-physician relationship includes a social contract: The physician, throughout history, has been expected to help, not to harm, and to act in the patient's best interests (not his or her own, or on behalf of others' interests). In addition, dimensions of this social contract have included justice/fairness of attention, distribution of resources, and, more recently, respect for the patient's autonomy and ability to give informed consent to treatment. Katz (1984) notes that the legal doctrine of informed consent dates only from the late 1960s, and that prior to that time, physician disclosure generally took the form of pragmatic efforts to get patients to do what physicians thought most useful. In recent years, the advent of consumerism, along with the civil rights and feminist

movements, has led, in Western countries, to the placing of greater value on patient autonomy than in previous generations or in other cultures.[1]

◆ What Common Situations Lead to Difficulties in Medical Interviews?

When difficulties arise between patient and physician, often the setting or circumstance of the interaction (e.g., noisy, interrupted settings such as emergency rooms) is to blame, but sometimes the problem lies in the physician's inability to surmount his or her own distress over the subject matter of the visit or social responses to the patient, disease, or problem. Physicians receive significantly less overt training in methods of self-reflection, personal awareness, and responses to patients than do workers in other clinical disciplines, such as nursing and counseling.

The subject of difficult patient encounters has engendered considerable writing (Groves 1978; Platt 1992) and many attempts at teaching and training physicians (Balint 1964; Brock and Salinsky 1993; Brock and Stock 1990; Scheingold 1988). In psychiatry, the patient who evokes a strong negative or positive response from the physician may be said to be eliciting *countertransference,* the physician's unconscious response to the patient based on the physician's prior life experiences with other, significant relationships (Stein 1985). However, an encounter may be difficult not only because of personality characteristics of the patient (or physician); other reasons might include the type of discussion, the uncertainty of the situation, and the physician's response to the mixed agenda of social and biomedical issues inherent in patient care.

In thinking about difficult interviews, it may be helpful to imagine what each participant might define as an ideal interaction. A patient might define an ideal patient-physician interaction as one that addresses concerns, builds the relationship, and allows discussion of preventive and therapeutic options. A physician might define an ideal interaction as one that is time and resource efficient and in which something can be done to aid the patient. A good interview may also be enjoyable. Below, we describe some specific challenges to good physician-patient interviews.

Bad news, or end-of-life issues. Many authors have studied and made recommendations about the difficulty of delivering bad news to patients. Because this is an emotionally difficult task, some authors have proposed guidelines for the humane breaking of bad news to patients (Garg, Buckman, and Kason 1997; Maynard 1997). The success of difficult discussions about advance directives, choices at life's end, and patient and family spiritual values and preferences, as well as the values of the physician, depend on the physician's willingness and capacity to engage with rather than withdraw from strong emotions.

HIV risk and sexuality. Discussions of patient sexuality are often difficult because of social taboos, shared by patients and physicians, concerning the discussion of sexual behavior, sexual orientation, and sexual dysfunction (Epstein et al. 1998). In addition, the awkwardness of physical examination and disclosure of personal information may lead to eroticization of the encounter (conscious or unconscious), particularly when either patient (due to a history of sexual abuse, for example) or physician (due to distress in marriage, for example) is unclear about boundaries in the interaction (Frankel and Williams 1997; McKegney 1993; Zoppi 1992).

Chemical dependency/addiction. Discussion of addiction or chemical dependency is difficult because resistance is a natural part of the disease process, failure can be shameful for both parties, and many physicians (as well as addicts' family members and friends, and the addicts themselves) may feel helpless in the face of such a powerful disease process (Fleming and Barry 1991).

Family violence. Partner violence, child abuse, sexual abuse, and rape are underdetected and underreported because of social norms and structures that reinforce the dominance of abusers, resistance to talking about violence in the families affected, and victims' seeming "collusion" with perpetrators to disguise the problem (Candib 1995; Hendricks-Matthews 1997). Social conventions and taboos that inhibit discussion as well as fear of involvement in legal proceedings may interfere with the physician's willingness to assess patients carefully.

Psychiatric diagnoses. The presence of psychiatric conditions, including common problems such as depression and anxiety, frequently engenders stigmatization. Patients therefore often present somatic symptoms preferentially and can bristle when psychological diagnoses are raised. A patient may perceive a physician's raising such issues as an attempt to describe symptoms as "all in the patient's head" or as a way of minimizing the patient's experience of somatic pain or illness (Epstein et al. 1998; McWhinney, Epstein, and Freeman 1997). The concept of mind-body interactions is relatively new to many people; some patients may find discussion of this concept more acceptable than others, depending on their family, social, cultural, and ethnic backgrounds.

Sociodemographics or social values. Differences between the patient and the physician on sociodemographic dimensions may not be discussed at all in the patient-physician interaction, but these differences can cause significant difficulties in communication. The research on cross-gender (Roter and Hall 1998; West 1993), cross-cultural (Cassata, Conroe, and Clements 1977; Stein 1990), and cross-group (Waitzkin 1990; Waitzkin and Stoeckle 1976) communication offers various views on the ways patients and physicians may attempt to bridge or fail to bridge the gaps caused by differences between them.

◆ What Is Known about the Structure and Process of the Medical Interview?

Most medical interviews are highly structured interactional events. Over time, interactions between a particular doctor and particular patient may vary but are likely to be highly patterned. The pattern typically includes the reviewing of sequences of events as well as similarity from visit to visit in both the proportions of time the physician and patient each speak and the patterns of who initiates and closes topics. Medical interviews are also marked by asymmetry in both disclosure and touch. During office visits, physicians spend proportionally more time talking than do patients; this is quite different from other therapeutic interviews, such as in psychotherapy (Ferrara 1994). Most physician time is spent asking questions, a strategy that preserves for the physician the right to question further. Much of this structure can be attributed to the relatively similar modeling physicians receive in the methods of using communication (essentially a set of social behaviors learned by native speakers in a culture) to accomplish certain tasks of examination, assessment, diagnosis, and treatment identification. Most often, this modeling is tacit and implicit; few clinicians reflect systematically on their patterns of communication.

In the medical encounter, the behaviors and skills that define professional competence often diverge from those that define social communicative competence. As medical students are trained, they learn the stages of the typical medical interview. Each stage has a defined task to be accomplished, with key goals and outcomes.

However, the typical medical encounter structure is not transparent to patients (Mishler 1984), although experienced patients often attempt to shape their responses in anticipation of the physician's structure (Korsch and Harding 1997).

In the patient-centered method, by contrast, the physician's activity should focus on the thorough elicitation of all patient concerns early in the interview (Stewart et al. 1995). The physician's role is to integrate both the patient's agenda and the physician's agenda into a (hopefully) seamless interview, by the end of which the patient's early concerns and hidden concerns have been addressed (Smith and Hoppe 1991). The physician attends carefully to both what is said and what is not said, and specifically to cues that might indicate the patient is not expressing all of his or her concerns overtly (Lang, Floyd, and Beine 2000; Levinson, Gorawara-Bhat, and Lamb 2000). This method specifically presumes that the active involvement of the patient, particularly early in the interview, will bring to the surface the patient's important concerns and will enable a more efficient interview, especially if it reduces the likelihood of later introduction of new issues. Each stage of the medical interview includes potential barriers to effective communication and particular tasks to be accomplished, as depicted in Table 18.2.

As in other types of interviews, the physician's task in the medical interview is generally to elicit information from the patient through the use of questions. Generally, open-ended questions and requests for elaborations elicit complex problems most efficiently. However, in the case of the medical interview, the patient's active seeking of help may also interfere with the physician's expectations about the way the interaction will occur. Whereas the physician's goal of gathering data may compel one sequence of events, the patient's way of thinking about and experiencing symptoms may lead her or him to another set of expectations about how to express concerns to the physician. Elliot Mishler (1984) elo-

Table 18.2   THE PATIENT-CENTERED MODEL AND TASKS OF THE MEDICAL INTERVIEW

Stages of the Interview	Tasks of the Patient-Centered Model
Greeting, introductions	Joining, developing rapport
Chief complaint	Eliciting the patient's and physician's agenda and expectations
History of present illness	Facilitating the patient's expression of concerns while gathering data to make a diagnosis
Past medical history	Understanding the previous illness context and its impact on the current situation
Family and social history	Understanding the patient's illness in life context
Review of systems	Data gathering about associated symptoms
Physical examination	Data gathering and communication of bodily empathy
Treatment plan	Reaching common ground with the patient about the problem and its treatment; patient education

quently terms these competing tasks the "voice of medicine" and the "voice of the lifeworld." In an integrated model, the tasks of the physician and patient are blended in a more fluid interaction, where both sets of agendas and goals are woven together to accomplish the goals of support, diagnosis, expression, examination, and discussion of plans.

In the first part of the interview, during the greeting and introduction phase, normal social ease may be disrupted by the patient's anxiety or by awkwardness arising from a physician's assumptions about the patient's preferred mode of address (Janeway 1980). After an initial social greeting, it is possible that with a new patient, the physician might ask the patient to describe him- or herself, or to talk a bit about topics other than medical concerns. In busy medical practices, however, it is much more common for physicians to initiate interactions with patients by asking questions such as "How can I help you?" or "How are you feeling?"

Most office visits begin with a general opening question. Quickly, however, the patient may begin to offer responses to the physician, stories and sequences being more common than lists. When a patient begins such a presentation, it is relatively rare that he or she is allowed sufficient time to complete the chronology. Research has found that during ambulatory visits, physicians redirect patients with specific follow-up questions only 18 to 23 seconds from the time the patients begin to respond to the physicians' initial solicitations (Beckman and Frankel 1984; Marvel et al. 1999). Early truncating of the patient's agenda may be presumed by the move of the physician from the general opening question to specific, closed-ended questions regarding specific symptoms.

In medical training, part of the process of history taking is the "funneling" of the chief complaint with specific questions concerning temporal characteristics of symptoms, localization of symptoms, and alleviating or aggravating circumstances (Stoeckle and Billings 1987). However, this approach presumes that patients arrive at the office visit with one major concern, which they present first in the sequence. Actually, given that multiple studies have found that patients have three to four major concerns at the average office visit, it is important to note that the chief complaint model does not allow full expression of all of these prior to the funneling of the chief concern. These additional concerns frequently address problems involving family members of the index patient (Medalie et al. 1998; Stange et al. 1998). This early change in the flow of the patient's story may actually "bury" patient concerns, resulting in patient dissatisfaction, early return visits, or increased anxiety, or the patient's changing of physicians (Stewart et al. 1999).

The review of systems is a structured set of topics, organized by organ system (e.g., cardiovascular, neurological, musculoskeletal, endocrine), that prompts the physician to ask questions that might reveal concomitant symptoms the patient has not associated with the presenting concerns. The additional data gathered in the review of systems and physical examination may sometimes lead the physician to offer a different view of symptoms that the patient has not previously considered.

The response of the physician to the expression of emotions by the patient is also a key aspect of the patient-centered approach. The average medical interview, despite the highly emotional nature of many illness experiences, is not replete with emotional expressions of distress, joy, humor, empathy, sadness, and anger. Instead, a compressed range of emotional expression is seen in most visits. However, patients have reported finding those visits where more emotional expression occurs to be more satisfactory, even when negative emotions, such as sadness, predominate (Kaplan et al. 1995, 1996; Levinson et al. 1993). A physician's premature assumptions about a patient's emotional state can be a consequence of projection rather than of empathy; thus physicians may appropriately delay the exploration of emotion and the expression of empathy (Roter et al. 1995).

Facilitation of expression of the patient's experiences requires specific skills on the part of the physician. The use of probes (questions that facilitate elaboration on a topic) such as those employed in many other types of interviews is not generally taught as a specific skill or technique and so appears variably in the medical interview. The use of such probes also may vary widely among physicians according to their differing beliefs about the importance of the psychosocial dimension of their task, or according to personality (Kaplan et al. 1995, 1996; Roter et al. 1995).

The physical examination is a unique aspect of the medical encounter: it is rare for any other professional interview to include physical touch other than a handshake. "Palpation" implies a professional detachment in the act of touching that in other circumstances would be considered intimate or embarrassing. Such touch is, of course, generally nonmutual; the rare instance of mutual contact, or physical contact initiated by the patient, is usually restricted to the opening or closing of the interview, with social greeting contact such as a handshake the norm (Heath 1986).

One interesting dimension of medical training and socialization is that students are slowly "desensitized" to the violation of routine social norms through their training, which includes anatomic dissection, exchanges of exams (usually restricted to eyes, ears, nose, and throat examination or musculoskeletal examination of peers), and practice examinations using standardized patients (actors or previous patients hired to "be" patients). In addition, student physicians receive feedback during training that, as Joan Emerson (1970) puts it, enables them to behave as though "nothing unusual is happening here." Thus the normal social behaviors that guide interaction are supplanted with a set of professional social behaviors that enable the physician and, hopefully, the patient to avoid the embarrassment or shame that might be associated with physical contact. In addition, the professional stance toward physical examination (for example, including a nurse or colleague in the room during breast or urogenital examinations) protects the patient and physician from the potential for inappropriate behavior or misinterpretation of the touch (Zoppi 1992).

One very crucial but often neglected aspect of the medical encounter is the post-physical examination phase, in which the physician identifies a diagnosis and outlines a potential treatment plan for the patient. In research on the medical interview, this critical phase of the interaction is often the briefest and often consists of only the physician's explication of the treatment plan, with no thorough exploration between physician and patient of how the plan fits with the patient's beliefs, economic or logistic constraints, and motivations.

The patient-centered model proposes an alternative framework for this phase in which patient and physician work toward common ground about their expectations for the treatment plan and follow-up care. This approach, which is effective in increasing patient satisfaction and adherence, is even more critical when the treatment plan is ambiguous, involves a range of possible choices (Quill and Townsend 1991), or involves changes to patient health behaviors or habits (Botelho 1998). In this phase, assumptions regarding the model of patient-physician relationship may be vividly expressed by the way the physician includes the patient.

Physicians and patients have two major tasks at the end of the interview: to engage in a social farewell and to complete such tasks as the scheduling of future visits and the writing of prescriptions. This is also a time when unmet needs are often expressed. An "Oh, by the way . . ." comment by the patient at the end of the encounter may invoke dread in the physician, especially if the patient's newly raised concern is potentially serious and cannot be deferred to a future visit (White et al. 1997).

The affective dimensions of the interaction, nonverbal exchanges, and vocal cues may account for more of the patient's perceptions of having been treated well, attended to, and heard than either the content or the actual structure of the interview. These dimensions profoundly affect such aspects of the experience as perceptions of time, tension or relaxation, and intangible feelings of connection during the visit. Empirical studies using thin-slice analysis support the hypothesis that the quality of the interview depends far more on the process and affective dimensions than on what is actually done or said in the interview (Ambady, Bernieri, and Richeson 2000; Ambady, LaPlante, et al. 2000). In this research method, observers notice nonverbal affect by examining very brief segments of speech, often filtered to render the content unintelligible. This method has been more powerful in allowing observers to predict patient dissatisfaction and malpractice suits than qualitative discourse analysis or quantitative coding analysis of the content of the same medical interviews.

In addition to these dimensions, both parties in any interaction participate simultaneously in metaprocessing, including self-awareness, the tracking of process and content, and mindfulness (Santorelli 1999; Stein 1985). These tasks of metaprocessing are the keys that enable the physician to change course in midstream, to become aware of the reactions of the patient or his or her own reactions, to inquire about them, and, ultimately, to use such self- and other-awareness consciously and toward therapeutic ends (Epstein 1999).

◆ How Do the People, Settings, and Health Care System Affect the Ways Patients and Physicians Work with Each Other?

The patient and the physician are usually considered the most important figures in the drama of the medical encounter; however, about one-third of primary care visits to physicians include another person, usually a member of the patient's family (Stange et al. 1998). In educational settings, additional people may include learners such as medical students. The presence of another person in the encounter changes the dynamics radically. For example, patient confidentiality standards require that the physician have specific patient consent for release of information about diagnosis, prognosis, or treatment, even if the person to whom the information is released is present in the examination room. In group practices, managed-care organizations, and other institutional settings, the involvement (either directly or indirectly) of administrators, utilization review coordinators, and insurance workers can affect the relationship between patient and physician.

PEOPLE

Below, we describe briefly several types of relationships and encounters in which patients and physicians are commonly involved; we also offer some comments regarding the issues raised by each of these for the nature of the interview and patient care.

Patient-physician. In the typical dyadic encounter it is possible to conceive of each person as both a unique individual and the "embodiment" of the family and social experiences he or she has had. Past family and social experiences can have powerful influence over how individuals work with each other (McDaniel, Campbell, and Seaburn 1990; Stein 1985). Although the care of the patient is focal in medicine, the biopsychosocial (Engel 1977) and family systems models have begun to persuade physicians that the identified patient in a system is not the only patient in the relationship. However, much of medical care still fails to include family members or significant others in patient-physician discussions, whether they are present or not.

Patient-family member-physician. In a landmark study of the practices of family physicians across the United States, Kurt Stange and his colleagues (1998) found that most visits included discussion about the concerns of or the presence of a family member in the encounter. Yet many medical offices do not routinely plan for the presence of a family member or for engaging a support person in the patient's direct medical care. The addition of another party to the encounter raises significant issues about management of the agenda: Aside from the patient and physician, does the family member also have an agenda for the visit? What confidentiality should be preserved between patient and physician? For example, in the case of a patient who is experiencing domestic violence, the co-presence of a family member is often intended to preserve silence about the violence; it is not a cue about family support. The physician and all other members of the health care team need to be both vigilant and inclusive, an odd combination for managing the interview. In some cultural subgroups, both confidentiality and the role of family may vary greatly from the assumptions of many American caregivers, so clinicians must assess cross-cultural dimensions of family communication as well as provider-patient interaction.

Patient-physician-student/learner, or patient-physician-supervisor. In many educational settings, the presence of another person (a medical student or resident, or other another health professional student) or a faculty supervisor of the practicing physician (often a physician faculty or behavioral science supervisor) may also participate in the interview. Permission for this other person to be present should be requested of the patient, but sometimes is not.

Patient-physician-interpreter. The use of a language interpreter (including a sign language interpreter, in the case of a hearing-impaired patient) offers some potential for additional difficulties and issues about confidentiality in the interview. An interpreter who comes with the patient may have a social or family relationship with him or her that the physician may find difficult to assess in the course of observation. Use of an interpreter who is unknown to the patient, such as those often employed by large hospitals and health care systems, may maintain better confidentiality and clearer communication on the patient's behalf, but may leave the patient feeling isolated and unsupported in the interaction. Institutionally based interpreters may also have little preparation for their job, whereas certified interpreters are better prepared but scarce (Witte and Kuzel 2000).

Physician-physician. The collegial level of interaction implies consultation or another level of interaction over or about the patient. Ronald Epstein (1998) details the complexities for physicians of engaging colleagues in the mutual care of a patient without offering the patient multiple and contradictory messages about care decisions. These interactions are particularly challenging for primary caregivers, who may have to orchestrate the input of multiple other physicians in the care of complex patient cases. These colleagues may have their own strong ideas about medical management or decision making.

Physician-other health professional. In the management of complex medical and social problems, or medical problems with multiple consequences for patient functioning, the physician's coordination of professionals from multiple disciplines is often essential. These other professionals, some with training and licensure requirements of their own, frequently find that physicians have been socialized to see their role as team captain. However, this model may reduce the effectiveness of colleagues from psychology, marriage and family therapy, social work, nursing, and physical and occupational therapy in the care of the patient. Newer models of collaboration and

partnership are increasingly being taught to maximize the effectiveness of care delivery by teams. Contact is particularly poor between physicians and practitioners of integrative, complementary, or alternative medicine (Eisenberg et al. 1998).

Physician-administrator. Administrators may communicate with physicians about patient care, institutional responsibilities, system functioning and constraints, malpractice, risk management, and personnel management and resources. In many systems, utilization review coordinators, who deal with financial and insurance liability for managed-care groups, hospitals, or insurers, may have direct interaction with patients independent of medical providers. Issues of insurance and reimbursement may motivate them to talk differently to patients about care than they would if their priorities were based on medical management alone. The potential for physician and patient to become adversaries increases with such triangulation (Emanuel and Brett 1993).

SETTINGS

Settings for medical encounters can include physicians' offices, patients' homes, hospitals, and other institutional settings, such as nursing homes and prisons. Different settings offer differing contexts and sometimes contradictory views of the patient and his or her problems. When an interview or patient contact occurs in a setting that is different from the usual setting, dramatic differences in the content, flow, and structure of the interview may be observed. In particular, patients seen on their own turf may behave more assertively and may be willing to share information or concerns they have not expressed in the physician's office or the hospital.

Office. Physician's office contacts are brief and orchestrated. Patients come to the office having groomed themselves, sometimes at great effort, for brief and sometimes intense encounters. These visits may be anxiety provoking, in that much activity needs to be compressed into a short period of time. The presence or inclusion of family members or significant others depends on the physician's specialty or style, on clinic organization, and on patient preferences, more than on the patient's disease.

Home visits. Home visits are still a part of many physicians' practices. Although still very common in Europe, in North America home visits are often reserved for posthospitalization, home-bound patients, terminally ill patients, and patients who require extensive or comprehensive social assessment. One benefit of the home visit is that it offers the professional an opportunity to assess the patient's physical functioning in the daily home setting (e.g., a physician may recognize safety hazards in the home of a patient at risk of falling that the patient may not have noticed). Likewise, the home visit offers the physician an opportunity to observe the patient's social and family functioning in a more realistic setting. Home visits can be coordinated among several professionals, such as home health nurses, social workers, and physical therapists, to assure comprehensive care. They can also enable physicians to assess certain aspects of patients' lives that patients may not disclose, such as how family members interact, what types of food are usually consumed, and what kinds of environmental hazards are daily experiences of the patient. Patients often value home visits because they allow patients some "social ground" and dignity that may be lacking in office visits. Home visits do not typically accommodate full physical examinations or procedures.

Hospital. Contacts between physicians and patients in the hospital are usually very brief, but often quite dramatic and meaningful. As the acuity of care increases, a patient's being in the hospital for any reason is usually indicative of severe and serious health concerns, and/or can be a marker of unmanageable social circumstances. Patients' primary care physicians may not always be accessible in the hospital setting, so often patients can feel removed from the security that comes with knowing their doctors. Hospitals can feel inhospitable to patients, with disruptions of routines, sleep, and typical food; however, some hospitals are more open to the involvement of patients' family members than are some outpatient offices.

Emergency room. Physician-patient contacts in emergency rooms may be highly structured, with physicians relying on protocols to triage the urgency of patient care needs and diagnostic processes.

TYPE OF VISIT

The type of visit can also determine the type of interaction likely to occur. In an urgent or acute visit, the physician generally expects to deal with highly focused concerns of the patient, whereas in chronic or routine visits, the patient may be more actively involved in defining his or her own progress and plans to the physician. In a routine visit, particularly with a patient who has chronic illness(es), the physician may act as coach to the patient, who is responsible for management of medications, health habits, and other regimens. When an acute condition is present, the patient's expectation is that the physician will act definitively to select a course of treatment and provide relief.

Compared with patients in a highly technical subspecialty treatment center, patients in a free clinic may experience significantly different types of interactions with professionals; such different settings will also differ in numbers of support staff, functions of the health care team, and other aspects of practice that have to do with economics and clinical parameters. For example, patients coming for a medical visit to a community health center might routinely meet with a public health nurse, an intake coordinator, a child-welfare program coordinator, and a social worker. When appropriate, patients might also meet with a mental health counselor, a dentist, a nutritionist, and other staff, depending on the nature of the patients' problems. This complete spectrum of care in one setting, although emulated by community-based centers, is rarely offered as part of the typical physician's office practice.

LENGTH OF VISIT

Although the length of the physician visit is believed to be related to patient satisfaction with care, an issue that has arisen in recent years concerns whether a managed-care focus is forcing a decrease in the average visit length. In a multisite, cross-sectional study done using the 1991-92 National Ambulatory Medical Care Survey, the average duration of the medical visit was found to be 16.3 minutes (SD ±9.7 minutes) (Blumenthal et al. 1999). Recent studies have attempted to determine whether adequate patient-centered interviewing can be done successfully in a short time. Work conducted by researchers at the University of Western Ontario indicates that a 10-minute interview threshold may exist with regard to patient satisfaction (Brown, Stewart, and Weston 1997). Yet in the average family practice office, a typical interview receives a 15-minute slot, which, by necessity, includes all pre- and postvisit paperwork (Dugdale, Epstein, and Pantilat 1999). It may be more crucial for researchers to investigate what factors (such as pacing and affect) contribute to patients' and physicians' perceptions of time during the visit (e.g., not feeling hurried or rushed, feeling that adequate closure has occurred; Epstein 2000). Perceptions of the passage of time vary greatly, probably due to the flow of the process and the synchrony/rapport of the parties to the interaction (Zoppi 1994).

◆ How Is the Medical Interview Linked to Important Health Outcomes?

The variables discussed below, which implicate communication skills and behaviors, may have some influence on the outcomes of medical care (Beckman, Kaplan, and Frankel 1989).

Treatment options and clinical decision making. Choices of treatment options have been found to affect health care outcomes. There is increasing evidence that, although physicians may not consciously assess patients based on social assumptions (about race, education, socioeconomic status), in fact they offer their patients different diagnostic and treatment options that correlate with such social judgments. This must be mediated by the process of social interaction, but the manner in which such clinical judgments and impressions are managed is not clear (Fiscella et al. 2000).

Patient satisfaction. Patient satisfaction has been employed as a measure of the effectiveness of interaction between patient and physician, but it may, in fact, be only a proxy measure of the affective tone of the exchange. Patient satisfaction research indicates that most individual patients are, in fact, satisfied with the quality of their own interactions with their individual physicians, but that satisfaction with health care received is not generally high (Hall and Dornan 1988).

Communication process. The effect of the physician-patient communication process on health functioning and status is confounded by relationship to the type of diagnosis and treatment (because some conditions may improve regardless of treatment). In one study that examined 100 visits of patients with headache to family physicians in Canada, the most important predictor of patient improvement at *one year* after the initial visit (regardless of headache type/cause or treatment) was found to be the patient's perception that he or she had fully expressed his or her concerns to the physician at the index visit (Headache Study Group of the University of Western Ontario 1986). The Medical Outcomes Study found that patients with diabetes, hypertension, and breast cancer all had significantly better health outcomes when they were seen by providers who were trained in participatory methods that included and involved patients in active management of their disease process and treatment (Kaplan, Greenfield, and Ware 1989). The potential link between patient-physician communication process and health status improvement is an area with considerable research potential and promise.

Patient adherence to treatment recommendations. Patient compliance (and lack of compliance) with treatment recommendations has been studied in both chronic and acute illnesses, and in relation to patient health behaviors and prevention. Increased attention to the steps of behavioral change has resulted in increased interest in motivational approaches to patient interviewing (Prochaska and DiClemente 1982). These approaches recognize the importance of physicians' eliciting patient health beliefs (Eraker, Kirscht, and Becker 1984) and the use of explanatory models (Kleinman 1983) in facilitating patient behavioral change. Diabetes management using a patient-centered approach has been demonstrated to improve patient outcomes (Steele and Susman 1998).

Continuity of care. Different researchers have studied and defined continuity of care differently. When defined as the majority of care given by the same provider(s), it has been associated with decreased unnecessary test ordering, increased diagnosis of psychological problems such as depression, and increased satisfaction for both pro-

vider and patient (Hjortdahl and Borchgrevink 1991).

Physician satisfaction. Physician satisfaction may be both a cause and an effect of good interactions with patients. It has been demonstrated that physicians' enjoyment of dealing with patients' psychosocial concerns is linked to greater longevity in practice. Suchman et al. (1993) examined physician satisfaction with primary care office visits and found that physicians who were more effective in dealing with psychosocial problems were more likely to remain in practice.

Malpractice suits. In studies of malpractice suits filed against physicians, Wendy Levinson and her colleagues found significant differences in the predictors of malpractice suits for primary care physicians and surgeons (see Levinson 1994; Levinson et al. 1997). Lawsuits against primary care physicians were more likely when the physicians were less skilled in educating patients, when they did not encourage or facilitate patients' expressions of concerns or opinions, and when humor or laughter was minimal in physician-patient interactions. Visit length was 20 percent longer in the no-claims group. Nonverbal expressions of affect held the strongest predictive value of any variable in a study of malpractice prediction using thin-slice analysis (Ambady, LaPlante, et al. 2000).

◆ What Research Methods Can Effectively Answer These Questions?

Early research on the process and structure of medical interviews was developed by researchers in psychiatry (Scheflen 1973; Hopkinson, Cox, and Rutter 1981; Cox, Holbrook, and Rutter 1981; Cox, Rutter, and Holbrook 1981, 1988; Rutter and Cox 1981) and by practitioners who were curi-

Table 18.3   METHODS OF DATA COLLECTION AND FORMS OF REPORTING ABOUT MEDICAL INTERVIEWS

Method	Typical Forms of Reporting
Direct observation	Qualitative or descriptive reports Case studies Interpretive or narrative accounts Ethnographies
Videotaping	Coding schemes (distributional analysis; correlation or regression analysis) Thin-slice analyses (observer perception/impression) Conversation analysis (transcription and analysis)
Audiotaping	Transcription and discourse analysis Transcription and conversation analysis Coding systems (distributional analysis; correlation or regression analysis)
Focus groups	Qualitative or thematic analysis; description of patient preferences
"Exit" interviews of patients, physicians	Comparison of patient-physician agreement, perceptions of time, and so on
Stimulated recall	Qualitative descriptions; teaching skill changes or self-observation
Standardized patients	Measurement of skill acquisition, performance
Surveys: health outcome, patient satisfaction, health status	Correlational analysis with sociodemographics of patient population

ous about the effectiveness of the communication process (Francis et al. 1969). Others, such as Gregory Bateson and his colleagues, contributed to the methods used to study the encounter through work on psychiatric interviews. The breadth of research efforts has been summarized effectively by others (e.g., Inui and Carter 1995); our point here is that research efforts have been developed largely independent of theories or models of the encounter and have generally used either qualitative or quantitative approaches to the study of interaction. Usually, such studies examine only one visit in a series, constituting a point in time in a developing or evolving relationship. Some researchers have looked at both first visits and return visits; most include a mixture of both types of visits in the research sample. Few, however, have employed the method of studying multiple encounters between

the same physician and patient over time (Boon and Stewart 1998). Such longitudinal research would be useful for defining the variations over time that may be characteristic of the life course of both a relationship and an illness, for example. Patients and physicians who behave in one way during an acute illness or exacerbation might behave quite differently in the quiescent phase of an illness, or near the end of life.

The data collection methods employed in the study of the patient-physician relationship have shaped our view of the interaction. The methods of data collection used most frequently are described in Table 18.3.

Qualitative or *descriptive* approaches are often employed to characterize medical encounters. Methods used most commonly include case descriptions or narrative accounts. In the ethnographic tradition of anthropology or sociology, meaning is inferred through a study of language and the expertise of the observer and informants.[2]

Conversation analysis and *discourse analysis* are two distinct methods in which researchers use detailed transcription to analyze the social interaction and structural features of the medical interview. These methods preserve the sequential development of speech patterns in the interactions between patients and physicians. These methods have in common the use of detailed transcripts from tapes, with descriptive decision rules about the common ways speakers engage in the mutual production of a conversation. Researchers compare social conversational norms with the patterns of interaction in medical encounters and use social norms to examine the joint production of interaction. Some researchers employ sociolinguistic methods (Labov and Fanshel 1977), whereas others use conversation analysis, following the tradition of Harvey Sacks and his colleagues (Maynard and Heritage forthcoming; Halkowski forthcoming; Roter and Frankel 1992; West and Frankel 1991; West 1984). Discourse analysis (Todd 1989; Mishler 1984; Waitzkin 1990) includes models for transcription and interpretation as well as an emphasis on sequential analysis and the degree to which interpretations are considered representative of the type of interaction being discussed.

Conversation analysis, for example, has been used to illustrate the differences between social encounters in which bad news is shared and medical encounters in which bad news is shared (Maynard and Frankel, forthcoming). Whereas social exchanges might enable givers and recipients of bad news to use a variety of methods for the breaking of news and for emotional expression afterward, the pattern is not the same for medical encounters. Because there is no reciprocity in the medical encounter, the physician often previews the announcement of bad news ("There is a problem") and then gives the news to the patient.

Virginia Gill and Douglas Maynard (forthcoming) have examined the ways in which physicians construct responses to patients' offers of explanations of health problems. Their findings point to the importance of physicians' complete elicitation of patients' beliefs and explanations early in the interview; patients sometimes offer their perspectives late in the interview, and physicians' responses to these offers are variable. Gill and Maynard explicate the typical types of physician responses and their consequences in the interaction. Conversation analysis provides a method of observing and describing patterns and sequences of interaction that can reveal the basic structure of the medical encounter.

Conclusions from this type of work have been dramatic for clinician-consumers, but much of this body of literature is known more to the social science community than to the clinical community.[3] Although case study format research is abundant in medicine, the absence of generalizable conclusions from this type of research can remove it from the very clinical readership that might find it applicable to the care of patients.[4] Because qualitative research on patient-physician interaction can uncover information that quantitative methods cannot, such as sequential structure, linguistic or lexical patterns, and other features of the interaction, it is important that such conclusions be accessible to clinical readers. Some research, such as work on the breaking of bad news (Maynard 1997), has been more widely used in prescriptive educational work for clinicians (Buckman 1992; Garg et al. 1997).

Research employing *coding schemes* offers the potential for researchers to assess the medical interview using distributional analysis (e.g., How much time does the physician speak? How much does the patient speak? How many questions does each ask?), but until recently has removed sequential features of the discourse from examination. Early research on the patient-physician encounter employed transcription and coding as methods of analysis

(Byrne and Long 1976; Korsch et al. 1968). Much of the research on patient-physician communication done using large data sets has employed coding schemes. Debra Roter (1984; Roter and Frankel 1992) has employed a revised version of Bales's (1950) interaction process analysis (a coding system for analysis of group process), which has been widely used as a framework for analysis. It relies on categories that distinguish task and relationship aspects of the content of the interview. An early coding system developed by Stiles and Putnam (1989) was more complex and based on sociolinguistics; it examined the conversational implications of verbal offers by patient or physician, using verbal response modes. Both coding systems resulted in distributional analyses, not sequential analyses.

More recently, Edward Callahan and Klea Bertakis (1991) developed a behavioral observation system for the medical interview (the Davis Observation Code system, or DOC) that identifies frequent occurrences in the interview as predictors of visit outcomes as well as distributional analyses. The representational validity of coding systems, particularly for measures attempting to code the patient's perspective, requires further research (Street 1992). In a recent study of patient-centered measures, health outcomes of interviews were coded with a patient-centered scheme that correlated well with patient perceptions of finding common ground; these, in turn, were correlated with improved health status and predicted decreased utilization of referrals and tests (Stewart et al. 2000).

As indicated above, qualitatively oriented researchers have criticized the lack of sequential analysis as a methodological shortcoming of coding systems. However, in communication research, methods for analysis of both the sequential and the distributional features of interaction are possible, but until recently have not been applied routinely to patient-physician discourse (Epstein et al. 1998).

Process analysis (e.g., relational coding schemes) that pays attention to the coding of both the process and the content of interaction was attempted in early research by Gregory Bateson, Paul Watzlawick, and others. Their approach to the analysis of discourse was to identify the relational level of message exchange, although the methods of analysis used were not applied until recently to patient-physician discourse. This approach has not been used widely in the analysis of patient-physician communication (Cecil 1998).

Thin-slice analysis is a promising method that employs brief excerpts of interactions to evoke observers' judgments about the quality of interactions/relationships. The study of impression management processes led to this method, which uses brief (10-second) clips of videotape, with or without audio. Research using this method has found that observers of such brief clips were able to make predictions about malpractice suits with high reliability (Ambady, Bernieri, and Richeson 2000; Ambady, LaPlante, et al. 2000).

Physiological responses have largely been overlooked in interview studies; there is a paucity of research demonstrating the physiological effects of interaction between patient and physician. The application of physiological measurement such as in marital research has not yet been done in medical interviewing research.

◆ What Future Directions in the Study of the Patient-Physician Interview Will Be Useful?

Research on patient-physician communication has been somewhat fragmented, in part because of the relative absence of multimethod research and a common theoretical framework. In research on the patient-physician relationship, studies of the communication process have been largely reductionist and often atheoretical, either selecting short segments of a relationship for study or selecting only certain features of communication process and structure for examination.

Few research studies have integrated both quantitative and qualitative approaches. Such integration can make distributional and sequential analyses possible and preserve the layers of nonverbal or "intangible" levels of interaction, along with the verbal, that researchers need to offer conclusive information about what is effective as well as what is teachable. However, questions remain concerning whether such skills can, in fact, be taught and what methods might be effective in teaching them.

In the view of thin-slice researchers, collections of observers can make accurate judgments about the quality of interactions based on very brief excerpts of those interactions. This may imply that the affective aspects of care truly "frame" the patient's experience, and that research methods that focus attention on content are not only obsolete but may be misleading about what is important to the patient's experience. Given that research has demonstrated significant disparities between participant and observer perceptions of the same medical encounters, and that the patient's experience likely determines outcomes, research methods that highlight and focus on the patient's experience and voice are particularly desirable (Street 1992).

Research to date has highlighted the areas in which medical interviews fall short of their potential: Patients have concerns that are often truncated or not expressed in the interview; patients' expertise and concerns are often minimized or not acknowledged; emotional expression is limited but powerful in its consequences; good interviews are important to patient health and to physician satisfaction; bad interviews may lead to poor outcomes for the individuals and the health care system. Although there have been several recent studies of exemplary physicians' communication styles (Marvel et al. 1999; Shoemaker 1986), we don't yet know why good interviews "work."

Some communication skills and styles are changeable and can be taught (Kaplan et al. 1997; Roter et al. 1995); we do not yet know what interventions are most effective for changing interactional behavior, or whether physician-only or dyadic/relational interventions are likely to be more successful. We do not know the physiological sequelae of either good or bad interviews, immediately or in the long term. And we do not know what research methods best capture the intangible elements of interpersonal chemistry that observers can see (even when they can't "hear" the content, as in thin-slice analysis) but that we cannot explain articulately. These and other research avenues remain open to those interested in the medical encounter.

■ Notes

1. Howard Brody (1992) provides a thorough discussion of the implicit cultural expectations of physicians, including altruism and nonabandonment of patients (especially of the terminally ill).

2. Examples are Arthur Kleinman's (1986) work on the cross-cultural presentation of depression in China and Western medicine using immersion and Charles Bosk's (1979) work using interviews to describe the ways errors were handled in a hospital. D. J. Walker, I. D. Griffiths, and C. M. Leon (1991) have explored the meanings of somatic illness to patients through analysis of therapy. Ronald Epstein and his colleagues (1998) discuss the avoidance and awkwardness that accompanies HIV-related topics.

3. An example from conversation analysis is the finding of Howard Beckman and his colleagues (1985), later replicated by M. Kim Marvel et al. (1999), that physicians interrupted patients to ask specific follow-up questions within an average of 18-23 seconds. Readers who are interested in the substantial body of work that has been generated by conversation analysts are referred to Douglas Maynard and John Heritage's forthcoming edited volume *Practicing Medicine: Talk and Action in Primary Care Encounters*. The book's contributors apply conversation analysis to all stages of the medical encounter, analyzing the structure and sequential production of each part of the visit. In addition,

researchers have used conversation analysis to look at a wide range of clinical encounters, including AIDS counseling.

4. See, for example, the case studies published each week in the *New England Journal of Medicine.*

■ *References*

Ambady, N., F. J. Bernieri, and J. A. Richeson. 2000. "Toward a Histology of Social Behavior: Judgmental Accuracy from Thin Slices of the Behavioral Stream." Pp. 1-126 in *Advances in Experimental Social Psychology,* Vol. 32, edited by M. P. Zanna. New York: Academic Press.

Ambady, N., D. LaPlante, T. Nguyen, N. Chaumeton, R. Rosenthal, and W. Levinson. 2000. "Thin Slice Judgments of Physicians' Affect: Vocal Cues Associated with Malpractice Claims among Primary Care Physicians and Surgeons." Unpublished manuscript.

Bales, R. F. 1950. *Interaction Process Analysis.* Reading, MA: Addison-Wesley.

Balint, M., ed. 1964. *The Doctor, His Patient, and the Illness.* New York: International Universities Press.

Barsky, A. J. 1981. "Hidden Reasons Some Patients Visit Doctors." *Annals of Internal Medicine* 94:492-98.

Beckman, H. B. and R. M. Frankel. 1984. "The Effect of Physician Behavior on the Collection of Data." *Annals of Internal Medicine* 101:692-96.

Beckman, H. B., R. M. Frankel, and J. Darnley. 1985. "Soliciting the Patient's Complete Agenda: A Relationship to the Distribution of Concerns" (abstract). *Clinical Research* 33:714A.

Beckman, H. B., S. H. Kaplan, and R. M. Frankel. 1989. "Outcome-Based Research on Doctor-Patient Communication." In *Communicating with Medical Patients,* edited by M. Stewart and D. L. Roter. Newbury Park, CA: Sage.

Berry, D. S. and J. W. Pennebaker. 1993. "Nonverbal and Verbal Emotional Expression and Health." *Psychotherapy and Psychosomatics* 59(1):11-19.

Blumenthal, D., N. Causino, Y. Chang, L. Culpepper, W. Marder, D. Saglam, R. Stafford, and B. Starfield. 1999. "The Duration of Ambulatory Visits to Physicians." *Journal of Family Practice* 48:264-71.

Boon, H. and M. Stewart. 1998. "Patient-Physician Communication Assessment Instruments: 1986-96 in Review." *Patient Education and Counseling* 35:161-76.

Bosk, C. L. 1979. *Forgive and Remember.* Chicago: University of Chicago Press.

Botelho, R. J. 1998. "Negotiating Partnerships in Healthcare: Contexts and Methods." Pp. 19-50 in *Partnerships in Healthcare: Transforming Relational Process,* edited by A. L. Suchman, R. J. Botelho, and P. Hinton-Walker. Rochester, NY: University of Rochester Press.

Brock, C. D. and J. V. Salinsky. 1993. "Empathy: An Essential Skill for Understanding the Physician-Patient Relationship in Clinical Practice." *Family Medicine* 25:245-48.

Brock, C. D. and R. D. Stock. 1990. "A Survey of Balint Group Activities in U.S. Family Practice Residency Programs." *Family Medicine* 22:33-37.

Brody, H. 1992. *The Healer's Power.* New Haven, CT: Yale University Press.

Brown, J. B., M. Stewart, and W. W. Weston. 1997. "The Patient Centered Clinical Method: Clinical Outcomes." Presented at the annual meeting of the Society of Teachers of Family Medicine, April, Boston.

Buckman, R. 1992. *How to Break Bad News: A Guide for Health Care Professionals.* Baltimore: Johns Hopkins University Press.

Byrne, P. and B. Long. 1976. *Doctors Talking to Patients: A Study of the Verbal Behavior of General Practitioners Consulting in Their Surgeries.* Exeter: Royal College of General Practitioners.

Callahan, E. J. and K. D. Bertakis. 1991. "Development and Validation of the Davis Observation Code." *Family Medicine* 23:19-24.

Candib, L. M. 1995. "Violence against Women, Not Family Violence." Pp. 56-80 in L. M. Candib, *Medicine and the Family: A Feminist Perspective.* New York: Basic Books.

Carroll, J. G. 1995. "Evaluation of Medical Interviewing: Concepts and Principles." In *The Medical Interview: Clinical Care, Education, and Research,* edited by M. Lipkin, Jr., S. M. Putnam, and A. Lazare. New York: Springer-Verlag.

Cassata, D. M., R. M. Conroe, and P. W. Clements. 1977. "A Program for Enhancing Medical Interviewing Using Video-Tape Feedback in the Family Practice Residency." *Journal of Family Practice* 4:673-77.

Cassell, E. J. 1985. *Talking with Patients,* Vol. 2, *Clinical Technique.* Cambridge: MIT Press.

Cecil, D. W. 1998. "Relational Control Patterns in Physician-Patient Clinical Encounters: Continuing the Conversation." *Health Communication* 10:125-49.

Cecil, D. W. and I. Killeen. 1997. "Control, Compliance, and Satisfaction in the Family Practice Encounter." *Family Medicine* 29:653-57.

Cox, A., D. Holbrook, and M. Rutter. 1981 "Psychiatric Interviewing Techniques VI. Experimental Study: Eliciting Feelings." *British Journal of Psychiatry* 139:144-52.

Cox, A., M. Rutter, and D. Holbrook. 1981. "Psychiatric Interviewing Techniques V. Experimental Study: Eliciting Factual Information." *British Journal of Psychiatry* 139:29-37.

———. 1988. "Psychiatric Interviewing Techniques. A Second Experimental Study: Eliciting Feelings." *British Journal of Psychiatry* 152:64-72.

Crabtree, B. F. and W. L. Miller. 1992. "Primary Care Research." In *Doing Qualitative Research,* edited by B. F. Crabtree and W. L. Miller. Newbury Park, CA: Sage.

DiMatteo, M. R. and H. S. Friedman, eds. 1979. "Interpersonal Relations in Health Care" (special issue). *Journal of Social Issues* 35(1).

Doherty, W. J. and M. A. Baird. 1983. *Family Therapy and Family Medicine: Toward the Primary Care of Families.* New York: Guilford.

Dugdale, D. C., R. Epstein, and S. Z. Pantilat. 1999. "Time and the Patient-Physician Relationship." *Journal of General Internal Medicine* 14(Suppl. 1):34-40.

Eisenberg, D. M., R. B. Davis, S. L. Ettner, S. Appel, S. Wilkey, M. Van Rompay, and R. C. Kessler. 1998. "Trends in Alternative Medicine Use in the United States, 1990-1997: Results of a Follow-Up National Survey." *Journal of the American Medical Association* 280:1569-75.

Emanuel, E. J. and A. S. Brett. 1993. "Managed Competition and the Patient-Physician Relationship. *New England Journal of Medicine* 329:879-82.

Emanuel, E. J. and L. L. Emanuel. 1992. "Four Models of the Physician-Patient Relationship." *Journal of the American Medical Association* 267:2221-26.

Emerson, J. P. 1970. "Behavior in Private Places: Sustaining Definitions of Reality in Gynecological Examinations." Pp. 74-97 in *Recent Sociology,* Vol. 2, edited by H. P. Dreitzel. London: Collier-Macmillan.

Engel, G. L. 1977. "The Need for a New Medical Model: A Challenge for Biomedicine." *Science* 196:129-36.

Epstein, R. M. 1996. "The Patient-Physician Relationship." Pp. 105-32 in *Fundamentals of Clinical Practice: A Textbook on the Patient, Doctor, and Society,* edited by M. B. Mengel and W. L. Holleman. New York: Plenum Medical.

———. 1998. "Communication between Primary Care Physicians and Consultants." Pp. 171-85 in *Partnerships in Healthcare: Transforming Relational Process,* edited by A. L. Suchman, R. J. Botelho, and P. Hinton-Walker. Rochester, NY: University of Rochester Press.

———. 1999. "Mindful Practice." *Journal of the American Medical Association* 282:833-39.

———. 2000. "The Science of Patient-Centered Care." *Journal of Family Practice* 49:805-7.

Epstein, R. M., D. S. Morse, R. M. Frankel, L. Frarey, K. Anderson, and H. B. Beckman. 1998. "Awkward Moments in Patient-Physician Communication about HIV Risk." *Annals of Internal Medicine* 128:435-42.

Eraker, S. A., J. P. Kirscht, and M. H. Becker. 1984. "Understanding and Improving Patient Compliance." *Annals of Internal Medicine* 100:258-68.

Ferrara, K. W. 1994. *Therapeutic Ways with Words.* New York: Oxford University Press.

Fiscella, K., P. Franks, M. R. Gold, and C. M. Clancy. 2000. "Inequality in Quality: Addressing Socioeconomic, Racial, and Ethnic Disparities in Health Care." *Journal of the American Medical Association* 283:2579-84.

Fleming, M. F. and K. L. Barry. 1991. "A Three-Sample Test of a Masked Alcohol Screening Questionnaire." *Alcohol and Alcoholism* 26(1):81-91.

Folger, J. and M. S. Poole. 1982. "Relational Coding Schemes: The Question of Validity." In *Communication Yearbook 5,* edited by M. Burgoon. New Brunswick, NJ: Transaction.

Francis, V., B. M. Korsch, and M. J. Morris. 1969. "Gaps in Doctor-Patient Communication: Patients' Response to Medical Advice." *New England Journal of Medicine* 280:535-40.

Frankel, R. M. and S. Williams. 1997. "Sexuality and Professionalism." In *Behavioral Medicine: A Primary Care Handbook,* edited by M. Feldman and T. Christensen. New York: Appleton & Lange.

Freidin, R. B., L. Goldman, and R. R. Cecil. 1980. "Patient-Physician Concordance in Problem Identification in the Primary Care Setting." *Annals of Internal Medicine* 93:490-93.

Garg, A., R. Buckman, and Y. Kason. 1997. "Teaching Medical Students How to Break Bad News." *Canadian Medical Association Journal* 156:1159-64.

Gill, V. T. and D. W. Maynard. Forthcoming. "Patients' Explanations for Disease and Physicians' Responsiveness in the Medical Interview." In *Practicing Medicine: Talk and Action in Primary Care Encounters,* edited by D. W. Maynard and J. Heritage. Cambridge: Cambridge University Press.

Greenfield, S., S. H. Kaplan, and J. E. Ware, Jr. 1985. "Expanding Patient Involvement in Care: Effects on Patient Outcomes." *Annals of Internal Medicine* 102:520-28.

Groves, J. E. 1978. "Taking Care of the Hateful Patient." *New England Journal of Medicine* 298:883-87.

Halkowski, T. Forthcoming. "Realizing the Illness: Patients' Narratives of Symptom Discovery." In *Practicing Medicine: Talk and Action in Primary Care Encounters,* edited by D. W. Maynard and J. Heritage. Cambridge: Cambridge University Press.

Hall, J. A. and M. C. Dornan. 1988. "Meta-analysis of Satisfaction with Medical Care: Description of Research Domain and Analysis of Overall Satisfaction Levels." *Social Science and Medicine* 27:637-44.

Headache Study Group of the University of Western Ontario. 1986. "Predictors of Outcome in Headache Patients Presenting to Family Physicians: A One Year Prospective Study." *Headache* 26:285-94.

Heath, C. 1986. *Body Movement and Speech in Medical Interaction.* Cambridge: Cambridge University Press.

Hendricks-Matthews, M. K. 1997. "A Survey of Family-Violence Curricula in Virginia Medical Schools and Residencies at University Medical Centers." *Academic Medicine* 72(1):54-56.

Hjortdahl, P., and C. F. Borchgrevink. 1991. "Continuity of Care: Influence of General Practitioners' Knowledge about Their Patients on Use of Resources in Consultations." *British Medical Journal* 303:1181-84.

Hopkinson, K., A. Cox, and M. Rutter. 1981. "Psychiatric Interviewing Techniques III. Naturalistic Study: Eliciting Feelings." *British Journal of Psychiatry* 138:406-15.

Inui, T. S. and W. B. Carter. 1985. "Problems and Prospects for Health Services Research on Provider-Patient Communication." *Medical Care* 23:521-38.

———. 1995. "A Guide to the Research Literature on Doctor/Patient Communication." In *The Medical Interview: Clinical Care, Education, and Research,* edited by M. Lipkin, Jr., S. M. Putnam, and A. Lazare. New York: Springer-Verlag.

Jaén, C. R., K. C. Stange, and P. A. Nutting. 1994. "Competing Demands of Primary Care: A Model for the Delivery of Clinical Preventive Services." *Journal of Family Practice* 38:166-71.

Janeway, E. 1980. *Powers of the Weak.* New York: Alfred A. Knopf.

Kaplan, C. B., B. Siegel, J. M. Madill, and R. M. Epstein. 1997. "Communication and the Medical Interview: Strategies for Learning and Teaching." *Journal of General Internal Medicine* 12(Suppl. 2):49-55.

Kaplan, S. H., B. Gandek, S. Greenfield, W. Rogers, and J. E. Ware, Jr. 1995. "Patient and Visit Characteristics Related to Physicians' Participatory Decision-Making Style: Results from the Medical Outcomes Study." *Medical Care* 33:1176-87.

Kaplan, S. H., S. Greenfield, B. Gandek, W. Rogers, and J. E. Ware, Jr. 1996. "Characteristics of Physicians with Participatory Decision-Making Styles." *Annals of Internal Medicine* 124:497-504.

Kaplan, S. H., S. Greenfield, and J. E. Ware, Jr. 1989. "Assessing the Effects of Physician-Patient Interactions on the Outcomes of Chronic Disease." *Medical Care* 27(Suppl.):S110-27. (Erratum appears in *Medical Care* 27:679.)

Katz, J. 1984. *The Silent World of Doctor and Patient.* New York: Free Press.

Kleinman, A. 1983. "The Cultural Meanings and Social Uses of Illness." *Journal of Family Practice* 16:539-45.

———. 1986. *Social Origins of Distress and Disease: Depression, Neurasthenia, and Pain in Modern China.* New Haven, CT: Yale University Press.

———. 1988. *The Illness Narratives: Suffering, Healing, and the Human Condition.* New York: Basic Books.

Kleinman, A., L. Eisenberg, and B. Good. 1978. "Culture, Illness, and Care: Clinical Lessons from Anthropologic and Cross-Cultural Research." *Annals of Internal Medicine* 88:251-58.

Korsch, B. M., E. K. Gozzi, and V. Francis. 1968. "Gaps in Doctor-Patient Communication 1: Doctor-Patient Interaction and Patient Satisfaction." *Pediatrics* 42:855-70.

Korsch, B. M. and C. Harding. 1997. *The Intelligent Patient's Guide to the Doctor-Patient Relationship.* New York: Oxford University Press.

Labov, W. and D. Fanshel. 1977. *Therapeutic Discourse: Psychotherapy as Conversation.* New York: Academic Press.

Lang, F., M. R. Floyd, and K. L. Beine. 2000. "Clues to Patients' Explanations and Concerns about Their Illnesses: A Call for Active Listening." *Archives of Family Medicine* 9:222-27.

Lazare, A. 1995. "The Interview as Clinical Negotiation." In *The Medical Interview: Clinical Care, Education, and Research,* edited by M. Lipkin, Jr., S. M. Putnam, and A. Lazare. New York: Springer-Verlag.

Lazare, A., S. M. Putnam, and M. Lipkin, Jr. 1995. "Three Functions of the Medical Interview." In *The Medical Interview: Clinical Care, Education, and Research,* edited by M. Lipkin, Jr., S. M. Putnam, and A. Lazare. New York: Springer-Verlag.

Levinson, W. 1994. "Physician-Patient Communication: A Key to Malpractice Prevention." *Journal of the American Medical Association* 272:1619-20.

Levinson, W., R. Gorawara-Bhat, and J. Lamb. 2000. "A Study of Patient Clues and Physician Responses in Primary Care and Surgical Settings." *Journal of the American Medical Association* 284:1021-27.

Levinson, W., D. L. Roter, J. P. Mullooly, V. T. Dull, and R. M. Frankel. 1997. "Physician-Patient Communication: The Relationship with Malpractice Claims among Primary Care Physicians and Surgeons." *Journal of the American Medical Association* 277:553-59.

Levinson, W., W. B. Stiles, T. S. Inui, and R. Engle. 1993. "Physician Frustration in Communicating with Patients." *Medical Care* 31:285-95.

Marvel, M. K., R. M. Epstein, K. Flowers, and H. B. Beckman. 1999. "Soliciting the Patient's Agenda: Have We Improved?" *Journal of the American Medical Association* 281:283-87.

Matthews, D. A., A. L. Suchman, and W. T. Branch, Jr. 1993. "Making "Connexions": Enhancing the Therapeutic Potential of Patient-Clinician Relationships." *Annals of Internal Medicine* 118:973-77.

Maugans, T. A. and W. C. Wadland. 1991 "Religion and Family Medicine: A Survey of Physicians and Patients." *Journal of Family Practice* 32:210-13.

May, W. F. 1995. "Code, Covenant, Contract, or Philanthropy?" *Hastings Center Report* 5(6):29-38.

Maynard, D. W. 1997. "How to Tell Patients Bad News: The Strategy of 'Forecasting.' " *Cleveland Clinic Journal of Medicine* 64(4):181-82.

Maynard, D. W. and R. M. Frankel. Forthcoming. "On the Edge of Rationality in Primary Care Medicine: Bad News, Good News and Uncertainty." In *Practicing Medicine: Talk and Action in Primary Care Encounters,* edited by D. W. Maynard and J. Heritage. Cambridge: Cambridge University Press.

Maynard, D. W. and J. Heritage, eds. Forthcoming. *Practicing Medicine: Talk and Action in Primary Care Encounters.* Cambridge: Cambridge University Press.

McDaniel, S. H., T. L. Campbell, and D. B. Seaburn. 1990. "Working Together: Collaboration and Referral to Mental Health Professionals." In S. H. McDaniel, T. L. Campbell, and D. B. Seaburn, *Family-Oriented Primary Care: A Manual for Medical Providers.* New York: Springer-Verlag.

McKegney, C. P. 1993. "Surviving Survivors: Coping with Caring for Patients Who Have Been Victimized." *Primary Care: Clinics in Office Practice* 20:481-94.

McWhinney, I. R. 1997. "Illness, Suffering, and Healing." In *A Textbook of Family Medicine,* 2d ed., edited by I. R. McWhinney. Oxford: Oxford University Press.

McWhinney, I. R., R. M. Epstein, and T. R. Freeman. 1997. "Rethinking Summarization." *Annals of Internal Medicine* 126:747-50.

Medalie, J. H., S. J. Zyzanski, D. M. Langa, and K. C. Stange. 1998. "The Family in Family Practice: Is It a Reality? Results of a Multifaceted Study." *Journal of Family Practice* 46:390-96.

Millar, F. E., L. E. Rogers-Millar, and J. A. Courtwright. 1979. "Relational Control and Dyadic Understanding." In *Communication Yearbook 3*, edited by D. Nimmo. New Brunswick, NJ: Transaction.

Miller, W. R. and S. Rollnick. 1991. *Motivational Interviewing: Preparing People to Change Addictive Behavior.* New York: Guilford.

Mishler, E. G. 1984. *The Discourse of Medicine: Dialectics of Medical Interviews.* Norwood, NJ: Ablex.

Platt, F. W. 1992. "Empathy: Can It Be Taught?" (letter). *Annals of Internal Medicine* 117:700 (comment p. 701).

Polanyi, M. 1974. *Personal Knowledge: Toward a Post-critical Philosophy.* Chicago: University of Chicago Press.

Prochaska, J. O. and C. C. DiClemente. 1982. "Transtheoretical Therapy: Toward a More Integrative Model of Change." *Psychotherapy Theory, Research and Practice* 19:276-88.

Quill, T. E. 1983. "Partnerships in Patient Care: A Contractual Approach." *Annals of Internal Medicine* 98:228-34.

———. 1989. "Recognizing and Adjusting to Barriers in Doctor-Patient Communication." *Annals of Internal Medicine* 111:51-57.

Quill, T. E. and P. Townsend. 1991. "Bad News: Delivery, Dialogue, and Dilemmas." *Archives of Internal Medicine* 151:463-68.

Rogers, C. R. 1961. "The Characteristics of a Helping Relationship." In C. R. Rogers, *On Becoming a Person: A Therapist's View of Psychotherapy.* Boston: Houghton Mifflin.

Roter, D. L. 1984. "Patient Question Asking in Physician-Patient Interaction." *Health Psychology* 3:395-409.

Roter, D. L. and R. M. Frankel. 1992. "Quantitative and Qualitative Approaches to the Evaluation of the Medical Dialogue." *Social Science and Medicine* 34:1097-1103.

Roter, D. L. and J. A. Hall. 1998. "Why Physician Gender Matters in Shaping the Physician-Patient Relationship." *Journal of Women's Health* 7:1093-97.

Roter, D. L., J. A. Hall, D. E. Kern, R. L. Barker, K. A. Cole, and R. P. Roca. 1995. "Improving Physicians' Interviewing Skills and Reducing Patients' Emotional Distress: A Randomized Clinical Trial." *Archives of Internal Medicine* 155:1877-84.

Rudebeck, C. E. 1992. "Humanism in Medicine: Benevolence or Realism?" *Scandinavian Journal of Primary Health Care* 10:161-62.

Rutter, M. and A. Cox. 1981. "Psychiatric Interviewing Techniques IV. Experimental Study: Four Contrasting Styles." *British Journal of Psychiatry* 138:456-65.

Santorelli, S. 1999. *Heal Thy Self: Lessons on Mindfulness in Medicine.* New York: Bell Tower.

Scheflen, A. E. 1973. *Communicational Structure.* Bloomington: Indiana University Press.

Scheingold, L. 1988. "Balint Work in England: Lessons for American Family Medicine." *Journal of Family Practice* 26:315-20.

Shoemaker, W. C. 1986. "Resuscitation of the Critically Ill Patient: Use of Branched-XX Chain Decision Trees to Improve Outcome." *Emergency Medicine Clinics of North America* 4:655-94.

Smith, R. C. and R. B. Hoppe. 1991. "The Patient's Story: Integrating the Patient- and Physician-Centered Approaches to Interviewing." *Annals of Internal Medicine* 115:470-77.

Smith, R. C., J. S. Lyles, J. Mettler, B. E. Stoffelmayr, L. F. Van Egeren, A. A. Marshall, J. C. Gardiner, K. M. Maduschke, J. M. Stanley, G. G. Osborn, V. Shebroe, and R. B. Greenbaum. 1998. "The Effectiveness of Intensive Training for Residents in Interviewing: A Randomized, Controlled Study." *Annals of Internal Medicine* 128:118-26.

Stange, K. C., S. J. Zyzanski, S. A. Flocke, R. Kelly, C. R. Jaén, W. L. Miller, B. F. Crabtree, E. J. Callahan, W. R. Gillanders, J. C. Shank, J. Chao, J. H. Medalie, V. Gilchrist, M. A. Goodwin, and D. M. Langa. 1998. "Illuminating the 'Black Box': A Description of 4454 Patient Visits to 138 Family Physicians." *Journal of Family Practice* 46:377-89.

Starfield, B., D. Steinwachs, I. Morris, G. Bause, S. Siebert, and C. Westin. 1979. "Patient-Doctor Agreement about Problems Needing Follow-Up Visit." *Journal of the American Medical Association* 242:344-46.

Starfield, B., C. Wray, K. Hess, R. Gross, P. S. Birk, and B. C. D'Lugoff. 1981. "The Influence of Patient-Practitioner Agreement on Outcome of Care." *American Journal of Public Health* 71:127-31.

Steele, D. J. and J. L. Susman. 1998. "Integrated Clinical Experience: University of Nebraska Medical Center." *Academic Medicine* 73(1):41-47.

Stein, H. 1985. *The Psychodynamics of Medical Practice: Unconscious Factors in Patient Care.* Berkeley: University of California Press.

———. 1990. *American Medicine as Culture.* Boulder, CO: Westview.

Stephens, G. G. 1994. "A Family Doctor's Rules for Clinical Conversations." *Journal of the American Board of Family Practice* 7(2):179-81.

Stewart, M., J. B. Brown, H. Boon, J. Galajda, L. Meredith, and M. A. Sangster. 1999. "Evidence on Patient-Doctor Communication." *Cancer Prevention Control* 3(1):25-30.

Stewart, M., J. B. Brown, W. W. Weston, I. R. McWhinney, C. L. McWilliam, and T. R. Freeman. 1995. *Patient-Centered Medicine: Transforming the Clinical Method.* Thousand Oaks, CA: Sage.

Stewart, M., J. B. Brown, A. Donner, I. R. McWhinney, J. Oates, and W. W. Weston. 2000. "The Impact of Patient-Centered Care on Patient Outcomes." *Journal of Family Practice* 49:796-804.

Stiles, W. B. and S. M. Putnam. 1989. Analysis of Verbal and Nonverbal Behavior in Doctor-Patient Encounters. In *Communicating with Medical Patients,* edited by M. Stewart and D. L. Roter. Newbury Park, CA: Sage.

Stoeckle, J. D. and J. A. Billings. 1987. "A History of History-Taking: The Medical Interview." *Journal of General Internal Medicine* 2:119-27.

Street, R. L., Jr. 1992. "Analyzing Communication in Medical Consultations: Do Behavioral Measures Correspond to Patients' Perceptions?" *Medical Care* 30:976-88.

Street, R. L., Jr. and J. N. Cappella, eds. 1985. *Sequence and Pattern in Communicative Behavior.* Baltimore: Edward Arnold.

Suchman, A. L., R. J. Botelho, and P. Hinton-Walker, eds. 1998. *Partnerships in Healthcare: Transforming Relational Process.* Rochester, NY: University of Rochester Press.

Suchman, A. L., K. M. Markakis, H. B. Beckman, and R. M. Frankel. 1997. "The Patient-Physician Relationship: A Model of Empathic Communication in the Medical Interview." *Journal of the American Medical Association* 277:678-82.

Suchman, A. L., D. L. Roter, M. Green, and L. Lipkin. 1993. "Physician Satisfaction with Primary Care Office Visits." *Medical Care* 31:1083-92.

Szasz, T. S. and M. H. Hollender. 1956. "The Basic Models of the Doctor-Patient Relationship." *Archives of Internal Medicine* 97:585-92.

Todd, A. 1989. *Intimate Adversaries: Cultural Conflict between Doctors and Women.* Philadelphia: University of Pennsylvania Press.

Tresolini, C. and the Pew-Fetzer Task Force. 1994. *Health Professions Education and Relationship Centered Care.* San Francisco: Pew Health Professions Commission.

Waitzkin, H. 1990. "On Studying the Discourse of Medical Encounters: A Critique of Quantitative and Qualitative Methods and a Proposal for Reasonable Compromise." *Medical Care* 28:473-88.

Waitzkin, H. and J. D. Stoeckle. 1976. "Information Control and the Micro Politics of Health Care: Summary of an Ongoing Research Project." *Social Science and Medicine–Oxford* 10:263-76.

Walker, D. J., I. D. Griffiths, and C. M. Leon. 1991. "Referrals to a Rheumatology Unit: An Evaluation of the Views of Patients, General Practitioners, and Consultants." *Annals of the Rheumatic Diseases* 50:926-29.

Watzlawick, P., J. H. Beavin, and D. D. Jackson. 1967. *Pragmatics of Human Communication: A Study of Interaction Patterns, Pathologies, and Paradoxes.* New York: Norton.

West, C. 1984. *Routine Complications: Troubles with Talks between Doctors and Patients.* Bloomington: Indiana University Press.

———. 1993. "Reconceptualizing Gender in Physician-Patient Relationships." *Social Science and Medicine* 36(1):57-66.

West, C. and R. M. Frankel. 1991. "Miscommunication in Medicine." In *"Miscommunication" and Problematic Talk,* edited by N. Coupland, H. Giles, and J. M. Wiemann. Newbury Park, CA: Sage.

White, J. C., C. Rosson, J. Christensen, R. Hart, and W. Levinson. 1997. "Wrapping Things Up: A Qualitative Analysis of the Closing Minutes of the Medical Visit." *Patient Education and Counseling* 30:155-65.

Williams, G. C., G. C. Rodin, R. M. Ryan, W. S. Grolnick, and E. L. Deci. 1998. "Autonomous Regulation and Long-Term Medication Adherence in Adult Outpatients." *Health Psychology* 17:269-76.

Witte, T. N. and A. J. Kuzel. 2000. "Elderly Deaf Patients' Health Care Experiences." *Journal of the American Board of Family Practice* 13(1):81-83.

Zinn, W. 1993. "The Empathic Physician." *Archives of Internal Medicine* 153:306-12.

Zoppi, K. A. 1992. "Sexuality in the Patient-Physician Relationship." *Journal of the American Medical Association* 268:3142-46.

———. 1994. "Communication about Concerns in Well-Child Visits." Ph.D. dissertation, University of Michigan.

19

THERAPY INTERVIEWING

♦ Gale Miller
Steve de Shazer
Peter De Jong

To say that therapy interviews are organized to remedy personal and family problems is, no doubt, to state the
obvious. That is why people are referred to,
and participate in, therapy. Less obvious,
however, is how people's problems are
shaped by therapy interviewing strategies
and interactions (Gubrium 1992; Miller
and Silverman 1995; Silverman 1997;
Peräkyla 1995). In this chapter we focus on
the latter issue by emphasizing the following question: What happens to people's
problems when people seek the services of,
or are referred to, therapists? We focus on
the ways in which personal and family
problems are given practical meaning in
therapy interviews. We also ask: How do
therapists, patients, and clients arrive at appropriate solutions to patients' and clients'
problems that are socially constructed in
therapy interviews? The word *appropriate*

is a key part of this question. Different
therapy approaches emphasize different
standards in determining what are appropriate solutions to patients' and clients'
problems.

♦ Analytic Perspective

We analyze therapy interviews as distinctive sites within the interviewing society
(Atkinson and Silverman 1997; see also
Gubrium and Holstein, Chapter 1, this volume). For example, therapy interviews are
conducted for reasons that are different
from those behind journalistic and research
interviews, which are designed to gather
relevant "facts" so that those "facts" can be
conveyed to members of the general public
and to specialized academic audiences, re-

♦ 385

spectively. Journalistic and research interviews may be analyzed as part of two different story-constructing processes. A major purpose of journalistic and research interviewing is the collection of information that may be useful in the development of news stories and academic publications. The concrete "fact"-gathering procedures used by journalistic and research interviewers are inextricably linked to these purposes (but see also Altheide, Chapter 20, this volume). Although gathering "facts" is part of therapy interviewing, therapists' "fact" gathering is linked to therapists' interest in changing the life circumstances of their patients and clients. Informing the public and specialized professional audiences about these "facts" is a secondary consideration in therapy interviewing. This is one of several ways in which therapy interviews and other clinical interviews are distinctive sites in the interview society.

In this chapter, we stress how therapy, journalistic, research, and other approaches to interviewing are related to diverse assumptions, concerns, and practices that form the social contexts or auspices within which particular interviewing practices are justified and evaluated. Indeed, interviewing practices that might be judged disingenuous and manipulative in one site might be treated as fundamental and necessary to interviewing in another site. Further, although it might be said that all interviews are concerned with "getting to know" the person being interviewed, different interviewing contexts orient to different ways of knowing the interviewee. Getting to know the interviewee, in other words, is directly related to the task at hand.

We find it useful to analyze therapy interviews as "homes for meaning" (Pitkin 1972). Therapy interviews are social contexts within which some aspects of patients' and clients' lives are stressed over other aspects, and in which patients' and clients' experiences are given distinctive meaning. Different approaches to therapy interviewing are different homes for assigning meanings to patients' and clients' lives. Further, the meanings that are socially constructed in therapy interviews have practical implications for patients and clients, and often for others as well. Each approach stresses some definitions of patients' and clients' problems over other definitions and emphasizes some solutions to the problems as more appropriate than other solutions. Thus the decision to seek the services of a therapist is only the first of two decisions an individual must make about solving his or her personal and family problems. The second involves what kind of therapist to contact. The second decision is as important as the first.

◆ Worlds of Therapy

Raymond Corsini and Danny Wedding (1995) estimate that there are at least 400 different approaches to psychotherapy, only a few of which are well-known and widely practiced. For example, Corsini and Wedding limit the discussion in their edited volume to psychoanalysis, Adlerian psychotherapy, analytic psychotherapy, person-centered therapy, rational emotive behavior therapy, behavior therapy, cognitive therapy, existential psychotherapy, reality therapy, multimodal therapy, Asian psychotherapies, psychodrama, and bioenergetic analysis. The therapy scene gets more complicated, however, when we consider that some of the therapists included in Corsini and Wedding's overview do not classify themselves as psychotherapists.

Most notably, many family therapists reject the psychotherapy designation, pointing out that family therapy was invented as an alternative to psychoanalysis (de Shazer 1991). Family therapists note that where many psychotherapists focus on the intrapsychic sources of persons' problems, family therapists orient to the family systems within which troubled persons live (Hoffman 1981; Hansen and L'Abate 1982; Goldenberg and Goldenberg 1991).

There are also the so-called postmodern therapies, which do not fit within either psychotherapy or family therapy (White and Epston 1990; Anderson 1997). Although they differ in many of their assumptions and strategies, postmodern therapies in general emphasize how problems and solutions are *discourses.* Problems and solutions are stories that people tell about their own and others' lives. Thus postmodern therapists draw from different intellectual sources than do psychotherapists and family therapists.

Some of the differences that distinguish therapy approaches are related to the terminology that therapists use in talking about the people they serve. The two major designations therapists use for these people are *patients* and *clients.* The term *patient* suggests a medical orientation to therapy relationships, one in which the therapist is the expert and the patient is a person who suffers from a problem that he or she cannot manage and probably does not understand. It is the therapist's professional responsibility, then, to diagnose and solve the patient's problem in professionally appropriate ways. Consider, for example, the following description of the psychiatric interview:

> The psychiatrist is considered an expert in the field of interpersonal relations and, accordingly, the patient expects to find more than a sympathetic listener. Any person seeking psychiatric help justifiably expects expert handling in the interview. The psychiatrist demonstrates his expertise by the questions he both asks and does not ask and by certain other activities. (MacKinnon and Michels 1971:5)

The language of *client,* on the other hand, is used to emphasize therapists' provision of services to others. These therapists focus on their clients' concerns and desires in conducting therapy interviews. Thus they use their professional expertise differently than do therapists who orient to others as patients. Therapists who work with clients also talk about their interactions with clients in distinctive ways, often portraying these interactions as conversations within which therapists and clients collaboratively address clients' concerns (Berg and De Jong 1996). Therapy interviews are, in other words, conversations about changing clients' lives, not about diagnosing patients' problems (de Shazer 1991, 1994).

The distinction between *patient* and *client* is a starting point for examining the various auspices under which therapy interviews are conducted. These words are associated with different therapist interests in patients/clients and in how therapy interviews are conducted. Different therapy approaches involve different orientations to patients'/clients' problems, different arrangements of therapy roles and responsibilities, and different therapy goals. We develop these themes in the rest of the chapter by discussing three major approaches to therapy interviewing: psychiatric, strategic, and solution-focused interviewing. Because psychiatric interviewing is practiced by a variety of contemporary therapists (not just psychiatrists), we refer to psychiatric interviewers as psychotherapists.

Although psychiatric, strategic, and solution-focused approaches do not begin to exhaust the full range of therapy interviewing strategies practiced in the contemporary world, these approaches are well-known and widely practiced around the globe. They are also exemplars of three different therapy orientations: to therapist-patient/client relationships, to problems and solutions, and to the purposes of therapy. Psychiatric interviewing is a medical approach to psychotherapy, strategic therapy interviewing is a major approach within family therapy, and solution-focused therapy interviewing involves conversations about how clients might use their existing knowledge, skills, and resources to build new lives, despite their problems. These three approaches are different homes for constructing meaning in therapy. Behaviors, statements, and relationships that outside observers might describe as virtually the same are assigned very different meanings in psychiatric, strategic, and solution-focused interviewing contexts.

In the following sections, we begin by briefly reviewing the fundamentals of psychiatric and strategic therapy interviewing. We then compare and contrast these approaches by discussing how they are different homes for the social construction of meanings in therapy interviews. We next turn to solution-focused interviewing techniques and strategies. This discussion is followed by an analysis of how solution-focused interviews are similar to and different from psychiatric and strategic therapy interviews.

◆ Psychiatric Interviewing

Perhaps the clearest statement of the purpose of psychiatric interviewing is offered by Shawn Christopher Shea (1998), who states that it is an art or craft concerned with the "the formidable task of understanding another human" (p. 3). Developing such understanding is the distinctive responsibility—and expertise—of psychotherapists in psychiatric interviews. Shea explains that the psychiatric interview is a dialogue that involves both verbal and nonverbal aspects. Or, as William U. Snyder and B. June Snyder (1961) state, the psychiatric interview is a kind of social relationship. Shea (1998:6-7) describes the psychiatric interview as involving an interviewer (the psychotherapist) who asks questions designed to "achieve specific goals" and another person (the patient) who answers the interviewer's questions. The major goals to which psychiatric interviews orient, then, are defined by the psychotherapist.[1]

Psychiatric interviewers ask questions that focus attention on how patients are troubled persons who are suffering from intrapsychic—and perhaps other—disorders (Hersen and Turner 1994; Perry, Frances, and Clarkin 1990; Polatin 1966; Reid 1989). This focus is basic to the mental status examinations that are part of many psychiatric interviews. The purpose of mental status examinations is to evaluate the mental conditions of patients based on observations made by psychiatric interviewers during interviews (Sommers-Flanagan and Sommers-Flanagan 1999). Hagop S. Akisal and Kareen Akisal (1994) recommend that the mental status examination include assessment of the patient's appearance, behavior in the interview, attitude toward the psychotherapist, psychomotor activity, emotional state, perceptual disturbances, and problems in speech, thought, and orientation.

Psychotherapists often describe the psychiatric interview as a step-by-step process. Shea (1998) breaks the process down into seven steps (see also Cormier 1985; Lazare 1979; Morrison 1993; Sommers-Flanagan and Sommers-Flanagan 1999; Storr 1980). In the first step, the psychiatrist makes the patient feel safe and respected, thus building the patient's confidence in the psychiatrist's ability to understand the patient's problems. Second, the psychiatrist collects information about the history of the patient's problems and about the patient's orientation to therapy.

Psychiatric interviewers are especially interested in patients' hidden agendas for therapy and proclivity for resisting their therapists. In the third step, the psychiatrist develops a compassionate understanding of the patient's perspective in order to see the world from the patient's point of view and to detect the patient's unconscious distortions of reality. During the fourth and fifth steps, the psychiatrist makes an initial diagnosis of the problem and develops a treatment plan based on the diagnosis. Sixth, the psychiatrist works to decrease the patient's anxiety, such as by acknowledging that going to therapy is an anxiety-provoking experience and by giving the patient a chance to talk about his or her anxieties. The psychiatrist also encourages the patient to adopt a hopeful attitude toward life and toward therapy. Finally, the psychiatrist makes certain that the patient will return for the next appointment.

Ekkehard Othmer and Sieglinde C. Othmer (1994) categorize psychiatric questions into two types: insight oriented and symptom oriented. They explain that these types address two separate, but related, aspects of psychiatric interviews. Insight-oriented interviewing focuses on the deep-seated conditions associated with patients' intrapsychic conflicts, distorted perceptions, and maladjusted behavior. The goal of insight-oriented interviewing is to reveal and explain these conditions to patients, thus making it possible for patients to resolve their conflicts, correct their perceptions, and change their behavior. Psychiatric interviewers' interest in developing patient insight is an important indicator of the profound influence that Sigmund Freud's writings have had on psychiatric interviewing (Brill 1938; Roazen 1968).

One way in which psychotherapists encourage patient insight is by asking questions that explore the gap between the patient's current level of insight into his or her situation and what the psychiatrist considers to be full insight. Psychotherapists treat the gap as a measure of the patient's level of reality distortion. Othmer and Othmer (1994) provide a useful example of how psychiatric interviewers assess patients' levels of reality distortion in discussing how interviewers should respond to patients whom they believe are suffering from hallucinations. Othmer and Othmer recommend that interviewers assume that patients have no insight into how the hallucinations are a problem. They also suggest that interviewers should be skeptical about patient denials about experiencing hallucinations. Specifically, Othmer and Othmer state that psychiatric interviewers should follow patient denials by asking the kinds of questions shown in the following exchange (in which I is the interviewer and P is the patient). Note how the interviewer responds to the patient's denial

of ever hearing voices or of hearing them in the past two or three months.

I: Did you hear voices recently?

P: No.

I: When was the last you heard them?

P: About 2 or 3 months ago when I was in the hospital.

I: You have not heard them since?

P: [hesitates] No, I don't think so.

I: Tell me, what did these voices tell you this morning?

P: They told me everything I should do and they told me not to talk about it. (Othmer and Othmer 1994:132)

Symptom-oriented interviewing is concerned with identifying signs of patients' disorders in order to classify them within the categories provided by the fourth revised edition of the *Diagnostic and Statistical Manual of Mental Disorders* (*DSM-IV-R*), published by the American Psychiatric Association (2000). *DSM-IV-R* provides psychotherapists with diagnostic categories for classifying patients' disorders; it describes the typical pattern of development of each disorder and suggests appropriate responses. Diagnosing the patient's disorder and assessing its current stage of development, then, are necessary parts of the development of treatment plans in psychiatric interviews (Forman, Jones, and Frances 1995; Perry et al. 1990; Reid 1989). It is difficult to overstate the importance of *DSM* categories in psychiatric interviews. As Linda Denise Oakley and Claudette Potter (1997) note: "Crying can be a symptom of any number of experiences such as stress, alcohol withdrawal, anxiety, depression, fear, confusion, or anger. Only by applying DSM-IV criteria is it possible to measure, rather than assume, the actual diagnostic significance of symptoms" (p. 19).

Although it is possible for psychotherapists to conduct interviews that orient only to developing patient insights or to diagnosing patients' symptoms, psychotherapists frequently combine these purposes. As Othmer and Othmer (1994) note, many patients suffer from multiple problems that call for differing psychotherapist responses, and in treating patients for psychiatric disorders, psychotherapists may revive, expose, or magnify patients' intrapsychic conflicts. Thus it is useful for psychotherapists to orient to both insights and symptoms in their interactions with patients, although they might emphasize one orientation over the other in any particular therapy session. Each interviewing strategy is designed to provide psychotherapists with different kinds of information about patients' lives and problems. For example, insight-oriented interviewing techniques are especially useful for identifying unconscious defense mechanisms that may give rise to patient resistance to therapy.

One area in which psychiatric interviews often combine insight-oriented and symptom-oriented concerns involves patients who are experiencing hallucinations. Hallucinating patients pose potentially complex diagnostic problems for psychiatric interviewers because these interviewers often conceptualize hallucination as a developmental process. It is important, then, that psychotherapists assess the level of each patient's hallucinating in order to develop appropriate strategies for increasing patient insight and treating the patient's problem. Othmer and Othmer discuss hallucination as involving five stages of development, recovery, and patient insight. These range from patients who currently hear voices and act on what the voices tell them to do (Stage 5) to patients who no longer hear voices and recognize that hearing voices is a problem (Stage 1). Between these stages, patients are classified based on whether they act on the voices that they report hearing (Stage 4), whether they are willing to

talk about their hallucinations (Stage 3), and whether they believe that the voices are real (Stage 2).

Othmer and Othmer (1994) also recommend different interviewing strategies for patients at each stage. For example, they describe Stage 5 as the point at which patients may suffer from persecutory delusions and even react in dangerous ways to psychotherapists and others who challenge their positions. Othmer and Othmer recommend a nonconfrontational interviewing strategy for a psychotherapist dealing with a patient at this stage. This involves the psychotherapist's inviting the patient to explain the situation and then just listening to the patient's explanation. Othmer and Othmer suggest different strategies for dealing with patients at other hallucinatory stages, including the psychotherapists' sometimes challenging patients' statements in order to assess whether patients have developed true insight or are saying what they think their psychotherapists want to hear. Often, the challenges presented by psychotherapists to these patients involve asking patients to clarify and elaborate on their prior statements. Consider, for example, the following psychiatric interview exchange between a patient (P) and a psychotherapeutic interviewer (I):

P: I think I'm getting crazy again.

I: Why?

P: I believe some people use waves to transmit their voices into my ears.

I: Is it crazy for you to hear these voices?

P: Not for me, only for others. (Othmer and Othmer 1994:133)

Through these psychiatric interviewing strategies and practices, psychotherapists and patients produce a distinctive kind of therapy relationship and transform patients' problems into issues that are understandable and treatable from a psychiatric standpoint. Very different therapy relationships, understandings, and treatments are produced by family therapists who use strategic interviewing techniques. We now turn to this approach to therapy interviewing.

◆ Strategic Therapy Interviewing

The concept with which family therapy is most associated is that of the *family system* (Goldenberg and Goldenberg 1991; Hansen and L'Abate 1982; Hoffman 1981). This approach emphasizes how families are made up of interrelated member activities, including the usual ways in which family members assign meanings to aspects of their lives and relationships. Family systems are structured by the recurring activities that link family members to one another. For family therapists, observable and predictable patterns of family life form the social environments within which problems sometimes emerge and persist in people's lives. Problems persist and evolve into increasingly serious matters when family system members become locked into destructive patterns of relationship to which each family member contributes in various and, often, unrecognized ways. Family therapists induce changes in one or a few areas of patients' family systems and then watch how these changes reverberate through the systems.

Family therapy is also distinguished by the use of therapy teams, the members of which often observe ongoing therapy sessions through the use of one-way mirrors, although not all family therapists make use of such tools (Hoffman 1981). Brian W. Cade and Max Cornwell (1983) discuss this development as an evolution that started with the one-way mirror observation used in therapists' training. Eventually, family therapy evolved into a team activity in which one therapist met with the family while other team members watched from

behind the mirror and sometimes intervened in the therapy sessions by telephoning the interviewing therapist or by joining the sessions. Family therapy teams also developed the therapy break, in which the interviewing therapist goes behind the mirror to meet with other team members in order to decide what to do next (Palazzoli et al. 1978).

Strategic therapy applies and extends these themes in family therapy by treating problems as useful information for assessing the organization of ongoing struggles over power and control in patients' family systems (Haley 1963, 1986; Watzlawick and Weakland 1977; Watzlawick, Weakland, and Fisch 1974).[2] Strategic therapists further state that therapists must control the therapy process in order to create change in patients' family systems. Richard Fisch, John H. Weakland, and Lyn Segal (1982) explain that "the client is not in a position to know how his problem should best be approached—if he did, why would he be seeking professional help?" (p. 22). Strategic therapists describe their interest in controlling the course of treatment as a matter of establishing *therapist maneuverability* (Fisch et al. 1982). This involves maximizing therapists' involvement in responding to patients' problems.

Although both psychiatric interviewers and many strategic therapy interviewers use the word *patient* in referring to the people they interview, the concept of patient has different meaning in strategic interviews. Indeed, some strategic therapy interviewers reject the concept of patient altogether. Strategic and psychiatric interview- ers' differing uses of the term *patient* are related to their differing orientations to patients' problems (Haley 1963). Strategic therapists stress how their patients' problems are embedded in the patients' troubled family systems and assert that solving patients' problems involves changing the patients' family systems (Haley 1963; Watzlawick et al. 1974; Watzlawick, Beavin, and Jackson 1967). Psychotherapists, on the other hand, are much more likely to treat patients' problems as individual problems that psychiatric interviews are designed to uncover, diagnose, and solve.

A related issue involves psychiatric and strategic therapy interviewers' orientations to the purposes and length of therapy. Psychotherapists take a longer-term approach, orienting to the underlying causes of patients' disorders, whereas strategic therapists stress that therapy interviews should be as efficient and effective as possible. Thus strategic therapy is sometimes called brief therapy (Fisch et al. 1982).

Jay Haley (1976) discusses the strategic therapy interviewing process as unfolding in the following way. First is the *social stage,* in which the therapist asks all family members to voice their concerns about the family's situation and observes family members' interactions with one another. Next is the *problem stage,* which focuses on the family members' desires for change, including what they want to change, how they wish the change to happen, and how fast they want change to occur. Third is the *interaction stage,* in which family members discuss their problems and the therapist further observes how the family system operates, particularly how family members communicate with each other and how their power struggles are organized as coalitions and power hierarchies. Finally, the *goal-setting stage* focuses on the concrete issues that the strategic therapist and family members will work to change in therapy.

Each stage in the strategic therapy interviewing process involves different therapist strategies. For example, Haley (1976) describes the problem stage as calling for a therapist attitude of helpful concern about the family's situation and a primary interest in listening to and observing family members in interaction. Thus it is important that strategic therapists make certain that all family members are encouraged to talk during this interview stage. Strategic therapists should also avoid giving advice to patients during this phase of the interview. It is appropriate, however, for strategic therapists

to ask for clarification from patients about issues that are unclear or confusing to the therapists.

Haley (1976) recommends a different therapist strategy for the goal-setting stage. This is the stage at which strategic therapists and patients develop "therapy contracts," that is, agreements about the problems that they will work to change. The therapy contract focuses the therapy relationship on one or a few issues, and it defines the criteria to be used in assessing whether the therapist has done a good job. During this stage, the therapist is concerned with defining a goal for change that is desired by family members and is solvable through strategic therapy. This requires that the therapist assertively guide therapy interviews toward discussion of symptoms that are observable, countable, or otherwise measurable. Haley recommends that the therapist ask the following types of questions about symptoms during goal setting in strategic therapy:

> Is it there all the time, or does it come intermittently? Is it unexpected when it arrives, or predictable? Does it go away suddenly or drift away? Is it more intense at some times or at others? Is day or night the most frequent time of occurrence, or the weekday or the weekend? How many times an hour does it occur? If something like bedwetting, does it happen early in the sleep, late, or just before waking up? As with all symptoms, asking what has been tried already clarifies the nature of the problem as well as provides guidance as to what to do. (P. 41)

Strategic therapists' interest in defining therapy goals that are solvable is related to their orientation to problem solving in therapy as the therapist's responsibility (Fisch et al. 1982; Haley 1980; Watzlawick et al. 1974; Weakland et al. 1974). The strategic therapist can and should be evaluated based on whether or not the agreed-upon change happens. Thus goal setting is only one step in the strategic therapy interviewing process. There is also the matter of intervening in patients' family systems to create change. Of course, one way that strategic therapists do this is by assertively guiding patients toward clear and achievable goals. This shift alone may radically change how patients orient to their lives and relationships, thus changing the family system. Strategic therapists also sometimes respond to patients' descriptions of their problems and family systems by reframing them (Fisch et al. 1982; Watzlawick et al. 1974; Weakland et al. 1974). Reframing involves restating a situation so that it may be perceived in a new way; for example, the therapist might suggest that the family's "troublemaker" is making positive contributions to the family through her seemingly troublesome behavior.

Many strategic therapy interviews conclude with therapists giving patients tasks to do after their sessions. The tasks are designed to disrupt ongoing system patterns and to create new information about how patients' family systems function. Sometimes, strategic therapists give tasks that are direct commands to patients about what to do or not do about recurring events in patients' family systems. A therapist might, for example, tell parents to ignore their children's temper tantrums, to act as if nothing unusual is happening. A more frequent strategy of strategic therapists involves giving patients indirect—often paradoxical—tasks (Fisch et al. 1982; Watzlawick et al. 1967, 1974). One example of a paradoxical intervention is the symptom prescription task (Weakland et al. 1974), in which the therapist tells the patient to do more of the problem behavior. Strategic therapists use this task when they think that patients will decide that they don't want to do the problem behavior anymore. Sometimes patients reject their therapists' recommendations right away, but other times it takes several therapy sessions.

The following paradoxical instruction is an example of how strategic therapists sometimes intervene in patients' family systems by emphasizing the dangers of improvement. It was given in a therapy session involving a married couple who were concerned about the wife's drinking problem. Therapists often use this intervention strategy in responding to patients who do not comply with the therapists' directives.

My colleagues are equally impressed by the skillful way both of you undermined this program, to sabotage the program. They felt, and I wondered, if there is something about resolving the problem that might, at some level—unconscious or slightly unaware level—that the simple resolution of the problem has some hidden threat or danger to the two of you. Now I've raised this question before, asking how much either or both of you are aware of any disadvantages of resolving the very problems that you're coming in about, and have been seeing a previous therapist about for about a year. . . . If there is some danger or threat, to either or both of you, in being able to set aside drinking as a problem—while I asked about it before, and we had some discussion, it's their feeling that there had not been given enough thought about it and that before proceeding with anything—we all feel strongly, there is just too much coincidence. And I have to agree—before proceeding with any further item, the two of you need to give some very searching thought to this question: "What in the resolution of this problem, however it may be solved—what would you be likely to face? What would be the full impact?" And I'd say it would be best not to narrow your thinking by being too concrete, or thinking too practically, because you might overlook some important considerations. Instead, to address the question by letting your imagination run free. (Fisch et al. 1982:163-64)

◆ Similarities and Differences

Psychiatric and strategic therapy interviews are similar in their treatment of therapy as problem solving. Patients suffer from problems that psychotherapists and strategic therapists take responsibility for solving. Both interviewing approaches cast therapists as experts at assessing problems and at developing solutions to the problems. Patients follow their therapists' leads by providing information (sometimes unwittingly) about themselves, their lives, and their relationships. Both psychiatric and strategic therapy interviewers are also sensitive to the ways in which patients sometimes resist therapists' attempts to help them. "Patient resistance" is any therapist assessment that a patient is inadequately participating in therapy (Erickson, Rossi, and Rossi 1976; Shea 1998). It is a therapist construct that does not require agreement from patients, who may disagree or be unaware of their therapists' assessments.

To focus only on the similarities between psychiatric and strategic therapy interviewing, however, is to miss the several important ways in which they are different. We have already noted how psychiatric and strategic therapy interviews involve different orientations to therapist-patient roles and relationships as well as to patients' problems and to therapy as problem solving. Psychiatric interviewers ask questions that are designed to help them "look into" their patients' troubled perspectives and psyches. Strategic therapy interviewers take a different approach that treats patients' problems as family system dysfunctions. They look for the sources of patients' problems "inside" patients' family systems by asking questions that focus on the patterns of activities and relationships that constitute patients' family systems (de Shazer 1991).

The differences between psychotherapy and strategic therapy are associated with several other important issues, which may be expressed as the following questions: What is a treatable problem for psychiatric and strategic therapy interviewers? What kinds of information are the interviewers' questions designed to elicit? How and why do psychotherapists and strategic therapists exert influence and control in therapy interviews? What are the typical solutions that psychotherapists and strategic therapists use in responding to their patients' problems? We develop these issues in the rest of this section by considering three major differences between psychiatric and strategic therapy interviewing.

The first contrast is found in the issue of who is the patient in psychiatric and strategic therapy interviews. One way of seeing this difference between the two kinds of interviewing is to return briefly to Shea's (1998) characterization of psychiatric interviewing as a process of understanding another person. This orientation assumes that each patient can be treated as a more or less separate and discrete individual. That is, even though individual patients are connected to many other people in their everyday lives, psychiatric interviewers assume that they can adequately assess patients' behavior, problems, and perspectives without investigating these various social connections. This assumption is central to the diagnostic categories of *DSM-IV-R,* which often include references to familial (especially hereditary) factors but emphasize patient symptoms. In treating *DSM* categories and diagnoses as central to psychiatric interviewing, then, psychotherapists cast their patients' problems as largely individual disorders and minimize the relevance of family system factors in the interviews. This is one example of how some "facts" are more likely to be stressed and honored than other "facts" in diverse therapy interviews.

Strategic therapy interviews, on the other hand, constitute a different therapy home for meaning involving a very different orientation to what counts as a relevant "fact" in therapy. The difference is centered in strategic therapists' assumption that each patient's seemingly individual problems are related to the patients' disordered family systems. Where psychiatric interviewers strive to understand their patients as individuals, strategic therapy interviewers orient to understanding the structure and operations of family systems. These systems might even be analyzed as the patient in strategic therapy interviews. Just as psychiatric interviewers have developed a language for diagnosing their patients' individual pathologies, so strategic therapy interviewers share a language for discussing system disorders. Consider, for example, the following description of schizophrenia offered by a prominent strategic therapist:

> This language can be used to describe the family situation in which communication . . . becomes more and more cryptic in the mutual attempt to avoid exposure. They learn how to skillfully avoid any *patent* contradiction and become expert in the use of paradox, taking advantage of that possibility specific to man, to communicate simultaneously on the verbal and the non-verbal level, jumping from one logical class to a member of that class, as if they were the same thing, thus becoming acrobats in the world of Russellian paradox. (Weakland 1974:275)

It is significant that the author of the above statement never discusses the schizophrenic person, but emphasizes how schizophrenia is a family situation involving problematic communication patterns. Schizophrenia is an interactional pattern, not a condition of one person (Bateson et al. 1956; Watzlawick 1963; Watzlawick et al. 1967; Watzlawick and Weakland 1977). Thus diagnosing schizophrenia involves closely observing the communication patterns of family members in therapy sessions. The treatment of schizophrenia in strategic therapy interviews focuses on the disruption and change of troublesome communication patterns.

A second major difference between psychiatric and strategic therapy interviewing is found in the two approaches' orientations to symptoms (Othmer and Othmer 1994; Watzlawick et al. 1967). This difference might seem a bit confusing at first, given that both interviewing approaches stress problem solving and that psychiatric and strategic therapy interviewers share an interest in identifying symptoms of problems in their interactions with patients. The key difference lies in how psychiatric and strategic therapy interviewers define the concept of symptom. A symptom might be defined in at least two different ways: It can be a patient behavior or statement that the therapist takes as a sign of an underlying problem that must be addressed in therapy, or the problematic behavior or statement might be treated as a problem in and of itself. In the latter case, the symptom is the problem.

Psychiatric interviewers emphasize the first definition of symptom; they usually treat symptoms as evidence of underlying problems. John Weakland calls this the iceberg theory of problems (see Weiner-Davis 1993), and it is related to psychiatric interviewers' reliance upon medicine as a model for doing therapy. Consider the following example. Suppose that you go to your doctor complaining of a pain on the left side of your abdomen. You know that it hurts, but you don't know why it hurts. You probably also assume that the problem cannot be fixed without a medical diagnosis that establishes a cause for the pain. The pain could, for example, be a sign of appendicitis, kidney stones, or urinary tract infection, each of which calls for a particular treatment program. You also assume that your doctor is an expert at diagnosing the cause of your pain and can prescribe an appropriate treatment program that will eradicate the symptom and its underlying cause simultaneously.

This line of thinking is consistent with the medical model. It is used to positive effect in medical settings around the world. Thus our purpose in mentioning the medical model is not to reject it as a useful approach to symptoms and problem solving; rather, our point is that this general line of thinking is central to psychiatric interviewing, and it is not central to strategic therapy interviewing. Psychiatric interviews are organized to treat patient complaints as symptoms of underlying mental and physical pathologies that psychotherapists must diagnose. It is the psychiatric interviewer's professional responsibility to observe the patient and to ask questions the answers to which will be useful in making a diagnosis. Psychiatric interviews are also designed to help the psychotherapist identify an appropriate treatment program that will address the underlying cause of the patient's problem.

Strategic therapy interviewers take a very different approach to symptoms and problems. The difference is related to the strategic therapist's skepticism about using a treatment model that was developed to address biological problems in dealing with other kinds of human problems. Strategic therapists ask, for example, Is it useful to think about family conflict or children's problems in school as illnesses? Of course their answer to this question is no. Instead, strategic therapy interviewers focus on the problematic patterns of behaviors, relationships, and orientations that patients report on in therapy sessions. These patterns are the problem for strategic therapists, and changing the patterns is the focus of strategic therapy interventions.

An important part of strategic therapy interviews involves the "mapping" of problematic patterns so that strategic therapists and other therapy team members can envision the everyday activities of family members (de Shazer 1982). The maps are described by scriptions of troublesome events in patients' family systems. They focus on when, where, and how troubles emerge, how troubles escalate, and what family members usually do about them, including what family members do that does not work. Strategic therapy interviewers guide their patients' mapping of problems by asking the patients to describe concretely family members' activities, interactions, and typical interpretations of everyday events. For strategic therapists, the maps developed in therapy interviews are the problems to be solved.

The third major difference between psychiatric and strategic therapy interviewers is found in their orientations to change. A major emphasis in psychiatric interviewing is the development of patient insight, which is defined as helping patients to see the reality of their situations so that they can change their troublesome behavior and perceptions (Othmer and Othmer 1994). Thus psychiatric interviewers ask questions that focus on the gap between patients' "flawed" insights about their lives and the "appropriate" insights preferred by the interviewers. Insight is achieved when patients traverse the gap and achieve "appropriate" understanding of their circumstances. Strategic therapy interviewers treat change as a process of developing binocular vision (Bateson 1979). This involves linking two different images in order to create a new understanding of the situation. Gregory Bateson (1979) stresses that we can make sense of new images only if they are compatible with our existing perspectives —that is, if they are sufficiently similar that we can integrate the new and existing images into a new pattern that makes sense to us. In strategic therapy interviewing, change centers on resolution of the differences between two related (but different) images of reality (Watzlawick 1978; Watzlawick et al. 1967, 1974).

"Binocular vision" is central to strategic therapy interviewers' interest in mapping patients' problems. Interviewers and other therapy team members use the patients' maps to understand the patterns of behaviors, relationships, and interpretations that organize life in patients' families. Strategic therapy intervention strategies are designed to be compatible with patients' orientations while introducing something that is new and different into the family system. We have already discussed some of the major ways in which strategic therapy interviewers and team members create change through the application of binocular vision. The strategies range from very clever interventions (such as paradoxical messages and tasks) to simple suggestions to patients that they consider different interpretations (reframings) of their lives and family relationships.

◆ Solution-Focused Therapy Interviewing

Although solution-focused therapy interviewing is greatly influenced by aspects of strategic therapy interviewing, it is still a separate and distinct orientation to creating change through therapy (Ray and de Shazer 1999). For example, many solution-focused therapists continue the family therapy tradition of using one-way mirrors and therapy teams. These solution-focused therapists also take breaks from ongoing therapy interviews to meet with other team members in order to develop parting messages for clients. On the other hand, solution-focused therapy interviewers differ from strategic therapy interviewers in their orientations to clients' problems and to how change happens (Miller 1997a, 1997b). Solution-focused therapists also share strategic therapists' interest in doing brief therapy—that is, in conducting interviews that are as efficient and effective as possible.

A useful way of beginning to see the differences between solution-focused and strategic therapy interviews is to look at the

social contexts in which solution-focused therapy interviewing emerged. Solution-focused therapy did not begin as a broad-based philosophical strategy, but as a series of practical solutions to situations that early solution-focused therapists observed in therapy interviews (de Shazer 1985, 1991, 1994). One particular interview proved to be especially significant in the development of solution-focused therapy. The interview was conducted by Steve de Shazer (1985) with a five-member family. During the family's first session, family members identified 27 different problems, none of which they regarded as more important than the others. Each time de Shazer asked about the patterns surrounding a particular difficulty, another family member interrupted and identified yet another problem.

During the therapy break, the therapy team could not formulate an appropriate problem-solving intervention message or task for the family. Team members decided, instead, to take a different approach. First, they decided to state the intervention message in terms as vague as those the clients had used in describing their concerns and problems. Second, they wondered what was holding the family together and decided to develop a therapy task that addressed this issue. Here is the message that the team constructed for the family:

> Between now and next time we meet, we would like you to observe, so that you can describe to us next time, what happens in your family that you want to continue to have happen. (de Shazer 1985:137)

The family returned two weeks later and described 27 different aspects of family life that they wished to continue. In describing what was better, family members agreed that the problem that brought them to therapy was solved and that they did not have to return. The clients' response surprised the therapists and stimulated discussions about new ways of thinking about and conducting therapy interviews.

FROM PROBLEM SOLVING TO SOLUTION BUILDING

Perhaps the most fundamental change made by early solution-focused therapists was to abandon the assumption that clients have objectively identifiable problems that must be assessed in detail and then treated with scientifically based interventions (de Shazer 1988, 1991, 1994). Instead, solution-focused therapists assume that their clients already have the capacity to change in desired ways (Berg and Miller 1992; De Jong and Berg 1996; Furman and Ahola 1992). The emphasis in solution-focused therapy interviewing, then, is on discussing how clients want their lives to be different and on identifying existing client strengths, knowledge, and resources that clients might use to create desired change (Berg and De Jong 1996; De Jong and Berg 1996).

These differences in orientation have important implications for how solution-focused therapy interviews are conducted (Miller and de Shazer 1998, 2000). For example, solution-focused therapy interviews are designed to construct solutions, not to solve problems (De Jong and Berg 1996; George, Iveson, and Ratner 1990; Berg and Miller 1992). Solution-focused therapists explain that the assumption that change requires problem solving is not borne out in actual practice. Personal change often happens without concerted efforts at problem solving, including without inquiry into the causes of people's problems. Change happens all the time and for many different reasons, even for what may appear to be no reason at all. Solution-focused therapists argue that constructing solutions is easier, faster, and simpler than problem solving. Thus solution-focused therapists' interest in solution building remains practical.

Solution-focused therapists' interest in building solutions pervades their inter-

viewing practices. This interest is central to their concern for finding out how clients want their lives to change. The focus of solution-focused therapists' concern is on identifying concrete signs of change that clients might notice and build on in constructing new lives for themselves. Solution-focused therapists' interest in solution building is also basic to their questioning of clients about what the clients already know how to do (Berg and Miller 1992; Berg 1994; de Shazer et al. 1986; Miller and Berg 1995). Solution building is a process of constructing new lives out of the resources and experiences that are already present in clients' lives. Solution-focused therapists orient to their clients as competent people who are capable of deciding what their goals should be and of identifying the most appropriate means of achieving their goals.

These emphases in solution-focused interviewing require that conventional therapist-patient roles be rearranged. The rearrangement transforms patients into clients and therapy interviews into conversations. The conversations involve therapists asking questions that are designed to help clients talk about their lives in new ways (de Shazer 1991, 1994; Berg and De Jong 1996). Clients use their expertise about their lives and about themselves to answer the therapists' questions. By describing and explaining what they want from life and what they already know how to do, clients construct goals for change and strategies for attaining their goals. This is how solution-focused interviews are designed to build solutions within the contexts of clients' lives. According to solution-focused therapists, once these solutions are built, clients' problems will go away on their own.

Solution-focused therapists' preference for describing interviewing as conversation points to another distinctive feature of this therapy approach. Solution-focused therapists orient to therapy interviewing as a language game, not as a step-by-step process of moving from one clearly defined stage to another (de Shazer 1988, 1991, 1994; de Shazer and Berg 1992). Drawing on Wittgensteinian philosophy (Wittgenstein 1958), solution-focused therapists stress how people socially construct problems and solutions by using language in different ways (Miller and de Shazer 1998, 2000; Miller 1997a, 2001). As de Shazer (1991) explains:

> Language games are culturally shared and structured activities that center on people's uses of language to describe, explain, and justify. Language games are activities through which social realities and relationships are constructed and maintained. The signs (or moves) during the game consist of sentences (or signs), which are made up of words, gestures, facial expressions, postures, thoughts, etc. Since this is a system complete in itself, any particular sign can only be understood within the context of the pattern of activities involved. Thus, the meaning of any one word depends entirely on how the participants in the language game use that word. If the context were significantly different, that game would be played; it would be a different language altogether. (P. 73)

Solution-focused therapists assert that, because problems and solutions are different language games that are associated with different social contexts, constructing solutions involves engaging new language games. There is no need to explore the deep-seated causes of clients' problems, nor is diagnosis necessary (de Shazer 1991, 1994). For solution-focused therapists, extended discussions about clients' problems and their causes is a language game that frequently makes problems even more overwhelming to clients. Solution-focused interviewing is the language game that therapists and clients "play" to make the shift from problem-focused to solution-focused contexts.

SOLUTION-FOCUSED CONVERSATIONS

The questions asked by solution-focused therapy interviewers orient to three general issues (Berg 1994; De Jong and Berg 1996; de Shazer and Molnar 1984; Miller and Berg 1995). The first of these focuses on what clients would like to be doing instead of what they are doing now. For solution-focused therapists, doing something new and more satisfying is the solution for clients. The second emphasis in on identifying resources that clients might use in changing their lives and on developing ideas about how clients might actually use these resources to create change. Ironically, the plans for change that often emerge in solution-focused therapy interviews frequently involve doing more of some of the behaviors that clients are already doing or have done in the past. Third, solution-focused therapy interviews orient to how far clients have come in achieving their desired changes. This is a major topic in second and subsequent solution-focused therapy interviews, which usually begin with the therapist asking, "What's better?" (de Shazer 1994; De Jong and Berg 1996). But solution-focused therapists also raise this issue in first sessions. The rationale for these questions is that, because clients are already competent people who know how to live satisfying lives, it is possible that clients are overlooking some of the ways they are already achieving some of their goals.

Clients frequently begin their first meetings with solution-focused therapists by stressing their problems, frustrations, and concerns about the future. The problems are the reasons the clients have come to therapy. Solution-focused therapists listen to clients' initial problem talk and often voice sympathy for clients' circumstances and expressions of hopelessness. As soon as possible, however, solution-focused therapists shift the conversation away from the problems language game and into the solutions language game. One way that solution-focused therapists initiate this shift is by asking clients, "What needs to happen here today, so that you can say that it was worthwhile coming here (or that it was not a waste of time)?" This question is designed to focus the interview on what needs to be done in the immediate future, not on what has happened or is happening in clients' lives. Also notice what the question does not say or promise. It does not say that solution-focused interviews will solve clients' problems, or that solution-focused interviewers will make clients' lives better. Solution-focused therapy interviews are designed so that clients build their own solutions within and between therapy sessions.

Solution-focused therapists also ask about exceptions to clients' problems (De Jong and Berg 1996). For example, they may ask, "So, are there any times when things are just a little bit better?" When clients reply that better times have happened, solution-focused therapists ask for details about these times and about what was different then. A major focus of such questions is on what clients were doing that helped make these times better. Solution-focused therapists may ask about exceptions to any client problem, including circumstances that others might assume are clear-cut evidence of serious pathology (de Shazer 1988). Consider the following example of how a solution-focused therapy interviewer might respond to a client who reports hearing voices. Notice that the therapist follows the exception question by asking the client, "How do you do that?"

Therapist: So I am a little confused. How are these voices a problem for you? . . .

Client: Well, these voices tell me that people are after me and that I'd better be careful.

Therapist: That could be good advice in some cases. So how are they a problem? . . .

Client: Well, people at my residence hall are telling me that I am acting pretty weird and paranoid.

Therapist: Oh, so the problem is that you act differently and then people treat you differently?

Client: Yeah, they are getting real suspicious of me.

Therapist: So, are there times when you do not listen to the voices or you do not act that way? . . .

Client: Well, the voices are there all the time.

Therapist: So, do you listen to them all the time?

Client: No, not all the time. Sometimes, I am just too busy or I trust my own opinion rather than the voices.

Therapist: So, sometimes you trust your own opinion and you act differently. Those times go more the way you like? . . .

Client: Yes.

Therapist: How do you do that? . . . (Walter and Peller 1992:95-96)

A third kind of question frequently asked by solution-focused therapists is the "miracle question" (de Shazer 1991, 1994). Solution-focused therapists ask clients to imagine a time in the near future when their problems have disappeared and to describe the concrete signs that will tell the clients that their miracles have happened. Thus the focus is not on the miracles themselves, but on the clients' imagining observable changes that will signal to the clients that their miracles have happened. Consider the following example taken from an interview with a married couple who had been referred to therapy by the Department of Social Services. The department's concerns included the couple's past drug abuse, drug dealing, domestic violence, housing evictions, and child neglect. The couple's previous treatments included psychiatric services, in-home family preservation services, and individual, family, and substance abuse therapies.

Therapist: I want to ask you a strange question, probably a question you have never heard before. Let's say, that after we meet today, you do whatever you do the rest of the day, and tonight when everybody is sleeping, *a miracle happens.* And the miracle is that you don't have to put up with social service at your door—the problems that have all these people coming at your family are all gone [pause]. But of course everyone is sleeping, so you don't know that this has happened. So when you wake up tomorrow morning, what will be the first small clue to you that [pause] whoa, something is different?

Father: You mean everything's gone: the kids [pause] everything? [laughter]

Therapist: It was there, but it's all gone now. Overnight.

Mother: To tell you the truth, I probably don't know how [pause] we're waiting on that day.

Therapist: You are. So when you sort of come out of sleep in the morning, and you look around and see, what will let you know, [pause] "Wow, today is a different day, something is different, something happened?"

Father: The gut feeling. The inside feeling. The monkey off the back so to speak.

Therapist: So after this miracle tonight, the problems are all solved, what would be different in your gut feeling?

The miracle question is designed to address several solution-focused therapy concerns at once. Specifically, interviewers use the miracle question in shifting therapy conversations away from problem talk and toward talk about solutions (Miller 1997a, 1997b). Clients' answers to the miracle question frequently include references to observable behaviors (such as hugging) or other observable changes about which solution-focused therapists might make further inquiries. They might ask, "So, after you hug your wife, what will she do?" or "When was the last time that your husband hugged you?" The first question extends and elaborates on clients' previous answers by describing some of the concrete ways in which clients' lives will be different in the future. The second question links clients' answers to the miracle question with solution-focused inquiries about exceptions in clients' lives.

The second question also links the future with the past. Solutions that are first imagined as possibilities for the future are shown to have their roots in clients' past lives. Therapists' asking about when clients have achieved a little bit of their miracles in the past can also be useful for the assessment of how far clients have moved toward building solutions. Unlike other therapy approaches, however, assessments of progress in solution-focused interviews are made by clients. Solution-focused therapists find out whether progress has been made, how it has been made, and how much clients have progressed by asking clients to tell them. One way that solution-focused therapy clients assess their progress is by answering scaling questions (Berg and de Shazer 1993; De Jong and Berg 1996; Berg and Miller 1992). Consider the following example, which is taken from the interview with the family discussed above.

Therapist: Let's say on a scale of one to ten that one means when your family was having one of those hell days, and the ten stands for the miracle. How close are you to the ten right now?

Father: I think we're over the hump.

Mother: Yeah, six or seven.

Therapist: Six or seven, [to Father] do you agree with that?

Father: Uh huh. I mean a lot has changed in the past year, I mean, we went from being to a point where we weren't really sure just what was happening, what was gonna happen, or where we were going to be today . . . right now. Maybe in the last two or three months we've come a long way.

Therapist: You said you were over the hump. What tells you that?

Father: That we're able to see the future a little bit. Able to make plans. Um.

Mother: And [pointing to the children] the way they play with each other, the way they hug each other, and the way that they sit with each other. To know that they've learned that no matter how much they hurt each other, that I know that, like Mike right there a while ago he would have never have had anything to do with her. To where you know that their relationships, brother and sister, have become more treasured to each other.

This exchange also shows how solution-focused therapists respond to clients' assessments of their lives as improved by asking clients to discuss observable signs of change in their lives. These questions are designed to give concrete meaning to clients' reports of progress and to encourage clients to expect that their lives are moving in desired directions. Solution-focused therapy interviewers often respond to clients' answers by asking, "What needs to happen next?" or "What needs to happen

to move from six or seven to seven or eight?" or "What will be different when you are at seven or eight?" Solution-focused therapy interviewers sometimes give this interviewing technique an ironic twist in talking with clients who state that they are at zero or that nothing is getting better. They might do this by asking, "So, what are you doing to keep things from being even worse than they already are?"

SOLUTION-FOCUSED MESSAGES

In both psychiatric and strategic therapy interviews, interviewers use their diagnoses and assessments of patients' problems to develop therapy interventions that are intended to solve patients' problems. The interventions may range from prescriptions for medications to paradoxical messages that patients must resolve between interviews. This is a major way in which psychiatric and strategic therapy interviewers meet their professional responsibility to direct therapy interviews toward problem solving. By contrast, solution-focused therapy interviews are designed to develop clients' solution-building resources (Miller and Berg 1995; De Jong and Berg 1996; de Shazer 1988). Clients are responsible for building their own solutions, thus in solution-focused interventions, therapists do not tell clients how to change their lives.

Parting messages in solution-focused therapy interviews summarize the solution-focused high points of the conversation and often suggest issues that clients might think about or activities clients might do between interviews. For example, solution-focused therapists sometimes suggest to clients that, if the clients want to, they might try beginning one day in the next week by pretending that their miracles have happened. Therapists might also ask the clients to notice what is different about the day on which they pretend that their lives are better. The messages given to clients at the end of most solution-focused therapy interviews are composed of compliments that emphasize the clients' strengths and successes, a bridging statement that affirms whatever clients have said is important to them, and one or a few suggestions (de Shazer 1988; De Jong and Berg 1996). Bridging statements may also include rationales for the interviewers' suggestions. The following solution-focused message was given to the family discussed above:

Therapist: I had a little time to think about what you all told me. And I just am absolutely amazed by you two. You have survived and have survived. Eight years of what you have put up with. Absolutely amazing! And, not only have you survived it, but also you have done a darn good job. Your children are very nice kids, considering all this stuff that's been going on. And they are all well behaved here. You can tell they are very nice kids!

Mother: Thank you.

Therapist: So, obviously in the midst of all this, in spite of all of this, you two have done something quite right. Lots of things are working. What makes it even more amazing is that in the middle of all this, you feel that you are over the hump. And that's a huge accomplishment. So I think that, ah, there must be more than love, there must be more than your background, there must be more than the will to make it together. I don't know what it is. Something has kept you going and still keeps you going. Even now, with all these people interfering. Amazing! So, I guess now that you are over the hump, what you need to do is stay over the hump. Stay there. The first thing you need to do is stay there.

Father: Right. Stay focused.

Therapist: Stay focused. So, what I would like you to keep in mind between now and the next time we meet is, I would like the two of you to pay special attention to what each of you do to stay over the

hump. That's the first part. The second part is pay attention to what the other person is doing to stay over the hump, little things each one of you and all of you're family are doing. And then when we come together again we'll discuss that.

Most subsequent solution-focused interviews begin with the "What's better?" question; otherwise, they are usually very similar to first interviews. Depending on clients' answers, solution-focused therapy interviewers use some or all of the questions asked in first sessions. Solution-focused therapists explain that every interview is a new and different interactional context, thus it is impossible for them to ask exactly the same question twice. The focus in all solution-focused therapy interviews is on identifying how clients already know how to build their own solutions and the extent to which they are already building solutions.

◆ Further Comparisons

Clearly, there are more similarities between solution-focused therapy and strategic therapy interviews than there are between solution-focused therapy and psychiatric interviews. We have already noted how early solution-focused therapy was influenced by aspects of strategic interviewing, and how many solution-focused therapists continue to use therapy teams and observation. Solution-focused therapy interviewers are also similar to strategic therapy interviewers in their rejection of the iceberg theory of symptoms and in their lack of interest in diagnosing clients' intrapsychic disorders or developing client insight into the causes of clients' problems. These shared aspects of solution-focused therapy and strategic therapy interviews point to these therapists' mutual rejection of the medical model as a useful basis for therapy interviewing.

It would be a mistake, however, to conclude that strategic and solution-focused therapy interviews are simply variations on a common theme. They are distinguished by some fundamental differences that have implications for therapist-client roles and relationships, for determining who is primarily responsible for creating change in therapy interviews, and for how interviewers orient to language use in therapy. Therapist-client roles and relationships in strategic therapy interviews are similar to traditional professional-client roles and relationships in Western society. The logic of these relationships is perhaps best expressed in the following statement made by Everett C. Hughes (1963):

> Professionals *profess*. They profess to know better than others the nature of certain matters, and to know better than their clients what ails them or their affairs. This is the essence of the professional idea and the professional claim. (P. 656)

Within the traditional professional-client model, the patient seeks the help of the therapist, who is an expert at problem solving. It is the therapist's role to fix the problem and the patient's job to follow the therapist's advice in this therapy relationship.

We have already discussed several ways in which strategic therapy interviews reflect the traditional professional-client relationship, including in the interviewers' assumption that they must solve their patients' problems (Fisch et al. 1982; Haley 1976). This assumption is related to strategic therapists' interest in directing therapy interviews toward topics that are useful to the therapists in mapping patients' problems. The assumption is also consistent with strategic therapy interviewers' use of paradoxical and other intervention strategies designed to create binocular vision (Bateson 1979). These intervention strategies require that patients resolve their differences between two compatible, but different, orientations to their problems.

Solution-focused therapy interviewers, on the other hand, emphasize how clients are consumers of therapy services. Clients are, in other words, capable of making their own decisions about how they want their lives to change. In this relationship, clients are the experts on what they need to do to create desired changes and on the most appropriate pace at which the changes should happen. Therapists' primary responsibility is to aid clients in identifying options for change and in deciding how to proceed toward clients' goals. One of the most important ways in which solution-focused therapy interviewers aid their clients is by asking questions that help clients to notice how the beginnings of solutions are already evident in their lives (De Jong and Berg 1996; de Shazer 1988, 1991). We have discussed several such questions in this chapter, including questions about exceptions, scaling questions, and the miracle question.

Defining clients as consumers is related to solution-focused therapists' shift away from trying to solve clients' problems to using therapy interviews to build solutions. The consumer imagery is one of many basic and far-reaching changes that accompanied this shift in interviewer orientation. The shift to solution building involved a reconfiguration of the therapist-client relationship and an inversion of conventional therapist-client responsibilities in therapy relationships. Clients are responsible for doing most of the work of creating change in solution-focused therapy interviews as well as for determining when it is time to terminate the therapy relationship. Indeed, many solution-focused therapists end therapy interviews by asking their clients, "Do you want to meet again?" It is the clients' choice.

Further, if clients are consumers, then solution-focused therapists are consultants to their clients. Therapists are resources that clients use in deciding how to create change in their lives. One way of seeing the practical significance of this emphasis in solution-focused therapy interviews is to contrast it with strategic therapists' interest in increasing therapist maneuverability. Strategic therapy interviewers explain that they create therapist maneuverability by maximizing their options in dealing with patients' problems (Fisch et al. 1982). Therapist maneuverability is important to strategic therapists because it is their responsibly to initiate change during interviews. Solution-focused therapy interviews invert this situation by emphasizing client maneuverability. This shift in orientation is consistent with the consumer-consultant imagery that organizes solution-focused therapy. Because clients are responsible for deciding when, how, and at what pace change will happen, it is important that they have as many options as possible in creating change. It is therapists' responsibility to assist in expanding clients' maneuverability.

Solution-focused therapists assist their clients by asking questions that focus on exceptions to clients' problems, how clients cope with their problems, how clients would like their future lives to be different from their present lives, and the concrete steps that clients might take to move toward their goals for the future. These questions might be described as aspects of mapping solutions in solution-focused therapy interviews. This is another difference between strategic and solution-focused therapy interviews. Strategic therapy interviewers ask questions in order to build maps about patients' problems. They then use these maps in developing strategies for solving patients' problems. Mapping solutions, on the other hand, centers on asking questions that help clients to envision new possibilities for their future lives, to see how the beginnings of solutions are already evident in clients' lives, and to decide upon the first steps they will take to initiate further changes in their lives (Miller and de Shazer 1998).

Finally, although both strategic and solution-focused therapy interviewers stress the importance of language in therapy, they do so from different orientations. Paying attention to patients' and clients' use of language is a major professional responsibility of both strategic and solution-focused therapists. The importance of language in strategic therapy interviews is evident in our previous discussion of schizophrenia. Where psychiatric interviewers treat schizophrenia as a disorder of individuals, strategic therapy interviewers define it as a pattern of communication within patient family systems. Schizophrenia is, in other words, a kind of pathological communication in strategic therapy interviews (Watzlawick et al. 1967). It is an observable pattern that can be disrupted and changed through strategic intervention.

For strategic therapy interviewers, then, patients' use of language is part of larger patterns of communication. What people say and how they say it reflects the communication system of which that language is a part. Further, once dominant communication patterns are in place, they tend to endure over time. The patterns produce recurrent social interactions that maintain the ongoing patterns of relationship, be they functional or pathological patterns. The dominant communication patterns also have implications for family system members who are constrained by the possibilities provided to them within the patterns. Dominant communication patterns shape what kinds of social roles, relationships, and choices are available to family system members. To paraphrase Paul Watzlawick and his colleagues (1967:73), within strategic therapy interviews a schizophrenic is a person who is caught in a family system dominated by the language of "schizophrenese."

Solution-focused therapy interviewers' interest in language is related to their treatment of problems and solutions as language games (Wittgenstein 1958). Problems and solutions are different ways of talking about our lives and what is possible in the future (de Shazer 1994; Miller and de Shazer 1998). Neither language game is a problem in itself, given that we frequently talk with others about problems and we still continue to manage our lives effectively.

We are able to envision and talk about solutions despite our problems. But sometimes, we get stuck in only talking about problems. We become problem focused and are unable to notice that we also know how to cope with our problems. Problem-focused talk, then, is a language of ever-present troubles that we are powerless to manage. It is a language game in which we define ourselves only in terms of our problems (Miller 2001).

Solution-focused therapy interviews constitute a different language game, one that is designed to help clients talk in new ways about their lives and selves. The point of solution-focused interviews is not to disrupt existing patterns of pathological communication, but to raise questions that allow clients to talk about their lives in new ways. Solution-focused therapists ask clients to notice how their lives are less problem saturated than they have previously assumed, to describe how they would like their lives to change in the future, and to identify the resources they might use to initiate change. Thus there is no need to diagnose clients' pathological communication patterns. It is sufficient to find new ways of talking about clients' present and future lives. Solution-focused therapists assert that once clients make this linguistic shift, they will do whatever they deem necessary to get on with their lives. At that point, they no longer need a therapist.

In sum, solution-focused therapy interviews involve a more fluid orientation to language in therapy than do strategic therapy interviews. Problems are not enduring conditions that are embedded in systemic patterns. Rather, problems are typical ways of talking that are not useful to clients. The emphasis in solution-focused therapy interviews, then, is on developing new ways of talking that will be more useful to clients.

◆ Conclusion

We have considered three major approaches to therapy interviewing in this chapter. Our emphasis has been on the ways in which psychiatric, strategic therapy, and solution-focused therapy interviews are distinctive homes for meaning. They involve very different orientations to patients' and clients' problems, to therapy roles and relationships, and to how therapy interviewing fosters change. We conclude by briefly considering a different issue: What might other interviewers learn from the experiences of therapy interviewers?

For us, the most important lesson to be drawn from studying therapy interviews involves the focus of such interviews on fostering change in patients' and clients' lives. This is why therapy interviews are conducted in the first place. The emphasis in therapy interviews may be contrasted with other sites in the interview society that are designed to achieve other purposes. We are especially taken by the contrast between therapists' concern for fostering change and the historical emphasis in research interviewing on developing standardized procedures for collecting data. In its extreme form, standardized data collection is designed to get information from interviewees while not significantly changing their lives, as in standardized survey research, for example (see Singleton and Straits, Chapter 3, this volume). Another way of thinking about the differences between these interviewing approaches is to imagine the differing responses of a therapist and a research interviewer to news that their interviewing processes had helped to create change in their interviewees' lives. What would be a compliment for one interviewer would be a cause for concern for the other.

One lesson that research interviewers might draw from therapy interviews is that there is always something more involved in interviews than just the collection of information (see also Schaeffer and Maynard, Chapter 28, this volume). All interviews are occasions for building social relationships and for constructing social realities (see Baker, Chapter 37, this volume). James Holstein and Jaber Gubrium (1995) make a similar point in discussing their approach to "active interviewing":

> To say that the interview is an interpersonal drama with a developing plot is part of a broader claim that reality is an ongoing interpretive accomplishment —a matter of practice. Ethnomethodological sensibilities underpinning this position draw our attention to the interactionally artful methods—the *hows*—through which meaning is produced and made visible. (P. 16)

We would extend this orientation to other interview settings by asking interviewers to consider what some therapists call "between-session change." That is, the significance of therapy interviews for patients and clients frequently becomes clear only at subsequent meetings. The intervening time is a period for patients and clients to think about the issues discussed and recommendations made by their therapists during therapy sessions. It is also a time when many patients and clients discuss their therapy interviews with others. Some patients and clients even report experimenting with new ways of living their lives. To use Holstein and Gubrium's (1995) language, these and other postinterview activities are part of the "interpersonal drama" and "ongoing interpretive accomplishment" of diverse interview settings.

In sum, we believe that a useful next step in exploring the interview society is to look at what happens after diverse interviews are completed. We are especially interested in how this strategy might inform social science research interviews. Many of these interviews focus on issues that are nearly as personal and troublesome as therapy interviews. Do social science research interviewees return to their lives and activities without any noticeable changes, or are they changed in some way? How do they make sense of the interview experience and explain it to others? We might also ask interviewees who report change to describe how it happened. This would be a useful strategy for developing a sociology of interviewing. It is a perspective that treats interviews as socially organized events having potentially significant implications for interviewees' lives, and often for interviewers, too.

■ Notes

1. For a detailed linguistic analysis of a psychotherapy interview, see William Labov and David Fanshel's (1977) *Therapeutic Discourse.*

2. It is important to note that the concept of family systems is defined in very different ways in family therapy, and that the differences have practical implications for how therapy interviewing is done. For example, Salvador Minuchin's (1974) structural approach to family therapy interviewing assumes that therapists know the characteristics of "normal" and "functioning" families. Structural interviewers assess the extent to which their patients' families "deviate" from this normative standard and initiate changes intended to help reorganize the families in more "normal" ways. Strategic therapy interviewers, on the other hand, take a more empirical approach to family systems. They focus on developing descriptions of the distinctive patterns that define each patient's family system. Thus there is not single normative standard for "proper" family functioning in strategic therapy.

■ References

Akisal, H. S. and K. Akisal. 1994. "Mental Status Examination: The Art and Science of the Clinical Interview." Pp. 25-54 in *Diagnostic Interviewing*, 2d ed., edited by M. Hersen and S. M. Turner. New York: Plenum.

American Psychiatric Association. 2000. *Diagnostic and Statistical Manual of Mental Disorders.* 4th ed., rev. Washington, DC: Author.

Anderson, H. 1997. *Conversation, Language, and Possibilities: A Postmodern Approach to Therapy.* New York: Basic Books.

Atkinson, P. and D. Silverman. 1997. "Kundera's *Immortality:* The Interview Society and the Invention of Self." *Qualitative Inquiry* 3:304-25.

Bateson, G. 1979. *Mind and Nature: A Necessary Unity.* New York: Dutton.

Bateson, G., D. D. Jackson, J. Haley, and J. H. Weakland. 1956. "A Note on the Double Bind." *Behavioral Science* 1:251-64.

Berg, I. K. 1994. *Family-Based Services: A Solution-Focused Approach.* New York: Norton.

Berg, I. K. and S. de Shazer. 1993. "Making Numbers Talk: Language in Therapy." Pp. 5-24 in *The New Language of Change: Constructive Collaboration in Psychotherapy,* edited by S. Friedman. New York: Guilford.

Berg, I. K. and P. De Jong. 1996. "Solution-Building Conversations: Co-constructing a Sense of Competence with Clients." *Families in Society* 77:376-91.

Berg, I. K. and S. D. Miller. 1992. *Working with the Problem-Drinker: A Solution-Focused Approach.* New York: Norton.

Brill, A. A., ed. 1938. *The Basic Writings of Sigmund Freud.* New York: Modern Library.

Cade, B. W. and M. Cornwell. 1983. "The Evolution of the One-Way Screen." *Australian Journal of Family Therapy* 4:73-80.

Cormier, W. H. 1985. *Interviewing Strategies for Helpers.* 2d ed. Monterey, CA: Brooks/Cole.

Corsini, R. and D. Wedding, eds. 1995. *Current Psychotherapies.* 5th ed. Itasca, IL: F. E. Peacock.

De Jong, P. and I. K. Berg. 1996. *How to Interview for Client Strengths and Solutions.* Pacific Grove, CA: Brooks/Cole.

de Shazer, S. 1982. *Patterns of Brief Family Therapy: An Ecosystemic Approach.* New York: Guilford.

———. 1985. *Keys to Solution in Brief Therapy.* New York: Norton.

———. 1988. *Clues: Investigating Solutions in Brief Therapy.* New York: Norton.

———. 1991. *Putting Difference to Work.* New York: Norton.

———. 1994. *Words Were Originally Magic.* New York: Norton.

de Shazer, S. and I. K. Berg. 1992. "Doing Therapy: A Post-Structural Re-Vision." *Journal of Marital and Family Therapy* 18:71-81.

de Shazer, S., I. K. Berg, E. Lipchik, E. Nunnally, A. Molnar, W. J. Gingerich, and M. Weiner-Davis. 1986. "Brief Therapy: Focused Solution Development." *Family Process* 25:207-22.

de Shazer, S. and A. Molnar. 1984. "Four Useful Interventions in Brief Family Therapy." *Journal of Marital and Family Therapy* 10:297-304.

Erickson, M. H., E. L. Rossi, and S. I. Rossi. 1976. *Hypnotic Realities: The Induction of Clinical Hypnosis and Forms of Indirect Suggestion.* New York: Irvington.

Fisch, R., J. H. Weakland, and L. Segal. 1982. *The Tactics of Change: Doing Therapy Briefly.* San Francisco: Jossey-Bass.

Forman, L. M., C. Jones, and A. Frances. 1995. "The Multiaxial System in Psychiatric Treatment." Pp. 3-21 in *Treatment of Psychiatric Disorders,* 2d ed., edited by G. O. Gabbard. Washington, DC: American Psychiatric Press.

Furman, B. and T. Ahola. 1992. *Solution Talk: Hosting Therapeutic Conversations.* New York: Norton.

George, E., C. Iveson, and H. Ratner. 1990. *Problem to Solution: Brief Therapy with Individuals and Families.* London: Brief Therapy.

Goldenberg, I. and H. Goldenberg. 1991. *Family Therapy: An Overview.* Pacific Grove, CA: Brooks/Cole.

Gubrium, J. F. 1992. *Out of Control: Family Therapy and Domestic Disorder.* Newbury Park, CA: Sage.

Haley, J. 1963. *Strategies of Psychotherapy.* New York: Grune & Stratton.

———. 1976. *Problem-Solving Therapy.* New York: Harper & Row.

———. 1980. *Leaving Home.* New York: McGraw-Hill.

———. 1986. *Uncommon Therapy: The Psychiatric Techniques of Milton H. Erickson, M.D.* New York: Norton.

Hansen, J. C. and L. L'Abate. 1982. *Approaches to Family Therapy.* New York: Macmillan.

Hersen, M. and S. M. Turner, eds. 1994. *Diagnostic Interviewing.* 2d ed. New York: Plenum.

Hoffman, L. 1981. *Foundations of Family Therapy: A Conceptual Framework for Systems Change.* New York: Basic Books.

Holstein, J. A. and J. F. Gubrium. 1995. *The Active Interview.* Thousand Oaks, CA: Sage.

Hughes, E. C. 1963. "Professions." *Daedalus* 92:655-68.

Labov, W. and D. Fanshel. 1977. *Therapeutic Discourse: Psychotherapy as Conversation.* New York: Academic Press.

Lazare, A. 1979. *Outpatient Psychiatry: Diagnosis and Treatment.* Baltimore: Williams & Wilkins.

MacKinnon, R. A. and R. Michels. 1971. *The Psychiatric Interview in Clinical Practice.* Philadelphia: W. B. Saunders.

Miller, G. 1997a. *Becoming Miracle Workers: Language and Meaning in Brief Therapy.* New York: Aldine de Gruyter.

———. 1997b. "Systems and Solutions: The Discourses of Brief Therapy." *Contemporary Family Therapy* 19:5-22.

———. 2001. "Changing the Subject: Self-Construction in Brief Therapy." Pp. 64-83 in *Institutional Selves: Troubled Identities in a Postmodern World,* edited by J. F. Gubrium and J. A. Holstein. New York: Oxford University Press.

Miller, G. and S. de Shazer. 1998. "Have You Heard the Latest Rumor about . . . ? Solution-Focused Therapy as a Rumor." *Family Process* 37:363-77.

Miller, G. and S. de Shazer. 2000. "Emotions in Solution-Focused Therapy: A Re-examination." *Family Process* 39:5-24.

Miller, G. and D. Silverman. 1995. "Troubles Talk and Counseling Discourse: A Comparative Study." *Sociological Quarterly* 36:725-47.

Miller, S. D. and I. K. Berg. 1995. *The Miracle Method: A Radically New Approach to Problem Drinking.* New York: Norton.

Minuchin, S. 1974. *Families and Family Therapy.* Cambridge, MA: Harvard University Press.

Morrison, J. R. 1993. *The First Interview: A Guide for Clinicians.* New York: Guilford.

Oakley, L. D. and C. Potter. 1997. *Psychiatric Primary Care.* St. Louis, MO: C. V. Mosby.

Othmer, E. and S. C. Othmer. 1994. *The Clinical Interview Using DSM-IV,* Vol. 1, *Fundamentals.* Washington, DC: American Psychiatric Press.

Palazzoli, M. S., L. Boscolo, G. Cecchin, and G. Prata. 1978. *Paradox and Counterparadox: A New Model in the Therapy of the Family in Schizophrenic Transaction.* New York: Jason Aronson.

Peräkyla, A. 1995. *AIDS Counselling: Institutional Interaction and Clinical Practice.* Cambridge: Cambridge University Press.

Perry, S., A. Frances, and J. Clarkin. 1990. *A DSM-III-R Casebook of Treatment Selection.* New York: Brunner/Mazel.

Pitkin, H. F. 1972. *Wittgenstein and Justice: On the Significance of Ludwig Wittgenstein for Social and Political Thought.* Berkeley: University of California Press.

Polatin, P. 1966. *A Guide to Treatment in Psychiatry.* Philadelphia: J. B. Lippincott.

Ray, W. A. and S. de Shazer, eds. 1999. *Evolving Brief Therapies: In Honor of John H. Weakland.* Iowa City: Geist & Russell.

Reid, W. H. 1989. *The Treatment of Psychiatric Disorders.* New York: Brunner/Mazel.

Roazen, P. 1968. *Freud: Political and Social Thought.* New York: Alfred A. Knopf.

Shea, S. C. 1998. *Psychiatric Interviewing: The Art of Understanding.* 2d ed. Philadelphia: W. B. Saunders.

Silverman, D. 1997. *Discourses of Counselling: HIV Counselling as Social Interaction.* London: Sage.

Snyder, W. U. and B. J. Snyder. 1961. *The Psychotherapy Relationship.* New York: Macmillan.

Sommers-Flanagan, R. and J. Sommers-Flanagan. 1999. *Clinical Interviewing.* 2d ed. New York: John Wiley.

Storr, A. 1980. *The Art of Psychotherapy.* New York: Methuen.

Walter, J. L. and J. E. Peller. 1992. *Becoming Solution-Focused in Brief Therapy.* New York: Brunner/Mazel.

Watzlawick, P. 1963. "A Review of the Double Bind Theory." *Family Process* 1:132-55.

———. 1978. *The Language of Change: Elements of Therapeutic Communication.* New York: Basic Books.

Watzlawick, P., J. H. Beavin, and D. D. Jackson. 1967. *Pragmatics of Human Communication: A Study of Interaction Patterns, Pathologies, and Paradoxes.* New York: Norton.

Watzlawick, P. and J. H. Weakland, eds. 1977. *The Interactional View.* New York: Norton.

Watzlawick, P., J. H. Weakland, and R. Fisch. 1974. *Change: Principles of Problem Formation and Problem Resolution.* New York: Norton.

Weakland, J. H. 1974. "The 'Double Bind Theory' by Self-Reflexive Hindsight." *Family Process* 13:259-77.

Weakland, J. H., R. Fisch, P. Watzlawick, and A. Bodin. 1974. "Brief Therapy: Focused Problem Resolution." *Family Process* 13:141-68.

Weiner-Davis, M. 1993. *Divorce Busting: A Revolutionary and Rapid Program for Staying Together.* New York: Summit.

White, M. and D. Epston. 1990. *Narrative Means to Therapeutic Ends.* New York: Norton.

Wittgenstein, L. 1958. *Philosophical Investigations.* Translated by G. E. M. Anscombe. New York: Macmillan.

20

JOURNALISTIC INTERVIEWING

◆ David L. Altheide

*There is almost no circumstance under which an American doesn't like to be interviewed.
... We are an articulate people, pleased by attention, covetous of being singled out.*

A. J. Liebling

Journalism is as useful as its interviewing practices are sound. In this chapter, I examine how the interview has been transformed into an entertainment vehicle driven by media logic that has developed since the early days of print journalism. My main focus is on the use of the interview in contemporary journalism, on talk shows, in the tabloid press, on "reality TV," in movies, and, of course, in political reporting. I pay particular attention to television as a key constructive player in institutionalizing the criteria for a "good interview." My basic thesis is that a major reason interviewing is so relevant and popular today is its transformation from an information orientation to an impact orientation that is more characteristic of our media culture. These points are set forth in sections examining the growth of media logic, the postjournalism turn, the changing context of interviews in journalism, information technology and entertainment, the professionalism of journalism, and prime-time TV interviewing.

In the modern age, it is journalists who have used interviews the most and whose work contributes significantly to how social scientists, reformers, and other investigators employ interviews. We should bear this in mind when some social scientists suggest that cultural observers are "journalists" (Marcus 1997). Contemporary interviewing is about the "mix of answers," given that texts are nearly always edited to illustrate certain themes that were known about in advance of the interview. The implications of such changes for social science research methods are addressed in other chapters in this *Handbook*. As I am concerned here with contemporary journalism, I will focus on how the institutional framework of journalism, including its commercial environment, changing information technologies, and adoption of entertainment formats, has led to important changes in the meaning and use of interviews. With its emphasis on evocative answers and the fleshing out of questions that will provide the kinds of answers that fit entertainment formats, contemporary journalism is not isolated in its use of such techniques. Key methodological issues regarding validity and competence are raised when more audience members are also involved in research projects.

◆ Media Logic

The form and content of communication are much different although quite related. The ways in which messages are mediated and formatted shape their character. How we communicate in daily interaction is a fundamental statement about social order. What we communicate, or the nature of the specific content, helps define specific situations. The key analytic terms *mediation, media logic,* and *format* are useful for understanding how elements of communication contribute to social order (Couch 1984; McLuhan and Fiore 1967; Simmel 1964; Weingartner 1962). Cultural change is signaled in part by the appearance, style, organization, and use of various media. A plethora of research studies demonstrate that formats of communication constitute the selection, organization, presentation, and content of messages (Altheide 1985, 1995; Altheide and Snow 1979, 1991; Ericson, Baranek, and Chan 1987, 1989).

Mediation refers to the channeling, transport, and molding of information as experience. Mediation is intuitively associated with major mass media, such as newspapers and television, and a distinction is made between "print" and "electronic" on the one hand and the various organizational cultures that shape and mold information on the other. *Media logic* refers to the assumptions and processes applied to the construction of messages within particular media. These include rhythm, grammar, and format. Format, a feature of media logic, is singularly important; in this context *format* refers to the rules or "codes" used for defining, selecting, organizing, presenting, and recognizing information as one thing rather than another. The evening news, for instance, is not formatted to be a situation comedy or a parody of news. An example of the latter can be found on the entertainment program *Saturday Night Live*, which presents parodies of news in the news format, but it is the inclusion of the news format within the more specific entertainment format of *Saturday Night Live* that is important. It is the distinctive media logic and format of television news reports that separate them from newspaper reports. More specifically, the former deal with electronic visuals in "time," whereas newspapers deal with linear print representations in space. Television news reports signal importance temporally, by where in the newscast an item is placed and by how much time is allotted. Newspapers, and print media in general, show importance by location (e.g., front page), column space allotted, and the presence of photos.

Media logic influences how organizations operate, particularly communications media. Media logic is most easily recognized through shifts in culture, when something new seems to be added to a previous experience or activity. For example, sports arenas now feature big-screen video monitors on which the audiences attending events can watch replays, advertisements, and even TV programs. These visual materials are now incorporated into the rhythm and flow of athletic contests. Indeed, "time-out" commercial breaks during basketball and football games are now taken for granted; the contests are altered to accommodate the commercial messages being sent to mass audiences while those who are actually attending the events "live" are presented other commercial messages in the stadiums.

Virtually every aspect of life in the United States, and an increasingly large part of the rest of the world, is influenced by media logic. Popular culture is the arena where media logic plays out, but popular culture is being transformed and integrated into most major institutions, including politics, education, religion, business, health care, and family. These impacts entail not only "mere technology," such as the use of computers in daily life, but temporal and spatial orientation, rhythm, and pacing, and, above all, a major expectation: entertainment. And most of this "looks like" television. Marked by an emphasis on evocative meanings—as opposed to more linear-oriented "referential formats"—the emergence of the entertainment format, and the technologies that have transformed it and normalized its presence, heralds the most fundamental, yet often subtle, changes in postindustrial life. Journalism in general, and especially journalistic interviewing, is in the middle of these fundamental shifts.

◆ The Postjournalistic Turn

In stressing how interviewing has changed for journalists, I wish to emphasize that this is due mainly to other changes in the context of information gathering, preparation, and delivery. Not only has the organizational end of journalism undergone major changes, but so has the audience, or rather "audiences," whose expectations of information have become linked with entertainment, or "infotainment." It is the context of information and news that has changed, but of course the practice of journalism and the mass media in general have contributed to these changes. I refer to the complex interaction of technology, communication patterns, and social activities as an "ecology of communication" (Altheide 1995).

Media logic has transformed journalistic interviewing from what was primarily a "discovering" or "information-gathering" enterprise into an aspect of entertainment. As journalistic practices and perspectives as well as entertainment formats became more widely understood, the line separating journalists from their interviewees began to fade. One consequence was that interviews began to be set up to complement the interviewees' own messages and emphases. Interviewing changed when politicians and other organizational shills became aware of some of the format changes noted above.

The postjournalistic turn fundamentally challenged the autonomy and relevance of professional journalism's training, ethics, and truth claims (Altheide and Snow 1991). As students of communication worked with advertisers and politicians, for example, the robustness of the media logic that underpins most broadcasting as well as major print media became apparent. The emphasis on entertainment formulas of visual, dramatic action meant that straight interviews providing referential information would take too long and would violate the media logic canon. As journalists and sources shared the media logic and formats for what constituted a good story, a good interview, the occupational and perspective lines that had separated them became blurred. With the rise of this postjournalism era, the interview became a tool for quick answers, narratively induced emotion, and purposes other than obtaining detailed specifics about particular questions.

As TV news heralded the visual, and especially the entertainment-oriented visual, sources soon mastered the relatively simple logic for "getting airtime." They would simply provide the kinds of events that journalistic formats preferred. Experts on journalistic interviewing contributed to the booming public relations industry (Ailes and Kraushar 1988). By the 1970s, most companies and politicians had followed presidential candidates' leads and hired "media consultants," "advisers," and "trainers" (Martin 1977). Much of the emphasis was on how to prepare for interviews, how to cover oneself, how to duck tough questions, and the like. The underlying thesis was that interviews could be damaging to interviewees and should be managed. News sources concentrated on how to shape events and interviewing opportunities to suit themselves. All they needed to do was provide the right mix of visual opportunities and, of course, timing. Michael Deaver, Ronald Reagan's media adviser, was one of the best at using media logic to take control of interviews. He later described his approach in an editorial in the *Washington Post*:

> My own contribution to campaign innovation resulted from observing the medium as we prepared for the 1976 presidential race. I noted how the people who run television news were reducing a candidate's thoughtful and specific speech on an issue, say, an upturn in the economy, to a 10-second sound-bite, which was then followed on the screen by an effective visual of someone, usually in the Midwest, "whose life remains untouched by the prosperity claimed by President Ford," as the voice-over told us. The point is that rather than inventing the effective visual or the 30-second sound-bite, we simply adapted an existing TV news technique that was already widely used.... So, in our morning issues conference, a meeting much like those held in the editorial offices of newspapers and television networks and stations all over the country, I decided to "lead" with the housing story. But rather than have White House Press Secretary Larry Speakes hold up charts or issue a

> press release, and thereby bury the story in the business segment, we took the president to a construction site. There, wearing a hard hat and standing in front of homes under construction, he announced the housing start numbers and what that meant to the American people and the national economy. Naturally, the story played big on the evening news. (Deaver 1988:C7)

The changing context and auspices of interviewing surely contributed to this change.

◆ The Changing Auspices of Journalistic Interviewing

In this section I will discuss briefly how other social changes, including the rise of new electronic media, contributed to the changing use, character, and meaning of journalism and interviewing. Some general comparisons are offered in Table 20.1. The content of communication is reflexive of the form and process of communication. All modes of inquiry are influenced by the dominant institutions of the day as well as by information technologies and the role and significance of certain communication formats (Couch, Maines, and Chen 1996). Putting information processes and information-gathering techniques in context, then, raises questions about the underlying logic, control, sponsorship, and oversight or auspices of interviewing. When viewed as part of an ecology of communication, or the communication process in context, the fate and utility of journalistic interviews is unsettling (Desmond 1978). The meaning, use, and significance of interviewing by journalists reflect changes in mass media, popular culture, organizational frameworks, marketing, and the professionalism of journalism (Bensman and Lilienfeld 1973). Together, these suggest some guidelines for tracking the changing auspices of interviewing. Some of these changes are

Table 20.1   THE CHANGING AUSPICES OF JOURNALISTIC INTERVIEWING

Interviewing Steps and Process	Newspapers and Print Media ("Traditional")	Television and Other Electronic Media
Information technology	Linear and referential: collect complete interviews; "get the facts"	Visual, reflexive, and evocative: collect thematic interviews; get some feelings and "emotions"
Formats	Inverted pyramid; narrative report	Entertainment; drama, action, and emotion
Time to gather information	Extended	Short
Use of interview in report	Extensive	Very brief
Interviewee's knowledge and experience	Usually minimal, especially prior to TV	Extensive; local officials
Audience's knowledge and expectation	Limited to previous news reports	Extensive; previous reports, movies, and personal experience
Perceived impact of interview	Limited to report and issues	Issues, personal, and legal implications
Impact on interviewing	Moderate	Major

due mainly to the rise of electronic media that are visual and operate according to entertainment formats, such as TV news. Newspapers and magazines have adjusted their own approaches to fit more closely with these formats (Altheide and Snow 1991; Bailey and Hale 1998; Maines and Couch 1988). Table 20.1 summarizes some of the changes discussed in the following sections. Contrasts are drawn between the more referentially oriented "newspapers" and the more evocatively oriented TV styles. Journalistic interviewing now reflects shifts in information technology, formats, time, and work schedules to gather information; the use of entertainment-oriented themes to set the stage for what will be used in interviews; and the impacts that journalists want interviews to have on audiences.

There are several important differences that suggest changes in contexts as well. Some general contrasts in the nature and use of the journalistic interview can be observed through the comparison of newspaper interviews with TV interviews. Whereas the larger context involved development and elaboration of "markets" within and between print and "electronic" journalism, interviewing practices oriented to getting the "right" message out differed in more profound ways. As workers in a print-based medium, journalists historically embraced the tools of writing and the market orientations of paper news (including magazines). Reporters worked by finding people who could tell them about events. They would pose questions, write down the answers, and then draw on those notes and impressions in writing stories. The writing would be descriptive, attempting to set a tone that would interest readers. This took time.

The relationship between the interviewer and his or her subject has changed in the age of television. Primarily due to adjustments in commercialism, entertainment formats, and reporters' responsibilities to produce more reports in less time, journalists seldom spend as much time interviewing as in the past. Previously, interviewing involved more discovery, with the reporter gathering information, refining a perspective, and perhaps learning more about the subject matter before undertaking further questioning. This changed in the era of instant electronic journalism.

◆ Information Technology and Entertainment

Changes in information technology and entertaining news formats from print to electronic have altered the nature and extent of interviewing. Interviewing orientations during the print era were informed by entertainment values, but, as noted, there was an emphasis on using the interview to learn about the events in question. Although journalists may have had particular biases about where their stories would go before they conducted interviews, it was not uncommon for them to adjust their views following revealing interviews. However, this could not happen unless interviewers had a certain orientation and attitude toward their subject matter. And although print journalists also faced space restrictions on the length of their articles, TV journalists, with few exceptions, faced even more severe limitations in terms of time.

The use of electronic technology in news gathering permitted and stressed visuals over aural information, impact and emotion over referentially derived meaning, and brevity over development. As news formats emerged that essentially began with the climax of the report in order to keep the viewer watching for parts to be filled in, writing styles became even more inverted than the approach used in headline writing in newspapers. The development of videotape recording and editing equipment meant that two or more visuals could even be superimposed at the same moment, set to dramatic tempo. Items selected for reporting and the nature of reporting changed accordingly.

TV journalists are trained to focus on certain themes and angles of topics for interviews. This means that a journalist enters an interview with a well-defined sense of what the story is and what the parts will be; with exceptions, the individual being interviewed is understood to be merely playing a part in completing the picture. Interviews on television are done in ways that fit prevailing formats. As noted previously, when TV news and other mass-media programs adopted the entertainment format based on assumptions about audience members' limited attention spans, emphasis was placed on selecting events and persons for interviews and coverage and presenting them in certain ways.

Presentation began to stress short, visual, action-oriented reports. This meant camera motion, the display of compelling emotions, and evocative presentation throughout. When typical news reports last less than two minutes, there is not much time to capture, let alone explain and elaborate, complex points. The journalist who conducts the interview knows this and seeks to elicit key points from the interviewee in a very brief time, focusing on the most emotional bases. Although an interview may actually last an hour or more, the interviewee cannot expect to see more than 30 seconds of comment in the aired report. And as many interviewees have witnessed, those portions that are used may not be the most significant points made during the interview, or the complete version of the point that the interviewee was trying to get across. This is the bane of referential information: Limited time and a focus on emotionally salient material cut out most information. Exceptions are interviews with well-known personalities and celebrities, which are seen throughout the barren TV landscape.

The format of many TV news reports calls for a "response," "other side," or "expert view" on a topic. The interviewee is approached with particular questions and answers in mind. The main role of the interviewee is to provide the appropriate piece within a limited time. For example, I am known as a person who is critical of news practices, and I am asked occasionally to provide a statement about a particular aspect of news coverage. When the U.S. Marines "invaded" Somalia in December 1992 and were met by an army of journalists, cameras, and so on, some people were outraged, calling for harsh actions against these interlopers. Of course, the entire operation had been set up by the Pentagon, and that is why the media people knew where and when to be on the beach. When the news department of a local network affiliate asked for my views on this, the reporter's initial questions suggested that I would be critical and would attack the news media for being so crass and interfering. The reporter was surprised when I stated that the media were doing exactly what was expected of them, and that the Pentagon helped stage the entire operation in order to try to enhance the image of the military and to obtain public approval for this very questionable military adventure. The report that aired that night on the evening news used an even smaller segment of my statement than usual.

The organization of interviews changed as well with the rise of television news. What individuals said and meant generally suffices for print journalists; they get information, interpret it, and write reports in a linear, narrative fashion. Their reports are referentially based, even though they may be emotional reports. This changed in the age of television. With more emphasis on entertainment, on capturing emotionally charged aspects of a topic, and less time in which to produce the report, there is no compelling reason to invest time in one or two interviews, excerpts of which may play for 15 seconds. Emphasis shifted to getting emotional signatures or reactions to accompany reports.

Radio and television have brought the emotional contexts of interviews to audiences. Capturing a sob, showing tears flowing down cheeks, and looking "into the eyes" of the interviewee through tight camera shots emerged as critical features of the message and, in some cases, the most important part of the report. It did not take long for "spin doctors" to realize that how something is said can be as important and compelling as what is said. In general, interviewers and interviewees have come to treat the interview as a vehicle for conveying entertaining and profitable images.

Taking this a step farther, entertainment-oriented interviewing has produced what may be termed the "talk for pay" syndrome, or the assumption that famous or important people deserve to be paid for having a conversation before an audience. Numerous actors have requested and received pay for talking, although the price tags grew with personalities such as Frank Sinatra, who reportedly turned down $250,000 for an interview (Brady 1976). The point is that the interface of interviewer and interviewee has become a viable format for profit in the changing face of our media age.

Some journalists, such as Barbara Walters, are known for conducting interviews with well-known people. In Walters's case, and to her credit, these occasionally include world leaders, but most are important popular culture icons, including movie stars, TV talk-show hosts, and professional athletes. The interview topics are virtually always personal, relating to careers, domestic conflicts, and promotions for interviewees' projects. The broadcasts of such interviews are well advertised, and the interviews may be aired over days in several parts. There is a very clear sense in such interviews that the interviewer is helping the interviewee tell his or her story, and, indeed, is providing a valuable service to him or her as well as to the audience.

The "inside" look at power and fame remains a compelling fiction of our popular culture industry. One commentator suggests that the depth, detail, and slow-moving coverage of programs such as C-Span's

Booknotes illustrate how things have changed in interviewing and the journalistic turn away from history:

> The broadcast network interviewers ask mostly about emotions and feelings. On many of the cable talk shows, the host is the star so the questions are really rococo essays that render the answers superfluous. And when you cast your eye out to the broader culture, you see even more than curiosity about simple facts has been submerged amidst the more sophisticated interest in theory and perceptions. (Brooks 1999:22)

Celebrity talk can be expensive, but in the big picture of TV production expenses, talk is cheap. Having a well-paid talk-show host thrust celebrities into the spotlight to benefit a movie premiere or upcoming event may cost mere thousands of dollars, compared with the several-million-dollar price tags that accompany most prime-time shows. Talk-show interviewers have adopted pure entertainment formats, so much so that many shows have evolved into comedy, such as *Rowan & Martin's Laugh-In* and, a decade or so later, *Saturday Night Live*. Politicians show their "accessible" selves, their "human" selves, by appearing to have senses of humor. Even Richard Nixon appeared as himself in a *Laugh-In* segment. Other presidents would travel the last third of the 20th century by stepping on quips and sitting in "guest" chairs usually reserved for movie stars and athletes. Presidential candidate Bill Clinton played a saxophone on a late-night talk show. The 2000 presidential campaign offered the opportunity for a program such as *The Tonight Show with Jay Leno* to develop regularly appearing segments featuring Angela Marie Ramos seeking hugs from the candidates. And David Letterman, in his "Campaign 2000" segment, issued a standing invitation for the presidential candidates to debate on his *Late Night* talk show, with Letterman serving as interviewer/moderator.

Recalling that the basic formula for most popular culture programs is to pursue those formats and topics that attract the largest audiences for the least amount of money, it comes as no surprise that talk shows have flourished. Most are relatively inexpensive to produce and, depending on their emphasis, such shows can attract relatively large audiences. The most salient point for this discussion, however, is that talk shows use interviews to promote entertainment via personality exposure. Talk as action is merged with onstage fighting for the enjoyment of all on some programs, such as *The Jerry Springer Show*. The interview in TV land has become a pretext for emotional display, even violence (Gamson 1998). Such staged battles have then been discussed even further on other talk shows, where more interviews are used to exploit the topic.

◆ The Impact of Journalism's Becoming a Profession

Interviewing also changed when journalism became more professional. In the past, print journalists often did not attend journalism school; rather, they learned their craft as apprentices, moving up through the ranks. The interview as a method of information gathering was not so much an option as a necessity for print-oriented journalists; everyone used it, and apprentice reporters just did it, learned how to get better at it, and made adjustments. News stories were greatly shaped by what people told reporters. Studs Terkel (1974) has given this account of his approach:

> I realized quite early in this adventure that interviews, conventionally conducted, were meaningless. Conditioned clichés were certain to come. The question-and-answer technique may be of some value in determining favored detergents, toothpaste and de-

odorants, but not in the discovery of men and women. There were questions, of course. But they were casual in nature—at the beginning; the kind you would ask while having a drink with someone; the kind he would ask you. The talk was idiomatic rather than academic. In short, it was conversation. In time, the sluice gates of damned up hurts and dreams were opened. (P. xxv)

As noted above, this kind of work took time.

As journalism became part of major media conglomerates and helped expand information-for-profit, the entertainment formats and communication styles that attracted audiences and commercial advertisers contributed to changes in interviewing. Changes in journalism also accompanied the fragmentation of large markets into smaller niches controlled by a few conglomerates. There was more competition for audiences who had more choices, among them cable TV, specialty magazines, and on-line attractions. Journalism schools had to adjust to new technologies and job markets. Students had to know how to write, of course, but also how to conduct interviews in different contexts in varied media. "J schools" expanded the point stressed by Joseph Bensman and Robert Lilienfeld (1973) about taking the audience into account:

The journalist, hemmed in by the periodicity of publication, and by the fact that he is selling some kind of media or publication, is forced to anticipate the response of his audience in terms of what the journalist calls newsworthy, or "human interest." He must anticipate what will excite, stimulate, and titillate an audience at the time of publication. This means that the flow of his attention must be consistent with the "natural flow of attention of his audience." He must drop stories and his interest in events as events themselves shift either in their dramatic impact on audiences,

or in the journalist's estimate of the audience's rhythm of interest. (P. 208)

Acquiring information remained important, but the meaning and message had to be curtailed, cut short, and acquired in less time. Many journalism schools do not even require students to take courses in interviewing, often combining these with more general courses on information-gathering techniques. Interviewing's distinctive edges have been melted to accommodate the faster, more evocative visual formats required by the new professions of journalism. This does not mean that quality journalistic interviews do not appear; they do. Nor should it be taken to imply that there are no very good interviewers working in journalism today; there are. It does suggest that the changing character of the look of information, and access to it, has had profound impacts on how journalists gather information, assess it, and reflect on related ethical practices.

The filing of false reports is a case in point. When journalists submit stories featuring supposedly real persons who are actually composites made up out of material gathered from various interviews, or simply make up cases in others, there is far more than mere ethics of reporting involved; there is a crack opening up into the epistemic contradictions of journalism practice involving interviewing. Every case of false reporting with which I am familiar involves fictitious detailed accounts and understanding of everyday life situations that resonate with thoroughly executed interviews. The stories that are being offered, made up as they are, are reflexive of a process of data gathering that, were it carried out, might paint similar pictures. In those false cases that win awards (e.g., Janet Cooke's 1980 Pulitzer Prize-winning fictitious account of an 8-year-old heroin addict, "Jimmy's Story"), there is an even sharper implication that authentic interviewing is the kind of reporting journalists should strive for, in this depth, detail, and understanding (Eason 1986).

Fortunately, journalism's ethics and standards continue to insist that no matter how compelling the printed version, no matter how essentially it touches on the typical scenarios and processes, it is not good enough if it is not real, if there was not an actual exchange between an interviewer and interviewee, if the former did not learn the latter's experience and then fashion it through an interpretive framework designed to capture the spirit and emotion in a narrative form. Indeed, an editorial about "Jimmy's Story" that ran in the *Washington Post* on April 16, 1981, included an assertion about journalistic credibility:

> In fact, it will be an error and a shame if serious students and critics of the press take the "Jimmy" episode as the model of what's wrong with us or as evidence that stories are largely fabrications. The fact is that the shortcomings we in this business are continually fighting against, the shortcomings that can threaten our prized credibility and that we recognize in all their danger are far more subtle and insidious than some out-and-out made-up story. (P. A18)

In other words, the line between the interviewer and the interviewee is a pragmatic substitute for authenticity. In the journalistic perspective, it separates reality from other alternatives, no matter how true they may be. That line is more distinct in a print and linear world than in an electronic age that operates more temporally than spatially, more emotionally than rationally.

◆ Interviewing as a Cultural Phenomenon

Interviews are everywhere in postindustrial society (see Gubrium and Holstein, Chapter 1, this volume). Interviews are seen and heard throughout popular culture. As suggested throughout this chapter, popular culture changed interviewing from a method of data gathering to inform a conclusion to an evocative presentation of another story. As more audience members witnessed hundreds of interviews and saw the collaboration that existed between interviewers and interviewees, the meaning and utility of the interview changed. Compromised veracity accompanied this shift. Whereas the question asked always has implications for the answer, and the face-to-face situation carries nuances that may inform the exchange, things are now different due to the impact of the situation and the occasion of the interview itself. This is now meaningful and has spilled over into the content.

Another significant change that has governed the use of interviews by journalists is that commercialism has contributed to the blurring of the distinction between journalist and entertainer. Interviewing has multiple meanings in popular culture, and those meanings are not as clear when someone is doing what looks like an interview but is really a promotion of someone or something. More is involved than merely whether the subject is serious or nonserious. The issue concerns what happens to the interview when it works both sides of the street, so to speak. This is one consideration that opens up the big issue about the nature of the interview itself and suggests that in popular culture, the interview is several things. Although interviewing is merely a vehicle for other purposes, it is so ingrained in our culture as a framework (Atkinson and Silverman 1997) for the acquisition of information that I would argue that the interview has contributed to the expansion of popular culture and has lent its credibility as an information vehicle to the transformation of news and the blending of other kinds of media programs.

Interview participants and audiences in earlier periods also differ in interviewing experience and expectations compared with the contemporary electronic scene. Most of the people interviewed in a primarily print-oriented culture may never have been interviewed previously, and certainly have not experienced a lot of interview presentations, except for perhaps something read in a newspaper. In our age, the situation is very different. The question-and-answer session with a clear purpose of being read or heard by others is familiar in everyday life. Most people are aware of the utilitarian side of interviews, namely, that what interviewees say can have consequences for jobs, families, organizations, and policies. One consequence is that newspaper audiences differ from television news viewers. The former's base of experience for reading and understanding news reports is everyday life and other newspaper experiences. TV audiences see many interviews on news programs and magazine shows—where "stars interview stars"—as well as in television entertainment programs and movies.

The meaning of interviews changed as people acquired the broader meaning of what they were. Not only was the utility of the interview involved (e.g., Will I get the job?), but the significance of power and identity as well. The person asking the questions is acting from a position of power, even if he or she is employed by another for this purpose. As more people became aware of interview procedures and the way interviewees' answers could be edited, interviewees began to add an "editing" perspective to answers, especially when interviews were conducted by journalists. Framing answers, considering different interpretations, and avoiding strong adjectives and specific times and places in answers became the hallmarks of this new awareness. This is particularly true of politicians and public officials, who are frequently interviewed. For example, when a "reporter" from Comedy Central's *Indecision 2000* program asked Republican presidential candidate John McCain if the Confederate flag controversy in South Carolina would lead him to support a call to remove the flag from a car in the TV show *Dukes of Hazzard,* McCain actually mustered a reply. According to one journalist, "He [McCain] started waxing nostalgic about lessons he's learned from Rosco P. Coltrane

[a character on the TV show]. . . . He doesn't miss a beat" (Goodykoontz 2000, p. E1).

Many organizations with public relations and image concerns have responded to the new understanding of the interview by establishing press relations officers, public relations arms, and the like to provide information and "commentary" when contacted by journalists. Many contemporary organizations such as police departments permit only designated officials to be interviewed by reporters. This, of course, has further interpretive consequences. Such personnel have come to be known as "spin doctors," and their comments are now widely acknowledged to be less than accurate, self-promoting, and always utilitarian.

Hunter Thompson's "gonzo" approach to journalism explicitly took into account how interviews would be arranged and managed so that interviewees could control the outcomes. One of his favorite strategies was to telephone "movers and shakers" in the early morning hours:

> In Washington, the truth is never told in daylight hours or across a desk. If you catch people when they're very tired or drunk or weak, you can usually get some answers. So I'd sleep days, wait till these people get their lies and treachery out of the way, let them relax, then come on full speed on the phone at two or three in the morning. You have to wear the bastards down before they'll tell you anything. (Thompson, quoted in Brady 1976:8)

In view of the multiple interests that may enter a journalistic interview, it seems cogent to ask about different meanings called forth by a particular interview. Keeping in mind that most people who are interviewed by journalists have themselves witnessed numerous interviews and, in many cases, have been interviewed on numerous occasions themselves, what does the interview tap? When one considers that the interviewee may have various agendas, different audiences in mind for each one, and perhaps a history with a particular interviewer, it is not altogether clear what answer a particular question will call forth. For example, most claim makers fashion their opportunities for journalistic interviews toward particular decision-making audiences of perhaps four or five people. They are not interested in merely going on record, feeding the public information in some way; rather, they target their responses to decision makers, who often view television newscasts to get a sense about what people in general are thinking.

Awareness of these contexts makes it imperative that we be able to unravel and identify their potential and actual relevance for specific interviews. As decades of social science methodology have taught, interview answers reflect much more than simply the questions and the truth of the matter (Cicourel 1964). This is particularly important when researchers are using interviews as a method of data collection and interview transcripts as data. Indeed, this is why it is often very risky for social scientists to use interview transcripts alone in attempting to capture what individual interviewees "really, really" think about a certain issue (although such transcripts are legitimate data sources for researchers attempting to delineate public information and reports about particular topics).

◆ Prime-Time Television Interviewing

As it is used in entertainment programs as well as in news "infotainment" programs, interviewing is powerful because it is evocative. Shaped by media logic, media interviews cut to the chase, ask the big question, help the audience anticipate the answer, and evaluate the answer. As one colleague of mine puts it, in prime time, testimony becomes evidence. This perspective can be seen in several genres of news and public information shows. All feature the interviewer as star.

The development of the "evocative interview," and the perspective that fostered its use by stars and, in turn, its adaptation by audiences, is a major event in the history of interviewing. It was the widespread adaptation of media logic and entertainment formats that fostered such a perspective and orientation among actors as well as audiences. In becoming more evocatively packaged and presented, the interviewing practices of many journalists have shifted from an emphasis on information gathering to an emphasis on production values stressing impact, shock, morality play scenarios, and "big conclusions." This has led journalists to push for the "big question" before they have obtained the necessary background information to recognize what a range of appropriate questions might be. Such questions often emerge from lengthy conversations, from the interviewer's engaging the interviewee in learning about his or her world and experiences and then locating an initial journalistic interest in this context. This takes time and experience. It is an approach that experienced journalists and other ethnographers cultivate. (There is also a style of interviewing that has developed from such practices, sometimes referred to as "deep background" and also variously called "depth interviewing," "focused interviewing," and the "active interview." See Holstein and Gubrium 1995; see also Johnson, Chapter 5, this volume.) Veteran journalist Daniel Schorr (1993) reflects on this increasingly unfamiliar look of journalism:

> I have this sense that somehow journalism has to separate itself from the media. I'm not sure how it is going to happen. But reporters have to somehow draw back from being part of the great performance and say there are responsibilities that we have. (P. 20)

Television news formats do not permit time for the presentation of more than a few minutes of interviews. Interviews may be used in TV reports if they are tied to entertainment formats. The focus is on impact, and on TV, impact must be seen, heard, and "felt" by the audience. One genre developed to permit this is the "newsmagazine," an example of which is *60 Minutes*. Such shows are known for probing controversial topics and for presenting "bombshell" interviews. These shows employ substantial teams of field producers and reporters who develop report ideas, pursue them, engage in preliminary interviewing with subjects, and basically set forth scripts based on a lot of background work for the stars (e.g., Mike Wallace) to use when they conduct the interviews. However, viewing audiences see only the star reporters asking a few probing questions for which the answers are usually already known. Like the tip of an iceberg, what the audience sees is only part of the illusion of showbiz, not the bulk that supports it. These programs present to their audiences edited investigations and interviews, essentially camera work, not the complex series of interviews and other background work that provides the essential understanding for "show time."

The programs within this genre focus on perhaps a half dozen investigative reports during 30 to 60 minutes of airtime. This approach has several advantages over conventional newscasts. First, reporters and producers have more time to prepare and present their reports. Because they do not focus on breaking news, they can plan interviews with various parties in advance. Second, the genre permits the airing of longer reports than can be aired on regular newscasts. This affords the reporters and producers the opportunity to present longer excerpts of interviews. Another strength of this approach for entertainment purposes is that the segments are cast as investigative reports, often focusing on social problems, but more typically focusing on some aspect of corruption that can be personalized or located in and around particular organizations, offices, or individuals.

Although only segments of longer interviews might be broadcast, the segments used tend to be provocative; often they are "smoking gun" interviews, filmed with tightly framed camera shots of the subjects' faces. With exceptions, the intent is to pursue an angle as part of a more general theme, such as corruption.

In most journalistic enterprise, the preparation and background work of actually collecting information is not presented as part of a report. This helps the credibility of journalism because it hides the fact that most news content can be described as "information transmission" or "information mechanics" rather than information gathering, sifting, challenging, interpreting, and then presenting. If the typical interviewing process were shown, the readers or viewers would see that reports frequently come from institutional news sources such as businesses, government agencies, and especially law enforcement agencies. Viewers would see that journalists receive press releases or monitor police radio transmissions and then select events and activities to cover. Their sources are often quite mundane.

Of course, investigative journalism did not begin with TV investigative reports, but TV has added the visual dimension of compelling pictures of the "guilty look." A key part of this presentation is to "open up" part of the interviewing process for viewers to see as part of the context of the overall message of guilt and guile. Newsmagazines incorporate into the presentation those parts of the interviewing process that are consistent with the theme of the report. This is sometimes done through the "ambush interview," in which a subject who has not granted an interview will be surprised by a reporter who pursues the subject for an interview as the person is leaving home early in the morning or emerging from a parking garage. With the reporter thrusting the microphone in front of the target, the two (or three or four, depending on the size of the crew) will verbally spar as they walk. Startled, and still not wanting to be interviewed, the individual will frequently say something in a defensive way or act in an untoward manner—perhaps pushing away the camera operator—that could be seen as evidence that he or she is an uncooperative person, with something to hide. Showing this process becomes part of the overall report, and it is consistent with another underlying theme of some newsmagazine shows: that reporters are helping us, the viewers.

Accompanying the economic and cultural power of television as a major aspect of popular culture has been the rise of news shows and related genres. The latter include an expanding universe of news analysis programs and programs featuring discussion with "newsmakers." The push for evocative formats that attract the audience, along with the widespread availability of technologies that permit "action news" or "going live" to an expanding range of events and activities, has led to the creation of numerous such TV shows. The hosts of these shows, often respected journalists in their own right, all suffer the metamorphosis of successful mass media: They come to believe their own propaganda, or, more directly, they begin to see themselves, rather than their interviewees, as the central figures in interviews.

A prime example is *ABC News Nightline,* a popular late-night news show that focuses on both current events and issues raised in the news media. The show began in 1979 to provide daily updates on the situation following the taking of Americans hostages from the American embassy in Teheran, Iran. Initially titled *The Iran Crisis: America Held Hostage,* the 444-day run of the hostage crisis seemingly revealed that late-night audiences are interested in news. The host, Ted Koppel, was a good interviewer who, during a relatively brief on-air conversation, could ask provocative but basic questions that often clarified issues and moved the discussion beyond the mere headlines of the topic. This skill and emphasis gradually merged into a more directive role when it came to interviewing. By

the mid-1990s, *Nightline* had become a more active player in events, not merely reporting on them but actively seeking resolutions. *Nightline* became entertainment. The sense of a public mission was invoked on numerous occasions as Koppel evolved from an energetic, curious journalist seeking information to one approaching omniscience and, in several cases, blatant arrogance. This all transpired through interviews.

A case in point is Koppel's approach to the story of "kids shooting kids." In the aftermath of the shootings at Columbine High School in Colorado in 1999, Koppel and his crew returned to Jonesboro, Arkansas, which had been the scene of similar violence some 13 months earlier. On April 22, 1999, the *Nightline* crew met in a church with several dozen Jonesboro residents, including the mother of one of the boys who did the shooting and the husband of a teacher who was killed. *Nightline*'s self-proclaimed role was to promote healing by letting the residents of the community who had previously been through a tragedy talk with those who had more recently experienced similar events. Emotions were running high, and they became more intense when the husband of the slain Jonesboro teacher objected to the presence in the church of the youthful shooter's mother, indicating that he had been "sandbagged" by *Nightline*. He went on to explain that he had never received an apology from the mother, even though he was aware of how bad the parents of the shooters felt, how devastated their families were. The few excerpts from a transcript of the program that appear below show what ensued. They also illustrate what has happened to the journalistic role, the use of interviews in evocative formats, and the active participation of the journalist in the event being covered. The discussion includes several speakers, including Mitchell Wright, the husband of the slain teacher, and Gretchen Woodard, the mother of one of the assailants. I have added italics to the transcript where appropriate to emphasize the strong, directive role the journalist takes in promoting a particular answer.

Ted Koppel: You said at the outset that it's been 13 months and you have not received any kind of direct communication or apology from either of the families. Mrs. Woodard would like a chance to get up and speak. I don't want you to feel blindsided again. May I call on her?

Mitchell Wright: I don't mind you doing that, but here's the thing. Just like I said earlier, don't, in Colorado, don't make the victims have to ask for an apology.

Ted Koppel: I heard you and I hear you now. Mrs. Woodard?

Gretchen Woodard: I guess I feel I need to say that I did not come here and I would not [want] words from me to ever hurt anyone any more than anyone has already suffered. I do know that I come here with good intentions and to let the people know that we all do have to work through this and we take a day at a time and sometimes it's a minute at a time. I have really struggled with coming here tonight because I did not want to cause any pain. I just did feel it was very important to know that there are people all over this world that are scared, that took five minutes of their busy life to say that we're also in their thoughts and prayers. And it's enough when I look in my other children's eyes to know we do have to go on. Where in the world would we ever go? You know, this went national. Someone wouldn't know . . .

Ted Koppel: But I can't begin to know what Mr. Wright is going through. I don't pretend to know what you're going through. I really don't. *But I do know that I've just heard an anguished cry from one man saying it's been 13 months and I haven't heard an apology yet and I, I don't, I don't want to be the one to lead you to it. That wouldn't be appropriate*

either. If you don't feel it, you shouldn't say it.

Gretchen Woodard: No. And I can't help what someone feels in their heart and I don't begin to know what Mr. Wright has gone through either. I do know what I live with every day of my life and like I said the rest of my family does and I guess that I don't feel it is my right to be here and cause any more hard feelings and it is important to me to say that standing here and pointing fingers at someone and saying you're a bad person or you're this or you're that, there isn't a quick fix answer.

Note here that Mrs. Woodard has made her point, but it is not a sufficiently evocative reply for this interview format, which is framed by Koppel's intent to be a "healer." The interview continues:

Ted Koppel: I don't think anyone was asking for a quick fix. *I'm going to ask one more time, do you feel it is appropriate, right, to say to the families of those who were killed by your son . . .*

Gretchen Woodard: Yes . . .

Ted Koppel: And how sorry you are?

Gretchen Woodard: I have [said] many times and I have in the papers and I have in the local media. There were many times.

Although conciliatory, Mrs. Woodard's contrition is still not strong enough for the dramatic finality called for by the entertainment interview. Koppel continues:

Ted Koppel: But not to them.

Gretchen Woodard: I haven't reached out . . .

Ted Koppel: I mean I'm not saying, I'm not saying that that's necessarily something you should do, but clearly Mr. Wright feels you should.

Gretchen Woodard: And I do feel that with my heart and I have said many times that I'm sorry. I don't know what I could say or do to help. Is there words? I mean there just isn't and I just know that it did take all the strength I had to come here tonight and

Ted Koppel: That I surely believe. I really do and I know a lot of you do.

Here, Koppel becomes aware of how painful this is for Mrs. Woodard and seems to sense that he is breaching a traditional journalist's interviewing role, so he retreats and Woodard continues.

Gretchen Woodard: And I am very sorry. My family's very sorry and my son lives with this every day, struggles with this, Mitchell does.

Ted Koppel: All right.

Gretchen Woodard: And that is the most I guess I can say.

Gretchen Woodard is clearly not an experienced interviewee, and she is not "performing" according to *Nightline*'s preferred grammar and flow of the interview; she is struggling to convey her feelings, but they are not emerging as Koppel had hoped. It is the entertainment format that matters most here, and Woodard does not take her "cue" to bring the interview to a dramatic climax.

Following other comments, which included various parents thanking Koppel for letting them speak, *Nightline* signed off. Cringing at the crass sensationalism of this production, I crossed the line from being a media analyst to being a media critic—very directly. I sent an e-mail to the *Nightline* producer:

From: David.Altheide
Sent: Friday, April 23, 1999, 12:04 PM

The Nightline show on Thursday, Apr. 22, 1999, was one of the worst displays of sensationalism on TV news that I've seen. You just dug the infotainment hole deeper and helped articulate further our postjournalism condition —where the line disappears between those covering an event/story and the event itself. As a longtime viewer of Nightline (remember, America Held Hostage, Day X?), I am chagrined that Ted K. and company sought to out-springer Jerry Springer and the soap opera emotional shows by trying to set up a confrontation between the mother of one of the Jonesboro "shooters" and the husband of one of the deceased, who skillfully plays out a TV victim role. And, in a church? Have the egos and media logic supporting this program gotten so bold as to think that you can "heal" something? Reverend Ted! Faaantastic!

David Altheide

A senior producer for *Nightline* responded:

We have had an unusually high volume of e-mails following our two-hour town meeting from Jonesboro, Arkansas. They have been thoughtful, provoking and very constructive. Please understand how difficult it is to answer each one individually. Please know each one is read.

Our objective was to perform a public service in the midst of crisis—to allow the people of Littleton, Colorado to hear from members of a community who had gone through a similarly horrific event thirteen months ago. What can they expect? What do you tell the kids about returning to school? What do you do about the media circus that puts down its tent after every one of these tragedies?

It was one of the most intense experiences anyone connected with NIGHTLINE has been through. The people in Jonesboro recently marked the first anniversary of the school shooting at Westside Middle School, churning up emotions and when the Littleton shootings erupted on Tuesday, it sent Jonesboro reeling, forcing the community to relive its worst nightmare.

Our fear was that by going to Jonesboro at this vulnerable moment, we would be adding to their burden. But many people told us they wanted to turn their grief into something positive and were eager to provide whatever help they could to the people of Littleton. In fact, the people in Littleton were so touched by the folks in Jonesboro that they stayed after the two-hour broadcast to talk with NIGHTLINE correspondent John Donvan. Their conversation was so riveting, it will be broadcast tonight.

The most common complaint we heard from our viewers was the frequent breaks for commercials, forcing Ted to interrupt some of the guests. It is irritating and frustrating, but the nature of the beast. The commercials allow us to send a team of people to Jonesboro and produce a two-hour town meeting with 36 hours notice. Can we make a more graceful transition to commercials at times? Of course, but understand on a live broadcast packed with emotion with all kinds of chatter in Ted's ear, it can be rocky at times.

As always, we value and encourage your feedback. Hopefully, we will act on your suggestions in a way that conforms to your vision for NIGHTLINE.

There are several points about this production that can also serve as summary points for this chapter about the changing contexts of interviewing and the impacts of the changes on interviewing's relevance for "truth seeking." I list these points below and then "sign off" with some concluding remarks.

1. Media people see that an opportunity to let the people speak can be beneficial to us all and, of course, to them. This is significant because *Nightline*, like most national media programs, seldom moves beyond a handful of locations and resources in its coverage of many issues and virtually never lets "regular people" express their views.

2. The entertainment format of drama, emotion, and confrontation is there, as *Nightline* draws on relatively recent formats found in daytime shows, such as *The Jerry Springer Show*, of staging confrontations or having conflicting parties apologize face-to-face. It is about generating conflict, drama, and emotion that will touch audiences and let them participate. It is a public degradation ritual. It is about ratings and money. A statement by the Jonesboro school superintendent, who remained silent during the *Nightline* telecast from a church in Jonesboro, sums this up nicely: "It stirred up emotions that were becoming lightened. We'll have to deal with that tomorrow. But they [ABC-TV] made their money" (quoted in Yozwiak, 1999, p. A1).

3. Even the "accuser," who dislikes the media setup of the confrontation—having an individual present whom he obviously blames for the tragedy—is cooled out by Koppel's questionable assertion that he did not know she would be present.

4. The *Nightline* producer refers to the commercial enterprise that promotes the program as an element in why commercials have to be aired in the midst of the program's emotional outpourings. We are given a glimpse of the real motivation and foundation for the coverage in the first place.

5. The victim role that is beneficial to public and evocative dramatizations of suffering is celebrated and promoted, as several actors (e.g., Mitchell Wright) repeat their performances. The spatial, temporal, and symbolic lines and spaces separating public from private are smashed. Sense making, reconciliation, and the all-too-human quest for meaning, comfort, and solace are appropriated by the visual coverage so that we all can share in their suffering.

6. Placing this event and its coverage in context is challenging but necessary, because "what it is" is largely a feature of the meanings and definitions that are made of it. The interviews by Koppel did not do this. There is much to be said about the event(s) themselves, but I can mention only a few points here, including the role of the high school social structure, in that some kids were not shot, presumably, because they had better relationships with the shooters, including the possibility that they were also the butt of an oppressive high school social structure. Anyone with a genuine interest in understanding the situation would consider the perspectives and findings of social scientists and clinicians who could conduct relevant field studies and interviews to provide scenarios describing possibilities for how these events emerged. Although no single cause would be found, understanding would be developed that might help inform others seeking to avoid similar situations.

◆ Conclusion

Journalistic interviewing reflects changes in culture, information technology, marketing and commercial interests, and the ways in which these have been folded into an ecology of communication guided by media logic. Entertainment formats rule the day in politics, sports, religion, education, and journalism.

I stated at the outset that journalism remains as useful as its interviewing practices are sound. Journalistic interviewing practices are sound for the things they reflect. Journalism is very useful for making money. It is very useful for getting public attention and for having a very focused impact, but it is less useful for understanding social problems and keeping audiences informed about their everyday lives and how they operate. The nature and meaning of interviewing have changed profoundly over the past 70 years, and journalism provides a paradox of interviewing in our media age. The journalistic interview has been transformed via media logic so that it now provides evocative scenarios that are quite effective. Such changes make interviews more interesting and more entertaining, but, with exceptions, such evocative approaches are less useful for truth seeking.

With changes in information technology, particularly TV news, and the mushrooming growth of popular culture industries, journalism has become more entertainment oriented. Preference for entertaining formats is less compatible with interviewing as a major form of information gathering, but is very useful for presentation and impact. The use of interviews to fill in established thematic points or to complete a "requisite role," such as that of expert, is well established and likely to continue. Interviews as referential points for anything other than personality interviews or for material to be incorporated into a documentary format are not likely to be very common. Yet there remains an audience for serious, even slower-moving analysis and discussion, a penchant for media "places" where audiences can tune in, learn, reflect, and participate.

> Indeed, when you step back far enough you begin to appreciate that C-SPAN is so far out of tune with the times that it has become an intellectual counterculture. Especially on the weekends, the people who fill its screens seem quaintly and bravely out of step. . . .

C-SPAN is factual in a world grown theoretical. It is slow in a world growing more hyper. It is word-oriented in an era that is visually sophisticated. With its open phone lines, it is genuinely populist in a culture that preaches populism more than it practices it. (Brooks 1999:22)

However, it seems clear that interviewing has a steadfast hold on entertainment and "infotainment" as well as a host of "reality shows," where "real people" tell their stories about "real problems" and often act out their differences in "real violence."

The credibility of journalism hinges in part on the place of interviewing in the craft. It is no coincidence that the decline in public respect for journalism has been accompanied by a fundamental shift in interviewing techniques and uses. Notwithstanding that false reports, propaganda, and distorted views of reality can always come from selecting sources of information

no matter how "well" they are interviewed, it is the interviewing process as a way of engaging and confronting social life more directly that greases the way journalism will slide in the future. To reiterate the *Washington Post* editorial statement quoted previously, the shortcomings of journalism "are far more subtle and insidious than some out-and-out made-up story."

When audience members and performers have experience with standards and criteria for what makes a good interview, how to conduct one, and how to participate as a competent member of popular culture, interviewing moves beyond the occupational borders of journalists, social scientists, and others into the popular culture. Interviewing in this context becomes a social activity to be done right, grounded in effective dramaturgy of everyday life. Useful information may occasionally be provided, but it can be evaluated only within the criteria appropriate to its time, place, and manner.

■ *References*

Ailes, R. and J. Kraushar. 1988. *You are the Message: Secrets of the Master Communicators.* Homewood, IL: Dow Jones-Irwin.

Altheide, D. L. 1985. *Media Power.* Beverly Hills, CA: Sage.

———. 1995. *An Ecology of Communication: Cultural Formats of Control.* Hawthorne, NY: Aldine de Gruyter.

Altheide, D. L. and R. P. Snow. 1979. *Media Logic.* Beverly Hills, CA: Sage.

———. 1991. *Media Worlds in the Postjournalism Era.* Hawthorne, NY: Aldine de Gruyter.

Atkinson, P. and D. Silverman. 1997. "Kundera's *Immortality:* The Interview Society and the Invention of Self." *Qualitative Inquiry* 3:304-25.

Bailey, F. and D. Hale. 1998. *Popular Culture, Crime, and Justice.* Belmont, CA: West/Wadsworth.

Bensman, J. and R. Lilienfeld. 1973. *Craft and Consciousness; Occupational Technique and the Development of World Images.* New York: John Wiley.

Brady, J. J. 1976. *The Craft of Interviewing.* Cincinnati: Writer's Digest.

Brooks, D. 1999. "Brian Lamb's America: In Praise of C-Span, Our National Historian." *Weekly Standard,* November 8, pp. 21-25.

Cicourel, A. V. 1964. *Method and Measurement in Sociology.* New York: Free Press.

Cooke, J. 1980. "Jimmy's World: Eight-Year-Old Heroin Addict Lives for a Fix." *Washington Post,* September 28, p. A1

Couch, C. J. 1984. *Constructing Civilizations.* Greenwich, CT: JAI.

Couch, C. J., D. R. Maines, and S.-L. Chen. 1996. *Information Technologies and Social Orders.* New York: Aldine de Gruyter.

Deaver, M. 1988. "Sound-Bite Campaigning: TV Made Us Do It." *Washington Post,* October 30, p. C7.

Desmond, R. W. 1978. *The Information Process: World News Reporting to the Twentieth Century.* Iowa City: University of Iowa Press.

Eason, D. L. 1986. "On Journalistic Authority: The Janet Cooke Scandal." *Critical Studies in Mass Communication* 3:429-47.

Ericson, R. V., P. M. Baranek, and J. B. L. Chan. 1987. *Visualizing Deviance: A Study of News Organization.* Toronto: University of Toronto Press.

———. 1989. *Negotiating Control: A Study of News Sources.* Toronto: University of Toronto Press.

Gamson, J. 1998. *Freaks Talk Back: Tabloid Talk Shows and Sexual Nonconformity.* Chicago: University of Chicago Press.

Goodykoontz, B. 2000. "Candidates and Comedy: Who's Winner?" *Arizona Republic,* April 2, p. E1.

Holstein, J. A. and J. F. Gubrium. 1995. *The Active Interview.* Thousand Oaks, CA: Sage.

Maines, D. R. and C. J. Couch. 1988. *Communication and Social Structure.* Springfield, IL: Charles C Thomas.

Marcus, G. E. 1997. *Cultural Producers in Perilous States: Editing Events, Documenting Change.* Chicago: University of Chicago Press.

Martin, D. 1977. *The Executive's Guide to Handling a Press Interview.* New York: Pilot.

McLuhan, M. and Q. Fiore. 1967. *The Medium Is the Massage.* New York: Bantam.

Schorr, D. 1993. "The Theodore H. White Lecture on Press and Politics." Presented at the Joan Shorenstein Center on the Press, Politics and Public Policy, Kennedy School of Government, Harvard University.

Simmel, G. 1964. *The Sociology of Georg Simmel.* Edited and translated by K. H. Wolff. New York: Free Press.

Terkel, S. 1974. *Working.* New York: Encyclopedia Americana/CBS News Audio Resource Library.

Weingartner, R. H. 1962. *Experience and Culture: The Philosophy of Georg Simmel.* Middletown, CT: Wesleyan University Press.

Yozwiak, S. 1999. "Massacre Disrupts Mending Process." *Arizona Republic,* April 25, p. A1.

21

FORENSIC INVESTIGATIVE INTERVIEWING

◆ Ian K. McKenzie

For the police and others responsible for conducting criminal investigations, there are two categories of individuals whose observation of, and knowledge about, the crime in question are key elements in obtaining information about what happened, to whom, and when: the witness and the suspect. In criminal justice systems that seek to protect those assisting the police from coercive manipulation, constraints are imposed on the behavior of investigators, the aim of which is to ensure that proper procedures are followed during the questioning process. The vast majority of these rules of due process are intended to protect suspects from the most coercive elements of evidence gathering. However, in some societies there remains the strongly held belief that the coercion of both suspects and witnesses is a legitimate and effective way of getting at the truth.

Coercion may be both physical and psychological. In addition, each type of coercion may produce effects that are sometimes unanticipated and are often misunderstood. It is now well-known that coercion and the unintentional manipulation of both witnesses and suspects may lead to erroneous evidence being presented in court. In the worst cases, the presentation of such evidence may result in gross miscarriages of justice, sometimes with fatal consequences.

In the past, for official law enforcement bodies, particularly those in democratic countries, the gathering of evidence from suspects and the gathering of evidence from witnesses were seen as distinct activities. For witnesses, the process was referred to as *interviewing* and was considered to be a straightforward evidence-gathering exercise in which witnesses were asked questions about what they saw, heard, and, sometimes, touched, tasted, or smelled. This was considered to be a rather mechanical process, and the success of the interview was believed to depend on the skill of the investigator. The process was not viewed as methodologically or morally problematic; it was merely a matter of asking the right questions. We now know this to be incorrect. As I will discuss more fully later in the chapter, considerable research evidence exists to show that questioning techniques and in some cases the questions themselves may have the effect of distorting the information gathered, sometimes to the extent that a picture very far from the truth emerges.

For suspects, the process of evidence gathering was and in some jurisdictions still is very different from that applied to witnesses. Commonly referred to as *interrogation,* suspect interviewing may still be typified as a search for the truth, but too frequently it is truth defined by the investigator.[1] Traditionally, the aim of interrogation was to obtain a confession from the suspect and to establish, *to the satisfaction of the interrogators,* that the person suspected of the crime was the same as the culprit, the one who actually committed the crime.[2] The decision to seek a confession from a suspect was often based on evidence gathered from other sources, including witnesses, and because there was a specific aim to obtain a confession, interrogation was likely to include the application of "tricks, ploys and tactics" (Irving 1980).

Currently, forensic researchers recognize that similar problems arise in the process of evidence gathering from both witnesses and suspects. Similar psychological dynamics underlie both, and some criminal justice systems are seeking to put into place rules and regulations (often in the form of "codes of practice") whose goal is to control the most coercive elements of *both* kinds of evidence gathering. Because of their similarities, these evidence-gathering procedures are now referred to, together, as *forensic investigative interviewing,* or FII. FII may be defined as the processes and procedures employed in the gathering of evidence from those involved in crime or illegal activity as either suspects or witnesses. The aim of FII is to produce the most accurate or "best-quality" account of what took place for presentation in court in accordance with the rules of law or practice relating to the admissibility of evidence.

My purpose in this chapter is to examine the procedural issues identified in the application of forensic interviewing techniques. Following some attention to the dynamics of witness interviewing, I give primary consideration to suspect interviewing or interrogation. I discuss the efforts made to limit and control the worst kinds of coercion in interrogation. For comparative purposes, I focus on the differences between the United States and the United Kingdom in the constraints placed on investigative interviewing; my aim is to show how the national auspices of due process inform and shape the investigatory process.

◆ Witness Interviewing

First, a few comments are in order on witness interviewing and what studies say about how the outcomes of such interviews are affected by the practices of investigators. It should be noted, initially, that, as Eric Shepherd and Rebecca Milne (1999) point out, "great reliance is placed upon the integrity of police representations of what a witness said. Ill-conceived and ill-judged editing has major implications, given the influence of the police record over the direction of investigation and the subsequent interviewing, charging and prosecution of an identified suspect" (p. 124). However, in major studies of the practice of police interviewing with witnesses, it has been established that despite the fact that detectives investigating a crime asked interviewees to give "free narrative" accounts of an incident, the detectives then interrupted the witnesses, on average, after only 7.5 seconds (Fisher, Geiselman, and Raymond 1987). The interviews were formulaic and agenda driven. They aimed at the production of subsequent statements and not at obtaining the best recall from witnesses. Interruptions were in the main for the purpose of asking questions in a form likely to produce answers supporting the investigators' theories. Questioning was directive, rapid-fire, and pressured. Officers used jargon and stylized language and made judgmental comments, evoking a high frequency of "don't know" responses (Fisher et al. 1987; for a review of the research, see also Shepherd and Milne 1999).

Richard George's (1991) research revealed that, in addition, there was a tendency for investigators' questions to be predominantly either closed-ended or extension/clarification inquiries. Furthermore, there were more leading questions than open questions, and pauses were very rare. Maxwell McLean (1992) found many similar problems, including the fact that more than half the questions asked by investigators were counterproductive; there were serious errors of omission in the final written statements made for presentation in evidence for the court.

Elizabeth Loftus has summarized the results of these observations of real-time interviewing, coupled with Loftus and John Palmer's (1974) laboratory studies, and their extensions in more recent work, as follows:

> It was an important experiment because it showed not only that the way you ask questions can affect the answer people give you, but also that ripple effects take place. That you can influence people's answers to other questions that you ask later: if you use the word "smashed" in a question and they give a higher estimate of speed, then later on, they are more likely to tell you they saw broken glass that wasn't there.[3] (Quoted in McKenzie 1999:80)

(For an outline of Loftus and her associates' work in this and related areas, see McKenzie 1999.)

Loftus and her colleagues' research led them to conclude that such "misleading" questions could "cause an alteration or transformation, a contamination, of a person's memory" (quoted in McKenzie 1999:82). Loftus has noted that she

> started seeing these misleading questions as just a tool for contaminating memory, a pretty good tool too, because sometimes they can be pretty subtle, especially when you slip the misinformation into a relative clause like, "How fast was the white sports car going when it passed the barn while travelling along the country road?" While you are thinking about the speed of the car, we slip in the information that there was a barn there, when there wasn't. (Quoted in McKenzie 1999:82)

These studies have shown that people do not seem to notice that such insertions have taken place because they are busy and distracted by another part of the question. The ease with which witnesses' reported memories may be distorted through inept questioning is matched only by the extent to which these distortions become embedded in memory in such a way that they become part of it (see Loftus 1979).

◆ Suspect Interviewing: Interrogation

There are similar issues with suspect interviewing or interrogation, but here there is the added matter that the individual in question can also easily be viewed as a culprit and coerced to "confess." In the following discussion, note in particular how national context, in this case the United Kingdom or the United States, mediates due process.

THE THIRD DEGREE

The expression *the third degree* refers to a particular level of questioning used during the Spanish Inquisition. The least coercive degree is simple, direct questioning, the second degree is questioning with threats of force, and the third degree is questioning with the application of force. Philip Zimbardo (1967) quotes the framers of the India Evidence Act of 1872 in describing with considerable irony the potential advantage of the application of the third level: "It is easier to sit comfortably in the shade rubbing pepper into some poor devil's eyes than to go out in the sun and gather evidence."

Some organizations now expressly prohibit the third degree, yet may nonetheless condone its psychological equivalent. For example, the U.S. *Army Field Manual, 30-15 Intelligence Interrogations,* notes in Section II:

> The use of force as an aid to interrogation is prohibited by law and international agreements and is not authorized by the United States Army. Experience indicates that the use of force is not necessary to gain the co-operation of subjects of interrogation. At best, the use of force is a poor technique since it may induce the subject to tell what he thinks the interrogator wants to hear. . . . This leads to doubt as to the truth of the information obtained and may cause more harm than good. The use of force is not to be confused with the application of psychological techniques to assist the interrogator in the successful interrogation of difficult subjects. (Quoted in Krousher 1985:1)[4]

Whether or not there is any real distinction between the physical coercion of suspects toward an anticipated outcome and the use of "psychological techniques to assist the interrogator" will be discussed further below.

In 1930, the American Law Association wrote, "We can only say that the 'third degree' in the sense of rigid and severe examination of men under arrest by police officers or prosecuting attorneys, or both, is in use almost everywhere if not everywhere in the United States" (Lavine 1930; quoted in Skolnick and Fyfe 1993:45). This was a view supported by the Wickersham Commission a year later (Wickersham 1931). The commissioners suggested that inflicting pain, whether physical or mental, to extract confessions or statements was widespread and concluded that the harsher forms of the third degree amount to torture. Jerome Skolnick and James Fyfe (1993) point out that, at the time, police interrogation remained true to the model of the Spanish Inquisition. It started with questioning, moved to "relays of examiners who would badger the suspect until his energies were depleted and his resistance overcome," and culminated in "fists, blackjacks, and rubber hoses, [the latter] preferred because they left no marks" (p. 45).

Despite such commonly expressed concerns, there was limited judicial activity on the matter until 1936, when the U.S. Supreme Court, in *Brown v. Mississippi,* declared that the use of confessions obtained with the application of physical violence was a "clear denial of due process."[5] The ground was set for some changes, which in the United States were destined to produce a series of U.S. Supreme Court decisions, the purpose of which was to police the police, who were felt to be out of control. In the United States, third-degree tactics were eventually declared unlawful. However, as we shall see, the resulting decisions left much to be desired from a psychological point of view.

CRIME CONTROL VERSUS DUE PROCESS

There is a widespread belief that policing and hence the processes of dealing with suspects of crime are undertaken with greater propriety in England than in the United States.[6] The United States is seen as operating in a more "freewheeling" manner (Reiner 1985, 1991). In practice, the distinction is more complicated. In England, there actually is a history of impropriety in dealing with suspects, noted in observations made, for example, by Sir Robert Mark (1978), a former commissioner of the London Metropolitan Police. In his memoirs, Mark describes a detective sergeant who, in Mark's early career as a detective, regularly commenced his dealings with suspects with the question, "Will you talk or be tanned?"[7] If the suspect did not comply, he was taken to a toilet, his head placed into the bowl, and the toilet repeatedly flushed until he agreed to make a "voluntary" confession.[8]

It might be argued that such practices spring from the nature of English law, which has a model of "crime control" as its underlying principle. A crime-control model allows the police considerable leeway in dealing with crime and criminals. By contrast, in the United States, criminal investigation is often described as having a built-in "due process" expectation. Strict adherence to the rules of a due process system ostensibly places limits on the more flexible, less restrictive practices found in a crime-control environment.

However, these models are idealized polarities. In practice, there are elements of both models in both systems. Although polarities have a certain appeal in making national comparisons, the reality in the United States is a complex interweaving of the two models, such that the coercive practices of a crime-control model are hedged, but not eliminated, by procedural expectations. Although the American criminal justice system is firmly based upon a written constitution, the full impact of the due process requirements embedded within that constitution was not seen until well after *Brown v. Mississippi* (1936). It did not fully develop until the U.S. Supreme Court's "due process revolution" of the late 1950s and early 1960s. Still, despite the Court's decisions, there remains in policing circles considerable opposition to notions of due process. In addition, in many cases, state courts and the U.S. Supreme Court have endorsed the application of more subtle coercive techniques, which,

although not of the third degree, nonetheless allow crime-control values to exist within a due process framework.

In a series of cases, the effects of which are well-known, if only through the popular media, the U.S. Supreme Court defined a series of rules of conduct for law enforcement officials, the most powerful of which comes out of *Miranda v. Arizona* (1966). This case, coupled with the earlier *Escobedo v. Illinois* (1964), set an increasingly recognizable due process tone for crime investigators in the United States. The procedural outcomes of *Miranda* are familiar: Suspects have their rights read to them when they are taken into custody; they are informed of their right to remain silent and are warned that anything they say may be used against them in court; they are also informed of their right to consultation with counsel (under the Fifth Amendment to the U.S. Constitution, which stipulates that "no person shall be compelled to be a witness against himself") and told that the opportunity to have such legal advice will be provided free of charge.

Less well-known is the rationale for the *Miranda* decision. *Escobedo* had left some unsatisfactory elements in respect to its practical application, and the Court declared its intention to ensure that, in the future, statements obtained from suspects during custodial interrogation were truly the product of free choice. Gerald Robin (1980) explains:

> The major portion of the Miranda decision is devoted to making and substantiating a single critical point; regardless of the circumstances under which it occurs, regardless of who the examiners are, regardless of who the suspects are, custodial interrogation is inherently coercive. . . . Custodial interrogation makes any statements obtained from suspects during this period "compelled" and thus "not voluntary beyond a reasonable doubt." (P. 116)[9]

As Kurt Danziger (1976) points out, interrogation "provides quite exceptional opportunities for the manipulation of interpersonal communication" (p. 26).[10] Thus, in the face of *Brown*, law enforcement specialists started to develop techniques of interrogation that moved away from the crude third-degree methods to take advantage of the "opportunities for manipulation" described in the growing literature on the psychology of human communication. By the time of the key U.S. Supreme Court decisions outlined above, manuals of interrogation with just these aims had sprung into being (Inbau and Reid 1962, 1967; O'Hara 1970; Royal and Schutt 1976). These and their later revisions were, and still are, held in high esteem by serving police officers in the United States and are used as source material for training courses in such techniques (McKenzie 1982).

John Kleinig (1996) argues that the purpose of the *Miranda* rules was to "create a bit of breathing space between the suspect and his/her accusers, to bring some equality into the relationship between the state and the arrested person" (p. 140). However, the interrogation manuals, particularly those written by Fred Inbau and John Reid (1962, 1967) and, later, Inbau, Reid, and John Buckley (1986), concentrated on the psychological manipulation of suspects in a manner more related to a crime-control model of jurisprudence than to one based on due process. Early on, Inbau and Reid (1967) wrote that "although both 'fair' and 'unfair' interrogation practices are permissible, nothing shall be done or said to the subject that will be apt to make an innocent person confess" (p. 218). This endorsement of unfair methods as being permissible as long as they do not make "an innocent person confess" flies in the face of any criminal justice system that has as its cornerstone the notion of "innocent until proven guilty." It is only a court of law that can find a person guilty, not the police or the prosecutor. The logical conclusion is that, for the police, any unfairness in inter-

rogation practice dissipates like mist when a finding of guilt is expected. Putting it crudely, the police might well say to themselves, "As long as it isn't violence, why not give it a try. You can only get into trouble if the suspect is found not guilty."

Before turning to a discussion of psychological manipulation, I would like to offer a few more words in comparison about the situation in England and Wales. As noted earlier, historically, the model of English law was firmly that of crime control: flexible practices driven by a desire to ensure convictions, sometimes at the cost of civil rights. Sir Kenneth Newman (1984), former commissioner of the Metropolitan Police, has indicated how in addition to the extensive use of stop-and-search powers and the likelihood of abrasive street contacts between the police and citizens, there is also embedded in a crime-control model of criminal justice an associated "casual attitude towards civil rights" (p. 68).

In 1906, the police themselves raised concerns about ensuring that confessions made by suspects were admissible in court. The lord chief justice responded to these concerns with advice that, many years later, was further developed by the judges of the Queen's Bench Division, who produced a set of recommendations known as the Judges' Rules. These rules provided advice to the police about a wide range of investigative matters, including the taking of written confessions.[11] The Judges' Rules went through a number of revisions, but, importantly, until the advent of the Police and Criminal Evidence Act of 1984, these remained only "rules of practice, not rules of law," having little or no legal clout and certainly setting no sanctions for violation (McKenzie and Gallagher 1989). In the context of the hard-nosed, crime-control values of many, if not all, police officers in England and Wales, the rules were seen as advisory and not mandatory, observed more in their violation than in their proper application. Apart from the advice that a person being arrested should be "cautioned," there were few controls on interrogation or detention practice beyond a general expectation that confessions would be "voluntary."

In 1980, following some years of concern about an identified series of miscarriages of justice, the British government set up the Royal Commission on Criminal Procedure to examine the processes of the criminal justice system. The commission's principal remit was to deal with preventing and/or controlling the likelihood of false confessions, that is, confessions made by suspects later found to have been innocent of the crimes of which they were accused. Included in the Royal Commission's evidence gathering was a declared intention to commission empirical research into police interrogation in the United Kingdom. In contrast to the United States, Barrie Irving (1980), who was commissioned to conduct this research, found that there was a complete absence of interrogation training for the police of England and Wales. Irving conducted research based upon the hypothesis that even in the absence of training, police officers would use the same sorts of techniques found in Inbau and Reid's books. He suggested that they would do so for the pragmatic reason that they work; they produce confessions (McKenzie 1989; Irving and McKenzie, 1989). The hypothesis was supported.

◆ Ploys and Tactics of Interrogation

Irving (1980) describes how in the past in England and Wales, interrogating officers have used a range of communicative tactics, echoing those advocated in the United States by Inbau and Reid. These tactics serve to influence suspects to provide information or to offer admissions of guilt. The various categories of these tactics are outlined below; each is described and discussed more fully in Irving's book.

POLICE DISCRETION

The police are "experts" in the processes of detention, case construction, and the courts. Irving (1980) explains that there are three aspects of police discretion that make use of this expertise. One is discretion regarding the nature of the charges. The police might, for example, make a suggestion to the suspect, either veiled or overt, that a confession and additional full information regarding the alleged offense could result in a lower charge (e.g., a charge of theft rather than of burglary). "Tell us everything and we'll go easy on you," they might claim. Alternatively, officers may suggest that the suspect might wish to admit to offenses other than those that are the subject of the interrogation, on the grounds that the admission of other offenses will not lead to additional charges but will be taken into consideration by the court under special rules that allow the books to be cleared. "Get it all off your chest and there won't be extra charges," they might explain. Or the interrogators might suggest that some party, an accomplice or possibly the suspect's spouse, partner, son, or daughter, who is potentially involved in prosecution would become the subject of a lesser charge if the suspect confesses.

A second aspect of police discretion centers on release and bail. The suggestion, veiled or overt, might be made during the interview that the consequence of failure to confess could be continued detention or could result in an application by the police for a remand in custody. Alternatively, it might be suggested that a full confession will result in a more rapid processing of the case, quick release, or an immediate court appearance.

A third aspect of police discretion relates to continuing investigation and police protection. Officers might suggest, either directly or in more subtle ways, that the suspect's failure to confess will result in other parties—such as the suspect's friends, relatives, and spouse—becoming suspects, being arrested, or being held in police cells and interrogated. Conversely, officers might point out that if a confession is not made, parties already in custody might be refused bail, or that if a confession is made, people potentially involved might not become the subject of inquiries.

THE PROVISION OF EXPERT KNOWLEDGE

For the suspect, the police are, as Irving (1980) puts it, also a "source of expert knowledge" about a poorly understood administrative apparatus, which offers a place for another category of ploys and tactics. In exchange for a confession, the police are able to provide information about court procedures or about the alleged value of "telling the truth" in a subsequent decision by the court (or, conversely, the potential procedural damage incurred by lying). They can offer advice about the degree to which "cooperation" with the police will mitigate the suspect's case. They can hint at the possibility of "special sentences" (suspended or deferred) or about the provision of specialist medical or psychiatric care that a suspect might obtain as a direct result of making a confession. In some cases, officers might make the threat of an immediate custodial sentence (including care orders) as a consequence of failure to confess. Finally, officers might suggest that if the suspect were to admit to additional offenses, such admissions probably would not increase the sentence.

THE PERSONAL CONSEQUENCES OF CONFESSION

A third category of ploys and tactics pertains to confession's alleged beneficial personal consequences. Suspects, particularly those who are naive, are often confused or uncertain about how they or others will be affected personally if they make confessions. Manipulation of the suspect's self-image, which is made possible by a growing rapport between the suspect and the interrogator, is a potent and effective tactic. The officer might, for example, stress the practical interpersonal advantages (or disadvantages) of confession for the suspect or for his or her friends and relatives. In this regard, the officer might explain, for example, that "help is at hand," "the offense is trivial," "you're upsetting your family," or "things will improve if you own up." Alternatively, the conversation might turn to the social consequences of admission or denial, exemplified by comments such as "You'll look stupid or childish," "You can start a new life with a clean slate," and "What will your family think?" The officer's aim might be to play directly into the suspect's self-esteem: "The victim/loser will think positively about you if you get it off your chest"; "Honesty is manly"; "You'll feel better"; and so on.

INFORMATIONAL BLUFFS

Sometimes, when the evidence in a case is weak, officers will lie and suggest that the opposite is true. Officers will intimate that, for the suspect, the decision of whether or not to confess is meaningless because there is no decision to be made. The proposition is floated that the police have the knowledge, evidence, and technical expertise to ensure victory in the case. Alleged evidence from forensic sources, ostensible evidence from witnesses, and, most significant, claims of evidence from accomplices all fall within the ambit of these ploys, which Irving (1980:145) refers to as "informational bluffs."

For example, officers might make unfounded suggestions about the existence of forensic evidence such as fingerprints, foot marks, or glove prints. They may make claims about eyewitness identification, or they might claim that an accomplice has "grassed" and made a statement. Not surprisingly, for the innocent suspect, who comes to believe that there is no other avenue to freedom, this is a powerful tactic. As Irving (1980) notes: "Informational bluffs are . . . used in a more sophisticated manner than any other single kind of interviewing tactic. When properly used, their *effectiveness in obtaining confessions is beyond doubt*" (p. 149; emphasis added).

The subtlety and power of informational bluffs are often underrated. Saul Kassin and Kenneth McNall (1991) point to the tactics known as "maximization," in which the interrogator exaggerates the strength of evidence against the suspect, and "minimization," in which the interrogator plays down the seriousness of the crime. Both have been shown to affect the suspect *and* a mock jury hearing them on tape or reading them in transcript. For the suspect, maximization implies a severe sentence in the same way as an explicit threat of punishment. Minimization implies a low sentence in the same manner as an overt offer of leniency. Each has its effect in pushing the unwilling suspect, guilty or not, toward a confession. Even more worrisome, although the mock jurors in the research disapproved of maximization, declaring it to be coercive, they accepted without question confessions elicited by the minimization technique. The mock jurors indicated that they would determine significantly more convictions in the case of the latter tactic, apparently choosing to ignore the "hope of advantage" held out by a person in authority and veiled within the technique. The mock jurors, apparently, similarly ignored the possibility that such a simple ploy could coerce the innocent. Coercion and the potential miscarriage of justice move hand in hand.

PROACTIVE USE OF CUSTODIAL CONDITIONS

Finally, as the U.S. Supreme Court recognized in *Miranda,* detention and the conditions of custody themselves have a powerful coercive effect on suspects. As Irving (1980) notes, custody "involves certain conditions that are likely to have a psychological effect on the suspect" (p. 146). At any time during an interview, an officer can return the suspect to a cell to "think about things," with the hope, overtly or covertly expressed, that the suspect will become more cooperative after a period of further confinement. ("Let's give you some more time to think about things." "Tell the officer when you're ready to talk to us again.") Interrogators assert their authority merely by word or gesture. They exercise physical control over suspects by keeping them from smoking, waking them up, or delaying the provision of meals. All such custodial tactics are designed to demonstrate to suspects that there is little point in continued resistance.

◆ The Psychology of Confessions

If the ploys and tactics described above are gossamer light in their application in comparison to the third degree, they can be pernicious in their effects. For example, the application of the U.S. military model is, because of its endorsement of "psychological methods," an iron fist in a seemingly velvet glove. The Inbau and Reid model, no less powerfully, manipulates suspects toward predetermined outcomes. The superficial creation of the appearance of "benign custody" produces a "plausible conformity" (J. R. Jarrett, personal communication, 1999) by apparently complying with *Miranda* and other proscriptions against coercive tactics while breaching them in practice.

Manuals of advice for interrogators contain specific guidance about the psychological techniques they may use to elicit confessions. Inbau and Reid (1967), for example, are specific in their insistence that "the interrogator must always remain in psychological control of the situation." Among other things, they advise that "after the interrogation is underway, the interrogator should move his chair in closer, so that, ultimately, one of the subject's knees is just about in between the interrogator's two knees." The reason for this is that "distance or the presence of an obstruction of any sort constitutes a serious psychological barrier, and also affords the subject a degree of relief and confidence, not otherwise obtainable" (p. 27). This is just a small part of the working psychology of interrogation. Putting it in the vernacular, the search by the interrogator is for "lie signs" and "buy signs," those subtle verbal and behavioral clues that suggest a person is lying or that intimate, as to a salesman, that the suspect is about to buy into the pitch and capitulate.

THE EVIDENCE

The evidence shows, however, that in many instances, including the manipulation of interpersonal distance, the effects of such ploys and tactics may have little or nothing to do with actual guilt. Although it is now well established, for example, that "interpersonal distance can be used to communicate intimacy and associated information about liking and status" (Hogg and Vaughan 1998:549), it is also the case that "inappropriate interpersonal distance can be very stressful" in principle (pp. 549-50). The invasion of interpersonal space has both physiological and psychological effects. It has been demonstrated, for instance, that when subjects are approached to a distance of less than one meter, they become "more aroused" (as assessed through galvanic skin responses and measurements of sweating). A similar effect occurs when the approach is made from the front as opposed to the side (McBride, King, and James 1965). According to Michael Argyle (1975:313), other studies have noted an increase in the number of gestures indicative of stress that people make at such times. Even if, according to interrogation advisers, such signs of arousal are possible evidence of dissimulation, there remains the important *general* question of why such effects occur—because of guilt or because of the situated activity of the interrogator?

James Baxter and Richard Rozelle (1975) focused on a simulated police interview in which the distance between an officer and a police suspect was systematically varied. Guilt aside, they found that when the distance between the two parties was reduced to less than two feet, the "suspect's" speech time and frequency became disrupted and disorganized, eye movements and gaze aversion became more pronounced, head movements increased, and foot movements diminished. These behaviors are strikingly similar to those identified by police officers and their interrogation advisers as the signs of guilt, suspicion, and deception—the so-called buy signs and lie signs.

Variations in performance also are associated with diurnal body rhythms (Colquohoun, Blake, and Edwards 1968), with cumulative sleep deprivation (Poulton 1970), and with "being awakened during the night" (Langdon and Hartman 1961). Thus the time of day (body rhythms), interruption of the suspect's normal sleep pattern (being awakened), and the length of time in custody (cumulative sleep deprivation) may affect the suspect's ability to respond effectively to questions.[12]

Evidence from social psychology that individuals are readily manipulated by those in authority is of additional critical importance. Drawing upon earlier research, Irving (1987) was able to show that the dynamics of deindividuation (Zimbardo 1970), compliance (Milgram 1963, 1964a, 1964b, 1965), conformity (Asch 1958a, 1958b), and the exercise of authority (Milgram 1963, 1964a, 1964b, 1965) all play their part.[13] Subsequent work by Gisli Gudjonsson (1992) and Isabel Clare and Gudjonsson (1993) has demonstrated that some people, including the mentally handicapped and the mentally ill, but not exclusively so, are likely to be more affected by such tactics. According to Gudjonsson, they are more suggestible, making them more likely to "confess" because of the sort of persons they are rather than because of what they might or might not have done.[14] These processes are highly effective in producing an atmosphere that, especially for the naive and psychologically vulnerable, is a powerful determining factor leading to "confession."

Recommendations that interrogators use such tactics constitute a scandalous application of psychological findings. In a critique of the first edition of Inbau and Reid's (1962) book, which remains little changed in later editions (Inbau and Reid 1967; Inbau et al. 1986), Zimbardo (1967), one of the principal social psychologists of the 20th century, has written:

> It is my professional opinion as a psychologist concerned with the experimental modification of attitudes and behavior, that current police techniques present a highly sophisticated application of psychological principles which for many are more compelling and coercive than physical torture. [The methods] are not only likely to make a guilty man incriminate himself against his will but I am convinced that they will also lead to false confessions by the innocent and to voluntary and unintentional false testimony by witnesses. (Pp. 456-57)[15]

◆ American and British Responses to the Problem

C. Ronald Huff, Arye Rattner, and Edward Sagarin (1986) suggest that annually there may be as many as 6,000 miscarriages of justice in the United States. A similar level (0.5 percent of the annual cases) has been mentioned by Sagarin and quoted by Michael Israel (1994).[16] Hugo Bedau and Michael Radelet (1987) note that false confessions are a "major source" of miscarriages of justice in America. Decades ago, Zimbardo (1971:503) noted that the police claimed that as many as 80 percent of their cases were solved by confession. There is little reason to think that the incidence of confessions used to "solve" cases has fallen since then. However, let us allow that this was a bit of police braggadocio and that the figure is nearer 60 percent. Even if the figure is half that, there remains a problem.

Although there are no directly comparable figures in England and Wales, a report published in 1989 by the organization Justice estimated that up to 15 defendants per year who are sentenced to four years or more on indictment have been wrongly convicted. Clive Walker (1993) points out that such a calculation at crown court level (equivalent to superior court level in the United States) allows one to conclude that wrongful conviction of defendants sentenced to other penalties may amount to more than 1,000 per year. The figure remains unestimated at the lower court (magistrates' court) level, where more than 90 percent of the cases are disposed of. The causes of these erroneous convictions may vary, but a significant number, particularly prior to adjustments for permissible detention and interviewing practices, were the result of false (induced) confessions.

Since the mid-1970s, concern has grown over the frequency with which coercive methods of interrogation have led to miscarriages of justice.[17] In 1981, the Royal Commission on Criminal Procedure in the United Kingdom, for example, went head-to-head with the problem. The issue was dealt with through the introduction of primary legislation (the Police and Criminal Evidence Act of 1984) that had the effect of placing a series of due process clauses at the core of a crime-control model of justice. Let us consider the relevant case law in both the British and the American contexts in greater detail.

THE AMERICAN RESPONSE

A. Louis DiPietro (1993) points out:

> A confession is probably the most damaging and probative evidence that can be admitted against a defendant. To be admissible, due process mandates [requires] that a confession be voluntary and the product of an essentially free and unconstrained choice by the maker. (P. 27)

In *Miranda,* the U.S. Supreme Court acknowledged that

> the process of custody and interrogation of persons accused of crimes contains inherently compelling processes that work to undermine the individual's will to resist and compel him to speak where he would not otherwise do so freely.

The key question for an American court of law is whether, following the interview of a person suspected of a crime who has made a confession, that confession should be admissible in court. Supreme Court decisions in *Haynes v. Washington* (1963) and *Fikes v. Alabama* (1957) define the test for admissibility, to be applied on a case-by-case basis, in such a way that the *totality of the circumstances* that precede a confession must be considered. The question to be considered is whether these circumstances deprived the defendant of the "power of resistance."

In deciding whether a defendant has been deprived of his or her power of resistance, "some courts may tolerate an officer's limited use of lies, promises or threats, so long as they do not overcome the free will of the suspect. However, other courts find an officer's use of such interrogation tactics *per se* violative of due process" (DiPietro 1993:27). Such an ill-defined application of discretion leads, inevitably, to bizarre and sometimes contradictory conclusions.

Skolnick and Richard Leo (1992) suggest that physical force, threats of harm or punishment, lengthy or incommunicado interrogation, denial of food and/or sleep, and promises of leniency are "presumptively coercive." [18] But the case law has been mixed in response to various disputed conditions of interrogation. In *United States v. Pelton* (1987/1988), it was held that a disputed claim of intoxication did not render a confession involuntary. Nor did broken wrists, seasickness, language difficulties, poor accommodations, and repeated interrogations lead to a rejection of a voluntary statement (*United States v. Yunis* 1988). Neither did a period of extended time without sleep (*People v. Hendricks* 1986) render a confession inadmissible.

In *Florida v. Cayward* (1989/1990), which has become a key case, the court drew a distinction between the false verbal indication that there is forensic evidence against the accused and the production of fictitious documentation in support of that concocted assertion. In suggesting that the production of fabricated documents allegedly establishing that semen stains on a victim's underwear were those of the accused and rendered the subsequent confession inadmissible because "police conduct overstepped the line," the court endorsed the practice of lying (to a more limited degree) to a suspect about the existence of fictitious forensic evidence.

In the *Miranda* decision, the majority of the Supreme Court justices "deplored a catalogue of manipulative and potentially coercive psychological tactics employed by the police to elicit confessions from unrepresented defendants" (Skolnick and Leo 1992:9). Since that case, an interrogation has been presumed to be coercive in the absence of a valid waiver. Once such a waiver is obtained, however, and also when a lawyer who does not advise silence is present, many if not all of the psychological tactics deprecated by the justices may be available to the interviewer(s).

Although the waiver of *Miranda* rights must be knowing, voluntary, and intelligent (see *Miranda v. Arizona* 1966), lies, trickery, and deception do not always render a subsequent confession inadmissible (DiPietro 1993:28). Suggestions of the existence of evidence beyond what really exists are not considered to interfere with "free and deliberate choice." For example, deliberate lies to a suspect by the police that a witness had seen a vehicle belonging to the accused at the scene of the crime, that a victim had identified the accused, and that nonexistent forensic evidence existed did not result in exclusion of a confession. In *Frazier v. Cupp* (1969), the U.S. Supreme Court accepted as legitimate the police practice of falsely telling a suspect that an accomplice had confessed. This and numerous other case outcomes have led DiPietro (1993) to suggest that "lies that merely relate to a suspect's connection to a crime often do not render a confession involuntary," although trickery relating to external considerations is "far more likely to invalidate a confession" (p. 28).[19]

Even in those cases in which presumptively coercive manipulations take place, exclusion of confessions may not be automatic. The U.S. Supreme Court has recently held that coerced confessions may be "harmless error" (*Arizona v. Fulminante* 1991). Even in the face of growing psychological evidence of the error of the "harmless error" (Kassin and Sukel 1997; Kassin and Neumann 1997), case law in the United States has continued to approve methods of interrogation that are at worst manifestly coercive and at best grossly unfair. Gudjonsson (1992) has summarized the injustice of this:

> Inbau, Reid, and Buckley do not consider the possibility that anyone who retracts a previous confession could possibly be innocent. They work on the misguided assumption that their tactics *never* induce a person to falsely confess [*sic*]. There are sufficient numbers of proven cases of innocent persons retracting false confessions to demonstrate that this belief . . . is unfounded. (P. 222)

THE BRITISH RESPONSE

The law in England and Wales has taken a different path. Following the deliberations of the Royal Commission on Criminal Procedure, legislation was passed in the form of the Police and Criminal Evidence Act of 1984. Largely because of concerns about miscarriages of justice and the coercive and manipulative tactics of the police in obtaining confessions, the act provides a due process spine to the existing crime-control model of criminal justice.

Under Section 66 of the Police and Criminal Evidence Act of 1984, codes of practice have been formulated that lay down guidelines about related police activity. These codes cover, among other things, the rules and regulations in respect to "the detention, treatment, and questioning of persons by police officers" (Code C).[20] Code C lays down some fundamental principles about the nature of police interrogation. The code defines an interview as "the questioning of a person regarding his involvement or suspected involvement in a criminal offence or offences." It should be noted that there is no suggestion that the purpose of the interview is to obtain a confession.[21]

The code requires that the interview be conducted within a framework of rules, some of which are considerably complex. For example, these rules do the following, among other things:

◆ Specify the maximum period of detention (36 hours without the approval of a court and 96 with it)

◆ Indicate that, as a rule, interviews should not take place with those who are intoxicated or unfit due to drugs (Code C, para. 12.3)[22] or at a time when the interviewee would normally be sleeping (8 hours of rest must be made available in every 24 hours) (Code C, para. 12.2)

◆ Require that juveniles, the mentally ill, the mentally handicapped, and those who are illiterate (Code C, paras. 1.6, 3.6, 16.4) be treated as "at-risk" subjects and provided with the support of an "appropriate adult" who will act to ensure the fairness of the proceedings (Code C, paras. 11.14-16)

◆ Require that interpreters be provided for people who do not speak English and for those who are hearing or sight impaired (Code C, para. 13.1 et seq.)

◆ Require that food be supplied (subject to certain provisos) at recognized mealtimes (Code C, para. 12.7)

◆ Require that short breaks in the interview be taken at "intervals of approximately two hours" (Code C, para. 12.7).

However, by far the most stringent requirement placed upon the police is that mandating the "contemporaneous recording" of interviews. In the early days of the Police and Criminal Evidence Act, police officers fulfilled this requirement by writing down in longhand each and every utterance of both the suspects and themselves (I have described this process in some detail elsewhere; see Irving and McKenzie 1989; McKenzie 1994). More recently, however, contemporaneous recording has been completed through the application of the Code of Practice for the Tape Recording of Interviews with Suspects (1992). It is now a requirement (a) that "an accurate record must be made of each interview with a person suspected of an offence, whether or not the interview takes place at a police station," and (b) that the record "be made on the forms provided for this purpose, or in the officer's pocket-book [notebook] or in accordance with the code of practice for the tape recording of interviews with suspects" (Code C, para. 11.5). Save in excep-

tional circumstances, the record must be made "during the course of the interview." This, in effect, requires that, as a general rule, interviews with suspects will be electronically recorded in all cases, except in instances where handwritten contemporaneous records are the only feasible method of record keeping.

As noted above, Zimbardo (1971) and Irving (1980) have both written of the extent to which the psychological and physiological effects of incarceration can make a person more "malleable." In the United Kingdom, the Codes of Practice and the Police and Criminal Evidence Act of 1984 make particular provision to ensure that suspects are not adversely affected by the conditions of custody or by the circumstances of their interviews. Those arrested are allowed to retain personal possessions, including money. They must be provided with food at recognized mealtimes (Code C, para. 12.7). Cells are to be ventilated and adequately lit. Blankets, mattresses, and bedding of "a reasonable standard and in a clean and sanitary condition" must be provided. Each police station at which suspects are detained is required under the legislation to have a police officer designated as the "custody officer" who is responsible for the good order of the cell block. Importantly, this officer can be found guilty of an offense under Police Discipline Regulations if he or she does not comply with the Codes of Practice. The "good order" of the cell block thus is ensured through the threat of sanctions.

In contrast with the United States, with its crime-control practices embedded in a due process philosophy, in England and Wales the Police and Criminal Evidence Act of 1984 and the Codes of Practice have been formulated to ensure that suspects are physically and mentally fit to deal with interviews. Furthermore, the failure of a police officer to abide by the contents of the Codes of Practice constitutes a disciplinary offense; this is a far cry from the unsatisfactory and almost toothless character of the Judges' Rules.

As mentioned earlier, the English courts have taken a forthright stance in the interpretation of legislation, declaring unacceptable many tactical approaches to the elicitation of confessions on the grounds that they tend to produce unreliability in confessions rather than that they are coercive per se (although they may well remain so). In *R. v. Mason* (1987), the judges of the Court of Appeal firmly declared inadmissible a confession obtained following a fictitious statement made to an arson suspect (and his solicitor) by the interviewing officers. The police officers falsely told the suspect that bits of glass bottle known to have contained flammable liquid and found at the scene bore the suspect's fingerprints. More recently, the practice of falsely telling a suspect that eyewitnesses have identified him or her as the culprit has been similarly declared to be unacceptable, albeit as part of a parcel of "problems" with a confession (McKenzie 1994), and rendered a subsequent confession to murder inadmissible.

In the United Kingdom, the Codes of Practice have barred the discussion, promise, or denial of bail as a "tactic" to be used in eliciting a confession. Similarly, discussion of the nature of the charge is prohibited. Not only may the police not initiate such exchanges, but they are constrained by guidelines about the responses they can make if suspects raise such issues themselves.[23] It seems that here, in the application of unethical or deceptive practices, the growing distinction between English and American jurisprudence may most readily be seen.

◆ Alternative Interviewing Methods

As a result of the recognition of problems associated with the gathering of evidence from both witnesses and suspects using traditional methods, there has been a substantial search for alternative procedures. The research conducted thus far has been concerned with finding methods that both limit the distortions inherent in inappropriate questioning techniques and eliminate the possibility that suspects will be coerced into making (false) confessions.

The British police have, since the beginning of the 1990s, moved to a model of interviewing known as the "investigative interview." The principles of the investigative interview are based on the underlying precept that there is a need for "ethicality" in the interviewing process, regardless of the status of the person being interviewed. Police officers are given specific training to develop their investigative interviewing skills. The interviewing techniques are laid out in two booklets produced by the Central Planning and Training Unit (1992a, 1992b).[24] These documents and a more recent revision give clear and comprehensive guidance and explanations of "best practice" and essential psychological issues related to memory and human communication (Shepherd and Milne 1999:137).

The recognition that traditional methods of interviewing those involved in or suspected of crime are flawed and may contribute substantially to the problem of miscarriages of justice has led to a specific movement in English law. This has, on the one hand, initiated a series of due process requirements in relation to the most coercive elements of arrest, detention, and interrogation. On the other hand, it has required that officers be adequately trained and understand the psychological dynamics of the interrogation process. Officers are trained to view forensic interviewing as aimed not at obtaining confessions or at "shaping" the evidence of witnesses to match a case theory espoused by an investigator, but at ensuring that all those caught up in criminal activity—whether by mistake or by design—be dealt with fairly and properly. At the same time as the due process elements discussed above have developed, so has the practice of tape-recording interviews. Tape recording is, to all intents and purposes, mandatory in England and

Wales. It is only when such a requirement exists that observers can truly make judgments about whether or not suspects have been treated fairly, whether police tactics are legitimate, and whether mandatory procedures and prohibited practices have or have not occurred.

◆ Conclusion

I want to emphasize that the observations made above are not, in any way, intended to be viewed as a claim that the English legal system has now gotten it right. There are still many flaws in the system. However, by contrast with current English practice, the application of interviewing and interrogation practices in the United States is caught in a time warp, one that is based on a model of humankind that is close to 100 years out of date.

There is a strongly and popularly held belief that it is the strength of an individual's personality—his or her willpower—that allows the individual to resist the blandishments of those who would otherwise be successful in seducing, manipulating, or coercing that person. Underlying this belief is the assumption that individual decision making is based on a fundamental principle of free will. This model, which is close to the hearts of many lawyers, judges, and police officers, takes for granted that a person who has not committed a crime will not confess to it. The corollary is that a person who has witnessed a crime is either a good witness or a bad witness, never a witness whose recollection has been distorted or whose memory may have been rearranged by the very process of information gathering. In the minds of those who make these assumptions, there is little possibility that a person might be coerced into producing a false confession for a crime or might give erroneous evidence because of the manner in which he or she was questioned in the first place.

However, as we have seen, in the psychological dynamics of interviewing and interrogation there are many circumstances in which individuals may be manipulated toward the production of false confessions or into giving false or at least mistaken evidence. My own view, from a police perspective, is that often such manipulation is undertaken for the best, rather than the basest, reasons. Sometimes the activities described in this chapter are referred to as police interrogator "abuse," and there is no doubt that some cases involving false confessions are, like the fabrication of evidence, the result of the deliberate exercise of abuse on the part of the police. But, again based on my own observations and experience, I believe that very often the police are little better than naive members of the public in understanding the dynamics of human communication and persuasion. Moreover, police officers commonly bring to their work their own self-concepts as crime fighters and the moral language of defeating evil in the war against crime.[25] It is from this view of the world, in the context of limited education and general blue-collar background, that officers see themselves as properly encouraging people whom they "know" to be guilty toward confession. This, when combined with assumptions about the autonomy of the individual, leads directly to the stance many interrogators and interviewers take toward witnesses—that they hold little responsibility for the outcome of their questioning.

In the United States, the consequence of this has been that, under the guise of a due process criminal justice system, there lies a substantial crime-control flaw. By contrast, English law, although not without fault, has recognized the extent to which unconscious manipulation and overt coercion are both possible and has built into a crime-control model of criminal justice a substantial, and in some cases quite restrictive, due process core.[26]

If legislators, civil rights experts, and judges are truly committed to ensuring the propriety of criminal investigation, there are two important avenues they can follow for improvement. The first and most obvious is that of education. A clear responsibility rests firmly upon criminal justice educators, forensic psychologists, enlightened senior police officers, and lawyers, both defense and prosecution, to take every possible step to ensure that the dynamics of interviewing and interrogation are understood. They must also ensure that, where necessary, safeguards are built into the system such that investigatory propriety is assured, as in the law of England and Wales.

The second avenue is to recognize the role that the courts, including the U.S. Supreme Court, must play in ensuring compliance. There is substantial evidence to suggest that the Police and Criminal Evidence Act of 1984 in England has been largely successful in achieving its aims. This would not have been so if a number of early cases in which breaches of the Codes of Practice came to light had not resulted in cases being dismissed by the courts. A 25-year police background, coupled with close to 40 years of observation and analysis of police behavior, leads me to conclude that there is no more effective way for the courts to encourage police officers to toe the line than by throwing out cases in which they have breached procedures. This is not an easy path. If adopted, it would be the subject of considerable resistance and may take many years to achieve. But, as somebody famous once said, "just because it's difficult doesn't mean it's not worth trying."

■ Notes

1. Skolnick and Fyfe (1993) suggest that this is to be expected in a system that requires probable cause for arrest. *Probable* implies guilt.

2. The distinction between the suspect (the person arrested by the police) and the culprit (the person who committed the crime) is important. The police can deal only with suspects; it is

the work of a court to decide if a suspect is the culprit. The assumption by the police that the individual being interviewed has moved from one category to the other is at the heart of coercive interviewing practices.

3. For example, it was demonstrated that the strength of a verb (e.g., *hit, crashed,* or *smashed*) placed in a question asking subjects who had been shown a film of an automobile accident, "How fast was the red car going when the cars [hit/crashed/smashed/etc.]?" affected estimates of the speed by up to 30 percent.

4. Despite this quotation and the observation that "we do not advocate the use of torture on human beings," but on the grounds that "regardless of the Geneva Convention and other laws and protocols, each commander must decide whether the use of force to obtain information from a hostile source is appropriate, based upon the circumstances at hand," Richard Krousher (1985) continues, "If a commander feels that he must use torture, we think he should understand the techniques available to him, and especially understand the dangers inherent in each technique" (pp. 2-3). Krousher then proceeds to outline such procedures as humiliation through stripping; the application of "spit, piss, and shit"; humiliation through the use of "the sex act," including forced fellatio and rape; confinement and restraint, including binding and flogging; burial alive; suspension and the rack; and the application of techniques leading to severe hunger and thirst. Other techniques mentioned include intrusion into body orifices, abrasion, beating, burning, skinning alive, and the use of insects and animals.

5. The defendants in *Brown v. Mississippi* (1936) were three African Americans who were suspected of murder. One of them, Arthur "Yank" Ellington, refused to confess in the absence of any evidence of his involvement in the crime and was, thereupon, first hanged with a rope from a tree and let down alive. He continued to deny his involvement in the crime and was again suspended alive from the tree. He was then whipped and still would not confess. Two days later, the sheriff told Ellington that he would whip him again until he confessed. Ellington complied. The other two men, Ed Brown and Henry Shields, were whipped and pummeled until "the blood ran" and they confessed. The deputy, Cliff Dial, told the court of original jurisdiction in Kemper County, Mississippi, that the beatings were "not too much for a nigger."

6. For the purposes of this chapter, England includes Wales, the only other part of the United Kingdom where English law applies. The law is different in Scotland and Northern Ireland.

7. *Tanned* is a northern England euphemism for *beaten*.

8. In my own early police career in west London, I saw a rape suspect treated in a similar manner.

9. There are, of course, dissenters from this view. Shortly after the *Miranda* decision, Congress passed the U.S. Code in an attempt to overrule the mandates of the U.S. Supreme Court in respect to the "irrefutable presumption against confessions made without prior warnings" (Redlich 1999). It includes a list of factors, similar to those in the *Miranda* ruling, that the courts must consider in deciding if a confession is voluntary, based on the view that the presence or absence of a factor is not conclusive evidence of "voluntariness" (Redlich 1999). Although there has been debate about the lawfulness of a congressional decision that seeks to overrule a U.S. Supreme Court decision, the appeals courts in a recent case (*United States v. Dickerson* 1999) has noted that as *Miranda* warnings are not specifically required by the U.S. Constitution, Section 3501 is good law. Because this is a decision by the Fourth Circuit of the U.S. Court of Appeals, it affects only federal cases in that jurisdiction. Nevertheless, the ground has been set for a legal battle over this matter.

10. It is the element of manipulation that distinguishes the "interview" from the "interrogation," as well as the bulk of the literature on the sociological aspects of interviewing from that to which psychological research applies.

11. The rules required, for example, that people should at the time of their arrest be told, "You are not obliged to say anything unless you wish to do so, but what you say may be written down and used in evidence." Later, before making a written statement of confession, the person should be read and should be asked to sign his or her name to a document that states, "I make this statement of my own free will. I have been told that I need not say anything unless I wish to do so, but that what I say will be taken down and may be given in evidence." Contrast these crime-control wordings with the explicit advice and warning of the language of *Miranda*: "You have the *right* to remain silent . . . *right* to an attorney . . . used in evidence against you" (emphasis added).

12. Irving (1980) found that nearly half (41 percent) of the suspects he observed being interviewed were in an "abnormal state." About 18 percent were intoxicated, hung over, or suffering from the effects of drugs. Irving also noted that 14 percent of the suspects were interviewed between 10:00 p.m. and 6:00 a.m., times when most people would normally be sleeping.

13. *Deindividuation* refers to the loss of a sense of individuality as a result of the procedure and practices of detention, *compliance* refers to doing as one is told, and *conformity* refers to doing what others do.

14. Irving (1987) has argued that the dynamics of suggestibility are little more than a reassessment of the dynamics of conformity, compliance, and obedience. Although Gudjonsson (1992) has strongly refuted this suggestion, it remains the case that there is considerable similarity between the notion of suggestibility and the distinctions drawn by David Krech, Richard Crutchfield, and Egerton Ballachey (1962) in their studies of the conformist, the anticonformist, and the nonconformist. Gudjonsson has provided valuable forensic tools, such as the Gudjonsson (1992) Suggestibility Scales, but there is insufficient space here for me to detail fully all of the related arguments in respect to the meaning and categorization of the behaviors and concepts in question.

15. Zimbardo (1967) concludes that the application and approval of such techniques is a disgraceful slur on the American criminal justice system.

16. Israel (1994) points out, however, that these estimates are misleading, because they include only those who have entered pleas of guilty. If the figure is recast to cover also those who plead not guilty but are the subject of guilty verdicts, the figure is about 5 percent.

17. See Walker (1993) for full details of these cases in England and Wales.

18. There are physiological reasons food and sleep deprivation must be taken into account in the assessment of the application of interrogation methods. In particular, depletion of blood sugar levels may lead to growing confusion and tractability. In combination with the verbal and nonverbal techniques outlined above, such deprivation may be key to understanding why innocent persons confess.

19. External considerations are exemplified by cases in which suspects have been told they are likely to lose welfare benefits and custody of

their children if they do not confess, coupled with offers of leniency in return for confession (*Lynumn v. Illinois* 1963); in which it has been suggested to suspects that confession is a now-or-never option and that failure to confess will lead to the loss of any advantage to be obtained from cooperation (*United States v. Anderson* 1991); and in which police have told suspects that some third party will suffer as a consequence of their failure to confess (*Spano v. New York* 1959). Compare each of these with Irving's list of tactical categories.

20. The "other things" are the powers to stop and search people and to search premises in matters associated with the identification of persons suspected of crime.

21. An earlier version of the Codes of Practice (1986, Code C, para. 12A) suggested that the purpose of an interview was to obtain from a suspect an "explanation" of his or her behavior. Even this language was considered too strong.

22. Following the introduction of the Police and Criminal Evidence Act of 1984, Barrie Irving and I conducted research in which we found that one year after the introduction of the

legislation, interviews with "abnormal" suspects had fallen to 13 percent of the total. Those who were "intoxicated, hung over, or suffering from the effects of drugs" accounted for only 4 percent of the total (Irving and McKenzie 1989).

23. A two-phase study examining the effects of the Police and Criminal Evidence Act of 1984, 6 and 18 months after the act's commencement, found that there was no evidence this proscription had been unsuccessful (Irving and McKenzie 1989).

24. The Central Planning and Training Unit is a Home Office (British government) body with general responsibilities for the development of police training in England and Wales.

25. Sincere thanks to James R. Jarrett for drawing my attention to this.

26. It remains the case that there are some individuals within the English criminal justice system (for example, undercover police officers in general) who still do not recognize the extent to which individuals may be manipulated, coerced, cajoled, or otherwise pushed toward a required, if not predetermined, outcome.

■ References

Argyle, M. 1975. *Bodily Communication*. London: Methuen.

Arizona v. Fulminante, U.S. LEXIS 1854 (1991).

Asch, S. 1958a. "Effects of Group Pressure on Modification and Distortion of Judgements." In *Readings in Social Psychology,* edited by E. E. Maccoby, T. M. Newcombe, and E. L. Hartley. New York: Holt, Rinehart & Winston.

———. 1958b. "Studies of Independence and Conformity: A Minority of One against a Unanimous Majority." *Psychological Monographs* 70(Whole No. 416).

Baxter, J. C. and R. M. Rozelle. 1975. "Nonverbal Expression as a Function of Crowding during a Simulated Police-Citizen Encounter." *Journal of Personality and Social Psychology* 32:40-54.

Bedau, H. and M. Radelet. 1987. "Miscarriages of Justice in Potentially Capital Cases." *Stanford Law Review* 40:21-179.

Brown v. Mississippi, 207 U.S. 278 (1936).

Central Planning and Training Unit, Home Office. 1992a. *A Guide to Interviewing*. London: Author.

———. 1992b. *The Interviewers Rule Book*. London: Author.

Clare, I. and G. H. Gudjonsson. 1993. "Interrogative Suggestibility, Confabulations and Acquiescence in People with Mild Learning Difficulties (Mental Handicap): Implications for Reliability during Police Interrogations." *British Journal of Clinical Psychology* 32:295-301.

Code of Practice for the Tape Recording of Interviews with Suspects. 1992. London: Her Majesty's Stationery Office.

Colquohoun, W. P., M. J. Blake, and R. S. Edwards. 1968. "Experimental Studies of Shift Work: In Stabilized Eight Hour Shift Systems." *Ergonomics* 11:527-56.

Danziger, K. 1976. *Interpersonal Communication*. Oxford: Pergamon.

DiPietro, A. L. 1993. "Lies, Promises, or Threats: The Voluntariness of Confessions." *FBI Law Enforcement Bulletin* 62(7):27-32.

Escobedo v. Illinois, 378 U.S. 478 (1964).

Fikes v. Alabama, 352 U.S. 191 (1957).

Fisher, R. P., E. Geiselman, and D. Raymond. 1987. "Critical Analysis of Police Interviewing Techniques." *Journal of Police Science and Administration* 15:177-85.

Florida v. Cayward, Fla. 2d Dist. (1989), review dismissed; 562 So.2d 347 (Fla. 1990).

Frazier v. Cupp, 394 U.S. 731 (1969).

George, R. 1991. "A Field Evaluation of the Cognitive Interview." Master's dissertation, Polytechnic of East London.

Gudjonsson, G. H. 1992. *The Psychology of Interrogations, Confessions and Testimony.* Chichester: John Wiley.

Haynes v. Washington, 373 U.S. 503 (1963).

Hogg, M. A. and G. M. Vaughan. 1998. *Social Psychology.* 2d ed. Hertfordshire, England: Prentice Hall.

Huff, C. R., A. Rattner, and E. Sagarin. 1986. "Guilty until Proven Innocent: Wrongful Conviction and Public Policy." *Crime and Delinquency* 32:518-44.

Inbau, F. E. and J. E. Reid. 1962. *Criminal Interrogation and Confessions.* Baltimore: Williams & Wilkins.

———. 1967. *Criminal Interrogation and Confessions.* 2d ed. Baltimore: Williams & Wilkins.

Inbau, F. E., J. E. Reid, and J. P. Buckley. 1986. *Criminal Interrogation and Confessions.* 3d ed. Baltimore: Williams & Wilkins.

Irving, B. 1980. *Police Interrogation: A Case Study of Current Practice* (Royal Commission on Criminal Procedure, Research Study No. 2). London; Her Majesty's Stationery Office.

———. 1987. "Interrogative Suggestibility: A Question of Parsimony." *Social Behaviour* 2:19-28.

Irving, B. and I. K. McKenzie. 1989. *Regulating Custodial Interviews.* London: Police Foundation.

Israel, M. 1994. "Convicting the Innocent: Due Process and the Natural Law Legacy." Presented at the annual meeting of the Academy of Criminal Justice Sciences, March, Chicago.

Justice. 1989. *Miscarriages of Justice.* London: Author.

Kassin, S. M. and K. McNall. 1991. "Police Interrogations and Confessions: Communicating Promises and Threats by Pragmatic Implication." *Law and Human Behavior* 15:233-51.

Kassin, S. M. and K. Neumann. 1997. "On the Power of Confession Evidence: An Experimental Test of the Fundamental Difference Hypothesis." *Law and Human Behavior* 21:469-84.

Kassin, S. M. and H. Sukel. 1997. "Coerced Confessions and the Jury: An Experimental Test of the 'Harmless Error' Rule." *Law and Human Behavior* 21:27-46.

Kleinig, J. 1996. *The Ethics of Policing.* Cambridge: Cambridge University Press.

Krech, D., R. S. Crutchfield, and E. L. Ballachey. 1962. *Individual in Society.* New York: McGraw-Hill.

Krousher, R. W. 1985. *Physical Interrogation Techniques.* Port Townsend, WA: Loompanics Unlimited.

Langdon, D. E. and B. Hartman. 1961. "Performance upon Sudden Awakening." School of Aerospace Medicine Report No. 62-17, Brooks Air Force Base.

Lavine, E. H. 1930. *The Third Degree: A Detailed and Appalling Expose of Police Brutality.* New York: Vanguard.

Loftus, E. F. 1979. *Eyewitness Memory.* Cambridge, MA: Harvard University Press.

Loftus, E. F. and J. C. Palmer. 1974. "Reconstruction of Automobile Destruction: An Example of the Interaction between Language and Memory." *Journal of Verbal Learning and Verbal Behavior* 13:585-89.

Lynumn v. Illinois, 372 U.S. 528 (1963).

Mark, R. 1978. *In the Office of Constable.* London: Collins.

McBride, G., G. M. King, and J. W. James. 1965. "Social Proximity Effects on Galvanic Skin Responses in Adult Humans." *Journal of Psychology* 61:153-57.

McKenzie, I. K. 1982. "Non Verbal Communication in Interrogation." M.Phil. thesis, University of Exeter.

———. 1989. "Regulating Custodial Interviews." Ph.D. thesis, University of Bath.

———. 1994. "Regulating Custodial Interviews: A Comparative Study." Presented at the annual meeting of the Academy of Criminal Justice Sciences, March, Chicago.

———. 1999. "Making Difficult Science Easy: An Interview with Professor Elizabeth F. Loftus." *International Journal of Police Science and Management* 2(1):78-87.

McKenzie, I. K. and G. P. Gallagher. 1989. *Behind the Uniform: The Police of Britain and America.* Brighton, England: Harvester Wheatsheaf.

McLean, M. 1992. "Obtaining Witness Statements: Best Practice and Proposals for Innovation." *Medicine, Science and the Law* 35:116-22.

Milgram, S. 1963. "Behavioral Study of Obedience." *Journal of Abnormal and Social Psychology* 67:371-78.

———. 1964a. "Group Pressure and Action against a Person." *Journal of Abnormal and Social Psychology* 69:137-43.

———. 1964b. "Issues in the Study of Obedience: A Reply to Baumrind." *American Psychologist* 19:848-52.

———. 1965. "Some Conditions of Obedience and Disobedience to Authority." *Human Relations* 18:57-76.

Miranda v. Arizona, 384 U.S. 436 (1966).

Newman, K. 1984. *Report of the Commissioner of Police of the Metropolis for 1983.* London: Her Majesty's Stationery Office.

O'Hara, C. E. 1970. *Fundamentals of Criminal Investigation.* 2d ed. Springfield, IL: Charles C Thomas.

People v. Hendricks, 495 NE.2d 85 (1986).

Police and Criminal Evidence Act 1984 (sec. 66): Codes of Practice. 1992. London: Her Majesty's Stationery Office.

Poulton, E. L. 1970. "Skilled Performance and Stress." In *Psychology and Work,* edited by P. B. War. Harmondsworth: Penguin.

R. v. Mason, Times Law Reports (May 23, 1987).

Redlich, J. W. 1999. "Old Law Learns New Tricks; Court Finds *Miranda* Loophole." *Police Chief* 66(6).

Reiner, R. 1985. *The Politics of the Police.* Brighton, England: Harvester Wheatsheaf.

———. 1991. *The Politics of the Police.* 2d ed. Hemel Hempstead, England: Harvester Wheatsheaf.

Robin, G. D. 1980. *Introduction to the Criminal Justice System.* New York: Harper & Row.

Royal, R. F. and S. Schutt. 1976. *The Gentle Art of Interviewing and Interrogation: A Professional Manual and Guide.* Englewood Cliffs. NJ: Prentice Hall.

Royal Commission on Criminal Procedure. 1981. *Report* (Cmnd. 8092). London: Her Majesty's Stationery Office.

Shepherd, E. and R. J. Milne. 1999. "Full and Faithful: Ensuring Quality Practice and Integrity of Outcome in Witness Interviews." In *Analysing Witness Testimony,* edited by A. Heaton-Armstrong, E. Shepherd, and D. Wolchover. London: Blackstone.

Skolnick, J. H. and J. J. Fyfe. 1993. *Above the Law: Police and the Excessive Use of Force.* New York: Free Press.

Skolnick, J. H. and R. A. Leo. 1992. "The Ethics of Deceptive Interrogation." *Criminal Justice Ethics* 11(1):3-12.

Spano v. New York, 360 U.S. 315 (1959).

United States v. Anderson, 929 F.2d (2nd Circuit 1991).

United States v. Dickerson, 1666 F.3d 667 (1999).

United States v. Pelton, 835 F.2d 1067 (4th Circuit 1987), cert. denied; 108 S. Ct. 1741 (1988).

United States v. Yunis, 859 F.2d 953 (DC Circuit 1988).

Walker, C. 1993. "Introduction." In *Justice in Error,* edited by C. Walker and K. Starmer. London: Blackstone.

Wickersham, G. W. 1931. *Report on Lawlessness in Law Enforcement: National Commission on Law Observance and Law Enforcement.* Washington, DC: Government Printing Office.

Zimbardo, P. G. 1967. "The Psychology of Police Confessions." In *Readings in Psychology Today.* Del Mar, CA: CRM.

———. 1970. *The Human Choice: Individuation, Reason and Order versus Deindividuation, Impulse and Chaos.* In *Nebraska Symposium on Motivation,* edited by W. J. Arnold and D. Levine. Lincoln: University of Nebraska Press.

———. 1971. "Coercion and Compliance: The Psychology of Police Confessions." Pp. 492-508 in *The Triple Revolution Emerging: Social Problems in Depth,* edited by R. Perrucci and M. Pilisuk. Boston: Little, Brown.

22

INTERVIEWING IN EDUCATION

◆ William G. Tierney
Patrick Dilley

nterviews played a central role in educational research throughout the 20th century. Like other fields of inquiry, education experienced pitched debates about the relative strengths and weaknesses of qualitative and quantitative methodologies. Perhaps in no other field, however, has qualitative inquiry in general, and the qualitative interview in particular, become so prevalent in research and in theoretical and policy-related discussions as in education. Indeed, some of the preeminent qualitative researchers, such as Egon Guba, George Spindler, Yvonna Lincoln, Elliot Eisner, and Shirley Heath, either consider education to be their primary area of study or have produced breakthrough educational texts.

A cursory review of prominent texts that deal with educational settings is equally re-vealing of the strength of qualitative methods. Courtney Cazden, Vera John, and Dell Hymes's *Functions of Language in the Classroom* (1972) and Shirley Heath's *Ways with Words* (1983) are landmark works in how language functions to promote or to disable learning. Sara Lawrence Lightfoot's *Worlds Apart* (1978) and Margaret Mead's *The School in American Culture* (1951) focus on the interrelationships between formal and informal schooling processes. Michael Scriven's "Objectivity and Subjectivity in Educational Research" (1972) and Patti Lather's "Research as Praxis" (1986) are hallmark discussions in the ongoing debate about the epistemological assumptions surrounding educational research. Jonathan Kozol's *Savage Inequalities* (1991) and Tracy Kidder's *Among Schoolchildren* (1989) are two of the most

AUTHORS' NOTE: We wish to acknowledge the helpful advice of Julia Colyar, Michelle Crockett, Yvonna Lincoln, Susan Talburt, Harry Wolcott, and the editors.

◆ 453

widely read books in education of the last generation, and both make extensive use of qualitative interviews.

Obviously, we could go on at length about the various texts that have employed interviews in the field, and different readers might proffer suggestions about authors who are more prominent or well regarded than those we have mentioned. Our point is not to create a who's who of educational research or to suggest the prominence of one text over another. Rather, we mean to underscore the observation that, unlike other fields of social research, education has utilized the interview as a central tool in its research efforts for more than a century and has experienced a quantum leap in the use of its qualitative versions in the past few decades. The manners in which such research has been carried out have varied greatly, depending upon the interests of the researchers, the theoretical frameworks called upon, and the questions put forth. Rather than taking a "one-size-fits-all" approach to interviews, educational researchers have been remarkably diverse in the ways they have applied the interviewing process.

Qualitative interviewing can be used to gather information that cannot be obtained using other methods. Surveys might offer mass data about a particular issue, but they lack the depth of understanding that a qualitative interview provides. Observation can certainly lead to insights about, say, interactional styles of teachers with students or patterns of behavior in a classroom, but without interview data gathered directly from the participants/actors, observation is akin to watching silent movies. For these reasons alone, the interview has become the most common qualitative tool that researchers employ in education (Glesne and Peshkin 1992; Merriam 1998).

This chapter has an important epistemological theme, centering on the increasing use of qualitative methods and the associated openness and flexibility in views of educational research in general and on the conceptualization and conduct of interviewing and the interview subject in partic-

ular. As opposed to some areas of study that have become more doctrinaire or narrow in applying particular theoretical or methodological models, educational research has widened its scope. Although educational psychology and statistics achieved prominence in schools of education immediately prior to World War II, qualitative methods and interviewing nonetheless continued to be important research tools for educators. In the past 20 years, educational researchers have applied and experimented with qualitative methods of all kinds. One of our purposes in this chapter is to delineate the epistemological shifts that have accompanied this change.

The chapter is divided into four major parts. We begin with a discussion of why researchers interview in educational settings and then consider changing notions about the category of the respondent. In the third section, we briefly survey the various interview formats used in education as well as the forms of presentation used for interview material. Finally, we discuss the challenges that interviewing researchers will face in the future. Our goal in this chapter is not so much to persuade our readers to consider interviewing as a tool for data collection, but instead to encourage them to think of interviews as sites for discourse and social analysis, for gathering data about educational practices and identities, and for the production of these practices and identities.

◆ The Purposes of Interviewing

Interviewing in education has as many purposes as it does in other fields. The purposes vary in significance, however, depending on disciplinary context. Here, we stress the most prominent of these purposes in education.

THE POLICY INTERVIEW

The policy interview is of primary importance in education and generally is held at a meta-level. It seeks information that will enable the interviewer to explain why a particular plan, strategy, or model has been employed in school systems. Policy interviews may be conducted with state-level agencies that accredit teacher education, coordinating committees for public higher education, school boards, or superintendents' offices in large school districts. One researcher might interview state bureaucrats in a study about organizational change and barriers in the implementation process. Another researcher might speak with agency directors about their views of leadership in order to discern the differences between internal and external views of what accounts for a good leader. A third researcher might interview individuals within a school building in order to understand how overall policies inhibit or promote particular actions. Much of the work on charter schools, for example, employs interviews at the policy level in seeking to answer questions concerning why charter reform is necessary and what it is trying to solve (e.g., Wong and Tierney forthcoming).

A great many texts report on research applying policy interviews. Some of the researchers involved have utilized interviews in attempting to learn how particular policies function (Donmoyer and Kos 1993; Goodlad, Soder, and Sirotnik 1990). Still others report the results of interviews with policy leaders in their quest to understand changes taking place across different states (Johnson and Pajares 1996; Richardson et al. 1998; Spillane 1998; Tierney 1988, 1991, 1997; Twombly 1992). This has been and continues to be an important area of interview research in education.

INTERVIEWING TO UNDERSTAND THE SOCIAL CONTEXTS OF LEARNING

A second form of interview is less concerned with policies and more concerned with improving our understanding of the social contexts of learning. Most often, these contexts are organizations or units within organizations, such as schools or classrooms. However, contexts also transcend traditional educational settings and may include a low-income housing community, an abortion clinic, a church, a homeless shelter, or a museum as each bears on educational concerns. Dorothy Smith (1999) suggests that contexts can also be interpreted more abstractly, as what she calls "relations of ruling." Understanding context in this approach means exploring contextual experience, actions, and relationships from within the interview process rather than merely describing behaviors or objectifying the subject. Regardless of the context, the purpose of the interview remains the same: The interviewer hopes to understand the setting—the relationships among the components and members of particular institutions or groups—from the respondent's viewpoint.

The focuses of such interviews can vary quite widely. Some researchers may conduct interviews to represent a social context from as many different viewpoints as possible; others concentrate on one group of individuals. Still others pursue particular interactional understandings that involve more than one group. An ethnography or case study of a school or college (French 1993; Moffatt 1989; Tierney 1988; Wolcott 1970, 1973) offers comments from multiple actors about the educational context in which they work and/or learn. For example, Kevin Coyne (1995) presents a narrative case study of a year at Notre Dame, whereas Robert Rhoads (1998) offers briefer vignettes of several sites of student activism. Michael Ruhlman (1996) presents the results of a year's shadowing and interviewing of students, teachers, and the headmaster of an all-boys day school. Thomas French (1993) lived with and interviewed seniors at a suburban Florida high school; his work reveals the multiple sets of identities and challenges facing those preparing to leave secondary education. Patricia Hersch (1998) spent four years going to school with adolescents in a suburban Virginia school system. She participated in activities with her subjects that were certainly not sanctioned by any school and were clearly unknown to many parents, and her portraits of the students reflect a wide spectrum of voices and concerns. Hugh Mehan and his colleagues (1996) also looked at some of the challenges facing high school students and, in particular, examined school-based untracking efforts and their impact on student success. Like Smith (1999), Mehan and his associates were interested in the social, contextual constructions of reality and how these affected student performance. For each of these researchers, student lives were prime sites for qualitative investigations; the researchers used interviews in their case studies to gain a sense of the different realities with which students and educators approach the classroom and the learning process.

An ethnography need not be based on interviews from a single institution or field site. For example, aiming to draft a schema of cultures and committees in higher education, William Tierney and Estela Bensimon (1996) convey the experiences of professors, department chairs, and academic leaders related to issues of promotion and tenure. Dorothy Holland and Margaret Eisenhart's *Educated in Romance* (1990) is a study of a specific group of women college students whom the researchers interviewed about their opinions and impressions of college life. Similarly, Peggy Orenstein (1994) examines how issues of self-esteem and self-confidence, or lack thereof, affect the schooling of young women. Ruth Sidel (1994) takes up issues of diversity from the perspective of students' individual attempts to build identity and community on a number of college campuses. Patrick Dilley (2000) maps the changing identities of nonheterosexual college men in the United States during the latter half of the 20th century, using intense interviews similar to those utilized by Rhoads (1994). Barbara Schneider and Da-

vid Stevenson (1999) analyze teenagers' ambitions and motivations through their presentation of qualitative interview data from a national study of U.S. adolescents conducted in the 1990s.

CASE STUDIES

The third form of interview focuses on a localized group of actors or, in the case of a life history, a single individual. Rhoads (1998) offers several case studies built on students' perceptions of their actions, activism, and attempts to create cultural diversity on specific campuses. William Finnegan (1998) spent six years in four communities gathering data on the lives of young Americans who were not part of, or were only peripherally involved in, traditional pipelines of education. Finnegan completed individual interviews with respondents at a number of different institutions within a relatively short period of time and buttressed this approach with the use of other methodologies, such as participant observation and artifact analysis. This combination of techniques constituted a solid method of investigating student lives and cultures.

The work of Harry Wolcott (1983, 1990, 1997) provides fine examples of the life history case method. In a series of life history interviews, Wolcott sought to understand how education (both the process and the system) shaped the lives of individual adolescents. In each study, the adolescent neither comments on educational policies nor discusses a specific context. Instead, the reader learns about the life of the youth and, in this light, discovers particular aspects of how education functions, or does not function, in the United States. Wolcott was one of the first researchers to use interviews to examine students who were not educational success stories.

Subsequently, researchers have presented ample case material that shows how interviewing can reveal in rich detail what occurs in the "black box" of education. Jay MacLeod's *Ain't No Makin' It* (1987) is not intended simply to define the context of the interviews, which is a low-income housing project; rather, its purpose is to take the reader directly into the lives of the "hallway hangers" and the "brothers" in order to portray how low-income youth learn to level, rather than raise, their aspirations. Similarly, LeAlan Jones and Lloyd Newman (1997) interviewed young residents of housing projects on Chicago's South Side; their work highlights the effects of the economics of daily survival for these youths. These interviews bring to life how income frames what an individual hopes to become, regardless of the educational contexts or policies that are developed.

INTERVIEWING ORIENTED TO EDUCATIONAL REFORM

The final interview category pertains to educational reform. A researcher might want to know why educational reform does not take place and might assume that interviews with policy analysts will shed light on challenging obstacles. Another researcher might choose to analyze how students learn in order to solve a particular theoretical conundrum about learning styles. Still another might wish to study a rural church or an AIDS clinic as a way to rethink basic notions about where people learn. Or a researcher might take issue with a particular theoretical proposition about educational opportunity and set out to interview individuals and groups in order to advance his or her own theoretical notions.

Each of these examples stops short of the researcher's offering actual plans for reform. However, some research interviewers begin with the premise that the data gathered through their interviews should ultimately serve to specify ways in which educational practices and contexts might be reformed. James Traub (1994) and Gene Maeroff (1998) are quite different in their political vantage points, but both make particular suggestions based on information gleaned from interviews. In Traub's case study of City College of New York, he at-

tempts to demonstrate, through interviews with students and faculty, that remedial education in a college setting has significant flaws. In many respects, Traub's work is the precursor to New York City policies that led to the elimination of remedial education at City College. Maeroff's work focuses on how students from low-income households who take college preparation courses have a higher chance of succeeding than those children who simply take "mainstream" classes in public school. Maeroff's interviews with policy analysts, teachers, program directors, families, and students led to recommendations for how public schools can better prepare students for postsecondary education.

Some interviewing research oriented toward reform has distinct theoretical resonances. For example, those who subscribe to Marxist critiques of schooling (e.g., Apple 1990, 1995; Varenne & McDermott 1998) or critical and postmodern theories (e.g., Tierney 1997; McLaren 1999) frequently seek to move educational research away from one way of viewing schools and colleges toward another, based on the assumption that theories frame how one conceptualizes and sees the world. If one utilizes a different theoretical lens, one will develop different policies, actions, and contexts.

Interviews with a reform orientation can serve a pedagogical function for the interviewed as well as for the interviewer. Paulo Freire's (1997) work of "consciousness-raising" among peasants, for example, takes the interview in this direction. The interviewer's purpose here is to open the respondent's eyes, as it were, by turning the interview in unfamiliar directions in order to prompt the respondent to think in alternative terms. The interview itself becomes a tool of educational reform.

◆ Interview Respondents

Educational interviews also vary in terms of their respondents. Especially important in this regard is the issue of who is considered a potential respondent. If particular groups are excluded from the pool of respondents in a study, this raises the possibility that a prejudicial, or at least perhaps biased, slant exists. For example, in research looking at why students drop out of school, the question of who is interviewed takes on enormous significance. If the interviews focus on children and parents, is one to conclude that the "problem" resides with them rather than with the schools and the educational process? If the interviews focus on educators and administrators, how does one weigh the roles of personal determination and responsibility in learning? If the interview protocol targets social and economic factors, what solutions can one realistically recommend to parents, students, educators, or administrators?

Michelle Fine (1991) has conducted research that bears directly on the respondent definition issue. She used interviews in a deconstructive way to understand the category of "dropouts." Her point of departure was an orientation from which the individual and the family were viewed as neither victim nor problem. Rather, the challenge was to understand how educational structures frame the idea of dropouts. Her work shows how, even before related interviewing actually occurs, the researcher can go a long way toward defining the answers that will be given by uncritically incorporating established categories of respondents.

PARENTS

Educational researchers work with three "received" categories of interview respondents. One of these is students' families, especially their parents. For example, during the second half of the 20th century, a great volume of work was produced that involved the families of Native American students. Daniel McLaughlin's (1992, 1993) studies of how literacy functions in Native American classrooms and Bryan Brayboy and Donna Deyhle's (forthcoming) study of the challenges of Native American youth place an emphasis on the opinions and beliefs of Native American families. Indeed, in the past 25 years, many researchers have focused their energy on interviewing the families of those students who have been especially disenfranchised by education (Heath and McLaughlin 1993; Tierney 1992).

STUDENTS

A second category of respondent would seem naturally to include those who are ostensibly most affected by the educational process—the students. In addition to the works cited earlier, several significant studies of student life have employed interviewing methods to great advantage. For example, Michael Moffatt (1989) provides information about student cultures from a case study of Rutgers College. Paul Loeb (1994) highlights the contrast between students' apathy and action on American campuses. Schneider and Stevenson (1999) challenge many of Loeb's findings, employing a combination of qualitative and quantitative research on the motivations and goals of American teenagers. Many other examples are available; one need do little more than a simple database search to find numerous studies in which students of all ages have served as key informants (see Eder and Fingerson, Chapter 9, this volume).

This explosion of student interviews, which aims to garner and represent the words and worlds of students and their peers, has been part of a movement to include the voices of those being educated in the learning process. (Oddly enough, as central as these respondents are now thought to be, their voices were once viewed as insignificant in matters of schooling and policy formation.) Behind this movement is an epistemological shift that continues to take place in educational research. Regardless of the purposes or contexts of the interviews, educational researchers assume that they will be able to define the nature of the objects they study. For researchers tied to positivist frameworks, the challenge has been to approximate the reliability and validity found in scientific laboratory settings. As researchers have moved toward more social constructionist frameworks, however, the nature of the objects of study has shifted (Guba and Lincoln 1994; Vidich and Lyman 1994). Questions especially about who defines reality have surfaced, and these bear significantly on the categorization of respondents (see Gubrium and Holstein, Chapter 1, this volume).

Few marginalized individuals participated in educational interviews in the first half of the 20th century because researchers assumed that those individuals would be unable to define their own realities. This assumption extended to individuals who might have been drawn from mental institutions, schoolhouses, prisons, or adult literacy classes. However, as the idea of the social construction of reality has taken hold, educational researchers have revised their research designs to include those who actually experience the educational process, regardless of their ostensible social or cognitive status. Depending upon one's epistemological standpoint, such interviews either add to the researcher's own understanding of reality or provide the definition of reality itself; the latter perspective became more and more important in the late decades of the century.

Our aim here is not to detour into a discussion of the nature of reality, but merely to observe that the inclusion of students as key interview informants was not an obvious methodological choice. Such an "obvious" choice requires an epistemological shift that continues to take shape, one that seeks an appreciation of the ordinary voices of all participants in the learning process. We are now seeing interviews with mentally retarded individuals about the nature of their learning (Szepkouski 1993), with families of students with disabilities (Turnbull et al. 1993), with elementary school students about their likes and dislikes (Spindler 1982), with adult learners about their perceptions of literacy classes (Varenne and McDermott 1998), and with students of color regarding their experiences within predominantly white educational settings (Freeman 1999; Johnsrud and Sado 1998). In each instance, the epistemological turnabout has led researchers to assume that in order to understand the particular problem under investigation, they must interpret the words and ideas of those who experience the reality in question.

TEACHERS, ADMINISTRATORS, AND POLICY MAKERS

A third category of interview subjects includes those who have been the most interviewed in educational research: teachers, administrators, and policy makers. These persons have traditionally been viewed as being "in the know" and, as a result, have been considered to be the general respondents of choice in educational interview studies.

Although one might also make the point with regard to this category that it has been affected by definitions-of-reality concerns, an equally interesting point is that the focus of interviewing with individuals in this category has changed over the years. Teachers were the primary informants for interviews a generation ago, as they are today, and policy makers will continue to be interview subjects for the foreseeable future. However, rather than assuming that policy analysts or school principals can define the educational context, researchers now focus in their interviews on understanding these respondents' interpretations of reality. Educational leadership, for example, has been an important area of investigation (Bensimon and Neumann 1993; Guido-DiBrito 1995; Johnson and Pajares 1996; Tierney 1991). Researchers in this area now less commonly assume that respondents will be able to define precisely the attributes of a good leader, say, and are just as likely to consider their responses as data about the rhetoric of good leadership.

Interviews with policy analysts about legislation are often conducted with similar intent. To be sure, one of the researcher's purposes may be to understand the nature of the legislation, but an equally important challenge may be to understand the ordinary cognitive processes involved—in particular, how the interviewee utilizes varied frameworks of knowledge and language to make sense of, and to account for, his or her world and experience. Although the individuals interviewed in this category remain the same, the epistemological stances of interviewers toward their interview data are rather different.

ABSENT RESPONDENTS

Those who have been historically absent from educational interviews make up the final category of respondent we wish to discuss. Take Native American children as an example. If one were to look at research conducted during the development of policies toward these children during the first part of the 20th century, one would be hard-pressed to find interviews with either the children or their parents. Educational researchers at that time presumed that the views of the children and parents were relatively unimportant for the improvement of schooling for Native Americans. Similarly, until a generation ago, the massive quantity of research on schools and postsecondary education did not include interviews conducted with gay students or gay faculty (e.g., Crew 1978; McNaron 1997; Tierney and Dilley 1998; see also Kong, Mahoney, and Plummer, Chapter 12, this volume). And, as we noted earlier, disabled individuals were also often overlooked.

Students, faculty, and administrators in settings of lesser status as well as nontraditional students are also among the absent respondents. In the world of postsecondary education, many more interviews have been conducted on four-year college and university campuses than in community colleges or proprietary institutions. Far more tenure-track faculty members have been interviewed than non-tenure-track faculty (Tierney and Bensimon 1996). Although more than 50 percent of students in postsecondary education are over 21 years of age, well under 20 percent of the research on college students reflects that age group. What is one to conclude when a review of the "worlds" of education does not include groups of nontraditional students? Are these individuals unimportant or nonexistent?

Those who are overlooked are often overlooked for particular reasons. How individual researchers define education, students, and educational settings is widely varied and determined by a mix of sociocultural forces. Far too often, researchers assume that words have definite meanings that are static and understood by everyone, regardless of time, culture, or locale. An analysis of those who are not interviewed tells us a great deal about how changing meanings have affected categorization in this area.

Over the last generation, for example, a number of researchers have studied the nature of race in schooling. Minority students have now become respondents and are being interviewed about what it means to be a minority member in a school system or about the nature of the racism they have experienced throughout their educational careers (Freeman 1999; Johnsrud and Sado 1998; Livingston and Stewart 1987). Far fewer interviews have been done that investigate the nature of whiteness in schooling (Graham 1992; Morawski 1997; Powell 1997), the assumption being that those who are defined as students of color attend to race as a social and cultural marker, whereas white students, who are taken to be race blind in this regard, have nothing to say about the subject. Such an assumption places white students at the "neutral" center of research on schooling while defining others in relation to the "noncolored" center (see Dunbar, Rodriguez, and Parker,

Chapter 14, this volume). Curiously enough, this has been supported by a *lack* of pertinent interview data rather than by interviews or other investigations of the broader cultural contours of the category of respondent.

The same might be said about students who are either impoverished or privileged. Educational theorists have often worked from a deficit model concerning the ability to learn. As a result, much more is known about the problems that exist in low-income schools than about problems in more affluent schools. When researchers frame the issue in terms of deficits, those in privileged positions tend to escape notice and analysis. This stems from the use of research questions framed in terms such as "Why do poor students succeed less often in schools?" instead of "Why do wealthy students succeed more often in schools?" The broader issue, of course, is still "What factors in school foster success, and for whom?" but the actual lives and experiences that researchers study shape the answers by influencing with whom researchers speak about these matters.

Over time, we predict that researchers will further problematize "the" respondent. Rather than accept as "fact" that school is the primary educational site, say, or that a teacher is the key informant, researchers will turn more and more to the sorts of individuals who have previously been overlooked. As research moves into postmodern and postcolonial inquiries concerning the discursive and rhetorical parameters of power, new questions will inevitably arise that will necessitate researchers' rethinking who is to be interviewed and who is not, as well as how to put questions to unknown respondents.

◆ Interview Formats and Forms of Presentation

Educational researchers use a variety of formats for interviewing and present their interview results in different ways. These, too, have changed considerably over the years, extending well beyond the traditional face-to-face interview encounter and "scientific" representation.

INTERVIEW FORMATS

The most widely used format remains the *individual interview,* in which a researcher uses a tape recorder, a laptop computer, or pen and paper (or all three) to record an individual's answers to particular questions. The interview might be done either in person or over the telephone (see Shuy, Chapter 26, this volume). In qualitative inquiry, the researcher interviews a small but theoretically significant number of individuals in the course of the study (see Warren, Chapter 4, this volume). Holland and Eisenhart (1990), for example, interviewed 23 women about their views on status and achievement, and Dilley (2000) interviewed 57 gay men about identity formation in college.

A second interview format, the *focus group,* has been acknowledged by researchers for some time, but has only recently come into its own as a significant educational research tool (see Morgan, Chapter 7, this volume). Focus group interviews achieved high utility in marketing research more than a generation ago. Recently, however, the use of focus groups has become popular among educational researchers because such groups enable them to call upon larger numbers of individuals than is possible with serial individual interviews. The work of David Morgan (1998), in particular, has helped researchers to understand the focus group interview process. This process has proven to be a reliable, efficient, and economical way for researchers to generate information for the broad public (Krop et al. 1998; Throgmorton 1999).

A third interview format, the *life history,* was used throughout the 20th century. Indeed, one might argue that the life history (or life story) was the hallmark of social research in its early years (Bruner 1987; Cohler 1998; Langness and Frank 1981; see also Atkinson, Chapter 6, this volume). Over the past decade, researchers have rediscovered the usefulness of the life history interview for helping them to understand respondents' identities and cultures, and related interviewing has grown in huge proportions. Previously, the life history was seen as a conduit to the detailed texture of culture and identity; now, however, the life history is conceived as a way for researchers and ultimately their readers to make sense of the multiple identities that individuals can hold, create, and manage over the course of a lifetime (Frank 1980; Freeman 1992; Polkinghorne 1995; Stewart, Franz, and Layton 1988).

The resulting case studies based on life story interviewing have been very well received in education. Wolcott (1983), for example, undertook life history interviewing with an adolescent in order to detail just how education shapes an individual's identity. Alexander Jun (2000) conducted five life history interviews with minority youths to see how schooling and community interact to enable or disable students' success in college. Tierney (1993) spent the better part of a year with a gay faculty member who had AIDS in order to understand the multiple identities that a teacher inhabits and the impact of illness on those identities.

The three formats we have mentioned have been used to a greater or lesser extent throughout the 20th century and into the 21st, and they continue to evolve, especially in relation to new technologies, one result of which has been the *virtual interview*. Researchers are discovering that Internet technology, specifically e-mail, creates opportunities for interviews with far-flung respondents (Dilley 2000; Goldman-Segall, Willinsky, & Halff 1997; Hedges 1995; McNaron 1997; see also Ryen, Chapter 17, this volume). The Internet enables researchers to utilize e-mail to conduct interviews either in "real time" or through series of interactive ques-

tions and answers. Interviewees might be single individuals, a series of individuals, or a number of individuals in a chat room. Because the technology is new, however, issues of reliability, validity, and trustworthiness are still problematic (see Mann and Stewart, Chapter 29, this volume).

FORMS OF PRESENTATION

The manner in which interview results are presented is undergoing a sea change (Herrington and Curtis 1990; Krieger 1985; Tierney 1997). To be sure, traditional presentation styles are still being used; Nancy Lesko's (1986) and Ken Kempner's (1990) presentations of their interview findings, for example, feature the common omniscient researcher behind their texts. Other researchers, however, have moved in the direction of "full disclosure," so to speak. For example, in the presentation style employed by Adel Assal and Edwin Farrell (1992) and Jacqueline Wade (1984), the interviewer's questions and the respondent's answers are made available to the reader verbatim. Some researchers take a highly narrative approach. Use of the first person, as in Deyhle's (1986) insertion of the first-person singular in her work ("The students asked if I was a new teacher"; p. 111) and Tierney's (1991) first-person voice ("It is early in the fall semester and I am interviewing faculty"; p. 19), is now in evidence in publications. Tense, too, varies in the presentation of results, with many researchers now using a very vivid present tense. Authors such as Anna Neumann (1992) develop their texts in this way, as if the story were unfolding in front of the eyes of the reader. Other researchers, such as Betty Tutt (1989) and Nancy Smith-Hefner (1993), continue to apply the more distant past tense.

Although we fully expect to continue to see texts that offer interview data in both the vivid present and the past tense, as well as from standpoints of the first person, third person, and omniscient narrator, we also suspect that future educational interview products will have an expanding narrative horizon. Instead of two or three narrative voices, we anticipate that experimentation, especially in postmodern ethnography or performance-based texts, will bring a multitude of narrative voices to the page (Bensimon et al. 1997; Lather & Smithies 1997; Sanders 1999; Slattery 1999; Tanaka 1997; Tanaka and Cruz 1998). As fictional literature has multiple narrative venues, so too will educational interviews (see Rosenblatt, Chapter 43, this volume). And as postmodern narratives themselves develop, creative interviewers will find additional ways to (re)present interview material (see Fontana, Chapter 8, this volume).

Of course, film has been utilized to document ethnographic projects and cultural sites for decades, especially in anthropology, but advances in electronic data collection and their presentational capabilities will allow for incredible connections among data, analysis, and representation. We envision ethnographic projects with interactive capabilities, such as hypertext links connecting filmed and/or audio data files, interview material, the researcher's field notes, the researcher's analyses, and relevant literature from other authors. The physical tools interviewers use will also reflect technical changes. Personal tape recorders already are approaching the size of an ink pen; transcription programs will ease the burden of preparing data; and compact discs will store large quantities of data that earlier required much more physical storage space.

All of this is possible within the limits of current state-of-the-art technology; we can only imagine what technological advancements will bring as the 21st century marches on. The epistemological base that grounds educational research is also undoubtedly going to continue to change, and this too will add to the presentational brew. The associated new methodologies will hasten the demise of standardized research methods, and the explosion of experimental, performance-based, nonlinear textual strategies suggests an unsettled future.

A generation ago, one would not have had to take the time to define the educational interview, its respondents, and its forms of presentation. Today, defining these terms is itself contentious, and their categorization is being expansively reformulated (see the contributions to Part VI of this volume). Changes are taking place neither incrementally nor in a linear chain, as if one piece of information leads logically to the next. Instead, the breakdown of a cohesive worldview is leading to multiple perspectives and experiments that attack once virtually sacred, standardized notions of what counts for knowledge, how one studies it, and how one presents it.

◆ Key Challenges for the Future

Attempts to predict the future often go awry. For example, 30 years ago, no one would have predicted that something called the Internet or the World Wide Web would be utilized not merely as a data gathering tool but as a way to think about the nature of data. New groups have also entered into educational research as the definition of the respondent has broadened. Thus we offer the following not as a checklist of issues that await resolution, but rather as challenges that educational interviewers are likely to encounter in the near future.

THE CHANGING CONTEXT OF LEARNING

For the past century the social context for learning has been remarkably static: A teacher works in a classroom with students. True, the identities of teachers and students have expanded; more minority students, for example, populate postsecondary education. And the manner in which teaching and learning takes place has been altered. For example, collegial seminars are more popular today than they were a century ago. The development of alternative learning strategies, such as video instruction, computer-assisted instruction, and Web-based instruction, has also generated a great deal of inquiry about what can be accomplished pedagogically.

However, in our view, no change in the 21st century will be as significant or as wide-ranging as distance learning. Our purpose here is neither to celebrate nor to bemoan the anticipated pedagogical developments. We do wish, however, to emphasize how distance learning will dramatically reconfigure virtually every aspect of educational interviewing. Rather than the pool of interview subjects being made up of those whose primary relationships have developed face-to-face in classroom settings, for example, interview respondents might never have seen their teachers apart from video transmission. Instead of addressing texts or activities for which all participants are physically present, interview participants will discuss activities that involve individuals who have never met one another or even heard one another's voices. Indeed, interviews themselves might not require that interviewers even sit beside respondents; instead, interviews may take place in "real time" in cyberspace. The initial steps and challenges that electronic mail presented for interviewers in the last decade of the 20th century are insignificant compared to the issues that will be raised when the technology of distance learning comes of age.

We noted earlier that the 20th century experienced an explosion of nontraditional educational interviewing. Whereas education once was thought of as taking place in a classroom, today's educational researchers might conduct their interviews in community centers, mental health institutions, adult learning centers, and prisons, among an increasingly wide array of locales. Not surprisingly, researchers in other, nontraditional educational fields are providing solid interview data that "official" educational researchers often have difficulty obtaining (Chandler 1995; Due 1995; Finnegan 1998; French 1993; Hersch 1998; Jones & Newman 1997).

The expansion of these new educational contexts will increase exponentially as distance learning grows. Corporate universities, for-profit educational organizations, and schools, colleges, and adult learning centers that are based entirely on the World Wide Web will at a minimum expand, and are likely to shift, the nature of inquiry in this area that prevailed in the 20th century. Again, we view such changes as neither good nor bad; we simply encourage researchers to consider how such innovations will restructure the educational interview.

SHIFTING INTERVIEW PERSPECTIVES AND PRACTICES

Debate related to identity politics was voluminous at the close of the 20th century (Arthur & Shapiro 1995; McCarthy & Crichlow 1993). Many have argued, for example, that people of color were excluded from earlier qualitative research in large part because white researchers overlooked minority interests (Sleeter 1993; Stowe 1996). The realization that those on the margins of society often face exclusion or misinterpretation has forced researchers to rethink the purposes of their work and how it is conducted (Dilley 1999; Hudak 1993).

Indeed, as members of minority groups themselves become researchers and interviewers rather than just respondents, the relationships among researchers, the researched, and the activities of research are changing (Brayboy & Deyhle forthcoming). As research utilizes theories informed by constructivist or relativist epistemologies, the standpoint of the researcher as irrelevant is being rejected (Lincoln & Denzin 1994; see also Briggs, Chapter 44, this volume). Postmodern, postcolonial, constructivist, and other related theories have highlighted the charged relationship a researcher/interviewer has to the research project and interviewees. One cannot help but assume that as different individuals undertake interviews, different kinds of authority, methods, and findings will be created.

Obviously, a heterosexual researcher who approaches homosexuality from the lens of deviance will conduct interviews in a manner different from that of someone who is openly gay and seeks to deconstruct normalizing dichotomies that suggest "straight equals normal, gay equals abnormal" (see Kong et al., Chapter 12, this volume). One interviewer might view the dropout problem in high school as one that resides with the children who cannot be retained; someone who identifies with those children might also examine the issue in terms of the larger social contexts in which the children live and attend (or do not attend) school.

The point here is not just that different individuals have different perspectives, but that as interviewers continue their work, we expect that the premises of what an interviewer does, how he or she constructs and conducts the interview, and the final product will change. An underlying premise throughout this chapter has been that interviews do not exist in epistemological vacuums; further to the point, interview practices are not set in methodological stone. Epistemological shifts have practical consequences. In a turbulent environment, the object of inquiry itself is sure to change.

Practice extends to everyday research life as well, and can reflect back on epistemological matters. Whereas an educator's tenure and promotion, for example, were once predicated on that person's ability to conduct research that would be publishable in refereed journals, a variety of additional questions and struggles are sure to surface in the coming years that are bound to affect how researchers conduct interviews. Funded research was never imperative for social researchers in general, or for interviewers in particular. When researchers received external funding, their epistemological positions were not often brought into question; it was assumed that a good interviewer, for example, would conduct good interviews regardless of the source of the funding for the project. Researchers who wanted to pursue nonfunded studies were able to do so under the aegis of academic freedom.

But as fiscal compression continues in universities, obtaining external funding could become compulsory rather than simply helpful. This may curb the efflorescence in interviewing techniques and representational strategies we have seen recently. If researchers need to be dependent on external funding, the nature of the interviews and the interviewers themselves will change. The kind of researcher who is adept at gaining external funds might not want to take the same kinds of methodological risks as someone who wishes to undertake interviews free from outside interference. Some issues are interesting to funding agents and others are not. Who pays for the research becomes a point of interest when one accepts that standard notions of validity and reliability are impossible to attain in a world that is socially constructed. As researchers recognize the need for external funding, what they have gained in expanding methodological horizons may start to work backward, exerting pressure on researchers to revert to earlier interviewing practices.

EMPOWERING RESPONDENTS

The final challenge concerns the outcomes of educational interviewing. These outcomes have been used in two ways in the past century: (a) Interviewers have gathered data as a way to discover topics that are rarely investigated and poorly, if at all, understood; and (b) researchers have used interviews to understand particular aspects of given theoretical puzzles, attempting to refine theories based upon interview data centered on respondents' experiences. Although we fully anticipate that such uses will continue to be of interest to researchers, some researchers will experience fundamental shifts in how they employ interview techniques and use the results. One direction researchers might take will be to offer policy resolutions based on interview data rather than to generate new questions or discover unknown information. We make this suggestion with an eye toward the need and demand for investigations to be more relevant to policy issues, for research to examine specific issues that policy makers and funding agencies find important. We expect that qualitative research, and interviewing in particular, will take a primary role in making educational policy relevant and responsible to constituents.

Another likely shift will be toward a more active respondent. We expect that researchers with critical predilections will try to create a closer relationship between the interview process and research findings, and will attempt to foster interview respondents' abilities to alter their personal or educational situations if they wish to do so. Rather than assuming that only experts, policy analysts, and researchers are capable of implementing changes based on interview material, those with the power to enact and enforce educational reform will increasingly rely upon interview narrators as change agents. Those who were previously objects of study will be increasingly empowered and become actively involved in reforming education.

◆ Conclusion

If in this chapter we have described critically the traditional purposes of educational interviews, the category of the respondent, and how interviews are organized, we have also attempted to look forward to anticipate new trends and future possibilities. In many respects, anyone now looking ahead to conducting educational research must be ready to disavow past notions of acceptable interview practice. The world is too fluid, technological changes are too rapid, and theoretical advances are too voluminous for researchers to settle on traditional methodological bromides.

One might approach such changes with regret for the loss of how interviews once were done or with trepidation over uncertainty about how to conduct and present future interviews. We encourage researchers to view the changes we have outlined with neither discouragement nor pessimism, but with a renewed sense of excitement and enthusiasm for the challenges yet to come. Educational interviews are undergoing a dramatic transformation today; virtually every aspect of the interview process is now under reformulation. Such rapidly changing times afford researchers unique opportunities for experimentation and risk taking, even while there are forces in place that might work against them. From experiments such as these, great advances often occur, changing the ways individuals think about particular practices, theories, and designs. Rather than relying upon or superficially reforming past practices that have perhaps become more routine than insightful, interviewers are now facing the challenge of inventing new styles and methods for the new century.

■ References

Apple, M. W. 1990. *Ideology and Curriculum.* 2d ed. New York: Routledge.
———. 1995. *Education and Power.* 2d ed. New York: Routledge.

Arthur, J. and A. Shapiro, eds. 1995. *Campus Wars: Multiculturalism and the Politics of Difference.* Boulder, CO: Westview.

Assal, A. and E. Farrell. 1992. "Attempts to Make Meaning of Terror: Family, Play and School in Time of Civil War." *Anthropology and Education Quarterly* 23:275-90.

Bensimon, E. M. and A. Neumann. 1993. *Redesigning Collegiate Leadership: Teams and Teamwork in Higher Education.* Baltimore: Johns Hopkins University Press.

Bensimon, E. M., M. Soto, M. C. Brown II, M. Clarke-Yapi, and B. Palmer. 1997. "Blacks and Jews: The (Dis)Uniting of a 'Model' Campus." Presented at the conference "Reclaiming Voice: Ethnographic Inquiry and Qualitative Research in a Postmodern Age," June 21, Los Angeles.

Brayboy, B. M. and D. Deyhle. Forthcoming. "Insider to Outsider and Outsider to Insider: The Role and Dilemmas of Researchers in American Indian Communities." *Theory into Practice.*

Bruner, J. 1987. "Life as Narrative." *Social Research* 54:11-32.

Cazden, C., V. John, and D. Hymes, eds. 1972. *Functions of Language in the Classroom.* New York: Teachers College Press.

Chandler, K. 1995. *Passages of Pride: Lesbian and Gay Youth Come of Age.* New York: Random House.

Cohler, B. 1998. "The Human Studies and Life History." *Social Science Review* 62:552-75.

Coyne, K. 1995. *Domers: A Year at Notre Dame.* New York: Viking Penguin.

Crew, L., ed. 1978. *The Gay Academic.* Palm Springs, CA: ETC.

Deyhle, D. 1986. "Break Dancing and Breaking Out: Anglos, Utes and Navajos in a Border Reservation High School." *Anthropology and Education Quarterly* 17:111-27.

Dilley, P. 1999. "Queer Theory: Under Construction." *International Journal of Qualitative Studies in Education* 12:457-72.

———. 2000. "A Qualitative, Typological History of Non-heterosexual Men in College in the U.S., 1945 to the Present." Ph.D. dissertation, University of Southern California.

Donmoyer, R. and R. Kos. 1993. *At-Risk Students: Portraits, Policies, Programs, and Practices.* Albany: State University of New York Press.

Due, L. 1995. *Joining the Tribe: Growing Up Gay and Lesbian in the '90s.* Garden City, NY: Anchor.

Fine, M. 1991. *Framing Dropouts: Notes on the Politics of an Urban Public High School.* Albany: State University of New York Press.

Finnegan, W. 1998. *Cold New World: Growing Up in a Harder Country.* New York: Random House.

Frank, G. 1980. "Life Histories in Gerontology: The Subjective Side to Aging." In *New Methods from Old Age Research: Anthropological Alternatives,* edited by C. L. Fry and J. Keith. Chicago: Loyola of Chicago University Press.

Freeman, K. 1999. "HBCs or PWIs? African American High School Students' Consideration of Higher Education Institution Types." *Review of Higher Education* 23:91-106.

Freeman, M. 1992. "Self as Narrative: The Place of Life History in Studying the Life Span." Pp. 15-43 in *The Self: Definitional and Methodological Issues,* edited by T. M. Brinthaupt and R. P. Lipka. Albany: State University of New York Press.

Freire, P. 1997. *Pedagogy of the Oppressed.* Rev. 20th anniversary ed. New York: Continuum.

French, T. 1993. *South of Heaven: Welcome to High School at the End of the Twentieth Century.* Garden City, NY: Doubleday.

Glesne, C. and A. Peshkin. 1992. *Becoming Qualitative Researchers: An Introduction.* White Plains, NY: Longman.

Goldman-Segall, R., J. Willinsky, and L. Halff. 1997. "On-Line Collaborative Research: Web Constellations Meets a Book Called *Points of Viewing Children's Thinking.*" Presented at EdMedia '97, the International Conference for Educational Multimedia, June, Calgary, Alberta. Available Internet: http://www.merlin.ubc.ca/publications/olcr/index.html

Goodlad, J. I., R. Soder, and K. A. Sirotnik, eds. 1990. *Places Where Teachers Are Taught.* San Francisco: Jossey-Bass.

Graham, S. 1992. " 'Most of the Subjects Were White and Middle Class': Trends in Published Research on African Americans in Selected APA Journals, 1970-1989." *American Psychologist* 47:629-39.

Guba, E. G. and Y. S. Lincoln. 1994. "Competing Paradigms in Qualitative Research." Pp. 105-17 in *Handbook of Qualitative Research,* edited by N. K. Denzin and Y. S. Lincoln. Thousand Oaks, CA: Sage.

Guido-DiBrito, F. 1995. "Student Affairs Leadership and Loyalty: Organizational Dynamics at Play." *NASPA Journal* 32:223-31.

Heath, S. B. 1983. *Ways with Words: Language, Life, and Work in Communities and Classrooms.* New York: Cambridge University Press.

Heath, S. B. and M. W. McLaughlin, eds. 1993. *Identity and Inner City Youth: Beyond Ethnicity and Gender.* New York: Teachers College Press.

Hedges, A. J. 1995. "Computer-Mediated Communication and College Student Development: A Discussion of the Internet's Potential Impact Using Lesbian, Gay, and Bisexual Students as Examples." Seminar paper, University of Maryland, College Park. Available Internet: http://www.efficacy.net/cmcandcsd.html

Herrington, A. J. and M. Curtis. 1990. "Basic Writing: Moving the Voices on the Margin to the Center." *Harvard Educational Review* 60:489-96.

Hersch, P. 1998. *A Tribe Apart: A Journey into the Heart of American Adolescence.* New York: Fawcett Columbine.

Holland, D. C. and M. A. Eisenhart. 1990. *Educated in Romance: Women, Achievement, and College Culture.* Chicago: University of Chicago Press.

Hudak, G. M. 1993. "Technologies of Marginality: Strategies of Stardom and Displacement in Adolescent Life." Pp. 172-87 in *Race, Identity, and Representation in Education,* edited by C. McCarthy and W. Crichlow. New York: Routledge.

Johnson, M. J. and F. Pajares. 1996. "When Shared Decision Making Works: A 3-Year Longitudinal Study." *American Educational Research Journal* 33:599-627.

Johnsrud, L. K. and K. C. Sado. 1998. "The Common Experience of 'Otherness': Ethnic and Racial Minority Faculty." *Review of Higher Education* 21:315-42.

Jones, L. and L. Newman, with D. Isay. 1997. *Our America: Life and Death on the South Side of Chicago.* New York: Scribner.

Jun, A. 2000. "Tracking the Odds: A Qualitative Examination of Access, Mobility, and Resilience for Historically Under-represented Minorities in Education." Ph.D. dissertation, University of Southern California.

Kempner, K. 1990. "Faculty Culture in the Community College: Facilitating or Hindering Learning?" *Review of Higher Education* 13:215-35.

Kidder, T. 1989. *Among Schoolchildren.* Boston: Houghton Mifflin.

Kozol, J. 1991. *Savage Inequalities: Children in America's Schools.* New York: Crown.

Krieger, S. 1985. "Beyond 'Subjectivity': The Use of the Self in Social Science." *Qualitative Sociology* 8:309-24.

Krop, C., D. Brewer, S. Gates, B. Gill, R. Reichardt, M. Sundt, and D. Throgmorton. 1998. "Potentially Eligible Students: A Growing Opportunity for the University of California." RAND Corporation, Santa Monica, CA. Unpublished manuscript.

Langness, L. L. and G. Frank. 1981. *Lives: An Anthropological Approach to Biography.* Novato, CA: Chandler & Sharp.

Lather, P. 1986. "Research as Praxis." *Harvard Educational Review* 5:257-77.

Lather, P. and C. Smithies. 1997. *Troubling the Angels: Women Living with HIV/AIDS.* Boulder, CO: Westview.

Lesko, N. 1986. "Individualism and Community: Ritual Discourse in a Parochial High School." *Anthropology and Education Quarterly* 17:25-39.

Lightfoot, S. L. 1978. *Worlds Apart: Relationships between Families and Schools.* New York: Basic Books.

Lincoln, Y. S. and N. K. Denzin. 1994. "The Fifth Moment." Pp. 575-86 in *Handbook of Qualitative Research,* edited by N. K. Denzin & Y. S. Lincoln. Thousand Oaks, CA: Sage.

Livingston, M. and M. Stewart. 1987. "Minority Students on a White Campus: Perception Is Truth." *NASPA Journal* 34:39-49.

Loeb, P. R. 1994. *Generation at the Crossroads: Apathy and Action on the American Campus.* New Brunswick, NJ: Rutgers University Press.

MacLeod, J. 1987. *Ain't No Makin' It: Leveled Aspirations in a Low-income Neighborhood.* Boulder, CO: Westview.

Maeroff, G. I. 1998. *Altered Destinies: Making Life Better for Schoolchildren in Need*. New York: St. Martin's.

McCarthy, C. and W. Crichlow, eds. 1993. *Race, Identity, and Representation in Education*. New York: Routledge.

McLaren, P. 1999. *Schooling as Ritual Performance: Toward a Political Economy of Educational Symbols and Gestures*. 3d ed. Lanham, MD: Rowman & Littlefield.

McLaughlin, D. 1992. *When Literacy Empowers: Navajo Language in Print*. Albuquerque: University of New Mexico Press.

———. 1993. "Personal Narratives for School Change in Navajo Settings." Pp. 95-118 in *Naming Silenced Lives: Personal Narratives and the Process of Educational Change*, edited by D. McLaughlin and W. G. Tierney. New York: Routledge.

McNaron, T. A. H. 1997. *Poisoned Ivy: Lesbian and Gay Academics Confronting Homophobia*. Philadelphia: Temple University Press.

Mead, M. 1951. *The School in American Culture*. Cambridge, MA: Harvard University Press.

Mehan, H., I. Villanueva, L. Hubbard, and A. Lintz. 1996. *Constructing School Success: The Consequences of Untracking Low-Achieving Students*. New York: Cambridge University Press.

Merriam, S. B. 1998. *Qualitative Research and Case Study Applications in Education*. San Francisco: Jossey-Bass.

Moffatt, M. 1989. *Coming of Age in New Jersey: College and American Culture*. New Brunswick, NJ: Rutgers University Press.

Morawski, J. G. 1997. "White Experimenters, White Blood, and Other White Conditions: Locating the Psychologist's Race." Pp. 13-28 in *Off White: Readings on Race, Power, and Society*, edited by M. Fine, L. C. Powell, L. Weis, and L. M. Wong. New York: Routledge.

Morgan, D. L. 1998. *Planning Focus Groups*. Thousand Oaks, CA: Sage.

Neumann, A. 1992. "Double Vision: The Experience of Institutional Stability." *Review of Higher Education* 15:417-27.

Orenstein, P. 1994. *Schoolgirls: Young Women, Self-Esteem, and the Confidence Gap*. Garden City, NY: Doubleday.

Polkinghorne, D. E. 1995. "Narrative Knowing and the Study of Lives." Pp. 77-99 in *Aging and Biography: Explorations in Adult Development*, edited by J. E. Birren, G. M. Kenyon, J. E. Ruth, J. J. F. Schroots, and T. Svensson. New York: Springer.

Powell, L. C. 1997. "The Achievement (K)not: Whiteness and Black Underachievement." Pp. 3-12 in *Off White: Readings on Race, Power, and Society*, edited by M. Fine, L. C. Powell, L. Weis, and L. M. Wong. New York: Routledge.

Rhoads, R. A. 1994. *Coming Out in College: The Struggle for a Queer Identity*. Westport, CT: Bergin & Garvey.

———. 1998. *Freedom's Web: Student Activism in an Age of Cultural Diversity*. Baltimore: Johns Hopkins University Press.

Richardson, R., K. Bracco, P. Callan, and J. Finney. 1998. *Higher Education Governance: Balancing Institutional and Market Influences*. Washington, DC: National Center for Public Policy and Higher Education.

Ruhlman, M. 1996. *Boys Themselves: A Return to Single-Sex Education*. New York: Henry Holt.

Sanders, J. H., III. 1999. "Dissertation as Performance [Art Script] (Take Three)." *International Journal of Qualitative Studies in Education* 12:541-62.

Schneider, B. and D. Stevenson. 1999. *The Ambitious Generation: America's Teenagers—Motivated but Directionless*. New Haven, CT: Yale University Press.

Scriven, M. 1972. "Objectivity and Subjectivity in Educational Research." In *Philosophical Redirection of Educational Research: The Seventy-first Yearbook of the National Society for the Study of Education*, edited by L. G. Thomas. Chicago: University of Chicago Press.

Sidel, R. 1994. *Battling Bias: The Struggle for Identity and Community on College Campuses*. New York: Viking Penguin.

Slattery, P. 1999. "10,000 Ejaculations: Learning from/with(in) the Body." Presented at the conference "Reclaiming Voice II: Ethnographic Inquiry and Qualitative Research in a Postmodern Age," June 4, Irvine, CA.

Sleeter, C. E. 1993. "How White Teachers Construct Race." Pp. 157-71 in *Race, Identity, and Representation in Education,* edited by C. McCarthy and W. Crichlow. New York: Routledge.

Smith, D. E. 1999. *Writing the Social.* Toronto: University of Toronto Press.

Smith-Hefner, N. J. 1993. "Education, Gender, and Generational Conflict among Khmer Refugees." *Anthropology and Education Quarterly* 24:135-58.

Spillane, J. P. 1998. "State Policy and the Non-monolithic Nature of the Local School District: Organizational and Professional Considerations." *American Educational Research Journal* 35:33-63.

Spindler, G., ed. 1982. *Doing the Ethnography of Schooling: Educational Anthropology in Action.* New York: Holt, Rinehart & Winston.

Stewart, A. J., C. Franz, and L. Layton. 1988. "The Changing Self: Using Personal Documents to Study Lives." In "Psychobiography and Life Narratives" (special issue), edited by D. P. McAdams and R. L. Ochberg. *Journal of Personality* 56(1).

Stowe, D. W. 1996. "Uncolored People: The Rise of Whiteness Studies." *Lingua Franca* 7:68-77.

Szepkouski, G. M. 1993. " 'I'm Me Own Boss!' " Pp. 177-97 in *Naming Silenced Lives: Personal Narratives and the Process of Educational Change,* edited by D. McLaughlin and W. G. Tierney. New York: Routledge.

Tanaka, G. 1997. "Pico College." Pp. 259-304 in *Representation and the Text: Re-framing the Narrative Voice,* edited by W. G. Tierney and Y. S. Lincoln. Albany: State University of New York Press.

Tanaka, G. and C. Cruz. 1998. "The Locker Room: Eroticism and Exoticism in a Polyphonic Text." *International Journal of Qualitative Studies in Education* 11:137-53.

Throgmorton, D. W. 1999. "Perceptions and Persistence: The Experiences of First-Year African American and Chicano/Latino Students at the University of California, Irvine." Ph.D. dissertation, University of Southern California.

Tierney, W. G. 1988. *The Web of Leadership: The Presidency in Higher Education.* Greenwich, CT: JAI.

———. 1991. "Utilizing Ethnographic Interviews to Enhance Academic Decision-Making." *New Directions for Institutional Research: Using Qualitative Methods in Institutional Research* 7:7-22.

———. 1992. *Official Encouragement, Institutional Discouragement: Minorities in Academe—The Native American Experience.* Norwood, NJ: Ablex.

———. 1993. "Self and Identity in a Postmodern World: A Life Story." Pp. 119-34 in *Naming Silenced Lives: Personal Narratives and the Process of Educational Change,* edited by D. McLaughlin and W. G. Tierney. New York: Routledge.

———. 1997. "Organizational Socialization in Higher Education." *Journal of Higher Education* 68:1-16.

Tierney, W. G. and E. M. Bensimon. 1996. *Promotion and Tenure: Community and Socialization in Academe.* Albany: State University of New York Press.

Tierney, W. G. and P. Dilley. 1998. "Constructing Knowledge: Educational Research and Gay and Lesbian Studies." Pp. 49-71 in *Queer Theory in Education,* edited by W. F. Pinar. Mahwah, NJ: Lawrence Erlbaum.

Traub, J. 1994. *City on a Hill: Testing the American Dream at City College.* Reading, MA: Addison-Wesley.

Turnbull, A. P., J. M. Patterson, S. K. Behr, D. L. Murphy, J. G. Marquis, and M. J. Blue-Banning. 1993. *Cognitive Coping, Families, and Disability.* Baltimore: Paul H. Brookes.

Tutt, B. R. 1989. "Report of a Pilot Study in Girlfriending: An Ethnographic Investigation of a Women's Poker Group." *Anthropology and Education Quarterly* 20:23-35.

Twombly, S. B. 1992. "The Process of Choosing a Dean." *Journal of Higher Education* 63:653-83.

Varenne, H. and R. McDermott. 1998. *Successful Failure: The School America Builds.* Boulder, CO: Westview.

Vidich, A. J. and S. M. Lyman. 1994. "Qualitative Methods: Their History in Sociology and Anthropology." Pp. 23-59 in *Handbook of Qualitative Research,* edited by N. K. Denzin and Y. S. Lincoln. Thousand Oaks, CA: Sage.

Wade, J. E. 1984. "Role Boundaries and Paying Back: Switching Hats in Participant Observation." *Anthropology and Education Quarterly* 15:211-24.

Wolcott, H. F. 1970. "An Ethnographic Approach to the Study of School Administrators." *Human Organization* 29:115-22.

———. 1973. *The Man in the Principal's Office: An Ethnography.* New York: Holt, Rinehart & Winston.

———. 1983. "Adequate Schools and Inadequate Education: The Life History of a Sneaky Kid." *Anthropology and Education Quarterly* 14:3-32.

———. 1990. "On Seeking—and Rejecting—Validity in Qualitative Research." Pp. 121-52 in *Qualitative Inquiry in Education: The Continuing Debate,* edited by E. W. Eisner and A. Peshkin. New York: Teachers College Press.

———. 1997. "Validating Reba: A Commentary on 'Teaching about Validity.' " *International Journal of Qualitative Studies in Education* 10:157-59.

Wong, M. P. A. and W. G. Tierney. Forthcoming. "Reforming Faculty Work: Culture, Structure, and the Dilemma of Organizational Change." *Teachers College Record.*

23

CONTEXT AND THE EMPLOYMENT INTERVIEW

◆ Gary P. Latham
Zeeva Millman

The employment interview takes place in the interaction between one or more interviewers and interviewees, the purpose of which is to determine (a) the applicant's fit with an organization's culture or values and (b) the applicant's knowledge, skills, and ability to advance the organization's strategy. Empirical research on this form of interviewing has a long history in industrial and organizational psychology. Ralph Wagner (1949) provided one of the first literature reviews of research in this area. Among other things, he found that the reliability and validity of the interview was low and concluded that the interview must be structured if interview decisions are to be reliable and valid.

Some 15 years after Wagner's study, little progress had been made in improving the interview as a selection instrument. Eu-

gene Mayfield's (1964) review of the literature showed that the job interview continued to have low reliability and validity. Mayfield suggested that, in addition to structure, attention needed to be paid to the decision-making process. A year later, a second review of this literature reiterated the low reliability and validity of the employment interview; Lynn Ulrich and Don Trumbo (1965) stressed the need to examine the information gathered in the interview as a way of understanding why interview decisions lacked reliability. Further, following Wagner (1949), Ulrich and Trumbo concluded that the interview must be structured in order to improve its reliability and validity. These literature reviews led to a series of studies by Edward Webster (1964) and his doctoral students on decision-making biases, such as first-impressions errors and stereotyping, that attenuate the effectiveness of the employment interview as a psychometrically sound selection instrument.

Almost 20 years afterward, Richard Arvey and James Campion (1982) again reviewed the employment interview literature and reached several conclusions. They found that the subject of bias in the interview had received increased attention. They found that research on the interview continued to be microanalytic in nature, yet overlooked related research on person perception. A significant recommendation was that research should focus on behavioral processes if the interview was ever to become a useful selection tool.

In the 1980s, significant advances were made in increasing the reliability and validity of the employment interview. Several interview techniques were developed, including the situational interview, or SI (Latham et al. 1980); the patterned behavior description interview, or PBDI (Janz 1982); Jerry Hedge and Mark Teachout's (1992) walk-through interview; and Michael Campion, Elliott Pursell, and B. K. Brown's (1988) comprehensive selection battery, of which the SI was a major component. Consistent with Wagner's recommendation, these interview procedures are structured. That is, all candidates or applicants are asked the same questions, which, in turn, are derived from a job analysis. Other ways of structuring employment interviews include using behavioral rating scales in the scoring of answers and ensuring consistency in administration. The advantages of structured over unstructured interviews are that they are more likely to replicate and are easier to meta-analyze to determine their transportability to different jobs and work settings. Moreover, structuring minimizes the role of interviewer experience and skill by shifting the emphasis to how well the interview content is constructed (Dipboye and Jackson 1999; Hough and Oswald 2000; Pulakos et al. 1996).

The two primary types of questions used in structured interviews are situational questions and patterned behavior descrip-

tion questions (Harris 1999). Consistent with earlier suggestions (Mayfield 1964; Ulrich and Trumbo 1965), the SI and the PBDI specify the types of questions that are to be asked of applicants in order to minimize interviewer biases. Both techniques focus on behavior, as recommended by Arvey and Campion (1982). The SI is based on the theory that intentions predict behavior (Latham et al. 1980). A job analysis is performed to identify the behaviors that are relevant to a person's effectively completing the job. Critical incidents gathered in the job analysis are used to develop situational questions that contain dilemmas. Applicants are asked to state what they would do in each job-related dilemma. It is the dilemma within each situation that "forces" interviewees to state their true intentions rather than offer socially desirable responses (Latham and Sue-Chan 1999). Responses are evaluated using a behavioral scoring guide. The scoring guide minimizes interviewer biases and increases interobserver reliability.

The PBDI is based on the premise that past behavior predicts future behavior (Janz 1982). Questions are developed from the same job analysis used by advocates of the situational interview, namely, the critical incident technique (Flanagan 1954). Interviewees are asked to recall a time when they demonstrated behavior that exemplifies a core competency identified through the job analysis. Next, they are asked to describe exactly what they did in that situation, as well as the resulting outcome.

All in all, meta-analyses have shown that structured interviews have greater reliability and validity than unstructured interviews (Harris 1989; Huffcutt and Arthur 1994; McDaniel et al. 1994; Wiesner and Cronshaw 1988). Moreover, a recent meta-analysis found the SI to be a useful employment interview technique across jobs, participants, performance criteria, and countries (Latham and Sue-Chan 1999).

At the end of the 20th century, fully 50 years after the start of critical reflection on research in the area, Richard Posthuma, Frederick Morgeson, and Michael Campion (1999) once more reviewed the employment interview literature and found that, although the interactive dynamics of this form of interviewing had received extensive attention, there had been little work done on the effects of contextual factors on the validity of the employment interview. They pointed to the need to examine the effects of factors such as an organization's geographic location and labor market conditions on interview content, the decision-making process, and subsequent reliability and validity. Contextual factors may act as moderator variables that enhance or attenuate reliability and validity.

Our purpose in this chapter is to discuss these contextual factors as moderator variables; we aim to add to the knowledge about, or provide specific directions for researching, how these "auspices" of interviewing shape the interview process. We begin with a discussion of external organizational factors, move to an examination of the internal context of organizational interviews and job-related decision making, and conclude with some observations about general directions for future research.

◆ External Organizational Factors

External organizational factors that can influence the employment interview include national culture, legal requirements, labor market conditions, and industry sector. We discuss each of these external factors below, as evidence suggests they can influence the interview process and its outcomes.

NATIONAL CULTURE

Cultural variables are likely moderators of the validity of employment interviews (Hough and Oswald 2000). A nation's cul-

ture influences the values, assumptions, and beliefs of the people within it and, consequently, the behavior of employment candidates (see Ryen, Chapter 17, this volume). For example, Yoshihisa Kashima and Harry Triandis (1986) found that, relative to American students, Japanese students attribute more failure and less success to themselves. Relatedly, P. S. Fry and Ratha Ghosh's (1980) research suggests that Indian children attribute much of their success to luck, whereas in comparison Anglo-Saxon children attribute their success to their own ability and effort. These findings indicate that members of different ethnic groups respond differently to employment interview questions. Research is needed to determine whether interview questions that are valid in one culture are also valid in another, and whether cultural sensitivity training will enhance the quality of the information gathered by interviewers and hence increase the validity of the employment interview within or across cultures.

Because of cultural differences, it might be hypothesized, for example, that Indians downplay their accomplishments and emphasize their responsibility for failures. Japanese might take less credit for their accomplishments in a PBDI than North American applicants. This would result in different validity coefficients being calculated from the same interview questions, reflecting primarily differences in culture rather than differences in applicants' ability to perform well in an organization. Interview content that is shown to be a valid predictor of performance in North America may not generalize to other cultures, where different predictor and criterion constructs are relevant.

LEGAL REQUIREMENTS

Cultural values are reflected in a nation's laws. Countries such as Canada and the United States are democracies where emphasis is placed on equality. To ensure equal opportunity in the hiring process, employment laws in both countries determine the questions that prospective employers are and are not allowed to ask of candidates. The Civil Rights Act in the United States and the Charter of Rights and Freedoms in Canada prohibit employers from asking potential employees questions regarding race, color, religion, sex, marital status, national origin, and physical or mental disability. The questions asked in an employment interview must focus solely on bona fide job requirements. Not surprisingly, unstructured employment interviews account for the majority of federal court cases in the United States involving disputes regarding employers' selection decisions (Hough and Oswald 2000).

Interview questions in both Canada and the United States should be based on information identified in a job or work analysis as critical for a person's performing the job well. Work analysis takes into account the ever-changing nature of work and thus focuses on tasks and the cross-functional skills of employees, as opposed to a traditional job analysis, where the assumption is often made that tasks are static (Cronshaw 1998; Hough and Oswald 2000).

In short, legal requirements largely prescribe the areas of questioning that an interview may tap and, consequently, the nature of the information that is obtained. Research is needed to determine the extent to which such laws enhance or attenuate interview validity. Two ideal locations to conduct this kind of research would be Germany and Austria, because the geographic and cultural proximity of these two countries has led to their having all-but-identical legal frameworks for the recruitment and hiring of employees. As in North America, employment law in Austria and Germany prohibits employers from making decisions on the basis of sex or race. However, the laws are strictly enforced in Germany, whereas in Austria organizations may hire and promote people with minimum legal interference.

LABOR MARKET CONDITIONS

Changing labor market conditions affect the size of the applicant pool, which in turn can influence an employment interviewer's judgment (Webster 1982). In the late 1980s there was a tremendous economic boom in North America. As a result, organizations were confronted by a shortage of labor talent. As organizations experienced growth, they hired many employees; consequently, the applicant pool shrank. Under such circumstances, the scarcity of qualified employees influences the behavior of interviewers, who tend to "sell the company" to applicants (Arvey and Campion 1982). When there is a perceived lack of talent available, organizational decision makers frequently reduce hiring criteria (Thurow 1975), omit drug screening (Bennett, Blum, and Roman 1994), and resort to intensive recruitment techniques (Hanssens and Levien 1983). Thus candidates who are interviewed when few applicants exist often receive inflated ratings.

In the early 1990s, in contrast, North America experienced a widespread economic recession. Thousands of employees lost their jobs, resulting in an abundance of job applicants. When such an abundance exists, interviewer ratings may reflect negative leniency (Eder and Buckley 1988). Thus it would appear that labor market conditions are a moderator of interview validity. Research is needed to identify appropriate employment interview training for interviewers who are working in tight versus abundant labor markets. When every applicant is given the same rating (high or low), employment interviews, no matter how well structured, will be all but useless for identifying individuals who are truly qualified for the jobs in question.

An issue that cuts across cultural values, legal requirements, and labor market conditions is diversity. With the exception of research on the situational interview, little attention has been given to the relationship between the employment interview and diversity of the labor force. Companies such as J. P. Morgan, for example, are currently at the forefront of active efforts to encourage homosexuals to apply for jobs. The resistance of the SI to interviewer bias has been investigated in regard to race, age, and ethnicity (Latham and Skarlicki, 1996; Lin, Dobbins, and Farh 1992), but researchers have yet to examine ways to overcome interviewer bias regarding applicants' sexual orientation.

INDUSTRY SECTOR

Whether an organization is in the service sector or the manufacturing sector seems to affect the relative importance that organizational decision makers place on the use of valid selection practices. David Terpstra and Elizabeth Rozell (1993) found that a stronger relationship exists between the use of effective staffing practices and organizational performance in the labor-intensive service sector than in less labor-intensive industries. The employment interview for a service sector position focuses on questions designed to gather information on a variety of interpersonal as well as technical skills. Here the question that needs to be addressed is, Does industry sector systematically influence the validity coefficients of the employment interview?

◆ Internal Organizational Factors

Internal organizational variables that may moderate the reliability and validity of the interview can be divided into macro and micro conditions. Internal macrovariables include the organization's culture, strategy, size, structure, internal labor market, technology, and union presence. Internal microvariables include the character of the job, the interview medium, interviewee perceptions of the recruiter, interviewer training, and characteristics of the interviewer and interviewee.

ORGANIZATIONAL CULTURE

Organizational culture is an internal macrovariable that involves the shared values, beliefs, and assumptions that guide organizational conduct (Ott 1989). An organization's culture influences the organization's definition of core technical and interpersonal competencies (Brockbank 1997). Organizational leaders naturally want to hire people who fit both the organization's culture and the job in question. If the cultures of two organizations differ, the knowledge, skills, and abilities of those holding identical positions in the two organizations are also likely to differ. Culture influences the interview questions that are organizationally relevant. Cultural differences influence the knowledge, skills, and abilities that are identified in a job analysis and, consequently, the subsequent job behaviors that are critical for a person's performing well in a given organizational environment.

For example, a sales representative in an organization with a short-term marketing perspective is required to generate sales quickly. The person is evaluated on a monthly or quarterly basis, with a focus on the volume of sales generated. A sales representative in an organization with a long-term focus is required to cultivate customer relationships in order to generate repeat business. Evaluation of that employee may occur only once or twice a year, with emphasis on the number of clients and relationships he or she has developed. Both employees are sales representatives whose jobs emphasize selling, but because their two organizations' cultures differ, so do their jobs. Thus organizational culture should be taken into account in the interview questions asked of applicants to evaluate their likelihood of success in a particular organizational environment. Research is needed to determine whether the employment interview can predict organizational fit in this regard, as well as to examine people's ability to shift from one role to another (Latham and Sue-Chan 1998).

ORGANIZATIONAL STRATEGY

Organizational strategy is the way in which an organization positions itself in relation to its stakeholders given its resources, capabilities, and missions (McShane 1998:481). Organizations can generally be categorized as using one of four organizational strategies: reactor, defender, analyzer, and prospector (Miles and Snow 1978). Reactor and defender organizations tend to be fairly passive toward changes in the environment. Analyzer organizations scan the environment for changes and then try actively to benefit from these changes. Prospector organizations exploit opportunities in attempts to create their own environments. Because prospector organizations are usually growing in size, they are especially concerned with recruitment (Olian and Rynes 1984); they willingly hire people with little experience and then train them (Peck 1994).

The hiring criteria and the job-relevant questions that predict who will do well on those criteria are likely to differ based on organizational strategy. Research is needed to determine whether the interview is more valid when one type of strategy is dominant over another in the organization. Research is also needed to explore whether the interview is more effective in predicting performance on training criteria, which in turn are used to predict performance on the job, as opposed to predicting performance on the job without taking into account any training that is provided. For example, in organizations that are characterized by innovation, there is considerable work uncertainty (Quinn 1978). The ability to deal with uncertainty and ambiguity is a critical job requirement in such organizations, and interviewers in these organizations should include questions centering on uncertainty and ambiguity in their employment interviews. Will responses to these questions subsequently predict performance? Will they do so as effectively as responses to interview questions that predict performance in relatively stable work environments? Currently, we know little about how to enhance workforce flexibility (Johns 1998). How well, therefore, can we predict it?

Business strategies affect organizations' selection of chief executive officers. Deepak Datta and James Guthrie (1994) found that where firm growth is the goal and profits are low, CEOs are selected from the external environment. Where the focus is on research and development, CEOs with technical/functional backgrounds and high levels of education are selected. Is interview validity for predicting CEO success equally high in these different contexts? Here, again, there is room for research.

ORGANIZATIONAL SIZE

Another variable that may moderate the effectiveness of the employment interview is the size of the organization. Human resources management practices vary with organizational size. For example, large organizations often employ several people in the same capacity, and recruiting can thus be done in groups. When this is the case, organizational decision makers may perceive as worthwhile the cost and time required to develop a valid employment interview. Large organizations also rely less on temporary staff (Davis-Blake and Uzzi 1993), hence they want valid staffing techniques for hiring relatively permanent employees (Terpstra and Rozell 1993). However, even in large organizations there is a growing trend toward outsourcing and the hiring of temporary staff at professional levels as well as for lower-level jobs. Is the interview as valid a selection tool for predicting the performance of these people as it is for predicting the performance of those who work in full-time positions? The SI, for example, predicts the organizational citizenship behavior of full-time employees (Latham and Skarlicki 1995), but can it do so for part-time workers? How easily can a teleworker exhibit organizational citizenship behavior (Johns 1998)? These are all questions for which answers are needed.

ORGANIZATIONAL STRUCTURE

Organizational structure is another internal macrovariable that can be important in the employment interview process. Organizational structure comprises the ways in which the organization is divided and how those divisions interact to implement the organization's strategy (Field and House 1995). The structure of the organization influences the flow of information (Cohen, March, and Olsen 1972). For example, in a matrix organization, employees report to both functional and product supervisors. This creates the need for coordination and hence requires people with strong interpersonal skills. Susan Jackson, Randall Schuler, and J. Carlos Rivero (1989) have argued that organizations that use a functional form are more likely than those with divisionalized structures to emphasize results rather than process. Interview questions in functional organizations thus focus on skill; in product organizations, they focus on product knowledge; and in matrix organizations, they focus on interpersonal and organizations skills. We need more research to determine whether these interview questions vary in their ability to predict performance in different types of organizations.

Another dimension along which organizational structures differ is the extent to which employees work primarily in teams or as individuals. Richard Klimoski and Robert Jones (1994) suggest that recruitment for team-based organizations may differ from recruitment for other structures. In support of this argument, a meta-analysis found that task success correlated with group homogeneity (Galarza and Dipboye

1996). Deborah Ancona and David Caldwell (1992) found that successful team performance was related to skills such as conflict management, ability to coordinate, and ability to give feedback in ways that are constructive and minimize defensiveness. This suggests that predicting the performance of a team member requires interview questions that are different from those used to predict the performance of an individual who works relatively independently. Here again, research is needed to determine whether the validity coefficients of applicant responses to these different types of interview questions differ in these two contexts.

INTERNAL LABOR MARKET

The internal labor market is made up of the individuals currently employed by an organization who qualify as candidates for other positions within the organization. In large organizations, internal labor markets may be sizable and may provide a number of candidates for any job. As a result of this existing pool of candidates, the influence of the external market over employment decisions is reduced (Cappelli and Shearer 1991). Research is needed to determine whether interview validity coefficients differ when the candidates are employees from within the organization as opposed to candidates from outside it.

TECHNOLOGY

Scott Snell and James Dean (1992) found that organizations that use advanced technologies are more likely to practice selective hiring than are those that use traditional technologies. They found a negative relationship between the use of "just-in-time" inventory control and the selectiveness of staffing. This invites the question of how the technology used by a company moderates the validity of its employment interviews.

UNION PRESENCE

In a comparison of unionized versus nonunionized business units, Jackson et al. (1989) found that unionized businesses were more likely to use assessment centers for the purposes of job appraisal and promotion. Included in assessment center evaluations is the selection interview. In addition, these organizations were more likely to include drug testing and physical and aptitude tests in the selection process. Hourly unionized employees were more likely to receive formalized performance appraisals than were hourly employees in nonunionized environments (Jackson et al. 1989). This leads to the question of whether unionization is a moderator variable of interview validity.

CHARACTER OF THE JOB

Among internal organizational microvariables, an important one is the character of the job. Due to the fluid character of many jobs, Steve Cronshaw (1998) advocated that organizations downplay traditional approaches to job analysis in favor of holistic work profiling. The work performed by employees in many organizations in the 21st century is not static; rather, it changes continuously. Thus work profiling should facilitate the prediction of person-organization fit. The extent to which various employment interview methods can predict adaptability and flexibility in behavior in the context of continuous change is in need of exploration. The extent to which methods can do so under conditions of extensive outsourcing and limited contracts is yet to be determined, however.

THE MEDIUM

In a global economy where there is a "war for talent," the most talented people will not necessarily be found in a local applicant pool. Employment interviews are now being conducted through teleconferencing and electronic conferencing. The extent to which this technology moderates the validity of the interview also has yet to be determined (relatedly, see in this volume Shuy, Chapter 26; Couper and Hansen, Chapter 27; Mann and Stewart, Chapter 29).

PERCEPTION OF RECRUITER

As a first consideration, the applicant's perceptions of the interviewer's behavior may affect the amount of information gathered in the employment interview. Michael Harris and Laurence Fink (1987) found a positive relationship between the perceived competence and informativeness of the recruiter and the applicant's perception of the job. Further, they found a negative relationship between the perceived aggressiveness of the recruiter and the perceived attractiveness of the job. Harris and Fink also found that applicants' perceptions of interviewer characteristics influence applicants' intentions to accept the job. It is likely that applicants who perceive the job favorably will provide as much information about themselves as possible, whereas applicants who, as a result of the recruiter's aggressiveness, do not perceive the job as attractive may withhold information or present themselves in a less desirable manner so as not to have to contend with a job offer. As personnel officers vary in their characteristics, we might well consider whether the validity of the same interview questions is higher, for example, when they are asked by human resource personnel, line personnel, or a combination of the two. Research is needed to test these hypotheses.

TRAINING OF INTERVIEWERS

Orientation training aimed at clarifying the task required of the interviewer appears critical for hiring people in complex jobs (Eder 1999). Interviewers who are given detailed information regarding the jobs for which they will be selecting people make decisions with high interobserver reliability.

The training of interviewers in ways that increase their objectivity influences the validity of selection decisions. For example, training in note taking can improve interviewers' attention, encoding, recall, and evaluation of interview information focusing on behavior (Burnett et al. 1998). Elliott Pursell, Dennis Dossett, and Gary Latham (1980) found that subsequent to a job analysis, the validity coefficient for the selection process was not significantly different from zero; only subsequent to the supervisors' being trained in ways to increase their objectivity was the validity coefficient significant.

Cynthia Kay Stevens (1998) examined the relationship between interviewer training and information management. Compared with untrained interviewers, interviewers who were trained digressed less often into non-job-related topics during the interview and asked a higher percentage of differentiating questions. Thomas Dougherty, Ronald Ebert, and John Callender (1986) found that training interviewers to elicit useful information increased the validity of their assessments.

Jack Howard and Gerald Ferris (1996) found that trained interviewers evaluate applicants who display self-promotion behaviors less favorably than those who do not display these inappropriate behaviors. This is because training increases the interviewers' awareness of irrelevant factors that influence the decision process favorably, and this in turn minimizes bias. The result is the collection of valid information. To what extent is the training of interviewers a solution for moderator variables that attenuate interview validity? Are some moderator variables more easily removed through training than others? Relatedly, it is important to bear in mind that the training moderator is difficult to assess. Typically, a study of interviewer training involves a group that receives training and a control group that does not. Validities

are then compared. However, some of the "untrained" interviewers may have what amounts to the same training gained through on-the-job experience or self-learning.

INTERVIEWER AND INTERVIEWEE CHARACTERISTICS

Stevens (1998) found that interviewers who are recruitment oriented speak more and ask fewer questions than do interviewers with a screening orientation. Recruitment-oriented interviewers gather less information than do screening-oriented interviewers.

A related factor is the similarity between interviewer and interviewee. With respect to selection practices used in hiring CEOs, a powerful board of directors is likely to select a new CEO who possesses a demographic profile similar to the board members'. In contrast, where the board is less powerful than the outgoing CEO, the board is less likely to make changes regarding CEO characteristics (Zajac and Westphal 1996). To what extent does this behavior affect the validity of the interview?

Interview decisions are social judgments (Johns 1998). In this context, interpersonal accountability would seem to be an important factor that can affect interviewers' behavior. The nature of the relationship between the interviewer and the applicant —for instance, whether the applicant is a current employee, a former employee, or a personal friend—has yet to be investigated in regard to its impact on the interview process and selection decision (Eder and Harris 1999).

Social accountability affects the applicant as well. The interview is an information exchange between interview participants, yet the preponderance of studies on this subject have focused on the validity of the interview for predicting applicant-organization job fit from the point of view of the employer. Few, if any, studies have examined validity—that is, the meaning of interview questions and related recruitment decisions—from the applicant's point of view (see Shuy, Chapter 26, this volume). This raises a number of important questions, such as, What types of questions should the interviewee ask in the job interview? To what extent is accountability to others, such as friends, family members, and dependents, a moderator?

◆ Summary and Conclusions

We can summarize our discussion in this chapter in the following ways. In the first half of the 20th century, responses to an employment interview were poor at predicting an applicant's performance on the job. Early reviews frequently found that the validity of the employment interview was near zero; the correlation between the job interview and job performance was not statistically significant. This is because different interviewers often asked different questions, the questions were usually not job relevant, and when the questions were job relevant, the interviewers seldom agreed on what constituted acceptable answers. Hence inter-interviewer reliability and criterion-related validity were low if not nonexistent.

In the second half of the 20th century, scientific knowledge about the employment interview accumulated through systematic research testing in the field. The findings and an evolving social climate led to a number of changes. First, the interview became more structured. Second, the questions asked were based on job analyses that identified the behaviors or core competencies critical to successful job performance. Third, legislation was passed in some countries, beginning with the United States and subsequently in Canada, Australia, and the United Kingdom, that made it illegal for prospective employers to ask questions that they might use to deny equal opportunity to applicants because of their age, race, sex,

or other characteristics. Fourth, training programs were developed that increased the objectivity of interviewers. Finally, at least two interview techniques have been developed that focus the interviewer's attention on the applicant's behavior, namely, the PBDI and the SI. Related to the change in social climate, the latter has been shown to minimize bias regarding the applicant's age, race, sex, and ethnicity (e.g., Anglophone versus Francophone job applicants in Canada). The result has been an increasingly valid employment interview—a selection tool that identifies the applicant who will do well at the job.

The task for researchers at the start of this new millennium is to examine contextual variables that may moderate the direction or strength of the relation between responses to the interview and performance in the organization. Currently, we do not know much about the extent to which various contextual variables increase or decrease the validity of the interview, as the many questions we have raised in this chapter indicate. Acquisition of this knowledge is becoming increasingly critical as the interview continues to be the primary basis upon which selection decisions are made and business activity across national borders increases the demand on the interview to predict cross-cultural and global competencies (Latham and Sue-Chan 1998). The globalization of markets and the growing intensity of worldwide competition have created an equally intense demand for sound human capital.

As organizations conduct business across borders, the complexity of the interview context increases. European and Asian companies with relatively homogeneous workforces often fill positions with employees from within the companies who express willingness to relocate to another country. The question is, Can the interview predict the extent to which such individuals will succeed in cultures foreign to them?

Multinational companies with diverse workforces often place employees who reside in the companies' host countries in key positions. Requirements for the job success of local employees vary from country to country and may differ from those required in the company's corporate headquarters. Cultural variances reflected in the behavior of applicants may influence the validity of the interview.

Most validity studies of the employment interview have been conducted in North America. However, globalization requires that research attention be given to a number of new questions. To what extent should interview content be uniform across cultures so as to ensure uniformity in commitment to, and implementation of, an organization's business plan? Is validity enhanced or attenuated if the structure of the interview remains constant (as in an SI) while the content is adapted to the local situation so as to tap cultural differences? Equality of opportunity and equality at the starting line do not imply overlooking individual differences in the selection process. The purpose of the interview is to identify and measure differences among individuals to ensure that the best person or persons are hired. Should we assume that differences among national cultures can be ignored without harm to interview validity?

Finally, as we have noted, research emphasis needs to be given to the other half of the interviewing equation, namely, the applicant. The contextual variables that influence the interviewer to decide to make an employment offer are not necessarily the same contextual variables that influence the applicant to apply for and accept the job. Research is needed on the interviewee as a decision maker and as an information processor. We need to know more about the structure of the interview questions that the interviewee him- or herself should pose and the variables that moderate the validity of a correct fit from the interviewee's perspective. There is a need for a research-based job applicant's interview handbook to balance the effects of available employment interview handbooks. The result of such egalitarian influences may be a quantum leap rather than an incremental increase in the validity of the employment interview.

■ *References*

Ancona, D. G. and D. F. Caldwell. 1992. "Bridging the Boundary: External Activity and Performance in Organizational Teams." *Administrative Science Quarterly* 37:634-65.

Arvey, R. D. and J. E. Campion. 1982. "The Employment Interview: A Summary and Review of Recent Research." *Personnel Psychology* 35:281-322.

Bennett, N., T. C. Blum, and P. M. Roman. 1994. "Presence of Drug Screening and Employee Assistance Programs: Exclusive and Inclusive Human Resource Management Practices." *Journal of Organizational Behavior* 15:549-60.

Brockbank, W. 1997. "HR's Future on the Way to a Presence." *Human Resource Management* 36:65-69.

Burnett, J. R., C. Fan, S. J. Motowidlo, and T. DeGroot. 1998. "Interviewer Notetaking and Judgement Accuracy in the Structured Selection Interview." *Personnel Psychology* 51:375-96.

Campion, M. A., E. D. Pursell, and B. K. Brown. 1988. "Structured Interviewing: Raising the Psychometric Properties of the Employment Interview." *Personnel Psychology* 41:25-42.

Cappelli, P. and P. D. Shearer. 1991. "The Missing Role of Context in OB: The Need for a Meso-Level Approach." Pp. 55-110 in *Research in Organizational Behavior,* Vol. 13, edited by L. L. Cummings and B. M. Staw. Greenwich, CT: JAI.

Cohen, M. D., J. G. March, and J. P. Olsen. 1972. "A Garbage Can Model of Organizational Choice." *Administrative Science Quarterly* 17:1-25.

Cronshaw, S. F. 1998. "Job Analysis: Changing Nature of Work." *Canadian Psychology* 39:5-13.

Datta, D. K. and J. P. Guthrie. 1994. "Executive Succession: Organizational Antecedents of CEO Characteristics." *Strategic Management Journal* 15:569-77.

Davis-Blake, A. and B. Uzzi. 1993. "Determinants of Employment Externalization: A Study of Temporary Workers and Independent Contractors." *Administrative Science Quarterly* 38:195-223.

Dipboye, R. L. and S. L. Jackson. 1999. "Interviewer Experience and Expertise Effects." In *The Employment Interview Handbook,* edited by R. W. Eder and M. M. Harris. Thousand Oaks, CA: Sage.

Dougherty, T. W., R. J. Ebert, and J. C. Callender. 1986. "Policy Capturing in the Employment Interview." *Journal of Applied Psychology* 71:9-15.

Eder, R. W. 1999. "Contextual Effects." In *The Employment Interview Handbook,* edited by R. W. Eder and M. M. Harris. Thousand Oaks, CA: Sage.

Eder, R. W. and M. R. Buckley. 1988. "The Employment Interview: An Interactionist Perspective." *Research in Personnel and Human Resources Management* 6:75-107.

Eder, R. W. and M. M. Harris, eds. 1999. *The Employment Interview Handbook.* Thousand Oaks, CA: Sage.

Field, R. H. G. and R. J. House. 1995. *Human Behaviour in Organizations: A Canadian Perspective.* Toronto: Prentice Hall.

Flanagan, J. C. 1954. "The Critical Incident Technique." *Psychological Bulletin* 51:327-58.

Fry, P. S. and R. Ghosh. 1980. "Attributions of Success and Failure: Comparisons of Cultural Differences between Asian and Caucasian Children." *Journal of Cross-Cultural Research* 11:343-64.

Galarza, L. and R. L. Dipboye. 1996. "The Effect of Group Heterogeneity on Group Performance: A Meta-analysis." Presented at the 11th Annual Meeting of the Society for Industrial and Organizational Psychology, April, San Diego, CA.

Hanssens, D. M. and H. A. Levien. 1983. "An Econometric Study of Recruitment Marketing in the U.S. Navy." *Management Science* 29:1167-84.

Harris, M. M. 1989. "Reconsidering the Employment Interview: A Review of Recent Literature and Suggestions for Future Research." *Personnel Psychology* 42:691-726.

———. 1999. "What Is Being Measured?" In *The Employment Interview Handbook,* edited by R. W. Eder and M. M. Harris. Thousand Oaks, CA: Sage.

Harris, M. M. and L. S. Fink. 1987. "A Field Study of Applicant Reactions to Employment Opportunities: Does the Recruiter Make a Difference?" *Personnel Psychology* 40:765-84.

Hedge, J. W. and M. S. Teachout. 1992. "An Interview Approach to Work Sample Criterion Measurement." *Journal of Applied Psychology* 77:453-61.

Hough, L. and F. L. Oswald. 2000. "Personnel Selection: Looking Toward the Future—Remembering the Past." *Annual Review of Psychology* 55:630-64.

Howard, J. L. and G. R. Ferris. 1996. "The Employment Interview Context: Social and Situational Influences on Interviewer Decisions." *Journal of Applied Social Psychology* 26:112-36.

Huffcutt, A. I. and W. Arthur, Jr. 1994. "Hunter and Hunter (1994) Revisited: Interview Validity for Entry-Level Jobs." *Journal of Applied Psychology* 79:184-90.

Jackson, S. E., R. S. Schuler, and J. C. Rivero. 1989. "Organizational Characteristics as Predictors of Personnel Practices." *Personnel Psychology* 42:727-86.

Janz, T. 1982. "Initial Comparisons of Patterned Behavior Description Interviews versus Unstructured Interviews." *Journal of Applied Psychology* 67:577-80.

Johns, G. 1998. "The Nature of Work, the Context of Organizational Behaviour, and the Application of Industrial-Organizational Psychology." *Canadian Psychology* 39:149-57.

Kashima, Y. and H. C. Triandis. 1986. "The Self-Serving Bias in Attributions as a Coping Strategy." *Journal of Cross-Cultural Research* 17:83-97.

Klimoski, R. J. and R. G. Jones. 1994. "Suppose We Took Staffing for Effective Group Decision Making Seriously?" In *Team Decision Making Effectiveness in Organizations,* edited by R. A. Guzzo and E. Salas. San Francisco: Jossey-Bass.

Latham, G. P., L. M. Saari, E. D. Pursell, and M. A. Campion. 1980. "The Situational Interview." *Journal of Applied Psychology* 65:422-27.

Latham, G. P. and D. Skarlicki. 1995. "Criterion-Related Validity of the Situational and Patterned Behaviour Description Interviews with Organizational Citizenship Behaviour." *Human Performance* 8:67-80.

———. 1996. "The Effectiveness of the Situational, Patterned Behaviour and Conventional Structured Interviews in Minimizing In-Group Favoritism of Canadian Francophone Managers." *Applied Psychology: An International Review* 45:177-84.

Latham, G. P. and C. Sue-Chan. 1998. "Selecting Employees in the 21st Century: Predicting the Contribution of I-O Psychology to Canada." *Canadian Psychology* 39:14-22.

———. 1999. "A Meta-analysis of the Situational Interview: An Enumerative Review of Reasons for Its Validity." *Canadian Psychology* 40:56-67.

Lin, T. R., G. H. Dobbins, and J.-L. Farh. 1992. "A Field Study of Race and Age Similarity Effects on Interview Ratings in Conventional and Situational Interviews." *Journal of Applied Psychology* 77:363-71.

Mayfield, E. C. 1964. "The Selection Interview: A Reevaluation of Published Research." *Personnel Psychology* 17:239-60.

McDaniel, M. A., D. L. Whetzel, F. L. Schmidt, and S. D. Maurer. 1994. "The Validity of Employment Interviews: A Comprehensive Review and Meta-analysis." *Journal of Applied Psychology* 79:599-616.

McShane, S. L. 1998. *Canadian Organizational Behaviour.* Toronto: McGraw-Hill Ryerson.

Miles, R. E. and C. C. Snow. 1978. *Organizational Strategy, Structure, and Process.* New York: McGraw-Hill.

Olian, J. D. and S. L. Rynes. 1984. "Organizational Staffing: Integrating Practice with Strategy." *Industrial Relations* 23:170-83.

Ott, J. S. 1989. *The Organizational Culture Perspective.* Pacific Grove, CA: Brooks/Cole.

Peck, S. 1994. "Exploring the Link between Organizational Strategy and the Employment Relationship: The Role of Human Resources Policies." *Journal of Management Studies* 31:715-36.

Posthuma, R. A., F. P. Morgeson, and M. A. Campion. 1999. "The Employment Interview: A Review of Recent Research and Examination of Trends over Time." Working paper.

Pulakos, E. D., N. Schmitt, D. Whitney, and M. Smith. 1996. "Individual Differences in Interviewer Ratings: The Impact of Standardization, Consensus Discussion, and Sampling Error on the Validity of a Structured Interview." *Personnel Psychology* 49:85-102.

Pursell, E. D., D. L. Dossett, and G. P. Latham. 1980. "Obtaining Valid Predictors by Minimizing Rating Errors in the Criterion." *Personnel Psychology* 33:91-106.

Quinn, R. E. 1978. "Towards a Theory of Changing: A Means End Model of the Organizational Improvement Process." *Human Relations* 31:395-416.

Snell, S. A. and J. W. Dean, Jr. 1992. "Integrated Manufacturing and Human Resource Management: A Human Capital Perspective." *Academy of Management Journal* 35:467-504.

Stevens, C. K. 1998. "Antecedents of Interview Interactions, Interviewers' Ratings, and Applicants' Reactions." *Personnel Psychology* 51:55-85.

Terpstra, D. E. and E. J. Rozell. 1993. "The Relationship of Staffing Practices to Organizational Level Measures of Performance." *Personnel Psychology* 46:27-48.

Thurow, L. 1975. *Generating Inequality.* New York: Basic Books.

Ulrich, L. and D. Trumbo. 1965. "The Selection Interview since 1949." *Psychological Bulletin* 63:100-116.

Wagner, R. 1949. "The Employment Interview: A Critical Summary." *Personnel Psychology* 2:17-46.

Webster, E. C. 1964. *Decision Making in the Employment Interview.* Montreal: Eagle.

———. 1982. *The Employment Interview: A Social Judgment Process.* Schomberg, Ontario: SIP.

Wiesner, W. and S. F. Cronshaw. 1988. "A Meta-analytic Investigation of the Impact of Interview Format and Degree of Structure on the Validity of the Employment Interview." *Journal of Occupational Psychology* 61:275-90.

Zajac, E. J. and J. D. Westphal. 1996. "Who Shall Succeed? How CEO/Board Preferences and Power Affect the Choice of New CEOs." *Academy of Management Journal* 39:64-90.

Part IV

TECHNICAL ISSUES

Interviewing in the 21st century employs an immense variety of technical innovations designed to improve research procedures and findings. This part of the *Handbook* discusses several technical advances that add new dimensions to the collection and management of interview data.

At one time, face-to-face interviewing was the only practical means available to researchers who wanted to "learn from strangers." Many respondents simply did not have telephones by which questions could be asked and answered. The rapid deployment of telephones to individual households following World War II gradually turned the matter of asking and answering questions, especially research interview questions, to the issue of whether face-to-face interviewing is necessary to obtain useful responses or whether this can be accomplished using cheaper telephone technology. Researchers have investigated the relative adequacy of face-to-face and telephone interviewing and continue to explore the nuances of the differences between the two methods (see in this volume Platt, Chapter 2; Singleton and Straits, Chapter 3; Shuy, Chapter 26; Couper and Hansen, Chapter 27). Although, by and large, telephone interviewing is cheaper, findings on the informational utility of the two techniques are mixed; the differences depend on, among other things, the nature of the questions asked and how cut-and-dried the answers are expected to be, as well as on the sensitivity of the issues being explored. For interviewing in which questions are likely to elicit brief and fairly straightforward responses, the telephone can be adequate, usually suiting the purposes of large-scale surveys. In fact, the greater expense of in-person as opposed to telephone interviewing, regardless of the research findings in this area, has made the real difference in the long run, so that telephone interviewing is now commonplace in the survey industry.

The use of the telephone was the first major technological leap forward for survey interviewing, and it was accompanied, at the data management and analysis stages, by the rapid expansion of electronic information processing. The now seemingly primitive punch card and card sorter were replaced by the computer and data management software, which are capable of handling masses of short and straightforward bits of data quickly and with the analytic sophistication researchers desire. The industry standard has become the telephone survey tied to computerized data monitoring and data management technology (see Schaeffer and Maynard, Chapter 28, this volume).

A second major technological leap forward in this area is currently upon us; this advancement centers on the Internet and its potential to allow researchers to learn from strangers. Although this change is also computer driven, curiously enough, in some ways it offers the possibility of returning the survey interview to some of the openness, if not also the charms, of the face-to-face interview (see Mann and Stewart, Chapter 29, this volume). The richly textured exchanges that are more likely to be accepted in the in-person interview are now the stock-in-trade of many Internet sites, where chat-room proceedings and virtual on-line individual and group interviews can be very detailed. And these exchanges can also be immediately turned into codable transcripts at fairly low cost. This eliminates the expense and complication of actually doing on-site interviews, which can sometimes be prohibitive (see Ryen, Chapter 17, this volume). This, of course, is balanced by the expense entailed in providing computers and Internet access to all interview participants. Although little actual research has yet been conducted on the comparative informational utility of the Internet over other vehicles for interviewing (see in this volume Mann and Stewart, Chapter 29; Couper and Hansen, Chapter 27), it seems safe to say that cost again will be a critical factor in decision making at this technological forefront.

If some of the issues considered in this section of the *Handbook* would seem to suggest that technological innovations respond mainly to cost and efficiency, three cautions are in order. One relates to the growing popularity of qualitative interviewing. For qualitative researchers, the vehicle for conducting interviews has always been less important than the provision to the respondent of the opportunity to tell his or her own story. The informational utility of lengthy and complex narratives is paramount, overshadowing the cost-effectiveness and efficiency of the questioning- and-answering process, although these are undoubtedly also of some concern. All studies, after all, have budgets of some kind, and there always are time constraints. There seems to be no substitute for in-person interviewing for many qualitative researchers, who seek the sort of information from respondents that would allow researchers, among other things, to trace narrative themes and tie these to biographical particulars; to represent in the respondent's own words the narrative contours of attitudes, sentiments, and conduct; or to relate accounts to the broader going concerns surrounding individual narrative presentations (see the contributions to Parts V and VI of this volume).

A second caution relates to nonresearch interview settings. The pertinent question here is whether the interviewing that is undertaken in sites such as medical clinics, schools, and employment settings can be evaluated solely in terms of the efficiency of data gathering technologies. Cost-containment concerns in many nonresearch sites for interviewing work against the institutional and professional ideologies that would lengthen and complicate the interview encounter, even while costs cannot be ignored. The narrative thrust of "patient-centered medicine," for example, would seem to operate counter to quick-and-efficient data gathering technologies (see Zoppi and Epstein, Chapter 18, this volume). It would be difficult to imagine how telephone and Internet interviewing could replace the in-person encounters typical of forensic investigation and therapy interviewing, where bodily and emotional presence is crucial (see in this volume McKenzie, Chapter 21; Miller, de Shazer, and De Jong, Chapter 19). In nonresearch sites there is always something else at stake besides informational utility, including what needs to be accomplished immediately with the information—whether that is healing, counseling, hiring, or interrogating.

A third and final caution relates to the central theme of this *Handbook,* which is that methodology in general, and interview methods in particular, is not just a means of gathering information but a part of society. Michel Foucault figures significantly here, as he points us to the constructive character, not just the efficiencies, of technology. Foucault combines the two to argue that the "technologies" in question—whether face-to-face or telephonic, paper and pencil or computer assisted, in-person or Internet mediated—construct and rationalize with various degrees of sophistication what technology otherwise seems merely to access differentially. It is important to consider that what takes place in the telephone interview, for example, is not only the efficient gathering of facts of experience and the containment of costs, but simultaneously the construction of a subject who formulates the experiences needed by an information-hungry, but time-conscious, interview society. Experience is thus produced and comes to us in bits and bytes, because the technologies in place serve it up in ways their sponsoring environments readily accept and can use (see in this volume Gubrium and Holstein, Chapter 1; Denzin, Chapter 40). This, of course, is not to denigrate technical matters and their immense successes and advances; rather, the argument is that technology always does more than technicians can properly admit.

24

ELICITATION TECHNIQUES FOR INTERVIEWING

◆ Jeffrey C. Johnson
◆ Susan C. Weller

How does an interviewer get informants to reveal what they know, feel, think, or believe? There are a variety of impediments to tapping into an informant's knowledge. Aside from the more obvious issues of rapport and personal style, the manner in which questions are framed and the use of supportive materials in the interview process are equally important in getting informants to provide reliable, comparable, and valid responses. But individuals vary in their ability to recall and report what they know, and this affects the value of traditional unstructured and semistructured interviewing. In particular, informants' knowledge or other data of interest may be tacit and difficult for them to explicate in simple discourse. This is where elicitation techniques come in—the aim of these techniques in general is to uncover unarticulated informant knowledge.

The elicitation interviewing methods discussed in this chapter have been variously referred to by anthropologists as "systematic data collection techniques" (Weller and Romney 1988) and "structured interviewing methods" (Bernard 1994). Although they are certainly structured, elicitation methods should not be confused with structured interviews, such as those found in survey research. Although both generally involve asking questions in a stan-

AUTHORS' NOTE: This work was sponsored in part by a grant from the National Science Foundation, Office of Polar Programs and Cultural Anthropology Program.

dard way, elicitation methods have more of an exploratory or emergent character in their attempts to reveal tacit subjective understandings in some cultural domain. Most of the elicitation methods described here assume no a priori knowledge of informant understandings on the part of the researcher; thus researchers can use them to describe informant responses while minimizing the amount of researcher bias introduced into the research process (Weller and Romney 1988).

When we speak of *responses* here, we mean a variety of things that people actually are able to report on with some degree of accuracy, including beliefs, attitudes, perceptions, judgments, emotions, feelings, and decisions, as well as responses focused on particular areas of experience, such as specific cultural, technical, environmental, or biological matters. Researchers have employed elicitation techniques in various attempts to construct mental models, cultural models, task or process models, and any number of other forms of descriptive and explanatory models of tacit knowledge, the goal of which is to understand how this knowledge is structured and how it is shared in a population.

In the next section of this chapter, we briefly describe the breadth of application of elicitation techniques across disciplines and in relation to research strategy, focusing on anthropology, where many of the techniques originated. Following that, we provide a glimpse of the origins of these techniques in anthropology, the disciplinary home of "elicitation methods," and relate these origins to a study's overall research strategy. We then move on to discuss the specific usages of elicitation techniques at various stages of research. Finally, we present a sampling of commonly used semistructured and structured techniques for eliciting informant knowledge, including methods for probing, question framing, use of visual stimuli, and traditional approaches, such as folk taxonomies and free-recall listing.

◆ Breadth of Application

The search for models of tacit knowledge has involved researchers from a vast array of disciplines and backgrounds, including anthropologists, linguists, computer scientists, psychologists, statisticians, economists, sociologists, accountants, political scientists, product developers, and market researchers, to name just a few. All share a reliance on these techniques in the pursuit of human-knowledge-based research problems. For example, economists may be concerned with the elicitation of the relative values of things (Holms and Kramer 1995), accountants may wish to elicit descriptions of accounting processes (Abdolmohammadi and Wright 1992), statisticians may be interested in eliciting prior knowledge for the construction of Bayesian models (Kadane 1996), and linguists may want to elicit knowledge concerning language production (Menn and Ratner 2000).

Computer scientists have employed elicitation methods in order to model expert knowledge concerning software and hardware development. Sometimes referred to as "knowledge engineering," elicitation methods are used to aid in expert knowledge acquisition through the identification of domain content, reasoning strategies and modes, and explanations of domain processes and relations on the part of informants (e.g., experts, hardware engineers, and pilots). Ultimately, the goal is to create a formal model of an expert system, a model of a user-system interface, or a model of the software and hardware development process. Elicitation methods are especially critical for the elicitation of unarticulated personal experience, in this case forms of expert knowledge that are often tacit and difficult to obtain through normal interviews or from simple descriptive discourse. (A good example of this kind of work on expert systems, undertaken by psychologists, can be found in Hoffman 1992.)

In contrast to modeling often rather esoteric expert knowledge and improving related complex decision-making information, elicitation methods also may be used to assess the "needs" of a community or a specific group. The success of a project or activity can depend upon how well it meets the group's unarticulated needs. Thus an important first step for the researcher is to obtain an accurate description of these needs. Rather than assuming from the start that he or she knows what might be best for the group or what should be offered, the researcher applies elicitation techniques to elicit subjective understandings. When trying to determine community needs, the best or the most accurate approach a researcher can take is to elicit the needs directly from community members through a needs assessment study. Techniques such as the free-recall listing interviews described below, conducted either with individuals or with groups, are extremely useful for eliciting concerns, problems, and unmet needs that can be incorporated into action strategies.

Even survey researchers and psychologists who rely on highly structured questionnaires (multiple-choice, checklist, and rating scale formats) integrate elicitation methods into their instruments. Initially, researchers may use open-ended interviews to elicit items for study. Then, after a questionnaire is designed, they may conduct additional exploratory interviews to discover respondents' understandings and interpretations of instructions, questions, and even their own responses. Understanding is a key element in interviewing: All participants must understand the task, understand each question, have the same interpretation of each question, and organize their responses accordingly (Fowler 1995). In order for researchers to combine responses across individuals and make meaningful comparisons between groups, all informants must interpret all questions in the same way.

Although we note the existence of this rather large and disparate body of work, we deal here primarily with examples from the social sciences, mostly from anthropology, where it all began, so to speak. However, we wish to emphasize the high degree of overlap with regard to problems, techniques, and modes of analysis among the various disciplines that use these techniques; we encourage the reader to examine this extensive body of literature for creative solutions that are especially pertinent in particular disciplinary areas.

◆ Origins and Research Strategies

Many elicitation techniques grew out of the empirical problems of early cognitive anthropology. Componential analysis, folk taxonomies, and frame elicitation techniques all are early examples of methods that anthropologists have employed to reveal various types of tacit knowledge held by informants in societies or social contexts whose cultural particulars were unknown (D'Andrade 1995). The general purpose of these methods was the elicitation of informants' subjective understanding of some given domain or well-bounded body of cultural knowledge. Researchers used the elicited information, for example, to develop formal models or ethnographic descriptions.

Good examples of elicitation in the descriptive mode come from James Spradley's work and his various ethnographies of such groups as cocktail waitresses (Spradley and Mann 1975) and urban nomads (Spradley 1970). In the course of ethnographic description of men on skid row, for example, Spradley used structured questions to obtain information from informants about social processes ("ways to beat a drunk charge"), locations ("places to be busted within jail"), and activities ("hustling"). He also used a number of different elicitation interviewing techniques in both group and one-on-one settings. Spradley was inter-

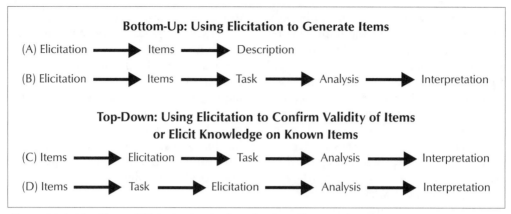

Figure 24.1. The Place of Elicitation Methods in the Overall Research Sequence

ested in all aspects of life on skid row; in fact, he changed his research focus and the labels he used for the men he studied, from an outsider label of *alcoholics* to *urban nomads,* owing to his growing appreciation for how they themselves figured their worlds.

An early example of the use of elicitation techniques to produce more formal models of cultural knowledge is found in Roy D'Andrade's (1976) propositional analysis of U.S. beliefs about illness. Dissatisfied with attempts at eliciting beliefs about illness with taxonomies (described below) and componential approaches that identified important distinctive features, D'Andrade used "sentence frames" to ask relational questions about the properties of illnesses. He was particularly concerned with the logical relations among diseases and their properties as perceived by informants. He used in-depth interviews to elicit statements about illnesses and their properties, such as "You can catch influenza from other people." By removing references to specific illnesses in such statements, D'Andrade produced sentence frames that could be compared across all disease terms, such as "You can catch _____ from other people." In this way, D'Andrade used an initial stage of interviewing to elicit information on illnesses and their culturally relevant properties; in a subsequent set of inter-

views he collected systematic comparisons of illnesses with illness properties in sentence frames. Further analysis led to a model of those relations.

Another important feature of D'Andrade's study concerns the place of elicitation techniques in the overall data collection and analysis process. In Spradley's work on skid row, elicitation led directly to ethnographic description—from the ground up, as it were. However, in D'Andrade's case, elicitation was one element in a long sequence of data collection, analysis, and model development and interpretation. Spradley used elicitation methods initially to explore the structure of experience in many related domains. He presented informants with diagrams of topic-specific structures and then used the information he gathered to create an integrated description. D'Andrade's work, in contrast, represents a more focused inquiry. D'Andrade attempted to model informants' underlying assumptions that could potentially generate behavior. He used elicitation methods to get relevant material from informants, in a manner similar to Spradley, and then used additional structured questions and statistical models to help him further interpret his informants' beliefs about illness.

Figure 24.1 shows four different data collection and analysis sequences and the place of elicitation methods within them. It summarizes how elicitation methods figure in different overall research strategies. The first two methods (A and B) represent the processes described above, with the Spradley example most similar to sequence A and the D'Andrade example most similar to sequence B. Both Spradley and D'Andrade used interviewing in the initial stages of their projects expressly to learn the subjective contours of their respective topics in the most rudimentary sense. The less a researcher knows about a topic, the more appropriate is the use of open-ended and less structured interviewing techniques. This is a bottom-up approach similar to that recommended by advocates of "grounded theory" (see Charmaz, Chapter 32, this volume).

As the researcher attains greater cultural understanding, the use of interview techniques with more structure is appropriate. The bottom two sequences in Figure 24.1 (C and D) represent cases where the items or categories in a domain are already substantially documented, where the researcher may have already studied the topic but seeks to elicit further or to reelicit properties, features, or reactions that are directly and/or indirectly relevant to the content area. Researchers undertake these more top-down approaches for a variety of reasons. Often, they use such approaches to explore the meaning or validity of previous work. For example, Roberta Baer (1996) conducted descriptive interviews to elicit understandings and possible responses to questions used in a national survey regarding mental health (the National Survey of Health and Stress). The survey was originally thought to contain questions that assessed symptoms indicative of depression, but Baer's results suggest that the questions may not be valid indicators of depression among Hispanics in the United States. Her in-depth interviews with a Hispanic sample indicated that although her informants' responses appeared to be consistent with the biomedical symptoms of depression, the responses could be attributed to the informants' work (hard physical labor) and lifestyle conditions, not necessarily to depression. Informants' understanding of the questions and their own responses indicated that the survey would report many false positives for Hispanics on mental illness.

The descriptive interview technique is used especially by psychologists and survey developers to ensure that survey questions are reliable and valid. Such researchers select a preliminary sample and ask the individuals in that sample about the meanings and possible responses to each survey question (Fowler 1995). Based on the answers, they can then make modifications to the questionnaire to ensure that all respondents interpret questions in the same way, and that their interpretations are consistent with the researchers' intended meanings (see Singleton and Straits, Chapter 3, this volume).

Of course, research practice can lead researchers to combine strategies in various ways. The place of elicitation methods in the research process and the particular data collection and analysis sequence used depend on just what is being studied (e.g., domain type) and the nature of the research population (e.g., literate versus nonliterate), among other contingencies of a project. Spradley (1970) makes the point in describing his research with men on skid row:

> Participant observation and recording casual conversations among these men made it possible to formulate many hypotheses and hunches which were later the basis for more formal ethnographic interviews. Specific question frames were then developed along with a variety of sorting tasks for testing the adequacy of these hypotheses. The result presented here is an ethnographic description which approaches the way insiders of this culture define their own identity, environment, and life style. Although listening, engaging in participant observation, formulating hypotheses, and testing these hypotheses with specific eliciting techniques were all

used throughout the research, some tended to precede others. In this chapter the formal questioning and sorting tasks will be discussed in some detail but it should be understood they were used in gathering and analyzing the data presented in later chapters also. (Pp. 69-70)

◆ Specific Uses at Various Stages of Research

Elicitation techniques may be useful at different stages in a research project. Researchers can employ these methods as exploratory or explanatory mechanisms to aid in the development of theory, to supplement other information or enhance an ethnographic description, to test hypotheses, and to elaborate and construct models. In addition, researchers can use such methods in an exploratory-explanatory sequence, where the results of earlier elicitation help to determine later elicitation approaches used in the testing of hypotheses (see Johnson 1998). Probably the best source on getting started with interviewing using these methods is Spradley's book *The Ethnographic Interview* (1979). We rely heavily on it here and recommend that beginners consult the original work.

GETTING STARTED

The very first step in interviewing is the selection of a topic area for exploration. It is easier for researchers to study areas in which they have little or no experience, because familiarity with a topic may cause them to overlook details about which they assume they are already informed. Also, researchers who are familiar with their topics of study may give informants the impression that the researchers already know the answers to the questions they ask; informants may feel that the researchers are testing them. When interviewing in an unfamiliar area, it is generally easier for a researcher to take the role of a student and orient to learning from the informant.

After selecting at least a general topic, the researcher must find an informant. Jeffrey Johnson (1990) describes several strategies for selecting informants. For exploratory interviews, researchers might select informants using random or nonrandom strategies. Random strategies are typically used when a random, representative sample has been drawn for interviewing with a questionnaire and in-depth interviews are to be conducted with a subset of the larger sample. In that case, a randomly selected subset may be taken or individuals can be identified by their personal characteristics (social class, gender, and so on) and then interviewed further.

Usually, however, nonrandom strategies are used for exploratory interviewing. A nonrandom or convenience sample does not necessarily imply that informants were not chosen without a prior plan. In fact, there are a variety of types of convenience samples. Informants may be chosen haphazardly or truly without a prior plan, or they may be chosen for theoretical reasons. For example, a researcher might select informants or groups of informants by using a stratified convenience sample (Johnson 1990), where important variables such as gender, social class, and role may be used to guide the selection. Some studies focus on social networks or the location of influential individuals and so may best use a "snowball" sampling technique, where individuals who are interviewed name other individuals for interviewing.

Although it is important that the selection of informants be guided by the theoretical requirements of the study, the development of fruitful relationships with informants, in practice, also depends upon the individual characteristics of the informant and the researcher. Spradley (1979: 46-54) outlines the characteristics that are important in an informant. An informant should have expertise in the area that the researcher wishes to study or learn about. This means that the person(s) identified for interviewing should have at least a year or more of full-time experience or three to four years of part-time experience in the topic area. The more experience an informant has, the better. The informant should be currently involved in the activity or area of interest and not retired or withdrawn from it. An informant also should have time to speak with the researcher. Although some busy people may make time to sit and talk, it is necessary that an informant be able to devote a few sessions of one hour or more to the project. Finally, an informant needs to be able to speak as a member of the culture in the usual language, and not overly interpret or analyze from some imagined outsider's perspective, so that the researcher can obtain an "insider's" knowledge of the topic.

The next stage is to get started with the interview itself. Spradley (1979) describes several steps in conducting exploratory interviews. After choosing a topic and locating informants, the researcher's next step is to begin interviewing with broad, descriptive questions before moving to more focused questions to understand local perceptions and categorizations of experience. Elicitation at this stage is broad and exploratory. As the researcher learns more about a topic and a group, relevant questions regarding meaningful areas for exploration become clearer and questions become more focused. This step may involve detailed elicitation of items relevant to a specific topic. Finally, with a complete set of (insider) terminology relevant to a particular topic or domain, the researcher can apply more highly structured interview techniques.

Spradley (1979:85-89) presents some introductory interviewing procedures that he refers to categorically as the "grand tour" and the "mini tour." For the researcher who is a novice to the topic, asking an informant for a grand tour can be especially informative. A grand-tour question is one that asks for a description of a place;

the informant does not necessarily literally take the researcher on a tour, but may do so. The researcher might also ask an informant to describe a "typical" day, a "typical" procedure, or how he or she did something last night or on some other occasion. This form of questioning also helps to establish the informant-ethnographer relationship and aids in putting both interviewer and informant at ease. The mini tour is a similar type of information gathering, but focused on a smaller area of activity, such as a specific part of a typical day.

Spradley describes several techniques for establishing the informant-ethnographer relationship and reducing anxieties on the part of both. An important starting point is the interviewer's explaining the reason for the interview and the purpose of the project. This also establishes the interview as different from an ordinary conversation. Throughout the interview, the ethnographer may need to repeat the explanation of the interview's purpose in different ways, along with expressions of his or her own ignorance, thus conveying to the informant that the ethnographer's purpose in conducting the interview is to learn. This helps to explain the asymmetry in the talking and asking of questions (see Briggs, Chapter 44, this volume). In a conversation, participants take turns; each person gets to ask and answer questions. In an interview, turn taking is unbalanced, with the interviewer asking many questions and the informant being encouraged to explain, describe, and give examples. To justify this, the ethnographer may need to express ignorance repeatedly, as well as interest in the topic and what the informant is saying.

FOCUSING ON SPECIFIC TOPICS

Mastery of local terminology and knowing what issues and questions to broach allow the ethnographer to focus on a specific topic. An essential part of moving ahead depends upon the researcher's knowing what questions are good ones. The important thing is that a question should ask about a relevant topic in a *subjectively* meaningful way.

An example of a more structured interviewing technique is the *taxonomic* approach. The purpose of taxonomic interviewing is to elicit both topical terminology and structure. Interview questions are structured to elicit categories, with set and subset relationships among items. Initial questions can be as simple as "What's that?" possibly followed by "What kind of _____ is it?" or "Are there other kinds of _____?" (Metzger and Williams 1966). Subsequent questions explore relations among items (possible set-subset relations), with further elicitation focused on types of items. Although this may seem to be an artificial method in terms of imposing categories upon the informant, in fact it is a very natural method of interviewing; a researcher might use it when trying to understand how someone does something or the nature of the materials the person uses, especially in the role of a learner.

Specific questions like "What kinds of _____ are there?" can be used to elicit domain items. A domain is a set of things that go together. This may be a set of attributes that something has or a set of types or examples of a specific thing, or it may be a set of sequences or developmental stages of something. Joseph Casagrande and Kenneth Hale (1967; cited in Spradley 1979: 110) list all the different types of relationships that a set may have. In exploratory interviewing, one of the interviewer's purposes is to obtain as complete a list as possible in local terms and to understand the meaning of each term. And, of course, the interviewer strives to understand informants' understandings of how the things are interrelated.

"Domain definition" interviews are known by a variety of names and involve a variety of procedures across the social sciences. In anthropology, researchers may use interviews with individuals or groups (focus groups) to collect and learn about things related to the topic of interest. In psychology, such interviews are called "item generation" interviews, the purpose of which is to elicit as many items on a given topic as possible. Psychologists use the results of such interviews to write items/questions for tests and attitude scales. Sociologists also conduct such "pilot" interviews to help them write more meaningful questions on surveys. They also may conduct such interviews using questions from existing surveys to understand the many ways respondents interpret survey questions and multiple-choice answers.

The many methods available for eliciting domain items differ mainly in style and in the amount of effort required to summarize responses. We have already mentioned the taxonomic interview, in which informants are asked to explain a domain in depth, listing the items in the set and their relationships to one another. Another direct interviewing technique is *free-recall listing* (discussed in detail below), in which informants are asked to list all of the things they can think of on a given topic. This technique is very efficient in terms of both the interviewer's and the informant's time. Because each informant is asked to provide a full list, fewer informants are needed to establish the set of relevant items than if each person provided only a few items. Also, because of the usual simple structure of questions and responses, the responses are generally quite readily tabulated across informants. Free-recall lists can be collected in one-on-one interviews or in groups (if collected prior to group discussion).

Some researchers prefer to study the actual texts of interviews (see in this volume Schaeffer and Maynard, Chapter 28; Baker, Chapter 37). Although such studies can be particularly informative (see Quinn's 1996 study of the use of metaphors and the development of a model of American marriage), the transcription alone is extremely time-consuming (see Poland, Chapter 30, this volume). Many researchers combine methods and do not rely solely on any one technique. Thus some may conduct free-recall listing but tape-record the interviews to check on the accuracy of their notes and to obtain details they may have missed. Tape-recorded interviews may provide more detailed accountings of case descriptions than the interviewers' notes alone.

ADDING STRUCTURE TO THE INTERVIEW

Researchers use elicitation interviewing techniques to gain rudimentary knowledge of specific topics about which their informants have considerable expertise. When a researcher has developed sufficient understanding of the topic area and has elicited items relevant to the topic or domain, he or she may be interested in moving to a more structured approach. A next step, for example, would be for the researcher to design an interview using the results of previous interviews.

A disadvantage in relying solely upon the results of open-ended interviews is that this makes it difficult for the researcher to make reasonable and valid comparisons across informants. To make comparisons across people and to summarize the results in a meaningful way, the researcher must ask all informants the same questions. With the open-ended procedures that we have described, all interviews may begin with the same question or may have similar skeleton outlines of questions to be asked, but each informant may need different probes and may be encouraged to explain in more or less detail at different points in the interview. Initial elicitation interviews are more flexible, with the goal of teaching the investigator about the material. This can result in considerable bias in the results. Some informants talk a lot or offer greater detail in their remarks. Some talk briefly, providing little detail and instead focusing on general issues. It is important for researchers to understand that they cannot conclude that their informants know nothing about a subject, or that the subject is not important to

them, just because the informants may say little about it. What informants say is a function of many factors in addition to knowledge, including the broader attributed relevance of the topic, memory, and even the informants' perceived self-worth.

The advantages of conducting open-ended interviews are found in the uses to which researchers can put the results. Researchers can use the information gathered in such interviews to develop psychological scales, to improve question wording in survey questionnaires, to study the categories informants use to classify and think about items in particular topic areas, and to develop relevant questions for the study of informants' specific beliefs about those items. In a bottom-up approach, the researcher interviews a small sample of individuals to gain an understanding of the topic and to gather items relevant to the topic of study. Some researchers do not go further than that initial set of exploratory interviews (see Figure 24.1A). Such findings, however, can only be suggestive, owing to the kinds of response bias that can affect open-ended interviews. In a variation on this approach, the researcher uses responses from the open-ended interviews to construct a meaningful interview protocol for use in exploring concepts that were suggested in the elicitation interviews (Figure 24.1B).

A number of different kinds of structured questions can be created from the results of open-ended interviews. Some examples include questions about informants' sociodemographic characteristics or behaviors, questions designed to gather information on informants' specialized knowledge, and questions about informants' perceptions, classifications, and beliefs concerning a particular domain (for a related discussion, see Weller 1998). Researchers in many fields rely upon open-ended interviewing techniques as a first step in moving toward greater structure. Psychologists, sociologists, and anthropologists all use open-ended interviewing techniques to gain understanding of particular topic areas, even if for somewhat different purposes. Anthropologists may also use domain items eventually to study the categorization of those items. Researchers usually create response categories themselves, naming and defining categories of responses and then coding informants' responses into those categories, but an alternative and preferable way to do this is for researchers to collect data directly from informants as to their categorization of items and then use that category system in the interpretation of responses.

Procedures for discovering informants' own categorizations of items are called *similarity data collection tasks.* These include techniques such as pile sorting, in which the researcher asks informants to judge which items go together into categories (we discuss pile sorting in greater detail below; see also Weller and Romney 1988:chap. 3). Another, related interviewing technique, sentence-frame elicitation, relies on direct statements and allows for the study of multiple sets of items (we also discuss sentence-frame elicitation below; see also Weller and Romney 1988:chap. 9).

The same elicitation methods can be used to ensure the reliability and validity of existing survey questions or other structured interview materials. The most important part of any study based on interviews that attempt to combine responses across people is that each and every respondent should have the same understanding/interpretation of the questions, and that interpretation should be the same as that intended by the researcher. After interview materials have been designed, the researcher can conduct top-down elicitation interviews, in which participants are not asked to answer the questions per se but instead are asked what the questions mean to them, what the possible responses might be, and why (Figure 24.1C or 24.1D). These interviews, whether conducted with individuals or groups, are a very important part of ensuring that questions are clear, that interpretations are the same across informants, that the response categories are appropriate and complete, and that respon-

dents' interpretations are consistent with the intended meaning of the questions.

◆ A Sampling of Techniques

We will now focus in greater detail on a sampling of commonly used elicitation techniques, several of which we have mentioned above. We present these techniques in the order in which they may be most appropriate in a research project. We pay particular attention to the theoretical question of interest, how the method contributes to the research project, the kinds of analyses appropriate for the data collected, and any possible drawbacks and problems with the methods as employed.

TAXONOMIC ELICITATION

As we have noted, the less that is known about a topic, the more appropriate are broad, general questions. Grand-tour and mini-tour questions are especially appropriate for getting started. Spradley (1979) illustrates the use of such questions with examples from his own work. He provides a verbatim excerpt of a conversation he had with a waitress in which he asked her to describe a typical night at work. Within the larger grand tour, he asked her a mini-tour question, namely, to describe what "setting up a tray" is. In his work with urban nomads, he used grand-tour questions to get descriptions of the city jail, for example. In a study of hunters and fishermen, Michael Orbach (1977; cited in Spradley 1979) elicited descriptions of the parts of a tuna boat from informants. A grand tour of a tuna boat oriented Orbach to the parts of the boat and indicated which parts or categories were important to the fishermen. Researchers' initial interviews should focus on discovering such categories and the terminology used by people in the setting to classify their thoughts and experiences.

In order to describe some aspect of culture or experience from the point of view of the informant, it is essential that the researcher understand the local dialect. A researcher might ask, for example, "What do they call _____?" or "What are your names for _____?" Thus during the initial stages of the project, the researcher's focus is on learning the local names for things, becoming familiar with local concepts, and, most important, uncovering locally relevant questions. Taxonomically structured questions are excellent for helping the researcher gain an organized understanding of a new topic.

A taxonomy is a structured set of inclusive relations among categories and items, such as set and subset relations among items. For instance, Steven Tyler (1969) discusses folk taxonomies and the features that distinguish categories. Charles Frake (1961) presents a detailed taxonomy of kinds of illnesses relevant to the Subanum in the Philippines. Although Frake had no initial interest in ethnobotany or illnesses, he found that these were among the top three topics of conversation among the Subanum. By asking, "What kinds of illnesses are there?" he elicited 134 words for illnesses. Subsequently, by applying more structured interviewing techniques, he also elicited the relations among the illnesses, including diagnostic criteria, and stages of progression of different illnesses.

FREE-RECALL ELICITATION

As the researcher learns more from informants about a topic, interviewing methods can become more structured and focused. Free-recall listing is related to taxonomic interviewing, except that in the free-recall method the interviewer requests only a single set of related items. When conducting taxonomic interviews, researchers explore items, categories, and subset relationships among items in order to flesh out much broader areas. In contrast, free-recall listing focuses on a single level of contrast, such that all items are members of the same set and there are no set or subset relations among them. In general, a researcher needs to have a basic understanding of the broader taxonomy in order to ask focused free-recall questions. Specifically, the researcher needs to know what questions are likely to elicit the category members. This type of elicitation is called *free-recall* because informants are asked to recall as much as they can on a topic without being given specific examples. It is referred to as a *listing* task because the purpose is to get an exhaustive list from each informant rather than a few short answers. The interviewer may use probes to increase the numbers of things recalled. These probes are generally of two types, and they serve two purposes: First, by repeating the question, the interviewer can emphasize the message that he or she is seeking an exhaustive list of items; second, by reading the last two to four items the informant has mentioned, the interviewer can improve the informant's memory or recall for more items.

The advantage of getting more information from each informant is that the researcher will then need fewer informants to obtain a complete mapping or listing of domain items. Although free-recall listing interviews may be conducted with individuals or with groups, individual interviews are more efficient. If a single question can generate approximately 10 to 20 responses from each informant and there is considerable overlap in responses among informants, as there often is, then a small sample of informants (10-20) may be adequate for the researcher to collect the most important items in a set. (For more detail on free-recall lists, see Weller and Romney 1988:chap. 2.) Focus groups retrieve about 60 percent as many items as do individual interviews (Fern 1982). With high agreement across groups (redundancy in items), a minimum of four groups with about eight people in each may suffice (Morgan 1996; see Morgan, Chapter 7, this volume). But in either case, the key factor that determines sample size is the point at which the set of items becomes "stable," meaning that few new items are being added to the set.

Frake's (1961) study of illnesses is a relatively simple and straightforward example of the elicitation of a full set of items. Illnesses constitute a coherent domain that is readily identified by informants. In a comparative study of illness concepts in Guatemala and the United States, Susan Weller (1984) wanted to be sure that the illness terms she selected for use in her study were recognized and understood by her informants, so she began her study with free-recall listing of illness terms from both a Guatemalan sample and a U.S. sample. In each sample, informants were asked to "name all the illnesses that they could think of." After listing the illnesses, each person was also asked to describe each illness.

Other domains must be elicited with series of related or contrasting questions. In a study measuring the attributes of success and of failure, Kimball Romney, Howard Freeman, and their colleagues asked informants to think of five friends and then describe the ways in which each was successful and/or a failure (Romney et al. 1979; Freeman et al. 1981). James Young (1980) was interested in why people sought health care from various sources in an indigenous community in Mexico. He could have asked, "Why do you or would you go to a doctor?" and "When would you go to a pharmacist?" However, contrasting questions such as "Could you tell me why you would go to a doctor and not a pharmacist?" and "Why would you go to a pharmacist and not a doctor?" revealed much more detailed and specific information. Young used questions that systematically compared all sources of health care and then asked about each pair.

In a study examining the reasons women choose either to breast-feed or to bottle-feed their infants, Susan Weller and Claibourne Dungy (1986) asked women to list all the reasons they might want to breast-feed, the reasons they might want to bottle-feed, and all the advantages and disadvantages of breast- and bottle-feeding. Weller and Dungy used a series of free-recall listing questions to elicit the reasons women choose a particular infant feeding method. Because they wanted to understand all of the reasons the women might have so that they could study the related decisions of individuals in the population, they used several questions to tap the broader set of reasons.

In a variation on the use of contrasts, in a study comparing adolescents' perceptions of adult/parental disciplinary actions, Weller, Romney, and Donald Orr (1987) elicited two related sets of items. First, they asked adolescents about things they might "do wrong" or things that teenagers might "do wrong." Then, for each item that was mentioned, they asked for a new list of possible adult/parental responses to that infraction. Because the purpose of the study was to examine the perceptions of possible physical abuse among ethnic groups, the researchers also took some items from the description of abuse in the emergency room of a university hospital to use in the next stage of their study in conjunction with items obtained from the free-recall lists.

Finally, free-recall listing can help researchers in validating or modifying existing questionnaires and tests. For example, C. E. Lewis, J. M. Siegel, and M. A. Lewis (1984) wanted to measure "stress" among children, but existing stress scales had been developed for adults, and it was not clear whether such scales would be meaningful when applied to children. This problem parallels the kinds of problems encountered by cross-cultural psychologists, who often wish to apply scales or tests developed through research on a particular group to groups in different countries or different ethnic groups (see in this volume Ryen, Chapter 17; Tierney and Dilley, Chapter 22; Latham and Millman, Chapter 23). Lewis and his colleagues conducted interviews with children, both individually and in groups, and asked them about all the things that make them "feel bad." From the lists of responses, the researchers could see whether there was a correspondence between existing adult scales for stress and the items relevant for children. The results indicated that children listed different items, and so the researchers developed a new stress scale for children.

INTEGRATING APPROACHES

An integration of these approaches can be seen in exploratory interviews conducted to discover cultural models for social support, for example. In the social sciences, *social support* refers to the support and assistance individuals might need from their social networks in various situations. Because it is unclear whether members of the general population share this concept, the researcher's initial questions might explore the problem area generally. The researcher might find a few folk taxonomy interviews useful for exploring the meaning of the concept, specifically to find out how to phrase questions in a meaningful way.

After discovering that words like *help, assistance,* and *support* do seem to have general meaning, the researcher might ask, "Sometimes things happen to people and they need some kind of help, support, or advice. Can you tell me situations in which someone might need some help, support, or advice?" Here, the goal would be to elicit the kinds of situations in which someone might require "social support." Then, in order to understand these situations better, the researcher might elicit another set of responses using questions such as "You mentioned [a particular situation]; what kind of help or support might be offered in that situation?" After eliciting this second set, the researcher might elicit a third set to find out about sources of support, such as could be drawn from the question, "You mentioned [a particular kind of help]—who or what might be the best person or place to do that?"

However, if initial interviews on the topic reveal that the meaning of the concept in question is not straightforward, the researcher's first task would be to find out if the concept even exists among members of the study population. It may turn out that the researcher needs to modify the whole initial plan for the interviews, so that respondents are asked, instead, "What people might offer you help or advice if you needed it?" From there, the researcher would move on to specific examples of the help offered by each person named. Such questions would help to elicit the cultural definition of social support through the use of specific examples.

Commonly, researchers then use such elicited items in further interviews or in conjunction with other elicitation tasks to increase understanding of the area of cultural knowledge under study. For example, in the study of social support, the next phase of the project might involve the researcher's using the elicited situations or scenarios where people need social support to study community beliefs about social support, to describe community behaviors and the kind of social support people actually have, or to see if there are relationships among community beliefs about social support, individual resources for social support, and health status.

A study conducted by William Dressler, Mauro Balieiro, and José dos Santos (1997) illustrates how these different kinds of interviews and data can be integrated. These researchers used ethnographic and case history information about social support to create a structured interview task about scenarios in which social support is needed. They asked informants about possible persons (parents, spouses, and others) who might fill particular needs. Dressler and his colleagues derived a cultural model of social support from a small sample of informants and then used a larger sample to test the relations among personal reports of social support resources, the cultural "ideal," and blood pressure.

SENTENCE-FRAME ELICITATION

Some structured interview tasks involve full statements rather than simply terms or other descriptors to be sorted by informants. Prime examples are psychological tests in which informants are asked about their agreement with various statements. These tests use sentence frames that allow for systematic comparison of one set of items, such as illnesses, with another set, such as illness attributes. An initial step in the research leading to the creation of such tests is the elicitation of the items and their properties. The researcher then uses another informant sample to collect the sentence-frame substitution data, which systematically compare each item with each property. The researcher then analyzes and interprets the response data.

Sentence-frame elicitation can be used in exploratory interviews and eventually re-applied in more highly structured tasks. For example, Jeff Johnson and M. L. Miller (1983) and Johnson and Ben Finney (1986) have described the importance of the presence of certain social roles in creating group cohesion and harmony in small to moderate-sized groups. Based on this earlier research, Johnson, James Boster, and Larry Palinkas (1991) sought to test hypotheses concerning the relationships among social roles, group cohesion, and well-being in isolated Antarctic work groups. An important element of the study was the elicitation of social roles relevant to a group of this kind. The study site was the Amundsen-Scott South Pole Station, which is located at 90 degrees south latitude.

Because the researchers had not been to the station prior to the study, they needed to interview individuals who had previously "wintered-over" (8.5 months of isolation) at the station in order to elicit statements concerning the types of culturally relevant informal social roles found in such small groups. During the period of the research, the winter-over crews at the station consisted of between 20 and 28 individuals. The researchers compiled an extensive list of previous winter-over crew members from South Pole Station and made arrangements to interview seven individuals in depth concerning their experiences during their winter-overs, particularly with respect to the informal social roles of various group members.

Because the number of crew members was relatively small, the researchers asked each informant to list the members of his or her winter-over crew, either by their initials or by their first names. Upon completing the list, the informant was asked to describe "how each individual crew member got along with others in the group" and to discuss the "types of roles each played in the group." The following extract is from one of the interviews with a female scientist we will call Pat. The italicized portions of the transcript are examples of the types of statements the researchers identified as pertinent to the informal roles in question.

Interviewer: Why don't we get the initials of the people?

Pat: All 20 of them? There's me; that's P.D., R.T., F.M, G.S., T.F., N.P., L.T., I.B., B.L., L.S., S.H., K.D., D.T., T.C., L.S2., R.K., K.R., R.B.

Interviewer: We'll come back to you last. Describe how these people interacted in the group, the kind of roles they played in the group—if they hindered things, if they helped things. How about R.T.?

Pat: *This was your class clown you're looking for or suggesting as part of the group. He was definitely one of the motivating people on station.* He was one of the science people, and most of the science crew out here was quite young, and I think that had a lot to do with the fact that we all got along so well, because we were around the same age. *But he was the motivator*—maybe not the motivator, but if you said, "P., we're going to do this," he was there for it. *He was very good professionally as well as personality-wise, very* intelligent and he was fun, a good person.

Interviewer: You said he was always there, he was always there to help you if you needed that?

Pat: Yeah, when he could. He was always more concerned with his project than anyone else's, obviously, because his grant was very important to him. *His work was very, very important to him.* But in time of "Hey, we've decided we're going to watch James Bond movies all night, it's going to be James Bond night," P. would be making popcorn for the event and saying, "Yeah, that's a good idea. Let's do that." *He may never have initiated something or made a suggestion, but he was always there for the event and made sure he supplied something,* whether it's just a hilarious night of—I don't even know, joking, running around, shaving his hair off except for down the middle . . .

Interviewer: What about F.M.?

Pat: He was a NOAA [National Oceanic and Atmospheric Administration] officer. I hope you get to meet him this evening; he's supposed to be coming down to dinner with us. F.'s a *very quiet person,* until you get to know him or until he has sort of a punch line to the story, and then he'll just blurt out and then continue doing what he's been doing. *So he was the person who everyone got along with.* If there was a problem, you knew F. wasn't part of it. And if—we just had a reunion recently, and the woman who was sending out the invitations for the reunion, most of them she put her name on to respond to, and about four or five of them she put "Respond to F.," because he was just the guy that everybody liked. There wasn't anything spectacular about him except for the fact that he—I've seen him angry once, I think—and *he was proba-*

bly the stable person on the base. I think we had two of those.

The interview continued until all crew members, including the informant, were discussed in depth. The interviews were then transcribed and two of the researchers took on the task of identifying all statements in the interviews relating to either the informal role characteristics or the social interaction characteristics of winter-over crew members (the italicized portions in the extract). Each of the researchers compiled a complete list of statements and then the two compared their lists for overlaps. Those statements that were most often identified by both researchers were then identified and sorted by similarity. For example, the statements "so he was a person who everyone got along with" and "he was the guy everybody liked" would have been seen as similar in intent.

Once the researchers had identified categories of roles, they selected the statement that best represented a category for inclusion in the final list of sentence frames. Table 24.1 shows the 11 frames that were finally used in the study. Sentence frame 7, for example, was chosen as the frame best reflecting the types of informal roles concerning someone "everyone got along with" and "everybody liked."

It is important to note that there are a number of other considerations for selecting frames that may relate to wording or the negative or positive valence of a statement. In this study, the researchers excluded statements of either a negative or valued (e.g., like or dislike) nature in favor of more value-neutral items. In preliminary tests of the frames and other questions, Johnson et al. discovered that the crew members felt too self-conscious making judgments concerning liking or even degrees of friendship due to the interactive intensity of the group setting.

Because the informants in this case were highly literate, the sentence completion task was done with paper and pencil. With a nonliterate group, an interviewer could

Table 24.1   FINAL SET OF SENTENCE ELICITATION FRAMES CONCERNING THE INFORMAL ROLE PROPERTIES OF CREW MEMBERS

1. _____ is a natural leader in getting things done around station.
2. _____ is a leading organizer of parties and other social events.
3. _____ is one of the station entertainers or comedians.
4. _____ is a good listener and serves as a counselor or confidant for a number of people on station.
5. _____ always volunteers to pitch in and help out whenever s/he can.
6. _____ is particularly involved in and committed to his/her work.
7. _____ doesn't just hang out with one group but is really everybody's buddy.
8. _____ is someone who you can really count on to come through in a jam.
9. _____ is fun to tease or joke with, s/he takes it in stride.
10. _____ is a good storyteller.
11. _____ serves as a peacemaker, is very good at helping people resolve their differences.

have read each of the sentence frames as well as each of the crew members' names (items). In any case, it is important that researchers recognize how potentially demanding this kind of task can be, particularly in face-to-face interviews. For example, if there are 20 crew members (items) and 11 sentence frames, an informant will have to evaluate 220 individual statements.

Data of this type are amenable to a number of analytic techniques that will help to reveal underlying structure and allow the researcher to assess patterns of agreement among informants to determine overall consensus. Volney Stefflre (1972), for example, who refers to data matrices constructed from sentence elicitation tasks as "item-by-use matrices," used a method that sorts the rows and columns of a matrix according to row and column similarities. Boster and Johnson (1989) used hierarchical clustering, correspondence analysis, and multidimensional Guttman scaling in analyzing the similarities and logical relations between and among fish (items) and their characteristics (sentence frames). (Weller and Romney 1990 provide an excellent background discussion of appropriate analytic methods for data of this type.)

A common problem in the elicitation of names is the omission of names due to limits on human recall. Invariably, even in the relatively small groups (20-28) under consideration in Johnson et al.'s study, informants would forget to list some fellow crew members. This was not a big problem in the winter-over project, because the researchers' probing and reading through the lists helped facilitate the recall of all members of this rather limited domain. But what about domains that are larger and less well bounded? We discuss this problem in a later section of this chapter, where we consider the use of various techniques for eliciting names in the study of social networks.

ELICITATION OF STATEMENTS FOR STUDIES OF BELIEFS

Many elicitation studies focus on belief structures. In one such study, Jeffrey Johnson and David Griffith (1996) were interested in understanding the intracultural variation of knowledge concerning the toxicological risks of eating seafood in the United States. A primary portion of the overall research effort involved the elicitation of statements from informants concerning the risks of eating seafood as part of a cultural consensus analysis (Romney, Weller, and Batchelder 1986). Cultural consensus analysis is a formalization of the notion of culture as consensus. In such analysis, the researcher first tests whether responses to a series of related questions exhibit a single pattern or theme and thus can be considered to reflect a single set of beliefs for those questions. The researcher then uses the same method to estimate the group's aggregated responses to the questions and how much each individual's responses agree with those of the group.

In the study under consideration, Johnson and Griffith initially selected a purposive sample of expert informants for the elicitation of free-recall lists of different types of pollution. They asked the informants to "list all the possible types of pollution that can be found in the sounds, bays, and nearshore waters of the Atlantic Coast" (e.g., coastal erosion and acid rain). They then asked the informants to list all the possible problems that might have been caused by these types of pollution (e.g., deformities in sea life or diseases in fish) and to list all estuarine and marine species they know about that might be affected by the different types of pollution elicited in the first step (e.g., tuna, clams, crabs). Based on these initial interviews, Johnson and Griffith identified 12 types of pollution, 11 causes of pollution, and 10 species for use in a further set of interviews.

Johnson and Griffith conducted a second set of elicitation interviews with a convenience sample of informants that included people in the coastal plain of North Carolina who had some environmental and ecological knowledge of the coast. The informants were commercial fishermen and longtime coastal residents of various ethnic backgrounds. The researchers typed up cards showing the different kinds of pollution, the problems these types of pollution might cause (e.g., deformities in sea life), and the species affected (e.g., swordfish, oysters) and presented the cards to each of the informants individually. They asked

each informant to (a) sort the types of pollution into piles according to their similarity, (b) link each of the pollutants to the possible problems they cause, and (c) identify which of the species the pollutants would affect the most. The researchers also asked each informant to explain his or her answers. The interviews were taped and later transcribed, and the researchers conducted a search for statements in a process much like that used in the frame elicitation analysis discussed earlier.

Three researchers independently reviewed the transcribed interviews and listed all statements that dealt with informants' descriptions of the relationships among seafood, pollutants, human health, and other risks. Those statements with the highest reliability (those identified by most or all of the researchers) were considered for use in the study. Statements that were redundant were removed, and the remaining statements were edited for clarity, but not so much as to alter the intent and language of the informants' original statements. About half of the statements selected were positive (e.g., "Heavy metals cause sores on both fish and people") and about half were negative (e.g., "Heavy metals are necessary nutrients for both fish and people"). The researchers balanced the statements this way to avoid possible response-set bias patterns in subsequent data collection (e.g., a lot of yes or a lot of no answers). Table 24.2 lists a sample of 8 of the 53 statements eventually used in the study.

The researchers administered the final statements to a random sample of 142 informants who were interviewed face-to-face and stratified on the basis of rural versus urban residence, coastal versus inland residence, ethnic identity, and socioeconomic status. Two comparison subsamples consisted of university students and marine scientists. The interviewers asked the informants to state whether each of the 53 statements was true or false, and to take a guess if uncertain about any of them. The researchers analyzed the data using the cultural consensus model (Romney et al.

Table 24.2 **EXAMPLES OF STATEMENTS ELICITED FROM INFORMANTS FOR USE IN THE CULTURAL CONSENSUS ANALYSIS**

1. If a seafood is being sold in a supermarket or restaurant, it must be okay.

2. Seafood that have shells are more protected from the effects of pollution than those that don't.

3. The dumping of human and industrial waste in the coastal waters can cause sores and lesions in some marine species.

4. We rarely eat contaminated fish, since they usually die before they even get caught.

5. Sea life can swallow trash, causing them to die.

6. Although not always directly lethal, pesticides can affect the reproductive success of many marine organisms.

7. Most people don't think much about the possible dangers of eating seafood.

8. Much of the pollution dumped into coastal and ocean waters has no effect on the flavor of seafood.

1986) to determine the level of agreement within and across the subsamples and to estimate each group's preferred answer to each question.

Parenthetically, this is a good example of a hybrid combination of research sequences A and D from Figure 24.1, in which the researchers used the elicitation of items (pollutants, problems, and marine species) in a structured task (i.e., a pile sort) to help them to discern statements about the relationships among the items. This would have been difficult to achieve through the use of less structured interview methods. The researchers then used the elicited statements in a more structured interview format in order to understand and compare systematically the informants' knowledge about marine pollution and seafood safety.

NETWORK ELICITATION

Researchers concerned with the study of social networks usually need to elicit the names and characteristics of a large number of informant ("ego") alters, including friends, family members, sex partners, and needle-sharing partners (McCarty et al. 1997; Brewer, Garrett, and Kulasingam 1998; Brewer, Garrett, and Rinaldi 1999). An important concern, particularly with respect to comparisons across egos, is the informant's ability to recall accurately all the alters in a given context. This is similar to free-recall listing, but here the lists contain names rather than cultural items of one kind or another.

There is an important distinction between the two methods, however, in that there are different consequences in terms of issues of reliability and validity. As we noted earlier with respect to the free-recall listing of cultural items, knowledge is by definition shared among informants; this implies that only a few interviews should elicit a valid list of cultural items. On the other hand, the elicitation of names of acquaintances from an individual informant involves knowledge that is unique to that informant alone; therefore problems of reliability and validity are relegated to each individual interview. The comparability and validity of interviews will depend on the interviewer's ability to elicit an exhaustive list from each informant. (There is a long-standing debate on the validity of retrospective data of this kind. For reviews of this issue with respect to social networks, see Bernard et al. 1984; Johnson 1994.)

Although there are limitations and constraints on individuals' ability to recall people, events, and behaviors, there are a number of things interviewers can do to help informants to recall items of interest. To illustrate some of these methods, we use an example from the research of Devon Brewer and his colleagues (1998, 1999) on the elicitation of the names of sexual and drug injection partners. Accurate information on the numbers and frequency of both sexual contacts and drug injection partners of infected individuals is critical for the understanding and control of the spread of HIV and other sexually transmitted diseases. The problem in question is that of getting informants to recall the names of individuals who may vary widely in relational strength (close versus distant), length of interaction (limited versus frequent contact), and time of last contact (recent versus distant past). In addition, there is a need to control for what is called forward telescoping of the recall of events (e.g., sexual partners) that may have actually happened before the recall period of interest.

In the elicitation of the names of an ego's friends, family members, sex partners, and others, the extent to which responses will be reliable and accurate will depend to some degree on the recall period of interest and the skills of the interviewer in helping the informant to remember. Brewer and his associates describe how interviewer prompting of the informant by reading back the list of names several times improved recall by about 10 percent. (Note that this kind of probe parallels one of those recommended for free-recall listing.) Returning to name elicitation at later points in a longer interview improved recall an additional 2 percent.

To improve informants' ability to recall people, some researchers employ different types of cues (e.g., social proximity, chronology, location, social role) or anchoring (i.e., providing a mnemonic point of refer-

ence) in which further information is gathered on those already recalled that might help to improve the informant's recall ability (e.g., Brewer et al. 1999; Fraser and Hawkins 1984). In the use of social proximity cues, the informant is asked to provide information about other persons the elicited individuals may know or interact with. The informant is then asked to recall if he or she had interacted in specific ways (e.g., had sex, injected drugs) with anyone in the set of newly listed people but had forgotten to mention them earlier. In addition to social proximity, interaction contexts or locations and social roles can be used as cues to aid in enhancing recall. Brewer et al. (1999) describe this process this way:

> To assess the list of location and role cues, we first noted all the responses our subjects gave to the questions about locations where subjects interacted with partners and partners' role relationships. Then we compiled a list of all the locations and roles mentioned by two or more subjects to ensure that the locations were not idiosyncratic. . . . To administer these cues, the interviewer says each location/role (in an individually randomized order) and asks the subject to think of all persons with whom she or he has interacted/had sex/injected drugs in that location or has that kind of relationship. The interviewer then asks the subject to list any of these other persons if she or he had sex/injected drugs with them during the recall period but forgot to mention before. (P. 5)

This is a nice example of how a series of questions can help in the overall elicitation of more complete, and hence more accurate, information, particularly for the types of idiosyncratic knowledge discussed here. The elicitation sequence involves the generation of names, prompting through the repetition of responses, followed by various cues as references, and in turn by further elicitation of names in relation to the cues. As in sequence B in Figure 24.1, these elicited names can subsequently be used in more structured interviews (e.g., survey) that target information on particular aspects of the social relations themselves.

VISUAL ELICITATION

Sometimes verbal questioning is inadequate for eliciting data of interest. In such cases, visual approaches may be more effective. Photographs, artifacts, actual items of interest, or virtually anything that can be visualized can be used in the elicitation process.

William Foote Whyte (1984) refers to such visual stimuli as projective aids or devices. Projective devices are appropriate for use in a wide range of settings, especially when the subject matter or domain defies the use of strictly verbal or written approaches, such as cards with the names of items on them. This can be the case when the nature of the subject matter of interest is especially difficult to characterize in linguistic terms or when informants themselves lack written language or are preliterate, as in the case of young children (Johnson et al. 1997).

There are numerous examples of the use of such devices in the literature. They include plant and animal specimens (Boster 1987), pictures of preschool children (Johnson et al. 1997), maps (Johnson 1990), drawings of occupations and rituals (Ericksen and Hodge 1991-92), and photographs of different types of processed meats found in grocery stores (Johnson and Griffith 1998). Visual items can be treated in the same manner as the verbal stimuli discussed in previous examples. Researchers can ask informants to relate items, determine the subjective similarity among them, describe what they see, or express any emotions they feel about the visual content.

Johnson (1990), for example, was interested in informants' subjective understanding of social class and status in the context of the small midwestern community where they lived. Understanding community ideas concerning social class posed a challenging problem, because these concepts were not easily articulated. The solution, in part, involved the use of visual materials and the interviewing of community experts. Johnson took photographs of the houses of 30 informants who had been interviewed earlier as a part of an ethnography of food consumption in the community. The 30 photographs were numbered, and each was encased in plastic for greater durability. Figure 24.2 shows two of these photos, which are representative of houses that were literally on "opposite sides of the tracks."

Johnson visited real estate agencies and city hall in attempts to identify and interview experts who would have knowledge about housing in the community. He presented the photographs to real estate agents, city housing inspectors, and code enforcement officers, focusing the interviews on housing values, neighborhood characteristics, and other types of information that would help him to understand the social and economic statuses of the original 30 informants and their households. Johnson asked the experts to sort the photographs into piles, as many or as few as they liked, and to make sure that photographs in given piles were similar to one another in "some way"—the nature of the similarities was left totally up to each informant (such a technique is often referred to in the literature as an *unconstrained judged similarity task*). Upon completion of the sorting task, Johnson asked each expert to explain in detail the reasoning for his or her placements. These explanations contained information that helped Johnson to discern not only the hierarchical nature of community organization itself, but also the relationship between status within the community and status in the world outside of it. As one expert informant put it in explaining one of the groupings, "Upper-class within the community, but nationwide would only be up-

Figure 24.2. Examples of Informants' Houses
NOTE: Houses A and B are literally "on different sides of the tracks" in the community.

per-middle-class." The data collected were both quantitative and qualitative. The pile sort of house photographs could be compiled and the relationship among photographs visualized using multidimensional scaling, and the qualitative descriptions could be used in ethnographic description and the interpretation of analytic results (see Johnson and Griffith 1998).

Ever-improving photographic technology facilitates researchers' use of visual devices in the study of a wide range of subjects. For example, digital cameras place picture taking, development, and production almost entirely in the hands of the researcher, making this an especially practical approach for elicitation, even in the remotest areas.

REPERTORY GRID ANALYSIS

A final approach is particularly noteworthy because it parallels many of the issues discussed in this chapter. Repertory grid analysis (Kelley 1955; Bell 1990) comes originally from psychology, but has spread to organizational research, computer science and knowledge acquisition, psychiatry, and nursing. Like some of the ap-

proaches discussed above, repertory grid techniques can be primarily qualitative or exploratory (e.g., using narratives), primarily quantitative or explanatory (e.g., applying computerized interviewing), or a blend of the two. Ultimately, however, as with all elicitation methods, the approach aims to identify the subjective understandings of individuals concerning some aspect of the world around them.

The main idea of repertory analysis interviewing is similar to free-recall listing, but the researcher's ultimate goal is to find elements of a domain that are subjectively viewed in a bipolar manner, leading to what are termed *constructs*. This stems from psychologist George Kelley's (1955) early work on personal construct theory. For example, the different social roles and role attributes elicited for the South Pole study (see Table 24.1) could also have been elicited with respect to bipolar distinctions or constructs, such as hard worker versus slacker. The initials of the winter-over crew members elicited in the interview with the informant Pat could have been written on cards. Pat then would have been asked to compare the individuals represented by the cards in triads (i.e., groups of three), possibly drawn at random, and asked to explain who is most different among the three cards or which two out of three are the most similar. She would then have been asked to explain the bases for her distinctions. The interview itself would have elicited social roles and role characteristics similar to what were elicited using a simple list. The following is an example of how 2 of the 11 roles and role attributes could be formatted in terms of bipolar constructs:

Hard worker—slacker
Count on—undependable

These constructs would serve eventually to uncover each informant's subjective assessment of the degree to which each other member of the winter-over crew was a hard worker or a slacker, and so on for other polarities. The resulting data would then be put into a grid or matrix in which values across the rows containing constructs show the subjective placement of each of the winter-over crew members on the various bipolar continua, possibly on a five-point scale. The resulting data could then be analyzed in many of the same ways as data gathered using other elicitation techniques, including the application of multivariate methods, such as multidimensional scaling or principal-components analysis. (Johnson and Griffith 1995 briefly discuss the similarities between grid techniques and sentence-frame elicitation techniques in their study of travel agents' perceptions of tourism destinations in the Caribbean. For a more in-depth discussion of repertory grid techniques, see Fransella and Bannister 1977.)

◆ Conclusion

As we have seen, elicitation techniques can be applied at many points in the research process. Researchers can use such techniques at the questionnaire design stage of a project, to support the interpretation of questionnaire responses, to help them to interpret interview transcripts, to enhance ethnographic description, to aid them in the modeling of subjective understandings, or any combination of these. Ultimately, elicitation techniques, no matter where in the research process they are employed, serve to curb researcher biases and to increase the production of reliable and valid findings.

We have presented and discussed several examples of elicitation interviewing techniques used by researchers today. Preparing such a review might appear to be a daunting task, given the vast array of disciplines and fields of study that are currently incorporating these techniques, but despite differences in researcher backgrounds and interests, all elicitation techniques have a similar aim: Almost universally, researchers employ them so that they can better understand, describe, capture, and model tacit knowledge. Whether researchers' use of such techniques is exclusively qualitative, exclusively quantitative, or a combination, elicitation interviewing is central to improving our understanding of how people see the world.

■ References

Abdolmohammadi, M. J. and A. Wright. 1992. "A Multi-attribute Investigation of Elicitation Techniques in Tests of Account Balances." *Behavioral Research in Accounting* 4.

Baer, R. D. 1996. "Health and Mental Health among Mexican American Immigrants: Implications for Survey Research." *Human Organization* 55:58-66.

Bell, R. C. 1990. "Analytic Issues in the Use of Repertory Grid Technique." *Advances in Personal Construct Psychology* 1:25-48.

Bernard, H. R. 1994. *Research Methods in Anthropology.* Walnut Creek, CA: AltaMira.

Bernard, H. R., P. D. Killworth, D. Kronenfeld, and L. Sailer. 1984. "The Problem of Informant Accuracy: The Validity of Retrospective Data." *Annual Review of Anthropology* 13:495-517.

Boster, J. S. 1987. "Agreement between Biological Classification Systems Is Not Dependent on Cultural Transmission." *American Anthropologist* 89:914-19.

Boster, J. S. and J. C. Johnson. 1989. "Form or Function: A Comparison of Expert and Novice Judgements of the Similarity of Fish." *American Anthropologist* 91:866-89.

Brewer, D. D., S. B. Garrett, and S. Kulasingam. 1998. "Forgetting as a Cause of Incomplete Reporting of Sexual and Drug Injection Partners." *Sexually Transmitted Diseases* 26(3):166-76.

Brewer, D. D., S. B. Garrett, and G. Rinaldi. 1999. "Patterns and Recall of Sexual and Injection Partners." Paper presented at the Third Biannual Meeting of the Society for Applied Research in Memory and Cognition, July, Boulder, CO.

Casagrande, J. B. and K. L. Hale. 1967. "Semantic Relationships in Papago Folk-Definitions." In *Studies in Southwestern Ethnolinguistics: Meaning and History of the Languages of the American Southwest,* edited by D. H. Hymes and W. E. Bittle. The Hague: Mouton.

D'Andrade, R. 1976. "Propositional Analysis of U.S. American Beliefs about Illness." In *Meaning in Anthropology,* edited by K. H. Basso and H. A. Selby. Albuquerque: University of New Mexico Press.

———. 1995. *The Development of Cognitive Anthropology.* Cambridge: Cambridge University Press.

Dressler, W. W., M. C. Balieiro, and J. E. dos Santos. 1997. "The Cultural Construction of Social Support in Brazil: Association with Health Outcomes." *Culture, Medicine, and Psychiatry* 21:303-35.

Ericksen, K. P. and R. W. Hodge. 1991-92. "Occupations and Ritual in Contemporary Egypt." *Journal of Quantitative Anthropology* 3:207-27.

Fern, E. F. 1982. "The Use of Focus Groups for Idea Generation: The Effects of Group Size, Acquaintanceship, and Moderator on Response Quantity and Quality." *Journal of Marketing Research* 19:1-13.

Fowler, F. J., Jr. 1995. *Improving Survey Questions: Design and Evaluation.* Thousand Oaks, CA: Sage.

Frake, C. O. 1961. "The Diagnosis of Disease among the Subanum of Mindanao." *American Anthropologist* 63:113-32.

Fransella, F. and D. Bannister. 1977. *A Manual for Repertory Grid Technique.* London: Academic Press.

Fraser, M. and J. D. Hawkins. 1984. "Social Network Analysis and Drug Misuse." *Social Service Review* 58:81-97.

Freeman, H. E., A. K. Romney, J. Ferreira-Pinto, R. E. Klein, and T. Smith 1981. "Guatemalan and U.S. Concepts of Success and Failure." *Human Organization* 40:140-45.

Hoffman, R. R. 1992. *The Psychology of Expertise.* New York: Springer-Verlag.

Holms, T. P. and R. A. Kramer 1995. "An Independent Sample Test of Yea-Saying and Starting Point Bias in Dichotomous-Choice Contingent Valuation." *Journal of Environmental Economics and Management* 29:121-32.

Johnson, J. C. 1990. *Selecting Ethnographic Informants.* Newbury Park, CA: Sage.

———. 1994. "Anthropological Contributions to the Study of Social Networks: A Review." In *Advances in Social Network Analysis: Research in the Social and Behavioral Sciences,* edited by S. Wasserman and J. Galaskiowicz. Thousand Oaks, CA: Sage.

———. 1998. "Research Design and Research Strategies." Pp. 131-71 in *Handbook of Methods in Cultural Anthropology,* edited by H. R. Bernard. Walnut Creek, CA: AltaMira.

Johnson, J. C., J. S. Boster, and L. Palinkas. 1991. "Social Structure, Agreement and Conflict in Groups in Extreme and Isolated Environments." Grant proposal submitted to the National Science Foundation.

Johnson, J. C. and B. R. Finney. 1986. "Structural Approaches to the Study of Groups in Space: A Look at Two Analogs." *Journal of Social Behavior and Personality* 1:325-47.

Johnson, J. C. and D. C. Griffith. 1995. "Promoting Sportfishing Development in Puerto Rico: Travel Agents' Perceptions of the Caribbean." *Human Organization* 54:295-303.

———. 1996. "Pollution, Food Safety, and the Distribution of Knowledge." *Human Ecology* 24:87-108.

———. 1998. "Visual Data: Collection, Analysis, and Representation." In *Using Methods in the Field,* edited by V. de Munck and E. Sabo. Walnut Creek, CA: AltaMira.

Johnson, J. C., M. Ironsmith, A. L. Whitcher, G. M. Poteat, and C. W. Snow. 1997. "The Development of Social Networks in Preschool Children." *Early Education and Development* 8:389-406.

Johnson, J. C. and M. L. Miller. 1983. "Deviant Social Positions in Small Groups: The Relation between Role and Individual." *Social Networks* 5:51-69.

Kadane, J. B. 1996. *Bayesian Methods and Ethics in a Clinical Trial Design.* New York: John Wiley.

Kelley, G. 1955. *The Psychology of Personal Constructs.* New York: Norton.

Lewis, C. E., J. M. Siegel, and M. A. Lewis. 1984. "Feeling Bad: Exploring Sources of Distress among Preadolescent Children." *American Journal of Public Health* 74:117-22.

McCarty, C., H. R. Bernard, P. D. Killworth, G. A. Shelly, and E. C. Johnsen. 1997. "Eliciting Representative Samples of Personal Networks." *Social Networks* 19:303-23.

Menn, L. and N. B. Ratner, eds. 2000. *Methods for Studying Language Production.* Mahwah, NJ: Lawrence Erlbaum.

Metzger, D. G. and G. E. Williams. 1966. "Some Procedures and Results in the Study of Native Categories: Tzeltal Firewood." *American Anthropologist* 68:389-407.

Morgan, D. L. 1996. "Focus Groups." *Annual Review of Sociology* 22:129-52.

Orbach, M. K. 1977. *Hunters, Seamen and Entrepreneurs: The Tuna Seinermen of San Diego.* Berkeley: University of California Press.

Quinn, N. 1996. "Culture Contradictions: The Case of America's Reasoning about Marriage." *Ethos* 24:391-425.

Romney, A. K., T. Smith, H. E. Freeman, J. Kagan, and R. E. Klein. 1979. "Concepts of Success and Failure." *Social Science Research* 8:302-26.

Romney, A. K., S. C. Weller, and W. Batchelder 1986. "Culture as Consensus: A Theory of Culture and Informant Accuracy." *American Anthropologist* 88:313-38.

Spradley, J. P. 1970. *You Owe Yourself a Drunk: An Ethnography of Urban Nomads.* Boston: Little, Brown.

———. 1979. *The Ethnographic Interview.* New York: Holt, Rinehart & Winston.

Spradley, J. P. and B. J. Mann. 1975. *The Cocktail Waitress: Women's Work in a Man's World.* New York: John Wiley.

Stefflre, V. J. 1972. "Some Applications of Multidimensional Scaling to Social Science Problems." In *Multidimensional Scaling: Theory and Applications in the Behavioral Sciences,* Vol. 2, edited by R. N. Shepard, A. K. Romney, and S. B. Nerlove. New York: Seminar.

Tyler, S. A. 1969. *Cognitive Anthropology.* New York: Holt, Rinehart & Winston.

Weller, S. C. 1984. "Cross-Cultural Concepts of Illness: Variation and Validation." *American Anthropologist* 86:341-51.

———. 1998. "Structured Interviewing and Questionnaire Construction." Pp. 365-410 in *Handbook of Methods in Cultural Anthropology,* edited by H. R. Bernard. Walnut Creek, CA: AltaMira.

Weller, S. C. and C. I. Dungy. 1986. "Personal Preferences and Ethnic Variations among Anglo and Hispanic Breast and Bottle Feeders." *Social Science and Medicine* 23:539-48.

Weller, S. C. and A. K. Romney. 1988. *Systematic Data Collection.* Newbury Park, CA: Sage.

———. 1990. *Metric Scaling: Correspondence Analysis.* Newbury Park, CA: Sage.

Weller, S. C., A. K. Romney, and D. P. Orr. 1987. "The Myth of a Sub-culture of Corporal Punishment." *Human Organization* 46:39-47.

Whyte, W. F., with K. K. Whyte. 1984. *Learning from the Field: A Guide from Experience.* Beverly Hills, CA: Sage.

Young, J. C. 1980. "A Model of Illness Treatment Decisions in a Tarascan Town." *American Ethnologist* 7:106-31.

25

THE RELUCTANT RESPONDENT

◆ Patricia A. Adler
Peter Adler

Although it is nearly a sociological maxim that people like to talk about themselves, researchers occasionally find that potential respondents are reluctant to be interviewed. This may have nothing to do with the character of the social scientist or the intended subject, but may be rooted in social patterns that are understandable and analyzable. Researchers generally encounter two types of reluctance, involving issues of *access* and *resistance*. These are lodged in different stages of the data gathering enterprise. Individuals who are reluctant to grant access will withdraw, be reticent, or demur when the interview is initially requested. They may be hard to find and even harder to secure for permission to study. Other people may agree to be interviewed, but then resist opening up or discussing certain kinds of topics. They may not be forthcoming during part or all of the interview.

The reluctance of respondents has been noted since the earliest days of recorded reflections on social scientific interviewing. More than 30 years ago, Howard Becker and Blanche Geer (1969) addressed respondents' inability or unwillingness to discuss certain matters:

> Frequently, people do not tell an interviewer all the things he might want to know. This may be because they do not want to, feeling that to speak of some particular subject would be impolitic, impolite, or insensitive, because they do not think to and because the interviewer does not have enough information to inquire into the matter, or because they are not able to. (P. 326)

Becker and Geer noted that social scientists had already begun to devise strategies to overcome such resistance, from experimenting with different approaches during the interview to probing for inconsistencies or illogicalities, to reacting to submerged data, when unearthed, in a matter-of-fact manner (see Becker 1954; Rose 1945). When resistance is not detected and overcome, they remarked, it is likely to result in significant data gaps. Further, other problems and areas of potential interest may remain undiscovered, and this can damage scholars' understanding of empirical issues and the theoretical extrapolations deriving from this base.

◆ Social Context

Now, more than ever, the reluctance of respondents may have developed into a problem of great magnitude. American society, as Jack Douglas (1971) long ago noted, is immense, highly complex, and pluralistic, composed of myriad different subgroups and subcultures, each having its cohesion and loyalty focused inward, away from the dominant, overarching society. Functioning in society's mass bureaucracy involves navigating through rules and regulations that are often more profitably skirted. Many groups operate within the context of opposition groups or movements, those who would critique, oppose, or eliminate their actions. This necessitates researchers' moving beyond the simplistic cooperation model of research to grapple with some of the characteristics of a conflictful view of social order (Douglas 1976). As a result, groups separate their terrain and knowledge into that which is publicly accessible —available to outsiders—and that which is accessible only to select companies of insiders. This may be the case for even the most seemingly innocuous groups, from informal collectives to formal organizations.

The rise of secrecy in U.S. society has been exacerbated by the expansion of litigation, as people increasingly use lawsuits as tools to force disclosures and redress grievances. To protect themselves against such damaging intrusions and costs, groups have become even more hidden. This has been made more difficult by advances in technology, which enable ever-greater surveillance over citizens (Marx 1988). Concealed audio and video devices record behavior, phone calls may be monitored and taped, Internet communication may be invaded, and secure documents and systems hacked. Records of individuals' lives, in this information age, are readily accessible to those with the necessary technological expertise, and privacy consequently has been diminished. All of these factors exacerbate individuals' reluctance to reveal too many aspects of their selves to others.

ETHICAL AND POLITICAL DEVELOPMENTS AFFECTING RELUCTANCE

In past times, research codes of ethics, both those informally taught and those formally codified by professional social science associations, privileged researchers' protection of the human subjects they studied. Scholars in training were taught through rhetoric and example that they should give careful regard to the welfare of the populations they studied. Social scientists routinely employed rules of confidentiality, safeguarding the identities of respondents in their published work. They widely practiced self-censorship (see Adler and Adler 1993), withholding information that could identify or harm respondents. They held strong loyalty tenets that allied them with the people who had opened up their lives to them and shared intimate details and experiences through their research relationships. They resisted pressures to reveal information that could threaten those relationships. For example, during John Van Maanen's (1983) study of the police, an incident occurred on a night when Van Maanen was doing a ride-along in a patrol car: A black man, in the course of being arrested, was beaten up. A dispute arose in which the man claimed he had been a victim of police brutality and the officers involved claimed he had resisted arrest. Investigators turned to Van Maanen, wanting to see if his field notes could shed some light on the competing charges. But Van Maanen withheld his notes, feeling that the loyalty bonds between his subjects and himself overrode other concerns. The research community sided with Van Maanen, and he safeguarded his subjects and data. Of course, such dilemmas can end up being quite complicated, because all sorts of legal, ethical, and moral concerns enter into the picture when researchers observe actions that are reprehensible. There may be times, therefore, when appeals to higher loyalties must supersede the protection of the people being researched.

Yet other research in the past exploited subjects for the gain of expanding scientific knowledge. Classic horror stories surfaced that generated alarm about the unchecked behavior of scientists. Among the most infamous examples are the U.S. government's medical experiments on the progression of syphilis, in which treatments that became known during the course of the research that could have reversed the fatal effects of the disease were withheld in order to preserve the original experimental design (Jones 1981), and psychological experiments on college students in which researchers tested compliance to authority by ordering subjects to administer (secretly fake) electric shocks to others strapped into electrode chairs to see how far people could be pushed to (allegedly) harm or kill others (Milgram 1965). These cases led a tide of change in public opinion, and the government sought to intervene into research behavior, turning formerly private decisions into public ones. Institutional review boards (IRBs), groups of individuals assigned to review research proposals with the intent of protecting human subjects, began to be formed in the 1970s, but this practice did not really take hold until the 1990s, when many universities mandated that all proposed research be approved by committee. IRBs privileged the moral good

of the country, the power of the law, and the protection of institutions sponsoring research (universities) from lawsuits over the informal loyalty ties between researchers and subjects. As a result, subjects could no longer be protected in the same ways as before (on the problems of protecting respondent confidentiality, see Picou 1996).

Some of the first test cases that came to national prominence in sociology shocked the research community. Mario Brajuha, a graduate student at the State University of New York at Stony Brook, was studying a restaurant when it burned down because of a fire of suspicious origin. When the police subpoenaed Brajuha's field notes, he refused to turn them over (Brajuha and Hallowell 1986). Rik Scarce, a graduate student at Washington State University, was studying animal rights activists when an animal research laboratory was invaded, equipment destroyed, and the animals "liberated." When the police subpoenaed Scarce's field notes, he refused to comply (Scarce 1994). In both of these cases, the researchers were denied the ability to shield their subjects from police inquiry, and the IRBs sided with the law. Brajuha was stripped of all rights, endured lengthy and expensive court battles, lost all his money as well as his family, and quit the field of sociology. Scarce, who was found to be in contempt of court, also experienced lengthy and expensive court battles and spent six months in jail.

A wave of concern washed over the research community as the new guidelines took effect. Researchers were mandated to place the public good over their moral obligations to respondents and deputized as agents of the state, required to report illegal and immoral behavior. As a result, when Eleanor Hubbard undertook an interview study of battered women who resisted their abuse by fighting back, she was clearly instructed that she should be vigilant in observing these "violent" women's behaviors; if they could strike their husbands, they might strike their children. She was ordered to report them to social service agencies should she see any indications of such tendencies. She was also instructed that she had to caution potential respondents, prior to obtaining their permission for interviews, that if they said anything that indicated they had taken part in illegal or immoral behavior, she was required to report them (Hubbard 1992).

Like Hubbard, all researchers now must caution respondents that the researchers' first loyalty lies with the state, and that respondents should regard researchers as deputized agents of the state. This declaration has a potentially chilling effect on research. It cannot help but exacerbate the reluctance of respondents who worry that their revelations might be used against them or their friends, colleagues, or family members. As a result, access to such respondents has been significantly diminished (Hamm and Ferrell 1998).

◆ The Spectrum of Reluctance

The variety of respondents who may feel some reluctance to be interviewed can be seen as falling along a spectrum of degrees of aversion to revealing aspects of self and/or being part of social scientific research. Depending upon their needs for secrecy or privacy, their fear of detection, and a host of other factors, individuals may want to guard themselves from talking to researchers, journalists, and a variety of other inquirers. Below, we discuss the range of respondents who might be particularly hesitant to be interviewed.

At the most anxious end of the spectrum of reluctance, more unwilling respondents, those we address specifically in this chapter, are scattered throughout society. They tend to cluster, however, around the top and bottom of the power, prestige, and socioeconomic hierarchies. In a cogent review of people who research "sensitive" topics, Claire Renzetti and Raymond Lee (1993) state:

It is probably possible for *any* topic, depending on context, to be a sensitive one. Experience suggests, however, that there are a number of areas in which research is more likely to be threatening than in others. These include (a) where research intrudes into the private sphere or delves into some personal experience, (b) where the study is concerned with deviance and social control, (c) where it impinges on the vested interests of powerful persons or the exercise of coercion or domination, and (d) where it deals with things sacred to those being studied that they do not wish profaned. (P. 6)

SECRETIVE RESPONDENTS

Some causes of reluctance can be found in individuals scattered across the wider spectrum of society. Especially fearful of being researched are people with secrets. Omnipresent in society, people with secrets live in fear that what they are hiding will be revealed to public attention. Despite the near-universal edict among social scientists that the identities of those they study must be protected, respondents who hold secrets are concerned about information leaking out. Most obvious among these are people who belong to secret societies (see Bellman 1984). This has often been an issue for anthropologists, who venture into indigenous cultures and sometimes find themselves among clandestine groups. For instance, Pamela Brink (1993) discusses the problems she encountered in studying the Annang, a covert women's cohort in a small, isolated African community. Like most secret societies, the Annang imposed sanctions against persons who revealed their secrets. This put Brink's respondents as well as Brink herself at personal risk of being "punished" several times for revealing the group's private matters.

Researchers need not venture onto foreign soil to confront such situations, however. Renée Anspach (1993) refers to the physicians in the neonatal intensive care unit she studied as members of a "closed" society. Much like a secret tribe, Anspach observes, these doctors had their own language, customs, and decisions that they sought to protect. Given the life-and-death judgments they were constantly making, these specialists feared retribution, lawsuits, or public humiliation if Anspach revealed information that was sensitive in nature. Even more radical in their secrecy were the Roman Catholic nuns who were the subjects of a study by Mary Anne Wichroski (1997). Wichroski had the challenging task of penetrating female monastic communities that practice codes of silence in truly cloistered societies. Beyond these extreme cases, many ordinary people hold secrets about themselves and others that they guard carefully, and that might be damaging to reveal.

SENSITIVE RESPONDENTS

Respondents who are being asked about delicate or sensitive topics may also display reluctance. Any personal issue that might cause embarrassment could fall into the "delicate or sensitive" category. Traditionally, people have been loath to discuss with interviewers their financial matters, health or disease issues, sexual conduct, drug use, and relational problems. Interestingly, Robert Weiss (1994:76) notes that survey researchers claim that income is, surprisingly, even more difficult to ask about than sex. Raquel Bergen (1993) endeavored to study marital rape, a highly sensitive topic about which women do not like to speak. Because obtaining access to women who had been raped in their marriages demanded that Bergen go through institutional channels, she had to obtain permission from the directors of appropriate women's organizations to do her research. Despite her gender and her background as a rape counselor, she was rejected by the vast majority of the institutions she contacted. Ironically, once she fi-

nally gained access to women for the interviews, she had little trouble getting them to open up. Similarly, Rosalind Edwards (1993) found that asking women about their private family lives was difficult. She referred to her respondents as putting "invisible walls" around their family lives (p. 186).

In our own research on upper-level drug dealers and smugglers (Adler 1985), we would not have been able to get these people to talk about their drug use had we not admitted (and, in fact, shared with them) our own patterns of use. Because of the illicit nature of the activity under study, respondents had an obvious mistrust of anyone prying into their business. However, as K. J. Day (1985; cited in Renzetti and Lee 1993:6) avers, there is no fixed private sphere. Areas of social life commonly shielded from others include sexual and financial matters. Concerning the former, a number of researchers have attempted to uncover the sexual proclivities of Americans. In the most recent major study, Edward Laumann and his colleagues (1994) included numerous checks and balances to try to ease the way for respondents to discuss the intimacies of their bedroom behavior. Despite such assurances, surveys concerning sexual practices have repeatedly been attacked or questioned by others regarding respondents' veracity (see, especially, Ericksen 1999). Particularly disturbing to social researchers is the notion that all people, not just members of certain groups or people discussing specific subjects, have confidences that they would prefer remain unrevealed. In this regard, almost all potential respondents should be treated as reluctant.

THE ADVANTAGED

Yet another group of people who have commonly been difficult for social scientists to access are the advantaged, those in positions of wealth, status, and power (see Odendahl and Shaw, Chapter 15, this volume). As Rosanna Hertz and Jonathan Imber (1995) note: "Few social researchers study elites because elites are by their very nature difficult to penetrate. Elites establish barriers that set their members apart from the rest of society" (p. viii).

Susan Ostrander (1984, 1995a) is one of the few sociologists who has successfully studied the upper class. Despite her success in this area, she has described in detail the arduous steps she has had to take to accomplish her various studies of elites (Ostrander 1995b). Because of their privileged position in society, upper-class individuals can parry the forays of social scientists trying to infiltrate their midst. Unlike members of downtrodden populations, who can often muster few protections to prevent people from intruding on and studying them, aristocrats in American society have many layers of shields that can keep social scientists at bay. Ostrander has proved that there are ways around these, but the relative paucity of research on the upper class serves as testimony to the difficulties researchers encounter in the field. Louis Corsino (1987) experienced some problems while he was trying to study the inner workings of political campaigns. With the knowledge and permission of the campaign managers, he researched the mayoral campaigns of Kevin White in Boston and Pete Wilson in San Diego. Despite his initial entrée, he was constantly under intense scrutiny regarding his political and research motives. Politicians, too, have been a group underresearched by sociologists, mainly because they have maintained the sanctity of access to their inner circles.

Celebrities. Another group of advantaged individuals who have traditionally been reluctant to be studied is made up of people with high visibility, such as celebrities, athletes, and opinion leaders. Used to being in the public eye and fearful of media exploitation or tabloid sensationalism, these people assiduously work to avoid being interviewed or portrayed in a negative light.

This makes gaining access to them extremely trying for social scientists. Joshua Gamson (1994), one of the few relatively successful researchers into this domain, has studied entertainment industry elites (entertainers, agents, managers). Hollywood types such as these are so wary of publicity seekers that they may see the social scientist merely as another gossipmonger. Our own research on a major college basketball team offers another example (Adler and Adler 1991). Entering the scene before the team's success and celebrity had struck, we were able to gain access and full insider status. At the same time, Peter gained celebrity status during the course of the research through his membership role with the team (Adler 1984). So necessary was it for us to establish a role that approximated the lifestyle of the players and coaches that Peter became swept up in the media attention, popularity, and stardom that was bestowed on other members of this scene, and he had to work to shield himself from the prying eyes and questions of outsiders.

Malcolm Spector (1980) has also discussed a similar problem: researching public figures. In his case, he was in the midst of two public controversies involving psychiatry in which the respondents drew the attention of the media. Because of the notoriety these people had accrued, they were wary of any incursion into their lives or opinions. People in the center of a well-publicized storm are not likely to give access to social scientists or others. We noted this as residents of Boulder, Colorado, in the 1990s, when swarms of media personnel descended on the community in relation to the JonBenet Ramsey murder case and the Columbine High School killings.

Organizations and corporations. Other powerful groups in society that desire to protect themselves from social researchers are organizations and corporations. Because corporate managers must safeguard organizational goals, they serve as gatekeepers, effectively keeping out unknown or nosy intruders. Robert Thomas (1995), who has conducted several studies of corporate executives, makes the point that, even though these elites are highly visible to their shareholders and employees, this visibility is not the same as accessibility: "Gaining access can be a tough proposition, even when the point of getting in is innocuous, well-intentioned, or attractive to key people in the organization itself. One reason is that business elites are quite good at insulating themselves from unwanted disturbances" (p. 4). Thus, through a variety of methods, corporate executives strive to keep in place the kinds of shields that will keep social researchers at bay.

Michael Useem (1995) also discusses the difficult times he had in trying to interview corporate executives. Many people he wanted to interview declined to receive him, were "unavailable" when he was able to see them, or were simply not very responsive to his questions. Years ago, we attempted to study a professional football team about momentum in sport, in the wake of having done interviews with the local professional baseball team (Adler 1981). Despite the fact that we had some people on the inside who could vouch for us, the football team denied us access because another author (not a social scientist) had previously written an exposé about drug use among team members. With corporate espionage, paranoid management, and industrial takeovers so prevalent in organizational life in the global business community today, social scientists are at a disadvantage in trying to study the elite circles of large companies.

Those vulnerable to litigation. The final group of elites who are wary of social scientific researchers are people with exposure to lawsuits. For example, one of Anspach's (1993) doctors in the neonatal ward said to her: "And for your notes, this is a very difficult ethical problem, iatrogenesis. I'm not particularly anxious to be called into court, and it is not in my self-interest to have this baby survive" (p. 185). Obviously, he was well aware of her presence, afraid of the ramifications of her report, and careful to warn her that she had better protect his interests. In our ethnography of a Hawaiian resort hotel, we worked for a year and a half to get management permission to conduct research (Adler and Adler 1999). After several years in the setting, however, two lawsuits were brought by employees against the resort. After that, our research access was systematically diminished, with approval being required for management interviews and that approval increasingly denied. Many of the kinds of elites discussed above, such as public figures, "deep-pockets" corporations, people under restraining orders, and those fearful of libel suits may be equally circumspect about allowing themselves to be interviewed or to become part of a research project.

THE DISADVANTAGED

The disadvantaged make up the final group in which reluctant respondents are likely to be found. These people, who lack the power to withdraw from researchers, may simply distrust the intentions and meanings of academic research. The poor, for instance, who may be more accessible and easier to find than the rich, still have many reasons to be careful about what social scientists discover about them. One particular group of people who have frequently come under the scrutiny of sociologists are those engaged in illegal activities, such as criminals and revolutionaries, and other "hidden" populations. W. Wayne Weibel (1990) defines these individuals: "The term 'hidden populations' refers here to a subset of the general population whose membership is not readily distinguished or enumerated based on existing knowledge and/or sampling capabilities" (p. 4). Most often associated with research on deviant groups, studies of such hidden populations are characterized by the difficulty involved in locating subjects (but for discussions of the facilitative aspects of gaining access to deviant groups, see Anderson and Calhoun 1992; Tewksbury and Gagné 1997). Ralph

Weisheit (1998) discusses how difficult it was for him to locate marijuana growers in rural areas. Not only were these people secretive about their activities, they were extremely scattered, living in remote locations.

Much criminological research is conducted with incarcerated populations, in part because active offenders are, as John Irwin (1972) notes, "hard to locate because they find it necessary to lead clandestine lives. Once located, they are *reluctant,* for similar reasons, to give accurate and truthful information about themselves" (p. 117; emphasis added). Bruce Jacobs (1998) describes how much difficulty he had in locating urban crack dealers. We encountered similar problems in our study of upper-level drug dealers and smugglers (Adler 1985). Although we were fortunate to have a next-door neighbor who became our key informant, we virtually had no other way to meet people than through the associates to whom we were introduced. Whenever respondents sense that the research might be threatening to them, they are likely to be cautious about allowing the inquiry to continue. Whether this is because much research deals with private aspects of people's lives, because of the possibility for information released to be incriminating, or because research impinges on political alignments in the community, social scientists can normally expect that people engaged in illegal activities will be loath to offer access (Lee 1993).

In contrast to elites who worry about lawsuits, less powerful people may be afraid of exposure to censure if they reveal too much to researchers. Subordinates in organizations who are bringing lawsuits against their employers might want to discuss their situations, but they may be under "gag orders" that prohibit them from engaging in this kind of disclosure. For example, in our study of a resort hotel, we interviewed a chef who was charging the resort with racial discrimination. While the lawsuit was pending, he could not discuss any aspects of the case or the treatment he received from the hotel's management. Less powerful people suing large corporations or governments may be concerned about getting "SLAPPed" (Pring and Canan 1996) back—that is, being sued by the organization for defamation, libel, or any action that they bring to make the group look bad. These people also need to be careful in talking to outsiders such as researchers. Thus disgruntled employees, angry citizens, and other people dissatisfied with the status quo might make interesting respondents, but they are frequently not allowed to be interviewed about their involvement.

Finally, people who may be at risk, especially because of their subordinate status, are likely to be reluctant respondents. Ramona Asher encountered this problem in her study of women married to alcoholics. Although the wives often wanted to talk about the emotional traumas they faced, the husbands, paranoid that something unseemly about them might be revealed, attempted to block these interviews (see Asher and Fine 1991). Similarly, a lower-level pastry chef at our resort, referred to us by mutual friends, declined our request for an interview because he had heard at work that talking to us might not be good for his job. Whenever employees are in a vulnerable position because of fear about losing their jobs, they may be disinclined to grant interviews. People who have been victimized may also be afraid to talk to researchers for fear of retaliation. Julia Brannen (1988:560) provides a number of examples in which her respondents feared negative reactions from their husbands in her study of marital difficulties. Finally, as Lee (1995) points out, potential subjects who are in dangerous situations—whether physical, financial, emotional, or relational—may be well-advised to keep their mouths shut.

NONWARY RESPONDENTS

Lest readers come away with the mistaken impression that all respondents are reluctant, we should point out that John

Dean, Robert Eichhorn, and Lois Dean (1969) provide a useful guide of types of respondents at the other end of the reluctance spectrum—those who are not reticent to talk to researchers. The "nouveau-statused," for instance, are people who have just been promoted or changed positions and are likely to want to open up about their experiences. "Old-timers" are respondents who no longer have a stake in the operations of the setting or who are so secure that they do not feel they will be jeopardized by what they say. "Frustrated" people may be rebels or malcontents who want to vent about their positions or the ill treatment they are receiving. "Rookies," or naive informants, may not even realize that they are revealing intimacies of the setting. They may be so new to the place that they have inadequate knowledge of and stake in the system to protect it. "Outsiders" may be people who are somewhat connected to a scene, but have a unique vantage point external to the culture or community. "Needy" members of a scene may fasten onto researchers because they crave attention or support and will talk to any sympathetic ear. "Subordinates," although discussed above as wary respondents, may sometimes be so hostile that they are willing to speak no matter the consequences. Finally, individuals on the "outs" are people who have lost power but may still be "in the know." Members of any of these groups of people may be particularly open to being interviewed.

◆ Overcoming Reluctance

In an attempt to provide some guidelines for researchers who need to overcome reluctance on the part of respondents, we outline various strategies below. Basically, these techniques are related to the two types of reluctance noted earlier: access and resistance. Problems related to getting access to subjects have plagued social scientists since formal research procedures were established. There is a wide range of possible conditions, and different researchers have arrived at some divergent, opposing viewpoints on how to overcome reluctance.

APPROACHING RESPONDENTS

Brannen (1988) asserts that researchers' success in attaining interviews, especially about sensitive topics, may be influenced by the *relationship between researchers and respondents*. She argues that researchers may facilitate their access to respondents if they cast the interviews within a "one-off" relationship (a transitory, as opposed to in-depth association, which assures anonymity). Respondents will have less fear, and therefore will be more forthcoming, if they believe they will never cross paths with the researchers again. According to this view, there is an ironic security in detachment, which creates anonymity and more likelihood for self-disclosure on the respondents' part. Irving Seidman (1991), too, asserts that the easier the access to interviewees, the more complicated the interview. This builds on the assumption in psychiatry that people can more openly disclose to others who are uninvolved in their lives. However, this opinion goes against the philosophy of other researchers, who believe that trust is best forged between a researcher and a respondent when a more personal relationship is established (see in this volume Warren, Chapter 4; Johnson, Chapter 5). Barbara Laslett and Rhona Rapoport (1975) suggest that repeated interviews will yield the best results, because this allows for the establishment of such relationships.

By returning to the same respondents several times, researchers may be able to broach more sensitive topics, and deeper intimacy may result. Some postmodern ethnographers have advocated interactive interviewing, in which respondents and researchers share personal and social experiences in a collaborative communication process that involves multiple interview situations (see Ellis, Kiesinger, and Tillmann-Healy 1997; see also Ellis and Berger, Chapter 41, this volume). Almost all current practitioners of ethnography have now adopted similar ideas about the importance of membership roles, contact with subjects, and in-depth involvement in subjects' lives (Adler and Adler 1987).

Feminist researchers have been at the forefront of the call to *empower respondents*. Criticizing the passive role of respondents in traditional interview situations, Ann Oakley (1981) asserts that methods such as coauthorship and collective consciousness-raising between researchers and respondents can give subjects more of a stake in the research process. Many researchers are now experimenting with various types of collaborative research ventures in which respondents are brought into the planning and analysis phases of the research (Clough 1994; Collins 1992; Smith 1989). Researchers may reduce problems of access to difficult-to-penetrate groups by entrusting group members with a say in what is written. As Bergen (1993) notes, "Research participants are empowered because they understand that their personal experiences are no longer raw material for the data mill but that they are active in sharing their stories with others and evoking change" (p. 202).

Heeding a similar cry, postmodern ethnographers believe that respondents should be given "voice" in their own stories (Denzin 1997). Merging notions of poststructuralism, feminism, and new journalism, these authors join with their respondents to produce polyvocal, subjective, poetic, and dramatic prose that incorporates equally the lives of researchers and respondents (see in this volume Fontana, Chapter 8; Denzin, Chapter 40; Ellis and Berger, Chapter 41; Richardson, Chapter 42). Central to all of these studies is the self, squarely situated in the research and openly available for inspection by those being studied (Clough 1992; Denzin 1997; Richardson 1997). Respondents are

also given an opportunity to see what the researcher has written, to respond to it, and to change what gets reported (Duelli Klein 1983; Ellis et al. 1997; Tripp 1983). Elliot Liebow (1993), for instance, went to great trouble to include what the homeless women he studied thought of his analysis, even to the extent of omitting materials to which they objected. Thus, through a variety of methods, postmodern ethnographers are bringing researchers into closer proximity to respondents, providing more mutual trust and intensifying the relationships between them. The expectation is, then, that problems of access are reduced in the process.

On a more traditional front, researchers have been debating for years the benefits of *providing goods, services, payments, or gifts* to respondents in order to gain access to them. Particularly important in research about organizations, payoffs can serve to cement the commitment that gatekeepers have to the continuation of a research project. According to Peter Yeager and Kathy Kram (1995), "The research must have an identifiable 'payoff' for the organization, and it must be presented in terms neither threatening to the organization's purpose nor foreign to its culture" (p. 46). Without some identifiable "profit," Yeager and Kram argue, organizations are not likely to welcome researchers. In studying deviant groups, often the only way researchers can get interviews is by making some monetary payoffs. Much of the research done on inner-city drug use, for instance, has relied on researchers' offering small pecuniary incentives to respondents (Hamid 1990; Johnson et al. 1985; Dunlap et al. 1990).

Survey researchers have long favored the use of incentive fees to gain the cooperation of reluctant respondents. For example, in their comprehensive study of the sexual practices of Americans, Laumann et al. (1994) found that "the judicious use of incentive is cost efficient since so much of the expense is due to interviewer travel time and costs incurred returning to residences" (p. 56).

Exchanges can be other than financial, however. For instance, Irwin (1972) frequently provided loans, transportation, accommodations, and other favors to the nonincarcerated criminals he studied. We, too, were often in the position of offering our services as baby-sitters to the drug dealers we studied to secure the research bargain (Adler 1985). By putting ourselves out and going beyond the standard relationship, we enhanced our ability to get access to dealers. In studying children, Gary Fine felt that, at times, there were benefits to be gained by offering services, such as companionship, educational expertise, praise, food, and monetary loans, to child informants (Fine and Sandstrom 1988:24). We did the same in our study of college athletes, feeding them, helping them with their studies, and providing short-term loans (Adler and Adler 1991).

However, there is not universal agreement that providing goods and services to respondents is advantageous to research projects (see Lee 1993). William Yancey and Lee Rainwater (1970) have argued that gifts or loans from affluent researchers to poor respondents can reinforce paternalistic roles and feelings of inequality. Richard Berk and Joseph Adams (1970) have warned that researchers who provide gifts to respondents may be getting "suckered." As Gary Fine and Kent Sandstrom (1988) express it: "A danger exists in providing services, even those that are not monetary. Researchers may become accepted for what they provide, not for what they are. The relationship may become commodified and instrumental" (p. 25). Thus the tying of respondents to researchers by payoffs of any kind may not necessarily produce the most trusting relationships. This issue remains highly controversial among social scientists today.

There are a number of *practical strategies* that interviewers can use to assure access to respondents. In most qualitative interviewing situations, the interviewer's goal is to be informal, nondirective, and freewheeling, because most qualitative researchers believe that a less structured atmosphere enhances rapport with subjects. They argue that it is especially important not to hurry respondents into interview situations prematurely. We made this mistake in our study of drug dealers and smugglers. Having thought that we had established a trusting relationship with one dealer's "old lady," we asked if we could interview her. Although we had not been overly specific about the scope of our research interests, we thought that she liked and trusted us and that, as a graduate student in cultural anthropology, she understood and respected academic research. However, as soon as the interview began, we realized that she felt uncomfortable discussing the drug trafficking of her friends: She ducked our questions, feigned sleepiness, and avoided direct answers. We politely left and lost all future access to her. Similarly, if researchers are too aggressive in their requests, they may scare or threaten respondents.

In order to counteract this problem, some authors have suggested that interviewers use "shallow cover" (Fine and Sandstrom 1988:19), or the "sin" of omission. Here, researchers are overt about their intentions but remain oblique or vague about their specific purpose. In Fine's (1987) case, he told the Little Leaguers he studied only that he was interested in observing the behavior of preadolescents; he did not go into any further detail about the exact nature of his study. Although this kind of approach did not work for us, it allowed Fine to remain more flexible in the research bargain and prevented him from possibly scaring off some of the children or their parents.

SPONSORSHIP

Perhaps the strategy researchers most commonly use to gain access to diffident groups is sponsorship. Made famous in sociology by such notables as Doc in *Street Corner Society* (Whyte 1943), the eponymous Tally (Liebow 1967), and Herman, the janitor whom Elijah Anderson (1976) met at Jelly's (the bar-liquor store he studied), sponsors act "in a bridging or a guiding role, serv[ing] indirectly to facilitate acceptance of the researcher" (Lee 1993: 131). One function a sponsor can serve is as a referral to others in the setting, vouching for the researcher. For instance, in our research with drug dealers, Dave, our key informant, introduced us to a wide spectrum of his associates and guaranteed our trustworthiness. Because we had housed Dave after he was imprisoned, his colleagues trusted us. These referrals were priceless, as there would have been no other way for us to gain access to members of such a concealed group. Having the backing of trusted individuals in the setting can greatly ease researchers' access. For example, Jeffrey Sluka (1990) had relatively little problem getting into a Catholic enclave in Belfast (despite the highly political and violent nature of the setting) because he initially contacted a local and trusted priest who vouched for him. Yeager and Kram (1995) found that developing a number of liaison relationships with internal groups of managers early on in their research allowed them the necessary access to sites in the banking and high-technology industries because these people referred them to others who were aware of their relationships with the sponsors.

Among some groups that are very difficult to penetrate, it may be tantamount to professional suicide for researchers not to have sponsorship networks to exploit. In explaining how he gained access to dignitaries in Hollywood, for example, Gamson (1995) states that "an outside researcher who does not tap into a relationship network, and one with a powerful individual at its center, is going to have terribly restricted access to the higher-ups in the industry elite" (p. 86). Similarly, Joan Hoffman (1980) used the sponsorship of her social ties, people she knew personally or who knew members of her family, to gain access to hospital boards of directors and their upper-class members. Without these connections, she never would have

been granted permission to interview the people she did.

If all else fails, and access is either not forthcoming or summarily denied, researchers may need to "send out feelers" (Henslin 1972:63) to establish contact with the groups they want to study. Using his role as a college professor, for example, Henslin (1972) recommended that students in his classes conduct research on abortion, a highly secretive practice at the time. He encouraged anyone who had a friend or acquaintance who had had an abortion to pursue these lines. In this way, he found respondents who otherwise would have been closed off to him.

RELATIONAL GROUNDWORK

A chief difference between ethnographers and those who practice survey research or qualitative interviewing unsupported by participant observation is the kind of groundwork that ethnographers can lay in their settings (see in this volume Warren, Chapter 4; Johnson, Chapter 5). Jennifer Platt (1981) suggests that researchers interview peers with whom they already have established relationships, and Robert Burgess (1991) urges researchers to develop friendships to gain access to the groups in which they are interested. In his studies of educational settings, he became friendly with administrators and teachers in various schools. He notes that, rather than causing problems in the collection of data,

> these friendships facilitated entry to groups that would otherwise have been difficult to enter. Secondly, these friendships provided access to a different range of perspectives on the school. Thirdly, my acknowledged friendships with particular individuals gave rise to a situation where other teachers wanted to give me their views on particular matters. (P. 51)

Ethnographers have long argued that they have a greater likelihood of securing interviews if they take the time to get to know the people they are studying, to develop relationships with them, and to build trust between respondents and themselves. Ethnographers believe that laying the relational groundwork for future interviews not only enhances their access to study populations, but, based on depth, commitment, and trust, these longitudinal associations may lead to research that yields richer portraits of the subjects. Long-term, meaningful, in-depth involvement with subjects, these researchers argue, yields a greater likelihood that respondents will be available, honest, and soul-searching in discussing the research topic.

JOINT MEMBERSHIP

Finally, we and others have argued that having a membership role in a setting increases a researcher's likelihood of gaining interview access (see, e.g., Adler and Adler 1987). Ethnographers have practiced this technique for decades, but Jeffrey Riemer (1977) was the first to highlight it in his discussion of "opportunistic" research sites. Many studies have been conducted by researchers who have had access to particular groups because they were already members. For example, researchers can *take advantage of unique circumstances or timely events* to select their topics of study. Lawrence Ouellet (1994) carried out his study of truck drivers while he drove a cross-country truck route to pay his bills during graduate school. Julius Roth's (1963) research on long-term medical patients was the result of his own hospitalization. Our own work on young children's car pools began when we found ourselves ferrying kids back and forth to preschool (Adler and Adler 1984).

Researchers can also *take advantage of familiar situations* to select topics for research. In studying preadolescents, we began by observing our own children and their friends (Adler and Adler 1996). As parents in the community, we already were interested in the lives of these children. Turning this into a research setting was a natural outgrowth of our parental roles. We were accepted and trusted by many in the setting because, as parents, we had a natural reason to be there and shared membership-related concerns and interests.

Similarly, researchers may *take advantage of their own special expertise* in selecting their research topics. Ned Polsky (1967) was an avid billiards player when he began his study of pool hustlers, and Marvin Scott (1968) was a frequent visitor at horse-racing tracks, leading him to study that world. Some autoethnographers focus primarily on their own experiences. Examples include Carolyn Ellis's (1995) study of the death of her husband, as both she and he chronicled the last months before he died of emphysema; David Karp's (1996) study of people who suffer from manic depression, a condition with which he was afflicted; and Carol Ronai's (1995) poignant study of incest survivors, of which she was one. The advantage of all such opportunistic approaches is that they facilitate entry into the setting, because the researcher already has a legitimate purpose for being there.

Not all ethnographers, of course, "exploit" their own biographies to expedite access to a research population. Often, researchers do not establish their membership in a setting until well after they have arrived there. One of the most creative examples of this is Nancy Mandell's (1988) "least-adult" role. In order to study preschool children, Mandell minimized the physical, cognitive, intellectual, and social differences between herself and the children by literally getting into the sandbox with them, putting herself eyeball to eyeball with them, ignoring their deviances and transgressions, and generally approximating, as best she could, the stance of a child. Although distrustful at first, the children came to see Mandell as much closer to them than other adults. Her observations and discussions with the youngsters were thus greatly enhanced.

At times, researchers who study social movements or proselytizing religious groups may be recruited by members (Grills 1994; Rochford 1985). Although such recruitment may ease the researcher's entry into the group, it may also prohibit the researcher from gaining access to respondents other than through being seen as a potential convert.

◆ Overcoming Resistance

Once a researcher has gained entrée to a group, the arduous task of actually conducting the interviews ensues. There are a host of problems that may arise once interviews are granted, particularly with respondents who are reluctant to talk in the first place. Researchers hope for full and complete disclosure on the part of respondents, but there may be many reasons respondents are not forthcoming with information. Below, we outline some of the typical problems interviewers face and some strategies they might use to overcome these obstacles.

SETUP ISSUES

In arranging and negotiating interviews, interviewers' *demographic characteristics* may serve as an important link to respondents (Weiss 1994). Thus if there is an overlap between the interviewer and the interviewee in such areas as age, gender, social class, ethnicity, and general appearance, a reluctant respondent may be more prone to openness during the interview. Bergen (1993), for instance, found that her gender was a major advantage in her interviewing women about marital rape. Martin Weinberg, Colin Williams, and Douglas Pryor (1994) recruited volunteers from the Bisexual Center and the Institute for Advanced Study of Human Sexuality to conduct the interviews in their San Francisco study of bisexuals. They had hoped that this would make their respondents more comfortable

with talking about their sexual orientations. However, as they note, this approach is not without its drawbacks:

> The danger of having organizational members conduct the interviews lay in the possible *reluctance* of people being interviewed to disclose something negative about being bisexual, the Bisexual Center itself, a mutual acquaintance, and the like. Similarly, there was always the chance that persons being interviewed might exaggerate their sexual history to impress a bisexual interviewer or provide acceptable responses with perceived interviewer effects. (P. 24; emphasis added)

Nevertheless, Weinberg et al. found that their respondents did prefer to discuss these intimate issues with like-minded people.

The *location* of the interview is another factor that can be important in assuring that reluctant respondents will feel comfortable. When interviews deal with highly emotional, sensitive, or private topics, it is often best if they can be conducted in places that are as secluded as possible, such as the respondents' homes. Bergen (1993) found this to be the case in her study of marital rape; she notes that "interviewing women in their homes was an important aspect of establishing a relationship and fully understanding the emotional and physical trauma that these women have suffered" (p. 207). Interviewing in a respondent's home casts a guest ambience over the researcher's presence and imbues the researcher with an aura of friendship. Other topics are best brought up in the workplace, particularly when respondents do not want to talk around other people in their homes, or when they are used to entertaining reporters at their places of business. Most critically, it is essential that researchers meet respondents at the times and places that are convenient to the respondents (Thomas 1995). For instance, in his study of Hollywood elites, Gamson (1994) conducted most interviews at respondents' workplaces, but others felt more comfortable at public meeting places, such as cafés or restaurants.

CONDUCT

The conduct of the interviewer during the course of the interview is a crucial determinant of how comfortable the respondent will be. Interviewers who are assiduous in providing reassurances can make even reluctant respondents feel at ease. John Brewer (1993) used humor, ribaldry, and self-deprecation to court and relax the police he studied in Northern Ireland. The interviewer's phrasing of the questions, too, is important; carefully worded questions can make a respondent feel less threatened, especially when the interview concerns hard-to-discuss topics such as sex. Numerous rape researchers, for example, have found that women are more likely to be willing to respond to questions about "forced or unwanted sexual intercourse" than to discuss "rape" (see Bergen 1993; Finkelhor and Yllo 1985; Russell 1990; Walker 1989). Richard Tewksbury and Patricia Gagné (1997) found that by reminding their transgendered respondents that they were not being seen as "freaks," they could greatly enhance their interviews with these respondents: "During interviews and other interactions when our research motives have been questioned or respondents have become defensive or reticent, we have been able to reestablish empathy by explaining that we believe gender is socially constructed and exists along a continuum" (p. 143).

In a similar vein, Hoffman (1980) found that "deflection" was a useful technique to use with subjects who were anxious about personal exposure. That is, although they were uncomfortable when they perceived themselves to be the objects of study, they talked more freely on generic or "external" topics. Marsha Rosenbaum (personal communication, 1999) has told us that in interviewing drug users about their behavior, she always started the conversation by asking, "Say, what sort of drugs do people use around here?" rather than asking them their drugs of choice. Anything that deflects attention away from respondents as the main target of study can be useful for promoting conversation. Using plural and personal pronouns with respondents is yet another way to facilitate rapport and break down barriers. John Johnson (1975:108) suggests that an interviewer's using words such as *we, us, they,* and *them* can convince respondents that the interviewer is actually *of* them, not apart from them.

A common ploy that interviewers use involves "normalizing perceived deviance" (Johnson 1975). That is, interviewers are well-advised not to raise their eyebrows, change their tone of voice, or seem dismayed when respondents discuss deviant activities. For instance, in our study of preadolescents, we were frequently in a position to hear about the transgressions of young teenagers, such as cigarette smoking, cutting school, and early sexual exploits. Rather than expressing moral indignation, we either nodded affirmatively or seemingly ignored the situation. If we had reacted any differently, these youngsters would not have felt comfortable telling us about these activities.

Qualitative interviews are, by definition, flexible. Researchers are permitted to allow respondents to shape the contours of the interview. At times, this may mean that respondents ask questions about the intimate lives of interviewers; this can result in appropriate and beneficial transactions that can ease respondent reluctance (but see Weiss 1994, who questions whether self-disclosure is an effective facilitative technique). The practice of postmodern and feminist ethnographers suggests that when respondents and researchers share information, the interview context is more comfortable and the hierarchical gap between researchers and respondents is diminished (Cook and Fonow 1986; Ellis et al. 1997). Rosalind Edwards (1993), for instance, was asked to "self-disclose" about her own family life in her study of mature mother-students seeking higher education. She felt that her own revelations aided the respondents in telling her their life stories. In our study of drug dealers, we often talked about the one day that Peter had spent in jail. Although this was a rather fleeting stay, we were able to milk this piece of our history to get respondents to open up about their own prison experiences or fears about arrest. With any sensitive topic, the more researchers can indicate that they share respondents' pain or have experienced similar feelings, the more likely it is that respondents will open up (Daniels 1983).

Lee (1995), in a useful manual about dangerous fieldwork, suggests that conducting open and *simultaneous fieldwork* with other, even opposing, parties may be helpful to researchers studying controversial topics. For instance, in their study of a nude beach, Jack Douglas and Paul Rasmussen (1977) found that their talking openly to all participants in disputes concerning the beach—such as nudists, police, and property owners—made those on each side want to tell their story. So as not to be left out or misunderstood, divided factions in disagreements may become less reluctant to talk. David Gilmore (1991) refers to this as the "competition of communication," wherein each side tries to convince the researchers of the justice of its cause, increasing the amount of data made available.

Ostrander (1995b) describes several ploys that she has found to be beneficial in getting elites to let their guard down. It is easy to feel intimidated by these people, she notes, especially given that they are used to being in charge of most social situations. However, counterintuitively, she recommends that interviewers not be too deferential or overly concerned about establishing positive rapport with elite respondents; rather, interviewers should take some visible control over the situation. In one example from her studies, she was invited to breakfast at a fancy restaurant selected by a respondent. She arrived early, before he did, and although this immediately put him off guard, he eventually deferred to her. Another simple strategy she has employed is to choose a particular spot to place her tape recorder, so that this gives her an excuse to take charge of where she and the respondent sit during the interview. Finally, Ostrander recommends that interviewers give elites the opportunity to respond directly to criticisms others have of them, thereby allowing them to express frustrations or to defend themselves.

RELATIONSHIPS

Similar to their role in affecting research access, researchers' relationships with respondents may overcome resistance during the course of interviews. "One-off" advocates continue to maintain that detachment fosters the greatest reduction of resistance, whereas those who believe that researchers should conduct multiple interviews with the same respondents and that researchers should forge relationships with respondents prior to interviewing champion greater intimacy and connection.

Researchers may also lessen respondent resistance by trying to equalize the status differentials and power inequalities between themselves and their respondents. In the difficult task of "studying up," Hoffman (1980) notes, the onus is on researchers to elevate their status and power. This earns them greater respect from respondents and a greater feeling of ease. Conversely, researchers who investigate the downtrodden and powerless should balance differences as well. In trying to get reluctant respondents to talk, interviewers should try not to appear overly above or below them. Researchers should avoid obvious displays of affluence or position and should look for areas of other personal overlap between respondents and themselves where they might forge rapport. Thus in our study of college athletes we tried to minimize the differences between our often black, inner-city, young, and inexperienced respondents and ourselves. They initially felt extremely deferential toward us, in part because of our age, race, social class, education, and position as faculty members; they called Peter "Coach" and Patti "Miss Patti." After a while, our unpretentious and unconventional behavior, and our clear desire to support them in the setting, led them to relax and treat us more as friends. They then felt more comfortable cursing in our presence, revealing their behavior and relationships, and expressing their feelings about others in the setting to us. Although many researchers agree that such status equalization diminishes interview reluctance, it cannot be overlooked that researchers can also purposely use their greater status and power in the interview setting to steamroll respondents, pushing them into answering questions without giving them the opportunity to be reticent. This occurs rarely, however.

◆ Conclusion

The litigious nature of U.S. society today and the politicization of research have influenced the core, basic character of interviewing. Compared with the past, there are now many more reasons, organizational and individual, for people to be wary of being studied. In particular, formal factors have been added to informal ones, escalating people's reluctance. As a result, some groups may be entirely lost to researchers' views, and aspects of the lives of some others may remain hidden. Still, thoughtful and sensitive researchers can still accomplish much fruitful research. Interviews, especially when they are deep and unstructured, fundamentally remain a potentially enjoyable medium of interaction and exchange, where social scientists' interests in people and their lives can stimulate respondents to share their experiences and insights in a way that leaves all participants mutually enriched.

As society changes, it is possible that the nature of resistance might change as well. With increasing degrees of protection built into the research relationship and the increasing education of the populace, perhaps respondents in the future will be better assured that their interests will be protected. It is more likely, however, that researchers will have to continue to deal with reluctant respondents, no matter the sociohistorical times or the context of the research. Although we do not envision a time when respondent reluctance will disappear entirely, we can hope that, for the future of social science, informed respondents will be less taciturn than they are in the fairly paranoid environment in which we currently live. Thus, although the strategies described in this chapter might need to be amended in the future, researchers will always need to aware of the cautionary feelings of the people they study.

■ References

Adler, P. 1981. *Momentum: A Theory of Social Action*. Beverly Hills, CA: Sage.
———. 1984. "The Sociologist as Celebrity: The Role of the Media in Field Research." *Qualitative Sociology* 7:310-26.
Adler, P. A. 1985. *Wheeling and Dealing: An Ethnography of an Upper-Level Drug Dealing and Smuggling Community*. New York: Columbia University Press.
Adler, P. A. and P. Adler. 1984. "The Carpool: A Socializing Adjunct to the Educational Experience." *Sociology of Education* 57:200-210.
———. 1987. *Membership Roles in Field Research*. Newbury Park, CA: Sage.

———. 1991. *Backboards and Blackboards: College Athletes and Role Engulfment.* New York: Columbia University Press.

———. 1993. "Ethical Issues in Self-Censorship: Ethnographic Research on Sensitive Topics." Pp. 249-66 in *Researching Sensitive Topics,* edited by C. M. Renzetti and R. M. Lee. Newbury Park, CA: Sage.

———. 1996. "Parent-as-Researcher: The Politics of Researching in the Personal Life." *Qualitative Sociology* 19:35-58.

———. 1999. "Transience and the Postmodern Self: The Geographic Mobility of Resort Workers." *Sociological Quarterly* 40:31-58.

Anderson, E. 1976. *A Place on the Corner.* Chicago: University of Chicago Press.

Anderson, L. and T. C. Calhoun. 1992. "Facilitative Aspects of Field Research with Deviant Street Populations." *Sociological Inquiry* 62:490-98.

Anspach, R. R. 1993. *Deciding Who Lives: Fateful Choices in the Intensive-Care Nursery.* Berkeley: University of California Press.

Asher, R. and G. A. Fine. 1991. "Fragile Ties: Shaping Research Relationships with Women Married to Alcoholics." Pp. 196-205 in *Experiencing Fieldwork: An Inside View of Qualitative Research,* edited by W. B. Shaffir and R. A. Stebbins. Newbury Park, CA: Sage.

Becker, H. S. 1954. "A Note on Interviewing Tactics." *Human Organization* 12:31-32.

Becker, H. S. and B. Geer. 1969. "Participant Observation and Interviewing: A Comparison." Pp. 322-31 in *Issues in Participant Observation,* edited by G. J. McCall and J. L. Simmons. Reading, MA: Addison-Wesley.

Bellman, B. L. 1984. *The Language of Secrecy.* New Brunswick, NJ: Rutgers University Press.

Bergen, R. K. 1993. "Interviewing Survivors of Marital Rape: Doing Feminist Research on Sensitive Topics." Pp. 197-211 in *Researching Sensitive Topics,* edited by C. M. Renzetti and R. M. Lee. Newbury Park, CA: Sage.

Berk, R. A. and J. M. Adams. 1970. "Establishing Rapport with Deviant Groups." *Social Problems* 18:102-17.

Brajuha, M. and L. Hallowell. 1986. "Legal Intrusion and the Politics of Fieldwork: The Impact of the Brajuha Case." *Urban Life* 14:454-78.

Brannen, J. 1988. "The Study of Sensitive Topics." *Sociological Review* 36:552-63.

Brewer, J. D. 1993. "Sensitivity as a Problem in Field Research: A Study of Routine Policing in Northern Ireland." Pp. 125-45 in *Researching Sensitive Topics,* edited by C. M. Renzetti and R. M. Lee. Newbury Park, CA: Sage.

Brink, P. J. 1993. "Studying African Women's Secret Societies." Pp. 235-48 in *Researching Sensitive Topics,* edited by C. M. Renzetti and R. M. Lee. Newbury Park, CA: Sage.

Burgess, R. G. 1991. "Sponsors, Gatekeepers, Members, and Friends: Access in Educational Settings." Pp. 43-52 in *Experiencing Fieldwork: An Inside View of Qualitative Research,* edited by W. B. Shaffir and R. A. Stebbins. Newbury Park, CA: Sage.

Clough, P. T. 1992. *The End(s) of Ethnography: From Realism to Social Criticism.* Newbury Park, CA: Sage.

———. 1994. *Feminist Thought: Desire, Power and Academic Discourse.* Cambridge, MA: Blackwell.

Collins, P. H. 1992. "Transforming the Inner Circle: Dorothy Smith's Challenge to Sociological Theory." *Sociological Theory* 10:73-80.

Cook, J. A. and M. M. Fonow. 1986. "Knowledge and Women's Interests: Issues of Epistemology and Methodology in Feminist Sociological Research." *Sociological Inquiry* 56:2-27.

Corsino, L. 1987. "Fieldworker Blues: Emotional Stress and Research Underinvolvement in Fieldwork Settings." *Social Science Journal* 24:275-86.

Daniels, A. K. 1983. "Self-Deception and Self-Discovery in Fieldwork." *Qualitative Sociology* 6:195-214.

Day, K. J. 1985. "Perspectives on Privacy: A Sociological Analysis." Ph.D. dissertation, University of Edinburgh.

Dean, J. P., R. L. Eichhorn, and L. R. Dean. 1969. "Fruitful Informants for Intensive Interviewing." Pp. 142-44 in *Issues in Participant Observation,* edited by G. J. McCall and J. L. Simmons. Reading, MA: Addison-Wesley.

Denzin, N. K. 1997. *Interpretive Ethnography: Ethnographic Practices for the 21st Century.* Thousand Oaks, CA: Sage.

Douglas, J. D. 1971. *American Social Order.* New York: Free Press.

———. 1976. *Investigative Social Research.* Beverly Hills, CA: Sage.

Douglas, J. D. and P. K. Rasmussen, with C. A. Flanagan. 1977. *The Nude Beach.* Beverly Hills, CA: Sage.

Duelli Klein, R. 1983. "How to Do What We Want to Do: Thoughts about Feminist Methodology." Pp. 99-121 in *Theories of Women's Studies,* edited by G. Bowles and R. Duelli Klein. New York: Routledge & Kegan Paul.

Dunlap, E., B. D. Johnson, H. Sanabria, E. Holliday, V. Lipsey, M. Barnett, W. Hopkins, I. Sobel, D. Randolph, and K. Chin. 1990. "Studying Crack Users and Their Criminal Careers: The Scientific and Artistic Aspects of Locating Hard-to-Reach Subjects and Interviewing Them about Sensitive Topics." *Contemporary Drug Problems* 17:121-44.

Edwards, R. 1993. "An Education in Interviewing: Placing the Researcher and the Research." Pp. 181-96 in *Researching Sensitive Topics,* edited by C. M. Renzetti and R. M. Lee. Newbury Park, CA: Sage.

Ellis, C. 1995. *Final Negotiations: A Story of Love, Loss, and Chronic Illness.* Philadelphia: Temple University Press.

Ellis, C., C. E. Kiesinger, and L. M. Tillmann-Healy. 1997. "Interactive Interviewing: Talking about Emotional Experience." Pp. 119-49 in *Reflexivity and Voice,* edited by R. Hertz. Thousand Oaks, CA: Sage.

Ericksen, J. A., with S. A. Steffen. 1999. *Kiss and Tell: Surveying Sex in the Twentieth Century.* Cambridge, MA: Harvard University Press.

Fine, G. A. 1987. *With the Boys: Little League Baseball and Preadolescent Culture.* Chicago: University of Chicago Press.

Fine, G. A. and K. L. Sandstrom. 1988. *Knowing Children: Participant Observation with Minors.* Newbury Park, CA: Sage.

Finkelhor, D. and K. Yllo. 1985. *License to Rape: Sexual Abuse of Wives.* New York: Holt, Rinehart & Winston.

Gamson, J. 1994. *Claims to Fame: Celebrity in Contemporary America.* Berkeley: University of California Press.

———. 1995. "Stopping the Spin and Becoming a Prop: Fieldwork on Hollywood Elites." Pp. 83-93 in *Studying Elites Using Qualitative Methods,* edited by R. Hertz and J. B. Imber. Thousand Oaks, CA: Sage.

Gilmore, D. D. 1991. "Subjectivity and Subjugation: Fieldwork in the Stratified Community." *Human Organization* 50:215-24.

Grills, S. 1994. "Recruitment Practices of the Christian Heritage Party." Pp. 96-108 in *Doing Everyday Life,* edited by M. L. Dietz, R. Prus, and W. B. Shaffir. Mississauga, Ontario: Copp Clark Longman.

Hamid, A. 1990. "The Political Economy of Crack-Related Violence." *Contemporary Drug Problems* 17:31-78.

Hamm, M. S. and J. Ferrell. 1998. "Confessions of Danger and Humanity." Pp. 254-72 in *Ethnography at the Edge: Crime, Deviance, and Field Research,* edited by J. Ferrell and M. S. Hamm. Boston: Northeastern University Press.

Henslin, J. 1972. "Studying Deviance in Four Settings: Research Experiences with Cabbies, Suicidees, Drug Users, and Abortionees." Pp. 35-70 in *Research on Deviance,* edited by J. D. Douglas. New York: Random House.

Hertz, R. and J. B. Imber. 1995. "Introduction." Pp. vii-xi in *Studying Elites Using Qualitative Methods,* edited by R. Hertz and J. B. Imber. Thousand Oaks, CA: Sage.

Hoffman, J. E. 1980. "Problems of Access in the Study of Social Elites and Boards of Directors." Pp. 45-56 in *Fieldwork Experience: Qualitative Approaches to Social Research,* edited by W. B. Shaffir, R. A. Stebbins, and A. Turowetz. New York: St. Martin's.

Hubbard, E. A. 1992. "Of Course I Fight Back: An Ethnography of Women's Use of Violence in Intimate Relationships." Ph.D. dissertation, Department of Sociology, University of Colorado at Boulder.

Irwin, J. 1972. "Participant-Observation of Criminals." Pp. 117-38 in *Research on Deviance,* edited by J. D. Douglas. New York: Random House.

Jacobs, B. A. 1998. "Researching Crack Dealers: Dilemmas and Contradictions." Pp. 160-77 in *Ethnography at the Edge: Crime, Deviance, and Field Research,* edited by J. Ferrell and M. S. Hamm. Boston: Northeastern University Press.

Johnson, B., P. J. Goldstein, E. Preble, J. Schmeidler, D. S. Lipton, B. Spunt, and T. Miller. 1985. *Taking Care of Business: The Economics of Crime by Heroin Abusers.* Lexington, MA: Lexington.

Johnson, J. M. 1975. *Doing Field Research.* New York: Free Press.

Jones, J. H. 1981. *Bad Blood: The Tuskegee Syphilis Experiment.* New York: Free Press.

Karp, D. A. 1996. *Speaking of Sadness: Depression, Disconnection, and the Meanings of Illness.* New York: Oxford University Press.

Laslett, B. and R. Rapoport. 1975. "Collaborative Interviewing and Interactive Research." *Journal of Marriage and the Family* 37:968-77.

Laumann, E. O., J. H. Gagnon, R. T. Michael, and S. Michaels. 1994. *The Social Organization of Sexuality.* Chicago: University of Chicago Press.

Lee, R. M. 1993. *Doing Research on Sensitive Topics.* Newbury Park, CA: Sage.

———. 1995. *Dangerous Fieldwork.* Thousand Oaks, CA: Sage.

Liebow, E. 1967. *Tally's Corner: A Study of Negro Street Corner Men.* Boston: Little, Brown.

———. 1993. *Tell Them Who I Am: The Lives of Homeless Women.* New York: Penguin.

Mandell, N. 1988. "The Least-Adult Role in Studying Children." *Journal of Contemporary Ethnography* 16:433-68.

Marx, G. T. 1988. *Undercover.* Berkeley: University of California Press.

Milgram, S. 1965. "Some Conditions of Obedience and Disobedience to Authority." *Human Relations* 18:57-76.

Oakley, A. 1981. "Interviewing Women: A Contradiction in Terms?" Pp. 30-61 in *Doing Feminist Research,* edited by H. Roberts. London: Routledge & Kegan Paul.

Ostrander, S. A. 1984. *Women of the Upper Class.* Philadelphia: Temple University Press.

———. 1995a. *Money for Change: Social Movement Philanthropy at Haymarket People's Fund.* Philadelphia: Temple University Press.

———. 1995b. " 'Surely You're Not in This Just to Be Helpful': Access, Rapport, and Interviews in Three Studies of Elites." Pp. 133-50 in *Studying Elites Using Qualitative Methods,* edited by R. Hertz and J. B. Imber. Thousand Oaks, CA: Sage.

Ouellet, L. 1994. *Pedal to the Metal: The Work Lives of Truckers.* Philadelphia: Temple University Press.

Picou, J. S. 1996. "Sociology and Compelled Disclosure: Protecting Respondent Confidentiality." *Sociological Spectrum* 16:209-32.

Platt, J. 1981. "On Interviewing One's Peers." *British Journal of Sociology* 32:75-91.

Polsky, N. 1967. *Hustlers, Beats, and Others.* Chicago: Aldine.

Pring, G. and P. Canan. 1996. *SLAPPS: Getting Sued for Speaking Out.* Philadelphia: Temple University Press.

Renzetti, C. and R. M. Lee. 1993. "The Problem of Researching Sensitive Topics: An Overview and Introduction." Pp. 3-13 in *Researching Sensitive Topics,* edited by C. M. Renzetti and R. M. Lee. Newbury Park, CA: Sage.

Richardson, L. 1997. *Fields of Play: Constructing an Academic Life.* New Brunswick, NJ: Rutgers University Press.

Riemer, J. 1977. "Varieties of Opportunistic Research." *Urban Life* 5:467-77.

Rochford, E. B. 1985. *Hare Krishna in America.* New Brunswick, NJ: Rutgers University Press.

Ronai, C. R. 1995. "Multiple Reflections of Child Sex Abuse: An Argument for a Layered Account." *Journal of Contemporary Ethnography* 23:395-426.

Rose, A. M. 1945. "A Research Note in Interviewing." *American Journal of Sociology* 51:143-44.

Roth, J. 1963. *Timetables.* Indianapolis: Bobbs-Merrill.

Russell, D. E. H. 1990. *Rape in Marriage.* Rev. ed. Bloomington: Indiana University Press.

Seidman, I. 1991. *Interviewing as Qualitative Research: A Guide for Researchers in Education and the Social Sciences.* New York: Teachers College Press.

Scarce, R. 1994. "(No) Trial, (but) Tribulations: When Courts and Ethnography Conflict." *Journal of Contemporary Ethnography* 23:123-49.

Scott, M. B. 1968. *The Racing Game.* Chicago: Aldine.

Sluka, J. A. 1990. "Participant Observation in Violent Social Contexts." *Human Organization* 49:114-26.

Smith, D. E. 1989. "Sociological Theory: Methods of Writing Patriarchy." Pp. 34-64 in *Feminism and Sociological Theory,* edited by R. A. Wallace. Newbury Park, CA: Sage.

Spector, M. 1980. "Learning to Study Public Figures." Pp. 98-109 in *Fieldwork Experience: Qualitative Approaches to Social Research,* edited by W. B. Shaffir, R. A. Stebbins, and A. Turowetz. New York: St. Martin's.

Tewksbury, R. and P. Gagné. 1997. "Assumed and Perceived Identities: Problems of Self-Presentation in Field Research." *Sociological Spectrum* 17:127-55.

Thomas, R. J. 1995. "Interviewing Important People in Big Companies." Pp. 3-17 in *Studying Elites Using Qualitative Methods,* edited by R. Hertz and J. B. Imber. Thousand Oaks, CA: Sage.

Tripp, D. 1983. "Co-authorship and Negotiation: The Interview as Act of Creation." *Interchange* 14:32-45.

Useem, M. 1995. "Reaching Corporate Executives." Pp. 18-39 in *Studying Elites Using Qualitative Methods,* edited by R. Hertz and J. B. Imber. Thousand Oaks, CA: Sage.

Van Maanen, J. 1983. "The Moral Fix: On the Ethics of Fieldwork." Pp. 269-87 in *Contemporary Field Research: A Collection of Readings,* edited by R. M. Emerson. Boston: Little, Brown.

Walker, L. E. A. 1989. *Terrifying Love: Why Battered Women Kill and How Society Responds.* New York: HarperCollins.

Weibel, W. W. 1990. "Identifying and Gaining Access to Hidden Populations." Pp. 4-11 in *The Collection and Interpretation of Data from Hidden Populations,* edited by E. Y. Lambert. Rockville, MD: National Institute on Drug Abuse.

Weinberg, M. S., C. J. Williams, and D. W. Pryor. 1994. *Dual Attractions: Understanding Bisexuality.* New York: Oxford University Press.

Weisheit, R. A. 1998. "Marijuana Subcultures: Studying Crime in Rural America." Pp. 178-204 in *Ethnography at the Edge: Crime, Deviance, and Field Research,* edited by J. Ferrell and M. S. Hamm. Boston: Northeastern University Press.

Weiss, R. S. 1994. *Learning from Strangers: The Art and Method of Qualitative Interview Studies.* New York: Free Press.

Whyte, W. F. 1943. *Street Corner Society: The Social Structure of an Italian Slum.* Chicago: University of Chicago Press.

Wichroski, M. A. 1997. "Breaking Silence: Some Fieldwork Strategies in Cloistered and Noncloistered Communities." Pp. 265-82 in *Reflexivity and Voice,* edited by R. Hertz. Thousand Oaks, CA: Sage.

Yancey, W. L. and L. Rainwater. 1970. "Problems in the Ethnography of the Urban Underclass." Pp. 78-97 in *Pathways to Data,* edited by R. W. Habenstein. Chicago: Aldine.

Yeager, P. C. and K. E. Kram. 1995. "Fielding Hot Topics in Cool Settings: The Study of Corporate Elites." Pp. 40-64 in *Studying Elites Using Qualitative Methods,* edited by R. Hertz and J. B. Imber. Thousand Oaks, CA: Sage.

26

IN-PERSON VERSUS TELEPHONE INTERVIEWING

◆ Roger W. Shuy

In the process of gathering data, social science researchers expend considerable time and effort that can make in-person interviewing impractical. Doing fieldwork —interviewing, observing, carrying out surveys and other kinds of data gathering —is often the most difficult and time- consuming part of the research task. Because time is valuable, researchers may try to figure out ways to reduce their work, short-cutting the data gathering or finding other ways to meet deadlines and get their projects done. One method of reducing fieldwork time that researchers may consider is to conduct interviews by telephone instead of meeting with subjects in person.

In this chapter I will consider the issue of in-person versus telephone interviews as it arises in the contexts of both traditional research surveys and everyday practical interviews, such as those conducted by hearings officers, doctors, lawyers, and journalists. Certain advantages and disadvantages are associated with each type of interviewing, and researchers who decide to use the telephone may benefit from realizing what they gain and lose in the process.

Many types of research interviews, such as surveys, whether conducted by telephone or in person, entail two different tasks for the researcher. The first task is to persuade the respondent to agree to be interviewed; the second is to elicit the information desired. In everyday practical interviews, the first task is usually unnecessary, because practical considerations make respondents willing to participate.

Studies of the persuasive aspect of research interviewing have focused on issues such as cost-efficiency, interviewer bias, response rates, questionnaire uniformity, and how researchers can best obtain subject compliance. Researchers have also examined how the voice characteristics of interviewers, such as rapid speech, loudness, varied intonation, and Standard English pronunciation, impinge on respondent confidence and refusal rates. No such research, however, has looked at these same speech characteristics in respondents (Oksenberg and Cannell 1988; Holstein and Gubrium 1995). It should also be noted that the studies examining speech characteristics of interviewers have been based on psycholinguistic laboratory research using only male voices (Brown 1973), leaving the voice characteristics of female interviewers, as well as female respondents, unexamined.

My focus here will be on comparing the advantages and disadvantages of telephone and in-person interviewing as carried out both by research interviewers and by those who interview as part of their everyday practical occupations. It is my hope that researchers using both methodologies can learn from this discussion of these strengths and weaknesses.

I will also emphasize the fact that most of the research on interviewing has concentrated on the interviewer rather than on the respondent. Reports on the advantages of telephone interviewing tend to stress matters such as interviewer bias, uniformity of questions and interviewer delivery, standardization of questions, interviewers' personal safety, and how interviewers can ask questions more sensitively. Very little is said about respondents' language and comfort. Communication consists of a sender, a message, and a receiver. By analyzing only the sender (interviewer) and the message (question), most researchers examining interviewing practices have overlooked the third major component, the person who answers the questions.

As in almost every other area of life, compromises in the interviewing task can lead to unanticipated problems. Some kinds of information may be gathered from respondents just as well by means of the telephone as in person. But researchers should know in advance, or at least should anticipate, the extent to which the quality and type of information they acquire can be affected by the mode they choose for gathering it.

After I review below the advantages and disadvantages of both telephone and in-person interviewing, I will present a case study of interviewing in an everyday practical context in order to illustrate many of the consequences of the differences between these two modes of interviewing.

◆ Criteria for Deciding between Telephone and In-Person Interviewing

Following are some of the criteria that researchers and others have set forth for deciding whether interviews should be conducted by telephone or face-to-face—whether the interviewing is done in relation to the everyday practical work of life or in relation to targeted surveys or polls:

◆ The type of interview to be carried out (e.g., research, polling, medical, journalistic)

◆ The type of information sought (e.g., demographic, personal, sensitive)

◆ The attitudinal variability, safety, and workload of the interviewers

◆ The need for consistency and/or uniformity among multiple interviewers

◆ The social variability of individual participants (e.g., gender, race, age)

◆ The need for contextual naturalness of response and setting

◆ The need to let participants generate responses with little or no influence from the questions

◆ The complexity of the issues and questions

◆ The economic, time, and location constraints of the project

◆ Research on Telephone versus In-Person Interviewing

The telephone interview has swept the polling and survey industry in recent years and is now the dominant approach (see Singleton and Straits, Chapter 3, this volume). There have been a few comprehensive comparisons of telephone and face-to-face interviewing, but even fewer studies comparing identical items and similar populations under the same conditions (Stokes and Yeh 1988). There have also been very few studies comparing telephone and in-person interviewing practices in practical, nonresearch settings. The reasons for the lack of comparisons are simple: (a) Such studies are very difficult to carry out, (b) they are very expensive, and (c) there has been little reason for those who interview as an integral part of their everyday work lives to veer from the traditional in-person interview. But there has been some movement to substitute telephone interviewing for in-person interviewing in bureaucratic settings of various sorts. This development has permitted a preliminary and somewhat limited comparison of telephone and face-to-face interviews, but one that allows us to compare the advantages and disadvantages of each mode.

Most of the available comparisons between telephone and in-person research interviewing concentrate on the interviewer. Some give attention to the attitudes of respondents, but even these typically focus on things that influence nonresponse (Groves 1979). Quality and quantity of responses are the focus of one report; Edith de Leeuw and Johannes van der Zouwen (1988) examined 28 studies that compared the summarized content (not the specific language) of telephone versus in-person interviews. They carried out a meta-analysis on the quantity and quality of data found in the studies, looking only at five indicators. Four of these five indicators—absence of social desirability bias (answers considered more acceptable in society), quantity of information given (responses to open questions), nonresponse to items (including "don't know"), and similarity of content of response in both modes (telephone and in person)—favored in-person interviewing, albeit with only a slight advantage. This confirms a finding from an earlier study that had concluded that the tilt of research findings is toward better-quality data in personal interviews, although the meaning of *quality* was not probed very deeply. Another comparison study found that respondents were more acquiescent, evasive, and extreme in their responses in telephone interviews than when they were interviewed face-to-face (Jordan, Marcus, and Reeder 1980).

It is difficult to assess the appropriateness of telephone interviewing versus in-person interviewing in all potential contexts. Researchers in different disciplines use interviewing for quite different purposes and seek distinct kinds of information. Some linguists, for example, interview with no particular content in mind. They simply want to obtain samples of natural, continuous speech, no matter what the respondents talk about. They place a premium on letting respondents ramble on at will, with as little participation and as few preset questions as possible from the interviewer. Ethnographers also carry out a version of this approach as relatively minor participants in the verbal exchanges they observe and analyze. In contrast, public opinion researchers focus almost totally on the content of what their respondents have to say. Their aim is often to keep respondents' verbal input to a minimum through the use of highly focused and consistent sets of questions.

The degree to which a researcher should consider either in-person or telephone interviewing more appropriate depends on many variables based on and growing out of the criteria noted above. It is possible to discern some of the advantages and disadvantages of these two interviewing modes from what is known and reported in the literature. In the following sections, I review the claimed advantages of both telephone and in-person interviewing practice.

◆ Advantages of Telephone Interviewing

Those who carry out surveys or polls for which it appears to be economically impractical to do in-person interviewing claim that there are certain advantages to telephone interviewing, as described below.

Reduced interviewer effects. Despite the lack of convincing comparisons of telephone and in-person interviewing, telephone interviewing appears to allow for fewer interviewer effects, largely because such effects can be monitored in centralized telephone research facilities (Lavrakas 1993; Frey 1989; de Leeuw and van der Zouwen 1988). The very presence of telephone interviewers together in the same facility offers them opportunities to learn from each other, in contrast to the face-to-face interviewer's conventional isolation.

Better interviewer uniformity in delivery. The vocal tone and delivery of interviewers has also been suggested as a reason telephone interviewing can be more successful than the in-person mode, because interviewer training can be more easily implemented and more successful (Oksenberg and Cannell 1988). Likewise, the shorter data collection period of telephone interviewing lends itself to closer monitoring of interviewer performance (Aquilino and LoSciuto 1990). But such findings leave unanswered the question of why in-person in-

terviewers cannot be trained with the same efficiency.

Greater standardization of questions. Survey researchers point out that using telephone interviewing provides researchers with control over quality: "When properly organized, interviewing done by telephone most closely approaches the level of unbiased standardization that is the goal of all good surveys" (Lavrakas 1993:5). This observation is undoubtedly accurate when the goal is to have every question asked in exactly the same way.

Researcher safety. Some researchers believe that by using telephone interviewing, they can safely reach respondents in difficult-to-visit or dangerous neighborhoods, especially late at night (Groves and Kahn 1979; de Leeuw and van der Zouwen 1988).

Greater cost-efficiency and fast results. If the research goal is limited to obtaining a completed interview in a short amount of time and in a cost-effective manner, there is little reason to question that telephone interviewing should be favored over face-to-face interviews. Robert Groves (1978) notes that the speed of questioning is greater in telephone interviews than in in-person interviews, but he also observes that the faster pace is linked to shorter answers to open-ended questions. Aside from cutting down on the travel time required for in-person interviews, using the telephone results in slightly shorter actual interview events. Groves (1989) estimates that questionnaires administered over the telephone take 10 to 20 percent less time than the same questionnaires administered in person. Speed in gathering the data required in some research other than opinion surveys is also faster when the telephone is used.

In the 1990s, computer-assisted telephone interviewing and computer-assisted personal interviewing increased the efficiency of telephone interviewing (see Couper and Hansen, Chapter 27, this volume). These techniques increase efficiency because the use of computers eliminates the researcher's need to generate a sampling pool, reduces noncoverage and nonresponse errors, reduces measurement errors associated with the wording of the questionnaire and the questioner's language, and assists in the data processing of the responses.

◆ Advantages of In-Person Interviewing

In contrast with the suggested advantages of telephone interviewing, the following advantages of face-to-face interviewing over in-person interviewing have been reported.

More accurate responses owing to contextual naturalness. Naturalness comes in many shapes. What is natural in most people's use of language is the freedom to introduce topics, change the subject, interrupt, and otherwise speak in the way they do in most of their everyday conversations. Answering questions posed by an interviewer is also natural, but because most people spend very little of their talking lives being interviewed, such language behavior occupies a very minor part of their existence. This explains, in part, why many people freeze up when asked questions by teachers, physicians, or lawyers.

The problem of a lack of naturalness in telephone interviewing may not be in the telephone per se, given that much of everyday telephone conversation is not a series of questions and answers. If the in-person interview consists of only the same questions and answers that are exchanged by telephone, little is gained in terms of adapting to the more natural mode of language interaction. But face-to-face interaction compels more small talk, politeness routines, joking, nonverbal communication, and asides in which people can more fully

express their humanity. And naturalness leads to open expression and comfort.

Recent research on interviewing in various professional settings, such as law (Conley and O'Barr 1998) and medicine (Roberts 1999; see also Zoppi and Epstein, Chapter 18, this volume), shows that when the goal is to elicit accurate information, natural conversation and narrative discourse are preferable to more rigid question-and-answer approaches. Judges, lawyers, and physicians often object to this notion, claiming that their time is too precious for them to wait for information to be unfolded before them in a way that is preferred by, and more natural to, witnesses and patients. Thus in the courts and in doctors' offices, natural conversation is normally subordinated to a more rigid question-and-answer format. The focus on what the lawyer or doctor wants to know, in the manner and sequence the lawyer or doctor wants it to unfold, seldom allows for witnesses or patients to tell their own stories. The above-cited researchers make a compelling case that the necessary and accurate information sought by the courts and doctors using a rigid question-and-answer format is not always revealed.

Greater likelihood of self-generated answers. It is the nature of questions to influence responses. For example, a tag question such as "You voted for Jones, didn't you?" gives the respondent very little latitude to disagree. Even yes/no questions influence answers, because they set the boundaries of answers to only two possibilities and assume that a simple yes or no represents the variability of responses that all people have. "Wh-" (what, who, what, where, when) questions are somewhat less influential, although they still focus the area of response on only the what, who, when, or where of the question, whereas the respondent may be more concerned about other things that these questions rules out. Open-ended questions influence answers the least, because they give respondents considerable leeway to take their answers wherever they want. Perhaps out of necessity, telephone interviewing tends to employ highly structured, closed-ended questions. To be sure, in-person interviews can also fall into this same pattern, asking only questions that focus the respondent on issues that are of concern to the interviewer. The virtue of the in-person interview, however, is that it has the context potential of simulating natural everyday conversation; a respondent may provide more than brief, underdeveloped answers to an interviewer's questions. The face-to-face approach encourages more self-generated responses.

Symmetrical distribution of interactive power. One of the characteristics of everyday conversation (as opposed to most interviews) is that it is mutually interactive. Both parties have the opportunity to raise topics, request clarification, change the subject, interrupt, and otherwise act conversationally normal. When one person is the designated question asker, the power of the interaction clearly falls to that person. The respondent is thus placed in a subordinate relationship to the questioner. Although question asking is central to interviewing and may have all the advantages noted above, including economy of the researcher's time, standardization of questions, and uniformity and sequencing of questions to avoid ordering effects, it also has the clear disadvantage of lack of naturalness and unequal distribution of interactive power. Just as patients and pupils who are questioned by physicians and teachers have little or no interactive power, so respondents in interviews are placed in a subordinate position. Again, not all face-to-face interviews avoid this problem, for if the in-person interaction is framed only as a version of the same questioning found in telephone interviews, little may be gained in terms of sharing power. But the face-to-face interview at least has the potential of escaping such asymmetry, largely because the in-person setting is more clearly like that of two people in everyday conversation than is the telephone interview. People expect differ-

ent things from different modes of interaction.

Greater effectiveness with complex issues. When the topic of research involves issues that require complex questions and answers, it is often more difficult to accomplish interviews over the telephone. As Paul Lavrakas (1993) notes, "It is tiresome to keep the average person on the telephone for longer than 20-30 minutes, especially for many senior citizens" (p. 6). Once again, one cause of such impatience is the absence of interactive naturalness. Whereas people do not become as fatigued or impatient in face-to-face settings, 20 minutes can seem like a long time on the telephone. When an interview requires the respondent to review documents, as in an administrative hearing interview, for example, use of the telephone can be a distinct disadvantage.

Better for older or hearing-impaired respondents. Even though some hearing-impaired individuals now have telephones equipped with amplification devices, this does not resolve all the communication issues raised by telephone interviewing. For example, linguists have found that average persons, regardless of hearing acuity, avoid requesting clarification or repetition as long as possible in conversation, choosing instead to infer meaning in the hope that they will eventually figure out what the other person has said. In the face-to-face interview, visual clues to a respondent's puzzlement or difficulty in understanding are available to the interviewer, who can then clarify without the respondent's needing to make an embarrassing request for him or her to do so.

On the other hand, A. Regula Herzog and Willard Rogers (1988), in a survey of older Americans on issues of politics, attitudes, health, well-being, and life satisfaction, found almost no difference in response distribution obtained from telephone and in-person interviews. In this study, respondents in two age groups, over 60 and under 60, were first interviewed face-to-face and then reinterviewed by telephone, so that the researchers could compare the two modes across age levels. Herzog and Rogers admit, however, that the older respondents were given more help by the interviewers in the telephone mode than they received face-to-face (see also Wenger, Chapter 13, this volume).

More thoughtful responses. Some researchers have noted that the faster pace of telephone interviews leads to less thoughtful responses (Sykes and Collins 1988). Again, the absence of visual clues is central. In face-to-face interaction there are many visual signs to encourage respondents to elaborate, clarify, or amend what they say. These visual signs are not available by telephone.

More accurate results owing to lower interviewer workload. Lavrakas (1993) asserts that the workload of telephone interviewers is higher than that of face-to-face interviewers, leading to less efficiency and less accurate results. A 20-minute telephone interview is more exhausting for both respondent and interviewer than is a 20-minute face-to-face meeting.

Better response rates. Some researchers have found that response rates for telephone interviews are typically lower than those for in-person interviews (Thornberry 1987; Lavrakas 1993; Groves and Kahn 1979; Groves, Miller, and Cannell 1987). Lavrakas (1993), in fact, notes a constant decrease in telephone response rates over the past two decades. Some effort has been made to increase telephone response rates with callbacks, but this actually can backfire by increasing the refusal rate and, in callback cases where the respondent agrees to respond, tends to result in inferior data.

Noting that there is lower cooperation on the telephone than in in-person interviews, Groves (1979) found that face-to-face respondents preferred the in-person

interview, whereas fewer telephone respondents said they preferred to be interviewed over the telephone. To help assure the cooperation of respondents in telephone interviews, Groves (1979) suggests that "perhaps the first few moments of the interaction should be designed to request no information but rather to attempt to develop trust of the interviewer by the respondent" (p. 204). This sounds very much like advice to engage in the kind of natural, everyday conversation that helps reduce asymmetrical power of the interactants discussed earlier.

Better for marginalized respondents. William Aquilino and Leonard LoSciuto (1990) found that whereas telephone and in-person interviews of white respondents concerning drug use yielded about the same responses, African Americans gave higher estimations of their marijuana and alcohol consumption in the face-to-face mode than over the telephone. There was no substantive difference between the modes, however, in questions about tobacco use, suggesting that the more sensitive the question, the more African Americans differ in their responses in the two modes of interviews. In an earlier study measuring depression among residents of Los Angeles, Carol Aneshensel and her associates (1982) found that both African Americans and Hispanics reported less depression in telephone interviews than they did in face-to-face contacts. Apparently there are different social norms among different ethnic groups about which researchers should be aware when they are planning interview research.

In his edited volume comparing National Center for Health Statistics face-to-face survey data with the Survey Research Center's telephone surveys on health issues, Owen Thornberry (1987) concludes that the lower response rates for telephone interviewing correlate with the poorly educated, younger adults, and the elderly. In a comparison of nine national surveys (five conducted in person and four by telephone), Herzog, Rodgers, and Richard Kulka (1983) found that the telephone surveys underrepresented elderly people, who were less likely to participate by telephone and were more likely to experience the telephone interview as lengthier than the in-person mode.

Better for research involving sensitive questions. Groves and Robert Kahn (1979) suggest that in the telephone mode there may be less likelihood that respondents will cast their answers to sensitive or threatening questions in the most positive light, despite the fact that the reason for this may be that telephone responses are usually briefer than in-person ones. In surveys conducted following both telephone and in-person interviews, Groves and Kahn found that a larger proportion of telephone respondents reported uneasiness about answering items on such topics as income, racial attitudes, income tax returns, health, jobs, voting behavior, and political opinions. In the case of questions about income, for example, the nonresponse rate was between two and three times greater in the telephone interviews than in the in-person interviews. It is difficult to reconcile these two rather conflicting findings about responses to sensitive questions.

In contrast, Aquilino (1994) reports that respondents in his survey of 18- to 45-year-olds in Los Angeles varied in their admissions to using illicit drugs. He found the respondents more likely to admit using marijuana, cocaine, or crack in face-to-face interviews than over the telephone. But he also found relatively similar admission rates about alcohol abuse in both modes. Perhaps the most interesting finding of Aquilino's research is that there are apparent degrees of sensitivity, with drug use being the strongest and other topics, such as alcohol abuse, less so. He concludes that confidentiality and trust factors appear to be harder for respondents to judge on the telephone. The results of this study contrast with those of an earlier survey of drinking behavior in Great Britain, in which the researchers found that telephone interviews revealed greater amounts of alcohol consumption than did face-to-face interviews (Sykes and Collins 1988).

Timothy Johnson, J. Hougland, and R. Clayton (1989) report a similar finding among college students who were asked questions about substance abuse in telephone and face-to-face modes. The students were much more open in their responses when interviewed in person. In a follow-up report, the researchers note that there were few differences in the students' reports of their use of nonillegal substances, such as tobacco and alcohol, by either males or females, but males were not as likely to report substance abuse over the telephone, suggesting that telephone interviews are not as reliable for such topics (Johnson, Hougland, and Moore 1991). On the other hand, female respondents were found to be less likely to agree to be interviewed in person about their drug use.

◆ Weighing the Advantages and Disadvantages

In the preceding sections, I have tried to indicate that a researcher's decision to carry out telephone versus face-to-face interviewing should depend on the nature of the requirements of the task, the type and depth of the responses desired, the relative need for standardization of questions, the need for cost-efficiency, the complexity of the information required, and the overall identity and makeup of the respondents.

With perhaps some justification, most comparisons of telephone interviewing and in-person interviewing have focused on the researcher's skills and on the effectiveness and standardness of the questionnaire. These are, of course, important considerations, not to be treated lightly. It is apparent, however, that most research comparing these two modes has not focused on variations in respondents' uses of language. As noted earlier, every communication is made up of a sender, a message, and a receiver. Focusing on the sender and the message covers only two-thirds of the communicative triad, whether the interviewing is conducted by telephone or in person. Traditional interview research often overlooks the receiver, with the exception of demographic information gathered before or during the interview. But such a broad demographic picture says nothing about the respondent's personal or social interactional needs, styles, patterns, or preferences. If these are discovered at all, it is during the course of the interview, often when it may be too late for the researcher to make use of the information.

Because the approaches of survey research consider the respondent and the answer to a given question to be the salient units of analysis, it would seem all the more likely that the individual and group variability of respondents should be more deeply probed, even when economic considerations make it difficult for the researcher to consider any mode of interviewing other than the telephone.

Researchers in other fields, such as anthropology, linguistics, law enforcement, medicine, and some of the other social sciences are often more concerned with variability of responses, especially those that are natural and self-generated rather than induced by a standard questionnaire. In these fields the face-to-face interview is generally considered appropriate, at least for the initial basic research. Once a researcher has found general patterns of specific answer features in smaller populations through in-person interviews, it is sometimes then useful to test these features on a larger population by telephone. For example, William Labov (1982) carried out a number of individual face-to-face interviews with a sample of the New York City population in an effort to determine the diagnostic features of New York City speech. Once he discovered salient distinctive fea-

tures through these interviews, he extended his population through telephone interviews with a larger number of New Yorkers, focusing only on these few selected features.

◆ A Case Study

The following case study shows how all three members of the sender-message-receiver triad can be examined in the interview process. It also provides some evidence of the role of gender differences in both the interviewer and the interviewee, and the advantages of in-person interviewing for getting better responses to sensitive items, reducing the social distance between interviewer and respondent, and letting respondents self-generate what is on their minds.

In 1970, the U.S. Supreme Court held that a person's statutory entitlement to welfare benefits cannot be terminated without a predetermination interview hearing, which would satisfy the requirement of due process (*Goldberg v. Kelly* 1970). Since that time, more and more of the requirements of government agencies have come under due process protection. This means that an individual recipient of benefits can request an agency interview concerning any loss or reduction of his or her benefits. The agency conducts such an interview both to comply with the rulings and to be fair to the beneficiary—to provide the beneficiary the opportunity to challenge the agency's decision and to supplement or explain the information on which the agency has based its decision.

As early as 1987, Medicare's proposal to substitute telephone hearings for in-person interviews in terminating benefits met stiff opposition from Congress, attorneys for the elderly, and the Association of Administrative Law Judges. The concerns of Congress ultimately led to the defeat of the proposal. By the 1990s, however, things had changed and Medicare Part B hearings began to be conducted in both telephone and in-person interviews, depending on the wishes of the beneficiaries, but still without the research that Congress had found lacking in the 1980s. Concern over this lack of research, coupled with a suspicion that older Medicare recipients might not be being treated fairly or accurately, led the Senior Citizens Law Center (SCLC) to propose a comparison of whatever extant tape recordings of telephone hearing interviews were available with in-person interviews (Shuy and Staton 1994; Shuy 1998).

Interviewing in practical work contexts, of necessity perhaps, needs to stress respondent conduct and well-being as much as interviewer behavior. In the case study material, however, those who managed the interviewing in question appeared to be somewhat undecided about whether to switch from conventional in-person interviewing to telephone interviewing, primarily for economic considerations. The growing number of established in-person interview hearings required by law became an issue of cost-effectiveness. Some bureaucrats argued that the interviews could be carried out by telephone. Unfortunately, there was no research evidence that various agencies could consult to find out what they would gain or lose by switching from an in-person to a telephone mode. Nevertheless, various agencies of the federal and state governments began encouraging the use of the telephone for hearing interviews, although they left the final choices to their regional or local offices. Some interviewers chose the telephone; some chose to continue interviewing in person. Fortunately, tape recordings were made of a small sample of the telephone interviews, so that it was possible to compare these with observed in-person events. The following describes an effort made by the SCLC (in association with the Gray Panthers) to answer the question of which mode would be most appropriate for Medicare Part B interviews (Shuy 1998).

DESIGN AND PURPOSE OF THE STUDY

The research design of this study hardly qualifies as rigorous. It was possible to locate 17 previously tape-recorded telephone interviews for comparison with 8 concurrently tape-recorded in-person interviews. No effort could be made to be random or representative. The 25 beneficiaries were from California, Iowa, Oregon, Maryland, and Virginia. The interviews were carried out by 11 female and 7 male hearing officers.

Issues that commonly concern traditional researchers comparing the two modes of interviewing were not foremost in this study. This research was not concerned with determining a profile of the recipients' attitudes, beliefs, or knowledge. Instead, the goal was to assess such issues as fairness of treatment, the comfort of both parties, and their mutual understanding of the success or failure of the interview. To accomplish these goals, the research examined the language and communicative styles of the various participants. In short, the focus was to determine, for both the interviewers and the beneficiaries, how communicative language and style differ between telephone and in-person interviews. The type and purpose of the interviews were held constant. Also unlike past research on this topic, this study focused on the receiver of the message as well as the sender and the message itself. Of particular importance were the issues of how and if clients were permitted to present their own agendas, whether they had conversational rights, whether they were being listened to and treated fairly, and the extent to which status, age, and gender of the respondents and interviewers affected the quality of the interviews.

Such research questions are very different from issues of standardization of questionnaire and interviewer uniformity. To a lesser extent, interviewer bias was observable in this study, but not in the same way that past research has described. Underlying the study, of course, was the important question of cost-effectiveness, for this was the government's concern in the first place. It was assumed from the outset that it is less expensive to do telephone interviews than to carry out individual meetings, but at what cost to the beneficiaries and at what cost to accuracy of the transmission and exchange of information?

Applying the research discussed previously concerning the advantages of both telephone and face-to-face interviewing, I summarize the results of this study below. It should be noted, however, that among the advantages of telephone interviewing mentioned above, those related to interviewer bias, standardization of questionnaire, response rates, and safety of the interviewer are not relevant for comparison, for various reasons. Interviewer monitoring was not possible in this context, nor did a standard questionnaire exist. Response rates are irrelevant, because the beneficiaries initiated the interviews. And the safety of the interviewer was not an issue here, whether the interviews were conducted by telephone or in person.

ACHIEVING COST- AND TIME-EFFICIENCY

Contrary to the literature reporting that in-person interviews take longer than those done by telephone, no substantive elapsed time difference was found between the two modes in this study. In two of the telephone interviews, the beneficiary was represented by an attorney, and these interviews took longer than interviews with beneficiaries alone. But even including these two interviews, there was no substantive difference between telephone and in-person modes in the time taken to complete interviews.

It is likely that the cost of in-person interviews for administrative hearings is somewhat greater than that of telephone interviews, simply because of the time required for travel to the designated interview location (usually a Social Security office). But there was no distinguishable difference in elapsed time for the interviews themselves between the telephone and in-person modes.

ENSURING INTERVIEWER UNIFORMITY

Surprisingly, the greatest uniformity found among interviewers was based on gender, both of the interviewer and of the interviewee. Female telephone interviewers were consistent in reframing the interview from the formal to the informal register, in making use of language markers of the informal register (such as address forms, contractions, personal comments, feedback markers, and varying intonation patterns), in being polite through indirectness rather than directness, in making use of positive speech acts such as advising (males tended to use the more negative speech act of warning), in avoiding challenges to the beneficiary, in sharing power rather than exploiting it, in avoiding power asymmetry (by not using the first-person pronoun *I* and by avoiding *my* statements), in letting the beneficiary generate his or her own story, in avoiding displays of authority and knowledge, and in taking the beneficiary's perspective. This practice by the female interviewers contrasted sharply with that of the male interviewers, but *only* in the telephone interviews. In the face-to-face interviews, male interviewers used the language forms just noted in approximately the same manner as the female interviewers. This suggests something very interesting about the use of the telephone mode. Female interviewers seemed to be more comfortable with it than males and used it to accomplish most of the agency's stated goals for the interaction, whereas male interviewers accomplished these goals best in face-to-face interactions.

The gender of the beneficiary was also noteworthy in terms of uniformity. When females interviewed female beneficiaries, the above-noted language features were symmetrically distributed. But when males interviewed male beneficiaries by telephone, these features were even more conspicuously sparse. Power, including language power, was evident in the language of the male interviewers, and even more so when male interviewers spoke with male beneficiaries rather than with female beneficiaries. Male interviewers appeared to be concerned with winning disputed points, defending mistakes of the agency, and challenging the points made by the male beneficiaries. Interestingly, the quantity of power moves made by male interviewers was lower when male interviewers met with male or female beneficiaries face-to-face. This contrast would suggest that male interviewers are more likely to use the language advantages of the female interviewers when engaged in face-to-face interviewing, but much less so in telephone exchanges.

GETTING RESPONSES TO SENSITIVE QUESTIONS

Groves and Kahn (1979) found that in telephone surveys, direct questions about income yield the largest missing-data rates in the research. To reduce this problem, they suggest that interviewers use an unfolding procedure when respondents are reluctant to provide exact income figures, in which respondents are asked to indicate into which one of three broad income categories their incomes fall. But even with this unfolding technique, the proportion of missing data on such questions is still higher in telephone surveys than in face-to-face interviews.

Why is it that in-person interviewing yields better response rates on more sensitive items than the telephone approach? For one thing, physical presence is naturally more intimate, even for people meeting for the first time, than is nonpresent telephone communication. The personal distancing from intimacy found in telephone interviewing has advantages. For example, small talk is less necessary, saving valuable interview time. On the other hand, there can be no doubt that physical presence provides the interviewer with a larger inventory of communicative tools, including those that allow the type of intimacy that promotes answers to sensitive questions. In addition, physical presence makes obvious the answers to some sensitive questions, such as those involving the respondent's physical and/or emotional state, and so eliminate the interviewer's need to ask; such answers are also difficult for respondents to refute with vague or inaccurate responses.

Another advantage of in-person interviewing is that physical presence makes available obvious communicative clues to the respondent's confusion, reluctance to answer, or discomfort, enabling the interviewer to rephrase a question or reframe the context in order to convert a no-answer response into a salvageable answer. This advantage was especially obvious in this study, where instances of respondents' confusion or anger were mitigated in the personal interviews much better than in the telephone mode. Once again, however, it should be noted that female telephone interviewers were much better at this than male telephone interviewers. Of course, if the point of the research is to follow the set questionnaire exactly, this is not an advantage after all.

OBTAINING CONTEXTUAL NATURALNESS

It is easy to overlook the obvious fact that the interview is only one of the many types of human communication. People engage actively in different types of communication daily, such as talk between friends and family members, talk between strangers, and talk with providers of goods and services. In most of these talking events the participants are more or less equal in power, status, and knowledge. The interview event, simply because one person asks all the questions, is fraught with the asymmetry of power. As such, it is a marked communicative episode in the respondent's day of otherwise symmetrical talk.

It would seem reasonable that interviewers would want to reduce this asymmetry as much as possible, especially because the interview is so different from the respondent's daily communication patterns. In the conventional interview event, power, status, and knowledge reside in the questioner, not in the respondent. In the administrative interviews in this study, the beneficiaries were supplicants, requesting redress for what they considered to be unfair treatment by the agency. They were the subordinates and the interviewers were the superordinates. In short, the interviews had a high probability of unequal role assignment.

Some of the administrative interviews met the agency's goal of permitting the beneficiaries to supplement or explain information in a fair way that could produce a more accurate picture of their situations. Others did not. The language of the more successful interviews can be characterized as producing an informal conversational style, sharing or giving up perceived power, letting the respondents self-generate topics, defusing the legal format, taking the beneficiary's perspective, and avoiding displays of knowledge (Shuy 1998). These qualities permitted respondents to initiate their own topics, disagree, give directives, and even ask questions. In short, the more successful interviewers reframed and reformatted the conventional question-answer interview to make the interview event more like the type of everyday conversation with which respondents were familiar, recontextualizing it and making it more natural to them. They took the respondents' perspectives and made them feel important. These interviewers let the beneficiaries be teachers while the interviewers took on the

role of learners, adopting what some field-workers have called the "one down" position (Agar 1980).

SELF-GENERATING RESPONSES

In the hearing interviews that met the agency's goal—unveiling the respondents' perceived new and important information as accurately and fairly as possible—the interviewers permitted, even encouraged, the respondents to bring up whatever topics they wanted, ask any questions they wanted, and otherwise talk as they might in natural, everyday conversation. It is clear that the open-ended question was highly valued as a topic introducer, with "wh-" questions used as follow-ups. For example, the female interviewers began with open-ended requests such as "Tell me anything that you would like to help me make a decision in your favor" and "I will give you the floor and you go on into what it is you wish to give me." As a side note, even when male telephone interviewers employed open-ended questions, they often posed them negatively; for example, "Why do you disagree with the denial you got from the agency?" This question, although open-ended, appears to reflect the competitive approach of the male interviewers who conducted their interviews by telephone. Curiously enough, this competitive aspect was far less evident among the male interviewers in the face-to-face mode.

One might predict that encouraging self-generated responses from interviewees would greatly extend the duration of the interviews, but as it turned out, this did not happen, except in two telephone interviews in which beneficiaries were accompanied and represented by attorneys. Those interviews took on the formulaic interview context of the courtroom, where information is unwrapped slowly and in a fashion comfortable only to lawyers. The beneficiaries in those cases played very minor roles in the interviews.

DISTRIBUTING
POWER EQUALLY

Respondents' lack of power in many interview situations can be intimidating to them, and can often result in their providing imperfect, ambiguous, incomplete, or otherwise unsuccessful representations of their actual knowledge and opinions. When interviewers permit respondents to participate in setting the agenda, to ask questions, and to change the direction of things, they surrender personal power and help to distribute power more equally between the participants.

But there is also more that interviewers can do to ensure symmetry of power, whether interviewing by telephone or in person. For example, an interviewer can make explicit statements about how important the interviewee is, tactfully demonstrating the equal status of respondent and interviewer; some of the hearing officers in this study took this approach. One positive way for an interviewer to promote equality, as noted above, is to use casual, conversational language rather than the normally more formal interview language. The use of casual address forms, contractions, added personal comments, abundant feedback markers (such as "uh-huh" uttered during responses), and conversational intonation aids this endeavor.

One significant finding of this case study is that the interviewers who managed to share power and take the perspective of the respondent were able to elicit necessary information faster and more completely than were those who did not do so. Among the remarks the interviewers made that show this perspective taking are the following:

I can appreciate your point that you've done everything you could to find out what the guidelines were and to adhere to them.

Sometimes that's the only route that you have open to you.

I can understand that since your doctor prescribed it, you feel that you know your condition.

There are also status pitfalls that interviewers can avoid, such as the use of "I" power statements ("I want you to . . ." or "I'll send you a . . . ,"); interviewers can substitute passive-voice equivalents for such statements. Once again, this study revealed that male interviewers used "I" power statements far more frequently on the telephone (but not in person) than did female interviewers, suggesting a mode weakness of the telephone interview, at least for male interviewers.

ADDRESSING COMPLEX ISSUES

In the interviews conducted in this study, it was sometimes necessary for the participants to refer to previous correspondence and/or regulations found in beneficiary handbooks. When this happened during telephone interviews, interviewers and respondents spent considerable time trying to locate documents or to refer to exact pages. When a beneficiary did not have the necessary documents at hand, the interviewer had to read relevant passages aloud. This increased the time spent and introduced the additional problem of the comprehensibility of orally read materials. Interviews that did not require such searches for documentation were smooth and quick, often taking no longer than 20 or 30 minutes. When such problems arose, however, the interviews lasted up to 10 minutes longer. In contrast, during face-to-face interviews, the needed documents were immediately available for both parties to see and discuss on the spot, with little or no time added to the event.

DEALING WITH OLDER OR
HANDICAPPED RESPONDENTS

In this study, the respondents were all older and/or handicapped, so a comparison between telephone and in-person interviewing is salient. In the telephone interviews, the interviewers had to ask more questions about the respondents' physical conditions than did interviewers in the in-person interviews. In addition, in-person interviewers were able to see whether hearing-impaired respondents were straining to hear what was being said and so could adjust the clarity and volume of their speech, often eliminating the respondents' need to request that they repeat questions.

◆ Related Studies of Practical Interviewing

Related research comparing telephone and in-person interviewing in the practical work context provides other information. In the 1970s, the California Unemployment Insurance Appeals Board (CUIAB) faced the problem of conducting interviews for applicants for benefits who had moved to another location, requiring split interviewing in two different sites. It was decided that experiments should be conducted to determine whether or not telephone interviews could replace this difficult task. After a lawsuit brought by an employee denied unemployment compensation had been rejected, the case was taken up the appeals ladder to the California Court of Appeals. The judge who wrote the decision supported the lower court's denial of the application, but continued to favor in-person interviews when possible (when the parties were within an hour's driving distance).

An entity called the Fair Hearing Project attempted to assist CUIAB by carrying out research on the reactions and attitudes of participants in both in-person and telephone hearing interviews. This study found that both interviewers and interviewees believed that the concerns about due process were met by the telephone interview, but, when asked to compare the two modes, the respondents were much less certain about their preference. Of the respondents surveyed, 44 percent felt that the telephone interviews provided a less extensive opportunity for the participants to question and rebut; 64 percent of the interviewers felt that telephone interviewing required more extensive preparation than the in-person mode, believed that the process of asking questions to obtain the necessary information was more difficult over the telephone, and felt that telephone hearings were more difficult to manage. A major conclusion of this research was that whenever possible, such interviews should be conducted in person (Corsi and Hurley 1979a). In a follow-up report, the researchers propose that the telephone might be substituted for in-person interviews in certain areas, especially when the claimant is represented by an attorney, but they still maintain that in-person interviews are preferable to telephone interviews (Corsi and Hurley 1979b).

Similar research by the Fair Hearing Project was carried out in the 1980s concerning a four-year study of telephone versus in-person interviewing for unemployment and welfare appeals in New Mexico (Corsi et al. 1984). It was found that appeals were more likely to be denied in telephone interviews and that the "somewhat artificial" setting caused by the telephone resulted in claimants' being less able to express themselves and more intimidated than in face-to-face interviews. Even so, 73.7 percent of the claimants reported being satisfied with the telephone interview, whereas 61.9 percent of those who were interviewed in person expressed such satisfaction. A clear conclusion of this study was that the telephone mode created savings in cost and time related to productivity improvement.

The partially conflicting findings of both the research of the Fair Hearing Project and the findings of the SCLC are due, at least in part, to the differences in what was studied and in the ages of the respondents. Whereas the SCLC (Gray Panther) study examined tape recordings of the actual language used by the parties, the Fair Housing Project concerned itself with self-reported reflections and feelings of the participants. Although both types of data can be useful, insights obtained from the actual language used during the interviewing event are seldom examined, nor were they by the Fair Hearing Project. Likewise, the ages of the interviewees, although not reported, are another likely source of difference in findings. The younger respondents in the Fair Hearing Project were likely more familiar with using the telephone and possibly more comfortable with telephone interviewing than were the senior citizen respondents in the SCLC interviews.

◆ Summary of Relative Benefits

I began this chapter by saying that different kinds of interviews use different criteria for success and that the decision to interview by telephone or face-to-face depends on many factors. It is not my purpose to claim that one mode is better than the other for research interviewing. Factors of expedience, cost, and time may dictate the mode to be used, despite whatever else may be compromised in the process. My purpose, rather, is to point out the relative benefits of both modes and to make as clear as possible the advantages and disadvantages that are present. These can be summarized as follows:

◆ *Cost:* In most cases, research interviewing by telephone is less expensive than face-to-face interviewing.

◆ *Control:* Research has shown that situational variables are easier to control in telephone interviews than in face-to-face interviews.

◆ *Quantification of results:* For research that seeks specific responses to specific questions, telephone interviewing lends itself more readily to ease in coding and

quantification of results. This is not to say that quantitative analysis is not possible with data collected in face-to-face interviews. Such analysis, however, is more difficult and time-consuming to manage, because responses are not given in a prescribed order, making eventual coding more time-consuming. Computer-assisted telephone interviewing makes such quantification even easier.

◆ *Completion time:* Although the time expended during face-to-face interviews is roughly equal to that expended during telephone interviews, in-person interviewing requires additional time for interviewers to make arrangements and travel to the interview sites.

◆ *Naturalness:* Advantages gained through telephone interviewing may be negated if it is important for the researcher to get the type of response accuracy provided by the everyday communication context found in face-to-face interaction.

◆ *Response rates:* From reports of past comparisons, it appears that better response rates are achieved in face-to-face interviewing than in telephone interviewing.

◆ *Thoughtfulness of responses:* If the goal is to probe deeply and to elicit thoughtful answers, then interviewers' letting respondents self-generate whatever is on their minds is superior to having probes controlled by a standardized set of questions, whether this is done in person or by telephone.

◆ *Complexity of issues:* Face-to-face interaction appears to be better suited than telephone interviewing for handling complex issues.

◆ *Marginalized respondents:* In-person interviewing is clearly superior to telephone interviewing with older, hearing-impaired, and minority respondents.

◆ *Sensitive questions:* Past research clearly shows that face-to-face interviews are better than telephone interviews for eliciting answers to the most sensitive questions, such as those concerning substance use, personal income, and sometimes even drinking patterns.

◆ Unresolved Issues

A number of issues remain unresolved concerning the advantages and disadvantages of telephone and in-person interviewing. As noted above, relatively little research has been done on the actual language used in interviews conducted in either mode. Researchers have looked at summaries of respondents' answers and at respondent attitudes, but few have undertaken detailed analyses of the ways interviewers and interviewees talk during interviews (see Schaeffer and Maynard, Chapter 28, this volume). Representations of attitudes, knowledge, and beliefs are always interesting self-report information, but such data are still at least a step away from much of the information discoverable in the actual language interaction. A good way for researchers to discover this information is by studying audiotapes of the spoken language and, if possible, videotapes of nonverbal aspects of in-person interviews. Because language goes by so fast and is so complex, researchers interested in studying language use in interviews will need to record interviews on video- or audiotape and then review the tapes many times for different features. Although the gap here is beginning to be filled, missing in most of the existing research comparing the two modes of interviewing is attention to the respondents' language and comfort. Perhaps it is only natural that research on interviewing would start with the sender of the message and the message itself. But with the knowledge that has been accumulated thus far, it is now important for researchers to give more attention to the receiver of the interviewer's questions.

For researchers to know exactly what they may be missing or gaining when they carry out telephone interviews rather than in-person interviews, they need reliable information based on detailed comparisons between the two modes. Also, in light of the findings of the research on the power of questioning cited above, it would be useful for future research to compare the advantages of highly structured, standardized question sequences with the responses obtained through freer and more natural forms of discourse. If the experience of linguistics and anthropology is in any way helpful, it may show that respondents who give single answers to directed interview questions may respond quite differently if given the chance to generate their own information. Realizing that the collaborative nature of communication is compromised when the major role of one party is to answer the questions of another (Cicourel 1964; Holstein and Staples 1992), we need to know more about how telephone and face-to-face interviewing each suit this human condition.

Finally, we need to know considerably more about the role of gender in interviewing. Some past research has pointed out gender differences in respondents, particularly with respect to sensitive topics, such as substance abuse (Cahalan 1968; Johnson et al. 1991; Murphy and Binson 1988). In a consumer attitude survey, Groves and Nancy Fultz (1985) analyzed the effects of interviewer gender on response rates and found that female interviewers were more successful at getting responses than were male interviewers. However, the results were confounded, as Groves and Fultz admit, by the fact that the male interviewers were less experienced than the females. In any case, the sole focus was on response rate rather than on quality or type of response. Judson Landis, Daryl Sullivan, and Joseph Sheley (1973), in analyzing questions about women's rights, found that male interviewers got more feminist responses from female respondents than did female interviewers. It is clear that some question topics elicit responses that vary depending on the gender of the interviewer. It would be useful to know more about how gender-based responses are the same or different in telephone versus in-person interview contexts.

■ References

Agar, M. 1980. *The Professional Stranger: An Informal Introduction to Ethnography.* New York: Academic Press.

Aneshensel, C. S., R. R. Fredrichs, V. A. Clark, and P. A. Yokopenic. 1982. "Measuring Depression in the Community: A Comparison of Telephone and Personal Interviews." *Public Opinion Quarterly* 46:110-21.

Aquilino, W. S. 1994. "Interview Mode Effects in Surveys of Drug and Alcohol Use: A Field Experiment." *Public Opinion Quarterly* 58:210-40.

Aquilino, W. S. and L. A. LoSciuto. 1990. "Effects of Interview Mode on Self-Reported Drug Use." *Public Opinion Quarterly* 54:362-95.

Brown, R. 1973. *A First Language: The Early Stages.* Cambridge, MA: Harvard University Press.

Cahalan, D. 1968. "Correlates of Respondent Accuracy in the Denver Validity Survey." *Public Opinion Quarterly* 32:606-21.

Cicourel, A. V. 1964. *Method and Measurement in Sociology.* New York: Free Press.

Conley, J. M. and W. M. O'Barr. 1998. *Just Words: Law, Language, and Power.* Chicago: University of Chicago Press.

Corsi, J. R. and T. L. Hurley. 1979a. "Attitudes toward the Use of the Telephone in Administrative Fair Hearings: The California Experience." *Administrative Law Review* 31:247-83.

———. 1979b. "Pilot Study Report on the Use of the Telephone in Administrative Fair Hearings." *Administrative Law Review* 31:485-524.

Corsi, J. R., L. B. Rosenfeld, G. D. Fowler, K. E. Newcomer, D. C. Niekerk, and J. D. Bell. 1984. "Major Findings of the New Mexico Experiment of Teleconferenced Administrative Fair Hearings." *University of Miami Law Review* 38:647-55.

de Leeuw, E. D. and J. van der Zouwen. 1988. "Data Quality in Telephone and Face-to-Face Surveys: A Comparative Meta-analysis." Pp. 283-300 in *Telephone Survey Methodology,* edited by R. M. Groves, P. P. Biemer, L. E. Lyberg, J. T. Massey, W. L. Nicholls II, and J. Waksberg. New York: John Wiley.

Frey, J. H. 1989. *Survey Research by Telephone.* 2d ed. Newbury Park, CA: Sage.

Goldberg v. Kelly, 397 U.S. 254 (1970).

Groves, R. M. 1978. "On the Mode of Administering a Questionnaire and Responses to Open-Ended Items." *Social Science Research* 7:257-71.

———. 1979. "Actors and Questions in Telephone and Personal Interview Surveys." *Public Opinion Quarterly* 43:190-205.

———. 1989. *Survey Errors and Survey Costs.* New York: John Wiley.

Groves, R. M. and N. H. Fultz. 1985. "Gender Effects among Telephone Interviewers in a Survey of Economic Attitudes." *Sociological Methods & Research* 14:31-52.

Groves, R. M. and R. L. Kahn. 1979. *Surveys by Telephone: A National Comparison with Personal Interviews.* New York: Academic Press.

Groves, R. M., P. V. Miller, and C. F. Cannell. 1987. "Differences between the Telephone and Personal Interview Data." Pp. 11-19 in *An Experimental Comparison of Telephone and Personal Health Interview Surveys* (Vital and Health Statistics Series 2, Data Evaluation and Methods Research, No. 106), edited by O. T. Thornberry. Hyattsville, MD: U.S. Department of Health and Human Services.

Herzog, A. R. and W. L. Rodgers. 1988. "Interviewing Older Adults: Mode Comparison Using Data from a Face-to-Face Survey and a Telephone Resurvey." *Public Opinion Quarterly* 52:84-99.

Herzog, A. R., W. L. Rodgers, and R. A. Kulka. 1983. "Interviewing Older Adults: A Comparison of Telephone and Face-to-Face Modalities." *Public Opinion Quarterly* 47:405-18.

Holstein, J. A. and J. F. Gubrium. 1995. *The Active Interview.* Thousand Oaks, CA: Sage.

Holstein, J. A. and W. G. Staples. 1992. "Producing Evaluative Knowledge: The Interactional Bases of Social Science Findings." *Sociological Inquiry* 62:11-35.

Johnson, T. P., J. G. Hougland, and R. R. Clayton. 1989. "Obtaining Reports of Sensitive Behavior: A Comparison of Substance Use Reports from Telephone and Face-to-Face Interviews." *Social Science Quarterly* 70:174-83.

Johnson, T. P., J. G. Hougland, and R. W. Moore. 1991. "Sex Differences in Reporting Sensitive Behavior: A Comparison of Interview Methods." *Sex Roles* 24:669-80.

Jordan, L. A., A. C. Marcus, and L. G. Reeder. 1980. "Response Styles in Telephone and Household Interviewing: A Field Experiment." *Public Opinion Quarterly* 44:210-22.

Labov, W. A. 1982. *The Social Stratification of English in New York City.* Washington, DC: Center for Applied Linguistics.

Landis, J. R. 1973. "Feminist Attitudes as Related to Sex of Interviewer." *Pacific Sociological Review* 16:305-14.

Lavrakas, P. J. 1993. *Telephone Survey Methods: Sampling, Selection, and Supervision.* 2d ed. Newbury Park, CA: Sage.

Murphy, P. A. and D. Binson. 1988. "Who Says 'No' to Whom: Respondent Interaction in Refusal to Sensitive Questions." Presented at the annual meeting of the American Association of Public Opinion Research, Toronto.

Oksenberg, L. and C. F. Cannell. 1988. "Effects of Interviewer Vocal Characteristics on Nonresponse." Pp. 257-69 in *Telephone Survey Methodology*, edited by R. M. Groves, P. P. Biemer, L. E. Lyberg, J. T. Massey, W. L. Nicholls II, and J. Waksberg. New York: John Wiley.

Roberts, F. D. 1999. *Talking about Treatment: Recommendations for Breast Cancer Adjuvant Therapy.* New York: Oxford University Press.

Shuy, R. W. 1998. *Bureaucratic Language in Government and Business.* Washington, DC: Georgetown University Press.

Shuy, R. W. and J. J. Staton. 1994. "A Linguistic Comparison of Telephone and In-Person Hearings." Pp. 1-87 in *Telecommunications and Public Benefit Hearings*, edited by B. Brewer, A. J. Chiplin, Jr., and B. D. Fretz. Washington, DC: National Senior Citizens Law Center.

Stokes, L. and M.-Y. Yeh. 1988. "Searching for Causes of Interviewer Effects in Telephone Surveys." Pp. 357-62 in *Telephone Survey Methodology*, edited by R. M. Groves, P. P. Biemer, L. E. Lyberg, J. T. Massey, W. L. Nicholls II, and J. Waksberg. New York: John Wiley.

Sykes, W. and M. Collins. 1988. "Effects of Mode of Interview: Experiments in the UK." Pp. 301-20 in *Telephone Survey Methodology*, edited by R. M. Groves, P. P. Biemer, L. E. Lyberg, J. T. Massey, W. L. Nicholls II, and J. Waksberg. New York: John Wiley.

Thornberry, O. T., ed. 1987. *An Experimental Comparison of Telephone and Personal Health Interview Surveys* (Vital and Health Statistics Series 2, Data Evaluation and Methods Research, No. 106). Hyattsville, MD: U.S. Department of Health and Human Services.

27

COMPUTER-ASSISTED INTERVIEWING

◆ Mick P. Couper
Sue Ellen Hansen

Computer-assisted data collection methods are having a profound effect on survey interviewing. In this chapter we explore several themes related to this impact. Although computer-assisted telephone interviewing (CATI) has been around for several decades (see Shuy, Chapter 26, this volume), the revolution in survey methods began to be felt with the introduction of computer-assisted personal interviewing (CAPI) in the early 1990s (see Couper and Nicholls 1999). More recently, with the development of methods that reduce the role of the interviewer (e.g., audio computer-assisted self-interviewing) or eliminate the interviewer entirely (e.g., Web surveys), renewed attention has been focused on the role of the survey interviewer in an automated data collection environment. Despite major changes in the survey process over the past several years, only recently has research attention been focused on the effects of the introduction of computers on the interviewing situation and on the role and task of the survey interviewer.

In this chapter we review the effects of the data collection revolution on survey interviewers and respondents. We explore how the work of interviewers has changed under computer-assisted interviewing (CAI). Our central thesis is that CAI and paper-and-pencil (P&P) surveys differ in many ways for both interviewers and respondents, and for the interaction between the two. This does not mean that one technology (paper or computer) is necessarily better than the other; rather, the two are qualitatively different. Furthermore, we believe that many of the effects of technology may be mediated by the particular design or implementation of a survey, rather than by fundamental features of the technology. These design differences may in turn reflect organizational philosophies (e.g., related to control of interviewers), constraints of particular software used (in the case of CAI), or design choices on the part of those implementing the survey (whether on paper on computer). To understand the effects of CAI on interviewers and respondents, it is important to understand the contexts in which particular survey instruments are created.

We begin with a brief review of the recent history of computer-assisted methods and their impacts on the survey endeavor. We then turn to an examination of the effects of the new technology on interviewers and on interactions between interviewers and respondents. We end with a discussion of some of the newer methods of data collection that includes some speculation on their possible impacts on the role of the survey interviewer.

We preface this discussion with a note that computer-assisted interviewing is widely viewed as a tool of standardized survey interviewing (see Singleton and Straits, Chapter 3, this volume). In other words, CAI is seen as a means to ensure greater control over the interview process or to increase standardization. However, this is not an inherent feature of computer assistance, and instruments can be designed to provide interviewers with more (rather than less) flexibility (see, e.g., Conrad and Schober 1999; Belli, Shay, and Stafford 1999). It is not our goal to join this debate; we merely want to note that standardized interviewing is the dominant viewpoint from which CAI has been developed and evaluated.

◆ Computer-Assisted Interviewing Methods

Computer-assisted telephone interviewing, first used in 1971, was the earliest form of computer-based survey data collection to gain widespread use. Improved data quality was among the potential benefits that early proponents claimed for the new technology. Such data quality was to come through (a) systematic control over the scheduling of calls and callbacks, (b) automatically tailored wording of complex questions based on prior responses, (c) computer-controlled branching between questions or sections of the instrument, (d) automatic range and consistency checks, and (e) careful monitoring of interviewer performance (Nicholls 1988). CATI also permitted study (and thereby control or improvement) of interviewer behavior and performance through its audio and video monitoring capabilities and automated call records (Couper and Nicholls 1999). Although these are now all standard features of most CAI surveys, the evidence of their effects on data quality is relatively modest.

Even before the advent of laptop computers, survey research realized the potential of extending computer assistance to face-to-face or personal-visit interviewing. In the late 1980s, computer-assisted personal interviewing was used for the first time in the Netherlands, and soon thereafter it was rapidly adopted in the United States and Europe. Today, most large-scale government and academic surveys in the United States are conducted using CAPI. During the progression from the early mainframe-based CATI days to PC-based CAPI systems, the software and interviewing systems became increasingly complex, to a point where many CAI surveys can no longer be replicated on paper. These complexities include features such as randomization of question order, tailored text (fills), on-line range and consistency checks, complex branching or skip instructions, links to external databases, on-line coding, and presentation of multimedia content. As a result, much of the development and testing effort has focused on program correctness or functionality rather than on optimal design from the interviewer's viewpoint, or usability.

Despite the rapid technological advances in survey data collection over the past few decades, most of the research has examined the quality of the resultant data rather than the process of data collection itself. For all the supposed benefits CAI was to bring in terms of data quality, a thorough review of the literature on data quality comparisons between CAI and paper-and-pencil interviewing led William Nicholls, Reginald Baker, and Jean Martin (1997) to conclude that data quality has been largely unaffected or only marginally improved by the introduction of CAI.

There are several indicators of data quality that researchers can examine to compare P&P and CAI methods. The first is the effect on skip errors. We should expect that, if the instrument is programmed correctly, skip errors would be eliminated in computer-assisted interviewing. In an early comparison of CATI and P&P, Robert Groves and Nancy Mathiowetz (1984) found that in one complex sequence of items (containing 28 questions and 42 possible paths), 1.8 percent of CATI entries were inappropriate, compared to 8.8 percent of non-CATI entries. Randy Olsen (1992), reporting results from the CAPI versus P&P experiment in round 12 of the National Longitudinal Survey—Youth Cohort, found that the percentage of invalid skips went from an already low 0.97 percent in P&P to 0.02 percent in CAPI. Gary Catlin and Susan Ingram (1988) compared discrepancy (or edit failure) rates between CATI and P&P in the Canadian Labor Force Survey. For the relatively straightforward household docket portion of the interview, the discrepancy rates were similar (0.7 percent in CATI and 0.6 percent in P&P), whereas for the more complex labor force questionnaire, the rates were significantly lower in CATI (1.8 percent in CATI, 4.6 percent in P&P). These findings suggest that the benefits of skip error or edit failure reductions in CAI are realized only when the instrument is very complex. Even so, these interviewer mistakes are not a large source of overall error in P&P surveys.

Given the evidence of general respondent indifference toward the technology used (which we will discuss later in this chapter), we would not expect large differences in the proportions of "don't know" and "refused" responses, and the research evidence bears this out. Groves and Mathiowetz (1984), for example, found comparable levels of item nonresponse for demographic and income questions in CATI and P&P. Jean Martin, Colm O'Muircheartaigh, and John Curtice (1993) similarly found proportions of "don't knows" and refusals to be identical in P&P and CAPI.

Another early concern in the transition to CAI was related to the length and quality of responses to open-ended questions. It was believed that interviewers could not type as fast as they could write. The evidence from comparisons on labor force surveys in France and Canada suggest these fears were unfounded. Bernard (1989) compared industry and occupation questions in CAPI and P&P and found no differences in the average length or number of words in the recorded responses. She also found identical coding rates for the two approaches. Catlin and Ingram (1988) obtained similar results in their comparison of CATI and P&P. Again, the conclusion of these studies is that CAI does no worse than paper-and-pencil interviewing.

A further source of initial concern was the possibility of keying errors associated with an interviewer's typing in a number to correspond with the selected answer in CAI, as opposed to checking a box in P&P. John Kennedy, Jennie Lengacher, and Loren Demerath (1990) found an average of only 0.62 percent keying errors over four CATI surveys, but did not collect comparable data from P&P surveys. Lynn Dielman and Mick Couper (1995) examined keying errors in a CAPI survey and found only 16 such errors out of more than 16,000 questions examined, for an error rate of 0.095 percent. James Lepkowski and his colleagues (1995) used behavior and error coding to examine responses to an even larger number of comparable CATI and P&P questions in the Panel Survey of

Income Dynamics. They found recording error rates to be identical at 0.1 percent. As we shall see later, some studies have found keying errors to be not a fundamental feature of CAI surveys, but rather a consequence of particular instrument design decisions. However, in general, entry errors appear to be no more (or less) of a concern in computer-assisted interviewing than in paper-and-pencil surveys.

Finally, a number of studies have compared the substantive distributions obtained from CAI and P&P surveys. Generally the distributions are similar, and where significant differences are found, these do not lend themselves to easy interpretation (e.g., Olsen 1992). Thus, despite the early claims of improved data quality resulting from the switch to computer-assisted methods, it is probably fair to say that, in general, data quality is no worse in CAI than it is in P&P interviewing. (There are two notable exceptions in which dramatic improvements in data quality have come from extensions of computer-assisted methods—audio computer-assisted self-interviewing, or audio-CASI, and dependent interviewing in panel surveys, in which data collected in a previous wave are fed back to respondents for review and confirmation.)

Where substantive differences have been found in comparisons of CAI with equivalent P&P surveys, the post hoc explanation in many cases has been that the designs or layouts of the two versions differed (e.g., Baker, Bradburn, and Johnson 1995; Bergman et al. 1994; see also Nicholls et al. 1997). Although many of these are seemingly innocuous changes of layout (e.g., separation of items across screens in CAI) rather than wording, they nonetheless convey different expectations of what kinds of information are required and thereby influence the responses obtained.

When the technology (i.e., paper or computer) alone is considered, rather than the technology with any concomitant change in instrument design, there has been found to be remarkably little change in the quality of the data collected. This should not be taken to imply that the advent of CAI has had minimal impact on interviewers and their work. Rather, it may suggest that although the *process* of interviewing has changed, the *outcome* is largely unaffected by the switch, at least as a result of computer assistance per se. This should not come as a big surprise, as many CAI surveys have been designed to be as comparable as possible to their P&P predecessors, in many cases to preserve the integrity of lengthy time series of trend data. One explanation may thus be the explicit efforts researchers have made to keep designs equivalent or comparable. Another may be that well-trained interviewers are compensating for instrument design flaws (in both paper-and-pencil and computer-assisted methods) in ways that mask the effects of the technologies. We should thus look more closely at the effects of computer assistance on the process of data collection, and particularly on the role of interviewers and their interactions with survey respondents.

◆ *Effects of CAI on Interviewers and Respondents*

Concerns about interviewers' use of computer software have been raised since the early days of CATI. Key among these is the problem of "segmentation," first identified by Robert Groves, Marianne Berry, and Nancy Mathiowetz (1980; see also House and Nicholls 1988). Segmentation arises from the fact that, because of the limited screen real estate in CAI, the interviewer sees only a small segment of the instrument at a time. Although this may have the benefit of focusing the interviewer on the immediate task at hand, the interviewer may lose a sense of the "big picture" of the interview, making his or her navigation (movement) through the instrument (other than the regular forward movement dictated by the program) more difficult and providing the interviewer little feedback on his or her progress through the instrument. As Groves et al. (1980) note: "With a paper questionnaire, no one has to explain to the interviewer how to flip backwards a page or two. But the designer of the on-line questionnaire must anticipate such needs and make explicit provision for them" (p. 519). Although some progress has been made in reducing the segmentation effect through judicious software design (see Sperry et al. 1999), this issue remains a common complaint of CAI interviewers.

With the advent of CAPI, additional concerns were raised about the effects of the new technology on interviewers. This was especially true of hardware and ergonomic issues, such as the heavy weight of the computer, low battery life, small screen size and low visibility, and slowness of the computer. The early machines did indeed suffer from a number of these limitations, but improvements in hardware and software over time appear to have eased these burdens for interviewers. With some exceptions (e.g., doorstep interviews and exit polls), concern about the feasibility of the current generation of laptop computers for CAPI surveys has waned. As a consequence, it seems, more attention is now being paid to software issues, some of which have been with us since the early days of CATI. Furthermore, as graphical user interfaces (e.g., Windows) become more common, increasing the range of options available to survey designers, the issue of software design is again becoming prominent in CAPI as well as in CATI.

Despite these concerns, both empirical and anecdotal evidence suggests that interviewers have adopted CAPI with enthusiasm (e.g., Baker and Wojcik 1992; Couper and Burt 1994; Edwards et al. 1993). Most of the initial concerns about in-person interviewers' ability to conduct computer-assisted interviews were unfounded. The reasons most often given for the positive reactions to the new technology relate to a sense of increased professionalism, of being on the cutting edge (see Nicholls and Groves 1986; Weeks 1992).

Interviewers using computers also report being relieved that they no longer have to worry about following complex skips, and being happy with the fact that their work is done when the interview is completed. In the days of P&P interviewing, an interviewer had a great deal of clerical work to perform before and after each interview. In some surveys (such as the Current Population Survey, or CPS), this involved transcribing details from previous waves of data collection onto the interviewing form, using optical mark recognition "bubbles." Similarly, after completing an interview, the interviewer had to clean up the questionnaire to prepare it for coding and keying, including at times rewriting or expanding upon hastily scribbled marginal notes. Many interviewers viewed these tasks as tedious and uninteresting, and certainly less important than their real task of interacting with sample respondents. Mick Couper and Geraldine Burt (1993) asked CPS interviewers in an open-ended question what they liked most about using a computer for interviewing: 47 percent mentioned the elimination of editing and transcription activities, 19 percent mentioned the ease or efficiency of interviewing, 18 percent mentioned the reduction of paperwork, and 16 percent mentioned the automation of skips and branching. On the other hand, 36 percent of the interviewers mentioned slow speed as the feature they enjoyed least about CAPI; this was followed by battery problems (19 percent), backing up to change answers in the instrument (11 percent), and weight of the computer (10 percent). In response to a later set of closed-ended questions, 81 percent agreed that using a computer enhanced the professional image of interviewers, and 39 percent agreed that using a computer slowed the interview down relative to paper and pencil (Couper and Burt 1994). Brad Edwards and his colleagues (1993) found that almost 40 percent of interviewers surveyed preferred P&P over CAPI for correcting errors.

Although interviewers generally express enthusiasm for CAPI, the number of interviewer complaints about features of the hardware and software suggest that optimal CAI design has not yet been achieved, and there is room for improvement of the interviewing systems being used. Increasingly, research attention has moved way from issues of feasibility (Is CAPI possible?) to issues of usability (How can the systems be optimized for the task?).

Respondent reactions to CAI appear equally as positive as those of interviewers. Several researchers have asked respondents how they feel about CAPI in sets of debriefing questions at the ends of interviews (e.g., Baker and Wojcik 1992; van Bastelaer, Kerssemakers, and Sikkel 1987).[1] We caution against overinterpretation of the results of such research, as the demand characteristics of the interview situation may make it hard for respondents to express negative attitudes to interviewers about an experience they just went through. Nonetheless, there is no evidence that suggests overt negative reactions to CAPI on the part of respondents. Furthermore, the introduction of CAI has appeared to have no effect on survey refusal rates (e.g., Bergman et al. 1994; de Leeuw and Nicholls 1996), suggesting that respondents are, at the very least, indifferent about the use of computers for interviewing. But, as we have already implied, the effects of the introduction of computers on respondents may be felt indirectly through changes in the behavior of the interviewer or the process of the interview. After all, the interviewer serves as intermediary between the computer and the respondent, and so any effects on the respondent (other than direct reactions to the presence of the computer) are likely to be mediated through the interviewer. For this reason, most of our work has focused on the interviewer's interactions with the CAI system.

◆ CAI Design and Interviewer-Computer Interaction

It is clear from our own work that the design of the computerized instrument has an impact on the way the interview is conducted. This is not a particularly new idea, but it is one that has received little research attention until recently. It has long been accepted that the design or layout of paper questionnaires can affect the data collection process. Several nonexperimental studies have demonstrated this for both interviewer-administered and self-administered surveys (e.g., Sanchez 1992; Smith 1995). Despite this, theory development on design issues other than question wording has been slow.[2] Furthermore, it appears to be presumed that in interviewer-administered surveys, well-trained interviewers can compensate for poor design, and in any case format, layout, and other design issues are not worthy of research attention. With the advent of CAPI, and particularly the range of design features made possible by the introduction of graphical user interfaces, this issue is becoming more salient in computer-assisted surveys. But this has already been recognized by Carol House and William Nicholls (1988), who note that a change to CAI "modifies the role of both survey interviewer and questionnaire designer. The interviewer becomes more dependent on the work of the designer" (p. 421).

That design is an important element of computer-assisted surveys (and indeed surveys of all types) is supported by evidence of several different types. The evidence provided by Maria Sanchez (1992) and Tom Smith (1995) comes from natural experiments of unintended layout changes in paper questionnaires. Sanchez (1992) examined the results when the layout of the same series of questions was changed in two similar surveys. She found that for one question, the number of "not ascertained" responses declined from 9 percent to 2 percent; for another, the number of interviewer failures to probe declined from 8.8 percent to 0.8 percent as a result of the changed designs. Similarly, Smith (1995) found wide variation (1.7 percent to 11.8 percent) in the number of missing answers to a follow-up question on religion across years of the General Social Survey. He concludes that placement of the identically worded questions contributed to this variation. In the surveys with high rates of missing data, the follow-up question appeared at the top of the reverse side of a page, making it more likely to be skipped.

Early indicators of possible design difficulties in CAI came from interviewer reports from debriefing surveys. For example, in response to Couper and Burt's (1993) questionnaire, 60 percent of CPS interviewers reported difficulties backing up and changing answers in the CAPI instrument. In fact, 52 percent reported having difficulty with a particular feature of the CAPI instrument that prevented them from backing up to the household roster once the roster had been completed.

Another source of information about interviewer difficulties in interacting with CAI instruments lies in keystroke or trace files. These automatic by-products of many CAI software systems provide records (with varying levels of detail across different software systems) of the functions used or keys pressed by interviewers during the interview. Studies have generally found that interviewers use certain CAI functions (e.g., on-line help and backup) less frequently than might be expected. For example, Mick Couper and Jay Schlegel (1998) found that CAPI interviewers in the National Health Interview Survey (NHIS) rarely used on-line help, with only 9 percent of all interviews showing any help access and an average use of 14 times per 100 interviews. The relatively infrequent use of on-line help parallels the findings of other researchers (Baker 1992; Couper, Sadosky,

and Hansen 1994; Sperry et al. 1999). What this does not reveal is why interviewers do not use on-line help. Do they not need the information? Do they not find the available information useful? Or do they not know how to access help during an interview?

Similar results have been found for interviewers' backing up during interviews. Although backing up one item at a time is a common procedure familiar to most interviewers, "jumpback" functions (which allow an interviewer to return to an earlier point in the interview) are extremely rare. Couper and Schlegel (1998) found that whereas 78 percent of the interviews they examined contained at least one single-item backup, less than 3 percent contained jumps back. Perhaps more illuminating from their keystroke file analysis is an examination of the targets of these backups and the reasons the interviewers backed up. We return to a few illustrative examples later.

Couper, Sue Ellen Hansen, and Sally Sadosky (1997) found that function key errors were not uncommon. In some cases, interviewers pressed a function key instead of the adjacent key, or instead of the equivalent numeric key on the laptop keyboard, indicating possible problems remembering the functions or dealing with the compact laptop keyboard in a live interviewing environment.

In general, the studies reveal that although, overall, interviewers appear quite comfortable with CAPI, there are instances where instrument design may lead to problems that can be revealed only through more detailed examination of the process. For example, the item illustrated in Figure 27.1 was found to be the target of a disproportionately large number of backups in the NHIS (about 13 backups for every 100 times the screen was accessed; see Couper and Schlegel 1998). At first blush this item appears unremarkable, until we note that it was the fifth in a series in which the previous four items all had two response op-

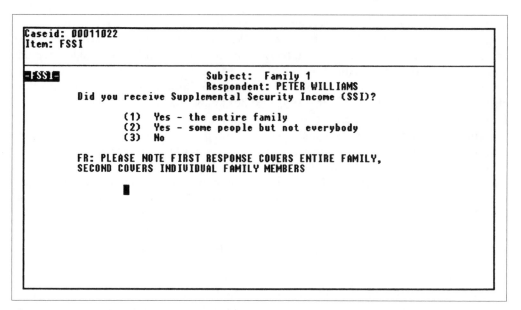

Figure 27.1. Example of Question Producing Large Number of Backups

tions: (1) Yes and (2) No. The fifth item changed response format as shown. It was found that 87 percent of the backups to this item were from a follow-up question asked only of those who answered 2. Of these, 97 percent returned to this item and changed the answer from 2 to 3. This suggests that changing the pattern of response options (i.e., inconsistent design) in this series of questions produced errors that were detected only because the follow-up question did not make sense for a "no" answer.

Harley Frazis and Jay Stewart (1998) report on a similar effect for the following question in the Current Population Survey:

Did you ever get a High School diploma by completing High School OR through a GED or other equivalent?

1. Yes, completed High School
2. Yes, GED or other equivalent
3. No

Again, there is nothing remarkable about this question, unless one again considers that the rest of the instrument uses 1 for yes and 2 for no. This question is asked only of those with less than high school education,

and of these, 12 percent selected option 2. Using external data, Frazis and Stewart estimate that almost all of these responses are spurious, and the true population estimate for these additional GEDs is closer to 400,000 than the 4.8 million estimated using the question above.

These examples show how the shift from paper to CAI has changed the interviewer data entry task from checking boxes closely associated with response options to entering numbers not necessarily visually associated with response options. A change in response option codes should have little or no effect on data quality in a paper interview, but can have a dramatic effect in CAI.

Another example comes again from the NHIS (see Hansen, Couper, and Fuchs 1998). In usability laboratory observations of NHIS interviews, we found one screen to be particularly problematic (see Figure 27.2). The interviewer's task is to read the first three names displayed, press [Shift-F6] to activate the bottom screen, then [PgDn] to see the remaining names to be read. The interviewer is then to return to the top of the initial screen to finish reading the question and enter the responses. In only 5 of the 18 usability interviews we observed in

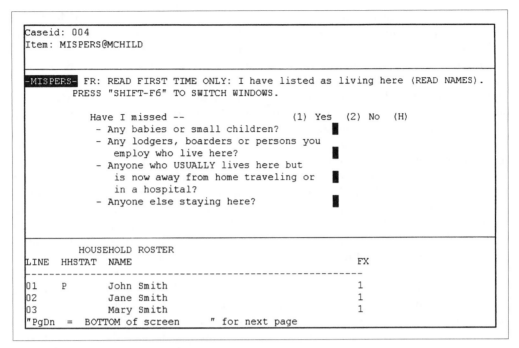

```
Caseid: 004
Item: MISPERS@MCHILD


-MISPERS-  FR: READ FIRST TIME ONLY: I have listed as living here (READ NAMES).
           PRESS "SHIFT-F6" TO SWITCH WINDOWS.

               Have I missed --                    (1) Yes  (2) No  (H)
               - Any babies or small children?          ▮
               - Any lodgers, boarders or persons you
                 employ who live here?                   ▮
               - Anyone who USUALLY lives here but
                 is now away from home traveling or      ▮
                 in a hospital?
               - Anyone else staying here?               ▮



          HOUSEHOLD ROSTER
LINE  HHSTAT  NAME                                    FX
-------------------------------------------------------
01    P       John Smith                              1
02            Jane Smith                              1
03            Mary Smith                              1
"PgDn  =  BOTTOM of screen      " for next page
```

Figure 27.2. Example of Complex Interviewer Function

which there were more than three family members was there an attempt to use the [Shift-F6] function to see the remaining names, and in all 5 cases the attempt was unsuccessful. Later trace file analysis of more than 16,000 interviews from the field revealed that in households with four or more persons, the [Shift-F6] function was used less than 6 percent of the time it was required. This clearly indicates a function that is not working as intended, a fact that could only have been revealed by an examination of the process of the interview rather than the resulting data.

We found many other examples like these in the NHIS (an instrument we have studied in some detail). In all of these examples, the interviewers had been using the CAPI survey instruments for several months before these observations were made, and so the blame for the difficulties cannot be placed on interviewer inexperience. Some of the problems were identified through usability evaluations of the instruments, whereas others were revealed through trace file analysis of field inter-

views. Together with a growing body of evidence from other surveys, this suggests that the design of CAI surveys does affect the interviewer's interaction with the instrument (see Couper 1999b). Some elements of an interviewer's work have been eliminated or improved under CAI, whereas other interviewing tasks may have become more difficult. It is important for researchers to understand what these are and to find ways to overcome these obstacles to smooth and effective administration of a survey instrument.

In summary, the design of survey instruments (both paper and computer) affects the conduct of the interview in ways that the field is only now beginning to explore systematically. In paper surveys, interviewers have to handle the complex tasks of following skip patterns and judging the appropriateness of answers. On the computer, branching and edit checks are now invisible to the interviewer. This means the interviewer must place trust in the designer to make the correct decisions and to anticipate all possible contingencies that may occur in the field. Although some interviewing tasks have been automated, freeing the interviewer of these concerns, the computer typically exercises greater control over the flow of the interview, and interviewer flexibility in dealing with unusual situations may have been reduced. This also means that there are circumstances in which the interviewer may be completely unaware of problems, as in the example above from Frazis and Stewart (1998). In other words, there may be both advantages and disadvantages to computerization of the survey interview. Design and research activities should focus on maximizing the potential benefits of CAI while minimizing the drawbacks.

Thus far we have examined only the interviewer-computer interaction. In the next section, we bring the third player in the interaction—the respondent—into consideration and examine the impact of CAI on the interviewer-respondent interaction and the triadic relationship among interviewer, computer, and respondent (see also Schaeffer and Maynard, Chapter 28, this volume).

◆ Effect of CAI on Interviewer-Respondent Interaction

Previous research has tended to focus on the interviewer-respondent interaction and on the respondent's cognitive processes in answering survey questions (see Schwarz and Sudman 1996; Sirken et al. 1999; Sudman, Bradburn, and Schwarz 1996). In contrast, the interaction between the interviewer and the survey instrument (whether paper or computer based) and the effects of instrument design on the interaction between interviewer and respondent have been largely unexplored. The survey instrument itself places cognitive demands on the interviewer, and these may interfere with the communication demands of interacting with the respondent. However, in

CAI additional cognitive demands may be placed on the interviewer. The interviewer's focus of attention is divided between the computer and the respondent and so tends to shift between the two throughout the survey interview. Depending on the cognitive demands of one, the interviewer may be more or less able to attend to the cognitive demands of the other. Computer assistance may further divide the interviewer's attention between the task at hand (e.g., recording the respondent's answer) and how to perform that task (e.g., typing the number associated with the response and pressing the [Enter] key). Thus an interviewer's attention in a computer-assisted interview may be divided in multiple ways. Interaction with the computer involves the interviewer's reading questions from the computer screen and entering data at the computer keyboard, and also attending to how the computer supports those tasks. The interviewer is also simultaneously attending to the respondent's answers and, if necessary, engaging in extended conversational turns with the respondent in order to elicit codable responses to enter on the computer. The computer may also serve to divide the respondent's attention, which may be focused either on the interviewer's questions and other contributions to conversation or on the interviewer's actions in relation to the computer. The interviewer's success in managing these multiple tasks as well as the survey instrument's design, which may or may not facilitate or support the interviewer, may well affect the interviewer's ability to collect the information desired in the manner prescribed.

We present a model of this three-way interaction in Figure 27.3 (see also Couper 1999a; Hansen 2000). The separate bidirectional interactions between interviewer and computer and between interviewer and respondent may affect one another, as represented by the curved and dashed bidirectional line. The interviewer, respondent, and computer all have potential impacts on the interviewing tasks of

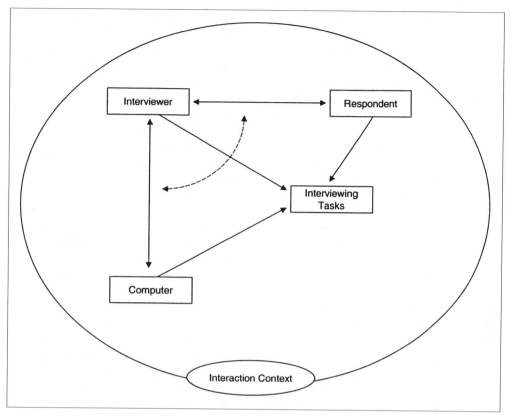

Figure 27.3. Computer-Interviewer-Respondent Interaction

each (for example, ask question, understand question, respond, record response, deliver next question) and the question-response outcome, and each is affected by the environment or survey setting, including mode and method of survey administration. For example, the interaction contexts or environments of personal and telephone interviews differ and thus may differ in how they affect interaction. The personal interview is conducted face-to-face by an interviewer using a laptop computer, and takes place in a setting that may make the presence, and hence effect, of the computer more salient. On the other hand, a telephone interview is typically conducted by an interviewer using a desktop computer, with larger keyboard and screen display than are available in a laptop, making it easier for the interviewer to interact with the computer, and the respondent sees neither the computer nor the interviewer.

This model of interaction in the computer-assisted survey interview could be generalized to represent other types of interactions involving the focused exchange of information between two people, one of whom is using a computer in the performance of a job (for example, a bank teller or emergency dispatch operator). Within this class, interactions vary in terms of who initiates the interaction, the participants' understanding of their respective roles, and external constraints placed on interaction. In the survey interview, the interviewer initiates interaction and may have a clearer understanding of the respondent's role than does the respondent, and standardization places considerable constraints on the behavior of the participants that are typically not present in other interactions of this type.

These types of interactions have generally received little attention in the literature on human-computer interaction or in the literature on computer-supported cooperative work (see Couper 1999a). Two exceptions are David Greatbatch and his colleagues' work on doctor-patient interactions before and after the introduction of desktop computers for record keeping (Greatbatch et al. 1993, 1995a, 1995b) and Jack Whalen's (1995a, 1995b) analysis of calls to an emergency dispatch center that used a computer-aided dispatch (CAD) system.

Greatbatch et al. (1993) found that both computer-assisted and paper-based records create a "tool-saturated" environment, dividing the doctor's attention between the interaction with the patient and the tools used to review and update patient records and to prescribe treatments. However, computers lack the "ecological mobility" of paper and pen, and thus change the nature of doctor-patient consultations in ways similar to what we have observed in interviewer-respondent interactions (see Hansen 2000).

Whalen (1995b) demonstrates how the features and structural properties of the CAD system can both facilitate and constrain interaction. The data entry form used by the emergency call takers he studied was designed to "standardize and routinize the recording of information and the processing of emergencies." However, Whalen notes that, rather than being a neutral, standardized instrument, the CAD system could be "characterized as a kind of ubiquitous and obligatory work instrument that call-takers must . . . manage and come to terms with over the course of each and every phone call," and that "call-takers must do this while they are simultaneously engaged in interaction with citizen callers" (p. 192).

Our research is finding parallels with these studies in the computer-assisted survey interview setting. For example, we have observed in a series of laboratory-based interviews that the complex situation described above and illustrated in Figure 27.2 led interviewers to adopt a variety of strategies in order to complete the task required by the computer, at times soliciting respondents' help in repeating the names of household members.

Another set of examples focused on the effect of CAI on standardization. As we have discussed, CAI is believed to help enforce standardization in two ways: by standardizing question wording through the programmed tailoring of questions to fit a respondent's characteristics and by eliminating skip errors through the enforced display of all appropriate questions. The goal of these programming efforts is to ensure that the interviewer both reads the appropriate question and does so in the prescribed manner, exactly as worded (e.g., Fowler and Mangione 1990). Despite the large amount of programming effort that goes into tailoring "fills" in CAI to facilitate the reading of the question text, there is little empirical evidence on its efficacy—that is, on the extent to which tailoring text facilitates the interviewer's reading of questions.

In a series of analyses based on coding of videotaped survey interactions, Hansen (2000) has explored the effect of these instrument design features on two indicators of standardization: not asking a question and not reading a question as worded. She found that, contrary to expectation, computer assistance did not decrease the likelihood of an interviewer's having problems reading a question, relative to paper and pencil. Regardless of technology, features of the question, such as name fills, emphasis, parenthetical text, alternative wording, and other customization features, had significant effects on interviewers' problems with reading questions as worded.

Computer assistance also did not appear to increase the likelihood of an interviewer's asking questions. However,

Hansen's analysis of items not asked showed that a large number of questions not asked were in the household roster section of the interview and could be linked to design decisions that introduced problems in interviewer-respondent interaction. When household roster items were removed from analysis, computer assistance significantly decreased questions not asked, as expected. These results, and others from the qualitative analysis of these interactions (Hansen et al. 1998; Hansen, Fuchs, and Couper 1997), reveal that when computer-assisted instruments are not designed to accommodate the interviewer's tasks, rather than increasing standardization (relative to paper and pencil) as expected, they may actually impede the interviewer's execution of the tasks as intended, leading to changes in the interviewer-respondent interaction.

Thus, contrary to the expectation that CAI will help achieve the explicit goals of standardization, we have seen numerous instances of interviewers departing from standardization or scripted interaction and customizing the interaction with the respondent to deal with some of the constraints placed on them by the survey instrument (such as not asking awkward questions that the computer delivers, or not reading questions as automatically tailored by CAI). As currently implemented in most surveys, CAI is less flexible than paper instruments, requiring (we believe) greater ingenuity on the part of the interviewer to balance the demands of interacting with the respondent and meeting the data needs of the researcher (as embodied in the CAI program).

We have seen the presence of the computer in CAI affect the interaction in survey interviews in several ways. First, on the outbound computer-interviewer communication, the instrument may affect the way the interviewer asks the question (as noted above from Hansen's analysis). Second, on the inbound interviewer-computer interaction, the instrument may affect the way the

interviewer enters the response provided by the respondent (see our earlier examples regarding inconsistent response options). Third, the computer (especially in CAPI) may indirectly affect the interviewer-respondent interaction, with increased attention of the interviewer to the computer (particularly when interviewer-computer interaction breaks down) leading to loss of eye contact or other changes in rapport between interviewer and respondent. Similar effects have also been noted in paper-and-pencil surveys. Further research is needed to determine when and how such effects may lead to differences in the quality of the data collected through computer-assisted surveys.

◆ Changes in Survey Interviewing

We end this chapter with a brief look at other trends in computer-assisted survey data collection that may affect survey interviewing, particularly the role of the survey interviewer. As early as 1984, the European Society for Market Research (ESOMAR) held a conference with the title "Are Interviewers Obsolete?" With recent developments in automated self-administered methods, such as audio-CASI, interactive voice response, and Web surveys, this question continues to be raised (see, e.g., Baker 1999).

The proponents of the new methods claim that interviewers are not only expensive but prone to make errors and influence respondents in the responses given, especially to socially sensitive questions. Some see computers as a replacement technology (e.g., Black 1998) that indeed has the potential to make interviewers obsolete. This view focuses primarily on the limitations of survey interviewers rather than on their strengths for survey data collection. It also gets at the heart of the standardization debate (see Beatty 1995). If standardization simply means reading the question exactly as worded with the same tone and inflection every time, this could be done better by a computer than by a human. Similarly, computers may eliminate skip errors (to the extent they are programmed correctly) and may not exert the same social influences on a respondent as a live interviewer. This implies that standardization of the stimulus is important, rather than standardization of the meaning of the questions.

But this ignores the important role that interviewers play in gaining cooperation from sample persons, in motivating them throughout what are often long and complex interviews, in explaining and clarifying complex concepts and ambiguous questions, in probing inadequate answers, and so on. Although it may be true that many questions, and indeed many surveys, may be administered by computers without a major loss of data quality (ignoring the nonresponse problem), there remains a large class of surveys for which interviewer administration seems essential and is likely to remain so for some time to come.

The newer methods of data collection have evolved to meet a variety of specialized needs or to seize opportunities offered by new technological developments. An example of the former is audio-CASI. The development of this method stemmed from the recognition that answers to sensitive questions are subject to social desirability biases when the questions are administered by an interviewer (Sudman and Bradburn 1982). For many years, paper-and-pencil surveys on sensitive topics such as sexual behavior and illicit drug use have included self-administered components for the most sensitive items. The effectiveness of this approach for increasing reports of socially undesirable behavior is well established. But this method still presents a threat in that others (e.g., family members) could possibly see the respondent's answers being recorded. An early precursor of audio-CASI involved the respondent's using a personal stereo cassette player (e.g., a Walkman) to listen to a tape on which the questions were recorded and enter responses onto an answer sheet that was devoid of the question wording (Camburn, Cynamon, and Harel 1991).[3] This approach had the advantage of increased privacy and reduced literacy requirements (respondents could listen to the questions, rather than having to read them). However, the prerecorded nature of the tape made it extremely difficult to implement skips or conditional questions, or to tailor wording based on previous answers. Hence audio-CASI, in which the respondent listens to the questions on a headset plugged into the computer and answers by entering responses on the computer screen, was developed at approximately the same time. Initially, audio-CASI made use of the multimedia capabilities of the Apple Macintosh laptop (Johnston and Walton 1995); the technology was then adapted for use with DOS-based laptop computers (O'Reilly et al. 1994). This method is now widely used in surveys on sensitive topics, with demonstrated gains in data quality (see Tourangeau and Smith 1996, 1999; Turner et al. 1999).

As currently implemented, audio-CASI remains part of an interviewer-administered survey. The interviewer gains cooperation from the selected household, selects a random sample person, and typically administers a large part of the interview. In preparation for the audio-CASI portion of the interview, the interviewer sets up the equipment, explains the operation to the respondent, and remains available in case the respondent needs assistance while completing the self-administered portion. In a large number of cases, the interviewer may actually administer the questions him- or herself or assist the respondent more directly than is intended (see Couper and Rowe 1996; Couper and Stinson 1999). The interviewer thus remains an integral part of the data collection operation. Nonetheless, there are questions about how long the self-administered part of the interview can or should be—some suggest the entire interview should be self-administered, with the interviewer's only role being to obtain cooperation and then to drop off and pick up the equipment.

Other newer methods of automated data collection obviate the need for an interviewer altogether. These methods are the functional equivalent of mail surveys, but computer assistance can offer the power and complexity of an interviewer-administered survey without the cost and unreliability, some claim. The most powerful of these at present are surveys on the World Wide Web (for a review, see Couper 2000; see also Mann and Stewart, Chapter 29, this volume). Web surveys are proliferating at a rate unprecedented in the survey industry, but at a pace quite in line with the general move toward Internet use. Often these new technologies are being adopted more for reasons of competitiveness than quality. Proponents of Web surveys are claiming, as have the proponents of many new technologies, that the new methods will replace traditional survey methodologies such as random-digit dialing telephone surveys and make interviewers obsolete (Black 1998). We believe that such pronouncements of the imminent demise of interviewers are premature. Instead, we expect to see an increasing fragmentation of the survey industry, with some sectors (dominated by market research) embracing Internet-based methods and others (mainly government and academic surveys) staying largely with interviewer-administered surveys for household populations. It is unclear where the smaller academic research centers and political polling organizations (both dominated by low-margin, rapid-turnaround telephone surveys with high turnover of interviewing staff) may fall.

These are either the best of times or the worst of times for survey interviewers. We predict that although the interviewing profession may appear to be under threat, it will certainly not disappear. Rather, interviewers will become more specialized—as well as better trained and better paid—as more and more is being asked of them. The straightforward surveys that could just as easily be administered by computers can be,

and are being, moved to automated methods, leaving the difficult, complex, intrusive surveys requiring a high degree of accuracy to be administered by a smaller cadre of well-trained interviewers. Thus the ranks of survey interviewers may well shrink over the next few years, but those who remain will be better trained, better paid, and better motivated—in other words, more professional.

If this is the case, then the issue of control versus flexibility, and the role of the computerized instrument therein, becomes even more salient. The model under which the computer controls the interaction is one in which there is little trust in the interviewer's ability to administer a standardized survey instrument appropriately while trying to adapt the interview to the needs, interests, and abilities of the respondent. Under this model, the interviewer simply carries out the instructions of the designer as embodied in the computer program. The program typically leaves the interviewer (and thereby also the respondent) with little flexibility to accommodate answers or situations that are outside the "normal range" anticipated by the designer. However, there are efforts under way to design CAI instruments that facilitate the task of the interviewer and provide greater flexibility (e.g., Conrad and Schober 1999; Belli et al. 1999).

Along with an increasing awareness of the professionalism of survey interviewers, we may see a growing recognition that CAI systems need to be designed to facilitate, rather than control, the task of interviewing. Rather than controlling the interview flow and interaction, well-designed CAI software could give the interviewer more freedom to execute the goals of the survey rather than blindly follow the successive commands presented by the computer. If standardization of meaning or understanding is the goal, then any effort that could accommodate the varying needs of respondents and assist in the variety of interviewing situations that develop is desirable. The CAI system should assist the interviewer in a manner that motivates the respondent to provide the most honest and accurate information possible, with minimal burden.

In summary, then, the introduction of computer-assisted interviewing has had profound effects on survey data collection and continues to do so. Although many researchers made the transition to CAI some time ago, there is still much we do not know about the role of the computer in the survey interview. Our work, consistent with that of Greatbatch et al. (1993) and Whalen (1995b), has shown that the computer is not a passive, neutral tool; rather, it is an active part of the survey interaction. We look forward to further research on this topic.

■ Notes

1. There is not likely to be much effect in CATI, as respondents are generally unaware of the technology being used by the interviewer at the other end of the telephone. Where comparisons have been made, few respondent differences have been found (e.g., Groves and Mathiowetz 1984).

2. Cleo Jenkins and Don Dillman (1997) have articulated a set of theoretical propositions regarding self-administered paper surveys, but this has not yet led to much empirical work on the issue.

3. This approach is still in use at the U.S. Bureau of the Census (see Bass and Downs 1999).

■ References

Baker, R. P. 1992. "New Technology in Survey Research: Computer-Assisted Personal Interviewing (CAPI)." *Social Science Computer Review* 10:145-57.

———. 1999. "The CASIC Future." In *Computer Assisted Survey Information Collection,* edited by M. P. Couper, R. P. Baker, J. Bethlehem, C. Z. F. Clark, J. Martin, W. L. Nicholls II, and J. M. O'Reilly. New York: John Wiley.

Baker, R. P., N. M. Bradburn, and R. A. Johnson. 1995. "Computer-Assisted Personal Interviewing: An Experimental Evaluation of Data Quality and Costs." *Journal of Official Statistics* 11:415-31.

Baker, R. P. and M. S. Wojcik. 1992. "Interviewer and Respondent Acceptance of CAPI." Pp. 613-21 in *Proceedings of the Bureau of the Census 1992 Annual Research Conference.* Washington, DC: U.S. Bureau of the Census.

Bass, L. E. and B. A. Downs. 1999. "What Can the SPD Adolescent SAQ Tell Us about the Well-Being of Adolescents in the Aftermath of the 1996 Welfare Reform Act?" Presented at the annual meeting of the Population Association of America, New York.

Beatty, P. 1995. "Understanding the Standardized/Non-standardized Interviewing Controversy." *Journal of Official Statistics* 11:147-60.

Belli, R. F., W. Shay, and F. Stafford. 1999. "Computerized Event History Calendar Methods: A Demonstration of Features, Functions and Flexibility." Presented at the annual meeting of the American Association for Public Opinion Research, May, St. Petersburg Beach, FL.

Bergman, L. R., K.-E. Kristiansson, A. Olofsson, and M. Säfström. 1994. "Decentralized CATI versus Paper and Pencil Interviewing: Effects on the Results in the Swedish Labor Force Surveys." *Journal of Official Statistics* 10:181-95.

Bernard, C. 1989. *Survey Data Collection Using Laptop Computers* (Report No. 01/C520). Paris: INSEE.

Black, G. S. 1998. "The Advent of Internet Research: A Replacement Technology." Presented at the annual meeting of the American Association for Public Opinion Research, May, St. Louis, MO.

Camburn, D., D. Cynamon, and Y. Harel. 1991. "The Use of Audio Tapes and Written Questionnaires to Ask Sensitive Questions during Household Interviews." Presented at the National Field Technologies Conference, San Diego, CA.

Catlin, G. and Ingram, S. 1988. "The Effects of CATI on Costs and Data Quality: A Comparison of CATI and Paper Methods in Centralized Interviewing." Pp. 437-52 in *Telephone Survey Method-*

ology, edited by R. M. Groves, P. P. Biemer, L. E. Lyberg, J. T. Massey, W. L. Nicholls II, and J. Waksberg. New York: John Wiley.

Conrad, F. G. and M. F. Schober. 1999. "A Conversational Approach to Text-Based Computer-Administered Questionnaires." In *Proceedings of the Third ASC International Conference, Edinburgh, September 22-24,* edited by R. Banks et al. Chesham, England: Association for Statistical Computing.

Couper, M. P. 1999a. "The Application of Cognitive Science to Computer Assisted Interviewing." In *Cognition and Survey Research,* edited by M. G. Sirken, D. J. Herrmann, S. Schechter, N. Schwarz, J. M. Tanur, and R. Tourangeau. New York: John Wiley.

———. 1999b. "Usability Evaluation of Computer Assisted Survey Instruments." In *Proceedings of the Third ASC International Conference, Edinburgh, September 22-24,* edited by R. Banks et al. Chesham, England: Association for Statistical Computing.

———. 2000. "Web Surveys: A Review of Issues and Approaches." *Public Opinion Quarterly* 64(4): 464-494.

Couper, M. P. and G. Burt. 1993. "The Impact of Computer-Assisted Personal Interviewing (CAPI) on Interviewer Performance: The CPS Experience." Pp. 189-93 in *Proceedings of the Joint Statistical Meeting of the American Statistical Association, Section on Survey Research Methods, 1992.* Alexandria, VA: American Statistical Association.

———. 1994. "Interviewer Attitudes toward Computer-Assisted Personal Interviewing (CAPI)." *Social Science Computer Review* 12:38-54.

Couper, M. P., S. E. Hansen, and S. A. Sadosky. 1997. "Evaluating Interviewer Performance in a CAPI Survey." In *Survey Measurement and Process Quality,* edited by L. E. Lyberg, P. P. Biemer, M. Collins, E. D. de Leeuw, C. Dippo, N. Schwarz, and D. Trewin. New York: John Wiley.

Couper, M. P. and W. L. Nicholls II. 1999. "The History and Development of Computer Assisted Survey Information Collection." In *Computer Assisted Survey Information Collection,* edited by M. P. Couper, R. P. Baker, J. Bethlehem, C. Z. F. Clark, J. Martin, W. L. Nicholls II, and J. M. O'Reilly. New York: John Wiley.

Couper, M. P. and B. Rowe. 1996. "Evaluation of a Computer-Assisted Self-Interview (CASI) Component in a CAPI Survey." *Public Opinion Quarterly,* 60:89-105.

Couper, M. P., S. A. Sadosky, and S. E. Hansen. 1994. "Measuring Interviewer Behavior Using CAPI." Pp. 845-50 in *Proceedings of the Joint Statistical Meeting of the American Statistical Association, Section on Survey Research Methods, 1993.* Alexandria, VA: American Statistical Association.

Couper, M. P. and J. Schlegel. 1998. "Evaluating the NHIS CAPI Instrument Using Trace Files." Presented at the annual meeting of the American Association for Public Opinion Research, May, St. Louis, MO.

Couper, M. P. and L. L. Stinson. 1999. "Completion of Self-Administered Questionnaires in a Sex Survey." *Journal of Sex Research* 36:321-30.

de Leeuw, E. D. and W. L. Nicholls II. 1996. "Technological Innovations in Data Collection: Acceptance, Data Quality and Costs." *Sociological Research Online* 1(4):1-19. Available Internet: http://www.socresonline.org.uk/socresonline/1/4/leeuw.html

Dielman, L. and M. P. Couper. 1995. "Data Quality in a CAPI Survey: Keying Errors." *Journal of Official Statistics* 11:141-46.

Edwards, B., D. Bittner, W. S. Edwards, and S. Sperry. 1993. "CAPI Effects on Interviewers: A Report from Two Major Surveys." Pp. 411-28 in *Proceedings of the Bureau of the Census 1993 Annual Research Conference.* Washington, DC: U.S. Bureau of the Census.

Fowler, F. J., Jr. and T. W. Mangione. 1990. *Standardized Survey Interviewing: Minimizing Interviewer-Related Error.* Newbury Park, CA: Sage.

Frazis, H. and J. Stewart. 1998. "Keying Errors Caused by Unusual Keypunch Codes: Evidence from a Current Population Survey Test." Pp. 131-33 in *Proceedings of the Joint Statistical Meeting of the American Statistical Association, Section on Survey Research Methods, 1997.* Alexandria, VA: American Statistical Association.

Greatbatch, D., C. Heath, P. Campion, and P. Luff. 1995a. "How Do Desk-Top Computers Affect the Doctor-Patient Interaction?" *Family Practice* 12(1):32-36.

Greatbatch, D., C. Heath, P. Luff, and P. Campion. 1995b. "Conversation Analysis: Human-Computer Interaction and the General Practice Consultation." In *Perspectives on HCI: Diverse Approaches,* edited by A. F. Monk and G. N. Gilbert. London: Academic Press.

Greatbatch, D., P. Luff, C. Heath, and P. Campion. 1993. "Interpersonal Communication and Human-Computer Interaction: An Examination of the Use of Computers in Medical Consultations." *Interacting with Computers* 5:193-216.

Groves, R. M., M. Berry, and N. A. Mathiowetz. 1980. "Some Impacts of Computer Assisted Telephone Interviewing on Survey Methods." Pp. 519-24 in *Proceedings of the Joint Statistical Meeting of the American Statistical Association, Section on Survey Research Methods, 1979.* Alexandria, VA: American Statistical Association.

Groves, R. M. and N. A. Mathiowetz. 1984. "Computer Assisted Telephone Interviewing: Effect on Interviewers and Respondents." *Public Opinion Quarterly* 48:356-69.

Hansen, S. E. 2000. "Asking Questions with Computers: Interaction in the Computer Assisted Standardized Survey Interview." Ph.D. dissertation, University of Michigan.

Hansen, S. E., M. P. Couper, and M. Fuchs. 1998. "Usability Evaluation of the NHIS Instrument." Presented at the annual meeting of the American Association for Public Opinion Research, May, St. Louis, MO.

Hansen, S. E., M. Fuchs, and M. P. Couper. 1997. "CAI Instrument Usability Testing." Presented at the annual meeting of the American Association for Public Opinion Research, May, Norfolk, VA.

House, C. C. and W. L. Nicholls II. 1988. "Questionnaire Design for CATI: Design Objectives and Methods." Pp. 421-26 in *Telephone Survey Methodology,* edited by R. M. Groves, P. P. Biemer, L. E. Lyberg, J. T. Massey, W. L. Nicholls II, and J. Waksberg. New York: John Wiley.

Jenkins, C. R. and D. A. Dillman. 1997. "Towards a Theory of Self-Administered Questionnaire Design." In *Survey Measurement and Process Quality,* edited by L. E. Lyberg, P. P. Biemer, M. Collins, E. D. de Leeuw, C. Dippo, N. Schwarz, and D. Trewin. New York: John Wiley.

Johnston, J. and C. Walton. 1995. "Reducing Response Effects for Sensitive Questions: A Computer-Assisted Self Interview with Audio." *Social Science Computer Review* 13:304-9.

Kennedy, J. M., J. E. Lengacher, and L. Demerath. 1990. "Interviewer Entry Error in CATI Interviews." Presented at the International Conference on Measurement Errors in Surveys, November, Tucson, AZ.

Lepkowski, J. M., S. A. Sadosky, M. P. Couper, L. Carn, S. Chardoul, and L. J. Scott. 1995. "Exploring Mode Differences in Interviewer Entry Errors." Pp. 521-26 in *Proceedings of the Joint Statistical Meeting of the American Statistical Association, Section on Survey Research Methods, 1979.* Alexandria, VA: American Statistical Association.

Martin, J., C. O'Muircheartaigh, and J. Curtice. 1993. "The Use of CAPI for Attitude Surveys: An Experimental Comparison with Traditional Methods." *Journal of Official Statistics* 9:641-62.

Nicholls, W. L., II. 1988. "Computer-Assisted Telephone Interviewing: A General Introduction." Pp. 377-86 in *Telephone Survey Methodology,* edited by R. M. Groves, P. P. Biemer, L. E. Lyberg, J. T. Massey, W. L. Nicholls II, and J. Waksberg. New York: John Wiley.

Nicholls, W. L., II, R. P. Baker, and J. Martin. 1997. "The Effect of New Data Collection Technologies on Survey Data Quality." Pp. 221-48 in *Survey Measurement and Process Quality,* edited by L. E. Lyberg, P. P. Biemer, M. Collins, E. D. de Leeuw, C. Dippo, N. Schwarz, and D. Trewin. New York: John Wiley.

Nicholls, W. L., II and R. M. Groves. 1986. "The Status of Computer-Assisted Telephone Interviewing: Part I. Introduction and Impact on Cost and Timeliness of Survey Data." *Journal of Official Statistics* 2:93-115.

Olsen, R. J. 1992. "The Effects of Computer-Assisted Interviewing on Data Quality." Working Paper No. 36, European Scientific Network on Household Panel Studies, University of Essex.

O'Reilly, J. M., M. Hubbard, J. Lessler, P. P. Biemer, and C. F. Turner. 1994. "Audio and Video Computer Assisted Self-Interviewing: Preliminary Tests of New Technologies for Data Collection." *Journal of Official Statistics* 10:197-214.

Sanchez, M. E. 1992. "Effect of Questionnaire Design on the Quality of Survey Data." *Public Opinion Quarterly,* 56:206-17.

Schwarz, N. and S. Sudman, eds. 1996. *Answering Questions: Methodology for Determining Cognitive and Communicative Processes in Survey Research.* San Francisco: Jossey-Bass.

Sirken, M. G., D. J. Herrmann, S. Schechter, N. Schwarz, J. M. Tanur, and R. Tourangeau, eds. 1999. *Cognition and Survey Research.* New York: John Wiley.

Smith, T. W. 1995. "Little Things Matter: A Sampler of How Differences in Questionnaire Format Can Affect Survey Responses." Pp. 1046-51 in *Proceedings of the Joint Statistical Meeting of the American Statistical Association, Section on Survey Research Methods, 1994.* Alexandria, VA: American Statistical Association.

Sperry, S., B. Edwards, R. Dulaney, and D. E. B. Potter. 1999. "Evaluating Interviewer Use of CAPI Navigation Features." In *Computer Assisted Survey Information Collection,* edited by M. P. Couper, R. P. Baker, J. Bethlehem, C. Z. F. Clark, J. Martin, W. L. Nicholls II, and J. M. O'Reilly. New York: John Wiley.

Sudman, S. and N. M. Bradburn. 1982. *Asking Questions: A Practical Guide to Questionnaire Design.* San Francisco: Jossey-Bass.

Sudman, S., N. M. Bradburn, and N. Schwarz. 1996. *Thinking about Answers: The Application of Cognitive Processes to Survey Methodology.* San Francisco: Jossey-Bass.

Tourangeau, R. and T. W. Smith. 1996. "Asking Sensitive Questions: The Impact of Data Collection Mode, Question Format, and Questions Context." *Public Opinion Quarterly* 60:275-304.

———. 1999. "Collecting Sensitive Information with Different Modes of Data Collection." In *Computer Assisted Survey Information Collection,* edited by M. P. Couper, R. P. Baker, J. Bethlehem, C. Z. F. Clark, J. Martin, W. L. Nicholls II, and J. M. O'Reilly. New York: John Wiley.

Turner, C. F., B. H. Forsyth, J. M. O'Reilly, P. C. Cooley, T. K. Smith, S. M. Rogers, and H. G. Miller. 1999. "Automated Self-Interviewing and the Survey Measurement of Sensitive Behaviors." In *Computer Assisted Survey Information Collection,* edited by M. P. Couper, R. P. Baker, J. Bethlehem, C. Z. F. Clark, J. Martin, W. L. Nicholls II, and J. M. O'Reilly. New York: John Wiley.

van Bastelaer, R. A., F. Kerssemakers, and D. Sikkel. 1987. "A Test of the Netherlands' Continuous Labor Force Survey with Hand-Held Computers: Interviewer Behavior and Data Quality." Pp. 37-54 in *Automation in Survey Processing,* edited by R. J. Mokken et al. Voorburg/Heerlen: Netherlands Central Bureau of Statistics (CBS Select 4).

Weeks, M. F. 1992. "Computer-Assisted Survey Information Collection: A Review of CASIC Methods and Their Implications for Survey Operations." *Journal of Official Statistics* 8:445-65.

Whalen, J. 1995a. "Expert Systems versus Systems for Experts: Computer-Aided Dispatch as a Support System in Real-World Environments." Pp. 161-83 in *The Social and Interactional Dimensions of Human-Computer Interaction,* edited by P. J. Thomas. Cambridge: Cambridge University Press.

———. 1995b. "A Technology of Order Production: Computer-Aided Dispatch in Public Safety Communications." Pp. 187-203 in *Situated Order: Studies in the Social Organization of Talk and Embedded Activities,* edited by P. ten Have and G. Psathas. Washington, DC: University Press of America.

STANDARDIZATION AND INTERACTION IN THE SURVEY INTERVIEW

◆ Nora Cate Schaeffer
Douglas W. Maynard

Survey interviews conduct measurement by question. That is, surveys use questions to collect measurements from a sample in order to estimate characteristics of a population (see Singleton and Straits, Chapter 3, this volume). The "objective" data obtained by survey interviews are achieved in the interaction between respondents and interviewers who have been trained to behave in a standardized manner. Over the years, both critics (e.g., Briggs 1986; Cicourel 1974; Mishler 1986; Suchman and Jordan 1990) and practitioners (e.g., Cannell and Kahn 1968) of standardized survey interviewing have considered how the fundamentally social nature

of the interview affects the data produced there. Both groups view the interaction between the interviewer and the respondent as critical to judgments about the quality of the data (e.g., Cicourel 1982; Schuman 1982). Thus critics have presented examples of the awkward, and even bizarre, interactions that sometimes occur in survey interviews as evidence that the resulting data cannot be valid. Practitioners view such individual incidents as resulting from unusual circumstances or "bad" survey questions, and they consider adherence to rules of standardization to improve the quality of the data in the aggregate (e.g., Cannell, Lawson, and Hausser 1975). Prac-

AUTHORS' NOTE: We would like to thank Colm O'Muircheartaigh, Jennifer Dykema, Frederick Conrad, and Michael Schober for their comments on an earlier version of this chapter.

titioners and critics of surveys both view respondents' answers as constructed during the interaction, but they evaluate the effects on the resulting data differently (see Holstein and Gubrium 1995; Tourangeau, Rasinski, and Rips 2000).

In the past decade, survey researchers and other social scientists have revisited the debate about standardization (e.g, Beatty 1995), a debate that has a long history (see O'Muircheartaigh 1997). The latest round of the debate has been accompanied by a new set of studies of interaction in the survey interview. Some of these studies extend traditional methods used by survey researchers for studying the interview by experimenting with styles of interviewing and analyzing detailed coding of the interaction between the interviewer and respondent. Other studies, deriving from a tradition of studies of work and the production of scientific knowledge, have used concepts and methods from ethnomethodology and conversation analysis.

In this chapter, we first review the justification for standardization in the survey interview; we summarize recent debates, discuss different varieties of standardization, and consider standardization's limits and limitations. As we consider the limits of standardization, we focus on the role of *tacit and commonsense knowledge* in the conduct of the survey interview. In the second main section of the chapter, we argue for studying interaction in the survey interview using an approach we call *analytic alternation*. Because of the tension between the procedures for social measurement and the practices of talk and interaction, interviewers *alternate* between following the rules of standardization and using the tacit knowledge available to competent social actors who must solve problems that arise as their work tasks unfold. *Analytic* alternation means following the situated oscillations between formal rule following and tacit practices that interviewers enact in concert with survey respondents. Following this procedure, we outline the role of tacit knowledge in survey interviewing and

consider, as an illustration, the *interviewing sequence* by which the survey instrument is administered.

In the third major section of the chapter we review recent studies of survey interaction. Some of these studies involve coding behavior so that the effects of different techniques for questioning or probing can be examined; other studies are experiments that test how the style of interviewing affects the respondent's motivation, understanding, and other phenomena; and a third group of studies use ethnomethodological and conversation-analytic approaches to examine the detail of situated work methods and the practices of talk and social interaction. Finally, we consider the challenges this research poses for improving measurement in the social sciences.

◆ Standardization: Why and What

The justification for standardization lies in the logic of scientific measurement applied to social phenomena. Investigators who analyze survey data would like the variation they observe in data to result from variation in the concept being measured. For example, if different respondents report different levels of self-esteem, the different levels of self-esteem recorded in the data should reflect true differences between respondents in their levels of self-esteem. If interviewers behave differently with different respondents, however, the distribution of answers may reflect variation in the behavior of interviewers rather than variation in levels of self-esteem among respondents.

In addition, interviewers can introduce errors—by their expectations that respondents will have consistent attitudes or that respondents with specific social characteristics will have certain beliefs—that can affect the accuracy of responses. This is sometimes referred to as *biasing* answers. The model that divides total error into variance and bias has dominated the way statisticians think about error: "Interviewer variance represents the error about the 'expected value' for all the interviewers, while net interviewer bias represents the deviation of this expected value from the true population mean" (Hyman et al. [1954] 1975:322).

The varied practices that researchers refer to as *standardization* evolved in response to early studies, such as those described by Herbert Hyman and his colleagues ([1954] 1975), that demonstrated how the behavior of interviewers affects "error" in survey estimates. Hyman et al. found that ratings made by interviewers and the numbers of responses recorded to open questions were substantially affected by interviewer variance (p. 257; see also the summary in Groves 1989:380-81). Individual studies also found substantial gross errors (for example, those introduced through the expectations or reactions of the interviewer) that could affect many interviewers but not increase inter-interviewer variation (Hyman et al. [1954] 1975:252-74). Hyman et al. summarize the effects of the interviewer on the distribution of answers as follows: "The only reasonable answer seems to be that absolutely anything can happen" (p. 271).

Standardization addresses both components of interviewer error. The rules of standardization attempt to hold the behavior of the interviewer constant, thereby to reduce variable error. Recent studies in centralized telephone facilities where standardization is practiced, for example, have found that the component of variance due to differences in the behavior of the interviewer across respondents (interviewer variability) is usually quite small for most types of survey items (e.g., Mangione, Fowler, and Louis 1992; Groves and Magilavy 1986). This is so even though there are many lapses in achieving the ideal of standardization (see, e.g., Oksenberg, Cannell, and Kalton 1991). When standardization is successful, it makes the net effect of the interviewer in the aggregate very small, in the specific sense that it re-

duces the interviewer's contribution to variance. Standardization also reduces bias by reducing the number of opportunities for the interviewer's expectations or opinions (for instance) to intrude on the process by which the respondent's answer is generated, interpreted, or recorded.

Standardization does not eliminate the effect of the interviewer on the individual respondent. An interviewer who follows the rules of standardization might react to a respondent's ambiguous answer by repeating all the response categories, for example, instead of using his or her own beliefs about the respondent's likely answer to choose which response categories to repeat. The standardized practice of repeating the response categories not only affects how respondents express their answers, but over the course of the interview probably has the desirable effect of training respondents to choose a category from among those offered as part of subsequent questions. Nevertheless, if standardization were comprehensive and perfectly implemented, we could say that the interviewer did not affect the respondent—in the very specific sense that the effect of any interviewer would be the same as the effect of any other interviewer.

THE RECENT DEBATE ABOUT STANDARDIZATION

In advocating standardization, Hyman et al. ([1954] 1975:21) still worried that researchers might focus on improving reliability and neglect the more difficult problem of increasing validity. Decades later, Lucy Suchman and Brigitte Jordan (1990) argued that standardization is itself a substantial threat to the validity of the resulting data (see also Briggs 1986; Mishler 1986). They presented illustrations in which the rigidities of standardization led to awkward interactions and answers that might be inaccurate. They proposed letting both the respondent and the interviewer see the instrument and allowing "the interviewer to talk about the questions, to offer clarifications and elaborations, and to engage in a limited form of recipient design and common-sense inference" (p. 240; we discuss recipient design later in the chapter).

Subsequent discussions of standardization among survey practitioners have been influenced by studies that examine social-information-processing models of the process of answering a survey question (see, e.g., Sudman, Bradburn, and Schwarz 1996; Tourangeau et al. 2000). Much of the research developed within this framework has focused on improving the respondent's comprehension of survey questions and increasing the accuracy of the information a respondent retrieves from memory. Some of this research has experimented with relaxing the constraints of standardization to improve retrieval (e.g., Means et al. 1991). More recent studies have modified standardization with the aim of helping respondents understand survey concepts (we discuss this research later in the chapter).

Nevertheless, suggestions for loosening the constraints of standardization raise the anxieties of many survey researchers. The concerns of survey practitioners include, for example, that questions about events and behaviors require different measurement practices than questions about subjective things such as attitudes; that a system of standardization must be suitable for the requirements of recruiting, training, and supervising interviewers for very large surveys; and that innovations not increase interviewer variance. Discussions about standardization in the past decade have focused researchers' attention on several topics that have been examined in the studies we review later: how standardized interviewers actually behave, how their behavior affects the answers given by respondents, how conversational practices from other sorts of talk might be used in standardized interviewing, and how standardization might be changed to improve both the quality of the interaction and the quality of the resulting data.

STANDARDIZATION: VARIETIES AND PRACTICES

In debates about interviewing, "standardization" is sometimes assigned the role of "straw object"—as though there were one method of standardization that all survey researchers agree is best, that provides guidelines for all situations that an interviewer might encounter, and that interviewers could implement perfectly even when questions are poorly written. The reality has always been more complex than this caricature. There are no received tablets on which the rules of standardization are inscribed, and the practices of standardization have developed at various sites, each of which has its own traditions.

The rules that Floyd Fowler and Thomas Mangione codify in *Standardized Survey Interviewing* (1990) are comprehensive, grounded in the rationale for standardization, and refined through many years of practice and observation. Fowler and Mangione describe four principles of standardized interviewing:

1. Read questions as written.
2. Probe inadequate answers nondirectively.
3. Record answers without discretion.
4. Be interpersonally nonjudgmental regarding the substance of answers. (P. 35)

These principles would probably be almost universally accepted among survey researchers, but the specific practices derived from these principles can vary. At various sites, researchers and staff charged with supervising field operations have developed their own specifications for training interviewers derived from general principles (see Viterna and Maynard forthcoming).

The rules of standardization assembled by Michael Brenner (1981:19-22) illustrate this variation. Brenner allows the interviewer to "show an interest in the answers given by the respondent," to "volunteer" clarification "when necessary," and to "obtain an adequate answer by means of nondirective probing, repetition of the question or instruction, or nondirective clarification" when the respondent gives an inadequate answer. If a respondent asks for clarification, the interviewer must provide clarification, but nondirectively, by using "predetermined clarifications." These clarifications appear to be similar to the information that is sometimes provided to interviewers in "question-by-question specifications" or to the interviewers in the experiments on "flexible" or "conversational" interviewing described below (Schober and Conrad 1997; Conrad and Schober 2000). Both practices offer a contrast to Fowler and Mangione's recommendations for restraining the discretion of interviewers.

The variability in the practice of standardization can also be seen in the differing ways in which Fowler and Mangione's first principle is implemented. Although the general principle that the question must initially be read exactly as worded is probably the basic technique of standardization, and is even part of a variant method variously labeled *flexible* or *conversational* interviewing (Schober and Conrad 1997; Conrad and Schober 2000), some survey centers also accept a process that has been called *verification* as a legitimate technique of standardization. Verification acknowledges that respondents sometimes provide information before the interviewer asks for it, and that if an interviewer ignores the fact that he or she has already heard the answer to a question, the interaction may be awkward for both the interviewer and the respondent. For example, when the interviewer has already been told the respondent's age in one context, instead of asking a later, scripted question about the respondent's age, the interviewer might say, "I think you said earlier that you were 68 years old. Is that correct?"

The second principle, to probe nondirectively, can also be implemented in differ-

ent ways. So, for example, Fowler and Mangione (1990:39-40) require interviewers to repeat all the response categories when they probe closed questions. There is substantial research showing that the meaning of any individual category depends on the entire set of categories (see, e.g., Schaeffer and Charng 1991; Smit, Dijkstra, and van der Zouwen 1997) to support this stipulation. But Johannes van der Zouwen (forthcoming) describes a practice he calls "tuning" in which the interviewer needs to repeat only the categories that appear to be in the vicinity of the respondent's answer. Tuning is itself similar to a technique called "zeroing in" that Fowler and Mangione (1990:41) describe for numerical answers.

Furthermore, practitioners recognize that there are situations in which the behavior of the interviewer cannot be completely standardized, such as the probing of "don't know" answers. Such answers, which require that the interviewer diagnose the "reason" for the "don't know," are a source of interviewer variation (Fowler and Mangione 1990:44; Mangione et al. 1992). When investigators train interviewers using "question-by-question specifications" of objectives, they recognize that the interviewer may need this information, the application of which cannot be prespeci- fied, to diagnose and correct respondents' confusions and misunderstandings. That interviewers become less standardized when they actually use the information provided to them during training is part of the tension latent in traditional styles of standardization.

THE LIMITS OF STANDARDIZATION: ALTERNATION TO THE TACIT REALM

Listening to a survey interview, it is easy to conclude both that standardization is essential and that it will never be implemented perfectly and comprehensively, because no set of rules can cover every contingency. For example, when survey practitioners first documented how interviewers followed respondents' answers with feedback, the researchers' impulse was to standardize that feedback. Controlled feedback (e.g., "thank you," "that information is helpful") is intended to provide positive reinforcement for thoughtful behavior by the respondent without evaluating the content of the answer. Some experiments with controlled feedback suggest that it may improve the accuracy of reports (Cannell, Miller, and Oksenberg 1981; but see also Miller and Cannell 1982), possibly because it teaches respondents what kinds of effort and answers the interviewer wants. This tactic extends the reach of standardization, and the use of feedback could be enhanced by an understanding of the features of various acknowledgment tokens (Maynard and Marlaire 1992). But, despite researchers' best efforts, interviewers may vary in how they use feedback, respondents may perceive that feedback evaluates the content of their answers, and respondents may react to feedback in unpredictable ways.

Survey practitioners often must accept data produced in "messy" interactions as good enough for the purposes and budget at hand. Survey practitioners explicitly or implicitly recognize that interviewers inevitably must alternate between the rules of standardization and supplementing those rules. By using the term *alternate*, we mean that interviewers deploy resources of an "interactional substrate"—basic skills for engaging meaningfully with respondents —in pursuit of answers. These skills are presumed by, and yet are largely ignored in, the rules of standardized interviewing (Marlaire and Maynard 1990; Maynard and Marlaire 1992). The reliance of survey researchers on the interactional competence of interviewers acknowledges that *tacit knowledge* is required to implement and supplement formal, standardizing rules.

◆ Tacit Knowledge and Interaction in the Survey Interview

Before we discuss the problem of tacit knowledge, we need to define an approach to the survey interview called *critical remediation* (Maynard and Schaeffer 2000). The approach derives from work done by researchers who have studied the survey interview from a critical, "qualitative" methodological orientation (e.g., Cicourel 1974; Suchman and Jordan 1990; Briggs 1986; Mishler 1986).

CRITICAL REMEDIATION

Some qualitative researchers have suggested that survey researchers do not understand respondents' commonsense knowledge. From the critics' perspective, utterances or questions in the survey interview are never self-evident in terms of meaning; they are always occasioned and gain their sense only against a background of unspoken meanings and aspects of settings (Cicourel 1974: 196). In Elliot Mishler's (1986:22) terms, the problem is that survey research is a "context-stripping procedure" in which investigators "pretend" that the context does not affect the meaning of questions and answers. Context and meaning comprise actors' commonsense ways of thinking, conversing, acting, and deciding, or, in a phrase, their "essential sociocultural grounds of meaning" as these reside in the "life setting" of the respondent (Mishler 1986:23). These matters are particularly important when there are variations in respondents' cultural backgrounds (see also Briggs 1986). This is the "critical" part of critical remediation.

Qualitative researchers have also argued that, because the interview involves the use of language, "structural and transformational linguistics, cognitive psychology, developmental psycholinguistics, and linguistically oriented anthropological works on componential analysis and the ethnography of speaking" need to be taken into account in the design of survey interviews (Cicourel 1964:108, 198). In addition, "retrospective talk" as it occurs in a survey interview is very different from speech events in day-to-day experience (Cicourel 1974:179). Linguistic, psycholinguistic, and sociolinguistic investigations, it is argued, could redress survey researchers' neglect of language use and interaction. This is the "remedial" part of critical remediation. These perspectives would enable investigators to appreciate more fully the character of talk in the interview.

Although such discussions of the survey interview raise important points, many of these issues have been recognized and studied within the survey methodological tradition itself. For example, more than 45 years ago, Robert Kahn and Charles Cannell (1957:16) argued that interviews are a "specialized pattern of verbal interaction," and, more recently, Louise Kidder (1981: 146) has suggested that surveys rely on "verbal reports" whose properties require investigation. In proposing that survey researchers should better appreciate *respondents'* life worlds, some qualitative investigators have bypassed the concerns of survey methodologists and have been preoccupied with what survey researchers miss, how they distort, and what they should do better. Such preoccupations mean that some critics have done with respect to interviewers precisely what they accuse survey researchers of doing with respect to respondents: They have ignored and misrepresented the *interviewers'* life worlds—or everyday work worlds—and failed to comprehend that the survey interview enterprise is a complex set of actions and activities. In other words, such critics have avoided immersion in the world of the researcher and interviewer in the way they recommend that the researcher and interviewer should enter the world of the respondent.

ANALYTIC ALTERNATION

To enter the world of the interviewer, we draw on the "Ethnomethodological Studies of Work" program in the arena of science studies and other professional endeavors (Heritage 1984b; Lynch 1992; see Maynard and Schaeffer 2000). The thrust of this research is to comprehend analytically the concreteness, specificity, and detail involved in actual work, including how practitioners use technologies. If we become concerned with the *survey interviewer's* work, we take a new approach to studying the survey interview. We consider the survey enterprise as a kind of "formal analytic" inquiry, providing a vast set of instructions for how investigations can proceed. These instructions—including procedures for standardization, as used in specific instances—necessarily and repeatedly raise an ethnomethodological question. To paraphrase Harold Garfinkel (1996:19): What more is there to instructions and instructed actions than a survey center—with its manuals, procedures, instruments, and other kinds of instructions—can provide? The "what more" question points to the tacit knowledge that interviewers use to handle the problems that emerge during the interview.

Analytic alternation, in the context of the survey interview, is a means of investigating practitioners' work. Practitioners' work involves both adherence to formal inquiry—the use of rules, procedures, and instruments for conducting the interview—and the exercise of taken-for-granted, tacit skills. Practitioners *alternate* from one orientation and set of competencies to the other. These skills are exhibited in the produced, orderly detail of everyday talk and embodied action that reflexively supports and helps achieve the accountability of the formal inquiry. *Accountability* means that the interview gets done in ways that are acceptably—for all practical purposes—standardized and scientific.

A straightforward example of interviewer alternation is to be found in a glance at any survey research center: We can observe interviewers engaged in computer-aided telephone interviewing to be gazing at and reading verbatim to their respondents from scripted interviews on the screens in front of them, with hands and fingers tethered to keyboards on the desks, and entering codes for heard responses that correspond to the proper categories as displayed on the screens. The interviewers, for some duration, appear to be formal analytic or standardized homunculi, enacting what the survey instruments on their computer screens tell them to do as they talk, listen, and type.

At singular and unpredictable moments, however, interviewers will glance away from the screens, move their hands from the keyboards, and gesture more or less expansively, producing talk that is neither scripted nor otherwise predesigned, in order to handle some departure from the routine, with the aim of being able to return to that routine. For example, an interviewer may find it necessary to gesture while explaining something learned during training about the survey to a respondent. Although the gesturing is not something that the respondent sees, it might help the interviewer in articulating a point, or in emphasizing a significant piece of talk, or some other aspect of the verbal presentation. When the point has been made, the interviewer returns gaze and hands back to the computer and keyboard. At these moments of departure, interviewers alternate from the formal to the tacit realm and engage practices designed to provide for alternation again back to the formal.

This is only a more visible manifestation of what we mean by alternation, for even when they read scripts more or less verbatim, interviewers, in interaction with re-

spondents, are engaged in performances that improvise on those scripts. For example, the script does not tell the interviewer how to manage turn taking with the respondent; instead, interviewer and respondent use a familiar "interviewing sequence" (which we discuss below). *Analytic* alternation refers to studying departures from, and improvisations on, scripts as orderly practices. That is, interactions, as manifestations of tacit and commonsense knowledge, are sites of pattern and organization and therefore need to be appreciated analytically in their own terms. Recent studies of interaction in the interview are beginning to provide such an appreciation. Tacit knowledge is not only necessary and inescapable; beyond this, it inescapably shapes social measurement.

THE "INTERVIEWING SEQUENCE" IN THE SURVEY AND OTHER ENVIRONMENTS

One form of tacit knowledge exhibited in the survey is the question-answer-acknowledgment series of turns—the "interviewing sequence"—that participants produce. In analyzing this sequence as a generic form, we are reminded that the survey is only one type of "interview." Dictionary definitions, for example, suggest that the interview is a "formal consultation" used to evaluate qualifications or "a meeting at which information is obtained (as by a reporter, television commentator, or pollster) from a person" (*Merriam-Webster's Collegiate Dictionary,* 10th edition). Accordingly, the survey has a relationship to other interviews, all of which embody the interviewing sequence but, as we discuss below, with "third-turn acknowledgments" of various configurations. For example, physicians and nurses often interview their patients to obtain medical histories (see Zoppi and Epstein, Chapter 18, this volume), teachers and psychologists interview students as part of teaching and testing (see in this volume Tierney and Dilley, Chapter

22; Miller, de Shazer, and De Jong, Chapter 19), employers interview prospective employees in making hiring decisions (see Latham and Millman, Chapter 23, this volume), and newscasters interview government officials and others as part of their programming (see Altheide, Chapter 20, this volume). The survey can be compared to these other kinds of interviews to specify some of its distinctive characteristics.

A comparison of survey interviews and other interviews is instructive. For example, a prominent feature of the medical interview is how questioning builds in certain biases. Physicians and other health professionals do not exhibit the disinterest and objectivity required of survey interviewers; instead, during history taking they "build their questions so as to convey a form of relatedness and concern for the welfare of the patient" (Boyd and Heritage forthcoming). Questions in medical interviews are built with presuppositions and preferences that suggest optimistic, "no problem" answers. Medical personnel do not ask questions such as "Is your father dead?" but rather "Is your father alive?" They would not ask, "Are your bowel movements problematic?" but rather "Are your bowel movements normal?" Similarly, British health visitors in interaction with mothers who have recently given birth construct their questions about the process of childbirth in ways that favor "no problem" responses, stringing together proposals to the mother about having a "normal pregnancy" and a "normal delivery," saying "she's bottle-feeding?" and the like in a way that suggests they expect positive answers. Heritage (forthcoming) calls this the principle of optimization.

Interview questions in medical contexts also embody what Harvey Sacks, Emanuel Schegloff, and Gail Jefferson (1974) call "recipient design," which refers to a "multitude of respects in which the talk by one party in a conversation is constructed or designed in ways which display an orientation and sensitivity to the particular other(s) who are the coparticipants" (p. 727). Such recipient design is exhibited in the following questions from a physician to a 50-year-old divorced woman whom the doctor knows to have had a tubal ligation procedure: "Are you using any contraception? Is that necessary for you?" These questions exhibit the physician's understanding of the women's circumstances (Boyd and Heritage forthcoming). Heritage (forthcoming) demonstrates that health visitors' questions to new parents also exhibit such recipient design. By contrast with social surveys and medical interviews, the standardized survey interview is designed to obviate any practices of optimization or recipient design that would increase the likelihood of obtaining biased answers from respondents. Standardized survey interviews are, in Heritage's (forthcoming) phrase, built to be "essentially anonymous" (on the anonymous way in which survey participation is solicited, see also Maynard and Schaeffer 1997).

ACKNOWLEDGMENT TURNS

One contribution of a comparison of surveys with other forms of interviewing is that it makes our understanding of what standardization overcomes—such as optimization and recipient design—more specific. A second contribution is that it describes issues surrounding the third, "acknowledgment," turn of the interviewing sequence. Acknowledgments are what survey researchers refer to as *feedback*. Acknowledgments include subtle forms of interviewer behavior, which may be influential, as well as the more formal tokens that interviewers use after a respondent has produced an answer to a survey question. Research on educational testing and occupational and news interviews shows how this third turn contributes to making the "outputs" from such diverse interviews *collaborative productions*.

Viewing interview outputs as collaborative productions goes against stimulus-response and other bipartite models of the in-

A

```
S:  1→    .hh When do you get out. Christmas week or the week before Christmas.
              (0.3)
G:  2→    Uh::m two or three days before Ch[ristmas.]
S:  3→                                     [Oh:,    ]
```

B

```
T:  1→    ((Holding up card)) This is the long word. Who knows what it says?
S:  2→    Cafeteria.
T:  3→    Cafeteria, Audrey, good for you!
```

terviewer-interviewee relationship that presume that interviewers are neutral conduits of questions that interviewees answer according to their own abilities, willingness to disclose, and so on. Research that examines interaction shows how the interviewer enters into the answering behavior and products of interviewees. Just one example from an educational testing situation illustrates how this happens. Children often learn from the examination experience itself, and from such patterns as the pacing of questions, the parsing of stimulus items, and the reactions of test administrators, whether their answers are on the right track. On the way to producing answers, using these cues, they can modify what they end up saying and fashion answers that more or less reflect the social environment as much as their own solitary efforts (Marlaire and Maynard 1990; Maynard and Marlaire 1992; Mehan 1973; Mehan, Hertweck, and Meihls 1986). Collaborative production of "answers" also occurs in teaching (as opposed to testing) environments, and it is a feature that Michael Schober and Frederick Conrad (forthcoming) argue is present in the survey interview.

The more formal forms of feedback described in interactional research are third-turn acknowledgments. In conversation, such third turns follow information-seeking question-answer sequences (turns 1 and 2) and register that the information is informative to the questioner (Heritage 1984b: 285-86). Turns in Excerpt A are labeled with numbers.

The "Oh" in turn 3 indicates a "change of state" in the answer recipient's knowledge (Heritage 1984a). In educational settings, question-answer or "instructional" sequences involve teachers asking "known-information" questions, as in Excerpt B, from Hugh Mehan (1979:52-53). In such instructional sequences, the third-turn response evaluates a student's answer.

In contrast with conversational and educational settings, there are other institutional settings in which questioners *withhold* third-turn responses of either variety (indicating a change of knowledge state or evaluation of an answer). Prominent among these are courtrooms (Atkinson and Drew 1979), job interviews (Button 1987), and news interviews (Heritage and Greatbatch 1991). These venues have in common that interviewers (lawyers or employers or newscasters, as the case may be) are soliciting answers for an *overhearing audience* of some kind who may do their evaluations of interviewees and their answers at some distance from the interview itself. By refraining from any kind of postanswer commentary, interviewers exhibit themselves as conduits for those answers to flow to those audiences—who are then in the position of supplying that commentary in another social context aside from the interview itself.

A rule that forbids third-turn responses may be clearer than protocols under which interviewers are not enjoined from such productions but are still not supposed to comment on the content of the answers.

This dilemma of being permitted to respond but in restricted ways characterizes the survey interview, and it is also present in educational testing interviews. Indeed, the protocols for tests such as the Woodcock-Johnson Psychoeducational Battery may warn administrators, "Be careful that your pattern of comments does not indicate whether answers are correct or incorrect" (Mehan et al. 1986:96-97). Administrators may produce "neutral" acknowledgments ("okay," "thank you," and the like) after a child has answered a test item. However, research demonstrates that administrators sometimes alter their third-turn responses *systematically,* using "good" when an answer is correct and "okay" when it is incorrect, for example; they may also give encouraging nonvocal signals by smiling or nodding when a child's answer is right and appearing more taciturn when it is wrong (Maynard and Marlaire 1992).

The concern that most survey centers have in regard to third-turn "feedback" is no doubt well placed. Survey researchers have long recognized that fine gradations in such responses potentially influence the answers of respondents (Marquis, Cannell, and Laurent 1972). Although most survey centers have protocols that attempt to standardize the use of feedback, such standards are by no means uniform *across* survey centers (Viterna and Maynard forthcoming). Practitioners agree on the principle that feedback should not evaluate the content of the answer, but specific rules about the frequency, content, and purpose of feedback vary (whether it should be used to sustain motivation, to take notice of the respondent's level of effort, to take notice that the respondent's answer meets task requirements, to provide reassurance, and so on).

CONVERSATION WITH A PURPOSE

The survey interview has long been described as a "conversation with a purpose" (Bingham and Moore 1924, cited by Cannell and Kahn 1968; see also Schaeffer, 1991). In this regard, it is like interviewing behavior in other settings, including both conversation (where participants may go on fact-finding excursions) and institutional settings such as schools, courtrooms, and news organizations. Both parties to an interview use tacit knowledge and taken-for-granted procedures to produce and answer interview questions; the interviewer uses these skills to respond or withhold responses in particular ways. The survey interview shares generic practices for asking, answering, and acknowledging answers with other interview forms. The survey interview is relatively distinctive in its practices for maintaining the anonymity of questions and acknowledging answers without evaluating their content. Studies of interaction in the survey interview, such as those we review next, implicitly or explicitly recognize the interviewing sequence as the base form for the interview.

◆ Recent Studies of Interaction in the Survey Interview

In the past decade, the methods used to study what happens during the survey interview and the goals of this research have become increasingly more diverse (on earlier studies, see Schaeffer 1991). Explicitly or implicitly, these various research efforts recognize how tacit knowledge is embedded in the conduct of a survey interview. The research we review here includes studies that have described and coded the behavior of standardized interviewers and respondents, experiments that have compared the effects of different styles of interviewing, and investigations that we will characterize roughly as ethnomethodological and conversation analytic. Studies in the last group have examined details of the interaction between the interviewer and respondent in order to map the interactional resources participants use to create survey data. But the other studies can also contribute to our understanding of how interviewers and respondents alternate between following the rules of standardization and using daily interactional competence. The studies we summarize vary in whether they are primarily descriptive or attempt to show how the participants' behavior affects the quality of survey data.

CONCEPTUAL MODELS

Social-information-processing models have motivated research that has increased and complicated our understanding of how respondents answer survey questions. However, we still lack a general conceptual framework that focuses on the interaction in the interview and that could guide research about how the interviewer's behavior affects the respondent and subsequently the respondent's answers. Early research about interviewing invoked concepts such as "rapport," acquiescence, and social desirability to speculate about the mechanisms that might intervene between the interviewer's behavior and the respondent's answer (see, e.g., Goudy and Potter 1975; Weiss 1968, 1970). But that research did not explicate what these mechanisms might actually look like in the interaction.

An attempt to incorporate the interaction in the interview appears in Johannes van der Zouwen, Wil Dijkstra, and Johannes Smit's (1991:420) model of interviewing "style" and the experiments they based on this model. The model specifies that interviewing style, which consists of specific behaviors, can affect the "respondent's willingness to provide adequate answers" and the adequacy of the cues the interviewer provides the respondent. The effect of the interviewer's behavior is modified by the respondent's certainty about his or her answer (a respondent who is more uncertain will pay more attention to cues provided by the interviewer's behavior) and the difficulty of the task (the style of in-

terviewing will have little impact if questions are easy and do not present many possibilities for suggesting answers). Questions that are difficult, but for which the interviewer cannot suggest answers, are likely to benefit from a personal style of interviewing because it increases the respondent's motivation to be accurate and complete. For questions that are easy (and so do not require as much motivation) but susceptible to suggestions by the interviewer, a formal style of interviewing may obtain higher-quality data.

We have taken a less formal approach to describing how the interaction in the interview affects the data (Schaeffer and Maynard 1996). Drawing on discussions of "social cognition" and studies of interaction in other contexts, we have argued that social-information-processing models of the response process are limited. We have illustrated how part of what these models label as "cognitive processing" is actually accomplished in the interaction between the interviewer and the respondent, and not inside the respondent's head. That "processing" also relies on aspects of the way language is used in interaction (e.g., Clark and Schober 1992).

More complete models of how the interaction in the interview affects responses could help researchers consider alternatives to strict standardization more systematically, just as the van der Zouwen et al. model directs our attention to assessing the motivation of the respondent and the adequacy of the cues provided by the interviewer. Both these projects—developing better models and designing variants of traditional standardization—could benefit from a better understanding of what interviewers and respondents actually do in survey interviews.

An initial list of the activities we observe interviewers performing that researchers should take into account in devising styles of standardization might include the following: reading questions, repeating information the respondent has given earlier as a "verification" of an answer to a current question, responding to comments respondents make about the survey question, responding to other comments made by respondents, proposing solutions to a possible comprehension problem, proposing a change in the structure of the task, proposing further choices or actions to the respondent, and providing acknowledgment or acceptance. Each of these activities can be analyzed as part of tasks that might be the subject of interviewing rules and training.

For example, the observation that interviewers sometimes propose a solution to a possible comprehension problem or propose a change in the task can lead to an examination of what situations lead to interviewer intervention, what behavior of respondents' interviewers treat as indicating problems in comprehension, what behavior of respondents' interviewers treat as indicating problems with the structure of the question-and-answer task, what techniques interviewers use to clarify questions or modify the task, and so on. Thus we can observe survey interviewers treating respondents' delays in answering and their "reportings" of material related to the topic of the question as though these behaviors indicate some problem in comprehension (we provide an example of this later). Interviewers may then "remedy" these problems by providing preemptive probes, repeating the question, and so on (Schaeffer and Maynard forthcoming; see also Schaeffer, Maynard, and Cradock 1993). The effectiveness of the techniques interviewers use can be tested in experiments, and those found to be successful can be used to expand the repertoire of survey interviewing.

DESCRIBING THE BEHAVIOR OF STANDARDIZED INTERVIEWERS

The justification for rules of standardization continues to receive support from recent studies that examine interviewer effects (e.g., Mangione et al. 1992). Research also shows how departures from standardization can affect the validity of answers. For example, Smit, Dijkstra, and van der Zouwen (1997) used a question that evoked a response before the response categories were presented to compare experimentally the effects of three different ways of having interviewers present the response categories. After the respondent "interrupted" with an answer, the interviewer presented (a) the three categories adjacent to the category the respondent's answer suggested, (b) a single category in the direction suggested by the respondent, or (c) the category that seemed closest to the answer given by the respondent. The results suggest that respondents are more likely to choose the category mentioned by the interviewer; in addition, the relationship of the item with the respondent's age varied depending on which technique the interviewer used. In an additional experimental manipulation that compared neutral and suggestive probes, Smit et al. found that the probes influenced the subsequent answer in one of two cases they examined. This finding complements that of an earlier experiment that showed that when interviewers briefly expressed an opinion on a topic related to the survey questions, the distribution of answers was affected (Dijkstra 1987).

Research that examines the behavior of standardized interviewers suggests, however, that departures from standardization sometimes increase the accuracy of answers. Jennifer Dykema, James Lepkowski, and Steven Blixt (1997) analyzed a study of health-related events and experiences that included a record check of respondents' answers for several questions. For only 1 of 10 items was there a relationship between reading the question exactly as worded and the accuracy of the answer—and for that case the relationship was not in the predicted direction. Dykema and her colleagues note that there may be something about the specific items involved that accounts for this finding. Furthermore, the deviations from standardization that account for this relationship when it occurs are unlikely to be random or haphazard alterations of question wording. The effect is likely to be due either to wording changes that are tailored to the situation in some way or to other interviewer behaviors that happen to be correlated with question wording changes. (For example, experienced interviewers may be both most likely to alter the wording of questions and most adept at identifying when respondents misunderstand questions.) In later analyses of these data, Robert Belli and colleagues find evidence that when interviewers modify the wording of the question, accuracy is improved for younger, but not for older respondents (Belli, Weiss, and Lepkowski 1999). Some of the mechanisms that produce these results may be those examined in recent experiments that let interviewers depart from standardization to try to improve respondents' comprehension of questions (see our later discussion).

EXPERIMENTING WITH THE STYLE OF INTERVIEWING TO IMPROVE SURVEY DATA

Experiments that compare styles of interviewing presume an analysis that identifies the components of interviewing "style." Such an analysis identifies behaviors of the interviewer—such as those discussed earlier—that could distinguish styles of interviewing and that are expected to affect the validity or reliability of resulting data. Experimental variations of interviewing styles can focus on any of the goals of standardized measurement, including reducing error variation and increasing the accuracy of individual answers. Borrowing from social-information-processing models of the question-answering process, one might propose modifying practices of standardization to improve the respondent's comprehension of survey concepts, improve the respondent's recall, clarify the format in which the response is to be provided, motivate the respondent to be accurate, and so on.

The goal of improving recall has long been a focus of experiments with interviewing techniques, such as controlled feedback, anchoring dates to fix reference periods, beginning the interview with a "free-flowing discussion" of the topic, and using various techniques to stimulate recall of events. Some of the techniques in these experiments could be used in standardized interviews (e.g., controlled feedback), but others involve substantially loosening the practices of standardization (e.g., varying the order of topics, free recall) (for examples, see discussions in Cannell, Marquis, and Laurent 1977; Means et al. 1989; Oksenberg et al. 1992). Many—perhaps most—of these techniques have not found their way into large-scale production interviewing. This is probably at least partly because they pose challenges (and additional expense) for the training and supervising of interviewers and for the recording and processing of data.

The motivation of the respondent has also been addressed in experiments with interviewing techniques. When respondents are asked to sign a form on which they commit themselves to working hard, reporting appears to improve (see, e.g., Cannell et al. 1981). In Dijkstra's (1987) comparison of formal and personal (elsewhere labeled "socioemotional"; see Dijkstra and van der Zouwen 1988) interviewing, both styles are essentially standardized, but the personal style attempts to increase the respondent's motivation by telling the interviewer during training that a good relationship with the respondent is important for getting accurate information and by allowing the interviewer to express sympathy toward the respondent (e.g., "How nice for you!"). Respondents interviewed in the personal style performed better on a map-drawing task, provided more irrelevant information, and had lower social desirability scores than did respondents interviewed in the formal style. Respondents in the two styles were similar in the amount of relevant information they provided and in their tendency to be influenced by an opin-

```
43   IV:   .hhh Naow (0.3) Last week
44         (0.5)
45   IV:   did you (.) do any work at all including work for pay or
46         other types of compensation
47   FR:   N:ow are you asking this of me? [personally?  ]
48   IV:                                   [You yeah ub] you
49         personally .hh be[cause] I'm speaking with=
50   FR:                    [(    )]
51   IV:   =you pers- and then the next question will be (.)
52         concerning (.) your husband=
53   FR:   =Oh um
54         (0.7)
55   IV:   [So do y-]
56   FR:   [I'm on ma]ternity lea- maternity leave right now=
57   IV:   =Okay so nother words you are .hhh w- last week you
58         actually did not work [right?  ]
59   FR:                         [No did] not work=
60   IV:   =O:kay (.) for any pay
61   FR:   Right
```

ion the interviewer provided (as part of an experimental treatment) during the course of the interview.

Subsequent analyses of this experiment examined how participants behaved in the two styles of interviewing. Interviewers in the formal and personal styles appeared similar in how often they deviated from the wording of the question in the questionnaire and in how often they "chose" an answer based on information provided by the respondent, but interviewers in the personal style were more likely to emit "irrelevant behaviors" and more likely to "hint" at an answer (asking leading questions or suggesting an answer) (Dijkstra and van der Zouwen 1988). Analyses of the interaction sequences indicate that interviewers trained in the personal style are more likely than interviewers trained in the formal style to use leading probes, and that these probes are usually "in line" with information already provided by the respondent. Respondents are likely to accept suggestions made by the interviewer, particularly when the interviewer uses the personal style (van der Zouwen et al. 1991).

Another important goal of interviewing, suggested by models of the response process, is to improve the respondent's understanding of the task. Survey questions can never apply perfectly to every respondent's situation. Thus interviewers regularly encounter respondents who have trouble classifying themselves using the available response categories. These problems occur when respondents present situations that the researcher expected to be infrequent in the sample or did not anticipate in the design of the instrument. The interactional trajectory of these occasions shows that correctly classifying the respondent using survey concepts is the interviewer's, not the respondent's, business, as the interaction between an interviewer (IV) and female respondent (FR) shown illustrates (see Schaeffer and Maynard forthcoming).

At line 56, the respondent produces a "report" of information relevant to the question, but does not provide a formatted answer. Paul Drew (1984) has shown that in other contexts, it is up to the recipient of a report to gather the upshot, as this interviewer does beginning at line 57.

The sort of directive probe used by this interviewer is probably unacceptable in most versions of standardization. We speculate, however, that at least some investigators would be comfortable with an intervention that presented a portion of the concept definition tailored for this respondent, such as, "And did you get paid for that maternity leave?" or "Did you have a job to which you expected to return after your maternity leave?" or whatever the relevant distinction might be. The clarification the interviewer presents at lines 48-52 is tailored in this way: She uses a contrast with "your husband" (he is presumably in the "common ground" of the interview) to clarify that "you" means only the respondent.

Under the strongest version of the flexible style of standardization examined by Schober and Conrad (1997; Conrad and Schober 2000) in their innovative series of experiments, the initiative shown by this interviewer in diagnosing the source of the difficulty would be within the range of acceptable behavior, as would the directive probe (M. F. Schober, personal communication, March 1, 2000). Schober and Conrad tested the impact of allowing interviewers to determine when they should help respondents by clarifying survey concepts and authorizing interviewers to define survey concepts in their own words, sometimes in combination with instructions to respondents that explained that survey concepts could differ from everyday concepts and encouraged respondents to ask for help. Respondents are much more likely to ask for clarification in the flexible style of interviewing (of the questions that mapped onto respondents' situations in complicated ways, 2 percent elicited questions in standardized interviews and 34 percent did so in conversational interviews; see Bloom and Schober 1999), which began with extensive instruction about the importance of asking for clarification (see also Schober, Conrad, and Fricker 1999). Either the respondents' requests or the initiative

taken by the interviewer, or the combination, appears to be effective: Respondents with complicated situations were significantly more likely to give accurate answers when they were interviewed with the flexible style. The increased accuracy comes at an increased cost (which is sometimes substantial) in interview time for both straightforward and complex situations (Schober et al. 1999).

The technique of authorizing interviewers to diagnose and intervene to correct possible problems in understanding and applying survey concepts faces a number of challenges. It is true that instruments cannot always anticipate or handle all situations respondents might present. However, instruments should be designed to handle complex situations that affect significant proportions of the sample. Because situations that instruments cannot handle will always arise, training interviewers in how to intervene properly could increase validity, even if it took more interviewing time for the affected cases.

The operational problems these techniques face in gaining acceptance include the cost of having the interviewer take the initiative when it might not be needed and the cost of training interviewers to use these techniques in surveys in which there are many concepts. There are also other unknowns: whether respondents will continue to ask questions and indicate when they need help during long interviews, whether interviewers can retain concepts over long field periods in which any given definition may be required only rarely, how the techniques might be applied to questions about subjective things (or how interviewers might manage alternating between strict standardization for subjective questions and flexible interviewing for other questions), how interviewers might be monitored and supervised in their use of these techniques, and what the impact on interviewer variance in a full-scale study might be (see also Schaeffer and Royston 1999).

ETHNOMETHODOLOGICAL AND CONVERSATION-ANALYTIC STUDIES OF INTERACTION

Many recent studies of interaction in the survey interview draw on ethnomethodology and conversation analysis, two interrelated subfields in sociology that regard concrete activities of participants in everyday life as a site of intelligible organization that is available for close scientific analysis (Maynard and Clayman 1991; see also Garfinkel 1967, 1996; Heritage 1984b). Ethnomethodology started with a concern for members' "accounting practices," or the devices by which intelligibility is sustained in and through concrete concerted actions. It has made large contributions to the study of practices in the workplace and in scientific laboratories (Lynch 1992). Consequently, it has implications for the study of survey interviewing as a work practice (Maynard and Schaeffer 2000; Lynch forthcoming).

Conversation analysis describes and analyzes the orderly properties of conversational interaction as the achievements of participants. Rather than being a product of external influence, processes of conversational interaction have their own internal constraints, or are under *local control* (Zimmerman 1988:408). For instance, Sacks et al. (1974) note that in taking turns at talk, participants have three ordered options: (a) a current speaker may select the next speaker, (b) a next speaker may self-select, or (c) a current speaker may continue. With this system of turn taking in conversation, participants have an *intrinsic* motivation for listening to one another, independent of other motivations including interest, deference, or politeness.

Potential next speakers must listen to a current speaker to find out whether they have been selected to take the next turn, to discover when the current turn ends and it is appropriate to start speaking, and to know what they may be constrained to say next, given what has been said in the turn of talk under way. This intrinsic motivation for listening means that conversation is largely self-governing with respect to the orderly achievement of mutual understanding. If the displayed understanding in that next turn does not align with the speaker's own, then the *next* turn of speaker can be devoted to correcting the matter. *Repair* of all kinds of conversational trouble usually exhibits sequentially systematic properties (Schegloff, Jefferson, and Sacks 1977). Robert Moore and Douglas Maynard (forthcoming) discuss how conversation repair intertwines with the *probing* of uncodable answers to survey questions. Turn-taking and repair mechanisms are part of the *local* control mechanisms for maintaining orderliness in conversational interaction.

Conversational and Interactional Sequencing

As we discussed earlier, Suchman and Jordan (1990) have observed that the survey interview is under external control. Survey design governs both what participants in the interview talk about and how they talk (through question-answer sequences). This means that ordinary resources for establishing shared understanding in conversation are prohibited in the interview. For instance, whereas participants in conversation are free to elaborate on what their presumptive worldviews are, what their utterances mean, and what the sources of any misunderstandings are, interviewers and respondents are severely constrained from such elaboration.

The critique of Suchman and Jordan (1990) and others (see our earlier discussion) focuses on how the survey interview differs from, and is inferior to, conversation in the establishment of mutual understanding and meaning, rather than on what characterizes the performance of the survey interview *as a standardized interview* for purposes of social measurement. Schegloff (1990), in a response to Suchman and Jordan, suggests that inquiry is possible "into the features of the survey interview as an organized occasion of talk in interaction" (p. 249; see also Schegloff forthcoming). Such inquiry would recognize that "all talk-in-interaction faces certain generic organizational problems, and will perforce adopt some organized solution to them." Such generic organizational problems include procedures for allocating turns of talk; interactional constraints on coherence; repair of troubles in speaking, hearing, understanding, and so on; an overall structural organization; and a variety of other matters depending on the nature of the survey and its substantive topic.

"Preference structures" provide an example of interactional constraints. The concepts of "preference" and "preference structure" in conversation refer to ways in which agreement (preferred) and disagreement (dispreferred) and other paired conversational actions (acceptance/rejection, offering/requesting, and so on) are asymmetrical in terms of their conversational enactment. Even when participants may "want" to disagree with someone, they often display their disagreements in a *dispreferred* fashion. Thus the term *preference* refers to structural properties of and systematic practices in conversation (see Pomerantz 1984; Sacks 1987). Nora Cate Schaeffer (1991) has argued that preference structure may intrude on the survey interview in a way that affects respondents' answers.

Because the fundamental framework for doing conversation analysis is sequential organization, the organization of question-answer sequences, which dominate the survey interview, is of natural interest. We have referred to the sequence in which an interviewer asks a question as written and a respondent answers in the format requested as *paradigmatic* (Schaeffer and Maynard 1996). This ideal sequence presumes that the cognitive processing required to produce an answer occurs "inside the respondent's head." But, as discussed earlier, we have shown how the *concerted*

participation in the interview radically enters into the cognitive processes researchers often assign to the respondent (Schaeffer and Maynard 1996). Respondents do not simply react to the wording of the survey questions, and interviewers are not only a conduit of the questions. Attention to question-answer sequences and ways in which respondents solicit interviewer help, or in which interviewers offer help, reveals a more complicated and interactive picture.

Monograph Studies of Interaction in the Survey Interview

Hanneke Houtkoop-Steenstra's book *Interaction and the Standardized Survey Interview* (2000) is the most extensive conversation-analytic study to date of question-and-answer sequences during the survey interview. Houtkoop-Steenstra's empirical investigation starts with a consideration of "participant roles" in the interview, suggesting that the interview implicates more than just an "interviewer" and a "respondent." Using Erving Goffman's (1979) concept of "footing," which refers to the stances that participants take in relation to their talk, Houtkoop-Steenstra describes how interviewers exhibit themselves as "animators" (Goffman 1979) or "relayers" (Levinson 1988) of text that is designed by others, the "author" (Goffman 1979) or "formulator" (Clark 1996). Accordingly, when respondents ask for clarification or have other difficulties, interviewers comment in ways that indicate such a participation status, such as "I just ask questions here." Or, in other circumstances, interviewers may refer to distant participants who design the instrument items, with phrases such as "They're asking . . . ." From time to time, interviewers may step out of their animating stance altogether, saying (for example) "I'm sorry" when a respondent reports a sad incident.

Elsewhere in her book, Houtkoop-Steenstra addresses the topics of redundant questions, the structure of question turns, and the field coding of questions. Redundant questions are those for which a respondent has already provided relevant information in response to a previous question. Although some centers use the "verification" procedure we described earlier, there are circumstances in which redundant questions still pose problems. In such circumstances, it appears that the Dutch survey interviewers Houtkoop-Steenstra studied become more "conversational," whereas U.S. interviewers may be stricter in following rules of standardization. Houtkoop-Steenstra also addresses the organization of question turns in interviews (see also Houtkoop-Steenstra forthcoming). Survey researchers have observed that when a "question" is followed by a definition, respondents may interrupt before the definition is read (e.g., Cannell et al. 1989); Schaeffer (1991) has shown how work by conversation analysts could be used to understand why such a question might frequently be interrupted.

Using specifications provided by Sacks et al.'s (1974) foundational work on turn taking, Houtkoop-Steenstra (2000) describes how many survey questions are vulnerable to interruption because they can be heard to implicate a response from the respondent before the scripted question is complete. Realizing this, interviewers often modify such questions in the course of producing them, although this reduces standardization. In the final chapter of *Interaction and the Standardized Survey Interview,* Houtkoop-Steenstra deals with "field coding" of answers to open questions, arguing that, in a variety of ways, interviewers are prompted to modify such questions, sometimes, for example, producing candidate answers on behalf of their respondents, who can confirm such candidates. Although this may compromise standardization, features of interaction may naturally occasion such interviewer behavior.

Another major conversation-analytic work on the survey is Robert Moore's (1999) doctoral dissertation on "repair" and its relation to "probing" in the survey interview. Moore discusses respondents' requests for repeats and clarifications of survey questions and interviewers' queries about inadequately formulated answers. A phenomenon related to repair, and to Houtkoop-Steenstra's consideration of question structure, is how interviewers handle "premature" answers or those that occur before a question has been completely read because respondents figure they have enough information. It is important to note that repair in conversation is related to the achievement of understanding (Schegloff et al. 1977), but in the survey interview, standardization may impede practices of repair and therefore interfere with such understanding (see also Moore and Maynard forthcoming).

Finally, Maynard et al. (forthcoming) have edited a collection of studies on interaction in the survey interview. Topics covered include theoretical orientations toward studying such interaction, the organization of questions and interviewing sequences, and data quality.

Recruiting Survey Participants

Robert Groves, Robert Cialdini, and Mick Couper (1992) propose that interaction is also one of the critical elements in a theory of survey *participation*. Conversation-analytic investigations add to other studies of survey interview openings that attempt to identify the tacit means by which scripted introductions are made to work on behalf of recruiting respondents to the interview. In one article, we have examined the practices by which interviewers open their encounters with potential respondents and make requests for participation, as well as the complementary means by which call recipients accept or decline such requests (exercising their "gatekeeping" capacity) and the methods by which both participants close and terminate the encounter when a respondent refuses the request (Maynard and Schaeffer 1997; see also Maynard and Schaeffer forthcoming-a).

Groves et al. (1992) introduce the concept of "tailoring" for understanding the work of soliciting participation. Successful interviewers, they argue, tailor the scripted instructions for recruiting participants to specific concerns and objections that potential survey respondents may raise. They search for cues about a householder who answers the door or telephone and should be able to size up a situation quickly and apply the appropriate persuasive messages. Couper and Groves (forthcoming) show some suggestive evidence that the more interviewers tailor their introductions, the more likely they are to get cooperation. And we have examined in detail the real-time devices of talk and embodied behavior by which an interviewer "tailors" the callback to a selected respondent who had previously refused participation in a survey and successfully obtains participation of the household, if not that particular respondent (Maynard and Schaeffer forthcoming-b). Through a variety of tacit and persuasive methods, the interviewer obtains permission to call back later, and, upon making that callback, the interviewer obtains a completed interview.

◆ Conclusion

The questions used in survey measurement are similar to everyday questions—which are a resource in many familiar types of talk. As a result, however, survey interviews are prey to a tension between the everyday task of "getting information" and the scientific task of "measurement." In resolving this tension, interviewers alternate between following the rules of standardization and, for circumstances such rules cannot foresee or prescribe how to handle, deploying their tacit knowledge and interactional competence in pursuit of survey answers.

Recent studies of interaction in the survey interview have documented the limits of standardization but also the resourcefulness of interviewers in pushing those limits in pursuit of answers. For example, detailed studies of interaction from a conversation-analytic standpoint describe ways that interviewers diagnose problems in comprehension (Schaeffer and Maynard forthcoming). Subsequent studies suggest that the validity of survey data might be enhanced if interviewers are authorized to intervene with clarifications when they determine that respondents do not understand survey concepts. Such innovations could improve the quality of survey data if they are shown to reduce total error—considering effects on both reliability and validity.

The fate of the innovative methods of interviewing examined by past research, however, suggests that improving survey measurement will require that researchers grapple with the operational issues involved in putting a "prototype" style of interviewing into "production." The challenges include devising methods that large field staffs can be trained to use reliably at an acceptable cost. New interviewing methods also will require guidelines for monitoring the quality of interviewers' behavior as well as appropriate instruments and data processing procedures.

In addition to their contribution to our understanding of the survey interview, the findings of the studies examined here may have implications for our understanding of how the interviewer affects what is observed in other sorts of interviews. The controls provided by standardization make the survey interview a useful site in which to observe features of social life operating (e.g., Schuman and Ludwig 1983). For example, race-of-interviewer effects in studies of racial attitudes are not methodological artifacts, but a reflection of the way respondents consider the race of the person with whom they are speaking when they talk about race. Respondents' sensitivity to the race of the person with whom they are speaking is a feature not only of survey interviews, but of social life, and one that researchers can describe systematically—if somewhat "thinly"—by examining its operation in survey interviews (see also Dunbar, Rodriguez, and Parker, Chapter 14, this volume). Similarly, the tacit knowledge that people require to interact at all forms the necessary grounding of social measurement and interviews of any sort. Tacit knowledge is necessary and inescapable, and it inescapably shapes social measurement.

■ References

Atkinson, J. M. and P. Drew. 1979. *Order in Court: The Organization of Verbal Interaction in Judicial Settings*. London: Macmillan.

Beatty, P. 1995. "Understanding the Standardized/Non-standardized Interviewing Controversy." *Journal of Official Statistics* 11:147-60.

Belli, R. F., P. S. Weiss, and J. M. Lepkowski. 1999. "Dynamics of Survey Interviewing and the Quality of Survey Reports: Age Comparisons." Pp. 303-26 in *Cognition, Aging, and Self-Reports*, edited by N. Schwarz, D. Park, B. Knauper, and S. Sudman. Philadelphia, PA: Psychology Press.

Bingham, W. and B. Moore. 1924. *How to Interview*. New York: Harper & Row.

Bloom, J. E. and M. F. Schober. 1999. "Respondent Cues That Survey Questions Are in Danger of Being Misunderstood." In *Proceedings of the Joint Statistical Meeting of the American Statistical Association, Section on Survey Research Methods, 1998*. Alexandria, VA: American Statistical Association.

Boyd, E. A. and J. Heritage. Forthcoming. "Taking the Patient's Personal History: Questioning during Verbal Examination." In *Practicing Medicine: Talk and Action in Primary Care Encounters*, edited by J. Heritage and D. W. Maynard. Cambridge: Cambridge University Press.

Brenner, M. 1981. "Aspects of Conversational Structure in the Research Interview." Pp. 19-40 in *Conversation and Discourse*, edited by P. Werth. London: Croom Helm.

Briggs, C. L. 1986. *Learning How to Ask: A Sociolinguistic Appraisal of the Role of the Interview in Social Science Research*. Cambridge: Cambridge University Press.

Button, G. 1987. "Answers as Interactional Products: Two Sequential Practices Used in Interviews." *Social Psychology Quarterly* 50:160-71.

Cannell, C. F. and R. L. Kahn. 1968. "Interviewing." Pp. 526-95 in *Handbook of Social Psychology*, Vol. 2, edited by G. Lindzey and E. Aronson. Reading, MA: Addison-Wesley.

Cannell, C. F., G. Kalton, L. Oksenberg, and K. Bischoping. 1989. *New Techniques for Pretesting Survey Questions* (Final Report, Grant No. HS 05616). Washington, DC: National Center for Health Services Research and Health Care Technology Assessment.

Cannell, C. F., S. A. Lawson, and D. L. Hausser. 1975. *A Technique for Evaluating Interviewer Performance*. Ann Arbor: University of Michigan, Survey Research Center of the Institute for Social Research.

Cannell, C. F., K. H. Marquis, and A. Laurent. 1977. *A Summary of Studies of Interviewing Methodology* (Vital and Health Statistics Series 2, Data Evaluation and Methods Research, No. 69). Rockville, MD: National Center for Health Statistics.

Cannell, C. F., P. V. Miller, and L. Oksenberg. 1981. "Research on Interviewing Techniques." Pp. 389-437 in *Sociological Methodology 1981*, edited by S. Leinhardt. San Francisco: Jossey-Bass.

Cicourel, A. V. 1964. *Method and Measurement in Sociology*. New York: Free Press.

———. 1974. *Theory and Method in a Study of Argentine Fertility*. New York: John Wiley.

———. 1982. "Interviews, Surveys, and the Problem of Ecological Validity." *American Sociologist* 17:11-20.

Clark, H. H. 1996. *Using Language*. Cambridge: Cambridge University Press.

Clark, H. H. and M. F. Schober. 1992. "Asking Questions and Influencing Answers." Pp. 15-48 in *Questions about Questions: Inquiries into the Cognitive Bases of Surveys*, edited by J. M. Tanur. New York: Russell Sage Foundation.

Conrad, F. G. and M. F. Schober. 2000. "Clarifying Question Meaning in a Household Telephone Survey." *Public Opinion Quarterly* 64:1-28.

Couper, M. P. and R. M. Groves. Forthcoming. "Introductory Interactions in Telephone Surveys and Nonresponse." In *Standardization and Tacit Knowledge: Interaction and Practice in the Survey Interview,* edited by D. W. Maynard, H. Houtkoop-Steenstra, J. van der Zouwen, and N. C. Schaeffer. New York: John Wiley.

Dijkstra, W. 1987. "Interviewing Style and Respondent Behavior: An Experimental Study of the Survey Interview." *Sociological Methods & Research* 16:309-34.

Dijkstra, W. and J. van der Zouwen. 1988. "Types of Inadequate Interviewer Behavior in Survey-Interviews." Pp. 29-35 in *Data Collection and Scaling,* edited by W. E. Saris and I. N. Gallhofer. New York: St. Martin's.

Drew, P. 1984. "Speakers' Reportings in Invitation Sequences." Pp. 129-51 in *Structures of Social Action: Studies in Conversation Analysis,* edited by J. M. Atkinson and J. Heritage. Cambridge: Cambridge University Press.

Dykema, J., J. M. Lepkowski, and S. Blixt. 1997. "The Effect of Interviewer and Respondent Behavior on Data Quality: Analysis of Interaction Coding in a Validation Study." Pp. 287-310 in *Survey Measurement and Process Quality,* edited by L. E. Lyberg, P. P. Biemer, M. Collins, E. D. de Leeuw, C. Dippo, N. Schwarz, and D. Trewin. New York: John Wiley.

Fowler, F. J., Jr. and T. W. Mangione. 1990. *Standardized Survey Interviewing: Minimizing Interviewer-Related Error.* Newbury Park, CA: Sage.

Garfinkel, H. 1967. *Studies in Ethnomethodology.* Englewood Cliffs, NJ: Prentice Hall.

———. 1996. "Ethnomethodology's Program." *Social Psychology Quarterly* 59:5-21.

Goffman, E. 1979. "Footing." *Semiotica* 25:1-29.

Goudy, W. J. and H. R. Potter. 1975. "Interview Rapport: Demise of a Concept." *Public Opinion Quarterly* 39:529-43.

Groves, R. M. 1989. *Survey Errors and Survey Costs.* New York: John Wiley.

Groves, R. M., R. B. Cialdini, and M. P. Couper. 1992. "Understanding the Decision to Participate in a Survey." *Public Opinion Quarterly* 56:475-95.

Groves, R. M. and L. J. Magilavy. 1986. "Measuring and Explaining Interviewer Effects in Centralized Telephone Surveys." *Public Opinion Quarterly* 50:251-66.

Heritage, J. 1984a. "A Change-of-State Token and Aspects of Its Sequential Placement." Pp. 299-345 in *Structures of Social Action: Studies in Conversation Analysis,* edited by J. M. Atkinson and J. Heritage. Cambridge: Cambridge University Press.

———. 1984b. *Garfinkel and Ethnomethodology.* Cambridge: Polity.

———. Forthcoming. "Ad Hoc Inquiries: 'Routine' Question Design in an Open Context." In *Standardization and Tacit Knowledge: Interaction and Practice in the Survey Interview,* edited by D. W. Maynard, H. Houtkoop-Steenstra, J. van der Zouwen, and N. C. Schaeffer. New York: John Wiley.

Heritage, J. and D. Greatbatch. 1991. "On the Institutional Character of Institutional Talk: The Case of News Interviews." Pp. 93-137 in *Talk and Social Structure: Studies in Ethnomethodology and Conversation Analysis,* edited by D. Boden and D. H. Zimmerman. Berkeley: University of California Press.

Holstein, J. A. and J. F. Gubrium. 1995. *The Active Interview.* Thousand Oaks, CA: Sage.

Houtkoop-Steenstra, H. 2000. *Interaction and the Standardized Survey Interview: The Living Questionnaire.* Cambridge: Cambridge University Press.

———. Forthcoming-b. "Questioning Turn Format and Turn-Taking Problems in Standardized Survey Interviews." In *Standardization and Tacit Knowledge: Interaction and Practice in the Survey Interview,* edited by D. W. Maynard, H. Houtkoop-Steenstra, J. van der Zouwen, and N. C. Schaeffer. New York: John Wiley.

Hyman, H. H., W. J. Cobb, J. J. Feldman, C. W. Hart, and C. H. Stember. [1954] 1975. *Interviewing in Social Research.* Chicago: University of Chicago Press.

Kahn, R. L. and C. F. Cannell. 1957. *The Dynamics of Interviewing: Theory, Technique, and Cases.* New York: John Wiley.

Kidder, L. H. 1981. *Research Methods in Social Relations.* New York: Holt, Rinehart & Winston.

Levinson, S. 1988. "Putting Linguistics on a Proper Footing: Explorations in Goffman's Concepts of Participation." Pp. 161-227 in *Erving Goffman: Exploring the Interaction Order,* edited by P. Drew and A. Wootton. Boston: Northeastern University Press.

Lynch, M. 1992. "Extending Wittgenstein: The Pivotal Move from Epistemology to the Sociology of Science." In *Science as Practice and Culture,* edited by A. Pickering. Chicago: University of Chicago Press.

———. Forthcoming. "The Living Text: Written Instructions and Situated Action in Telephone Surveys." In *Standardization and Tacit Knowledge: Interaction and Practice in the Survey Interview,* edited by D. W. Maynard, H. Houtkoop-Steenstra, J. van der Zouwen, and N. C. Schaeffer. New York: John Wiley.

Mangione, T. W., F. J. Fowler, Jr., and T. A. Louis. 1992. "Question Characteristics and Interviewer Effects." *Journal of Official Statistics* 8:293-307.

Marlaire, C. L. and D. W. Maynard. 1990. "Standardized Testing as an Interactional Phenomenon." *Sociology of Education* 63(2):83-101.

Marquis, K. H., C. F. Cannell, and A. Laurent. 1972. *Reporting Health Events in Household Interviews: Effects of Reinforcement, Question Length, and Reinterviews* (Vital and Health Statistics Series 2, Data Evaluation and Methods Research, No. 45). Rockville, MD: U.S. Department of Health and Human Services.

Maynard, D. W. and S. E. Clayman. 1991. "The Diversity of Ethnomethodology." *Annual Review of Sociology* 17:385-418.

Maynard, D. W., H. Houtkoop-Steenstra, J. van der Zouwen, and N. C. Schaeffer, eds. Forthcoming. *Standardization and Tacit Knowledge: Interaction and Practice in the Survey Interview.* New York: John Wiley.

Maynard, D. W. and C. L. Marlaire. 1992. "Good Reasons for Bad Testing Performance: The Interactional Substrate of Educational Exams." *Qualitative Sociology* 15:177-202.

Maynard, D. W. and N. C. Schaeffer. 1997. "Keeping the Gate: Declinations of the Request to Participate in a Telephone Survey Interview." *Sociological Methods & Research* 26:34-79.

———. Forthcoming-a. "Opening and Closing the Gate: The Work of 'Optimism' in Recruiting Survey Respondents." In *Standardization and Tacit Knowledge: Interaction and Practice in the Survey Interview,* edited by D. W. Maynard, H. Houtkoop-Steenstra, J. van der Zouwen, and N. C. Schaeffer. New York: John Wiley.

———. Forthcoming-b. "Standardization and Its Discontents: Standardization, Interaction, and the Survey Interview." In *Standardization and Tacit Knowledge: Interaction and Practice in the Survey Interview,* edited by D. W. Maynard, H. Houtkoop-Steenstra, J. van der Zouwen, and N. C. Schaeffer. New York: John Wiley.

———. 2000. "Toward a Sociology of Social Scientific Knowledge: Survey Research and Ethnomethodology's Asymmetric Alternates." *Social Studies of Science* 30:323-70.

Means, B., A. Nigam, M. Zarrow, E. F. Loftus, and M. S. Donaldson. 1989. *Autobiographical Memory for Health-Related Events.* Rockville, MD: National Center for Health Statistics.

Means, B., G. E. Swan, J. B. Jobe, and J. L. Esposito. 1991. "An Alternative Approach to Obtaining Personal History Data." Pp. 167-84 in *Measurement Errors in Surveys,* edited by P. P. Biemer, R. M. Groves, L. E. Lyberg, N. A. Mathiowetz, and S. Sudman. New York: John Wiley.

Mehan, H. 1973. "Assessing Children's Language Using Abilities: Methodological and Cross Cultural Implications." Pp. 309-43 in *Comparative Social Research: Methodological Problems and Strategies,* edited by M. Armer and A. D. Grimshaw. New York: John Wiley.

———. 1979. *Learning Lessons.* Cambridge, MA: Harvard University Press.

Mehan, H., A. Hertweck, and J. L. Meihls. 1986. *Handicapping the Handicapped: Decision-Making in Students' Educational Careers.* Stanford, CA: Stanford University Press.

Miller, P. V. and C. F. Cannell. 1982. "A Study of Experimental Techniques for Telephone Interviewing." *Public Opinion Quarterly* 46:250-69.

Mishler, E. G. 1986. *Research Interviewing: Context and Narrative.* Cambridge, MA: Harvard University Press.

Moore, R. J. 1999. "Achieving Understanding in the Standardized Interview: A Conversation Analytic Study of Talk in Telephone Surveys." Ph.D. dissertation, Department of Sociology, Indiana University.

Moore, R. J. and D. W. Maynard. Forthcoming. "Achieving Understanding in the Standardized Survey Interview: The Organization of Repair." In *Standardization and Tacit Knowledge: Interaction and Practice in the Survey Interview*, edited by D. W. Maynard, H. Houtkoop-Steenstra, J. van der Zouwen, and N. C. Schaeffer. New York: John Wiley.

Oksenberg, L., T. Beebe, S. Blixt, and C. F. Cannell. 1992. *Research on the Design and Conduct of the National Medical Expenditure Survey Interviews.* Ann Arbor, MI: Institute for Social Research.

Oksenberg, L., C. F. Cannell, and G. Kalton. 1991. "New Strategies for Pretesting Survey Questions." *Journal of Official Statistics* 7:349-65.

O'Muircheartaigh, C. A. 1997. "Measurement Error in Surveys: A Historical Perspective." Pp. 1-25 in *Survey Measurement and Process Quality*, edited by L. E. Lyberg, P. P. Biemer, M. Collins, E. D. de Leeuw, C. Dippo, N. Schwarz, and D. Trewin. New York: John Wiley.

Pomerantz, A. 1984. "Agreeing and Disagreeing with Assessments: Some Features of Preferred/Dispreferred Turn Shapes." Pp. 57-101 in *Structures of Social Action: Studies in Conversation Analysis*, edited by J. M. Atkinson and J. Heritage. Cambridge: Cambridge University Press.

Sacks, H. 1987. "On the Preferences for Agreement and Contiguity in Sequences in Conversation." Pp. 54-69 in *Talk and Social Organization*, edited by G. Button and J. R. E. Lee. Clevedon, England: Multilingual Matters.

Sacks, H., E. A. Schegloff, and G. Jefferson. 1974. "A Simplest Systematics for the Organization of Turn-Taking for Conversation." *Language* 50:696-735.

Schaeffer, N. C. 1991. "Conversation with a Purpose—or Conversation? Interaction in the Standardized Interview." Pp. 367-91 in *Measurement Errors in Surveys*, edited by P. P. Biemer, R. M. Groves, L. E. Lyberg, N. A. Mathiowetz, and S. Sudman. New York: John Wiley.

Schaeffer, N. C. and H.-W. Charng. 1991. "Two Experiments in Simplifying Response Categories: Intensity Ratings and Behavioral Frequencies." *Sociological Perspectives* 34:165-82.

Schaeffer, N. C. and D. W. Maynard. 1996. "From Paradigm to Prototype and Back Again: Interactive Aspects of Cognitive Processing in Standardized Survey Interviews." Pp. 65-88 in *Answering Questions: Methodology for Determining Cognitive and Communicative Processes in Survey Research*, edited by N. Schwarz and S. Sudman. San Francisco: Jossey-Bass.

———. Forthcoming. "Occasions for Intervention: Interactional Resources for Comprehension in Standardized Survey Interviews." In *Standardization and Tacit Knowledge: Interaction and Practice in the Survey Interview*, edited by D. W. Maynard, H. Houtkoop-Steenstra, J. van der Zouwen, and N. C. Schaeffer. New York: John Wiley.

Schaeffer, N. C., D. W. Maynard, and R. Cradock. 1993. "Negotiating Certainty: Uncertainty Proposals and Their Disposal in Standardized Survey Interviews." Working Paper No. 93-25, Center for Demography and Ecology, University of Wisconsin–Madison.

Schaeffer, N. C. and P. Royston. 1999. "Exploring the Interview Process." In *A New Agenda for Interdisciplinary Survey Research Methods: Proceedings of the CASM II Conference*, edited by M. Sirkin, T. Jabine, G. Willis, M. Elizabeth, and C. Tucker. Hyattsville, MD: Centers for Disease Control and Prevention, National Center for Health Statistics.

Schegloff, E. A. 1990. "Discussion of Suchman and Jordan: 'Interactional Troubles in Face-to-Face Survey Interviews.'" *Journal of the American Statistical Association* 85:248-50.

———. Forthcoming. "The Survey Interview as a Form of Talk in Interaction." In *Standardization and Tacit Knowledge: Interaction and Practice in the Survey Interview*, edited by D. W. Maynard, H. Houtkoop-Steenstra, J. van der Zouwen, and N. C. Schaeffer. New York: John Wiley.

Schegloff, E. A., G. Jefferson, and H. Sacks. 1977. "The Preference for Self-Correction in the Organization of Repair in Conversation." *Language* 53:361-82.

Schober, M. F. and F. G. Conrad. 1997. "Does Conversational Interviewing Reduce Survey Measurement Error?" *Public Opinion Quarterly* 61:576-602.

———. Forthcoming. "A Collaborative View of Standardized Survey Interviews." In *Standardization and Tacit Knowledge: Interaction and Practice in the Survey Interview*, edited by D. W. Maynard, H. Houtkoop-Steenstra, J. van der Zouwen, and N. C. Schaeffer. New York: John Wiley.

Schober, M. F., F. G. Conrad, and S. S. Fricker. 1999. "When and How Should Survey Interviewers Clarify Question Meaning?" In *Proceedings of the Joint Statistical Meeting of the American Statistical Association, Section on Survey Research Methods, 1998.* Alexandria, VA: American Statistical Association.

Schuman, H. 1982. "Artifacts Are in the Mind of the Beholder." *American Sociologist* 17:21-28.

Schuman, H. and J. Ludwig. 1983. "The Norm of Even Handedness in Surveys as in Life." *American Sociological Review* 48:112-20.

Smit, J. H., W. Dijkstra, and J. van der Zouwen. 1997. "Suggestive Interviewer Behavior in Surveys: An Experimental Study." *Journal of Official Statistics* 13:19-28.

Suchman, L. and B. Jordan. 1990. "Interactional Troubles in Face-to-Face Survey Interviews." *Journal of the American Statistical Association* 85:232-41.

Sudman, S., N. M. Bradburn, and N. Schwarz. 1996. *Thinking about Answers: The Application of Cognitive Processes to Survey Methodology.* San Francisco: Jossey-Bass.

Tourangeau, R., K. Rasinski, and L. Rips. 2000. *The Psychology of Survey Response.* Cambridge: Cambridge University Press.

van der Zouwen, J. Forthcoming. "Why Study Interaction in Survey Interviews?" In *Standardization and Tacit Knowledge: Interaction and Practice in the Survey Interview,* edited by D. W. Maynard, H. Houtkoop-Steenstra, J. van der Zouwen, and N. C. Schaeffer. New York: John Wiley.

van der Zouwen, J., W. Dijkstra, and J. H. Smit. 1991. "Studying Respondent-Interviewer Interaction: The Relationship between Interviewing Style, Interviewer Behavior, and Response Behavior." Pp. 419-37 in *Measurement Errors in Surveys,* edited by P. P. Biemer, R. M. Groves, L. E. Lyberg, N. A. Mathiowetz, and S. Sudman. New York: John Wiley.

Viterna, J. S. and D. W. Maynard. Forthcoming. "Varieties of Standardization: Practice in Academic Survey Centers." In *Standardization and Tacit Knowledge: Interaction and Practice in the Survey Interview,* edited by D. W. Maynard, H. Houtkoop-Steenstra, J. van der Zouwen, and N. C. Schaeffer. New York: John Wiley.

Weiss, C. H. 1968. "Validity of Welfare Mothers' Interview Responses." *Public Opinion Quarterly* 32:622-33.

———. 1970. "Interaction in the Research Interview: The Effects of Rapport on Response." In *Proceedings of the Meeting of the American Statistical Association, Section on Social Statistics, 1969.* Alexandria, VA: American Statistical Association.

Zimmerman, D. H. 1988. "On Conversation: The Conversation Analytic Perspective." Pp. 406-32 in *Communication Yearbook 11,* edited by J. A. Anderson. Newbury Park, CA: Sage.

29

INTERNET INTERVIEWING

◆ Chris Mann
Fiona Stewart

Interviews provide ready access to human experience in our everyday world. Now researchers in the 21st century are challenged by the simultaneously familiar yet mysterious worlds that lie "behind the screen" of the computer. They are the three-dimensional worlds of friends, colleagues, and strangers manifested in onscreen text. They are also the virtual worlds of on-line communities with their own images, rules, and interpersonal dynamics created in text. Sitting at a computer, using the Internet, researchers can interview disembodied people from across the earth and also the personae who frequent the imagined environments of cyberspace.

In this chapter we discuss interviewing using widely available Internet technology. First, we describe the key characteristics of computer-mediated communication and identify pioneering studies that have used

this medium for interviewing (also see Couper and Hansen, Chapter 27, this volume). We then consider some of the more important costs and benefits of conducting interviews on-line. Next, we discuss in detail the different kinds of expertise that researchers might need in order to conduct quantitative and qualitative interviews on-line. Finally, we consider options that might become available to researchers using the Internet as an interviewing medium in the future.

◆ Computer-Mediated Communication

Computer-mediated communication (CMC) allows computer users to interact directly with each other, using text, via keyboards.

◆ 603

Text-based CMC is available in two main modes. Asynchronous CMC, the feature of most e-mail messaging systems, allows users to type extended messages that are then electronically transmitted to recipients who can read, reply, print, forward, and file them at any time they choose. Synchronous CMC, or "real-time chat," involves the interchange of messages between two or more users simultaneously logged on at different computers or computer terminals.

CMC systems also divide into semiprivate and public arenas. The former include e-mail, one-to-one discussions using "chat" software, and conferences/forums (asynchronous discussion groups). These systems allow the interviewer (and participants) some level of control with regard to the nature and content of interaction. Public areas of CMC, in contrast, are beyond the direct control of the interviewer, and interaction may be extremely volatile (McLaughlin, Osborne, and Smith 1995). The main public arenas using CMC are bulletin board systems (BBSs) and news groups, such as those found in Usenet, the WELL, and ECHO, and undirected real-time chat systems such as those found in most Internet relay chat (IRC) and MU* environments.[1] Whichever modes they adopt for interviewing, researchers are becoming aware that CMC has characteristics that do not fit within more traditional modes of data collection (Mann and Stewart 2000); these characteristics are challenging some standard assumptions about language (Herring 1996), interpersonal relationships (Walther 1996), and group dynamics (Lea 1992; Garton, Haythornthwaite, and Wellman 1999).[2]

Although Internet use is still evolving, the potential of CMC as an interviewing medium has already been recognized, and pioneering studies have begun to identify the possibilities and pitfalls of Internet interviewing. Some researchers adopt CMC as an interviewing medium because it seems the "logical" (O'Connor and Madge 2000), indeed "the only authentic and congruent" (Smith-Stoner and Weber 2000) method of investigating Internet usage. Research has focused on the demographics of Internet use (Kehoe and Pitkow 1996) and also many aspects of on-line experience. Some investigations are associated with discussions of Internet culture (Baym 1995; Turkle 1995) and the impact of this culture, or variations of this culture (Shields 1996), on debates around identity (Bruckman 1992; Reid 1991), gender (Matheson 1992; Bannert and Arbinger 1996; Spender 1995), race (Burkhalter 1999), and cross-cultural relations (Hantrais and Sen 1996).

Other interviewers have investigated the experiences of people engaged in such on-line activity areas as distance learning (Salmon 2000; Smith-Stoner and Weber 2000), gay men's chat (Shaw 1997), virtual worlds (Correll 1995), use of Web sites (O'Connor and Madge 2000) and e-mail-mediated help services (Hahn 1998), virtual focus groups (Sweet 1999), on-line versions of a subculture (Hodkinson 2000), rural women's use of interactive communication technology (Daws 1999), and the empowering use of technology for people with disabilities (Seymour, Lupton, and Fahy 1999).

In addition, as Joseph Walther (1999) has pointed out, interviewers may use "computer-based tools and computer-accessible populations to study human behavior in general" (p. 1). Some examples of researchers who have used CMC to interview people about off-line experiences are Fiona Stewart, Elizabeth Eckerman, and Kai Zhou (1998), who collected data on a range of health issues and practices using on-line or "virtual" focus groups involving participants from the Fiji Islands, China, Australia, and Malaysia; Elizabeth Anders (2000), who conducted an international study of issues faced by women with disabilities in higher education; Anne Ryen and David Silverman (2000), who undertook a case study of an Asian entrepreneur in Africa; and Chris Mann, who looked in depth at factors that might relate to differences in academic performance among undergraduates (this research is discussed in Mann and Stewart 2000).

In these studies, the researchers chose CMC because it eliminated constraints that would have made face-to-face (FTF) research impractical. It allowed researchers to interview participants on different continents, to maintain day-by-day contact with many students throughout the course of work on their degrees, and to reach people who would have been unable to participate face-to-face because of disability, financial difficulties, and/or language and communication differences. Yet other interviewers have capitalized on the anonymity of the technology to access the voices of members of socially marginalized communities, such as gay fathers (Dunne 1999) and men who might have avoided discussing emotions if interviewed face-to-face (Bennett 1998). Psychologists are also beginning to explore CMC as a research medium (Senior and Smith 1999). For instance, on-line discussion groups have enabled researchers to access and then interview individuals with specific disorders, such as panic attacks (Stones and Perry 1998).

Clearly, CMC interviewing has a great deal to offer, but is it an interviewing medium suitable for all inquiries and all potential interviewees? This question can be answered only with reference to the methodological choices made in any research study. Research questions may focus on the form/nature or the extent/prevalence of phenomena. Generally, nonstandardized qualitative interviews, conducted with individuals or groups, investigate the former; standardized quantitative interviews map the latter. As other chapters in this book describe, qualitative and quantitative methods have costs and benefits at both practical and methodological levels. A particularly significant factor in this context is that the majority of conventional qualitative interviews are conducted face-to-face, whereas larger-scale quantitative interviews are frequently self-administered (see in this volume Warren, Chapter 4; Shuy, Chapter 26; Couper and Hansen, Chapter 27). These issues will come into play in the next section, where we discuss whether CMC increases the benefits and/or reduces the costs associated with off-line research.

◆ Some Costs and Benefits of Internet Interviewing

The costs and benefits of Internet interviewing can be assessed along a number of dimensions, some of which parallel traditional interviewing concerns and some of which are unique to the Internet medium. Let us begin by considering the first challenge that faces all interviewers: gaining access to participants.

SAMPLING AND RECRUITMENT

There is no doubt that the unrepresentativeness of current Internet access remains the greatest problem for data collection on-line. Given that only approximately 0.01 percent of the world's population was on-line at the start of 2000, it is not surprising that some writers focus on the "cyberspace divide" (Loader 1998) and the ascendancy of the literate and the computer literate in this mode of communication. Microsoft's Bill Gates (1997) has admitted that, in terms of the Internet, the problem of "the haves versus the have-nots has many dimensions: rich versus poor, urban versus rural, young versus old, and perhaps most dramatically, developing countries versus developed countries" (p. 34). Interviewers need to be aware that access to and use of the Internet is a matter not only of economics, but also of one's place in the world in terms of gender, culture, ethnicity, and language (Mann and Stewart 2000).

The patchiness of Internet access has clear implications for interviewing approaches that seek representative sampling. In statistical terms, large samples (which are certainly possible with e-mail-based and, in particular, Web-page-based surveys) do not mean anything unless they are representative of a target population, a goal that currently would clearly be difficult to attain except for specialized populations. With regard to the latter, Georgia Tech University's Graphics, Visualization, and Usability (GVU) Center's series of World Wide Web surveys attempted to identify the demographics of the Internet population itself (Kehoe and Pitkow 1996).[3] E-mail surveys have also been used to study small-scale homogeneous groups of on-line users (Parker 1992; Smith 1997; Tse et al. 1995; Winter and Huff 1996). Resourceful use of the Internet can expand the boundaries of how such interviewees may be identified. A variety of on-line formats, such as chat rooms, mailing lists, BBSs, and conferences, focus on specific topics, drawing together geographically dispersed participants who may share interests, experiences, or expertise. With a growing total of more than 25,000 news groups accessible to more than 40 million users (Kennedy 1998), the Internet is an extremely convenient way of identifying people with similar interests.

These same arenas are also available to qualitative researchers who seek purposive rather than representative samples of participants. The virtuality of the medium offers unprecedented possibilities for extending the range of participants beyond those who are available for FTF interviewing, such as mothers at home with small children, shift workers, and people with disabilities. The Internet also offers researchers a possible means of communicating with people in sites to which access is restricted (such as hospitals, religious communities, prisons, government offices, the military, schools, and cults).

The technology can offer interviewers practical access to sites previously "closed" to researchers with visible attributes that would make them stand out within the population of interest, such as age, gender, ethnicity, or even physical "style" (bikers, surfers, Goths, punks, jet-setters and so on)—although there are ethical considerations surrounding researchers' disguising their identities to become acceptable to insiders. CMC also extends the possibilities of conducting research in politically sensitive or dangerous areas (see Lee 1993). Physical distance and the possibility of anonymity offer protection to both researchers and participants (see, for instance, Coomber's 1997 study of illicit drug dealers). Political and religious dissidents or human rights advocates might feel able to participate in on-line interviews without excessive risk. Researchers can access censored and/or politically or militarily sensitive data without needing to be physically in the field. They can interview people living or working in war zones, or sites of corruption or criminal activity, or places where diseases are rife, without needing to grapple with the danger—and the bureaucracy —involved in actually visiting the area. The disembodiment of CMC also allows researchers to distance themselves physically from ideological camps, reducing the likelihood of suspicion and innuendo that might alienate some participants. Researchers could communicate, for instance, with both police and criminals without being seen visiting either; or researchers could interview both Israelis and Palestinians, say, without leaving themselves open to charges of spying.

Many interviewers recruit on-line participants using the Internet itself; another option for recruitment is to include a contact e-mail or Web address when advertising the research more conventionally in publicity leaflets and journals. Recruiting individual participants involves acquiring their e-mail addresses, either through earlier interaction (on- or off-line) or by soliciting responses from Internet users. Placing a request for contacts or information when logging onto appropriate Internet sites is one possibility (Kehoe and Pitkow 1996). Some researchers also target individuals by writing to their e-mail addresses, which are generally attached to postings in many public CMC environments. However, this can create problems if the researcher moves directly to sending research materials without first gaining a user's consent. Cooperative participants can also assist with recruitment by "snowballing" messages using the "forwarding" option provided by e-mail software (Hodkinson 2000).

Other options for interviewers are to invite participation passively by posting recruitment messages that set out to attract anyone who happens to "surf" or "lurk" around chat rooms and conference areas linked to particular Web sites, or to set up their own Web sites with "hotlinks" that draw in potential participants (O'Connor and Madge 2000). However, a certain degree of proactivity is needed to attract participants. Interviewers who advertise their research need a "hook" that will gain attention. For instance, Ross Coomber (1997) targeted drug dealers in news groups by using the subject headline "Have You Ever Sold Powdered Drugs? If So, I Would Like Your Help." Coomber also suggests that recruitment messages should be posted on a weekly basis, as news group posts are gradually replaced and sites attract new visitors all the time.

Why should individuals participate in on-line interview research at all? As with conventional research, they may be attracted by material reward or may have altruistic reasons. However, once interviewees are recruited, CMC offers them many bonuses. They can participate at their convenience from their own homes or places of work. Women, older people, and members of socially marginalized groups can communicate from familiar and physically safe environments. CMC is also experienced as relatively trouble-free, eliminating the "hassle" of finding pen and paper, buying stamps, and keeping FTF appointments. It is possible that low technical skills, particularly keyboarding skills, may marginalize some participants. On the other hand, CMC is generally informal and conversational in style and thus accessible to the everyday writer.

Sustaining CMC interaction over time, in view of both Internet "churn" (loss of access to the technology) and the ease with which participants can disappear without a trace into cyberspace, presents researchers with a new challenge. Early evidence suggests that, as in conventional research, the participants' commitment to the research purposes is a paramount factor in ensuring continuity of communication (Mann and Stewart 2000).

EXPENSE AND TIME

The lower cost of Internet research in relation to other modes is one of its most powerful advantages (and one that may increasingly encourage research sponsors to inquire whether conventional fieldwork could not be conducted through CMC). Once the necessary computer equipment has been acquired, the principal expenses for users of standard CMC are Internet service provider fees and telephone costs. In some parts of the world, phone calls for Internet use are already free, and, in a highly competitive and rapidly changing market, free Internet access is becoming increasingly available. For users with institutional access to the Internet, the cost to researchers or projects may be zero.

However, low-cost access to the on-line community has different implications for virtual versions of FTF and self-administered interviews. With conventional FTF interviewing, time and travel expenses can lead to compromises regarding where interviews are held and with whom. These problems are compounded as the research extends further afield. Interstate or interregional comparisons increase time and expense as the researcher and/or participants have to travel to different locations and conduct multiple sessions. In addition, venues for FTF interviews need to be easily accessible to participants in terms of location, timing (before work, in the evening, after children are dropped at day care), lifestyle (some participants may require child-care facilities, others may need on-site venues in businesses, schools, or hospitals), and physical access. Interviewers will also have their own requirements for FTF venues, depending upon the nature of the research (such as on-site if the research concerns a nursing home, or in a neutral location if it concerns abused wives). The requirements of researcher and participants can lead to costs in terms of the time to organize (and frequently reorganize) interview venues as well as the usage costs themselves.

In contrast, CMC is a practical and cost-efficient way of conducting in-depth interviews with individuals or groups who are geographically distant, and it also facilitates collaboration between colleagues who may be at different sites, even on different continents (Cohen 1996). With on-line participation, the venue becomes the sites at which CMC is available. There may still be site-related hire costs (such as usage rates in cybercafés), and there will still be considerations about the impacts of the venue (e.g., is computer access in a public, professional, or home context?). In practical terms, however, many of the difficulties and financial considerations associated with organizing FTF venues disappear. A further consideration is that, with on-line research, interaction results in the immediate production of a text file. Unlike in research using FTF interviews, the researcher has no need to budget for recording equipment, transcribing equipment, or transcription costs, and delays caused by transcription are eliminated.

The Internet also offers researchers the potential for substantial financial savings when their studies involve self-administered interviews (Bachmann, Elfrink, and Vazzana 1996; Mehta and Sivadas 1995).

E-mail and Web-page-based surveys eliminate paper, are cheap to send, and, once initial start-up costs have been met, involve minimal costs for implementation and analysis (Sheehan and Hoy 1999). Apart from the benefit to researchers of direct access to large numbers of people, the speed of response in such surveys offers substantial time-cost savings. Comparative studies confirm that e-mail questionnaires are returned faster than their paper equivalents (Schaefer and Dillman 1998; Comley 1996). Web-page-based surveys can speed up responses even further (Comley 1996; Smith, 1997); studies have shown that hundreds of responses may be generated over a single weekend (Sheehan and Hoy 1999), and there are anecdotal accounts of "thousands of responses" being received within a few hours (Gjestland 1996). However, savings are not automatic. E-mail surveys can consume time if the researcher has to search around for addresses, if many addresses turn out to be invalid, and if the form of the survey has to be explained to participants. There are also hidden costs associated with the level of technology involved. As we shall discuss below, researchers may need to set aside a considerable period for coping with the technical challenges and problems that might be involved in implementing on-line surveys (Couper, Blair, and Triplett 1999).

WORKING WITH DIGITAL DATA

Working with digital data offers researchers substantial benefits but also presents them with great challenges. There is no doubt that the technological base of the interviewing medium complements the computerized practices that are becoming so familiar to researchers. Individual interviews and even large databases from CMC surveys can be moved effortlessly into other computer functions. Electronic messages can be recalled on a computer monitor, saved and accessed in word-processing packages, and stored either as hard-copy printouts or on computer diskettes or compact discs.

The analysis of interview data can also benefit from the development and convergence of technologies. For instance, interview data can be moved directly into qualitative or quantitative analysis software packages (Creswell 1997; Fielding and Lee 1998; Tesch 1990) that might themselves interconnect (some qualitative software packages already have SPSS export facilities). There is likely to be a huge increase in such interconnection of digital processes in the future.

On the other hand, working with digital data in a virtual environment, researchers cannot avoid engaging with legal and ethical issues that are still in a state of flux. Research projects may involve interviewers in the processes of

> authentication (checking that someone is who he claims to be, or a website what it seems to be); authorisation (controlling access in a sophisticated ... way); confidentiality (keeping private information private); integrity (ensuring that information has not been tampered with); and non-repudiation (being sure the terms of a transaction are binding and legitimate). ("Future of the Internet," 1999:35)

Many of these areas require further legal definition and link in with other issues of intellectual property, security (including personal security from virtual assault, harassment, and stalking), encryption, digital signatures, and certification (see Kramarae and Kramer 1995; Thomas, Forcht, and Counts 1998). Researchers cannot overlook these issues, as some countries are establishing laws concerning, for instance, data protection and/or encryption that would apply to data generated in academic as well as commercial research.

The confusion about the legal implications of on-line research is matched by a lack of clarity about "good practice" on-line. There is little agreement about how to proceed ethically in a virtual arena, and few research practice conventions are available. Researchers are just beginning to grapple with the implications of the legal and ethical minefield and to discuss issues of confidentiality, participant risk, and informed consent in on-line research (Mann and Stewart 2000). As funding bodies and institutional review boards are adopting mandatory good-practice norms for on-line research, it would be politic for interviewers who intend to work on-line to give time to these issues and to find out at early stages of their research about current discussions that may have impacts on their research designs.[4]

◆ Technical Skills and Standardized Interviews

Dorothy Myers (1987) suggests that there are two kinds of experts on-line: the technically astute and the "relationally" astute (that is, the social experts who nurture and direct on-line relationships and create interpersonal bonds). On-line interviewers certainly need competence in both these areas, but do they need expertise? A great deal depends on the type of interview. As we shall discuss, conducting standardized interviews on-line is technically taxing. In a review of on-line surveys, Christine Smith (1997) concludes that "the lack of standardization among operating systems, servers, and browsers creates a challenging milieu in which a researcher must be technologically savvy as well as methodologically sound." For nonstandardized qualitative interviews, the technology may be more accessible but the acquisition of relational expertise is emphasized. Face-to-face, the human interviewer "can be a marvelously smart, adaptable, flexible instrument who can respond to situations with skill, tact, and understanding" (Seidman

1991:16); the challenge is to transfer these qualities on-line.

The technical challenges faced by researchers who have attempted structured interviews on-line have been documented more extensively than the work of researchers using qualitative approaches. Studies of self-completion surveys conducted on-line began to be published around the end of 1995 (for reviews, see Comley 1996; Couper et al. 1999; Witmer, Colman, and Katzman 1999) and offer considerable practical insights for any researcher who intends to use CMC in this way. We next consider the demands for technical expertise placed on researchers conducting standardized interviews using e-mail and the World Wide Web.

E-MAIL SURVEYS

In an e-mail survey, the questions are usually sent to respondents as the text of a conventional e-mail message. To complete the survey, respondents use the "reply" facility of their e-mail system and add their answers to the text of the returned message. The answers received can then be typed into an analysis program in the same way as for a conventional survey. Alternatively, a program can be written that will interpret the e-mailed responses and read the answers directly into a database; this approach offers significant savings in terms of data entry. Commercial survey-creation programs are available that, as well as assisting in producing the text of a survey, can carry out this interpretation of replies, provided the survey has been completed correctly (see also Smith 1997).[5]

Text-based e-mail surveys are convenient for respondents because they require no facilities or expertise beyond those the respondents use in their day-to-day e-mail communication. However, technical problems still arise. The size of the survey may also be a difficulty. Peter Comley (1996), for instance, had to split his survey into two

e-mails. Some organizations use e-mail systems that convert messages over a certain size (such as questionnaires) into attachments. In one study a number of employees reported that they had received attachments but didn't know what to do with them (Couper et al. 1999).

A further drawback is that a text survey can appear dry and uninteresting. E-mail in its simplest form does not allow formatting of text (e.g., use of boldface, italics, different fonts). In addition, the researcher has no control over the format of the responses. There is nothing to prevent a respondent from answering outside the boxes, selecting three choices where only one is required, or deleting or altering questions. In a study conducted by Mick Couper and his associates (1999), 21 percent of all e-mail respondents did not make use of the reply feature as intended, but used a word processor or text editor instead. In such cases, researchers may still be able to interpret what respondents mean, as with badly completed paper questionnaires, but the need to edit responses removes the advantages of automated data entry and can greatly increase per case costs.

If all potential respondents are using relatively modern e-mail systems that can understand HTML, the researcher can alleviate some design problems by using an HTML-based e-mail survey.[6] Because HTML uses only standard text characters, the survey is still sent as the text of an e-mail. But because the e-mail system interprets HTML commands, the message can be laid out in an attractive way. In addition, the researcher has control over participants' responses: Answers can be typed only in text-entry boxes, and if only one choice is required, only one will be accepted. HTML-based e-mail combines these advantages (usually associated with Web-based surveys) with the direct response advantage of e-mail. However, until HTML-enabled e-mail systems become more common, these benefits are possible only if the survey participants are within a defined population where the researcher knows what systems they are using.

A further possibility is for the researcher to present the survey not in the body of the e-mail message itself but as a file (for example, a word processor document or a spreadsheet) attached to the e-mail. The respondent opens the attached file, completes the survey using the relevant program, saves the file, and then attaches the saved file to a return e-mail. This gives the researcher control over the appearance of the survey, but completion and return require that respondents have more technical ability. In addition, respondents must all have access to the program (such as Microsoft Word or Microsoft Excel) in which the attached document was created. As with HTML-based mail, the approach is suitable only for a defined population where the researcher knows the abilities of the respondents or can provide them with training and support. In addition, some organizations may prohibit users from receiving e-mail attachments because of fears about viruses.

Researchers can overcome some of these problems by using survey-creation software to produce self-contained interactive survey programs.[7] The software allows researchers to create elegant, responsive, and efficient surveys, and the survey programs can produce formatted answer files that can be mailed back to interviewers for automated input to a database. However, such programs have a number of limitations. For example, a program created for the Windows operating system will not run on a Macintosh, and vice versa. Even with a single operating system, researchers may run into unexpected technical difficulties when trying to run their programs on the wide range of computers likely to be used by respondents; Couper et al. (1999) found problems with all seven of their pretest subjects. For instance, the program files produced may be large (in the case of Couper et al.'s study, approaching one megabyte),

which may result in unacceptable volumes of Internet traffic and may be beyond the size permitted for incoming e-mail attachments. Because of such problems, most of the e-mail surveys reported to date have used the straightforward text-based route. However, Couper et al. (1999) "remain optimistic about the potential for e-mail as an alternative to the traditional mail survey" (p. 54).

WEB-PAGE-BASED SURVEYS

David Schaefer and Don Dillman (1998) note that their experiment with e-mail surveys "revealed the possibility that [these] represent only an interim surveying technology" (p. 392). Many researchers are turning their attention to the World Wide Web as a more suitable medium for administering questionnaires (for further information, see Comley 1996; Kehoe and Pitkow 1996; Coomber 1997; O'Connor and Madge 2000; for a comparison with e-mail surveys, see Patrick, Black, and Whalen 1995). However, the main drawback of the Web approach is the high level of technical expertise that researchers must acquire or have available to them. This includes the knowledge of HTML required to create the Web pages. Survey-creation programs, as discussed previously, can provide "what you see is what you get" editing of pages, removing much of the mystery of HTML, but identifying and learning a suitable program presents another hurdle to be overcome. Once the pages have been created, they must be uploaded to a host Internet server, another technically complex procedure (Mann and Stewart 2000).[8]

Why might researchers grapple with the challenges attendant on using the Web to interview? A Web-page-based survey has the advantage that it appears identical (subject to the browser used) to all respondents. Through the use of text formatting, colors, and graphics, the survey can be given an attractive appearance. Web-page-based surveys are also easy for respondents to complete, typically by selecting responses from predefined lists or entering text in boxes and then simply clicking a "submit" button when finished. The data received by the researcher are in a completely predictable and consistent format, making automated analysis possible without the editing that may be necessary with text-based e-mail surveys.

Despite the technical challenges involved, Christine Smith (1997) has predicted that Web-based survey software will soon become an indispensable research tool, "along with or even instead of analytical tools like SPSS." The significant advantages that Web-page-based surveys offer suggest they will become more and more common, especially for commercial market research. It may not be long before the creation of Web survey pages is routinely taught in social science research methods courses.

◆ Relational Skills and Nonstandardized Interviews

In nonstandardized interviews, the focus moves from the preformulated ideas of the researcher to "the meanings and interpretations that individuals attribute to events and relationships" (May 1993:94). It is this emphasis that leads many practitioners to refer to such interviews as qualitative, and it is to the relational skills required in such interviews that we now turn.

SOFTWARE OPTIONS IN NONSTANDARDIZED INTERVIEWS

Researchers are familiar with the methodological reasons that might inform a decision to interview one-to-one or in groups (Mann and Stewart 2000; see also in this volume Warren, Chapter 4; Johnson, Chapter 5; Morgan, Chapter 7). However, when interviewing is conducted on-line,

the decision to use in-depth interviews or "virtual" focus groups involves further issues relating to temporality—that is, whether interviews should take place synchronously (with delayed response) or in "real" or synchronous time. There are various forms of software available:

Individual Interview
Options Software

◆ *E-mail:* E-mail allows asynchronous interviews one-to-one.

◆ *Real-time one-to-one chat:* Software such as AOL's Instant Messenger and ICQ (I Seek You; see www.icq.com) allows users to chat in real time one-to-one (or with groups of people).

Group Interview
Options Software

◆ *Real-time many-to-many chat:* This is communication in which messages are written and read at the same time, although in different places. What one person types is visible to everyone else on the same "channel." Chat software can range from "shareware" (software programs that are freely downloadable, such as mIRC; see www.mirc.com) to licensed software packages such as Hotline Client and FirstClass Conferencing, which are ideal for moderated real-time focus groups.[9] Typically, a chat program will have a conversation flow area, where a participant can read all contributions, as well as a separate composition area, where participants can write their own messages.

◆ *Asynchronous many-to-many conferencing:* In this form of communication, as in e-mail, participants can respond to messages from other participants at some time in the future. Unlike e-mail, however, conferencing is conducted at a "conference site" (as opposed to individual e-mail addresses), which can have restricted or public access. A typical conference site may be a type of folder, like the one that appears on both Macintosh and Windows computer screens. Conferencing provides an effective means of conducting non-real-time on-line focus groups. Conferencing systems include FirstClass (from SoftArc, Inc.) and CoSy (from Softwords Research International). In addition, both Microsoft and Netscape have their own systems and distribute them widely in combination with software and system packages. Conferencing systems are also known as groupware systems, of which Lotus-Notes (from Lotus) is perhaps the best known.

CMC AND THE DEVELOPMENT OF RAPPORT IN NONSTANDARDIZED INTERVIEWS

Generating textual data using e-mail or chat software is rarely a technical challenge (although group software involves extra complications). However, nonstandardized interviews also require researchers to acquire "relational" expertise. Successful qualitative interviewing depends upon interviewers' developing rapport with participants (Fontana and Frey 1994). Traditionally, this has been associated with a mutual reading of presentation of self. In any social situation, each party makes a swift appraisal of the other's age, gender, and ethnicity; of accent, dress, and personal grooming; of conventionality, eccentricity, and subcultural markers; of confidence levels, physical attractiveness, and friendliness or restraint. In addition, oral dimensions of language (pitch, tone, and so on) might identify whether what is said is spoken from a position of confidence, doubt, irony, and so forth. The sense of the other attained by such means allows each person to assess (a) how others are interpreting what he or she says and (b) the genuineness of intent in queries and responses.

If, as a result of this delicate interaction, participants come to trust in the sincerity and the motivation of the interviewer, they may be prepared to share in-depth insights into their private and social worlds (see in this volume Warren, Chapter 4; Johnson, Chapter 5). At the same time, the interviewer will increasingly be able to sense the appropriateness of questions and the meaningfulness of answers. Reading signs of the other is a human characteristic that many FTF qualitative researchers develop to the level of a skill. But is it possible to "connect" at these emotional and mental levels when communicating on-line?[10] Is it possible for an interviewer to develop rapport with participants whom he or she may never have seen or heard? We posed these questions to two researchers who had conducted qualitative e-mail interviews. They responded differently:

Generating an atmosphere of rapport online can be a problem, and given the lack of tone or gesture and the length of time between exchanges it can lead to something of a formal, structured interview. This is in contrast to the spontaneous speeding up, slowing down, getting louder, getting quieter, getting excited, laughing together, spontaneous thoughts, irrelevant asides etc. etc. which I have experienced in off-line interviews. The best words I can think of to separate off-line from E-mail interviews then, are FLOW, and DYNAMICS, both of which, in my view are liable to contribute to greater depth and quality of information in an off-line interview than over e-mail. (P. Hodkinson, e-mail communication, March 1999)

Is rapport online possible? Absolutely!!!! Rapport comes from being very up front with what you are doing and responding as you would with anyone. Laughing, listening and connecting are the key. (M. J. Smith-Stoner, e-mail communication, March 1999)

These perspectives reflect current debates about in-depth communication on-line. In one view, CMC cannot achieve the highly interactive, rich, and spontaneous communication that can be achieved in FTF interviewing. Communication differences between media are often conceptualized in terms of bandwidth, or the "volume of information per unit time that a computer, person, or transmission medium can handle" (Raymond 1993, cited in Kollock and Smith 1996:15). CMC is said by some to have a narrow or lean bandwidth, in contrast to the "rich" bandwidth of FTF interaction (see Sala 1998). As it allows insufficient transmission of social cues to establish the human "presence" of the other, CMC is seen as impersonal and distancing (Hewson, Laurent, and Vogel 1996; Kiesler, Siegel, and McGuire 1984; Short, Williams, and Christie 1976). Particularly in groups, the psychological distances separating participants and the depersonalization of "the other" that can result may lead to various kinds of unsociable behavior, such as flaming (Dubrovsky, Kiesler, and Sethna 1991). When CMC is seen as an "impoverished" communication environment (Giese 1998), it is not surprising that it is mainly considered appropriate for tasks requiring little social interaction or intimacy (Rice and Case 1983). Walther's (1992) review of this literature sums up the implications for research if CMC is viewed in this way: If investigations seek "information that is ambiguous, emphatic, or emotional . . . a richer medium should be used" (p. 57).

If CMC is indeed a "lean" communication medium that is neither conducive to establishing good interpersonal relationships nor capable of addressing delicate information, then it is clear that the work of the on-line qualitative interviewer will be challenging, if not doomed to failure from the beginning. However, relational devel-opment theorists have challenged these findings, pointing out that most assumptions about interpersonal relationships (such as the need for physical proximity) predate CMC and may not be fully applicable to on-line settings (Lea and Spears 1995; Parks and Floyd 1996). In his review of nonexperimental studies of CMC, Walther (1992) found evidence that warm relationships can and do develop on-line. He points out that the same motives that drive people in other contexts drive them in CMC. People want to interact, they seek social reward, they want to be liked. Thus research interactants, like communicators in any context, will "desire to transact personal, rewarding, complex relationships and . . . they will communicate to do so" (p. 68). We shall now consider factors that might contribute to the successful development of rapport on-line.

USING TECHNOLOGY TO CREATE RAPPORT

Some on-line interviewers use linguistic conventions available in CMC to help convey the mood of the communication and to make social and emotional connections. Electronic paralanguage consists of repetitions, abbreviations, and verbal descriptions of feelings and sounds, such as "hehehe" for laughter, "lol" for "lots of laughs," and "LJATD" for "let's just agree to disagree" (discussion going nowhere).

"Emoticons"—such as :-) for smiling/happy and :-o for surprise/shock—offer interviewers another textual means to show feelings and to soften the potentially distancing abruptness of some CMC messages by adding humor or whimsicality (Murphy and Collins 1997). However, the use of emoticons is not transparent in communicative terms. First, emoticons may reflect the social and communicative practices of a subculture (see Baym 1995). Second, emoticons may not always work cross-nationally. In Japan, where signs of respect are finely graduated and where relationships develop in indirect ways, a highly complex system of emoticons attempts to parallel some of the delicacy of FTF interaction. However, these emoti- cons are not familiar to most Western interviewers. Such emoticons are read in a traditional horizontal format rather than sideways: -o-) for "I'm sorry"; (^o^;) for "excuse me!"; (^o^) for happy; (^-^;; for awkward (see Aoki 1994).

Emoticons may also be "read" in different ways by participants in a research project. To some, they may indicate a friendly but rather impersonal approach (Aycock and Buchignani 1995). To others, as with varying responses to such friendship gestures as handshakes and open body language in FTF research, they may seem an inappropriate way of "doing research." They can also be seen as lazy and unimaginative, possibly alienating some members of sophisticated on-line communities. As Stacy Horn (1998) has warned, it is possible that "people will assume that you are without language, or conversation and suggest that you go back to America Online (a place known for its liberal use of emoticons)" (p. 63). It would seem that interviewers should use electronic paralanguage judiciously. Even if they do, in the opinion of one participant in Mann's study of academic performance at the University of Cambridge, CMC will never be subtle enough to compare to FTF interaction:

> You'll see people annotate their mails using smilies, HTML-style tags, capital letters, etc., but even so there is no reliable way of conveying tone. How you say something is often more important than what you say—and e-mail doesn't have this dimension. (Quoted in Mann and Stewart 2000:14)

Clearly, qualitative interviewers who seek to establish rapport on-line need to look beyond electronic paralanguage. In the following sections we discuss factors that have seemed of most importance in interview studies.

IMPORTANCE OF SHARED RESEARCH AGENDA FOR RAPPORT

Participants with a superficial interest in the research topic may be initially intrigued and attracted by the option of interacting on-line, but this might not be enough to sustain their ongoing interest without the impetus of enthusiasm and focus that can be injected in the FTF setting by a skilled interviewer who is "firing on all cylinders." On-line, interviewers may not be able to offer enough verbal "dazzle" to compensate for the charm or charisma that can be so effective face-to-face. If participants have no particular vested interest in a study or a low boredom threshold, there may be a tendency for less involved participants to drop away:

> The longest of my e-mail interviews has been a few weeks . . . usually I found that people lost interest before I am able to get to the same degree of detail as a face to face interview. (P. Hodkinson, e-mail communication, March 1999)

However, a shared research agenda and/or being given an opportunity to be "heard" in a meaningful way can "lead virtual relationships to become very personal very quickly" (Smith-Stoner and Weber 2000). In these circumstances, interest in the interaction is sustained.

> Respondents often spoke of the value of our dialogues for helping them to make sense of their lives. They remarked on the time they had taken in thinking through their responses (some taking several hours) and messages were usually very long. (Dunne 1999:3)

Marilyn Smith-Stoner and Todd Weber (2000), who report having had excellent rapport with their participants, point out that the women they interviewed were very enthusiastic about the research topic: It did not "require any selling at all." Not only did these women want to tell their stories, they "expressed deep satisfaction with the process and were grateful to be able to do in online." A similar overlap of appreciating methodological and personal factors ensured the effectiveness of O'Connor's real-time focus group discussions with new parents:

> The interviews all provided high levels of self-consciousness, reflexivity and interactivity. Whether it was owing to the nature of the interviewees (self-selected, motivated, frequent on-line users), or owing to the nature of the subject matter, clearly very close to the hearts of the women involved, it is difficult to judge. (O'Connor and Madge 2000:4)

ESTABLISHING TRUST AS A BASIS FOR RAPPORT

It is generally recognized that mutual trust is the basis for the development of rapport in interviews. One way for researchers to dispel respondents' feelings of caution and to increase trust is to be as open as possible about the purposes and processes of the research. For semistructured interviews, the researcher can do this by making an interview schedule available well before the interview and inviting clarifying questions. Another way for the researcher to display "openness" would be to inform participants fully about the time frame of the interaction. Some researchers may conclude that in-depth research, particularly regarding sensitive topics, would benefit if people met face-to-face before attempting to conduct an on-line relationship.

There are, however, precedents for researchers' conducting deeply personal interviews without ever meeting the respondents in person. One means of establishing trust, and bridging the geographic and perhaps personal distance that may characterize on-line interviews (Moore 1993), is for interviewers and participants to share information about themselves (Murphy and Collins 1997). Richard Cutler (1995) has suggested that the more an individual discloses personal information on-line, the more others are likely to reciprocate, and the more individuals know about each other, the more likely it is that trust, satisfaction, and a sense of being in a safe communication environment will ensue. Caroline Bennett (1998), in her in-depth e-mail interviews, sought to establish relationships that would "nurse" equal degrees of self-disclosure between herself and her coinvestigators. She made initial disclosures about herself to encourage this pattern of discourse, and her participants responded in kind.

Technical ease of contact in CMC gives researchers the option of repeating interview interactions over time. There is evidence that trust and warmth in CMC relationships increases over extended interactions (Walther 1992). As Nancy Baym (1995) notes, "In CMC, as in real life, relationships take time to build" (p. 158). This has been the experience of qualitative researchers who have used sequential one-to-one e-mail interviews (Bennett 1998; Dunne 1999; Mann and Stewart 2000). However, findings from sequential interviews using e-mail suggest that the outcomes in terms of intimacy are not predictable. In part, this reflects differences in research design. In Gill Dunne's (1999) study of gay fathers, it was the participants' strong desire to be "heard" that led spontaneously to interviewer-participant closeness. This continued after the formal closure of the research and, in some cases, led to FTF meetings. In other studies, the development of long-term relationships was a part of the research design (see Mann and Stewart 2000; Ryen and Silverman 2000; Bennett 1998). Both

Bennett and Anne Ryen and David Silverman (2000) sought to strengthen relational bonds through on-line disclosure, phone calls, exchange of photographs, and, in Ryen's case, some FTF meetings. In Chris Mann's research into experiences of higher education, extended relationships were the inevitable result of Mann's contacting students regularly over the course of their work on their degrees. There, the aim was to establish mutual trust rather than intimacy, thus Mann did not initiate talk about herself, nor did she see students face-to-face. This was not a misguided attempt to claim research "neutrality"; rather, Mann accepted that she was a very minor part of the students' lives and preferred to keep the focus of the interaction on the issues and students' perspectives on the issues.

In all these studies, the interviewers may be presumed to have different agendas. It is perhaps unsurprising that this should lead interviewers to different conclusions about whether electronic communication can sustain personal relationships over time. For Bennett and Ryen, the intensity of the relationship with participants seemed to peak and then falter somewhat, leading Bennett to admit that "maintaining long-term relationships is much more difficult than it appears" (e-mail communication, March 1999). In Bennett's study the frequency of on-line interaction over a seven-month period might explain a participant's disengagement due to pressures of time and a (sometimes reluctant) need to prioritize other commitments. Another possibility might have been a sense (from the participant's point of view) that all that could be said had been said. Ryen suggests that, as the novelty of the research project wears off, a participant might use the interaction for more instrumental purposes. In her case study, Ryen's e-mail correspondent seemed to move from commitment to the research process to a general desire to keep in touch because the interviewer might prove a possible useful contact in his business world. In Mann's study, a "slow and steady" approach to developing relationships within a time-limited, albeit extensive (three- to four-year) period was required. The interviewer-student relationships lacked the intensity of the relationships in Bennett's and Ryen's studies, but, perhaps for that very reason, most of the relationships were sustained for the duration of the research.

Considering these differing research patterns, it seems likely that human relationships have the same kind of variability on-line as they do in "real life." Some remain at a constant level of good neighborliness, whereas others reach deeper levels of intimacy that must increase (which would alter the research relationship), change in nature, or diminish. Although the ease and availability of CMC allows for extended communication, it does not follow that the technology can circumvent those life patterns.

INTERACTIVE SKILLS

There are several key areas where on-line interviewers may have to adapt expertise gained in FTF interviews in order to increase rapport in a virtual venue. We discuss these areas briefly below.

Reassurance

Cooperating in research in general, and on-line research in particular, may be a new and challenging experience for many people. Working one-to-one, participants may need regular confirmation that they are communicating in appropriate ways, that their contributions are valued, and that the faceless researcher is trustworthy. In on-line groups, participants may become anxious about how the group is operating or about what is expected of them, and facilitators have to be alert to signs of confusion or withdrawal into silence (Sweet 1999). It seems that in most on-line interviews participants benefit from frequent and explicit verbal assurances from the researcher.

Listening

An attentive pause to listen is a key feature in FTF interviewing skills. However, this may be a luxury in some CMC contexts. For instance, the characteristic rapid fire of chat can preclude pausing, whether it be for thought or for effect. In addition, participants may experience an interviewer's pause to listen not as attentiveness but as indifference, as absence. Cues that an interviewer is listening reassure participants of continuing interest. An interviewer who listens too much (read as being absent from the screen) may cause participants in focus groups to feel "leaderless and uncomfortable" (Gaiser 1997). Similarly, interviewers in turn may be unsure whether "silences" in real-time chat are "owing to the fact that the participant is thinking, is typing in a response and has not yet hit the return button, or has, in fact, declined to answer the questions" (O'Connor and Madge 2000:2).

Nonresponse in a virtual venue can undermine a developing sense of rapport. It is clear that on-line listening needs to be expressed as words, not silence. An interviewer may express listening with interest by "responding promptly to questions, overtly expressing interest in particular points made, asking follow up questions, or perhaps enthusiastically sharing similar experiences to that described by the interviewee" (P. Hodkinson, e-mail communication, March 1999). Meanwhile, the interviewer is also "listening" to the written script created by participants. The researcher needs to be alert to changes in the tone of the conversation, to any fracture in the flow of a response that might point to a reluctance to speak or a failure to understand language or concepts, and to verbal "cues" that might suggest that participants would be happy to talk more about something if asked. Marilyn Smith-Stoner notes

ways in which participants flag that they are prepared to talk in more detail:

> Often they put a tag line at the end of the phrase—"let me know if you want to know more"—or they bring the subject up more than once. I think many people need to be invited to expound on a topic, they are courteous about people's time and don't want to abuse it. (E-mail communication, March 1999)

Verbal Expertise

Sustaining rapport depends upon an interviewer's skill in dealing with sensitive issues and/or potentially embarrassing or conflictual interaction. How can researchers negotiate delicate interaction on-line? As with reassurance, language has to be explicit. Nuances in tone of voice, facial expression, and subtlety of gesture are unavailable. However, the use of mild imperatives (for example, "You may want to check out") and mitigation ("if you'd like") show how the skillful choice of words can avoid making presumptions about the reader (Galegher, Sproull, and Kiesler 1998:517). In real-time interaction, interviewers have to make rapid choices about how to handle sensitive issues. For Henrietta O'Connor and Clare Madge (2000), who interviewed together, the interaction felt abstracted from real life, and on-line language use often seemed inadequate: "There were occasions when we were 'lost for words,' taking some time to decide on what to send as a message, because we felt like our written comments sounded banal or our questions too direct and leading" (p. 3).

E-mail allows more time for interviewers to choose their words in one-to-one or asynchronous group interactions. For instance, in Wendy Seymour et al.'s (1999) asynchronous long-term conferencing study, in which the participants had disabilities, an exacerbation of a disability could interrupt the process of some interviews:

These events required gentle and sensitive communication to ensure that participants did not feel pressured to continue, so that they felt valued, and so that they would feel welcome to continue with the project once the episode had passed. (P. 3)

Anne Ryen was afraid that sensitive issues might arise when she was conducting interviews over a long period with someone on another continent (Tanzania/Kenya versus Norway) and from another culture (Asian versus Norwegian). Her approach was to try to clear the ground at an early stage in the interaction, as she did in the following e-mail communication with a research subject:

Well, I am very happy indeed that you will go on with the interview. If there are questions you find odd, or that you do not "appreciate," please do not hesitate to tell me. That is the only way to make me learn or to avoid repeating the mistake . . . (e-mail 10.12.98). (Quoted in Ryen, e-mail communication, March 1999)

This direct approach, where the interviewer makes no attempt to disguise the possibility that questions might come across as crass or impertinent, may also be a way to negotiate the questions themselves. This is an approach Mann has used in her own research: "I should like to ask you more about something you said, but if you feel my question is too intrusive please do not bother to reply to this—I shall not bring it up again" (see Mann and Stewart 2000).

Explaining Absences

Finally, absence, in terms of long gaps in communication in asynchronous studies, can be deeply unsettling for both interviewers and participants. Committed participants may take time to explain irregular messages. In Ryen's study, her correspondent's laptop broke down while he was traveling. However, he phoned to inform her of this. In Mann's study, students frequently e-mailed to explain that work had taken over their time. Similarly, Mann alerted students when she would be away at conferences. Interviewers have greater responsibility than participants to explain absences, even though, as Bennett (1998) discovered, this can be a taxing process:

For example, when I was ill in bed I still had to check in with my co-investigators; write replies, explain that I was ill and that my conversations would only be short, but thus maintaining the link between us. Whilst this may seem to make online interaction appear both tenuous and transient, I would argue that it is simply the nature of the environment that makes it so, and not the people who are involved. (P. 39)

However, as Bennett points out, neglecting to explain absences can seriously jeopardize the rapport that has been built up in earlier interactions.

RELATIONAL EXPERTISE IN GROUP DISCUSSIONS

In one-to-one investigations, qualitative researchers who ask questions are usually referred to as interviewers. However, asking questions in groups requires additional skills, as suggested by such titles as *moderator* and *facilitator*. David Morgan (1988) has argued that the key role of the focus group moderator is "to control the assembly and the running of the session" (p. 15). This is a task with multiple strands, and it is clearly a challenge to transfer these skills on-line. In another view, a moderator is a "person who reminds, tracks, clarifies, prompts, reviews, distills, negotiates, mitigates, mediates, arbitrates" (Davis and Brewer 1997:70). In the fast-paced and hectic environment of real-time chat, flexibility and patience (with everyone involved) are definite virtues (Sweet 1999).

From a human relations perspective, the task of moderating/facilitating groups has two principal aspects: (a) developing rapport between all interactants and (b) providing a noncontentious atmosphere for all—even at the cost of exerting control over the few. We discuss these issues next.

DEVELOPING RAPPORT AMONG MULTIPLE PARTICIPANTS

Many of the participants who are prepared to join on-line group discussions already have experience in chat rooms, so they are adept at creating on-line relationships quickly. However, as Casey Sweet (1999) reports, the guided group discussion "draws participants out and personalities begin to emerge, thereby creating a dynamic that develops during the group and varies just like in-person groups. . . . The amount of interaction between online participants can vary and may be influenced by the topic and moderator" (p. 3).

The initial moments of an on-line focus group are perhaps the most crucial, as this is when introductions are made and group rapport is first attempted. In the Young People and Health Risk study (Stewart et al. 1998), rapport was encouraged in two ways. First, the facilitator posted a welcome message in a non-real-time conference center ahead of time. This message sought to set the tone and atmosphere for the on-line groups to follow. Second, as the group facilitator, Stewart entered the young women's real-time focus group with the following lines:

Fiona Stewart: Welcome Yellow Beijing—I am fiona the controller, please introduce yourselves and tell the other girls about your hobbies, your subjects at school and then we can proceed. Have you read the welcoming message?

It was anticipated that messages such as this would create a sense of personal connection among the young people participating, who resided in four different countries. An-other approach that facilitators can use to encourage group rapport is to ask all participants about their immediate physical environments (Sweet 1999).

CONTROL IN GROUPS

In a face-to-face focus group, a facilitator may choose to be passive, exercising "mild, unobtrusive control over the group" (Krueger 1988:73), but in an on-line focus group this is rarely possible. Certain procedures have been shown to ensure the smooth running of group interviews (Sweet 1999; Mann and Stewart 2000). First, by establishing their expectations, facilitators can minimize participant confusion and enhance adherence to both subject matter and protocol. Second, facilitators need to state some ground rules. In cyberspace, arguments and disagreements "can erupt with little warning" (Horn 1998:56), and facilitators do not have the option of ignoring outrageous, patently false, or volatile comments. Rules are one means by which facilitators can manage the potential for conflict, although it can rarely be eliminated. Some listowners, such as Horn (1998), in ECHO, develop "mission statements" as the baseline rule of conduct. This can prove an effective mechanism for facilitating discussion and containing conflict, although its ongoing implementation is not without problems.

Rule setting is important for managing the volatility of real-time groups. It also acts as a means of encouraging effective group self-management, which is particularly important in asynchronous groups. Rules make explicit the ways in which participants may engage in the on-line discussion and can set a positive tone for the interaction. However, there is also a risk that the facilitator may inadvertently create a hostile and unwelcoming environment by seeking to establish behavioral guidelines. The facilitator's challenge is to introduce rules in a way that is positive and acceptable to participants.

Facilitators also rely on text to maintain order in on-line groups. Because a facilitator cannot use body language, such as shuffling papers or turning away (Krueger 1988:84), the style of the textual communication must be clear and precise. Such facilitation can range from subtle to more assertive and formal approaches. Sweet has found that subtle approaches can sometimes be more successful on-line than face-to-face:

> I find in FTF groups that some dominators can push a position over and over and over again even after I, as moderator, have repeated it to them and asked them to indicate if I have heard correctly. Online, I find they can fizzle out, or if I put it in print that, "I understand your point of view to be . . . ," or "you dislike the idea because . . . ," they seem to back off. They don't seem to have the same impact on the group as FTF. (E-mail communication, March 1999)

Facilitator intervention on-line may seem overbearing when compared with FTF conventions, but it is sometimes the only response to a fast-moving situation. Real-time groups are characterized by high interactivity, and a facilitator may not be able to intervene quickly enough to prevent an outburst of flaming. Even if the facilitator steps in promptly, there is no guarantee that intervention will be successful. The example below is taken from the Young People and Health Risk study (Mann and Stewart 2000:147). In this extract, although flaming did not occur, the young male participants did need to be reprimanded. As facilitator, however, Stewart was not sure that her request for an apology would be honored. She was thankful when it was.

Facilitator: Does anyone know what the health pyramid is?

Red Beijing: We know many good jokes

Facilitator: Red oz why don't you explain what the health pyramid is?

Red Australia: i don't like fiona

Facilitator: I beg your parden red oz

Facilitator: you should apologise for saying that

Red Australia: can you tell me a joke?

Red Australia: sorry

Red Beijing: the health pyramid is the meaning of different food. for example, bread meat milk

As we see, the need to reprimand participants can detract from the quality of the discussion. In the on-line environment there is no such thing as a quiet word in the ear of an individual participant. What is more, in the middle of attempting to obtain a public apology, the facilitator may need to repeat a particular question, even if this means spending more time than anticipated on a particular subject. In the example above, it was only after the facilitator pursued a line of questioning about the health pyramid that the participants contributed meaningfully to the dialogue. This was despite the fact that discussion and the flow of the dialogue had been disrupted for only a moment.

◆ Conclusion

In this chapter we have focused on the costs and benefits of using the Internet to interview and the skills that researchers may require to interview effectively on-line. As we have seen, researchers who consider conducting interviews on-line have many factors to weigh in the balance. The excitement of working with an interviewing medium that is not constrained by boundaries of time and space, and that offers digital data literally at one's fingertips, is matched by the growing realization that the virtual venue makes practical, legal, ethical, and interpersonal demands that move beyond the knowledge and expertise that researchers may have acquired in conducting off-line interview studies.

In addition, as long as CMC remains a text-based interchange, there are factors—such as the nature of language use on-line and the implications of disembodiment for issues of identity and/or power relations in cyberspace—that many researchers would wish to consider in designing their studies (Mann and Stewart 2000). It could be argued that using CMC to conduct interviews calls for such intensification of technical and interpersonal skills that only interviewers with considerable expertise in conventional research could feel confident about moving to a virtual venue. However, although pioneering researchers have alerted prospective on-line interviewers to some of the challenges of the medium, the majority of these pioneers have retained their initial excitement with regard to Internet interviewing. Most seem determined to develop the skills needed to conduct on-line interviewing in current circumstances and also to keep abreast of rapid technological developments that promise to extend interviewing possibilities in terms of both scope and style.

As we have discussed, the main barrier to more widespread participation in on-line interviews lies in the hardware and (in some countries) infrastructure costs associated with the desktop computer/modem/landline technology that currently dominates Internet access. Truly global access will require the development of other technologies, and the shape of these is becoming clear. Already, some mobile phones can be used to send and receive e-mail (Alanko et al. 1999). E-mail will also soon be offered as an offshoot of digital television (in conjunction with a telephone connection). Phones and other mobile devices, such as personal organizers or Palm Pilots, will use wireless application protocol to "gain access to the Internet using a 'microbrowser,'

which displays web pages specially formatted for tiny screens" ("Future of the Internet" 1999:30). If such devices follow the pattern of mobile voice telephony, we can expect that hardware costs will drop dramatically after the first couple of years (although usage costs may remain high) and that these devices will prove especially popular in countries (not only developing countries) where conventional telephone services are inadequate or unreliable.

For researchers, these developments offer the exciting prospect of Internet-based communication (and hence research) with a far wider spectrum of socioeconomic groups and nationalities than is currently available. They also hold the promise of new forms of interviewing. Text-based CMC may eventually be seen as one of many ways to interview using the Internet, and as new technologies develop, new interviewing skills will develop to meet them.

■ Notes

1. ECHO and WELL (Whole Earth 'Lectronic Link) are on-line towns emanating from New York and California. MU* environments, which include MUDS and MOOs, are multiuser, text-based, role-playing areas of CMC.

2. See Mann and Stewart (2000) for discussion of these issues.

3. The GVU Center uses repeat participation in Web surveys to map current and changing Internet user characteristics and attitudes (see Kehoe and Pitkow, 1996; see also www.gvu.gatech.edu/user_surveys/). More than 55,000 respondents were involved in the first five surveys, and new versions of the survey are sent out biannually.

4. The Economic and Social Research Council, which is a core funding body for social science research in the United Kingdom, has already responded to European Union data protection legislation with a guidance document relating to copyright and confidentiality. The Scientific Freedom, Responsibility and Law Program within the American Association for the Advancement of Science convened a workshop in 1999 to examine the challenges facing scien-

tists conducting Internet research involving human subjects. The outcomes of the workshop deliberations were used to draft a chapter for the *Guidebook for Institutional Review Boards on Internet Research,* produced by the NIH Office for Protection from Research Risks in 2000. The latest information is available at the AAAS Web site (see www.aaas.org/spp/dspp/sfrl/projects/intres/main.htm).

5. As of March 2000, available survey-creation programs included

MaCATI (www.senecio.com),
Survey Internet (www.aufrance.com),
Survey Said (www.surveysaid.com),
Survey Select (www.surveyselect.com),
SurveySolutions (www.perseus.com),and
SurveyTracker (www.surveytracker.com).

MaCATI's editing program is for the Macintosh only, and it has versions of its data collection program for the Mac, Windows, and Java. All of the other programs listed run under Windows only. Smith (1997) has pointed out that although Web survey development software is increasingly available, packages have huge variations in terms of price, functions, and server compatibility. It remains to be seen which, if any, of these packages will become the standard.

6. HTML stands for HyperText Markup Language, which is the coding system used to create pages that can be displayed by Web browsers. It consists of a series of "tags" that give instructions to the browser about how to display the text. For example, the text "<b>bold words<bsb> and <i>italic words<bsi>" would be displayed by a Web browser (or HTML-enabled e-mail system) as **bold words** and *italic words.* However, if the same text were read using a standard e-mail system, all the characters would be displayed exactly as typed: <b>bold words<bsb> and <i>italic words<bsi>. Originally, authors created HTML documents by typing the tags using a text editor. However, it is increasingly common to create HTML using "what you see is what you get" editing programs, where the author applies the formatting required (such as bold or italic) and the program automatically adds the relevant tags.

7. An example of such software is Perseus SurveySolutions Interviewer (www.perseus.com).

8. In this context, a server is a large computer that forms part of the worldwide network of permanently connected computers that is the Internet. Your pages are held on your host server. When someone requests a page, the request is routed to your host server and the page information is passed back to the requester's computer via the network.

9. FirstClass Conferencing has real chat and asynchronous conferencing options.

10. Patricia Wallace (1999) provides an excellent psychological framework for asking these questions.

■ *References*

Alanko, T., M. Kojo, M. Liljeberg, and K. Raatikainen. 1999. "Mobile Access to the Internet: A Mediator-Based Solution." *Internet Research: Electronic Networking, Applications and Policy* 9:58-65.

Anders, E. 2000. "Women with Disabilities: Higher Education, Feminism and Social Constructions of Difference." Ph.D. thesis, Deakin University, Melbourne.

Aoki, K. 1994. "Virtual Communities in Japan." Presented at the Pacific Telecommunications Council Conference.

Aycock, A. and N. Buchignani. 1995. "The E-Mail Murders: Reflections on 'Dead' Letters." Pp. 184-231 in *CyberSociety: Computer-Mediated Communication and Community,* edited by S. G. Jones. Thousand Oaks, CA: Sage.

Bachmann, D., J. Elfrink, J., and G. Vazzana. 1996. "Tracking the Progress of E-Mail vs. Snail-Mail." *Marketing Research* 8:30-35.

Bannert, M. and P. Arbinger. 1996. "Gender-Related Differences in Exposure to and Use of Computers: Results of a Survey of Secondary School Students." *European Journal of Psychology of Education* 11:269-82.

Baym, N. 1995. "The Emergence of Community in Computer-Mediated Communication." Pp. 139-63 in *CyberSociety: Computer-Mediated Communication and Community,* edited by S. G. Jones. Thousand Oaks, CA: Sage.

Bennett, C. 1998. "Men Online: Discussing Lived Experiences on the Internet." Honors dissertation, James Cook University, Townsville, Queensland, Australia.

Bruckman, A. 1992. "Identity Workshops: Emergent Social and Psychological Phenomena in Text-Based Virtual Reality." MIT Media Laboratory. Unpublished manuscript. Available from author (e-mail): Bruckman@media.mit.edu

Burkhalter, B. 1999. "Reading Race Online: Discovering Racial Identity in Usenet Discussions." Pp. 60-75 in *Communities in Cyberspace,* edited by M. A. Smith and P. Kollock. London: Routledge.

Cohen, J. 1996. "Computer Mediated Communication and Publication Productivity among Faculty." *Internet Research: Electronic Networking, Applications and Policy* 6(2-3):41-63.

Comley, P. 1996. "The Use of the Internet as a Data Collection Method." Presented at the ESOMAR/EMAC Symposium, Edinburgh.

Coomber, R. 1997. "Using the Internet for Survey Research." *Sociological Research Online* 2(2). Available Internet: http://www.socresonline.org.uk/socresonline/2/2/2.html

Correll, S. 1995. "The Ethnography of an Electronic Bar: The Lesbian Cafe." *Journal of Contemporary Ethnography* 24:270-98.

Couper, M. P., J. Blair, and T. Triplett. (1999). "A Comparison of Mail and E-Mail for a Survey of Employees in US Statistical Agencies." *Journal of Official Statistics* 15:39-56.

Creswell, J. W. 1997. *Qualitative Inquiry and Research Design: Choosing among Five Traditions.* Thousand Oaks, CA: Sage.

Cutler, R. H. 1995. "Distributed Presence and Community in Cyberspace." *Interpersonal Communication and Technology: An Electronic Journal for the 21st Century* 3(2):12-32. Available Internet: http://jan.ucc.nau.edu/~ipct-j/1995/n2/cutler.txt

Davis, B. H. and J. P. Brewer. 1997. *Electronic Discourse: Linguistic Individuals in Virtual Space.* Albany: State University of New York Press.

Daws, L. 1999. "Cattle, Special Education, Old Hats and Rain: Investigating Rural Women's Use of Interactive Communication Technologies." Center for Policy and Leadership Studies, Queensland University of Technology, Kelvin Grove. Unpublished manuscript. Available from author (e-mail): l.daws@qut.edu.au

Dubrovsky, V. J., S. Kiesler, and B. N. Sethna. 1991. "The Equalization Phenomenon: Status Effects in Computer-Mediated and Face-to-Face Decision-Making Groups." *Human-Computer Interaction* 6:119-46.

Dunne, G. 1999. "The Different Dimensions of Gay Fatherhood: Exploding the Myths." Report to the Economic and Social Research Council, London School of Economics.

Fielding, N. G. and R. M. Lee. 1998. *Computer Analysis and Qualitative Research.* Thousand Oaks, CA: Sage.

Fontana, A. and J. H. Frey. 1994. "Interviewing: The Art of Science." Pp. 361-76 in *Handbook of Qualitative Research,* edited by N. K. Denzin and Y. S. Lincoln. Thousand Oaks, CA: Sage.

"The Future of the Internet." *Economist,* November 13, 1999.

Gaiser, T. 1997. "Conducting On-Line Focus Groups." *Social Science Computer Review* 15:135-44.

Galegher, J., L. Sproull, and S. Kiesler. 1998. "Legitimacy, Authority, and Community in Electronic Support Groups." *Written Communication* 15:493-530.

Garton, L., C. Haythornthwaite, and B. Wellman. 1999. "Studying On-Line Networks." In *Doing Internet Research: Critical Issues and Methods for Examining the Net,* edited by S. G. Jones. Thousand Oaks, CA: Sage.

Gates, W. 1997. "Keynote Address." In *The Harvard Conference on the Internet and Society.* Cambridge, MA: O'Reilly.

Giese, M. 1998. "Self without Body: Textual Self-Representation in an Electronic Community." *First Monday* 3(4) [On-line]. Available Internet: http://www.firstmonday.dk/issues/issue3_4/giese/

Gjestland, L. 1996. "Net? Not Yet." *Marketing Research* 8:26-29.

Hahn, K. L. 1998. "Qualitative Investigation of an E-Mail Mediated Help Service." *Internet Research: Electronic Networking, Applications and Policy* 8:123-35.

Hantrais, L. and M. Sen. 1996. *Cross-National Research Methods in the Social Sciences.* Guildford, England: Biddles.

Herring, S. C., ed. 1996. *Computer-Mediated Communication: Linguistic, Social and Cross-Cultural Perspectives.* Amsterdam: John Benjamins.

Hewson, C., D. Laurent, and C. Vogel. 1996. "Proper Methodologies for Psychological and Sociological Studies Conducted via the Internet." *Behavior Research Methods, Instruments and Computers* 28:186-91.

Hodkinson, P. 2000. "The Goth Scene as Trans-Local Subculture." Ph.D. dissertation, Center for Urban and Regional Studies, University of Birmingham.

Horn, S. 1998. *Cyberville: Clicks, Culture, and the Creation of an Online Town.* New York: Warner.

Kehoe, C. M. and J. E. Pitkow. 1996. "Surveying the Territory: GVU's Five WWW User Surveys." *World Wide Web Journal* 1(3):77-84.

Kennedy, A. 1998. *The Internet and the World Wide Web: The Rough Guide.* London: Penguin.

Kiesler, S., J. Siegel, and T. McGuire. 1984. "Social Psychological Aspects of Computer-Mediated Communication." *American Psychologist* 39:1123-34.

Kollock, P. and M. Smith. 1996. "Managing the Virtual Commons: Cooperation and Conflict in Computer Communities." Pp. 109-28 in *Computer-Mediated Communication: Linguistic, Social and Cross-Cultural Perspectives,* edited by S. Herring. Amsterdam: John Benjamins.

Kramarae, C. and J. Kramer. (1995). "Legal Snarls for Women in Cyberspace." *Internet Research: Electronic Networking, Applications and Policy* 5(2):14-24.

Krueger, R. A. 1988. *Focus Groups: A Practical Guide for Applied Research.* Newbury Park, CA: Sage.

Lea, M., ed. 1992. *Contexts of Computer-Mediated Communication.* Brighton, England: Harvester-Wheatsheaf.

Lea, M. and R. Spears. 1995. "Love at First Byte? Building Personal Relationships over Computer Networks." In *Under-studied Relationships: Off the Beaten Track,* edited by J. T. Wood and S. Duck. Thousand Oaks, CA: Sage.

Lee, R. M. 1993. *Doing Research on Sensitive Topics.* Newbury Park, CA: Sage.

Loader, B. D., ed. *Cyberspace Divide: Equality, Agency and Policy in the Information Society.* London: Routledge.

Mann, C. and F. Stewart. 2000. *Internet Communication and Qualitative Research: A Handbook for Researching Online.* London: Sage.

Matheson, K. 1992. "Women and Computer Technology: Communicating for Herself." Pp. 66-88 in *Contexts of Computer-Mediated Communication,* edited by M. Lea. Brighton, England: Harvester-Wheatsheaf.

May, T. 1993. *Social Research: Issues, Methods and Processes.* Buckingham: Open University Press.

McLaughlin, M. L., K. Osborne, and C. Smith. 1995. "Standards of Conduct in Usenet." Pp. 90-112 in *CyberSociety: Computer-Mediated Communication and Community,* edited by S. G. Jones. Thousand Oaks, CA: Sage.

Mehta, R. and E. Sivadas. 1995. "Comparing Response Rates and Response Content in Mail versus Electronic Mail Surveys." *Journal of the Market Research Society* 37:429-39.

Moore, M. 1993. "Theory of Transactional Distance." In *Theoretical Principles of Distance Education,* edited by D. Keegan. London: Routledge.

Morgan, D. L. 1988. *Focus Groups as Qualitative Research.* Newbury Park, CA: Sage.

Murphy, K. L. and M. P. Collins. 1997. "Communication Conventions in Instructional Electronic Chats." *First Monday* 2(11) [On-line]. Available Internet: http://www.firstmonday.dk/issues/issue2_11/murphy/

Myers, D. 1987. "Anonymity Is Part of the Magic: Individual Manipulation of Computer-Mediated Communication Context." *Qualitative Sociology* 10:251-66.

O'Connor, H. and C. Madge. 2000. "Cyber-Parents and Cyber-Research: Exploring the Internet as a Medium for Research." Center for Labour Market Studies, University of Leicester. Unpublished manuscript.

Parker, L. 1992. "Collecting Data the E-Mail Way." *Training and Development,* July, pp. 52-54.

Parks, M. and K. Floyd. 1996. "Making Friends in Cyberspace." *Journal of Communication* 46(1):80-97.

Patrick, A. S., A. Black, and T. E. Whalen. 1995. "Rich, Young, Male, Dissatisfied Computer Geeks? Demographics and Satisfaction from the National Capital FreeNet." Pp. 83-107 in *Proceedings of*

Telecommunities 95: The International Community Networking Conference, edited by D. Godfrey and M. Levy. Victoria, BC: Telecommunities Canada. Available Internet: http://debra.dgbt.doc. ca/services-research/survey/demographics/vic.html

Raymond, E., ed. *The New Hacker's Dictionary.* 2d ed. Cambridge: MIT Press.

Reid, R. 1991. "Electropolis: Communication and Community on Internet Relay Chat." Honors thesis (electronically distributed version), Department of History, University of Melbourne.

Rice, R. E. and D. Case. 1983. "Electronic Message Systems in the University: A Description of Use and Utility." *Journal of Communication* 33(1):131-52.

Ryen, A. and D. Silverman. 2000. "Marking Boundaries: Culture as Category Work." *Qualitative Inquiry* 6:107-27.

Sala, L. 1998. "The Paradox: Megabandwidth and Micromedia." Presented at the International Sociology Conference. Montreal.

Salmon, G. 2000. *E-Moderating: The Key to Teaching and Learning Online.* London: Kogan Page.

Schaefer, D. and D. A. Dillman. 1998. "Development of a Standard E-Mail Methodology: Results of an Experiment." *Public Opinion Quarterly* 62:378-97.

Seidman, I. 1991. *Interviewing as Qualitative Research: A Guide for Researchers in Education and the Social Sciences.* New York: Teachers College Press.

Senior, C. and M. Smith. 1999. "The Internet . . . A Possible Research Tool?" *Psychologist* 12:442-44.

Seymour, W., D. Lupton, and N. Fahy. 1999. "Negotiating Disability, Technology and Risk: Towards a New Perspective." Report, School of Social Work and Social Policy, University of South Australia, Magill.

Shaw, D. 1997. "Gay Men and Computer Communication: A Discourse of Sex and Identity in Cyberspace." Pp. 133-46 in *Virtual Culture: Identity and Communication in Cybersociety,* edited by S. G. Jones. Thousand Oaks, CA: Sage.

Sheehan, K. B. and M. G. Hoy. 1999. "Using E-Mail to Survey Internet Users in the United States: Methodology and Assessment." *Journal of Computer-Mediated Communication* 4(3) [On-line]. Available Internet: http://www.ascusc.org/jcmc/vol4/issue3/sheehan.html

Shields, R., ed. 1996. *Cultures of Internet: Virtual Spaces, Real Histories, Living Bodies.* London: Sage.

Short, J., E. Williams, and B. Christie. 1976. *The Social Psychology of Telecommunication.* London: John Wiley.

Smith, C. B. 1997. "Casting the Net: Surveying an Internet Population." *Journal of Computer-Mediated Communication* 3(1) [On-line]. Available Internet: http://www.ascusc.org/jcmc/vol3/issue1/ smith.html

Smith-Stoner, M. J. and T. A. Weber. 2000. "Developing Theory Using Emergent Inquiry: A Study of Meaningful Online Learning for Women." Ph.D. dissertation, California Institute of Integral Studies. Available from authors (e-mail): mssrn@aol.com

Spender, D. 1995. *Nattering on the Net: Women, Power and Cyberspace.* Melbourne: Spinifrex.

Stewart, F., E. Eckerman, and K. Zhou. 1998. "Using the Internet in Qualitative Public Health Research: A Comparison of Chinese and Australian Young Women's Perceptions of Tobacco Use." *Internet Journal of Health Promotion,* December 29 [On-line]. Available Internet: http://www. monash.edu.au/health/IJHP/1998/12

Stones, A. and D. Perry. 1998. "Preliminary Evaluation of the World Wide Web as a Tool for Data Collection in the Area of Panic Research." Presented at the Computers in Psychology Conference, April, University of York.

Sweet, C. (1999) "Anatomy of an On-Line Focus Group." *Quirk's Marketing Research Review,* December. Available Internet: http://www.quirks.com/articles

Tesch, R. 1990. *Qualitative Research: Analysis Types and Software Tools.* New York: Falmer.

Thomas, D. S., K. Forcht, and P. Counts. (1998). "Legal Considerations of Internet Use: Issues to Be Addressed." *Internet Research: Electronic Networking, Applications and Policy* 8:70-74.

Tse, A. C. B., K. C. Tse, C. H. Yin, C. B. Ting, K. W. Yi, K. P. Yee, and W. C. Hong. 1995. "Comparing Two Methods of Sending Out Questionnaires: E-Mail versus Mail." *Journal of the Market Research Society* 37:441-46.

Turkle, S. 1995. *Life on the Screen: Identity in the Age of the Internet.* London: Weidenfeld & Nicolson.

Wallace, P. 1999. *The Psychology of the Internet.* New York: Cambridge University Press.

Walther, J. B. 1992. "Interpersonal Effects in Computer-Mediated Interaction: A Relational Perspective." *Communication Research* 19:52-90.

———. 1996. "Computer-Mediated Communication: Impersonal, Interpersonal, and Hyperpersonal Interaction." *Communication Research* 23:3-43.

———. 1999. "Researching Internet Behavior: Methods, Issues and Concerns." Presented at the National Communication Association Summer Conference on Communication and Technology, July, Washington, DC.

Winter, D. and C. Huff. 1996. "Adapting the Internet: Comments from a Women-Only Electronic Forum." *American Sociologist* 27:30-54.

Witmer, D., R. Colman, and S. Katzman. 1999. "From Paper-and-Pencil to Screen-and-Keyboard: Toward a Methodology for Survey Research on the Internet." Pp. 145-63 in *Doing Internet Research: Critical Issues and Methods for Examining the Net,* edited by S. G. Jones. Thousand Oaks, CA: Sage.

30

TRANSCRIPTION QUALITY

◆ Blake D. Poland

The transcription of audiotaped interviews as a method for making data available in textual form for subsequent coding and analysis is widespread in qualitative research. Yet, until relatively recently, little attention had been paid to methodological aspects of transcription, despite the theoretical and interpretive consequences of various approaches to defining and attending to transcription quality.

In this chapter, I explore the issue of transcription quality from a number of vantage points. I take the emerging literature on this topic as my point of departure, noting that the researcher is frequently exhorted to be ever more vigilant in the application of a growing number of possible conventions and measures to ensure that transcripts are verbatim facsimiles of what

was said in interviews (Edwards and Lampert 1993; Du Bois et al. 1993; Psathas and Anderson 1990). In the opening sections, I review several potential challenges to transcription quality, together with a number of suggested notational conventions that have been devised to assist transcribers in catching features of interest in the translation from spoken to written word.

A second vantage point from which to examine these issues takes inspiration from the postmodern turn in the social sciences. A growing number of voices in the emerging methodological literature on transcription call for a more explicitly reflexive stance vis-à-vis the inherently representational and interpretive nature of transcription (Mishler 1991; Lapadat and Lindsay 1999; Kvale 1996). These authors question

AUTHOR'S NOTE: The views expressed here do not necessarily represent those of the University of Toronto and remain the sole responsibility of the author. I am grateful to Norman Denzin, Joan Eakin, and two anonymous reviewers for comments on earlier drafts of this chapter.

not only the possibility of the verbatim transcript, but the implicit ontological and epistemological baggage that this kind of method talk conceals. Thus in subsequent sections of the chapter, I will problematize and deconstruct the notion of "verbatim" to reveal the nature of the transformations it frequently imposes on the data. In other words, data are (re)constructed in the process of transcription as a result of multiple decisions that reflect both theoretical and ostensibly pragmatic considerations. These vital insights, however, are typically accompanied by few suggestions for rigor in this aspect of qualitative research other than the general call to reflexivity. Thus I conclude the chapter by considering what the reflexive qualitative researcher might do to enhance the quality of transcription as a vital aspect of rigor in qualitative research.

My focus in this chapter is on the issues involved in the production of transcripts that are meant to be analyzed primarily for *what* is said, rather than *how* it is said. At several points I will make reference to the unique notational conventions and transcription requirements of conversation analysis, the preoccupation of which is the sequential development of talk. However, the latter is not my primary focus.

◆ Getting It Right

Many qualitative researchers, it would appear, do not give transcription quality a second thought. If they do, their concern is most often with ensuring the accuracy of verbatim accounts by minimizing sources of error in the transcription process. Insofar as these preoccupations are embedded in what Jaber Gubrium and James Holstein (1997) refer to as the "idiom" of "naturalistic method talk," it reflects a bias toward a realist ontology that is particularly evident, for example, in qualitative research in the health sciences. That is to say, from a naturalistic idiom, it is typically (if tacitly) assumed not only that the research interview

adequately captures social reality as it is experienced and expressed by respondents, but that the translation to audiotape and then text is not inherently problematic, so long as careful attention is given to ensuring accuracy of transcription.

Although the importance of ensuring that interview or focus group transcripts are verbatim accounts of what transpired is widely acknowledged (e.g., McCracken 1988; Patton 1990), it does not yet appear to be standard practice for qualitative researchers to consider transcription quality prior to their undertaking the analysis of textual data. A literature review conducted in 1995 of more than a decade of *Qualitative Sociology,* back issues of *Qualitative Health Research,* and more than a dozen frequently cited qualitative research textbooks and sourcebooks revealed very little substantive discussion of strategies for monitoring and improving transcription quality.[1]

Several resources have become available since 1995 (see Kvale 1996; Lapadat and Lindsay 1999; Seale 1999), but this literature is still relatively new. I would argue that, with the possible exception of the literature on transcription notation in conversation analysis, systematic and comprehensive attention to issues of transcription quality has yet to become routine practice in qualitative research. Of particular note is the absence of discussion of these issues in much of the literature on the rigor of qualitative research.[2]

CHALLENGES TO
TRANSCRIPTION QUALITY

In this subsection I consider several challenges to transcription quality and their possible origins. This is not intended as an exhaustive treatment of the subject; rather, I offer this discussion to stimulate reflection on and examination of these issues as they affect the quality of qualitative research.

Table 30.1   EXAMPLES OF TRANSCRIPTION "ERRORS"

As Recorded on Transcript	As Recorded on Audiotape
. . . it's kind of been a tough function but we, you would go with whatever the problems with health policies are . . .	it's been kind of a tacit assumption that we would go with whatever the province's health policies are . . .
. . . the government is almost saying to non-smokers well, you know, you were taught, like you either—	the government is almost saying to non-smokers "Well, you know, here its law. Its OK to stand up and give smokers hell"
. . . a broken cigarette is an (awful?) game. Now that's a proactive message	"A broken cigarette is a little freedom gained": now that's a proactive message.
You got to inhale all the diesel fumes. And that's worse, the way I see it anyway.	You've got to inhale all the diesel fumes. And that's worse than any cigarette ever will be.
I have no doubt that communities are the way to God!	I have no doubt that communities are the way to go.
. . . I think we we're a blast with a really good investigative team . . .	. . . I think we were blessed with a really good investigative team . . .
. . . a more direct interactive community confrontation model . . . and intimate health promotion projects don't recognize that need, that we've got to build in a consultation more process more	. . . a more direct interactive community consultation model . . . and community health promotion projects have recognized that need and have tried to build in a consultation process
I think unless we want to become like other countries, where people have, you know, democratic freedoms . . .	I think unless we want to become like other countries, where people have no democratic freedom . . .

SOURCE: Poland (1993).

My observations regarding challenges to transcription quality and strategies for addressing them arose initially from my dissertation research (Poland 1993; Poland et al. 1994).[3] As part of that research, the Brantford study, I reviewed interview transcripts on a computer screen while the interview or focus group tapes were running so as to identify and correct what I perceived as discrepancies between what was recorded in writing and what I felt fairly certain had actually been said during the interviews, as well as to refamiliarize myself with the material prior to coding. (I had been the interviewer/facilitator for all of the interviews and focus group discus-

sions.) At first, I kept a running tally of the number of discrepancies and maintained a cut-and-paste file of them that contained both versions of each—the excerpt as it appeared in the transcript and as I felt it should have appeared. Table 30.1 displays some examples from the entries in this file. I reviewed every transcript in my collection, and although the process of maintaining such a file became overly time-consuming and I eventually discontinued it, the information that I compiled helped me to generate the typology of challenges to transcription quality discussed below.

Even when a transcriber attempts to produce a verbatim account by remaining faithful to the original language and flow of the discussion, and even when the transcriber has a suggested syntax to follow in transcription (more on this later), there are a number of logistical and interpretive challenges to the translation of audiotape conversation into textual form. Drawing on my review of transcription quality in the aforementioned Brantford study, I have identified transcribers' problems with sentence structure, the use of quotation marks, omissions, and mistaking words or phrases for others. Each of these challenges is briefly discussed below.

Because people often talk in run-on sentences (actually, the concept of "sentence" does not translate well into oral tradition, or vice versa), transcribers must make judgment calls during the course of their work about where to begin and end sentences. The insertion of a period or a comma can sometimes alter the interpretation of the text. For example, "I hate it, you know. I do" carries a different meaning from "I hate it. You know I do." Although the original meaning and intent may be clear from the intonation and pacing of speech in the audiotape, it may be much less so in the transcript, unless these features are meticulously cataloged as well (see the discussion of notation systems to follow).

A second challenge identified in the Brantford study involved the failure of transcripts to indicate when people are paraphrasing or mimicking others, or when respondents quote things they told themselves or others told them. In these cases, the intonation and context of the testimony help, but transcribers who do not have a stake in the content of the material and are struggling word for word to get the material committed to paper may not catch what is going on, or may not judge the distinctions to be significant. The danger in a transcriber's failing to include quotation marks and/or annotations such as "(mimicking voice)" is that what a respondent was trying to convey as being someone else's thinking or reaction appears in the written text as if it were the respondent's own.

A third challenge revealed by the Brantford study involved omissions that occur when transcribers go forward and backward in the tape when they need to listen to a passage more than once, with the danger that they do not pick up exactly where they left off and pieces are lost. For example, in one case "I lost a very close friend to cancer" should have read "I lost a very close friend to lung cancer." The omission of the word "lung" was significant given the focus of the study on smoking cessation.

A fourth challenge for transcribers is the mistaking of words for other similar words that may or may not make sense in the context of what is being said. This is particularly apt to happen in passages that are difficult to discern due to problems of poor tape quality (more on this later). But it was not limited to those occasions alone in the Brantford study. On a number of occasions, transcribers' misinterpretations reversed the meaning of what was said. For example, in one case "consultation" was substituted for "confrontation," and "an evaluation model" became "and violation of the model" (see Table 30.1).

In some cases the mistaken wording made some sense (was plausible, although perhaps unlikely) in the immediate context of the sentence in which it was located, but not in the wider context of the interview. In other cases what was written in the transcript seemed bizarre and nonsensical even within the particular sentence or paragraph in which it appeared. In the most ambiguous places, researchers interpolate what makes sense to them as being what was likely uttered during the course of an interview.[4]

To discern the more plausible of several possible readings of an audio passage, then, the transcriber and/or researcher draws on powerful, if implicit, social conventions about the organization of speech and communicative competence to interpolate or adjudicate such apparent anomalies, under the assumption (when passages are unclear) that alternate bizarre phrasings would not have been intended and were therefore not uttered. In essence, confirmation is sought in terms of the coherence (see Hodder 1994) of the utterance with the phrases immediately preceding and following it, as well as with the rest of the respondent's testimony and whatever other knowledge the researcher has about the respondent and his or her social location and biography. The trustworthiness of such corroborating evidence, in turn, is ascertained in terms of prolonged engagement and other aspects of credibility, as described by Egon Guba and Yvonna Lincoln (1989) and others. A transcriber struggling to decipher what is being said from one utterance to the next cannot generally be expected to keep track of the larger context of what is being said as a basis for assessing the plausibility of alternate assessments of what is being said. Furthermore, when the substantive focus is quite outside the experience and/or expertise of the transcriber, such interpolation becomes less likely.

Many challenges associated with transcription quality can be attributed to the poor quality of some tape recordings (more on this later). Transcriber fatigue and lack of familiarity with the topic area can also contribute to the number of errors that creep into the transcription. Less controllable, but sometimes also a factor, is the clarity, speed, and accent of speech used by interviewees. With increasing ethnic and racial diversity in our populations and mounting pressure on researchers to include (and researchers' interest in including) diverse cultural perspectives in research studies, a number of challenges associated with cross-cultural research will also need to be addressed. For example, in cases where minority community members or translators are hired to interview (or assist in the interviewing of) respondents in languages other than those spoken by the principal investigator or the majority of the research team, the translation of audiotaped information or of interview transcripts must be considered. This introduces yet another layer of interpretation in the interview-tape-transcript interface.

ETHICAL CONSIDERATIONS

One of the most disconcerting moments in my dissertation research came when I reviewed several of the transcripts that had been completed by someone the project's primary transcriber had enlisted to assist her. This person (a legal secretary) took it upon herself to tidy up the discussion so that it would *read* better, just as she would have been expected to do with dictated correspondence at work. Michael Patton (1990) tells a similar story about an experience of one of his graduate students. And a colleague of mine recently discovered that her transcribers found the interview material they were working on so depressing and traumatic that they were altering the testimonies of respondents to make them sound more upbeat.[5] Such deliberate attempts to manipulate the data generally reflect transcribers' honest desires to be helpful, based on their own notions of what the transcripts should look like.

Verbal interactions follow a logic that is different from that for written prose, and therefore tend to look remarkably disjointed, inarticulate, and even incoherent when committed to the printed page. Inherent differences between the spoken tongue and the written word mean that transcripts of verbal conversations do not measure up well to the standards we hold for well-crafted prose (or even formal speeches), with the result that participants often come across as incoherent and inarticulate (Kvale 1988).

Ironically, this impression may be reinforced by an insistence on verbatim transcription in which all pauses, broken sentences, interruptions, and other aspects of the messiness of casual conversation are faithfully reproduced, despite what this messiness might lead one to presume about the participants. Some transcribers (particularly those accustomed to preparing correspondence based on dictated notes) find it difficult to resist the impulse to tidy up their transcriptions so that the participants do not appear so thoroughly inarticulate. The disjuncture between what coheres in natural talk and what demonstrates communicative competence in written prose comes as a shock to many respondents when they are asked or are offered the opportunity to review the transcripts of their interviews. Speaking from experience, I should add that interviewers themselves can find their own contributions, committed to paper, a rude awakening.

The potential for respondents (or classes of respondents) to be made to appear inarticulate as a result of the liberal use of verbatim quotes in the published results of a study has important ethical implications. In addition, verbatim quotes often make for difficult reading. The impact of quotes from respondents can often be greater if the researcher subjects them to a little skillful editing, without substantially altering the gist of what was said. Frequently, colleagues and I have been asked by editorial reviewers to tidy up quotes used in our publications. Usually, we consent in the interest of providing a more readable text. However, it is my opinion that although the tidying of quotations may be appropriate when an author is writing up qualitative research for publication, this should occur after the analysis has taken place and should be done by the researcher (not the transcriber), who should take care that what is removed does not appreciably alter the meaning of what was said (see Morse 1994:232). The author may wish to note in the text that "some transcription details have been omitted in the interest of readability" as a way of indicating to colleagues that the original transcripts paid closer attention to detail.

On the other hand, in cases where transcripts will be examined by a number of investigators and students who are part of a research team (which is increasingly the case in multidisciplinary research), ethical considerations might call for identifying information to be removed from transcripts prior to analysis. This is particularly the case when transcripts are made available for secondary analysis at a later date—for example, as part of a student dissertation after project funding has expired. The removal of identifying information becomes potentially problematic when this includes not simply the elimination of names but also the removal of other information that might allow analysts to identify individual respondents by virtue of their locations, social networks, job titles, organizations of employment, or other distinguishing features. The risk here is that removing too much identifying information could compromise future researchers' ability to contextualize the testimony of the respondents adequately as a basis for analysis, even though this practice may be defensible on ethical grounds.

Ethical issues also attend the unintentional misrepresentation of respondents, as when, for example, testimony is misunderstood or errors in transcription substantially alter the gist of what was intended, as is the case in several of the examples in Table 30.1. Giving study participants the opportunity to verify the transcripts or initial analyses may be one way for researchers to address this possibility. However, it is preferable that researchers forewarn respondents in these cases about how they are likely to appear on paper, for reasons that are elaborated above. (I discuss some other complications that may arise during member checking in a subsequent section of this chapter.)

I have noticed that a number of researchers today are including in the research proposals they submit for ethical review the stipulation that interview audiotapes will be erased as soon as transcripts are completed. This reflects a laudable concern for respondent confidentiality, but I am concerned that the erasure of audiotapes at an early stage in a research project will ensure that many decision points—regarding how difficult passages were transcribed and the application of the anointed syntax in practice, for example—will become irretrievable.

◆ *Problematizing "Verbatim"*

As previously noted, the transcript, as text, is frequently seen as unproblematic and given a privileged status in which its authority goes unquestioned (see Denzin 1994). This position may even be enhanced by an emphasis on accuracy of transcription. The conventional understanding of transcription error is in terms of the discrepancy between the written record (transcript) and the audiotape recording of the research interview upon which it is based. The notion of a verbatim transcript, therefore, is limited to a faithful reproduction of the oral record, the latter being taken as the indisputable record of the interview (problems with tape quality excepted).

However, many aspects of interpersonal interaction and nonverbal communication are not captured in audiotape records, so that the audiotape itself is not strictly a verbatim record of the interview. In other words, concern with ensuring that transcripts are accurate may unreflexively conflate lived experience of the one-on-one conversation with recorded speech (tapes), and this speech with the written word (transcript). In the words of Ann Oakley (1981), "Interviewing is rather like a marriage: everybody knows what it is, an awful lot of people do it, and yet behind each closed door there is a world of secrets" (p. 41). Those "secrets" include many nonverbal aspects of the interview context that are often not recorded on tape: body language, facial expressions, eye gazes (Bloom and Lahey 1978, cited in Lapadat and Lindsay 1999), nods, smiles or frowns (Kvale 1996), the physical setting, the ways participants are dressed, and other factors affecting the tone of the interview (Fontana and Frey 1994). Raymond Gorden (1980) identifies four types of nonverbal communication that are salient in this context:

> *Proxemic* communication is the use of interpersonal space to communicate attitudes; *chronemic* communication is the use of pacing of speech and length of silence in conversation; *kinesic* communication includes any body movements or postures; and *paralinguistic* communication includes all the variations in volume, pitch and quality of voice. (P. 335)

Even when aspects of emotional context are expressed with an oral component, such as intonation of voice, pauses, sighs, and laughter, these are not easily or straightforwardly translated into the written record. There may also be considerable variability in the extent to which verbal cues such as abandoned utterances, garbles, and verbal disruptions (Hughes, McGillivray, and Schmidek 1997, cited in Lapadat and Lindsay 1999) are adequately captured in transcription. These may require a standardized syntax for reliable encoding in the transcript, as well as a fuller accounting of the interview context that draws on field notes.[6]

Further, the dialogue that is captured on tape is framed not only by the immediate microcontext of the research interview (a stilted environment itself), but by a broader macrocontext of historically and socially located events. Because context is both "infinitely delicate and infinitely expandable" (Cook 1990, cited in Lapadat and Lindsay 1999:72), its apprehension is inherently incomplete and selective (on the importance of context, see also Kvale 1996).

We might do well then to ask, echoing Steinar Kvale (1995), "What is a valid translation from oral to written language?" (p. 27). The socially constructed nature of the research interview as a coauthored conversation-in-context must be acknowledged, instead of a quasi-positivist reification of the transcript as data about the interviewee, frozen in time (and space) (Kvale 1988; Richardson 1993). As text, the transcript is also open to multiple alternative readings, as well as reinterpretation, with every fresh reading (Denzin 1995; Kvale 1995).

The central issue, then, is what kind of text we envisage a transcript to be. How do we construct the transcript as an object of research? As recorded conversation? Phenomenological experience? Literary text? Linguistic data set? Dialogue? Narrative? (See Kvale 1988.) The reification of the transcript as synonymous with the interview, but also as a privileged text revealing the truth about the researched, glosses over these important distinctions (Kvale 1995). A modernist obsession with transcription accuracy, which problematizes transgressions in the privileged written text while simultaneously concealing the author in the writing up of interviews in conventional scientific prose, constructs issues of validity and reliability in terms of findings rather than tellings (Richardson 1993; see also Denzin 1994; Kvale 1995; Richardson, Chapter 42, this volume).

A number of authors have articulated and advanced alternative criteria for evaluating the quality of qualitative research (Lincoln and Guba 1985; Guba and Lincoln 1989; Corbin and Strauss 1990; Altheide and Johnson 1994; Hall and Stevens 1991), although none has addressed specifically the issue of transcription quality. Taken together, however, these authors raise issues of voice, representation, authenticity, audience, positionality, and reflexivity. This raises the possibility that our fixation on the depth interview and its textual representation in the form of transcripts is blinding us to the possibility and value of other ways of capturing voice, such as through self-stories and personal experience stories (Denzin 1995; see also Ellis and Berger, Chapter 41, this volume). In this context, theatrical and poetic (see Richardson, Chapter 42, this volume) representations of research data and/or findings are particularly well suited to convey the emotional content of the material.

I would therefore suggest that we can usefully focus our attention on the trust-worthiness of transcripts as research data by examining how faithfully they reproduce the oral (tape) record, while also being mindful of the limitations of these media to portray the full flavor of the interview. We must also take into account the potential for contested meanings and divergent interpretations of the gist and significance of what is being said, particularly when speech is garbled or poorly captured on tape. This may encourage us to examine reflexively our assumptions about transcription (and transcription quality) and its role in the research process, as well as to take the steps necessary to ascertain and document the trustworthiness of transcription as an aspect of rigor in qualitative research.

No doubt there are readers who will see these perspectives (error as real and yet also individually and socially constructed and contestable) as fundamentally contradictory. I think it is possible, indeed reasonable and defensible, to attend to many straightforward determinants of transcription quality (e.g., quality of audiotape recording, use of notational syntax to capture aspects of interaction more consistently, training of transcribers) while simultaneously maintaining a reflexive skepticism regarding the multiple interpretive acts that constitute the transcription process and their impact on the process of translating (re-presenting) the interview as audio recording and then as textual data. Putting it differently, I might say that such a position approximates that described by Martin Hammersley (1992) as subtle realism, or by David Altheide and John Johnson (1994) as analytic realism, in which it is assumed that knowable phenomena can be known only in cultural, social, politically situated ways (as situated human construction). Thus, by implication, researchers must consider the relationships among substance, observer, interpretation, audience, and style. This is broadly consistent with a critical realist stance. Indeed, this observation underscores the indivisibility of methodological issues (namely, transcription) from theoretical and epistemological ones.

◆ Strategies for Maximizing Transcription Quality

As with other aspects of qualitative research, there may be no singular approved approach to transcription divorced from the context and aims of the research project. However, several strategies are available for qualitative researchers to consider employing or adapting to their situations for the purpose of enhancing transcription quality. These include strategies for maximizing the audio quality of tape recordings, for using notation systems, for working with transcribers, for reviewing the quality of transcription, for using member checks, for flagging ambiguity in the interview, for using field notes or other sources as corroborating evidence in the interpolation of difficult passages, and for reporting on transcription quality in published research findings. Each of these is discussed below.

TAPE QUALITY

Much aggravation (for both researcher and transcriber) can be prevented by the interviewer's ensuring the quality of the original tape recording. Excessive background noise, weak batteries, a dirty recording head, placement of the recording device or microphone too far away from the respondent, the use of low-quality cassettes, and people speaking too softly to be heard well are all factors in the quality of the audio recording. Several suggestions for ensuring the audio quality of tape recordings are outlined in Table 30.2.

NOTATION SYSTEMS AND CONVENTIONS FOR TRANSCRIPTION

By failing to establish a priori a clear and consistent syntax for transcribers to use in recording pauses, laughter, interruptions, intonations, and so forth in the written text, the researcher does little to encourage consistency in the way these are handled within and between transcripts. Several notation systems have been developed and proposed over the years (Edwards and Lampert 1993; Psathas and Anderson 1990; Silverman 1993). Which one a researcher selects (or whether and how a researcher adapts an existing system or develops one for his or her own use) depends on which features the researcher considers important to capture, given the inevitable trade-off between level of detail and the resources required to achieve it. Thus it is neither appropriate nor possible to specify a priori what constitutes the most appropriate (or rigorous, or highest-quality) universal notation system. The researcher's decisions about what to include and how to do so must be informed by the theoretical stance and empirical focus of the study, as well as by such pragmatic considerations as the availability of sufficient resources.

Those researchers who are interested in detailed, turn-by-turn conversation analysis (CA) are especially concerned with pauses, overlaps, stretched sounds, intonations, partial words, and expressions of agreement, acknowledgment, surprise, and so on (see Atkinson and Heritage 1984). Such details of talk assume great significance because they reveal *how* things are said (and not only *what* is said). In these cases, even more careful precision in transcription is required, including the insertion of special codes to convey details that normally do not get committed to paper during the transcription process.

CA is concerned with the methods by which people produce orderly social interaction. This includes the ways in which conversation is structured, not only by implicit cultural norms (regarding appropriate turn taking and the like), but by the institutional and/or situational context of interaction, which may invoke competing discourses and opportunities for the display of social competence (see Silverman 1993). David Silverman and his colleagues provide a convincing demonstration of the

Table 30.2   STRATEGIES FOR ENSURING HIGH-QUALITY TAPE RECORDING

I. Equipment
   a. Use electrical outlet and outside mike whenever possible.
   b. If you use batteries, check them.
   c. Clean tape recorder heads regularly.
   d. Take along extra tape cassettes (and batteries).

II. Before interview
   a. Choose a place that's quiet and free from interruptions.
   b. Place microphone close to respondent, then speak loud enough so we hear what you're saying; most important, we want to hear the answer.
   c. Set recorder on stable surface.
   d. Test the recording system.

III. During interview
   a. Speak clearly and not too fast—respondent is likely to do the same.
   b. Ask respondent to speak clearly.
   c. Make test with respondent, then rewind and listen so respondent can hear whether she/he is speaking distinctly; if not, say, "The recorder does not seem to be picking up well. Could you speak up a little?" Whether the problem is mechanical or personal, correct it before continuing.
   d. Avoid using voice activation feature (if available), as it may fail to record the first few words spoken after each pause (also, lengths of pauses cannot be judged).
   e. Don't rustle papers, cups, bottles, and so on near the microphone.
   f. Watch for tape breakage and tangling.
   g. Repeat test if tape change is necessary.
   h. At end of interview, say, "This is the end of interview with . . . ."

IV. After interview
   a. Listen to tape—make notes, list proper names (or pseudonyms) and unfamiliar terminology.
   b. Label tapes and return them to appropriate containers.
   c. Keep tapes and recorder in good condition—do not touch tape or expose it to extreme temperatures.
   d. Consider making backup copies of tapes before turning them over to the transcriber.

SOURCE: Adapted from Patton (1990).

potential benefits of going beyond verbatim transcription to the use of the syntax of conversation analysis in terms of the sometimes profound effects this had on the way the transcripts were coded by the research project team (see Clavarino, Najman, and Silverman 1995; Silverman 1993). Similarly, Elliot Mishler (1991) compares the yield and impact of the use of several different approaches to notation and representation (poetic, narrative, discursive). And, taking the discussion in a different direction, Candace West (1996) points out the need to fit both transcription conventions and analytic questions to the level of detail that can possibly be recorded.

Detailed CA notation systems can help resolve some ambiguities in interpretation. To illustrate, the careful inclusion of pregnant pauses and interjections such as "yes-mm" and "uh-huh" could indicate receipt or assent (or resistance, in the case of refusals to provide the usual affirming responses to the speech of another). These subtleties (which can be significant) tend to be missed in less stringent transcription practices, particularly when they are overlaid with the speech of another. Without

Table 30.3   SAMPLE TRANSCRIPTION NOTATION SYSTEM ORIENTED TO CONVERSATION ANALYSIS REQUIREMENTS

[Mo:	C2: quite a [while [yea	Left brackets indicate the point at which a current speaker's talk is overlapped by another's talk.
=	W: that I'm aware of= C: =Yes. Would you confirm that?	Equal signs, one at the end of a line and one at the beginning of the next, indicate no gap between the two lines.
(.4)	Yes (.2) yeah	Numbers in parentheses indicate elapsed time in silence in tenths of a second.
(.)	to get (.) treatment	A dot in parentheses indicates a tiny gap, probably no more than one-tenth of a second.
::	O:kay?	Colons indicate prolongation of the immediately prior sound. The length of the row of colons indicates the length of the prolongation.
WORD	I've got ENOUGH TO WORRY ABOUT	Capitals, except at the beginnings of lines, indicate especially loud sounds relative to the surrounding talk.
.hhhhh	I feel that (.2) .hh	A row of h's prefixed by a dot indicates an inbreath; without a dot, an outbreath. The length of the row of h's indicates the length of the in- or outbreath.
( )	future risks and ( ) and life ( )	Empty parentheses indicate the transcriber's inability to hear what was said.
(word)	Would you see (there) anything positive	Parenthesized words are possible hearings.
(( ))	confirms that ((continues))	Double parentheses contain author's descriptions rather than transcriptions.
.,?	What do you think?	Punctuation indicates speaker's intonation.

SOURCE: Adapted from Silverman (1993).

clear direction from the research team on how to handle these situations, transcribers are faced with determining on a case-by-case basis which interjections are consequential enough to be included—a situation that can be fraught with uncertainty (yielding inconsistent results).

Gail Jefferson is generally credited with developing the core features of CA transcription conventions (see Jefferson 1984; see also Sacks, Schegloff, and Jefferson 1974; Atkinson and Heritage 1984; Psathas 1995). Drawing on these and other sources, Silverman (1993) has produced a more concise rendition that remains true to

the original objectives; Silverman's recommendations are displayed in Table 30.3.

On the other hand, this level of attention to detail can prove exhausting for transcribers and researchers alike. There is a limit to the degree of painstaking attention to detail that can be demanded of a transcriber in applying an elaborated system of codes. Whether or not this is warranted depends entirely on what the researchers wish to get out of the transcription. In studies with large sample sizes (60-100+ interviews), when analysis may be more superficial and limited to the cataloging of opinions or experiences, close attention to conversational dynamics may be unnecessary. On the other hand, in studies where sample sizes are smaller and where the features of interaction will be scrutinized (especially in naturally occurring talk such as the analysis of doctor-patient communication), it may be vitally important to employ notational systems of the type described in Table 30.3.

In Table 30.4, I offer an abbreviated set of instructions for transcribers that might be an alternative to Silverman's syntax of conversation analysis. Again, which of these, or which of several other conventions, a researcher uses will depend on the hypotheses, theoretical orientation, and nature of the data at hand. The schema in Table 30.4 calls for less detail in some areas than is stipulated in CA transcription. For example, short pauses are indicated by a series of dots (. . .) and longer ones by the word *pause* in parentheses; in CA, pauses are timed to tenths of a second. In addition to a formalized notation system for capturing these elements, Lori d'Agincourt-Canning and Susan Cox (2000) recommend that researchers give transcribers lists of jargon or special terms, with correct and phonetic spellings, to help them handle any terminology with which they may be unfamiliar.

SELECTING TRANSCRIBERS

The discussion in this chapter assumes that transcription is being done by individuals hired specifically for that purpose, rather than by the interviewers or researchers themselves. This practice is increasingly common in naturalistic qualitative inquiry, particularly in the health sciences, in contrast to conversation analysis, where the painstaking work of transcription is invariably undertaken by the researcher. The contracting out of transcription to paid employees presents a number of unique challenges with respect to transcription quality, although many of the issues raised in this chapter also pertain to transcription undertaken by interviewers and researchers.

Given the interpretive work involved in transcription, researchers need to consider carefully who might be the most appropriate persons to undertake this task. This is particularly so when the roles of interviewer, transcriber, analyst, and primary author of publications arising from a research study are embodied by different people. One might well ask whether persons with secretarial training and experience but little prior involvement in, or understanding of, qualitative research are appropriate candidates for making the myriad interpretive decisions involved in the transcription process, despite these persons' considerable technical skills.

It has been my observation that such divisions of labor (paid interviewer, transcriber, student/staff analyst, and principal investigator or coinvestigator) are increasingly common in large, externally funded research projects in the health sciences. The disruption of the continuity that might previously have been expected as a result of the same individual's embodying these roles has the potential for ruptures in understanding to occur in the process of translating data across media. I would suggest that such ruptures also attend the loss of intimacy with the fullness of the context of the data that occurs when investigators (or students or others undertaking secondary analysis) work directly from the transcripts without prior involvement in the interview or transcription phases, and often without having listened to any of the interview audiotapes.

WORKING WITH TRANSCRIBERS

Transcriber training should probably include at least one session in which the researcher introduces the syntax to be used and goes over a section of tape with the transcriber(s), answering questions that may arise in the course of applying the guidelines to an actual study interview.[7]

Table 30.4   ALTERNATIVE ABBREVIATED INSTRUCTIONS FOR TRANSCRIBERS

It is important for qualitative research that transcripts be verbatim accounts of what transpired in the interview; that is, they should not be edited or otherwise "tidied up" to make them "sound better."

Pauses	Denote short pauses during talking by a series of dots (. . .), the length of which depends on the amount of time elapsed (e.g., two dots for less than half a second, three dots for one second, four dots for one and a half seconds). Denote longer pauses with the word pause in parentheses. Use "(pause)" for two- to three-second breaks and "(long pause)" to indicate pauses of four or more seconds.
Laughing, coughing, etc.	Indicate in parentheses; for example, "(coughs)," "(sigh)," "(sneeze)." Use "(laughing)" to denote one person, "(laughter)" to denote several laughing.
Interruptions	Indicate when someone's speech is broken off midsentence by including a hyphen (-) at the point where the interruption occurs (e.g., "What do you-").
Overlapping speech	Use a hyphen to indicate when one speaker interjects into the speech of another, include the speech of the other with "(overlapping)," then return to where the original speaker was interrupted (if he or she continues). For example: R: He said that was impos- I: (overlapping) Who, Bob? R: No, Larry.
Garbled speech	Flag words that are not clear with square brackets and question mark, if guessing what was said (e.g., "At that, Harry just [doubled? glossed?] over"). Use x's to denote passages that cannot be deciphered at all (number of x's should denote approximate number of words that cannot be deciphered). For example, "Gina went xxxxx xxxxx xxxxx, and then [came? went?] home."
Emphasis	Use caps to denote strong emphasis; for example, "He did WHAT?" (Do not use boldface or underlining because such formatting is often lost when text files are imported into qualitative analysis software programs.)
Held sounds	Repeat the sounds that are held, separated by hyphens. If they are emphasized, capitalize them as well. For example, "No-o-o-o, not exactly" or "I was VER-r-r-y-y-y happy."
Paraphrasing others	When an interviewee assumes a voice that indicates he or she is parodying what someone else said or is expressing an inner voice in the interviewee's head, use quotation marks and/or indicate with "(mimicking voice)." For example: R: Then you know what he came out with? He said (mimicking voice) "I'll be damned if I'm going to let YOU push ME around." And I thought to myself: "I'll show you!" But then a little voice inside said "Better watch out for Linda." Sure enough, in she came with that "I'm in control now" air of hers.

The researcher should also make an attempt to review several of the initial transcripts, so that misunderstandings can be cleared up early in the process. I would recommend that researchers meet at regular intervals with all transcribers, in addition to reviewing their work early on in the process to ensure comparability (if there is more than one transcriber) and dependability.

In my experience, I have found that it helps if transcribers are informed about the nature and purpose of the research. It is even better if those doing the transcription have themselves undertaken social science research (perhaps as students), so that they are generally knowledgeable about the process. The tenets of hermeneutic science are often difficult to identify and convey adequately to transcribers without postsecondary education in the relatively short orientation periods available. Transcribers with primarily secretarial backgrounds have the technical skills required but find it harder to understand the research enterprise and topics under investigation than do transcribers with more education. In my experience this is reflected in the nature of the interpretive decisions such transcribers make in the course of transcription. On the other hand, they may have insights into the life worlds of the researched that are unavailable to the study investigators by virtue of their class location, race, and/or gender.

Indeed, researchers should not overlook the opportunity to involve transcribers in the study beyond their function as recorders. After all, other than the interviewers and one or two study investigators, transcribers are the only people to be exposed to the interviews in their entirety. In the Brantford study, the transcriber was encouraged to provide feedback (typically in writing at the end of the interview file) about her reactions to the interview—not only its content, but also her perceptions of the nature and quality of interaction between interviewer and interviewee (the time she took to provide her reactions was included as paid time). The quality of the transcriber's contributions in this vein was variable, but I frequently found her input to be worthwhile.[8] It may also be useful for researchers to contact transcribers for regular debriefings, by phone or in person, particularly when the material being transcribed is emotionally charged (d'Agincourt-Canning and Cox 2000). If the project employs more than one transcriber, and resources allow for it, the researcher may have the opportunity to engineer some overlap in the transcribers' workloads so as to identify and explore some of the differences that may arise in transcription of the same interview tape(s). There may be yet other ways in which researchers may engage the transcriber-as-hired-hand in making suggestions and modifications to the transcription syntax, the coding of data, the data entry of codes (when using computer analysis software), and so forth. In other words, researchers should not overlook opportunities to engage transcribers more fully in their research projects. Of course, in these cases it is important for researchers to remember to acknowledge the contributions of the transcribers in conference presentations and publications (d'Agincourt-Canning and Cox 2000).

REVIEWING TRANSCRIPTION QUALITY

It is unlikely that all discrepancies in interpretation between transcriber and interviewer/investigator regarding the translation of data from audiotape to written text can be prevented, even with well-trained transcribers working from high-quality recordings and supported by clear guidelines for transcription. On the other hand, reviewing all transcripts is time-consuming and expensive, and may not be justified. Transcription costs alone average $100 (for four to six hours) per interview (more for focus group discussions), depending on length and complexity, to which one would have to add at least another $50 of paid research staff time for reviewing transcription quality (unless this is done by the study investigators, for whom time is also at a premium).

For many studies, the addition of an extra step of this nature would represent a significant increase in costs and a setback in time. Given these limitations, two alternatives seem appropriate in this context, and these are not mutually exclusive. One option is for the researchers to consider not having all of the interviews transcribed in their entirety. Investigators (or research staff) could listen to the interview tapes and identify sections (using tape counter numbers) for subsequent transcription, for example. This would have the added benefit of ensuring that research staff/investigators involved in analysis (but who did not complete some or all of the interviews themselves) will have listened to the audiotapes of all the interviews. Alternatively, the researchers could review a subset of transcripts (selected purposefully or randomly) to highlight themes and phenomena around which subsequent (selective) transcription efforts (and analysis) would be focused. This would also help the researchers avoid the possibility (in larger studies) of their being overwhelmed by the volume of material to be analyzed.[9]

A second option (which may be exercised in concert with the first) is for the researchers to be selective in their review of transcript quality. They could review a small proportion of the transcripts, randomly or purposively selected, to gauge the quality of transcription overall. They should bear in mind, however, that transcription quality can be highly variable, as I found it to be in the Brantford study. Some transcripts (notably where the quality of the tape recording was poor) had errors affecting up to 60 percent of passages, whereas I judged many others to be virtually error-free. Such variability calls into question the viability of the practice of selecting a small (e.g., 10 percent) random sample of transcripts for closer scrutiny on the assumption that what holds for those will generally hold for the others. On the other hand, the effort required to assess transcription quality and effect remedial action will usually preclude an exhaustive review of all transcripts. One strategy a researcher might use would be to gravitate toward examining those texts that transcribers themselves identify as having been particularly difficult to produce. The researcher could select these plus a small sample of other transcripts for review onscreen while the interview tape is rolling. Keeping a tally of the number of minor (semantic) and major (meaning-reversing) errors will help the researcher to determine the extent of the problem and to decide whether a full review of the remainder of the transcripts is called for. In many cases, a researcher's documenting the quality of transcription in a sample of transcripts will itself be a marked improvement over conventional practice.

MEMBER CHECKING

The nature of transcription as an interpretive activity surfaces the possibility that multiple interpretations will not be easily resolved and that different people checking transcription quality may generate different versions of the interview transcript. Although the documentation of these differences may be instructive, the argument might be made that the interviewer (using his or her field notes and other recollections of the interview experience) should be the one to review the transcript, rather than a relative newcomer to the study hired for this purpose. In some cases, respondents themselves may also be of assistance in sorting out particularly ambiguous passages, as Guba and Lincoln (1989) advocate under the rubric of member checks for establishing the credibility of research (see also Bloor 1983).

This strategy presents other challenges, however. Despite the many merits of checking back with respondents, either on a routine or an ad hoc basis, the use of this strategy for the validation of the trustworthiness of transcription is potentially problematic. When a researcher presents a transcript to a respondent for review, what he or she typically gets back are not only corrections to (perceived) errors in transcribing, depending on the person's recollections of what was said, but also attempts to clarify, justify, or perhaps even revoke or alter aspects of what was said (Hoffart 1991). Such member checking may be an important and valued addition or component of the research process. It allows for the gathering of additional information, permits respondents to validate or clarify the intended meaning behind certain statements, or comment on the overall adequacy of the interview (Lincoln and Guba 1985). This highlights the ways in which respondents may reinterpret or try to alter their testimonies upon further reflection or later in time.

Some researchers also value an ethical stance in which respondents retain ultimate control over how their stories are reported and interpreted, regardless of the number of changes they request or the nature of those requests. Although giving respondents the power to revoke or alter their testimony is laudable, researchers need to be aware of the anxiety they may help to create in respondents when they give those who have been interviewed the opportunity to see their words in print. In my experience, no matter how many times promises of confidentiality and anonymity are repeated, when respondents see their own words in print, the possibility of sensitive material being made available to others seems to be highlighted. This appears to be particularly so for professionals who may have made comments about their colleagues or employers that could be damaging if revealed. I suspect that this is partly because we typically associate print material with dissemination and communication (i.e., text is printed for the purpose of sharing with others), and because most professionals in North America are acutely aware of the dangers of particular materials falling into the wrong hands. Stories of leaked confidential memos pepper the popular press, and this does little to reassure respondents when they see their own testimony in print.

Nevertheless, the distinction between what was originally intended and what was actually said (let alone what the respondent wishes to change or retract) is not addressed by a focus on transcription quality per se (i.e., ensuring that what was said—and how it was said—is accurately committed to paper). But the clarification of intended meaning may be as important as (or more important than) the establishment of the accuracy of transcripts as privileged texts. These observations reinforce a point made earlier—that transcripts are, at best, partial accounts of the encounters between researcher and researched, rather than simply windows into the lives of the researched (Kirk and Miller 1986; Kvale 1988).

FLAGGING AMBIGUOUS MATERIAL IN THE INTERVIEW

Ideally, some of the ambiguities that are most salient to the research study will be flagged during the interview. The interviewer can create opportunities within the interview for the respondent to clarify earlier statements or to validate the initial interpretations of the interviewer, rather than wait until after the interview is complete and the transcript in hand.

USE OF FIELD NOTES AND OBSERVATIONAL DATA

As noted above (in the context of the interpolation of meaning in difficult passages), field notes may also help researchers to clarify some aspects of the interview context (see Atkinson and Coffey, Chapter 38, this volume). Details pertinent to the setting or other aspects of the respondent's life, the researcher's relationship with the researched, and so forth may have a bearing on how statements in the interviews are heard or interpreted. Of course, this assumes that field notes are not a gold standard against which to assess transcription, but are themselves necessarily partial interpretive accounts. Indeed, researchers must pay attention to what conventions will guide what is transcribed "in the field," including how to represent conversation (see West 1996).

REPORTING ON TRANSCRIPTION QUALITY

The suggestions contained in this chapter have a number of implications for how research might be carried out as well as how it might be reported and written up. One could envisage a "methods" section of a research paper or report containing a description of the steps taken to ensure audiotape quality, the directions provided to transcribers, and an assessment of the trustworthiness of the transcription based on a review of selected transcripts, in the context of an explicit acknowledgment of the interpretive nature of the transcription process. As with other aspects of the qualitative research process, researchers should ideally provide sufficient information to allow others to assess the trustworthiness of the data and subsequent interpretations, although there will typically be limited space in peer-review journal articles in which to do so.

◆ The Future of Transcription

New technologies may eclipse or transform the transcription process as we know it. It is possible, for example, that voice-recognition software will improve sufficiently in accuracy to permit the automation of transcription. This could represent a considerable savings in both time and money, and would remove some of the drudgery (albeit drudgery that earns many

people a living) associated with preparing interview data for analysis. However, because this software is not designed to represent many aspects of the verbal record that might be of interest to researchers (e.g., pauses, sighs, intonations, laughter), programs would have to be adapted for use in qualitative research (perhaps to suit particular notational conventions, such as a particular program for conversation analysis). In any case, it is noteworthy that automation cannot do away with the many interpretive issues that normally arise in the course of transcription; however, it may make them more arbitrary and less visible or available for scrutiny.

It is possible that new information technologies will allow researchers to skip transcription altogether. As storage media increasingly permit the collection of larger sound files (spurred by developments of MP3 and other resources on the World Wide Web), it may be possible to develop qualitative analysis software that will work directly with audio material. Audio passages (and perhaps even video passages) could be coded and retrieved for analysis in presumably much the same manner that sections of transcript text currently are, with much more of the interaction preserved for analysis. A combination of voice-recognition software and audiovisual storage capabilities might even allow for streaming video images alongside the automatically generated transcript text (simultaneous code and retrieve). Indeed, such capabilities are already to be found in the KIT program (see Tesch 1990; Kvale 1996). To quote Kvale (1996), in the KIT program,

> the tape recording is transferred to a compact disk, converted into digital form, and stored in the computer. During replay the speech can be coded on the monitor, comments on the passages can be written down, and central passages for later reporting can be transcribed. The coded passages can be retrieved for relistening, or recoding and

other functions of the analysis program can be conducted—in this case, by working directly with the recorded interview instead of with the transcripts. (Pp. 174-75)

Although Kvale is optimistic that "many methodological and theoretical problems of transforming oral speech into written texts are simply bypassed when the analyst works directly on recordings of the live conversations" (p. 175), Judith Lapadat and Anne Lindsay (1999) remain skeptical of this claim. As long as scientific results are disseminated in written form (which continues to be the primary, although no longer the only, medium), transcription of at least some material is virtually inevitable, although at least with systems like KIT, more of the data in their raw form are available in the analysis phase. Nevertheless, audio passages (and even streaming video) do not capture all elements of the interview experience. Rather than being embedded in transcription notation conventions, many of the decisions regarding what to capture and how to do so would conceivably simply be deferred to the coding phase, with potentially unsatisfactory results (less predictable or uniform, for example). In other words, it is unlikely that technology will enable researchers to bypass the thorny issues of interpretation involved in the preparation of data for analysis. Would we really want it any other way?

■ Notes

1. The qualitative research sourcebooks examined in this review included *Analyzing Everyday Explanation* (Antaki 1988), *In the Field* (Burgess 1984), *Doing Qualitative Research* (Crabtree and Miller 1992), *Interpretive Interactionism* (Denzin 1989), *Handbook of Qualitative Research* (Denzin and Lincoln 1994), *Ethnography: Step by Step* (Fetterman 1989), *The Interpretation of Cultures* (Geertz 1973), *Using Computers in Qualitative Research* (Fielding and Lee 1991), *The Long Interview* (McCracken 1988), *Qualitative Data Analysis* (Miles and Huberman 1984), *Successful Focus Groups* (Morgan 1993), *Qualitative Evaluation and Research Methods* (Patton 1990), *Everyday Understanding* (Semin and Gergen 1990), *Qualitative Methodology and Sociology* (Silverman 1985), *Interpreting Qualitative Data* (Silverman 1993), *Qualitative Analysis for Social Scientists* (Strauss 1987), and *An Introduction to Qualitative Research Methods* (Taylor and Bogdan 1984). Of these, only David Morgan's (1993) edited collection and Michael Patton's (1990) volume make more than passing reference to the issue of transcription quality, and both are cursory and selective in their treatment of the topic.

2. I have consulted the following sources on rigor in qualitative research: Cobb and Hagemaster (1987), Strauss and Corbin (1990), Daly and McDonald (1992), Engel and Kuzel (1992), Guba and Lincoln (1989:chap. 8), Hall and Stevens (1991), Hammersley (1992:chap. 4), Italy and McDonald (1992), Kuzel and Like (1991), LeCompte and Goetz (1982), Lincoln and Guba (1985:chap. 11), Morse (1991a, 1991b), Silverman (1993:chap. 7), and West (1990).

3. An earlier paper on the issue of transcription quality was published in *Qualitative Inquiry* (Poland 1995) and was subsequently revised and updated for inclusion in this volume.

4. Such interpolations should probably be identified as such in transcripts through the use of square brackets ([. . .]) and/or question marks, or some other consistent syntax (see Table 30.3).

5. Exposing transcribers to potentially traumatic testimonies also raises ethical considerations, insofar as the provision of emotional supports should be considered.

6. Others argue that researchers must entertain entirely different approaches to data representation if they are to convey adequately the emotional content of the lived experience of study participants (regarding poetic representations, for example, see Richardson, Chapter 42, this volume).

7. Ideally, there might be more than one such session and more than one tape used (pulling, for example, from a recording judged to be difficult to understand or from different types of interviews or topic areas), particularly where a fairly detailed syntax is to be used.

8. This was so even, or perhaps especially, when her assessment of an interview was at odds

with mine, forcing me to reexamine my assumptions or conclusions about the interview.

9. Kvale (1988) discusses the ways in which the combination of large (excessive?) data sets and computer analysis software may compromise the research by seducing the researcher into substituting the search and retrieval of character strings for a more carefully thought-out analysis plan (when plans for the analysis of interview material are formulated after a large number of transcripts have been amassed).

■ *References*

Altheide, D. L. and J. M. Johnson. 1994. "Criteria for Assessing Interpretive Validity in Qualitative Research." Pp. 485-99 in *Handbook of Qualitative Research,* edited by N. K. Denzin and Y. S. Lincoln. Thousand Oaks, CA: Sage.

Antaki, C., ed. 1988. *Analyzing Everyday Explanation: A Casebook of Methods.* Newbury Park, CA: Sage.

Atkinson, J. M. and J. Heritage, eds. 1984. *Structures of Social Action: Studies in Conversation Analysis.* Cambridge: Cambridge University Press.

Bloom, L. and M. Lahey. 1978. *Language Development and Disorders.* New York: John Wiley.

Bloor, M. J. 1983. "Notes on Member Validation." Pp. 156-72 in *Contemporary Field Research: A Collection of Readings,* edited by R. M. Emerson. Boston: Little, Brown.

Burgess, R. G. 1984. *In the Field: An Introduction to Field Research.* London: George Allen & Unwin.

Clavarino, A. M., J. M. Najman, and D. Silverman. 1995. "The Quality of Qualitative Data: Two Strategies for Analyzing Medical Interviews." *Qualitative Inquiry* 1:223-42.

Cobb, A. K. and J. N. Hagemaster. 1987. "Ten Criteria for Evaluating Qualitative Research Proposals." *Journal of Nursing Education* 26(4):138-43.

Cook, G. 1990. "Transcribing Infinity: Problems of Context Representation." *Journal of Pragmatics* 14:1-24.

Corbin, J. and A. L. Strauss. 1990. "Grounded Theory Research: Procedures, Canons, and Evaluative Criteria." *Qualitative Sociology* 13:3-21.

Crabtree, B. F. and W. L. Miller. 1992. *Doing Qualitative Research.* Newbury Park, CA: Sage.

d'Agincourt-Canning, L. and S. M. Cox. 2000. *Mere Words on a Page? Transcription as Embodied Labor.* Presented at the Sixth Annual Qualitative Health Research Conference, Banff, Alberta.

Daly, J. and I. McDonald. 1992. "Covering Your Back: Strategies for Qualitative Research in Clinical Settings." *Qualitative Health Research* 2:416-38.

Denzin, N. K. 1989. *Interpretive Interactionism.* Newbury Park, CA: Sage.

———. 1994. "The Art and Politics of Interpretation." Pp. 500-515 in *Handbook of Qualitative Research,* edited by N. K. Denzin and Y. S. Lincoln. Newbury Park, CA: Sage.

———. 1995. "On Hearing the Voices of Educational Research." *Curriculum Inquiry* 25:313-30.

Denzin, N. K. and Y. S. Lincoln, eds. 1994. *Handbook of Qualitative Research.* Newbury Park, CA: Sage.

Du Bois, J. W., S. Schuetze-Coburn, S. Cumming, and D. Paolino. 1993. "Outline of Discourse Transcription." Pp. 45-87 in *Talking Data: Transcription and Coding in Discourse Research,* edited by J. A. Edwards and M. D. Lampert. Hillsdale, NJ: Lawrence Erlbaum.

Edwards, J. A. and M. D. Lampert, eds. 1993. *Talking Data: Transcription and Coding in Discourse Research.* Hillsdale, NJ: Lawrence Erlbaum.

Engel, J. and A. Kuzel. 1992. "On the Idea of What Constitutes Good Qualitative Inquiry." *Qualitative Health Research* 2:504-10.

Fetterman, D. M. 1989. *Ethnography: Step by Step.* Newbury Park, CA: Sage.

Fielding, N. G. and R. M. Lee, eds. 1991. *Using Computers in Qualitative Research.* Newbury Park, CA: Sage.

Fontana, A. and J. H. Frey. 1994. "Interviewing: The Art of Science." Pp. 361-76 in *Handbook of Qualitative Research,* edited by N. K. Denzin and Y. S. Lincoln. Newbury Park, CA: Sage.

Geertz, C. 1973. *The Interpretation of Cultures: Selected Essays.* New York: Basic Books.

Gorden, R. L. 1980. *Interviewing: Strategy, Techniques, and Tactics.* 3d ed. Homewood, IL: Dorsey.

Guba, E. G. and Y. S. Lincoln. 1989. *Fourth Generation Evaluation.* Newbury Park, CA: Sage.

Gubrium, J. F. and J. A. Holstein. 1997. *The New Language of Qualitative Method.* New York: Oxford University Press.

Hall, J. M. and P. E. Stevens. 1991. "Rigor in Feminist Research." *Advances in Nursing Science* 13(3):16-29.

Hammersley, M. 1992. *What's Wrong with Ethnography? Methodological Explorations.* London: Routledge.

Hodder, I. 1994. "The Interpretation of Documents and Material Culture." Pp. 393-402 in *Handbook of Qualitative Research,* edited by N. K. Denzin and Y. S. Lincoln. Newbury Park, CA: Sage.

Hoffart, N. 1991. "A Member Check Procedure to Enhance Rigor in Naturalistic Research." *Western Journal of Nursing Research* 13:522-34.

Hughes, D., L. McGillivray, and M. Schmidek. 1997. *Guide to Narrative Language: Procedures for Assessment.* Eau Claire, WI: Thinking Publications.

Italy, J. and I. McDonald. 1992. "Covering Your Back: Strategies for Qualitative Research in Clinical Settings." *Qualitative Health Research* 2:416-38.

Jefferson, G. 1984. "Caricature versus Detail: On Capturing the Particulars of Pronunciation in Transcripts of Conversational Data." *Tilberg Papers on Language and Literature No. 31,* University of Tilberg, Netherlands.

Kirk, J. and M. L. Miller. 1986. *Reliability and Validity in Qualitative Research.* Newbury Park, CA: Sage.

Kuzel, A. and R. Like. 1991. "Standards of Trustworthiness for Qualitative Studies in Primary Care." In *Primary Care Research: Traditional and Innovative Approaches,* edited by P. Norton. Newbury Park, CA: Sage.

Kvale, S. 1988. "The 1000-Page Question." *Phenomenology + Pedagogy* 6(2):90-106.

———. 1995. "The Social Construction of Validity." *Qualitative Inquiry* 1:19-40.

———. 1996. *InterViews: An Introduction to Qualitative Research Interviewing.* Thousand Oaks, CA, Sage.

Lapadat, J. C. and A. C. Lindsay. 1999. "Transcription in Research and Practice: From Standardization of Technique to Interpretive Positionings." *Qualitative Inquiry* 5:64-86.

LeCompte, M. D. and J. P. Goetz. 1982. "Problems of Reliability and Validity in Ethnographic Research." *Review of Educational Research* 52(1):31-60.

Lincoln, Y. S. and E. G. Guba. 1985. *Naturalistic Inquiry.* Beverly Hills, CA: Sage.

McCracken, G. 1988. *The Long Interview.* Newbury Park, CA: Sage.

Miles, M. B. and A. M. Huberman. 1984. *Qualitative Data Analysis: A Sourcebook of New Methods.* Beverly Hills, CA: Sage.

Mishler, E. G. 1991. "Representing Discourse: The Rhetoric of Transcription." *Journal of Narrative and Life History* 1:255-80.

Morgan, D. L., ed. 1993. *Successful Focus Groups: Advancing the State of the Art.* Newbury Park, CA: Sage.

Morse, J. M. 1991a. "Evaluating Qualitative Research." *Qualitative Health Research* 1:283-86.

———. 1991b. "On the Evaluation of Qualitative Proposals." *Qualitative Health Research* 1:147-51.

———. 1994. "Designing Funded Qualitative Research." Pp. 220-35 in *Handbook of Qualitative Research,* edited by N. K. Denzin and Y. S. Lincoln. Newbury Park, CA: Sage.

Oakley, A. 1981. "Interviewing Women: A Contradiction in Terms?" Pp. 30-61 in *Doing Feminist Research,* edited by H. Roberts. London: Routledge & Kegan Paul.

Patton, M. Q. 1990. *Qualitative Evaluation and Research Methods.* 2d ed. Newbury Park, CA: Sage.

Poland, B. D. 1993. "From Concept to Practice in Community Mobilization for Health: A Qualitative Evaluation of the Brantford COMMIT Intervention For Smoking Cessation." Ph.D. dissertation, McMaster University.

———. 1995. "Transcript Quality as an Aspect of Rigor in Qualitative Research." *Qualitative Inquiry* 1:290-310.

Poland, B. D., S. M. Taylor, J. Eyles, and N. F. White. 1994. "Qualitative Evaluation of the Brantford COMMIT Intervention Trial: The Smokers' Perspective." *Health and Canadian Society* 2:269-316.

Psathas, G. 1995. *Conversation Analysis: The Study of Talk-in-Interaction.* Thousand Oaks, CA: Sage.

Psathas, G. and T. Anderson. 1990. "The 'Practices' of Transcription in Conversation Analysis." *Semiotica* 78:75-99.

Richardson, L. 1993. "Poetics, Dramatics, and Transgressive Validity: The Case of the Skipped Line." *Sociological Quarterly* 34:695-710.

Sacks, H., E. A. Schegloff, and G. Jefferson. 1974. "A Simplest Systematics for the Organization of Turn-Taking in Conversation." *Language* 50:696-735.

Seale, C. 1999. *The Quality of Qualitative Research.* Thousand Oaks, CA, Sage.

Semin, G. R. and K. J. Gergen, eds. 1990. *Everyday Understanding: Social and Scientific Implications.* Newbury Park, CA: Sage.

Silverman, D. 1985. *Qualitative Methodology and Sociology.* Aldershot, England: Gower.

———. 1993. *Interpreting Qualitative Data: Methods for Analysing Talk, Text and Interaction.* London: Sage.

Strauss, A. L. 1987. *Qualitative Analysis for Social Scientists.* New York: Cambridge University Press.

Strauss, A. L. and J. Corbin. 1990. *Basics of Qualitative Research: Grounded Theory Procedures and Techniques.* Newbury Park, CA: Sage.

Taylor, S. J. and R. Bogdan. 1984. *An Introduction to Qualitative Research Methods.* 2d ed. New York: John Wiley.

Tesch, R. 1990. *Qualitative Research: Analysis Types and Software Tools.* New York: Falmer.

West, C. 1996. "Ethnography and Orthography: A Modest Proposal." *Journal of Contemporary Ethnography* 25:327-52.

West, P. 1990. "The Status and Validity of Accounts Obtained at Interview: A Contrast between Two Studies of Families with a Disabled Child." *Social Science and Medicine* 30:1229-39.

31

COMPUTER-ASSISTED ANALYSIS OF QUALITATIVE INTERVIEW DATA

◆ Clive F. Seale

Social researchers have long appreciated the usefulness of computers for data analysis. Statistical software run on increasingly powerful personal computers has automated mathematical calculations on large data sets to the extent that quantitative analysis can be increasingly interactive. Analysts can run procedures and get instant feedback on the results, freeing up time for the creative interplay of ideas and research data. In the humanities, the development of software based on various elaborations of string searches for content analysis has led to new conceptions of what

is possible in linguistic analysis (Miall 1990). Computer-assisted qualitative data analysis software (CAQDAS) for social research data is a more recent development that, unlike statistical or string-search software, has depended largely on the proliferation of personal computers since the early 1980s. In this chapter, I assess the contribution that CAQDAS can make to a variety of analytic approaches to interview data. As far as possible, I use examples from completed research studies to illustrate what is feasible. Additionally, I argue that CAQDAS should not be viewed in isola-

AUTHOR'S NOTE: Many people helped me with this chapter by sending published and unpublished materials for review. I am particularly grateful to Jenny Brightman, Russell Bernard, Katie Buston, James Carey, Alan Cartwright, Susanne Friese, Harshad Keval, Odd Lindberg, Kati Rantala, Anna Triandafyllidou, Birrell Walsh, and Mitchell Weiss. A special thanks to Ann Lewins and her associates, whose contribution through the University of Surrey CAQDAS Networking Project has been important both in the writing of this piece and in supporting an international community of CAQDAS users over several years.

tion; other forms of computer-assisted data analysis (including the ones mentioned above) have a great deal to offer if used in combination with CAQDAS.

Initially, I outline the history of CAQDAS in social research and summarize the key procedures enabled by this family of software. I do not attempt to provide the finer details of individual programs, as these change from one release to the next. Suffice it to say that programs vary, and if particular features are unavailable on one, they are available on another. (For those readers who wish to explore particular packages, I provide a list of some useful resources following the endnotes to this chapter.) I then consider actual usage of these features in published, and some unpublished, social research involving interview data. It will become clear that, as in statistical software, users of CAQDAS generally exploit only the basic features of packages, with advanced usage being less common. As well as demonstrating the advantages that CAQDAS offers, I discuss some of its limitations. Finally, I consider examples of more advanced usage, linking this with a discussion of changing conceptions of the links between social theory and contemporary research practice.

Computer programs are both technical tools and rhetorical devices. The rhetorical presence of CAQDAS is exploited both by software designers in their marketing and by users in their strategic presentations to grant-making bodies, readers of research reports, and the like. Many features of the software serve as symbols to address the subcultural preoccupations of different groupings within the research community. In particular, CAQDAS programs address the quantitative/qualitative divide by presenting features appealing to scientific conceptions of rigor on the one hand and promising theoretical sophistication on the other. The fact that many of these features are not much used in actual research studies should give us pause for reflection on software design as a system for symbolic representation.

◆ The Development of CAQDAS

The chief contribution of CAQDAS is automation of the retrieval of text segments (for instance, sections of an interview) that have been categorized as examples of some analytic concept. Such categorization of data is often called *coding,* although some—for example, the creators of the CAQDAS program NUD*IST—prefer the term *indexing* on the grounds that *coding* carries with it unwelcome empiricist connotations (Kelle 1997). To appreciate the difference computers make to code-and-retrieve operations, it is instructive to consider what preceded the development of CAQDAS.

As Nigel Fielding and Ray Lee (1998) point out, the coding of responses to open questions in survey data was a well-described procedure in market research for some time before methodolo- gists dealing with unstructured qualitative data gave accounts of coding. Additionally, in the 1940s, market researchers began to explore the possibilities of coding less structured interview material. Fielding and Lee observe that the first sustained sociological discussion of coding unstructured data is found in publications associated with Howard Becker et al.'s *Boys in White* (1961). However, it is clear that basic indexing operations were used before this. For example, William Foote Whyte (1981), in his appendix to the third edition of *Street Corner Society* (first published in 1943), describes his initial difficulty in deciding whether to organize his field notes "topically, with folders for rackets, the church, the family, and so on" (p. 308), or according to the different social groups he was observing. Eventually, as the volume of material "grew beyond the point where my memory would allow me to locate any given item rapidly" (p. 308), Whyte devised what he calls "a rudimentary indexing system" (p. 308), which served both to reduce his data and to remind him what was in the folders. Other researchers have used card indexes, different colored pens, scissors and tape, and a host of other manual devices to organize masses of otherwise unwieldy materials.

Becker (1970), however, is rightly identified as expounding a more systematic approach to coding and retrieval, which coincided with his concern to address with methodological rigor the problems of inference and proof from fieldwork data. Becker wanted researchers to be able to avoid anecdotalism, identify negative instances, produce quasi-statistics, and thereby represent without analytic bias the full range of phenomena in a data set. To this end, he recommended that coding should be done inclusively, so that all instances of a relevant phenomenon would be made available for inspection and perhaps further analysis.

At around the same time, Barney Glaser and Anselm Strauss (1967) were developing their approach to grounded theorizing (see Charmaz, Chapter 32, this volume). Like Becker, they built on earlier attempts at imposing analytic rigor on qualitative data (for example, analytic induction) and on an appreciation of developments in quantitative data analysis that involved a creative interaction between theoretical ideas and data (e.g., Lazarsfeld and Rosenberg 1955). The rigor and system made available by procedures such as the constant comparison of properties and their categories to generate theory, all of which were based on a fundamental code-and-retrieve logic, had a wide appeal that continues to this day. Aside from the real analytic gains, a generation of qualitative researchers learned the strategic advantages of citing grounded theory on grant application forms. Early CAQDAS programs (such as the Ethnograph and NUD*IST) were designed in large part to relate to the analytic logic of grounded theorizing, so that the basic procedures they make available reflect this tradition in sociological ethnography.

The advantages of automated code and retrieval, compared with manual versions of the same thing, can be illustrated with an example from my own use of the Ethnograph on data derived from interviews with people recalling the last year of life of deceased relatives or friends. This was an unusually large data set for the Ethnograph—in the version I was using then, only 80 interviews could be processed at any one time (I had a total of 639), so I had to repeat many operations several times. Nevertheless, computerized retrieval saved me a lot of clerical work that would have been necessary with manual methods. Using the "filter" operation, which enables the user to select interviews according to the values of "face sheet" variables (for example, the age or gender of the interviewee), I was able to carry out selective retrievals of coded segments. Thus I compared people who had died in hospitals with people who had died in private homes, selecting the segments where interviewees described learning of the deaths. Respondents whose deceased relatives or friends had lived alone at home and had died there often described finding the person dead; in hospitals, on the other hand, people were never "found dead" in this way, as hospital personnel ensured that relatives and friends "learned" of deaths before they witnessed the bodies (Seale 1995a). In this and other publications, I was also able to present counts of the numbers of times particular respondents said particular kinds of things, regardless of where the sentiments were expressed in the interviews (e.g., Seale 1995b, 1996). I made further comparisons of groups of interviewees (for instance, reports for people who had cancer were different in various respects from reports for people who had other kinds of illnesses) and identified negative instances, where particular examples ran counter to the majority picture. In this respect, the software's requirement that I code systematically and the tireless capacity of the computer to confront the analyst with all coded instances enforced a rigor that might otherwise have been daunting to achieve.

Aside from improving on manual methods, the basic procedures made feasible by the Ethnograph also demonstrate the advantages of dedicated CAQDAS programs compared with other software, such as databases and word processors. Anna Triandafyllidou (1999; Triandafyllidou and Fotiou 1998) has used FoxPro 2.0, a database management system, for the analysis of interviews and press reports on the topic of immigration policy. To include original text in the retrievals, however, Triandafyllidou had to type these into the database, because other links between the database and the raw transcripts were not feasible. Retrievals were therefore largely confined to the number of times a phenomenon occurred, with the user then having to locate relevant examples manually. Significantly, Triandafyllidou's research reports are thin on illustrative quotations, although theoretically the analysis is sophisticated. The macros in word processors can also be adapted to "spike" text segments that contain code words and store these in separate files (Bernard and Ryan 1998), but for researchers to undertake such do-it-yourself computer programming to mimic the most basic (code-and-retrieve) feature of a dedicated CAQDAS program seems unnecessarily time-consuming.

Beyond coding for retrieval, CAQDAS programs are capable of performing a variety of more advanced procedures; I will list these briefly here and, for the most part, illustrate them in use later in this chapter. Data entry varies from the restrictive to the inclusive. A restrictive program allows for text files only, shaped in a particular way and subject to a line limit, with additional restrictions as to the number of data files processed. An inclusive program allows users to import text files in any format (for example, downloaded from the Internet, with graphics and colors in place) as well as to attach, code, and search audio, video, and scanned images. Inclusivity also allows for the coding of "off-line" documents (such as handwritten notes stored in a filing cabinet but not scanned into a computer file) so that the phenomena occurring in these are reported in search operations. For specialist transcription, it is helpful if transcripts can be linked to audio files, so that the user can play these back while reading the transcripts; it is also helpful if the program allows the user to designate special characters and sections of transcript separately from the rest (so that they are not reported in string searches, for example). Brian Torode (1998) notes that his use of Code-A-Text for conversation analysis was greatly facilitated by such features. A program's ability to recognize special characters is also helpful if the researcher is working with a non-Western alphabet.[1] Allowing the user to edit original text without disturbing attached codes is also a feature of some more recent CAQDAS programs. Most programs allow users to attach analytic memos, in which they may explore emerging ideas, or definitions of code words.

I have noted above CAQDAS programs' capacity to search for segments according to "filter" variables, as demonstrated in the example from my own research; this is a basic feature of a code-and-retrieve program. Beyond this, programs can feature a variety of Boolean search combinations. For example, I might have asked the Ethnograph to show me segments in which respondents discussed the quality of health care and the topic of pain so that I could investigate the adequacy of care for this problem. This would have involved a simple overlap between two codes. Other kinds of Boolean searches involve manipulation of "and," "or," and "not in" commands to specify the conditions under which segments should be retrieved. Alternatively, users can specify proximity searches—that is, searches for differently coded segments that occur within specified distances of each other. Such searches can help an analyst to test hypotheses; for example, a researcher may ask whether event A always precedes event B, or whether this sequence occurs only under certain conditions of C.

The results of searches can be displayed as segments of original data, and some programs allow for both expanded and restricted views of these. At times, the researcher may need to see the text that occurs on either side of a coded segment, in order to see its context (an expanded view). Statistical output is another way to view the results of searches, and the ability to create data matrices amenable to statistical analysis by other software is now a common feature of CAQDAS programs. For example, such a feature would have allowed me to compare the number of statements made by men and women indicating satisfaction or dissatisfaction with the quality of care for various symptoms. Alternatively, I might have searched for word strings and compared the incidence of adjectives to describe, say, the experience of pain between different groups of interviewees.

The analytic operations developed in the humanities computing tradition for linguistic analysis are increasingly supported by CAQDAS programs for social research data. The capacity to do automatic searches for strings of letters (and therefore words) is fundamental to these operations. Some CAQDAS program developers remain suspicious of such "autocoding," as it raises the specter of automatic thinking. The Ethnograph, for example, stops at each "hit" of a string and requires the user to indicate whether a code should be applied in each case. This means that "I had a pain here" can be coded differently from "the doctor was a pain in the ass." Other developers feel that this approach is unnecessarily restrictive. NUD*IST, for example, will index every segment containing the word *pain* and retrieve these for inspection in one sweep; winMAX generates "key word in context" (KWIC) lists from such searches; and Code-A-Text allows for user-defined dictionaries, so that the user can identify counts of the percentages of words in each segment that belong to specific word groups. Other features of string searches that are useful include the use of "wild-card" letters (so that "coug*" returns "cough," "coughing," "coughed," and so on) and pattern searching, whereby a particular pattern of characters is identified

(for example, all words ending with "ing" and no more than 10 characters long). These latter features, however, are more likely to be found in specialist software for linguistic content analysis, such as concordance programs, which are relatively underused in qualitative social research, in spite of a "turn to language" in the contemporary social theories that increasingly influence social researchers (see Fontana, Chapter 8, this volume).

A further advanced feature of some CAQDAS programs is the capacity to draw conceptual maps that assist the development of theoretical models. Concepts can be linked with various kinds of connecting lines to indicate different kinds of relationships (for example, A causes B, A is a strategy for doing B, A loves B). Freestanding graphical modelers exist, but some CAQDAS programs (e.g., ATLAS.ti, NVivo) incorporate this feature, with the added advantage that elements of the model are linked to data files. Researchers can also use graphical modeling to represent and compare the "cognitive maps" of individual interviewees, and some specialist software exists for this purpose.

◆ CAQDAS in Use

For this section, I draw on a collection of studies that have used CAQDAS on interview data. I generated the list of studies by visiting the Web sites of CAQDAS developers, by conducting on-line searches of bibliographic databases in which CAQDAS programs are mentioned as well as a fairly random perusal of journals reporting social research, and by making announcements that I was searching for such material in e-mail discussion groups. Fielding and Lee (1998) report the first study of the CAQDAS-using community, based on focus groups involving researchers. I felt that the next step would be to analyze (mostly) published studies reporting on interview data and using CAQDAS, to see the extent to which CAQDAS has influenced analytic style as well as to assess whether the features made available by the software are used in practice.

Fielding and Lee (1995) conducted an analysis of the Ethnograph network licenses and found that the largest group of users was in educational research, followed by nursing research, sociology, anthropology, other health disciplines, and psychology. Additionally, in their 1998 study of users in the United Kingdom, Fielding and Lee found that data derived from interviews were the most common form of data on which CAQDAS was used. The use of CAQDAS to analyze purely observational or documentary data was rare; such data sources were more often used in combination with interviews. Fielding and Lee also found little use being made of the more advanced features of CAQDAS described in the preceding section. In particular, any "theory building" occurred "off-line," if at all. I had no trouble finding articles involving qualitative interviews done by educational and nursing researchers that involved basic code-and-retrieve procedures. In what follows, I first discuss the enhanced rigor that CAQDAS can help deliver and then give an account of typical code-and-retrieve usage before going on to less common studies.

ANALYTIC RIGOR

One of the major potential advantages of CAQDAS is that the approach encourages (but does not enforce) rigor. As an early enthusiast, Michael Agar (1983) exemplifies this in his report of interviews with drug users. Exploring the opinions his respondents expressed about other people in their lives, he compared an earlier "intuitive," or manual, analysis with an approach supported by CAQDAS. The computer search confronted him with more negative instances than he had uncovered in his manual analysis, because "the computer coding forced a more careful reading

and recall of the interview, though perhaps I would have picked up the additional material with another direct reading of the transcript" (p. 23). He concludes that CAQDAS "doesn't get tired and miss sections of data" (p. 26). Agar also mentions that CAQDAS displays data in a publicly falsifiable way, a theme taken up by Fielding and Lee (1998), who argue that by forcing researchers to become explicit about the underlying operations of data analysis, CAQDAS creates an auditable trail that ought to enhance the credibility of findings.

Reports of interrater reliability exercises supported by CAQDAS serve to emphasize the contribution it can make to rigor and public accountability (Carey, Morgan, and Oxtoby 1996; Northey 1997). Significantly, however, William Northey (1997) takes a step back from a traditional conception of such reliability exercises by abstaining from the view that disagreements between coders should always be reconciled. Instead, using examples generated from interviews with family members about their conflicts, he recommends that researchers use NUD*IST simply to display instances of segments included under a code, so that auditors or readers have a chance to see the kinds of instances that contribute to a category. He thus performs the familiar balancing act of retaining constructivist credentials while addressing scientific concerns, precisely the discursive terrain that CAQDAS programs as a whole must negotiate.

Agar (1983) mentions colleagues who made disparaging references to the "science points" he was earning by using a computer for qualitative analysis. More serious extensions of this sentiment are expressed in the generalized fear that the search for CAQDAS-inspired rigor might impose a rigid, quasi-positivist analytic style (Hesse-Biber 1995; Buston 1997). In part, these fears reflect the traditional paranoia of qualitative researchers that quantification will take over, fueled by the capacity of CAQDAS to generate counts of code words. Some CAQDAS studies are indeed little more than extensions of quantitative work, and certain kinds of CAQDAS may build in such assumptions. For example, the U.S. Centers for Disease Control developed CDC EZ-Text for use in analyzing responses to open questions in structured interviewing studies. The program depends on all respondents' having been asked the same questions, and users must record missing data if this has not been done (Carey et al. 1998).

At the opposite extreme, however, some studies using CAQDAS programs seem to show no sign of any influence toward systematic analysis. Examples include Sue Middleton's (1996) report on interviews with teachers in New Zealand and Blake Poland's (1995) account of the experience of restrictions on smoking in Canadian public places. Both of these studies used NUD*IST, according to information gleaned from the developer's Web site, yet they share a common characteristic, hard to convey without presenting the full report, of impressionistic and anecdotal reporting of data. Both Middleton and Poland focus on presenting general arguments or surveys of their topics—in Middleton's case a historical account of discipline in schools, and in Poland's an account of the growth and scope of antismoking policy. Both authors drop extracts from interviews into their text where the interviewees' personal experiences appear to support the authors' general narratives. Neither reports any coding, searching, or accounting for negative instances. It is, in theory, possible that these authors' general narratives are the products of more rigorous analytic procedures supported by CAQDAS and then hidden from view. Alternatively, these examples suggest that although CAQDAS can enhance analytic rigor, this is not an inevitability.

CODE-AND-RETRIEVE STUDIES

More commonly, however, researchers who have used CAQDAS report unstruc-tured or loosely structured qualitative interviewing with coding and retrieval of coded segments that vary in complexity. Retrieval, for example, can be based on a simple search of all instances of a code in a data set or can involve filtering and other operations. Coding varies from somewhat descriptive, "in vivo" concepts that rely on the categories that interviewees themselves appear to be using to codes derived from theoretical literature, codes based on prior hypotheses, and codes created with the help of some form of abductive reasoning that approximates grounded theorizing.[2] Some researchers exploit CAQDAS autocoding features; others do not. There is nothing in the design of CAQDAS programs that enforces in vivo coding, but in practice it is quite common because it is an obvious thing for a researcher to do when working from a commonsense conception of research practice.

A good example of in vivo coding is found in research conducted by Jillian MacGuire and Deborah Botting (1990), who interviewed 17 nurses about the introduction of a new way of organizing work in a hospital setting. The researchers' analysis, using the Ethnograph, focused on the impact of the change on nurses' knowledge of patients, on communication among staff, and on staff members' relationships with patients and relatives. MacGuire and Botting developed 58 codes to summarize the data. For example, they subcoded segments marked as being about "communication" according to five categories of persons with whom nurses said they communicated. They could then retrieve segments about communication with relatives separately from segments about communication with patients or other staff and summarize the main points made.

Katie Buston's (1997) use of NUD*IST in her interview study with 112 young people experiencing chronic illness represents a step up from this. The abductive nature of Buston's coding is clear in that she drew on concepts such as "loss of self" and "stigma" from the sociological literature and "denial" from psychiatric ideas, as well as such in vivo concepts as "money worries" and "thoughts about the future." Additionally, Buston reports the use of face sheet variables as filters; she compared people with different kinds of health problem, people of different genders, people in different age groups, and people with different scores on a standardized psychiatric measure. She found autocoding to be helpful for dealing with a common problem of emergent coding schemes: After 15 interviews had been coded, it became clear that many of the young people with asthma were concerned about a shortage of affordable nebulizers. A string search for "nebulizer" identified instances where this was discussed in the already-coded interviews, so that Buston could inspect and code these accordingly without having to read the entire transcript again.

Buston's study shows that as we move up in levels of sophistication in code-and-retrieve studies, CAQDAS use increasingly involves creative and flexible adaptation of software features. Lyn Richards (1995), reporting on interviews with women experiencing menopause, describes the insertion of code words at the data entry stage and how she used the automatic string-search feature of NUD*IST to find and index these at a later stage. Maree Johnson and her colleagues (1999), in a study of bilingual staff in health care settings, categorized interviewees according to their degree of fluency in their second language and the extent to which their jobs involved complex communication across languages. These became filter variables in later searches the researchers conducted using NUD*IST; this allowed them to examine how combinations of these qualities resulted in different kinds of experiences for the staff involved. Sharon Hoerr, David Kallen, and Marcia Kwantes (1995) clearly wanted to go beyond the limitations of their software (the Ethnograph) in comparing counts of particular words used by interviewees to describe obese friends and strangers. Although they could feasibly have used the

Ethnograph, Hoerr and her colleagues probably conducted such an analysis manually, as this program is limited in its string-searching capacities, although not in the filter operations that Hoerr et al. exploited at other stages of their analysis.

PATTERN ANALYSIS OR GROUNDED THEORIZING?

It is common for researchers doing this kind of work to claim that they are using grounded theory. Fielding and Lee (1998) report that in a bibliographic search, 31 percent of 163 articles cited John Seidel, the author of the Ethnograph, and also contained references to the writings of Glaser and Strauss (1967) on grounded theory methodology. The claim to having done grounded theory, however, is less than convincing in some cases, and clearly a rhetorical purpose is served by such announcements. It is helpful to distinguish between what might be termed the "pattern analysis" (L. Richards, personal communication) of studies like the code-and-retrieve ones described above and studies that really seem to have used the operations described in grounded theory methodology.[3]

Patricia Sharpe and Jane Mezoff (1995) present the results of an interview study in which Ethnograph was used; participants were 20 older women who were interviewed regarding their beliefs about diet and health. Sharpe and Mezoff claim that their "data coding and analysis were based on the constant comparison method" (p. 9) and discuss the generation of "higher order categories based on properties and dimensions the concepts share; and delineating relationships or themes among the categories" (p. 9). They also describe "a movement between inductive and deductive thinking" (p. 9) and cite Anselm Strauss and Juliet Corbin (1990). Their results, however, suggest a far less complex procedure, being a straightforward listing, with illustrative examples, of the main beliefs that were presented by interviewees. We learn, for example, that many of the women believed that eating fruits and vegetables and avoiding alcohol and sweets is a good way to stay healthy. Many of the women liked to cook and bake for their families and took pride in the compliments they received for this. Some of the diabetic women, however, had some ideas that were not in line with current dietary recommendations for this condition. It is hard to see how this worthy but descriptive pattern analysis required the conceptual operations of grounded theorizing.

John Lange and Sue Burroughs-Lange (1994), on the other hand, are more convincing in their claims to have used grounded theory. Their study involved the use of NUD*IST to analyze interviews with 12 teachers about how they gained their professional knowledge. Like Sharpe and Mezoff, Lange and Burroughs-Lange describe the use of constant comparison and refer to Strauss and Corbin (1990), specifically referring to "our grounded theory." NUD*IST "ensured that the mechanics of the field research did not draw attention away from the analytic process" (p. 620) and that it "greatly enhances the generating and testing of theorizing possibilities" (p. 621). Their analysis led them to a "transformational model of continuous professional learning" (p. 621) in which teachers moved from an initial state of professional certainty to one of "feeling comfortable" (p. 621). Realizing this transformation involved an initial perception of professional challenges triggered by a variety of encounters. Gradually gaining an understanding of the nature of these challenges, the teachers then drew on a variety of sources (their own experience, elements in the school context, or national educational initiatives) to meet these challenges and to develop strategies for resolving uncertainty and for moving on professionally. Lange and Burroughs-Lange lay out this simple sequential model of challenges, encounters, understanding, sources, resolutions, and professional growth as a series of concepts, each of which summarizes a num-

ber of subconcepts. They illustrate these with examples that demonstrate the plausibility of links they make between categories and properties in the model, so that their claim to have created a grounded theory appears fully justified.

The dividing line between computer-assisted grounded theorizing and pattern analysis is sometimes not easy to draw—I have chosen the examples above to make the distinction easy to perceive. The fuzziness of this boundary appears to encourage some authors to exploit the rhetorical advantages inherent in making grounded theory announcements, which are apparently all the more plausible if a "theory-building" CAQDAS program is also seen to be involved.

CONCEPTUAL MAPPING

It is difficult to find studies that show clear uses made of conceptual mapping software, a feature promoted by developers who wish to stress the theory-building aspects of their products. Lange and Burroughs-Lange (1994), Johnson et al. (1999), and Linda Kittell, Phyllis Mansfield, and Ann Voda (1998) present graphical models of the concepts emerging from their research, but it is clear that these were created on paper rather than with the use of mapping software. Kittell et al., for example, present a flowchart to summarize typical career patterns of the responses to menopausal change evident in their interviews with women. This is a device commonly used to summarize qualitative data (e.g., see Taraborrelli 1993; Seale 1998), and a computer is not needed to make such a drawing. Inclusion of this feature in CAQDAS programs clearly serves the rhetorical purposes of software developers.

In fact, I was able to collect only one example of the use of this feature: Susanne Friese's (1999) account of her interviews with shoppers exhibiting different degrees of addiction to compulsive buying. Using ATLAS.ti, Friese interviewed 55 shoppers about their behavior and analyzed the data so as to exploit a variety of CAQDAS features. She made links with quantitative measures and based filtering operations on scores on these variables. Counts of coded segments appear frequently in Friese's text, as well as numerous verbatim extracts to illustrate these. Figure 31.1 reproduces Friese's ATLAS-generated conceptual map summarizing the links made by addicted buyers that they perceived led to, or were associated with, episodes of impulse buying. Because Friese displays similar maps for less addicted buyers, the reader is presented with a quick comparative summary of how these people experienced and explained their behavior. The result of Friese's use of these CAQDAS-inspired analytic devices is a striking and evocative report.

REASONING WITH NUMBERS

Quantitative and qualitative data can be combined in a variety of ways (see Seale 1999:chaps. 8-9). This is increasingly done in research projects, because most practicing social researchers recognize the relative autonomy of their craft from the absolutist epistemological and theoretical debates that once appeared to divide them. CAQDAS programs generally provide support for quantification, and this has been used in interview studies in a variety of ways.

At the most straightforward level, CAQDAS can be useful in providing counts of events, whether these are code words attached to data files or words embedded in text data. The problem of anecdotalism, whereby analysts select illustrative examples that support a general point without saying how common equivalent examples are or mentioning any systematic skews in their distribution, can thereby be addressed. My own studies have exploited this element of CAQDAS, as shown in the following two extracts:

It was very common for the people living on their own to be described either as not seeking help for problems that they had (65 instances covering 48 people), or refusing help when offered (144 instances in 83 people). Accounts of this often stressed that this reflected on the character of the person involved, although other associations were also made. In particular, 33 speakers gave 44 instances where they stressed the independence this indicated: "(She) never really talked about her problems, was very independent. . . "; "(She) was just one of those independent people who would struggle on. She wouldn't ask on her own"; "She used to shout at me because I was doing things for her. She didn't like to be helped. She was very independent." Being "self sufficient," "would not be beaten," and being said to "hate to give in" were associated with resisting help. (Seale 1996:84)

More commonly, however, the event of telling [a diagnosis of terminal illness] was described in a positive light. A content analysis of adjectives and adverbs used in these descriptions shows how speakers used them to reflect on the character of the teller: nice, nicely or very nice (12 instances), kind or kindly (12), good, really, very or ever so good (8), sympathetic (6), understanding (5), compassionate (2), great (2), wonderful (2), caring or very caring (2) and well (2). There was one instance each for the following: friendly, tactful, professionally, concerned, marvellous, willing, excellent, lovely, forthcoming, gently, helpful and considerate. A typical comment was made by the wife of a man who had died of cancer:

They were very *kind,* they couldn't have done more. They made me a cup of tea and a young lady doctor —she was *lovely*—she stayed with me a while and told me . . . they

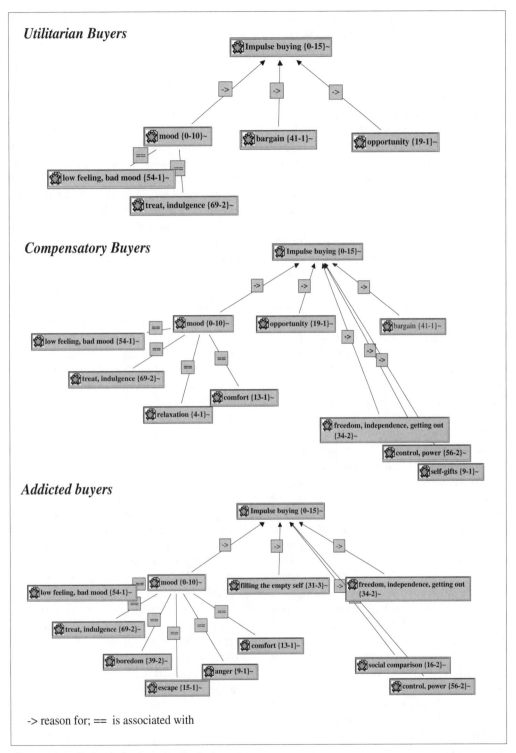

Figure 31.1 Reasons for Impulse Buying
SOURCE: Friese (1999).

couldn't do anything. I knew that really and I didn't blame them. (Seale 1995b:603)

The first of these relies on a count of code words, the second on a count of words generated by a string search of selected segments that shared a common code. In both cases the counts are designed to generate greater credibility, as readers would otherwise have to trust the author to have selected adjectives that were illustrative or common.

A step further toward quantitative methodology is represented by studies involving the use of measurement devices. For example, a sample survey might include qualitative data, derived either from unstructured interview data or from responses to open questions in structured survey instruments. R. Raguram et al. (1996) present a study of this sort, in which Textbase Alpha was used to analyze interviews with psychiatric patients in South India. Standardized quantitative measures showed that patients reporting depressive symptoms (for example, sadness, anxiety, fear) scored higher on a measure of stigma than did patients reporting somatoform symptoms (for example, limb and joint pain, headache). Qualitative analysis showed why and helped demonstrate the human impacts of the things that were being measured. Thus a patient who said, "I feel lonely . . . sad . . . like crying most of the time," also said, "I don't want anybody to know about my problem. I think others may say bad things about our family as a whole because of me. It would also affect my marriage." A patient who said, "If I walk I get pain in the back or thigh. I have pain all over," also said, "My friends know my problems. My in-laws, daughters all know about my aches and pains. The family understands my suffering" (p. 1047). The researchers, supported by systematic coding and retrieval, could generate lists of similar statements, filtered according to scores on the quantitative measures.

Causal reasoning in qualitative work is anathema to some, but others are less wary of it, and some specialist CAQDAS programs have been developed for this purpose. Conventional causal analysis through automated hypothesis testing is supported by HyperRESEARCH, which requires "factual" coding rather than "heuristic" indexing. For example, a heuristic coder might mark a text passage as being about the topic of religion; a "factual" coder might record whether or not the respondent indicates he or she believes in a god. Sharlene Hesse-Biber and Paul Dupuis (1995) give an example of hypothesis testing from a study of the causes of anorexia, testing the proposition that weight loss relates to certain antecedent conditions. A logical relationship between factual coding categories was written along the following lines: "*If* mother was critical of daughter's body image *and* mother-daughter relationship was strained *and* daughter experiences weight loss, *then* count as an example of mother's negative influence on daughter's self-image." Once particular interviews were identified as containing the codes involved, the researchers could retrieve the text for further examination in order to see whether support for this causal interpretation could be justified for each case.

"Qualitative comparison analysis" (Ragin 1987, 1995) is a method for causal reasoning that involves Boolean algebra. The relevant calculations are assisted by two CAQDAS programs: QCA and AQUAD. A detailed specification of this method is inappropriate here (for simplified explanations, see Seale 1999:chap. 9; Becker 1998:chap. 5); suffice it to say that from case study material the minimum conditions necessary to produce an outcome are specified through the analysis of "truth tables" that record the presence or absence of candidate causal factors. Thomas Schweizer (1991, 1996) used this in his secondary analysis of data from a Chinese village to establish what caused certain individuals to prosper and others to suffer during the momentous political and social changes that occurred in China between 1950 and 1980. Kati Rantala (1998) used QCA in an interview study of 14 teenagers attending art classes in Finland to establish a typology of their motivations for this activity.

Clearly, CAQDAS presents researchers with the possibility of incorporating numbers and statistical reasoning of various sorts. As in the examples discussed in the earlier section on rigor, it is clear that CAQDAS does not compel researchers to do this kind of work. But the encouragement to code systematically, as well as the capacity to search automatically for strings, places researchers in a position where quantification of qualitative events is made easy.

TURNING TO LANGUAGE

A variety of analytic approaches to research data driven by developments in social theory have emerged in recent years. Initially represented by conversation analysis and membership categorization work derived from the ethnomethodological tradition (for a review, see Silverman 1993; see also Baker, Chapter 37, this volume), more recently these have come to include several varieties of discourse analysis (Potter and Wetherell 1987; see also Schaeffer and Maynard, Chapter 28, this volume) and narrative analysis (Riessman 1993; see also Riessman, Chapter 33, this volume). These share an interest in the investigation of the effects of language, occurring either in talk or written texts, these commonly being either recordings or transcripts of interview material. CAQDAS remains relatively underused for these analytic purposes, so it is appropriate that I approach the topic of possible future developments by reviewing the possible role CAQDAS can play in this kind of work.

In one sense, of course, an interest in computerized analysis of language predates the development of CAQDAS programs for social research data. Linguists and literature specialists have long used computers to generate concordances and other string-search software to analyze literary style or language-in-use through quantitative content analysis. As noted earlier, some CAQDAS programs have features enabling elements of this approach. It is my belief that the intelligent use of CAQDAS could, in the future, assist in merging these linguistic analytic strategies with sociological concerns.

H. Russell Bernard and Gery Ryan (1998) express a similar conception in their useful review of approaches to text analysis. For them, the link is made in part through cognitive anthropology, which, among other things, has involved linguistic analysis in order to generate cognitive maps shared by people in a culture (see, e.g., Agar 1979, 1980; see also Johnson and Weller, Chapter 24, this volume). They report that this can involve the construction of what one author has called "personal semantic networks" (Strauss 1992), mapping the ideas that, say, interviewees express. Steve Cropper, Colin Eden, and Fran Ackermann (1990) describe software designed to assist the cognitive mapping of interview accounts; they use this technique in management consultancy exercises, citing personal construct theory as an antecedent. The software enables users to compare and combine the different maps generated in individual interviews, so that they can observe changes over time in a single person or group of people or make comparisons between people. Kathleen Carley and Michael Palmquist (1992), using STARTUP and CodeMap software, show how this can be applied in educational research, demonstrating how students' ideas (expressed in before-after interviews) about how they approach writing tasks change as a result of a course of instruction. The software is at one level a more elaborate version of the graphical mapping add-ons to conventional CAQDAS programs described earlier, but rather than being an end stage of analysis, it is used to generate more complex and revealing reports.

For Bernard and Ryan (1998), "schema analysis" represents a productive merging of the linguistic and sociological traditions. They illustrate this with anthropological studies of storytelling in Indian and Inuit cultures, but they could equally well have applied it to contemporary research interviews. Benjamin Colby (1966; Colby, Kennedy, and Milanesi 1991), for example, has developed a computer program (called SAGE) to analyze both the overall structural features and the linguistic content of stories. Initially, in work derived from interviews, he compared the words used by Zuni informants (a crop-growing group) with those used by Navajo (a sheepherding group). Crop growers are concerned with weather conditions above all; sheepherders are concerned with finding good grazing land and protection from stormy weather. Words concerning different forms of moisture (snow, rain, clouds) were accordingly found more often in Zuni stories than in Navajo stories, where storms, wind, and cold featured more frequently. Because traveling was more a feature of Navajo lifestyle, in Navajo stories home was depicted as a place of rest after a journey, and arrival home was often the end of the story; for Zuni, home was where things happened and events there occurred at the start of stories. Colby then became interested in identifying common structures in folktales and in using a computer to analyze the linguistic content of particular points in tales in order to reveal underlying cultural themes. In this respect his work develops that of Vladimir Propp (1968) on the structures of Russian folktales and of Catherine Riessman (1993) on the narrative structures of interview material.

Discussions of the uses of string searches appear from time to time in the CAQDAS literature. For example, Karl Moore, Robert Burbach, and Roger Heeler (1995), in a market research context, describe the use of CATPAC for the automated analysis of the language of interviews. They analyze answers to a question about breakdowns in contemporary family life, revealing systematic differences between respondents who blamed "internal" factors (divorce, money problems, and so on) and those who blamed "external" factors (the government, economy, crime).

The numerous messages posted by participants in e-mail discussion groups that support users of such CAQDAS programs provide more varied insights into the uses of string searching for linguistically oriented analysis. A recent exchange, involving John Seidel (the maker of the Ethnograph) and Lyn Richards (one of the developers of NUD*IST) focused on the merits and demerits of what the discussants called "autocoding." The use of this term to describe string searching is revealing, and predictably discussion focused initially on fears that this equated to automated thinking. Reference was made to the "shotgun correlations" that one sometimes sees in quantitative work, where a researcher generates a massive bivariate correlation matrix and selects the significant combinations on which to build an argument. The dangers of this were rapidly illustrated by subsequent discussants:

> [I attended] a seminar recently where . . . they counted the occurrences of key words in presidential addresses from the American Sociological Association and from the American Political Science Association. . . . They found that political scientists talk about politics and sociologists talk about society. Mmm. Then there was a set of words that both used. I wanted an analysis of the meanings, the use of argument, the structure of reasoning . . . but no, this was all too complex, let's just count the words! (Ezzard, personal communication 1999)

But this was then followed by users reporting instances of the usefulness of automated string searching. One user (Walsh) sensed that "opening doors" was an important metaphor for one interviewee in a study, and so used a string search to bring up rapidly all segments of her talk that contained this string, discarding false "hits." Another user (Downing) was interested in the way in which informants discussed "responsibility," as she was interested in how interviewees defined themselves as acting responsibly in the face of genetic risk, and so ran "check searches" on this word, its derivations, and related terms. Alan Cartwright, the developer of Code-A-Text, observed that a word concordance, if done at the outset of data analysis, could be useful in identifying themes that might not occur to the analyst by identifying key words, or those that were used very frequently. Walsh added that with string searches, one could find things where one least expected them, and this could have a suddenly great significance, like the Roman coins that someone once found in India.

Michael Fisher then reminded the discussants of his published example of the usefulness of string searches, in which he describes searching for word strings associated with "discipline" and "children" in a corpus of interviews in order to identify text segments in which parents discussed this aspect of their approach to child rearing (Fisher 1997). This is rather similar to the study reported by Anni George and Surinder Jaswal (1993), who describe how they searched for words associated with "honor" and "shame" in interviews with women in Bombay talking about their personal lives. Because these concepts rarely co-occurred in a text segment (unlike children and discipline), the researchers became aware of an important difference between public reputation and private morality. Fisher (1997) refers to this kind of analysis as "aerial reconnaissance" of data: It is useful for identifying broad patterns that deserve further detailed investigation "on the ground" but that might not be seen if the aerial view were not first taken.

The discussion ended with contributions pointing to the advantages offered to ana-

lysts of social research data of the more sophisticated aspects of the linguistic analysis tradition. Walsh described the need for semantic proximity software that could generate and sort a list of words in a document that are close in meaning to a chosen word. Peladeau announced that a beta version of WordStat that he was developing would do this, drawing on an electronically stored thesaurus. Klein referred to (unnamed) software that could detect negation automatically (thus distinguishing between "I like tea" and "I don't like tea"). For some, such contributions may once again raise the specter of automated thinking taking over analysis. A standard response to this kind of fear is that the technical tools of CAQDAS can take over only if the analyst allows them to do so.

HYPERTEXT

On a related issue, a development in CAQDAS that is explicitly derived from the preoccupations of contemporary social theory with linguistic representation is the exploitation of hypertext links. Although this builds on Ian Dey's (1993) earlier work, it is largely promoted by Paul Atkinson and his colleagues (Weaver and Atkinson 1995; Coffey, Holbrook, and Atkinson 1996), who draw on a poststructuralist critique of modes of representation in ethnographic writing (see, e.g., Atkinson 1990; see also in this volume Fontana, Chapter 8; Richardson, Chapter 42). This development addresses the complaint of some users of code-and-retrieve packages (e.g., Armstrong 1995; Sprokkereef et al. 1995) that these fragment data, encouraging the analyst to look across interviews rather than retain the whole context. Miriam Catterall and Pauline Maclaren (1997) develop this argument to say that coding and retrieval of segments out of their original context "freezes" the analysis of focus group data, making the analyst blind to the fact that participants often change their views during the course of a discussion —this change being the point of interest for many who run such groups.

Atkinson and his colleagues construct their work as a response to these concerns while drawing on a fashionable deconstruction of the conventional relationship between author and audience. Hypertext links allow the "analyst" of data, or the "reader" of an electronic report, to click on a highlighted word or icon and go instantly to some link that has been previously made. Thus a click on a code word might lead to an associated segment of text or to a picture or sound file illustrating the concept. This feature will be familiar to users of the Internet. It avoids decontextualization because the link does not retrieve a segment, but shows it in its original location, surrounded, for example, by the rest of the interview in which the segment of speech occurs. Additionally, the analyst can attach explanations, interpretations, and memos to particular links. Amanda Coffey and Paul Atkinson (1996) argue that, as an example, "we might also attach additional details, such as career details of particular respondents, their family trees, or details about their domestic lives" (p. 183). The reader is then able to explore original data in as much depth as he or she desires, and is thereby free of the need to attend to an overarching and exclusive presentation by a single author.

Although this is an interesting development in a new mode of presentation, it seems unlikely that readers will wish to do away with all modes of traditional representation in favor of such a deconstructable authorial presence. Many readers look to researchers for authoritative and concise statements delivered from a position of defensible expertise, based on a rigorous methodological approach that does not involve sharing methodological anxieties with the reader or pass over to them the hard work of drawing general conclusions about a disparate mass of loosely structured material.

◆ Conclusion

Many of the features of CAQDAS programs can be understood as rhetorical devices designed to appeal to both social scientists and social theorists. The more advanced features often seem to serve as symbols, helping software developers gain a foothold in the various cultures of qualitative work rather than being widely used in analysis. In this respect, however, CAQDAS is no different from other kinds of computer software. Like the word processor I am using to produce this text, CAQDAS programs have a basic core of frequently used procedures alongside a large variety of more advanced and more rarely used features. These core features—code-and-retrieve capabilities, automated string-search capabilities, and so on—have proven helpful to many qualitative researchers who have made the move to computer-assisted analysis.

Daniel Dohan and Martin Sanchez-Jankowski (1998) take the view that no single "killer app" has yet emerged from the CAQDAS scene. They define this as "a computer application that makes use of the computer irresistibly compelling by doing tasks unmanageable without computer assistance, in the fashion that spreadsheet programs *Visicalc* and *Lotus 1-2-3* motivated United States businesses to place personal computers on employees' desks" (p. 492). In part, they argue, this is due to the variety of conceptions of qualitative work that exist; those interested in exploring the "crisis of representation" brought about by postmodern critiques (Lincoln and Denzin 1994; see also Denzin, Chapter 40, this volume) pursue analytic directions that are rather different from those pursued by social researchers working in more pragmatic or scientifically oriented settings. Spreadsheets can solve common bureaucratic and organizational problems, but the problems faced by social researchers (such as issues of validity and reliability) cannot be resolved by computer programs because there are differing underlying conceptions about their nature and importance, as reflected in creative epistemological and political debates that characterize the research scene (Seale 1999). Social research can be conceived as a craft skill that draws on underlying philosophical and theoretical debates, using a variety of tools and procedures to explore particular research problems. CAQDAS is clearly something that can assist the craft of social research, as I hope has been demonstrated in this review, but it is unlikely and indeed undesirable that any single "killer app" should substitute for creative thinking about data analysis.

■ Notes

1. Developments in voice-recognition software seem set to transform the time-consuming business of interview transcription over the next few years. It is unlikely that CAQDAS programs will ever be able to transcribe automatically direct from tape, but transcribers who listen to tapes and speak the words into computers will work faster than typists once word recognition improves to an acceptable level.

2. I assume that it is by now a fairly well accepted point that pure induction cannot be plausibly proposed as a basis for grounded theory.

3. These involve theoretical sampling; constant comparison of categories and their properties, and how these interact; and open, axial, and selective coding (Glaser and Strauss 1967; Strauss and Corbin 1990).

■ Useful Web Resources

Details of how to join user discussion groups are available at the sites listed below. Demonstration versions of the packages can be downloaded from these sites or the links they provide. Scolari distributes CAQDAS programs in the United Kingdom.

ATLAS.ti: The Knowledge Workbench
(for ATLAS.ti):
    http://www.atlasti.de
CAQDAS Networking Project,
Surrey University:
    http://www.soc.surrey.ac.uk/caqdas
QSR International (for NUD*IST/NVivo):
    http://www.qsr.com.au
Qualis Research Associates
(for The Ethnograph):
    http://www.qualisresearch.com
Scolari: Sage Publications Software
(for CAQDAS programs):
    http://www.scolari.co.uk

■ References

Agar, M. 1979. "Themes Revisited: Some Problems in Cognitive Anthropology." *Discourse Processes* 2:11-31.

———. 1980. "Getting Better Quality Stuff: Methodological Competition in an Interdisciplinary Niche." *Urban Life* 9:34-50.

———. 1983. "Microcomputers as Field Tools." *Computers in the Humanities* 17:19-26.

Armstrong, D. 1995. "Finding a 'Role' for the ETHNOGRAPH in the Analysis of Qualitative Data." Pp. 63-80 in *Studies in Qualitative Methodology*, Vol. 5, *Computing and Qualitative Research*, edited by R. G. Burgess. Greenwich, CT: JAI.

Atkinson, P. A. 1990. *The Ethnographic Imagination: Textual Constructions of Reality*. London: Routledge.

Becker, H. S. 1970. "Problems of Inference and Proof in Participant Observation." Pp. 25-38 in H. S. Becker, *Sociological Work: Method and Substance*. Chicago: Aldine.

———. 1998. *Tricks of the Trade: How to Think about Your Research While You're Doing It*. Chicago: University of Chicago Press.

Becker, H. S., B. Geer, E. C. Hughes, and A. L. Strauss. 1961. *Boys in White: Student Culture in Medical School.* Chicago: University of Chicago Press.

Bernard, H. R. and G. W. Ryan. 1998. "Text Analysis: Qualitative and Quantitative Methods." Pp. 595-646 in *Handbook of Methods in Cultural Anthropology,* edited by H. R. Bernard. Walnut Creek, CA: AltaMira.

Buston, K. 1997. "NUD*IST in Action: Its Use and Its Usefulness in a Study of Chronic Illness in Young People." *Sociological Research Online* 2(3). Available Internet: http://www.socresonline. org.uk/socresonline/2/3/6.html

Carey, J. W., M. Morgan, and M. J. Oxtoby. 1996. "Intercoder Agreement in Analysis of Responses to Open-Ended Interview Questions: Examples from Tuberculosis Research." *Cultural Anthropology Methods* 8(3):1-5.

Carey, J. W., P. H. Wenzel, C. Reilly, J. Sheridan, and J. M. Steinberg. 1998. "CDC EZ-Text: Software for Management and Analysis of Semistructured Qualitative Data Sets." *Cultural Anthropology Methods* 10(1):14-20.

Carley, K. and M. Palmquist. 1992. "Extracting, Representing and Analyzing Mental Models." *Social Forces* 70:601-36.

Catterall, M. and P. Maclaren. 1997 "Focus Group Data and Qualitative Analysis Programs: Coding the Moving Picture as Well as the Snapshots." *Sociological Research Online* 2(1). Available Internet: http://www.socresonline.org.uk/socresonline/2/1/6.html

Coffey, A. and P. A. Atkinson. 1996. *Making Sense of Qualitative Data Analysis: Complementary Strategies.* London: Sage.

Coffey, A., B. Holbrook, and P. A. Atkinson. 1996. "Qualitative Data Analysis: Technologies and Representations." *Sociological Research On-line* 1(1). Available Internet: http://www.socresonline. org.uk/socresonline/1/1/4.html

Colby, B. N. 1966. "The Analysis of Culture Content and the Patterning of Narrative Concern in Texts." *American Anthropologist* 68:374-88.

Colby, B. N., S. Kennedy, and L. Milanesi. 1991. "Content Analysis, Cultural Grammars and Computers." *Qualitative Sociology* 14:373-84.

Cropper, S., C. Eden, and F. Ackermann. 1990. "Keeping Sense of Accounts Using Computer-Based Cognition Maps." *Social Science Computer Review* 8:345-66.

Dey, I. 1993. *Qualitative Data Analysis: A User-Friendly Guide for Social Scientists.* London: Routledge.

Dohan, D. and M. Sanchez-Jankowski. 1998. "Using Computers to Analyze Ethnographic Field Data: Theoretical and Practical Considerations." *Annual Review of Sociology* 24:477-98.

Fielding, N. G. and R. M. Lee. 1995. "Confronting CAQDAS: Choice and Contingency." Pp. 1-24 in *Studies in Qualitative Methodology,* Vol. 5, *Computing and Qualitative Research,* edited by R. G. Burgess. Greenwich, CT: JAI.

———. 1998. *Computer Analysis and Qualitative Research.* Thousand Oaks, CA: Sage.

Fisher, M. 1997. *Qualitative Computing: Using Software for Qualitative Data Analysis.* Aldershot, England: Ashgate.

Friese, S. 1999. *Self Concept and Identity in a Consumer Society: Aspects of Symbolic Product Meaning.* Marburg, Germany: Tectum.

George, A. and S. Jaswal. 1993. "An Example of Searching for Words Using GOfer." *Cultural Anthropology Methods* 5(3):12.

Glaser, B. G. and A. L. Strauss. 1967. *The Discovery of Grounded Theory: Strategies for Qualitative Research.* Chicago: Aldine.

Hesse-Biber, S. 1995. "Unleashing Frankenstein's Monster? The Use of Computers in Qualitative Research." Pp. 25-42 in *Studies in Qualitative Methodology,* Vol. 5, *Computing and Qualitative Research,* edited by R. G. Burgess. Greenwich, CT: JAI.

Hesse-Biber, S. and P. Dupuis. 1995. "Hypothesis Testing in Computer-Aided Qualitative Data Analysis." Pp. 129-35 in *Computer-Aided Qualitative Data Analysis: Theory, Methods and Practice,* edited by U. Kelle. London: Sage.

Hoerr, S. L., D. Kallen, and M. Kwantes. 1995. "Peer Acceptance of Obese Youth: A Way to Improve Weight Control Efforts?" *Ecology of Food and Nutrition* 33:203-13.

Johnson, M., C. Noble, C. Matthews, and N. Aguilar. 1999. "Bilingual Communicators within the Health Care Setting." *Qualitative Health Research* 9:329-43.

Kelle, U. 1997. "Theory Building in Qualitative Research and Computer Programs for the Management of Textual Data." *Sociological Research Online* 2(2). Available Internet: http://www.socresonline.org.uk/socresonline/2/2/1.html

Kittell, L. A., P. K. Mansfield, and A. M. Voda. 1998. "Keeping Up Appearances: The Basic Social Process of the Menopausal Transition." *Qualitative Health Research* 8:618-33.

Lange, J. D. and S. G. Burroughs-Lange. 1994. "Professional Uncertainty and Professional Growth: A Case Study of Experienced Teachers." *Teaching and Teacher Education* 10:617-31.

Lazarsfeld, P. F. and M. Rosenberg. 1955. *The Language of Social Research: A Reader in the Methodology of Social Research.* Glencoe, IL: Free Press.

Lincoln, Y. S. and N. K. Denzin. 1994. "The Fifth Moment." Pp. 575-86 in *Handbook of Qualitative Research,* edited by N. K. Denzin and Y. S. Lincoln. Thousand Oaks, CA: Sage.

MacGuire, J. M. and D. A. Botting. 1990. "The Use of the ETHNOGRAPH Program to Identify the Perceptions of Nursing Staff Following the Introduction of Primary Nursing in an Acute Medical Ward for Elderly People." *Journal of Advanced Nursing* 15:1120-27.

Miall, D. S., ed. 1990. *Humanities and the Computer: New Directions.* Oxford: Clarendon.

Middleton, S. 1996. "Uniform Bodies? Disciplining Sexuality in School 1968-1995." *Women's Studies Journal* 12(2):9-35.

Moore, K., R. Burbach, and R. Heeler. 1995. "Using Neural Nets to Analyze Qualitative Data." *Marketing Research* 7(1):35-39.

Northey, W. F. 1997. "Using QSR NUD*IST to Demonstrate Confirmability in Qualitative Research." *Family Science Review* 10:170-79.

Poland, B. D. 1995. "Smoking, Stigma and the Purification of Public Space." Pp. 208-25 in *Putting Health into Place: Landscape, Identity and Well-Being,* edited by R. A. Kearns and W. M. Gesler. Syracuse, NY: Syracuse University Press.

Potter, J. and M. Wetherell. 1987. *Discourse and Social Psychology: Beyond Attitudes and Behaviour.* London: Sage.

Propp, V. I. 1968. *The Morphology of the Folktale.* 2d rev. ed. Edited by L. A. Wagner. Austin: University of Texas Press.

Ragin, C. C. 1987. *The Comparative Method: Moving beyond Quantitative and Qualitative Strategies.* Berkeley: University of California Press.

———. 1995. "Using Qualitative Comparative Analysis to Study Configurations." Pp. 177-89 in *Computer-Aided Qualitative Data Analysis: Theory, Methods and Practice,* edited by U. Kelle. London: Sage.

Raguram R., M. G. Weiss, S. M. Channabasavanna, and G. M. Devins. 1996. "Stigma, Depression, and Somatization in South India." *American Journal of Psychiatry* 153:1043-49.

Rantala, K. 1998. "Art as Communicative Practice for Teenagers." *Young: Nordic Journal of Youth Research* 6(4):39-58.

Richards, L. 1995. "Transition Work! Reflections on a Three-Year NUD*IST Project." Pp. 105-40 in *Studies in Qualitative Methodology,* Vol. 5, *Computing and Qualitative Research,* edited by R. G. Burgess. Greenwich, CT: JAI.

Riessman, C. K. 1993. *Narrative Analysis.* Newbury Park, CA: Sage.

Schweizer, T. 1991. "The Power Struggle in a Chinese Community, 1950-1980: A Social Network Analysis of the Duality of Actors and Events." *Journal of Quantitative Anthropology* 3:19-44.

———. 1996. "Actor and Event Orderings across Time: Lattice Representation and Boolean Analysis of the Political Disputes in Chen Village, China." *Social Networks* 18:247-66.

Seale, C. F. 1995a. "Dying Alone." *Sociology of Health and Illness* 17:376-92.

———. 1995b. "Heroic Death." *Sociology* 29:597-613.

———. 1996. "Living Alone towards the End of Life." *Ageing and Society* 16:75-91.

———, ed. 1998. *Researching Society and Culture.* London: Sage.

———. 1999. *The Quality of Qualitative Research.* London: Sage.

Sharpe, P. A. and J. S. Mezoff. 1995. "Beliefs about Diet and Health: Qualitative Interviews with Low Income Older Women in the Rural South." *Journal of Women and Aging* 7(1-2):5-18.

Silverman, D. 1993. *Interpreting Qualitative Data: Methods for Analysing Talk, Text and Interaction.* London: Sage.

Sprokkereef, A., E. Lakin, C. J. Pole, and R. G. Burgess. 1995. "The Data, the Team and the ETHNOGRAPH." Pp. 81-104 in *Studies in Qualitative Methodology,* Vol. 5, *Computing and Qualitative Research,* edited by R. G. Burgess. Greenwich, CT: JAI.

Strauss, A. L. and J. Corbin. 1990. *Basics of Qualitative Research: Grounded Theory Procedures and Techniques.* Newbury Park, CA: Sage.

Strauss, C. 1992. "What Makes Tony Run? Schemas as Motive Reconsidered." Pp. 191-224 in *Human Motives and Cultural Models,* edited by R. G. D'Andrade and C. Strauss. Cambridge: Cambridge University Press.

Taraborrelli, P. 1993. "Becoming a Carer." Pp. 172-86 in *Researching Social Life,* edited by N. Gilbert. London: Sage.

Torode, B. 1998. "Narrative Analysis Using Code-A-Text." *Qualitative Health Research* 8:414-32.

Triandafyllidou, A. 1999. " 'Racists? Us? Are You Joking?': The Discourse of Social Exclusion of Immigrants in Greece and Italy." Pp. 186-205 in *Eldorado or Fortress? Migration in Southern Europe,* edited by R. King, G. Lazaridis, and C. Tsardanidis. London: Macmillan.

Triandafyllidou, A. and A. Fotiou. 1998. "Sustainability and Modernity in the European Union: A Frame Theory Approach to Policy-Making." *Sociological Research Online* 3(1). Available Internet: http://www.socresonline.org.uk/socresonline/3/1/2.html

Weaver, A. and P. A. Atkinson. 1995. *Microcomputing and Qualitative Data Analysis.* Aldershot, England: Avebury.

Whyte, W. F. 1981. *Street Corner Society: The Social Structure of an Italian Slum.* 3d ed. Chicago: University of Chicago Press.

Part V

ANALYTIC STRATEGIES

The analytic strategies presented in this part of the *Handbook* concentrate on qualitative data. Procedures for analyzing quantitative material have been well documented, with discussion typically centering on the multivariate statistical analysis of numerical data. Statistical innovations abound as researchers stretch the horizons of descriptive, inductive, and causal analysis (see Singleton and Straits, Chapter 3, this volume). Qualitative analytic strategies have evolved differently —and less systematically. A broader range of approaches is available, approaches that reflect the diverse theoretical aims and perspectives that qualitative researchers bring to their craft and material.

Each theoretical perspective implicates a set of procedures or ways of organizing, categorizing, and interpreting data. There is no single approach to qualitative analysis. Even though it might appear that a naturalistic field-worker, say, takes careful notes and interprets those notes in relation to a conceptual framework, much as a constructionist field-worker might do, these alternative perspectives suggest different analytic strategies. The naturalistic field-worker likely orients to the data as the facts of experience, whereas the constructionist field-worker emphasizes and aims to describe *how* those facts come into being in the first place. The methods themselves —observing, recording field notes, coding, categorizing, extrapolating, interpreting— belie what those methods are considered to be doing in relation to empirical material. In the case of the naturalist, for instance, method is seen as a matter of "gathering" data; constructionist methods orient more to the goal of revealing *how* social actions and interactions become data. This is a distinction that Kathy Charmaz makes in her chapter in this section on forms of grounded theory analysis; she challenges the view that grounded theory methodology is a single analytic strategy.

Of course, these perspectives are not completely distinct from one another, either; there can be considerable overlap in their analytic sensibilities. Studies of narrative, for example, center on stories in some form or other; they might be informed by interpersonal approaches at one end of a continuum (see Riessman, Chapter 33) and cultural or historical perspectives at the other (see Cándida Smith, Chapter 34). Yet they all typically aim to identify narrative themes or narrative structures. How they interpret themes and structures distinguishes them, but the fact that both have this aim, and not some alternative—membership categorization analysis, for example (see Baker, Chapter 37)—serves to group them as narrative strategies.

Another feature of qualitative analysis that makes it less uniform than its quantitative counterpart is the traditional goal of conceptualizing empirical material at close range and throughout the data collection process. Quantitative analysis is, by and large, a set of activities that come *after* the data are collected. Qualitative analysis, in contrast, applies from the very start and continues throughout the data collection process, as well as after it is completed. The emphasis is as much on concept formation, elaboration, and understanding as it is on testing particular hypotheses and empirical generalization. Closeness to empirical material also compels qualitative researchers to adapt their methods and analytic strategies to the ongoing observational and narrative contingencies of their data. This, too, adds to the greater variability in this area.

Although the chapters in this section do not cover the strategic waterfront of qualitative analysis, they do represent well-established options. One very popular strategy stems from Barney Glaser and Anselm Strauss's development in the 1960s of what has come to be called *grounded theory methodology* (see Charmaz, Chapter 32). Reacting to the post–World War II emphasis in social research on formal theory construction and hypothesis formation separate from the data, Glaser and Strauss developed an analytic strategy that views theoretical formulation as best conducted from the ground up, meaning in close and continuous relation to empirical material.

Charmaz's chapter presents this approach, which has grown immensely popular, especially in qualitative nursing and educational research. Charmaz adds a constructionist twist to the approach, drawing inspiration from the many perspectives in social research that now view social life as continuously created and not simply as empirically available.

Three chapters in this section—those by Catherine Kohler Riessman, Richard Cándida Smith, and Barbara Czarniawska—reflect the massive influence that narrative perspectives now have as analytic strategies. These perspectives approach empirical material in terms of their storylike qualities. Taking for granted that experience comes to us in the form of stories, the authors show what can be done with interview data from that point of view. Riessman focuses on personal stories, narratives that give shape to individual experience. Typically, she searches for the narrative strategies that storytellers use to formulate their experiences, such as compartmentalizing them by narrating them differently. Borrowing from literary analysis, Riessman points out the narrative importance of a variety of story elements, such as scene setting, characterization, emplotment, and thematization.

Not all narrative approaches take up personal stories. In their chapters, Cándida Smith and Czarniawska bring other disciplinary and theoretical sensibilities to bear on narrative material. Cándida Smith presents us with a way of orienting to oral history interviews. As he explains, there are a number of perspectives available, ranging from naturalistic efforts to represent historical events through personal stories (see Atkinson, Chapter 6, this volume) to constructionist views that take concerted account of the ways respondents make meaning by appropriating historical material for their own uses. Elaborating the latter view, Cándida Smith is not concerned in his analysis with the "mistakes" made in the narrative process, but rather with documenting the ways interviewees communicatively build their worlds out of the historical material available to them. Czarniawska also

takes narrative in a constructionist direction, focusing on organizational ("organizing") processes. In her view, organizations are not so much captured in their stories as they are brought to life through narrative. Indeed, as she presents her material, we come to learn that the analytic strategy presented takes the organization actually to be its manifold stories.

In their chapter in this section, Marjorie DeVault and Liza McCoy offer an analytic strategy for interview material originally formulated by Dorothy Smith, a Canadian feminist working at the intersection of institutions and everyday life. Although the strategy has come to be called *institutional ethnography*, the approach is not immediately recognizable as either institutional or ethnographic. As the subtitle of the DeVault and McCoy's chapter indicates, the approach orients to the use of "interviews to investigate ruling relations." According to DeVault, McCoy, and their colleagues, researchers can make institutional discourses and their lived normative preferences visible by approaching interviewees' responses as they are mediated by the relations of ruling in which the interviewees' experiences are embedded. Distinct traces of institutional relations of ruling can be uncovered in institutionally mediated interview material. The result is that researchers can use interviews to study institutional processes, revealing in individual testaments what traditional ethnographers might otherwise document from observational material.

The last chapter in this section, by Carolyn Baker, is less focused on the substance of interview material than it is on strategies for analyzing how respondents' use of categories gives meaning to what they say about their lives and experiences. Presenting various forms of what ethnomethodologists call "categorization analysis," Baker shows how member categorization (not the researcher's categories or codes for interview material) serves to make meaning. Here again, we are presented with respondents who actively construct their experiences, not merely report them in varied detail.

32

QUALITATIVE INTERVIEWING AND GROUNDED THEORY ANALYSIS

◆ Kathy Charmaz

Novices raise two fundamental questions about qualitative interviewing: (a) How do you do it? and (b) How do you analyze your interview data? In this chapter, I address how grounded theory methods shape qualitative interviewing in relation to personal narratives and guide analysis of interview data. Essentially, grounded theory methods consist of flexible strategies for focusing and expediting qualitative data collection and analysis. These methods provide a set of inductive steps that successively lead the researcher from studying concrete realities to rendering a conceptual understanding of them. The founders of grounded theory, Barney G. Glaser and Anselm L. Strauss (1967), aimed to develop middle-range

theories from qualitative data. Hence they not only intended to conceptualize qualitative data, but planned to demonstrate relations between conceptual categories and to specify the conditions under which theoretical relationships emerge, change, or are maintained.

Grounded theory methods consist of guidelines that aid the researcher (a) to study social and social psychological processes, (b) to direct data collection, (c) to manage data analysis, and (d) to develop an abstract theoretical framework that explains the studied process. Grounded theory researchers collect data and analyze it simultaneously from the initial phases of research. Researchers cannot know exactly what the most significant social and social

AUTHOR'S NOTE: Thanks are due to Jaber F. Gubrium, James A. Holstein, and Sally Hutchinson for their extensive critiques of an earlier draft of this chapter. I also thank Wanda Boda, Maureen Buckley, Noel Byrne, Scott Miller, Leilani Nishime, Tom Rosin, and Elisa Valesquez, participants in a Sonoma State University faculty writing seminar, for their comments on a preliminary statement of these ideas.

◆ 675

psychological processes are in particular settings, so they start with areas of interest to them and form preliminary interviewing questions to open up those areas. They explore and examine research participants' concerns and then further develop questions around those concerns, subsequently seeking participants whose experiences speak to these questions. This sequence is repeated several times during a research project. Hence grounded theory methods keep researchers close to their gathered data rather than to what they may have previously assumed or wished was the case. These methods give researchers tools for analyzing data as well as for obtaining additional focused data that inform, extend, and refine emerging analytic themes. Thus the interviews that grounded theory researchers conduct are focused; grounded theory methods create a tight fit between the collected data and analysis of those data.

In-depth qualitative interviewing fits grounded theory methods particularly well (see in this volume Warren, Chapter 4; Johnson, Chapter 5). At first glance, the advantages of qualitative interviewing for conducting a grounded theory analysis seem unassailable. An interviewer assumes more direct control over the construction of data than does a researcher using most other methods, such as ethnography or textual analysis. As John Lofland and Lyn Lofland (1984, 1995) have noted, the interview is a directed conversation. Grounded theory methods require that researchers take control of their data collection and analysis, and in turn these methods give researchers more analytic control over their material. Qualitative interviewing provides an open-ended, in-depth exploration of an aspect of life about which the interviewee has substantial experience, often combined with considerable insight. The interview can elicit views of this person's subjective world. The interviewer sketches the outline of these views by delineating the topics and drafting the questions. Interviewing is a flexible, emergent technique;

ideas and issues emerge during the interview, and the interviewer can then immediately pursue these leads.

Grounded theory methods depend upon a similar kind of flexibility. In addition to picking up and pursuing themes in interviews, grounded theorists look for ideas by studying data and then returning to the field to gather focused data to answer analytic questions and to fill conceptual gaps. Thus the combination of flexibility and control inherent in in-depth interviewing techniques fits grounded theory strategies for increasing the analytic incisiveness of the resultant analysis. Grounded theory interviewing differs from in-depth interviewing as the research process proceeds in that grounded theorists narrow the range of interview topics to gather specific data for their theoretical frameworks.

Throughout this chapter, I draw upon my earlier grounded theory studies of how adults with serious chronic illnesses experienced their conditions. After completing a doctoral dissertation in this area based on notes from 55 interviews (Charmaz 1973), I conducted 115 more intensive interviews, almost all of which were tape-recorded. These interviews focused on the effects of illness upon the self and relationships among self, time, and illness (Charmaz 1987, 1991a). The English language does not include a full, explicit, and shared vocabulary for talking about time. Thus the open-ended nature of grounded theory methods and the emphasis on emergent ideas in this approach proved especially helpful for the study of implicit meanings of time. My next project looked directly at what it means to have a chronically ill body; that work built upon earlier data and 25 new focused interviews for which there was a detailed interview guide, 12 of which were conducted with earlier participants (Charmaz 1995a, 1999).

In the past, most discussions of grounded theory have taken data collection practices for granted, giving them scant attention. Glaser and Strauss (1967; Glaser 1978) stressed the analysis and its resultant strengths. They redirected qualitative research to turn toward theoretical statements and reduced the distance between empirical research and theorizing. Yet data and theorizing are intertwined. Obtaining rich data provides a solid foundation for developing robust theories. Grounded theorists must attend to the quality of their data. Thus in the following pages I not only outline the logic of grounded theory but also attempt to show how researchers can obtain and use rich data with which to construct viable grounded theories.

◆ Variations on Grounded Theory

All variants of grounded theory include the following strategies: (a) simultaneous data collection and analysis, (b) pursuit of emergent themes through early data analysis, (c) discovery of basic social processes within the data, (d) inductive construction of abstract categories that explain and synthesize these processes, (e) sampling to refine the categories through comparative processes, and (f) integration of categories into a theoretical framework that specifies causes, conditions, and consequences of the studied processes (see Charmaz 1990, 1995b, 2000; Glaser 1978, 1992; Glaser and Strauss 1967; Strauss 1987, 1995).

Grounded theory methods have taken two somewhat different forms since their creation: constructivist and objectivist (Charmaz 2000). The constructivist approach places priority on the phenomena of study and sees both data and analysis as created from the shared experiences of researcher and participants and the researcher's relationships with participants (see Charmaz 1990, 1995b, 2000; Charmaz and Mitchell 1996, 2001). In this view, any method is always a means, rather than an end in itself. Methods do not ensure knowing; they may only provide more or less useful tools for learning. Construc-

tivists study how participants construct meanings and actions, and they do so from as close to the inside of the experience as they can get. Constructivists also view data analysis as a construction that not only locates the data in time, place, culture, and context, but also reflects the researcher's thinking. Thus the sense that the researcher makes of the data does not inhere entirely within those data.

Objectivist grounded theory, in contrast, emphases the viewing of data as real in and of themselves. This position assumes that data represent objective facts about a knowable world. The data already exist in the world, and the researcher finds them. In this view, the conceptual sense the grounded theorist makes of the data derives from the data: Meaning inheres in the data and the grounded theorist discovers it (see, e.g., Strauss and Corbin 1990; Glaser and Strauss 1967; Glaser 1978). This perspective assumes an external reality awaiting discovery and an unbiased observer who records facts about it. Objectivist grounded theorists believe that careful application of their methods produces theoretical understanding. Hence their role becomes more that of a conduit for the research process than that of a creator of it. Given these assumptions, proponents of objectivist grounded theory would argue for a stricter adherence to grounded theory steps than would constructivists.[1]

Objectivist grounded theorists also assume (a) that research participants can and will relate the significant facts about their situations, (b) that the researcher remains separate and distant from research participants and their realities, (c) that the researcher represents the participants and their realities as an external authority, and (d) that the research report offers participants a useful analysis of their situations. Interviewers who subscribe to these assumptions look for explicit themes, gather findings (i.e., facts), and treat their analytic renderings as objective.

The dual roots of grounded theory in Chicago school sociology and in positivism have produced both advantages and ambiguities. The Chicago school pragmatist, symbolic interactionist, and field research traditions that Anselm Strauss brought to grounded theory give this method its open-ended emphasis on process, meaning, action, and usefulness.[2] Barney Glaser's positivism imbued grounded theory with empiricism, rigorous codified methods, and its somewhat ambiguous specialized language.[3] Glaser and Strauss (1967) developed grounded theory methods to codify explicit procedures for qualitative data analysis and to construct useful middle-range theories from the data.

My approach to grounded theory builds upon a symbolic interactionist theoretical perspective with constructivist methods (Charmaz 1990, 1995b, 2000). I make the following assumptions: (a) Multiple realities exist, (b) data reflect the researcher's and the research participants'[4] mutual constructions, and (c) the researcher, however incompletely, enters and is affected by participants' worlds. This approach explicitly provides an *interpretive* portrayal of the studied world, not an exact picture of it (Charmaz 1995b, 2000; Guba and Lincoln 1994; Schwandt 1994).[5] The researcher aims to learn participants' implicit meanings of their experiences to build a conceptual analysis of them. A constructivist approach takes implicit meanings, experiential views, and grounded theory analyses as constructions of reality. A constructivist approach to grounded theory complements symbolic interactionism because both emphasize the study of how action and meaning are constructed.

◆ Grounded Theory Interviewing as Unfolding Stories

Interview data are useful for grounded theory studies that address individual experience. For example, many people experience disrupted lives because of grief, illness, marital dissolution, or financial crises, but they may not have sustained contact with other people who face similar troubles (Charmaz 1991a; Stephenson 1985). A researcher can create an interpretive analysis of their experiences through qualitative interviewing.[6] Grounded theorists aim to explain social and social psychological processes. In my work, such processes have included situating the self in time, disclosing illness, and adapting to impairment. In researching these processes, I had to identify the conditions and sequences surrounding what chronically ill people did and what happened to them as a result (see also Morse, Chapter 16, this volume). A hazard in such an undertaking is the possibility that the researcher will aim to define the analytic story at the expense of the participant's story. Thus the researcher needs to achieve a balance between hearing the participant's story and probing for processes.

A grounded theory interviewer's questions need to define and to explore processes. The interviewer starts with the participant's story and fills it out by attempting to locate it within a basic social process. The basic grounded theory question driving a study is, "What is happening here?" (Glaser 1978). In this case, the "happening" is the experience or central problem addressed in the research. Most grounded theory interview studies do not look at what is happening in the construction of the story during the interview. Objectivist grounded theorists view interview questions as the means for gathering "facts." In this view, interview questions are more or less useful tools to obtain these facts. In contrast, constructivist grounded theorists see an interview as starting with the central problem (which defines suitable participants for the study) but proceeding from how interviewer and subject co-construct the interview. Their constructions are taken as the grist of the study, but constructivists frame much of this material as "views," rather than hard facts. Constructivists emphasize locating their data in context. Thus they may attend to the context of the specific interview, the context of the individual's life, and the contextual aspects of the study and research problem within the setting, society, and historical moment.[7] Objectivists, in contrast, concentrate on the specific data they have and treat. Thus their analyses may glow with accuracy but fade in context. Both constructivist and objectivist grounded theorists try to get at key events, their contexts, and the processes that contribute to shaping those events.

The first question may suffice for the first interview if stories tumble out. Receptive "uh huhs" or a few clarifying questions or comments may keep a story coming when the participant can and wants to tell it. I choose questions carefully and ask them slowly to foster participants' reflections. Grounded theory researchers use in-depth interviewing to explore, not to interrogate (Charmaz 1991b). Framing questions takes skill and practice. Questions must both explore the interviewer's topic and fit the participant's experience. As is evident below, questions must be sufficiently general to cover a wide range of experiences as well as narrow enough to elicit and explore the participant's specific experience.

I list some sample questions below to illustrate how grounded theory interviewers frame questions to study process. These questions also reflect a symbolic interactionist emphasis on learning participants' subjective meanings and on stressing participants' actions. The questions are intended to tap individual experience. For a project concerning organizational or social processes, I direct questions to the collective practices first and then later attend to the individual's participation in and views of those practices (see also in this volume DeVault and McCoy, Chapter 36; Czarniawska, Chapter 35). The questions below are offered merely as examples. I have never asked all of them in a single interview, and often I do not get beyond the initial set of questions in one session. I sel-

dom take an interview guide with me into an interview, as I prefer to keep the interaction informal and conversational.

Researchers who are working on grounded theory studies of life disruptions or of deviant behaviors of some kind risk being intrusive. Participants may tell stories during interviews that they never dreamed they would tell. Their comfort should be of higher priority for the interviewer than obtaining juicy data. Thus concluding questions should be slanted toward positive responses, to bring the interview to closure on a positive note. No interview should end abruptly after the interviewer has asked the most searching questions or when the participant is distressed. The rhythm and pace of the interview should bring the participant back to a normal conversational level before the interview ends. The following examples of interview questions illustrate the above points.

EXAMPLES OF GROUNDED THEORY INTERVIEW QUESTIONS

Initial Open-Ended Questions

1. Tell me about what happened [or how you came to _____].

2. When, if at all, did you first experience _____ [or notice _____]?

3. [If so,] What was it like? What did you think then? How did you happen to _____? Who, if anyone, influenced your actions? Tell me about how he/she or they influenced you.

4. Could you describe the events that led up to _____ [or preceded _____]?

5. What contributed to _____?

6. What was going on in your life then? How would you describe how you viewed _____ before _____ happened? How, if at all, has your view of _____ changed?

7. How would you describe the person you were then?

Intermediate Questions

1. What, if anything, did you know about _____?

2. Tell me about your thoughts and feelings when you learned about _____.

3. What happened next?

4. Who, if anyone, was involved? When was that? How were they involved?

5. Tell me about how you learned to handle _____.

6. How, if at all, have your thoughts and feelings about _____ changed since _____?

7. What positive changes have occurred in your life [or _____] since _____?

8. What negative changes, if any, have occurred in your life [or _____] since _____?

9. Tell me how you go about _____. What do you do?

10. Could you describe a typical day for you when you are _____? [Probe for different times.] Now tell me about a typical day when you are _____.

11. Tell me how you would describe the person you are now. What most contributed to this change [or continuity]?

12. As you look back on _____, are there any other events that stand out in your mind? Could you describe it [each one]? How did this event affect what happened? How did you respond to _____ [the event; the resulting situations]?

13. Could you describe the most important lessons you learned about _____ through experiencing _____?

14. Where do you see yourself in two years [five years, ten years, as appropriate]? Describe the person you hope to be then. How would you compare the person you hope to be and the person you see yourself as now?

15. What helps you to manage _____? What problems might you encounter? Tell me the sources of these problems.

16. Who has been the most helpful to you during this time? How has he/she been helpful?

Ending Questions

1. What do you think are the most important ways to _____? How did you discover [or create] them? How has your experience before _____ affected how you handled _____?

2. Tell me about how your views [and/or actions depending on topic and preceding responses] may have changed since you have _____?

3. How have you grown as a person since _____? Tell me about your strengths that you discovered or developed through _____. [If appropriate] What do you most value about yourself now? What do others most value in you?

4. After having these experiences, what advice would you give to someone who has just discovered that he or she _____?

5. Is there anything that you might not have thought about before that occurred to you during this interview?

6. Is there anything you would like to ask me?

There is overlap in the questions above, and this is intentional. Such overlap allows the interviewer to go back to an earlier thread to gain more information or to winnow unnecessary or potentially uncomfortable questions. Taking notes on key points during the interview helps as long as it does not distract either interviewer or participant. Notes remind the interviewer to return to earlier points and suggest how he or she might frame follow-up questions.

Grounded theory researchers must guard against forcing data into preconceived categories (Glaser 1978). Interviewing, more than other forms of qualitative data collection, challenges researchers to create a balance between asking significant questions and forcing responses. An interviewer's questions and interviewing style shape the context, frame, and content of the study. Subsequently, a naive researcher may inadvertently force interview data into preconceived categories. Asking the wrong questions can result in the researcher's forcing the data, as can the way questions are asked, with which emphasis, and with what kind of pacing.

By asking the wrong questions, the interviewer will fail to elicit the participant's experience in his or her own language. Such questions superimpose the researcher's concepts, concerns, and discourse upon the subject's reality—from the start. Grounded theory analysis attempts to move inductively upward from data to theoretical rendering. When either forced or superficial questions shape the data collection, the subsequent analysis suffers. Thus researchers need to be constantly reflexive about the nature of their questions and whether they work for the specific participants.

The focus of the interview and the specific questions will likely differ depending on whether the interviewer adopts a constructivist or an objectivist approach. A constructivist would emphasize the participant's definitions of terms, situations, and events and try to tap the participant's assumptions, implicit meanings, and tacit rules. An objectivist would be concerned with obtaining accurate information about chronology, events, settings, and behaviors. Then, too, Glaser's (1978) influence would produce questions different from those likely to be used by proponents of Strauss and Corbin's (1990, 1998) version of grounded theory.

On a more general level, all interviewers need to be aware of the assumptions and perspectives they might import into interview questions. Consider the following:

◆ Tell me about the stressors in your situation.

◆ What coping techniques do you use to handle these stressors?

These questions might work well with a sample of research participants, such as nurses, who are familiar with the terms *stressors* and *coping techniques,* as long as the interviewer asks participants to define these terms at some point. However, the thought of identifying sources of stress and having explicit techniques for dealing with them may not have occurred to many other participants, such as elderly nursing home patients. The interviewer must pay attention to language, meaning, and participants' lives.

Like other skilled interviewers, grounded theory interviewers must remain active in the interview and alert for interesting leads (for suggestions, see Gorden 1987; Holstein and Gubrium 1995; Rubin and Rubin 1995; Seidman 1998). Sound interviewing strategies help the interviewer to go beyond commonsense tales and subsequent obvious, low-level categories that add nothing new. Any competent interviewer shapes questions to obtain rich material and simultaneously avoids imposing preconceived concepts on it. Keeping the questions open-ended helps enormously. When participants use expressions from the lexicon of their experience, such as "good days" and "bad days," the interviewer can ask for more detail. Consider the difference between these interview questions:

◆ Tell me what a "good" day is like for you.

◆ Do you feel better about yourself on a "good" day?

The first leaves the response open to the experiences and categories of the participant, inviting the participant to frame and explore his or her own views of a good day. The second closes down the discussion and relegates the answer to a yes or no. This question also assumes both the definitional frame and that participant and interviewer share it.

A basic rule for grounded theorists is, *Study your data.* Nonetheless, grounded theory interviewers must invoke another rule first: *Study your interview questions!* Being reflexive about how they elicit data, as well as what kinds of data they obtain, can help grounded theory interviewers to amass a rich array of materials.

◆ Multiple Sequential Interviews

Unfortunately, grounded theory studies have come to be identified with a "one-shot" interviewing approach (Creswell 1997). However, multiple sequential interviews form a stronger basis for creating a nuanced understanding of social process. Ethnography, case studies, historical research, and content analysis are also suitable methods for grounded theory analysis (see Charmaz and Mitchell 2001; see also Atkinson and Coffey, Chapter 38, this volume).

One-shot interviewing undermines grounded theory research in several ways. The logic of the grounded theory method calls for the emerging analysis to direct data gathering, in a self-correcting, analytic, expanding process. Early leads shape later data collection. Again, paying attention to language helps to advance a constructivist approach. Rather than glossing over a participant's meaning, a constructivist asks for definitions of it. For example, the interviewer's request above, "Tell me what a 'good' day is like for you," elicits the properties of a "good" day and how the participant constructs his or her definition. New questions arise as the researcher talks to more people and gains greater understanding of their situations. One useful way for the researcher to check leads and to refine

an analysis is to go back and ask earlier participants about new areas as these are uncovered. When interviewers rely on one-shot interviewing, they miss opportunities to correct earlier errors and omissions and to construct a denser, more complex analysis. Consequently, the contribution of the research to a theoretical rendering of the empirical phenomenon also has less power.

Interviewers who must use single interviews can attempt to mitigate these problems by ensuring that later interviews cover probing questions that address theoretical issues explicitly. An interview may capture a participant's views and preferred self-presentation at one point in time. Both can change. The present frames any view of the past (Mead 1932). As the present changes, so also may the participant's view of past events and of self. For example, one participant told me she had glossed over earlier events in a preceding interview because she could not face what they implied about her marriage. She had not acknowledged what an earlier set of medical tests indicated. At the time, her husband refused to drive her to the hospital for the tests and took little interest in their outcome. By downplaying the seriousness of the tests, she also diminished the significance of his actions.[8] Multiple interviews chart a person's path through a process. Conducting multiple interviews also fosters trust between interviewer and interviewee, which allows the interviewer to get closer to the studied phenomenon.

Multiple sequential interviews also permit independent checks over time. Through multiple interviews, the participant's story gains depth, detail, and resonance. Yet the significance of conducting multiple interviews transcends the simple aim of prompting a fuller story. Multiple interviews allow the researcher to hear about events when participants are in the middle of them, not only long afterward. For example, in my own research I was able to listen to a young woman's accounts of shifts in her definitions of trusted relationships as her experience changed over the course of years.

The logic of grounded theory demands that the interviewer successively ask more questions about participants' experiences that probe for theoretical insights. Through the early data analysis, the researcher's questions aim to explore leads about the studied process much more than about individual proclivities. The grounded theory interview develops through a shaped, but not determined, process.

Interviewers then have the opportunity to follow up on earlier leads, to strengthen the emerging processual analysis, and to move closer to the process itself. One-shot interviews often leave the researcher outside of the phenomenon and contribute to the objectivist cast of many grounded theory works. The interviewer may visit the phenomenon and at least peek at it, if not engage it, but he or she does not enter it and live in it. The one-shot interviewer need not sustain his or her gaze or become immersed in either the participant's realities or the participant's feelings (although listening to tapes and reading transcripts over and over may seem like immersion in the field). Grounded theory researchers often lay out general parameters of a topic as external observers but remain apart from it (Charmaz and Mitchell 2001).[9] The externality and objectivism in much grounded theory data collection and analysis has granted grounded theory credibility at the cost of the full realization of its phenomenological potential.[10]

◆ Grounded Theory Guidelines for Analyzing Data

Grounded theory provides researchers with guidelines for analyzing data at several points in the research process, not simply at the "analysis" stage.

CODING DATA

Coding is the pivotal first analytic step that moves the researcher from description toward conceptualization of that description. Coding requires the researcher to attend closely to the data. Nonetheless, the codes reflect the researcher's interests and perspectives as well as the information in the data. Researchers who use grounded theory methods do so through the prism of their disciplinary assumptions and theoretical perspectives.[11] Thus they already possess a set of "sensitizing concepts" (Blumer 1969; van den Hoonaard 1997) that inform empirical inquiry and spark the development of more refined and precise concepts. Symbolic interactionism provides a rich array of sensitizing concepts, such as "identity," "self-concept," "negotiation," and "definition of the situation." The idea of identity has served as a sensitizing concept for me, alerting me to look for its implicit meanings in the lives of participants (Charmaz 1987). In my research on the lives of the chronically ill, I saw identity and threats of the loss of identity as connected with a variety of participants' actions and concerns, such as identity goals, that formed an identity hierarchy. Participants moved up and down this identity hierarchy as their physical conditions and social circumstances changed.

Grounded theorists draw upon sensitizing concepts to begin coding their data, although usually they do so implicitly. Constructivist grounded theory encourages researchers to be reflexive about the constructions—including preconceptions and assumptions—that inform their inquiry. Objectivist researchers minimize this reflexivity to the extent that they treat the researcher as a tabula rasa who conducts inquiry without prior views or values. If researchers make their sensitizing concepts more explicit, they can then examine whether and to what extent these concepts cloud or crystallize their interpretations of data. Researchers can use sensitizing concepts if they spark ideas for coding and take the nascent analysis further and drop them if they do not. Questions that researchers might ask about sensitizing concepts include the following: (a) What, if anything, does the concept illuminate about these data? (b) How, if at all, does the concept specifically apply here? (c) Where does the concept take the analysis? As researchers answer such questions, they make decisions about the boundaries and usefulness of the sensitizing concept. Extant concepts are expected to earn their way into a grounded theory analysis (Glaser 1978).

From a grounded theory perspective, the first question to ask and to pursue is, "What is happening in the data?" (Glaser 1978). Constructivist grounded theorists acknowledge that they *define* what is happening in the data. Objectivist grounded theorists assume they *discover* what is happening in the data.

Grounded theory coding is at least a two-step process: (a) Initial or open coding forces the researcher to begin making analytic decisions about the data, and (b) selective or focused coding follows, in which the researcher uses the most frequently appearing initial codes to sort, synthesize, and conceptualize large amounts of data.[12] Thus coding entails the researcher's capturing what he or she sees in the data in categories that simultaneously describe and dissect the data. In essence, coding is a form of shorthand that distills events and meanings without losing their essential properties. During the coding process, the researcher (a) studies the data before consulting the scholarly literature, (b) engages in line-by-line coding, (c) uses active terms to define what is happening in the data, and (d) follows leads in the initial coding through further data gathering. Studying successive interviews helps the researcher to stay close to the studied empirical world and thus lessens the probability that he or she will force borrowed concepts on it (Glaser 1978, 1992; Melia 1996). Similarly, coding each line with active terms prompts the researcher to link specific interview statements to key processes that affect individuals or specific groups. After the grounded theorist defines these processes, he or she gathers more data about them. Grounded theory coding can lead the researcher in unanticipated directions; for example, the researcher may find that he or she needs to obtain new kinds of data from the participants or to increase the interview sample to include another type of participant.

Initial coding helps the grounded theory researcher to discover participants' views rather than assume that researcher and participants share views and worlds. Should ambiguities arise, the grounded theorist returns for another interview. Through additional interviews, the researcher can check whether and how his or her interpretations of "what is happening" fit with participants' views. In the sample of initial coding displayed in Table 32.1, the excerpt is from an interview with a woman I had interviewed over a seven-year period. She had become increasingly disabled during that time from the effects of lupus erythematosus and Sjögren's syndrome, combined with back injuries. I tried to understand how this woman's statements about her physical suffering affected her situation at work. Although I had conducted previous interviews with her, this one focused on her experiencing bodily limitations. Hence the interview questions frame the content, which, in turn, shapes the codes constructed in analysis of the data. Certainly my theoretical interests in the social psychology of time and of the self informed my coding of her experience. Note the specificity of the codes in relation to the interview statements.

The line-by-line coding in Table 32.1 generated several categories: "suffering as a moral status," "making a moral claim," and "having a devalued moral status because of physical suffering" (Charmaz 1999). Line-by-line coding prompts the grounded theorist not only to study the interviews, but to

Table 32.1   INITIAL CODING

Christine Danforth, a 43-year-old receptionist, had returned to work after eight recent hospitalizations and a lengthy convalescence from a flare-up of lupus erythematosus and Sjögren's syndrome (see Charmaz 1999). A statement from her interview and the initial coding of the statement appear below.

Initial Coding	*Interview Statement*

Recounting the events
Going against medical advice
 	
Being informed of changed rules
Suffering as a moral status
Accounting for legitimate rest time
Distinguishing between "free" and work
  time
Receiving an arbitrary order
Making a moral claim
Finding resistance; tacit view of worth
Having a devalued moral status because of
  physical suffering
Taking action
Learning the facts
 	
Making a case for legitimate rights
 	
Trying to establish entitlement
 	
Meeting resistance
 	
Comparing prerogatives of self and other
 	
Seeing injustice
 	
Making claims for moral rights of person-
  hood
	And so I went back to work on March 1st, even though I wasn't supposed to. And then when I got there, they had a long meeting and they said I could no longer rest during the day. The only time I rested was at lunchtime, which was my time, we were closed. And she said, my supervisor, said I couldn't do that anymore, and I said, "It's my time, you can't tell me I can't lay down." And they said, "Well you're not laying down on the couch that's in there, it bothers the rest of the staff." So I went around and I talked to the rest of the staff, and they all said, "No, we didn't say that, it was never even brought up." So I went back and I said, "You know, I just was talking to the rest of the staff, and it seems that nobody has a problem with it but you," and I said, "You aren't even here at lunchtime." And they still put it down that I couldn't do that any longer. And then a couple of months later one of the other staff started laying down at lunchtime, and I said, you know, "This isn't fair. She doesn't even have a disability and she's laying down," so I just started doing it.

examine how well the codes capture participants' implied and explicit meanings. By keeping these codes active, I preserve process and can later discern sequences after examining multiple interviews. By defining processes early in the research, the grounded theorist avoids limiting the analyses of interviews to typing people into simplistic categories. By conducting multiple sequential interviews, the researcher can establish the conditions under which individuals move between categories.

Grounded theory requires the researcher to make comparisons at each level

of analysis. Action codes show what is happening, what people are doing. These codes move the researcher away from topics, and if they address structure, they reveal how it is constructed through action. I try to make action in the data visible by looking at the data as action. Hence I use terms such as *going, making, having,* and *seeing.* Using action codes helps the researcher to remain specific and not take leaps of fancy. In addition, action codes help the grounded theorist to compare data from different people about similar processes, data from the same individuals at different times during the

Table 32.2   SELECTIVE OR FOCUSED CODING

Selective Coding	Interview Statement
Going against medical advice	And so I went back to work on March 1st, even though I wasn't supposed to. And then when I got there, they had a long meeting and they said I could no longer rest during the day. The only time I rested was at lunchtime, which was my time, we were closed. And she said, my supervisor, said I couldn't do that anymore, and I said, "It's my time, you can't tell me I can't lay down." And they said, "Well you're not laying down on the couch that's in there, it bothers the rest of the staff." So I went around and I talked to the rest of the staff, and they all said, "No, we didn't say that, it was never even brought up." So I went back and I said, "You know, I just was talking to the rest of the staff, and it seems that nobody has a problem with it but you," and I said, "You aren't even here at lunchtime." And they still put it down that I couldn't do that any longer. And then a couple of months later one of the other staff started laying down at lunchtime, and I said, you know, "This isn't fair. She doesn't even have a disability and she's laying down," so I just started doing it.
Suffering as a moral status	
Making a moral claim	
Having a devalued moral status because of physical suffering	
Making a case for legitimate rights	
Seeing injustice	
Making claims for moral rights of person-hood	

course or trajectory of the studied experience, new data with a provisional category, and a category with other categories (Charmaz 1983, 1995b; Glaser 1978, 1992; Strauss 1987).

In selective or focused coding, the researcher adopts frequently reappearing initial codes to use in sorting and synthesizing large amounts of data. Focused codes are more abstract, general, and, simultaneously, analytically incisive than many of the initial codes that they subsume (Charmaz 1983, 1995b; Glaser 1978). They also cover the most data, categorize those data most precisely, and thus outline the next phase of analytic work, as indicated in Table 32.2. Selective coding must take into account a careful study of the initial codes.

Note that I include the same data as displayed in Table 32.1 to show which codes I chose to treat in greater analytic detail.

These codes cut across multiple interviews and thus represent recurrent themes. In making explicit decisions about which focused codes to adopt, the researcher checks the fit between emerging theoretical frameworks and their respective empirical realities. Of the initial codes listed in Table 32.1, "suffering as a moral status" received analytic treatment. Within the same study, comparisons of different interviews netted similar statements about learning about having an impaired and unpredictable body and how to monitor it.

The reciprocal relation between the coding of data and the creation of analytic categories now becomes apparent: Grounded theorists develop categories from their focused codes. Subsequently, they construct entire analytic frameworks by developing and integrating the categories.

MEMO WRITING

Memo writing links coding to the writing of the first draft of the analysis; it is the crucial intermediate step that moves the analysis forward. Grounded theorists use memos to elaborate processes defined in their focused codes. Hence memo writing prompts them to raise their codes to conceptual categories. Through memo writing, researchers take these codes apart analytically and, by doing so, "fracture" the data. That is, they define the properties of each category; specify conditions under which each category develops, is maintained, and changes; and note the consequences of each category and its relationships with other categories. As researchers analyze categories, they ground them in illustrative interview excerpts included in their memos. Thus memos join data with researchers' original interpretations of those data and help researchers to avoid forcing data into extant theories. Memos can range from loosely constructed "freewrites" about the codes to tightly reasoned analytic statements.

Memo writing helps grounded theorists to do the following:[13]

◆ Stop and think about the data

◆ Spark ideas to check out in further interviews

◆ Discover gaps in earlier interviews

◆ Treat qualitative codes as categories to analyze

◆ Clarify categories—define them, state their properties, delineate their conditions, consequences, and connections with other categories

◆ Make explicit comparisons—data with data, category with category, concept with concept

The researcher's gains from memo writing go beyond the specific analytic procedures. Memo writing helps the researcher to spark fresh ideas, create concepts, and find novel relationships. This step spurs the development of a writer's voice and a writing rhythm. Memo writing is much like focused freewriting for personal use (see Elbow 1981). Memos should be written quickly—as fully as possible, but not perfectly. Aiming for perfection is a worthy goal for revising drafts. At the memo-writing stage, however, researchers need to explore their ideas and aim for spontaneity, writing down questions and musings for later checking. Memos may read like letters to a close friend rather than like stodgy scientific reports. Through memo writing, the researcher begins analyzing and writing early in the research process and thus avoids becoming overwhelmed by stacks of undigested data. This step keeps the researcher involved in research and writing. Furthermore, memos explicitly link data gathering, data analysis, and report writing. They provide the foundation upon which whole sections of papers and chapters can later be built. One latent benefit of memo writing is the increased sense of confidence and competence it can instill in the researcher (Charmaz 1999).

The excerpt below is the first section of an early memo from one of my studies; it is followed by a brief discussion of the published work that covers the same material (Charmaz 1991a). I wrote this memo quickly after comparing data from a series of recent interviews.

Example of a Grounded Theory Memo: "Suffering as a Moral Status"

Suffering is a profoundly moral status as well as a physical experience. Stories of suffering reflect and redefine that moral status. With suffering comes moral rights and entitlements as well as moral definitions—when suffering is deemed legitimate. Thus the person can make certain moral claims **and** have certain moral judgments conferred upon him or her.

> Deserving
> Dependent
> In need

Suffering can bring a person an elevated moral status. Here, suffering takes on a sacred status. This is a person who has been in sacred places, who has seen known what ordinary people have not. Their stories are greeted with awe and wonder. The self also has elevated status. . . .

Although suffering may first confer an elevated moral status, views change. The moral claims from suffering typically narrow in scope and in power. The circles of significance shrink. Stories of self within these moral claims may entrance and entertain for a while, but grow thin over time—unless someone has considerable influence or power. The circles narrow to most significant others.

The moral claims of suffering may only supersede those of the healthy and whole in crisis and its immediate aftermath. Otherwise, the person is less. WORTH LESS. Two words—now separate may change as illness and aging take their toll. They may end up as "worthless." Christine's statement reflects her struggles at work to maintain her value and voice.

> And so I went back to work on March 1st, even though I wasn't supposed to. And then when I got there, they had a long meeting and they said I could no longer rest during the day. The only time I rested was at lunchtime, which was my time, we were closed. And she said, my supervisor, said I couldn't do that anymore, and I said, "It's my time, you can't tell me I can't lay down." And they said, "Well you're not laying down on the couch that's in there, it bothers the rest of the staff." So I went around and I talked to the rest of the staff, and they all said, "No, we didn't say that, it was never even brought up." So I went back and I said, "You know, I just was talking to the rest of the staff, and it seems that nobody has a problem with it but you," and I said, "You aren't even here at lunchtime." And they still put it down that I couldn't do that any longer. And then a couple of months later one of the other staff started laying down at lunchtime, and I said, you know, "This isn't fair. She doesn't even have a disability and she's laying down," so I just started doing it.

Christine makes moral claims, not only befitting those of suffering, but of PERSONHOOD. She is a person who has a right to be heard, a right to just and fair treatment in both the medical arena and the workplace.

In the sections of the memo excerpted above, I addressed the following concerns: (a) establishing suffering as moral status, (b) explicating the tacit moral discourse that occurs in suffering, and (c) sketching a moral hierarchy. I realized that the term *stigma* did not capture all that I saw in key interviews. Subsequently, I recoded earlier interviews and talked further with select participants about these areas, then formed questions to ask other participants. In this way, I thought I might tap participants' unstated assumptions that would shape my developing categories. Objectivist grounded theory guidelines suggest that the direct relationship between data and categories generates definitive and obvious categories (Charmaz 1983; Glaser 1978, 1992;

Glaser and Strauss 1967). That may not be true. If researchers bring similar perspectives to the same data, they may define similar categories; otherwise, they may not. Categories denote researchers' ways of asking and seeing as well as participants' ways of experiencing and telling.

Slight differences from the memo above are evident in the more developed published version (Charmaz 1999). In the published work, I discuss a range of social conditions that affect the hierarchy of moral status in suffering and describe more empirical examples. In conducting my research, I find it helpful to include the exact wording of interview excerpts in my memos from the start. After exhausting the analytic potential of categories in a memo, I can take the memo further by relating it to relevant literatures.

THEORETICAL SAMPLING

Theoretical sampling—that is, sampling to develop the researcher's theory, not to represent a population—endows grounded theory studies with analytic power. Grounded theorists return to the field or seek new cases to develop their theoretical categories. Thus theoretical sampling builds a pivotal self-correcting step into the analytic process. Predictable gaps become apparent when researchers raise their codes to analytic categories and find that some categories are incomplete or lack sufficient evidence. Obtaining further data to fill these gaps makes the categories more precise, explanatory, and predictive. For example, I sought further data on the elevated moral status of suffering to flesh out that category. When categories are incomplete, grounded theorists interview select participants about specific key ideas to extend, refine, and check those categories. Thus I returned to earlier participants to learn more about bodily suffering and, later, sought new interviewees and read personal accounts to illuminate the categories.

Theoretical sampling helps grounded theorists to do the following:

◆ Gain rich data

◆ Fill out theoretical categories

◆ Discover variation within theoretical categories

◆ Define gaps within and between categories

Through theoretical sampling, a researcher can define the properties of a category, the conditions under which it is operative, and how and when it is connected with other categories. For example, I needed to explore "making moral claims" with a number of participants to discern to what extent the category was evident and when and how it fit into my emerging analytic framework and the participants' experience. That meant comparing interview excerpts from the same person to discover when he or she did or did not make moral claims, how this person may have learned to make such claims, what the properties of this experience were, and when, if at all, making moral claims reflected definitions of self. Then I compared different participants' interview excerpts. For example, when Christine says, "and I said, you know, 'This isn't fair. She doesn't even have a disability and she's laying down,' so I just started doing it," she is doing more than just recounting a past event; she is making moral claims.

Theoretical sampling relies on comparative methods. Through comparative methods, grounded theorists define the properties of categories and specify the conditions under which categories are linked to other categories. In this way, categories are raised to concepts in the emerging theory. By the time a researcher conducts theoretical sampling, he or she will have developed a set of relevant categories for explaining the data. Presumably, a grounded theorist will keep seeking data to check a category until it is "saturated" (i.e., no new information is found). In practice, saturation tends to be an elastic category that contracts and expands to suit the researcher's definitions rather than any consensual standard (see also Morse 1995).

After deciding which categories best explain what is happening in the study, the grounded theorist treats these categories as concepts. In this sense, these concepts are useful for understanding many incidents or issues in the data (Strauss and Corbin 1990). Strauss (1987) suggests that researchers conduct theoretical sampling early in the research, but I recommend conducting it later in order to allow relevant data and analytic directions to emerge without being forced. Theoretical sampling undertaken too early may bring premature closure to the analysis.

INTEGRATING THE ANALYSIS

Memo writing provides researchers with the material from which they can draft papers or chapters. Grounded theorists decide which memos to use on the basis of their analytic power for understanding the studied phenomenon; they may set aside other memos for later projects (Charmaz 1990). Theoretical sampling sharpens concepts and deepens the analysis. Then the work may gain clarity and generality that transcends the immediate topic. But how do the memos fit together?

Writing memos during each phase of the analysis prompts the researcher to make the analysis progressively stronger, clearer, and more theoretical. Each memo might be used as a section or subsection of a draft of a research paper. Some sets of memos fit together so well that ordering them seems obvious. The researcher's integration of the memos may simply reflect the theoretical direction of the analysis or stages of a process. But for many topics, researchers must create the order and make connections for their readers. How do the ideas fit together? What order makes most sense? The first draft of a paper may represent a researcher's first attempt to integrate a set of memos into some kind of coherent order.

Researchers go about integrating their memos in many ways, but the steps generally include sorting the memos by the titles of categories, mapping several ways to order the memos, choosing an order that works for the analysis and the prospective audience, and creating clear links between categories. When ordering memos, a grounded theorist may think about how a particular order reflects the logic of participants' experience and whether it will fit readers' experience. The grounded theorist will attempt to create a balance between these goals, which may mean collapsing categories for clarity and readability.

Grounded theory methods provide the researcher with powerful tools for honing an analysis. One inherent danger in using these tools is that the researcher may create a scientistic report overloaded with jargon. Like other social scientists, grounded theorists may become enamored of their concepts, especially because they provide a fresh handle on the data.

◆ Conclusion

A grounded theory interview can be viewed as an unfolding story. It is emergent although studied and shaped. It is open-ended but framed and focused. It is intense in content yet informal in execution—conversational in style but not casual in meaning. The relationship of the research participant to the studied phenomenon as well to the interviewer and the interview process also shapes the type, extent, and relative depth of the subsequent story. This unfolding story arises as interviewer and participant together explore the topic and imprint a human face upon it. The story may develop in bits and pieces from liminal, inchoate experience. It may tumble out when participants hold views on their experience but are not granted voices to express those views or audiences to hear them.

Interviews may yield more than data for a study. Research participants may find the experience of being interviewed to be cathartic, and thus the interviews may become significant events for them. Furthermore, participants may gain new views of themselves or their situations. Many participants gain insights into their actions, their situations, and the events that shape them. Simply telling their stories can change the perspectives participants take on the events that constitute those stories and, perhaps, the frames of the stories themselves. These shifts in perspective may range from epiphanies to growing realizations.

The kinds of research stories told are likely to differ between constructivist and objectivist renderings of data. The constructivist approach leans toward a story because it rests on an interpretive frame. Like a story, a constructivist grounded theory may contain characters and plots, although they reflect reality rather than dramatize it. Unlike a story such as an ethgraphic tale, with rich description of people and events, a constructivist grounded theory stresses the analytic and theoretical features of the study processes. An objectivist grounded theory study takes the form of a research report prepared by an unbiased observer. Thus it looks more like a traditional quantitative study than a story, emphasizing parsimony, clarity, comprehensiveness, and analytic power. Objectivist grounded theorists attempt to specify the applicability and limits of their analyses through explicit conditional statements and propositions, whereas constructivists weave these into the narrative.

Grounded theory interviews are used to tell a collective story, not an individual tale told in a single interview. The power of grounded theory methods lies in the researcher's piecing together a theoretical narrative that has explanatory and predictive power. Thus inherent tensions are apparent between the emphasis on the subjective story in the interview and the collective analytic story in grounded theory studies. Grounded theorists place a greater priority on developing a conceptual analysis of the material than on presenting participants' stories in their entirety.

Are these inherent tensions irresolvable? No, not if the researcher intends to follow grounded theory strategies and stays on the analytic path. Not if the researcher outlines the place of interview stories in the final report and the research participant agrees. Not if the researcher believes that reciprocities are possible between interviewer and participant during the interview process itself. Priorities may legitimately differ during data collection and analysis. So, too, may the roles of researcher and participant. Although roles are always emergent and may take novel turns, clarity about reciprocities and ethics can mitigate later dilemmas. The interviewer can minimize the hierarchical nature of the relationship between interviewer and participant through active involvement in that relationship (see also Fontana and Frey 1994). The interviewer can give full attention to what the participant wants to tell—even when it seems extraneous or requires additional visits. And the interviewer can pace the interview to fit the participant's needs first. During data collection, then, participants take precedence. During analysis and presentation of the data, the emerging grounded theory takes precedence.

Tensions between participants' stories and grounded theory analyses may be more academic than actual. Postmodernists who take a literary turn may argue for telling research participants' whole stories, yet participants may not. Whether participants wish to have themselves and their stories captured in prose and revealed in public remains an empirical question as much as an ethical issue. Not every participant finds the prospect appealing—especially if the story reveals private, unmanageable, or discreditable concerns.

Taking a different stance, there is no inherent reason grounded theorists cannot include fuller stories or, for that matter, move closer to a narrative style. Grounded theorists are not prevented from exploring and adopting other genres to some extent simply because earlier grounded theorists adopted the style of scientific reportage. The potential exists for discovery and innovation. In the meantime, grounded theorists need to remain reflexive during all phases of their research and writing. In this way, they may learn how their grounded theory discoveries are constructed.

■ Notes

1. For a more complete statement of contrasts distinguishing constructivist and objectivist grounded theory, see Charmaz (2000).

2. Robert Prus (1987, 1996) discusses a complementary approach for using symbolic interactionism as a guiding perspective for the development of conceptual analyses of data.

3. Since the foundational statements of grounded theory were made, Anselm Strauss and Juliet Corbin (1990, 1998) have added dimensionalizing, verification, axial coding, and the conditional matrix to the grounded theory lexicon. Glaser (1992) contends that these procedures subvert grounded theory analyses. Phyllis Noerager Stern (1994a) asserts that they erode grounded theory, and Linda Robrecht (1995) states that axial coding adds undue complexity. Ian Dey (1999) has examined the logic of grounded theory, and he notes that Glaser and Strauss use the term *categories* inconsistently in their works.

4. I use the term *participants* to indicate their contribution to the research.

5. Earlier major grounded theory statements took a more objectivist position (see Charmaz 1983; Glaser and Strauss 1967; Glaser 1978; Strauss and Corbin 1990, 1998).

6. If these individuals were to become involved with informal support groups or formal organizations that focus on their problem, then a combination of interviews and ethnographic research would be the best choice (see Gubrium and Holstein 1997).

7. Gale Miller (1997) provides a nice statement addressing the need for placing texts into contexts.

8. This example comes from data collected for the study reported in my book *Good Days, Bad Days* (Charmaz 1991a).

9. This difference suggests Henri Bergson's ([1903] 1961) distinction between two ways of studying phenomena: going around them as contrasted with entering them.

10. Holly Skodol Wilson and Sally Hutchinson (1991) provide a statement about the use of grounded theory and hermeneutic approaches. I argue for less fidelity to method and more fidelity to the studied phenomenon.

11. For other statements of the steps of the method in addition to those already cited, see the work of W. Carole Chenitz and Janice Swanson (1986), Stern (1994b), and Strauss and Corbin (1994).

12. Strauss and Corbin (1990, 1998) introduce a third step in coding, axial coding, which aims to code the dimensions of a property. For example, expanded time and spatial horizons are properties of a good day. Using axial coding would lead me to analyze further what expanded time and space include. Glaser (1992) views axial coding as unnecessary; I find that it adds complexity to the method but may not improve the analysis.

13. This list is adopted in part from Charmaz (1999:376-77).

■ References

Bergson, H. [1903] 1961. *An Introduction to Metaphysics*. Translated by M. L. Andison. New York: Philosophical Library.

Blumer, H. 1969. *Symbolic Interactionism: Perspective and Method*. Englewood Cliffs, NJ: Prentice Hall.

Charmaz, K. 1973. "Time and Identity: The Shaping of Selves of the Chronically Ill." Ph.D. dissertation, School of Nursing, University of California, San Francisco.

———. 1983. "The Grounded Theory Method: An Explication and Interpretation." Pp. 109-26 in *Contemporary Field Research*, edited by R. M. Emerson. Boston: Little, Brown.

———. 1987. "Struggling for a Self: Identity Levels of the Chronically Ill." Pp. 283-321 in *Research in the Sociology of Health Care*, Vol. 6, *The Experience and Management of Chronic Illness*, edited by J. A. Roth and P. Conrad. Greenwich, CT: JAI.

———. 1990. " 'Discovering' Chronic Illness: Using Grounded Theory." *Social Science and Medicine* 30:1161-72.

———. 1991a. *Good Days, Bad Days: The Self in Chronic Illness and Time*. New Brunswick, NJ: Rutgers University Press.

———. 1991b. "Translating Graduate Qualitative Methods into Undergraduate Teaching: Intensive Interviewing as a Case Example." *Teaching Sociology* 19:384-95.

———. 1995a. "Body, Identity, and Self: Adapting to Impairment." *Sociological Quarterly* 36:657-80.

———. 1995b. "Grounded Theory." Pp. 27-49 in *Rethinking Methods in Psychology*, edited by J. A. Smith, R. Harré, and L. van Langenhove. London: Sage.

———. 1999. "Stories of Suffering: Subjects' Stories and Research Narratives." *Qualitative Health Research* 9:362-82.

———. 2000. "Grounded Theory: Objectivist and Constructivist Methods." Pp. 509-35 in *Handbook of Qualitative Research*, 2d ed., edited by N. K. Denzin and Y. S. Lincoln. Thousand Oaks, CA: Sage.

Charmaz, K. and R. G. Mitchell. 1996. "The Myth of Silent Authorship: Self, Substance, and Style in Ethnographic Writing." *Symbolic Interaction* 19: 285-302.

———. 2001. "An Invitation to Grounded Theory in Ethnography." Pp. 160-174 in *Handbook of Ethnography*, edited by P. A. Atkinson, A. Coffey, S. Delamonte, J. Lofland, and L. H. Lofland. London: Sage.

Chenitz, W. C. and J. M. Swanson, eds. 1986. *From Practice to Grounded Theory: Qualitative Research in Nursing*. Reading, MA: Addison-Wesley.

Creswell, J. W. 1997. *Qualitative Inquiry and Research Design: Choosing among Five Traditions*. Thousand Oaks, CA: Sage.

Dey, I. 1999. *Grounding Grounded Theory: Guidelines for Qualitative Inquiry*. San Diego: Academic Press.

Elbow, P. 1981. *Writing with Power: Techniques for Mastering the Writing Process*. New York: Oxford University Press.

Fontana, A. and J. H. Frey. 1994. "Interviewing: The Art of Science." Pp. 361-76 in *Handbook of Qualitative Research*, edited by N. K. Denzin and Y. S. Lincoln. Thousand Oaks, CA: Sage.

Glaser, B. G. 1978. *Theoretical Sensitivity*. Mill Valley, CA: Sociology Press.

———. 1992. *Basics of Grounded Theory Analysis: Emergence vs. Forcing*. Mill Valley, CA: Sociology Press.

Glaser, B. G. and A. L. Strauss. 1967. *The Discovery of Grounded Theory: Strategies for Qualitative Research*. Chicago: Aldine.

Gorden, R. L. 1987. *Interviewing: Strategies, Techniques, and Tactics*. 4th ed. Homewood, IL: Dorsey.

Guba, E. G. and Y. S. Lincoln. 1994. "Competing Paradigms in Qualitative Research." Pp. 105-17 in *Handbook of Qualitative Research*, edited by N. K. Denzin and Y. S. Lincoln. Thousand Oaks, CA: Sage.

Gubrium, J. F. and J. A. Holstein. 1997. *The New Language of Qualitative Method*. New York: Oxford University Press.

Holstein, J. A. and J. F. Gubrium. 1995. *The Active Interview*. Thousand Oaks, CA: Sage.

Lofland, J. and L. H. Lofland. 1984. *Analyzing Social Settings*. 2d ed. Belmont, CA: Wadsworth.

———. 1995. *Analyzing Social Settings*. 3d ed. Belmont, CA: Wadsworth.

Mead, G. H. 1932. *Philosophy of the Present*. LaSalle, IL: Open Court.

Melia, K. M. 1996. "Rediscovering Glaser." *Qualitative Health Research* 6:368-78.

Miller, G. 1997. "Contextualizing Texts: Studying Organizational Texts." Pp. 77-91 in *Context and Method in Qualitative Research*, edited by G. Miller and R. Dingwall. Thousand Oaks, CA: Sage.

Morse, J. M. 1995. "The Significance of Saturation." *Qualitative Health Research* 5:147-49.

Prus, R. C. 1987. "Generic Social Processes: Maximizing Conceptual Development in Ethnographic Research." *Journal of Contemporary Ethnography* 16:250-93.

———. 1996. *Symbolic Interaction and Ethnographic Research: Intersubjectivity and the Study of Human Lived Experience.* Albany: State University of New York Press.

Robrecht, L. C. 1995. "Grounded Theory: Evolving Methods." *Qualitative Health Research* 5:169-77.

Rubin, H. J. and I. S. Rubin. 1995. *Qualitative Interviewing: The Art of Hearing Data.* Thousand Oaks, CA: Sage.

Schwandt, T. A. 1994. "Constructivist, Interpretivist Approaches to Human Inquiry." Pp. 118-37 in *Handbook of Qualitative Research,* edited by N. K. Denzin and Y. S. Lincoln. Thousand Oaks, CA: Sage.

Seidman, I. 1998. *Interviewing as Qualitative Research: A Guide for Researchers in Education and the Social Sciences.* 2d ed. New York: Teachers College Press.

Stephenson, J. S. 1985. *Death, Grief, and Mourning: Individual and Social Realities.* New York: Free Press.

Stern, P. N. 1994a. "Eroding Grounded Theory." Pp. 212-23 in *Critical Issues in Qualitative Research Methods,* edited by J. M. Morse. Thousand Oaks, CA: Sage.

———. 1994b. "The Grounded Theory Method: Its Uses and Processes." Pp. 116-26 in *More Grounded Theory: A Reader,* edited by B. G. Glaser. Mill Valley, CA: Sociology Press.

Strauss, A. L. 1987. *Qualitative Analysis for Social Scientists.* New York: Cambridge University Press.

———. 1995. "Notes on the Nature and Development of General Theories." *Qualitative Inquiry* 1:7-18.

Strauss, A. L. and J. Corbin. 1990. *Basics of Qualitative Research: Grounded Theory Procedures and Techniques.* Newbury Park, CA: Sage.

———. 1994. "Grounded Theory Methodology: An Overview." Pp. 273-85 in *Handbook of Qualitative Research,* edited by N. K. Denzin and Y. S. Lincoln. Thousand Oaks, CA: Sage.

———. 1998. *Basics of Qualitative Research: Techniques and Procedures for Developing Grounded Theory.* 2d ed. Thousand Oaks, CA: Sage.

van den Hoonaard, W. C. 1997. *Working with Sensitizing Concepts: Analytical Field Research.* Thousand Oaks, CA: Sage.

Wilson, H. S. and S. A. Hutchinson. 1991. "Triangulation of Qualitative Methods: Heideggerian Hermeneutics and Grounded Theory." *Qualitative Health Research* 1:263-76.

33

ANALYSIS OF PERSONAL NARRATIVES

◆ Catherine Kohler Riessman

It is a common experience for investigators to craft interview questions carefully only to have participants respond with lengthy accounts, long stories that appear on the surface to have little to do with the questions. I became aware of this in the early 1980s while researching the topic of divorce. After completing a household interview with a divorcing spouse, I would note upon listening to the tape that a respondent had gone "on and on." Asking a seemingly straightforward question (e.g., "What were the main causes of your separation?"), I expected a list in response but instead got a "long story." Those of us on the research team interpreted these stories as digressions.

Subsequently, I realized that participants were resisting our efforts to fragment their experiences into thematic (codable) categories—our attempts, in effect, to control meaning. There was a typical sequence to the moments of resistance: The long story began with the decision to marry, moved through the years of the marriage, paused to reenact especially troubling incidents, and ended often with the moment of separation (Riessman 1990a). If participants resisted our efforts to contain their lengthy narratives, they were nonetheless quite aware of the rules of conversational storytelling. After coming to the end of the long and complex story of a marriage, a participant would sometimes say, "Uh, I'm afraid I got a little lost. What was the question you asked?" With such "exit talk," the interviewer could move on to the next question.

Looking back, I am both embarrassed and instructed. These incidents underscore the gap between the standard practice of research interviewing on the one side and the life world of naturally occurring conversa-

AUTHOR'S NOTE: I thank Elliot Mishler, Paul Rosenblatt, Jay Gubrium, and Jim Holstein for comments on earlier versions of this chapter. The Narrative Study Group provided valuable input for my analysis of Gita's narrative.

tion and social interaction on the other (Mishler 1986). Although dehumanizing research practices persist, feminists and others in the social sciences have cleared a space for less dominating and more relational modes of interviewing that reflect and respect participants' ways of organizing meaning in their lives (DeVault 1999; see also Reinharz and Chase, Chapter 11, this volume). We have made efforts to give up communicative power and follow participants down their diverse trails. The current wellspring of interest in personal narrative reflects these trends.

◆ The Narrative Turn

The burgeoning literature on narrative has touched almost every discipline and profession. No longer the province of literary study alone, the "narrative turn" has entered history (Carr 1986; Cronon 1992; White 1987), anthropology and folklore (Behar 1993; Mattingly and Garro 2000; Rosaldo 1989; Young 1987), psychology (Bruner 1986, 1990; Mishler 1986, 2000b; Polkinghorne 1988; Rosenwald and Ochberg 1992; Sarbin 1986), sociolinguistics (Capps and Ochs 1995; Gee 1986, 1991; Labov 1982; Linde 1993), and sociology (Bell 1988, 1999, 2000; Chase 1995; Boje 1991; DeVault 1991; Frank, 1995; Holstein and Gubrium 2000; Williams 1984). The professions, too, have embraced the narrative metaphor, along with investigators who study particular professions. These include law ("Legal Storytelling" 1989), medicine (Charon 1986; Greenhalgh and Hurwitz 1998; Hunter 1991; Hydén 1997; Kleinman 1988), nursing (Sandelowski 1991), occupational therapy (Mattingly 1998), and social work (Dean 1995; Laird 1988). Storytelling, to put the argument simply, is what we do when we describe research and clinical materials, and what informants do with us when they convey the details and courses of their ex-

periences. The approach does not assume objectivity; rather, it privileges positionality and subjectivity.

Narrative analysis takes as its object of investigation the story itself. I limit discussion here to first-person accounts in interviews of informants' own experience, putting aside other kinds of narratives (e.g., about the self of the investigator, what happened in the field, media descriptions of events, or the "master narratives" of theory).[1] My research has focused on disruptive life events, accounts of experiences that fundamentally alter expected biographies. I have studied divorce, chronic illness, and infertility, and I draw on examples from my work throughout the chapter.

Narrative analysis, however, is not only relevant for the study of life disruptions; the methods are equally appropriate for research concerning social movements, political change, and macro-level phenomena (see in this volume Cándida Smith, Chapter 34; Czarniawska, Chapter 35). Because storytelling "promotes empathy across different social locations," regarding the U.S. abortion debate William Gamson (1999:5) argues, for example, that storytelling has counteracted excessive abstraction, bridging policy discourse and the language of women's life worlds; storytelling has fostered the development of constituencies—communities of action. Ken Plummer (1995:174) puts it vividly: "Stories gather people around them," dialectically connecting the people and social movements. The identity stories of members of historically "defiled" groups, such as rape victims, gays, and lesbians, reveal shifts in language over time that shape, and were shaped by, the mobilization of these actors in collective movements. Examples here are "Take Back the Night" and gay rights groups (see Kong, Mahoney, and Plummer, Chapter 12, this volume). "For narratives to flourish, there must be a community to hear; . . . for communities to hear, there must be stories which weave together their history, their identity, their politics" (Plummer 1995:87).

Storytelling is a relational activity that encourages others to listen, to share, and to empathize. It is a collaborative practice and assumes that tellers and listeners/questioners interact in particular cultural milieus and historical contexts, which are essential to interpretation. Analysis in narrative studies opens up forms of telling about experience, not simply the content to which language refers. We ask, "Why was the story told that way?" (Riessman 1993).

The study of personal narrative is a type of case-centered research (Mishler 2000b). Building on the kind of analysis articulated most vividly by C. Wright Mills (1959), the approach illuminates the intersection of biography, history, and society. The "personal troubles" that participants represent in their narratives of divorce, for example, tell us a great deal about social and historical processes—contemporary beliefs about gender relations and pressures on marriage at a junction of American history (Riessman 1990a). Similarly, coming out stories, in which narrators proclaim their gayness to themselves and to others, reveal a shift in genre over time; the linear, "causal" modernist tales of the 1960s and 1970s have given way in contemporary stories to identities that blur and change (Plummer 1995). Historical shifts in understanding and growing politicization occur in the stories of women with cancer whose mothers were exposed to diethylstilbestrol (DES) during their pregnancies (Bell 1999). Illness narratives reveal "deeply historicized and social view[s] of health and illness," as Vieda Skultans (1999:322) shows with post-Soviet women patients' accounts of hardship, whose explanations are erased in their physicians' biomedical definitions of problems. As Mills said long ago, what we call "personal troubles" are located in particular times and places, and individuals' narratives about their troubles are works of history as much as they are about individuals, the social spaces they inhabit, and the societies they live in. The analysis of personal narratives can illuminate "individual and collective action and meanings, as well as

the processes by which social life and human relationships are made and changed" (Laslett 1999:392).

◆ Defining Narratives for Analysis

There is considerable variation in how investigators employ the concept of personal narrative and, relatedly, in the methodological assumptions investigators make and the strategies they choose for analysis. These are often tied to disciplinary background. In one tradition of work, typical of social history and anthropology, the narrative is considered to be the entire life story, an amalgam of autobiographical materials. Barbara Myerhoff's (1978) work offers an early example of the life story approach and illustrates its potentials and problems. Myerhoff constructs compelling portraits of elderly Eastern European Jews who are living out the remainder of their lives in Venice, California. She builds these portraits from the many incidents informants shared with her during extended fieldwork. She artfully "infiltrates" her informants, "depositing her authorial word inside others' speech" to speak her truth without "erasing the others' viewpoint and social language" (Kaminsky 1992:17-18). In this genre, the stories that informants recount merge with the analyst's interpretation of them, sometimes to the point that stories and interpretation are indistinguishable.

In a very different tradition of work, the concept of personal narrative is quite restrictive, used to refer to brief, topically specific stories organized around characters, setting, and plot. These are discrete stories told in response to single questions; they recapitulate specific events the narrator witnessed or experienced. William Labov's (1982) work illustrates this approach. For example, Labov analyzes the common structures underlying a series of bounded (transcribed) stories of inner-city violence told in response to a specific question. Narrators recapitulate sequences of actions that erupt and bring the danger of death. The approach has been extended by others who include more than brief episodes to analyze a variety of experiences (Attanucci 1991; Bamberg 1997a; Bell 1988; Riessman 1990b).

In a third approach, personal narrative is considered to encompass large sections of talk and interview exchanges—extended accounts of lives that develop over the course of interviews. The discrete story as the unit of analysis of Labov's and others' approach gives way to an evolving series of stories that are framed in and through interaction. Elliot Mishler (2000b), for example, studied the trajectories of identity development among a group of artists/craftspersons that emerged from his extended interviews with them. The approach is distinguished by the following features: presentation of and reliance on detailed transcripts of interview excerpts, attention to the structural features of discourse, analysis of the coproduction of narratives through the dialogic exchange between interviewer and participant, and a comparative orientation to interpreting similarities and contrasts among participants' life stories (see also Bell 1999).

Despite differences in these approaches, most investigators share certain basic understandings. Narration is distinguished by ordering and sequence; one action is viewed as consequential for the next. Narrators create plots from disordered experience, giving reality "a unity that neither nature nor the past possesses so clearly" (Cronon 1992:1349).[2] Relatedly, narrators structure their tales temporally and spatially; "they look back on and recount lives that are located in particular times and places" (Laslett 1999:392). The temporal ordering of a plot is most familiar and responds to the characteristic Western listener's preoccupation with time marching forward, as in the question, "And then what happened?" But narratives can also be organized thematically and episodically (Gee 1991; Michaels 1981; Riessman 1987). Narrators use particular linguistic devices to hold their accounts together and communicate meaning to listeners (for a review, see Riessman 1993:18-19). Human agency and imagination are vividly expressed:

> With narrative, people strive to configure space and time, deploy cohesive devices, reveal identity of actors and relatedness of actions across scenes. They create themes, plots, and drama. In so doing, narrators make sense of themselves, social situations, and history. (Bamberg and McCabe 1998:iii)

If all talk in interviews is not narrative (there are questions and answers about demographic facts, listings, chronicles, and other nonnarrative forms of discourse), how does an investigator discern narrative segments for analysis? Sometimes the decision is clear: An informant signals that a story is coming and indicates when it is over with entrance and exit talk (Jefferson 1979). In my divorce interviews, for example, responding to a question about the "main causes" of separation, one man provided a listing and then said, "I'll clarify this with an example," an utterance that introduced a lengthy story about his judging a dog show, an avocation his wife did not share. He exited from the story many minutes later by saying, "That is a classic example of the whole relationship . . . she chose *not* to be with *me*." As the story was especially vivid, I used it along with others to theorize about gender differences in expectations of companionate marriage in the contemporary United States (Riessman 1990a:102-8).

Stories in research interviews are rarely so clearly bounded, however, and often there is negotiation between teller and listener about placement and relevance, a process that can be analyzed with transcriptions that include paralinguistic utterances ("uhms"), false starts, interruptions, and other subtle features of interaction. Deciding which segments to analyze and putting boundaries around them are interpretive acts that are shaped in major ways by the investigator's theoretical interests.

Deciding where the beginnings and endings of narratives fall is often a complex interpretive task. I confronted the problem in a study of stigma and infertility as I began to analyze a woman's narrative account of her multiple miscarriages. The research was conducted in Kerala, South India, and elsewhere I describe the fieldwork (Riessman 2000a, 2000b). At a certain point in the project, I began to focus on identity development for women beyond childbearing age, how older women construct identities that defy stigma and the master narrative of motherhood.

Below, I present a portion of an interview with a woman I call "Gita," who is 55 years old, married, childless, Hindu, and from a lower caste. Because of progressive social policies and related opportunities in Kerala, Gita is educated, has risen in status, and works as a lawyer in a small municipality. The interaction represented in this extract took place after she and I had talked (in English) for nearly an hour in her home about a variety of topics, most of which she introduced. These included her schooling, how her marriage was arranged, and her political work in the "liberation struggle of Kerala." We enter the interview as I reintroduce the topic of infertility. My transcription conventions are adapted from those recommended by James Gee (1986).[3]

Although Gita could answer my question "Were you ever pregnant?" directly with a yes, she chooses instead to negotiate a space in the interview to develop a complex narrative. She describes terminated pregnancies, going to a political demonstration, and coming home to her husband's anger, whereupon the scene shifts to the actions of her in-laws and her husband's refusal to be examined for infertility. This was unlike other women's accounts about failed pregnancies in my interviews. Although temporally organized, Gita's plot spans many years and social settings, and

emotions related to the events are absent. She makes no reference to sadness, disappointment, or other feelings common to narratives of miscarriage and infertility.

In an effort to interpret this segment of the interview, I struggled to define its boundaries. Initially, I decided to conclude my representation of the narrative with what seems like a coda at the end of Scene 4: "But afterwards I never became—[pregnant]." The utterance concludes the sequence about pregnancies—the topic of my initial question. Ultimately, however, I decided to include the next scene, which communicates various family members' responses and the reported speech of Gita's husband ("No, no, I will not go to a lady doctor"). The change in decision coincided with a theoretical shift in my thinking about identity construction. I became interested in how women in South India resist stigma when infertility occurs (Riessman 2000b). It was crucial, then, to include the episode about the in-laws, the interaction with the gynecologist, and the husband's response to the request that he be tested.

Although not my focus here, the narrative excerpt could have been analyzed as an interactional accomplishment, that is, as a joint production of the interviewer and the respondent. Such a focus would require retranscription so as to include all of my utterances (deleted and marked with == in the interview excerpt), the ways I elicited and shaped the narrative (for examples of this approach, see Bell 1999; Capps and Ochs 1995; Mishler 1997; Riessman 1987; see also Poland, Chapter 30, this volume). The narrative also could have been analyzed with a primary focus on cultural context, centering on the prominent role of the wife's in-laws, for example, in defining and managing infertility in India (for an example, see Riessman 2000a). And the narrative could have been analyzed in terms of problems it solves for the narrator—an angle into the text I will develop shortly—and other problems that narrative creates. Investigators interested in psychological processes, narrative therapy, and change

Cathy:	Now I am going to go back and ask some specific questions. Were you ever pregnant?	
Gita:	Pregnant means—You see it was 3 years [after the marriage] then I approached [name of doctor] then she said it is not a viable—[pregnancy].	Scene 1

==

So she asked me to undergo this operation, this D&C
and she wanted to examine him [husband] also.

Then the second time in 1974-in 75,   Scene 2
next time—four months.
Then she wanted [me] to take bed rest
advised me to take bed rest.

Because I already told you   Scene 3
it was during that period that [name] the socialist leader
led the gigantic procession against Mrs. Indira Gandhi,
the Prime Minister of India, in Delhi.

And I was a political leader [names place and party]
I had to participate in that.

So I went by train to Delhi
but returned by plane.
After the return I was in [name] Nursing Home
for 16 days bleeding.

And so he [husband] was very angry   Scene 4
he said "do not go for any social work
do not be active" this and that.
But afterwards I never became—[pregnant]

==

Then my in-laws, they are in [city]   Scene 5
they thought I had some defect, really speaking.
So they brought me to a gynecologist,
one [name], one specialist.

She took three hours to examine me
and she said "you are perfectly-[normal], no defect at all"
even though I was 40 or 41 then.
"So I have to examine your husband."

Then I told her [doctor] "You just ask his sister."
She was—his sister was with me in [city].
So I asked her to ask her to bring him in.
He will not come.
Then we went to the house
so then I said "Dr. [name] wants to see you."
Then he [husband] said "No, no, I will not go to a lady doctor."
Then she [sister-in-law] said she would not examine him
they had to examine the—what is it?—the sperm in the laboratory.
But he did not allow that.

(White and Epston 1990; Josselson and Lieblich 1993; McLeod 1997) might explore Gita's account of infertility for its closed, sealed-off features; Gita displays a set of understandings that seem to defy redefinition and change. Or silence about emotions might be a focus. These are just a few of the analytic strategies available.

Across the board, the discernment of a narrative segment for analysis—the representations and boundaries chosen—is strongly influenced by the investigator's evolving understandings, disciplinary preferences, and research questions. In all of these ways, the investigator variously "infiltrates" the text. Unlike some of the life story approaches mentioned earlier, especially Myerhoff's, my approach here includes detailed transcripts of speech so that readers can, to a much greater degree, see the stories apart from their analysis.[4] The selves of storyteller and analyst then remain separate (Laslett 1999).

◆ Analyzing Narrative as Performance

Personal narratives serve many purposes—to remember, argue, convince, engage, or entertain their audiences (Bamberg and McCabe 1998). Consequently, investigators have many points of entry. Personal narratives can be analyzed textually (Gee 1986; Labov 1982), conversationally (Polanyi 1985), culturally (Rosaldo 1989; Mattingly and Garro 2000), politically/historically (Mumby 1993; White 1987), and performatively (Langellier 1989).[5] It is the last of these analytic positions that I emphasize primarily here. A story involves storytelling, which is a reciprocal event between a teller and an audience. When we tell stories about our lives we perform our (preferred) identities (Langellier 2001).

As Erving Goffman (1959, 1981) suggests with his repeated use of the dramaturgical metaphor, social actors stage performances of desirable selves to preserve "face" in situations of difficulty, thus managing potentially "spoiled" identities. Relatedly, gender identity is performed, produced for and by audiences in social situations. To emphasize the performative element is not to suggest that identities are inauthentic, but only that they are situated and accomplished in social interaction.

Applying these insights to interviews, informants negotiate how they want to be known by the stories they develop collaboratively with their audiences. Informants do not reveal an essential self as much as they perform a preferred one, selected from the multiplicity of selves or personas that individuals switch among as they go about their lives. Approaching identity as a "performative struggle over the meanings of experience" (Langellier 2001:3) opens up analytic possibilities that are missed with static conceptions of identity and by essentializing theories that assume the unity of an inner self.

Personal narratives contain many performative features that enable the "local achievement of identity" (Cussins 1998). Tellers intensify words and phrases; they enhance segments with narrative detail, reported speech, appeals to the audience, paralinguistic features and gestures, and body movement (Bauman 1986). Analysts can ask many questions of a narrative segment in terms of performance. In what kind of a story does a narrator place herself? How does she locate herself in relation to the audience, and vice versa? How does she locate characters in relation to one another and in relation to herself? How does she relate to herself, that is, make identity claims about who or what she is (Bamberg 1997b)?

Social positioning in stories—how narrators choose to position audiences, characters, and themselves—is a useful point of entry because "fluid positionings, not fixed roles, are used by people to cope with the situations they find themselves in" (Harré and van Langenhove 1999:17). Narrators can position themselves, for example, as victims of one circumstance or another in their stories, giving over to other characters rather than themselves the power to initiate action. Alternatively, narrators can position themselves as agentic beings who assume control over events and actions, individuals who purposefully initiate and cause action. They can shift among positions, giving themselves active roles in certain scenes and passive roles in others. To create these fluid semantic spaces for themselves, narrators use particular grammatical resources to construct who they are. Verbs, for example, can frame actions as voluntary rather than compulsory. Other grammatical forms intensify vulnerability (Capps and Ochs 1995). These positionings of the self in personal narratives signify the performance of identity. They are enacted in an immediate discursive context, the evolving interview with a listener/questioner, and can be analyzed from detailed transcriptions.

I illustrate this approach by returning to Gita's narrative account in the transcript excerpt above. In the larger research project from which the transcript is taken, I show how the cultural discourse of gender defines women by their marital and childbearing status. In South India, married women face severe stigma when they cannot, or choose not to, reproduce (Riessman 2000b). Self-stigma was a recurring theme in my interviews, even as historical developments in contemporary India are enabling some women to resist the "master narrative" of motherhood. Gita deviated from the general pattern. She was beyond childbearing age, and the absence of motherhood did not seem to be a particularly salient topic for her (I was always the one to introduce it); she did not express sadness or negative self-evaluation about not having had children, as younger women did. It turned out that Gita had built a life around principles other than motherhood; she is a lawyer and political activist. Close examination of the narrative reveals precisely how she constructs this preferred, positive identity, solving the problem of stigma and subordination as a childless woman in South India. She resists the dominant cultural narrative about gender identity with an autobiographical account that transforms a personal issue into a public one (Richardson 1990).

Gita carefully positions the audience (me) and various characters in constructing her story, which is, as I noted earlier, a complex performance that I have represented in five scenes. Each scene offers a snapshot of action located in a particular time and setting. Unlike narratives in the discrete story approach (Labov 1982), Gita's narrative is complex in its organization. Attention to how scenes are organized within the performance is my analytic point of entry.

The first two scenes are prompted by an audience request ("Were you ever pregnant?"), my attempt to position Gita in a world of fertility. She reluctantly moves into the role of pregnant woman in these brief scenes, quickly chronicling two pregnancies several years apart (the outcomes of which I attempt to clarify, in lines deleted from the transcript). She does not provide narrative detail, elaborate meanings, or describe emotions associated with the miscarriages; the audience must infer a great deal. Gita constructs the first two scenes with only one character aside from herself, her doctor. She "approached" the doctor, who "asked" her to have a D&C. In a quick aside, she states that the doctor wanted to examine the husband, but we infer that this did not happen. With this utterance, Gita prefigures her husband's responsibility, anticipating the final scene and the moral of the narrative. Gita again casts the doctor as the active agent in Scene 2; she "wanted" and "advised" Gita to take bed rest. Through her choices of verbs and the positioning of characters, Gita constructs scenes in which she has a relatively minor role. From the lack of narrative detail, the audience assumes that the events in the plot up to this point are not particularly salient for Gita.

The narrator's position and the salience of the events change dramatically in the third scene. Gita shifts topics, from pregnancy "to what I already told you," which is the primacy of her political world. She now constructs a scene in which *she* is the central character, the agent of action, a "political leader" in her Kerala community who "had to" participate in a demonstration in Delhi against Mrs. Indira Gandhi, who was seeking reelection. Verbs frame the narrator's intentional actions, situated as political exigencies, and there is considerable narrative elaboration, which is a sharp contrast to the spare, "passive" grammar of the previous scenes, in which Gita was the object of the doctor's actions.[6] As Gita locates her private fertility story in the larger public story of India's socialist movement, the audience is not left wondering which is more important. Ignoring her doctor's advice "to take bed rest" during her second pregnancy, she traveled to Delhi to participate in a mass demonstration, which probably involved a three-day train trip in 1975. Despite her return by plane and a 16-day nursing home stay for "bleeding," the audience infers that Gita lost the pregnancy (a fact I confirm a few moments later in lines not included here). She constructs a narrative around oppositional worlds—family life on one side and the socialist movement of India on the other. The personal and the political occupy separate spheres of action and, as such, do not morally infringe upon each other.

Moving along, in the next two scenes Gita shifts the plot to the family world. In Scene 4, she again introduces her husband as a character and reports that he was "very angry" at her "social work," meaning her political activism. She communicates a one-way conversation; Gita does not give herself a speaking role. She positions herself only as the object of her husband's angry speech. We do not know what she said to him, if anything. Her passive positioning in this scene contrasts with her activity in the previous one. Is she displaying here the typical practice in South Indian families, which is that wives are expected to defer to their husbands' authority (Riessman 2000b)? If so, her choice of language is in-

structive; he said "this and that." Could she be belittling her husband's anger and directives? She concludes Scene 4 with a factual utterance: "But afterwards I never became —[pregnant]".

In the fifth and final lengthy scene, Gita introduces new characters—her parents-in-law, an infertility specialist, a sister-in-law—and an intricate plot before the narrative moves toward its moral point, which is that Gita's infertility is not her responsibility. The final scene is most elaborate, suggesting importance. Gita's performance of identity is quite vivid here. She begins by constructing a passive, stigmatized position for herself: Her in-laws "brought" her for treatment to a gynecologist in the major South Indian city where the parents live because "they thought I had some defect." As in earlier scenes involving pregnancy, others suggest or initiate action.[7] She intensifies meaning and thematic importance with repetition ("defect") in the next stanza; the gynecologist determined after a lengthy examination that Gita has "no defect at all." She is "perfectly" normal. Blame for her infertility, Gita intimates, resides elsewhere. Using the linguistic device of reported speech, she performs several conversations on the topic of getting her husband tested. Everyone is enlisted in the effort—gynecologist, sister-in-law—but he refuses: "No, no, I will not go to a lady doctor." Nor is he willing to have his sperm tested in a laboratory. (Gita returned several other times in our interview to his refusal to be tested.) The narrator has crafted a narrative performance in which she has no responsibility whatsoever.[8]

Readers might question Gita's attributions. She ignored her physician's advice to "take bed rest" during her second pregnancy, choosing to travel instead to Delhi. She gave primacy to political commitments, valuing work in the socialist movement over her gendered position in the home. She was also "40 or 41" years old when she was finally examined by a specialist. Age may have been a factor. Gita had conceived twice, but could not sustain pregnancies, implying a possible "defect." Gita's performance, however, suggests how she wants to be known as a "perfectly" normal woman "with no defect at all." The way she organizes scenes within the narrative performance, the choices she makes about positioning, and the grammatical resources she employs put forth the preferred identity of committed political activist, not disappointed would-be mother.

Later in the interview (in a portion not extracted here), she supported this interpretation. Resisting once again my positioning of her in the world of biological fertility, she said explicitly, "Because I do not have [children], I have no disappointments, because mine is a big family." She continued with a listing of many brothers, their children, and particular nieces who "come here every evening . . . to take their meals." With these words, she challenged my bipolar notions of parenthood—either you have children or you don't. Gita performs a gender identity that resists the master cultural narrative in place in her world: that biological motherhood is the central axis of identity for women. Elsewhere, I historicize Gita's life chances and locate her in an evolving cultural discourse about women's "proper" place in modern India, a "developing" nation that is formulating new spaces other than home and field in which women may labor (Riessman 2000b).

The analytic strategy I have illustrated is generalizable. Narrators can emplot events in their lives in a variety of ways. They "select and assemble experiences and events so they contribute collectively to the intended point of the story . . . why it is being told, in just this way, in just this setting" (Mishler 2000a:8). How narrators accomplish their situated stories conveys a great deal about the presentation of self (Goffman 1959). To make the process visible, we can analyze scenes in relation to one another, how narrators position characters and themselves, and we can "unpack" the grammatical resources they select to make their moral points clear to the listener. Interpretation

requires close analysis of how narrators position audiences, too, and, reciprocally, how the audience positions the narrator. Identities are constituted through such performative actions, within the context of the interview itself as a performance. Audiences, of course, may "read" events differently than narrators do, resulting in contested meanings.

◆ The "Truths" of Personal Narrative

I stated at the outset that my approach to narrative analysis assumes not objectivity but, instead, positionality and subjectivity. The perspectives of both narrator and analyst can come into view. As the Personal Narratives Group (1989) articulates, "truths" rather than "the" truth of personal narrative is the watchword.

Not all scholars who work with personal narratives would agree (see in this volume Atkinson, Chapter 6; Fontana, Chapter 8; Cándida Smith, Chapter 34). Daniel Bertaux (1995) believes that "every life story contains a large proportion of factual data which can be verified" (p. 2), for example, with respect to the dates and places of biographical events. Locating himself in the "realist" research tradition, Bertaux argues that informants' stories collected from the same milieu can serve as documentary sources for investigating the world "out there." Although acknowledging that informants do not "tell us the whole truth and nothing but the truth," Bertaux claims that by collecting many stories from the same milieu, a researcher can uncover "recurrent patterns concerning collective phenomena or share collective experience in a particular milieu" (p. 2).

Those working from social constructionist or performative perspectives approach the issue of truth differently. Verification of the "facts" of lives is less salient than understanding the changing meanings of events for the individuals involved, and how these, in turn, are located in history and culture. Personal narratives are, at core, meaning-making units of discourse. They are of interest precisely because narrators interpret the past in stories rather than reproduce the past as it was.

Returning to Gita's narrative account of infertility, it is irrelevant whether the events "really" occurred just as she reports them. Gita was one informant in a larger project about identity for childless women, and she clearly performs one strategic solution to the problem infertility poses for her; she is "perfectly" normal, with "no defect at all." As noted earlier, it is possible to question her causal attributions. It also goes without saying that the passage of time since the miscarriages has softened their emotional impact, and consequently she can be silent about her feelings. As all narrators do, Gita presents past events from the vantage point of present realities and values. Not unlike other women I interviewed who were beyond childbearing age, she minimizes the significance of biological motherhood and emphasizes, instead, occupational and political identities. The truths of narrative accounts lie not in their faithful representation of a past world, but in the shifting connections they forge among past, present, and future.

The complex relationships among narrative, time, and memory are currently a vital topic of research and theorizing (Freeman 1998, forthcoming; for a review, see Hinchman and Hinchman 1997). Storytelling among those with chronic illnesses offers a case in point (see Morse, Chapter 16, this volume). Serious illness interrupts lives (Charmaz 1991) and occasions the "call for stories" (Frank 1995:53). Friends want to know "what happened," and stories provide maps for the ill themselves "to repair the damage that illness has done to the ill person's sense of where she is in life, and where she may be going" (Frank 1995:53). Yet the storylines or plots into which the seriously ill pour their experience may be at variance with biomedical plots. Patients with incurable cancers, for example, construct "restitution" narratives that suggest positive end points, whereas others represent themselves in "chaos" narratives, where continuity between past and future is unclear (Frank 1995). Oncologists are often asked about time, and they construct narratives of hope for families that blur endings and leave the future ambiguous (Good et al. 1994). For both practitioner and patient, a storyline locates the threatening illness in an imagined life trajectory (Mattingly 1994; Riessman 1990b).

The meanings of life events are not fixed or constant; rather, they evolve, influenced by subsequent life events. According to Mishler (1999), "As we access and make sense of events and experiences in our pasts and how they are related to our current selves, we change their meanings" (p. 5). Ends beget beginnings, in other words (Mishler 2000a). Personal narratives—the stories we tell to ourselves, to each other, and to researchers—offer a unique window into these formations and reformations: "We continually restory our pasts, shifting the relative significance of different events for whom we have become, discovering connections we had previously been unaware of, repositioning ourselves and others in our networks of relationships" (Mishler 1999:5).

A useful way to see how identities can shift over time is to look at "turning points" in stories—moments when the narrator signifies a radical shift in the expected course of a life. For example, in my research on divorce, it was common for informants to report moments when they realized retrospectively, "This is it"—the marital relationship had crossed a line beyond repair. Such turning points often coincided with incidents of physical violence, directed toward either the spouse or a child. One woman said: "That was the last straw. You just don't hit me. . . . I wasn't going to stay around to be hit again." Another woman, who had been physically abused for years, spoke of "the final blow": Her husband "punched our oldest daughter across the

living room . . . if he was going to start doing that to the kids, that was it." A divorcing
man told a long narrative about his wife's
open infidelity, culminating in a moment
when he hit her. He said to himself, "This is
it . . . there wasn't any reason to be there
other than to hurt" (Riessman 1990a). Such
turning points fundamentally change the
meaning of past experiences and consequently individuals' identities. "They open
up directions of movement that were not
anticipated by and could not be predicted
by their pasts"—an insight Mishler
(1999:7-8) applies to the narratives of sexual abuse survivors. Past abuse is given new
significance as women move out of destructive relationships and construct new identities.

The "trustworthiness" of narrative accounts cannot be evaluated using traditional correspondence criteria. There is no
canonical approach to validation in interpretive work, no recipes or formulas. (For a
review of several approaches that may be
useful in certain instances, see Riessman
1993:64-69.)

◆ Conclusion

I began this chapter with an account of my
difficulty in doing research interviews with
individuals whose lives had been disrupted
and being initially annoyed at interviewees'
lengthy and convoluted responses. Since
then, many investigators have given a name
to my problem—these were "narratives"—and offered analytic solutions for
working with interview responses that do
not require fragmenting them. The field
now named *narrative analysis* has grown
rapidly, and no review can be complete and
summarize the many types of work that are
evident today. I have purposively bounded
the field, focusing on the personal narrative
and emphasizing the performative dimension, but I have also pointed the reader toward other perspectives. (For reviews and
typologies of research strategies, see

Cortazzi 1993; Langellier 1989; Mishler
1995; Riessman 1993.)

Narrative analysis has its critics, of
course (Atkinson 1997; Atkinson and
Silverman 1997). Its methods are not appropriate for studies of large numbers of
nameless, faceless subjects. The approach is
slow and painstaking, requiring attention
to subtlety: nuances of speech, the organization of a response, relations between researcher and subject, social and historical
contexts. It is not suitable for investigators
who seek a clear and unobstructed view of
subjects' lives, and the analytic detail required may seem excessive to those who
orient to language as a transparent medium.

Narrative methods can be combined
with other forms of qualitative analysis (for
an example, see Riessman 1990a), even
with quantitative analysis.[9] Some fancy
epistemological footwork is required, because the interpretive perspective that typically underlies narrative work is very different from the realist assumptions of some
forms of qualitative analysis and certainly
of quantification. Combining methods
forces investigators to confront troublesome philosophical issues and to educate
readers about them. Science cannot be spoken in a singular, universal voice. Any
methodological standpoint is, by definition, partial, incomplete, and historically
contingent. Diversity of representations is
needed. Narrative analysis is one approach,
not a panacea; it is suitable for some situations and not others. It is a useful addition
to the stockpot of social research methods,
bringing critical flavors to the surface that
otherwise get lost in the brew. Narrative
analysis allows for the systematic study of
personal experience and meaning. The approach enables investigators to study the
"active, self-shaping quality of human
thought, the power of stories to create and
refashion personal identity" (Hinchman
and Hinchman 1997:xiv).

Narratives are a particularly significant
genre for representing and analyzing identity in its multiple guises in different con-

texts. The methods allow for the systematic study of experience and, for feminist researchers such as myself, the changing meanings of conditions that affect women disproportionately, including domestic violence, reproductive illness, and poverty. Personal narratives provide windows into lives that confront the constraints of circumstances. Attention to personal narratives in interviews opens discursive spaces for research subjects, representing them as agents acting in life worlds of moral complexity.

■ Notes

1. There are, of course, narrative sites other than interviews (see Ochs, Smith, and Taylor 1989; Polanyi 1985; Gubrium and Holstein 2000).

2. There is lively philosophical debate in this area about whether primary experience is "disordered"—that is, whether narrators create order out of chaos (see Hinchman and Hinchman 1997:xix-xx).

3. I have grouped lines about a single topic into stanzas, which I have then grouped into scenes. Because of the narrative's direct performative reference, I have organized it into "scenes" rather than "strophes," as Gee (1986) does. I have deleted brief exchanges between Gita and me, questions I ask to clarify what she has said, which are marked ==.

4. Transcriptions, of course, are themselves theory-laden; how we choose to represent spoken dialogue is not independent of theoretical goals (see Ochs 1979; Mishler 1991; Kvale 1996:chap. 9; Poland 1995).

5. Lisa Capps and Elinor Ochs (1995) provide a compelling analysis of conversations with a single narrator over several years. They combine textual and conversational approaches in their study of the discourse of a woman suffering from agoraphobia (severe panic attacks).

6. The verb construction *had to* is, in fact, ambiguous. It might refer to others' expectations that Gita participate in the political demonstration, a consequence of her leadership role in the community, or it might refer to an "inner" compulsion to participate, arising out of her own political convictions and priorities. The narrative context supports the latter interpretation.

7. Infertility is a family event in the Indian context, and husbands' relatives often suggest and initiate treatment for daughters-in-law, including medical and religious cures (Riessman 2000a, 2000b).

8. The physiological responsibility for infertility in this and the other cases is unclear. India's infertility clinics require both spouses to be tested, and about a third of the time the problem lies in the sperm. Elsewhere, I have described Indian women's management of male responsibility; they do not disclose it to deflect stigma but, in an effort to keep families together, absorb the "fault" themselves (Riessman 2000b).

9. The material in this paragraph is adapted from Riessman (1993:70).

■ References

Atkinson, P. 1997. "Narrative Turn or Blind Alley?" *Qualitative Health Research* 7:325-44.

Atkinson, P. and D. Silverman. 1997. "Kundera's *Immortality:* The Interview Society and the Invention of Self." *Qualitative Inquiry* 3:304-25.

Attanucci, J. 1991. "Changing Subjects: Growing Up and Growing Older." *Journal of Moral Education* 20:317-28.

Bamberg, M. G. W., ed. 1997a. "Oral Versions of Personal Experience: Three Decades of Narrative Analysis" (special issue). *Journal of Narrative and Life History* 7(1-4).

———. 1997b. "Positioning between Structure and Performance." In "Oral Versions of Personal Experience: Three Decades of Narrative Analysis" (special issue), edited by M. G. W. Bamberg. *Journal of Narrative and Life History* 7:335-42.

Bamberg, M. G. W. and A. McCabe. 1998. "Editorial." *Narrative Inquiry* 8(1):iii-v.

Bauman, R. 1986. *Story, Performance, and Event: Contextual Studies of Oral Narrative.* Cambridge: Cambridge University Press.

Behar, R. 1993. *Translated Woman: Crossing the Border with Esperanza's Story.* Boston: Beacon.

Bell, S. E. 1988. "Becoming a Political Woman: The Reconstruction and Interpretation of Experience through Stories." In *Gender and Discourse: The Power of Talk,* edited by A. D. Todd and S. Fisher. Norwood, NJ: Ablex.

———. 1999. "Narratives and Lives: Women's Health Politics and the Diagnosis of Cancer for DES Daughters." *Narrative Inquiry* 9(2):1-43.

———. 2000. "Experiencing Illness in/and Narrative." In *Handbook of Medical Sociology,* 5th ed., edited by C. E. Bird, P. Conrad, and A. M. Fremont. Upper Saddle River, NJ: Prentice Hall.

Bertaux, D. 1995. "A Response to Thierry Kochuyt's 'Biographic and Empiricist Illusions: A Reply to Recent Criticism.' " *Biography & Society* (annual newsletter of Research Committee 38, International Sociological Association), pp. 2-6.

Boje, D. M. 1991. "The Storytelling Organization: A Study of Story Performance in an Office-Supply Firm." *Administrative Science Quarterly* 36:106-26.

Bruner, J. 1986. *Actual Minds, Possible Worlds.* Cambridge, MA: Harvard University Press.

———. 1990. *Acts of Meaning.* Cambridge, MA: Harvard University Press.

Capps, L. and E. Ochs. 1995. *Constructing Panic: The Discourse of Agoraphobia.* Cambridge, MA: Harvard University Press.

Carr, D. 1986. *Time, Narrative, and History.* Bloomington: Indiana University Press.

Charmaz, K. 1991. *Good Days, Bad Days: The Self in Chronic Illness and Time.* New Brunswick, NJ: Rutgers University Press.

Charon, R. 1986. "To Render the Lives of Patients." *Literature and Medicine* 5:58-74.

Chase, S. E. 1995. *Ambiguous Empowerment: The Work Narratives of Women School Superintendents.* Amherst: University of Massachusetts Press.

Cortazzi, M. 1993. *Narrative Analysis.* London: Falmer.

Cronon, W. 1992. "A Place for Stories: Nature, History, and Narrative." *Journal of American History* 78:1347-76.

Cussins, C. M. 1998. "Ontological Choreography: Agency for Women Patients in an Infertility Clinic." In *Differences in Medicine: Unraveling Practices, Techniques, and Bodies,* edited by M. Berg and S. Mol. Durham, NC: Duke University Press.

Dean, R. G. 1995. "Stories of AIDS: The Use of Narrative as an Approach to Understanding in an AIDS Support Group." *Clinical Social Work Journal* 23:287-304.

DeVault, M. L. 1991. "Talking and Listening from Women's Standpoint: Feminist Strategies for Interviewing and Analysis." *Social Problems* 37:96-116.

———. 1999. *Liberating Method: Feminism and Social Research.* Philadelphia: Temple University Press.

Freeman, M. 1998. "Mythical Time, Historical Time, and the Narrative Fabric of the Self." *Narrative Inquiry* 8(1):1-24.

———. Forthcoming. "The Presence of What Is Missing: Memory, Poetry, and the Ride Home." In *Between Fathers and Sons: Critical Incident Narratives on the Development of Men's Lives,* edited by R. J. Pellegrini and T. R. Sarbin. Thousand Oaks, CA: Sage.

Frank, A. W. 1995. *The Wounded Storyteller: Body, Illness, and Ethics.* Chicago: University of Chicago Press.

Gamson, W. A. 1999. "How Story Telling Can Be Empowering." Presented at the conference "Toward a Sociology of Culture and Cognition," November 12-13, Rutgers University, New Brunswick, NJ.

Gee, J. P. 1986. "Units in the Production of Narrative Discourse." *Discourse Processes* 9:391-422.

———. 1991. "A Linguistic Approach to Narrative." *Journal of Narrative and Life History* 1:15-39.

Goffman, E. 1959. *The Presentation of Self in Everyday Life.* Garden City, NY: Doubleday.

———. 1981. *Forms of Talk.* Philadelphia: University of Pennsylvania Press.

Good, M.-J. D., T. Munakata, Y. Kobayashi, C. Mattingly, and B. J. Good. 1994. "Oncology and Narrative Time." *Social Science and Medicine* 38:855-62.

Greenhalgh, T. and B. Hurwitz, eds. 1998. *Narrative Based Medicine: Dialogue and Discourse in Clinical Practice.* London: BMJ.

Gubrium, J. F. and J. A. Holstein, eds. 2000. *Institutional Selves: Troubled Identities in a Postmodern World.* New York: Oxford University Press.

Harré, R. and L. van Langenhove. 1999. "Introducing Positioning Theory." Pp. 14-31 in *Positioning Theory*, edited by R. Harré and L. van Langenhove. Malden, MA: Blackwell.

Hinchman, L. P. and S. K. Hinchman. 1997. "Introduction." In *Memory, Identity, Community: The Idea of Narrative in the Human Sciences*, edited by L. P. Hinchman and S. K. Hinchman. Albany: State University of New York Press.

Holstein, J. A. and J. F. Gubrium. 2000. *The Self We Live By: Narrative Identity in a Postmodern World*. New York: Oxford University Press.

Hunter, K. M. 1991. *Doctors' Stories: The Narrative Structure of Medical Knowledge*. Princeton, NJ: Princeton University Press.

Hydén, L. C. 1997. "Illness and Narrative." *Sociology of Health and Illness* 19:48-69.

Jefferson, G. 1979. "Sequential Aspects of Storytelling in Conversation." In *Studies in the Organization of Conversational Interaction*, edited by J. Schenkein. New York: Academic Press.

Josselson, R. and A. Lieblich, eds. 1993. *The Narrative Study of Lives*, Vol. 1, *The Narrative Study of Lives*. Newbury Park, CA: Sage.

Kaminsky, M. 1992. "Introduction." In B. Myerhoff, *Remembered Lives: The Work of Ritual, Storytelling, and Growing Older*. Ann Arbor: University of Michigan Press.

Kleinman, A. 1988. *The Illness Narratives: Suffering, Healing, and the Human Condition*. New York: Basic Books.

Kvale, S. 1996. *InterViews: An Introduction to Qualitative Research Interviewing*. Thousand Oaks, CA: Sage.

Labov, W. 1982. "Speech Actions and Reactions in Personal Narrative." In *Analyzing Discourse: Text and Talk*, edited by D. Tannen. Washington, DC: Georgetown University Press.

Laird, J. 1988. "Women and Stories: Restorying Women's Self-Constructions." In *Women in Families: A Framework for Family Therapy*, edited by M. McGoldrick, C. Anderson, and F. Walsh. New York: Norton.

Langellier, K. 1989. "Personal Narratives: Perspectives on Theory and Research." *Text and Performance Quarterly* 9:243-76.

———. 2001. " 'You're Marked': Breast Cancer, Tattoo, and the Narrative Performance of Identity." In *Narrative and Identity: Studies in Autobiography, Self, and Culture*, edited by J. Brockmeier and D. Carbaugh. Amsterdam: John Benjamins.

Laslett, B. 1999. "Personal Narratives as Sociology." *Contemporary Sociology* 28:391-401.

"Legal Storytelling" (special issue). 1989. *Michigan Law Review* 87(8).

Linde, C. 1993. *Life Stories: The Creation of Coherence*. New York: Oxford University Press.

Mattingly, C. 1994. "The Concept of Therapeutic 'Emplotment.' " *Social Science and Medicine* 38:811-22.

———. 1998. *Healing Dramas and Clinical Plots: The Narrative Structure of Experience*. New York: Cambridge University Press.

Mattingly, C. and L. C. Garro, eds. 2000. *Narrative and Cultural Construction of Illness and Healing*. Berkeley: University of California Press.

McLeod, J. 1997. *Narrative and Psychotherapy*. Thousand Oaks, CA: Sage.

Michaels, S. 1981. " 'Sharing Time': Children's Narrative Styles and Differential Access to Literacy." *Language and Society* 10:423-42.

Mills, C. W. 1959. *The Sociological Imagination*. New York: Oxford University Press.

Mishler, E. G. 1986. *Research Interviewing: Context and Narrative*. Cambridge, MA: Harvard University Press.

———. 1991. "Representing Discourse: The Rhetoric of Transcription." *Journal of Narrative and Life History* 1:255-80.

———. 1995. "Models of Narrative Analysis: A Typology." *Journal of Narrative and Life History* 5:87-123.

———. 1997. "Narrative Accounts in Clinical and Research Interviews." In *The Construction of Professional Discourse*, edited by B.-L. Gunnarsson, P. Linell, and B. Norberg. London: Longman.

———. 1999. "Time's Double Arrow: Re-presenting the Past in Life History Studies." Presented at Radcliffe Murray Center conference "Lives in Context: The Study of Human Development," November 12-13, Cambridge, MA.

———. 2000a. "Narrative and the Paradox of Temporal Ordering: How Ends Beget Beginnings." Presented at the Conference on Discourse and Identity, Clark University.

———. 2000b. *Storylines: Craftartists' Narratives of Identity*. Cambridge, MA: Harvard University Press.

Mumby, D. K. 1993. *Narrative and Social Control: Critical Perspectives*. Newbury Park, CA: Sage.

Myerhoff, B. 1978. *Number Our Days*. New York: Simon & Schuster.

Ochs, E. 1979. "Transcription as Theory." In *Developmental Pragmatics*, edited by E. Ochs and B. B. Schieffelin. New York: Academic Press.

Ochs, E., R. Smith, and C. Taylor. 1989. "Dinner Narratives as Detective Stories." *Cultural Dynamics* 2:238-57.

Personal Narratives Group. 1989. "Truths." In Personal Narratives Group, *Interpreting Women's Lives: Feminist Theory and Personal Narratives*. Bloomington: Indiana University Press.

Plummer, K. 1995. *Telling Sexual Stories: Power, Change and Social Worlds*. New York: Routledge.

Poland, B. 1995. "Transcription Quality as an Aspect of Rigor in Qualitative Research." *Qualitative Inquiry* 1:290-310.

Polanyi, L. 1985. "Conversational Storytelling." Pp. 183-201 in *Handbook of Discourse Analysis*, Vol. 3, edited by T. A. van Dijk. London: Academic Press.

Polkinghorne, D. E. 1988. *Narrative Knowing and the Human Sciences*. Albany: State University of New York Press.

Richardson, L. 1990. *Writing Strategies: Reaching Diverse Audiences*. Newbury Park, CA: Sage.

Riessman, C. K. 1987. "When Gender Is Not Enough: Women Interviewing Women." *Gender & Society* 1:172-207.

———. 1990a. *Divorce Talk: Women and Men Make Sense of Personal Relationships*. New Brunswick, NJ: Rutgers University Press.

———. 1990b. "Strategic Uses of Narrative in the Presentation of Self and Illness." *Social Science and Medicine* 30:1195-1200.

———. 1993. *Narrative Analysis*. Newbury Park, CA: Sage.

———. 2000a. " 'Even If We Don't Have Children [We] Can Live': Stigma and Infertility in South India." In *Narrative and Cultural Construction of Illness and Healing*, edited by C. Mattingly and L. C. Garro. Berkeley: University of California Press.

———. 2000b. "Stigma and Everyday Resistance Practices: Childless Women in South India." *Gender & Society* 14:111-35.

Rosaldo, R. 1989. *Culture and Truth: The Remaking of Social Analysis*. Boston: Beacon.

Rosenwald, G. C. and R. L. Ochberg, eds. 1992. *Storied Lives: The Cultural Politics of Self-Understanding*. New Haven, CT: Yale University Press.

Sandelowski, M. 1991. "Telling Stories: Narrative Approaches in Qualitative Research." *Image: Journal of Nursing Scholarship* 23(3):161-66.

Sarbin, T. R., ed. 1986. *Narrative Psychology: The Storied Nature of Human Conduct*. New York: Praeger.

Skultans, V. 1999. "Narratives of the Body and History: Illness in Judgement on the Soviet Past." *Sociology of Health and Illness* 21:310-28.

White, H. 1987. *The Content of the Form: Narrative Discourse and Historical Representation*. Baltimore: Johns Hopkins University Press.

White, M. and D. Epston. 1990. *Narrative Means to Therapeutic Ends*. New York: Norton.

Williams, G. 1984. "The Genesis of Chronic illness: Narrative Reconstruction." *Sociology of Health and Illness* 6:175-200.

Young, K. G. 1987. *Taleworlds and Storyrealms: The Phenomenology of Narrative*. Boston: Martinus Nijhoff.

34

ANALYTIC STRATEGIES FOR ORAL HISTORY INTERVIEWS

◆ Richard Cándida Smith

Two understandings of the past confront each other across the tape recorder. In the encounter between scholar and informant, oral history interviews juxtapose the oldest and newest forms of historical method. For millennia, communities created and preserved their understanding of the past through spoken accounts passed entirely by word of mouth. No less today than in the past, people create and sustain a shared imaginative life wherever they gather and converse, be it at the kitchen table, the tavern counter, the street corner, the wedding reception, or the office lunchroom. Oral history interviews tap into a continuous outpouring of words that provide matrices defining both community and individual identity.[1] Informal collective modes of knowledge permeate the background of contemporary oral history

interviews, even though academic researchers conduct interviews primarily to collect firsthand testimony that may assist them in describing historical events or the experience of social processes. In the unusual exchange that occurs specifically for an oral history interview, collectively generated popular understandings of the past enter scholarly discourse in a verbatim record accessible for scholarly analysis.[2]

In this chapter, I explore how scholars have used narrative analysis to understand more fully the historical foundations of the personal experience documented in oral history interviews. I begin with Luisa Passerini's (1987b) now classic model of interviews as drawing upon preexisting oral cultural forms that translate historical processes into symbolically mediated experiences. In the second section, I discuss how scholars have explored tensions and contradictions within narrative structures as the starting points for their analyses. In conclusion, I look at efforts to rethink the ways in which memory encodes historical processes into experience and the consequent possibilities for oral history interviews to augment historical understanding.

In common with other types of evidence, interviews contain a mix of true and false, reliable and unreliable, verifiable and unverifiable information. Details of accounts can often be incorrect. Interviews may contradict each other, and, occasionally, interviewees provide inconsistent accounts in different interview situations. Researchers need to approach oral sources with cautious skepticism. A good starting point for evaluating the veracity of oral testimony can be found in Paul Thompson's (1988:240-41) extrapolation to interviews of three basic principles fundamental to all historical research: (a) Assess each interview for internal consistency; (b) cross-check information found in interviews with as many other published, oral, and archival sources as possible; and (c) read the interview with as wide a historical and theoretical understanding of relevant subjects as possible.[3]

Narrative analysis allows for a historical interpretation of interview-based source material that is not dependent upon the ultimate veracity of the accounts provided. Even if only tacitly expressed, explanatory assumptions affect every aspect of an interview, from the organization of the story line or the plot to the presentation of personalities and events, to patterns of factual errors, omissions, and contradictions. The stories that interviewees share provide insight into the narrative and symbolic frameworks they use to explain why things turned out as they did. The first step in using interviews to reconstruct links among personal experience, collective memory, and broad historical processes is to address the role of storytelling in popular consciousness.

◆ Popular Memory and Oral Narratives: The Translation of History into Experience

In approaching interviews, whether unearthed in the course of archival research or taped specifically for one's own project, making them speak intelligibly can initially prove a frustrating challenge. Confronting the transcripts of the 67 interviews that constituted the core set of sources for the study reported in her book *Fascism in Popular Memory*, Luisa Passerini (1987b: 10-16) at first felt that there was an impassable gulf separating popular expression from scientific historical understanding. The interviews were full of anecdotes, irrelevancies, inaccuracies, contradictions, silences, and self-censorship, as well as out-and-out lies. The interviews contained plenty of colorful material, but the scattered recollections offered few immediately clear insights into the period or the effects of the fascist dictatorship on the lives of working-class Italians.

Passerini addressed her problem of making her interviews speak historically by doing some reading in anthropology and folklore. The perspectives she acquired helped her to think about how people use language to synthesize their experience into memorable images that make for interesting, often dramatic conversation. She looked for recurrent motifs in her interviews, many of which had documentable roots in Italian peasant folktales and folk songs. Everyday storytelling conventions might in themselves be historical evidence of past social relations.

Although the interviews were ostensibly firsthand testimony, personal experience dissolved into deeply rooted oral cultural forms that provided a ready set of stereotypes for structuring memories and filling them with meaning (see Narayan and George, Chapter 39, this volume). The interviews, Passerini concluded, provided evidence of how communities had talked about the past and arrived at collective conclusions as to what had happened to them all. With these insights, Passerini advanced a sophisticated reconstruction of recurrent patterns within her subjects' representations. Different interviewees used the same narrative structures to recount the stories of their lives, an understanding that syntagmatic analysis could decode. The same metaphors occurred across interviews, used to emphasize conclusions about the meanings of past events. The personalities narrators ascribed to themselves and to others involved stereotyped character traits. Through analysis of these and other paradigmatic elements, Passerini (1987b:1-4, 8-11, 51-52) focused on narrative forms present in all interviews and used to express judgments and relationships (see also Passerini 1988; Portelli 1991:1-26).

Passerini no longer viewed interviews as products of narrators' immediate, personal memories. They provided no privileged access to actual historical experiences. Without external supporting evidence, one could never be certain that even deeply emotional accounts were factual firsthand reports of events the interviewee had undergone. Narrators often borrowed available mythic forms to articulate emotional truths they had formed about their pasts. For all intents and purposes, the past disappeared into a narrative structure of plot turns and symbolic motifs that embedded speakers in a particular discursive community.

THE RECORD OF A CULTURAL FORM

The cornerstone of Passerini's (1987b) textual analysis is her definition of the oral history interview as the record of a cultural form. "When someone is asked for his life-story," she writes, "his memory draws on pre-existing storylines and ways of telling stories" (p. 8). Thus *memory*, as the term is used in the title of her book, is not a psychological category but the "transmission and elaboration of stories handed down and kept alive through small-scale social networks—stories which can be adapted every so often in a variety of social interactions, including the interview" (p. 19). Three critical elements follow from this definition:

1. Interviews are windows into collective thought processes; incidents and characters, even if presented in an individualized performative style, are conventionalized and shaped by a long history of responses to previous tellings.

2. Interviews draw upon a repertoire of oral-narrative sources that affect interviewees' selection of form and imagery; these sources include conversational storytelling, jokes, church sermons, political speeches, and testimonies given at Bible study groups and political party training schools.

3. Silences and other ruptures point to aspects of experience not fully mediated by group interpretation of past events.

The ideas, images, and linguistic strategies found in oral narratives constitute what Passerini (1987b) calls the "symbolic order of everyday life" (p. 67). What she means by this concept might be illustrated by an anecdote a woman factory worker recounted to Passerini about defending, in the years after World War II, her right to wear red overalls:

> [The management] asked me, "And is it because you like red or is it because you are a Communist?" I replied: "Because I like red, because I'm a Communist, because I wear what colour I like, and because G. doesn't give me overalls and

I don't want to spend money on his account. Why haven't I the right to wear
what colour I like?"

To which Passerini (1987b) comments,
"The girl's reply summarises rather better
than we could the multiplicity of meanings
that a red outfit could assume in the daily
struggle and balance of forces in the factory" (p. 106).

READING FOR
SYMBOLIC ORDER

Passerini argues that reading for the
symbolic order of her interviews illuminates an otherwise invisible subjective experience of the fascist period. Her aim is a
broader interpretation of subjectivity as a
historical rather than a natural phenomenon. She demonstrates the conventionalized nature of narratives by comparing
written and oral self-representations of
workers. When picking up pen to write
about their lives, working-class authors
typically adopt the literary conventions of
the classic novel. They focus their narratives on a process of education and growth,
a movement that dramatizes the hero's increasing competence in handling life's challenges. Passerini's narrators, on the other
hand, showed no growth but tended toward stereotypical, timeless, "fixed" identities that closely corresponded to age, gender, and skill levels. Women, for example,
particularly those born before 1900, often
presented themselves as "born rebels."
Men, however, described themselves as capable workers with "instinctive" or "natural" know-how, a convention that preserved traditional patriarchal and artisanal
virtues when such roles no longer had any
direct relationship to actual working conditions.

Such stereotypes are neither self-deceptions nor reductive but ultimately valid representations of reality. Passerini (1987b)
observes that many (although not all)

women who characterized themselves as
"born rebels" exhibited socially and politically conservative attitudes in their testimonies. The "rebel" self-appellation, she concludes, was part of a complex reaction to
the radical changes industrialization
brought to women's social roles:

The stereotypical notion of "having the
devil in her" justifies and explains certain innovative choices made in moments of crisis—the decision to marry
without her father's permission, the
wish to work in the factory even after
the birth of her son, the call for a different division of labor in the house. (P. 28)

The "rebel woman" image, deriving
from Italian folklore traditions about
women's supposed propensity for sweeping away conventions, is what Passerini
calls a "survival." Urban working-class
women reworked the tradition and
changed its content to fit the emotionally
ambiguous and unsettling circumstances of
their lives. The power of the image derived
precisely from its not being "true." The
symbol helped women narrate to each
other their confusions over female identity
in a changing society. Modern Italy remained oppressive of women but nonetheless demanded that they abandon stable relationships promising, even if not always
delivering, reciprocal responsibilities
within family relationships. A self-proclaimed character trait mitigated compulsory social transformations through an assumption of responsibility that, because it
was inborn rather than acquired, evaded
questions of choice and decision. The symbol allowed for the transmission of an
awareness of oppression and a sense of otherness from the social order within which
working-class women lived. It helped them
develop an openness to change, which they
nonetheless often resented, as they forged
new lifeways for themselves. Self-representation necessarily involves an individual's
acquiescence to the role his or her character

plays in supporting group interpretations of historical events and processes (Passerini 1987b:27-28).

Stereotypical self-representations typically lend themselves more readily to humorous accounts than to tragic accounts of the past. Retelling anecdotes about individuals' lives is a form of entertainment in which the community can identify and interpret factors shaping life patterns. There is room for both tears and laughter, but humor is more likely to succeed in providing a satisfactory resolution to the tensions crystallized in an anecdote. In a collective storytelling situation, response shapes the way an individual comes to tell an oft-repeated story, causing him or her to drop those elements that elicit indifference or antagonism and sharpen those that promote good company.

Passerini recorded several brutal accounts of fascist terror, but her subjects spoke of life under fascism much more frequently with humor, laughter, and even joviality. The absurd posturing and venality of the regime loomed larger in their collective memory than its viciousness. Were the interviews evidence of a more benign image of fascism than that presented by other sources? Hardly. Behind the laughter, Passerini uncovered a complex of social and psychological forces that etched a darker picture.

Passerini notes that the humor in her interviews conducted in the 1970s, as well as that found in police documents from the 1930s, most frequently took the form of self-ridicule. One could interpret this recurrent feature as a marker of shame and guilt, as even an uneasy admission of complicity when daily life required some form of cooperation with the rulers of the nation. Passerini (1987b:125) observes, however, that although any form of antifascist statement was dangerous, police authorities were more likely to be lenient if a violator of public order appeared to be a drunk, playing the fool and making statements in jest. Police records show that verbal antifascism evaded judicial proceedings if it took the form of regression to childhood language and humor.

In analyzing working-class humor, Passerini did not look for hidden political meanings. She understood humor as at once a symptom of the regimentation of life under fascism and a sign of resistance to it. In the fascist period, popular culture was a substitute for politics. A sense of self distinct from that of the oppressor could be expressed through jokes and laughter instead of through political action. When the world situation changed and the Allied invasion precipitated the collapse of Mussolini's government, laughter could suddenly turn into actual resistance, fueling an armed political warfare that previously would have been futile. The hidden side of humor suddenly became visible. Laughter and self-ridicule had all along been weapons of struggle, preserving identity against a hated regime intent on eradicating the rights of individuals to have personal opinions, to reflect on their lives, or to make judgments of any kind about the state of the nation. Humor helped express working-class self-identity, as well as a sense of pride in having endured and survived to have the last laugh.

Passerini's observations on Italian women's resistance of fascist demographic policy illustrate her use of oral sources to reveal the intersection of historical processes and personal experience in the generation of new possibilities for self-understanding. The natalist policies of the fascist regime subjected women to constant propaganda praising large families as a sign of femininity. Mothers were offered significant material inducements to bear additional children. Passerini's (1987b:155) interviews reveal that this propaganda had some continuing subjective effect: Even antifascist women praised themselves as being "fertile" and dismissed their enemies as "barren."[4] Nonetheless, birthrates continued to decline, and the number of illegal abortions, the most widespread form of birth control, continued to rise among the working classes. One-third of the women interviewed acknowledged having had abortions in those years, and Passerini assumed that other women interviewed for the project must also have had abortions but did not want to discuss this aspect of their past.

How had these women learned about birth control, given that they lived in a culture in which the practice was universally condemned? Passerini could not find evidence of underground traditions passed from mother to daughter, nor did she find evidence of working-class women's having access to or knowledge of middle-class birth control methods. Knowledge about abortion apparently spread clandestinely through social networks contained within the community and the age group most concerned about pregnancy. The choice to have an abortion was difficult and involved a radical break with community traditions. All dominant ideological institutions—the Fascist and Communist Parties and the Catholic Church—equally condemned abortion. A woman arrested for ending a pregnancy faced heavy legal penalties, with little likelihood of sympathy or support from anyone. Even 40 years later, the subject remained painful for the women who elected to share this part of their experience, although they defended their choice as an effort to make their lives better than those of their mothers or grandmothers. Passerini (1987b) concludes that, to some degree, their understanding of past behavior was influenced by feminist ideas of the 1970s retrospectively projected onto their actions in the 1930s. Still, she argues, "the fact that the meaning of actions is perceived with the wisdom of hindsight, when they had not been so clear and conscious for our subjects in the past, does not diminish the importance of their intuition in the present" (p. 181).

This aspect of Passerini's analysis suggests a model for understanding the subjective ground of ideological change. The women had recognized a need so strong that they ignored both universal ideological condemnation and heavy legal penalties. This new behavior, conflicting with preexisting community values, made the women particularly receptive to new ideas, new values, and new ideologies that might justify what self-interest had said was necessity. A tentative process of ideological shift had begun documented by a retrospective effort to justify past transgressions that subsequently could be more broadly recognized as heroic.

LINKING PERSONAL AND HISTORICAL TIME

The conceptual tools Passerini chose are particularly suitable for reading contradictions in interview texts. Silences, self-censorship, lies and exaggerations, an overabundance of insignificant episodes told in minutest detail, the reworking of the past in terms that serve present-day interests— these offer rich sources for historical insight because such narrative blemishes indicate areas of conflict: The individual and the group could not arrive at a satisfying way of narrating painful or contentious events. Symbolic turns within a text link personal and historical time. All oral history interviews, Passerini (1987a) has written, involve

> decision-making about the relationship between the self and history, be it individual history or general. . . . The problem is [to determine] what forms the idea of historical time takes at different levels of abstraction and in various philosophical or daily conceptions; and in what ways the idea of historical time is connected with historical narration and self-representation. (P. 412)

Two different but subjectively undifferentiated conceptions of time alternate in interviews. These modes of temporal experience are markedly more complex than the common observation that interviews involve a retrospective reworking of past experience into terms meaningful for the present. Interviews include a linear conception of change, and interviewees feel obligated to explain differences between the present and the past. Spiraling around efforts to understand change by narrating its causes and effects, however, is a condition of atemporality, in which a "fixed" identity locates the speaker in an eternal present. Passerini (1987a:420) argues that this combination reflects a desire to see change in the surrounding world but not in oneself, because recognition of personal temporality involves acceptance of death. The idea of personal time is inseparable from an idea of a tragic fate. A fixed identity is a narrative strategy, an imaginative leap that allows a speaker to talk about historical change and still repress confrontation with mortality.

Symbols fuse judgment of historical events with retreats into the imaginary. Analysis of the "symbolic order of everyday life" found in interviews allows historians to separate these two aspects of consciousness. Symbolization is the process that mediates the ongoing, continuous dislocation of the self between the real and the imaginary. Symbols through such mediation constitute subjective experience as both encounter and evasion of history. Reflection on individual historical experience takes on the forms of literary expression: Through metaphor and other verbal juxtapositions, interviews create their experience as symbolic expressions. In a particularly eloquent account, a woman told Passerini how the fascists administered castor oil to political opponents to humiliate them in front of their neighbors. She linked a number of distinct anecdotes about fascist terror by leaping from feces to menstrual blood to the blood of victims of politically motivated beatings. The connections between the episodes emerged in the narrator's metonymic stringing together of images linked by the transformation of bodily discharges. Feces, menstrual blood, and blood from beatings became symbols for each other, and the ensemble illuminated for Passerini a past

emotion that continued to live through a linguistic, aesthetic device. Tracing the shifts among these three symbols, she argues that shame, vulnerability, and rage still defined her interviewee's subjective experience of the fascist years. Metaphorical leaps are seldom arbitrary, even when clumsy, misguided, or fabulous. Narrative figures refer the listener (and subsequently the analyst) to an aspect of the speaker's mental representations that most clearly express her understanding of historical reality. Displaced meaning allows speakers to redescribe—in other words, reinterpret—experiences in ways that are more emotionally satisfying to them than usages that are more literal would allow.[5]

By focusing on oral narratives as cultural objects, Passerini shows that what one might dismiss as malapropism can be a key to reading oral texts. However, if metaphoric figures used by interviewees are never arbitrary, critical readings can easily be. Passerini locates the solution to this problem in the simple but fundamental observation that the structures of oral narratives arise to communicate ideas and feelings within a group. The narrative traditions of that group necessarily limit interpretations of figurative representations to what members of that group would likely find intelligible. Individuals push the boundary of sense at the risk of becoming incomprehensible. The guarantee that narrative structure must contribute to sense combines with the performative opportunities in every speech situation to generate a field of regularities and innovations vital to understanding the play of ideas within popular memory. Every interview contains within it a guide to the plotlines and symbolic structures of the interviewee's most important communities, as well as evidence of the social tensions narratives express and often displace. Passerini applied ethnographic and folkloric study of Italian working-class and peasant cultures along with psychological theory to decode the historically specific meaning of symbol systems used to narrate the experience of fascism.

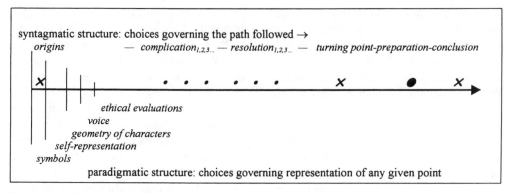

Figure 34.1. The Two Axes of Narratives

Underlying her method was a semiotic approach to language acts such as storytelling. Many scholars working with life history and oral history sources have found that before they can interpret the symbolic orders converting historical events into personal experience, they first need to analyze the narrative structures interviewees use to convey that experience.

◆ Syntagmatic and Paradigmatic Analysis: The Organization of Plot and Symbol

Contemporary thought on narrative is structured by two contradictory ideas: Language is a set of rules that impose categories of knowledge upon speakers, but all performative acts are unique expressions that push against boundaries established by genre, content, or form of expression. Researchers undertaking analysis of the linguistic aspects of interviews begin by identifying regular verbal and narrative patterns, knowing that performance will never be precisely regular. This distinction parallels the relation of speech to language in the semiotic theories of Ferdinand de Saussure, who held that languages are best understood not as they are actually spoken but as ideal forms comprising regular value

distinctions combined in predictable sets. These recurrent codings render historical forces into narrative symbols and meaningful explanatory narratives (Culler 1986; Gadet 1989; Harris 1988; Holland 1992).

Narratives have two axes. In Figure 34.1, syntagmatic structure appears as a horizontal arrow that represents the emplotted, temporal dimension of narration: how a story begins and what problem is posed, what complications mark change in the development of the problem, what the turning point is that makes the conclusion inevitable, how the story concludes, with what kind of resolution. Paradigmatic analysis focuses on recurrent images that can appear at any point in the story. It describes and explains symbolic vocabulary and the ways in which associational registers express both judgments and affective responses.

Both syntagmatic analysis and paradigmatic analysis look for coded regularities. Because these understandings expressed through regularities in the interview arise in communicative acts, repetition of storytelling motifs across interviews with different informants provides evidence of a shared construction of the past. Whether marked by individual variations or presented in a stereotyped form, narrative and symbolic structures tend to reappear in different interviews conducted in the same community. Recurrent images found in more than one interview reveal a storytelling language that provides a finite set of preferred expressive forms for the recollection of experience. Analysis of regularities across interviews can help define the boundaries of discursively defined communities—that is, of groups of people who may or may not know each other personally, but who are connected through shared languages (Joutard 1981; Joyner 1979; McMahan 1989:89-90; Tonkin 1992:97-112).

SYNTAGMATIC ANALYSIS

Syntagmatic analysis focuses on strategies of emplotment. Any story, whether a firsthand account of a specific event, a humorous anecdote, or a life history recounted across several sessions, must have a starting point, markers of transition, a turning point, and a conclusion. Emplotment involves the selection and highlighting of some events as most important. Other aspects may simply be dropped from the account altogether for the sake of narrative efficiency. Narrative form may also require the hypothetical construction of past events that may or may not have occurred but that the logic of the plotline demands. The conclusion determines that logic. Narratives are teleological, meaning that every story element flows from an effort to make the ending appear necessary and intelligible. Choices of significant details reveal "causes" that explain the inevitability of the conclusion. One may like the outcome or not, but narration enacts a process of coming to terms with the state of affairs that the narrator assumes characterize the conclusion.

One can find a clear example of syntagmatic analysis in Elliot G. Mishler's (1992) use of interviews to study career paths. Mishler categorizes an anecdote as articulating an "on-line" choice when the episode led to the narrator's taking another step toward his ultimate career goal. Even events that occur before the "turning point," the account in the story in which

the narrator becomes aware of his goal, take their meaning from the conclusion. Complications and resolutions account for an accretion of factors that ultimately made the final status of the narrator inevitable. Mishler categorizes anecdotes about events that took the narrator away from his goal as "off-line" choices. The alternation of on-line and off-line choices develops dramatic tension. Adjusting the tempo of alternation heightens or diminishes the tension by increasing or decreasing the feeling that a detour could have affected the ultimate outcome. Dramatic tension is a narrative effect, as the outcome, even if unknown to the audience, is pregiven. The sequence presents the factors that had to be addressed and the obstacles that had to be overcome for the outcome to occur. Interviews can be broken down into discrete sections, each of which is defined by its relation to the plot. Off-line choices present complications, whereas on-line choices present resolutions that allow the story to continue. The presentation of each episode underscores the "logic" of the outcome. Mishler's approach allows for analytic abstraction to replace a sequence of anecdotes with a structure of episodes, each articulating an important step in the movement to achieved identity (pp. 2-25, 28-33).

In Mishler's case study of a furniture craftsman, the outcome is satisfactory, and the story affirms the ability of the narrator to overcome his own confusions by taking a dramatic leap into a new line of work (see Table 34.1). Mishler identifies "intuition" as the causal factor the narrator uses to explain his ultimate ability to overcome a previous personal history determined more by chance events than by active decision making (see episode 7 in Table 34.1, the turning point). "Intuition" does not appear as a direct explanation in every episode, but each episode is presented in a way that supports the explanatory framework the interviewee has developed to explain his personal history. To understand a narrative is to have command of the rules governing the selection and ordering of events into a plot. The

Table 34.1 ACHIEVING A CRAFT IDENTITY: THE NARRATIVE OF AN ARTIST-FURNITURE MAKER

Narrative Episode	Identity Narrative: Interview Excerpts
1. Origins	"My beginnings were in—uh I did a little bit of woodworking when I was a kid, mostly with wooden boats."
2. Complication$_1$	"I'm one of those people really vague about what I wanted to do. I—I entered—I got accepted to college as a chemical engineer, because I was interested in plastics at the time."
3. Resolution$_1$	"I decided I wanted to do something else. . . . I started in an under-graduate program as an architect."
4. Complication$_2$	"And ah after school I had a job for a while with a firm. ah The firm . . . collapsed. Folded. And uh I met an architect, and he and I decided to design some geodesic domes, and do that kind of thing."
5. Resolution$_2$	"And I met a third-generation craftsman in Indiana, who uh allowed me to share his shop space with—And ah that's when I really started to do woodworking. . . . But he just knew so much technically, and I learned an awful lot."
6. Complication$_3$	"I felt like I was wasting all my—my ah schooling as a landscape architect. So [we] moved [and] I started working as a landscape architect. And I did that for five and a half years."
7. Turning point	"And ah it just wasn't what I wanted to do for the rest of my life. . . . So I did a search, and uh decided to go to graduate school in furniture. . . . I made the—ah the decision to ah, go into furniture. Just in that I had an intuitive sense about woodworking, which I didn't about landscape architecture."
8. Preparation	"So three years altogether, totally investing myself in—in ah the furniture world as a craftsman. Got a—degree in crafts, .hh ah treating furniture as an art form."
9. Conclusion	"I started teaching . . . I collected more equipment and set up the shop here. . . . Started doing some shows and commission work, and that all went pretty well."

SOURCE: Adapted from Mishler (1992:29-31).

events that serve as plotting points are symbols in that they merge description with ethical evaluation. The evaluation appears to be the result of examining consequences, but it flows from the principles that narrators assume can and do provide explanation of the concluding point.

This distinctly conservative aspect of narration reconciles narrators (and their communities) to the patterns of change they have experienced. At times, however, the conclusion can be unbearable. Utopian aspiration refuses reconciliation and prompts a reconstruction of memory so that possibilities for change are accentuated. In his essays "The Death of Luigi Trastulli: Memory and the Event" and "Uchronic Dreams: Working-Class Memory and Possible Worlds," Alessandro Portelli (1991:1-26, 99-116) analyzes patterns of narrative reconfiguration he found in interviews with working-class residents of Terni, Italy. Their reconstructions of the past were factually wrong. Their accounts merged or scrambled events and at times referred to events that never occurred. In effect, their collective stories had created an alternative chronology that allowed them to maintain their own historical experience.

Portelli argues that chronological inaccuracy in the narrative helped the community maintain a sense of continuing to have a future and retaining the possibility of political resurgence during a time of retreat. Notwithstanding modernization of economic structures, the growth of educational opportunities, and a growing differentiation occurring as a result of individuals' differing personal responses to a changing society, the community maintained its political cohesion. Portelli's analysis suggests that the community's ability to maintain identity rested on a utopian, historically inaccurate, but culturally effective myth of the past. The narratives kept alive an alternative future that preserved for several decades the possibility of independent, worker-based action, even if, for the most part, members of the community were actively participating in the reconstruction of Italian society around international markets.

Disjunction between discursive and pragmatic behavior may be quite widespread and could provide insight into discrepancies in the political, economic, social, and cultural actions of social groups. The disjunction between subjective and objective factors in social relationships is an area for which oral history documents provide ideal sources of evidence. Paul Ricoeur's (1983:52-87) model of threefold mimesis may help researchers to see how individual textual configurations (mimesis$_2$) found in oral history interviews intersect with collective processes of prefiguration (mimesis$_1$) and refiguration (mimesis$_3$). *Prefiguration* refers to the metaphorical transpositions that are normally available and allowed in a community, which for these purposes we can define as a group built around regularly shared communicative acts. *Refiguration* refers to the process of reconstruction of texts into experiences of meaning. In simplified terms, prefigured time (ideology) becomes refigured time (experience) through the mediation of configured time (narrative accounts).

Prefiguration sets limits as to what will be a refigurable text—that is, one that potential audiences will accept as meaningful. Nonetheless, prefigurative conventions do not predetermine the shape of any configured text. Texts are propositions that members of a community put forward to each other. Texts must convince others that the narration accounts for what a group accepts as fact. Texts prove their aptness as explanations by providing satisfying understandings of the present and by identifying key events that others will accept as suitable evidence for the conclusion proffered (Ricoeur 1973).

As individual performances of collective prefigurations circulate with varying degrees of success, ideology becomes a fluid part of individual lives and social relations. Accepted narratives create a temporal world within which people have "experiences" that they can continue to share; that is, they have a sense of actions that remain meaningful and related logically to conclusions understood as "necessary" or, less strongly, "probable." Action may not necessarily be dependent upon narrative explanations available to a group, but stories that people exchange and accept as satisfying help establish a sense of proper, effective action, which can then be configured into new narratives. The truth of narratives rests on their ability to instigate and sustain new action. One of the values of examining how oral history interviews emplot explanatory frameworks is the degree to which they can point researchers to preferred actions as well as to likely blockages, clues that will assist with the identification and reading of other sources.

PARADIGMATIC ANALYSIS

Paradigmatic analysis complements the study of emplotment by examining recurrent symbols and other expressive motifs that are the basic constructive units of narrative flow. Oral accounts in particular tend to synthesize complex series of events into readily comprehensible and expressible images. Symbols take their place within stories as instantiations of narrative logic (Allen 1982; Ashplant 1998; McMahan 1989:100-105; Tonkin 1992:126-30). For example, in my work on interviews recorded with painters in California (Cándida Smith 1989, 1995), I found that the special quality of light and climate in the state was a recurrent symbolic motif. Interviewees used the image to articulate a special condition that shaped their work and set them apart from painters in other parts of the world. The motif appeared to the interviewees as an indubitable natural fact that explained the particularities of painting in the region. In fact, the symbol as deployed in narratives had little to do with nature but appeared typically when interviewees wanted to encapsulate their sometimes pleasant, sometimes difficult relationship to society into a ready metaphor. In one interview recorded over several sessions, the narrator described California light as clarifying and liberatory to underscore the freedom he felt when he began painting and exhibiting. Several sessions later, he described California light as blinding and stultifying as he discussed a point when his career had reached a dead end. In either case, light was not a physical phenomenon but a symbolic displacement of professional self-representation. The value that the symbol expressed depended in both cases upon its location within a narrative plotline and the conclusion it had to reinforce (Cándida Smith 1989:3-4).

Symbols often appear in patterned relationships. Women painters in post-World War II California, for example, often found as they struggled to establish their careers that critics couched favorable reviews in highly sexualized terms. Joan Brown was "everybody's darling," according to one writer, who proceeded to describe her as a talented, energetic "receptacle of attitudes" for the "germinating" ideas of her (male) teachers. In the several oral history interviews conducted with Brown over a 30-year period, she alternated two distinctive voices as she recounted her life story. One voice used humorous hyperbole to accentuate the surreality of commerce and business and those who live within that world. This inflection drew a veil across painful elements of her life by rendering them into sharp, quick, brittle images designed to shock and get a laugh. The other voice used more expansive, philosophical language to express the wonder and excitement that a once young woman felt embarking on her career. Painting was explicitly a symbol for a journey of initiation that would ultimately result in wisdom and inner peace.

Brown never recursively marked the transition between these two voices. Her vocabulary and sentence structures changed unself-consciously as she went back and forth between the two modes of her career. She was, however, quite aware of a double self-representation that enacted her response to the sexualization of herself and her art. She used archly stereotypical sexual imagery to portray herself in interaction with the absurd world of career building. She presented herself as a compulsive liar who used dress and appearance to make fools of people she encountered. This mendacious, opportunistic character appeared in her accounts as a person who drank too much, participated in parties to excess, and let herself be carried to unspecified extremes by others. Opposed to a gendered, sexualized conception of self, another voice called within the interviews, invoking the deeper reality of an initiate who survived spiritually through recurrent journeys into the alternative worlds that painting realized for her. This self-consciously degendered self-representation gave her strength to stand her ground and make difficult practical career decisions that alienated critics, curators, and gallery owners (Cándida Smith 1995:172-89).

The recurrence of paradigmatic motifs across interviews and their structural logic suggests that they are not simply individual performative expressions. They help articulate the logic of a communication by stressing the justice of a conclusion. Self-representation is a privileged symbolic feature of oral narrations because it articulates the moral position that the speaker has taken on the turning point and its consequences. Eva M. McMahan (1989), building on the theoretical work of Livia Polanyi (1985), argues that the framing of a speaker's evaluative conclusions is particularly strong in oral narratives as they establish the relationship between speaker and listeners. McMahan (1989) states that

> the teller must constantly address the implicit evaluative response of the listener: "So what?" The teller must show that the story is both topical and meaningful—that it makes a point. Generally, the interviewee as storyteller is expected to "(a) tell a topically coherent story; (b) tell a narratable story—one worth building a prolonged telling around; (c) introduce the story so that the connection with previous talk is clear; (d) tell a story that begins at the beginning, that is, one in which time moves ahead reasonably smoothly except for flashbacks that seem to serve a justifiable purpose in the telling; and, (e) evaluate states and events so that it is possible to recover the core of the story and thereby infer the point being made through telling." (Pp. 80-82; McMahan quotes Polanyi 1985:200)

In oral accounts, bracketing sections are frequently introduced so that the narrator can comment explicitly on the ethical meaning of the story, just in case listeners do not quite intuit how to feel the symbols. The narrator may elicit responses from listeners, often by asking questions. By the end of the story, as the conclusion becomes inevitable, McMahan argues, ethical evaluation begins to merge with self-representation. How listeners respond to the story determines how they respond to the storyteller, and through the account an ethical

relationship has been proposed, if not established (pp. 89-92, 93-96).

Just as emplotment can lead to a reimagination and reordering of events to strengthen the inevitability of the conclusion, paradigmatic elements may be reworked to strengthen the moral evaluation and consequently the subject position that the storyteller takes in relation to his or her listeners. Mariano Vallejo, in his testimonial collected in 1874 for Hubert Bancroft's multivolume history of California, discussed at length a meeting he claimed took place in 1846, on the eve of the American invasion of Mexico. Subsequent historians have largely dismissed Vallejo's account as legendary and in the process missed the vital political content his possible fabulation conveys. As war loomed, Californio leaders convened to discuss their options. Nominally, they were citizens of Mexico, but since a local revolution in 1836, California had been for all practical purposes autonomous of the central government. Vallejo's story condensed a series of debates that occurred within Californio society over many years into the arguments of one evening. As Rosaura Sánchez (1995) has analyzed the anecdote, the participants in the debate represented four positions. Spokesmen for a liberal, federalist, republican future opposed those who were promonarchist. Liberals were evenly divided between those who favored immediate independence and those, like Vallejo, who sought annexation to the United States. The monarchists were divided between those who wanted British annexation and those who sought French intervention. The characters presented in the anecdote articulate a geometry of political positions. Whether or not the meeting actually occurred, the characters were paradigmatic inventions that allowed the speaker to articulate his evaluation of the meeting and its ultimate consequences.

Throughout his account, Vallejo editorialized on the strengths and weaknesses of each position. He linked the arguments to several practical issues for Californio society, such as trade and property regimes, while he ignored other issues entirely, such as slavery and implications for relations with the indigenous peoples. Vallejo's anecdote, however symbolic, articulated in crystalline form the competing ideological positions of his people in 1846 while explaining the political strategies that he and others followed. He defended his support for annexation to the United States by articulating his understanding of the American Revolution of 1776 and its, to his mind, still-universal promises of freedom, equality, and due process of law. He structured his account largely to convince his listeners, primarily the Anglo-American readers who would encounter him either directly in the transcript of his interview or indirectly through Bancroft's history, of their hypocrisy. His overall testimonial builds around his protest of the theft of the Californios' property and their political marginalization. American expansion had in fact betrayed the hopes that Vallejo and others had felt 30 years earlier. He wanted to convince his listeners that the outcome might have been very different had the Californios adopted policies opposed to annexation by the United States. Vallejo's account, motivated by moral fervor and foregrounding political and ideological choices of his people, still provides an important corrective to accounts that present westward expansion as a story with only American actors (Sánchez 1995:245-48).

◆ Recuperating Experience Back into History

In the context of narrative analysis, the "data" of interviews are first and foremost the ways in which a person has reconstructed the past to negotiate an ever-fluid process of identity construction. The subjective position in narration differs from psychological consciousness in its exterior manifestation and the element of self-reflective purpose. Vallejo's interview unfolds as a conscious effort to speak through his interviewers to a broad public. Although this is not uncommon, particularly in interviews with elite figures, many interviews remain within the local, intimate historical contexts that stories shared between friends help establish. In a world of close acquaintances, anecdotes convey possibly useful impressions about what individuals might expect in future encounters. The cues are couched in explanations that, however trivial in form, remove arbitrariness from the relationship. Fred will flame you at the least provocation because "he's always like that." Characterization in this case is more of a predication than an explanation, but it serves to warn those who must or might be exposed to Fred of what to expect (Cándida Smith 1995:xxi-xxvi; Clark, Hyde, and McMahan 1980; Frank 1979; Halbwachs 1993:38; Thompson 1988:150-65).

In reading emplotment and paradigm codes, scholars often must assign meanings and values to these images that they may not have had in their original context in order to make them speak to a broader historical context. Isabelle Bertaux-Wiame (1982:192-93), for example, analyzed interviews with migrants from the countryside into Paris and found recurrent patterns in the choices of pronouns used by the interviewees. Men typically used first-person singular forms to speak of themselves as actors making decisions and changing their lives and those of their families. Women, on the other hand, tended to avoid first-person singular forms and to speak more usually either with first-person plural forms or with the impersonal third-person pronoun *on* (one). This observation allowed Bertaux-Wiame to develop a rich psychological argument about gendered conceptions of power and historical action prevalent among the French working class at a particular historical conjuncture. She readily acknowledges that her categories would seem irrelevant and foreign to the narrators whose accounts stimulated her insight. Many historians might likewise question the validity of her interpretation. Gendered selection of pronouns became meaningful because Bertaux-Wiame turned to feminist theory for assistance in reading "data" that would otherwise be ignored. Interpersonal relations symbolized through the selection of pronouns would likely not register as relevant to the study of larger transpersonal social forces without a theoretical perspective that reread intimate interactions as dialectically constituted with political and economic structures.

The distinction between psychological consciousness and narrative self is foundational to the examination of regularities, whether syntagmatic or paradigmatic, within interviews. The narrative self takes shape in the unfolding stories within which it is deployed as one of several codes. Changes in self-representation do not provide evidence in and of themselves about how people "felt." Such studies trace instead how understandings of the self have grown from and altered in relation to other social and cultural phenomena *also* represented within a narrative.

Symbolic contradictions within narrative texts indicate areas of conflict about how to represent and understand the past. The storyteller and his or her group could not arrive at a satisfying way of narrating painful or contentious events, so they deflected issues into a variety of evasive symbolic strategies. Isolation of contradictory, confused, and evasive elements within a narrative has served historical analysis by highlighting areas of concern that communities have not been able to resolve narratively. Analysis presents a field of symbolic measures that in and of themselves are subject to multiple interpretations, but these areas of contention themselves reveal places for further historical contextualization and exploration. Careful analysis of the subject positions contained within these symbols in particular can elucidate a pattern of self-imagining that includes perceptions of the dangers that "others" pose (Passerini 1987a).

Conflicts between identity and subjectivity may be a recurrent paradigmatic feature in interviews. The challenge of reconciling differences between the subject position assigned a person due to his or her social classification with a more complex, varied sense of relationships may reveal itself at the paradigmatic level through such measures as Joan Brown's double self-representation. The challenge may also appear in performative tensions that undercut a narrator's ability to articulate either a clear ethical evaluation or a clear self-representation.

Feminist scholars in particular have worked with contradictions in self-representation to identify the translation of gendered power structures into historically situated experience of gender relations. Women's accounts of their lives negotiate, as Joan Brown's does with great elegance, the discrepancy between the self-image they have developed in the course of their everyday activities and the images of themselves that they receive from men. Kathryn Anderson and Dana C. Jack (1991) argue that women's oral history interviews usually have two channels working simultaneously across the episodes narrated. On the one hand, many women may tell their stories using dominant, masculinist emplotment and paradigmatic codes. They enunciate through the selection of complications, resolutions, turning point, and conclusion, as well as through the symbols used, concepts and values that affirm male supremacy, and the appropriateness of women's reduced social position. Within the performance, however, there may be a muted story that expresses painful disappointments and resentments as a set of ironies that suggest the purely fictional character of dominant values. Anderson and Jack advise that interviewers and analysts should focus on difficult choices that women have had to make in their lives, much as Passerini did when probing for information on birth control and abortion. They also advise paying careful attention to expressions of pain and subjects that address the margins of acceptable behavior, particularly feelings and behaviors that the interviewees themselves identify as "unwomanly." Stereotypes about women invoked in the interview provide the analyst with an opportunity to see efforts to reconcile derogatory images with an interviewee's positive self-images. In these areas, narrative structures will be less likely to effect a comfortable ethical evaluation that reconciles the interviewee and her listeners to the inevitability of the conclusion. Anecdotes and images that women use to address their weakness in a situation often lead to a layering of codes conveying the storyteller's intellectual and emotional conflict. In these situations, logic collapses and the storyteller abruptly tacks on a conclusion to a story that was headed in another direction. A pat ending realigns her account with dominant values in her community but does so in a way that signals an experience of tensions (see also Borland 1991; Passerini 1987b:138-49).

Catherine Kohler Riessman (1992), in her work on women's accounts of abusive marriages, has observed critical differences in how women relate stories of victimization and stories of resistance. At the beginning of the 1980s, stories about marital rape were difficult to narrate, in part because the term itself did not yet have currency. Neither laws nor social custom recognized a wife's right to refuse sexual relations with her husband. As a political movement developed to demand legal change, new narrative structures emerged that helped women transform brutal facts in their lives into communicable experience. In seeking security and the right to divorce, abused women learned to speak to each other, to counselors, and to lawmakers. A shared language allowed for crisp, articulate stories in which the pain endured was coded typically in inflections of speech patterns, such as the introduction of unusually long pauses. Stories of resistance typically became less articulate when self-defense was angry or violent. Not even the

women involved were sure that their efforts to protect themselves from further abuse were ethical. Riessman (1992) observes that the language structures surrounding abusive marriages provide "for women's depressed emotions but not for their rage" (p. 246). Consequently, narration of anger is more episodic and confused, as if the storyteller herself had to struggle to understand her emotions and actions, which are ostensibly out of character for a "good" woman. A political movement had succeeded by establishing one emplotment code, which then blocked positive reception of alternative narratives arriving at conclusions less consonant with the nobility of victimhood.

Emplotment structures as well as symbolic motifs established in one discourse are then available for use in other situations. Work on narrative plotlines, and the subject positions they entail, allows for analysis of individual narrating style. William R. Earnest (1992) has examined the relation of workplace narratives to typical patterns for the interviewee's life story. In an interview with an employee in an automobile factory, Earnest noticed a syntagmatic pattern that recurred across several sessions. A grievance about work conditions in the factory welled up with considerable bitterness, but then the issues in dispute found resolution through a pattern of "self-effacement, criticism of other workers, sympathy for management rationales, and then final absolution of management" of any responsibility for the problem (pp. 257-58). When the questioning turned to family background and personal life, Earnest heard the same syntagmatic pattern applied to the interviewee's relationship with his father. Whenever anger at paternal neglect flared up, the interviewee's story line displaced his rage into criticism of others in the family. Family stories paralleled workplace stories by concluding with the interviewee's acceptance of his father's rationales and affirmation of father-son identity. The interviewee was unconscious of this storytelling pattern. When told of it, he was surprised and doubtful, but he accepted the validity of the conclusion when shown the evidence. Confronting his experience as a narrative effect jolted him into reexamining his memories and his organization of his recollections into discrete episodes directing him to preordained conclusions. The interviewee was thrown out of experience into a historical reconsideration of how he had come to form his social relationships.

His self-reexamination began with his examination of the points in his narratives where he felt the most tension. The movement toward reevaluating the codes he used to create meaning arose, according to George Rosenwald's (1992) analysis of this case, from a conflict between identity and subjectivity that the interview process brought to the surface. Rosenwald contends that the culture-specific narrative rules ensuring intelligibility also govern identity. In opposition to the relatively stable and stabilizing patterns of self that arise as one talks in ways that are comprehensible to others, Rosenwald poses the force of subjectivity, which he defines as the "restlessness of desire" (p. 265). Recursive recognition of the rules of narration can allow normally repressed imagination of other ways of being to enter into the storytelling process.

The introduction of such self-reflection into oral history interviews is not common—at least not as a conscious aim of the interviewer and the narrator. Portelli (1997), however, in his recent work on genre in oral history, suggests that the encounter of historian and interviewee, each with such different strategies for understanding the past, must inevitably generate cognitive tension. One way interviewers have coped with this has been by effacing themselves and allowing narrators to tell their stories with a minimum of response or guidance. That strategy imposes highly artificial requirements upon dialogic exchanges. No matter how silent interviewers strive to be, they are not invisible, and the interview situation, although drawing upon narrative repertoires that interviewees have developed, has little in common with everyday conversation.

"What is spoken in a typical oral history interview has usually never been told *in that form* before," Portelli (1997:4) argues. Even if interviewees rely upon twice-told tales to answer questions posed to them, they have usually never previously strung their stories together in a single, extended account. Narrators are also aware, like Mariano Vallejo, that they speak through their interviewers to a larger audience. Portelli notes that this leap into an imagined public realm often involves a marked change in diction. Interviewees begin to speak in a formally correct style. Even more important, Portelli adds, "the novelty of the situation and the effort at diction accentuate a feature of all oral discourse—that of being a 'text' in the making, which includes its own drafts, preparatory materials, and discarded materials" (p. 5). The task that the narrator faces is new and not reducible to the rules of everyday conversation, even if words and anecdotes spring largely or exclusively from that source.

What distinguishes oral history from folklore, Portelli (1997) claims, is the move away from "storytelling," from the sharing of familiar accounts with workmates, friends, and family that help bind them together into communities. Narrators discover a genre of discourse that Portelli calls "history-telling" (p. 6). Flowing out of researchers' theoretical and analytic assumptions, interview questions challenge narrators to transform their personal anecdotes. The process provokes narrators to reflect consciously upon the larger historical and social meanings of what has happened to them as individuals.

The relationship at the heart of oral history, as Portelli describes it, is a groping toward mutual understanding that is equally taxing for both parties to the interview. Interviewers must work to understand the connections that narrators are providing as they consider additional lines of questioning that will build upon rather than cut short the dialogue. Historians' questions ask narrators to apply their experiences to frameworks that they may never have thought with before, but that they need to intuit if they are to respond with helpful and relevant information. An attempt to reconstruct memory so that it can speak to history proceeds within this dialectic, which if it breaks down leads to an interview lacking in either texture or information. Successful oral history interviews take on a special verbal quality that Portelli calls "thick dialogue," and the recorded conversation ceases to be a rehearsal of comfortable and conventional formulas and becomes a deeper probing of what happened and why.

Oral history has been part of a broader deontological trend in the social sciences. Collaboration between historian and narrator has helped generate greater understanding that personal experience has historical impact and is not simply an aftereffect of social process. The possibility of communication, and not simply translation, across quite different modes of representing the past rests in an understanding of the symbolic structures that narrators use to posit themselves as subjects who know the objects of their worlds—past, present, and future—in specific, practical, and community-based ways. A focus on the practical underpinnings of meaning systems reintegrates ethics, politics, and knowledge.

Memory and history confront each other across the tape recorder. Separately, both struggle with syntagmatic and paradigmatic codes that structure comprehension of what the present situation means. From their collaboration occasionally emerges a richer, more nuanced understanding of the past, the power of which lies in its having transcended the particular languages that engulf both participants in the interview. (On the alienation of both academic and community understandings of the past through the oral history process,

see Friedlander 1975:xxiii-xxvii.) The first step in analyzing oral history interviews is to recognize that they are not raw sources of information. Oral sources are themselves already analytic documents structured with complex codes and achieved meanings. An analyst can make visible neither the limitations nor the critical capacities of those meanings without delving into the text of the interview and beginning a process of dialogue with its narrator.

■ Notes

1. Jan Vansina's *Oral Tradition: A Study in Historical Methodology* (1965) is the classic text on oral tradition. On the relationship between oral tradition and oral history, see Elizabeth Tonkin (1992) and Isabel Hofmeyr (1992). On the selectivity of sources and the relation of oral traditions to documentary archives, see Michel-Rolph Trouillot (1995).

2. A large literature has developed on the social construction of memory. The classic sociological texts were written by Maurice Halbwachs prior to World War II. Lewis Coser has edited a selection of Halbwachs's work in a volume titled *On Collective Memory* (1993). See also the work of Alan Confino (1997), Susan Crane (1997), Noa Gedi and Yigal Elam (1996), Patrick H. Hutton (1993, 1997), Andreas Huyssens (1995), Iwona Irwin-Zarecki (1994), Jacques Le Goff (1992), Allan Megill (1989), Pierre Nora (1989), Jeffrey K. Olick and Joyce Robbins (1998), Michael Roth (1995), Michael Schudson (1995), David Thelen (1989), Frances Yates (1966), and James Young (1993).

3. For recent discussions of rules of evidence and verifiability in historical investigation after the narrative turn, see Joyce Appleby, Lynn Hunt, and Margaret Jacob (1994), Susan Stafford Friedman (1995), Lynn Hunt (1996), David Lowenthal (1989), Allan Megill (1998), and Peter Novick (1988). For classic discussions of the historical method, see Raymond Aron (1961), Lee Benson and Cushing Strout (1965), Marc Bloch (1953), Fernand Braudel (1980), R. G. Collingwood (1946), William Dray (1957), Louis Mink (1965, 1970), and Paul Veyne (1984).

4. Fascist demographic propaganda drew upon preexisting ideas and cultural expressions, which may explain to a degree the hold such ideas had on women, even those who did not act in conformity with older ideals of femininity.

5. For the classic account of displacement through narrative figures, see Aristotle's *Poetics* (1982:secs. 1451b5-6, 1458a18-23, 1457b6). See also Roland Barthes (1982), Seymour Chatman (1975), Leon Golden (1962), and Paul Ricoeur (1977).

■ *References*

Allen, B. 1982. "Recreating the Past: The Narrator's Perspective in Oral History." *Oral History Review* 10:33-45.

Anderson, K. and D. C. Jack. 1991. "Learning to Listen: Interview Techniques and Analyses." Pp. 11-26 in *Women's Words: The Feminist Practice of Oral History,* edited by S. B. Gluck and D. Patai. New York: Routledge.

Appleby, J., L. Hunt, and M. Jacob. 1994. *Telling the Truth about History.* New York: Norton.

Aristotle. 1982. *Poetics.* New York: Norton.

Aron, R. 1961. *Introduction to the Philosophy of History: An Essay on the Limits of Historical Objectivity.* Boston: Beacon.

Ashplant, T. 1998. "Anecdote as Narrative Resource in Working-Class Life Stories." Pp. 99-113 in *Narrative and Genre,* edited by M. Chamberlain and P. Thompson. London: Routledge.

Barthes, R. 1982. "Introduction to the Structural Analysis of Narrative." Pp. 251-95 in R. Barthes, *A Roland Barthes Reader.* New York: Hill & Wang.

Benson, L. and C. Strout. 1965. "Causation and the American Civil War: Two Appraisals." Pp. 74-96 in *Studies in the Philosophy of History: Selected Essays from History and Theory,* edited by G. H. Nadel. New York: Harper Torchbooks.

Bertaux-Wiame, I. 1982. "The Life History Approach to the Study of Internal Migration." Pp. 186-200 in *Our Common History: The Transformation of Europe,* edited by P. Thompson. London: Pluto.

Bloch, M. 1953. *The Historian's Craft.* New York: Alfred A. Knopf.

Borland, K. 1991. " 'That's Not What I Said': Interpretive Conflict in Oral Narrative Research." Pp. 63-76 in *Women's Words: The Feminist Practice of Oral History,* edited by S. B. Gluck and D. Patai. New York: Routledge.

Braudel, F. 1980. *On History.* Chicago: University of Chicago Press.

Cándida Smith, R. 1989. "Exquisite Corpse: The Sense of the Past in Oral Histories with California Artists." *Oral History Review* 17:1-34.

———. 1995. *Utopia and Dissent: Art, Poetry, and Politics in California.* Berkeley: University of California Press.

Chatman, S. 1975. "The Structure of Narrative Transmission." Pp. 213-57 in *Style and Structure in Literature: Essays in the New Stylistics,* edited by R. Fowler. Ithaca, NY: Cornell University Press.

Clark, E. C., M. J. Hyde, and E. M. McMahan. 1980. "Communicating in the Oral History Interview: Investigating Problems of Interpreting Oral Data." *International Journal of Oral History* 1:28-40.

Collingwood, R. G. 1946. *The Idea of History.* Oxford: Oxford University Press.

Confino, A. 1997. "Collective Memory and Cultural History: Problems of Method." *American Historical Review* 102:1386-1403.

Crane, S. 1997. "Writing the Individual Back into Collective Memory." *American Historical Review* 102:1372-85.

Culler, J. D. 1986. *Ferdinand de Saussure.* Ithaca, NY: Cornell University Press.

Dray, W. 1957. *Laws and Explanations in History.* London: Oxford University Press.

Earnest, W. R. 1992. "Ideology Criticism and Life-History Research." Pp. 250-64 in *Storied Lives: The Cultural Politics of Self-Understanding,* edited by G. C. Rosenwald and R. L. Ochberg. New Haven, CT: Yale University Press.

Frank, G. 1979. "Finding a Common Denominator: A Phenomenological Critique of Life History Method." *Ethnos* 7:68-94.

Friedlander, P. 1975. *The Emergence of a UAW Local, 1936-1939: A Study in Class and Culture.* Pittsburgh, PA: University of Pittsburgh Press.

Friedman, S. S. 1995. "Making History: Reflections on Feminism, Narrative, and Desire." Pp. 11-54 in *Feminism beside Itself,* edited by D. Elam and R. Wiegman. New York: Routledge.

Gadet, F. 1989. *Saussure and Contemporary Culture.* London: Hutchison Radius.

Gedi, N. and Y. Elam. 1996. "Collective Memory: What Is It?" *History and Memory* 8:30-50.

Golden, L. 1962. "Catharsis." *Proceedings of the American Philological Association* 43:51-60.

Halbwachs, M. 1993. *On Collective Memory,* edited by L. Coser. Albany: State University of New York Press.

Harris, R. 1988. *Language, Saussure, and Wittgenstein: How to Play Games with Words.* London: Routledge.

Hofmeyr, I. 1992. " 'Nterata'/'The Wire': Fences, Boundaries, Orality, Literacy." Pp. 69-92 in *International Annual of Oral History, 1990: Subjectivity and Multiculturalism in Oral History,* edited by R. J. Grele. New York: Greenwood.

Holland, N. N. 1992. *The Critical I.* New York: Columbia University Press.

Hunt, L. 1999. "Psychoanalysis, the Self, and Historical Interpretation," presented at the symposium "History and the Limits of Interpretation," March 15-17, Rice University, Houston. Available Internet: http://www.ruf.rice.edu/~culture/papers/hunt.html

Hutton, P. H. 1993. *History as an Art of Memory.* Hanover, NH: University Press of New England.

———. 1997. "Mnemonic Schemes in the New History of Memory." *History and Theory* 36:378-91.

Huyssens, A. 1995. *Twilight Memories: Marking Time in a Culture of Amnesia.* New York:

Irwin-Zarecki, I. 1994. *Frames of Remembrance: The Dynamics of Collective Memory.* New Brunswick, NJ: Rutgers University Press.

Joutard, P. 1981. "A Regional Project: Ethnotexts." *Oral History* 9:47-51.

Joyner, C. W. 1979. "Oral History as Communicative Event: A Folkloristic Perspective." *Oral History Review* 7:47-52.

Le Goff, J. 1992. *History and Memory.* New York: Columbia University Press.

Lowenthal, D. 1989. "The Timeless Past: Some Anglo-American Historical Preconceptions." *Journal of American History* 75:1263-80.

McMahan, E. M. 1989. *Elite Oral History Discourse: A Study of Cooperation and Coherence.* Tuscaloosa: University of Alabama Press.

Megill, A. 1989. "Recounting the Past: 'Description,' Explanation, and Narrative in Historiography." *American Historical Review* 94:627-53.

———. 1998. "History, Memory, and Identity." *History and the Human Sciences* 11:37-62.

Mink, L. 1965. "The Autonomy of Historical Understanding." *History and Theory* 5:24-47.

———. 1970. "History and Fiction as Modes of Comprehension." *New Literary History* 1:556-69.

Mishler, E. G. 1992. "Work, Identity, and Narrative: An Artist-Craftsman's Story." Pp. 21-40 in *Storied Lives: The Cultural Politics of Self-Understanding,* edited by G. C. Rosenwald and R. L. Ochberg. New Haven, CT: Yale University Press.

Nora, P. 1989. "Between Memory and History: *Les Lieux de mémoire.*" *Representations* 26:7-25.

Novick, P. 1988. *That Noble Dream: The "Objectivity Question" and the American Historical Profession.* Cambridge: Cambridge University Press.

Olick, J. K. and J. Robbins. 1998. "Social Memory Studies: From 'Collective Memory' to the Historical Sociology of Mnemonic Practices." *Annual Review of Sociology* 22:105-40.

Passerini, L. 1987a. "Documento autobiografico e tempo storico." *Rivista di Storia Contemporanea* 16:412-20.

———. 1987b. *Fascism in Popular Memory: The Cultural Experience of the Turin Working Class.* Cambridge: Cambridge University Press.

———. 1988. "Conoscenza storica e fonti orali." Pp. 31-66 in L. Passerini, *Storia e soggetività: Le fonti orali, la memoria.* Florence: La Nuova Italia.

Polanyi, L. 1985. "Conversational Storytelling." Pp. 183-201 in *Handbook of Discourse Analysis,* Vol. 3, edited by T. A. van Dijk. London: Academic Press.

Portelli, A. 1991. *The Death of Luigi Trastulli and Other Stories: Form and Meaning in Oral History.* Albany: State University of New York Press.

———. 1997. *The Battle of Valle Giulia: Oral History and the Art of Dialogue.* Madison: University of Wisconsin Press.

Ricoeur, P. 1973. "The Model of the Text: Meaningful Action Considered as a Text." *New Literary History* 5:91-117.

———. 1977. *The Rule of Metaphor: Multidisciplinary Studies of the Creation of Meaning in Language.* Toronto: University of Toronto Press.

———. 1983. *Time and Narrative,* Vol. 1. Chicago: University of Chicago Press.

Riessman, C. K. 1992. "Making Sense of Marital Violence: One Woman's Narrative." Pp. 231-49 in *Storied Lives: The Cultural Politics of Self-Understanding,* edited by G. C. Rosenwald and R. L. Ochberg. New Haven, CT: Yale University Press.

Rosenwald, G. C. 1992. "Conclusion: Reflections on Narrative Self-Understanding." Pp. 265-89 in *Storied Lives: The Cultural Politics of Self-Understanding,* edited by G. C. Rosenwald and R. L. Ochberg. New Haven, CT: Yale University Press.

Roth, M. S. 1995. *The Ironist's Cage: Memory, Trauma, and the Construction of History.* New York: Columbia University Press.

Sánchez, R. 1995. *Telling Identities: The Californio Testimonios.* Minneapolis: University of Minnesota Press.

Schudson, M. 1995. *Memory Distortion: How Minds, Brains, and Societies Reconstruct the Past.* Cambridge, MA: Harvard University Press.

Thelen, D. 1989. "Memory and American History." *Journal of American History* 75:117-29.

Thompson, P. 1988. *The Voice of the Past.* Oxford: Oxford University Press.

Tonkin, E. 1992. *Narrating Our Pasts: The Social Construction of Oral History.* Cambridge: Cambridge University Press.

Trouillot, M.-R. 1995. *Silencing the Past: Power and the Production of History.* Boston: Beacon.

Vansina, J. 1965. *Oral Tradition: A Study in Historical Methodology.* London: Routledge & Kegan Paul.

Veyne, P. 1984. *Writing History: Essay on Epistemology.* Middletown, CT: Wesleyan University Press.

Yates, F. 1966. *The Art of Memory.* Chicago: University of Chicago Press.

Young, J. E. 1993. *The Texture of Memory: Holocaust Memorials and Meaning.* New Haven, CT: Yale University Press.

35

NARRATIVE, INTERVIEWS, AND ORGANIZATIONS

◆ Barbara Czarniawska

It is customary to refer to Roland Barthes (1977) as the author who first postulated that the modern social sciences should pay attention to narratives, which are as central to modernity as they were to earlier eras. Barthes's appeal was adopted by Alasdair MacIntyre ([1981] 1990) and Richard Rorty (1991) in philosophy, by Hayden White (1973, 1978) in history, by Jean Matter Mandler (1984) and Jerome Bruner (1986, 1990) in psychology, by Walter Fisher (1984, 1987) in political science, and by Clifford Geertz (1980, 1988) in anthropology, among many others.

One of the first sociologists to emphasize the relevance of narrative to an understanding of social processes was Richard Harvey Brown, whose opus *A Poetic for Sociology* (1977) was inspired by the work of the Russian postformalist Mikhail Bakhtin (see Bakhtin and Medvedev [1928] 1991).

Brown (1977, 1987) formulated a perspective he called "symbolic realism," which postulates that people are creators of their own worlds, even as they insist on seeing every pragmatically constructed world as the real one, the one to act upon. Narratives of all kinds are very important tools in this construction.

Brown pointed out the proximity between literary metaphors and the notion of institutions, emphasizing that institutions are not just patterns of action. The taken-for-grantedness of institutionalized action sometimes leads to the mistaken conclusion that such action does not need to be justified or accounted for. In practice, an action, in order to be legitimate, requires an institutionalized account, which in fact is an inseparable part of action itself.

The uniqueness of Brown's (1987, 1989) way of espousing the narrative mode of knowing, and its consequent relevance for organization theory, was that he did not lose sight of the question of power. This is important, because there is much related criticism of constructionist theories (to which the narrative approach belongs), allegedly unmasking their apologetic character. However, there is nothing inherent in the narrative approach to warrant such criticism. A narrative has a world-creating force, but worlds thus created can allow more freedom to some than to others. "The 'rationalization of production' or the 'competition for foreign markets' may narrow the freedom of workers" (Brown 1987: 135), as power is really the *power to define* (Brown 1989). Brown's approach is a disavowal of the conventional critical stance that sees managerial narratives as pertaining to "false consciousness" rather than to "direct relations of reality as it is," and also a refusal to take any narrative for granted, if only because there are many competing ones.

◆ Narrative and Organization Studies

The process of organizing is also, and perhaps primarily, a process of narration. "Organizations" may be treated as a subgenre of a modern narrative, and each organizing process produces many such narratives. As such, organizational narratives deserve to be analyzed both as organizing tools and as the results of organizing.

Narrative enters organizational studies in at least four forms: (a) as organizational research that is written in a storylike fashion ("tales of the field," as John Van Maanen, 1988, characterizes them), (b) as organizational research that collects organizational stories ("tales from the field"), (c) as organizational research that conceptualizes the process of organizing as story making, and (d) as reflection on organization theory as a literary endeavor. In what

follows, I will focus on the first three of these, as the fourth is less pertinent to the present context and has been dealt with extensively elsewhere (see Czarniawska 1999).

The narrative form of organization research is easiest to find in case studies: research cases, educational cases, and fictive cases that all use chronology as the main organizing device. One recent example of such a "tale of the field" is Bent Flyvbjerg's (1998) study of a traffic project in the Danish city of Aalborg. Based mainly on interview material, the narrative case presentation is consequently elucidated along theoretical, not normative, lines, which is a common way of combining narrative with the logico-scientific mode of reporting. (On the distinction between the two, see Bruner 1986.)

But it is the attempt to collect stories *from* the field that drew the attention of organizational researchers to the narrative. Although the most common early references are to the work of Burton Clark (1972) and Ian Mitroff and Ralph Kilmann (1975), the institutionalization of the topic of organizational stories in organization theory can be safely located at some point in the early 1980s, and is best exemplified in the works of Joanne Martin and her collaborators (e.g., Martin 1982; Martin et al. 1983). Many researchers working in the 1980s, however, conceived of organizational narratives as artifacts forever petrified in organizational reality, "out there," so to speak, waiting to be "collected" (Boland and Tankasi 1995). In time, the convention grew broader and studies began to accentuate the process of story telling as the never-ending construction of meaning in organizations. The late 1990s witnessed a proliferation of such narrative studies, which I describe in more detail elsewhere (Czarniawska 1998b). Subsequently, the focus narrowed onto the ways narratives were collected.

It can be safely repeated, following Walter Fisher (1984, 1987), that narratives are a natural form of organizational communication, if the word *natural* is used in the sense of being unreflective and easily coming to mind. Fieldwork tends to reveal this in a somewhat paradoxical way. Trained in "scientific" techniques of data collection, most organizational researchers structure their interviews directively, their interest in the narrative notwithstanding. "What are the most acute problems you are experiencing today?" and "Can you compare your present situation with that of two years ago?" are typical questions. The researchers ask people in the field to compare, to abstract, and to generalize. But in my experience, although many respondents engage such questions, they also ramify them by adding, say, "Let me tell you first how it all started" or "You need some more background first." The result is the production of a rich narrative, which might or might not be finally summarized along the lines the interviewer had in mind (see Holstein and Gubrium 1995).

I must admit that this used to bring me to the verge of panic—How to bring them back to the point?—but now I have learned that this *is* the point. Karl Weick played an important role in my reaching this understanding. It was Weick (1979) who first pointed out the processual character of organizing and then the role of sense making in the process of organizing (Weick 1995). This shift had a decisive impact on my use of interviews in organization studies. Rather than treating them only as a means to, and also impediments to, obtaining information about "organizations out there," I rediscovered interviews as the sites for the production and distribution of narratives.

In what follows, I provide, first, an example of how a coherent narrative (a "tale of the field") can be self-consciously constructed out of the diverse thoughts and commentaries of interview material and, second, an example of how a researcher can analyze narratives that have been collected in interviews textually ("tales from the field"). The examples are drawn from my current research, which focuses on the management of big cities and in which

fieldwork has so far been conducted in three municipalities: Warsaw, Stockholm, and Rome.[1] In the last section of the chapter, I reflect briefly on the consequences of conceptualizing the process of organizing as story making and of taking a narrative approach to organization studies.

◆ A Tale of the Field: Governmental Reform in Warsaw

In my study of Warsaw, the change of the governance system was a project that attracted much of my respondents' attention. I have decided to re-present this project here from the original report (Czarniawska 1998a) as a story of the reform, based on the contents of 18 interviews, complemented by press releases and other documents.

My decision results from the fact that not all narratives are stories. For example, Mandler (1984) distinguishes stories, scripts (which I have renamed "serials" in my own work; see Czarniawska 1997), and scenes ("themes" in my vocabulary). A story contains a plot consisting of causally related episodes that culminate in a solution. The minimal plot, states Tzvetan Todorov ([1977] 1990),

> consists in the passage from one equilibrium to another. An "ideal" narrative begins with a stable situation, which is disturbed by some power or force. There results a state of disequilibrium; by the action of a force directed in the opposite direction, the equilibrium is re-established; the second equilibrium is similar to the first, but the two are never identical. (P. 111)

A story usually contains several stages that contribute to a final solution, albeit in a complex way, for example, by way of false solutions and the creation of new problems. Stories reveal a good deal about specific organizations, because it is precisely in the story context that actors improvise against the background of known rules (see Cándida Smith, Chapter 34, this volume). Stories have a clear chronological structure; each story has a beginning and an end. Serials, such as repeated reforms in the Swedish public sector (Czarniawska 1997), continue as long as they pass the test of popularity. Themes consist of minor scenes that are continually repeated. Stories combine traditional elements ("This is the way we do things here") with spontaneous features ("But does it actually apply in this case?") and creative aspects ("Now we do it this way instead"). Stories are about critical, dramatic events in the lives of the organization.

In the process of organizing, the recipe for a good story is very simple indeed: Mix well some random events, several attempts at control, and the corresponding amount of counter control; put the mixture in a warm place, and wait for results. A story begins because somebody has had an idea and wants to realize it, or the other way around, because something has happened and people in an organization feel they have to react to it. The stream of events is reported as a story that begins to flow from this, and, as all streams do, it encounters various obstacles along the way. In the traditional discourse of organizational theory, both researchers and organizational participants speak of "friction"—encounters between "the old" and "the new" result in "friction," which, in fact, is a recurring topic in the constructed story that follows.

CONTEXTUALIZING THE STORY

Consider, first, the context of the reform. Traditionally, context is understood as a kind of a scene within which organizing takes place. It is worth pointing out, however, that the word actually means "another text, a text that accompanies the main text." Indeed, a section within a report called "the background," "the context," "the scene," or something along these lines is usually, as in the case under consideration, based on texts that are not the main story material. It summarizes, briefly and nonproblematically, the piles of other texts that are not the focus of the narrator, as the following excerpt from the original report illustrates.

In response to an initiative that originated in the county governor's office and was supported by the Mayor of Warsaw, the Polish government appointed a proxy for the Public Administration Reform, while Warsaw's county governor, instructed by the Chief Minister of the Cabinet, appointed a group of experts who had to prepare a new bill sustaining the reform. The previous governance system of Warsaw was dysfunctional, claimed the reformers, mainly because of the multiplicity of governance areas, which made it difficult for Warsaw to function as the capital of the country, that is, to provide services for the central government, the diplomatic corps, and international contacts.

The Association of the Polish City Planners served as a consultant because the project focused primarily on changes in the city administrative division. The basic idea was to join the seven district municipalities into one municipality called Warsaw Centrum, surrounded by a ring of ten suburban municipalities, so as to enable a comprehensive finance management function, an overall city plan, and a coherent control over city services. One of the first problems was, of course, the boundary. Even though the idea guiding the project was to return to the prewar boundaries of Warsaw, the reformers, lured by what seemed a "natural" boundary, excluded "a big chunk of the decree terrain," as it was called in city language. A storm of protests ensued.

Opposition to the project as a whole was expressed in a "counter-project," or "district mayors' project" (so called because most of the district mayors participated in its preparation) and two lesser projects prepared by the opposition parties. A text of an Act changing the system has been formulated and sent on parliament's "preferential route," meaning that there was little social consultation about it. It is necessary to add that many projects were shepherded by the country government along the preferential route at that time, because the bills not yet approved had accumulated beyond any hope of tackling them in the foreseeable future. (Czarniawska 1998a:3-4)

Complications begin to take shape in this extract from the report. Action usually provokes counteraction, both in stories and in organizations. Here we already have most of the elements necessary for emplotment: Warsaw existed in a state of equilibrium until the county governor and his allies undermined it, defining it as "dysfunctional" (which brings to mind Brown's [1989] "power to define"). An action restoring equilibrium is needed, and the reform is such an action. Observe that, in constructing my story, I am mimicking the story making of the reformers.

STORY MAKING

Now for the next excerpt from the report:

The fact that the city mayor gave his support to the county governor's project, thereby acting against the district mayors, was widely mentioned. The majority of district mayors agreed that "the city mayor and his team have been stressing from the very beginning how difficult and problematic the collaboration with the district mayors is; as a matter of fact, he made a *cause célèbre*

out of it" (the expression "the city mayor's whining" circulated freely). The statements from the city mayor's office confirmed this impression. However, the disagreement did not refer so much to the fact that there were conflicts between district municipalities, as to the ways in which they should be resolved or should not be allowed to arise. (Czarniawska 1998a:4)

Earlier, I was speaking in one voice; there was only one story. In the preceding excerpt, however, it is obvious that there are different stories in the making. I mark this with the conventional device "[the voice of] the majority," but I minimize the differences by presenting them as variations of the same story.

The report continues:

The conflicts related, among other things, to the wealth of Srodmiescie district in comparison to other districts and, in particular, to the attitude of "an enlightened despot"—the district mayor of Srodmiescie—who, to the amusement of some and the dismay of others, either extended or refused help to other districts and the City as he saw fit. [Conflict also related] to the lack of cooperation from the districts not included directly in a common project (e.g. the subway) but forced to pay for it, to the difficulties of foreign contractors and clients (e.g. an ambassador who had to visit all the district municipalities looking for a suitable location for his embassy). The contestants of the reform argued that a different system of collecting the revenue stamps would curb the wealth of Srodmiescie, that time and again the typical rhetoric of particularism (natural in a situation of direct election) has been misconstrued as unwillingness to cooperate, and that the search for the diplomatic residences should be taken care of by the Ministry of Foreign Affairs and not by the respective ambassadors. In other words, that a mouse was being killed with a cannon. (Czarniawska 1998a:7)[2]

In this excerpt, the story I'm developing becomes slightly more dramatic as I allow the voices to be further distinguished, but, again, this is a conventional narrative device: There are "the main storytellers" and "the contestants" (a usual casting in connection with a reform). As the story proceeds, an aside of sorts is added:

> Many, perhaps most, of the practical questions—district and Centrum finances, relations between the municipalities, and so forth—were formulated vaguely in the project and included in that form in the text of the Act of the reform. During the period of my observation, "reading the Act" and interpreting its individual paragraphs became a systematic activity in the city government and the municipal service units. These "hermeneutic groups" exchanged interpretations and speculations about the possible meanings and tried to influence official interpretation of this key document. (Czarniawska 1998a:7)

The aside seemingly does not contribute to the plot. Yet it prepares the reader/listener for a complication that will be presented later. Also, observe another typical move: a substitution of a "metaphor of the field" with my own ("reading the Act"; "hermeneutic groups").

INCORPORATING OTHER NARRATIVE MATERIAL

The complete story of the reform appears in my article "Changing Organizations in a Changing Institutional Order: The Administrative Reform of the City of Warsaw" (Czarniawska 1998a). Below, I present two additional excerpts, to ramify the construction of "simple" story making out of the interview material. As in the orig-

inal report, the second main source of narrative material was the press, especially the daily *Gazeta Wyborcza* (*GW*), which faithfully and in great detail informed its readers about the vicissitudes of the reform. I wove my story from such sources, too, trying to preserve different voices and differing opinions. The first extract is an excerpt from my own writing:

> On the 17th of March [1994], there was a demonstration in front of the Parliament of those inhabitants of district municipalities who would soon be divided into "urbanites" and "suburbanites." Parliament approved the bill with amendments and sent the bill to the Senate. The Senate proposed an amendment according to which, from the moment the Act is approved, only those local government decisions taken prior to the publication of the Act may be carried out. The Act has been distributed for signing by the president of the country, who asked his council for the territorial self-government for an opinion. (Czarniawska 1998a:8)

Now, an excerpt from the daily press is incorporated, followed by excerpts from my own commentary again:

> The following consequences were listed as positive aspects of the Act: elimination of the particularism of the districts, empowerment of the city mayor, accelerated transformation of Warsaw from a typical, grayish city of "real socialism" into a western-type metropolis. . . . The negative aspects included the decreased role of local governments, strong opposition of the inhabitants due to the lack of consultation with them, a temporary destabilization of the municipal and district administration, the destruction of the historical boundaries of Warsaw, legislative vagueness in the division of tasks and competencies, the high cost of the operation, and lack of staff for the

newly created administrative offices. (*GW,* April 1, 1994)

* * *

Hopes and wishes dominated the list of the "positive aspects," while "negative aspects" were certain to be revealed. A witty journalist gave the article the title: "A Piece of Advice for the President: Be For, and Even Against." (Czarniawska 1998a:8)[3]

* * *

On March 25, 1994, the new Warsaw Governance System Act went into effect. On April 4, at the meeting with the district mayors, the county governor said: "All of us will have to sustain the costs. The county office will press the cabinet to allocate as much money as possible, but we know that they may have problems with it" (*GW,* April 8, 1994). Indeed, the cabinet refused to allocate any money from the state budget for the implementation of Warsaw's reform (*GW,* June 17, 1994).

The announcement of the Senate that the district municipalities will not be permitted to manage their estate provoked unusually intense real estate activity in the districts, some of which was invalidated later by the county governor. On April 28, the district mayor of Srodmiescie suggested that a signboard reading "The City is closed down for the change of the governance system" should be hung at the city gates. (Czarniawska 1998a:9)

These excerpts are a kind of "second-hand interview," in which I let journalists do my job for me. Not only did they interview many of the same people I did, but during the period I was conducting direct observation, I often witnessed the interviews given to the press. They differed not in the stories told (these were well exercised by constant repetition), but in the

richness of comments given to me and not to the press. Narratives were broadly the same, in other words, but I was given more interpretive clues to the events in question.

April through October 1994 was spent on the election of the city mayor, a part of the story that contained four false solutions, and there were many amusing details that cannot be reported here in full. On November 3, the council session elected a new city mayor, who was also the mayor of the municipality Centrum. The city treasurer prepared a budget. Thus the city took down the sign reading "Closed for the change of the governance system" and started reforming itself.

PLOT DEVELOPMENT

My story now moves to another plane, and the plot is further developed.

The new Warsaw governance system created 11 municipalities: Warsaw Centrum and 10 suburban municipalities. And while public opinion focused on the election of the mayor, the new municipalities were trying to put their act together. (Czarniawska 1998a:13)

The major confrontation started, as one can imagine, with the division of personnel. The situation varied across time and space: "Some of the districts and municipalities were able to do it without exceeding the 'normal sparking level.' Others made quite a hullabaloo but then they stopped." The mayor of one of the former district municipalities took what he considered to be the radical step of giving away all the employees the new municipalities needed. According to critical opinion, however, "he stripped the former district of all employees" (2-9). The most common attitude was probably "catch-as-catch-can," as the following extract from my (BC) interview with the municipal mayor (MM) shows.

MM: I asked for certain people but the answer was negative. I didn't want any other clerks because those I wanted didn't drink, they were valuable people, I didn't want any new ones. They said that they won't give other workers, and I said that I won't hire other ones and that's it. Maybe such stubbornness on my part wasn't necessary, but it was the same with other things. They still begrudge us the use of their premises.

BC: And what did you do about the clerks?

MM: I hired the new ones. I teach them here. I train them because it also happened that they eventually refused to train my employees, saying that they have learned enough. But if necessary I have a possibility to let them have training in other offices.

My respondent was not particularly worried, as he noted "I think that these are really petty things that we will overcome in a year. For a city office or a municipality, a year isn't a long time." Besides, as it turned out later on, "the enemy" wasn't totally in the wrong. The district started to refuse to transfer employees only after the new municipality "emptied" its financial department. (Pp. 14-15)

As these excerpts indicate, from happening in all places at once, the narrative becomes localized. Although it still moves from one locale to another, and it carries the same plot, it is more detailed. A subplot is introduced—the changes in personnel—that is subordinate to the main plot. The reform, an equilibrium-restoring action in the main plot, disturbs the equilibrium of

employment, which must be restored in turn.

As the plot develops, distinct voices are more clearly heard, although the cast of proponents and opponents is maintained. The district directors usually had an understanding attitude, but they were not willing to make sacrifices, as excerpts from their varied comments indicate:

Why do I have to give good clerks to the new municipality? Better yet, did the legislator oblige me to give good clerks to the new municipality? No. The legislator puts new organs, including the municipality we are talking about, under obligation to organize municipal services, and my task is to help them.

* * *

I can't force an employee of mine to move to the new municipality. However, I apply a certain procedure indicated by the law, which means that if a clerk who lives in that municipality presents to me a request to be transferred, I can talk in her name with the municipality. Or, the other way around, if the municipality talks to her and decides that this particular clerk interests them, then they ask me to transfer this clerk on the basis of the "agreement-between-employers" rule, which is the most convenient solution because she gets transferred with the same salary, which means that she can get a raise over there and doesn't lose various benefits.

* * *

One condition has to be satisfied, though. It has to be done properly. The things have to be concluded over here. If that clerk was doing a job here, she has to finish it and has to account for it. If the transfer of a clerk doesn't disrupt the work in my office, of course I approve.

* * *

So much from a district where the "sparking" was "normal." Sometimes the troubles were bigger, and the fault could be on both sides. The mayors of the municipalities have their "assembly" where they meet and discuss these sorts of things, even though the situation gets complicated somewhat by the fact that one of mayors is also the city mayor, while the assembly's goal is actually to work out a common strategy in dealings with him. (Pp. 13-16)

This is an example of a typical emplotment device in reform stories: the elaboration of events termed "friction." This time I replace the researcher's metaphor of "friction" with one more commonly used by my respondents, namely, "sparking." This is done for purely aesthetic reasons, to apply expressions used in the field. (And, besides, "friction" is by now a worn metaphor in organization studies.)

DISTINGUISHING STORY POINTS

As I proceeded through the interviews, I tried to establish some focus for the respondents' replies, as the following excerpt reveals:

When I asked what influence prolonged "mayorlessness" had on the destiny of the new municipalities, the respondents from those municipalities often answered that it was a blessing, although a mixed one. As one commented:

Between you and me, it proved useful for us not to have the city mayor for six months. It was useful because we could stay here and look

for a temporary seat. If those conflicts between the municipality and the district had had to be solved in a day or two, they would have been much more difficult to cope with. This way, we had to bide our time and they [the former municipality], too. However, the waste in the other matters is impossible even to begin to describe. The money transfer didn't work. The management of Centrum's finances didn't work, for there were no political decisions.

Continuing his opinion on the reform as a whole, this respondent said:

I have two points of view, one as a resident of municipality X and one as a resident of Warsaw. I believe that it was very disadvantageous for Warsaw. A mess has been created, and it will last for at least another two years, which means irrecoverable losses for the city. As far as the municipality of X is concerned, however, the reform was something good. The municipality will gain on this deal because most of the revenues in the previous district were actually produced here. (Czarniawska 1998a:16)

Thus I asked my interlocutor to provide the point of the story, which he did.

As is usually the case, however, I soon moved to another story point of my own. In doing so, I now step outside of the plot to comment on its development.

Two aspects struck me, as a long-standing student of public reforms, though I do not claim that they were exceptional. The first is that in spite of a heated, involved and long-lasting discussion about the pros and cons of the reform, not even once did anyone ask whether it was *the right moment* to carry out an administrative reform at all, whether Warsaw could afford reform? No reform achieves its goals exactly, but each reform costs, and costs more than was assumed. One can imagine less expensive methods of dealing with one or two "strong personalities" and poorly planned ways of redirecting City revenues. Will the reform eliminate conflicts between districts and municipalities? For the time being, there are many conflict-prone areas, both old and new ("They changed the City of Seven Boroughs into the City of Eleven Boroughs.") Conflicts can also disappear, but who can prove that they would not have disappeared even without the reform? (Pp. 25-26)

NARRATIVE PRIVILEGE

My concern here centers on the question of how to introduce another point to the story without questioning the one offered by my respondents. Am I incurring narrative privilege by confronting it with another story or stories? Presenting myself as a "long-standing student of public reforms," I am attempting to create an ethos of the author who has heard many such stories and therefore earned the right to summarize them all. As Howard Becker (1982) reminds us, the theoretician is the person who has traveled much. I could achieve a similar effect by referring to other authors and quoting them.

My text then raises another issue:

The second interesting aspect was that not a single one of my respondents, who, after all, implemented the reform, considered himself or herself the reform's promoter. Maybe the former City mayor proxy for the Municipality of Centrum would have considered himself that, even though he, like other district mayors, had definitely been against it before he was appointed as a proxy. The former City mayor, the county governor, and the official "au-

thors" of the reform, two public administration professors, were all outside the action net called city management when the reform was being implemented. The same phenomenon was to be found locally. It seemed to be a rule that the people directly affected by the local changes and adaptation projects were excluded during their preparation, especially when there were suspicions that they might react negatively to the project. A direct question confirmed my observation. It was assumed that a person whose interests could be threatened would try to stop the project, so that person had to be kept in the dark about the project as long as possible. (P. 26)

Here I comment critically on the making of my story of the field. I seem to be saying, on the strength of the authorial ethos built before: "It could have been made better! You had too many characters, too many authors, no clear director." But do I have the right to say this? Clearly, the fact that I attempt to build my authority does not mean that I succeed; despite what consultants in rhetoric tell everybody, the science of rhetoric is only probabilistic. No one knows what will succeed, but educated guesses can be made. Still, it does not answer the question of my narrative rights and duties. In order to discuss this matter, it is necessary to leave Warsaw and to take a more general view on what was happening while I was constructing my story.

NARRATIVE RESPONSIBILITY AND RESPECT

The traditional rendering of interview material consists of information gathered in fieldwork from which the researcher writes "the one true story" of what "really" happened in a clear, authoritative voice. This procedure is nowadays often considered anathema, but with a great degree of exaggeration. After all, there are many good reasons to make up a consistent narrative out of many partly conflicting ones, or out of an incomplete or fragmented one. The justice or injustice done to the original narratives depends on the attitude of the researcher and on the precautions he or she takes.

The main problem of rendering somebody else's story in one's own idiom is the political act of totalizing that this entails. This problem became acute in anthropology as literacy increased in previously oral societies (Lejeune 1989). The Other, who once was authoritatively "just described," took on the task of self-description and of questioning the descriptions of the anthropologists. What is considered a problem in one context, however, can turn into its own solution in another. It is precisely because respondents in organization studies especially are highly literate that the re-presentations undertaken by researchers are open to their comments and questions. The status of science, especially the social sciences, no longer stifles these protests and critiques. As I have pointed out at some length in other writing, the "voices of the field" reported in organization studies are as literate and eloquent as those of their reporters, and often have greater political clout (Czarniawska 1998b).

This does not absolve researchers from the responsibility for what they write and their duty to respect respondents. But this responsibility and respect do not have to be expressed in a literal repetition of what has been said. A researcher has a right, but also a professional duty, to do a "novel reading," to use an apt expression coined by Marjorie DeVault (1990) to refer to an interpretation by a person who is not socialized into the same system of meaning as the narrator but is familiar enough with it to recognize it as such. At any given time and place, DeVault notes, there are dominant and marginal readings of the same text, and, I may add, there are a number of narratives reporting the same developments but emplotting them in different ways. Some plots dominate whereas others are considered marginal, and it is not necessary that the researcher subscribe to the dominant plot. Agreement is not always the best way of expressing respect. It is the researcher's duty, however, to take the authorial responsibility for the narrative he or she constructs and also to admit to the existence of narrative opposition from respondents, if the researcher is aware of any. A colleague of mine described his version of events that took place in a Swedish municipality and sent the manuscript to the people he had interviewed. One of them, a minister at the time, sent him a letter threatening him with negative consequences if he published his book. My colleague described the letter, together with other kinds of feedback, in the book (Jacobsson 1987). This may be an extreme case, but I mention it because many times researchers' supposed respect for respondents hides a lack of courage to stand up for their own texts.

There are many other ways for researchers to pay respect in their texts. One is the multivocal story, recommended by many anthropologists (see, e.g., Marcus 1992). In the multivocal story there are many narratives, as in a postmodern novel; all tell the story, and the researcher does not have to take a stand on which is "right" or "wrong." Although there are increasing numbers of such accounts in scientific texts, I shall refer to a literary one, because of its exemplary character—Iain Pears's *An Instance of the Fingerpost* (1998), which is a novel about science. It contains four different narratives, each of which could serve as a model for a narrative to be collected in an interview. The author's role—which can be imitated by scientific writers—is not to say which story is correct, but to make the reader understand why the stories differ as they do.

It should be pointed out that such polyphony in a text is a textual strategy (Czarniawska 1999). The "voices of the field" do not speak for themselves; it is the author who makes them speak in polyphonic form. Therefore it is more adequate to refer (after Bakhtin) to the "variegated speech" of the field, and of leaving traces of different dialects, different idioms, and different vocabularies, rather than homogenizing them into a univocal "scientific text." Again, this textual strategy is not as drastically different from the authoritative story as it may seem. Even pasting together fragments of authentic narratives, taken straight from interview transcripts, decontextualizes them, but in return it also recontextualizes them as engrossing narratives (Rorty 1991). Alas, it is never a question of "authenticity," but always a question of creating an impression of authenticity, of recontextualization that is interesting ("novel"), credible, and respectful (see Briggs, Chapter 44, this volume).

◆ Tales from the Field: Analyzing Interview Narratives

There are basically two things the researcher can do with, and to, narratives elicited in interviews. The first thing the researcher can do, which I have reflexively discussed and illustrated in the preceding section, is to construct his or her own narrative out of them—that is, to write up, rewrite, or interpret field accounts. The second thing the researcher can do is to analyze such accounts as a corpus of texts in their own right. Let us now turn to how one might analyze "tales from the field." The latter is still a relatively new method of procedure in organization studies.

TEXTUAL ANALYSIS

An interview is a text, and as such can be submitted to textual analysis. One can ask, *What* does a text say? but one can also ask, *How* does it say it? There are many techniques of textual analysis and many manuals available that explain their use. For example, the analysis of personal narratives

derived from interviews is now at the center of attention of researchers such as Eliot Mishler (1986) and Catherine Kohler Riessman (1993; see also Riessman, Chapter 33, this volume). I intend to take up the most obvious alternatives and highlight the gains and losses connected with textual analysis as this relates to organizational narratives.

One now traditional way of analyzing a narrative is in structuralist terms, an enterprise close to semiology and formalism (see, e.g., Propp 1968; Barthes 1977; Todorov [1977] 1990). To quote Algirdas Greimas and Joseph Courtés (1982), two well-known French semiologists, narrative structures "or, more accurately, semio-narrative structures, [are] to be understood in the sense of deep semiotic structures (which preside at the generating of meaning and bear general forms of discourse organization)" (p. 317). According to Greimas and Courtés: "Deep structures are customarily opposed in semiotics to surface (or superficial) structures. While the latter ostensibly belong to the sphere of the observable, the former are considered as underlying the utterance" (p. 69). Just about the time this method acquired legitimacy in the social sciences, however, it was swept away by poststructuralism. It makes sense, however, to follow Raman Selden (1985) in his suggestion that "poststructuralists are structuralists who suddenly see the error of their ways" (p. 72). This statement is especially convincing when we observe that the leading poststructuralists were, in fact, leading structuralists, among them Barthes, Bakhtin, and Todorov. As Josue Harari (1979) notes, "The most fundamental difference between the structuralist and poststructuralist enterprises can be seen in the shift from the problematic of the subject to the deconstruction of the concept of representation" (p. 29). This shift led, inevitably, to the problematization of the "deep structure" concept.

In this context, one could say that the move from structuralism to poststructuralism meant abandoning the depths for the surface: If deep structures are demonstrable, they must be observable. Structures can no longer be "found," as they are obviously put into the text by those who read the text, including the author (after all, writing is reading anew). This meant abandoning the ideas of the universal structure of language, or of mind, and accepting the idea of a common repertoire of textual strategies that are recognizable to both the writer and the reader (Harari 1979). This relaxation of a basic assumption also leads to the relaxation of the related technique: As there is no one true deep structure to be discovered, various techniques can be applied to structure a text and therefore permit novel readings.

AN EXAMPLE: CONFRONTATIONAL POLITICS IN STOCKHOLM

Here I offer my own attempt at a structuralist-inspired reading of two narratives extracted from interviews I conducted in Stockholm. I use these examples because the respondents refer to the same development in two different voices. E stands for different equilibria, and F stands for forces (actions or events); 1M is the first respondent and 2W the second. Equilibria are the stable dynamic states attributed to the events in question, in this case E_1 being consensual and E_2 confrontational. Forces are changes in these states. The respective ways these respondents' voices form are presented in the following excerpts according to their different equilibria and depiction of forces.

Respondent 1M

E_2: Swedish politics is [now] very confrontational, perhaps among the most confrontational in Europe. There is so much talk about consensus, what consensus, bullshit, here we are enemies. If the liberals say anything the social democrats assume it is nonsense and the other way around.

E_1: The picture of consensus-grounded Swedish politics was launched by the Social Democrats. The very fact that they stayed in power so long before 1976 created a picture of much greater unity than it ever really was. There were conflicts even before 1976, but they have been suppressed. The foreign press wrote about The Swedish Model, but they interviewed Social Democrats only. The result was that people abroad believed that everybody in Sweden thought like a Social Democrat. This simply wasn't true.

F: After 1976, the first change of the regime, and especially after the next two or three government changes, Sweden became a normal European country. The social conflicts became more visible, and Social Democrats met with more opposition and lost their dominance. Swedish politics is today marked by a fierce fight about the basic ideology, about the way to look at the people, about the worldview that will dominate this country in the future. We are living through a dramatic paradigm change—economic, mental, and political—and nobody knows where we are going to land.

Respondent 2W

E_1: There was not a trace of confrontational politics when I joined the City Council in 1973.

E_2: But when I listen to the new Council members now, the only thing I hear is how they attack one another. Nothing constructive, no recognition of a job well done, no suggestion to do something together. I think this is a very sorry state of affairs. The way of talking when at the speaker's podium is truly unpleasant, stabbing one another until it hurts. No respect for differences in political opinion, a negative tone of discourse, just a confrontation, all the way through.

E_1: This is a very visible change. It was so much better before. It was a completely different style. Everything was different. Everybody came to the meetings well dressed, not necessarily elegant or formal, but respectful.

E_2: Now they dress as they please, this is a style in itself. It may seem insignificant, but this is a way to undermine the seriousness of the circumstances, of the work being done. Because it is important for citizens to see that their local government representatives perceive their jobs as important, as serious. Somebody who arrives with his shirt hanging outside his jeans can hardly expect respect from the citizens. And the way of behaving involves taking a lot of liberties that were unthinkable before.

$E_1 + F$: It does not mean that all old mores were perfect. There were many things that were necessary to change in order to modernize, but the part that was taken for granted was the way to behave, and that could well stay as it was?

E_2: Especially this habit of seeking confrontation all the time and avoiding collaboration even where it is obvious. There is no need to question every little thing, is there? There are issues that could pass unquestioned, without a debate. But as everything becomes a problematic issue, the Council meetings never end. The list of interpolations is limitless, nobody gives up, and this, rather than achieving the desired effect of publicity, bores the journalists to death.

My two respondents are experienced narrators. Respondent 1M uses a simple structure that achieves its effect by violat-

ing the logic of succession: "twisting" the order of occurrence in the order of telling (Goodman 1980). E_2 precedes E_1 (a flashback), and F contains traces of a flashforward, a mention of an unknown but different E_3. The narrator does not offer the reader/listener an obvious point. It is uncertain whether it is good or bad to have a confrontational style in politics, and to be a "normal" European country, but the inclusion of an obscenity ("bullshit") subtly suggests his standpoint. Other than this, the narrator is absent in this narrative, which contains collective characters only: the foreign press, the people abroad, the Social Democrats. The use of flashback, however, also suggests what should be considered a "normal" state of affairs.

Respondent 2W also begins with what she considers "normal." But here the similarity ends. Respondent 2W is present in her narrative both as a participant observer and as an author. The plotting strategy she uses is also different. She alternates E_1 with E_2, thus producing a series of flashbacks that illustrate the disadvantages of E_2, and makes the negative character of the transformation visible. The point here is clear: E_1 was "good," E_2 is "bad," and the reader/listener is invited to share the related feelings and the judgment of the narrator.

What happened between E_1 and E_2? A paradigm shift, or a modernization, which perhaps are one and the same? It is hard to judge, as they are described by their precedents and consequences rather than by their mechanism. Walter Fisher (1987) and Murray Edelman (1988) would consider this typical of the political narrative, where events are often naturalized. Unlike the managerial narrative, which revolves around intentional actions, often individual, the political narrative favors forces, events, or collective actions, as is appropriate for collective actors such as the party, the voters, or the government.

These extracts can be further distinguished according to whether they are presented as experientially "distant" or "involved" accounts. But perhaps the most interesting feature is that the two cases illustrate how, by using distinct textual strategies, one can construct two different narratives about the recognizably same course of events.

◆ The Point of This Story

Story making is by no means all there is to the process of organizing, and narratives are not all that is found in interviews. The process of organizing produces not only narratives, but also goods, services, fortunes, identities, and much more. There are, however, many advantages in conceptualizing organizing as story making. To begin with, organizations-as-stories are made of the same material and along the same lines as organization studies. Another important point is made by Weick (1995), who argues that sense making, of which story making is perhaps the most important device, engages much of the time and effort of organizers, a fact that has escaped the attention of traditional organization theory. And, last but not least in the present context, the narrative approach to the analysis of interviews permits researchers to exploit the potential of this technique to achieve better understanding of organizing in everyday communication.

The growing interest in narratives, however, has also raised warnings about two kinds of dangers. One of these, and one to worry about, is that by engaging in literary work, social scientists will become literary critics, thus problematizing the legitimacy of traditional endeavors and leading to the likelihood that they will lose out in competition with more seasoned literary theorists. This concern is a historical echo of a similar concern voiced when the social sciences quite unreflectively imitated the natural sciences, an imitation that, like every process of translation, brought about some

very interesting and some rather unfortunate results. No science is, or ever has been, autarchic, so the question is not whether to imitate, but who and how.

The question of "how" produces a concern of its own that can be signaled in ironicizing the ideas of "proper deconstruction" and "correctly applied structural analysis." These ideas actually provide the ground for a differentiation between a theory of literature and a theory of organizing (assuming anybody risks mistaking one for the other). Whereas students of literature must show themselves worthy apprentices of craftsmen such as Jacques Derrida and Roland Barthes, students of organizing must be able to say something significant about organizing. In order to accomplish that, they need to operate like all other readers, who, in Michel de Certeau's (1988) metaphor, "move across lands belonging to someone else, like nomads poaching their way across the fields they did not write, despoiling the wealth of Egypt to enjoy it themselves" (p. 174).

This brings me to the point of my own story. What I want to convey is my belief that there is no one thing that a researcher must, should, or can do with narratives as they relate to organizing. Every reading is an interpretation and every interpretation is an association tying the text that is interpreted to other texts, other voices, other times, and other places. Much more important than a specific interpretive or analytic technique is the result—an interesting recontextualization. Saying this, I betray my pragmatist preferences, and, indeed, I cannot but share Rorty's (1991) "desire to be as polymorphous in our adjustments as possible, to recontextualize for the hell of it" (p. 110).

■ Notes

1. This study, "Managing the Big City: A 21st Century Challenge to Technology and Administration," conducted at the Gothenburg Research

Institute, was initiated thanks to the generosity of the Rockefeller Foundation at the Bellaggio Center. The study of Warsaw has been funded by the Daimler-Benz Foundation. The studies of Stockholm and Rome have been supported by the Bank of Sweden Centenary Foundation. I would like to express my gratitude to all the sponsors and to my collaborators.

2. The revenue stamps mentioned in this extract are the fees for processing legal documents, which are collected by notaries and then paid to the state treasury.

3. The article's title came from an infamous expression of a president known for his malapropisms.

■ References

Bakhtin, M. M. and P. N. Medvedev. [1928] 1991. *The Formal Method in Literary Scholarship: A Critical Introduction to Sociological Poetics.* Baltimore: Johns Hopkins University Press.

Barthes, R. 1977. *Image-Music-Text.* Translated by S. Heath. New York: Hill & Wang.

Becker, H. S. 1982. *Art Worlds.* Berkeley: University of California Press.

Boland, R. J., Jr. and R. V. Tankasi. 1995. "Perspective Making and Perspective Taking in Communities of Knowing." *Organization Science* 6:350-72.

Brown, R. H. 1977. *A Poetic for Sociology: Toward a Logic of Discovery for the Human Sciences.* New York: Cambridge University Press.

———. 1987. *Society as Text: Essays on Rhetoric, Reason, and Reality.* Chicago: University of Chicago Press.

———. 1989. *Social Science as Civic Discourse: Essays on the Invention, Legitimation, and Uses of Social Theory.* Chicago: University of Chicago Press.

Bruner, J. 1986. *Actual Minds, Possible Worlds.* Cambridge, MA: Harvard University Press.

———. 1990. *Acts of Meaning.* Cambridge, MA: Harvard University Press.

Clark, B. R. 1972 "The Organizational Saga in Higher Education." *Administrative Science Quarterly* 17:178-84.

Czarniawska, B. 1997. *Narrating the Organization: Dramas of Institutional Identity.* Chicago: University of Chicago Press.

———. 1998a. "Changing Organizations in a Changing Institutional Order: The Administrative Reform of the City of Warsaw." *Studies in Cultures, Organizations and Societies* 4:1-27.

———. 1998b. *A Narrative Approach to Organization Studies.* Thousand Oaks, CA: Sage.

———. 1999. *Writing Management: Organization Theory as a Literary Genre.* Oxford: Oxford University Press.

de Certeau, M. 1988. *The Practice of Everyday Life.* Translated by S. F. Rendall. Berkeley: University of California Press.

DeVault, M. L. 1990. "Novel Readings: The Social Organization of Interpretation." *American Journal of Sociology* 95:887-921.

Edelman, M. 1988. *Constructing the Political Spectacle.* Chicago: University of Chicago Press.

Fisher, W. R. 1984. "Narration as a Human Communication Paradigm: The Case of Public Moral Argument." *Communication Monographs* 51:1-22.

———. 1987. *Human Communication as Narration: Toward a Philosophy of Reason, Value, and Action.* Columbia: University of South Carolina Press.

Flyvbjerg, B. 1998. *Rationality and Power: Democracy in Practice.* Chicago: University of Chicago Press.

Geertz, C. 1980. "Blurred Genres: The Refiguration of Social Thought." *American Scholar* 29(2):165-79.

———. 1988. *Works and Lives: The Anthropologist as Author.* Stanford, CA: Stanford University Press.

Goodman, N. 1980. "Twisted Tales; or, Story, Study, and Symphony." Pp. 99-116 in *On Narrative,* edited by W. J. T. Mitchell. Chicago: University of Chicago Press.

Greimas, A. J. and J. Courtés. 1982. *Semiotics and Language: An Analytical Dictionary.* Bloomington: Indiana University Press.

Harari, J. V. 1979. "Critical Factions/Critical Fictions." Pp. 17-72 in *Textual Strategies: Perspectives in Post-Structuralist Criticism,* edited by J. V. Harari. Ithaca, NY: Methuen.

Holstein, J. A. and J. F. Gubrium. 1995. *The Active Interview.* Thousand Oaks, CA: Sage.

Jacobsson, B. 1987. *Kraftsamlingen. Politik och företagande i parallela processer.* Lund, Sweden: Doxa.

Lejeune, P. 1989. *On Autobiography.* Minneapolis: University of Minnesota Press.

MacIntyre, A. [1981] 1990. *After Virtue.* London: Duckworth.

Mandler, J. M. 1984. *Stories, Scripts and Scenes: Aspects of Schema Theory.* London: LEA.

Marcus, G. E. 1992. "Past, Present and Emergent Identities: Requirements for Ethnographies of Late Twentieth-Century Modernity World-Wide." Pp. 309-30 in *Modernity and Identity,* edited by S. Lash and J. Friedman. Oxford: Blackwell.

Martin, J. 1982. "Stories and Scripts in Organizational Settings." Pp. 165-94 in *Cognitive Social Psychology,* edited by A. H. Hastrof and A. M. Isen. New York: Elsevier North-Holland.

Martin, J., M. Feldman, M. J. Hatch, and S. B. Sitkin. 1983. "The Uniqueness Paradox in Organizational Stories." *Administrative Science Quarterly* 28:438-53.

Mishler, E. G. 1986. *Research Interviewing: Context and Narrative.* Cambridge, MA: Harvard University Press.

Mitroff, I. and R. Kilmann. 1975. "Stories Managers Tell: A New Tool for Organizational Problem Solving." *Management Review* 64:13-28.

Pears, I. 1998. *An Instance of the Fingerpost.* London: Vintage.

Propp, V. I. 1968. *The Morphology of the Folktale.* 2d rev. ed. Edited by L. A. Wagner. Austin: University of Texas Press.

Riessman, C. K. 1993. *Narrative Analysis.* Newbury Park, CA: Sage.

Rorty, R. 1991. "Inquiry as Recontextualization: An Anti-dualist Account of Interpretation." Pp. 93-110 in R. Rorty, *Objectivity, Relativism and Truth: Philosophical Papers,* Vol. 1. New York: Cambridge University Press.

Selden, R. 1985. *A Reader's Guide to Contemporary Literary Theory.* Brighton, England: Harvester.

Todorov, T. [1977] 1990. *The Poetics of Prose.* Oxford: Blackwell.

Van Maanen, J. 1988. *Tales of the Field: On Writing Ethnography.* Chicago: University of Chicago Press.

Weick, K. E. 1979. *The Social Psychology of Organizing.* Reading, MA: Addison-Wesley.

———. 1995. *Sensemaking in Organizations.* Thousands Oaks, CA: Sage.

White, H. 1973. *Metahistory: The Historical Imagination in Nineteenth-Century Europe.* Baltimore: Johns Hopkins University Press.

———. 1987. *The Content of the Form: Narrative Discourse and Historical Representation.* Baltimore: Johns Hopkins University Press.

36

INSTITUTIONAL ETHNOGRAPHY

Using Interviews to Investigate Ruling Relations

◆ Marjorie L. DeVault
Liza McCoy

Social researchers use interviews in various ways, but they usually think of interviews as sources for learning about individual experience. In this chapter, we discuss interviewing as part of an approach designed for the investigation of organizational and institutional processes (see also Czarniawska, Chapter 35, this volume). In this alternative to conventional forms of interview research, investigators use informants' accounts not as windows on the informants' inner experience but in order to reveal the "relations of ruling" that shape local experiences (Smith 1996).

We use the term *institutional ethnography* (IE), following Canadian sociologist Dorothy E. Smith, to refer to the empirical investigation of linkages among local settings of everyday life, organizations, and translocal processes of administration and governance. These linkages constitute a complex field of coordination and control that Smith (1999) identifies as "the ruling relations"; these increasingly textual forms of coordination are "the forms in which power is generated and held in contemporary societies" (p. 79).

Smith (1987) introduced the term *institutional ethnography* in writing about a "sociology for women," illustrating with her studies of mothers' work at home in relation to their children's schooling, but she understands the approach as having wide application. Those who have followed Smith in developing IE have investigated many different social processes, including the regulation of sexuality (Smith 1998; Khayatt 1995; Kinsman 1996); the organization of health care (Campbell 1988, 1995, 1999; Diamond 1992; Mykhalovskiy 2000; Mykhalovskiy and Smith 1994; Smith 1995), education (Griffith 1984, 1992; Andre Bechely 1999; Stock 2000), and social work practice (de Montigny 1995; Parada 1998); police and judicial processing of violence against women (Pence 1997); employment and job training (K. M. Grahame 1998); economic restructuring (McCoy 1999); international development regimes (Mueller 1995); planning and environmental policy (Turner 1995; Eastwood 2000); the organization of home and community life (DeVault 1991; Luken and Vaughan 1991, 1996; Naples 1997); and various kinds of activism (Walker 1990; Ng 1996).

Over the past two decades, a loosely organized network of IE researchers has emerged in North America, the members of which meet regularly to share developing projects and refinements of these methods.[1] This chapter surveys the work of that network. In preparing the discussion that follows, we have examined published examples of IE research, interviewed practitioners (individually and in small groups), and collected accounts of research practices and reflections via e-mail. We understand IE as an emergent mode of inquiry, always subject to revision and the improvisation required by new applications. Thus we wish to emphasize that we do not intend any prescriptive orthodoxy. Rather, we hope to introduce this approach, provide practical information about it that is often unarticulated in published work, and reflect on unresolved issues of research practice. Because many of the specifics of IE interviews are the same as the "good practices" used by researchers conducting other kinds of interviews (methods of gaining access, building rapport, probing for specific accounts, listening carefully, and so on), we highlight distinctive practices associated with IE studies.

In the following section, we provide an introduction to this research approach and consider various uses of interviewing in IE

projects. Next, we discuss the conduct of interviews. The subsequent section foregrounds the key role of texts and institutional discourses in IE research, showing how interviews can be oriented toward these aspects of social organization. We then turn to analysis and writing in relation to IE interviews.

◆ Institutional Ethnography as a Mode of Inquiry

Dorothy Smith proposes IE as part of an "alternative sociology," an approach she describes as combining Marx's materialist method and Garfinkel's ethnomethodology with insights from the feminist practice of consciousness-raising. "In different ways, all of these ground inquiry in the ongoing activities of actual individuals" (Smith 1999:232, n. 5). Analytically fundamental to this approach is an ontology that views the social as the concerting of people's activities. This is an ontology shared by phenomenologists, symbolic interactionists, and ethnomethodologists. Smith expands this through the concept of social relations, which, as in Marx, refers to the coordinating of people's activities on a large scale, as this occurs in and across multiple sites, involving the activities of people who are not known to each other and who do not meet face-to-face.

In contemporary global capitalist society, the "everyday world" (the material context of each embodied subject) is organized in powerful ways by translocal social relations that pass through local settings and shape them according to a dynamic of transformation that begins and gathers speed somewhere else (e.g., if the local hospital closes, the explanation will not be wholly local). Smith (1990) refers to these translocal social relations that carry and accomplish organization and control as "relations of ruling":

They are those forms that we know as bureaucracy, administration, management, professional organization, and the media. They include also the complex of discourses, scientific, technical, and cultural, that intersect, interpenetrate, and coordinate the multiple sites of ruling. (P. 6)

A central feature of ruling practice in contemporary society is its reliance on text-based discourses and forms of knowledge, and these are central in IE inquiries (a topic we return to later).[2]

Building on this conception of ruling, Smith's notion of institution points to clusters of text-mediated relations organized around specific ruling functions, such as education or health care. *Institution,* in this usage, does not refer to a particular type of organization; rather, it is meant to inform a project of empirical inquiry, directing the researcher's attention to coordinated and intersecting work processes taking place in multiple sites. For example, when health care is considered as an institution, what comes into view is a vast nexus of coordinated work processes and courses of action—in sites as diverse as hospitals, homes, doctors' offices, community clinics, elementary schools, workplaces, pharmacies, pharmaceutical companies, advertising agencies, insurance companies, government ministries and departments, mass media, and medical and nursing schools. Obviously, institutions cannot be studied and mapped out in their totality, and such is not the objective of institutional ethnography. Rather, the aim of the IE researcher is to explore particular corners or strands within a specific institutional complex, in ways that make visible their points of connection with other sites and courses of action. Thus Tim Diamond is studying the organization of health benefits in the United States, which he examines in its character as a text-mediated relation connecting the activities of individuals, their employers, insurance companies, hospitals, pharmacies, and so on (focus group, August 1999).

Institutional ethnography takes for its entry point the experiences of specific individuals whose everyday activities are in some way hooked into, shaped by, and constituent of the institutional relations under exploration. The term *ethnography* highlights the importance of research methods that can discover and explore these everyday activities and their positioning within extended sequences of action. When interviews are used in this approach, they are used not to reveal subjective states, but to locate and trace the points of connection among individuals working in different parts of institutional complexes of activity. The interviewer's goal is to elicit talk that will not only illuminate a particular circumstance but also point toward next steps in an ongoing, cumulative inquiry into translocal processes. As Peter Grahame (1999) explains, "The field continuously opens up as the researcher explores the institutional nexus that shapes the local" (p. 7; see also P. R. Grahame 1998).

The researcher's purpose in an IE investigation is not to generalize about the group of people interviewed, but to find and describe social processes that have generalizing effects. Thus interviewees located somewhat differently are understood to be subject, in various ways, to discursive and organizational processes that shape their activities. These institutional processes may produce similarities of experience, or they may organize various settings to sustain broader inequalities (as explored in DeVault 1999:chap. 5); in either case, these generalizing consequences show the lineaments of ruling relations. For example, George W. Smith (1998) treated the gay young men he interviewed not as a population of subjects, but as informants knowledgeable about school life for gay youth. He explains:

The interviews opened various windows on different aspects of the organization of this regime. Each informant provides a partial view; the work of institutional ethnography is to put together an integrated view based on these otherwise truncated accounts of schools. (P. 310)

The general relevance of the inquiry comes, then, not from a claim that local settings are similar, but from the capacity of the research to disclose features of ruling that operate across many local settings.

IE studies can "fit together"—much like the squares of a quilt (Smith 1987)—because they share the same organizing ontology and the same focus on generalizing processes of ruling. Thus Janet Rankin's (1998) study of nurses' work and administrative categories in a British Columbia hospital extends the analysis in Eric Mykhalovskiy's (2000) study of health services research and hospital restructuring in Ontario, and both extend the analysis in Liza McCoy's (1999) study of accounting texts and restructuring in another area of the public sector in Canada. This does not mean that the three studies consciously locate their analyses in relation to one another, but that through the analytic frame they share they can be seen to be describing different moments and aspects of the same generalizing set of relations.

Dorothy Smith's work on the social organization of knowledge predates the emergence of feminist sociology, but her formulations gained increasing power as she situated them within a community of activist feminist scholars seeking a transformative method of inquiry (DeVault 1999). IE researchers generally have critical or liberatory goals; they undertake research in order to reveal the ideological and social processes that produce experiences of subordination. For example, in Smith's classic feminist text *The Everyday World as Problematic* (1987), the idea is to "begin from women's experiences" and to take as the problematic for the research the question of how such experiences are produced. This notion shares with much feminist writing an interest in women's previously excluded views, but it uses women's accounts only as a point of entry to a broader

investigation (see also Reinharz and Chase, Chapter 11, this volume). The idea is to shift from a focus on women themselves (as in a sociology "of women") to a kind of investigation that could be useful in efforts to change the social relations that subordinate women (and others).

IE researchers aim at specific analyses of social coordination; the liberatory potential of the approach comes from its specification of possible "levers" or targets for activist intervention. Some IE research has emerged directly from the researcher's position as activist (G. W. Smith 1990; Pence 1997); these projects may be driven and targeted directly toward questions arising from activist work. Some academic researchers work collaboratively with activists: Roxana Ng with garment workers' unions, Marie Campbell with people who have disabilities, and Mykhalovskiy and McCoy with AIDS activists, for example. And some academics (and other professionals) research processes that shape their own work settings, often exploring the peculiar ways in which they themselves are implicated in ruling relations despite their intentions (de Montigny 1995; Parada 1998). Whatever the position of the researcher, the transformative potential of IE research comes from the character of the analysis it produces; it is like a "map" that can serve as a guide through a complex ruling apparatus.

POSSIBLE SHAPES OF IE PROJECTS

Institutional ethnography is driven by the search to discover "how it happens," with the underlying assumptions that (a) social "happening" consists in the concerted activities of people and (b) in contemporary society, local practices and experiences are tied into extended social relations or chains of action, many of which are mediated by documentary forms of knowledge. IE researchers set out to provide analytic descriptions of such processes in actual settings.

There is no "one way" to conduct an IE investigation; rather, there is an analytic project that can be realized in diverse ways. IE investigations are rarely planned out fully in advance. Instead, the process of inquiry is rather like grabbing a ball of string, finding a thread, and then pulling it out; that is why it is difficult to specify in advance exactly what the research will consist of. IE researchers know what they want to explain, but only step by step can they discover whom they need to interview or what texts and discourses they need to examine. In the discussion that follows, we describe some common "shapes" or trajectories of IE research.

BEGINNING WITH EXPERIENCE

A common—even a "classic"—IE approach (recommended by Dorothy Smith 1987) begins with the identification of an experience or area of everyday practice that is taken as the experience whose determinants are to be explored. The researcher seeks to "take the standpoint" of the people whose experience provides the starting point of investigation. For example, George Smith (1988) begins from the experience of gay men who were arrested by police in a series of sweeping raids on gay bathhouses; Didi Khayatt (1995) begins from the experience of young lesbian women in high school; Campbell and her associates begin from the experience of people attempting to live independently with physical disabilities (see Campbell 1998, 1999); Diamond (1992) begins from the experience of people, mostly women, who work as nursing assistants in nursing homes for the elderly; and Susan Turner (1995) begins from the experience of community residents seeking to stop a developer from destroying a wooded ravine. In all of these studies, the researchers go on to investigate the institutional processes that are shaping that experience (e.g., the work of policing, the work of teaching and school administration, the organization of

home-care services, the administration of Medicare and nursing homes, the organization of municipal land-use planning). The research follows a sequence: (a) identify an experience, (b) identify some of the institutional processes that are shaping that experience, and (c) investigate those processes in order to describe analytically how they operate as the grounds of the experience.

The researcher can employ a range of data collection techniques to explore the experience that provides the starting place and identifies the problematic. Most common among these techniques are interviews and focus groups, participant observation, and the researcher's reflection on her or his own experience, all of which serve to generate descriptions of what people do in their everyday lives. The analytic enterprise is paramount, however, and ways of realizing it are diverse. Many IE researchers use individual and group interviews. For example, Khayatt (1995) conducted interviews with young lesbians. Campbell and her associates conducted interviews with people living with disabilities (see Campbell 1998). Paul Luken and Suzanne Vaughan (1998; Vaughan and Luken 1997), along with older women informants, generated oral histories regarding the women's housing activities. Dorothy Smith, Liza McCoy, and Paula Bourne (1995) conducted focus group interviews with girls in secondary school. And Darien Taylor and associates (forthcoming) conducted focus groups with men and women living with HIV/AIDS about their experience of looking after their health. Through informants' stories and descriptions, the researcher begins to identify some of the translocal relations, discourses, and institutional work processes that are shaping the informants' everyday work.

Some IE researchers spend considerable time at this point of entry (for it can take time to understand the complexity of an experience, and data from this exploration can provide material with much analytic potential). In other cases, a researcher may begin from an experience that he or she knows something about, or where the problematic is already clear (e.g., G. W. Smith 1990; Walker 1990). Eventually, however, the researcher will usually need to shift the investigation to begin examining those institutional processes that he or she has discovered to be shaping the experience but that are not wholly known to the original informants. Thus a second stage of research commonly follows that usually involves a shift in research site, although not in standpoint. Often, this shift carries the investigation into organizational and professional work sites. At this stage, other forms of research and analysis may come to be used. The researcher may employ observation and the analysis of naturally occurring language data to examine institutional work processes, for example. Or the researcher may use text and discourse analysis to examine the textual forms and practices of knowledge that organize those work processes. But interviews continue to play an important role here as well, whether as the primary form of investigation or as a way of filling in the gaps of what the researcher can learn through observation and document analysis.

A common aspect of IE research at this second stage involves the researcher's investigating institutional work processes by following a chain of action, typically organized around and through a set of documents, because it is texts that coordinate people's activity across time and place within institutional relations. For example, Turner (1995) traced the trajectory of a developer's planning proposal as it passed through a review process involving the city planning office, the local conservation authority, the railroad company, and a meeting of the city council.

RESEARCH FOCUSED ON "RULING" PROCESSES

In some IE research, the point of entry is in organizational work processes and the activities of the people who perform them.

Rather than arriving at these processes through an exploration of the experience of people who are the objects of that work or who are in some way affected by it, the researcher in this type of IE jumps right into the examination of organizational work sites. The researcher knows about a set of administrative or professional practices and sets about studying how they are carried out, how they are discursively shaped, how they organize other settings. For example, Mykhalovskiy (2000) investigated health services research and its use in health care restructuring. Dorothy Smith and George Smith (1990) researched the organization of skills training in the plastics industry. Elizabeth Townsend (1998) studied the work of professionals in the mental health system and the contradictions between their professional goal of empowering people and system processes organized to control deviance. And Alison Griffith (1998) investigated the legislative and policy bases for educational restructuring in Ontario. This type of IE emphasizes the detailed examination of administrative and professional work processes.

CONCEPTUALIZATION AND PLACE OF INTERVIEWING

Interviewing is present in some form in just about all IE studies. But "interviewing" in IE is perhaps better described as "talking with people," and IE uses of interviewing should be understood in this wide sense, as stretching across a range of approaches to talk with informants. At one end of the continuum are planned interviews, where the researcher makes an appointment with someone for the purpose of doing a research interview. Then there is the kind of "talking with people" that occurs during field observation, when the researcher is watching someone do his work and asks him to explain what he is doing, why he did what he just did, what he has to think about to do the work, where this particular document goes, and so on. "Informal," on-the-spot interviews can be combined with later "formal" or planned interviews, in which the researcher brings to the longer interview a set of questions or topics based on the earlier observation-and-talk. Yet in IE, investigation through "talking with people" is not necessarily confined to settings and occasions that occur during formal field research. Because IE researchers are investigating widespread institutional and discursive processes in which the researcher is located as well as the informants, opportunities to talk with people about institutional processes can arise for the researcher serendipitously, as it were, in her or his daily life of going shopping, talking with friends, seeking medical care, and so on, depending on the topic of the research (see also Atkinson and Coffey, Chapter 38, this volume).

Further, "talking with people" is not necessarily done one-to-one. At the planned end of the continuum, a number of recent IE studies have used focus groups to generate group conversations about shared experiences (Smith et al. 1995; Campbell 1999; Stock 2000; see also Morgan, Chapter 7, this volume). And Tim Diamond reports that his research into health insurance draws on collective interviews he holds with his students during class, in which participants collaborate in developing an account of how health care is covered in the news and on television (focus group, August 1999). Such an approach works in IE because institutional processes are standardized across local settings, so any group of informants encounters those processes in some way.

"Talking with people" is also a wide term in the sense that it includes more than the usual research format (whether formal or informal) of asking questions and listening to answers. Eric Mykhalovskiy comments: "Describing interviews as a set of questions doesn't get at the actual work involved. For me, analytic thinking begins in the interview. It's like an analytic rehearsal. I'm checking my understanding as it develops; I offer it up to the informant for confirma-tion or correction" (interview, September 1999; see also Charmaz, Chapter 32, this volume).

◆ Conducting IE Interviews

IE interviewing is open-ended inquiry, and IE interviewers are always oriented to sequences of interconnected activities. They talk with people located throughout these institutional complexes in order to learn "how things work." In many investigations, informants are chosen as the research progresses, as the researcher learns more about the social relations involved and begins to see avenues that need exploration. Given that the purpose of interviewing is to build up an understanding of the coordination of activity in multiple sites, the interviews need not be standardized. Rather, each interview provides an opportunity for the researcher to learn about a particular piece of the extended relational chain, to check the developing picture of the coordinative process, and to become aware of additional questions that need attention.

Dorothy Smith reports that when she conducted interviews jointly with George Smith, in their study of the organization of job training (Smith and Smith 1990), they thought of their talk with informants as a way to build "piece by piece" a view of an extended organizational process. Rather than using a standard set of questions, they based each interview in part on what they had learned from previous ones. She explains: "You have a sense of what you're after, although you sometimes don't know what you're after until you hear people telling you things. . . . Discovering what you don't know—and don't know you don't know—is an important aspect of the process" (interview, September 1999). As in any qualitative interviewing, there is a balance to be achieved between directing the interview toward the researcher's goals and encouraging informants to talk in ways that reflect the contours of their activity (see also in this volume Warren, Chapter 4; Johnson, Chapter 5). The distinctiveness of IE interviews is produced by the researcher's developing knowledge of institutional processes, which allows a kind of listening and probing oriented toward institutional connections. Again, Smith explains, "The important thing is to think organizationally, recognizing you won't know at the beginning which threads to follow, knowing you won't follow all possible threads, but noting them along the way."

IE researchers often think of interviewing as "coinvestigation." Such an approach is evident in Gary Kinsman and Patrizia Gentile's (1998) discussion of the oral history narratives they collected from gay men and lesbians affected by Canadian national security campaigns of the late 1950s and early 1960s. They see the first-person narratives as both a "form of resistance to the official security documents" (p. 8) and a basis from which to build a critical analysis of those documents. Because people were affected differently, the narratives took different shapes, and the researchers found that their providing some historical context often helped informants remember and reconstruct their experiences. They describe their interviewing as "a fully reflexive process in which both the participant and the interviewer construct knowledge together" (p. 58).

Most IE interviewers tape conversations with informants, both as an aid in making notes and to preserve details whose relevance may not be immediately obvious. Transcripts of interviews are important texts in themselves, facilitating analysis and providing a way for research participants to "speak" in published accounts of the research. Diamond, however, is concerned about privileging the textual representation over the embodied actuality of the research conversation. We are always in our bodies, he reminds us; in fact, Smith's concept of the "everyday" begins from that fundamental fact. People's descriptions of their work activities and lived experiences are often produced gesturally as well as verbally, and our understanding of that work and that experience arises for us, in part, through our bodily response to their gestures. "IE, in insisting on bodies being there, sensitizes us to bodies as part of the data. . . . It's not about just words but how the words live in embodied experience" (T. Diamond, personal communication, December 1999).

INTERVIEW STRATEGIES

IE interviewing is typically organized around the idea of work, defined broadly, or "generously" (Smith 1987). Whether it is the paid work of an organizational position, the activist work of challenging a regime, or some "everyday life work" such as parenting or managing an illness, the point of interest is the informant's activity, as it reveals and points toward the interconnected activities of others. The idea of work provides a conceptual frame and guides interview talk; the point is not to insist on the categorical status of any activity, but to hold in place a conception of the social as residing in the concerting of people's actual activities.

The generous understanding of work deployed by IE researchers is related to early feminist insights about women's unpaid and often invisible work—the recognition that although various kinds of work sustain social life, some are uncompensated, unacknowledged, or mystified as aspects of personality (e.g., women's "caring" work, as explored in DeVault 1991). An IE study aims at a picture that displays all the activity sustaining a particular institutional nexus or arena, and this analytic goal gives rise to several distinctive strategies for the conduct of interviews. In the following subsections, we identify several kinds of work and discuss strategies associated with each.

Work Practices of Everyday Life

Some researchers conduct IE interviews with a view to understanding the everyday/everynight experiences of people living particular lives—single mothers, people with AIDS or disabilities, older women, or immigrant women, for example. In these interviews researchers seek detailed accounts of activities: What do mothers do when their children have trouble at school? How do individuals work at managing their health? What work do older women do to maintain their housing? How do immigrant women seek employment, education, or training? Ellen Pence began her research by "talking to women who used the police and courts. I would ask what went right or wrong"; these conversations gave her a view of the efforts battered women made to seek help (focus group, August 1999). Similarly, Nancy Naples (1998) studied the implementation of the 1988 Family Support Act in an Iowa jobs program that allowed recipients to work toward a college degree. She collected interview, observational, and documentary data on the policy, but the grounding for her study came from interviews with women in the program. Her interviews produced accounts of the women's everyday routines, which she used to uncover the tensions between their lives as mothers and college students and the demands of the program—thus bringing an "everyday life" dimension to policy analysis.

Given the conceptual frame discussed above, the interviewer approaches these conversations as explorations of work practices in everyday life; the point is to learn about what the informant actually does. Informants may or may not think of what they do as a form of "work"; the interviewer may use the rubric of work in questioning, but there is no need to insist on explicit talk of work or agreement about the status of the activity. When Smith and Griffith interviewed mothers, for example, "It worked well to take them through the school day, to ask them what they did at each point, such as what is involved in getting the kids ready for school, getting them there on time." Smith finds that guiding the interview in this way often has the result of "training the informant": "I tell people what I'm interested in, things I'd like to hear about, rather than asking questions. . . . Some people happily go on at a level of expanding practice, and some don't. So that's maybe a good reason to do multiple interviews" (interview, September 1999). Similarly, Diamond elicits "stories" as the basis for his research into the organization of health care: "Sometimes I just say, I want to talk about health insurance in the U.S. People jump in with long stories. . . . Invariably people will talk about employment, because that's the intervening institution—people need to be employed or connected to someone employed to have health insurance" (focus group, August 1999). In a study of a public school choice program, Lois Andre Bechely interviewed parents using the program. She notes:

> Getting people to continue to talk about the details of their "work" can be a challenge. . . . And in the case of parents (and this is almost always the mothers), not all of them saw their involvement as work—it was just what they did—while others did actually use words like, "it's my job," etc. (E-mail communication, September 1999)

Taylor and associates (forthcoming) found that although the notion of work was useful to them, conceptually, in establishing the framework of their group interviews, it was counterproductive when used with informants, for whom it evoked a prevalent normative standard of the "good patient" who conscientiously works at "managing" his or her health, against which many informants perceived themselves as delinquent. The researchers had the delicate job of figuring out how to ask people what they did around their health without suggesting that they should have been doing more or otherwise.

Interviews about everyday life work may also be used to point toward the work practices of others. For example, George Smith (1998) emphasizes that the gay students he interviewed were not meant to be "objects of study"; although their narratives could be interpreted as accounts of "work" they do as students (e.g., to "fit in," or pass), he uses their stories as windows on the work processes that affect them—both the "everyday work" of students upholding a heterosexist regime through surveillance and gossip and the paid work of teachers and administrators, which was not organized to interrupt that regime and sometimes reinforced it.

Some IE researchers attempt to conduct such interviews with a view to more than data collection, seeking to share insights with informants in the course of interviewing. Diamond says of his interviews on health insurance, "Together we construct a critique of benefits" (focus group, August 1999). And Gerald de Montigny, commenting on his studies of youth in state care, reports:

> My big challenge is that when I do an interview, I do so not only as an ethnographer, but from the standpoint of wanting to be a skilled social work interviewer. . . . I do not feel that I am able to explicate in my interviews the complex social forces at play in these youth's lives, though as a social worker, I do try to help them to understand the play of forces across the landscape of the everyday experiences. (E-mail communication, September 1999)

Whether such dual goals are achievable —and if so, how—appears to be among the unresolved questions of IE interviewers.

Frontline Organizational Work

Frontline professionals, such as teachers, nurses, trainers, social workers, community agency personnel, and other bureaucrats, often become informants in IE research. Individuals in such positions are especially important because they make the linkages between clients and ruling discourses, "working up" the messiness of an everyday circumstance so that it fits the categories and protocols of a professional regime. In some studies, such individuals are interviewed as intermediary actors in an institutional complex: Kamini Maraj Grahame (1998, 1999), for example, interviewed intake workers who screened Asian immigrant women into job training, showing that funding formulas organized their work such that they tracked the women into employment streams compatible with local employers' needs. Similarly, Smith and Griffith's interviews with teachers showed how they are located between parents, concerned with particular children, and school district practices, designed for standardized processing of groups (Smith 1987). And Yoko Ueda (1995) interviewed human resource professionals to learn about corporate personnel policies that shaped the family work of Japanese expatriate wives in Toronto. In other studies, researchers may be more directly focused on the work situations of these frontline workers and concerned with the organization and control of such work. For example, Campbell's (1988, 1992; Campbell and Jackson 1992) studies of nursing work are designed to illuminate the mechanisms of managerial control that have increasingly limited nurses' autonomy in care work. Similarly, Ann Manicom's (1995) examination of "health work" undertaken by teachers in low-income schools explores how these teachers are drawn into work that goes beyond official accounts of their jobs.

Here again, IE researchers seek detailed accounts of work processes, but interviewing frontline workers presents its own distinctive challenges. These workers have been trained to use the very concepts and categories that IE researchers wish to unpack, and they are accustomed to speaking from within a ruling discourse. Thus the interviewer must find ways of moving the talk beyond institutional language to "what actually happens" in the setting. Campbell teaches such interviewing strategies in part by offering the following advice:

> Listen to the person tell her story. Pay attention to the sequencing. Then ask yourself, can you tell exactly how she gets from one point to another? If not, ask questions; clarify, so that you can. (Interview, January 2000)

Such strategies require practice, because "we're all very good at filling in the blanks." But the organizational orientation of IE researchers leads them, with practice, to see both gaps in these accounts and the kinds of filling in necessary for a fuller organizational analysis. The challenge of moving beyond institutional language is so central to IE interviewing that we return to it in the following section.

In some studies that are focused more explicitly on change, interviews might include discussion of possible modifications of frontline work. For example, Pence's (1997) study of safety for battered women involved interviews with the various workers who serve the women as advocates, hospital, and criminal justice workers. As she gained an understanding of the interlocking activities of these workers, she could see that women's safety was only one of the concerns that shaped their work and, in fact, was often subordinated to organizational imperatives. She and her team began to ask workers not only how the system operated, but also how it might be organized differently. She explains:

> We ask, "Is there something you don't have in your job, that if you did have, would help prevent that woman getting beat up?" "If you were going to build victim safety into this process, how would you do it?" . . .
> It's an eye-opener. People in an institution rarely get asked, do you want to change something as basic as a form you fill out every day. How would you change it? Usually people totally get into it. And when you ask them, "Why is this on the form?" or "Why does the form ask that?" they can be quite insightful [about how the form works in the system], even though they might never have thought about it that way before. (focus group, August 1999)

As with everyday experience interviews, then, some researchers orient toward the dual goals of analysis and change; but these intriguing possibilities require partnerships with activists and practitioners that are not easily established and may not always be feasible.

"Ruling" Work

IE researchers are always interested in moving beyond the interchanges of frontline settings in order to track the macroinstitutional policies and practices that organize those local settings. Thus interviews are often conducted with managers and administrators who work at the level of translocal policy making and implementation, and these interviews also require a distinctive orientation and strategy. Kamini Maraj Grahame (1998, 1999), who studied federally funded job training for immigrant women in the United States, emphasizes the complexity of this kind of institutional process and the amount of "legwork and conversation" required even to have a sense of where in the structure one might need to conduct interviews. She learned about various parts of the institutional complex of job training while working in and with community organizations, and eventually conducted interviews not only with clients of and workers in those organizations, but also with managers working in the local, state, and federal agencies that funded and oversaw the programs. With each interviewee, she focused on that worker's role in the overall job training system. She would ask, "What do *you* do?" Recognizing that she was interviewing each at a particular point in time, and therefore at a particular point in what she came to call "the training cycle," she would ask what the interviewee was doing that day or week, and then, "Why are you doing this now?" Whenever someone mentioned a document, she would ask to see a copy of it and then ask what the worker did with that document. In these ways, she built an accumulating understanding of how work processes were textually linked across sites and levels of administration. (We address this kind of textual coordination again below.)

Grahame found that she often had to proceed without a clear sense of where interviewing would take her: "Someone in the federal government says something I have no way of making sense of—seeing the relevance of—until I go back to an interview I did at a community organization. Then I can put it all together." Because the information gained in interviews requires this kind of synthesis, she feels it is very important to tape and transcribe whenever possible. "Taping allows me to go back and forth and have things make sense in a way they did not initially," she explains. "It's a very complex enterprise, and there's no time to go back and redo interviews" (focus group, August 1999).

Often, interviews with managers and administrators are conducted in the later phases of IE studies, so that researchers can use information gained from clients and frontline workers to direct the interviewing. For example, Lois Andre Bechely reports:

> As I got farther up the chain of command, I had already done preliminary analysis of parent interviews and policy documents and my questions were focused on trying to uncover the social and textual organization of school choice practices that parents encounter and participate in. (E-mail communication, September 1999)

Andre Bechely used her knowledge as a former teacher to organize questions for administrators, but the talk still proceeded in the searching and open manner characteristic of IE interviewing.

The openness of such interviewing allows informants to speak in the forms appropriate to their work. For example, McCoy's (1998, 1999) study of restructuring in Canadian community colleges and the forms of accounting coordinating that process is based on interviews conducted almost entirely with managers. Her informants often talked about new cost accounting documents by enacting speech situations, that is, reporting what was said in the past or what might be argued in future negotiations. McCoy (1998) points out:

> It is not to be supposed that these enactments exactly match what was said or what will be said; their usefulness as data in this kind of study lies in what they suggest about what can possibly or appropriately be [said], and especially, how what can be said depends on and is oriented to the textual forms through which events and activities are known in authoritative ways. (Pp. 416-17)

Such reports give a strong sense of the discursive character of the work of ruling in this kind of setting.

Processing Interchanges

IE researchers are especially alert to the points where work processes intersect, points that Pence (1997) has labeled "processing interchanges":

> Processing interchanges are organizational occasions of action in which one practitioner receives from another a document pertaining to a case (e.g., a 911 incident report, a warrant request, or a motion for a continuance), and then makes something of the document, does something to it, and for-

wards it on to the next organizational occasion for action. It is the construction of these processing interchanges coupled with a highly specialized division of labor that accomplishes much of the ideological work of the institution. Workers' tasks are shaped by certain prevailing features of the system, features so common to workers that they begin to see them as natural, as the way things are done and—in some odd way—as the only way they could be done, rather than as planned procedures and rules developed by individuals ensuring certain ideological ways of interpreting and acting on a case. (P. 60)

In her study of the processing of domestic violence cases, Pence attends to the spaces and tools that organize the tasks of workers—how dispatchers use computers, police use Dictaphones, and so on—and to the forms required at each point of connection. As she points out, it is not "the woman who was beaten who moves from one point to the next in the stages of case processing"; rather, the "file stands in for the woman who was assaulted" (p. 67). In studying how this extremely important file is produced, Pence watched workers in these processing interchanges and also asked them about their work, querying police officers, for instance, on "how they decide when to write a report, how they decide what to record in their narratives, and how much leeway they have in making these decisions" (p. 71). At each processing interchange, she explains, "an institutional investigation helps to determine how such an objective (i.e. accounting for victim safety) could be incorporated into the design at each of these occasions" (p. 89). Working with practitioners in the system, Pence has developed an "audit" procedure—basically, an IE investigation—to be used collaboratively to provide "a place for advocates and practitioners to work together" (p. 187).

Campbell (1998, 1999) has used a similar approach in her participatory research project on home support for people with disabilities. Her team used interview material to identify processing interchanges they wished to examine in detail, and Campbell and her assistants arranged for team members to conduct observations of these moments in the management of home support. Watching a scheduler work at a computer screen, for example, they asked questions to help her make explicit the kinds of choices she was making. "People think the computer does it," Campbell notes, "but that glosses the judgment involved in her work" (interview, January 2000). The researchers found that "continuity" in scheduling home support workers was important for people with disabilities and a goal shared by workers in the system. As they observed the scheduler, however, they found that "her talk open[ed] up the organizational priorities that interfere with the Client-focus of her work" (p. 6).

Both Pence and Campbell have found that working with a team to investigate interchanges provides opportunities for participants to come to a fuller shared understanding of organizational action. Campbell reports that team members would sometimes "clash" over differing perspectives: "The professionals would say, 'You're not seeing this right; this is what's happening.' And people with disabilities would say, 'But it doesn't feel that way; here's how it feels' " (interview, January 2000).

As facilitator, Campbell would let such discussion proceed, and then ask, "Now whose standpoint are we taking?" Team members could then respond, "Oh yes, the standpoint of people with disabilities" (interview, January 2000). In this kind of exchange, Campbell is reminding her research team of the way that a notion of "standpoint" anchors the research in the relevancies of a particular group. The point is not that "people with disabilities" share a determinate standpoint, or that the perspectives of the professionals should be ignored or discounted. Rather, the idea is to consider how the perspectives from different locations illuminate the relevant social relations while keeping in mind the questions focused by the concerns of people living with disabilities.

SELECTING INFORMANTS

The preceding discussion provides some context for understanding IE approaches to the selection of interviewees. Because IE researchers are not oriented toward descriptive reporting on a population, they do not think of informants as a "sample." Still, when exploring the ground of everyday experience, some IE investigators seek informants who can report on varied circumstances and situations. For example, Smith and Griffith (1990) interviewed both middle-class and working-class mothers; Manicom (1995) spoke with teachers in schools serving middle-class and poor students; Smith et al. (1995) sought high school girl informants in different kinds of school situations. Some researchers make special efforts to include perspectives they believe are missing: Didi Khayatt, for example, found it relatively easy to interview middle-class lesbians in Egypt, but had to make special efforts to find working-class informants (focus group, October 1999).

Such efforts are common to many kinds of interview studies. However, IE researchers aim not for categorical descriptions, but for analyses that trace how the people living in these different circumstances are drawn into a common set of organizational processes. Some report that attention to differences among informants can easily pull them toward the kinds of categorical analyses embedded in ruling process, as when Smith and Griffith (1990) found themselves thinking much like school administrators about the class composition of student groups. One solution is for researchers to conceive of this kind of selection in terms of diversity of experience rather than categorically. For example, when interviewing people living with

HIV/AIDS about their health work, Taylor and associates (forthcoming) thought about diversity among their informants' circumstances, reasoning that they needed to include women caring for children, people living in prison, people on welfare, and so forth.

As discussed above, IE studies are rarely based solely on such a group of interviews; rather, they almost always use such interviews as pointers toward informants working in other settings. Those interviewees might be chosen in more varied ways. Some researchers follow "chains of action" (e.g., McCoy 1998; K. M. Grahame 1999). Some choose informants located in and around sites of confrontation; George Smith (1990), for example, located the "field" of the AIDS bureaucracy through work with other activists attempting to gain access to treatments. And in some studies, it seems useful for researchers to select "good thinkers" as interviewees. When Pence interviewed police, for example, she sought those who wrote especially complete or useful reports:

> If you read 50 police reports, you can say, "I want to talk to the cop who wrote these four." But I also try to interview one dud, so I can see how much is the institutional process and how much is the person. (focus group, August 1999)

Often, as George Smith (1990) explains, researchers simply rely on informants they encounter as their investigations proceed, using each conversation to expand understanding of the terrain.

Clearly, the selection of informants is more open-ended in IE investigations than it is in more conventional positivist studies, but the process is not haphazard. Rather, fieldwork and interviewing are driven by a faithfulness to the actual work processes that connect individuals and activities in the various parts of an institutional complex. Rigor comes not from technique—such as sampling or thematic analysis—but from the corrigibility of the developing map of social relations. When George Smith (1990) was learning about placebo-controlled trials of experimental AIDS treatments, for example, he did not need to identify recurring "themes" in the accounts of multiple physician informants. Rather, he sought their help in filling in his knowledge of how such trials work, continuing to "check" the account he was building as he proceeded with the investigation, and returning to physician (and other) informants as needed when questions or inconsistencies arose.

◆ Interviewing about Textual Practices

A prominent aspect of institutional ethnography is the recognition that text-based forms of knowledge and discursive practices are central to large-scale organization and relations of ruling in contemporary society. To use an organic metaphor, textual processes in institutional relations are like a central nervous system running through and coordinating different sites. To find out how things work and how they happen the way they do, a researcher needs to find the texts and text-based knowledge forms in operation. Thus IE investigation often involves close attention to textual practices, and interviewing is an important strategy in this regard.

When IE researchers talk about texts, they usually mean some kind of document or representation that has a relatively fixed and replicable character, for it is that aspect of texts—that they can be stored, transferred, copied, produced in bulk, and distributed widely, allowing them to be activated by users at different times and in different places—that allows them to play a standardizing and mediating role. In this view, a text can be any kind of document, on paper, on computer screens, or in computer files; it can also be a drawing, a pho-

tograph, a printed instrument reading, a video or sound recording, and so on.

Much IE research has focused on standardized texts used in professional and bureaucratic settings, such as care pathway forms in hospitals (Mykhalovskiy 2000), intake forms and applications at an employment agency (Ng 1996), patients' charts (Diamond 1992), nursing worksheets (Rankin 1998), forms for calculating teachers' workloads (McCoy 1999), course information sheets used in competency-based education reform (Jackson 1995), and safety assessment forms used by child protection workers (Parada 1998). Other bureaucratic texts studied have included job descriptions (Reimer 1995) and developers' maps used in land-use planning (Turner 1995). Griffith (1998) and Ng (1995) have examined legislative texts. Sometimes IE researchers look at the creation or generation of texts, such as the work of producing a newsletter for doctors (Mykhalovskiy 2000), creating materials for job skills training (Smith and Smith 1990), or taking wedding photographs (McCoy 1987, 1995).

IE researchers are also interested in the text-mediated discourses that frame issues, establish terms and concepts, and in various ways serve as resources that people draw into their everyday work processes, for example, health services research (Mykhalovskiy 2000), the literature on child development (Griffith 1984, 1995), the literature on "deviant" sexuality as an aspect of the policing of gay men (Kinsman 1989), the terms of an international development regime (Mueller 1995), and popular cultural discourses of femininity (D. E. Smith 1990:chap. 6). Whatever the text or textual process, in IE research it is examined for the ways it mediates relations of ruling and organizes what can be said and done.

LISTENING FOR TEXTS

At the early stages of research, when researchers are just beginning to learn about the institutional processes that shape the relations they are studying, they are alert to catch informants' references to texts or text-mediated processes. Sometimes these are fairly easy to catch, as when an informant mentions a specific document and how it functions. In the following extract, for example, a college administrator talks about a bureaucratic "D form":

> Well, that's the problem. We mounted programs and the last thing that's looked at is the return. Because the ministry—when we mount a program—has a little clause at the bottom of the D form, that simply says, you've got to make this work, we're not going to give you any more money than the funding units for it. So, if you want to put it on, fine. It's a disclaimer by the ministry of any acceptance of any debts that this program mounting creates.

At this point, or perhaps later in the interview, the researcher might ask to see a copy of the D form and, if possible, get one to take away with her. She will also want to learn more about how the D form is used: When is it filled out? By whom? What resources and future activities depend on the D form? In this way, the researcher begins to see how local settings are tied into extended institutional relations and at the same time lays the groundwork for future interviews ("Who could I talk to about that?").

Sometimes the researcher suspects that a textual process lies behind the description an informant is giving. It is not uncommon for informants who work in bureaucratic settings to use glosses and metaphors, as in the following example, where a college administrator is describing the work of a committee that recommends "per diem prices":

> And they report to the College Committee presidents who agree or disagree with their recommendation. And then that's sent on to the Ministry of Skills Development who again have to nod their approval. And finally to the federal government who have to pay the per diem. And they nod their approval or whatever.

Experience suggests that this "nodding" occurs textually, and an IE researcher interested in this process might go on to ask explicitly what form the reporting and the approval take. She might also want to discover which office or person does the approving on behalf of the ministry.

Not all the texts mentioned will become focal in the analysis, but in the early stages of studies some researchers like to map out the main textual processes at work in an institutional setting. In some cases, "mapping" might precede the initial interviews. Pence explains:

> We get together a prep work of documents and legislation. We used to start by going out and blindly interviewing. Now we prepare. But we do find out things [about texts] when we interview that we didn't know were there. (focus group, August 1999)

ASKING ABOUT TEXTS

However texts come to be identified as central to the relations under study—whether through exploratory interviews, through prep work, or through the researcher's prior knowledge—the research at some stage may involve interviews with people who can talk in detail about a text or those aspects of a textual process they know. One effective way for an interviewer to structure such an interview is to sit down with the informant and the text in question and talk very concretely about what is in the text and how the informant works with it. Diamond reports: "I ask people to bring a pay stub to the interview, so we can look at that text. We explore together: Where is health care in this pay stub?" (focus group, August 1999).

If the document in question is a standardized form, some researchers like to do the interview around a form that has been completed, rather than a blank one, as that will result in more concrete description. For example, when Dorothy Smith was interviewing a probation officer about a presentencing investigation form, she worked from an actual, completed form to ask about the sources of information (predominantly textual) and the practices of judgment that went into filling it out (interview, September 1999). When McCoy (1987) was interviewing a wedding photographer, she and the photographer worked from a set of photographs he had recently taken; as they looked through the stack of proofs, he talked about how he had worked with actual people and actual equipment on that specific day to make those pictures.

In other cases, the text in question is not one the informant creates or completes, but one he or she activates in some way, such as a report or a memo. Here the interviewer might focus on practices of reading to learn how the text is taken up in an actual setting, within an accountable work process. A transcript excerpt provided by Eric Mykhalovskiy illustrates this:

Eric Mykhalovskiy: So when you get those reports, what are you looking for? . . . How do they inform your thinking?

Informant (hospital administrator): Hmm. Well, certainly we look at the average length of stay, the time line. So if all of a sudden, I mean, we're averaging around five days, so if all of a sudden we're up to six, then that would concern me.

What the researcher wants to learn about the text and the practices of making or using it will vary, depending on the nature of the text and the focus of the investigation, but in general IE researchers are after the following:

1. How the text comes to this informant and where it goes after the informant is done with it

2. What the informant needs to know in order to use the text (create it, respond to it, fill it out, and so on)

3. What the informant does with, for, and on account of the text

4. How this text intersects with and depends on other texts and textual processes as sources of information, generators of conceptual frames, authorizing texts, and so on

5. The conceptual schema that organizes the text and its competent reading.

THE PROBLEM AND RESOURCE OF INSTITUTIONAL LANGUAGE

Institutional work processes are organized by conceptual schemes and distinctive categories. These are the terms in which the accountability of the work is produced, and procedures of accountability provide one of the main ways that various local settings are pulled into translocal relations. IE therefore pays strong attention to institutional categories and the interpretive schemata that connect them.

In interviews, it is common—and understandable—that people in an institutional setting describe their work using the language of the institution. This is especially the case with people who have been taught a professional discourse as part of their training or people whose work requires them to provide regular accounts of institutional processes. "Some people do jobs where public relations is part of their job, so they are doing that work while talking to me" (K. M. Grahame, focus group, August 1999). The challenge for the institutional ethnographer is to recognize when the informant is using institutional language. Not to do so is to risk conducting interviews that contain little usable data beyond the expression of institutional ideology in action, because institutional language conceals the very practices IE aims to discover and describe. Dorothy Smith elaborates:

> These terms are extraordinarily empty. They rely on your being able to fill out what they could be talking about. During the interview, you do that filling in while you listen, but when you look at the transcript afterward, the description isn't there. (Interview, September 1999)

As an example, Ann Manicom reports:

> One challenge I've faced in interviewing professionals is . . . to get them beyond saying something like, "Well, I have a lot of ADHD kids" to getting them to actually describe day-to-day work processes. The discourses are of course also interesting and an important piece of the analysis, but shifting them out of the discourse is important for actual descriptions of the work process. (E-mail communication, September 1999)

An informant's comment that she has "a lot of ADHD kids" would not be treated by an IE researcher as a straightforward description of her work, although it does show the teacher using institutional concepts to make sense of and to talk about her day-to-day actuality. Within the institution of schooling, it is certainly a competent description—other teachers would nod in sympathy and feel that they knew exactly what the teacher was talking about. A school administrator would understand something about that classroom relevant to her work of allocating resources. This is because the term references a discourse and practice of knowledge operative within the institution. An interviewer who knows something about teaching and professional discourses might also find, as Smith suggests above, that she too knows what the teacher is talking about. An alert IE researcher, however, would try to get the teacher to describe, for example, what these "ADHD kids" are like: what they do or need, and in what ways their needs complicate or add to her teaching work. The researcher would try to learn how the teacher uses the ADHD concept to organize her work with the children and her conferences with their parents. Furthermore, the researcher might try to learn how ADHD as a category operates in the administration of schooling: for example, in some school districts, classroom assistants and other resources are allocated through a procedure that takes into account the number of students in a class who are entered in school records as having "special needs," such as ADHD. An IE researcher encountering institutional language has thus a twofold objective: to obtain a description of the actuality that is assumed by, but not revealed in, the institutional terms, and, at the same time, to learn how such terms and the discourses they carry operate in the institutional setting.

◆ Analysis and Presentation

As IE is fundamentally an analytic project, we cannot terminate this discussion of interviewing at the moment when the tape recorder is turned off and the researcher packs up her or his notes to go home. In this section we briefly address the work that comes after the interview has been taped and transcribed. The studies we have referred to and cited throughout the chapter provide further advice and models for analysis.

IE researchers tend not to use formal analytic strategies such as interpretive coding. Some use qualitative data analysis software to group chunks of transcript, sometimes pages in length, by theme or topic; others contend that the logic of these programs runs against that of the IE approach. The software seems to work best for IE analysis when the grouping is done rather simply, something like the indexing for a book (D. Smith, personal communication), sticking closely to topics of talk and references to institutional sites and processes. For example, a researcher might collect in one file everything informants said about using AIDS service organizations, in another the informants' stories about the work and challenges of finding suitable doctors, and so on. A researcher examining chains of action or process interchanges could use the software to group informants' comments around particular sites, texts, or moments in the process. This kind of computer-aided sorting works at a fairly primary level and offers researchers a manageable way to work with large numbers of interviews; it still leaves the analytic work to be done, as always, through writing, thinking, and discussion with collaborators and colleagues.

Just as projects have different shapes, IE researchers aim toward different kinds of analyses. Some use their data to map out complex institutional chains of action; others describe the mechanics of text-based forms of knowledge, elaborate the conceptual schemata of ruling discourses, or explicate how people's lived experience takes shape within institutional relations. John McKendy (1999), who interviewed men incarcerated for violent crimes, focuses his analysis on the informants' stories and the interview itself as a conversation, but in a way that makes visible the juxtaposition of primary narratives and ideological, institutionally oriented accounts:

> In doing the analysis now . . . I am on the lookout for segments of the interviews where "fault lines" can be detected, as the two modes of telling— the narrative and the ideological—rub up against each other. I want to examine how such junctures are occasioned within the flow of the interview, what kinds of narrative problems they pose for the speakers, and what methods speakers improvise to handle (over-

> come, resist, circumvent) these problems. (P. 9)

Townsend (1996, 1998) took her data —participant observation notes, interview transcripts, and documents—and addressed them through three analytic processes. First she "undertook the rather arduous task of describing the everyday world of occupational therapy" (1998:19). Then she "trac[ed] the social processes that connect the work being studied with the work of others. . . . Through a back-and-forth method of exploration, [she] traced connections between what occupational therapists do and the documentation and other processes that govern that work" (p. 21). Finally, she examined the "ideological character" of the institutional process: the ways that "occupational therapists and the people with whom occupational therapists work are conceptualized and categorized in mental health services, then coordinated and controlled through textual facts about these categories rather than through face-to-face supervision" (p. 24).

In general, IE analysts look at interview data as raising questions; according to Khayatt, the key is to ask, "How is it that these people are saying what they're saying?" She adds, "This methodology allows you to go back to a political-economic context for the answer" (focus group, October 1999). Ng and Griffith agree that analysis is always a matter of moving back and forth between collected speech and the context that produced it. For Ng (1996, 1999), whose research explores the work experiences of immigrant women, the analytic focus is how these women are drawn into institutional processes. She believes that conventional analyses of immigrants' lives often "produce ethnicity" through particular kinds of analytic work on interview data, linking informants' comments back to their "home cultures." Her goal, instead, is to find clues to "how things happen" for the people identified as immigrants in Canadian institutions. Griffith says of analysis: "It's never instances, it's always processes and coordination. It's all these little hooks. To make sense of it, you have to understand not just the speech of the moment, but what it's hooked into" (focus group, October 1999).

Many IE researchers find that they collect considerably more information than they use in a single analysis, because the analysis eventually follows some more specific thread of social organization. Dorothy Smith explains: "You don't have to use the whole interview. You can be quite selective, because you're not interested in all aspects of the institutional process" (interview, September 1999).

WRITING STRATEGIES

Two general strategies for presenting interview-based analyses can be discerned in published IE studies. In one, the writer uses interview data to produce a description, in the writer's voice, of the institutional processes under examination. Usually this account is a composite built up from multiple sources: people's explanations, documents, and so on. Knowledge gleaned through interviews with informants in different institutional locations is rolled together into a description of how a complex institution "works." The individual informants, however, do not "speak" in the text.

Researchers employing an alternative strategy use quoted excerpts from interviews to carry forward the description and analysis in the final text. George Smith (1998) uses the notion of the "exhibit" to specify a distinctive use of interview excerpts:

> As exhibits, the excerpts create windows within the text, bringing into view the social organization of my informants' lives for myself and for my readers to examine. Though what is brought into view emerges out of the dialogic relations of the interview, excerpts must not be read as extensions of my description. As exhibits, they make available the social organization of the everyday school lives of the individuals I interviewed. Dialogically they enter the actual social organization of schools into the text of the analysis. (P. 312)

Some writers combine these strategies, using composite accounts where analytically appropriate as well as bringing forward exhibits, descriptions, and life stories from the transcripts:

> In general, I use informants' descriptions when the matter is their actual work and the experience of doing it; I use my own description (based on multiple sources) when I am describing generalized relations or chains of action that transcend the local experience of any one informant. (McCoy 1999:47)

Institutional ethnographers try to maintain a focus on institutional relations not just during interviews, but in analysis and writing as well. This can be a challenge, because apparently minor features of presentation format, such as the identification of speakers, can support or interrupt that focus. For example, writing procedures that tag all quotes, regardless of topic, with the gender, race, and class status of the speaker risk inviting an individualizing line of analysis, in which class and ethnicity are treated as inherent in individuals rather than produced through coordinative social processes. Consequently, some IE writers suppress personal information about informants in order to keep the focus on the institutional processes they are describing; they identify quoted speakers only by their location in the institutional work process of which they speak (e.g., nurse, client, teacher, administrator). On the other hand, IE writers using life stories to examine an experience and elaborate a problematic usually find it analytically important to include biographical details and to distinguish speakers from each other through the use of pseudonyms (see also Atkinson, Chapter 6, this volume).

It is sometimes useful for writers to instruct their readers in how to read interview excerpts. Campbell (1999) introduces her team's report with some comments about how excerpts should be understood:

> Viewed from the standpoint of what might be called "the official work processes" of community health, people with disabilities are clients. . . . In Project Inter-Seed's research we found that the person on the receiving end is not passive but must claim his or her place as an active participant in health care. . . . We ask you to think differently about clients and to read the word client in this report as a *job title (i.e., Client)*. It signifies that Clients work, including conducting relationships with people in the health care system, orienting Home Support Workers, managing different workers in their home in order to work towards having their individual health needs met. The understanding of people with disabilities as actively engaged in Home Support work helps set the frame for our discussions. (Pp. 1-2)

As in most aspects of IE, there is no fixed writing format to which all practitioners adhere; instead, writers have the goal of keeping the institution in view and different ways of realizing that goal.

◆ Conclusion

In one view, our brief discussion here risks misrepresenting institutional ethnography, because of the artificiality of separating out the "interview" parts of the approach. For practitioners, IE always combines theory and method, and these are understood not as dichotomized "ingredients" for an analysis, but as constituting a coherent approach to "writing the social" (Smith 1999). We have also been concerned with the danger of reifying the approach as technique. (Indeed, the IE focus on "ruling" prompts de Montigny to ask, skeptically, "What social forces of funding, or recognition, or careers compel us to label and name that which we do as 'IE'?"; e-mail communication, September 1999.) These risks seem worth taking, however, because we believe that IE approaches offer distinctive advantages for researchers seeking to unmask the relations of ruling that shape everyday life.

Dorothy Smith's writing has been taken up in sociology as critique and revision of core theoretical concerns of the discipline, but the IE approach to empirical investigation has fit less comfortably within academic sociology, because its focus is not on theory building but on "what actually happens." [3] Much of the work we have discussed here, and much development of IE approaches, has occurred among professionals concerned with their relations to clients and the forces shaping their work or among activists working to understand the institutions they confront and seek to change. In addition, many IE researchers have found that the approach is a powerful teaching tool, because it can provide anyone with a strategy for investigating the lineaments of ruling (Naples forthcoming).

Institutional ethnography is one of the new modes of inquiry that have grown from the cracks in monolithic notions of "objective" social science, as women of all backgrounds, people of color, and others previously excluded from knowledge production have found space and "voice" to explore their experiences and pose questions relevant to their lives. In this context, the distinctiveness of IE lies in its commitment to going beyond the goal of simply "giving voice."

Ann Manicom reports that her feminist students—sensitized to the occlusion and misrepresentation of women's experience in so much traditional social science—

sometimes worry about "imposing" extended analyses:

> So the work to be done is to help them think more deeply, first about the notion of "women's voices," and secondly about the notion of going "beyond" voice. The first process makes problematic any simplistic notion of "experience" arising in any one of us as individuals; the second brings into view how the traces of social relations are already in women's accounts of their experience. Thus, what is called for in IE is not so much "going beyond" as it is tracing more intently what is already there to be heard. (E-mail communication, September 1999)

Such analyses are directed toward ruling processes that are pervasive, consequential, and not easily understood from the perspective of any local experience. But the IE approach suggests that an understanding grounded in such a vantage point is possible, and necessary, if we are to build upon excluded perspectives the kind of "map" of institutional processes that might be used in making changes to benefit those subject to ruling regimes.

■ Notes

1. The group includes several generations of Smith's students from the University of British Columbia and the Ontario Institute for Studies in Education (University of Toronto) and has attracted increasing numbers of other scholars.

During the past decade, informal meetings have evolved into more regular conferences at York University and OISE, including a 1996 workshop sponsored by the American Sociological Association's Sex and Gender Section. Members of the group have collected exemplars of the approach in publications such as Campbell and Manicom's (1995) edited collection; a special symposium in *Human Studies* titled "Institutions, Ethnography, and Social Organization" (1998); and a forthcoming special issue of *Studies in Cultures, Organizations and Societies* on institutional ethnography (Smith forthcoming).

2. Although this approach shares with Foucault an interest in texts, power, and governance, there are some central differences that are particularly significant for empirical research. In Foucault's work and in work taking up his approach, for example, the notion of discourse designates a kind of large-scale conversation in and through texts; Smith works with a wider notion of discourse that is consistent with her social ontology and her commitment to grounding inquiry in the activities of actual individuals. For Smith, *discourse* refers to a field of relations that includes not only texts and their intertextual conversation, but the activities of people in actual sites who produce them and use them and take up the conceptual frames they circulate. This notion of discourse never loses the presence of the subject who activates the text in any local moment of its use.

3. Smith's critique involves seeing the enterprise of theory building as implicated in ruling relations. The revision it calls for is one of orientation: Rather than building theory, the researcher seeks to explicate how the categories of social theory work, in concert with related institutional processes, to regulate activities in local sites.

■ References

Andre Bechely, L. N. 1999. "To Know Otherwise: A Study of the Social Organization of Parents' Work for Public School Choice." Ph.D. dissertation, University of California, Los Angeles.

Campbell, M. 1988. "Management as 'Ruling': A Class Phenomenon in Nursing." *Studies in Political Economy* 27:29-51.

———. 1992. "Nurses' Professionalism: A Labour Process Analysis." *International Journal of Health Services* 22:751-65.

———. 1995. "Teaching Accountability: What Counts as Nursing Education?" Pp. 221-33 in *Knowledge, Experience, and Ruling Relations*, edited by M. Campbell and A. Manicom. Toronto: University of Toronto Press.

———. 1998. "Research on Health Care Experiences of People with Disabilities: Exploring the Everyday Problematic of Service Delivery." Presented at the conference "Exploring the Restructuring and Transformation of Institutional Processes: Applications of Institutional Ethnography," October, York University, Toronto.

———. 1999. "Home Support: What We've Learned about Continuity and Client Choice." Discussion paper, Project Inter-Seed: Learning from the Health Care Experiences of People with Disabilities, University of Victoria and South Vancouver Island Resource Centre for Independent Living, Victoria, BC.

Campbell, M. and N. Jackson. 1992. "Learning to Nurse: Plans, Accounts and Action." *Qualitative Health Research* 2:475-96.

Campbell, M. and A. Manicom, eds. 1995. *Knowledge, Experience, and Ruling Relations*. Toronto: University of Toronto Press.

de Montigny, G. 1995. *Social Working: An Ethnography of Front-Line Practice*. Toronto: University of Toronto Press.

DeVault, M. L. 1991. *Feeding the Family: The Social Organization of Caring as Gendered Work*. Chicago: University of Chicago Press.

———. 1999. *Liberating Method: Feminism and Social Research*. Philadelphia: Temple University Press.

Diamond, T. 1992. *Making Gray Gold: Narratives of Nursing Home Care*. Chicago: University of Chicago Press.

Eastwood, L. 2000. "Textual Mediation in the International Forest Policy Negotiation Process." Presented at the conference "Making Links: New Research in Institutional Ethnography," May, Ontario Institute for Studies in Education, Toronto.

Grahame, K. M. 1998. "Asian Women, Job Training, and the Social Organization of Immigrant Labor Markets." *Qualitative Sociology* 21:75-90.

———. 1999. "State, Community and Asian Immigrant Women's Work: A Study in Labor Market Organization." Ph.D. dissertation, University of Toronto.

Grahame, P. R. 1998. "Ethnography, Institutions, and the Social Organization of Knowledge." *Human Studies* 21:347-60.

———. 1999. "Doing Qualitative Research: Three Problematics." *Discourse of Sociological Practice* 2(1):4-10.

Griffith, A. I. 1984. "Ideology, Education, and Single Parent Families: The Normative Ordering of Families through Schooling." Ph.D. dissertation, University of Toronto.

———. 1992. "Educational Policy as Text and Action." *Educational Policy* 6:415-28.

———. 1995. "Mothering, Schooling, and Children's Development." Pp. 108-21 in *Knowledge, Experience, and Ruling Relations*, edited by M. Campbell and A. Manicom. Toronto: University of Toronto Press.

———. 1998. "Educational Restructuring in Ontario." Presented at the conference "Exploring the Restructuring and Transformation of Institutional Processes: Applications of Institutional Ethnography," October, York University, Toronto.

"Institutions, Ethnography, and Social Organization" (symposium). 1998. *Human Studies* 21:347-436.

Jackson, N. 1995. " 'These Things Just Happen': Talk, Text, and Curriculum Reform." Pp. 164-80 in *Knowledge, Experience, and Ruling Relations,* edited by M. Campbell and A. Manicom. Toronto: University of Toronto Press.

Khayatt, D. 1995. "Compulsory Heterosexuality: Schools and Lesbian Students." Pp. 149-63 in *Knowledge, Experience, and Ruling Relations,* edited by M. Campbell and A. Manicom. Toronto: University of Toronto Press.

Kinsman, G. 1989. "Official Discourse as Sexual Regulation: The Social Organization of the Sexual Policing of Gay Men." Ph.D. dissertation, University of Toronto.

———. 1996. *The Regulation of Desire: Homo and Hetero Sexualities*. Montreal: Black Rose.

Kinsman, G. and P. Gentile. 1998. " 'In the Interests of the State': The Anti-gay, Anti-lesbian National Security Campaign in Canada." Preliminary research report, Laurentian University, Sudbury, Ontario.

Luken, P. C. and S. Vaughan. 1991. "Elderly Women Living Alone: Theoretical and Methodological Considerations from a Feminist Perspective." *Housing and Society* 18:37-48.

———. 1996. "Narratives of Living Alone: Elderly Women's Experiences and the Textual Discourse on Housing." Presented at the annual meeting of the Society for the Study of Social Problems, New York.

———. 1998. "Talk about Race and Housing." Presented at the annual meeting of the Society for the Study of Social Problems, San Francisco.

Manicom, A. 1995. "What's Health Got to Do with It? Class, Gender, and Teachers' Work." Pp. 135-48 in *Knowledge, Experience, and Ruling Relations,* edited by M. Campbell and A. Manicom. Toronto: University of Toronto Press.

McCoy, L. 1987. "Looking at Wedding Pictures: A Study in the Social Organization of Knowledge." M.A. thesis, University of Toronto.

———. 1995. "Activating the Photographic Text." Pp. 181-92 in *Knowledge, Experience, and Ruling Relations,* edited by M. Campbell and A. Manicom. Toronto: University of Toronto Press.

———. 1998. "Producing 'What the Deans Know': Cost Accounting and the Restructuring of Post-secondary Education." *Human Studies* 21:395-418.

———. 1999. "Accounting Discourse and Textual Practices of Ruling: A Study of Institutional Transformation and Restructuring in Higher Education." Ph.D. dissertation, University of Toronto.

McKendy, J. 1999. "Bringing Stories Back In: Agency and Responsibility of Men Incarcerated for Violent Offences." Unpublished manuscript.

Mueller, A. 1995. "Beginning in the Standpoint of Women: An Investigation of the Gap between *Cholas* and 'Women of Peru.' " Pp. 96-107 in *Knowledge, Experience, and Ruling Relations,* edited by M. Campbell and A. Manicom. Toronto: University of Toronto Press.

Mykhalovskiy, E. 2000. "Knowing Health Care/Governing Health Care: Exploring Health Services Research as Social Practice." Ph.D. dissertation, York University.

Mykhalovskiy, E. and G. W. Smith. 1994. *Getting Hooked Up: A Report on the Barriers People Living with HIV/AIDS Face Accessing Social Services.* Toronto: Ontario Institute for Studies in Education.

Naples, N. 1997. "Contested Needs: Shifting the Standpoint on Rural Economic Development." *Feminist Economics* 3:63-98.

———. 1998. "Bringing Everyday Life to Policy Analysis: The Case of White Rural Women Negotiating College and Welfare." *Journal of Poverty* 2:23-53.

———. Forthcoming. "Negotiating the Politics of Experiential Learning in Women's Studies: Lessons from the Community Action Project." In *Locating Feminism,* edited by R. Wiegman. Durham, NC: Duke University Press.

Ng, R. 1995. "Multiculturalism as Ideology: A Textual Analysis." Pp. 35-48 in *Knowledge, Experience, and Ruling Relations,* edited by M. Campbell and A. Manicom. Toronto: University of Toronto Press.

———. 1996. *The Politics of Community Services: Immigrant Women, Class and State.* Halifax, Nova Scotia: Fernwood.

———. 1999. "Homeworking: Dream Realized or Freedom Constrained? The Globalized Reality of Immigrant Garment Workers." *Canadian Woman Studies* 19(3):110-14.

Parada, H. 1998. "Restructuring Families and Children in the Child Welfare Bureaucracy." Presented at the conference "Exploring the Restructuring and Transformation of Institutional Processes: Applications of Institutional Ethnography," October, York University, Toronto.

Pence, E. 1997. "Safety for Battered Women in a Textually Mediated Legal System." Ph.D. dissertation, University of Toronto.

Rankin, J. 1998. "Health Care Reform and the Restructuring of Nursing in British Columbia." Presented at the conference "Exploring the Restructuring and Transformation of Institutional Processes: Applications of Institutional Ethnography," October, York University, Toronto.

Reimer, M. 1995. "Downgrading Clerical Work in a Textually Mediated Labour Process." Pp. 193-208 in *Knowledge, Experience, and Ruling Relations,* edited by M. Campbell and A. Manicom. Toronto: University of Toronto Press.

Smith, D. E. 1987. *The Everyday World as Problematic: A Feminist Sociology.* Boston: Northeastern University Press.

———. 1990. *Texts, Facts and Femininity: Exploring the Relations of Ruling.* New York: Routledge.

———. 1996. "The Relations of Ruling: A Feminist Inquiry." *Studies in Cultures, Organizations and Societies* 2:171-90.

———. 1999. *Writing the Social: Theory, Critique, Investigations.* Toronto: University of Toronto Press.

———, ed. Forthcoming. "Institutional Ethnography" (special issue). *Studies in Cultures, Organizations and Societies.*

Smith, D. E. and A. I. Griffith. 1990. "Coordinating the Uncoordinated: Mothering, Schooling, and Social Class." Pp. 25-44 in *Perspectives on Social Problems: A Research Annual,* edited by G. Miller and J. A. Holstein. Greenwich, CT: JAI.

Smith, D. E. and G. Smith. 1990. "Re-organizing the Jobs Skills Training Relation: From 'Human Capital' to 'Human Resources.' " Pp. 171-96 in *Education for Work, Education as Work: Canada's Changing Community Colleges,* edited by J. Muller. Toronto: Garamond.

Smith, D. E., L. McCoy, and P. Bourne. 1995. "Girls and Schooling: Their Own Critique." Gender and Schooling Paper No. 2, Centre for Women's Studies in Education, Ontario Institute for Studies in Education.

Smith, G. W. 1988. "Policing the Gay Community: An Inquiry into Textually-Mediated Social Relations. *International Journal of the Sociology of Law* 16:163-83.

———. 1990. "Political Activist as Ethnographer." *Social Problems* 37:629-48.

———. 1995. "Accessing Treatments: Managing the AIDS Epidemic in Ontario." Pp. 18-34 in *Knowledge, Experience, and Ruling Relations,* edited by M. Campbell and A. Manicom. Toronto: University of Toronto Press.

———. 1998. "The Ideology of 'Fag': The School Experience of Gay Students." *Sociological Quarterly* 39:309-55.

Stock, A. 2000. "An Ethnography of Assessment in Elementary Schools." Ph.D. dissertation, University of Toronto.

Taylor, D., M. Bresalier, L. Gillis, C. McClure, L. McCoy, E. Mykhalovskiy, and M. Webber. Forthcoming. "Making Care Visible: Exploring the Everyday Work of People Living with HIV/AIDS." Report for the AIDS Program Committee, Toronto.

Townsend, E. A. 1996. "Institutional Ethnography: A Method for Analyzing Practice." *Occupational Therapy Journal of Research* 16:179-99.

———. 1998. *Good Intentions Overruled: A Critique of Empowerment in the Routine Organization of Mental Health Services.* Toronto: University of Toronto Press.

Turner, S. M. 1995. "Rendering the Site Developable: Texts and Local Government Decision Making in Land Use Planning." Pp. 234-48 in *Knowledge, Experience, and Ruling Relations,* edited by M. Campbell and A. Manicom. Toronto: University of Toronto Press.

Ueda, Y. 1995. "Corporate Wives: Gendered Education of Their Children." Pp. 122-34 in *Knowledge, Experience, and Ruling Relations,* edited by M. Campbell and A. Manicom. Toronto: University of Toronto Press.

Vaughan, S. and P. C. Luken. 1997. "Here and There/Now and Then: The Social Organization of Women's Moving Experiences." Presented at the annual meeting of the Pacific Sociological Association, San Diego, CA.

Walker, G. A. 1990. *Family Violence and the Women's Movement: The Conceptual Politics of Struggle.* Toronto: University of Toronto Press.

■ *Interviews*

Campbell, Marie. Telephone interview with M. L. DeVault, January 2000.

Diamond, Timothy. IE focus group conducted by L. McCoy, Duluth, MN, August 1999.

Grahame, Kamini Maraj. IE focus group conducted by L. McCoy, Duluth, MN, August 1999.

Griffith, Alison I. IE focus group conducted by L. McCoy, Toronto, October 1999.

Khayatt, Didi. IE focus group conducted by L. McCoy, Toronto, October 1999.

Mykhalovskiy, Eric. Interview conducted by L. McCoy, Toronto, September 1999.

Ng, Roxana. IE focus group conducted by L. McCoy, Toronto, October 1999.

Parada, Henry. IE focus group conducted by L. McCoy, Duluth, MN, August 1999.

Pence, Ellen. IE focus group conducted by L. McCoy, Duluth, MN, August 1999.

Smith, Dorothy E. IE focus group conducted by L. McCoy, Duluth, MN, August 1999.

———. Interview conducted by M. L. DeVault and L. McCoy, Toronto, September 1999.

37

ETHNOMETHODOLOGICAL ANALYSES OF INTERVIEWS

◆ Carolyn D. Baker

Although ethnomethodology is not typically associated with interview research, in this chapter I demonstrate a number of ways in which ethnomethodological ideas can be applied in the analysis of interview data. Such analysis provides for readings of the data that go well beyond the conventional "content" or "thematic" explications, where interviewee talk is seen as information about interior or exterior realities. Instead, ethnomethodological analyses draw attention to the interactive work that occurs during the questioning and answering process, understood as a place in the social world equally as "real" as any other, and where the participants undertake conversational interaction using resources recruited from their memberships in other settings. Such analyses attend to *how* participants do the work

of conversational interaction, including how they make sense of each other, how they build a "corpus of interview knowledge," how they negotiate identities, and how they characterize and connect the worlds they talk about.

Ethnomethodology is a distinctive enterprise within the social sciences. Founded in the work of Harold Garfinkel (1967) and of Harvey Sacks, whose writings are collected in *Lectures on Conversation* (1992), ethnomethodology has been described as a "radical respecification" of the human sciences (Button 1991) because of the unique approach it takes to the study of social organization and social order. Most centrally, and most simply, ethnomethodologists are concerned with studying the resources and methods with which ordinary members go about making sense of the settings, the peo-

AUTHOR'S NOTE: I wish to thank Mike Brown, Mike Emmison, and Eleni Petraki for comments on an earlier draft of this chapter. I am grateful to Jay Gubrium, James Holstein, and David Silverman for their helpful reviews.

ple, and the events they encounter. John Heritage (1984) puts it this way:

> The term "ethnomethodology" . . . refers to the study of a particular subject matter: the body of common-sense knowledge and the range of procedures and considerations by means of which the ordinary members of society make sense of, find their way about in, and act on the circumstances in which they find themselves. (P. 4)

The reference to "ordinary" members is meant to draw attention to the sense-making accomplishments of any people anywhere and is a response and an alternative to sociologies that start with the assumptions of grand theories and/or assume that the (social) scientist's knowledge is of an inherently different order than the ordinary person's. Importantly, ethnomethodology does not compete with other sociologies for the mantle of explaining the social world. Ethnomethodology is concerned with *explicating how* things are *accomplished* by members to have the character that they do in any given site in the social world. Therefore, the topics that ethnomethodologists can study are limitless. Ethnomethodological inquiry is inspired by a sense of fascination with how people accomplish their identities, their activities, their settings, and their sense of social order.

An important recognition about ethnomethodology's interests in interview data is that ethnomethodologists do not use interviews to collect data in the manner that other social scientists do. Instead, ethnomethodologists study interviews as instances of settings—like other interactional events that are not interviews—in which members use interactional and interpretive resources to build versions of social reality and create and sustain a sense of social order. Interviews, then, are seen as a particular subset of interactional settings and as events that members make happen thoroughly inside and as part of the social

worlds being talked about, rather than as "outside" or "time out" from those social worlds. Understood this way, interviews are treated not so much as techniques for getting at information (although, commonsensically, people orient to them in this way), but more as in-their-own-right-analyzable instances of talk-in-interaction (see Baker 1997). Looked at and analyzed this way, interviews can yield new orders of insight about a range of matters, such as the production of situated identities and the moral work of accounting. This range of matters turns out to be (un)surprisingly large and, further, can connect in unanticipated ways with the topics of interviews (see Schaeffer and Maynard, Chapter 28, this volume).

In this chapter, I identify several keys to understanding the ethnomethodological approach to the analysis of interview data. These keys are as follows: (a) studying the interview as conversational interaction, (b) treating interview materials as accounts rather than reports, (c) looking for membership categorization work within the interaction and within accounts, (d) finding the production of identities, and, relatedly, (e) finding versions of worlds talked about in the interaction, in the accounts, and in the membership categorization work. These keys are connected, such that turning any one of them to open an analysis gives access to the next key, and the next. I use a number of extracts from different interview studies to demonstrate how to turn these keys. Although I have organized the chapter to focus on each of the five keys separately, each extract and discussion section contains reflections of the others.

◆ The Interview as Conversational Interaction

I discuss the first key in relation to an interview with a call taker for a technical support line for software users that took place in Sydney, Australia. Pam is a technician who answers calls from clients about their problems with computer software. The interviewer is Carolyn, a member of the research team present at the work site that is audiorecording calls to the help line and videotaping the call takers at work.[1] Interviews with call takers were organized spontaneously, and there was no set of guiding questions; call takers were simply asked to talk about their experiences as call takers and to share their insights into the work that they do. In the extract presented below, the interviewer's first turn captures precisely the ethnographic fact that the researchers have been witnesses to the work about which they will now interview the call takers.[2]

The first turns of this extract show the conversational work that is done by the participants in making the interview happen *as an interview*. Words are parts of utterances that are treated as activities (Turner 1974). The analysis of conversational interaction involves tracing the work that is done turn-by-turn by each speaker in relation to prior turns and in orientation to next turns. The sequential analysis of conversational interaction is most highly developed in the field known as conversation analysis (CA), which originated in the work of Harvey Sacks, Emanuel Schegloff, and Gail Jefferson (1974) and is closely related to ethnomethodology. Rather than drawing on the specialized terminology of CA here, I will provide a reading of each extract in less technical ethnomethodological terms.

We can focus first on the interviewer's work in talking with Pam, the technical support call taker. The first turn is an offer of a description characterizing the call taker's work, a selection of first topic, and an invitation for Pam to respond. It is also a selective characterization of what the researcher noticed as remarkable in Pam's work, and therefore a kind of self-description of the researcher's identity as a stranger to this form of work. Pam agrees with this description, but not with the same sense of awe offered by the interviewer;

Pam turns the remarkable into the mundane (turn 2). The interviewer then produces a comment that reinstates her initial assessment of the work as remarkable or extraordinary (turn 3). Pam responds by again downplaying the interviewer's characterization, and her response includes an account of how the long time is not so exceptional as to be marveled at (turn 4). The interviewer offers agreements over the course of Pam's ensuing talk (turns 5, 7, 9). After Pam concludes her account of why she does not mind long calls, the interviewer provokes some further talk about the nature of the calls by supplying yet more descriptions of Pam's work (turns 11, 13, 15), with which Pam agrees.

These comments—these "noticings"—are expressed as if from Pam's perspective. The interviewer is offering Pam some further descriptions of what her work might be like. Pam then begins a lengthy turn describing how she thinks during these long calls, describing her motivations and the callers' motivations and needs—a veritable jackpot of talk for the interviewer.

The first few lines of this extract show how deeply the interviewer has shaped the beginning of the interview. This shaping has involved characterizations of Pam and of the interviewer herself as a witness and a stranger to the work. It has involved finding things to marvel at, things that Pam makes unremarkable in her early accounts and disclaimers. Although there are no questions and no answers in this extract, as there are in many interviews, there is a clear initiation-reply format, and the exchange is oriented to by both speakers *as* an interview, as can be seen in the asymmetry of the talk, with the subject being Pam and her work. The study of *how* Carolyn and Pam converse to arrive at descriptions of Pam's work that might later be taken to be "interview data" shows that the social organization of the talk is fundamental to the production of such data. Any interview is by definition an instance of conversational interaction, and this is deeply consequential for what interviewers and interviewees

EXTRACT 1

Turn	Speaker	
1	Carolyn:	you spent a lot of time with some of those (0.2) people yesterday (.) a long time
2	Pam:	you learn patience haha
3	Carolyn:	boy
4	Pam:	ha well it's part of the job really (.) because if I wasn't on the phone to them (.) I'd be on the phone to another customer
5	Carolyn:	mm
6	Pam:	anyway like I'd be sitting there on the phone anyway
7	Carolyn:	yeah
8	Pam:	so (0.4) it doesn't really make it a lot different I'm happy to sit there as long as we fix the problem (0.4) it's like nice to 'cause if you're on a long call like that it's usually like troubleshooting rather than knowing the exact answer
9	Carolyn:	yep yep
10	Pam:	so (.) it's really good to (0.2) sit there and actually find out what does cause that problem (.) part of a learning process (1.0) so (0.4) that's (0.2) that's the reason I don't mind sitting on long calls
11	Carolyn:	and it's it's (0.2) there are all these gaps where (0.2) you know the person at the other end is trying something
12	Pam:	yeah
13	Carolyn:	and (.) and you sort of have to wait
14	Pam:	yeah
15	Carolyn:	and you don't know how long it's going to take
16	Pam:	no (0.6) you you while I'm doing that (.) I sometimes like if the computer's restarting and things like that .hh I try and figure out what to do next 'cause sometimes like you're just <u>boggled</u> like (0.4) one of those problems I had before where sh the refresh (.) the screen wasn't being refreshed .hh I just had (.) no idea what to do (0.2) and you just kinda try and sit there and <u>think</u> (1.0) and sometimes when customers ring up and they say I've got (0.2) this this this this problem (0.2) what do I do (0.2) and ((click of fingers)) they expect an answer straight away .hh and you're kind of and I just like .hh you've gotta get everything straight in your mind and I say to them just (0.8) hold on a moment just while I have a think about it and I just sit there and go if this happens this happens (0.4) okay (.) then I tell them to do something which is (.) probably sometimes irrelevant just so they think that they're doing something just (0.4) just stepping them through that I know by heart (0.4) just while I'm thinking about what could be causing the problem (0.4) and then I say (.) okay (.) just cancel that for the moment and then (0.2) tell them what to do (0.2) so they always like to be doing something 'cause then they think they get confidence in you (0.4) with what they're doing (.) if you say to them straight away .hh okay do this (0.2) they'll have more confidence in what you're doing than .hh (.) <u>um</u> (.) *alright* (.) <u>um</u> (.) hang on (.) um (.) like do you know what I mean (0.4) have more confidence

might say and hear. Relatedly, Mark Rapley and Charles Antaki (1998), who have studied interviewers' conversational work in "view-soliciting" open-ended interviews, conclude that "some of the things in interviewers' talk . . . do not so much solicit views as act positively to generate and shape them" (p. 605). An ethnomethodological analysis of interview talk calls into serious question the conventional social scientific characterization of interviewing as a form of data *collection*—which presumes that the data preexist the interview.

This first extract also illustrates what James Holstein and Jaber Gubrium (1997) call "active interviewing," during which "the active interviewer's role is to incite respondents' answers, virtually *activating narrative production* . . . by indicating—even suggesting—narrative positions, resources, orientations and precedents" (p. 123). The conduct of an active interview as proposed by Holstein and Gubrium (1997) is built on an appreciation that "any attempt to strip interviews of their interactional ingredients will be futile" (p. 114; see also Holstein and Gubrium 1995). These interactional ingredients are constitutive of the interview and are one key to analyzing the social organization of knowledge production in the interview (see also Schaeffer and Maynard, Chapter 28, this volume).

◆ Attention to Accounting

Ethnomethodological approaches to the analysis of interviews are characterized by the treatment of answers (and sometimes questions) as *accounts,* as distinct from reports about matters exterior to the interview or responses to questions. These accounts are best understood as sense-making work through which participants engage in explaining, attributing, justifying, describing, and otherwise finding possible sense or orderliness in the various events, people, places, and courses of action they talk about. In a first important sense, to be developed in the next section of the chapter, interviewees can be seen to account for themselves as competent members of the social category to which the interviewer has assigned them. That is, people are interviewed *as members* of some specific cate-

gory, or population, such as technical support line call takers or, as in the next example, *as* parents, teachers, or students. Accounting for oneself involves invoking a social world in which one's version of competent membership in a category could make sense. Accounting, then, is more than reporting or responding; it is a way of arranging versions of how things are or could be. It turns out that accounting is rife within interviews. As David Silverman (1993) puts it, "In studying accounts, we are studying displays of cultural particulars as well as displays of members' artful practices in assembling those particulars" (p. 114). This leads to the recognition that by "analyzing how people talk to one another, one is directly gaining access to a cultural universe and its content of moral assumptions" (p. 108).

The following transcribed example (see Extract 2), from a study I conducted with Jayne Keogh, comes from a set of interviews between parents and teachers held at a secondary school parents' night in Brisbane, Australia (see Baker and Keogh 1995). The interviews in this set are therefore not research interviews in the sense that they were conducted for research purposes; rather, they were conducted for school purposes and were recorded for research purposes. The interviews took place in a large room at the school that was set up with a number of stations where teachers sat at desks and additional chairs were provided for parents. Parents and, in most cases, the student who was the subject of the interview came to a teacher's desk, engaged in talk with the teacher, and left; then another family would come to the teacher. The following encounter involves the teacher, the student, Barry, and Barry's mother, although Barry does not speak in this exchange.

It can be seen that in turn 1 the teacher begins by addressing Barry ("how did you go?") and asking Barry for a look at (presumably) some report card or document that he holds. In turn 2, Barry's mother answers for him with a negative assessment of

EXTRACT 2

Turn	Speaker	
1	Teacher:	Right now <u>Barry</u>, (2.0) how did you go can I just have a look at that?
2	Mother:	Not real good actually [we're not really happy with it
3	Teacher:	[No
		(3.0)
	Teacher:	I think Barry's he's had a lot of activity
4	Mother:	Mm
5	Teacher:	with his um, er rap dance=
6	Mother:	=Yeah yeah=
7	Teacher:	the rock eisteddfod
8	Mother:	He's had the rock ((festival)) and he's had ((theatre group)), yeah I know, that's all finished now
9	Teacher:	Yeah, but that's good, I mean I don't think there's anything <u>wrong</u> with that and I think it might um perhaps, had something to do, perhaps, with his results
10	Mother:	Yeah

the report, followed by a three-second silence, after which the teacher addresses the mother by referring to Barry as "he," third person, which turns out to make Barry the third person in the interview. This observation led us to discuss the interviews that had this feature as talk designed for an overhearing audience, in this case the silent student (Baker and Keogh 1995; see also Silverman, Baker, and Keogh 1998).

Following this logic, we analyzed the interviews in terms of the accounting that parents and teachers did for the students' achievement (given that the students did not account for themselves) and in terms of their accounting for their competence *as teachers and parents* of the students. In this respect, we treated the interviews not as literal reports about the students, but as accounts about how parents and teachers invoked attributes of their respective categorical responsibilities and thus talked into being a version of how home-school communications should be arranged. Barry is audience to this work done by his mother and teacher.

It can be seen in this illustration how quickly the accounting begins: In turn 3,

the teacher finds a candidate reason for Barry's poor performance; the mother concurs with this account and then, in turn 8, claims responsibility for it ("that's all finished now"), which the teacher hears as a defense of her mothering practice ("Yeah, but that's good, I mean I don't think there's anything <u>wrong</u> with that"). An ethnomethodological approach to such interview data, using notions of membership categorization and accounting, treats the talk as much more than reports about Barry, showing how interinstitutional relations are produced from within the talk itself.

A further demonstration of this last point concerning turn design as context sensitive and context producing, is provided by closer investigation of the design of the first turn by the teacher. The teacher opens the talk; she thus claims to be the host of the interview. This makes sense given that the interview occurs at school, not in Barry's home, where Barry or a parent might be host. "Right now <u>Barry</u>" followed by a within-turn pause can be heard as representing Barry as one in a series of students whose parents the teacher will see that evening. (The converse, an opening along the lines of "Right now Miss X," spoken by Barry or a parent, would turn the relation around, so that Miss X becomes one in a series of teachers that the family will see that evening.) Barry, as *one in a series,* can account for the question that follows: "how did you go can I just have a look at that?" This account gets the teacher off the possible hook that she does not have at her fingertips all the relevant information about Barry, even though she is his teacher. So in this very first turn she is also doing a description of her conditions of work. Turn design, then, is sensitive to the institutional relations within which the talk occurs and that the talk simultaneously achieves. In interviews, then, there is always the display of appreciation of "who, situationally speaking, they are, and what, situationally speaking, they are up to" (Zimmerman 1992:50). Interviews are definitely not "time out" from the social worlds that the participants are talking about; rather, they are reflexive descriptions of those worlds. Heritage (1984) makes the point that "in designing the accounts which formulate their actions, actors address the unavoidable accounta- bility of their own accounting practices" (p. 177).

◆ Membership Categorization Work in Interview Talk

A powerful approach to uncovering the reflexive relation of speaker, audience, and topic in research interviews is found in the use of membership categorization work by speakers. Membership categorization analysis originated in the work of Harvey Sacks (1974, 1992) and has been developed by Lena Jayyusi (1984), Stephen Hester and Peter Eglin (1997), and David Silverman (1998). Sacks's (1974) initial writings on membership categorization proposed the idea that membership categories are resources with which people do reasoning.

Membership categories carry with them more or less tightly associated activities, or "predicates" (for example, babies are members who conventionally cry), and further, membership categories come in sets (for example, babies and mothers are two membership categories that are heard to belong to the same set, or "device," such as "family"). Membership categorization analysis turns on the identification of how speakers and hearers generate and use categories and membership categorization devices as ways of describing and making sense of events and situations. It turns out that interviews, as much as any other site of talk-in-interaction, are replete with the use of membership categorization work—reasoning with categories, reasoning from activities to categories, reasoning from categories to activities. Observing how categories are generated and elaborated within interview talk is a sensitive way of investigating how "particulars" are assembled into a social world and moral universe as described by speakers. I have summarized an approach to this way of examining interview talk in the following terms:

> Interview responses . . . are treated as accounts . . . by a member of a category for activities attached to that category. . . . in this accounting work, we look for the use of membership categorization devices by the interviewer and respondent, and show how both are involved in the generation of versions of social reality built around categories and activities. Further, in the work done with categories and activities, we see the local production in each case of versions of a moral order. (Baker 1997:131)

Researchers implicitly use membership categories to "collect" interviewees within or as representatives of a posited category of social actor. Interviewees are then made accountable members of that particular category in the sense that they then are meant to sound like members of that category and speak from within that particular, research-generated categorical incumbency and not some other. In this sense, they are accountable for speaking as competent members of that category might speak, and, for the most part, interviewees do this. One exception is found where the theory of the category in which incumbency is proposed is not shared, where an individual does not know how to sound like a member of the category. Such a situation arose on one occasion in my earlier studies of "adolescent-adult" interviews, when one interviewee did not produce items (particulars) that matched the cultural concept of "adolescent" in play within the questions (Baker 1984). Most of the people interviewed were able to (re)produce, as I put it, an adult theory of adolescence, and were therefore able to answer the questions in the interviewer's adult terms, and I suggested that "being" an adolescent amounted to displaying exactly that cultural knowledge of adult-adolescent relationships.

Going beyond this first matter of the categorical incumbency assigned to the interviewee, the use of membership categorization analysis can uncover much more within interview data. Taking as established the category membership from within which the interviewee is asked to speak, we can look further for the array of other, related categories that are generated in the interactive talk. These other categories are produced as a "cast of characters" *surrounding* the interviewee in the interviewee's accounts of membership of the category. These characters are introduced with and through associated predicates or attributes, and those attributes are specific to the interviewee's descriptions of his or her own conditions of work or life and, importantly, his or her own attributes within those descriptions. We read these other characters, then, as incumbents of other categories that connect with the research-relevant category and that are, in effect, elaborations of it.

The following segment of data (see Extract 3), from a study by Kathy Roulston

(2001) of interviews with itinerant primary school music teachers in Queensland, Australia, provides an illustration of this way of analyzing interview data. This extract comes from an interview that Roulston—herself an experienced primary school music teacher now undertaking higher-degree research—conducted with a teacher. In this interview, the teacher has been describing her relations with office staff in the various schools she visits (except for Roulston, pseudonyms are used in the transcript), who are variously "nice as pie," "down to earth," or "a real bitch" —clearly morally laden attributes variously assigned to members of the category. She moves from her discussion of them to identifying some new categories of persons she encounters during the week: groundsmen and cleaners.

This segment of interview talk is nicely "rounded" in that the teacher begins and ends with the same lineup of characters as being the ones who matter in her getting her job done. (At the end, a comparison is drawn with classroom teachers, who are made out *not* to be crucial to her coping with the job.) The office staff, groundsmen, and cleaners are given different degrees of precisely the attribute that the itinerant music teacher needs: helpfulness. In this respect, her remarks are an indirect way of stating what she needs, via description and valorization of those who give it.

Roulston (2001) makes the point that these characters are brought to life within accounts through the use of such devices as reporting their direct speech and other scenic practices, in which the interviewer (herself an experienced music teacher) can hear and appreciate the particulars that represent the pattern (as in turn 114, "Wow"). That the researcher and interviewee in this case share coincumbency of the category that is the focus of the research is of course not incidental to how the interview talk proceeds. The interviewer's "wow" in this (very) active interview (see Holstein and Gubrium 1995) signals coincumbency. After this assessment ("wow") the teacher goes further to imply that the groundsman

EXTRACT 3

Turn	Speaker	
104	Teacher:	but o:::h it's (.) yeah the office people (.) if you can get on with the office and the cleaners
105	Roulston:	I'll tell you what [that counts for a lot doesn't it=
106	Teacher:	[and the groundsman
107	Roulston:	=because they're the ones that you're working with really aren't they heh heh heh=
108	Teacher:	=you know I can go to Frank at um Varsity and say 'Oh Frank (.) 've
109		got a little job for you' he'd say 'Oh OK what is it' and I'll tell him and he said (.) you know one day I wanted a filing cabinet [moved from my block (.) two blocks over
110	Roulston:	[yeah
111	Teacher:	we're exchanging he said (1.0) 'OK when do you want it done' I said 'When- ever you
112		can' [you know 'I'll empty it' (1.0) and within five minutes he was there to do it
113	Roulston:	[yeah
114	Roulston:	Wow
115	Teacher:	you know 'Oh Frank I'd like the piano moved' heh heh ((mock annoyance))
116		I don't upaknow these pe(h)ople that wa(h)nt' heh heh you know but he always (.) he's always friendly about it (.) [the one at Roseview depends on what mood he's in=
117	Roulston:	[yeah
118	Roulston:	=yeah yeah=
119	Teacher:	=Austin don't have one (2.0) and the one at (.) Eldergrove (.) he's pretty good=
120	Roulston:	=yeah=
121	Teacher:	=he's only part-time he works twenty hours a week but if I've asked him to do something (.) he's he's done it he mightn't have been able to do it straight away (.)
122	Teacher:	but (.) he comes in and does things for me so (1.0) yeah but this is it get on with the cleaners the secretary (.) and the groundsman and your'er fine
123		(1.0)
124		You can cope with not getting on with the teachers [heh heh heh heh . . .
125	Roulston:	[Well that's it

Frank will even move the piano on a moment's notice. Whether or not Frank the groundsman even exists, the force of the teacher's account of his willingness to help is, to the researcher-audience, an effective and telling particular about the moral world of the music teacher's work. As Rod Watson and T. S. Weinberg (1982) put it:

> We are not aiming for a truth-functional approach to the content of the interlocutors' accounts. In no way are we attempting to assess the truth-value of these accounts; we are interested in how some aspects of the accounts are put together irrespective of their truth-value. (P. 57)

◆ The Production of Identities

In many studies, the persons interviewed might themselves be the "subjects" of the research. That is, rather than being talked with as witnesses to some scenes or events, or as commentators on some external situation, people might be interviewed about themselves as members of some particular category (see Baker 1997; Antaki and Widdicombe 1998; Widdicombe 1998). This is the case in a recent study of a 15-year-old girl named Hannah, one of several young people who were at the center of Michele Knobel's (1999) case studies of literacy learning at school. This study involved Knobel's observing and videotaping Hannah's classroom and interviewing Hannah, her teacher, and her mother in various locations at home and school. Hannah therefore knew that she was a prime subject of the research, and she knew that classroom observations, home visits, and talks with the researcher would form data for the study.

As I have proposed in a prior analysis of these materials (Honan et al. 2000), Hannah could be seen to be "representing herself" to the researcher throughout all the research activities and documenting for the researcher just who she is, what she is like, how she learns literacy, and so on. She knows that the researcher will eventually assemble bits and pieces of these observations and interviews into the ethnographic text of a case study. Whereas in many such studies researchers seek to draw from their scattered observations coherent portraits of the case study subjects, in this case the researcher was theoretically alert to competing ways in which Hannah might represent herself. However, the case study text is opened with the question "Who is Hannah?" and we might take it that Hannah also understood this to be the main research interest.

In this kind of ethnographic case study we can observe a version of the "documentary method of interpretation" (Garfinkel 1967; Watson and Weinberg 1982), in which "particulars" are interpreted with reference to an "underlying pattern" and in which both the particulars and the underlying pattern are open to revision in light of each other. Each thing that Hannah says and does could count as a "particular" that we might study against other particulars in order to locate some underlying pattern or, in this case, patterns. The ethnographic text is like a "documentary" film, showing us Hannah here and there, and others talking about Hannah. Hannah is a documentary subject, then, in three senses: (a) She is the subject of Knobel's research and later text, which documents the lives of each of several young people; (b) Knobel herself uses "particulars" and assembles them so as to point to "underlying patterns," as shown in the published text; and (c) Hannah can be seen to do the work of "documenting herself" to Knobel throughout the data collection period.

The documentary method of interpretation also can be found *inside* the course of interview talk undertaken as part of the study. Interview talk can be seen as one of many interactive events in which people accomplish a sense of identity. In the study from which these materials are drawn, the interviews can be seen as sites where Hannah, her teacher, and her mother, in talk with the researcher, accomplish the identity of Hannah (which in this research is the very point of the interviews). These others accomplish reflexively their own identities, speaking as teacher and mother. The interviewer is intimately engaged in the construction of these versions of Hannah through the questions she asks and through how she hears what is said.

Using an extract from an interview segment presented in Knobel's (1999) chapter on Hannah, I will show this documentary work undertaken by the interviewer,

EXTRACT 4

Turn	Speaker	
111	Michele:	Right OK OK. uhm, and what about your friends, Phon and Ha, did they come here as refugees, or they just moved over?
112	Hannah:	N:o, I think they were actually born here. I'm not too sure. I think Phon might have actually moved over here, and so did Ha. But I don't know- I don't know much, I just know that they- Ha's come from Vietnam. Phon's come from Cambodia. That's all I know.
113	Michele:	Right. That's all they've ever told you. Yeah yeah. And sometimes it's hard to ask people more
114	Hannah:	Well I've never even really thought about it ((smiles))
115	Michele:	Oh ((laughs)) No, no, I was just interested. Ok, and if you had three wishes in the whole world, what would you wish?
116	Hannah:	Oh I always thought about that. U:hmm, that all the violence goes away, that there were no pollution and that it would never happen again, a:nd that we used, that we did stuff like in the olden days
117	Michele:	Oh what do you mean by that?
118	Hannah:	Horse and cart, so we wouldn't cause pollution and, like, did stuff so it wouldn't cause pollution, or we used- just stuff that didn't cause pollution, we used stuff that didn't cause pollution
119	Michele:	Right. Uh-huh, what if you had three wishes just for yourself?

Michele, and Hannah. The exchange (Extract 4) begins at a point where Michele has asked Hannah how much she knows about the background of her two international friends. Hannah claims not to know much.

What we see is a brief interaction in which Hannah expresses her lack of knowledge of her friends' histories and in which the interviewer acknowledges that finding. However, there is much identity-production work occurring in this fleeting interaction. A first observation is that by asking the question in turn 111, the interviewer has done a description of Hannah by implying that Hannah could know this information; possibly, that she should know it. It is in this sense that no question is neutral in respect to the way it characterizes the person being interviewed. Hence the identity work that emerges in the interview is a product of the

questioning as much as it is a product of the answering. A second observation to be made is that Hannah's "lack of knowledge" is entirely a product of the question's having been asked in the first place. Otherwise, it would never surface as a "particular" about Hannah.

What is most compelling about the identity work in this fleeting segment, however, is the way in which the interviewer works with Hannah to account for her lack of knowledge and thus to recover her as a person who, on further reflection, might not be expected to know this information. The sequence involved in this "repair" work is quite elegant. Hannah completes her turn 112 with "That's all I know." If this interview were just about gathering information about Hannah from Hannah, this comment could have concluded the topic. That is, the interviewer could have moved on at that point to another question. Instead, the interviewer supplies *two* accounts while expressing agreement ("Yeah yeah"), accounts that effectively present some reasons Hannah might not know this kind of information.

The interviewer, in effect, is doing part of Hannah's identity work for her by supplying these reasons. Hannah is recovered as a competent person by the interviewer's offer of these reasons. These reasons imply that Hannah's lack of knowledge was due to the facts that (a) friends do not always tell you everything and (b) asking such questions—seeking the missing information—is a possibly delicate matter. This turn (113) is also the interviewer's description of Hannah: She is produced here as a member of a category of people who would appreciate this delicacy.

In documentary method terms, the "particular" that this sequence produced about Hannah—her not knowing the information about her friends—is adjusted from possibly pointing to a "lack" in Hannah to pointing to a different "underlying pattern" that the interviewer has intimated. This different pattern is an underlying competent Hannah in a world where we may not be expected to know such matters (even though the initial question in turn 111 intimated that these are things we should or could know).

But the identity work does not stop there. In turn 114 Hannah offers what could be a counterexplanation for her lack of knowledge and a counterparticular to offset the "particular" that the interviewer has just produced. Hannah says, "Well I've never even really thought about it" and smiles. In this turn she removes herself from the identity attribution that the interviewer has found for her and provides an alternative. The interviewer receives this alternative first as a surprise—"Oh"—and laughs. The second part of turn 115 includes the interviewer's disclaimer *and* an account: "No, no, I was just interested." What is being disclaimed? To what is the "No, no" directed?

The account, however, "I was just interested" (= "this is why I asked") seems to implicate Hannah's identity. We cannot know how Hannah heard it, but it seems the interviewer is characterizing the preceding talk, with its admission by Hannah that she never thought about the matter, as not important, or not consequential, thus resurrecting Hannah's competence once again. It seems that both interviewer and Hannah are engaged in positing and negotiating "particulars" about Hannah. Hannah's correction (turn 114) of Michele's generous offer (turn 113) is especially intriguing in terms of Hannah's position as a documentary subject and of her possibly speaking "for the record." We should note that after the "No, no" disclaimer, the interviewer changes the topic as appears in turns 116-119.

In response to the interviewer's question in turn 115, Hannah initially offers three wishes. The interviewer follows up in turn 119 with a second question, specifying "wishes just for yourself." This signals another order of wishes, "just for yourself," and retrospectively describes Hannah's first three wishes as in a category "not just for yourself." This respecification of the question asks Hannah to draw on her knowledge of this second category "just for yourself."

Hannah shows some difficulty with finding candidate "wishes" to fill this category (see Extract 5). This interview segment reads more like an interrogation, with the interviewer providing a lot of "why" questions. At turn 127, the interviewer appears to change the topic somewhat abruptly. This segment is reminiscent of other interviews with adolescents, in which the interviewer asks for lists of things that belong in particular categories (Baker 1984) and then hears candidate answers as not fitting those categories. This can lead to puzzlement, as might be present in turns 121-25. In such sequences the interviewer can be seen to be working very hard to make sense of what the interviewee is say-

EXTRACT 5

Turn	Speaker	
120	Hannah:	U:hmm. . . . u:hmm . . . that my scho:ol- that all my friends and all the people in my class and friends and stuff, that- and that my school was like in out in the country- we lived out in the country. So we're like based out in the country, and I still have all my friends and the teachers
121	Michele:	Why's that?
122	Hannah:	'Cause I'd like to live out there. Don't like living here
123	Michele:	Why- How come you [do-
124	Hannah:	[Oh I like- I like living here but, I like country better
125	Michele:	Why's that?
126	Hannah:	Well, I haven't actually lived there, and I like- I like to like, have fun and
127	Michele:	Oh is that right? What did you want to be when you leave school?

ing and how it can possibly fit into the presumably shared category system.

Within this segment, however, is a sequence that is recoverable in terms of the documentary work both interviewer and interviewee are doing. Hannah has said she would like it if her school and all of her friends and teachers could move to the country. This may or may not be an order of "wish" intended by the interviewer as a wish "just for herself." We could read Hannah's wish as ambiguous on this point. In any case, the interviewer pursues the ideas by seeking explanations in three consecutive turns (121, 123, and 125). These turns that seek explanations produce answers by Hannah in which she offers more particulars about herself: turn 122, she does not like living in the city; turn 124, she does like living in the city, but prefers the country; and turn 126, she has not "actually" lived in the country. Hannah produces two self-corrections in this segment, each prompted by a "why" question from the interviewer. It seems the interviewer is after some kind of accounting for Hannah's wish (Why do you not like living here? Why do you like the country better?). Hannah deflects the accounting in each case, once by withdrawing the grounds for the account (I do like living in the city) and once by correcting an implied claim (that she has lived in the country). She is revising the particulars of herself as a documentary subject in these turns.

These revisions are oriented to the possibility of Hannah's being held accountable. Michele has produced Hannah as a "theoretic actor" (McHugh 1970), as one who can be taken to know what she is doing and who can account for her activities in ways understood to be competent. Young children, for example, are not held to be theoretic actors in this sense. So here, Hannah is being held accountable for her "wishes."

In addition to using her status as a theoretic actor to revise her claims, Hannah calls on another membership category altogether as part of the production of herself at this moment in the interview. First she offers the confession or concession that she has not "actually" lived in the country (which may be hearable as a weakening of the rationality of her wish). She follows this with an appeal to herself as someone who "likes to have fun." This dramatically shifts who she is speaking as, from the "wish + reason producer" organized by the interviewer to something like "just a kid." In turn 127 the interviewer changes course. This is a pragmatic move that works to get Hannah off the other conversational hook.

Turn 127 produces Hannah as someone who has ideas about what to be when she leaves school. And the identity work goes on. The interviewer and Hannah could both take it that the point of having the interviews is to gain a sense of who Hannah is, but the interviews might more usefully be described as work that produces, for the participants and later readers, a sense of who Hannah could be. The turn-by-turn interactive work that has gone into proposing and managing "particulars" about Hannah shows how some items are withdrawn from the interview record whereas others are let stand. Most important, the version of Hannah that anyone could take away from this talk is produced by both participants. Hannah works to assemble a sense of herself at various points in the interview, hearing and dealing with the identity implications in Michele's talk. I would propose further that as Michele interviews Hannah, Hannah uses particulars of what Michele says to achieve a "sense of Michele" (see also Holstein and Gubrium 1995). I have not attempted that analysis here, but would offer the observation that any subject of an ethnographic case study who enters repeatedly into research conversations such as these would reflect back to an interviewer the sense that he or she has of the interviewer's identity and interests.

◆ Versions of Worlds

According to Gubrium and Holstein (1997), ethnomethodological studies focus on "how members accomplish, manage, and reproduce a sense of social structure, and themselves confer privilege on select versions. Research centers on the properties of practical reasoning and the constitutive work that produce the unchallenged appearance of a stable reality" (p. 44). By extension, ethnomethodological studies of interviews do the same thing. Some of the properties of practical reasoning—centrally, the use of membership categorization and of accounting—have been shown in rela-

tion to the transcript segments presented above, as has the constitutive work involved in producing identities. Interview participants can be seen to be engaging in a range of practices and procedures that make the interview happen as an accountable event in itself (see Silverman 1973; Watson and Weinberg 1982). They can also be seen to be engaging in a range of practices and procedures that assign structure, sense, rationality, and order to the worlds they describe. Accounts are central to this work. Silverman (1993) has pointed out Garfinkel's (1967) insistence that accounts are part of the worlds they describe and has further stated that interviewees "invoke a sense of social structure in order to assemble recognizably 'sensible' accounts which are adequate for the purposes at hand" (p. 114). Such assembling of recognizably "sensible" accounts raises the intriguing question of what kind of social world is posited such that the accounts are sensible displays of possible courses of actions within it.

A final transcript excerpt (see Extract 6) demonstrates how finely the work of assembling sensible accounts is organized in interviews and how the interview talk invokes a sense of social structure and order. In the study from which this extract is drawn, Greer Johnson and I invited elderly Italian Australians living in a regional community to tell their courtship and marriage stories to an interviewer for the purpose of a book to be written (see Baker and Johnson 2000). In analyzing conversational interaction in the interviews where the stories were told, we studied orientations that were evident in the opening turns of the storytelling. These included orientations to the written list of possible topics that might be addressed, orientation to the interviewer's indications of what kind of detail was wanted, and orientation to the destiny of the storytelling in a book. The extract shows the beginning of an interview conducted by Greer with Celia. In common with other interviews designed to encourage talk and elicit information, the inter-

EXTRACT 6

Turn	Speaker	

1   Greer: [This is an interview] with Celia Rosetti (.) on Sunday (.) the sixteenth of March nineteen ninety seven

               (6.0)

2   Celia: I first met my partner (.) in (0.8) in Caltabellotta where I was born (0.9) my parents (.) had a hotel (0.9) and he worked on the farm (.) which was the closest farm to the (.) to the ↑ town (0.4) he went ↑ past the hotel every time he had to ↑ go to town (.) therefore (.) he called into the hotel often (0.2) he then became friendly with my brother (.) and- ((at this point it sounds as if the recorder was turned off; Celia may have signaled to stop to have a drink))

3   Greer: So that was (.) Marco

4   Celia: Mmm mmm mmmm and we began going out together (0.4) [((laughs))

5   Greer: [Why are (hh) you laughing?

6   Celia: I'm laughing at it ↑ because our ↑ first date, when he asked to take me out to the pictures (.) we were making ravioli at the hotel that ↑ night and when you make them in the hotel it was about three or four hundred dozen you know (.) and ((laugh)) I put him down so that he spent the evening plac- ((cough/laugh)) placing the ravioli and counting them.

7   Greer: Oh for the next day?

8   Celia: ((cough/laugh)) Yes for the next day's function.

9   Greer: So that was the first [time

10   Celia: [(coughs) That was the first time (.) when he plucked up courage to ask could he take me to the pictures .hhh

11   Greer: And how old were you (.) when [you first

12   Celia: [A:h, I was about eighteen=

13   Greer: =Uh huh=

14   Celia: =And I was married when I was (0.2) arr nineteen and a half.

15   Greer: Uh huh

16   Celia: Um (1.0) we spent our courtship (0.2) by going to pictures (0.9) and to dances (0.8) entertainment was very limited at that time.

17   Greer: What were the dances like=

18   Celia: =O:h

19   Greer: that you went to

20   Celia: Oh well we went to the (0.2) dance at the (0.7) Italian Club in town (0.1) and went to the dances at Avola

21   Greer: Uh huh.

22   Celia: If it was too far out (.) we couldn't go because (0.9) ahh (0.9) we had to do our ↑ work before ↑ going and ah (0.1) Marco my brother (0.9) wouldn't wait sometimes ((laugh))

***   [turns 23-33 omitted]

34   Celia: But ah (0.2) that's about all we had the opportunity to do.

35   Greer: So your parents were happy ↑ about

36   Celia: Oh-yes (.) ye:ah going (0.6) they were (0.7) quite satisfied he was a hard worker (.) and um (0.1) then when it came to marriage (0.2) um (0.9) there was no way that we could build a house on the farm because it was a ↑ lease.

viewer provides prompts, checks, and questions.

An orientation to a list is observable in the reading of this extract; the reader can probably infer that the list included such matters as how you met your partner, the courtship, and the marriage. This is inferable because Celia shows her use of a list as an organizing device in her beginning following a six-second silence, and then at turns 14, 16, and 36. It can also be seen that Celia and the interviewer have shared knowledge of people and places. This shared knowledge is formulated at turn 3.

Both Celia and the interviewer know that Celia's brother is named "Marco," and they both know that they both know it. The significance of this turn, as we have described it, is to indicate to Celia how to balance the telling of a story to an insider with the telling of a story to outsider audiences, for the book, "for the record" (Baker and Johnson 2000). We can see that on the next mention of reference to this person, Celia in turn 22 uses the phrase "Marco my brother."

This sensitivity to the story's destiny concerning Marco in this case is equivalent to some of the other opening turns canvassed above (see Extract 1, turn 1; Extract 2, turn 1).

Each opening move by the interviewer contains an implicit description of the local, situated circumstances of the interview, which is a characterization of the world within which the interview is situated and of how the interview fits inside that world. As Watson and Weinberg (1982) put it, "Such interviews and our accounts of them involve many reflexivities; they constitute, in the phenomenological sense, the circumstances they describe" (p. 73).

The participants can also be seen to be engaging in a range of interpretive practices and procedures that assign structure, sense, rationality, and order to the worlds they describe. For example, as shown in turns 4-8, Celia uses laughter *as* an interpretive puzzle for the interviewer. In effect, she is inviting the interviewer to ask for an account of why she is laughing:

What sense of social structure provides for Celia's explanation to be seen as *sensibly* funny? How does Celia invoke that sense? She does this in part by calling on an understanding that first dates in courtship are meant to be private affairs for the couple and not immersion into a family's work. The interviewer, in turn 7, finds and offers a sensible account for why the event turned out as it did: The family needed the ravioli prepared "for the next day." Both interviewee and interviewer are engaged in "putting together a world that is recognizably familiar, orderly and moral" (Baker 1997:143).

◆ Conclusion: Connecting Talk and Topic

Conventional content or thematic reading or coding of interview data is aimed primarily at uncovering what people say about topics. As I have shown in this chapter, ethnomethodological interests extend very deeply into how people talk about those topics in the local, situated event that is the interview. Talk about a topic is understood as a display of practical and moral reasoning, not only about the topic of the interview, but about what a competent or sensible *interview account* of events, people, courses of action, and so on could sound like. In this "roundabout" way, interviews, like any other instances of talk-in-interaction, provide an order of data about how the social world is, or could be, put together *in everyday life*.

From this perspective, social order is not something imposed on interview data by analysts, but something assembled by the participants using their commonsense members' resources. Ethnomethodological analyses of interview talk show the deployment by *both* participants of routine ways of assembling what comes to be seen as rationality, morality, or social order, and by extension displays of "culture in action" (Hester and Eglin 1997).

The five sections I have presented in this chapter are meant to represent related dimensions of an ethnomethodological interest in interview data. The entry point of studying the interview as conversational interaction shows that, to an ethnomethodologist, the interview data *are* the social organization of talk between interviewer and interviewee. From that initial point I have worked through the topics of accounting activities, membership categorization work, and identity work toward two questions: What kind of social world are the speakers making happen in their talk? and What kind of social world must speakers assume such that they speak this way? These are some of the resources that researchers may use in investigating interview talk just like any other talk where members "make sense of, find their way about in, and act on the [interview] circumstances in which they find themselves" (Heritage 1984:4).

Studying the social organization of talk about, or around, a topic does not mean losing sight of what is said in terms of propositional "content" in terms of reports on realities external to the interview—for example, that Barry has been too active in theater events, or that Frank the groundsman moved a filing cabinet, or that Celia's family made hundreds of dozens of ravioli. Nor does it mean losing the "interior to persons" reports, such as that the software help-line call taker doesn't mind long calls or that Hannah has never thought about where her friends were born. However, there is much reason researchers should proceed with caution in treating these kinds of reports as "interview data" without looking closely at the specific local circumstances and conversational interactions that generated these reports.

In a more positive light, however, ethnomethodological analyses of interview data are interesting to generate because they represent a far more reflexive social science research practice than most other approaches. In such analyses it becomes impossible *not* to see the artful practices of interviewer and interviewee in making the interview happen, and consequently it becomes very difficult to unhitch "answers" from their (em)bedding in an actual, local situation of production. The investigation of the reflexivities involved leads to a continuously developing appreciation of how the social world is assembled and accounted for. Although researchers rarely conduct interviews with the intent of performing ethnomethodological analysis, interviews are replete with evidence of how relevant identities and memberships are assembled as part of the talk about the topic and of how the topic can accountably be talked about. Interviews can be opened to this distinctive order of interest with the use of the keys I have described, and fundamental aspects of social organization can be found there.

◆ Notes

1. This work was part of a study titled "The Social Organization of Expert-Lay Communication: A Micro-analytic Investigation of Calls to a Computer Software Help Line," conducted by Carolyn Baker, Mike Emmison, and Alan Firth and funded by an Australian Research Council Large Grant, 1999-2001.

2. Following are explanations of the notation symbols used in the transcript extracts in this chapter:

underlining	emphasis
(0.2)	silence or pause, timed in seconds
(.)	microsecond pause
((click))	transcriber's description of sound, item, or activity
=	no discernible gap between turns
[	talk of speakers overlaps at this point
o:::h	vowel sound extended
↑	rising intonation
(h)/(hh)	laughing sound
.hh	inbreath

■ References

Antaki, C. and S. Widdicombe. 1998. "Identity as an Achievement and as a Tool." Pp. 1-14 in *Identities in Talk*, edited by C. Antaki and S. Widdicombe. London: Sage.

Baker, C. D. 1984. "The 'Search for Adultness': Membership Work in Adolescent-Adult Talk." *Human Studies* 7:301-23.

———. 1997. "Membership Categorization and Interview Accounts." Pp. 130-43 in *Qualitative Research: Theory, Method and Practice*, edited by D. Silverman. London: Sage.

Baker, C. D. and G. Johnson. 2000. "Stories of Courtship and Marriage: Orientations in Openings." *Narrative Inquiry* 10(2):1-25.

Baker, C. D. and J. Keogh. 1995. "Accounting for Achievement in Parent-Teacher Interviews." *Human Studies* 18:263-300.

Button, G., ed. 1991. *Ethnomethodology and the Human Sciences*. Cambridge: Cambridge University Press.

Garfinkel, H. 1967. *Studies in Ethnomethodology*. Englewood Cliffs, NJ: Prentice Hall.

Gubrium, J. F. and J. A. Holstein. 1997. *The New Language of Qualitative Method*. New York: Oxford University Press.

Heritage, J. 1984. *Garfinkel and Ethnomethodology*. Cambridge: Polity.

Hester, S. and P. Eglin, eds. 1997. *Culture in Action: Studies in Membership Categorization Analysis*. Washington, DC: International Institute for Ethnomethodology and Conversation Analysis/ University Press of America.

Holstein, J. A. and J. F. Gubrium. 1995. *The Active Interview*. Thousand Oaks, CA: Sage.

———. 1997. "Active Interviewing." Pp. 113-29 in *Qualitative Research: Theory, Method and Practice*, edited by D. Silverman. London: Sage.

Honan, E., M. Knobel, C. D. Baker, and B. Davies. 2000. "Producing Possible Hannahs: Theory and the Subject of Research." *Qualitative Inquiry* 6:9-32.

Jayyusi, L. 1984. *Categorization and the Moral Order*. London: Routledge & Kegan Paul.

Knobel, M. 1999. *Everyday Literacies: Students, Discourse and Social Practice*. New York: Peter Lang.

McHugh, P. 1970. "A Common-Sense Perception of Deviance." Pp. 151-81 in *Recent Sociology*, Vol. 2, *Patterns of Communicative Behavior*, edited by H. P. Dreitzel. London: Macmillan.

Rapley, M. and C. Antaki. 1998. " 'What do you think about . . . ?': Generating Views in an Interview." *Text* 18:587-608.

Roulston, K. 2001. "Investigating the 'Cast of Characters' in a Cultural World." In *How to Analyse Talk in Institutional Settings: A Casebook of Methods*, edited by A. McHoul and M. Rapley. London: Continuum International.

Sacks, H. 1974. "On the Analysability of Stories by Children." Pp. 216-32 in *Ethnomethodology*, edited by R. Turner. Harmondsworth: Penguin.

———. 1992. *Lectures on Conversation*, Vols. 1-2. Edited by G. Jefferson. Oxford: Blackwell.

Sacks, H., E. A. Schegloff, and G. Jefferson. 1974. "A Simplest Systematics for the Organization of Turn-Taking in Conversation." *Language* 50:696-735.

Silverman, D. 1973. "Interview Talk: Bringing Off a Research Instrument." *Sociology* 7:31-48.

———. 1993. *Interpreting Qualitative Data: Methods for Analysing Talk, Text and Interaction*. London: Sage.

———. 1998. *Harvey Sacks: Social Science and Conversation Analysis*. Cambridge: Polity.

Silverman, D., C. D. Baker, and J. Keogh. 1998. "The Case of the Silent Child: Advice-Giving and Advice-Reception in Parent-Teacher Interviews." Pp. 220-40 in *Children and Social Competence: Arenas of Action*, edited by I. Hutchby and J. Moran-Ellis. London: Falmer.

Turner, R. 1974. "Words, Utterances and Activities." In *Ethnomethodology*, edited by R. Turner. Harmondsworth: Penguin.

Watson, R. and T. S. Weinberg. 1982. "Interviews and the Interactional Construction of Accounts of Homosexual Identity." *Social Analysis* 11:56-78.

Widdicombe, S. 1998. "Identity as an Analysts' and a Participants' Resource." Pp. 191-206 in *Identities in Talk,* edited by C. Antaki and S. Widdicombe. London: Sage.

Zimmerman, D. H. 1992. "Achieving Context: Openings in Emergency Calls." Pp. 35-51 in *Text and Context: Contributions to Ethnomethodology,* edited by G. Watson and R. M. Seiler. Newbury Park, CA: Sage.

Part VI

REFLECTION AND REPRESENTATION

The contributors to this concluding section of the *Handbook* look both backward and forward in examining the question of how to construe and represent interview material. Postmodern sensibilities now keep us from weighing alternatives simply in terms of truth and clarity. What might once have been considered a truly representative depiction of interview material now must wend its way through the social and cultural contingencies of truth.

The issues are manifold and complex. When respondents speak of their experiences, do we hear their "own" voices or the expressions of the social and cultural discourses that have influenced them? How might this be conveyed in writing? Do the sentiments of the popular culture industry mediate the "heartfelt" expressions of interviewees? How do researchers take this into account in conveying interview material? How does the sense of narrative ownership—which varies by institutional setting, generation, and culture, among other mediating conditions of speech—affect narrative expression? And how does power, as it percolates across the social statuses of interviewer and respondent, relate to what is and is not said in interviews? In what ways does this implicate representation?

Paul Atkinson and Amanda Coffey begin the discussion by revisiting a classic article published by Howard Becker and Blanche Geer in the 1950s, about the relative value of participant observation versus interviewing. Becker and Geer focus their comparison on the question of which method of obtaining data represents social life most accurately. Ultimately, they come down on the side of participant observation. For Becker and Geer, participant observation, or "being there," is the more direct or purer way of discerning the contours of social life. What the participant observer sees and hears is not mediated by biased retrospection, as is invariably the case with interview respondents.

Both Becker and Geer's presentation and the debate that followed publication of their article took for granted the essential distinction between empirical material and its representation. It is this assumption, not the methods' comparative accuracy, that becomes Atkinson and Coffey's point of departure. According to Atkinson and Coffey, in the context of postmodern epistemological sensibilities, the debate needs to be viewed in a much different light, embedded as it now must be in foundational issues of truthfulness and centering on a dialectic of reflection and representation.

Looking ahead, the chapters by Kirin Narayan and Kenneth George, by Norman Denzin, and by Charles Briggs take up several of the social and cultural contingencies of truth as they bear on the representation of interview material. Basing their discussion mainly on interviews conducted in South Asia, Narayan and George examine the representational difficulties of simply assigning interview material to individual respondents. Interview responses, they argue, are always about both individual biography and culture; researchers would be best served by articulating the interplay of biography and culture, documenting this in both individual and cultural terms. As Narayan and George point out, the idea of the "individual" interview cannot be taken for granted; individuality, as it bears on narrative relevance, is a representational issue.

In his chapter, Norman Denzin relates interviewing to the popular culture industry, arguing that the representational and discursive penetration of the visual media into everyday life requires us to figure that what has become a "cinematic society" can no longer be seen as separate from personal experience and reflection. What we reflect upon, both within and outside of interviews, and how we represent our thoughts, feelings, and actions, is likely to be drawn from the descriptive array of myriad cinematic images. Denzin maintains that researchers can turn to the mass media, especially cinema, for clues to some of the important representational options interviewees call upon in framing interview responses. As these images vary in content over time and within a field of developing representational genres, the moral contours of their messages shape who and what we are, and who we hope to be. Individualized truths, which are the procedural stock-in-trade of most interviewing, are reflexively linked with the prevailing means of self-description in cinema, one of the central representational apparatuses of contemporary society.

Drawing from his experience interviewing Mexicanos, Charles Briggs raises questions relating to power. He describes the differential social and cultural statuses of interview participants as these relate to both narrative expression and narrative representation. Differences in social status between the interviewee and interviewer, for example, play into the question of whether, and how, the proverbial passive "vessel of answers" that interviewees are often assumed to be will activate their subjectivity in the interview context. Power also bears on how interview material will be represented. This may relate to whether analytic writing, say, will display truths defined in terms of criteria such as procedural adequacy and sample representativeness or will take into account the representational acumen and preferences of respondents themselves.

Representing empirical material clearly is no longer just a matter of producing good, accessible writing. The leading question here is, Is it enough to be clear about *the* data, or do the many ways interview data are mediated by their social and cultural contingencies need to be given their due in the representation of the data in writing? The related question of whether standard scientific writing is adequate to the challenges of postmodern interview sensibilities is now itself at the forefront.

Carolyn Ellis and Leigh Berger address the writing problem in their chapter by extending the representation of interview material to researchers' deliberations about what the material means. Ellis and Berger offer us a view of the way ongoing reflections on the interviews in relation to interviewers' own experiences play into question formation and the interview process itself. They choose to present their material in a layered account, dividing their writing between their own deliberations as coresearchers and interviewers on the one hand and their interviewees' responses on the other. As we read the chapter, we find that this also may be too distinct a representational division, as each layer of text serves to inform the reader of the developing personal and conceptual relevance of the interview material "itself."

In her chapter, Laurel Richardson questions the advisability of representing interview material in standard prose. Her argument understandably irritates our "scientific" sensibilities; it raises the issue of whether scientific prose tends to encourage readings that are constrained by the analytic predispositions and categories of the researcher—at the expense of meanings that are closer to the respondent's lived experience. This broaches the possibility that competing modes of representation can render empirical material understandable in distinctly different terms. Poetry, Richardson argues, is a form of writing that encourages multiple readings and thus provides the writer with a means by which to build diverse facets into the voice of the respondent. Other viewpoints, not represented here, take additional directions, suggesting that performance and even song might also figure as incentives to multiple "readings" of interview material.

In his chapter, Paul Rosenblatt takes us to the border of fact and fiction, as he presents the potential of relaxing the border for increasing the credibility of accounts of interview material. Rosenblatt has written novels based on his research experience, integrating the knowledge gained from his interviews into poignant fictional texts. Scientific representational protocol makes it difficult for him to tell certain sides of his research stories, which are more compellingly told in fiction. At the same time, we learn from Rosenblatt how the experiences of a fiction writer enhance the plausibility of scientific prose; the cross-fertilization enriches both the science and the fiction of the material under consideration.

38

REVISITING THE RELATIONSHIP BETWEEN PARTICIPANT OBSERVATION AND INTERVIEWING

◆ Paul Atkinson
Amanda Coffey

In this chapter we propose a reevaluation of the relationship between participant observation and interviewing in sociological field research. Comparisons between these two methods of data collection have been part of the discourse of qualitative methodologists for more than four decades. The starting point for this reexamination is a paper published by Howard Becker and Blanche Geer in the 1950s in which they outline the relative merits of participant observation and interviewing (Becker and Geer [1957] 1970a). (The paper and its ensuing debate were reprinted in 1970 in a collection edited by William Filstead; page references here are to the version published in that anthology.) That paper was, and has remained, an influential

reference point for scholars engaged in field research. The subject matter and arguments presented in the paper remain valuable in their own right, as well as provide a means of tracing significant changes in how the conduct of field research is conceptualized.

In the first half of this chapter, we reread the paper by Becker and Geer through a contemporary lens, as a step to rethinking relationships between participant observation and interviewing. We consider briefly the use of the notion of triangulation to mediate the relationships between participant observation and interviewing. We then move on to propose a possible approach to ethnographic data that subsumes participant observation and interviewing. Developing our argument initially through a reconsideration of the classic position exemplified by Becker and Geer, we argue that field researchers must not assume that what is done should enjoy primacy over what is said, and that therefore observation and interviewing stand in opposition to one another. Actions, we argue, are understandable because they can be talked about. Equally, accounts—including those derived from interviewing—are actions. Social life is performed and narrated, and we need to recognize the performative qualities of social life and talk. In doing so, we shall not find it necessary to juxtapose talk and events as if they occupied different spheres of meaning. We thus propose an analytic stance that transcends some of the methodological puzzles that have appeared to confront qualitative methods for several decades.

◆ Rereading Becker and Geer

In the 1960s, sociologists in the interactionist tradition in the United States—and, to a lesser extent, elsewhere—were formulating a view of field research that was to become canonical. The authors who represented the "second Chicago school," as identified by Gary Alan Fine (1995), including Howard Becker, Blanche Geer, Everett Hughes, Anselm Strauss, and Leonard Schatzman, did much to promote empirical field research in a variety of institutional and other settings: hospitals, schools, colleges and universities, and other workplaces. Their interest in research methods was firmly grounded in their shared commitment to practical empirical research. They wrote from a blend of interests that reflected a shared intellectual culture: symbolic interactionism, social psychology, pragmatist epistemology, organizational and occupational sociology. Their starting point was normally the practice of social research rather than abstract epistemology. They blended their personal

experience of and commitment to field research with the desire to promote systematic and coherent research among their students and colleagues. The diaspora from Chicago itself led to the promotion of such methodological perspectives in various centers of excellence in the United States. The publication of various textbooks and edited collections helped to promote and disseminate the new methodological systems in the 1960s and early 1970s (Schatzman and Strauss 1973; Lofland 1971; McCall and Simmons 1969; Filstead 1970). Becker and Geer's paper "Participant Observation and Interviewing: A Comparison" was a key ingredient in this movement. It was anthologized and became part of the codification of research methods, incorporated into the craft knowledge of several generations of graduate students and researchers.

The advice offered by authors such as Becker and Geer, Schatzman, and Strauss was essentially sensible, straightforward, and practical. It bears all the hallmarks of the work of researchers who were thoroughly versed in the practical work of field research and who also appreciated the value of clear and systematic advice for their peers and their advanced students. The development and spread of qualitative research methods owes much to that particular generation of authors. However, with the benefit of hindsight, much of that methodological advice now looks dated, and the common sense of one generation can seem limited to another.

In the original paper, Becker and Geer compare the relative strengths and applications of participant observation and interviewing. The paper deals with both the relationships between these techniques and the possibility of complementarity. Although it would be quite unwarranted to accuse Becker and his colleagues of naïveté, from today's perspectives (and we use the plural here advisedly) one is struck by the extent to which the data collection methods are treated as relatively unproblematic in themselves. A closer reading of Becker and Geer is worthwhile, not merely for historical purposes, but in order to unpack some of the implicit assumptions that informed the original paper and understandings of field research that stemmed from them. It is helpful to reread the paper in conjunction with Martin Trow's ([1957] 1970) reply and the rejoinder by Becker and Geer ([1957] 1970b). We do so not in order to belittle the contributions of Becker and Geer or of their contemporaries. On the contrary, we think that the issues they raised remain worthy of fresh consideration. We would pay them least respect were we merely to treat their ideas as p845 art of a stock of taken-for-granted ideas.

A GOLD STANDARD?

Becker and Geer ([1957] 1970a) claim a specific advantage for participant observation over other kinds of data collection strategy, based in part on their own research on medical students (Becker et al., 1961). They suggest:

> The most complete form of the sociological datum, after all, is the form in which the participant observer gathers it: An observation of some social event, the events which precede and follow it, and explanations of its meaning by participants and spectators, before, during, and after its occurrence. Such a datum gives us more information about the event under study than data gathered by any other sociological method. Participant observation can thus provide us with a yardstick against which to measure the completeness of data gathered in other ways, a model which can serve to let us know what modes of information escape us when we use other methods. (P. 133)

Trow's ([1957] 1970) response challenges this apparent claim for participant observation's status as a gold-standard method for sociological data collection.

Trow reiterates the commonplace assumption that the choice of research methods should be dictated by the research problem, rather than the unchallenged superiority of one kind of strategy:

> It is with this assertion, that a given method of collecting data—any method —has an inherent superiority over others by virtue of its special qualities and divorced from the nature of the problem studied, that I take sharp issue. The authoritative view, and I would have thought this the view most widely accepted by social scientists, is that different kinds of information about man and society are gathered most fully and economically in different ways, and that the problem under investigation properly dictates the methods of investigation. (P. 143)

Here is not the place to divert attention to unpacking the value of this particular topos, except to note that in the world of real research, social scientists do not dream up "problems" to investigate out of thin air, divorced from concerns of theory and methodology, and only then search for precisely the right method. Clearly, problems and methods come as part of packages of ideas—whether or not one chooses to call them "paradigms." The notion that one can simply apply the best method to an independently derived problem is at best unrealistic. However, the rebuttal by Becker and Geer ([1957] 1970b) clarifies their original argument and helps sharpen our own focus. They point out that theirs was not a sweeping claim for the superiority of participant observation over all other methods in all cases. On the contrary, they stress their original emphasis on the observation and understanding of *events:*

> It is possible Trow thought we were arguing the general superiority of participant observation because he misunderstood our use of the word "event." We intended to refer only to specific and

> limited events which are observable, not to include in the term such large and complex aggregates of specific events as national political campaigns. (P. 151)

Contrary to some possible, glib readings of their paper, then, Becker and Geer are certainly not advocating the wholesale superiority of participant observation over interviewing, nor are they proposing participant observation as the only valid method for sociological fieldwork.

EVENTS AND COMPLETENESS

Becker and Geer claim that the significance of participant observation and its superiority over interviewing rests on the "completeness" of the data. They propose that observation of events in context yields a more *complete* record and understanding of *events* than reliance on interviewing *about those events* alone. Their comparison between participant observation and interviewing is not wholesale, therefore. Becker and Geer make specific claims. In some ways, the original argument—especially as clarified by Becker and Geer—is unremarkable. Indeed, as formulated it is virtually unassailable. It is hard to quarrel with the assertion that the study of observable events is better accomplished by the observation of those events than by the collection of retrospective and decontextualized descriptions of them. Clearly, Becker and Geer are advocating a holistic approach to data collection and its interpretation. They believe that the sociological understanding of a given social world is optimized by the deployment of participation, observation, and conversation (in the form of field interviews). What is remarkable, however, and what strikes us from a contemporary vantage point, is the extent to which Becker and Geer treat "events" as self-evident and the extent to which they assume that the observation of "events" is a primary goal of participant observation. In turn they also

seem to assume that interviews are primarily about events.

Their own illustration of the phenomenon is telling, and it bears reexamination. Their remarks on research methods were informed by their recent fieldwork with medical students at the University of Kansas (Becker et al. 1961). The example they give from their fieldwork is illuminating about the general perspective from which they wrote. Becker and Geer give an extract from their field materials in which they discuss medical students' perceptions of their teachers. Being in a subordinate position, the students, Becker and Geer ([1957] 1970a) argue, are likely to develop a kind of mythology about their teachers, and so to interpret their actions in a particular way: "Any such mythology will distort people's view of events to such a degree that they will report as fact things which have not occurred, but which seem to them to have occurred" (p. 138). In comparing participant observation and interviewing, therefore, Becker and Geer suggest that observation can be a corrective, allowing for adjudication of what "really" happened:

> The point is that things can be reported in an interview through such a distorting lens, and the interviewer may have no way of knowing what is fact and what is distortion of this kind; participant observation makes it possible to check such points. (P. 138)

The actual example Becker and Geer use to demonstrate this assertion strikes a false note with the contemporary reader. The medical students had, apparently, formed the view that particular resident physicians on the teaching staff would regularly humiliate the students. The extract of field notes reproduced in the paper shows either Becker or Geer (the author of the data extract is not specified) reflecting on his or her observations of a particular teaching episode and students' reflections on it. Following a particular encounter with one of the residents, a student reported to his fellow students that the resident had "chewed him out." The observer felt able to intervene and say that the resident had actually been "pretty decent." Another student disputed the observer's description and affirmed that such behavior by a resident was always "chewing out," no matter how "God damn nice" the resident might be. In evaluating this episode, Becker and Geer ([1957] 1970a) conclude:

> In short, participant observation makes it possible to check descriptions against fact and, noting discrepancies, become aware of systematic distortions made by the person under study; such distortions are less likely to be discovered by interviewing alone. (P. 139)

They add a caveat to this point, distinguishing between the descriptive content and the process of the interview:

> This point, let us repeat, is only relevant when the interview is used as a source of information about situations and events the researcher himself has not seen. It is not relevant when it is the person's behavior in the interview itself that is under analysis. (P. 139)

Notwithstanding that last proviso—to which we shall return later—Becker and Geer may strike the contemporary reader as naive, schooled as that reader now is in the complexities of accounts, actions, and interpretations, and at home amid the ambiguities of postmodern analysis (Gubrium and Holstein 1997; Silverman 1993; Atkinson 1996). They seem to be operating with a strangely unproblematic view of "events," and thus of the social world. They strongly imply that there are "events" that are amenable to definitive description and evaluation by sociological observers. Consequently, the observer can adjudicate between a true description of events and a distorted one, and can therefore evaluate degrees of "distortion" in such descriptions.

It is, incidentally, instructive to read the data extract used in the paper and to which we have referred here—a passage from processed field notes in narrative form, incorporating short verbatim quotes. It does not contain a description of the events that are under consideration and that are the subject of the disputed interpretation. The "events" that are described are the students' comments about the resident and the subsequent conversation between the observer and the students. The original interaction between the resident and the student, on which the latter's claim of being "chewed out" is based, is summarized in the most cursory fashion. Strikingly, it is totally impossible to reconstruct the original interaction from the data provided. Any adjudication as to the reasonableness of the student's complaint, the observer's corrective intervention, or the second student's reaffirmation of the students' perspective—their "mythology" as the authors describe it—is not possible.

In principle, this treatment of data is congruent with the general analysis that is enshrined in *Boys in White* (Becker et al. 1961). Becker and his colleagues do not actually base their account on "events" in the sense that they report and analyze much of what medical students or their teachers actually do. Their analysis is concerned with the development of students' perspectives rather than with, say, their embodied skills or their actual encounters with hospital patients. To that extent, Becker and Geer are consistent: The published monograph and their methodological prescriptions are congruent. The problems we raise, by contrast, reflect their treatment of observation, interviewing, accounts, and events as all rather unproblematic.

One might argue in defense of Becker and Geer that they use the data extract only by way of illustration, that the general argument is important rather than the details of a particular example. Yet this is not just an isolated incident or a minor discrepancy. It is thoroughly characteristic of the wider research project from which it is taken, which is in turn representative of a lot of work based on some combination of participant observation and interviewing, of a kind typical among the generation of researchers represented by Becker and Geer. Any reading of *Boys in White* (Becker et al. 1961), other than a most cursory one, will emphasize the problem. Although the Chicago research team spent a considerable amount of time engaged in participant observation with the medical students and their teachers, the book does remarkably little to report what these social actors actually did. We gain few glimpses of, say, the actual work with patients on hospital wards or in clinics. The "data" seem to consist primarily of what the students themselves *said about* their lives and work. The primary data, in practice, therefore seem to be conversations about events and actors' perspectives on events and happenings. At least, it is those data that are reported directly in the monograph.

A reexamination of the original formulation of the problem by Becker and Geer highlights some significant issues and problems. As we have seen, their argument is a very specific one that is extremely plausible. Even within their argument's restricted scope, Becker and Geer seem to establish a strong case for the value of participant observation. On closer inspection, however, the argument seems less straightforward, and raises some potentially intriguing issues that we shall attempt to address afresh in the final section of this chapter. Before that, in the next section we turn to consider another approach to the combination of participant observation and interviewing, through the notion of methodological triangulation.

◆ Triangulation

One of the key areas in which claims have been made for the productive *combination* of participant observation and interviewing is in the methodological discussion of *trian-*

gulation. Although authors such as Norman Denzin (1970) have certainly not intended to promote a naive or vulgar view of research methods and their proper relationships, the rhetoric of between-method triangulation clearly implies for many enthusiasts the possibility of combining participant observation and interviewing so as to capitalize on the respective strengths of these methods, or to counteract the perceived limitations of each.

Denzin's original formulation of methodological triangulation also conveys the impression that researchers could combine methods such as participant observation and interviewing to draw on the methods' complementary strengths and offset their respective weaknesses. Denzin's (1978) own summary of methodological triangulation captures the essence of this approach:

> In organizational studies, for example, it is extremely difficult to launch large-scale participant-observation studies when the participants are widely distributed by time and place. In such extractions participant observation may be adapted only to certain categories of persons, certain events, certain places, or certain times. The interview method can then be employed to study those events that do not directly come under the eyes of the participant observer. (P. 303)

Here interviewing is treated as a potential proxy for direct observation: It is implied that researchers can glean data about events and actors through indirect means in order to supplement the method of direct observation.

It is clear that Denzin's formulation of the relationships between methods is actually addressed to an issue that is slightly different from the one examined by Becker and Geer. But (in his early writings) Denzin too treats the methods themselves as relatively unproblematic. His early views of triangulation assume that research methods should be determined by research problems and that methods can be combined in terms of their respective strengths and weaknesses: "Methodological triangulation involves a complex process of playing each method off against the other so as to maximize the validity of field efforts" (Denzin 1978:304). Denzin emphasizes the degree to which the combination of methods is a matter of strategic decision making, and that research design and choice of methods are emergent features of concrete projects: "Assessment cannot be solely derived from principles given in research manuals—it is an emergent process, contingent on the investigator, the research setting, and the investigator's theoretical perspective" (p. 304).

Subsequent editions of Denzin's text reflect the changing character of methodological thinking and make explicit reference to potential, and actual, criticisms of this approach to triangulation. Denzin acknowledges that his accounts of the relationships between methods such as interviewing and observation were open to the interpretation, and the accusation, that they were unduly positivistic (for critiques of the early Denzin approach, see Silverman 1985, 1993). Indeed, Denzin did seem to imply that research problems are prior to and independent from methods, and that methods can be brought to bear on research problems in unproblematic ways. Although Denzin himself was clearly no naive positivist in intention, the implications of his text certainly seemed to suggest an easy accommodation between methods, and between methods and problems. The rhetoric of research problems driving the choice of methods too readily implied an independent and prior "list" of researchable topics divorced from the theories and methods that constructed those topics.

The simplest view of triangulation treats the relationships between methods as relatively unproblematic, and those methods themselves as even more straightforward in themselves. More sophisticated versions of triangulation may treat the relationships between methods in a less straightforward fashion—stressing the differences between them rather than complementarity—but can still be predicated on unproblematic views of the methods themselves. Current perspectives on methodology and epistemology incline toward a quite different view. Treatments of participant observation and interviewing would not try to privilege one over the other, or try to seek out ways simply to integrate them or treat their outcomes in an additive way.

REFLEXIVITY

The underlying problem with the simple or "optimistic" version of triangulation is that it treats the nature of social reality as unduly unproblematic and the relationships between the social world and the methods of investigating it as transparent. But we cannot assume a unitary and stable social world that can simply be viewed from different standpoints or from different perspectives. Rather, we have to pay due attention to the principle of reflexivity. *Reflexivity* is a term that is widely used, with a diverse range of connotations (and sometimes with virtually no meaning at all). Here we use it in a specific way: to acknowledge that the methods we use to describe the world are—to some degree—constitutive of the realities they describe (Hammersley and Atkinson 1995; Gubrium and Holstein 1997). In other words, the research methods we use imply or depend on particular kinds of transactions and engagements with the world. Each kind of transaction therefore generates a distinctive set of descriptions, versions, and understandings of the world. These are not arbitrary or whimsical. They are generated out of our systematic and methodical explorations of a given social world; they are not private fantasies. Equally, they are not purely contingent. There are systematic relationships between methods and representations, but they cannot be washed out or eliminated through simpleminded aggregation. Rather, we have to address what methods do construct and what sense we can make of those constructions. Such a realization does not deprive us of different modes of data collection and analysis. It does, however, require us to address the distinctive and intrinsic attributes of particular methods, to retain some fidelity to those methods and their products.

From this perspective, for instance, the status of interview data is especially problematic. In particular, the precise referential value of interviews is questionable. Interviews are not regarded as intrinsically worthless sources of data. Rather, as Silverman (1993) points out, we cannot approach interview data simply from the point of view of "truth" or "distortion," and we cannot use such data with a view to remedying the incompleteness of observations. By the same token, we cannot rely on our observations to correct presumed inaccuracies in interview accounts. On the contrary, it is argued that interviews generate data that have intrinsic properties of their own. In essence, we need to treat interviews as generating accounts and performances that have their own properties and ought to be analyzed in accordance with such characteristics. We need, therefore, to appreciate that interviews are occasions in which are enacted particular kinds of narratives and in which "informants" construct themselves and others as particular kinds of moral agents. Examples of this kind of approach include Margaret Voysey's (1975) analysis of parents' accounts of life with handicapped children and Nigel Gilbert and Michael Mulkay's (1980) analysis of natural scientists' accounts of scientific discoveries.

These and analyses like them by no means reject the utility of interview data, but they insist on a particular analytic strategy. The data are examined for their properties as accounts. Voysey, for instance, suspended the taken-for-granted view that the presence of a handicapped child disrupts normal family life; she examined, rather, how parents constructed moral accounts of

"normal" parenting and family conduct. Likewise, Gilbert and Mulkay document scientists' often inconsistent and contradictory accounting devices in their descriptions of scientific discovery, which construct science and scientists in distinctive ways. These are coherent and consistent ways of dealing with interview data. They do not, however, lend themselves to aggregation to observational data in order to achieve "triangulation" in any conventional sense.

From such perspectives, then, the analyst does not worry about whether "the informant is telling the truth" (Dean and Whyte 1958), if by that one understands the analyst's task to be that of distinguishing factual accuracy from distortion, bias, or deception. Similarly, ironic contrasts between what people do and what they say they do (see Deutscher 1973) become irrelevant. Rather, attention is paid to the coherence and plausibility of accounts, to their performative qualities, the repertoires of accounts and moral types that they contain, and so on. In the remainder of this chapter we address the implications of this position a little further. In essence, we argue that participant observation and interviewing are themselves distinctive forms of social action, generating distinctive kinds of accounts and giving rise to particular versions of social analysis. Each yields particular sorts of textual representation: There are other kinds of texts and other kinds of representation in and of social fields. If we cannot simply add them together and superimpose them to make a single coherent narrative or picture, what are the proper relations between them?

◆ Talk, Experience, and Action

Radical criticisms of the interview can treat naturally occurring social action as primary and talk about action as but a poor substitute for the observation of action, echoing Becker and Geer's original argument. From that perspective, we cannot take the interview as a proxy for action. Hence we cannot rely on it for information about what people do or what they have done; rather, it serves only as a mechanism for eliciting what people say they do. From this perspective, the interview inhabits a quite different universe from the observation of social action. One can readily move to the position that grants primacy to the recording of naturally occurring social interaction and relegates virtually everything else to the periphery of sociological interest. This particular view is sometimes accompanied by appeals for primary reliance on the analysis of permanent recordings of spoken activity, such as conversation analysis (Atkinson and Heritage 1984; Boden and Zimmerman 1991; Sacks 1992).

This is one possible position, but it is an unnecessary and unhelpful one. It is unduly insensitive to the variety of social action. It is also in danger of endorsing a particular kind of naturalism; the endorsement of one sort of action or activity over another implicitly attributes authenticity to one while denying it to others. It runs the risk of assuming that some sort of actions are "natural" whereas others are "contrived" (Hammersley and Atkinson 1995; Silverman 1985, 1993).

A more productive way of thinking about these relationships is to start from a more symmetrical perspective, rather than trying to privilege one source, or method, over another. This approach is, in one respect at least, more in keeping with contemporary epistemology. It is also antipathetic to the excesses of some recent enthusiasms that have rejected the study of action in situ in favor of an almost exclusive focus on interviews, narratives, and accounts (Atkinson and Silverman 1997). We can fruitfully begin to think of what we observe (and the work of observing) and the contents of interviews (and the work of interviewing) as incorporating social actions

of different kinds and yielding data of different forms. We can thus be released from trying to combine them to produce information from them about something else and concentrate more on the performance of the social actions themselves.

Indeed, we know enough about the performance of everyday social action to be thoroughly suspicious of methodological formulations that even appear to attach particular kinds of authenticity to it. All of Erving Goffman's work, for instance, is—with varying degrees of explicitness—concerned with rendering problematic such a naive view. Admittedly, some of Goffman's key insights might seem to suggest the contrary. His famous essay on role distance, for example, seems to imply a dichotomy, not a continuity, between an ironic distance and a wholehearted commitment (Goffman 1961). Likewise, some accounts that are thoroughly or partially indebted to Goffman, such as Arlie Hochschild's *The Managed Heart* (1983)— an account of the self-conscious management of emotional work among workers such as airline flight attendants—seem to imply a contrast between authentic and insincere social actions. Hochschild distances herself from Goffman's vision of the social self, and her analysis depends on the presence of a deep self that preexists and authors authentic and inauthentic performances. But if we take full and serious account of the performativity of social life (the dramaturgical metaphor), then it clearly makes no more sense to assume any action as inherently authentic, and thus to grant it priority.

Part of the reported comparison between participant observation and interviewing has revolved around the ironic contrast between what people do and what people say (they do). This has also fed into the equally hoary question posed to and by field researchers: How do you know if your informant is telling the truth? These related problems equally reflect the position we have characterized as naive: the contrasts between actions and accounts, and between truth and dissimulation.

INTERVIEWING AS ACTION

This approach to interviewing as action can be illustrated with reference to the topic of memory. One way of thinking about interviews and the data they yield is to think about informants producing descriptions of past events. In part, therefore, the interview is aimed at the elicitation of memories. Viewed from a naive perspective, it also follows that one of the main problems of this kind of data collection concerns the accuracy or reliability of such recollections. Such a perspective certainly presents pressing problems if—to return to the preoccupations of Becker and Geer— one is using the interview to gather information about "events." The same is true of the elicitation of "experiences." It is possible to view the interview as a means for the retrieval of informants' personal experiences—a biographically grounded view of memories and past events.

The analytic problems of memory and experience are equivalent from our point of view. It is possible to address memory and experience sociologically, and it is possible to address them through the interview (and through other "documents of life"). But it is appropriate to do so only if one accepts that memory and experience are social actions in themselves. They are both enacted. Seen from this perspective, memory is not (simply) a matter of individual psychology, and is certainly not only a function of internal mental states. Equally, it is not a private issue. (We are not denying the existence of psychological processes in general, or the personal qualities and significance of memories—ours is a methodological argument about the appropriate way of conducting and conceptualizing social research.) Memory is a cultural phenomenon, and is therefore a collective one. What is "memorable" is a function of the cultural categories that shape what is thinkable and

what is not, what is counted as appropriate, what is valued, what is noteworthy, and so on. Memory is far from uniquely (auto)biographical. It can reside in material culture, for instance: The deliberate collection or hoarding of memorabilia and souvenirs—photographs, tourist artifacts, family treasures, or other bric-a-brac—is one enactment of memory, for instance. Equally, memory is grounded in what is tellable. In many ways the past is a narrative enactment.

Memory *and* personal experience are narrated. Narrative is a collective, shared cultural resource (see in this volume Atkinson, Chapter 6; Cándida Smith, Chapter 34; Narayan and George, Chapter 39). Authors such as Ken Plummer (1995) have reminded us that even the most intimate and personal of experiences are constructed through shared narrative formats. The "private" does not escape the "public" categories of narrativity. Just as C. Wright Mills (1940) demonstrated that "motive" should be seen as cultural and linguistic in character, and not as a feature of internal mental states or predispositions, we must recognize that memories and experiences are constructed through the resources of narrative and discourse. Narratives and the resources of physical traces, places, and things—these are the constituents of biography, memory, and experience. When we conduct an interview, then, we are not simply collecting information about nonobservable or unobserved actions, or past events, or private experiences. Interviews generate accounts and narratives that are forms of social action in their own right.

EVENTS AND ACCOUNTS AS ENACTMENTS

At this point we return to the original formulation offered by Becker and Geer ([1957] 1970a). They refer to the study of "events," arguing that observation provides access to events in a way that interviews cannot. In one sense, that is self-evidently true. We can observe and we can make permanent recordings of events. On the other hand, we need to ask ourselves what constitutes an "event." Clearly an event is not merely a string of unrelated moments of behavior, nor is it devoid of significance. In order to be observable and reportable, events in themselves must have some degree of coherence and internal structure. An "event" in the social world is not something that just happens: It is made to happen. It has a beginning, a middle, and an end. It is differentiated from the surrounding stream of activity. Its structure and the observer's capacity to recognize it are essentially narrative in form. In that sense, therefore, a radical distinction between "events" that are observed and "accounts" that are narrated starts to become less stark, and the boundary maintenance becomes more difficult to sustain.

Does this mean that we still acknowledge the primacy of particular kinds of social actions? Not necessarily. By acknowledging that accounts, recollections, and experiences are enacted, we can start to avoid the strict dualism between "what people do" and "what people say." This is a recurrent topic in the methodological discourse of social science. It rests on the commonplace observation that there may be differences or discrepancies between observed actions and accounts about action. (This may be proposed as a rather vulgar counterargument against vulgar triangulation.) They are different kinds of enactments, certainly, but we would argue that the specific dualism that implicitly asserts an authenticity for what people (observably) do and the fallibility of accounts of action is both unhelpful and "untrue." By treating both the observed and the narrated as kinds of social action, we move beyond such simple articulations and instead reassert the methodological principle of symmetry.

We therefore bracket the assumption of authenticity, or the "natural" character of "naturally occurring" action, and the contrasts that are founded on that implicit du-

alism. If we recognize that memories, experiences, motives, and so on are themselves forms of action, and equally recognize that they and mundane routine activities are enacted, then we can indeed begin to deal with these issues in a symmetrical, but nonreductionist, way. In other words, it is not necessary to assert the primacy of one form of data over another, or to assert the primacy of one form of action over another. Equally, a recognition of the performative action of interview talk removes the temptation to deal with such data as if they give us access to personal or private "experiences." We need, therefore, to divorce the use of the interview from the myth of inferiority: the essentially romantic view of the social actor as a repository of "inner" feelings and intensely personal recollections. Rather, interviews become equally valid ways of capturing shared cultural understandings and enactments of the social world.

THE POSITION OF THE RESEARCHER

We have thus far said very little about the position of the researcher within these different kinds of research "events." One of the distinctions between participant observation and interviewing has pivoted on the relationship of the researcher to the field of study. In the case of observational work, claims have been made that participant observation enables the researcher to participate firsthand in the happenings of the setting; these claims have been countered, of course, by warnings that the researcher may affect (contaminate) the setting or become too much of a participant, and thereby lose the capacity to observe critically. In contrast, the interview has been perceived as an artificial enactment, with unequal relations and potentially less contamination between participants, and more recently as a site for collaboration and the genuine sharing of experiences.

Here we would wish to stress again the symmetry of the two broad approaches. This does not necessary imply complementarity or sameness, but recognizes the complexity of research experiences and relationships. Through both participant observation and interviewing there is the potential for "contamination," although this is a paralyzing and unhelpful way of characterizing the research process (and can actually render all research inadequate). Rather, through active reflexivity we should recognize that we are part of the social events and processes we observe *and* help to narrate. To overemphasize our potential to change things artificially swells our own importance. To deny our being "there" misunderstands the inherent qualities of both methods—in terms of documenting and making sense of social worlds of which we are a part (either through participant observation or as facilitators of shared accounts and narrative strategies).

The (auto)biographical work that is common to both approaches is also worth noting. Again, in digressing from Becker and Geer's assertion of the primary goal of describing events, we should recognize that the process of undertaking research is suffused with biographical and identity work (Coffey 1999). The complex relationships among field settings, significant social actors, the practical accomplishment of the research, and the researcher-self are increasingly recognized as significant to all those who engage in research of a qualitative nature (whether that be participant observation, interviewing, or some combination of the two).

◆ Conclusion

We began this chapter with a retrospective evaluation of Becker and Geer's ([1957] 1970a) original observations concerning the respective merits and weaknesses of participant observation and interviewing. We did so for two reasons. First, Becker and

Geer's paper is a locus classicus in the corpus of methodological writing in qualitative sociology. Second, it helps us to identify a particular constellation of assumptions concerning observation and interviewing characteristic of that period, during which many aspects of qualitative fieldwork were being codified. We repeat our acknowledgment that the scholars of that generation were responsible for the demystification of qualitative methods, providing practical advice manuals for the research community as well as acting as methodological advocates. Their contribution should not be underestimated, and it was never our intention to do so. However, we have reached a point that suggests a position very different from that articulated by Becker and Geer. This difference reflects a good deal of methodological change and development over the intervening years, not least in the burgeoning of qualitative methods texts and the increased acceptance and innovative use of the whole variety of qualitative research strategies.

For a long time, ethnographers and other qualitative researchers have relied on the ironic contrast between "what people do" and "what people say they do." That contrast is—as we have suggested—based on some further differences. It assumes that what people do is unproblematic and is amenable to direct observation and description; what people say, on the other hand, is treated as a much more unstable category. The relationship between action and talk is perceived as problematic because accounts can distort: Accounts can be motivated in various ways, and can function as excuses, legitimations, rationalizations, and so on. However, actors may falsify their accounts. Deliberate deception, wishful thinking, recipient design for difficult audiences—these can all affect the accuracy and reliability of actors' accounts (according to a well-established tradition). As a consequence, discussions of interviewing have often sought to address the question, How do you know if your informant is telling the truth? As we have now seen, however, these issues are radically changed if one abandons the initial presumption of difference. If we accept that interview talk is action—is performative—then ironic contrasts between "doing" and "acting" become increasingly redundant. Taken-for-granted distinctions between talk and action are erroneous and irrelevant when one recognizes that talk is action. In a performative view, interviews, and other accounts, need not be seen as poor surrogates or proxies for unobserved activities. They can be interrogated for their own properties—their narrative structures and functions (see Riessman, Chapter 33, this volume). Accounts are, or are composed of, speech acts and may therefore legitimately be regarded as games or types of action in their own right.

By the same token, actions or events, even observed firsthand, are not inherently endowed with meaning, nor is their meaning unequivocally available for inspection. The kinds of "events" that Becker and Geer ([1957] 1970a) discuss are recognized as such precisely because they are describable and narratable by participants and by onlookers, including ethnographers and other observers. After all, the "data" of participant observation are the events as narrated (written down, often retrospectively) by observers, and hence rely on the same culturally shared categories of memory, account, narrative, and experience. In retrospect, it seems odd that Becker and Geer felt able to legislate for "what really happened" and to discount the tellings of medical students. From our point of view, they could and should have paid much more attention to several things: how the "events" were performed; how the medical students narrated and evaluated the "events"; how certain events or classes of events were endowed with significance through the medical students' own tellings; and how they themselves, as observers, recorded and described the "events." They might thus have found themselves dealing with classes of performance and rhetoric, in different contexts, in different modes, rather than incommensurable kinds of phenomena. And once articulated in this way, their particular distinction between participant observation and interviewing, and the primacy of the former, becomes untenable. This does not deny the different qualities of these methods as data collection strategies. Rather, in emphasizing their commonalities in terms of social action and performance (and extinguishing the false dichotomy), we may actually be in a better, and certainly a more informed, position to "choose."

■ *References*

Atkinson, J. M. and J. Heritage, eds. 1984. *Structures of Social Action: Studies in Analysis.* Cambridge: Cambridge University Press.

Atkinson, P. 1996. *Sociological Readings and Re-readings.* Aldershot, England: Ashgate.

Atkinson, P. and D. Silverman. 1997. "Kundera's *Immortality:* The Interview Society and the Invention of Self." *Qualitative Inquiry* 3:304-25.

Becker, H. S. and B. Geer. 1970a. "Participant Observation and Interviewing: A Comparison." Pp. 133-42 in *Qualitative Methodology: Firsthand Involvement with the Social World,* edited by W. J. Filstead. Chicago: Markham. Reprinted from *Human Organization* 16 (1957):28-32.

———. 1970b. "Participant Observation and Interviewing: A Rejoinder." Pp. 150-52 in *Qualitative Methodology: Firsthand Involvement with the Social World,* edited by W. J. Filstead. Chicago: Markham. Reprinted from *Human Organization* 16 (1957):39-40.

Becker, H. S., B. Geer, E. C. Hughes, and A. L. Strauss. 1961. *Boys in White: Student Culture in Medical School.* Chicago: University of Chicago Press.

Boden, D. and D. H. Zimmerman, eds. 1991. *Talk and Social Structure: Studies in Ethnomethodology and Conversation Analysis.* Berkeley: University of California Press.

Coffey, A. 1999. *The Ethnographic Self: Fieldwork and the Representation of Identity.* London: Sage.

Dean, J. P. and W. F. Whyte. 1958. "How Do You Know If the Informant Is Telling the Truth?" *Human Organization* 17:34-38.

Denzin, N. K. 1970. *The Research Act.* Chicago: Aldine.

———. 1978. *The Research Act.* 2d ed. New York: McGraw-Hill.

Deutscher, E. 1973. *What We Say/What We Do: Sentiments and Acts.* Glenview, IL: Scott, Foresman.

Filstead, W. J., ed. 1970. *Qualitative Methodology: Firsthand Involvement with the Social World.* Chicago: Markham.

Fine, G. A., ed. 1995. *A Second Chicago School? The Development of a Postwar American Sociology.* Chicago: University of Chicago Press.

Gilbert, N. and M. Mulkay. 1980. *Opening Pandora's Box: A Sociological Account of Scientists' Discourse.* Cambridge: Cambridge University Press.

Goffman, E. 1961. *Encounters: Two Studies in the Sociology of Interaction.* Indianapolis: Bobbs-Merrill.

Gubrium, J. F. and J. A. Holstein. 1997. *The New Language of Qualitative Method.* New York: Oxford University Press.

Hammersley, M. and P. Atkinson. 1995. *Ethnography: Principles in Practice.* 2d ed. London: Routledge.

Hochschild, A. R. 1983. *The Managed Heart: Commercialization of Human Feeling.* Berkeley: University of California Press.

Lofland, J. 1971. *Analyzing Social Settings.* Belmont, CA: Wadsworth.

McCall, G. J. and J. L. Simmons, eds. 1969. *Issues in Participant Observation: A Text and Reader.* Reading, MA: Addison-Wesley.

Mills, C. W. 1940. "Situated Actions and Vocabularies of Motive." *American Sociological Review* 5:439-52.

Plummer, K. 1995. *Telling Sexual Stories: Power, Change and Social Worlds.* London: Routledge.

Sacks, H. 1992. *Lectures on Conversation,* Vols. 1-2. Edited by G. Jefferson. Oxford: Blackwell.

Schatzman, L. and A. L. Strauss. 1973. *Field Research: Strategies for a Natural Sociology.* Englewood Cliffs, NJ: Prentice Hall.

Silverman, D. 1985. *Qualitative Methodology and Sociology.* Aldershot, England: Gower.

———. 1993. *Interpreting Qualitative Data: Methods for Analysing Talk, Text and Interaction.* London: Sage.

Trow, M. 1970. "Comment on 'Participant Observation and Interviewing': A Comparison." Pp. 143-49 in *Qualitative Methodology: Firsthand Involvement with the Social World,* edited by W. J. Filstead. Chicago: Markham. Reprinted from *Human Organization* 16 (1957):33-35.

Voysey, M. 1975. *A Constant Burden.* London: Routledge & Kegan Paul.

39

PERSONAL AND FOLK NARRATIVE AS CULTURAL REPRESENTATION

◆ Kirin Narayan
Kenneth M. George

There is a thirst among the Paxtun women for autobiography. There is also a correct way to "seek the person out" with questions. One day, when my daughter's nanny had observed me eliciting a life story from someone, she later tried to correct me on the grounds that I did not know how to interrogate properly. "You foreigners don't know how to search [*latawel*] one another," she reproached me. "When we Pakistanis ask a person's story, we don't let a single detail go by. We dig in all the corners, high and low. We seek the person out. That's how we do things. We are storytellers and story seekers. We know how to draw out a person's heart." (Grima 1991:81-82)

As this outspoken Paxtun woman from Northwest Pakistan reminds us, asking people for and about stories is a widespread practice, even though the ways of asking and the kinds of stories told may vary. Indeed, most of us are already old experts at coaxing, inviting, or outright demanding stories in our everyday lives. From a child's wheedling "Tell me" to a friend's bright-eyed prod "And then what happened?" we regularly make and receive such requests.

In pursuing stories within an interview context, however, we create a frame of analytic reflection around storytelling transactions. The delights of a well-told tale may continue to sweep us along, but as interviewers we usually elicit and evaluate stories from the vantage points of particular

---

AUTHORS' NOTE: We extend our great thanks to Lila Abu-Lughod and Maria Lepowsky for their helpful critiques of this chapter.

professional agendas. Like Benedicte Grima's (1991) Paxtun critic, the people we seek to interview sometimes already have their own ideas about how a person should go about extracting stories. For them too, stories move about in a range of interpersonal and institutional settings, and the presence of a researcher eagerly seeking stories may provide yet another occasion for retellings. In addition to scholars, there are other specialists with their own purposes and methods for eliciting stories—therapists, shamans, lawyers, doctors, talk-show hosts, priests, immigration officers, police detectives, journalists, human rights workers, and so on. This interactive process of extracting and yielding stories plays an ongoing role in the shaping of social life.

Our task in this chapter is to describe interviewing for two sorts of stories: personal narratives and folk narratives. The distinction between these may seem commonsensical at first: Personal narratives are idiosyncratic, whereas folk narratives are collective. However, we will argue that the distinction is actually less clear. Second, we explore the process of eliciting stories in interviews, emphasizing the need for researchers to be aware of the social life of stories that extends beyond the interview. Third, we argue that it is important for researchers to supplement interviews *for* stories with interviews *about* stories in order to comprehend the interpretive frames that surround storytelling transactions. Finally, we point out the usefulness of critically examining interview transcripts in evolving practice.

Many excellent publications offering insights and guidelines for ethnographic interviewing, or folkloristic interviewing more generally, are already available (Atkinson 1998; Briggs 1986; Holstein and Gubrium 1995; Ives 1995; Jackson 1987; Langness and Frank 1981; Spradley 1979). Rather than rehash insights from these other works, we direct interested readers to them. Here we will draw on a selection of memorable examples of prior interviews for stories, working from the larger ethnographic record and also from our own fieldwork experiences.

◆ Folk Narrative and Personal Narrative

For the better part of the 20th century, most anthropologists, folklorists, and literary specialists assumed that personal narratives are uniquely individual, shaped more by the vagaries of experience than by the conventions of collective tradition. From this vantage point, experience appears to dictate the content and form of personal narrative, and so the teller is of central importance. In contrast, folk narratives have been seen as highly conventional, widely shared cultural representations mediated by the narrative community at large. As Franz Boas (1916) asserts, folk narratives, like myths, "present in a way an autobiography of the tribe" (p. 393). Yet, time and again, the people with whom anthropologists work have not made the same distinction between "personal" and "folk" in terms of the significance of stories to individuals' lives.

Personal stories are also shaped through the use of culturally recognized—and, sometimes, transculturally negotiated—narrative and linguistic conventions that are themselves differentially put to use by people positioned by gender, age, or class (see Atkinson, Chapter 6, this volume). As life story research in anthropology has shown, such stories are closely tied to cultural conceptions of personhood (Langness and Frank 1981). So, for example, when Renato Rosaldo (1976) asked his Ilongot "brother" Tukbaw to speak about his own life, he found that Tukbaw chose to build stories around the wise words and advice of his father rather than provide introspective vignettes about feelings or events. Or, when Grima (1991) went to Northwest Pakistan in the hope of researching Paxtun women's romance narratives, she soon learned that the stories the women themselves most liked to tell involved tragic tales of personal suffering—the more tragic the better. A woman who had not suffered was assumed not to have a life story. For example, a 30-year-old unmarried schoolteacher told Grima: "I have no story to tell. I have been through no hardships" (p. 84).

Similarly, in Northwest India, Kirin Narayan was also startled when Vidhya Sharma, an educated Kangra village woman, claimed that she had no life story. "Look, it's only when something different has happened that a woman has a story to tell," Vidhya said, speaking Hindi. "If everything just goes on the way it's supposed to, all you can think of is that you ate, drank, slept, served your husband and brought up your children. What's the story in that?" (Narayan n.d.:1). Building on cultural conceptions, individuals may also elaborate their own tastes and convictions about appropriate life stories. Ruth Behar (1993), for example, found that the Mexican peddler—Esperanza—whose life story she recorded followed a narrative structure that moved from suffering to rage to redemption and appeared to expect other women's narratives to follow this pattern too. When Behar proposed to ask other women for their life stories, Esperanza objected to Behar's choice of a respected schoolteacher, declaring, "But she, what has she suffered? I never heard that her husband beat her or that she suffered from rages" (p. 12).

The genre that anthropologists have developed to write about people's lives is labeled *life history,* but we prefer the term *life story* or even *life stories* because it draws attention to the fragmentary and constructed nature of personal narratives (see Peacock and Holland 1991). Sometimes, asking someone to tell a life story may appear altogether too overwhelming or foreign a request, whereas asking about particular eras or incidents may stimulate retellings. For example, Migdim, an old, semiblind Bedouin woman, waved off Lila Abu-Lughod's

(1993) request for her life story, stating, "I've forgotten all of that. I've got no mind to remember with any more." Migdim then proceeded to add some generalities about the past nomadic experiences of the group: "We used to milk the sheep. We used to pack up and leave here and set up camp out west" (p. 46). As Abu-Lughod points out, for this old woman, like others in the community, "the conventional form of 'a life' as a self-centered passage through time was not familiar. Instead there were memorable events, fixed into dramatic stories with fine details" (p. 46). As Abu-Lughod learned, when Migdim reminisced in the company of family members about particular past events, she was indeed a spirited storyteller with a sharp memory for things that had happened to her.

Whether entire life stories or passing anecdotes, personal narratives emerge within what is culturally "storyworthy." By looking at the subjects that people choose to dwell on in narrating their lives, we are in a position to see what most matters to them, from their point of view. Describing the hunting stories that Ilongot men of the Philippines love to tell, Rosaldo (1986) observes, "Narrative can provide a particularly rich source of knowledge about the significance people find in their workaday lives. Such narratives often reveal more about what can make life worth living than about how it is routinely lived" (p. 98).

In addition to being implicitly encoded in cultural practice, conventions for talking about lives can also be actively inculcated by institutional demands of various kinds (see Holstein and Gubrium 2000; Gubrium and Holstein 2001). As Kenneth George (1978) learned in his fieldwork with pastor John Sherfey, the religious doctrines of evangelical Protestant congregations in the United States require adherents to "testify" to their spiritual salvation through stories about their personal conversion experience (see also Harding 1987; Titon 1988; Titon & George 1977, 1978). Or as Carole Cain (1991) has argued, Alcoholics Anonymous teaches newcomers how to tell stories in which they are not just drinkers, but alco-holics who have hit rock bottom and need help. Through pamphlets, the examples of others' storytelling, and feedback from fel-low participants at A.A. meetings, people joining the group learn how to shape per-sonal experience along the lines of this key story form.

Ironically, the presence of conventions for telling the right stories about particular kinds of life experience means that people who have not actually lived through these experiences might nonetheless learn how to recount convincing stories of their own. So, for example, Bruce Jackson (1996) writes about meeting Jim, a "perfect infor-mant" who readily told long, detailed tales about his war experiences in Vietnam. Jim kept not only Jackson but other veterans spellbound. It eventually turned out, how-ever, that Jim had never been in Vietnam at all; he had so steeped himself in widespread accounts of being there that he told the sto-ries as his own. Other veterans had sniffed out the inconsistencies and exaggerations even before Jackson became aware of the hoax. Yet when Jackson asked them, "Why didn't you ever blow the whistle on him?" one of the veterans responded in a classic defense of a mesmerizing storyteller, "Wasn't doing me any harm. And he told such great stories. I loved listening to him tell those goddamned stories. I mean, I was *there* and I couldn't tell stories like that guy" (p. 220).

Even as personal narratives are shaped by shared conventions, folk narratives cir-culating within and across communities are personalized through retellings. After all, people remember and retell shared stories —myths, legends, folktales, parables, jokes, and so on—because these are personally as well as socially meaningful. Yet folk narra-tives have tended to be so analytically yoked to communities that many collec-tions and analyses have rarely mentioned tellers, or have alluded to them only by name—as though their existence is impor-tant only because they serve as conduits of traditional knowledge. Shifting attention

from traditional stories to the storytellers, it becomes clear that storytellers put their own creative and aesthetic stamp on folk narratives, personalizing them through retellings to fit particular occasions (Aza-dovskii 1974; Dégh 1969). As Swamiji, a Hindu holy man who delighted in making moral and spiritual points through stories once reflected to Narayan, people tell sto-ries according to their own feelings and the feelings of their audience. As Swamiji said: "When you tell a story, you should look at the situation and tell it. Then it turns out well. If you just tell any story any time, it's not really good. You must consider the time and shape the story so it's right. All stories are told for some purpose" (Narayan 1989:37).

Occasionally, tellers may make explicit links between their folk narratives and their lives. So, for example, Urmilaji, a woman in the Himalayan foothills, once compared hard times she had experienced to the wan-derings of an exiled king and queen in one of the folktales she had told Narayan. In making this explicit connection, Urmilaji was shedding light not just on her own life, but on the traditional tale as well. Similarly, when Urmilaji's family priest retold the same story, foregrounding the beleaguered king and downplaying the travails of his loyal wife, it became clear that both tellers were recasting the tale according to their own gendered experiences (Narayan 1997:121-24; see also Taggart 1990).

Reading life histories, one can occasion-ally sense the subject straining against an anthropologist's conceptions of appropri-ate "personal" content in an interview. So, for example, when the energetic !Kung woman Nisa suggested to Marjorie Shostak (1981), "Let's continue our talk about long ago. Let's also talk about the stories that the old people know" (p. 40), it is possible that Nisa was trying to include some of her rep-ertoire of traditional tales within the frame of her life stories. Sometimes, subjects are more emphatic. Julie Cruikshank (1990), for example, found that three Yukon women elders whose life stories she was recording insisted that their myths were *part* of their lives and so should be included along with their more personal reminiscences.

Breaking down the division between personal and folk narratives forces researchers to revise their assumptions about how to conduct interviews and about what they should include in their texts. Rather than suppressing the disjunction between the kinds of stories researchers might seek and the forms of discourse that they receive in interviews, exploring this gap between "analytic categories" and the locally conceived genres that index social power can be a source of creative scholarly insight and creativity (see Ben-Amos [1969] 1976; Bauman and Briggs 1992; Briggs 1986). As Michael Young (1983) admits in his prologue to *Magicians of Manumanua: Living Myth in Kalauna,* the book emerged from his attempt to make sense of the ritual expert Iyahalina's puzzling response to a request for his life history:

> Instead of telling me tales from his childhood, recounting the circumstances of his marriage, or enumerating his mature achievements, he narrated a sequence of myths and legends that described the activities of his ancestors. He concluded with a passionate peroration on the ritual duties they had bequeathed him, the central task of which was to "sit still" in order to anchor the community in prosperity. (Pp. 3-4)

As Young learned, Iyahalina and other hereditary guardians of myths on Goodenough Island identified with the heroes of their myths and drew on mythic themes to construct their own autobiographical narratives. At the same time, possession of these myths was a means of asserting status. Similarly, Maria Lepowsky (1994:126) found that in Vanatinai, New Guinea, women could also own authoritative versions of myths, a fact that she links to women's stature within this more gender-egalitarian society.

Whether folk or personal, narratives are not just a means of cultural representation; they are also potent tools in social interaction, a form of cultural work. By *cultural work,* we mean the ways that narrators and audiences use narrative resources for political and social ends. Although stories of different kinds certainly contain representations of cultural values, concerns, and patterns, we cannot forget that stories are also practices intended to get things done: to entertain, edify, shock, terrorize, intimidate, heal, comfort, persuade, testify, divulge, and so on. Narrative form, then, not only conjures up other worlds, whether imagined or remembered; it is also a way of artfully arranging words for social and political consequences in the immediacies of this world.

◆ Getting Stories

Alert researchers should ideally try to be present when stories are narrated as part of ongoing social life, and so be in a position to overhear spontaneously evoked commentaries, debates, revisions, and retellings. Yet researchers are not always so lucky as to be in the right place at the right time, to participate in the many varied moments when people tell or comment upon stories that circulate in everyday life. When researchers do have a chance to listen in, their very presence cannot help but shape different aspects of the storytelling occasion. Further, being present for a single narrative performance is usually not enough for a researcher to gain insight into the larger ongoing life of stories and storytelling encounters. Interviews, then, are a useful supplement to the ethnographer's taking part in social life in an engaged, observant way (see Atkinson and Coffey, Chapter 38, this volume).

Because all storytelling events are situationally unique, narratives heard or exchanged in interviews should not be carelessly confused with or substituted for narratives that take place outside of the interview context. All stories emerging from an interview will bear the mark of an interviewer's presence and the hierarchical dynamics of the interview situation. Yet we should not dismiss interview narratives as contrived or worthless. Like so many other social encounters, interviews are culturally negotiated events worthy of analysis (see Briggs 1986). Because the interview can be an invitation to narrate, it is a wonderful opportunity for the researcher to grasp—or at least begin to think about—the complexity of stories exchanged elsewhere in a community.

The word *interview* has roots in Old French, and at one time meant something like "to see one another." Although we cannot ignore the social hierarchies of inquiry, we want to underscore how "seeing one another" in interviews requires close attentiveness and an openness to the surprises of dialogue and exchange. How an interview runs its course depends very much on all participants involved. It is important for the interviewer to be flexible and ready to follow unexpected paths that emerge in the course of talking together with interviewees. In fact, in our experience, interviews often end up having less to do with structured questions or answers than with the animated exchange of stories. The interviewer's willingness to reveal his or her own stories can also add to the depth of an interview, inspiring the person being interviewed to open up, knowing that the interviewer is willing to be vulnerable too (see also in this volume Johnson, Chapter 5, and the contributions to Part II).

The ethnographic interview is a bid on the part of a researcher to get an interviewee to converse openly about a set of issues of concern to the researcher. The political conditions surrounding the consent and participation of interviewees in ethnographic interviews—and in the negotiated elicitation of stories—have been anticipated in human subjects protocols designed to hold in check the potentially coercive impulses of social scientific and humanistic inquiry. Setting up an interview becomes an invitation to narrate, albeit one that can be refused, subverted, or turned back on the interviewer.

Most basically, when looking for stories in interviews, researchers should keep in mind that all people are not equally skilled storytellers. Some people are energetic raconteurs who will use the interview as a welcome occasion to spin stories. Stories may pour toward the researcher in such dizzying numbers that all he or she need do is show engagement with nods or murmurs while the recording equipment rolls. In the presence of such practiced storytellers, an interviewer may have to struggle to direct the stories toward subjects suited to his or her specific interests. Sometimes, the interviewer may need to clarify details. But mostly, when a storyteller takes charge, an interviewer's work is to listen with attentive care so as to be able to formulate necessary questions when the retelling is over.

In other cases, the interviewer has to work harder. With some respondents, it may take a while for the interviewer to formulate the right questions that will inspire the telling of stories. Questions that can be answered with a simple yes or no are particular hazards, and can give an interviewer a sense of getting nowhere at all. Sometimes, a person is more willing to tell stories outside the formal context of an interview, without recording devices or notebooks at hand. Occasionally, a person being interviewed is willing to tell stories about some things, but not others. Here, for example, is a moment from Narayan's fieldwork in the Northwest Himalayan foothills: Suman Kumari (SK), a woman who had been animatedly telling stories about her grandmother's and mother's difficult lives, comes to a place in her narrative for which there no longer appears to be a clear prior story. Narayan had already been struggling to keep the stories flowing by asking what Suman's mother's brothers had made of Suman's father's not working. Finally, giving up on questions that received brief answers, Narayan (KN) asked as broad a question as possible.

KN: And after that?

SK: After that what can I say? What can I say, Bahenji? [Turns to her half sister, who, along with the mother, is listening in] After that—that's all: sons and all that, and daughters-in-law.

KN: [Seeing that SK is still speaking from the perspective of her mother, tries to turn the interview to SK's own life] And your earliest memories were of this place? What was your childhood like?

SK: [Looking at her sister again] What should I tell her about my childhood, Bahenji?

Sister: That you went to school in your childhood—that's just fine. [Both sisters laugh]

SK: What happened is that we went to school, we ate food. Sometimes there would be mangoes on the trees and we'd eat a lot. In the house, she [indicating her mother] would say, "Go to sleep." But as soon as she was asleep, then all three of us would run out!

In a cursory way, Suman Kumari spoke about collecting mangoes, of going to school, of knitting, yet her own life clearly did not have as much interest to her as did the lives of her mother and grandmother. Although Narayan tried to refuel the narrative with questions, these reminiscences soon sputtered to a halt.

Asking people to be more specific can sometimes be a good way of getting them to expand on stories. For example, if someone says, "Life was hard," the interviewer might ask in what ways life was hard, or if there are any particular moments that stand out as being especially hard; such probes can result in the unpacking of stories. However, the more an interviewer works at extracting a story, the less sure he or she can be that it is a story already present in the person's repertoire rather than one created only by the interview. This is one of the reasons it has been suggested that researchers should include the questions they asked interview respondents in their final published works; this information can be crucial to showing how the materials emerged as part of a dialogic process (Dwyer 1982).

Folklorists make the distinction between "active bearers" and "passive bearers" (von Sydow 1948:12-15). Active bearers are those who are actively engaged in transmitting folk knowledge; passive bearers are those who may know folklore, but who may not think of themselves as competent tellers to pass the folklore on. The distinction is fluid: Sometimes an active bearer may slip into a passive role, for example, with age and failing memory. Equally, a passive bearer might assume a more active role through various circumstances, such as growing seniority, migration, or the death of an active bearer. In some contexts, a perfectly competent active bearer of stories may be forced to defer to the authority of a storyteller who is socially recognized. In Kangra, for example, when Narayan worked with women's ritual tales, she found that many women were passive bearers of ritual tales. Yet it was the senior women in patrilineages, considered "very wise," who were called on to tell stories in the context of ritual worship. In cases where related, less senior women interrupted, telling their own versions, there were enormous tensions around these transgressions, with relatives of the older women sometimes advising Narayan to erase her tapes.

It is important, then, for researchers to ascertain where individual storytellers stand in relation to wider social conventions around narrative practices and how a storyteller might be evaluated within his or her own community. Also, researchers will find it valuable to reflect on the structural relations between interviewers and interviewees, and what motives may be built into the transmission of stories from the interviewees' side. For example, in Barbara Myerhoff's (1978) memorable ethnography about elderly American Jews, the retired tailor, Shmuel, seemed to hint at how vital transmitting his memories to the safekeeping of an ethnographer was for his own peace of mind. After recounting incidents from his childhood in Eastern Europe, he mused:

> For myself, growing old would be altogether a different thing if that little town was there still. . . . But when I come back from these stories and remember the way they lived is gone forever, wiped out like you would erase a line of writing, then it means another thing altogether for me to accept leaving this life. If my life goes now, it means nothing. But if my life goes, with my memories, and all that is lost, that is something else to bear. (P. 74)

Shmuel sent Myerhoff home with what he called "all this package of stories"; a day later, he died in his sleep. Shmuel's frank words remind us that sometimes interviews are of value not just to scholars. Transmitting memories to an eager audience, ensuring the survival of stories beyond a limited lifetime, an interviewee may also have a stake in the process.

The elicitation of stories in interviews may be subject to wider constraints around narrative practice. Examples abound in many Native American communities, where storytelling is often intimately linked to seasons, especially winter. Telling or eliciting stories at other times can be complicated. So, for example, if a storyteller among the Anishanaabe (Ojibwa) wishes to tell myths outside the winter months, he or she can put on a white weasel pelt, as though simulating snow. Exploring indigenous sacred traditions in highland Sulawesi, George (1996) found he had to adjust his interview work to take into account taboos that regulated the time and place for narrative activity. During the long months that stretched from the time of preparing rice fields to the time of harvest, communitywide prohibitions against storytelling and singing were in place and effectively prevented George from gathering and discussing narrative materials. Once the postharvest ritual season began, a period that extended for about two months, he was at liberty to record and discuss traditional songs and stories. Even then, certain taboos remained in effect, such as those that allowed *sumengo*—a genre of ritual song associated with head-hunting narratives—to be performed and discussed for only one week out of the year in any given community. As a result, George had to adjust his research, moving from community to community as sets of taboos came into effect in one and relaxed in another.

The kinds of stories appropriate to tell may vary not just with calendrical cycles, but with social location. Gender and age are particularly important factors to consider. For example, among Southeast Asia's Ilongot (Rosaldo 1986), Karo Batak (Steedly 1993), Meratus Dayak (Tsing 1993), and Pitu Ulunna Salu (George 1996) communities, personal stories about the experience of going on journeys figure as an especially prominent genre for adult males in both everyday and ritual life. Interestingly, many of the mythic and historical narratives in these regions feature male "culture heroes" whose journeys led to the foundation of the communities in question. Thus men's contemporary tales of personal journeys resonate well with the foundational narratives of any specific locale. Women in these same communities have less to say about personal journeys but comparatively more when it comes to talking about trance experience (George 1996; Steedly 1993; Tsing 1993). Although both men and women in these communities go on journeys and go into trance, in an important sense it is more relevantly male to make a story of personal travel and more relevantly female to talk about trance experience. The very familiarity and pervasiveness of this pattern makes it all the more striking when, for example, a woman recounts the dangers of a journey she has made. Her move into a typically "male" narrative terrain, then, is an exceptionally revealing and socially salient example of gender play and transgression.

Storytelling forms are not static. Like other genres, kinds of stories evolve within the play of power in ongoing social life and in dialogue with other genres (Bauman and Briggs 1992). This means that there may be shifts in the kinds of stories that are appropriate for different social groups to tell. In his long-term research among the Kwaio of the Solomon Islands, Roger Keesing (1985) at first found men ready to talk about their lives, whereas women "were fragmented and brief, distancing themselves from serious autobiography with reciprocal jests" (p. 29). On return visits, he found that men's efforts to codify cultural rules and conventions or *kastom* as a form of postcolonial resistance to outside influences had also inspired women to think of culture as an objectifiable "thing" and to lay claim to their own accounts of *kastom* in which women's importance was given its due. When Kwaio women finally spoke out, they did so in counterpoint to the men, who had previously been working with Keesing to codify *kastom*. Also, senior women recounted their lives *"as moral texts,* as exemplifications of the trials, responsibilities, virtues and tragedies of A Woman's Life" (p. 33). Speaking out, for Kwaio women, was a bid to power. While acknowledging the wider historical shifts that made women perceive their life stories as valuable texts to transact, Keesing also mentions the importance of what he terms "the politics of the elicitation situation" (p. 37)—that is, the particular interpersonal circumstances of the interview. That he was joined by a female field-worker during the time that he was finally able to record women's stories was also a key factor

in his coaxing Kwaio women who had previously been silent about their lives to become animated speaking subjects.

Anthropologists have typically addressed the self-revelatory content of one life story at a time. However, moving beyond one life story to compare several related life stories brings expected narrative forms and their transgressions into clearer focus. Oscar Lewis (1961) pioneered this method of juxtaposing life stories in his work with a poor Mexican family, where each family member recounted his or her own stories, revealing multifaceted, crosscutting, and even diverging perspectives on the same episodes. Other researchers have also used this method to show how positioned perspectives and gendered conventions pervade the shaping of life stories (see Mintz [1960] 1974; Viramma, Racine, and Racine 1997).

For folklorists, there is an implicit understanding that any retelling is a version rather than *the* story. To track the wider lives of entire stories and their constituent parts beyond particular iterations, folklorists have developed such tools as tale-type indexes and motif indexes. At the same time, attention to performance has revealed how stories emerge within the parameters of particular contexts rather than as perfect forms that float above social life. The same attention to the surfacing of versions in performance can be applied to life histories. So, for example, Laurel Kendall (1988) was able to record multiple versions of the stories that Yongsu's Mother, a Korean shaman, dramatically retold to Kendall, neighbors, and clients to make varied points about gender, about the power of gods, about dangers of ritual lapses, and so on.

We would like to emphasize how valuable it is for researchers to elicit several versions of folktales and life stories—from the same persons through time and from different individuals—so that they can see how the uniqueness of particular tellings emerges within larger patterns. Collecting multiple versions of folk narratives and life stories, and talking to different storytellers, is vital to researchers' understanding of how narrative traditions are creatively reworked by particular tellers for particular social ends. Also, situating the performance of different versions within social interactions reveals the role of storytelling in the exercise of power, authority, and identity.

◆ Interviews about Stories

Getting a story during an interview still leaves unfinished the intellectual work of making sense of the story. Many researchers have found that there are great rewards in engaging the subjects of their research in the interpretive process, through asking for their opinions on meaning and through dialogues exposing the interpretive biases of both the storytellers and the scholars.

For folklore scholarship, Alan Dundes (1966) has coined the term *oral literary criticism* to characterize the move beyond eliciting texts to also comprehending indigenous meanings. In Dundes's classic formulation, oral literary criticism involves the collection of (a) metafolklore, that is, folklore about folklore (for example, folktales about folktales) that gives a sense of how a genre is locally conceived; (b) asides and explanations during folklore performances; (c) systematic exegeses of texts by storytellers and their audiences; and (d) analysts' attempts to comprehend possibly unconscious symbols by also looking at other texts in which the same symbols are used (p. 507). In an article affirming the theoretical and methodological value of this method, Narayan (1995) also adds the elicitation of generalized testimonies about a genre of folklore, supplementing talk about particular texts. Thus if an interviewee finds it too revealing to explain *why* he or she tells a particular story, the interviewer can elicit valuable insights by asking about why people more generally tell sto-

ries, and what kinds of meanings certain sorts of stories might carry.

Narayan sought to put this method to work through a collaboration with Urmila Devi Sood, or "Urmilaji," the wise woman we met earlier. After hearing Urmilaji's tales, Narayan transcribed them, thought about them, and came back to talk more about texts in particular and what meanings they held, and about storytelling in general. Sometimes her questions mystified Urmilaji, and at other times Urmilaji expounded implicit meanings in the tales, self-evident to most Kangra people but perplexing to Narayan. Speaking with Urmilaji about her stories, Narayan also came to understand how stories can be associated with particular prior tellers, keeping their wisdom and influence alive. Urmilaji, for example, loved many of these tales because they had been gifts, lovingly imparted, by her father and ancient aunt-in-law.

In addition to interviewing storytellers, it is also valuable for researchers to interview a range of people about what particular stories mean to them. Kay Stone (1985), for example, interviewed Americans of all ages about their memories of and reactions to popular fairy tales, in particular the story of Cinderella. She found that the males tended not to remember fairy tales, whereas the females worked out their self-images partly in dialogue with fairy-tale characters. Girls and women sometimes chafed at the messages in fairy tales, and some also reworked the stories to carry alternate endings. So, for example, a 9-year-old girl who preferred the character of Jack in "Jack and the Beanstalk" to Cinderella suggested that perhaps Cinderella could recover her slipper from the prince, and then "maybe she doesn't marry him, but she gets a lot of money anyway, and she gets a job" (p. 144).

Talking to people about stories gives researchers a chance to learn how the stories work interpersonally and psychologically. Keith Basso (1996) has explored how, among the Western Apache, historical tales bearing moral points are associated with various sites in the landscape. A place called "Trail Goes Down between Two Hills" for example, is associated with a story about lascivious Old Man Owl and how he is tricked by two beautiful girls; one might tell this story to comment on how someone's behavior involves uncurbed appetites and so is laughable and offensive (pp. 113-20). By telling a story instead of speaking directly, an individual can imply criticism rather than state it directly. The moral points carried within stories become embodied within the geographic landscape, reminding people of occasions when places have been pointed out to them. As Nick Thompson, a spirited elderly Apache, explained to Basso, stories "go to work on your mind and make you think about your life" (p. 58). Using the metaphor of hunting to characterize how stories are aimed at appropriate quarry, Thompson went on to describe how, when a person acts inappropriately, someone goes hunting for that person:

> So someone stalks you and tells a story about what happened long ago. It doesn't matter if other people are around —you're going to know that he's aiming that story at you. All of a sudden it *hits* you! It's like an arrow, they say. Sometimes it just bounces off—it's too soft and you don't think about anything. But when it's strong it goes in deep and starts working on your mind right away. No one says anything to you, only that story is all, but now you know that people have been watching you and talking about you. They don't like how you've been acting. So you have to think about your life. (Pp. 58-59)

The messages, then, are reinforced by place: "You're going to see the place where it happened, maybe every day if it's nearby. . . . If you don't see it, you're going to hear its name and see it in your mind" (p. 59). Even when the original storyteller dies, the place will continue to stalk the person, reminding him or her how to live right. In this conception of storytelling, then, a good story pierces deep and transforms a person from inside even while its effects are continually reinforced by the outer landscape.

In some societies, much of the power of stories lies in the ways they are internalized and embodied—"living myth," as Young (1983) memorably puts it. Thus an interviewer's inviting someone to stand aside so that he or she can extract explicit meaning may have no cultural frame of reference and, indeed, may be annoying. As Elsie Mather, a Yup'ik teacher, forcefully wrote to Phyllis Morrow (1995) when the question of explication came up in the course of their collaboration in documenting Yup'ik oral traditions:

> Why do people want to reduce traditional stories to information, to some function? Isn't it enough that we hear and read them? They cause us to wonder about things, and sometimes they touch us briefly along the way, or we connect the information or idea into something we are doing at the moment. This is what the old people say a lot. They tell us to listen even when we don't understand, that later on we will make some meaning or that something that we had listened to before will touch us in some way. Understanding and knowing occur over one's lifetime. . . .
>
> Why would I want to spoil the repetition and telling of stories with questions? Why would I want to know what they mean? (P. 33)

Like Nick Thompson, Morrow reminds us how stories live in ongoing reverberations through lived practices, not just in analytic reflection. Asking people for meaning isolated from particular contexts of retelling or remembering is to fix meaning in inappropriate ways. As Margaret Mills (1991) found in her research in Afghanistan, storytellers may actually thrive on the ambiguity of storytelling and the intertextual relations among stories, as this allows them to make sly commentaries on the sociopolitical world beyond the stories.

The analytic stance that breaks up stories may be perceived as dangerous for other reasons, too. In a dramatic example of the dangers of a researcher's blithely asking about stories without being cognizant of their social role or power, Barre Toelken (1996) has traced different moments of "enlightenment" in his long-term research on Navajo Coyote tales. With growing understanding of these Coyote tales, he was told that the tales were not just entertainment for winter months, but were also used in Navajo healing ceremonies. As Toelken was discussing the use of these tales with an elderly Navajo singer one night, the singer asked him, "Are you ready to lose someone in your family?" Baffled, Toelken asked him to explain. That is the cost of taking up witchcraft, the singer told him. Without being aware of it, Toelken had gained a reputation among the Navajo as someone with an interest in witchcraft because of the sorts of questions he had asked, and this had potentially malevolent repercussions for the Navajo people around him. As Toelken (1996) writes:

> For just as the tales themselves in their narration are normally used to create a harmonious world in which to live, and just as elliptical references to the tales can be used within rituals to clarify and enhance the healing processes, so the tales can be dismembered and used outside the proper ritual arena by witches to promote disharmony and to thwart the healing processes. In discussing parts and motifs separately, by dealing with them as interesting ideas which might lead me to discoveries of my own, I had been doing something like taking all the powerful medicines to be found in all the doctors' offices in the land and dumping them by the bucketload out of a low-flying chopper over downtown Los Angeles. (P. 11)

For researchers, then, asking for help with interpretations is like walking a razor's edge: On one hand, in asking, researchers run the danger of making severe cultural faux pas, as Toelken did; on the other hand, in not asking, they risk attributing their own interpretive frames to their subjects. The same dangers hold for both folk narratives and personal narratives, although with personal narratives people may be even more sensitive to interpretations that researchers make without consulting them.

A powerful example of the conflict that can arise when informants do not share the interpretations with their interviewers is described in an essay by Katherine Borland (1991). Borland interviewed her grandmother, Beatrice Hanson, about events that had taken place in 1944 when Beatrice attended a horse race and bet against the wishes of her father. Borland then wrote a student essay in which she interpreted her grandmother's actions as enacting a female struggle for autonomy and, thus, as being feminist. Her grandmother, however, after reading the essay, wrote back a 14-page letter in which she pointedly objected to being theorized in her feminist granddaughter's framework and asked questions that all scholars would do well to heed:

> So your interpretation of the story as a female struggle for autonomy within a hostile male environment is entirely YOUR interpretation. You've read into the story what you wished to—what pleases YOU. That it was never—by any wildest stretch of the imagination—the concern of the originator of the story makes such an interpretation a definite and complete distortion, and in this respect I question its authenticity. The story is no longer MY story at all. The skeleton remains, but it has become your story. Right? How far is it permissible to go in the name of folklore [or scholarship generally] and still be honest in respect to the original narrative? (P. 70)

This disagreement resulted in a dialogue in which both grandmother and granddaughter explained the assumptions they were working from and the different associations they brought to the term *feminist*. In the process of this conflict and the ensuing discussion, each woman stretched to understand the other's position, and each was educated in the process.

Indeed, feminist work on life stories has been at the forefront of the exploration of issues of possible reciprocity amid the hierarchical imbalances of interviews and their outcomes (see Personal Narratives Group 1989; Gluck and Patai 1991). Sociologist Ann Oakley (1981), for example, long ago advocated replacing a distanced interviewing technique that seeks to deflect questions aimed at the interviewer with a "different role, that could be termed 'no intimacy without reciprocity,' " especially for in-depth interviewing through time. As she writes: "This involves being sensitive not only to those questions that are asked (by either party) but to those that are not asked. The interviewee's definition of the interview is important" (p. 49). Elaine Lawless (1991) has worked out a system of "reciprocal ethnography" that she used in eliciting the life stories of Pentecostal women ministers; even as she sought to interpret their personal narratives, she allowed the women to critique and reflect on her ethnographic practices. Such an openness to the perspectives of the people interviewed can radically reframe the scholarly project, enhancing accountability to the contradictions and inequalities of the real world.

◆ Reflecting on Interviews

We have found that researchers can learn much not just from looking to the work of others, but from looking back at their own interview practices, whether this involves listening again to tapes or studying transcripts. Most immediately, such a review can help a researcher to frame questions about stories already recorded, and so more self-consciously engage interviewees in an unfolding interpretive process. More generally, encountering one's own shortcomings can be very instructive for future practice. For example, interviewers may discover moments where they have asked questions that elicited yes or no responses instead of stories, moments where they have interrupted, or moments where they have radically misunderstood what someone was trying to say and taken an interview off on a new tangent. Bruce Jackson (1987) summarizes what many interviewers likely feel as they transcribe their own tapes: "The most important thing I learned was that I talked too much" (p. 81).

We now turn to a segment from an interview conducted by Narayan, who will reflect critically on her own practices. This interview was conducted in the fall of 1995, with a second-generation South Asian American called Zeynab (Z). At the time, Narayan (KN) was interviewing partly to comprehend second-generation South Asian American experience as an anthropologist and partly to construct a character for a novel she was writing. In her questions, she was striving to enter experience from within. In this segment, Zeynab has been talking about growing up in Southern California, and how her father's brother and his wife had come to live with the family, creating conflict and even urging Zeynab's father to divorce. Narayan's commentary appears in italics.

Z: And my mother didn't have anyone to talk to about these things.

KN: So she would talk to you? *[This query is based on Zeynab's having earlier told me that she was very close to her mother.]*

Z: Yeah. I still remember. I didn't understand exactly what was going on at the time. All I remember was my mother in the kitchen. Like I'll be doing the dishes and she'll be cleaning the floor and she'll be crying. And it wasn't ever that she told me, she never said that my sister-in-law was saying this and that, it was like, "I'm very alone, I have no one to talk to, I miss home." She did not have any intention of turning my father against his brother. So she just kept quiet. She took all of that in.

KN: When she said "home," what images came into your mind? *[Here my own agenda of understanding how second-generation South Asian Americans construct "home" is breaking in, redirecting the narrative flow. Ideally, I would have waited until a break in the larger narrative of growing up to ask this question.]*

Z: I guess for me, I had very strong images of when I was there as a child. Because my Nana [maternal grandfather] was still alive at that time.

KN: How old were you? Cause you were born here . . . *[Again, looking back, I am breaking in to ask for specification and possibly redirecting the story. I should have just kept my mouth shut, making affirmative sounds, then later asked her about her visits back to Pakistan.]*

Z: I was born in Los Angeles and maybe after a year or two we went back, and then every maybe year or two we would go back. My mother would take us. Some of my earliest memories are from there. My fondest memories too. We used to go to my Nana's house. It was a very nice house. One of the women who worked in the house, her husband was breeding pigeons on the roof. So we used to go up on the roof. Some of my NICEST memories are from that time. So . . .

KN: What did you see from the roof? *[In retrospect, I wish I could clap my hand over my mouth. With my desire to imaginatively participate in her experience, and my own strong visual sense, I am interrupting Zeynab from her own story.*

Zeynab, however, found her way back to what she was trying to say].

Zeynab responded, "I think it's more the air I remember. The color of the sky. You know, seeing the other rooftops from the distance." In her own construction of the story, what she saw from the roof was less key than her going up there to play with pigeons, and then returning to playing games with cousins, or going out to be treated to ice cream by her uncles. With time, Narayan hopes to have become more attentive to allowing stories to take shape without her intervention, learning to keep questions in her head until the teller has finished speaking. Narayan is also puzzling over whether her practice of turning off the tape recorder when an interviewee asks her questions (that is, when she tells stories about her own South Asian American experience) is appropriate or misleading. On the one hand, she is not interested in recording her own stories; on the other hand, might the inclusion of her own storytelling input in interview situations lessen the hierarchical imbalance?

Yet, as Narayan looks back at this exchange with Zeynab, she sees that there is something grand and lovely about the spaciousness she evoked with her hasty question about the views from that rooftop. Perhaps one of the most important lessons interviewers can learn from the mortifying process of looking back at their own interviews is to forgive themselves, make the best of what they have done, and look ahead to the next interview. In querying their own interview practices, researchers would do well to recall the poet Rainer Maria Rilke's (1984:34) stricture to "live the questions" rather than look for fixed and certain answers.

◆ Conclusions

The interest in "getting stories" has an institutional backdrop and a place within broader fields of everyday inquiry. As we stated at the opening of this chapter, it is not just scholars who want to obtain stories; police officers, medical and psychiatric diagnosticians, journalists, refugee agents, shamans, social workers, state and corporate bureaucrats, courts, and human rights workers want stories too. Interview narratives have been put to use not just by anthropologists and folklorists, but also by colonizers seeking to comprehend "the native mind," by nationalists wanting to mobilize support around an imagined "spirit of the people," and by those promoting regional and state articulations of identity.

The distinction between "personal" and "folk" narrative, we have argued, is often blurred in practice, and so cross-fertilizing methodologies and theories usually associated with one body of stories or the other may be sources of creative insight. We have emphasized the need for researchers to follow other people's own conceptions of stories, as speech genres and as interpersonal, politically charged transactions with lives outside an interview context. Paying attention to the kinds of people who are storytellers, the kinds of stories appropriate to tell within social locations, transformations in the kinds of stories told, and the shifting multiplicity of versions enhances researchers' appreciation for the specificity of stories that emerge within interviews.

We have underscored the value for researchers of talking about stories with both storytellers and listeners, in addition to gathering stories in interviews. Researchers' sensitivity to indigenous conceptions of the meanings and psychological impacts of stories can bring the researchers' own interpretive biases to light, where they can be transformed in constructive dialogues. Sometimes, cultural sensitivity may require that interviewers hold back on analytic questions that carve up stories into constituent elements, cutting them away from the ongoing flow of lived experience.

Finally, we have noted the fruits that researchers may glean by critically examining their own interview tapes or transcripts, learning to ask and to listen with greater skill. Often, being a good interviewer for stories involves not just asking the right questions, but sympathetically listening and holding back questions so the person being interviewed can shape stories in his or her own way. Equally, being a good interviewer may involve responding to questions from an interviewee, and so entering into a reciprocal exchange.

Telling and listening to stories is at the heart of social and cultural life. Much of what we understand as personhood, identity, intimacy, secrecy, experience, belief, history, and common sense turns on the exchange of stories between people. In receiving stories, we are often receiving gifts of self; it is incumbent on us as researchers to handle these gifts with respect as we pass them onward in our scholarly productions.

■ References

Abu-Lughod, L. 1993. *Writing Women's Worlds: Bedouin Stories.* Berkeley: University of California Press.

Atkinson, R. 1998. *The Life Story Interview.* Thousand Oaks, CA: Sage.

Azadovskii, M. 1974. *A Siberian Tale Teller.* Translated by J. Dow. Austin: University of Texas Press.

Basso, K. 1996. *Wisdom Sits in Places: Landscape and Language among the Western Apache.* Albuquerque: University of New Mexico Press.

Bauman, R. and C. L. Briggs. 1992. "Genre, Intertextuality and Social Power." *Journal of Linguistic Anthropology* 2:131-72.

Behar, R. 1993. *Translated Woman: Crossing the Border with Esperanza's Story.* Boston: Beacon.

Ben-Amos, D. [1969] 1976. "Analytical Categories and Ethnic Genres." Pp. 215-42 in *Folklore Genres,* edited by D. Ben-Amos. Austin: University of Texas Press.

Boas, F. 1916. *Tsimshian Mythology* (31st Annual Report of the Bureau of American Ethnology). Washington, DC: Smithsonian Institution.

Borland, K. 1991. " 'That's Not What I Said': Interpretive Conflict in Oral Narrative Research." Pp. 63-76 in *Women's Words: The Feminist Practice of Oral History,* edited by S. B. Gluck and D. Patai. New York: Routledge.

Briggs, C. L. 1986. *Learning How to Ask: A Sociolinguistic Appraisal of the Role of the Interview in Social Science Research.* Cambridge: Cambridge University Press.

Cain, C. 1991. "Personal Stories, Identity Acquisition and Self-Understanding in Alcoholics Anonymous." *Ethos* 19:210-53.

Cruikshank, J. with A. Sidney, K. Smith, and A. Ned. 1990. *Life Lived Like a Story: Life Stories of Three Yukon Native Elders.* Lincoln: University of Nebraska Press.

Dégh, L. 1969. *Folktales and Society: Story Telling in a Hungarian Peasant Community.* Translated by E. M. Schossberger. Bloomington: Indiana University Press.

Dundes, A. 1966. "Metafolklore and Oral Literary Criticism." *Monist* 60:505-16.

Dwyer, K. 1982. *Moroccan Dialogues: Anthropology in Question.* Baltimore: Johns Hopkins University Press.

George, K. M. 1978. " 'I Still Got It': The Conversion Narrative of John C. Sherfey." M.A. thesis, University of North Carolina, Chapel Hill.

———. 1996. *Showing Signs of Violence: The Cultural Politics of a Twentieth-Century Headhunting Ritual.* Berkeley: University of California Press.

Gluck, S. B. and D. Patai, eds. 1991. *Women's Words: The Feminist Practice of Oral History.* New York: Routledge.

Grima, B. 1991. "Suffering in Women's Performance of *Paxto.*" Pp. 78-101 in *Gender, Genre and Power in South Asian Expressive Traditions,* edited by A. Appadurai, F. J. Korom, and M. Mills. Philadelphia: University of Pennsylvania Press.

Gubrium, J. F. and J. A. Holstein, eds. 2001. *Institutional Selves: Troubled Identities in a Postmodern World.* New York: Oxford University Press.

Harding, S. 1987. "Convicted by the Holy Spirit: The Rhetoric of Fundamental Baptist Conversion." *American Ethnologist* 14:167-81.

Holstein, J. A. and J. F. Gubrium. 1995. *The Active Interview.* Thousand Oaks, CA: Sage.

———. 2000. *The Self We Live By: Narrative Identity in a Postmodern World.* New York: Oxford University Press.

Ives, E. D. 1995. *The Tape Recorded Interview: A Manual for Fieldworkers in Folklore and Oral History.* 2d ed. Knoxville: University of Tennessee Press.

Jackson, B. 1987. *Fieldwork.* Urbana: University of Illinois Press.

———. 1996. "The Perfect Informant." Pp. 206-26 in *The Word Observed: Reflections on the Fieldwork Process,* edited by B. Jackson and E. D. Ives. Bloomington: Indiana University Press.

Keesing, R. 1985. "Kwaio Women Speak." *American Anthropologist* 87:27-39.

Kendall, L. 1988. *The Life and Hard Times of a Korean Shaman: Of Tales and the Telling of Tales.* Honolulu: University of Hawaii Press.

Langness, L. L. and G. Frank. 1981. *Lives: An Anthropological Approach to Biography.* Novato, CA: Chandler & Sharp.

Lawless, E. 1991. "Women's Life Stories and Reciprocal Ethnography as Feminist and Emergent." *Journal of Folklore Research* 29:35-60.

Lepowsky, M. 1994. *Fruit of the Motherland: Gender in an Egalitarian Society.* New York: Columbia University Press.

Lewis, O. 1961. *The Children of Sánchez: Autobiography of a Mexican Family.* New York: Random House.

Mills, M. 1991. *Rhetorics and Politics in Afghan Traditional Storytelling.* Philadelphia: University of Pennsylvania Press.

Mintz, S. [1960] 1974. *Worker in the Cane.* New York: Norton.

Morrow, P. 1995. "On Shaky Ground." Pp. 27-51 in *When Our Words Return: Writing, Hearing and Remembering Oral Traditions of Alaska and the Yukon.* Logan: Utah State University Press.

Myerhoff, B. 1978. *Number Our Days.* New York: Simon & Schuster.

Narayan, K. 1989. *Storytellers, Saints and Scoundrels: Folk Narrative in Hindu Religious Teaching.* Philadelphia: University of Pennsylvania Press.

———. 1995. "The Practice of Oral Literary Criticism: Women's Songs in Kangra, India." *Journal of American Folklore* 108:243-64.

———. 1997. *Mondays on the Dark Night of the Moon: Himalayan Foothill Folktales* (assembled in collaboration with U. D. Sood). New York: Oxford University Press.

———. n.d. "Unspeakable Lives: Silences in the Life Stories of Women in Kangra, Northwest India." Unpublished manuscript.

Oakley, A. 1981. "Interviewing Women: A Contradiction in Terms?" Pp. 30-61 in *Doing Feminist Research,* edited by H. Roberts. London: Routledge & Kegan Paul.

Peacock, J. L. and D. C. Holland. 1993. "The Narrated Self: Life Stories in Process." *Ethos* 21:367-83.

Personal Narratives Group, ed. 1989. *Interpreting Women's Lives: Feminist Theory and Personal Narratives.* Bloomington: Indiana University Press.

Rilke, R. M. 1984. *Letters to a Young Poet.* Translated by S. Mitchell. New York: Random House.

Rosaldo, R. 1976. "The Story of Tukbaw: 'They Listen as He Orates.' " Pp. 121-51 in *The Biographical Process,* edited by F. Reynolds and D. Capps. The Hague: Mouton.

———. 1986. "Ilongot Hunting as Story and Experience." Pp. 97-138 in *The Anthropology of Experience,* edited by V. W. Turner and E. M. Bruner. Urbana: University of Illinois Press.

Shostak, M. 1981. *Nisa: The Life and Words of a !Kung Woman.* Cambridge, MA: Harvard University Press.

Spradley, J. P. 1979. *The Ethnographic Interview.* New York: Holt, Rinehart & Winston.

Steedly, M. M. 1993. *Hanging without a Rope: Narrative Experience in Colonial and Postcolonial Karoland.* Princeton, NJ: Princeton University Press.

Stone, K. 1985. "The Misuses of Enchantment: Controversies on the Significance of Fairy Tales." Pp. 125-45 in *Women's Folklore, Women's Culture,* edited by R. A. Jordan and S. J. Kalčik. Philadelphia: University of Pennsylvania Press.

Taggart, J. M. 1990. *Enchanted Maidens: Gender Relations in Spanish Folktales of Courtship and Marriage.* Princeton, NJ: Princeton University Press.

Titon, J. T. 1988. *Powerhouse for God: Speech, Chant, and Song in an Appalachian Baptist Church.* Austin: University of Texas Press.

Titon, J. T. and K. M. George. 1977. "Dressed in the Armor of God." *Alcheringa: Ethnopoetics* 3(2):10-31.

———. 1978. "Testimonies." *Alcheringa: Ethnopoetics* 4(1):69-83.

Toelken, B. 1996. "From Entertainment to Realization in Navajo Fieldwork." Pp. 1-17 in *The Word Observed: Reflections on the Fieldwork Process,* edited by B. Jackson and E. D. Ives. Bloomington: Indiana University Press.

Tsing, A. 1993. *In the Realm of the Diamond Queen: Marginality in an Out-of-the-Way Place.* Princeton, NJ: Princeton University Press.

Viramma, J. Racine, and J.-L. Racine. 1997. *Viramma: Life of an Untouchable.* London: Verso.

von Sydow, C. 1948. *Selected Papers in Folklore.* Copenhagen: Rosenhilde & Bagger.

Young, M. 1983. *Magicians of Manumanua: Living Myth in Kalauna.* Berkeley: University of California Press.

40

THE CINEMATIC SOCIETY
AND THE REFLEXIVE INTERVIEW

◆ Norman K. Denzin

We inhabit a secondhand world, one already mediated by cinema, television, and other apparatuses of the postmodern society. We have no direct access to this world; we experience and study only its representations. A reflexive sociology studies society as a dramaturgical production. The reflexive interview is a central component of this interpretive project.

In this chapter I examine the nexus of the cinematic society and the interview society. I show how postmodern society has become an interview society, how our very subjectivity "comes to us in the form of stories elicited through interviewing" (Holstein and Gubrium 2000:129; see also Atkinson and Silverman 1997). The interview, whether conducted by social researchers, mass-media reporters, television journalists, therapists, or counselors, is now a ubiquitous method of self-construction (Holstein and Gubrium 2000; see also in this volume Miller, de Shazer and De Jong, Chapter 19; Altheide, Chapter 20). I will discuss the concept of the active, dialogic interview, anchoring this complex formation in the postmodern, cinematic society (Holstein and Gubrium 1995; Gubrium and Holstein 1997; Jackson 1998; Denzin 1995a, 1995b, 1997; Scheurich 1995). The reflexive interview is simultaneously a site for conversation, a discursive method, and a communicative format that produces knowledge about the self and its place in the cinematic society—the society that knows itself through the reflective gaze of the cinematic apparatus. A cinematic sociology requires a concept of the reflexive interview.

A two-part question organizes my argument: First, how does the postmodern, cinematic world mediate the ways in which we represent ourselves to ourselves? And second, what is the place of the interview-interviewer relationship in this production process? I begin by outlining the central features of the postmodern, cinematic-interview society. I then show how the interview and the interviewer, as a voyeur, are basic features of this society. I thicken this argument by demonstrating how popular media representations shape and define situated cultural identities. I show how these representations become anchor points for the postmodern self; that is, how they occupy a central place in the background of our cultural consciousness. They mediate structures of meaning in the cinematic-interview society. A circular model of interpretation is thus created. Interviews, interviewers, and storytellers are defined in terms of these dominant cultural images and understandings. Thus does the cinematic society structure the interview society, and vice versa. I conclude with a series of epistemological observations on the significance of the relation between the cinematic society and the reflexive interview (see also Mishler 1986; Heyl 2001; Burawoy 1998; Bourdieu 1996).

◆ The Postmodern, Cinematic Society

Members of the postmodern society know themselves through the reflected images and narratives of cinema and television. On this, Altheide (1995) observes, "Culture is not only mediated through mass media . . . culture in both form and content is constituted and embodied by the mass media" (p. 59). The postmodern landscape is distinguished, as Simon Gottschalk (2000) argues, by "its constant saturation by multiple electronic screens which simulate emotions, interactions, events, desires. . . . From TV screens to computer terminals, from surveillance cameras to cell phones, we in-creasingly experience everyday life, reality . . . via technologies of spectacle, simulation and 'telepresence' " (p. 23).

Consider the following exchange between ESPN sports journalist Sal Paolantonio and Kurt Warner, quarterback of the St. Louis Rams, named Most Valuable Player in the 2000 Super Bowl:

Sal: There's a minute and 54 seconds left in the game. The Titans have just tied the score. Now look, let me show you your 73-yard winning pass to Isaac Bruce. Kurt, what were you thinking when Isaac caught that pass?

Kurt: [Looks up at replay] We'd called the same play earlier and Isaac was open. So we thought it would work. It was a go route. We thought we could get a big one right off the bat. I just thought it was meant to be, it was meant to work.

Sal: This has been a terrific year for you. Five years ago you were sacking groceries in the IGA. Two years ago you were playing arena football in Cedar Rapids, Iowa. This is better than a Hollywood script. Tell me how you feel about what has happened to you this year.

Kurt: I don't think of it as a Hollywood story. It's my life. I take it one day at a time.

Sal: It has not been easy, has it?

Kurt: I was getting to the point of thinking how much longer am I going to have before people say he is too old to give him an opportunity. It has been tough for us until this last year. Even when I was playing arena football we did all right, but a lot of tough decisions . . . When I first started dating my wife, she was on food stamps, and I was in between jobs. That is why I ended up stocking shelves; I had to do something at nights so I could work out and keep my chances in football. A lot of things like that have helped keep things in perspective, even though we are not making a million dollars, we are very fortunate to be where we are at, in this position, and don't look beyond that, don't take anything for granted.

Sal: Thanks Kurt. Is there anything else you want to say?

Kurt: I'm truly blessed. If I can be a source of hope to anybody, I'm happy to be a part of it. The good Lord has blessed me. I am on a mission. He has called me to do this. I can only share my testimony with others. Thank you Jesus. (*SportsCenter*, ESPN, January 31, 2000; see also Vecsey 2000)

Kurt's self-narrative is grafted onto the replay of the winning touchdown pass. Indeed, this Super Bowl victory symbolizes the larger-than-life triumph that he has experienced over the course of the preceding five years. Sal elicits this self-story by asking Kurt how he feels about his award-winning year, comparing it to a Hollywood script. Kurt complies by giving him a socially acceptable answer; indeed, Sal's questions establish Kurt's right to give this extended account of his life and what it means (see also Holstein and Gubrium 2000:129). The viewer vicariously shares in this experience.[1]

The ingredients of the postmodern self are modeled in the media. The postmodern self has become a sign of itself, a double dramaturgical reflection anchored in media representations on one side and everyday life on the other. These cultural identities are filtered through the individual's personal troubles and emotional experiences in interactions with everyday life. These existential troubles connect back to the dominant cultural themes of the postmodern era. The electronic media and the new information technologies turn everyday life into a theatrical spectacle where the dramas that surround the decisive performances of existential crises are enacted. This creates a new existential "videocy," a language of crisis coded in electronic, media terms.

The media structure these crises and their meanings. A 38-year-old male alcoholic is standing outside the door to a room where Alcoholics Anonymous (A.A.) meetings are held. He asks:

> How do I get into one of those A.A. meetings? What do I say? I seen them in the movies. That Michael Keaton in *Clean and Sober*. He went to one of them. He just stood up and said he was an alcoholic. Do I have to do that? I ain't even sure I am one, but I drank a fifth of Black Jack last night and I started up agin this mornin'. I'm scared. (Quoted in Denzin 1995b:260)

This is a postmodern story waiting to be heard, already partially told through the figure of Michael Keaton, himself an actor, playing a fictional character (Daryl Poynter) who goes to a fictional A.A. meeting in a Hollywood film. Texts within texts, movies, everyday life, a man down on his luck, A.A., a door into a room where meetings are held, anxiety, fear. The everyday existential world connects to the cinematic apparatus, and our drunk on the street hopes to begin a story that will have a happy ending, like Michael Keaton's.

◆ The Birth of Cinematic Surveillance

In the space of the period from 1900 to 1930, cinema became an integral part of American society. Going to the movies became a weekly pastime for millions of Americans. Motion pictures became a national institution. Hollywood stars became personal idols, fan clubs were formed, and movie theaters, with their lighted marquees, were a prominent part of virtually every American community.

The cinematic, surveillance society soon became a disciplinary structure filled with subjects (voyeurs) who obsessively looked and gazed at one another, as they became, at the same time, obsessive listeners, eavesdroppers, persons whose voices and telephone lines could be tapped, voices that could be dubbed, new versions of the spoken and seen self. A new social type was created; the voyeur, or Peeping Tom, who would, in various guises (ethnographer, social scientist, detective, psychoanalyst, crime reporter, investigative journalist, innocent bystander, sexual pervert), elevate the concepts of looking and listening to new levels.

With the advent of color and sound in films in the mid-1920s, there was a drive toward cinematic realism. This impulse to create a level of realism that mapped everyday life complemented the rise of naturalistic realism in the American novel and the emergence of hard-nosed journalistic reporting by major American newspapers and radio networks (Denzin 1997). During the same period, an ethnographic, psychoanalytic, and life history approach was taking hold in the social sciences and in society at large. Like journalists, sociologists, market researchers, and survey researchers were learning how to use the interview to gather and report on the facts of social life (Fontana and Frey 1994, 2000; Denzin 1997).

Robert E. Park (1950), a founder of the Chicago school of ethnographic research (Vidich and Lyman 1994), clarifies the relationships among journalism, social science, and the use of the interview:

> After leaving college, I got a job as a reporter. . . . I wrote about all sorts of things. . . .
>
> My interest in the newspaper had grown out of the discovery that a reporter who had the facts was a more effective reformer than an editorial writer. . . .
>
> According to my earliest conception of a sociologist he was to be a kind of

> super-reporter. . . . He was to report a little more accurately, and in a little more detail. (Pp. v, vii-ix)

And so although sociologists and journalists both used interviews, the duties and practices of the two occupational groups were separated, organizing surveillance in distinct ways.

THE INTERVIEW SOCIETY

The interview society emerges historically as a consequence, in part, of the central place that newspapers and cinema (and television) came (and continue) to occupy in daily life. Holstein and Gubrium (1995) invite us to

> think of how much we learn about contemporary life by way of interviews. Larry King introduces us to presidents and power brokers. Barbara Walters plumbs the emotional depths of stars and celebrities. Oprah . . . and Geraldo invite the ordinary, tortured and bizarre to "spill their guts" to millions of home viewers. (P. 1)

The media, human services personnel, market researchers, and social scientists "increasingly get their information via interviews" (Holstein and Gubrium 1995:1). The interview society has turned the confessional mode of discourse into a public form of entertainment (Atkinson and Silverman 1997; Holstein and Gubrium 2000). The world of private troubles, the site of the authentic, or real, self, has become a public commodity.

THE INTERVIEW GOES TO HOLLYWOOD

It remained for Hollywood to authorize the interview as a primary method of gathering information about social issues, selves, and the meanings of personal experience. Soon Hollywood was telling stories about newspaper reporters (*The Front Page*, 1931), detectives and private eyes (*The Maltese Falcon*, 1931, 1941), psychoanalysts and psychiatrists (*Spellbound*, 1945), spies and secret agents (*Saboteur*, 1942), and market researchers (*Desk Set*, 1957). More recently, the movies have offered spoofs of sociologists (*The Milagro Beanfield War*, 1988) and anthropologists (*Krippendorf's Tribe*, 1998).

Each of these film genres glamorized the interview as a form of interaction and as a strategy and technique for getting persons to talk about themselves and others (see Holstein and Gubrium 1995). Journalists, detectives, and social scientists were presented as experts in the use of this conversational form. Hollywood led us to expect that such experts will use this form when interacting with members of society. Furthermore, it led us to expect that persons, if properly asked, will reveal their inner selves to such experts.

And thus the key assumptions of the interview society were soon secured. The media and Hollywood cinema helped solidify the following cluster of beliefs: Only skilled interviewers and therapists (and sometimes the person) have access to the deep, authentic self of the person; sociologists, journalists, and psychoanalysts know how to ask questions that will produce disclosures, often discrediting, about the hidden self; members of the interview society have certain experiences that are more authentic than others, and these experiences are keys to the hidden self (these are the experiences that have left deep marks and scars on the person); adept interviewers can uncover these experiences and their meanings to the person; nonetheless, persons also have access to their own experiences, and this increases the value of first-person narratives, which are the site of personal meaning.

When probing for the inner self, or when seeking information from an individual, interviewers are expected to use some method to record what is said in the interview. In the film *True Crime* (1999), Clint Eastwood plays Steve Everett, a burned-out, alcoholic reporter who becomes convinced that Frank Beachum, a black man due to be executed within 24 hours, is innocent. Eastwood tracks down Mr. Porterhouse, the man whose testimony led to Beachum's conviction. Everett and Porterhouse meet in a café and the following exchange unfolds:

Everett: Let me get this straight, you didn't really see the murder?

Porterhouse: I never said I did.

Everett: What did you see?

Porterhouse: I can't tell you how many times I've been over this. I went into Pokeums to use the phone. My car had overheated. Beachum jumped up from behind the counter. He was covered with blood and had a gun in his hand. He was bending over, stealing her necklace. He got one good look at me and then he ran out the store. My concern was for the girl. So I immediately dialed 911. I figured why should I run after a killer, when the police should do their job.

Everett: And they sure did it, didn't they.

Porterhouse: Aren't you gonna take some notes, or somethin'? Or use a tape recorder? Usually when I'm talkin' to a reporter they wanta keep some sort of record of what I've been sayin'.

Everett: I have a photographic memory [points to head]. I have a notebook right here [pulls a notebook and pen out of his jacket pocket].

Everett refuses to write anything in his notebook, and Porterhouse challenges him: "I did some checking on you. You're the guy who led the crusade to get the rapist released. That lying what's his name? Had all your facts straight on that one too, didn't you?"

Everett next interviews Beachum in his prison cell. Beachum's wife, Bonnie, is there too. (The reporter who had originally been assigned to the case was killed in a car accident.)

Beachum: I guess you wanta hear how it feels to be in here.

Everett: Yeah, it's a human interest piece.

Beachum: I feel isolated. I feel fear, pain, fear of prison, fear of being separated from my loved ones. All those fears rolled up into one.

[Everett takes notebook out of pocket.]

Beachum: I want to tell everyone that I believe in Jesus Christ, our Lord and Savior.

[Everett scribbles on page of notebook: BLV, JC.]

Beachum: I came into my faith late in life. Did a lot of bad things. . . . I believe that the crooked road remains straight, that's what the Bible says.

[Everett scribbles on page of notebook: LORD, SAV, CARO, STRAIT.]

Beachum: Is there any more that you want?

Everett: You don't know me. I'm just a guy out there with a screw loose. Frankly I don't give a rat's ass about Jesus Christ. I don't even care what's right or wrong. But my nose tells me something stinks, and I gotta have my faith in it, just like you have your faith in Jesus. . . . I know there's truth out there somewhere. . . . I believe you.

Bonnie Beachum: Where were you?

Everett: It wasn't my story.

Beachum clearly expected Everett to ask him how he felt about being on death row. Beachum expected to tell a reporter a deeply personal story about what this experience means to his inner, authentic self. Indeed, Everett's presence in the prison elicits such a story from Beachum. To paraphrase Holstein and Gubrium (2000:129), the prison interview with a journalist is now a natural part of the death row identity landscape. But Everett, through his note taking, mocks this assumption. He has no desire to record the inner meaning of this experience for Beachum. This is unlike the desire illustrated in the excerpt from the *SportsCenter* interview above, in which Sal Paolantonio sought and got from Kurt Warner a self-validating, self-congratulatory story about hard work and success in American life.

THE INTERVIEW MACHINE AS AN EPISTEMOLOGICAL APPARATUS

The interview society uses the machinery of the interview to methodically produce situated versions of the self. This machinery works in a systematic and orderly fashion. It structures the talk that occurs in the interview situation. There is an orderly mechanism "for designating who will speak next" (Holstein and Gubrium 2000:125). Using the question-answer format, this mechanism regulates the flow of conversation. Talk occurs in question-answer pairs, for the asking of a question requires an answer. Turn taking structures this give-and-take. The rule of single speakership obtains: One persons speaks at a time. Interviews, in this sense, are orderly, dramaturgical accomplishments. They draw on local understandings and are constrained by those understandings. They are narrative productions; they have beginnings, middles, and endings.

The methodology of asking questions is central to the operation of this machine. Different epistemologies and ideologies shape this methodological practice. Four epistemological formats can be identified:

the objectively neutral format, the entertainment and investigative format, the collaborative or active interview format, and the reflexive, dialogic interview format.[2] In each format, the asking of a question is an incitement to speak, an invitation to tell a story; in this sense the interview elicits narratives of the self (Holstein and Gubrium 2000). The place of the interviewer in this process varies dramatically. In the *objectively neutral format*, the interviewer, using a structured or semistructured interview schedule, attempts to gather information without influencing the story that is being told. Holstein and Gubrium (2000) correctly observe that the demands of ongoing interaction make the " 'ideal' interview a practical impossibility, because the interview itself always remains accountable to the normative expectancies of competent conversation as well as to the demand for a good story to satisfy the needs of the researcher" (p. 131).

In the *entertainment and investigative format*, the interviewer often acts as a partisan, seeking to elicit a story that will sell as an entertainment commodity or can be marketed as a new piece of information about a story that is in the process of being told. In this format, the interviewer asks leading, aggressive questions as well as friendly questions, questions that allow the subject to embellish on a previous story or to give more detail on the meanings of an important experience (see Altheide, Chapter 20, this volume). Paolantonio's interview with Warner employs the entertainment format. This is a friendly interview that shows both Warner and Paolantonio in a good light. Steve Everett's interview with Mr. Porterhouse in *True Crime* illustrates the investigative version of this format. Everett is aggressive and hostile; he seeks to discredit Porterhouse as a witness.

In the *collaborative or active format*, interviewer and respondent tell a story together (see Holstein and Gubrium 1995:76-77). In this format a conversation occurs. Indeed, the identities of interviewer and respondent disappear. Each becomes a

storyteller, or the two collaborate in telling a conjoint story. The *SportsCenter* interview excerpt above also illustrates this format, as together Sal and Kurt tell a story about the meaning of this victory for Kurt's life.

In the *reflexive interview format*, two speakers enter into a dialogic relationship with one another. In this relationship, a tiny drama is played out. Each person becomes a party to the utterances of the other. Together, the two speakers create a small dialogic world of unique meaning and experience. In this interaction, each speaker struggles to understand the thought of the other, reading and paying attention to such matters as intonation, facial gestures, and word selection (see Bakhtin 1986:92-93).

Consider the following excerpt from the 1982 film *Chan Is Missing*, directed by Wayne Wang. Set in contemporary San Francisco, the film mocks popular culture representations of stereotypical Asian American identities. It also mocks social science and those scholars who point to language as an answer to cultural differences. The following Lily Tomlin-like monologue is central to this position. In the monologue, racial and ethnic identities are constructed. This construction is directly connected to the use of the objective interview format. The speaker is a female Asian American attorney. She is attempting to find Mr. Chan, who had an automobile accident just days before he disappeared. She is speaking to Jo, a middle-aged Chinese American cab driver, and Jo's young "Americanized" nephew, Steve. They are at Chester's Cafe. The young attorney is dressed in a black masculine-style suit, with a white shirt and dark tie.

> You see I'm doing a paper on the legal implications of cross-cultural misunderstandings. [nods head] Mr. Chan's case is a perfect example of what I want to expose. The policeman and Mr. Chan have completely different culturally related assumptions about what kind of communication [shot of Steve,

then Jo] each one was using. The policeman, in an English-speaking mode, asks a direct factual question—"Did you stop at the stop sign?" He expected a yes or a no answer. Mr. Chan, however, rather than giving him a yes or a no answer, began to go into his past driving record —how good it was, the number of years he had been in the United States, all the people that he knew—trying to relate different events, objects, or situations to what was happening then to the action at hand. Now this is very typical. . . . The Chinese try to relate points, events, or objects that they feel are pertinent to the situation, which may not to anyone else seem directly relevant at the time. . . . This policeman became rather impatient, restated the question, "Did you or did you not stop at the stop sign?" in a rather hostile tone, which in turn flustered Mr. Chan, which caused him to hesitate answering the question, which further enraged the policeman, so that he asked the question again, "You didn't stop at the stop sign, did you?" in a negative tone, to which Mr. Chan automatically answered, "No." Now to any native speaker of English, "No" would mean, "No I didn't stop at the stop sign." However to Mr. Chan, "No I didn't stop at the stop sign" was not "No I didn't stop at the stop sign" [Jo shakes head, looks away]. It was "No, I didn't not stop at the stop sign." In other words, "Yes I did stop at the stop sign." Do you see what I'm saying? [camera pans room]

Then, in a voice-over, Jo comments, "Chan Hung wouldn't run away because of the car accident. I'm feeling something might have happened to him" (see Denzin 1995a:105).

Here the speaker, the young attorney, attempts to dialogically enter into and interpret the meanings that were circulating in Mr. Chan's interview with the policeman. In so doing, she criticizes the concept of cross-cultural communication, showing through her conversation that meanings are always dialogic and contextual.

This text from Wang's film is an example of how the reflexive, dialogic interviewer deconstructs the uses and abuses of the interview—uses that are associated with the objectively neutral and entertainment/investigative formats. This text suggests that interpretations based on the surface meanings of an utterance sequence are likely to be superficial. To paraphrase Annie Dillard (1982:46), serious students of society take pains to distinguish their work from such interpretive practices.

At another level, reflexively oriented scholars, such as Mikhail Bakhtin, contend that there is no essential self or private, real self behind the public self. They argue that there are only different selves, different performances, different ways of being a gendered person in a social situation. These performances are based on different interpretive practices. These practices give the self and the person a sense of grounding, or narrative coherence (Gubrium and Holstein 1998). There is no inner or deep self that is accessed by the interview or narrative method. There are only different interpretive (and performative) versions of who the person is.

Steve Everett embodies one version of the reflexive interviewer. He has no interest in the inner self of the person he is interviewing, no interest in right or wrong. He only seeks the truth, the truth that says an injustice may have been done. Wang's Asian American attorney is another version of this interviewer; she understands that the self is a verbal and narrative construction.

THE INTERVIEW AND THE DRAMATURGICAL SOCIETY

The text from the Kurt Warner interview presented above suggests that the metaphor of the dramaturgical society (Lyman 1990), or "life as theater" (Brissett and Edgley 1990; Goffman 1959:254-55), is no longer a metaphor. It has become interactional reality. Life and art have become mirror images of one another. Reality, as it is visually experienced, is a staged, social production.

Jonathan Raban (1981) provides an example of how life and television coincide. In a TV ad "beamed by the local station in Decorah, an Iowa farmer spoke stiffly to the camera in testimony to the bags of fertilizer that were heaped in front of him" (p. 123). Here the personal testimony of the farmer, a hands-on expert, authorizes the authenticity and value of the product. This message is carried live, staged in the frame of the TV commercial; a real farmer says this product works. The farmer's awkwardness comes, perhaps, from the fact that he must look at himself doing this endorsement, knowing that if he sees himself looking this way, others will as well.

The reflected, everyday self and its gendered presentations are attached to the cinematic/televisual self. Herbert Blumer (1933) provides an example. An interview respondent connects her gendered self to the Hollywood screen:

> *Female, 19, white, college freshman.*—When I discovered I should have this coquettish and coy look which all girls may have, I tried to do it in my room. And surprises! I could imitate Pola Negri's cool or fierce look. Vilma Banky's sweet and coquettish attitude. I learned the very way of taking my gentlemen friends to and from the door with that wistful smile, until it has become a part of me. (P. 34)

Real, everyday experiences are judged against their staged, cinematic, video counterparts. The fans of Hollywood stars dress like the stars, make love like the stars, and dream the dreams of the stars. Blumer provides an example:

> *Female, 24, white, college senior.*—During my high-school period I particularly liked pictures in which the setting was a millionaire's estate or some such elaborate place. After seeing a pic-

ture of this type, I would imagine myself living such a life of ease as the society girl I had seen. My day-dreams would be concerned with lavish wardrobes, beautiful homes, servants, imported automobiles, yachts, and countless suitors. (P. 64)

With this dramaturgical turn, the technology of the media "disengages subjects from their own expressions. . . . Individuals become observers of their own acts. . . . Actions come to be negotiated in terms of a media aesthetic, both actor and spectator live a reality arbitrated by the assumptions of media technicians" (Eason 1984:60). David Altheide and Robert Snow (1991) provide an example from the Richard Nixon presidency. In a memo to H. R. Haldeman dated December 1, 1969, Nixon wrote:

> We need a part-or full-time TV man on our staff for the purpose of seeing that my TV appearances are handled on a professional basis. When I think of the millions of dollars that go into one lousy 30-second television spot advertising deodorant, it seems to me unbelievable that we don't do a better job of seeing that Presidential appearances [on TV] always have the very best professional advice. (quoted in Altheide and Snow 1991:105; see also Oudes 1989:46)

And because of the same media aesthetic, Kurt Warner has learned how to talk the form of sports talk that Ron Shelton mocks in his 1988 film *Bull Durham*. So, too, does Frank Beachum expect Steve Everett to record his moral story.

The main carriers of the popular in the postmodern society have become the very media that are defining the content and meaning of the popular; that is, popular culture is now a matter of cinema and the related media, including television, the press, and popular literature. A paradox is created, for the everyday is now defined by the cinematic and the televisual. The two can no longer be separated. A press conference at the 1988 Democratic National Convention is reported thus:

> A dozen reporters stood outside CBS's area, and as was so often the case at the convention, one began interviewing another. A third commented wryly on the interview: "Reporter interviews reporter about press conference." (Weiss 1988:33-34; also quoted in Altheide and Snow 1991:93)

Reporters are reporting on reporters interviewing reporters.

◆ Studying the Interview in Cinematic Society

The cinematic apparatuses of contemporary culture stand in a twofold relationship to critical inquiry. First, the cultural logics of the postvideo, cinematic culture define the lived experiences that a critical studies project takes as its subject matter. How these texts structure, and give meaning to the everyday must be analyzed. At the same time, critical ethnographies of the video-cinematic text must be constructed, showing how these texts map and give narrative meaning to the crucial cultural identities that circulate in the postmodern society.

Consider race, the racial self, and Hollywood cinema. Ana Lopez (1991) reminds us that "Hollywood does not represent ethnics and minorities; it creates them and provides an audience with an experience of them" (pp. 404-5). Consider her argument in terms of the following scene from Spike Lee's highly controversial 1989 film *Do the Right Thing*. Near the film's climax, as the heat rises on the street, members of each racial group in the neighborhood hurl vicious racial slurs at one another:

Mookie: [to Sal, who is Italian, and Sal's sons, Vito and Pino] Dago, wop, guinea, garlic breath, pizza slingin' spaghetti bender, Vic Damone, Perry Como, Pavarotti.

Pino: [to Mookie and the other blacks] Gold chain wearin' fried chicken and biscuit eatin' monkey, ape, baboon, fast runnin', high jumpin', spear chuckin', basketball dunkin' ditso spade, take you fuckin' pizza and go back to Africa.

Puerto Rican man: [to the Korean grocer] Little slanty eyed, me-no speakie American, own every fruit and vegetable stand in New York, bull shit, Reverend Sun Young Moon, Summer 88 Olympic kick-ass boxer, sonofabitch.

White policeman: You Goya bean eatin' 15 in the car, 30 in the apartment, pointy red shoes wearin' Puerto Ricans, cocksuckers.

Korean grocer: I got good price for you, how am I doing? Chocolate egg cream drinking, bagel lox, Jew asshole.

Sweet Dick Willie: [To the Korean grocer] Korean motherfucker . . . you didn't do a goddamn thing except sit on your monkey ass here on this corner and do nothin. (See Denzin 1991:129-30)

Lee wants his audience to believe that his speakers are trapped within the walls and streets of the multiracial ghetto that is the Bedford-Stuyvesant area of New York. Their voices reproduce current (and traditional) cultural, racial, and sexual stereotypes about blacks (spade, monkey), Koreans (slanty eyed), Puerto Ricans (pointy red shoes, cocksuckers), Jews (bagel lox), and Italians (dago, wop). The effects of these in-your-face insults are exaggerated through wide-angled, close-up shots. Each speaker's face literally fills the screen as the racial slurs are hurled.[3]

Lee's film presents itself as a realist, ethnographic text. It asks the viewer to believe that it is giving an objectively factual, authentic, and realistic account of the lived experiences of race and ethnicity. The film performs race and ethnicity, and does so in ways that support the belief that objective reality has been captured. The film "realistically" reinscribes familiar (and new) cultural stereotypes, for example, young gang members embodying hip-hop or rap culture. Lee's text functions like a documentary film.

THE CINEMATIC SOCIETY AND THE DOCUMENTARY INTERVIEW

It is this documentary impulse and its reliance on the objectively neutral interview format that I now examine through an analysis of Trinh T. Minh-ha's 1989 film *Surname Viet Given Name Nam*. This is a film about Vietnamese women, whose names change or remain constant depending on whether they marry foreigners or other Vietnamese. In this film, Trinh has Vietnamese women speak from five different subject positions, representing lineage, gender status, age status, leadership position, and historical period (see Trinh 1992). This creates a complex picture of Vietnamese culture.

The film is multitextual, layered with pensive images of women in various situations. Historical moments overlap with age periods (childhood, youth, adulthood, old age), rituals and ceremonies (weddings, funerals, war, the market, dance), and daily household work (cooking) while interviewees talk to offscreen interviewers. There are two voice-overs in English, and a third voice sings sayings, proverbs, and poetry in Vietnamese (with translations into English appearing as texts on the screen). There are also interviews with Vietnamese subtitled in English and interviews in English synchronized with the onscreen images (Trinh 1992). The interviews are reenacted in the film by Vietnamese actresses, who are then interviewed at the end of the film about their experiences of being performers in the film.

The film allows the practice of doing reflexive interviews to enter into the construction of the text itself, thus the true and the false, the real and the staged intermingle; indeed, the early sections unfold like a traditional, realist documentary film (Trinh 1992). The viewer does not know that the women onscreen are actresses reenacting interviews. Nor does the viewer know that the interviews were conducted in the United States, not Vietnam (this becomes apparent only near the end of the film).

In using these interpretive strategies, Trinh creates a space for the critical appraisal of the politics of representation that structure the use of interviews in the documentary film. In undoing the objectively neutral interview as a method for gathering information about reality, Trinh takes up the question of truth (see Trinh 1992). Whose truth is she presenting—that given in the onscreen interview situation or that of the women-as-actresses who are interviewed at the end of the film?

Trinh begins by deconstructing the classic interview-based documentary film that enters the native's world and brings news from that world to the world of the Western observer. In its use of the traditional, nondialogic interview method, documentary film, like Spike Lee's *Do the Right Thing*, starts with the so-called real world and the subject's place in that world. It uses an aesthetic of objectivity and a technological apparatus that produces truthful statements (images) about the world (Trinh 1991). Trinh (1991:39) argues that the following elements are central to this apparatus:

◆ The relentless pursuit of naturalism, which requires a connection between the moving image and the spoken word

◆ Authenticity—the use of people who appear to be real and locating these people in "real" situations

◆ The filmmaker/interviewer presented as an observer, not as a person who creates what is seen, heard, and read

◆ The capture only of events unaffected by the recording eye

◆ The capture of objective reality

◆ The dramatization of truth

◆ Actual facts presented in a credible way, with people telling them

Along with these elements, the film-interview text must convince spectators that they should have confidence in the truth of what they see. These aesthetic strategies define the documentary interview style, allowing the filmmaker-as-interviewer to create a text that gives the viewer the illusion of having "unmediated access to reality" (Trinh 1991:40). Thus naturalized, the objective, documentary interview style has become part of the larger cinematic apparatus in American culture, including a pervasive presence in TV commercials and news (Trinh 1991:40).

Trinh brings a reflexive reading to these features of the documentary film, citing her own texts as examples of dialogic documentaries that are sensitive to the flow of fact and fiction, to meanings as political constructions (see Trinh 1991). Such texts reflexively understand that reality is never neutral or objective, that it is always socially constructed. Filmmaking and documentary interviewing thus become methods of "framing" reality.

Self-reflexivity does not translate into personal style or a preoccupation with method. Rather, it centers on the reflexive interval that defines representation, "the place in which the play within the textual frame is a play on this very frame, hence on the borderlines of the textual and the extra-textual" (Trinh 1991:48). The film becomes a site for multiple experiences.

A responsible, reflexive, dialogic interview text embodies the following characteristics (Trinh 1991:188):

◆ It announces its own politics and evidences a political consciousness.

◆ It interrogates the realities it represents.

◆ It invokes the teller's story in the history that is told.

◆ It makes the audience responsible for interpretation.

◆ It resists the temptation to become an object of consumption.

◆ It resists all dichotomies (male/female and so on).

◆ It foregrounds difference, not conflict.

◆ It uses multiple voices, emphasizing language as silence, the grain of the voice, tone, inflection, pauses, silences, repetitions.

◆ It presents silence as a form of resistance.

Trinh creates the space for a version of the cinematic apparatus and the interview machine that challenges mainstream film. She also challenges traditional ethnography and its use of objective and investigative interview formats.

Reflexive texts question the very notion of a stable, unbiased gaze. They focus on the pensive image, on silences, on representations that "unsettle the male apparatus of the gaze" (Trinh 1991:115). This look makes the interviewer's gaze visible. It destabilizes any sense of verisimilitude that can be brought to this visual world. In so doing, it also disrupts the spectator's gaze, itself a creation of the unnoticed camera, the camera that invokes the image of a perfect, natural world, a world with verisimilitude. In using these interpretive strategies, Trinh creates the space for the viewer (and listener) to appraise critically the politics of representation that structure the documentary text.

CULTIVATING REFLEXIVITY

Learning from Trinh, I want to cultivate a method of patient listening, a reflexive method of looking, hearing, and asking that is dialogic and respectful. This method will take account of my place as a co-constructor of meaning in this dialogic relationship. As an active listener (Bourdieu 1996), I will treat dialogue as a process of discovery. I will attempt to function as an empowering collaborator. I will use the reflexive interview as a tool of intervention (Burawoy 1998). I will use it as a method for uncovering structures of oppression in the life worlds of the persons I am interviewing. As a reflexive participant, I will critically promote the agendas of radical democratic practice. In so doing, I hope to cultivate a method of hearing and writing that has some kinship with the kinds of issues Gloria Naylor (1998) discusses in the following passage:

> Someone who didn't know how to ask wouldn't know how to listen. And he coulda listened to them the way you been listening to us right now. Think about it: ain't nobody really talking to you. . . . Really listen this time; the only voice is your own. But you done just heard about the legend of Saphira Wade. . . . You done heard it in the way

> we know it, sitting on our porches and shelling June peas . . . taking apart the engine of a car—you done heard it without a single living soul really saying a word. (P. 1842)

But this is also a sociology that understands, here at the end, that when we screen our dreams and our crises through the canvases and lenses that the cinematic, electronic society makes available to us, we risk becoming storied versions of somebody else's versions of who we should be.

■ Notes

1. The underlying logic of the sports interview is mocked in the following dialogue from Ron Shelton's 1988 film *Bull Durham*. Kevin Costner, who plays an aging pitcher named Crash Davis, says to his protégé, played by Tim Robbins, "Now you are going to the Big Show. You have to learn how to talk to interviewers. When they ask you how it feels to be pitching in Yankee Stadium, you say, 'I just thank the good Lord for all his gifts. I owe it all to him. I just take it one game, one pitch at a time.' "

2. These interview formats blur with the three types of relationships between interviewer and interviewee that Mishler (1986) identifies: informant and reporter, collaborators, and advocates.

3. Although prejudice crosses color lines in this film, racial intolerance is connected to the psychology of the speaker (e.g., Vito). It is "rendered as the *how* of personal bigotry" (Guerrero 1993:154). The economic and political features of institutional racism are not taken up. That is, in Lee's film, "the *why* of racism is left unexplored" (Guerrero 1993:154).

■ References

Atkinson, P. and D. Silverman. 1997. "Kundera's *Immortality:* The Interview Society and the Invention of Self." *Qualitative Inquiry* 3:304-25.

Altheide, D. L. 1995. *An Ecology of Communication.* New York: Aldine de Gruyter.

Altheide, D. L. and R. P. Snow. 1991. *Media Worlds in the Postjournalism Era.* New York: Aldine de Gruyter.

Bakhtin, M. M. 1986. *Speech Genres and Other Late Essays.* Austin: University of Texas Press.

Blumer, H. 1933. *Movies and Conduct.* New York: Macmillan.

Bourdieu, P. 1996. "Understanding." *Theory, Culture & Society* 13:17-37.

Brissett, D. and C. Edgley, eds. 1990. *Life as Theater: A Dramaturgical Sourcebook.* 2d ed. New York: Aldine de Gruyter.

Burawoy, M. 1998. "The Extended Case Method." *Sociological Theory* 16:4-33.

Denzin, N. K. 1991. *Images of Postmodern Society: Social Theory and Contemporary Cinema.* London: Sage.

———. 1995a. *The Cinematic Society: The Voyeur's Gaze.* Thousand Oaks, CA: Sage.

———. 1995b. "Information Technologies, Communicative Acts, and the Audience: Couch's Legacy to Communication Research." *Symbolic Interaction* 18:247-68.

———. 1997. *Interpretive Ethnography: Ethnographic Practices for the 21st Century.* Thousand Oaks, CA: Sage.

Dillard, A. 1982. *Living by Fiction.* New York: Harper & Row.

Eason, D. 1984. "The New Journalism and the Image-World: Two Modes of Organizing Experience." *Critical Studies in Mass Communication* 1:51-65.

Fontana, A. and J. H. Frey. 1994. "Interviewing: The Art of Science." Pp. 361-76 in *Handbook of Qualitative Research,* edited by N. K. Denzin and Y. S. Lincoln. Thousand Oaks, CA: Sage.

———. 2000. "The Interview: From Structured Questions to Negotiated Text." Pp. 645-72 in *Handbook of Qualitative Research,* 2d ed., edited by N. K. Denzin and Y. S. Lincoln. Thousand Oaks, CA: Sage.

Goffman, E. 1959. *The Presentation of Self in Everyday Life.* Garden City, NY: Doubleday.

Gottschalk, S. 2000. "Escape from Insanity: 'Mental Disorder' in the Postmodern Moment." Pp. 18-48 in *Pathology and the Postmodern: Mental Illness as Discourse and Experience,* edited by D. Fee. London: Sage.

Gubrium, J. F. and J. A. Holstein. 1997. *The New Language of Qualitative Method.* New York: Oxford University Press.

———. 1998. "Narrative Practice and the Coherence of Personal Stories." *Sociological Quarterly* 39:163-87.

Guerrero, E. 1993. *Framing Blackness: The African American Image in Film.* Philadelphia: Temple University Press.

Heyl, B. S. 2001. "Ethnographic Interviewing." In *Handbook of Ethnography,* edited by P. A. Atkinson, A. Coffey, S. Delamonte, J. Lofland, and L. H. Lofland. London: Sage.

Holstein, J. A. and J. F. Gubrium. 1995. *The Active Interview.* Thousand Oaks, CA: Sage.

———. 2000. *The Self We Live By: Narrative Identity in a Postmodern World.* New York: Oxford University Press.

Jackson, M. 1998. *Minimia Ethnographica.* Chicago: University of Chicago Press.

Lopez, A. M. 1991. "Are All Latins from Manhattan? Hollywood, Ethnography, and Cultural Colonialism." Pp. 404-24 in *Unspeakable Images: Ethnicity and the American Cinema,* edited by L. D. Friedman. Urbana: University of Illinois Press.

Lyman, S. M. 1990. *Civilization: Contents, Discontents, Malcontents and Other Essays in Social Theory.* Fayetteville: University of Arkansas Press.

Mishler, E. G. 1986. *Research Interviewing: Context and Narrative.* Cambridge, MA: Harvard University Press.

Naylor, G. 1998. "Excerpt from *Mamma Day.*" Pp. 1838-42 in *Call and Response: The Riverside Anthology of the African American Literary Tradition,* edited by P. L. Hill. Boston: Houghton Mifflin.

Oudes, B. 1989. *From the President: President Nixon's Secret Files.* New York: Harper & Row.

Park, R. E. 1950. "An Autobiographical Note." Pp. v-ix in R. E. Park, *Race and Culture: Essays in the Sociology of Contemporary Man.* New York: Free Press.

Raban, J. 1981. *Old Glory: A Voyage down the Mississippi.* New York: Random House.

Scheurich, J. J. 1995. "A Postmodernist Critique of Research Interviewing." *International Journal of Qualitative Studies in Education* 8:239-52.

Trinh T. M. 1989. *Surname Viet Given Name Nam* (film). Women Make Movies, Museum of Modern Art, Cinenova, Idera, Image Forum.

———. 1991. *When the Moon Waxes Red: Representation, Gender and Cultural Politics.* New York: Routledge.

———. 1992. *Framer Framed.* New York: Routledge.

Vecsey, G. 2000. "Kurt Warner Gives Hope to Others." *New York Times,* February 1, p. C29.

Vidich, A. J. and S. M. Lyman. 1994. "Qualitative Methods: Their History in Sociology and Anthropology." Pp. 23-59 in *Handbook of Qualitative Research,* edited by N. K. Denzin and Y. S. Lincoln. Thousand Oaks, CA: Sage.

Weiss, P. 1988. "Party Time in Atlanta." *Columbia Journalism Review,* September/October, pp. 27-34.

41

THEIR STORY/MY STORY/OUR STORY

Including the Researcher's Experience in Interview Research

◆ Carolyn Ellis
Leigh Berger

I cull books on interviewing from my bookcases and arrange them alphabetically on an empty shelf, the product of the last few days of cleaning my office. Even the floor, my favorite storage area, is empty of the usual stacks of manuscripts and books. I feel free, excited to begin the chapter I'm writing with Leigh on including the researcher's experience in interview research. The task shouldn't be too difficult. The chapter is a continuation of what I've spent the last 15 years doing, which is using autoethnographic stories—stories written in an autobiographical genre about the relationship of self, other, and culture—in social science research. Since researchers now commonly discuss their own experience in

their research, this project seems timely. I smile contentedly as I think about the growing recognition and acceptance of autoethnography among interpretive ethnographers.

As I muse about autoethnography, I hear Leigh's car pull in to the driveway. I herd our four barking dogs into the bedroom, then open the front door. Once Leigh is seated in my office and has admired how tidy and organized it is, I let the dogs out of the bedroom. Without pausing, they fly up the stairs. By the time I get to my office, three of them surround Leigh, sniffing her clothes, while the fourth sits on her lap, licking her face. Leigh greets them warmly. They quickly settle down and claim their usual sleeping spots in my office.

AUTHORS' NOTE: We thank Arthur P. Bochner, Jim Holstein, Jay Gubrium, and two anonymous reviewers for their helpful reading and editing of the manuscript for this chapter.

Leigh sits beside me as I type notes from our conversation into the computer. "Okay, now let's think about what we have to do here," I start. "The paper isn't due for six months, so we have plenty of time."

"Oh, yes, plenty," Leigh agrees. "What exactly is our goal?"

"The idea is to look at the inclusion of the researcher's experience in interview research," I respond. "Not so much how we do it, but the different forms it can take and how this inclusion deepens and enriches what we know about our subjects of research. Maybe we'll try to move from lesser to greater degrees of involvement of the researcher and provide exemplars of the variety."

"So you mean a typology then?" Leigh inquires, laughing because I usually argue for stories and against typologies. "So what would we include?"

I too chuckle at the irony and continue, "I thought we'd select an excerpt from my piece with Lisa and Christine [Ellis, Kiesinger, and Tillmann-Healy 1997] on interactive interviewing where we talk about bulimia. And one from my chapter with Art [Ellis and Bochner 1992] on co-constructed narratives, where we discuss our decision to have an abortion early in our relationship."

"They both show the researcher as full participant," Leigh says thoughtfully, breaking through the emotions that arise as I think about including a selection from the abortion story. It's hard emotionally for me to confront that piece, but I want to include it because it provides an instructive exemplar of co-constructed narratives. "What will we do for exemplars that show inclusion to a lesser degree?" Leigh continues.

"That's where you come in," I respond. "Remember that interview you did with Karen, your informant at the Messianic Judaism congregation? The one where you reflect on what the interview makes you think about in terms of your own spiritual beliefs? How about an excerpt from that interview story?"

"I thought you didn't like the Karen I presented there," Leigh says.

"I don't. It always seemed to me that you needed to write in more of your reflections on spirituality as you wrote that story. More reflection would have deepened readers' understanding of Karen's beliefs and made her a more complex character. This is your chance to add more reflection, although the focus should remain on Karen."

"So we'll have three types then—interactive interviews, co-constructed narratives, and reflexive dyadic interviews?" Leigh asks, returning the focus to the paper rather than thinking more deeply about the difficulties of revealing her thoughts about her own spirituality, especially to an academic audience.

"No, there are four. Your interview with Karen parallels the interactive interview I did with Lisa and Christine. They're both interactive and emergent in that we're concerned with the stories created and evolving in each interview context. But while the three authors act as researchers and participants alike in the bulimia study, you as researcher stay focused on the experience of your participant, Karen."

"Okay, I see where you're going. And what's the parallel case to co-constructed narrative?"

"In our co-constructed narrative about abortion, Art and I focused exclusively on our story. We wrote our experiences separately and then came together to co-construct them into a collective story we could agree on. The parallel case would be one in which a researcher carries out the same process with another couple, staying focused on them but adding her reflections. I know you've wanted to interview a family member of someone who converted to Messianic Judaism. I'd like you to do a co-constructed interview with the convert and family member, if you're willing."

"I'd love to," Leigh says hesitantly. "But after thinking about it, I'm not sure it's a good idea to interview family members of Messianic Jews. Families seem to have so much animosity toward those who convert. I don't want to cause my participants any problems."

"But I have planned to interview the rabbi of the Messianic congregation and his wife about their roles in marriage," she continues, more enthusiastically. "I could conduct this as a co-constructed interview and include questions about how their families reacted to their conversion."

"That would work," I respond.

"Though I'm not sure the couple would be willing to write anything," Leigh cautions.

"You could interview them separately and tape record their individual stories and then work with them to co-construct their collective story."

"I can do that," Leigh responds. "I'll set up the interview. What needs to be done now?"

"Before turning to the cases, let's work on the literature review to show how some of the trends in the literature have guided us to where we are. This will set the stage for the reader."

◆ Literature Review

Many researchers, particularly feminists, have debunked the myth of value-free scientific inquiry (Cook and Fonow 1986; Reinharz 1992; Roberts 1981), calling for researchers to acknowledge their personal, political, and professional interests. Instead of insisting on a rigid separation of researcher and respondent, they have construed the interview as an active relationship occurring in a context permeated by issues of power, emotionality, and interpersonal process (Holstein and Gubrium 1995).

Interviews now are commonly understood as collaborative, communicative events that evolve their own norms and rules (Briggs 1986; Kvale 1996). As a result, researchers who use interviews should not focus solely on the outcomes—the words spoken by interviewees—but should examine the collaborative activities of interviewees from which these outcomes are produced (Chase and Bell 1994; Futrell and Willard 1994; Hertz 1995; Jorgenson 1995; Langellier and Hall 1989; Miller 1996; Mishler 1986; Suchman and Jordan 1992).

The literature is replete with examples of writers who draw attention to the relational aspects of the interview and the interactional construction of meaning in the interview context (Holstein and Gubrium 1995; Langellier and Hall 1989; Oakley 1981). This interaction is situated in the context of an ongoing relationship where the personal and social identities of both interviewers and interviewees are important factors (Collins 1986; DeVault 1990; Riessman 1987), and the relationship continually changes as each responds to the other (Jorgenson 1991, 1995). Thus interpretive scholars note the "double subjectivity" (Lewis and Meredith 1988) that abounds in interviewing: how each participant's attitudes, feelings, and thoughts affect and are affected by the emerging reciprocity between the participants.

Moving away from the orthodox model of distance and separation, interactive interviewers often encourage self-disclosure and emotionality on the part of the researcher (see Johnson, Chapter 5, this volume). Researcher involvement can help subjects feel more comfortable sharing information and close the hierarchical gap between researchers and respondents that traditional interviewing encourages (Bergen 1993; Cook and Fonow 1986; Douglas 1985; Hertz 1995; Oakley 1981), thus promoting dialogue rather than interrogation (Bristow and Esper 1988). In this interactive context, respondents become narrators who improvise stories in response to the questions, probes, and personal stories of the interviewers (Bruner 1986; Chase and Bell 1994; Holstein and Gubrium 1995; Mishler 1986; Myerhoff 1992; Riessman 1993).

The interactive interviewing context requires an interviewer who listens empathically (Mies 1983; Stanley and Wise 1983), identifies with participants, and shows respect for participants' emotionality (Mies 1983). Unlike traditional research, where feelings and private realms of experience often are avoided, interactive interviews assume that emotions and personal meanings are legitimate topics of research (Anderson et al. 1987). As a result, interactive interviewers explore sensitive topics that are intimate, may be personally discrediting, and normally are shrouded in secrecy (Renzetti and Lee 1993). When doing so, they pay close attention to ethical issues of privacy and confidentiality as they try to listen "around" and "beyond" the words (DeVault 1990), exploring the unsaid as much as the said (Ochberg 1996).

Research on sensitive and emotional topics has raised questions about the boundary between research interviewing and psychotherapy (Lieblich 1996; Miller 1996; see also Gale 1992; Maione and Chenail 1999). Writers ponder how a researcher should respond if a subject asks for help (Lieblich 1996; Miller 1996), and they question the morality of withholding information and assistance (Cook and Fonow 1986; Oakley 1981; Reinharz 1992; Webb 1984). Some researchers have voiced concern about the emotional harm that can be done to participants with whom they develop personal relationships (Stacey 1988) and about the emotional load such relationships can place on researchers who are not trained as psychotherapists (Brannen 1988; Edwards 1993). On the other hand, some writers emphasize the positive therapeutic benefits that can accrue to respondents and interviewers who participate in interactive interviews (Bloom 1996; Gale 1992; Hutchinson, Wilson, and Wilson 1994; Langellier and Hall 1989; Romanoff 2001; Rosenwald 1996).

Increasingly, research monographs are concerned with subjects' responses to what is written about them (see Agronick and Helson 1996; Apter 1996; Chase 1996; Josselson 1996). After spending time as an interviewee, Colleen Larson (1997) laments that she did not feel she was able to tell in the interview setting the complex

and authentic stories she needed and wanted to tell (see also Tillmann-Healy and Kiesinger 2000). Along with other researchers, especially those doing participatory and action research (e.g., Stringer 1996), Larson (1997) suggests a more collaborative and longitudinal approach that gives interviewees opportunities to reflect on, elaborate, and build on the stories they have told before, as well as to respond to and change what gets reported (see also Belenky et al. 1981-82; Duelli Klein 1983; Tripp 1983). Many interactive researchers have heeded the call for research that gives something useful back to respondents and their communities, rather than research that is pointed exclusively toward restricted academic audiences (Bochner and Ellis 1996; Finch 1984; Oakley 1981). Consequently, interviewers must now face their ethical responsibility to their respondents on both personal and policy levels (Bergen 1993).

Interactive interviews offer opportunities for self-conscious reflection by researchers as well as respondents. Some interviewers now discuss how they feel during interviews (Bar-On 1996; Berger 1997b; Kiesinger 1998; Markham 1998; Miller 1996) and how they use their feelings, experiences, and self-analysis to understand and interpret the experiences of others (DeVault 1999; Douglas 1985; Ellis 1998; Griffith and Smith 1987). Barbara Rothman (1986), for example, writes poignantly about the pain she suffered as she took on the feelings of women who had undergone amniocentesis. By immersing herself in the women's emotional worlds, she felt able to understand and to write about their experiences in a more powerful and empathic way than she could have by keeping herself emotionally distanced. Other researchers discuss how they gained insight into themselves and were changed in the process of interviewing others (Miller 1996). For example, Janet Yerby and Bill Gourd (1994) show how their interviews with members of a nontraditional family had a therapeutic effect on their own marital relationship. Kristin Langellier and Deanna Hall (1989), moreover, report that their research on mother-daughter storytelling strengthened their relationships with their own mothers.

Some writers now advocate that researchers interview peers with whom they have already established relationships (Platt 1981; Segura 1989) and that researchers make use of the everyday situations in which they are involved (Stanley and Wise 1983). Qualitative researchers have co-constructed narratives with family members and friends (Austin 1996; Berger 1997b; Bochner and Ellis 1992; Ellis and Bochner 1992; Fox 1996; Kiesinger 1992; Yerby and Gourd 1994). They have studied themselves reflexively in the process of observing, communicating with, and writing about others (Abu-Lughod 1995; Adler and Adler 1997; Angrosino 1998; Behar 1995; Blee 1998; Crapanzano 1980; Dumont 1978; Ellingson 1998; Goodall 1991, 1999; Jones 1998; Karp 1996; Kondo 1990; Lagerwey 1998; Lather and Smithies 1997; Linden 1993; Markham 1998; Myerhoff 1978; Mykhalovskiy 1997; Ponticelli 1996; Rabinow 1977; Richardson 1992, 1997; Rosaldo 1989; Tillmann-Healy 1996; Zola 1982b). They have conducted interactive interviews about emotional and personal topics (Ellis et al. 1997; Kiesinger 1998; Macleod 1999). And they have introspectively written about their own experiences and their own families as the focus of research (Behar 1996; Berger 1997a, 1997b, 1998; Bochner 1997; Clough 1999; Coyle 1998; Denzin 1999; Eisenberg 1998; Ellis 1993, 1995, 1996; Ellis and Bochner 1996, 2000; Jago 1996; Kolker 1996; Kulick and Willson 1995; Krieger 1991, 1996; Lewin and Leap 1996; Murphy 1987; Pacanowsky 1988; Paget 1993; Payne 1996; Perry 1996; Quinney 1996; Richardson 1997, 1998; Robillard 1997, 1999; Ronai 1992, 1995; Ross and Geist 1997; Shostak 1996; Tillmann-Healy 1996; Trujillo 1998; Williams 1991; Zola 1982a).

Following the trajectory suggested here, interviewing then changes in function as well as form (J. A. Holstein and J. F. Gubrium, personal communication). The interviewing process becomes less a conduit of information from informants to researchers that represents how things are, and more a sea swell of meaning making in which researchers connect their own experiences to those of others and provide stories that open up conversations about how we live and cope.

♦ Types of Collaborative Interviewing

The stories interviewers write about themselves range from descriptions of the researcher's positioning and experience with the subject at hand to reflections on the research process and the researcher's feelings about the subject being explored, to including the researcher as a central character in the story, to making the personal experience of the researcher the focus of the study. In this section, we organize these variations into several categories, which we call reflexive dyadic interviews, interactive interviews, mediated co-constructed narratives, and unmediated co-constructed narratives. We present an exemplar for each of these categories to illustrate how the different types of interviews unfold. After this discussion, we return to our introductory narrative and conclude with a co-constructed story that reflects on the methodological issues involved in the writing of this chapter and on how including the researcher's self in interviews deepens and enriches our understanding of our own research interests.

REFLEXIVE DYADIC INTERVIEWING: ACTS OF FAITH

Reflexive dyadic interviews follow the typical protocol of the interviewer asking questions and the interviewee answering them, but the interviewer typically shares personal experience with the topic at hand or reflects on the communicative process of the interview. In this case, the researcher's disclosures are more than tactics to encourage the respondent to open up; rather, the researcher often feels a reciprocal desire to disclose, given the intimacy of the details being shared by the interviewee. The interview is conducted more as a conversation between two equals than as a distinctly hierarchical, question-and-answer exchange, and the interviewer tries to tune in to the interactively produced meanings and emotional dynamics within the interview itself (Gubrium and Holstein 1997). When telling the story of the research, the interviewers might reflect deeply on the personal experience that brought them to the topic, what they learned about and from themselves and their emotional responses in the course of the interview, and/or how they used knowledge of the self or the topic at hand to understand what the interviewee was saying (see Johnson, Chapter 5, this volume). Thus the final product includes the cognitive and emotional reflections of the researcher, which add context and layers to the story being told about participants, such as in the exemplar discussed below.

* * *

Since January 1998, I (Leigh) have been conducting ethnographic fieldwork for my dissertation at Dalet Shalom Messianic Jewish Congregation. Messianic Jews believe that they can retain their cultural and ethnic ties to Judaism while recognizing Jesus (whom they refer to by the Hebrew name "Yeshua") as the Messiah. My dissertation research traces my own spiritual journey throughout the ethnographic process, showing how my stories and feelings about religion interact with the stories told by my participants.

The congregation's secretary, Karen, immediately became my main "informant," guiding me through the world of Messianic Judaism. Although I brought some questions to my first interview with Karen, I let the conversation evolve as naturally as possible. Karen spoke at length about her spiritual experiences over the course of her life and also asked me several questions about my own experiences, such as how often I had thought about Jesus and what my religious experiences were like as I was growing up. As we became more comfortable with each other, I began volunteering information, for example, pointing out similarities between our relationships with our grandparents. Although our taped interviews focused mainly on Karen, what she expressed during the interviews undoubtedly was dependent on "the particularities of the subject/researcher relationship" (Angrosino 1989:315-16). For example, my identity as a Jewish woman gave us several points of connection. Several times, Karen said, "Well, you understand what it's like to be Jewish," or "There are all these Jewish cultural things, but I know I don't have to explain all that to you."

An added dimension to our research relationship was that Karen wanted me to accept Yeshua as the Messiah. I felt uncomfortable about her desire for me to convert, while I simultaneously felt that my resistance disappointed her. These relational and emotional dynamics shaped our interview process. Kathleen Blee (1998) explains that the interaction between interviewer and respondent is intensely complex, shaped by positive and negative emotions, and that "just as researchers may try to invoke rapport to facilitate data collection in interviewing situations, so too respondents may attempt to create emotional dynamics to serve their strategic interests" (p. 395).

Karen's stories led me to reflect on my own experiences with and feelings about religion and spirituality. At times, I related to the story Karen told, able because of our similarities to appreciate her attachment to Jewish ritual. Other times, it was difficult for me to understand her transformation from a fairly liberal, secular Jew to an evangelical Messianic Jewish believer. I reflect on these many complexities within the story that follows.

I sip my herbal tea and place the cup back down on the small Formica café table. Karen and I have been in the Barnes and Noble coffee shop for about 15 minutes. "So, how did you find Dalet Shalom?" I ask her.

Karen adjusts her glasses and smiles, "A woman I know heard about it. I was telling her that I had been thinking a lot about Yeshua, but that I also knew I loved being Jewish. I could never change from being Jewish because that is so much a part of who I am. After this woman told me about it, I found the phone number in the phone book and called. I remember the rabbi spoke to me for about an hour. He was so warm and understanding! He told me to come to services on Saturday to see how I felt." She laughs at the memory. "I remember that I arrived late and the place was packed! I couldn't find a seat. Finally, I noticed there was one right up front—right under the rabbi's nose! So there I am, right up front, and . . ." Her eyes fill with tears in the pause before she continues, "I can't even name one of the songs I heard that day. I can't even tell you what the sermon was about. All I know is I was filled with emotion, and I couldn't stop crying. Finally, the rabbi asked if there was anyone who wanted to come know Yeshua, so I raised my hand. I was still crying, and as I moved to go up to the rabbi, I saw a male figure next to me wearing white. I felt this sense of comfort, as if I could just rest my head on his shoulder."

She picks up a napkin to wipe her eyes. "I felt the presence of his arm around me, and I knew it was Yeshua, welcoming me."

"Wow," I respond. I wonder what I would have done if I had ever felt a spiritual presence during a religious service. I wonder if I will ever experience during fieldwork the kind of visions of which Dalet Shalom congregants often speak.

"So were services at Dalet Shalom very different from what you were used to growing up?" I continue, seeking a point of contact.

She nods, "Yes. At home we basically celebrated Passover and Hanukkah."

I smile in recognition. "Yes, me too. At least in my parents' house. I mostly learned about religion from my grandparents because they were more observant. They kept kosher and my grandfather walked to synagogue."

Her eyes light up with familiarity. "Yes! Exactly! We have pictures of my grandfather saying the morning service prayers."

"So would you say your perspective on life has changed a lot since your conversion?"

"Oh, definitely! I can't even express how much happier I am, Leigh. One day you'll get to feel that too. I know that Yeshua is calling to you. Just don't be afraid of what the Lord has to offer you. Just ask Him what He wants. Have you had questions—questions you've wanted to ask God?"

I contemplate what she is asking me, feeling awkward about having to answer questions about my own beliefs. I know I shouldn't feel this uncomfortable. After all, she's been open to answering my questions. I decide that I owe her an honest response. "Yes, I suppose I have. Sometimes I wonder why certain things happen, like why my sister is deaf and diabetic, or why my father is mentally ill. And I wonder about why good things happen too, like what causes things to go extremely well."

She is quiet for a moment. "So, what do you think about Dalet Shalom?"

"Oh, there are many things I like about Dalet Shalom. I like the dancing and the praise and worship. I think the people are warm and inviting." I remain silent about the things that I do not feel comfortable with or agree with, such as their fundamental belief in the Bible, and their stance against homosexuality and abortion.

"Where do you think the Lord is taking you?" Karen pushes some strands of hair behind one ear.

"I don't know. That's not really a question I ever ask," I confess.

"Do you think about Yeshua a lot?"

I smile because doing this research has caused me to think of Yeshua almost daily.

"Of course. But thinking about Yeshua has always been scary for me." The image of Jesus I held in my mind prior to my excursions into the Messianic world was one of dangerous attraction. Salvation extends its hands of allure and promise, a sense of safety blanketed with acceptance. I have always been afraid of Jesus, a fact I hesitate to admit. After all, how can I fear the epitome of peace and kindness? But for me, Jesus was too complicated to face. I didn't know what to do with the concept of Him, and of salvation. I was fascinated by the ease with which some people seemed to believe—really believe—in their religion. Not only fascinated, but envious. Why couldn't it be that easy for me? Why was I constantly questioning, debating, doubting?

"Intellectualizing it makes it harder. I think that is where the fear comes from. But I've also seen a big change in you since you've been coming to services."

Surprised by this observation, I inquire, "What change?"

"You seem more peaceful. I think the Lord is trying to talk to you." She watches as some people order pastries and coffee. "I just can't imagine how I lived my life without Yeshua in it. I just . . . I am a completely different person now. I look at these people, and ask myself how they all do it." As she says this, I wonder if her real question is how I do it. "How do they live their lives without Him? Not having that belief . . ." Her voice breaks and tears slip from her eyes. "The thought of it just makes me so sad."

Witnessing her deep emotional reaction, I think about my own emotional discomfort when the conversation turned to me and my beliefs. Am I being dishonest by not telling her the things that trouble me? I know that I cannot convert to Messianic Judaism, so am I unfairly deceiving her by not directly telling her this?

In listening to and writing Karen's stories about faith and conversion, I come to understand more fully the complicated array of emotions that accompanies religious belief. By revealing her stories, Karen pres-

ents me with an opportunity to witness her religious experiences and try them on for size. When Karen begins to ask me questions about my beliefs, she opens a window into how she sees me and allows me to reflect upon how it feels to be an interviewee. This leaves me better able to understand Karen's emotions as a participant in my research. Rather than Karen's merely reporting information to me, the researcher, our emotions are produced in an unfolding conversation (Holstein and Gubrium 1995). Here, readers can connect to the story either through my perceptions or through Karen's, interpreting our experiences for themselves.

As a researcher, I do not dismiss Karen's beliefs as mere social constructions, but allow that she actually experienced something spiritually transcendent during her conversion. Although I am unable to relate fully to Karen's religious beliefs, I remain open to her descriptions and gain new insights into my own beliefs by questioning my faith and comparing it to her spiritual beliefs. Her descriptions of visions, in fact, cause me to reflect on whether or not I may someday experience something similar.

Although qualitative researchers often focus on how positive and empathic feelings shape their interactions in the field, my not being able to identify completely with Karen illuminates how negative or differing emotions can shape ethnographic relationships as well (Blee 1998). Both participant and researcher negotiate the emotional dynamics of any situation, positive or negative. Narrative's openness to multiple perspectives can successfully communicate the difficulties and dilemmas of studying those with whom we do not connect as well as those we do.

INTERACTIVE INTERVIEWS: EXPERIENCING BULIMIA

Sometimes interviewers desire to position themselves in a more self-consciously collaborative way than occurs in reflexive one-on-one interviews. The prototype of this approach is the interactive interview, which usually takes place in a collaborative, small group setting (Ellis et al. 1997). The goal of an interactive interview is for all those participating, usually two to four people, including the primary researcher, to act both as researchers and as research participants. Each is given space to share his or her story in the context of the developing relationships among all participants. Interactive interviewing works especially well when all participants also are trained as researchers (see, e.g., Ellis et al. 1997; Tillmann-Healy and Kiesinger 2000). Even if that is not the case, however, participants can be given an important role in determining the research process and its content, as well as in interpreting the meanings of the interviews (see, e.g., Macleod 1999). Likewise, the feelings, insights, and stories that the primary researcher brings to the interactive session are as important as those of other participants; the understandings that emerge among all parties during interaction —what they learn *together*—are as compelling as the stories each brings to the session. Ideally, all participants should have some history together or be willing to work to develop a strong affiliation. It is helpful for the researcher as well as coparticipants to have personal experience with the topic under investigation; if that is not the case, the researcher should be willing to take on the role and lived experience of other participants in this regard. This strategy is particularly useful when the researcher is examining personal and/or emotional topics that require reciprocity and the building of trust, such as eating disorders, as in the case elaborated below.

＊　＊　＊

The article "Interactive Interviewing: Talking about Emotional Experience" (Ellis et al. 1997) describes a project about the embodiment and meanings of bulimia. The research was conducted by three researchers: Lisa, at the time a Ph.D. candidate; Christine, a recent Ph.D.; and Carolyn, a

professor. Lisa and Christine have had direct personal experience with bulimia; I (Carolyn) have not. But we all share concerns about food and bodies that arise from women's immersion in cultural contradictions of thinness of bodies and abundance of food and commodities. Also, we share a desire to work within a methodological and theoretical orientation that privileges emotional and concrete details of everyday life and that critically interrogates traditional social science interviewing practices.

In this project, we were interested in learning more about bulimia and how we might methodologically access important bodily, emotional, and interactive details of the experience. Our final paper consisted of four stories, two written from transcripts of dyadic interviews between Christine and Lisa (Kiesinger 1995; Tillmann-Healy 1996), one from the numerous interactive sessions in which all three of us participated, and the last from a dinner at a restaurant written as a narrative ethnography. These accounts tell the story of the development of our interactive interviewing project, with each story adding another textured layer to the approach.

The excerpts below come from the story I wrote about our group discussions. I reflect from the position of a participant who did not engage in the bulimic behaviors we sought to understand. As an "outsider," I show how I consider the problems and risks in this kind of interview situation, how I attempt to get inside a world I know little about, and how Christine and Lisa move me to consider my own relationship to my body and food and to see the similarities between their world and mine.

Initially I do not understand that I am fashioning my story as well (Parry 1991). I hesitantly add my thoughts about food— how I too love to eat and am a "sugar junky," how I try to remember to pause after one helping to wait for fullness cues. I also speak of our differences—how my generation enjoyed adventure and being out of control, while theirs seems to want to have it all—adventure and control, fullness and thinness. . . .

They say that going out to dinner is their favorite activity. I admit it is one of mine too. They say they obsess about food. I deny that I do, but then think about how much food enters my consciousness on any given day. As Christine and Lisa say, working on this project makes me think more about food and my body. Is it healthy to concentrate so much on these details? "There's too much to accomplish to become consumed by these issues," I think. For me, perhaps, but not for young women like Christine and Lisa whose lives are intertwined so intricately with the subject. I wonder how our research can help us to refashion personal and cultural scripts about women's bodies.

Sometimes I think I understand their world so well, it frightens me. I imagine being them and purging, and then admiring my thin body. Then I recoil, knowing I won't engage in such an unhealthy activity. At age 45, health is more important than appearance. What about when I was 20? What if someone had suggested purging to me then? Were the diet pills I occasionally took so different?

I understand the desire to be physically attractive. In my sophomore year in college I lost 47 pounds by eating 500 calories a day. I wore contact lenses, even when I had to take Excedrin each time I inserted the lenses into my watery, itchy, red eyes. What really separates me from Lisa and Christine? Twenty years? Growing up in an earlier decade where those in my cohort rebelled against gender stereotypes and were less inclined to take on cultural labels? Coming of age in a decade where the thrill of "getting away with something" involved drugs and sex, not bingeing and purging? We all have our temptations.

Being thin is less important to me now than ever. Is that because other issues have my attention now, and I have a career I enjoy and a mate who loves and accepts me? Or is it only because a "beautiful" body is less attainable now? I remember a scene that I've never told anyone about. At a con-

ference a few years ago, I wore a bathing suit to the hotel pool and ran into Christine and her sister; their perfection moved me to wrap my body in a towel.

All these thoughts abound as I try to enter their worlds, become their bodies with their concerns. I neither can nor want to distance myself from this intimate, interactive situation. I try to normalize what they do, to take away some of the stigma of shit and vomit. That doesn't mean I support their self-destructive behaviors; it means I am willing to consider that they are not so different from the rest of us. All women are affected by cultural messages of abundance and thinness.

Prior to this study, I had some contact with women who were bulimic. Although I voiced concerns about the role that cultural expectations played in their behavior, I saw them as "other," as strange, different from me. The more they told me about themselves, in some ways the more other they became. It was only when I put myself in an interview situation with them and we talked in depth about our relationship to food that I started to see the similarities between them and me. It is only since then that I can admit how much food and the desire to be physically attractive have affected my life. As we share stories, we create deeper understandings in interaction with each other. I am no longer healthy and they sick; I am not their professor and they my students. We are three women together trying to understand an intimate part of our lives. We have taken different routes, but even those become more understandable as we trace our histories, think about the messages and values of the different eras in which we grew up, and discuss where we are in our lives now. By seeing myself as a subject as well as a researcher, I am able to move from the distanced observer to the feeling participant and learn things I could not learn before, both about them and about me.

Eating dinner together also provides another occasion for learning about eating disorders. The short excerpt below shows the co-construction from our three independent accounts of our collective story of eating together.

When Carolyn sits down across from her, Christine instantly is aware that they have never eaten together. Because she tends to synchronize her eating pattern with others, she panics. Will Carolyn eat quickly or slowly? Does she talk while eating? Is she a sharer? Will Carolyn, a seasoned ethnographer, be watching her every move?

Lisa's stomach growls continuously as they sit talking without picking up their menus. Why don't they order? When finally the waitress stops to ask if they want an appetizer, Carolyn looks questioningly at Lisa and Christine. Lisa can almost taste the salty-greasy choices—oozing processed-cheese nachos, fried mozzarella sticks, and hot chicken wings. But she's not feeling particularly "bad," and she knows Christine almost never eats appetizers. They shake their heads "no" simultaneously. Carolyn had considered ordering some for the table, but after their response, she thinks that she really shouldn't have them either.

Carolyn takes one of the menus tucked behind the salt and pepper shakers. Immediately Christine and Lisa reach for menus as well. It seems they have been waiting for Carolyn to make the first move. Right away, Carolyn knows what she wants. But Christine and Lisa grasp their menus tightly, immersed, reading line by line. For what seems like minutes to Carolyn, they say nothing. Carolyn continues holding her menu in front of her face so they don't feel rushed. She'd like to know what they're thinking. Minutes go by.

This excerpt portrays the impact of bulimia on how we thought, felt, and related as we ate a meal. These stories reveal our concerns about sharing food, our rules for eating with others, the inner dialogues that occupy us during dinner, our obsession with the food in front of us, our concerns about how we were being perceived by oth-

ers, and the similarities and differences in the eating experiences of women who do and do not have bulimia.

MEDIATED AND UNMEDIATED CO-CONSTRUCTED NARRATIVES

Researchers also may share their stories through co-constructed narratives, or tales jointly constructed by relational partners about epiphanies in their lives (see Bochner and Ellis 1996; Ellis and Bochner 1996). This approach may be *mediated,* meaning a researcher may monitor the conversation of two relational partners, or *unmediated,* meaning a researcher might study his or her own relationship with a partner or two researchers might study their relationship with each other. In either case, these stories show dyads engaged in the specific, concrete, and unique details of daily living. They cope with the untidy ambiguities, ambivalences, and contradictions of relationship life and try to make sense of their local situations. This type of research focuses on the interactional sequences by which interpretations of lived experiences are constructed, coordinated, and solidified into stories. The local narratives that are jointly produced thus display couples in the process of "doing" their relationships as they try to turn fragmented, vague, or disjointed events into intelligible, coherent accounts.

MEDIATED CO-CONSTRUCTED NARRATIVES: ONE FLESH

Mediated co-constructed narrative research is similar to conjoint marital therapy (Satir 1983), where couples participate together in therapy after providing their different perspectives on the same events. It also is related to interpersonal process recall (Elliott 1986; Gale 1992), where an interviewer asks two participants to watch a tape of their therapy session and rate and comment on meaningful moments. In mediated co-constructed narratives, a researcher serves as coordinator and moderator as a couple engages in a joint construction of an epiphany in their relationship. The researcher asks them to reflect on the event and to write, talk into a tape recorder, or be interviewed separately about the experience. Then, in the presence of the researcher, the participants hold a discussion about the event. Sometimes the participants are asked to exchange transcripts or stories written independently and read each other's constructions before the discussion, although this may not always be feasible. Nevertheless, the goal is to produce or co-construct a version of the event that takes into account each individual's perspective.

The researcher stays in the role of researcher as he or she take notes on (and/or tapes) the interaction. The researcher then writes the participants' story from the materials they provide as well as from his or her own observation of and participation in their co-construction. While writing their story, the researcher reflects on how he or she, as the researcher, views the participants and analyzes their conversational style and their negotiation of the co-construction of their separate stories. The researcher might describe events leading up to the interview, the physical and emotional environment of the interview, and his or her role in the interview (for example, what the researcher asked the participants, how he or she responded to them, and how the researcher possibly influenced the conversation). The account of the interview process becomes part of the story told. The researcher also might include his or her views on and experience with the topic at hand and discussion of how his or her views and feelings have developed and changed as a result of observation of and interaction with the participants. Including the researcher's experience helps readers understand more about the researcher's interest in the topic and provides background for how he or she interprets what is going on.

Although the researcher becomes a character in the story, his or her identity remains one of researcher rather than researcher-participant as in interactive interviewing. As shown below, the focus stays on the experience of the other research participants rather than on the interviewer.

* * *

As my (Leigh's) dissertation research continued, I wanted to interview a couple about the role of Messianic belief in married life. Every congregant I asked referred me to Rabbi Aaron Levinson and his wife, Rebecca. I was repeatedly told that they "really live up to biblical guidelines for marriage." Both Aaron and Rebecca had Messianic conversion experiences in the early 1970s. Aaron became very involved at the organizational level of the Messianic movement and opened Dalet Shalom in 1980. A few years later, he and Rebecca met and married. When I approached Aaron and Rebecca, they were happy to be interviewed, and I set up an appointment with them in June 1999.

Originally, I conducted two-hour taped interviews separately with Aaron and Rebecca about their marriage and Messianic expectations for marriage roles. I then conducted a follow-up joint interview once the initial interviews were transcribed. Ideally, I would have preferred that Aaron and Rebecca had had a chance to read and comment on one another's transcripts, but because of their schedules, we were not able to arrange for this. In addition, once I read the original transcripts, I realized that Aaron and Rebecca agreed with one another about every topic we had discussed. Asking them to comment on each other's individual stories most likely would not have produced stories any different from the ones they had already told me. I thought that I might be able to show the collaborative nature of their relationship by writing a story of our interview that included details about how they interacted.

In writing a story based on our follow-up joint interview session, I used what I already knew about Aaron and Rebecca, shaping their mannerisms and voices. I recalled the way Aaron had cried when he described first meeting Rebecca. I remembered Rebecca's blush at detailing their first telephone conversation, and how nervous she had been. Many times while volunteering in the Dalet Shalom office, I witnessed Aaron's romantic gestures toward Rebecca, such as unexpectedly buying her flowers. All of these elements filtered my understanding of their relationship prior to our interviews.

In this excerpt, I interview Aaron and Rebecca together, reflecting on their interaction with one another and the emotions present in the interview. In addition, I show how Rebecca's reflections on her family's reaction to her conversion cause me to reflect on my own family relationships. Unlike Karen, Aaron and Rebecca do not ask me questions about my own experiences; they remain focused on the questions I have for them.

I shuffle my transcripts and smile at Rabbi Aaron Levinson and his wife, Rebecca. "Well, I have the transcripts from the last interview here." I pat the papers beneath my hand. A few weeks earlier, I had interviewed Aaron about the role of men in Messianic theology, following that with a separate interview with Rebecca about women's roles. "And I must say that even though I interviewed you separately, there is no disagreement between the two of you."

They both smile, and Aaron takes Rebecca's hand in his own. "We're always together. We have to be, as it says in the Bible, one flesh." I notice the intimacy and genuine caring for one another that their gestures communicate.

"Well, I did have some questions about some things we didn't get to cover in our previous interviews."

"Yes?" *Aaron runs his hand over his white beard and adjusts his glasses. The sparkling*

brown eyes behind them inquisitively meet my own.

"How do you advise congregants about handling nonbelieving family members?" *In the Messianic world, non-Messianic followers (especially Jewish ones) are referred to as "nonbelievers."*

"Well, I'll let Rebecca handle that. She's dealt a lot with that issue." *Aaron willingly gives the floor to Rebecca, showing a trust and respect for her experience with this topic. This give-and-take, primarily orchestrated by Aaron, seems characteristic of much of their communication with one another.*

Pushing some of her curly brown hair behind her shoulders, Rebecca takes the floor without missing a beat. "How do you handle nonbelieving family members? First of all, you do so with love because love really does conquer all. I'll give you an example. I have a family member who lives in Israel, and who is an observant and religious Jew—not Messianic. When he addresses less observant family members, he pounds ideas into them: 'You have to do this, you have to do that.' The more he does that, the more the rest of the family resists worshiping the Lord. They see him as forcing beliefs on them. Now when Aaron and I go visit my family in Israel, we love them. We don't force any ideas on them, and because of that, they're more willing to be open to our ideas."

She pauses, contemplating her next words, and I wonder if she is considering whether or not to say anything else. I wait, allowing the silence to encourage further information. "I will say that when I first came to know the Messiah, I was very anxious about how this would be received in my family. I had all these questions about how to deal with my loyalty to my family, our rabbi, my friends . . ." *Her voice trails off, and I perceive that her eyes are focused somewhere on the past. Her gold bracelets quietly clink together as she adjusts her hair once again, and her expression is sad as she finds her voice.* "My family sat shivah [a

Jewish mourning practice for the dead] when I came to accept the Messiah. I was no longer a part of the family, and we didn't speak for a long time." Aaron reaches out to touch her shoulder, offering emotional support. She touches his hand and smiles, reassuring him that she is okay.

Sitting in my seat, I feel my chest tighten, and I wonder at the power of a newfound faith that allowed her to face this pain in exchange for her belief. I try to imagine my own family cutting me off for choosing an alternative belief system. If that were the fate that awaited me, how many of my choices in life would be different? Biting my lip, I think about how much my grandparents were opposed to family members' dating and marrying anyone outside of the Jewish faith. If they were still alive, would I be in a long-term relationship with a Christian man? I wonder if I would have crossed that line anyway, and what the results would have been. Although I cannot imagine my grandparents completely cutting me off, I cannot say for sure. I ponder whether anticipation of their deep disappointment might have been enough to dissuade me from dating men outside of Judaism.

I realize Rebecca has continued to talk, and I snap back to attention. "Eventually, someone in the Jewish community spoke to my parents. To this day, I have no idea what this person said to them, but whatever it was, I know she is resting in peace with the Lord because my family decided to ask me for forgiveness, and I was accepted back into the family again." *She says this quickly, as if to brush aside the emotions this story makes her recall.* "But I never ever push any of my beliefs on them. All I do is act with love, and show them through my loving actions and attitude how strong my dedication to the Lord is. And although at this time they do not know the Messiah as we know the Messiah, they see that Aaron and I are very observant. Their acceptance comes through our love and through us letting the fruit of our belief show." *She turns to Aaron for confirmation, and he smiles and nods at her words.*

I hesitate, wanting to probe further into this experience. Rebecca has tied things up a little too nicely, and I know that her feelings regarding her family's sudden "forgiveness" were probably not as simple as she describes. Certainly, she must have felt some residual anger for their rejection. Did she really "forgive and forget" that easily? But I don't want to force her into areas she may not be emotionally ready or willing to enter. I decide to let it go for now. Maybe there will be a better time or place for such questions later.

In the scene above, I am open with readers about my own thoughts and feelings during my conversation with Aaron and Rebecca. Letting readers know what I think and how I emotionally react to Aaron and Rebecca brings them into the interview context with me, allowing them to watch as the interview progresses and to imagine how they might respond in a similar situation. Some readers may draw conclusions that are different from mine, or may interpret Aaron's and Rebecca's words and actions in a different light.

Throughout our interview, Aaron and Rebecca enact marriage roles through actions rather than words. Although they hold more traditional views about marriage than I do, I am able to see and understand how and why these roles work for them. Their silent exchanges reinforce Messianic views on how spouses should interact: The man is considered the head of the household and the person who, after discussions with the wife, has the final say on all decisions. For example, even though Rebecca holds the floor when answering my question about non-Messianic family members, she does so only after Aaron has directed her to do so. Rebecca seeks Aaron's confirmation and support of what she says through nonverbal behaviors such as exchanging glances and touching. Aaron reassures her through actions such as nodding and placing a hand on her shoulder. Allowing their interaction to evolve more naturally reveals how Aaron and Rebecca's co-construction is beneath the surface of their words, in a conversational dance so skillfully performed that their give-and-take appears almost flawless.

UNMEDIATED: CO-CONSTRUCTED NARRATIVES: DECIDING ABOUT ABORTION

In unmediated co-constructed narratives, the focus turns directly to the self, as researchers examine their own relationships rather than the relationships of others. In such narratives, researchers use the same procedures as described above, except there is no outside researcher mediating the interview process. The two researchers, or a researcher and partner, write their stories separately, exchange them with each other, read them, and then discuss them. Then they attempt to co-construct a collective version. They might present the result in the form of a script, a short story, or an essay; or they might analyze or even perform their narrative for an audience. Other participants in the event might be asked to add their voices as well. Although the result is a collective interpretation, individual voices might be kept separate, as the exemplar below demonstrates.

* * *

"Telling and Performing Personal Stories: The Constraints of Choice in Abortion" (Ellis and Bochner 1992; see also Bochner and Ellis 1992) tells the story of a decision my partner, Art, and I (Carolyn) had to make upon discovering only 10 weeks into our relationship that I was pregnant. After much agonizing, I had an abortion. This experience had a profound impact on our relationship and our personal lives. For the next two months, we were numb, self-protective, and unable to express our thoughts and feelings about the abortion. When we finally broke through

our resistance, we realized how much the experience had affected us and how deeply we had ventured into our private and submerged registers of emotion.

With a self-consciously therapeutic motive, we decided to write a story about our experience to try to understand what had happened at a deep emotional level. We wanted to reveal ourselves to ourselves as we revealed ourselves to others. Hoping to provide companionship to others who may have been similarly bruised by the ambivalence and contradictions associated with the constraint of making such a choice, we attempted to share the complex emotions that were part of this experience so that readers might experience our experience—actually feel it—and consider how they might feel or have felt in similar situations. We tried to write in an open, revealing way that would connect us to readers, especially those who had themselves suffered the complexities of abortion. We hoped to tell enough in our story so that readers might, as Jaber Gubrium and James Holstein (1997) point out, connect our emotions to the cultures in which they arise.

In telling our story, we first independently constructed a detailed chronology of the emotions, events, decisions, and coping strategies that had taken place. After completing our individual accounts, we read each other's versions and began to co-construct a single story of what had happened. We took notes on our discussions and asked others with whom we had consulted during the decision making about the abortion to contribute to the narrative, thus producing a multivocal text.

We wrote our final story as a script that presented, in sequence, critical scenes in which we expressed our self-reflections, feelings, and analysis of the main events—the discovery and shock of the pregnancy, pre- and postdecision interactions, and the abortion procedure described side by side in both the female and male voices. Later, we performed this narrative at a professional social science conference, a step that became a vital part of our attempt to cope with and bring closure to this experience. The excerpt below details the abortion procedure in two voices, Ted's as Art's voice and Alice's as Carolyn's voice.

Alice: *The suction machine is turned on. I tighten my grip on Ted's wrists, he tightens his. I feel excruciating pain. I moan and scream. Everything speeds up. The nurse yells, "Deep breaths. Deep breaths." I try to, but the screams get in the way. Ted's face is now right next to mine. I hear his voice, sense his encouragement. I don't know what Ted is saying, but I'm glad he's here. There is confusion. I hear the suctioning noise, and then they're pulling out my whole uterus. I bear down, my nails sink into Ted's wrists. Then I am in the pain, going round and round like in a tangled sheet. I feel it being sucked out of my vagina. My god I can't stand the pain. I hear gut-wrenching screams. Then the doctor's voice, "Five more seconds, just five more seconds, that's all." I am comforted and know that I can stand anything for five seconds. I feel I am with friends. The nurse continues yelling, "Breathe. Breathe." And I try as hard as I can to breathe as I imagine one should when having a baby. Ted is encouraging, gripping. Then I feel another cutting as the doctor does a D&C to make sure nothing was missed. The pain takes over my full consciousness.*

Ted: *Suddenly I hear the rumble of the suction machine and I feel a vibration pass through Alice's body as the machine extracts the last remnants of the fetus. I see the blood and am repulsed by the horror of this crude technological achievement. I want to look away, but I can't. I am face-to-face with the terror of creation and destruction. Alice has a firm hold on my hands. I cannot turn away. She cannot escape the physical pain; I cannot feel it. I cannot evade the horror of what I see in front of me; she cannot witness it. My*

ears are ringing from the frenzied sound created by the simultaneous talking and screaming and rumbling that is engulfing the room. The action is fast and furious. Alice's ferocious cries submerge the sound of the machine. "Hold on, baby," I say. I clutch her hands as tight as I can. Her breathing intensifies, growing louder and louder. "Oh, god," she screams. "Oh, my god." Ironically, her cries and screams echo the sounds of orgasmic pleasure she released the afternoon this fetus was created.

Alice: *Then Quiet. The machine is turned off. "That's all," the doctor says. A nurse puts a pad between my legs and I have visions of blood gushing from my angry uterus. Ted's grip eases. I relax, but the leftover pain continues to reverberate through my body.*

Ted: *Then, abruptly, with no forewarning, the machine is turned off. Alice lies still, out of breath, quiet. The doctor's assistant whisks away the tray of remains covered by a bloody towel.*

In the literature on abortion, details of the emotional and communicative processes of the experience are obscure, leaving readers without a sense of the complexity, confusion, and vacillation often associated with the lived experience of abortion. The emotional trauma seems bleached of its most profound and stirring meanings. Most of the literature bypasses interpersonal and emotional conflicts in favor of political ideology or moral indignation. Because Art and I are both authors and subjects in our story, we have the freedom to explore emotional trauma as we experienced it separately and together. Although our own relationship may be vulnerable, we are not limited by concerns of doing emotional harm to other research participants or our fears about losing control of our words and experiences to another researcher. Thus we are able in our story to explore emotional complexities from both the female and male perspectives and to consider such graphic differences as those between Art's experience of grief and my experience of unworthiness or the meaning of my repeated use of the term *baby* juxtaposed against Art's references to *fetus*. These descriptive revelations lead us to contemplate further the significance of frames: grief versus self-contempt, physical pain juxtaposed against emotional pain, and the experience-near female voice compared to the more distanced male voice. Writing and discussing this story helps us to unify the past (the pregnancy and abortion) with an anticipated and hopeful future—to bring closure to this experience as one we might live with together.

◆ In the Middle of Flexibility and Confusion: Two or Three Things We Know for Sure (Allison 1995)

Books and papers cover my desk and surround my chair. Humming from the computer and printer fills the room. Staring at the screen, I feel walled in; the only way out is to finish this chapter. I pick up the stack of pages in front of me. The ragged edges, unevenly stapled paragraphs, and half sheets refute the order I try to impose by tapping all four sides of the stack on the desk. I read through the draft Leigh and I have written of "Their Story/My Story." It's already November 17th, I remind myself as I squint at the small date on my watch. I look again, just in case I've misread it. Jay Gubrium periodically reminds us of the December 1st deadline, and I don't want to be late. Besides, I need to move to all the other unfinished commitments I have taken on. I sigh. This chapter isn't coming together as we'd hoped.

Leigh and I have constructed a typology of kinds of interview studies that include the

researcher's experience and have used four exemplars from our own studies to demonstrate. The chapter works well enough in theory, but I'm not sure it's working in practice. Our interview exemplars don't quite match the ideal types we have described. And the continuum from lesser to greater involvement of the researcher—well, that hasn't worked either. What do we do now? It's too late to conduct other interviews or select other studies as exemplars.

I should have chosen my excerpts more carefully; Leigh and I should have worked more closely while she was doing her interviews for this chapter, I admonish myself. Now I have to rewrite my description of the types so that our exemplars are really exemplars. Or I will have to choose other excerpts, and Leigh will have to rewrite her interview stories to fit our types.

Choosing the former, I frantically start to edit our text. I glance again at my watch as I type. Leigh will be here in 30 minutes, and this is the only day this week I can work on our chapter. Next week is filled with dissertation defenses, proposal hearings, conference planning, and other deadlines. I type faster.

Suddenly a ray of light makes its way through a crack in the wall and a smile breaks over my face. I stop editing and start to type what I am thinking: In doing this chapter, Leigh and I are engaged in writing what we have called in the text an unmediated co-constructed narrative. She brings her (interview) stories and I bring mine, and we work to put them together in a co-constructed story we both agree on. We have written about how difficult these projects are to accomplish, how they never quite work out as you think they will, how it is important to leave room for improvisation, and how difficult it is for researchers to include their stories without taking over the stories of others. We agree that in our interview studies we're trying to reflect life as lived, not simply follow traditional social science procedures. But until now, we had forgotten to take our own advice in writing this chapter. Given our goals and flexible procedures, should it be a surprise that we are having trouble fitting our work into neat categories and traditional social science sections? Should it be a surprise that I feel compelled to include here our reflexive story of writing this chapter?

As I type this paragraph, Leigh pulls in to my driveway. I open the front door only a crack, so the dogs can't run out. Leigh squeezes through the narrow opening I provide and greets me and the barking dogs. "Quite a doorbell," she says, laughing.

I start to offer apologies for the noise, but instead just shrug, "I know. What can I say?"

As I fix glasses of tea, all four dogs take turns sniffing the smells of Leigh's dog hidden on her clothes. Our Australian shepherd Sunya, wide-eyed and poised in anticipation, drops a ball in front of Leigh, enticing her to play. Ande, our Jack Russell, jumps into her arms when she reaches down to pet Likker and Traf, the two rat terriers. As we move to my office, the dogs run in behind us. They knock the piles of books and papers across the floor, eliminating any possibility of organization, before they jump on Leigh and vie for attention. When I yell at them to be quiet, then squirt them with water from a bottle I keep in my office, they scamper playfully into the hallway, still barking. Apologizing to Leigh for the mess, I quickly close the office door. "There's no room," I yell as they whine and scratch on the wooden door.

I tell Leigh that our interview types and the excerpts we have chosen aren't quite fitting together. She seems disheartened and offers to rewrite her excerpts or to write other stories from her interviews. "Maybe it's okay that they aren't working," I offer. She looks at me quizzically, perhaps thinking that the herbal tea we're drinking has gone to my head. "Well, just think how you did your interviews," I say. "That summer we both were traveling. You also were writing your dissertation proposal and I was working on a book. We didn't have much

time to talk about how you'd do the interviews with your participants to fill in our last two 'cells.' "

Smiling at my use of the term cells, she replies, "I knew we were using your articles on co-constructed narratives and interactive interviews as two of our cases. So I reread those and then just let my interviews evolve."

"I know," I reply, "and often that's the best way to do it. Anyway, I didn't want to be too rigid about how you did them. I wasn't in the interview context with you, so there was much I didn't know. You also were using the interviews to gather data for your dissertation, not just this chapter."

"And my participants had their own constraints and agendas," Leigh says.

"As all participants do," I reply and we nod in agreement. "As we do in the writing of this chapter. Think how long it's taken us to find time to get together. That's the nature of research. Why should I have expected this to work exactly as planned? Why did I expect this situation to be any different?"

"So what's not working?" Leigh asks.

"Your dyadic interview. It doesn't really show you reflecting during the interview, like we say happens. Instead, you tell Karen's story and then you tell yours."

"Well, I was trying to show how Karen's story led me to reflect while I transcribed and wrote the interview. As Laurel Richardson [1994] says, writing served as a process of inquiry . . ."

"Just as in this piece we're writing now," I interrupt, "and it's all an evolving process."

Leigh nods and continues, "I also reflected during the interview process. But I was unsure of which reflective moment to focus on for the chapter. What else?"

I am impressed, as always, by her lack of defensiveness. Reminding myself that she is my student and this is the first time we have worked together as coauthors, I choose my words carefully. "Your interview participants in the co-constructed mediated narrative didn't read each others' individual transcripts before you met for a joint interview. I've always thought of that as an important part of the process."

"I asked them to, but when they said they didn't have time to read the transcripts before I came back for a second interview, well, I pushed a little, but I also didn't want to negatively impact my relationship with them because . . . well mainly because I care what they think. . . ."

"And it's not your style to be pushy . . . ," I interrupt, thinking about her reticence to push Rebecca on the emotions surrounding her family's sudden forgiveness of her conversion.

"No, it isn't," Leigh laughs. "Besides, Rabbi Aaron and Rebecca are authority figures in the temple. I needed them for my dissertation research. It didn't seem appropriate to push." (Similar to your relationship to me, I think.) "With Karen, it was different. We're peers and the interaction was on a different level."

I think about how different Leigh's interviews were from mine. Although both of us knew our respondents, my participants were close friends, long-term students, and loved ones. Leigh's interviews involved relationships made in the process of fieldwork that probably would not continue after her dissertation was done. My situation provided more latitude and, at the same time, less than hers did. In some ways, my participants and I could ask for more from each other and reveal more in the process because we knew each other so well. But because our lives were so intertwined, we also had a lot to lose if the interviews didn't go well. No matter the circumstances, though, my style was to push more than Leigh. I am reminded that we all have to find a comfortable interactive style in interviews that emphasizes relationship and communication.

"There didn't seem to be much to co-construct anyway," Leigh continues, breaking into my thoughts. "In the individual interviews, both of them said almost the same things and portrayed the same images in their stories about gender roles and reli-

gion. It was clear they had talked this over a lot."

"Even in the joint conversation," Leigh continues, "when I probed, they basically agreed. I took notice of the nonverbals, such as hand-holding and how they looked at each other, and they do seem to have a good relationship. But rather than both of them answering, each took over certain questions. That seemed to be where the agreement took place—they agreed on who should speak on which question. You can see how focused I am on dynamics in the interview."

"That explains, then, why your narrative doesn't have much of a co-constructed feeling," I say. "It's not so much they co-constructed a story as that they took turns telling individual stories . . ."

"Which, of course, is a form of co-construction," Leigh interjects.

I nod, pleased at her insight, and continue. "I think you might have gotten different stories had you asked them to discuss an epiphany that was yet unresolved, which may be necessary for this kind of interview to work best. What they gave you didn't center on a crisis or turning point that had not yet been processed, which is the idea."

As I talk, I think about my own unmediated co-constructed story with Art about abortion. "When Art and I wrote our stories, it was about an unresolved epiphany in our relationship. I couldn't wait to read his transcript and show him mine. The co-construction process we went through was very important. I wonder, then, why I chose an excerpt to present here that kept the two individual stories side by side instead of one that showed the co-construction process."

"There's also a problem with the portion I chose to demonstrate interactive interviews," I add, thinking that pointing out the problems in my cases will make Leigh feel more comfortable about the problems in hers. "It's all me and doesn't show Christine, Lisa, and me in interaction, and that's the whole point of interactive interviews

—that what happens in the interaction is as important as the stories each brings to the interview. Maybe I should show a different excerpt from both of these pieces or add a second."

"And I could always rewrite my story about Karen," Leigh offers, "to show how I reflected during the interview. But with Rebecca and Aaron . . . well how could I know ahead of time that they might not provide a good example of co-constructed narrative . . ." Her voice trails off. "I guess I should have concentrated more on an unresolved event, as you said, or pushed more in the interviews about their families' responses to their conversion." We stare at each other for a while. Then we simultaneously look at our watches, as though the gun is ready to go off to signify time to run toward the finish line.

"Well, we still have to be careful that we are trying to be truthful about what happened in the interviews, and not intruding too much into their stories," I respond. "At what point are we taking too much control over the stories that get told? Are we manipulating the 'data' to fit the categories and in doing so privileging our categories over the stories and the interview contexts? I'm concerned about that. I don't think I want to second guess the excerpts I initially chose from my published pieces, although I think I'll add an excerpt from my interaction with Christine and Lisa at dinner."

"Good idea," says Leigh. "I don't know how I could rewrite the story of Rebecca and Aaron to fit more with the way you describe co-construction in your article with Art."

"You can't. It's important for readers to see that this process doesn't always go the way you planned. Anyway, both excerpts, yours and mine, demonstrate that co-constructed stories sometimes retain individual voices, or sometimes never had them in the first place. But the co-constructed version presented is still the agreed-upon collective story."

"Good point. I do think, though, that there are good reasons to present another portion of Karen's story to show the reflec-

tion that went on during the interview process. I have all that in my notes, so it wouldn't be that difficult."

"I agree. I like that we're concentrating more on making our story work, flexibly dealing with what happened, rather than being too concerned with methodological rules."

"What do you think about using the conversation we're having as the conclusion to our chapter?" I ask suddenly. "Or is it too much of us, the authors, intruding into the research story?"

Leigh laughs, "It is interesting that the issues we deal with in writing this chapter are the same ones we encountered in doing our interview studies in the first place."

"Well, at least now I don't have to worry about our typology and our categories bleeding into each other. Instead we can view our schema as a heuristic device to introduce readers to the variety of ways interviewers can insert themselves into their interviews and the stories they write about others."

"Glad we resolved all that," Leigh says, breathing a sigh of relief.

"Not so fast. We still have the conclusion to write," I remind her, then silently remind myself not to dominate the conversation, as Leigh sometimes seems hesitant to challenge my authority. "What do we want to leave the readers with?"

"Well, the point of all this, other than showing the ways in which researchers can add their experiences to an interview, has been to show how what we learn in and about interviews can be deepened by our participation," Leigh offers.

"I agree. As I see it, the most important thing that happens is that you get a deeper understanding both of self and of others in this process, because you're not only exploring them, you're exploring you."

"Yes, as Jack Douglas [1985] and Michael Jackson [1989] emphasize, 'Understanding ourselves is part of the process of understanding others.' "

"And vice versa."

"That's certainly true for me," Leigh acknowledges. "For example, I understood

Karen's background by thinking about my own and how similar they were, and she made me examine my own religious beliefs, especially the possibility of believing in Jesus."

"And working with Christine and Lisa certainly helped me to understand bulimia on a cultural level and to reframe my own concerns with eating. In doing this," I continue, "I was drawn to how much we can come to understand by concentrating on our similarities with those we study, in addition to our differences. So often we see those we study as different from us but similar to each other. In this research, I was forced to consider how they and I were alike as well. I had to try on their worlds."

Leigh chimes in, "When I first decided to study Messianic Judaism, I was sure I would dislike the congregants and be angry with them for claiming to be both Jewish and believers in Jesus. Now after spending so much time with members and exploring my own feelings that come up in the interviews, I've come to understand the complexity of their beliefs and I connect to their ability to express and be in their emotions."

"So really what we're advocating here is mutual understanding as opposed to advocating that we, as all-knowing researchers, understand the other unidirectionally. It's similar to what happens in our day-to-day lives, where we try to understand others by comparing our experiences to theirs. We ask them, What do you think, do, what are your relationships like? Sometimes we tell stories about ours and wait to hear them compare their lives to ours. The exchange becomes more of a conversation than, as Holstein and Gubrium [1995] describe traditional interviews, information produced for the interviewer."

"I hope our texts also encourage readers to think about and feel their commonalities with our participants and with us," I continue. "As we examine ourselves, we invite readers to do the same, and to enter into their own conversations."

"I think the multiple voices in the text also play a part here."

"Yes, things are revealed and constructed in interaction that might not be accomplished with one voice."

"Well, there's that. But I was still thinking of readers," Leigh responds. "As Laurel Richardson and Ernest Lockridge [1998] remind us, multiple voices in co-constructed pieces give readers multiple places to stand and look. Some readers might relate to Rebecca and Aaron's relationship, where they seemingly agree on everything. Or they might relate to me as an outside observer trying to decipher from nonverbal cues whether something else might be going on."

"In letting them look with you as a researcher, you provide an interview frame for readers to enter, as you did with Rabbi Aaron and Rebecca. This allows readers to understand more fully what went on there or even to come up with alternate interpretations. They also can feel with you as a researcher. Or feel with you as a character in your story. That's what Art and I had in mind in the abortion piece. We wanted to present a version of both the female and male experience of abortion, within the context of our collective confusion, ambivalence, and feelings. These are feelings that other respondents most likely wouldn't reveal. And even if they did, it might not be ethical to ask them to. To be able to invite readers to enter our emotional, physical, and spiritual, as well as cognitive, experience—well, that's what can happen when you include yourself as a character. It opens up other realms of existence."

"As long as you can handle the vulnerability it entails," Leigh says quietly. "Our own emotionality, physicality, spirituality —these realms seem to bring with them a great deal more vulnerability than we're accustomed to in traditional social science."

"That's for sure," I respond. We sit silently, both contemplating the vulnerability in the stories we tell in this chapter. Simultaneously, we shake out of our reverie.

"I think we should retitle our chapter 'Their Story/My Story/Our Story,'" I say, typing the words as I speak them.

■ *References*

Abu-Lughod, L. 1995. "A Tale of Two Pregnancies." Pp. 339-49 in *Women Writing Culture,* edited by R. Behar and D. A. Gordon. Berkeley: University of California Press.

Adler, P. A. and P. Adler. 1997. "Parent-as-Researcher: the Politics of Researching in the Personal Life." Pp. 21-44 in *Reflexivity and Voice,* edited by R. Hertz. Thousand Oaks, CA: Sage.

Agronick, G. and R. Helson. 1996. "Who Benefits from an Examined Life? Correlates of Influence Attributed to Participation in a Longitudinal Study." Pp. 80-93 in *The Narrative Study of Lives,* Vol. 4, *Ethics and Process in the Narrative Study of Lives,* edited by R. Josselson. Thousand Oaks, CA: Sage.

Allison, D. 1995. *Two or Three Things I Know for Sure.* New York: Plume.

Anderson, K., S. Armitage, D. Jack, and J. Wittner. 1987. "Beginning Where We Are: Feminist Methodology in Oral History." *Oral History Review* 15:103-27.

Angrosino, M. V. 1989. "The Two Lives of Rebecca Levengstone: Symbolic Interaction in the Generation of the Life History." *Journal of Anthropological Research* 45:315-26.

———. 1998. *Opportunity House: Ethnographic Stories of Mental Retardation.* Walnut Creek, CA: AltaMira.

Apter, T. 1996. "Expert Witness: Who Controls the Psychologist's Narrative?" Pp. 22-44 in *The Narrative Study of Lives,* Vol. 4, *Ethics and Process in the Narrative Study of Lives,* edited by R. Josselson. Thousand Oaks, CA: Sage.

Austin, D. A. 1996. "Kaleidoscope: The Same and Different." Pp. 206-30 in *Composing Ethnography: Alternative Forms of Qualitative Writing,* edited by C. Ellis and A. P. Bochner. Walnut Creek, CA: AltaMira.

Bar-On, D. 1996. "Ethical Issues in Biographical Interviews and Analysis." Pp. 9-21 in *The Narrative Study of Lives,* Vol. 4, *Ethics and Process in the Narrative Study of Lives,* edited by R. Josselson. Thousand Oaks, CA: Sage.

Behar, R. 1995. "Writing in My Father's Name: A Diary of *Translated Woman's* First Year." Pp. 65-82 in *Women Writing Culture,* edited by R. Behar and D. A. Gordon. Berkeley: University of California Press.

———. 1996. *The Vulnerable Observer: Anthropology That Breaks Your Heart.* Boston: Beacon.

Belenky, M. F., B. M. Clinchy, N. R. Goldberger, and J. M. Tarule. 1981-82. "Listening to Women's Voices." *Newsletter, Education for Women's Development Project* (Simon's Rock of Bard College, Great Barrington, MA), no. 2.

Bergen, R. K. 1993. "Interviewing Survivors of Marital Rape: Doing Feminist Research on Sensitive Topics." Pp. 197-211 in *Researching Sensitive Topics,* edited by C. M. Renzetti and R. M. Lee. Newbury Park, CA: Sage.

Berger, L. 1997a. "Between the Candy Store and the Mall: The Spiritual Loss of a Father." *Journal of Personal and Interpersonal Loss* 2:397-409.

———. 1997b. "Sister, Sister: Siblings, Deafness, and the Representation of Signed Voice." M.A. thesis, University of South Florida, Tampa.

———. 1998. "Silent Movies: Scenes from a Life." Pp. 137-46 in *Fiction and Social Research: By Ice or Fire,* edited by A. Banks and S. P. Banks. Walnut Creek, CA: AltaMira.

Blee, K. M. 1998. "White-Knuckle Research: Emotional Dynamics in Fieldwork with Racist Activists." *Qualitative Sociology* 21:381-99.

Bloom, L. 1996. "Stories of One's Own: Nonunitary Subjectivity in Narrative Representation." *Qualitative Inquiry* 2:176-97.

Bochner, A. P. 1997. "It's About Time: Narrative and the Divided Self." *Qualitative Inquiry* 3:418-38.

Bochner, A. P. and C. Ellis. 1992. "Personal Narrative as a Social Approach to Interpersonal Communication." *Communication Theory* 2:165-72.

———. 1996. "Talking over Ethnography." Pp. 13-45 in *Composing Ethnography: Alternative Forms of Qualitative Writing,* edited by C. Ellis and A. P. Bochner. Walnut Creek, CA: AltaMira.

Brannen, J. 1988. "The Study of Sensitive Subjects." *Sociological Review* 36:552-63.

Briggs, C. L. 1986. *Learning How to Ask: A Sociolinguistic Appraisal of the Role of the Interview in Social Science Research.* Cambridge: Cambridge University Press.

Bristow, A. R. and J. A. Esper. 1988. "A Feminist Research Ethos." In *A Feminist Ethic for Social Science Research,* edited by Nebraska Sociological Feminist Collective. New York: Edwin Mellen.

Bruner, J. 1986. *Actual Minds, Possible Worlds.* Cambridge, MA: Harvard University Press.

Chase, S. 1996. "Personal Vulnerability and Interpretive Authority in Narrative Research." Pp. 45-59 in *The Narrative Study of Lives,* Vol. 4, *Ethics and Process in the Narrative Study of Lives,* edited by R. Josselson. Thousand Oaks, CA: Sage.

Chase, S. and C. Bell. 1994. "Interpreting the Complexity of Women's Subjectivity." Pp. 63-81 in *Interactive Oral History Interviewing,* edited by E. McMahon and K. L. Rogers. Hillsdale, NJ: Lawrence Erlbaum.

Clough, P. T. 1999. "And Now Writing." Presented at the annual meeting of the Society for the Study of Symbolic Interaction, August, Chicago.

Collins, P. H. 1986. "Learning from the Outsider Within: The Sociological Significance of Black Feminist Thought." *Social Problems* 33:14-32.

Cook, J. A. and M. M. Fonow. 1986. "Knowledge and Women's Interests: Issues of Epistemology and Methodology in Feminist Sociological Research." *Sociological Inquiry* 56:2-27.

Coyle, S. 1998. "Dancing with the Chameleon." Pp. 147-63 in *Fiction and Social Research: By Ice or Fire,* edited by A. Banks and S. P. Banks. Walnut Creek, CA: AltaMira.

Crapanzano, V. 1980. *Tuhami: Portrait of a Moroccan.* Chicago: University of Chicago Press.

Denzin, N. K. 1999. "Performing Montana: Part II." Presented at the annual meeting of the Society for the Study of Symbolic Interaction, August, Chicago.

DeVault, M. L. 1990. "Talking and Listening from Women's Standpoint: Feminist Strategies for Interviewing and Analysis." *Social Problems* 37:96-116.

———. 1999. *Liberating Method: Feminism and Social Research.* Philadelphia: Temple University Press.

Douglas, J. D. 1985. *Creative Interviewing.* Beverly Hills, CA: Sage.

Duelli Klein, R. 1983. "How to Do What We Want to Do: Thoughts about Feminist Methodology." Pp. 99-121 in *Theories of Women's Studies,* edited by G. Bowles and R. Duelli Klein. New York: Routledge & Kegan Paul.

Dumont, J.-P. 1978. *The Headman and I: Ambiguity and Ambivalence in the Fieldworking Experience.* Austin: University of Texas Press.

Edwards, R. 1993. "An Education in Interviewing: Placing the Researcher and the Research." Pp. 181-96 in *Researching Sensitive Topics,* edited by C. M. Renzetti and R. M. Lee. Newbury Park, CA: Sage.

Eisenberg, E. M. 1998. "From Anxiety to Possibility: Poems 1987-1997." Pp. 195-202 in *Fiction and Social Research: By Ice or Fire,* edited by A. Banks and S. P. Banks. Walnut Creek, CA: AltaMira.

Ellingson, L. 1998. " 'Then You Know How I Feel': Empathy, Identification, and Reflexivity in Fieldwork." *Qualitative Inquiry* 4:492-514.

Elliott, R. 1986. "Interpersonal Process Recall (IPR) as a Psychotherapy Process Research Method." Pp. 503-28 in *The Psychotherapeutic Process: A Research Handbook,* edited by L. Greeneberg and W. Pinsof. New York: Guilford.

Ellis, C. 1993. " 'There Are Survivors': Telling a Story of Sudden Death." *Sociological Quarterly* 34:711-30.

———. 1995. *Final Negotiations: A Story of Love, Loss, and Chronic Illness.* Philadelphia: Temple University Press.

———. 1996. "Maternal Connections." Pp. 240-43 in *Composing Ethnography: Alternative Forms of Qualitative Writing,* edited by C. Ellis and A. P. Bochner. Walnut Creek, CA: AltaMira.

———. 1998. "Exploring Loss through Autoethnographic Inquiry: Autoethnographic Stories, Co-constructed Narratives, and Interactive Interviews." Pp. 49-61 in *Perspectives on Loss: A Sourcebook,* edited by J. H. Harvey. Philadelphia: Taylor & Francis.

Ellis, C. and A. P. Bochner. 1992. "Telling and Performing Personal Stories: The Constraints of Choice in Abortion." Pp. 79-101 in *Investigating Subjectivity: Research on Lived Experience,* edited by C. Ellis and M. G. Flaherty. Newbury Park, CA: Sage.

———, eds. 1996. *Composing Ethnography: Alternative Forms of Qualitative Writing.* Walnut Creek, CA: AltaMira.

———. 2000. "Autoethnography, Personal Narrative, Reflexivity: Researcher as Subject." Pp. 733-68 in *Handbook of Qualitative Research,* 2d ed., edited by N. K. Denzin and Y. S. Lincoln. Thousand Oaks, CA: Sage.

Ellis, C., C. E. Kiesinger, and L. M. Tillmann-Healy. 1997. "Interactive Interviewing: Talking about Emotional Experience." Pp. 119-49 in *Reflexivity and Voice,* edited by R. Hertz. Thousand Oaks, CA: Sage.

Finch, J. 1984. " 'It's Great to Have Someone to Talk To': The Ethics and Politics of Interviewing Women." Pp. 70-87 in *Social Researching: Politics, Problems, Practice,* edited by C. Bell and H. Roberts. London: Routledge & Kegan Paul.

Fox, K. 1996. "Silent Voices: A Subversive Reading of Child Sexual Abuse." Pp. 330-47 in *Composing Ethnography: Alternative Forms of Qualitative Writing,* edited by C. Ellis and A. P. Bochner. Walnut Creek, CA: AltaMira.

Futrell, A. and C. Willard. 1994. "Intersubjectivity and Interviewing." Pp. 83-105 in *Interactive Oral History Interviewing,* edited by E. McMahon and K. L. Rogers. Hillsdale, NJ: Lawrence Erlbaum.

Gale, J. 1992. "When Research Interviews Are More Therapeutic Than Therapy Interviews." *Qualitative Report* 1 [On-line]. Available Internet: http://www.nova.edu/ssss/QR/QR1-4/gale.html

Goodall, H. L., Jr. 1991. *Living in the Rock 'n' Roll Mystery: Reading Context, Self, and Others as Clues.* Carbondale: Southern Illinois University Press.

———. 1999. *Writing the New Ethnography.* Walnut Creek, CA: AltaMira.

Griffith, A. and D. Smith. 1987. "Constructing Cultural Knowledge: Mothering as Discourse." Pp. 87-103 in *Women and Education,* edited by J. Gaskell and A. T. McLaren. Calgary, Alberta: Detselig.

Gubrium, J. F. and J. A. Holstein. 1997. *The New Language of Qualitative Method.* New York: Oxford University Press.

Hertz, R. 1995. "Separate but Simultaneous Interviewing of Husbands and Wives: Making Sense of Their Stories." *Qualitative Inquiry* 1:429-51.

Holstein, J. A. and J. F. Gubrium. 1995. *The Active Interview.* Thousand Oaks, CA: Sage.

Hutchinson, S., M. Wilson, and H. S. Wilson. 1994. "Benefits of Participating in Research Interviews." *Image: Journal of Nursing Scholarship* 26:161-64.

Jackson, M. 1989. *Paths toward a Clearing: Radical Empiricism and Ethnographic Inquiry.* Bloomington: Indiana University Press.

Jago, B. 1996. "Postcards, Ghosts, and Fathers: Revising Family Stories." *Qualitative Inquiry* 2:495-516.

Jones, S. H. 1998. *Kaleidoscope Notes: Writing Women's Music and Organizational Culture.* Walnut Creek, CA: AltaMira.

Jorgenson, J. 1991. "Co-constructing the Interviewer/Co-constructing 'Family.' " Pp. 210-25 in *Research and Reflexivity,* edited by F. Steier. London: Sage.

———. 1995. "Relationalizing Rapport in Interpersonal Settings." Pp. 155-70 in *Social Approaches to Communication,* edited by W. Leeds-Hurwitz. New York: Guilford.

Josselson, R. 1996. "On Writing Other People's Lives: Self-Analytic Reflections of a Narrative Researcher." Pp. 60-71 in *The Narrative Study of Lives,* Vol. 4, *Ethics and Process in the Narrative Study of Lives,* edited by R. Josselson. Thousand Oaks, CA: Sage.

Karp, D. A. 1996. *Speaking of Sadness: Depression, Disconnection, and the Meanings of Illness.* New York: Oxford University Press.

Kiesinger, C. 1992. "Writing It Down: Sisters, Food, Eating, and Body Image." Unpublished manuscript, University of South Florida, Tampa.

———. 1995. "Anorexic and Bulimic Lives: Making Sense of Food and Eating." Ph.D. dissertation, University of South Florida, Tampa.

———. 1998. "Portrait of an Anorexic Life." Pp. 115-36 in *Fiction and Social Research: By Ice or Fire,* edited by A. Banks and S. P. Banks. Walnut Creek, CA: AltaMira.

Kolker, A. 1996. "Thrown Overboard: The Human Costs of Health Care Rationing." Pp. 133-59 in *Composing Ethnography: Alternative Forms of Qualitative Writing,* edited by C. Ellis and A. P. Bochner. Walnut Creek, CA: AltaMira.

Kondo, D. K. 1990. *Crafting Selves: Power, Gender, and Discourses of Identity in a Japanese Workplace.* Chicago: University of Chicago Press,

Krieger, S. 1991. *Social Science and the Self: Personal Essays on an Art Form.* New Brunswick, NJ: Rutgers University Press.

———. 1996. *The Family Silver: Essays on Relationships among Women.* Berkeley: University of California Press.

Kulick, D. and M. Willson, eds. 1995. *Taboo: Sex, Identity, and Erotic Subjectivity in Anthropological Fieldwork.* London: Routledge.

Kvale, S. 1996. *InterViews: An Introduction to Qualitative Research Interviewing.* Thousand Oaks, CA: Sage.

Lagerwey, M. 1998. *Reading Auschwitz.* Walnut Creek, CA: AltaMira.

Langellier, K. and D. Hall. 1989. "Interviewing Women: A Phenomenological Approach to Feminist Communication Research." Pp. 193-220 in *Doing Research on Women's Communication,* edited by K. Carter and C. Spitzack. Norwood, NJ: Ablex.

Larson, C. L. 1997. "Re-presenting the Subject: Problems in Personal Narrative Inquiry." *International Journal of Qualitative Studies in Education* 10:455-70.

Lather, P. and C. Smithies. 1997. *Troubling the Angels: Women Living with HIV/AIDS.* Boulder, CO: Westview.

Lewin, E. and W. L. Leap. 1996. *Out in the Field: Reflections of Lesbian and Gay Anthropologists.* Urbana: University of Illinois Press.

Lewis, J. and B. Meredith. 1988. *Daughters Who Care: Daughters Caring for Mothers at Home.* London: Routledge & Kegan Paul.

Lieblich, A. 1996. "Some Unforeseen Outcomes of Conducting Narrative Research with People of One's Own Culture." Pp. 151-84 in *The Narrative Study of Lives,* Vol. 4, *Ethics and Process in the Narrative Study of Lives,* edited by R. Josselson. Thousand Oaks, CA: Sage.

Linden, R. R. 1993. *Making Stories, Making Selves: Feminist Reflections on the Holocaust.* Columbus: Ohio State University Press.

Macleod, V. A. 1999. " 'Getting It Off Our Chests': Living with Breast Cancer Survival." Ph.D. dissertation. Department of Interdisciplinary Education, University of South Florida, Tampa.

Maione, P. V. and R. J. Chenail. 1999. "Qualitative Inquiry in Psychotherapy: Research on the Common Factors." Pp. 57-88 in *The Heart and Soul of Change: The Role of Common Factors in Psychotherapy,* edited by M. A. Hubble, B. L. Duncan, and S. D. Miller. Washington, DC: American Psychological Association.

Markham, A. M. 1998. *Life Online: Researching Real Experience in Virtual Space.* Walnut Creek, CA: AltaMira.

Mies, M. 1983. "Toward a Methodology for Feminist Research." Pp. 117-39 in *Theories of Women's Studies,* edited by G. Bowles and R. Duelli Klein. New York: Routledge & Kegan Paul.

Miller, M. 1996. "Ethics and Understanding through Interrelationship: I and Thou in Dialogue." Pp. 129-47 in *The Narrative Study of Lives,* Vol. 4, *Ethics and Process in the Narrative Study of Lives,* edited by R. Josselson. Thousand Oaks, CA: Sage.

Mishler, E. G. 1986. *Research Interviewing: Context and Narrative.* Cambridge, MA: Harvard University Press.

Murphy, R. F. 1987. *The Body Silent.* New York: Holt.

Myerhoff, B. 1978. *Number Our Days.* New York: Simon & Schuster.

———. 1992. *Remembered Lives: The Work of Rituals, Storytelling, and Growing Older.* Ann Arbor: University of Michigan Press.

Mykhalovskiy, E. 1997. "Reconsidering Table Talk: Critical Thoughts on the Relationship between Sociology, Autobiography and Self-Indulgence." Pp. 229-51 in *Reflexivity and Voice,* edited by R. Hertz. Thousand Oaks, CA: Sage.

Oakley, A. 1981. "Interviewing Women: A Contradiction in Terms?" Pp. 30-61 in *Doing Feminist Research,* edited by H. Roberts. London: Routledge & Kegan Paul.

Ochberg, R. L. 1996. "Interpreting Life Stories." Pp. 97-113 in *The Narrative Study of Lives,* Vol. 4, *Ethics and Process in the Narrative Study of Lives,* edited by R. Josselson. Thousand Oaks, CA: Sage.

Pacanowsky, M. 1988. "Slouching towards Chicago: Fiction as Scholarly Writing." *Quarterly Journal of Speech* 74:453-68.

Paget, M. 1993. *A Complex Sorrow: Reflections on Cancer and an Abbreviated Life.* Philadelphia: Temple University Press.

Parry, A. 1991. "A Universe of Stories." *Family Process* 30:37-54.

Payne, D. 1996. "Autobiology." Pp. 49-75 in *Composing Ethnography: Alternative Forms of Qualitative Writing,* edited by C. Ellis and A. P. Bochner. Walnut Creek, CA: AltaMira.

Perry, J. 1996. "Writing the Self: Exploring the Stigma of Hearing Impairment." *Sociological Spectrum* 16:239-61.

Platt, J. 1981. "On Interviewing One's Peers." *British Journal of Sociology* 32:75-91.

Ponticelli, C. 1996. "The Spiritual Warfare of Exodus: A Postpositivist Research Adventure." *Qualitative Inquiry* 2:198-219.

Quinney, R. 1996. "Once My Father Traveled West to California." Pp. 349-74 in *Composing Ethnography: Alternative Forms of Qualitative Writing,* edited by C. Ellis and A. P. Bochner. Walnut Creek, CA: AltaMira.

Rabinow, P. 1977. *Reflections on Fieldwork in Morocco.* Berkeley: University of California Press.

Reinharz, S. 1992. *Feminist Methods in Social Research.* New York: Oxford University Press.

Renzetti, C. M. and R. M. Lee, eds. 1993. *Researching Sensitive Topics.* Newbury Park, CA: Sage.

Richardson, L. 1992. "The Consequences of Poetic Representation: Writing the Other, Rewriting the Self." Pp. 125-37 in *Investigating Subjectivity: Research on Lived Experience,* edited by C. Ellis and M. G. Flaherty. Newbury Park, CA: Sage.

———. 1994. "Writing: A Method of Inquiry." Pp. 516-29 in *Handbook of Qualitative Research,* edited by N. K. Denzin and Y. S. Lincoln. Thousand Oaks, CA: Sage.

———. 1997. *Fields of Play: Constructing an Academic Life.* New Brunswick, NJ: Rutgers University Press.

———. 1998 "Meta-Jeopardy." *Qualitative Inquiry* 4:464-68.

Richardson, L. and E. Lockridge. 1998. "Fiction and Ethnography: A Conversation." *Qualitative Inquiry* 4:328-37.

Riessman, C. K. 1987. "When Gender Is Not Enough: Women Interviewing Women." *Gender & Society* 1:172-207.

———. 1993. *Narrative Analysis.* Newbury Park, CA: Sage.

Roberts, H., ed. 1981. *Doing Feminist Research.* London: Routledge & Kegan Paul.

Robillard, A. B. 1997. "Communication Problems in the Intensive Care Unit." Pp. 252-64 in *Reflexivity and Voice,* edited by R. Hertz. Thousand Oaks, CA: Sage.

———. 1999. *Meaning of Disability: The Lived Experience of Paralysis.* Philadelphia: Temple University Press.

Romanoff, B. D. 2001. "Reclaiming Voice: Ethnographic Inquiry and Qualitative Research in a Postmodern Age." In *Meaning Reconstruction and the Experience of Loss,* edited by R. A. Neimeyer. Washington, DC: American Psychological Association.

Ronai, C. R. 1992. "The Reflexive Self through Narrative: A Night in the Life of an Erotic Dancer/Researcher." Pp. 102-24 in *Investigating Subjectivity: Research on Lived Experience,* edited by C. Ellis and M. G. Flaherty. Newbury Park, CA: Sage.

———. 1995. "Multiple Reflections of Child Sex Abuse: An Argument for a Layered Account." *Journal of Contemporary Ethnography* 23:395-426.

Rosaldo, R. 1989. *Culture and Truth: The Remaking of Social Analysis.* Boston: Beacon.

Rosenwald, G. 1996. "Making Whole: Method and Ethics in Mainstream and Narrative Psychology." Pp. 245-74 in *The Narrative Study of Lives,* Vol. 4, *Ethics and Process in the Narrative Study of Lives,* edited by R. Josselson. Thousand Oaks, CA: Sage.

Ross, J. L. and P. Geist. 1997. "Elation and Devastation: Women's Journeys through Pregnancy and Miscarriage." Pp. 167-84 in *Courage of Conviction: Women's Words, Women's Wisdom,* edited by L. A. M. Perry and P. Geist. Mountain View, CA: Mayfield.

Rothman, B. K. 1986. "Reflections: On Hard Work." *Qualitative Sociology* 9:48-53.

Satir, V. 1983. *Conjoint Family Therapy.* 3d ed. Palo Alto, CA: Science & Behavior.

Segura, D. 1989. "Chicana and Mexican Immigrant Women at Work: The Impact of Class, Race and Gender on Occupational Mobility." *Gender & Society* 3:37-52.

Shostak, A., ed. 1996. *Private Sociology: Unsparing Reflections, Uncommon Gains.* Dix Hills, NY: General Hall.

Stacey, J. 1988. "Can There Be a Feminist Ethnography?" *Women's Studies International Forum* 11:21-27.

Stanley, L. and S. Wise. 1983. " 'Back into the Personal'; or, Our Attempt to Construct 'Feminist Research.' " Pp. 20-62 in *Theories of Women's Studies,* edited by G. Bowles and R. Duelli Klein. London: Routledge & Kegan Paul.

Stringer, E. 1996. *Action Research: A Handbook for Practitioners.* Thousand Oaks, CA: Sage.

Suchman, L. and B. Jordan. 1992. "Validity and the Collaborative Construction of Meaning in Face-to-Face Surveys." Pp. 241-67 in *Questions about Questions: Inquiries into the Cognitive Bases of Surveys,* edited by J. M. Tanur. New York: Russell Sage Foundation.

Tillmann-Healy, L. M. 1996. "A Secret Life in a Culture of Thinness: Reflections on Body, Food, and Bulimia." Pp. 77-109 in *Composing Ethnography: Alternative Forms of Qualitative Writing,* edited by C. Ellis and A. P. Bochner. Walnut Creek, CA: AltaMira.

Tillmann-Healy, L. M. and C. Kiesinger. 2000. "Mirrors: Seeing Each Other and Ourselves Through Fieldwork." Pp. 81-108 in *The Emotional Nature of Qualitative Research,* edited by K. R. Gilbert. Boca Raton, FL: CRC.

Tripp, D. 1983. "Co-authorship and Negotiation: The Interview as Act of Creation." *Interchange* 14:32-45.

Trujillo, N. 1998. "In Search of Naunny's Grave." *Text and Performance Quarterly* 18:344-68.

Webb, C. 1984. "Feminist Methodology in Nursing Research." *Journal of Advanced Nursing* 9:249-56.

Williams, P. 1991. *The Alchemy of Race and Rights: Diary of a Law Professor.* Cambridge, MA: Harvard University Press.

Yerby, J. and W. Gourd. 1994. "Our Marriage/Their Marriage: Performing Reflexive Fieldwork." Presented at the annual Couch and Stone Symposium of the Society for the Study of Symbolic Interaction, University of Illinois, Urbana-Champagne.

Zola, I. K. 1982a. *Missing Pieces: A Chronicle of Living with a Disability.* Philadelphia: Temple University Press.

———. 1982b. *Ordinary Lives: Voices of Disability.* Watertown, MA: Applewood.

42

POETIC REPRESENTATION OF INTERVIEWS

◆ Laurel Richardson

How we write has consequences for ourselves, our disciplines, and the publics we serve. *How* we are expected to write affects *what* we can write about; the form in which we write shapes the content. Prose is the form in which social researchers are expected to represent interview material. Prose, however, is simply a literary technique, a convention, and not the sole legitimate carrier of knowledge.

For the past 15 years, I have been exploring alternative forms of presenting research texts (see Richardson 1990, 1997). My purposes have been several: to examine how knowledge claims are constituted in scientific writing, to write more engaged sociology, and to reach diverse audiences. In this chapter, after briefly addressing some poststructuralist writing issues, I discuss one alternative way of conveying interview material: by means of poetic representation. I consider both the long narrative poem and the short poem (formerly called the lyric poem). Then I offer suggestions, for beginners especially, and some examples of poetic representation. I draw heavily upon my own work because I am most familiar with its construction.

My goal in this chapter is not to compare poetic representation with other evocative or mimetic forms, but to discuss the poetic form on its own terms as it relates to the representational issues under consideration. Consequently, the reader may find that some of what I say applies to other forms for presenting research material; I don't view this as problematic or distressing. I do not contend that poetic representation is the only or even the best way to represent all social research knowledge. But I do claim (a) that for some kinds of knowledge, poetic representation may be preferable to representation in prose, and (b) that poetic representation is a viable method for seeing beyond social scientific conventions and discursive practices, and therefore should be of interest to those concerned with epistemological issues and challenges.

◆ Poststructuralist Writing Issues

My theoretical position is that of poststructuralism. The core of that position is the doubt that any discourse has a privileged place, any method or theory a universal and general claim to authoritative knowledge. Truth claims are suspected of masking and serving particular interests in local, cultural, and political struggles. Wherever truth is claimed, so is power; the claim to truth is also a claim to power. Once the veil of privileged truth is lifted, the opportunities for addressing how we think, who can legitimately think, and what we can think are legion; with this comes the possibility of alternative representations of research material.

Language is a constitutive force, creating a particular view of reality (see Foucault 1978). This is as true of writing as it is of speaking, and as true of science as it is of poetry (see Haraway 1988). Producing "things" always involves value—what to produce, what to name the productions, and what the relationship between the producers and the named things will be. Writing "things" is no exception. Writing always involves what Roland Barthes calls "the ownership of the means of enunciation" (quoted in Shapiro 1985-86:195). A disclosure of writing practices is thus always a disclosure of forms of power (Derrida 1982). No textual staging is ever innocent in that regard, including this one.

Social science writing, like all other forms of writing, is a sociohistorical construction that depends upon literary devices such as narrative, metaphor, imagery, invocations to authority, and appeals to audiences, not just for adornment, but for cognitive meaning (Lakoff and Johnson 1980). The truth value of social science writing depends upon a deep epistemic code regarding how knowledge in general is figured. Imminent in this prefiguring are metaphors so entrenched and familiar that they do their partisan work in the guise of neutrality, passing as literal (Derrida 1982).

For example, the grammatical split between subject and object goes wholly unnoticed as metaphor for the separation of "real" subjects and objects, for "objectivity" and a static world fixed in time and space. The temporal and human practices that reified the objects are rendered invisible, irrelevant. The technical mechanisms of explanation are quarantined from the human processes of interpretation. The actual linguistic practices in which the researcher/writer is engaged are hidden, but they are not eradicated.

A deep and totally unnoticed trope used by social researchers is the reporting of interview material in prose. In writing this chapter, I myself am using the prose trope and will for the next several pages. Its conventions allow me to stage my arguments in ways that are familiar to the reader, which is my goal here. The reader is not distracted by a different genre, and I am aided in my argument by the invisible power inherent in the adoption of conventional writing. Those conventions are particularly helpful for the making of abstract arguments, which I am rhetorically interested in doing before I demonstrate violations of those conventions.

In the routine work of the interviewer, the interview is tape-recorded, transcribed as prose, and then cut, pasted, edited, trimmed, smoothed, and snipped, just as if it were a literary text—which it is, albeit usually without explicit acknowledgment or recognition as such by the researcher. Underlying this process is the belief that the purpose of the text is to convey information, as though information consists of facts or themes, notions that are taken to exist independent of the context in which they are articulated, as if the story the researcher has recorded, transcribed, edited, and rewritten as snippets is the true one: a "research" story. The use of standard writing conventions, including the use of prose, conceals the handprint of the researcher who produced the written text.

According to the oral historian Dennis Tedlock (1983), however, when people talk, whether as conversants, storytellers, informants, or interviewees, their speech is closer to poetry than it is to prose. Nobody talks in prose. For example, everybody, including so-called literate and nonliterate people, adults and children, male and female, speaks using a poetic device, the pause. Indeed, in American speech, estimates are that about half of the time we are speaking, we are not; we are pausing. And some 25 percent of these pauses cannot be explained by physiological needs for breath or grammatical demands for closure, such as is required at the ends of sentences or for clauses (Tedlock 1983:198). Unlike prose, poetry writes in the pauses through the conventions of line breaks, spaces between lines and between stanzas and sections, and for sounds of silence.

"Poems exist in the realm of making (mimesis) rather than of knowing or doing; they are representations of human experience . . . not speech uttered by, or speech acts performed by individuals who happen to be poets" (Borroff 1993:1032). That is, poems are consciously constructed to evoke emotion through literary devices such as sound patterns, rhythms, imagery, and page layout. Even if the prosodic mind resists, the body responds to poetry. It is *felt*. To paraphrase Robert Frost, poetry is the shortest emotional path between two people.

These understandings also map onto semiotics (Eco 1979; Manning and Cullum-Swan 1994). Semiotics is an approach to texts, such as interview transcriptions, that emphasizes the centrality of the reader in the interpretation of texts, including the researcher-reader of the transcript. Readers find and name meanings; they clump meanings together, creating categories and codes. In this respect, texts are always subject to multiple readings; no singular reading is definitive (see Gilgun 1999).

Constructing interview material as poems does not delude the researcher, listener, or readers into thinking that the one and only true story has been written, which is a temptation attached to the prose trope, especially in a research context. Rather, the facticity of the findings as constructed is ever present. Moreover, because the poetic form plays with connotative structures and literary devices to convey meaning, poetic representations have a greater likelihood of engaging readers in reflexive analyses of their own interpretive labor, as well as the researcher's interpretive labor in relation to the speaker's interpretive labor. The construction of text is thus positioned as joint, prismatic, open, and partial.

Poetry belongs to both written and oral traditions. It can be read silently, read aloud, or performed. Unlike conventional social science writing, poetry is welcome in diverse settings and can bring theoretic understandings to life for audiences as diverse as those found in poetry bars, theaters, policy-making settings, literary conventions, street scenes, and the mass media.

Poetic representation also may be used as one of the discursive practices within other oppositional paradigms whose goals are to challenge the power relationships inscribed through traditional writing practices. Gregory Ulmer's (1989, 1994) "mystory" is one such paradigm. A mystory is writing that juxtaposes personal narrative, popular culture, and scholarly discourses. Mystories are published in academic journals, yet they dethrone academic writing. They honor a journey of discovery, a process of meaning construction, not only about the subject but about the self. Private and public knowledges are interlaced, but the reader assembles the connections. The collage created from interview studies would be intensified should one of the mystories—the respondent's or the researcher's—be a poetic representation.

Writing is never innocent. Writing always inscribes. One can write in ways that reinscribe the discourses of academia and social science as the only legitimate form of knowledge, or one can write in ways that empower those whose "ideas and beliefs are not cast in the rhetoric of science" (Danforth 1997:104-5). The inscriptions of academic discourse are not harmless

—words hurt. Academic discourse names, categorizes, and constructs others in racist, masculinist, and colonial texts. Those who speak in "nonscience" voices are marginalized (Danforth 1997:105; P. Smith 1999: 246). Poetic representation offers social researchers an opportunity to write about, or with, people in ways that honor their speech styles, words, rhythms, and syntax.

◆ The Long and the Short of It

Poststructuralism proposes that systems of knowledge are narratively constructed. Traditionally, ethnographies, oral histories, social histories, biographies, and other qualitatively oriented research are constructed with fairly straightforward, obvious, and visible plotlines. The author intends that the reader gets "the" story. "The" story is understood as taking place within, or reflecting, a particular experience or culture. Writing in-depth interviews as a long narrative poem, while transgressing representational practices, also can cohere with the narrative traditions of qualitative research and in-depth interview reporting. It, too, aims to convey "the" story, but leaves this open to interpretation. Such transgressive writings reinscribe the possibility of "the" story, even as they challenge the format through which the story is told. The narrative structure is familiar and comprehensible, but urges the reader to unsettle the truths under consideration.

I constructed a long narrative poem, "Louisa May's Story of Her Life" (1992; the poem is reproduced in whole in the appendix to this chapter). The poem, which I have presented to different audiences, is about an unwed mother. Listening to the poem, introduced as a sociology poem, altered people's ways of hearing; boundaries were broken. Poets in these audiences theorized about the social construction of normality, genre boundaries, and authorship.

Women's studies audiences theorized the poetry as a method for "demasculinizing" the production of social research. Culture studies audiences perceived a welcoming place for different cultural displays of, and claims to, knowledge. Oral historians saw this poetic representation as a method for capturing the "essence" lacking in their own reporting conventions. Folklorists saw it as another, legitimate, performance method. Social workers and policy makers claimed the poem altered their stereotypical thinking about unwed mothers.

When the goal of poetic representation is to re-present significant moments in lived experience, such as something epiphanous, the short poem and especially a sequence of short poems with an implied narrative works well. More than the long narrative poem, short poems focus and concretize emotions, feelings, and moods—the most private kind of feelings—in order to re-create moments of experience. The poem "shows" another person how it is to feel something.

Each short poem represents a candid photo, an episode, or an epiphany. People organize their sense of self around and through such epiphanous moments (Denzin 1989). Lived experiences are not primarily organized around the long biographical account, the epic poem, or the life history. Rather, people tell stories about *events* in their lives and the meanings of these events change through the invocation of different narratives. Not all events are stuffed into the same narrative. A life may indeed have a plotline, but not everything lived, or everything of significance to the person, fits neatly into a lengthy unfolding story. We are not characters. The points of our lives are not morals. Our lives are not even in-depth narratives.

Of course, cultures do provide prefabricated narratives that we use to assemble the events of our lives. As cultural studies and discourse analysis demonstrate, those narratives are multiple, contradictory, changing, and differentially available to us (Richardson 1988). But as agents in our own constructions, we artfully choose among available cultural stories and apply them to our experiences. We sometimes get stuck in an especially strong metanarrative, often operate with contradictory story lines, and sometimes seek plots that transgress the culturally condoned ones. Any or all of these processes through which the self is constructed and reconstructed may be going on simultaneously. A sequence of short poems can echo this complexity—the artful openness of the process and the shifting subjectivities by which we come to know and not to know ourselves, and then to know ourselves again, differently.

My own collection of poems titled "Nine Poems: Marriage and the Family" exemplifies this process (Richardson, 1994). Unlike in "Louisa May," in "Nine Poems" a narrative is only implied. Each of the nine poems is short, each is a mini-narrative, an episode, representing an emotionally and morally charged experience. The order of the poems implies a plot, but the spaces between the poems invite greater readerly response and interpretive work than would a long narrative poem. The nine poems could be reordered, implying yet different plots. Reversing the title and subsuming "Nine Poems" under the narrative rubric "Marriage and the Family" can imply a different metanarrative, the poetic co-construction of the two concepts "marriage" and "family," and a seeming relationship between them, "marriage *and* the family." The implied narrative would change again if, alternatively, "Nine Poems" were titled "Gender," "Maturing," "Socialization," "Treason," or "Paper Airplanes."

Constructing a series of short poems reflecting the chronological or thematic concerns of an interviewee can deepen the researcher's attachment to the interviewee and help the researcher see through preconceptions and biases. A series of alternatively arranged short poems offers the researcher the possibility of exploring other unexamined assumptions of interview representation, challenging accepted representational conventions such as the "ideal typical" portrait and snippets linked by theme (see Richardson 1997).

Poetic representation can both cohere and conflict with normative writing. It offers opportunities for alternative expressions of people's lives as well as opportunities for critical attention to knowledge claims about them.

◆ Constructing Poetic Representations

As both ethnomethodology and deconstruction have made clear, there is no way to provide a complete list of "how-tos" and "not tos" regarding any human enterprise. I certainly would not want to try to provide such a list for poetic representation, which I view as a creative, emergent, changing form. What I would like to do instead, especially for the beginner, is to share some recommendations and practices that I and others have found useful in constructing poetic representations from interviews and interview experiences.

PRELIMINARIES FOR THE BEGINNER

If you are a beginning poet, my strongest recommendation is that you take a class in poetry, attend poetry workshops and poetry readings, join a poetry circle, read contemporary poetry, and peruse extensively the books in the Poets on Poetry series published by the University of Michigan Press. Learning poetry is like learning a second language. The more you immerse yourself in it, the better you can communicate within it. Learning to write poetry will not result in your unlearning your ability to write social science prose, any more than learning any second language undoes a person's proficiency in the first one.

Most contemporary poets consider three elements: sound, sight, and ideation.

Sound refers to alliteration, assonance, rhythms, pauses, rhymes, and off-rhymes. Poems do not have to rhyme, and poems do not have to bounce (da-dah, da-dah, da-dah). *Sight* refers to images and imagery. This normally requires concrete language, similes, and metaphors that allow the reader to imagine what the poet is saying. *Ideation* is the feeling and thought behind, beneath, before, and after the poem—what the poet is trying to express. All the various poetic techniques are harnessed to support the communication of the idea at hand parsimoniously. Remind yourself:

A line
break does
not
a poem
make.

And revise, revise, revise. During the revision process, it helps to read the poem aloud. Listen to someone else read the poem aloud. Put the poem away for a while. And then revise some more. Write different poems about the material. Work toward a series of portraits, different angles on the same interviewee.

Do not imagine that all poetic transcriptions are publishable. Many will be drafts, never finished, perhaps because these particular poetic representations never please you or perhaps because they have served their purpose of opening your mind to alternative interpretations. Many experienced poets stash their work for years because, as they realize later, it is preparatory; the material is not ready to be closed down.

And do not imagine that your work cannot be published. Most qualitative journals at this point accept poetic representation. Nor need you imagine, if you are a student, that your adviser will not approve of your work. There are many advisers today who are open to alternative forms of representation. Usually their questions stem from their wanting to know about the "method" of representation and whether or not you can get a job. Refer them to this chapter or

to the second edition of the *Handbook of Qualitative Research* (Denzin and Lincoln 2000). Supply them with copies of the respected journals that publish poetic representations, such as *Sociological Quarterly, Symbolic Interaction, American Anthropologist, Journal of Contemporary Ethnography, Journal of Aging Studies, Qualitative Inquiry, Qualitative Research, International Journal of Qualitative Research in Education, Qualitative Studies in Psychology, Qualitative Sociology, Waikato Journal of Education,* and *Text and Performance Quarterly,* among others. The research annuals *Studies in Symbolic Interaction* and *Cultural Studies* showcase evocative writing. Publishers such as AltaMira, Routledge, University of Chicago Press, University of Michigan Press, Indiana University Press, Temple University Press, and Sage Publications regularly feature works that include poetry. Entire conferences are devoted to experimentation in social research representation, such as the recent "Redesigning Ethnography" conference held at the University of Colorado and the Year 2000 Couch-Stone Symbolic Interaction Symposium.

A final suggestion is one you should implement early in the research process. Because poems (and prose, too) are more interesting if they include metaphoric language, construct your interview schedule in such a way as to elicit images and similes. For example, you might ask the interviewee something like, "If you could be any animal, what would it be? And why?" Language is enriched when you probe images and metaphors. Corrine Glesne (1997) actually asked and probed an interviewee about what metaphor would best describe her, which led to this stanza: "I would be a flying bird. / I want to move so fast / so I can see quickly, everything. / I wish I could look at the world / with the eyes of God, / to give strength to those that need" (p. 202).

A writer of poetic representation can have different, often overlapping, intentions; he or she may start with one goal and find that another takes over. That is often the case with creative activity. It is as if the writing had a mind of its own, strange as that may sound. (I think what happens is that the censorious left brain gives up, and the more playful right brain takes over, so to speak.)

One can write poetic representations in order to (a) fulfill as best as possible both traditional research and traditional poetic criteria, (b) express the sense of the whole or the essence of the experience as constructed by the interviewer, (c) transform normative discourse and actions, (d) relieve emotional pressure, or (e) some combination of the above—or, as always, (f) for other reasons. I illustrate and discuss some poetic representations below, but I encourage the reader to explore the wealth of poetic representations and discussions of them that are now available (e.g., Austin 1996; Baff 1997; Brady 1998; Ellis and Bochner 1996; Hones 1998; Jones 1998, 1999; Poindexter 1998; L. Richardson 1995, 1996, 1997, 1999a, 1999b; M. Richardson 1998, 1999; Rinehart 1997; B. Smith 1999; Sommerville 1999; St. Pierre 1997; Travisano 1998, 1999).

LOUISA MAY'S STORY

My goal in writing the long narrative poem "Louisa May's Story of Her Life" was to meet both scientific and poetic criteria. As part of a research project on unwed mothers, I completed a five-hour interview with "Louisa May" (a pseudonym), transcribed the tape into 36 pages of prose, and then shaped the transcript into a five-page poem. Following social research protocol, I used only Louisa May's words, tone, and diction, but relied upon poetic devices such as repetition, off-rhyme, sounds, meter, and pauses to convey her narrative. The speech style is Louisa May's, the words are hers, but the poetic representation, including the ordering of the material, are my own.

Below, I present an extract from the beginning of the transcript of Louisa May's interview. I invite the reader to contrast it with its poetic representation, which appears in its entirety in the appendix. The reader will note that I have taken liberties with the placement of words, but not with Louisa May's language or her sense-making process. In constructing the poem, I have depended also upon the tape itself, which recorded Louisa May's accent, pauses, tempo, and asides; these are missing in the extract. Further, because Louisa May returns again and again to the idea of "normal life" in her interview, I use that as the central theme of the poem, featuring poetically what was of chief importance to her as she described her life to me. The extract follows, with her many pauses noted as ellipses.

> Well, most important to say in . . . terms of that is that I grew up in the South— which puts a definite stamp on what you think you are and what you think . . . you're going to be.
>
> [Louisa May looks at the tape recorder] I remember my origins when I hear . . . myself on tape—that Lady Bird kind of accent—and I think, "Oh my Lord. I'm from Tennessee." I had no idea I sounded like . . . that. In any event that [being Southern] shapes it and in . . . terms of . . . aspirations. I grew up in a very poor . . . with parents . . . who were uneducated but who lived in a very normal sort of . . . middle-class neighborhood where we rented a house. So my . . . friends were not in the same situation, but no one ever . . . suggested to me that anything might happen *with* my life. So . . . when I was 12, I suppose, and with my friends—and they . . . really, ah very nice, wonderful friends, some of whom I . . . still see. I remember thinking at the time that I would . . . want a large number of children.

Because scientific protocol usually requires information about the method of data collection, as the reader of the poem in the appendix will see, I constructed it to inscribe the interactional nature of the interview. Louisa May's responses were produced in a particular kind of speech context, which is the research interview. I am the implied listener throughout the poem. When Louisa May speaks to me, referring directly or indirectly to the interview process itself, her words are italicized. In that respect, the poem registers the interview conversation's research buttress, reminding the reader that this is the recording of a particular kind of speech performance.

How one talks and what one talks about is always circumscribed by the context in which speech unfolds. Louisa May's story arises in the context of an interview; the context is written into the poem. Because an interview is a jointly constructed text arising from the intersection of two subjectivities (see Mishler 1986), framing the findings as though they are independent of the method in which they were produced (a standard claims-making procedure of interview reporting) is falsifying and misleading. Framing the by-product as "results" tells the reader how the words were "found," ignoring how they were produced.

THE "ESSENCE"
OF DOÑA JUANA

Another example is drawn from Corrine Glesne's (1997) "poetic transcriptions" of interviews with Doña Juana, an 86-year-old professor of education at the University of Puerto Rico. These "transcriptions" are short poems written to meet both literary and scientific criteria with the intention of constructing an "essence." Glesne began her analysis by sorting interview material thematically, reducing data and segregating thoughts. But then, rather than progressively coding and categorizing, she reread the words she coded under a particular theme and reflected on them, trying to "understand the essence" of Doña Juana's words (p. 206).

In the process, Glesne discovered that the theme she had constructed was connected to other themes, that the orderliness of the usual analytic process needed to be superseded by a freer movement through the transcript. She searched to illuminate "the wholeness and interconnections of thoughts" (p. 206). Like a scientist showing us a table or graph, moreover, Glesne provides an example of a transcript page with selected words underlined, which then appear in a first version of a poem, and then in a second, where Glesne has drawn from other parts of the interview and taken more license with word forms. We can judge the "validity" of the resulting poem, should we care to, but we probably would not, at least not in the usual terms, because the emotional pull of the poem dominates, as illustrated by the "flying bird" stanza quoted earlier.

TESS'S TEACHING STORY

A third example comes from a remarkable dissertation based on an interview study of teachers on the cusp of retirement. In the dissertation, Judy Erskine Lawton (1997) deploys a variety of alternative representations. Her goal is to represent as truly as possible the life experiences of the teachers and to honor their advice for making the transition out of teaching less stressful.

Lawton tells tells the teaching story of "Tess"—Trudy Plummer—through narrative and lyric poetry, some culled directly from interviews and some chosen from "symbolic representations" provided by Plummer for Lawton's analysis. Plummer and Lawton at times, become co-authors.

In the interview, Tess spoke like a poet, in images, metaphors, symbols, sounds, and sights. To write her interview as other than a poetic representation, I think, would have been a violation of Tess's sensibility, Tess's way of communicating her world. Lawton recognizes the richness of Tess's language and capitalizes on it in both the construction and the discussion of Tess's story. For example, Tess envisions "the end of her career as the shadow of an umbrella, which Lawton describes as 'a vivid image conveying a shift from sunrise to sunset, a literal and symbolic awareness of a shadow at the end of a day, and maybe as Tess expressed it in symbolic representation . . . at the end of a life' " (p. 199).

Here is more of Tess's interview, this set to poetry that almost literally "pencils in" the minutiae of her classroom life.

Pencilling It In

The Schaefer is gone.
The gold-tipped Parker's
relegated to the drawer,
its decisive black
used only on checks.

The felt-tip is abandoned
as too indelible.

For a time the blue automatic pencil
shot words off its tip.
Now its occasional care and feeding,
its hardened eraser
are too much.
He has become a pencil person.
The Number Two is all he pockets.
Its yellow (eraser worn with indecision)
can be forgotten if dropped,
tapped to splinter
snapped in anger.

Light and hesitant, its words
make less and less impression,
weaken blurrily as they
reach the bottom
of a page
or a life.   (P. 189)

In the poem, Lawton enlists Tess's interview's central images as analytic guideposts —"the treadmill," "the downhill roller coaster," and "a hill to climb." Throughout her analysis, Lawton enlists Tess's metaphors as analytical guideposts, a truly remarkable blending of literary analysis with social scientific analysis; a sociopoetics that honors the interviewee and speaks to readers poetically and analytically.

FOOD TRUCK'S STORY

In an absolutely stunning long narrative poem, Phil Smith (1999) tells us the story of Food Truck, a 65-year-old developmentally disabled man who has been living for 40 years in Langdon, a facility for the "mentally retarded." Smith does not inform the reader of how he constructed the poem; he does not state that he wants to meet scientific and aesthetic criteria. What he does tell us, however, is that his journey into conventional scientific writing convinced him that an alternative representation was necessary to prevent his further harming Food Truck. Smith wanted his representation to be a "*nam shub*," as he calls it, a Sumerian term meaning "speech with magical force" (Stephenson 1992:211). He wanted to write a *nam shub* that would change how people thought about and acted toward persons with developmental disabilities.

In seven sections covering 11 pages, Smith takes us on a journey into Food Truck's world. In the process, we learn how Food Truck looks and moves; his routines; his words for people, things, and events that matter to him; his complex emotional life; the struggles of both Food Truck and Smith to communicate with each other; and Smith's indebtedness to Food Truck for being his teacher. The descriptive grace is apparent from the opening words of the poem—"He looks me square in the face, square as a man can whose head doesn't / ever stop bobbing and weaving, swooping and diving"—to the conclusion, which follows:

Food Truck looks up
he says quietly
in a voice falling apart
tumbling in on itself
Grandma's not feeling good
huge old man tears
flow out from his eyes

drip down his cheek
to make a small wet mark on his shirt.
All I can ever think to do
all I can ever do

is

rub

the back
of his
neck—

One surely cannot doubt that Smith engaged in ethnographic interviewing as an emotionally present witness to and advocate for Food Truck (see Behar 1996). Because Smith has mastered the sounds, sights, and images of poetic representation, we are taken into Langdon, walk in Food Truck's steps, take on his categories and words. We do all of this without judgment. We are changed by the writing; we feel differently about the developmentally disabled, the cultural narratives have been resisted. I believe this would not have happened if Smith had reported Food Truck's world in conventional social science writing, rather than in the *nam shub* that he did write.

CLAIRE PHILIP'S "LIFELINES"

In poststructuralist representational practice, not only are the interviewees subject to analysis, but so is the interviewer. A new genre and new specialty—the sociology of subjectivity—has emerged based on "interviews of the self" (Ellis and Flaherty 1992; Ellis 1991, 1995; Richardson 1992, 1994, 1997; St. Pierre 1997). Many of these self-interviews are published in prose or bricolage and are referred to as "autoethnography," but some are published as poems.

A moving example of the narrative of the self as poetic representation appears in social worker Claire E. Philip's (1995) "Lifelines," which includes her journal and her poems. For eight years, Philip kept a journal that was focused on her living with cancer. The journal served as a creative and therapeutic resource, a safe place for dialoguing with herself, a venue for writing about the ethical and interactional consequences of "self-disclosures." Whom should she let know about the diagnosis and her impending death? What would be the consequences of revelation? Of concealment? She wrote to untangle her complex emotions and to help fellow therapists deal with the comparable realities of their lives. In Philip's words, "The journal changed me as the cancer changed me, but throughout, the inner self was constant, recognizable, and reachable. . . . Creativity within the self seeks to connect and in doing so, transforms" (p. 267).

Philip transformed some of her thoughts, interactions, and experiences into poems. Many of the poems arose from interactions and "interviews" with her oncologist. Reading the poems puts the reader into Philip's experiences, evokes compassion and anger, engages and teaches in ways that a research or clinical account—or even poems written by an ethnographer about someone else—would not. Two of Philip's "doctor/patient" poems follow.

Hair

I have spent the last week
In my hospital room
Tidying up fallen hair.
Something to do, anyway.
Doctor, don't say to me
Your wig looks nice.
Rather, say something like
I'll bet you can't wait
Until your hair grows back.
You could say the wig's okay, though.
        (Dated 5/89) (P. 276)

Losing Faith

I tried to tell you how my husband holds
  his head
in his hands

and doesn't know it,
his despair more apparent each week.
Our shared stress ebbs and flows
while time
      moves forward
carrying us along. Bad or good,
test results will anchor this grief,
give it brief respite
      from uncertainty.
You sought to reassure, saying there's
 no proof yet
it's not working
or it is,
      implying his and my lack of faith
is perhaps premature.
You compare this to your wife's recent
 fear
during the storm
      that the electricity would go out.
It's not the same, doctor;
My husband worries his wife will
      go out.
                    (Dated 8/93) (P. 300)

Because Philip's journal has been published along with her poems, we can trace how she constructed the poems from her "field notes." Following her example, we quickly realize that poetry can be found in our own research and personal journals. Poetry's task is to re-present actual experiences—episodes, epiphanies, misfortunes, pleasures; to retell those experiences in such a way that others can experience and feel them. Poems, therefore, have the possibility of doing for social research what conventional social research representation cannot. Philip's "Lifelines" gives us a lifeline into methods for transforming field notes and personal notes into poetry that moves us.

◆ Conclusion

In literary writing and ethnographies of the self, the boundary line is personal; the boundary is between the foreign territory of one person's psyche and that of another. The Other that is the foreign territory, the *terra exotica,* is the inner experience, the inner life of the writer. Writing about the self as both subject and object distances the self from the usual codifications of ethnographic interviewing, even while the writing points out how the self depends upon social and cultural discourses to "know" itself, to position itself.

Poems have the capability of reducing the distance between the "I" and the "Other," and between the "writing-I" and "experiencing-I" of the writer. It can move us to rethink the boundaries between ourselves and our work, help us to feel how our work might be situated within the self (Krieger 1991; see also Rosenblatt, Chapter 43, this volume).

The research self is not separable from the lived self. Who we are and what we can be, what we can study, and how we can write about what we study are all tied to how a knowledge system disciplines its members and claims authority over knowledge. Needed are concrete practices through which we can construct ourselves as ethical subjects engaged in ethical research, even if that means challenging the authority of a discipline's cherished modes of representation. Poetic representation is one such practice.

Self-reflexivity brings to consciousness some of the complex political and ideological agendas hidden in the controls exercised over how interview materials are represented. Minorities entering academia—including members of nonmajority ethnic, class, racial, and postcolonial groups, gays and lesbians, the physically challenged, and returning students—are often tied to traditions, cultures, and meaning making that are in opposition to the conventions and discourses of hegemonic disciplinary practices. These students find the option of poetic representation beckoning and supportive, as they do other representations that honor the arts as a legitimate path to knowing and expressing truths about lived experiences (see Ellis and Berger, Chapter 41, this volume). Science is one lens, creative arts another. Do we not see more deeply through two lenses?

Alternative representational methods create a welcoming space in which to build a community of diverse, socially engaged researchers in which everyone profits. This new research community could, through its theory, analytic practices, and diverse membership, reach beyond academia to teach us about social injustice and methods for alleviating it. Poetic representation, I submit, is a practical and powerful, indeed transforming, method for understanding the social, altering the self, and invigorating the research community that claims knowledge of our lives.

◆ *Appendix*

Louisa May's Story of Her Life

i

The most important thing
to say is that
I grew up in the South.
Being Southern shapes
aspirations shapes
what you think you are
and what you think you're going to be.

> (*When I hear myself, my Ladybird*
> *kind of accent on tape. I think, "Oh Lord.*
> *You're from Tennessee.")*

No one ever suggested to me
that anything
might happen *with* my life.

I grew up poor in a rented house
in a very normal sort of way
on a very normal sort of street
with some very nice middle-class friends
    (*Some still to this day*)
and so I thought I'd have a lot of children.

I lived outside.

Unhappy home. Stable family, till it fell apart.
The first divorce in Milfrount County.

So, that's how that was worked out.

ii

Well, one thing that happens
growing up in the South
is that you leave.   I
always knew I would
I would leave.

> (*I don't know what to say . . .*
> *I don't know what's germane.*)

My high school sweetheart and I married,
went north to college.
    I got pregnant and miscarried,
and I lost the child.
> (*As I see it now it was a marriage*
> *situation which got increasingly horrendous*
> *where I was under the most stress*
> *and strain without any sense*
> *of how to extricate myself.*)

It was purely chance
that I got a job here,
and Robert didn't.
I was mildly happy.

After 14 years of marriage,
That was the break.

We divorced.

A normal sort of life.

iii

So, the Doctor said, "You're pregnant."
I was 41.   John and I
had a happy kind of relationship,
not a serious one.
But beside himself with fear and anger,
awful, rageful, vengeful, horrid,
Jody May's father said,
"Get an Abortion."

I told him,
"I would never marry you.
I would never marry you.
I would never.

"I am going to have this child.
I am going to.
I am.   I am.

"Just Go Away!"

But he wouldn't. He painted the nursery.
He slept on the floor. He went to therapy.
We went to LaMaze.
> *(We ceased having a sexual relationship*
> *directly*
> *after I had gotten pregnant and that has*
> *never again*
> *entered the situation.)*

He lives 100 miles away now.
He visits every weekend.
He sleeps on the floor.
We all vacation together.
We go camping.

I am not interested in a split-family,
her father taking her on Sundays.
I'm not interested in doing so.

So, little Jody Mae always has had a situation
which is normal.

Mother—bless her—the word "married" never
crossed her lips.
> *(I do resent mother's stroke. Other mothers*
> *have their mother.)*

So, it never occurs to me really that we are
unusual in any way.

No, our life really is very normal.
I own my house.
I live on a perfectly ordinary middle-class street.

So, that's the way that was worked out.

iv

She has his name. If she wasn't going to have a
father,
I thought she should have a father, so to speak.

We both adore her.
John says Jody Mae saved his life.

Oh, I do fear that something will change—

v

(Is this helpful?)

This is the happiest time in my life.

I am an entirely different person.

With no husband in the home there is less
tension.
And I'm not talking about abnormal families
here.
Just normal circumstances.
Everyone comes home tired.

I left the South a long time ago.
I had no idea how I would do it.

So, that's the way that worked out.

(I've talked so much my throat hurts.)

■ *References*

Austin, D. A. 1996. "Kaleidoscope: The Same and Different." Pp. 206-30 in *Composing Ethnography: Alternative Forms of Qualitative Writing*, edited by C. Ellis and A. P. Bochner. Walnut Creek, CA: AltaMira.

Baff, S. J. 1997. "Realism and Naturalism and Dead Dudes: Talking about Literature in 11th-Grade English." *Qualitative Inquiry* 3:468-90.

Behar, R. 1996. *The Vulnerable Observer: Anthropology That Breaks Your Heart.* Boston: Beacon.

Borroff, M. 1993. "Cluster on the Poetic: From Euripides to Rich." *Publications of the Modern Language Association of America* 108:1032-35.

Brady, I. 1998. "A Gift of the Journey." *Qualitative Inquiry* 4:463-64.

Danforth, S. 1997. "On What Basis Hope? Modern Progress and Postmodern Possibilities." *Mental Retardation* 35:93-106.

Denzin, N. K. 1989. *Interpretive Interactionism.* Newbury Park, CA: Sage.

Denzin, N. K. and Y. S. Lincoln, eds. 2000. *Handbook of Qualitative Research.* 2d ed. Thousand Oaks, CA: Sage.

Derrida, J. 1982. *Margins of Philosophy*. Translated by A. Bass. Chicago: University of Chicago.

Eco, U. 1979. *A Theory of Semiotics*. Bloomington: Indiana University Press.

Ellis, C. 1991. "Sociological Introspection and Emotional Experience." *Symbolic Interaction* 14:23-50.

———. 1995. *Final Negotiations: A Story of Love, Loss, and Chronic Illness*. Philadelphia: Temple University Press.

Ellis, C. and A. P. Bochner, eds. 1996. *Composing Ethnography: Alternative Forms of Qualitative Writing*. Walnut Creek, CA: AltaMira.

Ellis, C. and M. G. Flaherty, eds. 1992. *Investigating Subjectivity: Research on Lived Experience*. Newbury Park, CA: Sage.

Foucault, M. 1978. *The History of Sexuality,* Vol. 1, *An Introduction*. Translated by R. Hurley. New York: Pantheon.

Gilgun, J. F. 1999. "Fingernails Painted Red: A Feminist, Semiotic Analysis of a 'Hot' Text." *Qualitative Inquiry* 5:181-207.

Glesne, C. E. 1997. "That Rare Feeling: Re-presenting Research through Poetic Transcription." *Qualitative Inquiry* 3:202-21.

Haraway, D. J. 1988. "Situated Knowledges: The Science Question in Feminism and the Privilege of Partial Perspective." *Feminist Studies* 14:575-99.

Hones, D. F. 1998. "Known in Part: The Transformational Power of Narrative Inquiry." *Qualitative Inquiry* 4:225-48.

Jones, S. H. 1998. "Kaleidoscope Notes: Writing Women's Music and Organizational Culture." *Qualitative Inquiry* 4:148-77.

———. 1999. "Torch." *Qualitative Inquiry* 5:280-304.

Krieger, S. 1991. *Social Science and the Self: Personal Essays on an Art Form*. New Brunswick, NJ: Rutgers University Press.

Lakoff, G. and M. Johnson. 1980. *Metaphors We Live By*. Chicago: University of Chicago Press.

Lawton, J. E. 1997. "Reconceptualizing a Horizontal Career Line: A Study of Seven Experienced Urban English Teachers Approaching Career End." Ph.D. dissertation, Ohio State University.

Manning, P. K. and B. Cullum-Swan. 1994. "Narrative, Content, and Semiotic Analysis." Pp. 463-77 in *Handbook of Qualitative Research,* edited by N. K. Denzin and Y. S. Lincoln. Thousand Oaks, CA: Sage.

Mishler, E. G. 1986. *Research Interviewing: Context and Narrative*. Cambridge, MA: Harvard University Press.

Philip, C. E. 1995. "Lifelines." *Journal of Aging Studies* 9:265-322.

Poindexter, C. C. 1998. "Poetry as Data Analysis: Honoring the Words of Research Participants." *Reflections: Narratives of Professional Helping* 4(3):22-25.

Richardson, L. 1988. "The Collective Story: Postmodernism and the Writing of Sociology." *Sociological Focus* 21:199-208.

———. 1990. *Writing Strategies: Reaching Diverse Audiences*. Newbury Park, CA: Sage.

———. 1992. "The Consequences of Poetic Representation: Writing the Other, Re-writing the Self." Pp. 125-37 in *Investigating Subjectivity: Research on Lived Experience,* edited by C. Ellis and M. G. Flaherty. Newbury Park, CA: Sage.

———. 1994. "Nine Poems: Marriage and the Family." *Journal of Contemporary Ethnography* 23:3-13.

———. 1995. "Vespers." *Chicago Review* 41:129-46.

———. 1996. "Educational Birds." *Journal of Contemporary Ethnography* 25:6-15.

———. 1997. *Fields of Play: Constructing an Academic Life*. New Brunswick, NJ: Rutgers University Press.

———. 1999a. "Dead Again in Berkeley." *Qualitative Inquiry* 5:141-44.

———. 1999b. "Feathers in Our Cap." *Journal of Contemporary Ethnography* 28:660-68.

Richardson, M. 1998. "Poetics in the Field and on the Page." *Qualitative Inquiry* 4:451-62.

———. 1999. "The Anthro in Cali." *Qualitative Inquiry* 5:563-65.

Rinehart, R. 1997. "Concatenations: Three Lives . . . to Be Continued." *Cultural Studies* 11:169-90.

St. Pierre, E. A. 1997. "Nomadic Inquiry in the Smooth Spaces of the Field: A Preface." *International Journal of Qualitative Studies in Education* 10:363-83.

Shapiro, M. 1985-86. "Metaphor in the Philosophy of the Social Sciences." *Cultural Critique* 2:191-214.

Smith, B. 1999. "The Abyss: Exploring Depression through a Narrative of the Self." *Qualitative Inquiry* 5:264-79.

Smith, P. 1999. "Food Truck's Party Hat." *Qualitative Inquiry* 5:244-61.

Sommerville, M. 1999. *Body/Landscape Journals.* Melbourne: Spinifex.

Stephenson, N. 1992. *Snow Crash.* New York: Bantam.

Tedlock, D. 1983. *The Spoken Word and the Work of Interpretation.* Philadelphia: University of Pennsylvania Press.

Travisano, R. 1998. "On Becoming Italian American: An Autobiography of an Ethnic Identity." *Qualitative Inquiry* 4:540-63.

———. 1999. "Kansas City Woman." *Qualitative Inquiry* 5:262-63.

Ulmer, G. L. 1989. *Teletheory: Grammatology in the Age of Video.* New York: Routledge.

———. 1994. *Heuretics: The Logic of Invention.* Baltimore: Johns Hopkins University Press.

INTERVIEWING AT THE BORDER OF FACT AND FICTION

◆ Paul C. Rosenblatt

For many social scientists there is still a distinct boundary between fact and fiction in interviewing. For them, interviewing is a matter of finding the best ways to elicit true, valid, factual answers to interview questions. However, for ever more of us, the boundary between fact and fiction has blurred (Denzin 1997). We see the boundary not as a reality that transcends time and culture, but as a social construction, like other boundaries (Rosenblatt 1994). We live in a world of postmodernist thought in which, even if we are affirmatively postmodern (Rosenau 1992) and resist an anarchy of standards and the annihilation of anything that could be called truth, we understand that social science facts and truths are at best perspectival. We hear our interview respondents relating narratives about their lives that seem to be like what we read in novels (Polkinghorne 1988:163). We have come to recognize that what we write is fiction in the sense of having been fashioned by us (Clifford 1986). It no longer is clear that the voice of the social scientist has more claim to be heard than the voice of anyone else (Kenneth Gergen, cited in Gülerce 1995). It seems no longer to make sense to evaluate what we think we know against standards of predictive utility, empirical fact, or other criteria championed by positivists (Gergen 1988).

In this chapter, I use my own experiences as researcher and hopeful writer of fiction to inform my discussion of interviewing at the boundary of fact and fiction. Most of my interviewing research has focused on families or couples dealing with difficult issues. Among these studies are book-length qualitative works on business-owning families (Rosenblatt et al. 1985), farm families dealing with an economic crisis in farming (Rosenblatt 1990), multiracial couples (Rosenblatt, Karis, and Powell 1995), and married couples dealing with the death of a child (Rosenblatt 2000). As an aspiring fiction writer, I am in the midst of work on an action-adventure novel set in a nursing home and on the cotranslation of a novel from Korean to English. I have also drafted a detective novel that focuses on a farm family dealing with a death on the farm. These efforts at writing fiction, plus my research experience, converge to provide a basis for my comments here on the boundary between fact and fiction.

◆ Blurring the Boundary between Fact and Fiction

The postmodern interviewer understands that interviewing produces a social co-construction in which interviewer and interviewee are both players (Holstein and Gubrium 1995). The postmodern interviewer also understands that the language researchers use to communicate what they think they have learned creates, highlights, limits, and obscures what some people might consider to be fact and truth (see Gubrium and Holstein 1997). The postmodern interviewing world is one of standpoint perspectives (Smith 1987) and of cultural and experiential diversity, where a shift from one perspective to another can radically alter realities. We may still be influenced by Karl Popper (e.g., 1962) and Donald T. Campbell (e.g., 1988) to doubt systematically and to challenge our provisional truths as though we have faith that challenging will lead to truths that are ever more resistant to challenge. But in our awareness of the social construction of reality, the rhetoric of writing social research reports, and the inevitable limits, biases, and subjectivity (often covert) of research, we are ever more skeptical of the status of

the provisional truths we have to offer (see Fontana, Chapter 8, this volume).

We might be so modest as to call our truths suggestions, possibilities, or perspectives, but we may still seek grants on the promise of documenting something like truth. We often are published, read, and cited by people who think we have truths to offer. And many of us who are in some ways postmodernist are still using methodological approaches that were developed in the days when social science realities were real. Perhaps we use those methodologies because they are what we have or because they legitimate our work for important constituencies.

I am not uncomfortable that my interviewing approaches and ways of working with interview material are related to modernist research approaches because I think they help me to get at something like truth, and I still want to learn something like truth. I still think it is possible to be ignorant or wrong, and I want to be less ignorant and no longer wrong. I do my interview research because I think I can get closer to whatever is "right" by hearing what people have to say. I know I could do interviews simply to learn what people say—to do research on storytelling—but I still think what I hear in interviews gives me more than mere stories.

When, for example, bereaved parents tell me about their grieving and their closest relationships after their child's death, I believe I am learning something that is real and true for them. I am not simply learning their stories. When I hear similar stories from many bereaved parents, I think I am learning something about parent grief. I don't think I am learning immutable truths, but I think I am learning something important about many bereaved parents. With Robert Weiss (1994:148-49) and others who have written about qualitative research, I do not consider the truths I learn to be unambiguous, invariant, the whole truth and nothing but the truth. But I still feel I am doing the right thing in making something out of what I hear from interviewees.

We can also view the blurring of the boundary between fact and fiction from the perspective of the writers and readers of fiction. For some of them, the boundary between fact and fiction has been blurred if not destroyed in part because it is now clear that much of fiction has strong autobiographical, experiential, and observational elements. Also, many people read works of fiction as guides to life and as sources of insight. For them, there is truth in fiction. In fact, readers may find in fiction truths that are for them more profound, persuasive, and trustworthy than those they find in social science writings.

◆ Research Interviewing in Postmodern Hindsight

With postmodern blurring of boundaries and borders, what can we make, in hindsight, of research interviewing?

INTERVIEWEES' BELIEF IN TRUTH

Every person I have ever interviewed seemed to believe in truth and to try hard to deal with the truth. They were all psychological essentialists (Gergen 1994) in that they talked as though there is a real reality to be known and told (or withheld). So even if we as interviewers are postmodernists, the social construction of our interview interactions is to some extent driven by truth and essentialism. People think I want to know the truth. The context, and to some extent the language, of our interview interaction is a language of truth and falsity, of trying to get to accurate memories and accurate reports of events, feelings, and beliefs. In fact, some people I interview will telephone or write after an interview in order to give what they consider to be a

more accurate statement about something, to clarify something they said during the interview, or to add something they had forgotten.

Often an interviewee will interview me about what I think about something, what my experience has been, or what I have learned from others I have interviewed. An interviewee might, for example, ask me, "What do the parents you have talked with already say about how family members and friends treated them after the child's death?" Typically I reply with something that has a postmodern tone to it, for example: "I don't know. It's hard to say. Most parents I've talked with so far have said that they felt that after the funeral most family members and friends avoided them. But there are lots of ways of understanding that, and I don't know whether the family members and friends would say they were trying to avoid. It's difficult to generalize or to say what's true." But even if I offer my postmodern perspectives in the interviews, respondents always return to the modern language of truth and facts.

The interviews people give me are carried out in the context of their notions of reporters, detectives, medical researchers, pollsters, and others interviewees believe to seek the truth. Interviewees have the concept of the investigator searching for the truth and also believe that it is crucial to the investigator that the truth be given. I think they also believe that not giving the truth is, except in exceptional circumstances, immoral. Many people I have interviewed seem to me to feel an almost sacred obligation to provide the truth. So even if I am in a postmodern and perspectival world as I read and write social science, the people I interview offer me truth and push me to be like the reporters, detectives, and others they believe to be seekers of truth.

This naive realism influences me. Although I can frame what people say to me in terms that are quite foreign to them and quite compelling to me, I often write my social science in ways that honor their real realities. I don't want them to read what I have written and wonder where their realities went. I also don't want to abandon their realities because I think part of what I have to offer readers is what the people I interview seem to say is real and true.

ENTITLEMENT TO DECEIVE

Interviewees think that some people lie or mislead—for example, politicians and defendants in legal proceedings. I think they look down on those people and do not want to be like them. Still, I think often people feel entitled in an interview not to tell the whole truth and nothing but the truth. I think in my interviewing, the key "deceptions" or failures to tell the whole truth and nothing but the truth come from people wanting to avoid embarrassment and from the dynamics of family members being interviewed together who do not want to reveal something that might hurt, embarrass, or offend another family member.

Sometimes the "deception" comes from what is probably normal in the early part of an interview. Interviewees don't know if they can trust me; I haven't engaged them fully, they don't know how deep I want them to go, and they are using the etiquette they would use with strangers (which involves not disclosing anything that might make me think less well of them). I know there are "deceptions" early in interviews because sometimes as an interview unfolds things that were hidden earlier are brought out. For example, it may only be after an hour into an interview in which a couple has represented their marital relationship as problem-free that I discover that the wife has serious alcohol problems and her husband has often hit her.

In his advice to interviewers, based on his own experience as an interviewer and as a manager of interviewers, Weiss (1994) offers a number of suggestions for getting to what interviewees may have withheld. Perhaps the key suggestions are that the inter-

viewer should pick up on clues the interviewee may have dropped and should use good interviewing skills to build a rapport that will lead the interviewee to disclose more as the interview progresses. From a postmodern perspective, what constitutes a clue could be said to differ from interviewer to interviewer, and sometimes the clue is that something has not been mentioned at all. And from a postmodern perspective, the building of rapport may be understood as the interviewer building, with the interviewee, a sense of how embarrassing, emotional, or otherwise possibly difficult topics can be brought up and how they will be co-constructed. The processes of building rapport and what is gained and lost through the building of rapport in various ways are, I think, matters that we postmodern interview researchers should not take for granted but should study carefully and understand well.

ELICITING POSSIBLY CONTRADICTORY TRUTHS

I allow respondents great latitude to construct our relationship and to define what is important. Good postmodern qualitative interviewing is much less controlling and directive than is the model for positivist interviewing. But still I will push people to talk about what is important to them from various viewpoints. For example, I might ask a couple how their clergyman or -woman might think about something, or how they would have thought about something 10 years ago. Or I might ask a question that I hope will move an interviewee to a different way of thinking about an event (for example, feelings based versus biomedical versus religious versus legal). So, even though I expect that interviewees will tell me what they consider to be the truth and I honor their efforts to tell that truth, I do not accept that the truth they have just given me is the truth that others share or that will be the whole truth after they reply to my next question.

When interviewees signal me in some way that they have told all they know about something, I might stop digging and go on to my next question. But on important matters, I often return to a question that seemingly has already been answered completely. I might ask the question from another angle, or with different words, or with additional permission to the interviewee to say something that could be embarrassing or otherwise difficult. Or I might ask that the question be answered from another perspective. I might frame the renewed questioning as a matter of aiding interviewee memory, so the whole truth can be given. Or I might frame it as looking for additional specifics.

RESEARCHER OPENNESS TO DIVERSE REALITIES

A continuing challenge for the interviewer is to be open-minded, to decenter from one's own realities so as to be able to move into realities that are not only different from one's own but also surprising, alien, uncomfortable, a direct challenge to one's thinking, disgusting, horrifying, anxiety-provoking, boring, or otherwise difficult. If I had lived a totally realist life, without reading fiction, seeing films, having a rich fantasy life, or having come to know a diversity of people whose different realities have challenged me, it would be more difficult to be open. What Andrea Fontana and James H. Frey (1994) call "understanding the language and culture of the respondents" can be understood as learning culture and new languages, but I also think it is about being comfortable with realities that are new to one.

Good interviewing will draw out from interviewees what they would be reluctant to tell most people. Sometimes the reluctance arises from concerns that people will think what they have to say is a fiction. Perhaps it is their experience of spirit possession. Perhaps it is an allegation (inconsistent with what everyone else in the family believes and inconsistent with what the authorities have said) that a family death was murder, not an accident or a death by natural causes. Perhaps it is about communications they have received from the dead, about their past lives, about their experiences of prescience, or about their fantastic powers.

As I interview, I think about how I may construct the interview material I am hearing/seeing when I analyze the interview transcript and write up my research. I do not want these preliminary "takes" on the interview to swamp whatever respondents say. That is, I am still trying to write works that are empirically grounded (grounded in experiences not wholly my own). I am still open to learning that my preliminary interpretations are wrong, or wrong for particular respondents. So I try out my interpretations on the people I interview. I push as I interview for more information consistent and inconsistent with my emerging interpretations (Rosenblatt 1981) and try to elicit a great deal of concrete documentation on what seem ever more likely, as an interviewing study goes on, to be central interpretive points.

DOUBT AND THE ELICITATION OF NEW INFORMATION

Occasionally I think a respondent is not telling what she or he would consider to be the truth or the whole truth. When I think someone is hiding something, being evasive, making things up, I feel that I am on shaky ground. On the one hand, I think that I must accept that this person's claimed reality is her or his reality. On the other hand, when people seem to be outliers, are giving off verbal and nonverbal cues that I think are deceptive, are saying things that are internally inconsistent, are saying things that I doubt are their truths, I push for more.

It is my experience that when I probe in an area that seems to be one of untruth or not full truth, I sometimes learn that what I thought was fiction was fiction. For example, the person was too embarrassed to tell me at first that he drinks 6 to 12 cans of beer each day. And sometimes I learn that the fiction is, for the person, totally believable. For example, a widow believes that her deceased husband was a saint. Or, to take an example offered by Melvin Pollner and Lynn McDonald-Winkler (1985) and that I have come across in my own interviewing, parents believe that a child who is disabled and developmentally delayed at the extreme is very able.

NARRATIVES GOOD ENOUGH TO BE FICTION

As interviewees talk to me, I think about what will make for fascinating reading— for example, the vivid story, the powerful metaphor, the touchingly authentic statement of feelings, or the family battle that erupts with a *Who's Afraid of Virginia Woolf?* volcanic power. My sense of what will make good reading comes partly from my reading of fiction. I relish interview narratives that are as gripping as those in a powerful and moving work of fiction. I feel deep satisfaction on hearing an interviewee say something that I know will make a vivid, attention-grabbing, memorable quote in print. Thus my sense of what makes for good reading in fiction as well as in social research reports provides guidelines that are important to me in my interviewing.

I am not sure it is so different for the people being interviewed. I think many have a sense of what is a good story, and some delight in telling a story well. Some are obviously experienced storytellers who are telling me stories they have told on many previous occasions. However, not infrequently, individuals will say to me that they have never told their stories, or their whole stories, to anyone. They seem grateful for the opportunity to have somebody hear them out. They also seem grateful to hear the stories themselves and feel that they learned something from hearing what it is they had to say.

Another connection between fiction and research based on interviews that generate "good" narrative is that it is much easier to carry out interview research or to write fiction in areas in which people have passionate feelings and speak eloquently and at length. You do not see much fiction or interview research dealing with topics about which people are inarticulate or have almost nothing to say. In that sense, "Would it make good fiction?" is a good question to ask of a qualitative research interview. Qualitative research can be understood as constructed out of people's stories (Paget 1983). If people in good fiction would not speak these words because there is no story there, or no story that could interest anyone, perhaps there is not much to the interview.

IMAGINING THE INTERVIEWEE; IMAGINING THE INTERVIEWER

All research begins with imagined research subjects (Holstein and Gubrium 1995; see also Gubrium and Holstein, Chapter 1, this volume). We cannot decide on an issue to study or what data to gather without imagining the research subject. In qualitative interviewing, the interview schedule and the ongoing interaction with interviewees always involves our imagination of who the interviewees are, what is going on with them, and how they will react to various things we might ask or do. The process of constructing the subject begins prior to the interview, but it is modified during the course of an interview session, so once we begin the interview the imagined subject is co-constructed. And no matter how much we believe we know an interviewee or all the interviewees in a study we have carried out, we are still imagining them. Thus, when I said earlier that interviewees believe in truth, I was asserting as true what is a construction I believe I have reached with interviewees. But my belief does not make what is in a sense fiction into fact. However much we believe in constructed selves, they are still constructed and are capable of being constructed in other ways. Similarly, at times I try to "bracket" my presuppositions about interviewees in order to be as open as possible to their constructions of themselves. But that does not mean I have left the realm of constructed, construed, and, in a sense, fictional selves.

I think my reading and writing of fiction have made me a better interviewer because I bring a broader range of hypothesized selves and experiences to an interviewee and have more openness to possible interviewee selves and experiences. I am comfortable with the idea that an interviewee is in her 15th reincarnation, that God has sent me to her, that I am interviewing a married couple who have almost not spoken to each other in six years, or that an interviewee is right in believing that a powerful spirit has stopped my tape recorder from working.

I am also aware that the interviewee will have hypotheses about what I am up to and what is behind my questions (Alasuutari 1995). From that perspective, part of what goes on in the interview is that the interviewee tests out hypotheses about me and my questions. As the interview progresses, the interviewee is likely to develop a more precise sense of who I am and what I am up to, and, if correct, may do a better job by my standards of addressing the issues I want addressed in ways that I value.

INTERVIEWING AND WHAT IS DEEP INSIDE THE INTERVIEWER

So far, I have been writing as though I know what I am doing when I carry out qualitative interviews and as though I and most respondents are rational. But I assure you that there is much going on beneath the surface for me and, I think, for the people being interviewed, a great deal that is not rational or in awareness (Scheurich 1995).

One thing that persuades me that there is a great deal beneath the surface of interviewers is my experience doing studies with multiple interviewers. No matter how much I work at having us all understand the research questions and the interview guide in the same way, no matter how much we practice interviewing, no matter how much we cointerview before we solo, interviewers are inevitably quite different in their interviews. They differ in the kind of rapport they develop with respondents, how they ask certain questions, how they interact as they listen to respondents, what they pick up on, what they accept without questioning, how and what they probe, how much they allow the interviewee to go off on what could be taken as tangents, and how long their interviews run. One could say these things are a matter of social skills or research experience, but one can also take them as beneath-the-surface stuff. I have never done the research, but I believe that the differences among interviewers in what they pick up from respondents are related to differences in what is beneath the surface in the interviewers.

I think the interviewers who do the best are people who are comfortable with under-the-surface emotional matters related to the research. For example, if one is not comfortable with death and mortality issues, one will find it hard to draw bereaved people out, hear them out, and co-construct realities with them. (For further discussion about how some interviewers might not "click" with some interviewees, see Weiss 1994:136-41, 145-47.)

One can also take interviewer differences as connected to the inherent ambiguity in language (Scheurich 1995), which leaves interviewer and interviewee free, to some extent, to make any question or comment a projective test. I think repeatedly in an interview the respondent and the interviewer are choosing among many different possible understandings of things said. Interview transcripts map those choices and often give hints of possible alternative choices. An interviewee who is a recent widow might say, for example, "I read the newspaper every day, but I can't stand to look at the sports section." One interviewer might follow that comment up with a question about what the widow does like to read; another might ask why she can't stand the sports section. The former interviewer might learn about the widow's interest in local news and the television schedule. The latter interviewer might learn about the widow's sense that it was the sports section that her husband most liked, that it makes her feel sad to be reminded of him, and that she tries to avoid feeling sad by avoiding reminders of him. Perhaps the difference between the two interviewers would simply be a matter of what to do with the ambiguity of language, but my guess is that it might also have to do with their comfort with a widow's pain and with their own feelings connected to death.

DATA ANALYSIS AS PART OF AN INTERVIEW

Many sources on how to do qualitative interview research say that data analysis can and should begin during the interviewing phase of the research (e.g., Kvale 1996; Strauss and Corbin 1998; see also Charmaz, Chapter 32, this volume). Part of what they mean is that one should question based on what one thinks one has learned so far in the study. From a constructionist perspective (Holstein and Gubrium 1995), that means that one should be actively planful about one's part in cocreating truths with interviewees. In a sense that means that based on what one believes one has found out so far in the research, one should try to elicit words from interviewees that refute, support, or qualify one's developing interpretation. One may develop these preliminary analyses during one's interviews, by thinking things through by means of a field diary, by listening to interview tapes, or—what works best for me—by transcribing interviews immediately and analyzing as one goes what seems to be significant and what one wishes one had asked.

From another perspective, the process of analysis during the interview seems to me to blur the boundary between two texts—the "text" that is the verbal and non-verbal performance of the interview and the "text" that is the transcription of the interview. The interviewer's on-the-fly analysis of the former text cocreates that text, in a postmodern sense, and intrudes into the interview transcription text.

There was, however, a time in my life when I caught myself creating research findings that were more fictional than I was comfortable creating. At the time, I was a quantitative positivist researcher teaching experimental social psychology and modernist research methods. As a standard part of my research, I "debriefed" respondents. That is, after the data gathering part of the research was complete, I interviewed respondents about their experience of the research. Initially, I conducted such debriefing primarily to tell them about deceptions in the research and to be sure that they were not leaving the research setting in anger or pain. But my interviews with respondents led to them talking about how they understood my instructions to them, my experimental manipulations, and my paper-and-pencil psychological measures. I also began to interview "pilot" respondents in my sample survey studies about how they understood questions in my survey questionnaires and what their own responses meant to them. It was my qualitative interviewing at the end of experimental sessions and as part of piloting survey studies that set me on the road to being a qualitative researcher.

As I debriefed subjects in my experiments, I became aware of how arrogantly ignorant and wrong my assumptions were about the people I was researching. They often understood things differently and in more complex ways than I assumed. Similarly, with my survey questionnaires, my interviews showed that virtually all questions, even the questions I thought were most straightforward, were engaged by people in ways that made my interpreting their responses without knowledge of the complexities of their understandings a work of fiction. A simple question like "How much sleep did you have last night?" would be interpreted differently depending on what a respondent decided "sleep," "last night," and "night" meant, and depending on whether the respondent thought I really wanted to know about "last night" or about a typical night. Multiply such complexities by the number of questions in the survey, and it became clear to me that I might best become a qualitative interview researcher.

◆ *Writing Fiction*

I now turn to the writing experience and how a research context relates to the way findings are presented. I am especially concerned here with how fiction can inform the interpretation of interview findings.

FICTION AND THE WRITING UP OF QUALITATIVE INTERVIEW RESEARCH

When I write up qualitative interview research, there is again a blurred boundary between fiction and fact. Part of it is that when I write about my research methods, the conventions of writing about methods (Harré 1990), the rhetoric of research reporting (Gusfield 1976), and the page limits imposed by editors guarantee that I simplify in ways that could be misleading. Somebody could see such simplifying as necessary for reader sanity or see it as the essence of respectable research reporting. But in that simplifying, there is a kind of fictionalizing. By contrast, in the detective novel I have drafted about a researcher who specializes in qualitative interviewing and who has been recruited to help a farm family understand and deal with what may have been an accidental death or may have been murder, the researcher discusses the interview craft in detail. For example, he

talks about what he does when a speaker pauses or seems to change the topic of conversation, what he does with his anxiety during an interview, how he decides what to ask when he is not sure what to ask, and how he processes an interview in the hours following the interview.

Laurel Richardson (1994), in reviewing and commenting on experimental representations in qualitative research, shows how such representations grow out of postmodern irreverence, doubt, and impatience with standard reporting in qualitative research. In a sense, my detective novel is what she calls a "narrative of self," a self who provides unusual detail about the range of things to which he, as a researcher, attends. For example, in the fictional account, I talk about how people sit as they talk, what they ask me, how they smell, how their language changes as who is present changes, how their dogs are players in family experience, their use of facial tissues when they cry, how they slide by family disagreements during a family interview, the ways they can blithely and unapologetically be inconsistent, and how much they seem trapped by culture, neighbors, property ownership, and much else into thinking along certain lines and not others.

FICTION THAT TELLS WHAT HAS BEEN LEARNED IN RESEARCH

My detective novel is based on my interview studies of farm families who have lost a family member in a fatal farm accident (e.g., Rosenblatt and Karis 1993, 1993-94). Writing the novel has enabled me to give more context to the situations of the people I have interviewed and to describe characters with far greater texture than I ever could in a research publication. I can also detail the starts, stops, blind alleys, mistakes, and evolution of an investigative journey, as opposed to what I can do in research reports, which usually give only a picture of what is intended to be the end of the journey. In those ways, writing fiction enables me to be true to much that I can never report so honestly within the standard venues for publishing in the social sciences.

If I am providing readers with fictionalized accounts that seem to me to be reasonable representations of things I know about grieving families dealing with fatal accidents, how can the reader judge what I have written? Laurel Richardson and Ernest Lockridge (1998), in discussing the writing of fictional ethnography, explore several criteria. One is that the text inspires something—research, action, a change in the reader. A critic of fictional representations of research might argue that something invalid or inauthentic in the fiction could inspire, and what it inspires might be invalid or inauthentic. As a postmodernist, I squirm when a discussion turns to matters of validity and authenticity, because those terms imply certainties, criteria, and truths that I think are at best questionable.

Determining what readers derive from a text is a complex matter, because a text can be perceived and felt at many different levels and in many different ways (Ang 1985; Holland 1968). So a critic who considers something invalid in a text may miss that some people are picking up on something very different from what the critic sees in the text or sees as invalid. But even if a reader makes use of something a critic considers invalid, I see no problem with that. I think readers are fully capable of taking personally valid and authentic inspiration from texts that in some way are not valid or authentic by somebody's standards. So a critic who is concerned about what fiction might inspire would do well to focus on the reader, not the fiction. And, in fairness, the focus should also encompass readers of scholarly articles and books. I think we need studies of readers of social science and what they take from what they read. My suspicion is that we might find that readers will at times be stimulated to think thoughts they consider new and valuable

even by social science writings they, or others, consider to be flawed.

Another criterion explicated by Richardson and Lockridge (1998) for evaluating fictionalized research accounts is the "aesthetic." They include in the "aesthetic" the relationship between the reader and the writer, the integration of the writing, the sensory qualities of what is being written about (how it tastes, smells, sounds, looks, feels), the characters coming to life, and the conveying of profundity, mystery, magic, and possibility.

It seems to me that in the typical social science reporting mode, the writer is supposed to be aloof from the particulars, not supposed to be "distracted" by the details that do not speak directly to the research agenda. The writer is supposed to emphasize theory and ideas (in contrast to sensory qualities, characters coming to life, profundity, mystery, magic, and perhaps possibility). In such reporting, the aesthetic is very different from what it is for fiction. It is an aesthetic that makes the material much less accessible to most of the reading public. To the extent that I want what I have learned from carrying out my research to be accessible to a wide range of readers, fiction offers a much better venue for making the interview material and what I think of it accessible. If my fiction is written well, the characters and their experiences come alive. In my social science writing, I may be able to sneak in aesthetic qualities with interview quotes, but it is not a sustained vitality, as in fiction. My sense is that bad fiction will, by definition, fail to meet what Richardson and Lockridge consider to be aesthetic qualities, but it is much easier to meet those aesthetic qualities with fictionalized accounts than with standard research reports.

I have come to appreciate deeply social scientists who have written fiction that reflects what they have learned as scholars —for example, anthropologists such as Oliver La Farge (e.g., 1929) and Zora Neale Hurston (e.g., 1937) and womanists such as Charlotte Perkins Gilman (e.g., 1979). I no longer think of scholarly writing as something that necessarily communicates what I most want readers to know about what I have learned from my research. Also, I have been influenced by sociologists and psychologists such as Howard Becker, Kenneth Gergen, Michal McCall, and Marianne Paget, who have explored alternative means of communicating about social research (e.g., McCall et al. 1990).

As I have moved further into trying to write fiction, I have experienced most powerfully the realization that in creating fiction I have been freed to tell readers far more than I could while working within the constraints of conventional social science writing. At the same time, I worry a great deal about how to persuade myself and the reader that what I have to offer has some kind of validity and truth to it.

Writing fiction challenges me with the same concerns about validity as writing a research report. I still wonder whether what I say has validity by some standard, however imperfect, makes sense, and is understandable to the reader in ways that I intend it to be understood. I still worry about whether what I have the characters say fits what the text I write around those quotes says is going on with them.

Years of interviewing, transcribing interviews, checking transcriptions, coding transcriptions, and creating manuscripts that quote from transcriptions has given me, I think, a good sense of how people speak. Sometimes when I read fiction or watch drama or film, I marvel at the authenticity the writer has captured. But sometimes I think the writer is off base, missing something important about how people speak. You might think that my good sense of how people speak would be a benefit in my writing of fiction, and I think it is some of the time. But sometimes it is not. One way it is not is that I am lost when my fictional characters are supposed to say things that are remote from what I have heard, transcribed, and coded people saying. At that point, I am probably less equipped than most fiction writers to use the resources of my fantasy, because I have come to rely so much on my experience with research interviews.

The other way my experience with ordinary speech is not an advantage is that I know ordinary speech is ungrammatical, redundant, often unpunctuated, sometimes incoherent, filled with "you know," "uh," "er," and restarts, and often internally inconsistent. I also know that ordinary speech has rhythm and pitch variations that are impossible to represent in an ordinary written text. Those things are very tricky to incorporate into fictional dialogue on a sustained basis (and why some scholars [e.g., Paget (1993) 1995] have tried dramatic representations to disseminate their personal and research insights). I think to make fiction readable, a writer almost has to have fictional characters most of the time speak more clearly than ordinary people do.

As an aspiring novelist who is an experienced researcher, teacher of researchers, and reviewer for social science journals, I find that my writing of fiction is complicated in that I have never totally abandoned my modernist concern about evidence, validity, and certainty. My concern weighs me down like concrete shoes on a runner. It has the potential to make my writing process tedious and labored, and to make what I write ponderous to read. On the other hand, the kind of thinking I do as a researcher makes, I think, for mystery writing that is smart. In fact, the parallels between the detective in the detective novel genre (Alasuutari 1998; Hoppenstand 1987; Sanders 1974) and the researcher in the modern social research genre are clear. Both are learned and rational, both are smart about finding clues to help solve a puzzle, both are able to see what the untrained and inexperienced person cannot see, and both have worked hard to master a craft that enables them to seek and evaluate information.

However, the modern has been engulfed in the postmodern. Like me as a researcher, the fictional researcher who is acting as a detective in the novel I have written has epistemological and ontological concerns that have become in many ways postmodern. He searches for many different kinds of evidence and he questions the evidence given him, which are respectably modern things to do. But he is postmodern in that he also questions his and other people's categories of reality, the nature of certainty, and how he affects the realities that emerge through his investigating. And he is humble and provisional about what he knows.

My concerns as a researcher also show up in how much I research the fiction I may write. In preparing to write a novel about missionaries and the Spokane Indians they tried to convert in the 1830s, I have put in many hours reading ethnohistory, 19th-century diaries and letters, anthropological accounts, and Indian accounts. Writing a novel about Indians and missionaries in the 1830s is extremely difficult for me, because I cannot find writings that I am confident present the Indian perspective in the 1830s. In a sense, the problem I have is why I do interview research—to learn things that are not already in journals, books, and other repositories of knowledge. But the Spokane Indians in the 1830s are not available to be interviewed. And as a committed empiricist I can be exquisitely uncomfortable about making up the thoughts and conversations of people about whom I know too little. I fear they will sound like me, movie Indians, 19th-century Euro-American idealizations of Indians, modern-day Indians, or nobody in particular. At this point, the novel is emplotted; I know what I want to say. But I am too much anchored in my epistemological concerns to write, because I have not found what I consider to be reasonably authentic voices and perspectives for Indian characters.

The demands for something like truth in the writing of social science can be impossibly burdensome, but in some ways they make for easier writing than the writing of fiction. As a social scientist, I only have to say what I have research grounding to say,

meeting reasonable social science truth standards. When I do not know something, I can say that, or slide away from it. Not only do I not have to make things up, I must not. When writing fiction, I must write as though I know much. If I am not sure what a character would think or do, I have to come up with something that fits, seems plausible, and is interesting. It is a luxury for the social scientist not to know. The writer of fiction in some ways has a much tougher job.

QUALITATIVE INTERVIEWING IN TRANSLATING A WORK OF FICTION

I am currently collaborating with Sungeun Yang on translating into English the Korean novel *The Most Beautiful Farewell in the World*, by Hee Gyoung Noh. Yang is a native speaker of Korean, and I have no proficiency in the language. So our translation process involves my interviewing her intensively about her translation decisions and dilemmas. Using qualitative interviewing techniques, I recurrently question her about her choices of English words or what a word or phrase in Korean means to native speakers of Korean. During our interview discussions, she teaches me an enormous amount of what is truth for herself, for Koreans as she understands and represents them, and for the novel's author. I am learning a great deal that is outside of my experience and culture and that challenges the English language to do a reasonable rendering.

For example, in Korean there is a kind of respect that is paid to things that seems to me to be outside of how respect is talked about in American English. Also, the Korean language draws finer distinctions among kinds of danger than does American English. In this situation, I think that my qualitative interviewing skills do an excellent job of identifying the many challenges in the translation project and give Sungeun Yang and me a solid base for doing the best translation possible by at least one of the many standards for evaluating translations (Wilss 1982).

However, the best translation possible by the standard we have pursued (fidelity to what seems to us to be the original meanings, although not to the exact wording) involves fictionalizing in the sense that even the best translation is a painfully imperfect representation of the text in the original language. The translation loses what cannot easily be translated if translated at all, and even much of what can be translated becomes altered in subtle ways at many places in each chapter. A translated work of fiction may be experienced as a superb book, but it is not the same book as the original. And the qualitative interviewing I have done with Yang has made the imperfections of the translation crystal clear.

One can take the changes that happen when fiction is translated as an allegory for qualitative interviewing research. Perhaps the translations we make from interviewees' original understandings and narratives to our research reports are like translated works of fiction. At best we can hope for good, interesting writing, but the reports invariably lose things that cannot be "translated" into them and alter much else away from the meanings and understandings the interviewees thought they were conveying.

FACT AND FICTION
IN THE CONSUMPTION
OF RESEARCH FINDINGS

What happens when research reports are quoted in other research reports, in textbooks, and in the mass media? I believe that research findings are often fictionalized in such situations. Many of us have had the experience of having our published research findings distorted in textbooks or in the research reports of others, perhaps even to the point of being unrecognizable or of saying the opposite of what we thought we said. Similarly, the media interviews we give about our research often, perhaps al-

ways, come out in such selective and distorted ways that it is often an embarrassment to be quoted in the media as an expert (see Altheide, Chapter 20, this volume). Even speaking for oneself, using one's expertise about one's own research, in radio and television interviews is often a losing battle against the fictionalizing of that work. (For a fascinating account of such experiences, see Richardson 1987.) Many postmodernists would say that what an author intends to write has little or nothing to do with how that author's text can, will, or should be read (Rosenau 1992). But from my authorial perspective, at the level of consumption of research findings, there is not so much a blurred boundary between fact and fiction as there is a broken dam with a great torrent of something that is not fact threatening to inundate anything that might be a reasonable representation of what I want to communicate to others.

◆ Critical Views of
the Blurred Boundary

I have a postmodernist view of truth, and yet in my interview research, I never want to write fiction. I am afraid of eliciting fiction from interviewees and mistaking it for fact. I am afraid of analyzing and interpreting interview material in a way that makes the research reports I write into fiction. I hope to write truth, not *the* truth, but certainly a truth. My truths may be provisional, situation-bound, perspectival, even personal, but I work very, very hard to ground them empirically, rhetorically, and logically and to make them seem sound and persuasive to me and, I hope, to the reader.

Still, positivist critics may interpret this chapter to mean that qualitative interviewing is too subjective to be science or to be worth taking seriously. However, as the reader can gather from my discussion of my experiences doing qualitative interviewing as an adjunct to experimental social psychology and sample surveys, I think qualitative interviewing is good protection against the fictions of "objective," positivist research. From this perspective, refusing to force the world into a positivist social science template in which the researcher posits meanings and understandings for the people studied may have greater truth value than maintaining a strict fact-versus-fiction dichotomy.

I realize that critics of the perspectives I represent in this chapter may feel raging indignation about the ways the ideas represented here seem to slight scientific sociology and psychology. To understand and accept postmodern doubting is to end certainty and confidence about what is right and what is wrong. There are fascinating qualitative studies and novels to be written about any confrontation of doubt with orthodoxy, or of multiple realities with a monolithic reality. I think it is obvious why people would resist postmodern thinking. Who would want to give up certainty and a simple and unambiguous world if they had them? On the other hand, a person who brought certainty and an unambiguous view of the world to qualitative interview research would find it very hard to maintain certainty, orthodoxy, and a simple worldview. What people have to say in qualitative interviews challenges simple views of the world.

In all this, what is good interviewing and what is a good research report? If it is not unambiguous truth that we seek, what are we after? What if in my research reports (e.g., Rosenblatt 2000) I claim to analyze narratives (people's organized stories of experience), not objective, unambiguous, true, as-accurate-as-possible statements? The old questions, drawn from positivist research, about reliability and validity have a great deal of currency in the social sciences and are certainly matters that many of us, as qualitative researchers, write about. And yet the questions are not quite the right questions for disciplining qualitative interview research. We differ from positivist researchers in terms of the realities that we write about, the goals of our research, and our sense of reality. If we are at the boundary between fact and fiction, we need to think of reliability and validity in a different sense; perhaps we might use the words but change the meanings. What is reliable and valid becomes based not on objective truth but on what we believe to be fact (Denzin 1997:159, n. 5) established as well as we can from some perspective.

Questions of validity can be separated into questions about the quality of the interviews, questions about the quality of the texts created to represent the interviews (typically transcriptions; see Poland, Chapter 30, this volume), and questions about the quality of claims about the realities the researcher takes the interviews to represent (see Alasuutari 1995). For each of the three, there may be different grounds for doubting absolute truth or anything like firm validity. For each there may be different things a qualitative researcher can do to persuade self and reader that the research is worth taking seriously. To the extent that the data analysis and claims about the data are made on the basis of texts that others can know (for example, through interview quotes), it may be easiest to establish something like validity for the data analysis. As Pertti Alasuutari has noted: "Although we cannot assume that we get to the truth of the phenomenon talked about in interviews, we CAN make more or less valid, that is more or less clearly empirically grounded and defendable claims and interpretations about the interview text: e.g., how it is organized, what narrative structures the interviewee used, what discourses are evident in it, etc." (personal communication, December 1999).

Beyond that, validity involves writing in an interesting way, saying things that readers can believe to be true from some perspective, and saying things that help readers to see the world in new ways. It is valid if we can establish facticity in some way that makes sense within a community of others

(Denzin 1997) and if our narrative rings true enough by standards that are valued in that community. It is reliable if, going back into the same human morass, we, writers and readers, can see more or less the same things, the "facts," from the particular perspective we have been taking. And if it is not reliability and validity we are after—if using those terms does not ring true—how about using "memorable," "transforming," "entertaining," and "fascinating" as criteria?

Will writing fiction, or even imagining writing fiction, make one a better interviewer? I think anything that challenges an interviewer to think in new ways can be helpful. For me, the writing of fiction has given me a better ear for interviewer-interviewee dialogue and the dialogue among people being interviewed together. By a "better ear," I mean that I think I am more aware of the dialogue and the ways that one person does or does not connect well with what someone else said. I think I am more aware of how at some level the dialogue is a unit, not a collection of separate but more or less related statements. I also think I am more aware of what will read well when put into writing and what needs clarification or explication in order to be understood by a reader.

At another level, writing fiction has, I think, opened me to possibility. That is, something about going where fantasy happens to go has made me more willing to follow interviewees on tangents or even to push them out onto tangents. At times that seems to make me a less focused interviewer and makes for longer interviews and additional hours with the transcribing machine. Sometimes those tangents seem to me to be productive—another chapter in a social science research book, a new social research lead. Perhaps, once in a while, a tangent gets me thinking about something I might include, after considerable transformation, in a work of fiction. But sometimes those tangents seem to me more about my indulging my curiosity or an interviewee's

desire to go far away from my research interest, and then what I have is a lot of specifics about something I believe I will never write up for social science readers.

◆ Conclusion

In writing about the boundary between fact and fiction, I am doing what I think is always good for a researcher to do: to question recurrently and determinedly the fundamental philosophical grounds on which research rests. There is nothing sacred about specific research methods or conventions of research reporting. They are so embedded in culture, in the sociology of the academic world, in the sociology of American society, that those methods are limited and limiting in myriad ways. Nor do I think I escape limits when I question. This chapter, for example, is still very much embedded in culture, society, and orthodoxies. But by raising the questions I raise, I am at least asking qualitative interview researchers to examine their presuppositions.

The perspective I offer here on the blurring of the boundary between fact and fiction points out that fiction may be a legitimate outcome of qualitative interviewing research. It also points out that there may be much in social research that can be said to be fictional. But I do not think the blurring of the boundary between fiction and fact means that if one is doing qualitative interview research, anything goes. Interviewing at the border of fact and fiction, one still must be a craftsperson, a consummate interviewer, a doubter, a systematic explorer, and a careful reporter in ways that are responsive to a community of researchers (even if it includes many people one could label as doubters). And yet, looking at fiction and the writing of fiction can help one to think through what one is doing and what it means.

At the end of this, I want to speak to the reader who is depressed or angered at the thought that the idealism, security, safety, and disciplined honesty of social *science* may have been lost to an anything-goes chaos. I think that we always had an anything-goes chaos, but it was dressed up to look like honest, realist science. The move into multiple realities, an awareness of the ways that researcher subjectivity operates even when using the trappings of science, the exploration of alternative modes of representing what we know, and all else that seems to contribute to the new chaos are, I think, actually more honest—more true to the social world and to human psy-chology and sociology—than what went on in the past.

At the same time, I think the exploration of alternative modes of representing what we know has given us a blessed freedom to feel, know, and communicate. As I experience it, there is a sense of using parts of one's mind, language, and awareness that have been taboo to use in modernist social science. And with that freedom comes a power to ask the people we interview new and interesting questions, to know them, and to inform ourselves and our readers in ways that were blocked in the past.

■ *References*

Alasuutari, P. 1995. *Researching Culture: Qualitative Method and Cultural Studies.* London: Sage.
———. 1998. *An Invitation to Social Research.* London: Sage.
Ang, I. 1985. *Watching* Dallas: *Soap Opera and the Melodramatic Imagination.* London: Methuen.
Campbell, D. T. 1988. *Methodology and Epistemology for Social Science: Selected Papers.* Chicago: University of Chicago Press.
Clifford, J. 1986. "Introduction: Partial Truths." Pp. 1-26 in *Writing Culture: The Poetics and Politics of Ethnography,* edited by J. Clifford and G. E. Marcus. Berkeley: University of California Press.
Denzin, N. K. 1997. *Interpretive Ethnography: Ethnographic Practices for the 21st Century.* Thousand Oaks, CA: Sage.
Fontana, A. and J. H. Frey. 1994. "Interviewing: The Art of Science." Pp. 361-76 in *Handbook of Qualitative Research,* edited by N. K. Denzin and Y. S. Lincoln. Thousand Oaks, CA: Sage.
Gergen, K. J. 1988. "The Concept of Progress in Psychological Theory." Pp. 1-14 in *Recent Trends in Theoretical Psychology,* edited by W. J. Baker, L. P. Mos, H. V. Rappard, and H. J. Stam. New York: Springer Verlag.
———. 1994. "Mind, Text, and Society: Self-Memory in Social Context." Pp. 78-104 in *The Remembering Self: Construction and Accuracy in the Self-Narrative,* edited by U. Neisser and R. Fivush. New York: Cambridge University Press.
Gilman, C. P. 1979. *Herland.* New York: Pantheon.
Gubrium, J. F. and J. A. Holstein. 1997. *The New Language of Qualitative Method.* New York: Oxford University Press.
Gülerce, A. 1995. "An Interview with K. J. Gergen (Part 1): Culture and Self in Postmodern Psychology: Dialogue in Trouble?" *Culture and Psychology* 1:147-59.
Gusfield, J. 1976. "The Literary Rhetoric of Science: Comedy and Pathos in Drinking Driver Research." *American Sociological Review* 41:16-34.
Harré, R. 1990. "Some Narrative Conventions of Scientific Discourse." Pp. 81-101 in *Narrative in Culture: The Uses of Storytelling in the Sciences, Philosophy, and Literature,* edited by C. Nash. London: Routledge.
Holland, N. N. 1968. *The Dynamics of Literary Response.* New York: Oxford University Press.
Holstein, J. A. and J. F. Gubrium. 1995. *The Active Interview.* Thousand Oaks, CA: Sage.
Hoppenstand, G. C. 1987. *In Search of the Paper Tiger: A Sociological Perspective of Myth, Formula and the Mystery Genre in the Entertainment Print Mass Medium.* Bowling Green, OH: Bowling Green State University Popular Press.
Hurston, Z. N. 1937. *Their Eyes Were Watching God.* Philadelphia: J. B. Lippincott.

Kvale, S. 1996. *InterViews: An Introduction to Qualitative Research Interviewing.* Thousand Oaks, CA: Sage.

La Farge, O. 1929. *Laughing Boy.* Boston: Houghton Mifflin.

McCall, M. M., H. S. Becker, P. Meshejian, and R. A. Hilbert. 1990. "Performance Science." *Social Problems* 37:117-32.

Paget, M. A. 1983. "Experience and Knowledge." *Human Studies* 6:67-90.

———. 1995. "Performing the Text." Pp. 222-44 in *Representation in Ethnography,* edited by J. Van Maanen. Thousand Oaks, CA: Sage. (Reprinted from M. A. Paget, *A Complex Sorrow: Reflections on Cancer and an Abbreviated Life.* Edited by M. L. DeVault. Philadelphia: Temple University Press, 1993.)

Polkinghorne, D. E. 1988. *Narrative Knowing and the Human Sciences.* Albany: State University of New York Press.

Pollner, M. and L. McDonald-Winkler. 1985. "The Social Construction of Unreality: A Case Study of a Family's Attribution of Competence to a Severely Retarded Child." *Family Process* 24:251-54.

Popper, K. R. 1962. *Conjectures and Refutations: The Growth of Scientific Knowledge.* New York: Basic Books.

Richardson, L. 1987. "Disseminating Research to Popular Audiences: The Book Tour." *Qualitative Sociology* 10:164-76.

———. 1994. "Writing: A Method of Inquiry." Pp. 516-29 in *Handbook of Qualitative Research,* edited by N. K. Denzin and Y. S. Lincoln. Thousand Oaks, CA: Sage.

Richardson, L. and E. Lockridge. 1998. "Fiction and Ethnography: A Conversation." *Qualitative Inquiry* 4:328-36.

Rosenau, P. M. 1992. *Post-modernism and the Social Sciences: Insights, Inroads, and Intrusions.* Princeton, NJ: Princeton University Press.

Rosenblatt, P. C. 1981. "Ethnographic Case Studies." Pp. 194-225 in *Scientific Inquiry and the Social Sciences,* edited by M. B. Brewer and B. E. Collins. San Francisco: Jossey-Bass.

———. 1990. *Farming Is in Our Blood: Farm Families in Economic Crisis.* Ames: Iowa State University Press.

———. 1994. *The Metaphors of Family Systems Theory.* New York: Guilford.

———. 2000. *Parent Grief: Narratives of Loss and Relationship.* Philadelphia: Brunner/Mazel.

Rosenblatt, P. C., L. de Mik, R. M. Anderson, and P. A. Johnson. 1985. *The Family in Business: Understanding and Dealing with the Challenges Entrepreneurial Families Face.* San Francisco: Jossey-Bass.

Rosenblatt, P. C. and T. A. Karis. 1993. "Economics and Family Bereavement Following a Fatal Farm Accident." *Journal of Rural Community Psychology* 12(2):37-51.

———. 1993-94. "Family Distancing Following a Fatal Farm Accident." *Omega* 28:183-200.

Rosenblatt, P. C., T. A. Karis, and R. D. Powell. 1995. *Multiracial Couples: Black and White Voices.* Thousand Oaks, CA: Sage.

Sanders, W. B. 1974. *The Sociologist as Detective: An Introduction to Research Methods.* New York: Praeger.

Scheurich, J. J. 1995. "Interviewing." *International Journal of Qualitative Studies in Education* 8:239-52.

Smith, D. E. 1987. *The Everyday World as Problematic: A Feminist Sociology.* Boston: Northeastern University Press.

Strauss, A. L. and J. Corbin. 1998. *Basics of Qualitative Research: Techniques and Procedures for Developing Grounded Theory.* 2d ed. Thousand Oaks, CA: Sage.

Weiss, R. S. 1994. *Learning from Strangers: The Art and Method of Qualitative Interview Studies.* New York: Free Press.

Wilss, W. 1982. *The Science of Translation: Problems and Methods.* Tübingen, Germany: Gunter Narr Verlag Tübingen.

44

INTERVIEWING, POWER/KNOWLEDGE, AND SOCIAL INEQUALITY

◆ Charles L. Briggs

Back in 1986, I published a book titled *Learning How to Ask: A Sociolinguistic Appraisal of the Role of the Interview in Social Science Research.* Analyzing interviews that I had conducted during more than a decade's research in New Mexico, I argued that the interview is fairly unique and rather poorly understood as a communicative event. I was particularly interested in the asymmetries of power that emerge in interview situations and how they are embodied in what I referred to as "metacommunicative norms," principles that invest interviewers with control over the referential content of what is said (by posing questions), the length and scope of answers (by deciding when to probe or ask a new question), and the way that all participants construct their positionality with respect to the interview and the information it produces. Interview data have multiple

footings, to use Erving Goffman's (1981) term, being simultaneously rooted in the dynamics of the interview, the social spheres constructed by the responses, and the academic or other domains (theoretical and empirical) that give rise to the project and to which it contributes.

I argued that differences between contrasting sets of such norms often lead to problems that range from misunderstandings to resistance and conflict between interviewers and respondents. I suggested that interviewing deploys discourse that is highly adapted to producing the precise types of information that will be recontextualized in the books, articles, reports, media productions, and the like that are envisioned as the final product. When interviews provide the nation-state and its institutions with representations of marginalized populations, the possibilities for

◆ 911

constructing a "minority voice" that confirms the hegemonic status quo is thus acute.

My goal was not to suggest that researchers should abandon interviews, a position that would be as counterproductive as it would be unrealistic. Rather, I sought to bring into focus the discrepancy between the complex character of interview data as discursive phenomena and the way they are reified as reflections of the social phenomena depicted in questions and answers. I also attempted to demonstrate how deeply the power relations that emerge in interviews are embedded in the data they produce. Drawing on work in a number of fields, I suggested that this discursive mediation should not be viewed as a source of contamination but rather as a crucial source of insights into both interviewing processes and the social worlds they seek to document.

The present juncture provides an excellent moment to return to these questions. A great deal of work—inspired by post-structuralism; postmodernism; ethnic, cultural, and women's studies; subaltern studies; research on globalization; and other perspectives—has explored the way that discourses of difference lie at the center of producing and resisting structures of social inequality. At the same time, the social and political importance of interviews of many sorts has expanded greatly in the decade and a half since I published my study; we now live, as Paul Atkinson and David Silverman (1997) put it, in the interview society. In many countries, a populist aura attempts simultaneously to project the voice of the "average citizen" into the middle of electoral politics and to place the voices of candidates and officials as those of concerned citizens or political outsiders; this political agenda is closely tied to new communications technologies. Television and radio programs that specialize in interviews with persons who have special stories to tell, candidates, politicians, specialists, and celebrities have flourished. Political candidates use question-and-answer-based media events as central features of electoral campaigns, and polling increasingly guides who runs, what candidates say, and whom they address.

My goal in this chapter is to extend the discursive analysis of power relations in the interview that I began in *Learning How to Ask* in such a way as to connect it with approaches to discourse that emerge from these perspectives and historical developments. I hope to be able to provide some insight into why interviewing is playing such a profound role in shaping forms of knowledge and practices in contemporary society and how interviews are being used in legitimating the growing social inequality that characterizes a globalizing world. I argue that research on interviewing can deeply inform contemporary concerns with knowledge, power, and difference.

◆ Modernity, Knowledge, and Power

Zygmunt Bauman (1987) argues that modernity created pervasive asymmetries of knowledge and power and used them in recasting growing social inequality, which was being exacerbated by the emergent capitalist economy, as the product of individual differences. John Locke ([1690] 1959) played a key role in creating a new cartography of language, knowledge, and discourse that mapped social inequality. In his *Essay Concerning Human Understanding*, Locke sharply separated rational reflections on individual experience and the articulation of thought in "plain," serious speech from imprecise, shifting, ambiguous uses of words, which he associated with rhetoric, poetry, and the like. This linguistic cartography was projected onto a social one. Gentlemen, who had the leisure and training to reflect rationally on their use of language, exemplified ideal speech. Women, the poor, laborers, merchants, cooks, lovers, and rural folk, on the other hand, spoke in the imprecise ways that Locke condemned; such persons were largely incapable of developing greater rationality and linguistic precision by virtue of their lives. Inhabitants of the Americas provided Locke with an image of the linguistic baseline, the sort of knowledge of language that humans possess before their speech is shaped by civilization. Locke's discursive model of the modern subject—autonomous, disinterested, and rational—became the model of the scientist (see Shapin 1994), the citizen (see MacPherson 1962), and the public sphere (see Habermas [1962] 1989). At the same time, another fellow of the Royal Society, John Aubrey, was interviewing the traditional people of the countryside in constructing a portrait of the customs and language that defined modernity vis-à-vis its premodern opposite (see Aubrey 1972; Bauman and Briggs in press).

The productiveness of Locke's program seems to revolve around a central contradiction. His ideology projected an overtly egalitarian tone in that it constructed language as an essential part of the makeup of all human beings. At the same time, Locke authorized a set of standardizing practices and a powerful means of assessing the rationality of each individual and instituting gatekeeping mechanisms. Locke's ideology of language and politics naturalized both the emergent social and political structures of modernity and the idea that the degree to which individuals approximate the ideal of the modern subject naturally locates them within relations of inequality.

Zygmunt Bauman (1987) goes on to argue that this knowledge-inequality connection prompted the rise of "legislators" who exercise surveillance and control over the projected transformation of their social inferiors from premodern to modern ways of knowing. Arguing that we must examine how "effects of power circulate among scientific statements, what constitutes, as it were, their internal régime of power,"

Michel Foucault (1980:112) has pointed to the role of legislators in medical, legal, criminological, academic, and other institutions in producing discourses that create the objects they regulate.

The power invested in interviews to construct discourses that are then legitimated as the words of others points to their effectiveness as technologies that can be used in naturalizing the role of specialists in creating systems of difference. But we can also take a larger lesson from Foucault's work. Ian Hacking (1990) suggests that the systematic collection and publication of statistics by the nation-state regarding the lives of its citizens produced a revolution in the 19th century in terms of the way in which society was conceptualized and structured, one that centered on statistical definitions of the "normal" subject and its "abnormal" counterparts. We might suggest, following Foucault, that the growing ubiquity and visibility of interviewing in the 20th century has created a widely disseminated idea that both social similarity and difference can best be explained through the use of interviews to reveal individual social and intrapsychic worlds and to compare them, thereby identifying patterns of consensus and disagreement. Interviewing is thus a "technology" that invents both notions of individual subjectivities and collective social and political patterns and then obscures the operation of this process beneath notions of objectivity and science—or, in the case of journalistic and television interviews, of insight and art.

Although Foucault draws our attention to institutions as epistemological regimes, he does little to elucidate the social dynamics that render them such powerful sites for producing discourse. Drawing on sociolinguistic research (see Hymes 1974), Pierre Bourdieu (1991) argues that forms of communicative competence constitute symbolic capital, the acquisition of which is constrained by such gatekeeping institutions as schools and professional societies (see also Erickson and Shultz 1982). Members of dominant sectors use interviews in furthering institutionalized agendas, such as the compilation of census information and the use of surveying for purposes of enhancing consumption or devising political rhetoric. Bourdieu ([1972] 1979, 1990) suggests that polling creates the illusion of a "public opinion," creating images of national conversations that serve the interests of institutions whose legitimacy derives from the relations of class-based inequality that are reproduced in the supposedly inclusive nature of this "public." Drawing on Bourdieu, we can suggest that interviews create and sustain the power relations of modern society in a variety of ways, by producing representations of social life that are deeply and invisibly informed by class relations and by providing modes of screening individuals, through employment, counseling, social service, and other interviews, for the forms of competence that will position them in relation to institutions. Dominated communities are common targets for interview projects, providing both models of difference and objects of surveillance and regulation.

Having reflected more deeply on the work of Foucault and Bourdieu during the past 15 years, I would criticize my earlier study for rooting its analysis of power too directly in interview settings themselves. Applying these writers' perspectives suggests that it is the *circulation* of discourse among a range of institutional contexts that imbues interviews with the power to shape contemporary life. Nevertheless, neither Foucault nor Bourdieu is very helpful when it comes to identifying concretely the discursive and institutional means by which this circulation takes place and how we can trace it in particular instances. Here the totalizing thrust of viewing discourse as political technology or symbolic capital can be suitably complemented by a discourse-analytic perspective that explores textual and contextual dimensions of the production, circulation, and interpretation of interviews as grounded social practice.

◆ Heteroglossia and Recontextualization in Interviews

Hayden White (1978) argues that the power of historical narratives derives from the way their rhetoric achieves two contradictory effects. First, historians imagine past events, thereby creating schemes of social classification and forms of agency and causation. Interview researchers similarly imagine the social worlds depicted in the content of responses, creating images of political participation, family life, work experience, and so forth. But interview materials simultaneously imagine an intrapsychic world for the interviewee, a space inhabited by opinions, memories, emotions, plans, preferences, and desires. As I argued in *Learning How to Ask,* interviews are saturated by images of the social dynamics of the interview itself, projections of the social context in which it takes place, the roles and power dynamics of interviewer and respondent, and their respective agendas. But a fourth sphere is being constructed, that of the imagined texts that will be created through the use of interview data. This realm becomes explicit in statements on consent forms regarding the textual rights that participants are granting researchers. The disclaimers that interviewees frequently insert, such as "I don't want the people who read your book to get the impression that . . . ," suggest that respondents often shape their responses in keeping with imaginings of future texts and audiences. Not only are these four realms constructed simultaneously, but interviews are punctuated by the distinct and often competing imaginations of researchers and respondents.

Second, historical rhetoric converts the arbitrary into the real, casting imaginations as reflections of what actually took place, thereby hiding the imaginary and arbitrary character of such constructions. Although a variety of strategies for converting imaginations into reality are used in the wealth of different sorts of projects that rely on interviews, erasing the third and fourth realms constructed in interviews in favor of the first two is key. In other words, some researchers highlight opinions, memories, and other reflections of the mental worlds of the respondents; others foreground the social worlds that are represented. Both of these strategies revolve around obscuring the role of constructions of the social dynamics of the interview and the way projected uses of the data are embedded in responses.

The richest rhetorical resource for the erasure of these domains consists of techniques for eliminating "distortion" and "bias"—explicit signs of the effects of the interaction and perceptions of research agendas on interview content. Suggesting that interview data (including surveys) can be obtained in such a way that their contextual grounding can be factored out (through sampling, question wording, training of interviewers, and the like) constitutes simultaneously a claim to the epistemological marginality of these realms and a prohibition on allowing any explicit evidence of their presence to appear in texts that report interview data.

Feminist interviewing has often made the position of the interviewer in relationship to the respondent a central object of description and analysis (see DeVault 1990; Harding 1987; Reinharz 1992; see also in this volume Reinharz and Chase, Chapter 11; DeVault and McCoy, Chapter 36). A great deal of attention has focused on the use of narratives that emerge in interviews as means of drawing attention to the complex processes that shape the construction of identities in interviews (see, e.g., Bruner 1990; Chase 1995; Mishler 1986, 2000; Riessman 1993). Postmodern scholars have sometimes violated this prohibition systematically and explicitly, highlighting the interaction between the participants and their visions of how the materials will be used; Ruth Behar's (1993) *Translated Woman* provides a notable example. Norman Denzin (1989) and others have brought postmodern perspectives to bear on the issue of interviewing in general, questioning the privileged authority of the interviewer or researcher and urging a decentering of subject positions.

Such notions as bias, distortion, reliability, and validity reveal a great deal about the assumptions that commonly underlie interview-based research. Elliot Mishler (1986) argues that researchers commonly see interview data as behavior that can be analyzed using stimulus-response models associated with scientific experimentation. The information obtained in this manner is seen as a set of stable "social facts" that have an objective existence independent of the linguistic and contextual settings in which they are "expressed" (see Karp and Kendall 1982). Jaber Gubrium and James Holstein (1997) suggest that this epistemological stance of naturalism, the notion that the task of researchers is to richly and accurately document the "natural" environment of the social world without disrupting it, lies at the center of much qualitative research and inspires related concerns. The reductionism of received interview practices also springs from Western ideologies of language (see Joseph and Taylor 1990; Schieffelin, Woolard, and Kroskrity 1998; Kroskrity 2000) that treat verbal interaction in Lockean fashion as a transfer of referential content from one party to another, as if participants had no interests or communicative foci that interfere with their playing the roles of interviewer and respondent (see Back and Cross 1982; Clark and Schober 1992; Dijkstra and van der Zouwen 1977, 1982: 3-4; Foddy 1993: 13-14). Interviewing thus provides a valuable source of data on the ideologies of language that underlie social scientific research, particularly in that conceptions that have been banished from the realm of explicit theory are often preserved implicitly in "purely methodological" spheres.

The complexity of interviews does not emerge simply from the manner in which connections with distinct realms are imagined in the course of interviews. Rather, the process involves practices for extracting discourse from one social setting and inserting it in a range of other settings. In my work with Richard Bauman, we have argued that a vital part of the process of rendering discourse socially powerful involves gaining control over its recontextualization—rights to determine when, where, how, and by whom it will be used in other settings (Bauman and Briggs 1990; Briggs and Bauman 1992; see also Silverstein and Urban 1996). Interview discourse is maximally configured in terms of both form and content for recontextualization into the sorts of texts that the researcher anticipates creating—interviewees are granted very few rights over this process. Survey instruments and techniques for implementing them maximize the social control of interviewers by the researchers who direct the study as well of interviewees by interviewers, creating hierarchies of discursive authority that also include individuals responsible for coding data.

The recontextualization process provides another angle on the complexity of interview data. A statement that emerges in an interview is tied explicitly to the question that precedes it and generally indirectly to previous questions and responses, the broad range of texts, agendas, and contexts that shape questions and interviewing practices, and the anticipated uses of the data. Quotations or summaries taken from interviews used in publications are, of course, deeply entwined in this broad range of recontextualizations. As the work of Mikhail Bakhtin (1981) would suggest, this recontextualization process informs each word that is spoken, such that the different contexts, vocabularies, styles, subject positions, and the like are built into what is said and how it is uttered. Responses are like crossroads at which multiple paths converge, with signs pointing in all directions.

The power of researchers thus lies not only in their control over what takes place in the interview itself but particularly in their ability to use that setting as a site that is geared toward creating a broad field for the circulation of discourse.

At the same time that researchers attempt to control how material will move between different sites, they seek to render all save a few dimensions of this process invisible. In order to seem "unbiased" and to be suitable for recontextualization in a range of future settings, interview materials must be systematically decontextualized in various ways, leaving only minimal road signs that point in the direction of social or intrapsychic worlds. Otherwise, data and analyses are likely to be rejected by positivistic researchers either as biased or as being too complex and contextually specific to permit abstraction and generalization. Atkinson and Silverman (1997) observe that even many critical, revisionist approaches to interviewing attempt to empower individuals to create biographical, authentic voices, thereby reifying an individual and confessional approach to discourse that is also promoted by corporate media. The indexical signs that point, as it were, to the embedding of this process in larger social and material structures are thus largely erased.

One advantage in viewing interviews not as unified political technologies but as politically situated and interested practices for producing and recontextualizing discourse is that this perspective enables us to see that respondents often attempt to resist discursive relations that are stacked against them. The literature on interviewing abounds with advice regarding "uncooperative" respondents (see Adler and Adler, Chapter 25, this volume). Scholars seldom seem to recognize that individuals who decline to participate or to answer particular questions, or who plead ignorance, "mislead" the interviewer, and the like, may be pursuing strategies designed to disrupt the recontextualization process (see Dunbar,

Rodriguez, and Parker, Chapter 14, this volume).

I suggested in *Learning How to Ask* that the apparent failure of interviews I conducted early in my research on "Mexicanos" or Mexican Americans in New Mexico reflected precisely this type of contestation. The fact that I had a research project in hand and was asking reasonable questions of individuals who had detailed knowledge of the issues in question led me to believe that extensive answers would be forthcoming. My elderly respondents saw things differently. As the most authoritative sources of information on Mexicano cultural politics, they found it difficult to accept the idea that a young gringo should structure such discussions. Most of my initial questions were thus met with a jolting "¡Pues, quién sabe! [Well, who knows!]." By learning to respect these individuals' right to control the recontextualization of discourse about the past, I was able to gain insight not only into Mexican cultural politics but into the politics of memory and strategies of resistance to cultural and political-economic domination.

◆ Three Contradictions of Power and Knowledge in Contemporary Society

I alluded above to the way that differences in the distribution of knowledge came to be viewed as explaining social inequality in modern society. Locke clearly articulated a fundamental modernist contradiction as he simultaneously advanced the idea that common possession of capacities for language, rationality, and reflection render us all part of humanity and condemn most people to subordinate social categories on the basis of their purported failure to develop this potential. Two basic contradictions similarly seem to structure the relationship between knowledge and social inequality in late-capitalist societies, and I

suggest that interviewing plays a key role in mediating them.

Lisa Lowe (1996) argues that economic and political structures place people of color in a contradictory position in the United States. On the one hand, the need to maintain a pool of cheap laborers who enjoy few legal and occupational protections prompts the racialization of populations and their placement in subordinate social categories. Immanuel Wallerstein makes a similar argument for the economic underpinnings of the construction of racial categories worldwide (see Balibar and Wallerstein 1991). Nonetheless, U.S. political ideologies are based on the imagination of a shared cultural and political community; ascriptive barriers of race, gender, and class that create hierarchies of types of citizenship thus render it difficult to conceive of U.S. society as actually reflecting this privileged political ideology, at least when these obstacles become visible. The work of critical discourse analysts suggests that similar processes are at work in European nation-states (see Blommaert 1997; Blommaert and Verschueren 1998; van Dijk 1984; Wodak 1999).

By conducting interviews among, say, African Americans, or asserting that X percentage of survey respondents are Latinos, researchers can project the sense that "minorities" are included in national conversations about politics, economics, medicine, education, or whatnot—even when significant (and currently growing) barriers limit the participation of people of color in the institutions that regulate these domains. By the same token, by classifying respondents as members of racialized groups, researchers can create a synecdochic logic that suggests that an Asian American, for example, is speaking *as* an Asian American and is representing all Asian Americans, thereby confirming a sense of people of color as one-sided subjects. These practices also project interviews as capable of including racialized, subordinated voices in a seemingly equal position within national conversations. Whereas native-born, middle-class whites just naturally seem to be part of the dialogue, people of color and working-class persons can be portrayed as needing the mediation of researchers, journalists, or other professionals to make their voices heard on public stages. Here interviewing has assumed a crucial part of the role of the legislator identified by Bauman (1987).

Second, as globalization is augmenting social inequality, both within and between countries, a number of observers have sought to characterize its effects on the participation of populations on the so-called periphery. Arjun Appadurai (1996) argues that globalization is producing new modes of inclusion, suggesting that deterritorialization and denationalization disrupt centralization of control over global flows of capital, people, goods, culture, and information. He thus suggests that the United States no longer dominates "a world system of images but is only one node of a complex transnational construction of imaginary landscapes" (p. 31). Appadurai's vision of globalization is thus one of a global egalitarianism, in that even the poor and powerless can participate actively in shaping widely distributed practices of the imagination.

Other writers view globalization as largely *exclusionary,* as exacerbating social differences based on access to capital, commodities, information, and culture. Michel-Rolph Trouillot (1991) has pinpointed a key issue here in a brief but highly suggestive passage. Insofar as a universal transition is postulated from "modern" to "postmodern" or from "national" to "deterritorialized" ideologies and social forms, what are the implications for social segments that were deemed to have failed to be incorporated into *modern* social, cultural, and economic patterns? If this supposedly universal stage of globalized, postmodern culture is tied to a questioning of the "metanarratives" and cultural premises of modernization, it would seem to exclude people who never gained access to progress and modernity. Zygmunt Bauman

(1998) suggests that the production of social fragmentation, differentiation, and inequality so fundamental to globalization fixes some people in space and restricts access to the globally circulating capital and culture that others increasingly enjoy; getting localized while others get globalized "is a sign of social deprivation and degradation" (p. 2).

CNN provides a striking illustration of the power of interviewing in mediating this contradiction between the inclusive and exclusive effects of globalization. The cable television news network's broadcasts take the voices and images of East Timorese refugees or victims of Venezuelan floods and project them to audiences worldwide, creating the sense of a global conversation. Nevertheless, whereas experts, particularly those living in industrialized countries, can make broad pronouncements on global phenomena, poor victims of wars, epidemics, and disasters are called upon to speak about the most immediate and concrete dimensions of their own experience. Different segments of the same broadcast can present interviews with the president or prime minister of a rich and powerful nation-state, the CEO of a transnational corporation that has just completed a huge merger, and survivors of genocidal campaigns. The sense that the faces, songs, and stories of all people are included in these global flows is thus projected without attention being drawn to the increasingly monopolistic formations of capital and power that determine who gets to speak and when as well as what counts as a local voice.

The illusion of equality goes hand in hand with quite different constructions of historical agency as we view leaders and CEOs speaking about their roles as globalizing agents, as catalysts of changes that produce structural changes that lead to more globalized markets, transnational intervention into affairs of seemingly sovereign nation-states, and greater social inequality. Individuals constructed as localizing agents, on the other hand, are portrayed as experiencing the effects of such policies. Interviews animate the role of the legislator, who controls the production and circulation of public voices on a global basis while creating the illusion that he or she is simply a witness to conversations and events that shape history. Interviewing thus aids the large transnational corporations that own the global media in projecting images of a worldwide community of producers and consumers, and of the very different positions that they occoupy in relation to capital.

◆ Conclusion

David Harvey (1989) has argued that new technologies of transport and communication have effected a victory of time over space, producing time-space compression and continual fragmentations of time-space patterns that lead to the postmodern feeling of dislocation. The notion that global capital is undermining the power of nation-states and destroying our sense of place, identity, and authenticity has moved from scholarly discourse, where it has become increasingly criticized and qualified, into popular and corporate discourses. Such influential observers as Robert Putnam (1993) have argued that this process is undermining the foundations of democracy, which are described as resting in the face-to-face interactions that characterized civil society—as epitomized by small-town society. This postmodern nostalgia for a supposedly authentic and interactional past does not, of course, lead Putnam or the governments (including the U.S. government) that have taken up his cry to call for an end to global political intervention or corporate expansion. Rather, it creates a vast need to project what appear to be forms of face-to-face communication and decision making as forming the center of social and political processes.

Enter the interview, that archetype of dyadic communication. Whether inter-

views take place in interviewees' homes, on *The Oprah Winfrey Show,* or on *CNN Headline News,* or even when interlocutors are connected only by telephone lines, these encounters create vox populi that seemingly provide an interpersonal—rather than purely private or purely public and depersonalized—space for the articulation of individual perspectives. I argued in *Learning How to Ask* that this image is largely illusory, in that interviews are structured by power asymmetries and by conventions that produce discursively complex material that is geared toward the institutional ends for which it was created. I have argued here that construing the interview itself as the locus of knowledge production places audiences and analysts alike in the grip of a powerful illusion. I have suggested, rather, that the power of interviewing lies in the status of the interpersonal interaction as one site in a complex process of controlling the decontextualization and recontextualization of discourse, one that links broader scholarly, corporate, and political agendas; previously circulating messages (be they scholarly literatures or campaign slogans); forms of disciplinary authority or celebrity stature; and the creation of texts, media programs, Web sites, and the like that serve the interests of interviewers and their employers. The sense that the people have spoken through such venues is sustained by the heteroglossic nature of what is said, being shot through with the echo of the words and contexts that shaped its production and that guide its recontextualization.

We are now more thoroughly modern than ever, in the sense that the illusion of shared participation in discourse and the production of knowledge legitimates practices for creating social inequality and modes of exclusion that seem to spring naturally from differences in what individuals know and can project into the public sphere. Ironically, new technologies are reinvigorating desire for the sense that it is interpersonal interaction and self-expression that shape our identities and lives;

Internet chat rooms have taken a quite visible place alongside radio and television talk shows, call-ins by listeners and viewers, electronic "town meetings," and interviews by journalists in satisfying this longing. Corporations are increasingly requiring their employees to end service encounters with the briefest of interviews: "How was everything?"

Interviews played key roles in the political technologies of the modern era, being central to the power of the state to enumerate and imagine its citizens, of physicians to medicalize their patients' ills, of psychiatrists to illuminate madness and define sanity, of lawyers and courts to construct criminals and invent crimes, and so forth. As Foucault and many others have argued, these are powers of abstraction, disembodiment, and objectification. As postmodern angst and global insecurity create resistance to master narratives and faceless, bureaucratic control, the productive power of the illusion of social interaction and self-expression that fuels both scholarly and popular senses of interviews positions them even more crucially within the technologies and social relations of a globalized world. As tools are required for inventing new forms of social inequality and the practices needed to construe them as products of passivity in the face of global forces and/or as individual failings, uses of interviewing are sure to expand.

I called in 1986 for systematic inquiry into the discursive and political underpinnings of interviews and the need to dispense with the illusion that we know what they are and what functions they serve. This call was echoed in the same year by Mishler (1986). The scholarly debates and social, political-economic, and technological transformations that have emerged since that time suggest to me that the failure to devote substantive critical attention to interviews would place scholars as passive onlookers—or willing participants—in creating new practices of imagination for producing and legitimating social inequality in the 21st century. It thus seems clearer than ever that we must establish anew that systematic inquiry into interviewing is of far more than "merely methodological" significance. Just as a political economy of the production and circulation of interview materials and their role in shaping social representations and relations can fundamentally illuminate the dynamics of the historical moment in which we live, such critical perspectives are needed to help us avoid taking on the task of providing a key discursive machinery to be used in extending and naturalizing social inequality.

■ References

Appadurai, A. 1996. *Modernity at Large: Cultural Dimensions of Globalization*. Minneapolis: University of Minnesota Press.

Atkinson, P. and D. Silverman. 1997. "Kundera's *Immortality:* The Interview Society and the Invention of Self." *Qualitative Inquiry* 3:304-25.

Aubrey, J. 1972. *Three Prose Works*. Edited by J. Buchanan-Brown. Carbondale: Southern Illinois University Press.

Back, K. W. and T. S. Cross. 1982. "Response Effects of Role Restricted Respondent Characteristics." Pp. 189-207 in *Response Behaviour in the Survey-Interview*, edited by W. Dijkstra and J. van der Zouwen. London: Academic Press.

Bakhtin, M. M. 1981. *The Dialogic Imagination: Four Essays*. Edited by M. Holquist; translated by C. Emerson and M. Holquist. Austin: University of Texas Press.

Balibar, E. and I. Wallerstein. 1991. *Race, Nation, Class: Ambiguous Identities*. London: Verso.

Bauman, R. and C. L. Briggs. 1990. "Poetics and Performance as Critical Perspectives on Language and Social Life." *Annual Review of Anthropology* 19:59-88.

———. in press. *Modernizing Discourse: Language Ideologies and the Politics of Inequality.* Cambridge, UK: Cambridge University Press.

Bauman, Z. 1987. *Legislators and Interpreters: On Modernity, Postmodernity, and Intellectuals.* Ithaca, NY: Cornell University Press.

———. 1998. *Globalization: The Human Consequences.* New York: Columbia University Press.

Behar, R. 1993. *Translated Woman: Crossing the Border with Esperanza's Story.* Boston: Beacon.

Blommaert, J. 1997. "The Slow Shift in Orthodoxy: (Re)formulations of 'Integration' in Belgium." *Pragmatics* 7:499-518.

Blommaert, J. and J. Verschueren. 1998. *Debating Diversity: Analysing the Discourse of Tolerance.* London: Routledge.

Bourdieu, P. [1972] 1979. "Public Opinion Does Not Exist." Pp. 124-30 in P. Bourdieu, *Communication and Class Struggle,* Vol. 1. New York: International General.

———. 1990. "Opinion Polls: A 'Science' without a Scientist." Pp. 168-74 in P. Bourdieu, *In Other Words: Essays Towards a Reflexive Sociology.* Translated by M. Adamson. Cambridge: Polity.

———. 1991. *Language and Symbolic Power.* Translated by G. Raymond and M. Adamson. Cambridge, MA: Harvard University Press.

Briggs, C. L. 1986. *Learning How to Ask: A Sociolinguistic Appraisal of the Role of the Interview in Social Science Research.* Cambridge: Cambridge University Press.

Briggs, C. L. and R. Bauman. 1992. "Genre, Intertextuality, and Social Power." *Journal of Linguistic Anthropology* 2:131-72.

Bruner, J. S. 1990. *Acts of Meaning.* Cambridge, MA: Harvard University Press.

Chase, S. E. 1995. *Ambiguous Empowerment: The Work of Narratives of Women School Superintendents.* Amherst: University of Massachusetts Press.

Clark, H. H. and M. F. Schober. 1992. "Asking Questions and Influencing Answers." Pp. 15-48 in *Questions about Questions: Inquiries into the Cognitive Bases of Surveys,* edited by J. M. Tanur. New York: Russell Sage Foundation.

Denzin, N. K. 1989. *Interpretive Interactionism.* Newbury Park, CA: Sage.

DeVault, M. L. 1990. "Talking and Listening from Women's Standpoint: Feminist Strategies for Interviewing and Analysis." *Social Problems* 37:96-116.

Dijkstra, W. and J. van der Zouwen. 1977. "Testing Auxiliary Hypotheses behind the Interview." *Annals of Systems Research* 6:49-63.

———, eds. 1982. *Response Behaviour in the Survey-Interview.* London: Academic Press.

Erickson, F. and J. Shultz. 1982. *The Counselor as Gatekeeper: Social Interaction in Interviews.* New York: Academic Press.

Foddy, W. 1993. *Constructing Questions for Interviews and Questionnaires: Theory and Practice in Social Research.* Cambridge: Cambridge University Press.

Foucault, M. 1980. *Power/Knowledge: Selected Interviews and Other Writings, 1972-1977.* Edited by C. Gordon; translated by L. Marshall, J. Mepham, and K. Soper. New York: Pantheon.

Goffman, E. 1981. *Forms of Talk.* Philadelphia: University of Pennsylvania Press.

Gubrium, J. F. and J. A. Holstein. 1997. *The New Language of Qualitative Method.* New York: Oxford University Press.

Habermas, J. [1962] 1989. *The Structural Transformation of the Public Sphere: An Inquiry into a Category of Bourgeois Society.* Translated by T. Burger. Cambridge: MIT Press.

Hacking, I. 1990. *The Taming of Chance.* Cambridge: Cambridge University Press.

Harding, S., ed. 1987. *Feminism and Methodology: Social Science Issues.* Bloomington: Indiana University Press.

Harvey, D. 1989. *The Condition of Postmodernity.* Cambridge, MA: Blackwell.

Hymes, D. 1974. *Foundations in Sociolinguistics: An Ethnographic Perspective.* Philadelphia: University of Pennsylvania Press.

Joseph, J. E. and T. J. Taylor, eds. 1990. *Ideologies of Language.* London: Routledge.

Karp, I. and M. B. Kendall. 1982. "Reflexivity in Fieldwork." Pp. 249-73 in *Explaining Social Behavior: Consciousness, Human Action, and Social Structure,* edited by P. F. Secord. Beverly Hills, CA: Sage.

Kroskrity, P. V., ed. 2000. *Regimes of Language: Ideologies, Polities, and Identities.* Santa Fe, NM: School of American Research Press.

Locke, J. [1690] 1959. *An Essay Concerning Human Understanding,* 2 vols. New York: Dover.

Lowe, L. 1996. *Immigrant Acts: On Asian American Cultural Politics.* Durham, NC: Duke University Press.

MacPherson, C. B. 1962. *The Political Theory of Possessive Individualism: Hobbes to Locke.* Oxford: Oxford University Press.

Mishler, E. G. 1986. *Research Interviewing: Context and Narrative.* Cambridge, MA: Harvard University Press.

———. 2000. *Storylines: Craftartists' Narratives of Identity.* Cambridge, MA: Harvard University Press.

Putnam, R. D. 2000. *Bowling Alone: The Collapse and Revival of American Community.* New York: Simon & Schuster.

Reinharz, S. 1992. *Feminist Methods in Social Research.* New York: Oxford University Press.

Riessman, C. K. 1993. *Narrative Analysis.* Newbury Park, CA: Sage.

Schieffelin, B. B., K. A. Woolard, and P. V. Kroskrity, eds. 1998. *Language Ideologies: Practice and Theory.* New York: Oxford University Press.

Shapin, S. 1994. *A Social History of Truth: Civility and Science in Seventeenth-Century England.* Chicago: University of Chicago Press.

Silverstein, M. and G. Urban, eds. 1996. *Natural Histories of Discourse.* Chicago: University of Chicago Press.

Trouillot, M.-R. 1991. "Anthropology and the Savage Slot: The Poetics and Politics of Otherness." Pp. 17-44 in *Recapturing Anthropology: Working in the Present,* edited by R. G. Fox. Santa Fe, NM: School of American Research Press.

van Dijk, T. A. 1984. *Prejudice in Discourse: An Analysis of Ethnic Prejudice in Cognition and Conversation.* Amsterdam: J. Benjamins.

White, H. 1978. *Tropics of Discourse: Essays in Cultural Criticism.* Baltimore: Johns Hopkins University Press.

Wodak, R. 1999. "Discourse and Racism: European Perspectives." *Annual Review of Anthropology* 28:175-99.

AUTHOR INDEX

SUBJECT INDEX

ABOUT THE EDITORS

Jaber F. Gubrium is Professor of Sociology at the University of Florida. His research focuses on the descriptive organization of personal identity, family, the life course, aging, and adaptations to illness. He is the editor of the *Journal of Aging Studies* and author or editor of more than 20 books, including *Living and Dying at Murray Manor, Caretakers, Describing Care, Oldtimers and Alzheimer's, Out of Control,* and *Speaking of Life.*

James A. Holstein is Professor of Sociology in the Department of Social and Cultural Sciences at Marquette University. He has studied diverse people-processing and social control settings, including courts, schools, and mental health agencies. He is the author or editor of numerous books, including *Court-Ordered Insanity, Dispute Domains and Welfare Claims, Reconsidering Social Constructionism,* and *Social Problems in Everyday Life.* He is also coeditor of the research annual *Perspectives on Social Problems.*

As collaborators for more than a decade, Gubrium and Holstein have developed their distinctive constructionist approach to everyday life in a variety of texts, including *What Is Family? Constructing the Life Course, Aging and Everyday Life, The Active Interview,* and *The New Language of Qualitative Method.* They continue to explore the theoretical and methodological implications of interpretive practice as it unfolds at the intersection of narrative, culture, and social interaction. Their most recent works—companion volumes *The Self We Live By: Narrative Identity in a Postmodern World* and *Institutional Selves: Troubled Identities in a Postmodern World*—consider the impact on self-construction of a postmodern world of increasingly diverse institutional identities.

ABOUT THE CONTRIBUTORS

Patricia A. Adler and **Peter Adler** have written and worked together for more than 25 years. Patricia is Professor of Sociology at the University of Colorado. Peter is Professor of Sociology at the University of Denver, where he served as chair from 1987 to 1993. Their interests include qualitative methods, deviant behavior, drugs and society, sociology of sport, sociology of children, social theory, and work, occupations, and leisure. Together, they have published numerous articles and books, including *Momentum* (1981), *Wheeling and Dealing* (1985; second edition 1993), *Membership Roles in Field Research* (1987), *Backboards and Blackboards* (1991), and *Peer Power* (1998). They have served as editors of the *Journal of Contemporary Ethnography* (1986-94) and as the founding editors of *Sociological Studies of Child Development* (1985-92). Their coedited anthologies include *Constructions of Deviance*, now in its third edition, and *Sociological Odyssey*.

David L. Altheide is Regents' Professor in the School of Justice Studies at Arizona State University. He is a qualitative researcher, and his work has focused on the role of mass media and information technology for social control. His most recent theoretical and methodological statements on the relevance of the mass media for sociological analysis are *An Ecology of Communication: Cultural Formats of Control* (1995) and *Qualitative Media Analysis* (1996). He has also applied qualitative research designs to investigate the nature and process of educational reform, with particular emphasis on school context and culture. He is currently writing on the news media's constructions of a discourse of fear and its social consequences.

Paul Atkinson is Professor of Sociology at Cardiff University in Wales. He is currently directing two research projects on the social consequences of new genetic technologies and is completing an ethnographic study of an international opera company. His publications include the second edition of *Ethnography: Principles in Practice* (with Martyn Hammersley; 1995), *Sociological Readings and Re-readings* (1996), *Making Sense of Qualitative Data* (with Amanda Coffey; 1996), *Supervising the PhD* (with Sara Delamont and Odette Parry; 1997), and *The Doctoral Experience* (with Sara Delamont and Odette Parry; 2000). He is coeditor of the *Handbook of Ethnography* (2001) and of the journal *Qualitative Research*.

Robert Atkinson is Professor of Human Development and Director of the Center for the Study of Lives at the University of Southern Maine. He received his Ph.D. in cross-cultural human development from the University of Pennsylvania, has a background in philosophy, folklore, and counseling, and was a postdoctoral research fellow at the University of Chicago. He is the author of *The Life Story Interview* (1998) and *The Gift of Stories: Practical and Spiritual Applications of Autobiography, Life Stories, and Personal Mythmaking* (1995) and coauthor of *The Teenage World: Adolescent Self-Image in Ten Countries* (1988). With the help of his graduate students, he has built an archive of more than 500 life stories in the Center for the Study of Lives.

Carolyn D. Baker is a Reader in the Graduate School of Education at the University of Queensland, where she specializes in qualitative methodology, including ethnomethodology and conversation analysis. She has published widely on talk and interaction in institutional settings and in interviews. Her current research projects include studies of telephone calls to a computer software technical support line (with Mike Emmison, Queensland, and Alan Firth, Aalborg), studies of talk in interview narratives, and studies of talk at work in preschool and primary school classrooms. Her recent publications include "Membership Categorization and Interview Accounts" (in *Qualitative Research: Theory, Method and Practice*, edited by David Silverman, 1997); "Courtship and Marriage Stories: Orientations in Openings" (with G. Johnson; in *Narrative Inquiry*, 2000), and "A Child's Say in Parent-Teacher Talk at the Preschool: Doing Conversation Analytic Research in Early Childhood Settings" (with M. Leiminer; in *Contemporary Issues in Early Childhood*, 2000). She is currently preparing for publication a book titled *Conducting and Analyzing Interviews*.

Leigh Berger received her M.A. in sociology and is pursuing her Ph.D. in the Department of Communication at the University of South Florida in Tampa. Her dissertation research is a narrative ethnography of a Messianic Jewish congregation that explores how its spirituality is experienced and also illuminates the personal journey of the ethnographer. She hopes her writing invites the reader to observe ethnographic encounters, to participate in them, and to come away with a better understanding of both their social worlds and themselves.

Charles L. Briggs is Professor and Chair of the Department of Ethnic Studies at the University of California, San Diego. He has been awarded fellowships by the Andrew W. Mellon Foundation, the National Endowment for the Humanities, the John Simon Guggenheim Memorial Foundation, the Woodrow Wilson International Center for Scholars, and the Center for Advanced Studies in the Behavioral Sciences. His books include *Learning How to Ask: A Sociolinguistic Appraisal of the Role of the Interview in Social Science Research, The Wood Carvers of Córdova, New Mexico: Social Dimensions of an Artistic "Revival," Competence in Performance: The Creativity of Tradition in Mexicano Verbal Art, The Lost Gold Mine of Juan Mondragón* (with Julián Josué Vigil), and *Stories in Times of Cholera: The Transnational Circulation of Bacteria and Racial Stigmata in a Venezuelan Epidemic* (forthcoming).

Richard Cándida Smith is Professor of History at the University of Michigan. He is the author of *Utopia and Dissent: Art, Poetry, and Politics in California* (1995) and *Mallarmé's Children: Symbolism and the Renewal of Experience* (1999). He is currently working on a biography of the painter Jay DeFeo.

Kathy Charmaz is Professor of Sociology and Coordinator of the Faculty Writing Program at Sonoma State University. She assists faculty in writing for publication and teaches in the areas of sociological theory, social psychology, qualitative methods, health and illness, and aging and dying. Her books include two recent coedited volumes, *The Unknown Country: Death in Australia, Britain and the USA* and *Health, Illness, and Healing: Society, Social Context, and Self*. In addition, she has written *Good Days, Bad Days: The Self in Chronic Illness and Time*, which won awards from the Society for the Study of Symbolic Interaction and the Pacific Sociological Association. She currently serves as editor of *Symbolic Interaction*.

Susan E. Chase is Chair and Associate Professor of Sociology at the University of Tulsa. She also is a cofounder of the Women's Studies Program at the University of Tulsa. Her publications include *Mothers and Children: Feminist Analyses and Personal Narratives* (with Mary Rogers; 2001) and *Ambiguous Empowerment: The Work Narratives of Women School Superintendents* (1995).

Amanda Coffey lectures in sociology and research methods at Cardiff University in Wales. Her research interests focus on young people and citizenship, gender and education, and ethnographic representations. Her publications include *The Ethnographic Self* (1999), *Feminism and the Classroom Teacher* (with Sara Delamont; 2000), and *Education and Social Change* (2001). She is coeditor of the *Handbook of Ethnography* (2001).

Mick P. Couper is Senior Associate Research Scientist in the Survey Research Center and Adjunct Associate Professor in the Department of Sociology, both at the University of Michigan. He is also a Research Associate Professor in the Joint Program in Survey Methodology. He holds a Ph.D. in sociology from Rhodes University, an M.A. in applied social research from the University of Michigan, and an M.Soc.Sc. from the University of Cape Town. He is coauthor, with Robert Groves, of *Nonresponse in Household Interview Surveys* (1998) and chief editor of *Computer Assisted Survey Information Collection* (1999). His current research focuses on nonresponse, the role of the interviewer, and computer-assisted survey data collection (including CATI, CAPI, audio-CASI, and Web surveys).

Barbara Czarniawska holds the Skandia Chair in Management at Gothenburg Research Institute, School of Economics and Commercial Law, Göteborg University, Sweden. Her research focuses on control processes in complex organizations, most recently in the field of big-city management. Methodologically, she combines institutional theory with the narrative approach. She has published in the area of business and public administration in Polish, her native language, as well as in Swedish, Italian, and English. Among her many publications are *Narrating the Organization: Dramas of Institutional Identity* (1997), *A Narrative Approach to Organization Studies* (1998), *Writing Management* (1999), and *A City Reframed: Managing Warsaw in the 1990s* (2000). She is a member of the Royal Swedish Academy of Sciences.

Peter De Jong is Professor of Sociology and Social Work at Calvin College in Grand Rapids, Michigan, where he teaches courses on interviewing skills and individual and family practice. He also is on the teaching faculty of the Brief Family Therapy Center in Milwaukee. He has been an outpatient therapist and a foster care worker, and has led solution-focused training with practitioners from mental health, family service, and juvenile correction agencies and conducted outcome research on the model. In 1996, he wrote a strengths-based, solution-focused training program for the Family Independence Agency of the state of Michigan; this program is now being used for training throughout the state. He has coauthored articles and chapters in *Social Work, Families in Society, Handbook of Solution Focused Therapy,* and the *Social Worker's Desk Reference,* and is coauthor of *Interviewing for Solutions* (with Insoo Kim Berg). Currently, he is working with a family service agency to develop more effective ways to engage and work with mandated clients.

Norman K. Denzin is Distinguished Professor of Communications, College of Communications Scholar, and Research Professor of Communications, Sociology and Humanities, at the University of Illinois, Urbana-Champaign. He is the author of numerous books, including *Interpretive Ethnography: Ethnographic Practices for the 21st Century, The Cinematic Society: The Voyeur's Gaze, Images of Postmodern Society, The Research Act: A Theoretical Introduction to Sociological Methods, Interpretive Interactionism, Hollywood Shot by Shot, The Recovering Alcoholic,* and *The Alcoholic Self,* which won the Charles Cooley Award from the Society for the Study of Symbolic Interaction in 1988. In 1997 he was awarded the George Herbert Award from the Society for the Study of Symbolic Interaction. He is the coeditor of the *Handbook of Qualitative Research* (with Yvonna S. Lincoln; second edition, 2000). He is also editor of the *Sociological Quarterly,* coeditor of *Qualitative Inquiry,* and editor of the book series *Cultural Studies: A Research Annual* and *Studies in Symbolic Interaction.*

Steve de Shazer is cofounder of the Brief Family Therapy Center and a pioneer in the development of solution-focused brief therapy. He is internationally prominent as a teacher and an author. He has written numerous articles about solution-focused brief therapy as well as five books, the latest of which is *Words Were Originally Magic.*

Marjorie L. DeVault is Associate Professor of Sociology and a member of the Women's Studies Program at Syracuse University. She received her Ph.D. from Northwestern University and writes on women's work, household life, and qualitative and feminist research methodologies. She is the author of *Feeding the Family: The Social Organization of Caring as Gendered Work* and *Liberating Method: Feminism and Social Research.*

Patrick Dilley is Visiting Assistant Professor in the College of Education at the University of Washington. He received his Ph.D. in higher education policy and organization from the University of Southern California. His areas of specialization include qualitative methodologies, student development theories, the history of higher education, and queer theory in education.

Christopher Dunbar, Jr., is Assistant Professor in the Department of Educational Administration at Michigan State University. He received his Ph.D. in educational policy studies from the University of Illinois. His research interests include urban school leadership, ethnographic studies, alternative education, charter schools, and African American males and education. His work has been published in *Qualitative Inquiry, Cultural Studies,* and *Theory into Practice.* He teaches courses on schools, families and communities, organizational theory, and qualitative research.

Donna Eder is Professor of Sociology at Indiana University. She has written numerous journal articles and book chapters in the areas of gender, schooling, and women's culture. Her book *School Talk: Gender and Adolescent Culture* is an in-depth study of middle school peer cultures and the ways in which gender stereotypes are maintained and resisted. In her current research, she is conducting in-depth interviews with storytellers from different cultures to understand more fully the role of storytelling in teaching about social differences and social dynamics. She has also done group interviews with elementary students to identify how stories teach them to view differences across groups of people and cultures.

Carolyn Ellis is Professor of Communication and Sociology and Co-Director of the Institute for Interpretive Human Studies at the University of South Florida. She is the author of *Final Negotiations: A Story of Love, Loss, and Chronic Illness* and *Fisher Folk: Two Communities on Chesapeake Bay.* She is coeditor of *Composing Ethnography, Investigating Subjectivity, Social Perspectives on Emotion* (Volume 3), and the book series Ethnographic Alternatives. Her current research focuses on illness narratives, autoethnography, and emotional sociology.

Ronald M. Epstein is Associate Professor of Family Medicine and Psychiatry at the University of Rochester. He completed a residency in family medicine and received fellowship training in research on patient-physician communication, developing protocols for the care of HIV disease in primary care, and training in family therapy. He has lectured throughout North America and Europe about patient-physician communication, focusing on topics that practitioners find difficult to manage, such as HIV, end-of-life issues, and unexplained symptoms. He is the author of more than 50 articles and book chapters, and has received grants for his research from the Robert Wood Johnson Foundation, the National Institutes of Health, the Agency for Healthcare Research and Quality, and the Department of Health and Human Services, as well as a Fulbright Senior Lecturer's Award.

Laura Fingerson is Assistant Professor in Sociology at the University of Wisconsin–Milwaukee. Her research interests include the sociology of children and adolescents; gender, race, and class; and qualitative and quantitative methods. Her current research explores adolescent girls' and boys' discourses on the body and menstruation. Through individual and single-sex group interviews, she uncovers what boys and girls are saying about the body and menstruation; how they use language to construct their discourses; how they socially construct the body, masculinity, and femininity; and how they use their bodies as sites of power and agency. Her recent work also includes an analysis of girls' collective and collaborative talk about family television programs and a quantitative look at parents' influences on their children's sexual decision making.

Andrea Fontana is Professor of Sociology at the University of Nevada, Las Vegas. He received his Ph.D. from the University of California, San Diego, in 1976. He has published articles on aging, leisure, theory, and postmodernism. He is the author of the *Last Frontier: the Social Meaning of Growing Old*, coauthor of *Social Problems* and *Sociologies of Everyday Life,* and coeditor of *The Existential Self in Society* and *Postmodernism and Social Inquiry.* He is a former president of the Society for the Study of Symbolic Interaction and a former editor of the journal *Symbolic Interaction.* His latest published essays are a deconstruction of the work of the painter Hieronymus Bosch, a performance/play about Farinelli the castrato, and an ethnographic narrative about land speed records at the Bonneville Salt Flats.

Kenneth M. George is Professor of Anthropology at the University of Wisconsin–Madison and specializes in the cultural politics of religion, art, and violence in Indonesia. He is the author of *Showing Signs of Violence* (1996), which was awarded the 1998 Harry J. Benda Prize by the Association for Asian Studies. His current research centers on contemporary Islamic art in Southeast Asia and the Indonesian artist A. D. Pirous. His recent articles include "Signature Work: Bandung, 1994" (in *Ethnos*) and "Some Things That Have Happened to 'The Sun after September 1965': Politics and the Interpretation of an Indonesian Painting" (in *Comparative Studies in Society and History*).

Sue Ellen Hansen is a Research Investigator in the Survey Research Center at the University of Michigan. She holds an M.A. in applied social research and a Ph.D. in sociology from the University of Michigan. She has extensive knowledge of computer-assisted interviewing systems and has worked closely with users of such systems. Her primary research interests concern the design and evaluation of computer-assisted data collection systems, interviewer-respondent interaction in the computer-assisted interview, and interviewer training and performance evaluation.

Jeffrey C. Johnson is a Senior Scientist at the Institute for Coastal and Marine Resources and Professor in the Departments of Sociology, Anthropology, and Biostatistics, East Carolina University. He received his Ph.D. from the University of California, Irvine, and is currently working on a long-term research project supported by the National Science Foundation comparing the group dynamics of the winter-over crews at the American South Pole Station with those at the Polish, Russian, Chinese, and Indian Antarctic stations. His interests include interviewing techniques for the collection of data appropriate for constructing cognitive models of ecological knowledge. He is the author of *Selecting Ethnographic Informants* and has published extensively in anthropological, sociological, and marine journals. He is the founder and former editor-in-chief of the *Journal of Quantitative Anthropology.*

John M. Johnson is Professor of Justice Studies at Arizona State University. He regularly teaches classes in qualitative research methods, domestic violence, and theory. He has done qualitative research and interviewing on evangelical crusades, the military, welfare offices, battered women's shelters, churches, self-help groups for violent men, court orders of protection, police, prisons, drug programs, and the death penalty. He is a Past President of the Society for the Study of Symbolic Interaction and a former editor of the journal *Symbolic Interaction.*

Travis S. K. Kong completed his doctoral dissertation, titled "The Voices in Between . . . : The Body Politics of Hong Kong Gay Men," at the University of Essex. His article "The Seduction of the Golden Boy: The Body Politics of Hong Kong Gay Men" is forthcoming in *Body and Society.* His research interests include sexuality and gender studies, media studies, cultural studies, and postcolonial studies. He currently lectures in the Department of Applied Social Studies at the Hong Kong Polytechnic University.

Gary P. Latham is Secretary of State Professor of Organizational Effectiveness at the University of Toronto. He is a fellow of both the American Psychological Association and the Canadian Psychological Association, and in 1996 he was made a fellow of the Royal Society of Canada. He has served as President of the Canadian Psychological Association and consults widely in industry. Among his numerous publications are *Increasing Productivity through Performance Appraisal* (with K. N. Wexley), *A Theory of Goal Setting and Task Performance* (with E. A. Locke), *Developing and Training Human Resources in Organizations* (with K. N. Wexley), and *Goal Setting: A Motivational Technique That Works* (with E. A. Locke), the last of which has been translated into Hebrew and Japanese.

Dan Mahoney is a doctoral candidate in the Department of Sociology at the University of Essex in the United Kingdom. His dissertation is an investigation of how gay men construct notions of intimacy and belonging with friends, partners, or family members through the narrative practice of storytelling. His research interests are in the areas of intimacy, identity construction, sexuality, family relations, and qualitative research methods. He lectures at the Ryerson Polytechnic University in Toronto.

Chris Mann is employed by the University of Cambridge to conduct several innovative research studies that focus on equal opportunities issues in higher education. She is based in the Faculty of Social and Political Sciences and is a member of the Centre for Family Research. She is coauthor, with Fiona Stewart, of *Internet Communication and Qualitative Research: A Handbook for Researching Online* (2000).

Douglas W. Maynard is Professor of Sociology at the University of Wisconsin–Madison. He does research in the areas of ethnomethodology and conversation analysis, has interests in science and technology studies, and is particularly concerned with survey research as a set of technologies for the scientific study of society. With Hanneke Houtkoop-Steenstra, Nora Cate Schaeffer, and Hans van der Zouwen, he is coediting a book titled *Standardization and Tacit Knowledge: Interaction and Practice in the Survey Interview.* He also is coeditor (with John Heritage) of the forthcoming *Practicing Medicine: Talk and Action in Primary Care Encounters.* He has published extensively on "bad news" and "good news" in conversational and professional interaction and is the author of the forthcoming *Bad News, Good News, and the Benign Order of Everyday Life.*

Liza McCoy is Assistant Professor of Sociology at the University of Calgary in Alberta, Canada. Her research has looked at knowledge practices in the areas of health, education, management, and photographic representation.

Ian K. McKenzie is a forensic and occupational psychologist holding chartered status with the British Psychological Society (BPS). A former senior police officer with the Metropolitan Police in London, he is immediate past Honorary Secretary of the Division of Forensic Psychology of the BPS and immediate past Chair of the International Section of the Academy of Criminal Justice Sciences. He is the author of a large number of papers, book chapters, and articles dealing with the interface between psychology and the criminal justice system, many of them comparative studies of U.K./U.S. jurisprudence and policing. He is a former Director of the Institute of Criminal Justice Studies at the University of Portsmouth, England, and currently Director of Course Programmes for the Institute, which delivers a wide range of distance learning programs for criminal justice professionals. His principal, current research interest is an examination of the psychological effects of undercover police work.

Gale Miller is Professor of Sociology in the Department of Social and Cultural Sciences at Marquette University. He has devoted many years to studying everyday life in diverse human service institutions. Among his many publications is *Becoming Miracle Workers: Language and Meaning in Brief Therapy* (1997), which presents a comparative analysis of systemic and solution-focused therapy interviews.

Zeeva Millman received her Ph.D. in organizational behavior and human resources management from the University of Toronto School of Business and holds an M.B.A. degree from McGill University. She has published in the areas of training and development, job search, motivation, and change. Currently she is President of A&M Human Resources Consultants and provides executive coaching to clients such as the Niagara Institute, applicant screening services, and motivational training. She also writes a column for *Pharmaceuticals and Devices,* a pharmaceutical industry trade magazine.

David L. Morgan is Professor in the Institute on Aging and School of Community Health at Portland State University and is also affiliated with the Department of Sociology. He received his Ph.D. in sociology from the University of Michigan and did postdoctoral training at Indiana University. His research interests include the aging of the baby boom generation as well as the role that social networks play in individuals' coping with life-course transitions. He has a broad interest in research methods, and although he is best known for his work with focus groups, he has also used a wide variety of other methods. He is currently finishing a book on practical strategies for combining qualitative and quantitative methods.

Janice M. Morse, Ph.D. (nursing), Ph.D. (anthropology), D.Nurs. (honors), is Director of the International Institute for Qualitative Methodology and Professor with the Faculty of Nursing at the University of Alberta. She has published extensively in the areas of comfort, suffering, and qualitative methods and serves as editor of the bimonthly international, interdisciplinary journal *Qualitative Health Research.* She is editor of *Critical Issues in Qualitative Research Methods* (1994), *Completing a Qualitative Project* (1997), and, with Janice Swanson and Anton Kuzel, *The Nature of Qualitative Evidence* (2001).

Kirin Narayan is Professor of Anthropology and of the Languages and Cultures of Asia at the University of Wisconsin–Madison. Much of her work has addressed the place of stories in people's lives, whether in the form of folktales, oral histories, ballads, ethnographic narratives, or fiction. She is the author of *Storytellers, Saints, and Scoundrels: Folk Narrative in Hindu Religious Teaching* (1989), which won the 1990 Victor Turner Prize for Ethnographic Writing and was co-winner of the 1990 Elsie Clews Parsons Prize for Folklore. Working in collaboration with Urmila Devi Sood, a village woman in Northwest India, she is also author of *Mondays on the Dark Night of the Moon: Himalayan Foothill Folktales* (1997). She has published a novel, *Love Stars and All That* (1994), and has recently completed a second novel, *Becoming a Foreigner,* that builds from her fieldwork in the Himalayan foothills and interviews among second-generation South Asian Americans.

Teresa Odendahl is Executive Director of the National Network of Grantmakers in San Diego, California. She received her Ph.D. in anthropology from the University of Colorado. She has been a consultant and facilitator with grassroots nonprofit organizations, a director of development, the executive director of two women's foundations, and a professor of women's studies. She was Project Manager of the Foundation Formation, Growth and Termination study at Yale University's Program on Nonprofit Organizations. She is editor and contributor to *Women and Power in the Nonprofit Sector,* author of *Charity Begins at Home: Generosity and Self-Interest among the Philanthropic Elite,* and numerous other publications. She is currently co-principal investigator of a research project titled "Impact of Board and Staff Diversity in the Philanthropic Field." She serves on the boards of the Institute for Women's Policy Research and National Committee for Responsive Philanthropy in Washington, D.C., as well as on the editorial board of *Nonprofit and Voluntary Sector Quarterly* and the advisory committee of the Urban Institute Center on Nonprofits and Philanthropy.

Laurence Parker is Associate Professor in the Department of Educational Policy Studies at the University of Illinois. His areas of specialization are urban educational policy, critical race theory and education, and higher-education desegregation. His most recent publication is a coedited book titled *Race Is . . . Race Isn't . . . : Critical Race Theory and Qualitative Studies in Education.*

Jennifer Platt is Professor of Sociology at the University of Sussex. She has been President of the British Sociological Association and editor of its journal *Sociology,* and currently is a member of the Executive Committee of the International Sociological Association. Her research interests include the history of sociological research methods, the logic of case studies, intellectual migration and its consequences, and the social structure of social science nationally and internationally. Her publications include "Research Methods and the Second Chicago School" (in *A Second Chicago School?* edited by Gary Alan Fine), *A History of Sociological Research Methods in America, 1920-1960,* "Migration and Globalization in Intellectual Life: A Case Study of the Post-1956 Exodus from Hungary" (with Phoebe Isard, in *Global Future: Migration, Environment, and Globalization,* edited by A. Brah et al.), and *A Brief History of the ISA: 1948-1997.*

Ken Plummer is Professor of Sociology at the University of Essex. He is author or editor of several books, including *The Making of the Modern Homosexual* (1982), *Telling Sexual Stories* (1995), and *Documents of Life* (second edition, 2000). Currently, he is writing a book titled *Intimate Citizenship* and is the editor of the journal *Sexualities.*

Blake D. Poland is Associate Professor in the Department of Public Health Sciences at the University of Toronto. His research focuses primarily on community development as an arena of practice for health professionals and on lay perceptions of tobacco control. His work is informed by a critical-interpretive perspective and social justice orientation. He also has published on the methodological and epistemological aspects of qualitative research in *Qualitative Inquiry, Health Promotion International, Canadian Journal of Public Health,* and the *Operational Geographer,* as well as in several book chapters. He is lead editor of *Settings for Health Promotion: Linking Theory and Practice* (2000).

Shulamit Reinharz has been Professor of Sociology at Brandeis University since 1991, the first and only woman to hold that rank at the university. In 1992, she became Director of the Women's Studies Program and developed a graduate degree component along with a National Board, a program on domestic violence, and a program on women's health. Her publications include four books, *Feminist Methods in Social Research* (1992), *Qualitative Gerontology* (1987), *On Becoming a Social Scientist* (1979/84), and *Psychology and Community Change* (1984). She serves on the editorial boards of many sociology journals. In the field of Jewish women's studies, she has created an academic journal and is the editor of a book series.

Laurel Richardson is Professor Emerita of Sociology and Visiting Professor of Cultural Studies at the Ohio State University. Her recent book *Fields of Play: Constructing an Academic Life* was honored with the Society for the Study of Symbolic Interaction's Charles Horton Cooley Award. She continues to be interested in the applications of poststructural theory, exploring the boundaries of how claims to knowledge are constructed and communicated.

Catherine Kohler Riessman is Research Professor, Department of Sociology, Boston College. Her research has been in medical sociology, especially women's health, and in the narrative study of lives. Using narrative methods of interviewing and analysis, she has examined accounts of a variety of life events that disrupt individuals' assumptions about biographical order, specifically divorce, chronic illness, and infertility. She has conducted fieldwork in South India on childless women, supported by an Indo-American Fellowship (CIES). Her books include *Divorce Talk* (1990) and *Narrative Analysis* (1993). She has published articles in *Gender & Society, Narrative Inquiry, Women and Health*, and the *American Journal of Public Health*. She also has contributed chapters to edited books on narrative approaches in the social sciences.

Dalia Rodriguez is a graduate student in the Department of Educational Policy Studies at the University of Illinois. Her main research interests focus on the social context of education, with an emphasis in educational policy, including racial/ethnic inequality in the legal and educational contexts.

Paul C. Rosenblatt is Morse Alumni Distinguished Teaching Professor of Family Social Science at the University of Minnesota. His book-length works based on intensive interviewing include *Parent Grief: Narratives of Loss and Relationship, Multiracial Couples: Black and White Voices, Farming Is in Our Blood: Farm Families in Economic Crisis*, and *The Family in Business*. His current interview and writing projects using intensive interviewing deal with couples in which one partner is Chinese and the other Euro-American, with grief in African American families, with shame in Korean families, and with the circumstances in which bereaved parents use the present tense in talking about a child who has died.

Anne Ryen is Associate Professor at Agder University College and a Senior Researcher at Agder Research Foundation, Kristiansand, Norway. Her main interests are qualitative methodology, fringe benefits, and social security. She has conducted research in South Africa, Kenya, Tanzania, and Indonesia. She is currently leading three research clusters, on gender-related issues in Tanzania, on local government in developing countries, and on local government in Norway. She is also conducting research on social security in Indonesia and on fringe benefits in Norway. Her most recent publications are "Marking Boundaries: Culture as Category Work" (with David Silverman, in *Qualitative Inquiry*, 2000), and *Child Care, Ethics, and Methodology* (2001).

Nora Cate Schaeffer is Professor of Sociology at the University of Wisconsin–Madison, where she teaches courses in survey research methods and conducts research on issues in survey design and questionnaire development. Before receiving her doctorate from the University of Chicago, she worked at the National Opinion Research Center. She has taught questionnaire design at the Summer Institute of the Survey Research Center at the University of Michigan and through the University of Michigan–University of Maryland Joint Program in Survey Methodology. She has served on the Panel to Evaluate Alternative Census Methodology for the National Research Council of the National Academy of Science; on the National Science Foundation Advisory Committee for the Social, Behavioral and Economic Sciences; and on the governing Council of the American Association for Public Opinion Research. She has been a member of the editorial boards for *Public Opinion Quarterly, Sociological Methods & Research*, and *Sociological Methodology*.

Michael L. Schwalbe is Associate Professor of Sociology at North Carolina State University. He is the author of *Unlocking the Iron Cage: The Men's Movement, Gender Politics, and American Culture*

(1996) and *The Sociologically Examined Life* (1998). Currently, he is writing a biography based on the life histories of two working-class black men in the American South.

Clive F. Seale is Professor of Sociology at Goldsmiths College, University of London. His books include *Researching Society and Culture* (1998), *Constructing Death: The Sociology of Dying and Bereavement* (1998), and *The Quality of Qualitative Research* (1999). He is currently engaged in a study of media representations of health, illness, and health care.

Aileen M. Shaw is Research and Development Director at the National Network of Grantmakers (NNG) in San Diego, California. She has a B.A. in history from Trinity College Dublin and an M.A. from New York University. Currently, she is study director for a research project titled "Impact of Board and Staff Diversity in the Philanthropic Field," an examination of best practices for recruiting and retaining diverse foundation staff and trustees. She is the author of *Preserving the Public Trust,* a study of accountability, accessibility, and relations with grantees based on interviews with more than 100 foundation executives, managers, and trustees. Her research interests include gender, class, and cultural dynamics in the workplace. She has written organizational histories of NNG and the Western States Center in Portland, Oregon. She also has extensive experience as a development consultant for progressive, community-based, and women's organizations locally, nationally, and internationally.

Roger W. Shuy is Distinguished Research Professor of Linguistics at Georgetown University, where he founded and then directed the Sociolinguistics Program for 30 years, interrupted only by a term as Chair of the Linguistics Department. One of the founders of the American Association of Applied Linguistics, he has also served as its President. He has conducted research on regional and social dialects, literacy, medical discourse, classroom language, and, for the past 20 years, the intersection of language and law. Of his 27 books, the most recent are *Language Crimes: The Use and Abuse of Language Evidence in the Courtroom* (1996), *The Language of Confession, Interrogation, and Deception* (1998), and *Bureaucratic Language in Government and Business* (1998). Forthcoming is *A Few Months to Live,* an ethnographic study of terminally ill patients. Since his retirement from teaching in 1996, he continues to consult with attorneys on law cases and to carry out research from his Montana home.

Royce A. Singleton, Jr., is Professor of Sociology and Chair of the Department of Sociology and Anthropology at the College of the Holy Cross in Worcester, Massachusetts. He is the author of several articles spanning social psychology, race relations, research methodology, and undergraduate education. His most recent work, including an article in *Change* magazine on the Holy Cross First-Year Program (May/June 1998), focuses on program evaluation. He is the coauthor, with Bruce Straits, of *Approaches to Social Research* (third edition, 1999).

Fiona Stewart is Chief Knowledge Officer at Brands Online Ltd, an Australian on-line research company, and Director of Realworld Research & Communications. Her interests are currently focused upon the use of WAP technologies for consumer polling and on-line market research. She is coauthor, with Chris Mann, of *Internet Communication and Qualitative Research: A Handbook for Researching Online* (2000).

Bruce C. Straits is Associate Professor of Sociology, University of California, Santa Barbara. His research areas include social demography, cigarette smoking and cessation, the social psychology of research, personal networks, and research methodology. Currently, he is studying the influence of personal networks on individuals' attitudes and behavior.

William G. Tierney is Wilbur-Kieffer Professor of Higher Education and Director of the Center for Higher Education Policy Analysis at the University of Southern California. Previously, he was Professor of Education and Senior Scientist in the Center for the Study of Higher Education at the Pennsylvania State University. He earned a master's degree from Harvard University and holds a Ph.D. from Stanford University in administration and policy analysis. His research interests center on faculty work, issues of equity, and qualitative research. He is coeditor, with Yvonna S. Lincoln, of *Representation and the Text: Re-framing the Narrative Voice* (1997), a volume that deals with how authors construct texts. He has focused most recently on issues pertaining to life history methods and the role of the author in the text. The results of his research have appeared in numerous higher-education and anthropology journals. He is currently at work on a novel about academic life.

Carol A. B. Warren is Professor of Sociology at the University of Kansas. Among her research monographs are *Pushbutton Psychiatry: A History of Electroshock in America* (with Timothy Kneeland), *Madwives: Schizophrenic Women in the 1950s,* and *The Court of Last Resort: Mental Illness and the Law.* Her many methodological writings include *Gender Issues in Ethnography* (with Jennifer Hackney), "Gender and Fieldwork Relations" (in *Contemporary Field Research,* second edition, edited by Robert M. Emerson), and the entry "Ethnography" in the *Encyclopedia of Sociology.*

Susan C. Weller is a Medical Anthropologist at the University of Texas Medical Branch, Galveston. She received her training in the social sciences and specializes in the study of illness beliefs. Her recent work includes comparative studies of beliefs about biomedical and folk illnesses in four distinct Latino populations: Puerto Ricans in Hartford, Connecticut; Mexican Americans in Edinburg, Texas; Mexicans in Guadalajara, Jalisco; and Guatemalans on the Pacific Coastal Plain of Guatemala. Her work reflects a concern with obtaining accurate interview data and combining qualitative and quantitative methods in order to make valid generalizations from interview data. She is a co-developer, with A. K. Romney and W. Batchelder, of the Cultural Consensus Model and has authored *Systematic Data Collection* with A. K. Romney.

G. Clare Wenger is Professor of Gerontology, Director of CSPRD, Associate Director of IMSCAR, and Director of Postgraduate Studies in Gerontology at the University of Wales, Bangor. She has been involved in research in the aging field since 1978, including a 20-year study of the aging process in rural Wales. She contributes regularly to the doctoral program in gerontology of the Sanders-Brown Center for Aging at the University of Kentucky and is International Adviser to the Centre for Gerontology and Geriatric Medicine at the Medical Institute of Baharati Vidyapeeth Deemed University, India. She is on the editorial board of the *Journal of Cross-Cultural Gerontology* and has published widely in the field of aging. Her main areas of interest are the family sociology of older people, social networks, comparative transnational research, and the use of social research findings in social policy development.

Michelle Wolkomir is Assistant Professor of Sociology at Centenary College of Louisiana. Her current research project examines the lives of gay and ex-gay Christian men, focusing on how these men resolve the identity dilemmas that arise from the conflict between Christian doctrine and gay sexuality.

Kathleen A. Zoppi is Assistant Professor and Director of Educational Development and Fellowships at the Indiana University Department of Family Medicine. She received her Ph.D. in communication and her MPH in Health Education and Health Behavior from the University of Michigan, Ann Arbor. Her area of research centers on relational approaches to the study of patient-physician communication. She is currently involved in research projects on domestic violence and end-of-life training for residents. She has published on communication skills and on patient-physician interaction. She has taught residents and medical students at Bon Secours Hospital, Henry Ford Hospital, and Indiana University for the past 14 years.